Psychology

a journey

First Canadian Edition

Psychology

a journey

Dennis Coon

Patrick Brown
University of Western Ontario

Rajesh Malik
Dawson College

Susanne McKenzie
Dawson College

THOMSON

NELSON

Australia   Canada   Mexico   Singapore   Spain   United Kingdom   United States

THOMSON

NELSON

**Psychology: A Journey,
First Canadian Edition**

by Dennis Coon, Patrick Brown,
Rajesh Malik, and Susanne McKenzie

Editorial Director and Publisher:
Evelyn Veitch

Executive Editor:
Joanna Cotton

Marketing Manager:
Murray Moman

Developmental Editor:
Joanne Sutherland

Production Editor:
Bob Kohlmeier

Production Coordinator:
Hedy Sellers

Copy-Editor:
Valerie Adams

Proofreader:
Sarah Robertson

Creative Director:
Angela Cluer

Interior Design:
Lisa Delgado

Interior-Design Modifications:
Peter Papayanakis

Cover Design:
Anne Bradley

Cover Image:
Anne Bradley

Compositor:
Zenaida Diores

Indexer:
Jim Leahy

Printer:
Webcom

**National Library of Canada
Cataloguing in Publication Data**

Psychology : a journey /
Dennis Coon ... [et al.]. — 1st
Canadian ed.

Includes bibliographical references
and indexes.
ISBN 0-17-622400-9

1. Psychology.   I. Coon, Dennis

BF121 P8323 2003   150
C2002-904955-5

Brief Contents

Contents

Chapter 2   Brain and Behaviour   40

Chapter 5   States of Consciousness   165

Chapter 6 Conditioning and Learning 208

Chapter 7 Memory 247

Chapter 8   Cognition, Intelligence, and Creativity   283

Chapter 9   Motivation and Emotion   324

Chapter 10 Personality 368

Chapter 14 Social Behaviour 527

Using Psychology: Groupthink—Agreement at Any Cost   538

 Using Psychology: Buffering Television's Impact   560

About the Authors

After earning a doctorate in psychology from the University of Arizona, Dennis Coon taught for 22 years at Santa Barbara City College, California. Throughout his career, Dr. Coon has especially enjoyed the challenge of teaching introductory psychology. He and his wife, Sevren, recently returned to Tucson, where he continues to teach, write, edit, and consult.

Dr. Coon is the author of *Introduction to Psychology* and *Essentials of Psychology*. Together, these texts have been used by over two million students. Dr. Coon frequently serves as a reviewer and consultant to publishers, and he edited the best-selling trade book *Choices.* He also helped design modules for the *PsychNow!* interactive CD-ROM.

In his leisure hours, Dr. Coon enjoys hiking, photography, painting, woodworking, and music. He also designs, builds, and plays classical and steel-string acoustic guitars. His recent return to Arizona has made it possible for him to fulfill a lifelong dream of using operant conditioning to teach scorpions to tap dance.

Patrick Brown studied linguistics at the University of Ottawa and psychology at the University of Waterloo, receiving M.A. and Ph.D. degrees. During a postdoctoral fellowship in the Department of Neurology, College of Medicine, at the University of Florida, he studied the influence of brain damage on perception of, and memory for, emotion. He taught for three years at Laurentian University in Sudbury before going to the Department of Psychology at the University of Western Ontario, where he has taught cognition, research methods, and statistics since 1990.

Born and raised in India, Rajesh Malik arrived in Canada at the age of 20. He obtained his doctorate degree in psychology from Concordia University, and currently teaches in the Department of Psychology at Dawson College and in the Department of Education at Concordia University. He and his wife, Kamal, are the proud parents of a toddler named Vivaik. Without exaggeration, Rajesh feels that having a child is one of the best events of his life. He is passionate about classical music, reads literature and philosophy with deep interest, derives immense pleasure from taking long walks, and remains a committed vegetarian.

Sue McKenzie received a B.A. from Northwestern University and M.A. and Ph.D. degrees from McGill. She has been teaching psychology at Dawson College in Montreal since the college opened in 1969. She and her husband, Bob, who also teaches at Dawson, have three grown children. When not teaching, skiing, or singing in a women's barbershop chorus, she likes to weave. On a loom.

Preface

▶ To the Student—The Journey Begins

Psychology is at once familiar, exotic, surprising, and challenging. Most of all, psychology is changing. Indeed, this book is just a snapshot of a colourful passing scene. Yet change is what makes psychology fascinating: What could be more intriguing than our evolving understanding of human behaviour?

Psychology is about each of us. Psychology asks, "How can we step outside of ourselves to look objectively at how we live, think, feel, and act?" Psychologists believe the answer is through careful thought, observation, and inquiry, so those principles inform all that follows in this text.

Each chapter of this book takes you into a different realm of psychology, such as personality, abnormal behaviour, memory, consciousness, and human development. Each realm is complex and fascinating, with many pathways, landmarks, and detours to discover. The title of this book, *Psychology: A Journey,* reflects the fact that learning is an adventure. Like any journey of discovery, your tour of psychology will help you to better understand yourself, others, and the world around you. It's definitely a trip worth taking.

We hope you will find human behaviour as fascinating as we do. In the pages that follow, we have done all that we could to make your first journey through psychology enjoyable and worthwhile.

Getting Started

A special CD-ROM is included with this book to help you learn more about yourself and human behaviour. *Psychology: An Interactive Journey* makes it easier for you to study, review, test yourself, relate new ideas to your own life, and experience psychology directly through interactive exercises. You'll find valuable guidelines for effective reading, note-taking, test-taking, and time management. These skills will help you get the most out of this text and your psychology course. Additional tips tell how to use the Internet, electronic databases, and CDs.

We hope the delight we have found in our own students' curiosity, insights, imagination, and interests will be apparent to you as you explore psychology. Please view this book as a long letter from us to you. It is, in a very real sense, written about you, for you, and to you.

▶ To the Instructor—A Concise Survey of Psychology

Psychology: A Journey was written to provide a concise but complete first course in psychology. It is organized into 14 chapters so that the entire field can be covered in a single term, at the rate of one chapter per week. With that in mind, we were prompted to select only the best material from the vast quantity available. Nevertheless, the book manages to cover not only essential topics at the core of psychology but many others at the cutting edge of current knowledge.

The publication of the First Canadian Edition of *Psychology: A Journey* is a direct result of feedback from instructors and students. We want to read about research that was conducted and is currently happening in Canada, about statistics that are relevant to Canadians, and about examples that illustrate the diversity of Canadian cultural experience.

The result is a concise text that is readable, relevant, and motivating.

Text-Specific CD-ROM

Psychology: A Journey, is accompanied by an exciting new in-text CD-ROM called *Psychology: An Interactive Journey.* The CD was created by Content and Instructional Design Consultants D. L. Seagle and K. H. Trotter, to enliven students' learning experiences. Interactive, CD-based instruction is an ideal way to bring psychology to life for technologically attuned college students. In essence, *Psychology: An Interactive Journey* serves as a tour guide for students as they make their first foray into psychology. Professors Seagle and Trotter are enthusiastic users of instructional technologies in their own courses. Their expertise and talents are readily apparent in the CD they have produced. (The features of *Psychology: An Interactive Journey* are described later in this Preface.)

Readability and Narrative Emphasis

Selecting a textbook is half the battle in teaching a successful course. A good text does much of the work of imparting information to students. This frees class time for discussion, extra topics, or media presentations. It also leaves students asking for more. When a book overwhelms students or dampens their interest, teaching and learning suffer.

Growing numbers of students who enter introductory courses are poor or reluctant readers. No matter how interesting a text may be, its value is lost if students fail to read it. That's why we've worked hard to make this a clear, readable, and engaging text. We want students to read this book with genuine interest and enthusiasm, not merely as an obligation.

To encourage students to read, we made a special effort to weave narrative threads through every chapter. Everyone loves a good story, and the story of psychology is among the most compelling to be told. In every chapter of *Journey,* we have used intriguing anecdotes and running examples to propel reading and sustain interest. Near the end of each chapter, an Epilogue brings the narrative full circle. This provides closure and some final food for thought, as students complete their journey through each realm of psychology.

Practical Applications

An important question to ask about introductory psychology is, "What will students remember next year? Or in 10 years?" Consequently, *Psychology: A Journey* is designed to give students a clear grasp of major concepts without burying them in details. At the same time, it offers an overview that reflects psychology's rich heritage of ideas. We think students will find this book informative and intellectually stimulating. Moreover, we have emphasized the many ways that psychology relates to practical problems in daily life.

A major feature of this book is the Psychology in Action section found in each chapter. This high-interest discussion bridges the gap between theory and practical application. We believe it is fair for students to ask, "Does this mean anything to me? Can I use it? Why should I learn it if I can't?" The Psychology in Action features spell out how students can use psychology to solve problems and manage their own behaviour. This allows students to see the benefits of adopting new ideas, and it breathes life into psychology's concepts.

An Integrated Study Guide

The chapters of this text are divided into short segments by special features called Knowledge Builders. Each Knowledge Builder asks students to relate concepts to their own experiences, to quiz themselves, and to think critically about the principles they are learning. In addition, each chapter concludes with a feature called Chart Your Progress. The multiple-choice questions in Chart Your Progress provide a way for students to judge how well they are doing in their studies by taking a sample test at the end of the chapter.

Taken together, the Knowledge Builders and Chart Your Progress are essentially an integrated study guide. The text-specific CD that accompanies this book includes additional exercises and self-testing materials; these too are related closely to the text. For students who would like even more feedback and practice, printed Chapter Quizzes can be bundled with this text, a traditional printed Study Guide is available, and Web Tutor provides access to online quizzes and electronic flashcards.

Electronic Resources

To encourage further exploration, a section called Psychology on the Net is included at the end of each chapter of this book. The URLs listed there take students to interesting sites on the Internet. Each list also directs students to relevant articles in *InfoTrac® College Edition,* Nelson's exclusive online college library. All chapters include a list of relevant modules in *PsychNow!* and *Psyk.trek.* These excellent CD-ROMs offer an assortment of interactive learning experiences, animations, and simulations.

How Chapter Features Support the SQ4R Method

This text is designed around the SQ4R study-reading method. In addition to helping students learn psychology, its format promotes valuable study skills. Notice how the steps of the SQ4R method—*survey, question, read, recite, relate,* and *review*—are incorporated into the chapter structure.

SURVEY   Our goal in the initial pages of each chapter is to help students form a cognitive map of upcoming topics before they start reading. To begin, an entry in our own Psychologist's Journal serves as a high-interest preview of the chapter. The Psychologist's Journal presents anecdotes, personal observations, news clippings, or interesting quotations. These entries focus attention on upcoming topics, so that students will read with a purpose. In many cases, the Psychologist's Journal sets up running examples that are woven through chapters.

The Psychologist's Journal is followed by a list of Survey Questions that provide a more focused overview of the chapter. The same Survey Questions appear again in the main body of the text to help students structure their learning. Later, the Survey Questions are used to organize the chapter Summary, and they appear on the in-text CD and in the *Study Guide.* In this way, students are given a consistent framework to use as their knowledge grows.

QUESTION   Throughout each chapter, italicized Guide Questions serve as organizers that prompt students to look for important ideas as they read. These organizers promote active learning by combining studying and reading. Guide Questions also establish a dialogue that anticipates students' questions and reactions. This dialogue clarifies difficult points in a lively question-and-response format.

READ   In terms of formal readability measures, this is a highly readable text. To further aid comprehension, we've used a full array of traditional learning aids. These include: boldface terms (with phonetic pronunciations), bullet summaries, a robust illustration program, summary tables, a name index, a subject index, and a detailed glossary. As an additional aid, figure references in the text are marked with small coloured triangles. These bookmarks make it easy for students to return to the point where they interrupted their reading to view a figure.

A running glossary aids understanding by providing precise definitions in the page margins. In this way, students get clear definitions when and where they need them. The running glossary also makes it easier for students to find, study, and review important terms.

Several times per chapter, boxed highlights discuss recent research, human diversity, and how to apply psychology. These highlights are stimulating but non-intrusive supplements to the main text. They enrich the presentation and encourage students to think about what they are learning.

RECITE   Every few pages, a Knowledge Builder provides opportunities for students to test their understanding and recall of psychological principles. As noted earlier, Knowledge Builders are essentially a built-in study guide. Each includes a Learning Check, which is a short, non-comprehensive quiz. Learning Checks help students actively process information and assess their progress. Students who miss any questions are encouraged to backtrack and clarify their understanding before they read more. In this way, completing Learning Checks serves as a form of recitation to enhance learning.

RELATE   Cognitive psychologists tell us that elaborative rehearsal is one of the best ways to form lasting memories. Elaborative rehearsal increases the meaningfulness of new information by relating it to familiar knowledge. To help students use elaborative rehearsal, each Knowledge Builder includes a series of Relate questions. These questions encourage students to associate new concepts with meaningful personal experiences and prior knowledge.

A course in psychology naturally contributes to critical thinking. To further promote critical thinking abilities, each Knowledge Builder includes one or more Critical Thinking questions. These questions challenge students to think critically and analytically about psychology. Each is followed by a brief answer, which students can compare with their own thoughts. Many of the answers are based on research and are informative in their own right.

REVIEW   As noted above, all important terms appear in a running glossary, which aids review. As also noted, a Psychology in Action section completes each chapter. This feature shows students how psychological concepts relate to practical problems, including problems in their own lives. The information in the Psychology in Action features helps reinforce learning by illustrating psychology's practicality, and it also encourages students to review and extend the ideas they have learned.

To complete the review phase of the SQ4R method, the Chapter in Review section restates all of the major ideas presented earlier. This section includes Major Points, a list that summarizes the "take home" concepts—the ones that every student should be able to remember 10 years after reading this text. Next, a Summary provides a detailed synopsis of the chapter, point by point. As mentioned before, the Summary is organized around the same Survey Questions found at the beginning of the chapter. This brings the SQ4R process full circle and reinforces the learning objectives for the chapter. Every chapter concludes with Chart Your Progress, the brief multiple-choice test described earlier. Students who miss any questions are urged to review further, using various supplements available with this text.

New to the First Canadian Edition

Canadian research, examples and statistics have been integrated into every chapter of the text.

The following is a list of just some of the Canadian information and examples you will read about:

- Professional training and qualifications required for psychologists in Canada are discussed in Chapter 1.
- A discussion of new legislation governing the use and cultivation of marijuana for medical purposes is included in Chapter 5.
- Inuit Sign Language (ISL) is discussed in a new Human Diversity box in Chapter 8.
- A discussion of Pibloktoq, a mental disorder found among the Inuit, is included in Chapter 12.
- Information on the range of mental health resources that are available in Canada is discussed in Chapter 13.
- Research on how psychotherapy can be adapted to suit the cultural needs of First Nations clients is found in Chapter 13.
- The story of a young woman in Montreal who was injured and ignored for over three hours by employees in a nearby office building helps to illustrate the concept of bystander apathy in Chapter 14.

Some examples of Canadian statistics include:

- sleep patterns, insomnia, SIDS, and drug use, in Chapter 5
- obesity, in Chapter 9
- leading causes of death, in Chapter 11

- incidences of depression, in Chapters 11 and 12
- number of Canadians afflicted with various mental illnesses, in Chapter 12
- suicide rates among Canadians, in Chapter 12

Research from across the country is represented, including the following studies:

- University of British Columbia researcher Liisa Galea's study on neurogenesis (2001), in Chapter 2
- a study looking at the effects of daycare on attachment in infants and toddlers, by Margaret McKim of the University of Saskatchewan (1999), in Chapter 3
- the extensive research of Shephard Siegel and his colleagues at McMaster University on the role of classical conditioning in the development of tolerance to drugs (1999, 2000), in Chapter 6
- work by Daniel Yarmey at the University of Guelph on the accuracy of recall and recognition (1996), in Chapter 7
- leading researcher Ronald Melzack of McGill University on the psychological component of pain (1999, 2001), in Chapter 9
- research and statistics by Nancy Galambos of the University of Victoria on Canadian adolescents/young adults who engage in risky behaviours (1998), in Chapter 11

Human Diversity

Student populations increasingly reflect the multicultural, multifaceted nature of contemporary society. In *Psychology: A Journey* students will find numerous discussions of human diversity, including differences in race, ethnicity, culture, gender, abilities, sexual orientation, and age. Too often, such differences divide people into opposing groups. Our aim throughout this text is to discourage stereotyping, prejudice, discrimination, and intolerance. We've tried to make this book gender neutral and sensitive to diversity issues. All pronouns and examples involving females and males are equally divided by gender. In artwork, photographs, and examples, we have tried to portray the rich diversity of humanity.

Many topics and examples in this book encourage students to appreciate social, physical, and cultural differences and to accept them as a natural part of being human. Human Diversity boxes, in every chapter, highlight specific topics of interest.

Critical Thinking

The active, questioning nature of the SQ4R method is itself an inducement to think critically. Many of the Guide Questions that introduce topics in the text act as models of critical thinking. More important, Chapter 1 contains a brief discussion of critical thinking skills and a rational appraisal of pseudo-psychologies. In reality, the presentation of research methods in Chapter 1 is a short course on how to think clearly about behaviour. It is supplemented by suggestions about how to critically evaluate claims in the popular media. Chapter 8, "Cognition, Intelligence, and Creativity," discusses many topics that focus on thinking skills. Throughout the text, many boxed highlights promote critical thinking and healthy skepticism. As mentioned earlier, every Knowledge Builder includes Critical Thinking questions. The *Psychology: An Interactive Journey* CD identifies controversies in psychology and shows students how to use *InfoTrac College Edition* to investigate the underlying issues. Taken together, these features help students gain thinking skills of lasting value.

Positive Psychology

In January 2000, Martin E. P. Seligman and Mihaly Csikszentmihalyi coedited a special issue of *American Psychologist* devoted to optimal functioning, happiness, and "positive psychology." Over the past 100 years, psychologists have paid ample attention to the negative side of human behaviour. This is easy to understand, because we urgently need to find remedies for human problems. However, Seligman and Csikszentmihalyi have urged us to study positive psychology also. What do we know, for instance, about love, happiness, creativity, well-being, self-confidence, and achievement? Throughout this book, we have attempted to answer such questions for students. Our hope is that students who read this book gain an appreciation for the potential we all have for optimal functioning. Also, of course, we hope that they leave introductory psychology with emotional and intellectual tools they can use to enhance their lives.

Psychology: An _Interactive_ Journey CD-ROM

New technologies are making it possible for students to relate to information in ways that supplement or even transcend traditional textbook presentations. We are pleased that this book includes the new _Psychology: An Interactive Journey_ CD. This resource gives students a wonderful way to interact with ideas and concepts. The information in _Psychology: An Interactive Journey_ is closely coordinated with this text. Each chapter includes the following features: Introduction; Multiple-choice Pretest; Chapter Overview with electronic flashcards; Interactive Knowledge Builder; Interactive Exercises; Journal Activity; Crossword Puzzle; Search Online with InfoTrac; Multiple-choice Posttest; and Weblinks.

Psychology: An Interactive Journey also allows students to type and store notes as they are working and to send their responses to tests and exercises to their professors, via email. The SQ4R format of the text, combined with the interactivity of the CD, creates a powerful learning environment to help students realize their goals and maximize their potentials.

▶ A Complete Course—Teaching and Learning Supplements

A rich array of supplements accompanies _Psychology: A Journey,_ including several that make use of the latest technologies. These supplements are designed to make teaching and learning more effective. Many are available free to professors or students. Others can be packaged with this text at a discount.

Student Support Materials

Introductory students must learn a multitude of abstract concepts, which can make a first course in psychology difficult. The materials listed here will greatly improve students' chances for success.

STUDY GUIDE   To facilitate learning, the _Study Guide_ (ISBN: 0-17-622543-9) provides abundant opportunities for practice, self-testing, and rehearsal. The _Study Guide_ is structured around the SQ4R method and closely coordinated with this text. Each chapter includes the following sections: Chapter Overview (a concise chapter summary), Learning Objectives (a detailed list of what students need to know), Recite and Review (a survey of major terms and concepts), Connections (matching items), Check Your Memory (true–false items), Final Survey and Review (fill-in-the-blank questions) and a Mastery Test (multiple-choice questions similar to in-class test items). (The _Study Guide_ was adapted by Madeleine Côté of Dawson College.)

CHAPTER QUIZZES   This collection of self-administered quizzes (ISBN: 0-534-56884-X) can be packaged free with this text. It includes a 25-item multiple-choice quiz that students can use to evaluate their understanding and prepare for tests. An answer key is provided at the end of the booklet.

Multimedia CD-ROMs

Interactive CD-ROMs make it possible for students to experience directly some of the phenomena they are studying. The following CDs from Nelson provide a wealth of engaging modules and exercises.

PSYCHNOW! INTERACTIVE EXPERIENCES IN PSYCHOLOGY, VERSION 2.0   This highly interactive CD-ROM (ISBN: 0-534-59046-2) is perfectly matched to _Psychology: A_

Journey. At the end of each chapter of this text, students will find a list of *PsychNow!* modules they can access for additional, hands-on learning experiences.

PSYCHNOW! provides a dynamic multimedia experience that goes beyond the boundaries of the classroom, allowing students to explore psychology like never before. Stunning graphics and animations, interesting video clips, interactive exercises, and Web links bring psychology to life. With *PsychNow!*, students can do more than just read about a topic—they can read, watch, listen, react, and reflect on the meaning of their own responses. *PsychNow!*, which is available for Macintosh and Windows, contains fully interactive modules that pique students' curiosity and enhance their understanding.

PSYK.TREK 2.0: A MULTIMEDIA INTRODUCTION TO PSYCHOLOGY   This student tutorial CD-ROM for Windows and Macintosh (ISBN: 0-534-37062-4) is organized in 62 individual learning modules that parallel the core content of any introductory psychology course. Students using *Psyk.trek* will find studying fun, as they create illusions, run simulated experiments, view videos, and quiz themselves on the content of the introductory psychology course. *Psyk.trek* also includes an interactive study guide and a multimedia glossary with an audio pronunciation guide.

SNIFFY™ THE VIRTUAL RAT, LITE VERSION   There's no better way to master the basic principles of learning than working with a real laboratory rat. However, this is usually impractical in introductory psychology courses. *Sniffy the Virtual Rat* offers a fun, interactive alternative to working with lab animals. This innovative and entertaining software teaches students about operant and classical conditioning by allowing them to condition a virtual rat. Users begin by training Sniffy to press a bar to obtain food. Then they progress to studying the effects of reinforcement schedules and simple classical conditioning. In addition, special Mind Windows enable students to visualize how Sniffy's experiences in the Skinner Box produce learning. The Sniffy CD-ROM includes a Lab Manual that shows students how to set up various operant and classical conditioning experiments. *Sniffy™ the Virtual Rat, Lite Version,* may be packaged with this text for a discount (dual-platform CD-ROM, ISBN: 0-534-35869-1).

Internet Resources

The Internet is providing new ways to exchange information and enhance education. In psychology, Nelson is at the forefront in making use of this exciting technology.

INFOTRAC COLLEGE EDITION   *InfoTrac* is a powerful online learning resource, consisting of thousands of full-text articles from hundreds of journals and periodicals. Students using *Psychology: A Journey* receive four months of free access to the *InfoTrac College Edition* database. By doing a simple keyword search, students quickly generate a list of relevant articles from thousands of possibilities. Then they select full-text articles to read, explore, and print for reference or further study. *InfoTrac's* continually updated collection of articles can be useful for doing reading and writing assignments that reach beyond the pages of this text.

BOOK-SPECIFIC WEBSITE   As users of this text, you and your students have access to the *Psychology: A Journey* website (www.psychologyjourney.nelson.com). This Internet site includes the following features for instructors and students: online quizzes, interactive activities; links to relevant sites, Hot Topics, the Research and Teaching Showcase, and a downloadable Statistics Appendix in PDF format.

THOMSON WEB TUTOR   This online supplement helps students succeed by taking them into an environment rich with study and mastery tools, communication aids, and additional course content. For students, *Web Tutor* offers real-time access to a full array of study tools, including flashcards, quizzes and tests, online tutorials, exercises, asynchronous discussion, a whiteboard, an integrated email system, and a full glossary. Students will also have integrated access to this text's free website and *InfoTrac College Edition.*

Professors can use *Web Tutor* to offer virtual office hours, to post syllabuses, to set up threaded discussions, to track student progress on quizzes, and more. You can customize the content of *Web Tutor* in any way you choose, including uploading images and other resources, adding Web links, and creating course-specific practice materials. (*Web Tutor* on *WebCT*, ISBN: 0-17-640547-X; *Web Tutor* on *Blackboard*, ISBN: 0-17-640551-8.)

Essential Teaching Resources

As every professor knows, teaching an introductory psychology course is a tremendous amount of work. The supplements listed here should not only make life easier for you, they should also make it possible for you to concentrate on the more creative and rewarding facets of teaching.

INSTRUCTOR'S RESOURCE MANUAL The *Instructor's Resource Manual* (ISBN: 0-17-640544-5), adapted by Jill Esmonde Moore of Georgian College, contains learning objectives, discussion topics, lecture enhancements, role-playing scenarios, supplemental activities, suggestions for further reading, *InfoTrac* search terms, Web links, and media suggestions. In addition, the *Instructor's Resource Manual* includes general teaching strategies, references, and other helpful materials, such as handout masters. The manual's *Resource Integration Guide* will help you coordinate the many teaching and learning supplements available for this text.

MULTIMEDIA MANAGER FOR INTRODUCTORY PSYCHOLOGY: A MICROSOFT® POWERPOINT® LINK TOOL Free to adopters of this text, this CD-ROM presentation tool can be used to create engaging lectures that include art, graphics, CNN video clips, and animations. This one-stop, cross-platform lecture tool makes it easy to assemble, edit, publish, and present custom lectures for your introductory psychology course. Created by Joe Mior at Sir Sandford Fleming College, *Multimedia Manager for Introductory Psychology* utilizes Microsoft *PowerPoint* to let you bring together lecture outlines, graphics from many sources, and your own material—culminating in powerful, personalized, media-enhanced presentations (ISBN: 0-534-58025-4).

TEST BANK The printed *Test Bank* (ISBN: 0-17-640543-3), adapted by Jill Esmonde Moore and Tom Hanrahan (Canadore College), includes over 2500 multiple-choice questions organized by chapter and by Learning Objectives. All items are classified as factual, conceptual, or applied, and all include correct answers and page references from the text. To encourage students to study, 20 items per chapter in the *Test Bank* are drawn from Knowledge Builders in the text, the printed *Study Guide,* online Web quizzes, and the CD-ROM that accompanies this text. Every chapter of the *Test Bank* also includes 20 fill-in-the-blank and 20 essay/short-answer questions, with model answers.

MICROTEST III COMPUTERIZED TESTING All questions from the printed test items in Windows and Mac formats. MicroTest III allows instructors to create, deliver, and customize tests (both in print and online) in minutes with this easy-to-use assessment and tutorial system (ISBN: 0-17-640546-1).

INSTRUCTOR'S RESOURCE MANUAL FOR PSYCHOLOGY: AN INTERACTIVE JOURNEY CD-ROM This manual provides all the information necessary to take full advantage of the CD-ROM that accompanies this text. The CD is already closely integrated with the text, which makes it easy for students to use. The resource manual gives additional suggestions about assignments, how to incorporate the CD into your course, and how to use email to monitor students' work (ISBN: 0-534-56877-7).

TRANSPARENCY ACETATES Approximately 100 text-specific transparencies make it easy to display tables, graphs, charts, and drawings from this text—most of them in colour (ISBN: 0-17-640548-8).

Videotapes and Films

Nelson offers a variety of videotapes and films to enhance classroom presentations. Many video segments in this collection pertain directly to major topics in this text, making them excellent lecture supplements.

NELSON FILM AND VIDEO LIBRARY FOR INTRODUCTORY PSYCHOLOGY   Adopters can select from a variety of continually updated film and video options, including the exclusive CNN offerings described below. Contact your Nelson sales representative for details.

CNN TODAY **VIDEOS FOR INTRODUCTORY PSYCHOLOGY**   These one- to four-minute video clips, a Nelson exclusive, allow you to integrate the news-gathering and programming power of CNN into the classroom to show students the relevance of psychology to daily life. Organized by course topics, these compelling clips are ideal for launching lectures and encouraging discussion. Adopters receive one new, updated video each year.

Topics covered in the videos include: the brain, genetic mapping, sensation and perception, variations in consciousness, learning, human memory, language and thought, intelligence and psychological testing, gender and sexuality, diversity, human development, stress, health, psychological disorders, mental health, therapies, social behaviour, and more.

> *CNN Today: Introductory Psychology, Volume I* (ISBN: 0-534-36634-1)
> *CNN Today: Introductory Psychology, Volume II* (ISBN: 0-534-50420-5)
> *CNN Today: Introductory Psychology, Volume III* (ISBN: 0-534-50749-2)
> *CNN Today: Introductory Psychology, Volume IV* (ISBN: 0-534-50751-4)

THE BRAIN VIDEO, SECOND EDITION   Updated and expanded teaching modules from *The Brain* series offer your students extensive new footage of research into the inner workings of the brain. Segments cover the latest findings on Alzheimer's disease, schizophrenia, autism, Parkinson's disease, and many other topics. These modules can enhance classroom lectures on topics found throughout the introductory course, not just in the realm of biopsychology.

PSYCHOLOGY/CAREERS FOR THE TWENTY-FIRST CENTURY VIDEO   An exclusive agreement with the American Psychological Association provides this dynamic 13-minute video free to adopters of *Psychology: A Journey.* The video gives students an overview of the emerging growth opportunities in the field of psychology and advice on how to choose a career path (ISBN: 0-534-34293-0).

Summary

We sincerely hope that teachers and students will consider this book and its supporting materials a refreshing change from the ordinary. Creating it has been quite an adventure. In the pages that follow, we think students will find an attractive blend of the theoretical and the practical, plus many of the most exciting ideas in psychology. Most of all, we hope that students using this book discover that reading a college textbook can be entertaining and enjoyable.

▶ Acknowledgments

Psychology is a cooperative effort requiring the talents and energies of a large community of scholars, teachers, researchers, and students. Like most endeavours in psychology, this book reflects the efforts of many people.

To all the professional reviewers who gave their time and expertise we extend our sincere thanks. We wish to thank the following reviewers, whose sage advice helped make this concise, interactive text a reality: Tom Hanrahan, Canadore College; Joseph Mior, Sir Sandford Fleming College; Jill Esmonde Moore, Georgian College; Jean Brown, Cambrian College; David English, Durham College; John Jacquemain, Georgian College; Paul Johnson, Confederation College; Neil McGrenaghan, Humber College; Louis Pinel, Algonquin College; R. Bruce Tallon, Niagara College; and Mark Cummins, Dawson College.

Producing the first Canadian edition of *Psychology: A Journey* and its supplements was a formidable task, requiring the work of many talented people. We are especially indebted to Dennis Coon and the talented individuals at Wadsworth who collaborated to produce the original text on which this edition is based.

I would like to thank Joanna Cotton, Joanne Sutherland, and Pamela Duprey, all at Nelson, for inviting me to participate in this project and for not subsequently sticking pins in a voodoo doll with my face on it. It was a pleasure to work with them and with copy-editor Valerie Adams. I would also like to thank Louise and Stephanie for their unstinting support throughout this process.

Patrick Brown

First and foremost, my sincere thanks go to Linda Iarrera for helping to create the opportunity for me to be able to work on this book. Joanna Cotton, the Executive Editor at Nelson, deserves a special note of acknowledgment for believing in my abilities to take on this challenge. I would also like to thank Joanne Sutherland, the Senior Development Editor, for her tremendous patience and understanding. As I worked on the various drafts of the chapters, she was always there to answer my endless list of questions. Valerie Adams did an admirable job on the copy editing of the manuscript. My thanks also go to Bob Kohlmeier for making the proofreading process almost painless. Finally, a big thank-you to my family for putting up with my long absence as I prepared the manuscript during the winter and spring months of 2002.

Rajesh Malik

I am indebted to Joanne Sutherland and Joanna Cotton for support and encouragement throughout the process of preparing this Canadian adaptation. If good copy editors are worth their weight in rubies, Valerie Adams is a diamond; thank you for taking my words and making them clear and readable. And to my husband, Bob, special thanks for support, encouragement, and meals. This is the last time, I promise.

Sue McKenzie

And finally to our students—present, past, and future—this is really for you.

PSYCHOLOGY: THE SEARCH FOR UNDERSTANDING

Chapter 1

Psychologist's Journal

WHY STUDY PSYCHOLOGY?

(Dennis Coon) When I first meet someone, that person usually asks, "Why did you become a psychologist?" Because you and I are just getting acquainted, let me answer in this way:

You are a universe, a collection of worlds within worlds. Your brain is possibly the most complicated device in existence. Through its action you are capable of art, music, science, philosophy, love, hatred, and charity.

You are the most challenging riddle ever written, a mystery even to yourself at times. Your thoughts, emotions, and actions—and those of your family and friends—are the most fascinating subject I can imagine. I chose to study psychology because everything of interest and importance in the world is ultimately related to human behaviour.

Look around you. Newspapers, radio, magazines, television, and the Internet are loaded with psychological information. Psychology is an ever-changing panorama of people and ideas. Really, you can't call yourself educated without knowing something about it. And, while we might envy those who have walked on the moon or explored the ocean's depths, the ultimate frontier still lies closer to home. What could be more fascinating than a journey of self-discovery?

As you read this book, think of it as a travel guide. Ultimately, each person's path through life is unique. Nevertheless, psychology can show you much about human behaviour, so you will better understand yourself and others. Your guide awaits you. We hope you enjoy the journey.

Survey Questions

- ■ What is psychology? What are its goals?
- ■ How did psychology emerge as a field of knowledge?
- ■ What are the major trends and specialties in psychology?
- ■ Why is the scientific method important to psychologists?
- ■ How do psychologists collect information?
- ■ How is an experiment performed?
- ■ What other research methods do psychologists use?
- ■ What is critical thinking?
- ■ How does psychology differ from false explanations of behaviour?
- ■ How good is psychological information found in popular media?

▶ Psychology—Spotlight on Behaviour

Survey Question:
■ What is psychology? What are its goals?

Psychology touches many areas of our lives. Psychology is about memory, stress, therapy, love, persuasion, hypnosis, perception, death, conformity, creativity, learning, personality, aging, intelligence, sexuality, emotion, happiness, and many more topics.

Psychology is both a science and a profession. Some psychologists are scientists who do research to create new knowledge. Others are teachers who pass this knowledge on to students. Still others apply psychology to solve problems in mental health, education, business, sports, law, and medicine (Meltzoff, 1998). Later we will return to the profession of psychology. For now, let's focus on how knowledge is created. Whether they work in a lab, a classroom, or a clinic, all psychologists rely on information gained from scientific research.

Defining Psychology

The word *psychology* comes from the roots *psyche,* which means "mind," and *logos,* meaning "knowledge or study." However, when was the last time you saw or touched a "mind"? Because the mind can't be studied directly, **psychology** is now defined as the scientific study of behaviour and mental processes.

What does behaviour refer to in the definition of psychology? Anything you do—eating, sleeping, talking, or sneezing—is a behaviour. So are dreaming, gambling, watching television, learning Spanish, basket weaving, and reading this book. Naturally, we are interested in **overt behaviours** (observable actions and responses). But psychologists also study **covert behaviours.** These are private, internal activities, such as thinking, remembering, and other mental events (Kelly & Saklofske, 1994).

Empiricism

At various times in the last 100 years, experts have made statements such as these: "Heavier-than-air flying machines are impossible," "Radio has no future," "X-rays are a hoax," and "Computers will never serve any practical purpose." Obviously, all of these statements eventually proved to be false.

Where human behaviour is concerned, self-appointed "authorities" are also often wrong. Because of this, psychologists have a special respect for **empirical evidence** (information gained from direct observation and measurement). When possible, we study behaviour directly, by collecting **data** (observed facts) (Kimble, 1989). This allows us to compare observations and draw valid conclusions. Would you say it's true, for instance, that "You can't teach an old dog new tricks"? Why argue about it? A psychologist could simply get ten "new" dogs, ten "used" dogs, and ten "old" dogs and then try to teach them all a new trick to find out!

Psychology The scientific study of human and animal behaviour.

Overt behaviour An action or response that is directly observable.

Covert behaviour A response that is internal or hidden from view.

Empirical evidence Facts or information based on direct observation or experience.

Data Observed facts or evidence (*data:* plural; *datum:* singular).

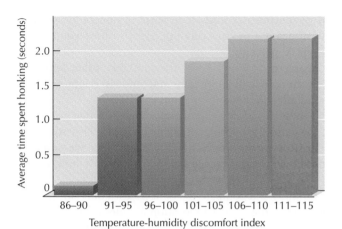

▶ Figure 1.1

Results of an empirical study. The graph shows that horn honking by frustrated motorists becomes more likely as air temperature increases. This suggests that physical discomfort is associated with interpersonal hostility. Riots and assaults also increase during hot weather. Here we see a steady rise in aggression as temperatures go higher. However, research done by other psychologists has shown that hostile actions that require physical exertion, such as a fistfight, may become less likely at very high temperatures. (Data from Kenrick & MacFarlane, 1986.)

Psychologists are highly trained professionals. In addition to the psychological knowledge they possess, psychologists learn specialized skills in counselling and therapy, measurement and testing, research and experimentation, statistics, diagnosis, treatment, and many other areas.

Scientific observation An empirical investigation that is structured to answer questions about the world.
Research method A systematic approach to answering scientific questions.

Basically, the empirical approach says, "Let's take a look" (Stanovich, 1998). Have you ever wondered if drivers become more hostile when it's blazing hot outside? Douglas Kenrick and Steven MacFarlane (1986) decided to find out. They parked a car at a green light in a one-lane intersection, in Phoenix, Arizona, in temperatures ranging from 88° to 116°F. Then they recorded the number of times other drivers honked at the stalled car, and how long they honked. The results are shown in ▶ Figure 1.1. Notice that when it was very hot, drivers spent more time leaning on the horn (which may be why cars have horns and not cannons).

Isn't the outcome of this study fairly predictable? In many studies, the results are surprising or unexpected. In this instance, you may have guessed how drivers would react. However, it's possible that drivers would become lethargic in hot weather, not more aggressive. Thus, the study tells us something interesting about frustration, discomfort, and aggression.

Psychological Research

Many fields, such as history, law, art, and business, are interested in human behaviour. How is psychology different? The great strength of psychology is that it applies the scientific method to study behaviour. True **scientific observation** is structured so that it answers questions about the world (Stanovich, 1998). This is also what separates scientific psychology from the "pop" psychology found in trendy books and magazines.

Sometimes ethical or practical concerns make it impossible to study a topic. More often, questions go unanswered for lack of a suitable **research method** (a systematic procedure for answering scientific questions). For example, at one time we believed people who said they never dreamed. Then the EEG (electroencephalograph, or brain-wave machine) was developed. Certain EEG patterns, and the presence of eye movements, can reveal when a person is dreaming. People who "never dream," it turns out, dream frequently. If they are awakened during a dream they vividly remember it. Thus, the EEG (see ▶ Figure 1.2) helped make the study of dreaming more scientific.

What kinds of topics do research psychologists study? Here's a sample of what various research psychologists might say about their work.

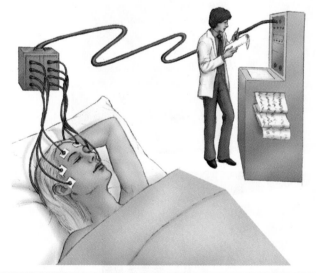

▶ Figure 1.2

The scientific study of dreaming was made possible by use of the EEG, a device that records the tiny electrical potentials generated by the brain as a person sleeps. The EEG converts these electrical signals to a written record of brain activity. Certain shifts in brain activity, coupled with the presence of rapid eye movements, are strongly related to dreaming. (See Chapter 5 for more information.)

Developmental psychologist
A psychologist interested in human growth and development from birth until death.

Learning theorist
A psychologist interested in variables affecting learning and in theories of learning.

Personality theorist
A psychologist who studies personality traits, dynamics, and theories.

Sensation and perception psychologist
A psychologist who studies the sense organs and the process of perception.

Comparative psychologist
A psychologist primarily interested in studying and comparing the behaviour of different species, especially animals.

Biopsychologist
A psychologist who studies the relationship between behaviour and biological processes, especially activity in the nervous system.

Social psychologist
A psychologist particularly interested in human social behaviour.

Cultural psychologist
A psychologist who studies the ways in which culture affects human behaviour.

"In general, **developmental psychologists** study the course of human growth and development, from conception until death. I'm especially interested in how young children develop the ability to think, speak, perceive, and act."

"I'm also interested in how people get to be the way they are. Like other **learning theorists,** I study how and why learning occurs in humans and animals. Right now I'm investigating how patterns of reward affect learning in pigeons."

"I'm a **personality theorist.** I study personality traits, motivation, and individual differences. I am especially interested in the personality profiles of highly creative college students."

"As a **sensation and perception psychologist,** I investigate how we come to know the world through our senses. I am using a perceptual theory to study how we are able to recognize faces."

"**Comparative psychologists** study and compare the behaviour of different species, especially animals. Personally, I'm fascinated by the echolocation abilities of porpoises."

"**Biopsychologists** are interested in how behaviour is related to biological processes, especially activities in the nervous system. I've been doing some exciting research on how the brain controls hunger."

"**Social psychologists** explore human social behaviour, such as attitudes, persuasion, riots, conformity, leadership, racism, and friendship. My own interest is interpersonal attraction. I place two strangers in a room and analyze how strongly they are attracted to each other."

"**Cultural psychologists** study the ways in which culture affects human behaviour. The language you speak, the foods you eat, how your parents disciplined you, what laws you obey, who you regard as 'family,' whether you eat with a spoon or your fingers—these and countless other details of behaviour are strongly influenced by culture."

This small sample should give you an idea of the diversity of psychological research. It also hints at some of the kinds of information we will cover later in this book.

The variety and complexity of human behaviour make psychological investigation challenging. How would you explain the behaviours shown here?

Some of the most interesting research with animals has focused on attempts to teach primates to communicate with sign language. Such research has led to better methods for teaching language to aphasic children (children with serious language impairment). (See Chapter 8 for more information.)

Animal model In research, an animal whose behaviour is used to discover principles that may apply to human behaviour.

Description In scientific research, the process of naming and classifying.

Understanding In psychology, understanding is achieved when the causes of a behaviour can be stated.

Prediction An ability to accurately forecast behaviour.

Control Altering conditions that influence behaviour in predictable ways.

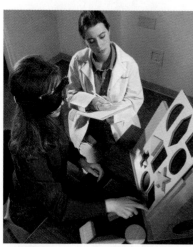

Some psychologists specialize in administering, scoring, and interpreting psychological tests, such as tests of intelligence, creativity, personality, or aptitude.

Animals and Psychology

Research involving animals was mentioned in some of the preceding examples. Why is that? It may surprise you to learn that psychologists are interested in the behaviour of any living creature—from flatworms to humans. Indeed, there are some comparative psychologists who have spent their entire careers studying rats, cats, dogs, turtles, or chimpanzees.

Animal models are used to discover principles that apply to human behaviour. Studying animals has helped us better understand obesity, memory, stress, psychosis, therapy, aging, and many other topics. Psychology also benefits animals. The care of endangered species in zoos, for example, relies on behavioural studies (Miller, 1985). Overall, about 8 percent of all psychological research is done with animals (McCarty, 1998).

Psychology's Goals

What do psychology's goals mean in practice? Assume that we would like to answer the following questions: What happens when the right side of the brain is injured? Is there more than one type of memory? Do autistic children react abnormally to their parents?

DESCRIPTION The answer to each of the preceding questions requires a careful description of behaviour. **Description,** or naming and classifying, is typically based on making a detailed record of behavioural observations.

But a description doesn't explain anything, does it? Right. Useful knowledge begins with accurate description, but descriptions fail to answer the important "why" questions. Why do more women attempt suicide, and why do more men complete it? Why are people more aggressive when they are uncomfortable? Why are bystanders often unwilling to help in an emergency?

UNDERSTANDING Psychology's second goal is met when we can explain an event. That is, **understanding** usually means we can state the causes of a behaviour. Take our last "why" question as an example: Research on "bystander apathy" has shown that people often fail to help when other possible helpers are nearby. Why? Because a "diffusion of responsibility" occurs. Basically, no one feels personally obligated to pitch in. Generally, the more potential helpers present, the less likely it is that help will be given (Darley & Latané, 1968). Now we can explain a perplexing problem.

PREDICTION Psychology's third goal, **prediction,** is the ability to forecast behaviour accurately. Notice that our explanation of bystander apathy makes a prediction about the chances of getting help. Anyone who has been stranded by car trouble on a busy freeway will recognize the accuracy of this prediction: Having many potential helpers nearby is no guarantee that anyone will stop to help.

CONTROL *Description, explanation, and prediction seem reasonable, but is control a valid goal for psychology?* Control may seem like a threat to your personal freedom. However, to a psychologist, **control** simply means altering conditions that influence behaviour in predictable ways. If someone suggests changes in a classroom that help children learn better, that person has exerted control. If a clinical psychologist helps a person overcome a terrible fear of heights, control is involved. Control is also an element of designing airplanes to reduce pilot errors. Clearly, psychology can change behaviour. However, psychological control must be used wisely and humanely (Kipnis, 1987).

In summary, psychology's goals are a natural outgrowth of our desire to understand behaviour. Basically, they boil down to asking the following questions:

- What is the nature of this behaviour? (description)
- Why does it occur? (understanding and explanation)
- Can we predict when it will occur? (prediction)
- What conditions affect it? (control)

Knowledge builder

THE SCIENCE OF PSYCHOLOGY

Relate

At first, many students think that psychology is primarily about abnormal behaviour and psychotherapy. Did you? How would you describe the field now?

Learning Check

To check your memory, see if you can answer these questions. If you miss any, skim over the preceding material before continuing, to make sure you understand what you just read.

1. Psychology is the _____ study of _____ and _____ processes.
2. Information gained through direct observation and measurement is called _____ evidence.
3. In psychological research, animal _____ may be used to discover principles that apply to human behaviour.
4. Which of the following questions relates most directly to the goal of understanding behaviour?
   a. Do the scores of men and women differ on tests of thinking abilities?
   b. Why does a blow to the head cause memory loss?
   c. Will productivity in a business office increase if room temperature is raised or lowered?
   d. What percentage of college students suffer from test anxiety?

Match the following research areas with the topics they cover.

_____ 5. Developmental psychology
_____ 6. Learning
_____ 7. Personality
_____ 8. Sensation and perception
_____ 9. Biopsychology
_____ 10. Social psychology
_____ 11. Comparative psychology

A. Attitudes, groups, leadership
B. Conditioning, memory
C. The psychology of law
D. Brain and nervous system
E. Child psychology
F. Individual differences, motivation
G. Animal behaviour
H. Processing sensory information

Critical Thinking

12. All sciences are interested in controlling the phenomena they study. T or F?

Answers:

1. scientific, behaviour, mental 2. empirical 3. models 4. b 5. E 6. B 7. F 8. H 9. D 10. A 11. G 12. False. Astronomy and archaeology are examples of sciences that do not share psychology's fourth goal.

▶ A Brief History of Psychology—Psychology's Family Album

Survey Question:
■ How did psychology emerge as a field of knowledge?

Stimulus Any physical energy that has some effect on an organism and that evokes a response.

Introspection To look within; to examine one's own thoughts, feelings, or sensations.

Psychology began centuries ago as a branch of philosophy, the study of knowledge, reality, and human nature. In many Canadian universities, psychology remained connected with philosophy departments until after World War II (Adair, Pavio, & Ritchie, 1996).

Psychology's history as a separate science began in 1879 in Leipzig, Germany. There, the "father of psychology," Wilhelm Wundt (VILL-helm Voont), set up the first psychological laboratory to study conscious experience. How, he wondered, do we form sensations, images, and feelings? To find out, Wundt observed and measured stimuli of various kinds (lights, sounds, weights). A **stimulus** is any physical energy that affects a person and evokes a response (stimulus: singular; stimuli [STIM-you-lie]: plural). Wundt then used **introspection,** or "looking inward," and careful measurement to probe his reactions to various stimuli. (If you stop reading right now and carefully examine your thoughts, feelings, and sensations, you will have done some introspecting.) Over the years, Wundt studied vision, hearing, taste, touch, memory, time perception, and many other subjects. By

Wilhelm Wundt, 1832–1920. Wundt is credited with making psychology an independent science, separate from philosophy. Wundt's original training was in medicine, but he became deeply interested in psychology. In his laboratory, Wundt investigated how sensations, images, and feelings combine to make up personal experience.

William James, 1842–1910. William James was the son of philosopher Henry James, Sr., and the brother of novelist Henry James. During his long academic career, James taught anatomy, physiology, psychology, and philosophy at Harvard University. James believed strongly that ideas should be judged in terms of their practical consequences for human conduct.

Structuralism The school of thought concerned with analyzing sensations and personal experience into basic elements.

Functionalism School of psychology concerned with how behaviour and mental abilities help people adapt to their environments.

Natural selection Darwin's theory that evolution favours those plants and animals best suited to their living conditions.

Behaviourism School of psychology that emphasizes the study of overt, observable behaviour.

Response Any muscular action, glandular activity, or other identifiable aspect of behaviour.

Conditioned response A reflex response that has become associated with a new stimulus.

insisting on careful observation and measurement, he answered some interesting questions and got psychology off to a good start.

Structuralism

Wundt's ideas were carried to North America by a man named Edward B. Titchener (TICH-in-er). Titchener called Wundt's ideas **structuralism** because they dealt with the structure of mental life. Essentially, the structuralists hoped to analyze experience into basic "elements" or "building blocks."

How could they do that? You can't analyze experience like a chemical compound, can you? Perhaps not, but the structuralists tried, mostly by using introspection. For instance, an observer might hold an apple and decide that she had experienced the elements "hue" (colour), "roundness," and "weight." Another example of the kind of question that might have interested a structuralist is, What basic tastes mix together to create complex flavours as different as liver, lime, bacon, and burnt-almond fudge?

It soon became clear that introspection was a poor way to answer many questions. Why? Because the structuralists frequently disagreed. And when they did, there was no way to settle differences. If two people came up with different lists of basic taste sensations, for example, who could say which was right? Despite such limitations, "looking inward" is still used in studies of hypnosis, meditation, problem solving, moods, and many other topics (Mayer & Hanson, 1995).

Functionalism

William James, an American scholar, broadened psychology to include animal behaviour, religious experience, abnormal behaviour, and other interesting topics. James's brilliant first book, *Principles of Psychology* (1890), helped establish the field as a serious discipline (Simon, 1998).

The term **functionalism** comes from an interest in how the mind functions to adapt us to our environment. James regarded consciousness as an ever-changing stream or flow of images and sensations—not a set of lifeless building blocks, as the structuralists claimed.

The functionalists admired Charles Darwin, who deduced that creatures evolve in ways that favour their survival. According to Darwin's principle of **natural selection,** physical features that help animals adapt to their environments are retained in evolution. Similarly, the functionalists wanted to find out how the mind, perception, habits, and emotions help us adapt and survive.

Behaviourism

Functionalism was soon challenged by **behaviourism,** the study of overt, observable behaviour. Behaviourist John B. Watson objected strongly to the study of the "mind" or "conscious experience." "Introspection," he said, "is unscientific." Watson realized that he could study animals even though he couldn't ask them questions, or know what they were thinking. He simply observed the relationship between stimuli (events in the environment) and an animal's **responses** (any muscular action, glandular activity, or other identifiable behaviour). Why not, he asked, apply the same objectivity to studying humans (Watson, 1994)?

Watson soon adopted Russian physiologist Ivan Pavlov's (ee-VAHN PAV-lahv) concept of conditioning to explain most behaviour. (A **conditioned response** is a learned reaction to a particular stimulus.) Watson enthusiastically proclaimed, "Give me a dozen healthy infants, well-formed, and my own special world to bring them up in and I'll guarantee to take any one at random and train him to become any type of specialist I might select—doctor, lawyer, artist, merchant-chief, and yes, beggarman and thief" (Watson, 1913).

John B. Watson, 1878–1958. Watson's intense interest in observable behaviour began with his doctoral studies in biology and neurology. Watson became a psychology professor at Johns Hopkins University in 1908 and advanced his theory of behaviourism. He remained at Johns Hopkins until 1920 when he left for a career in the advertising industry!

B. F. Skinner, 1904–1990. Skinner studied simple behaviours under carefully controlled conditions. The "Skinner box" you see here has been widely used to study learning in simplified animal experiments. In addition to advancing psychology, Skinner hoped that his radical brand of behaviourism would improve human life.

Cognitive behaviourism
An approach that combines behavioural principles with cognition (perception, thinking, anticipation) to explain behaviour.

Gestalt psychology
A school of psychology emphasizing the study of thinking, learning, and perception in whole units, not by analysis into parts.

Would most psychologists agree with Watson's claim? Today, most would consider it an overstatement. Just the same, behaviourism helped make psychology a natural science, rather than a branch of philosophy (Richelle, 1995).

One of the best-known modern behaviourists, B. F. Skinner (1904–1990), believed that our behaviour is controlled by rewards, or positive reinforcers. To study learning, Skinner created his famous conditioning chamber, or "Skinner box." With it, he could present stimuli to animals and record their responses (see Chapter 6, "Operant Conditioning"). Many of Skinner's ideas about learning grew out of work with rats and pigeons. Nevertheless, he believed that the same laws of behaviour apply to all organisms, including humans. As a "radical behaviourist," Skinner also believed that mental events are not needed to explain behaviour (Richelle, 1995).

Skinner was convinced that a "designed culture" based on positive reinforcement could encourage desirable behaviour. (Contrary to common belief, Skinner disliked the use of punishment.) It is essential, he said, to change our behaviour before overpopulation, pollution, or nuclear war shatters humanity. Too often, misguided rewards lead us into destructive actions.

COGNITIVE BEHAVIOURISM Strict behaviourists have been criticized for ignoring the role that thinking and other mental processes play in our lives. One critic even charged that Skinnerian psychology had "lost consciousness!" However, many criticisms have been answered by **cognitive behaviourism,** a view that combines cognition (thinking) and conditioning to explain behaviour (Sperry, 1995). For example, let's say you frequently visit a particular website because it offers free games. A behaviourist would say that you visit the site because you are rewarded by the pleasure of game playing each time you go there. A cognitive behaviourist would say that, in addition, you expect to find free games at the site. This is the cognitive component of your behaviour. Behaviourists deserve credit for much of what we know about learning, conditioning, and the proper use of reward and punishment.

Gestalt Psychology

Imagine that you just played "Happy Birthday" on a tuba. Next, you play it on a high-pitched violin. None of the tuba's sounds are duplicated by the violin. Yet, we notice something interesting: The melody is still completely recognizable—as long as the relationship between notes remains the same.

Now, what would happen if you played the notes of "Happy Birthday" in the correct order, but at a rate of one per hour? What would we have? Nothing! The separate notes would no longer be a melody. Perceptually, the melody is somehow more than the individual notes that define it.

It was observations like these that launched the Gestalt school of thought. **Gestalt psychologists** studied thinking, learning, and perception in whole units, not by analyzing experiences into parts. Their slogan was, "The whole is greater than the sum of its parts." (See ►Figure 1.3.)

►**Figure 1.3**

The design you see here is entirely made up of the two elements shown below it. If you stare at the design for a moment, you should quickly see that as a whole it contains patterns and complexities that greatly exceed the sum of its parts.

Max Wertheimer, 1880–1941. Wertheimer first proposed the Gestalt viewpoint to help explain perceptual illusions. He later promoted Gestalt psychology as a way to understand not only perception, problem solving, thinking, and social behaviour, but also art, logic, philosophy, and politics.

Unconscious The region of the mind that is beyond awareness—especially impulses and desires not directly known to a person.

Max Wertheimer (VERT-hi-mer), a German psychologist, was the first person to advance the Gestalt viewpoint. It is a mistake, he said, to analyze psychological events into pieces, or "elements," as the structuralists did. Like a melody, many experiences cannot be broken into smaller units. For this reason, studies of perception and personality have been especially influenced by the Gestalt viewpoint.

Were all the early psychologists men? So far, no women have been mentioned. For the most part, men dominated science and education at the beginning of the 20th century. Nevertheless, women have contributed to psychology from the beginning (Minton, 2000). Take a moment and read "Women in Psychology" for more information.

Psychoanalytic Psychology

As psychology grew more scientific, an Austrian doctor named Sigmund Freud was developing his own theories. Freud believed that mental life is like an iceberg: Only a small part is exposed to view. He called the area of the mind that lies outside of personal awareness the **unconscious.** According to Freud, our behaviour is deeply influenced by unconscious thoughts, impulses, and desires—especially those concerning sex and aggression. Freud's ideas opened new horizons in art, literature, and history, as well as psychology (Robins, Gosling, & Craik, 1998).

Sigmund Freud, 1856–1939. For over 50 years, Freud probed the unconscious mind. In doing so, he altered modern views of human nature. His early experimentation with a "talking cure" for hysteria is regarded as the beginning of psychoanalysis. Through psychoanalysis, Freud added psychological treatment methods to psychiatry.

HUMAN DIVERSITY   Women in Psychology

Women were actively discouraged from seeking advanced degrees in the late 1800s (Bohan, 1990). Even so, by 1906 in the United States about one psychologist in every ten was a woman. Who were these "foremothers" of psychology? Three who became well known are Mary Calkins, Christine Ladd-Franklin, and Margaret Washburn.

Mary Calkins did valuable research on memory. She was also the first woman president of the American Psychological Association, in 1905. Christine Ladd-Franklin studied colour vision. In 1906 she was ranked as one of the 50 most important psychologists in the United States.

In 1908, Margaret Washburn published an influential textbook on animal behaviour titled *The Animal Mind.*

The first woman to be awarded a Ph.D. in psychology was Margaret Washburn, in 1894. Over the next 15 years, many more women followed her pioneering lead. Today, two out of three graduate students in psychology are women. And, in recent years, nearly 75 percent of all college graduates with a major in psychology have been women. Clearly, psychology has become fully open to both men and women.

(Sources: Furumoto & Scarborough, 1986; Howard et al., 1986; Madigan & O'Hara, 1992; Martin, 1995.)

Mary Calkins, 1863–1930.

Christine Ladd-Franklin, 1847–1930.

Margaret Washburn, 1871–1939.

Table 1.1
The Early Development of Psychology

DATE	NOTABLE EVENTS
1875	• First psychology course offered by William James at Harvard University
1878	• First American Ph.D. in psychology awarded
1879	• Wilhelm Wundt establishes first psychology laboratory in Germany
1883	• First American psychology laboratory founded at Johns Hopkins University
1885	• First Canadian psychology textbook published by the Rev. William Lyall
1886	• First American psychology textbook published by John Dewey
1890	• James publishes *Principles of Psychology*
1891	• James Mark Badwin establishes the first psychology laboratory at the University of Toronto
1892	• American Psychological Association founded
1895	• Sigmund Freud publishes first studies
1898	• Edward Titchener advances psychology based on introspection
1900	• Freud publishes *The Interpretation of Dreams*
1906	• Ivan Pavlov reports his research on conditioning
1912	• Max Wertheimer and others advance Gestalt viewpoint
1913	• John Watson presents behaviouristic view
1939	• Canadian Psychological Association founded
1968	• Mary Wright elected first woman president of the Canadian Psychological Association

Repression
The unconscious process by which memories, thoughts, or impulses are held out of awareness.

Psychoanalysis
A Freudian approach to psychotherapy emphasizing the exploration of unconscious conflicts.

Psychodynamic theory
Any theory of behaviour that emphasizes internal conflicts, motives, and unconscious forces.

Humanism An approach to psychology that focuses on human experience, problems, potentials, and ideals.

Determinism The idea that all behaviour has prior causes that would completely explain one's choices and actions if all such causes were known.

Free will The idea that human beings are capable of freely making choices or decisions.

Freud theorized that many unconscious thoughts are threatening; hence, they are **repressed** (held out of awareness). But sometimes, he said, they are revealed by dreams, emotions, or slips of the tongue. ("Freudian slips" are often humorous, as when a student who is tardy for class says, "I'm sorry I couldn't get here any later.")

Freud believed that all thoughts, emotions, and actions are determined. In other words, nothing is an accident: If we probe deeply enough we will find the causes of every thought or action. Freud was also among the first to appreciate that childhood affects adult personality ("The child is father to the man"). Most of all, perhaps, Freud is known for creating **psychoanalysis,** the first "talking therapy." Freud's method of psychotherapy explores unconscious conflicts and emotional problems (see Chapter 13). Today, his ideas have been altered so much that few strictly psychoanalytic psychologists are left. However, Freud's legacy is still evident in various **psychodynamic theories,** which emphasize internal motives, conflicts, and unconscious forces (Westen, 1998).

Humanistic Psychology

Humanism is a view that focuses on understanding subjective human experience. As a group, humanistic psychologists are interested in human problems, potentials, and ideals.

How is the humanistic approach different from others? Carl Rogers, Abraham Maslow, and other humanists rejected the Freudian idea that personality is ruled by unconscious forces. They were also uncomfortable with the behaviourist emphasis on environmental control. Both views have a strong undercurrent of **determinism** (the idea that behaviour is determined by forces beyond our control). In contrast, the humanists stress **free will,** the ability to make voluntary choices.

Abraham Maslow, 1908–1970. As a founder of humanistic psychology, Maslow was interested in studying people of exceptional mental health. Such self-actualized people, he believed, make full use of their talents and abilities. Maslow offered his positive view of human potential as an alternative to the schools of behaviourism and psychoanalysis.

Self-image Total subjective perception of oneself.

Self-evaluation Positive and negative feelings held toward oneself.

Frame of reference A mental perspective used for judging and evaluating events.

Self-actualization The process of fully developing one's personal potential.

Of course, past experiences affect us. Nevertheless, humanists believe that people can freely choose to live more creative, meaningful, and satisfying lives.

Humanists helped stimulate interest in psychological needs for love, self-esteem, belonging, self-expression, creativity, and spirituality. Such needs, they believe, are as important as our biological urges for food and water. For example, newborn infants deprived of human love may die just as surely as they would if deprived of food.

How scientific is the humanistic approach? Humanists collect data and seek evidence to support their ideas. However, they tend to be less interested in treating psychology as an objective, behavioural science. Instead, they stress subjective factors, such as one's self-image, self-evaluation, and frame of reference. **Self-image** is your perception of your own body, personality, and capabilities. **Self-evaluation** refers to the positive and negative feelings you have about yourself. A **frame of reference** is a mental or emotional perspective used for evaluating events. Thus, humanists seek to understand how people perceive themselves and experience the world.

Maslow's concept of self-actualization is a special feature of humanism. **Self-actualization** refers to developing one's potential fully and becoming the best person possible. According to humanists, everyone has this potential. Humanists seek ways to help it emerge.

▶ Psychology Today—Five Views of Behaviour

Survey Question:
■ What are the major trends and specialties in psychology?

At one time, loyalty to each school of thought was fierce, and clashes were common. Today, viewpoints such as functionalism and Gestalt psychology have blended into newer, broader perspectives. Also, some early systems, such as structuralism, have disappeared entirely. Certainly, loyalties and specialties still exist. But today, many psychologists are *eclectic* (ek-LEK-tik: They draw from many sources and embrace a variety of theories). Even so, five major perspectives shape modern psychology. These are the psychodynamic, behaviouristic, and humanistic views, plus the increasingly important biopsychological and cognitive perspectives (see Table 1.2) (Robins, Gosling, & Craik, 1999).

Table 1.2
Five Ways to Look at Behaviour

PSYCHODYNAMIC VIEW
Key Idea: *Behaviour is directed by forces within one's personality that are often hidden or unconscious.* Emphasizes internal impulses, desires, and conflicts—especially those that are unconscious; views behaviour as the result of clashing forces within personality; somewhat negative, pessimistic view of human nature.
BEHAVIOURISTIC VIEW
Key Idea: *Behaviour is shaped and controlled by one's environment.* Emphasizes the study of observable behaviour and the effects of learning; stresses the influence of external rewards and punishments; neutral, scientific, somewhat mechanistic view of human nature.
HUMANISTIC VIEW
Key Idea: *Behaviour is guided by one's self-image, by subjective perceptions of the world, and by needs for personal growth.* Focuses on subjective, conscious experience, human problems, potentials, and ideals; emphasizes self-image and self-actualization to explain behaviour; positive, philosophical view of human nature.
BIOPSYCHOLOGICAL VIEW
Key Idea: *Human and animal behaviour is the result of internal physical, chemical, and biological processes.* Seeks to explain behaviour through activity of the brain and nervous system, physiology, genetics, the endocrine system, biochemistry, and evolution; neutral, reductionistic, mechanistic view of human nature.
COGNITIVE VIEW
Key Idea: *Much human behaviour can be understood in terms of the mental processing of information.* Concerned with thinking, knowing, perception, understanding, memory, decision making, and judgment; explains behaviour in terms of information processing; neutral, somewhat computer-like view of human nature.

Donald O. Hebb (1904–1985). Born in Nova Scotia, Hebb received a B.A. from Dalhousie University and worked as a school principal while studying for a M.A. at McGill. After receiving a Ph.D. from Harvard, he worked at the Montreal Neurological Institute and Queen's University before returning to McGill as a Professor of Psychology. His book *The Organization of Behavior* (1949) paved the way for the current emphasis on understanding the brain. His ideas continue to have a major influence on both cognitive psychology and cognitive neuropsychology.

Biopsychology is a fast-growing area. Eventually, biopsychologists expect to explain all behaviour in terms of physical mechanisms, such as brain activity and genetics. Their optimism is based on exciting new insights about how the brain relates to thinking, feelings, perception, abnormal behaviour, and other topics (Robins, Gosling, & Craik, 1998).

Cognitive science is another rapidly expanding area. In fact, over the last 10 years, a "cognitive revolution" has taken place in psychology. Cognition means "thinking" or "knowing." **Cognitive psychologists** study thoughts, expectations, memory, language, perception, problem solving, consciousness, creativity, and other mental processes. With all this renewed interest in thinking, it could be said that psychology recently "regained consciousness" (Robins, Gosling, & Craik, 1999).

Cognitive psychology
The area of psychology concerned with human thinking and information processing.

SUMMARY As you can see, it is helpful to view human behaviour from more than one perspective. This is also true in another sense. We are rapidly becoming a multicultural society, made up of people from many different nations. How has this affected psychology? The next section explains why it is important for all of us to be aware of cultural differences.

▶ Human Diversity—Appreciating Social and Cultural Differences

Jerry, whose parents came to Canada from Japan, is married to Anne, whose family arrived in Quebec during the Irish potato famine. They live in Vancouver with their children. Last year, this is how they spent New Year's Day.

> We woke up in the morning and went to Mass at St. Brigid's, which has a gospel choir. . . . Then we went to the Japanese Community Centre for the Oshogatsu New Year's program and saw Buddhist archers shoot arrows to ward off evil spirits for the year. Next, we ate traditional rice cakes as part of the New Year's service and listened to a young storyteller who was visiting from Japan. On the way home, we stopped in Chinatown for tea and after that we ate poutine. (adapted from Njeri, 1991)

Jerry and his family reflect the Canadian social reality: Cultural diversity is the norm. According to the 1996 census, in Vancouver, more people listed their origin as east or southeast Asian than as European (Statistics Canada, 2002, June 18).

The Impact of Culture

In the past, psychology was based mostly on the cultures of North America and Europe. Now, we must ask, Do the principles of Western psychology apply to people in all cultures? Are some psychological concepts invalid in other cultures? Are any universal? As psychologists have probed such questions, one thing has become clear: Most of what we think, feel, and do is influenced in one way or another by the social and cultural worlds in which we live (Segall, Lonner, & Berry, 1998).

Cultural relativity The idea that behaviour must be judged relative to the values of the culture in which it occurs.

Norms Rules that define acceptable and expected behaviour for members of a group.

CULTURAL RELATIVITY   Imagine that you are a psychologist. Your client, Linda, who is a Native Canadian, tells you that spirits live in the trees near her home. Is Linda suffering from a delusion? Is she abnormal? Obviously, you will misjudge Linda's mental health if you fail to take her cultural beliefs into account. **Cultural relativity** (the idea that behaviour must be judged relative to the values of the culture in which it occurs) can greatly affect the diagnosis of mental disorders (Alarcon, 1995). Cases like Linda's teach us to be wary of using inappropriate standards when judging others or comparing groups.

A BROADER VIEW OF DIVERSITY   In addition to cultural differences, age, ethnicity, gender, religion, disability, and sexual orientation all affect the **norms** that guide behaviour. (Norms are rules that define acceptable and expected behaviour for members of various groups.) All too often, the unstated standard for judging what is "average," "normal," or "correct" is the behaviour of white, middle-class males. To fully understand human behaviour, psychologists need to know how people differ, as well as the ways in which we are all alike. For the same reason, an appreciation of human diversity can enrich your life,

Knowledge builder

HISTORY AND MAJOR PERSPECTIVES

Relate

Which school of thought most closely matches your own view of behaviour? Do you think any of the early schools offers a complete explanation of why we behave as we do? What about the five contemporary perspectives? Can you explain why so many psychologists are eclectic?

Learning Check

Match:

_____ **1.** Philosophy

_____ **2.** Wundt

_____ **3.** Structuralism

_____ **4.** Functionalism

_____ **5.** Behaviourism

_____ **6.** Gestalt

_____ **7.** Psychodynamic

A. Against analysis; studied whole experiences

B. "Mental chemistry" and introspection

C. Emphasizes self-actualization and personal growth

D. Interested in unconscious causes of behaviour

E. Interested in how the mind aids survival

F. First woman Ph.D. in psychology

G. Studied stimuli and responses, conditioning

_____ **8.** Humanistic

_____ **9.** Cognitive

_____ **10.** Washburn

_____ **11.** Biopsychology

H. Part of psychology's "long past"

I. Concerned with thinking, language, problem solving

J. Used introspection and careful measurement

K. Relates behaviour to the brain, physiology, and genetics

L. Also known as engineering psychology

12. Cultural relativity refers to the fact that some universal behaviour patterns are not related to culture. T or F?

13. Universal norms exist for judging the behaviour of people in various cultural and social groups. T or F?

Critical Thinking

14. Modern sciences like psychology are built on observations that can be verified by two or more independent observers. Did structuralism meet this standard? Why or why not?

Answers:

1. H 2. J 3. B 4. E 5. G 6. A 7. D 8. C 9. I 10. F 11. K 12. F 13. F 14. No, it did not. The downfall of structuralism was that each observer examined the contents of his or her own mind—which is something that no other person can observe.

as well as your understanding of psychology (additional sources: Denmark, 1994; Graham, 1992; Sampson, 1993; Shweder, 1999; Tomes, 1998).

In a moment, we will further explore what psychologists do. First, here are some questions to enhance your learning.

▶ Psychologists—Guaranteed Not to Shrink

QUESTION: *What is the difference between a psychologist and a psychiatrist?*

ANSWER: *About $30 an hour. (And going up.)*

In the film *Good Will Hunting*, Robin Williams plays a psychologist who physically assaults a defiant patient played by Matt Damon. Such dramatic scenes are typical of the way psychologists and psychotherapy are misrepresented in the media.

What are the differences among various kinds of mental health professionals? Certainly, they're not all "shrinks." Each has a specific blend of training and skills.

A **psychologist** is highly trained in the methods, factual knowledge, and theories of psychology. Psychologists usually have a master's degree or a doctorate. These degrees typically require from three to eight years of postgraduate training. Psychologists may teach, do research, give psychological tests, or serve as consultants to business, industry, government, or the military. In most industrialized nations, the number of professional psychologists continues to grow (Rosenzweig, 1999).

Public impressions of psychologists are often inaccurate. Perhaps this occurs because so many stereotyped images appear in movies and on television. For example, in the film *Good Will Hunting*, a psychologist angrily chokes his rebellious young patient. No ethical therapist would ever engage in such behaviour, yet it is not unusual in the movies. Such characters may be dramatic and entertaining, but they seriously distort public perceptions of responsible and hardworking psychologists (Sleek, 1998).

Even without media distortions, misconceptions about psychologists and what they do are common. In reality, not all psychologists are therapists in private practice. They are also employed by schools, businesses, governments, and social agencies.

One public perception of psychologists is accurate: Most do help people in one way or another. Psychologists interested in emotional problems specialize in clinical or counselling psychology. **Clinical psychologists** treat psychological problems or do research on psychotherapy and mental disorders. **Counselling psychologists** treat milder emotional and behavioural disturbances. Counselling psychology used to be limited to problems such as poor adjustment at work or school. Now, many counselling psychologists are doing psychotherapy. As a result, differences between counselling and clinical psychology are beginning to fade.

To enter the profession of psychology, it is best to have a doctorate (Ph.D. or Ed.D.). Many clinical psychologists hold a Ph.D. degree and follow a **scientist-practitioner model,** in which they are trained to do either scientific research or therapy (O'Sullivan & Quevillon, 1992). Many do both. The Psy.D. (Doctor of Psychology) degree, which emphasizes therapy skills rather than research, is not currently offered at any Canadian universities, but in 1998 the Canadian Psychological Association established a task force to study the possibility of offering this degree.

Other Mental Health Professionals

A **psychiatrist** is a medical doctor who specializes in treating mental disorders. Most psychiatrists are "talking doctors" who primarily do psychotherapy. However, they may also prescribe drugs, which is something a psychologist cannot do (Foxhall, 1999).

To be a **psychoanalyst,** you must have a moustache and goatee, spectacles, a German accent, and a well-padded couch—or so the TV and movie stereotype goes. Actually, to become a psychoanalyst, you must have an M.D. or Ph.D. degree plus further specialized training in the theory and practice of Freudian psychoanalysis. In other words, either a physician or a psychologist may become an analyst by completing more training in a specific type of psychotherapy.

Psychologist A person highly trained in the methods, factual knowledge, and theories of psychology.

Clinical psychologist A psychologist who specializes in the treatment of psychological and behavioural disturbances or who does research on such disturbances.

Counselling psychologist A psychologist who specializes in the treatment of milder emotional and behavioural disturbances.

Scientist-practitioner model A view that holds that clinical psychologists should be skilled both as scientists and as therapists.

Psychiatrist A medical doctor with additional training in the diagnosis and treatment of mental and emotional disorders.

Psychoanalyst A mental health professional (usually a medical doctor) trained to practise psychoanalysis.

Counsellor A mental health professional who specializes in helping people with problems not involving serious mental disorder (e.g., marriage counsellors, career counsellors, or school counsellors).

Psychiatric social worker A mental health professional trained to apply social science principles to help patients in clinics and hospitals.

Psychiatric nurse A nurse with specialized training in mental health.

Basic research Scientific study undertaken without concern for immediate practical application.

Applied research Scientific study undertaken to solve immediate practical problems.

Counsellors may also do mental health work. A **counsellor** is an adviser who helps solve problems with marriage, career, school, work, or the like. Counsellors may be trained in practical helping skills, and may do family or sex therapy, for example, but generally do not treat serious mental health problems and they may not practise as "psychologists." The term "psychologist" is reserved for people licensed in their province or territory to practise psychology. Different provinces require different levels of education for licensing: doctoral degrees are required in British Columbia and Saskatchewan, while all other provinces and the Northwest Territories require at least a masters degree in psychology or a related field. Most provinces also require a period of supervised practical training, with the length of training depending on whether the person has a masters or doctoral degree.

Psychiatric social workers and psychiatric nurses play an important role in many mental health programs. **Psychiatric social workers** apply social science principles to help patients in clinics and hospitals. Many social workers hold an M.S.W. (Master of Social Work). **Psychiatric nurses** may also provide counselling and other mental health services, in addition to nursing care. Both social workers and nurses may assist psychologists and psychiatrists as part of a team. Their typical duties include evaluating patients and families, conducting group psychotherapy, or visiting a patient's home, school, or job to alleviate problems.

Specialties in Psychology

Do all psychologists do therapy and treat abnormal behaviour? No. Although many are clinical and counselling psychologists, the rest are found in other specialties. At present, the Canadian Psychological Association has 23 divisions, each reflecting special skills or areas of interest. These areas are listed in Table 1.3. Many psychologists are employed full-time at colleges or universities, where they teach and do research, consulting, or therapy. Some do **basic research,** in which they seek knowledge for the sake of knowledge. For example, a psychologist might study memory purely out of a desire to understand how it works. Others do **applied research** to solve immediate practical problems, such as finding ways to improve the memory of eyewitnesses to crimes. Some do research of both types.

In a moment we'll take a closer look at how research is done. Before that, here's a chance to do a little research on how much you've learned.

Table 1.3 Sections of the Canadian Psychological Association

Adult Development and Aging	History and Philosophy
Brain and Behaviour	Industrial/Organizational
Clinical	International and Cross-Cultural
Clinical Neuropsychology	Military
Community	Perception, Learning and Cognition
Counselling	Psychopharmacology
Criminal Justice	Religion
Developmental	Social and Personality
Psychologists in Education	Students
Environmental	Teaching
Family	Women and Psychology
Health	

Knowledge builder

PSYCHOLOGISTS AND THEIR SPECIALTIES

Relate

You're going to meet four psychologists at a social gathering. How many would you expect to be therapists in private practice? Odds are that only two will be clinical (or counselling) psychologists and only one of these will work in private practice. On the other hand, at least one out of the four (and probably two) will work at a college or university.

Learning Check

See if you can answer these questions before continuing.

1. Which of the following can prescribe drugs?
   a. a psychologist *b.* a psychiatrist *c.* a psychotherapist
   d. a counsellor

2. A psychologist who specializes in treating human emotional difficulties is called a _____ psychologist.
3. Roughly 40 percent of psychologists specialize in counselling psychology. T or F?
4. Who among the following would most likely be involved in the detection of learning disabilities?
   a. a consumer psychologist *b.* a forensic psychologist
   c. an experimental psychologist *d.* a school psychologist

Critical Thinking

5. If most psychologists work in applied settings, why is basic research still of great importance?

Answers:

1. b 2. clinical or counselling 3. F 4. d 5. Because practitioners benefit from basic psychological research in the same way that physicians benefit from basic research in biology. Discoveries in basic science form the knowledge base that leads to useful applications.

▶ Scientific Research—How to Think Like a Psychologist

Survey Question:
■ Why is the scientific method important to psychologists?

Observation Gathering data directly by recording facts or events.

Scientific method Testing the truth of a proposition by careful measurement and controlled observation.

Hypothesis The predicted outcome of an experiment or an educated guess about the relationship between variables.

Operational definition Defining a scientific concept by stating the specific actions or procedures used to measure it. For example, "hunger" might be defined as "the number of hours of food deprivation."

Observation, or carefully recording facts and events, is the heart of all sciences. To be scientific, observations must be systematic, so that they reveal something about behaviour (Stanovich, 1996). To use an earlier example, little would be gained if you drove around a city during the summer and made haphazard observations of aggressive horn honking.

The Scientific Method

The **scientific method** is based on careful collection of evidence, accurate description and measurement, precise definition, controlled observation, and repeatable results (Schick & Vaughn, 1995). In its ideal form the scientific method has six elements:

1. Observation
2. Defining a problem
3. Proposing a hypothesis
4. Gathering evidence/testing the hypothesis
5. Publishing results
6. Theory building

HYPOTHESIS TESTING *What exactly is a hypothesis?* A **hypothesis** (hi-POTH-eh-sis) is a tentative explanation of an event or relationship between events. In common terms, a hypothesis is a testable hunch or educated guess about behaviour. For example, you might hypothesize that "Frustration encourages aggression." How could you test this hypothesis? First you would have to decide how you are going to frustrate people. (This part might be fun.) Then you would need to find a way to measure whether or not they become more aggressive. (Not so much fun if you plan to be nearby.) Your observations would then provide evidence to confirm or disconfirm the hypothesis.

OPERATIONAL DEFINITIONS Because we cannot see or touch frustration, it must be defined operationally. An **operational definition** states the exact procedures used to represent or measure a concept. Operational definitions allow abstract ideas to be tested in real-world terms. (See ▶Figure 1.4.) For example, you might define frustration as "interrupting an adult before he or she can finish a puzzle and win a $100 prize." And aggres-

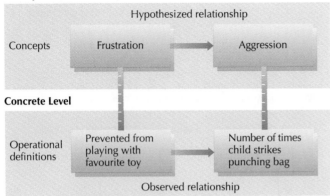

Conceptual Level

Concrete Level

▶**Figure 1.4**

Operational definitions are used to link concepts with concrete observations. Do you think the examples given are reasonable operational definitions of frustration and aggression? Operational definitions vary in how well they represent concepts. For this reason, many different experiments may be necessary to draw clear conclusions about hypothesized relationships in psychology.

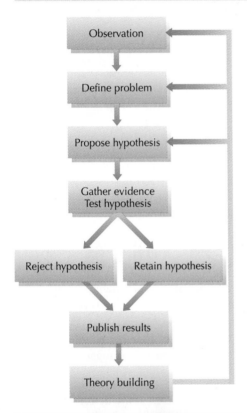

▶**Figure 1.5**

Psychologists use the logic of science to answer questions about behaviour. Specific hypotheses can be tested in a variety of ways, including naturalistic observation, correlational studies, controlled experiments, clinical studies, and the survey method. Psychologists revise their theories to reflect the evidence they gather. New or revised theories then lead to new observations, problems, and hypotheses.

Theory A system of ideas designed to interrelate concepts and facts in a way that summarizes existing data and predicts future observations.

sion might be defined as "the number of times a frustrated individual insults the person who prevented work on the puzzle."

CLEVER HANS   Several steps of the scientific method can be illustrated with the story of Clever Hans, a famous "wonder horse" (Rosenthal, 1965). Clever Hans seemed to solve difficult math problems, which he answered by tapping his hoof. If you asked Hans, "What is 12 times 2, minus 18," Hans would tap his hoof six times. This was so astonishing that a scientist (Oskar Pfungst) decided to find out if Hans really could do arithmetic. Assume that you are Pfungst and that you are just itching to discover how Hans really does his trick.

Can a Horse Add?

Your investigation of Hans's math skills would probably begin with careful observation of both the horse and his owner. Assume that these observations fail to reveal any obvious cheating. Then the problem becomes more clearly defined: What signals Hans to start and stop tapping his hoof? Your first hypothesis might be that the owner is giving Hans a signal. Your proposed test would be to make the owner leave the room. Then someone else could ask Hans questions. Your test would either confirm or deny the owner's role. This evidence would support or eliminate the cheating hypothesis. By changing the conditions under which you observe Hans, you have controlled the situation to gain more information from your observations.

Incidentally, Hans could still answer when his owner was out of the room. But a brilliant series of controlled observations revealed Hans's secret. If Hans couldn't see the questioner, he couldn't answer. It seems that questioners always lowered their heads (to look at Hans's hoof) after asking a question. This was Hans's cue to start tapping. When Hans had tapped the correct number, a questioner would always look up to see if Hans was going to stop. This was Hans's cue to stop tapping!

THEORIES   *What about theory formulation?* Since Clever Hans's ability to do math was an isolated problem, no theorizing was involved. However, in actual research, a **theory** acts as a map of knowledge (Meltzoff, 1998). Good theories summarize observations, explain them, and guide further research (see ▶ Figure 1.5). Without theories of forgetting, personality, stress, mental illness, and the like, psychologists would drown in a sea of disconnected facts (Stanovich, 1996).

PUBLICATION   Scientific information must always be publicly available. The results of psychological studies are usually published in professional journals. (See Table 1.4.) That

**Table 1.4
Outline of a
Research
Report**

- **Abstract** Research reports begin with a very brief summary of the study and its findings. The abstract allows you to get an overview without reading the entire article.
- **Introduction** The introduction describes the question to be investigated. It also provides background information by reviewing prior studies on the same or related topics.
- **Method** This section tells how and why observations were made. It also describes the specific procedures used to gather data so that other researchers can duplicate the study to see if they get the same results.
- **Results** The outcome of the investigation is presented. Data may be graphed, summarized in tables, or statistically analyzed.
- **Discussion** The results of the study are discussed in relation to the original question. Implications of the study are explored and further studies may be proposed.

way, anyone willing to make appropriate observations can see whether or not a claim is true (Schick & Vaughn, 1995).

SUMMARY Now let's summarize more realistically. All the basic elements of the scientific method are found in the example that follows.

Observation: Susanne, a psychologist, observes that some business managers seem to experience less work-related stress than others do.

Defining a Problem: Susanne's problem is to identify the ways in which high-stress and low-stress managers are different.

Observation: Susanne carefully questions managers about how much stress they experience. These additional observations suggest that low-stress managers feel they have more control over their work.

Proposing a Hypothesis: Susanne hypothesizes that having control over difficult tasks reduces stress.

Gathering Evidence/Testing the Hypothesis: Susanne designs an experiment in which [two groups of] people must solve a series of very difficult problems. One group is required to solve the problems at a pace dictated by Susanne. The other group is allowed to set its own pace. While working, the second group reports lower stress levels than the first. This suggests that Susanne's hypothesis is correct.

Publishing Results: In a scholarly article, Susanne carefully describes the question she investigated, the methods she used, and the results of her experiment. The article is published in the *Canadian Journal of Experimental Psychology*.

Theory Building: Drawing on the results of similar experiments, Susanne and other psychologists create a theory to explain why having control over a task helps reduce stress.

Research Methods

Psychologists gather evidence and test hypotheses in many ways: They observe behaviour as it unfolds in natural settings (**naturalistic observation**); they make measurements to discover relationships between events (**correlational method**); they use the powerful technique of controlled experimentation (**experimental method**); they study psychological problems and therapies in clinical settings (**clinical method**); and they use questionnaires to poll large groups of people (**survey method**). Let's see how each of these is used to advance psychological knowledge.

Naturalistic observation Observing behaviour as it unfolds in natural settings.

Correlational method Making measurements to discover relationships between events.

Experimental method Investigating behaviour through controlled experimentation.

Clinical method Studying psychological problems and therapies in clinical settings.

Survey method Using questionnaires and surveys to poll large groups of people.

Survey Question:
■ How do psychologists collect information?

▶ Naturalistic Observation—Psychology Steps Out!

▶ **Figure 1.6**

A special moment in Jane Goodall's naturalistic study of chimpanzees. A chimp uses a grass stem to extract a meal from a termite nest. Goodall's work also documented the importance of long-term emotional bonds between chimpanzee mothers and their offspring, as well as fascinating differences in the behaviour and "personalities" of individual chimps (Goodall, 1990). (Photo by Baron Hugo van Lawick. © National Geographic Society.)

Instead of waiting for a chance encounter, psychologists may actively observe behaviour in a **natural setting** (the typical environment in which a person or animal lives). The work of Jane Goodall provides a good example. She and her staff have been observing chimpanzees in Tanzania since 1960. A quote from her book *In the Shadow of Man* captures the excitement of a scientific discovery:

Quickly focusing my binoculars, I saw that it was a single chimpanzee, and just then he turned my direction. . . . He was squatting beside the red earth mound of a termite nest, and as I watched I saw him carefully push a long grass stem into a hole in the mound. After a moment he withdrew it and picked something from the end with his mouth. I was too far away to make out what he was eating, but it was obvious that he was actually using a grass stem as a tool (▶Figure 1.6). (Van Lawick-Goodall, 1971)

Notice that naturalistic observation only provides descriptions of behaviour. In order to *explain* observations, we may need information from other research methods. Just the same, Goodall's discovery helped us realize that humans are not the only tool-making animals (Lavallee, 1999).

Chimpanzees in zoos use objects as tools. Doesn't that demonstrate the same thing? Not necessarily. Naturalistic observation allows us to study behaviour that hasn't been tampered with by outside influences. Only by observing chimps in their natural environment can we tell if they use tools without human interference.

Limitations

Doesn't the presence of human observers in an animal colony affect the animals' behaviour? Yes. A major problem is the **observer effect,** which refers to changes in a subject's behaviour caused by an awareness of being observed. Naturalists must be very careful to keep their distance and avoid "making friends" with the animals they are observing. Likewise, if you were interested in differences between aggressive and non-aggressive school children, you couldn't simply stroll onto a playground and start taking notes. As a stranger, your presence would probably change the children's behaviour. Whenever possible, this problem is minimized by concealing the observer. Another solution is to use hidden recorders. For example, a recent naturalistic study of playground aggression was done with video cameras and remote microphones (Pepler, Craig, & Roberts, 1998).

Observer bias is a related problem in which observers see what they expect to see or record only selected details. Teachers in one study were told to watch elementary school children (all normal) who had been labelled as learning disabled, mentally retarded, emotionally disturbed, or normal. The results were troubling: Teachers gave the children very different ratings, depending on the labels used (Foster & Ysseldyke, 1976). In some situations, observer bias can have serious consequences. An example is studies of the effectiveness of psychotherapy, where therapists tend to get better results with the type of therapy they favour (Lambert, 1999).

THE ANTHROPOMORPHIC ERROR   A special trap that must be avoided while observing animals is the **anthropomorphic fallacy** (AN-thro-po-MORE-fik). This is the error of attributing human thoughts, feelings, or motives to animals—especially as a way of explaining their behaviour (Blumberg & Wasserman, 1995).

Why is it risky to attribute motives or emotions to animals? The temptation to assume that an animal is "angry," "jealous," "bored," or "guilty" can be strong, but it can lead to false conclusions. If you have pets at home, you probably already know how difficult it is to avoid anthropomorphizing.

Recording Observations

Psychologists doing naturalistic studies make a special effort to minimize bias by keeping a formal log of data and observations, called an **observational record.** As suggested in

Natural setting The environment in which an organism typically lives.
Observer effect Changes in behaviour brought about by an awareness of being observed.
Observer bias The tendency of an observer to distort observations or perceptions to match his or her expectations.
Anthropomorphic fallacy The error of attributing human thoughts, feelings, or motives to animals, especially as a way of explaining their behaviour.
Observational record A detailed summary of observed events or a videotape of observed behaviour.

the study of playground aggression, videotaping often provides the best record of all (Pepler & Craig, 1995).

Despite its problems, naturalistic observation can supply a wealth of information and raise many interesting questions. In most scientific research it is an excellent starting point.

▶ Correlational Studies—In Search of the Perfect Relationship

Correlation The existence of a consistent, systematic relationship between two events, measures, or variables.

Correlational study A non-experimental study designed to measure the degree of relationship (if any) between two or more events, measures, or variables.

Coefficient of correlation A statistical index ranging from +1.00 to –1.00 that indicates the direction and degree of correlation.

Positive correlation A statistical relationship in which increases in one measure are matched by increases in the other (or decreases correspond with decreases).

Negative correlation A statistical relationship in which increases in one measure are matched by decreases in the other.

Causation The act of causing some effect.

Let's say a psychologist notes an association between the IQs of parents and their children, or between beauty and social popularity, or between anxiety and test performance, or even between crime and the weather. In each instance, two observations or events are **correlated** (linked together in an orderly way).

A **correlational study** finds the degree of relationship, or correlation, between two existing traits, behaviours, or events. First, two factors of interest are measured. Then a statistical technique is used to find their degree of correlation. For example, we could find the correlation between the number of hours slept at night and afternoon sleepiness. If the correlation is large, knowing how long a person sleeps at night would allow us to predict his or her degree of sleepiness in the afternoon. Likewise, afternoon sleepiness could be used to predict the duration of nighttime sleep.

Correlation Coefficients

How is the degree of correlation expressed? The strength and direction of a relationship can be expressed as a **coefficient of correlation.** This is simply a number falling somewhere between +1.00 and –1.00. If the number is zero or close to zero, the association between two measures is weak or nonexistent. For example, the correlation between shoe size and intelligence is zero. (Sorry, size 12 readers.) If the correlation is +1.00, a perfect positive relationship exists; if it is –1.00, a perfect negative relationship has been discovered.

Correlations in psychology are rarely perfect. But the closer the coefficient is to +1.00 or –1.00, the stronger the relationship. For example, identical twins tend to have almost identical IQs. In contrast, the IQs of parents and their children are only generally similar. The correlation between the IQs of parents and children is .35; between identical twins it's .86.

What do the terms "positive" and "negative" correlation mean? A **positive correlation** shows that increases in one measure are matched by increases in the other (or decreases correspond with decreases). For example, there is a positive correlation between high-school grades and college grades; students who do better in high school tend to do better in college (and the reverse). In a **negative correlation,** increases in the first measure are associated with decreases in the second (▶ Figure 1.7). We might observe, for instance, that students who watch many hours of television get lower grades than those who watch few hours. (This is the well-known TV zombie effect.)

Would that show that watching TV too much causes lower grades? It might seem so, but we cannot be sure without performing an experiment.

CORRELATION AND CAUSATION Correlational studies help us discover relationships and make predictions. However, correlation does not demonstrate **causation** (a cause-and-effect relationship) (Meltzoff, 1998). It could be, for instance, that students who are uninterested in their classes have more time for TV. If so, then their lack of study and lower grades would both result from disinterest, not excessive TV watching. Just because one thing appears to be related to another does not mean that a cause-and-effect connection exists.

Here is another example of mistaking correlation for causation: What if a psychologist discovers that the blood of schizophrenic patients contains a certain chemical not found in normal people? Does this show that the chemical causes schizophrenia? It may seem so, but schizophrenia could cause the chemical to form. Or, both schizophrenia and the chemical might be caused by some unknown third factor, such as the typical diet in mental hospitals. Just because one thing appears to cause another does not confirm that it does. The best way to be confident that a cause-and-effect relationship exists is to perform a controlled experiment. You'll learn how in the next section.

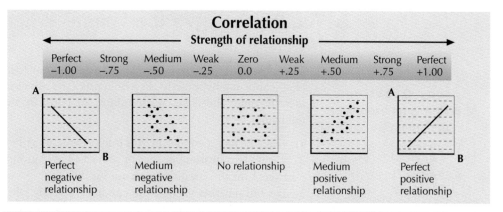

Correlation
Strength of relationship

Perfect −1.00	Strong −.75	Medium −.50	Weak −.25	Zero 0.0	Weak +.25	Medium +.50	Strong +.75	Perfect +1.00

| Perfect negative relationship | Medium negative relationship | No relationship | Medium positive relationship | Perfect positive relationship |

▶ Figure 1.7

The correlation coefficient tells how strongly two measures are related. These graphs show a range of relationships between two measures, A and B. If a correlation is negative, increases in one measure are associated with decreases in the other. (As B gets larger, A gets smaller.) In a positive correlation, increases in one measure are associated with increases in the other. (As B gets larger, A gets larger.) The centre-left graph ("medium negative relationship") might result from comparing anxiety level (B) with test scores (A): Higher anxiety is associated with lower scores. The centre graph ("no relationship") would result from plotting a person's shoe size (B) and his or her IQ (A). The centre-right graph ("medium positive relationship") could be a plot of grades in high school (B) and grades in college (A) for a group of students: Higher grades in high school are associated with higher grades in college.

Knowledge builder

RESEARCH METHODS, NATURALISTIC OBSERVATION, AND CORRELATION

Relate

You probably hypothesize daily about why people act the way they do. Do you seek to verify your hypotheses? Usually we closely observe others to determine if our "educated guesses" about them are correct. But casual observation can be misleading. To really test a hypothesis, systematic observation and formal research methods are necessary.

Learning Check

1. Most of psychology can rightfully be called common sense because psychologists prefer naturalistic observation to controlled observation. T or F?
2. A hypothesis is any careful observation made in a controlled experiment. T or F?
3. Two major problems in naturalistic observation are the effects of the observer and observer bias. T or F?

4. The _____ fallacy involves attributing human feelings and motives to animals.
5. Correlation typically does not demonstrate causation. T or F?
6. Which correlation coefficient represents the strongest relationship?
   a. −0.86   *b.* +0.66   *c.* +0.10   *d.* +0.09

Critical Thinking

7. Can you think of some additional "common-sense" statements that contradict each other?
8. Attributing mischievous motives to a car that is not working properly is a thinking error similar to anthropomorphizing. T or F?
9. Adults who often ate Frosted Flakes cereal as children now have half the cancer rate seen in adults who never ate Frosted Flakes. What do you think explains this strange correlation?

Answers:

1. F 2. F 3. T 4. anthropomorphic 5. T 6. *a* 7. There are many examples. Here are a few more to add to the ones you thought of: "You can't make a silk purse out of a sow's ear," versus "Clothes make the man (or woman)." "He (or she) who hesitates is lost," versus "Haste makes waste." "Birds of a feather flock together," versus "Opposites attract." 8. True. It appears to be difficult for humans to resist thinking of other species and even machines in human terms. 9. The correlation is related to an age bias in the group of people studied. Older adults have higher cancer rates than younger adults, and Frosted Flakes weren't available during the childhoods of older people. Thus, Frosted Flakes appear to be related to cancer, when age is the real connection (Tierny, 1987).

▶ The Psychology Experiment—Where Cause Meets Effect

Survey Question:
■ How is an experiment performed?

The most powerful research tool is an **experiment** (a formal trial undertaken to confirm or disconfirm a hypothesis). Psychologists carefully control conditions in experiments to identify cause-and-effect relationships. To perform an experiment you would do the following:

1. Directly vary a condition you think might affect behaviour.
2. Create two or more groups of subjects. These groups should be alike in all ways except for the condition you are varying.
3. Record whether varying the condition has any effect on behaviour.

Assume that you want to find out if hunger affects memory. First, you would form two groups of people. Then you could give the members of one group a memory test while they are hungry. The second group would take the same test after eating a meal. By comparing average memory scores for the two groups, you could tell if hunger affects memory.

As you can see, the simplest psychological experiment is based on two groups of **experimental subjects** (animals or people whose behaviour is investigated). One group is called the *experimental group;* the other becomes the *control group.* The control group and the experimental group are treated exactly alike except for the condition you intentionally vary. This condition is called the *independent variable.*

Variables and Groups

A **variable** is any condition that can change and that might affect the outcome of the experiment. Identifying causes and effects in an experiment involves three types of variables:

1. **Independent variables** are conditions altered or varied by the experimenter, who sets their size, amount, or value. Independent variables are suspected causes for differences in behaviour.
2. **Dependent variables** measure the results of the experiment. That is, they reveal the effects that independent variables have on behaviour. Such effects are often revealed by measures of performance, such as test scores.
3. **Extraneous variables** are conditions that a researcher wishes to prevent from affecting the outcome of the experiment.

We can apply these terms to our hunger/memory experiment in this way: Hunger is the independent variable—we want to know if hunger affects memory. Memory (defined by scores on the memory test) is the dependent variable—we want to know if the ability to memorize depends on how hungry a person is. All other conditions that could affect memory scores are extraneous. Examples are the number of hours slept the night before the test, intelligence, or difficulty of the questions.

As you can see, an **experimental group** consists of subjects exposed to the independent variable (hunger in the preceding example). Members of the **control group** are exposed to all conditions except the independent variable.

Let's examine another simple experiment. Suppose you notice that you seem to study better while listening to music. This suggests the hypothesis that music improves learning. We could test this idea by forming an experimental group that studies with music. A control group would study without music. Then we could compare their scores on a test.

Is a control group really needed? Can't people just study with music on to see if they do better? Without a control group it would be impossible to tell if music had any effect on learning. The control group provides a point of reference for comparison with scores of the experimental group. If the average test score of the experimental group is higher than the average of the control group, we can conclude that music improves learning. If there is no difference, it's obvious that the independent variable had no effect on learning.

Experiment A formal trial undertaken to confirm a fact or principle.

Experimental subjects Humans or animals whose behaviour is investigated in an experiment.

Variable Any condition that changes or can be made to change; a measure, event, or state that may vary.

Independent variable In an experiment, the condition being investigated as a possible cause of some change in behaviour. The values that this variable takes are chosen by the experimenter.

Dependent variable In an experiment, the condition (usually a behaviour) that is affected by the independent variable.

Extraneous variables Conditions or factors excluded from influencing the outcome of an experiment.

Experimental group In a controlled experiment, the group of subjects exposed to the independent variable or experimental condition.

Control group In a controlled experiment, the group of subjects exposed to all experimental conditions or variables *except* the independent variable.

In this experiment, the amount learned (indicated by scores on the test) is the dependent variable. We are asking, Does the independent variable affect the dependent variable? (Does music affect or influence learning?)

EXPERIMENTAL CONTROL   *How do we know that the people in one group aren't more intelligent than those in the other group?* It's true that personal differences might affect the experiment. However, they can be controlled by randomly assigning people to groups. **Random assignment** means that a subject has an equal chance of being in either the experimental group or the control group. Randomization evenly balances personal differences in the two groups. In our musical experiment, this could be done by simply flipping a coin for each subject: Heads, and the subject is in the experimental group; tails, it's the control group. This would result in few differences in the number of people in each group who are geniuses or dunces, hungry, hung over, tall, music lovers, or whatever.

Other *extraneous,* or outside, variables—such as the amount of study time, the sex of subjects, the temperature in the room, the time of day, the amount of light, and so forth—must also be prevented from affecting the outcome of an experiment. But how? Usually this is done by making all conditions (except the independent variable) exactly alike for both groups. When all conditions are the same for both groups—except the presence or absence of music—then a difference in the amount learned must be caused by the music (▶Figure 1.8).

CAUSE AND EFFECT   Now let's summarize more formally. In an experiment, two or more groups of subjects are treated differently with respect to the independent variable. In all other ways they are treated the same. That is, extraneous variables are equalized for all groups in the experiment. The effect of the independent variable (or variables) on some behaviour (the dependent variable) is then measured. In a carefully controlled experiment, the independent variable is the only possible *cause* for any effect noted in the dependent variable. This allows clear cause-and-effect connections to be identified (▶Figure 1.9).

> **Random assignment** The use of chance (for example, flipping a coin) to assign subjects to experimental and control groups.

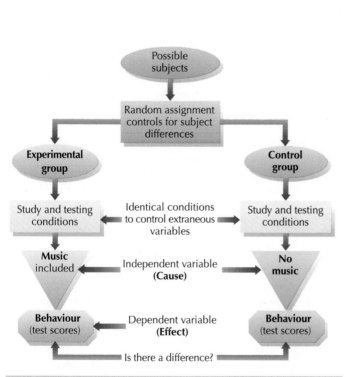

▶Figure 1.8

Elements of a simple psychological experiment to assess the effects of music during study on test scores.

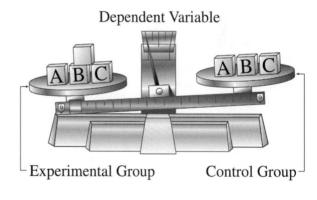

Extraneous Variables
Independent Variable

▶ Figure 1.9

Experimental control is achieved by balancing extraneous variables for the experimental group and the control group. For example, the average age (A), education (B), and intelligence (C) of group members could be made the same for both groups. Then we could apply the independent variable to the experimental group. If their behaviour (the dependent variable) changes (in comparison with the control group), the change must be caused by the independent variable.

▶ Placebo Effects—Sugar Pills and Saltwater

Let's do an experiment to see if caffeine (a stimulant) affects learning: Before studying, members of our experimental group take a caffeine pill. Control group members get nothing. Later, we assess how much each subject learned. Does this experiment seem valid? Actually, it is seriously flawed.

Why? The experimental group took the drug and the control group didn't. Differences in the amount they learned must have been caused by the drug, right? No, because the drug wasn't the only difference between the groups. People in the experimental group swallowed a pill, and control subjects did not. Without using a placebo (plah-SEE-bo), it is impossible to tell if the drug affects learning. It could be that those who swallowed a pill expected to do better. This alone might have affected their performance, even if the pill didn't.

What is a placebo? Why would it make a difference? A **placebo** is a fake pill or injection. Inert substances such as sugar pills and saline (saltwater) injections are common placebos. Thus, if a placebo has any effect, it must be based on suggestion, rather than chemistry (Quitkin, 1999).

The **placebo effect** (changes in behaviour caused by belief that one has taken a drug) can be powerful. For instance, a saline injection is 70 percent as effective as morphine in reducing pain. That's why doctors sometimes prescribe placebos—especially for complaints that seem to have no physical basis. Placebos have been shown to affect pain, anxiety, depression, alertness, tension, sexual arousal, cravings for alcohol, and many other processes (Kirsch & Lynn, 1999).

How could an inert substance have any effect? Placebos alter people's expectations about their own emotional and physical reactions. These expectancies, in turn, influence bodily activities. For example, placebos that relieve pain do so by causing the pituitary gland to release endorphins. These powerful chemicals are similar to painkilling opiate drugs such as morphine (ter Riet et al., 1998). (See Chapter 2 for more information.)

Controlling Placebo Effects

To control for placebo effects, we could use a **single-blind experiment.** In this case, subjects do not know if they are receiving a real drug or a placebo. All subjects get a pill or injection. People in the experimental group get a real drug and the control group gets a placebo. Because subjects are blind as to whether they received the drug, their expectations are the same. Any difference in their behaviour must be caused by the drug.

Keeping subjects "blind" is not necessarily enough, however. In a **double-blind experiment** neither subjects nor experimenters know who has received a drug and who has taken a placebo. This keeps researchers from unconsciously influencing subjects. Typically, someone else prepares the pills or injections so experimenters don't know until after testing who got what. Testing of this type has shown that about 50 percent of the effectiveness of antidepressant drugs such as Prozac is due to the placebo effect (Kirsch & Sapirstein, 1998).

The Experimenter Effect

How could a researcher influence subjects? The **experimenter effect** (changes in behaviour caused by the unintended influence of an experimenter) is a common problem in psychological research. In essence, experimenters run the risk of finding what they expect to find. This occurs because humans are very sensitive to hints about what is expected of them (Rosenthal, 1994).

The experimenter effect even applies outside the laboratory. Psychologist Robert Rosenthal (1973) reports an example of how expectations can influence people: At the U.S. Air Force Academy Preparatory School, 100 airmen were randomly assigned to five different math classes. Their teachers did not know about this random placement. Instead, each teacher was told that his or her students had unusually high or low ability. Students in the classes labelled "high ability" improved much more in math scores than those in "low-ability" classes. Yet, initially, all of the classes had students of equal ability.

Placebo An inactive substance given in the place of a drug in psychological research.

Placebo effect Changes in behaviour due to expectations that a drug (or other treatment) will have some effect.

Single-blind experiment An arrangement in which subjects remain unaware of whether they are in the experimental group or the control group, although the researcher knows.

Double-blind experiment An arrangement in which both subjects and experimenters are unaware of whether subjects are in the experimental group or the control group.

Experimenter effect Changes in subjects' behaviour caused by the unintended influence of an experimenter's actions.

Knowledge builder

THE PSYCHOLOGY EXPERIMENT

Relate

In a sense, we all conduct little experiments to detect cause-and-effect connections. If you are interested in gardening, for example, you might try adding plant food to one bed of flowers but not another. The question then becomes, Does the use of plant food (the independent variable) affect the size of the flowers (the dependent variable)? By comparing unfed plants (the control group) to those receiving plant food (the experimental group), you could find out if plant food is worth using. Can you think of at least one informal experiment you've run in the last month? What were the variables? What was the outcome?

Learning Check

1. To understand cause and effect, a simple psychological experiment is based on creating two groups: the _____ group and the _____ group.
2. There are three types of variables to consider in an experiment: _____ variables (which are manipulated by the experimenter); _____ variables (which measure the outcome of the experiment); and _____ variables (factors to be excluded in a particular experiment).

3. A researcher performs an experiment to learn if room temperature affects the amount of aggression displayed by college students under crowded conditions in a simulated prison environment. In this experiment, the independent variable is which of the following?
   a. room temperature *b.* the amount of aggression *c.* crowding *d.* the simulated prison environment
4. A procedure used to control both the placebo effect and the experimenter effect in drug experiments is
   a. the correlation method *b.* extraneous prophecy *c.* double-blind technique *d.* random assignment of subjects

Critical Thinking

5. There is a loophole in the statement, "I've been taking vitamin C tablets, and I haven't had a cold all year. Vitamin C is great!" What is the loophole?
6. How would you determine if sugary breakfasts affect children's activity levels and their ability to learn in school?
7. People who believe strongly in astrology have personality characteristics that actually match, to a degree, those predicted by their astrological signs. Can you explain why this occurs?

Answers:

1. experimental, control 2. independent, dependent, extraneous 3. *a* 4. *c* 5. The statement implies that vitamin C prevented colds. However, not getting a cold could just be a coincidence. A controlled experiment with a group given vitamin C and a control group not taking vitamin C would be needed to learn if vitamin C actually has any effect on susceptibility to colds. 6. An actual experiment on this question used a double-blind design in which children were given a breakfast drink containing either 50 grams of sucrose (sugar), a placebo (aspartame), or only a very small amount of sucrose. Observed changes in activity levels and in scores on a learning task did not support the view that sugar causes major changes in children's behaviour (Rosen et al., 1988). 7. Belief in astrology can create a self-fulfilling prophecy in which people alter their behaviours and self-concepts to match their astrological signs (van Rooij, 1994).

Self-fulfilling prophecy A prediction that prompts people to act in ways that make the prediction come true.

Case study An in-depth focus on all aspects of a single person.

Apparently, the teachers subtly communicated their expectations to students. Most likely, they did this through tone of voice, body language, and by giving encouragement or criticism. Their "hints," in turn, created a **self-fulfilling prophecy** that affected the students. A self-fulfilling prophecy is a prediction that prompts people to act in ways that make the prediction come true. In short, people sometimes become what we prophesy for them. It is wise to remember that others tend to live up or down to our expectations for them (Jussim & Eccles, 1992; Madon, Jussim, & Eccles, 1997).

▶ The Clinical Method—Data by the Case

Survey Question:
■ What other research methods do psychologists use?

Natural clinical test A natural event that provides data on a psychological phenomenon.

Many experiments are impractical, unethical, or impossible to do. In instances such as these, information may be gained from a **case study** (an in-depth focus on all aspects of a single subject). Clinical psychologists rely heavily on case studies.

Case studies may sometimes be thought of as **natural clinical tests** (accidents or other natural events that provide psychological data). Gunshot wounds, brain tumours, accidental poisonings, and similar disasters provide much information about the human brain. One remarkable case from the history of psychology is reported by Dr. J. M. Harlow (1868). Phineas Gage, a young foreman on a work crew, had a 6-kilogram steel rod blown

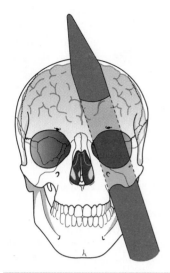

Some of the earliest information on the effects of damage to frontal areas of the brain came from a case study of the accidental injury of Phineas Gage.

through the front of his brain by a dynamite explosion (see ▶ Figure 1.10). Amazingly, he survived the accident. Within two months Gage could walk, talk, and move normally. But the injury forever changed his personality. Instead of the honest and dependable worker he had been before, Gage became a surly, foul-mouthed liar. Dr. Harlow carefully recorded all details of what was perhaps the first in-depth case study of an accidental frontal lobotomy (the destruction of front brain matter).

Not all people would have the same reaction to a similar injury. This is why psychologists prefer controlled experiments and often use lab animals for studies of the brain. Case studies lack formal control groups. This, of course, limits the conclusions that can be drawn from clinical observations. Nonetheless, when a purely psychological problem is under study, the clinical method may be the *only* source of information.

Case studies can provide special opportunities to answer interesting questions. For instance, how do you know what kind of person you are? Would your self-image change if you lost your memory for past events? To answer these questions, psychologists did a case study of W. J., an 18-year-old female college student. After she suffered a head injury, W. J. had amnesia for about a month. During that time, W. J. could recall little of what had occurred during the previous six months. Nevertheless, her ratings of her own personality appeared to be unaffected by her memory loss. This suggests that an awareness of one's own personal characteristics is based on memories that are more lasting than those for everyday events (Klein, Loftus, & Kihlstrom, 1996).

The careful recording of cases like W. J.'s is essential to psychology. Case studies often provide insights into human behaviour that couldn't be obtained by any other method (Edwards, 1998).

▶ Survey Method—Here, Have a Sample

Sometimes psychologists would like to ask everyone in the world a few well-chosen questions: "Do you drink alcoholic beverages? How often per week?" "What form of discipline did your parents use when you were a child?" "What is the most creative thing you've done?" The answers to such questions can reveal much about people's behaviour. But because it is impossible to question everyone, doing a survey is often more practical.

In the **survey method** public polling techniques are used to answer psychological questions. Typically, people in a representative sample are asked a series of carefully worded questions. A **representative sample** is a small group that accurately reflects a larger population. A good sample must include the same proportion of men, women, young, old, occupations, ethnicity, political affiliation, and so on, as found in the population as a whole.

A **population** is an entire group of animals or people belonging to a particular category (for example, all college students or all married women). Ultimately, we are interested in entire populations. But by selecting a smaller sample, we can draw conclusions about the larger group without polling each and every person. Representative samples are often obtained by *randomly* selecting who will be included. (Notice that this is similar to randomly assigning subjects to groups in an experiment.)

How accurate is the survey method? Surveys conducted by firms such as Decima Research and Léger and Léger are usually quite accurate. However, if a survey is based on a biased sample, it may paint a false picture. A **biased sample** does not accurately reflect the population from which it was drawn. Surveys done by magazines, websites, and online information services can be quite biased. Surveys on the use of illicit drugs done by *Cosmopolitan* and *Rolling Stone* would probably produce very different results—neither of which would represent the general population. That's why psychologists using the survey method go to great lengths to ensure that their samples are representative. Fortunately, people can often be polled by telephone, which makes it easier to obtain large samples. Also, recent studies have shown that even if one person out of three refuses to answer survey questions, the results are still likely to be valid (Krosnick, 1999).

Social Desirability Even well-designed surveys may be limited by another problem. If a psychologist were to ask you detailed questions about your sexual history and current sexual behaviour, how accurate would your replies be? Would you exaggerate? Would you

Survey method The use of public polling techniques to answer psychological questions.

Representative sample A small, randomly selected part of a larger population that accurately reflects characteristics of the whole population.

Population An entire group of animals or people belonging to a particular category (for example, all college students or all married women).

Biased sample A subpart of a larger population that does not accurately reflect characteristics of the whole population.

Courtesy bias The tendency to give "polite" answers—especially the tendency to alter answers so as not to hurt an interviewer's feelings.

be embarrassed? Replies to survey questions are not always accurate or truthful. Many people show a distinct **courtesy bias** (a tendency to give "polite" or socially desirable answers). For example, answers to questions concerning sex, drinking or drug use, income, and church attendance tend to be less than truthful. Likewise, the week after an election, more people will say they voted than actually did (Krosnick, 1999).

Summary   Despite their limitations, surveys frequently produce valuable information. For instance, the survey method was used to find out how often sexual harassment occurs and to raise public awareness about the problem (Janus & Janus, 1993). To sum up, the survey method can be a powerful research tool. Like other methods, it has limitations, but new techniques and strategies are providing valuable information about our behaviour (Krosnick, 1999).

▶ Summary—Science and Critical Thinking

Survey Question:
■ What is critical thinking?

Is so much emphasis on research really necessary in psychology? In a word, yes. As we have seen, science is a powerful way of asking questions about the world and getting trustworthy answers. Your awareness of this fact should help make you a more critical observer of human behaviour. Table 1.5 summarizes many of the important ideas we have covered.

Most of us would be skeptical when buying a used car. But all too often, we may be tempted to "buy" outrageous claims about topics such as dowsing, the occult, the Bermuda Triangle, UFOs, Tarot cards, healing crystals, and so forth. Likewise, most of us easily accept our ignorance of subatomic physics. But because we deal with human behaviour every day, we tend to think that we already know what is true in psychology.

Critical thinking An ability to evaluate, compare, analyze, critique, and synthesize information.

For these and many more reasons, learning to think critically is one of the lasting benefits of a college education. **Critical thinking** refers to an ability to evaluate, compare, analyze, critique, and synthesize information. Critical thinkers are willing to ask the hard questions, including those that challenge conventional wisdom. For example, many people believe that punishment (a spanking) is a good way to reinforce learning in children. Actually, nothing could be further from the truth. That's why a critical thinker would immediately ask: "Does punishment work? If so, when? Under what conditions does it not work? What are its drawbacks? Are there better ways to guide learning?" (Halonen, 1986).

Table 1.5
Comparison of Psychological Research Methods

	ADVANTAGES	DISADVANTAGES
Naturalistic observation	Behaviour is observed in a natural setting; much information is obtained, and hypotheses and questions for additional research are formed	Little or no control is possible; observed behaviour may be altered by the presence of the observer; observations may be biased; causes cannot be conclusively identified
Correlational method	Demonstrates the existence of relationships; allows prediction; can be used in lab, clinic, or natural setting	Little or no control is possible; relationships may be coincidental; cause-and-effect relationships cannot be confirmed
Experimental method	Clear cause-and-effect relationships can be identified; powerful controlled observations can be staged; no need to wait for natural event	May be somewhat artificial; some natural behaviour not easily studied in laboratory (field experiments may avoid these objections)
Clinical method	Takes advantage of "natural clinical trials" and allows investigation of rare or unusual problems or events	Little or no control is possible; does not provide a control group for comparison; subjective interpretation is often necessary; a single case may be misleading or unrepresentative
Survey method	Allows information about large numbers of people to be gathered; can address questions not answered by other approaches	Obtaining a representative sample is critical and can be difficult to do; answers may be inaccurate; people may not do what they say or say what they do

Thinking about Behaviour

The core of critical thinking is a willingness to actively *evaluate* ideas. Critical thinkers analyze the evidence supporting their beliefs and probe for weaknesses in their reasoning. They question assumptions and look for alternative conclusions. True knowledge, they recognize, comes from constantly revising and enlarging our understanding of the world.

Critical thinking is built upon four basic principles (Gill, 1991; Shore, 1990):

1. *Few "truths" transcend the need for empirical testing.* It is true that religious beliefs and personal values may be held without supporting evidence. But most other ideas can be evaluated by applying the rules of logic and evidence.
2. *Evidence varies in quality.* Judging the quality of evidence is crucial. Imagine that you are a juror in a courtroom, judging claims made by two battling lawyers. To decide correctly, you can't just weigh the amount of evidence. You must also critically evaluate the quality of the evidence. Then you can give greater weight to the most credible facts.
3. *Authority or claimed expertise does not automatically make an idea true.* Just because a teacher, guru, celebrity, or authority is convinced or sincere doesn't mean you should automatically believe him or her. It is unscientific and self-demeaning to just take the word of an "expert" without asking, "What evidence convinced her or him? How good is it? Is there a better explanation?"
4. *Critical thinking requires an open mind.* Be prepared to consider daring departures and go wherever the evidence leads. However, it is possible to be so "open-minded" that you simply become gullible. Critical thinkers try to strike a balance between open-mindedness and healthy skepticism. Being open-minded means that you consider all possibilities before drawing a conclusion. It is the ability to change your views under the impact of new and more convincing evidence.

To put these principles into action, here are some questions to ask over and over again as you evaluate new information (Bartz, 1990):

1. What claims are being made?
2. What test of these claims (if any) has been made?
3. Who did the test? How good is the evidence?
4. What was the nature and quality of the tests? Are they credible? Can they be repeated?
5. How reliable and trustworthy were the investigators? Do they have conflicts of interest? Do their findings appear to be objective? Has any other independent researcher duplicated the findings?
6. Finally, how much credibility can the claim be given? High, medium, low, provisional?

A course in psychology naturally enriches thinking skills. To add to the process, all upcoming chapters include Critical Thinking questions like the ones you have seen here. Tackling these questions will sharpen your thinking abilities and make learning more lively. For an immediate thinking challenge, let's take a critical look at several non-scientific systems that claim to explain behaviour.

Pseudo-psychology Any false and unscientific system of beliefs and practices that is offered as an explanation of behaviour.

▶ Pseudo-psychologies—Palms, Planets, and Personality

Survey Question:
■ How does psychology differ from false explanations of behaviour?

What are false psychologies? Why do they sometimes seem to work? A **pseudo-psychology** (SUE-doe-psychology) is any unfounded system that resembles psychology. Many pseudo-psychologies give the appearance of science but are actually false. (*Pseudo* means "false.") Pseudo-psychologies change little over time because their followers avoid evidence that contradicts their beliefs (Kelly & Saklofske, 1994). Scientists, in contrast, actively look for contradictions as a way to advance knowledge. They are skeptical critics of their own theories (Woodward & Goodstein, 1996).

Palmistry False system that claims to reveal personality traits and to predict the future by "reading" lines on the palms of the hands.

Phrenology False and antiquated system based on the belief that personality traits are revealed by the shape of the skull.

Graphology False system based on the belief that handwriting can reveal personality traits.

Astrology False system based on the belief that human behaviour is influenced by the position of stars and planets.

Unlike the real thing, pseudo-psychologies are not based on scientific testing. For instance, **palmistry** is a false system that claims lines on the hand reveal personality and predict the future. Despite the overwhelming evidence against this, palmists can still be found separating the gullible from their money in many cities. A similar false system is **phrenology,** which claims that personality traits are revealed by the shape of the skull (▶Figure 1.11). Phrenology was popularized in the 19th century by Franz Gall, a German anatomy teacher. Modern research has long since shown that bumps on the head have nothing to do with talents or abilities. In fact, the phrenologists were so far off that they listed the brain area for hearing as a centre for "combativeness"!

At first glance, a pseudo-psychology called **graphology** might seem more reasonable. Graphologists claim that personality traits are revealed by handwriting. Based on such claims, some companies use graphologists to select job candidates. This is troubling because graphologists score close to zero on tests of accuracy in rating personality (Ben-Shakhar et al., 1986). In fact, graphologists do no better than untrained college students in rating personality and job performance (Neter & Ben-Shakhar, 1989; Rafaeli & Klimoski, 1983). (By the way, graphology's failure at revealing personality should be separated from its proven value for detecting forgeries.) (See ▶Figure 1.12.)

Graphology might seem harmless enough. However, this false system has been used to determine who is hired, given bank credit, or selected for juries. In these and similar situations, pseudo-psychologies do, in fact, harm people (Barker, 1993; Beyerstein & Beyerstein, 1992).

If pseudo-psychologies have no scientific basis, how do they survive and why are they popular? There are several reasons, all of which can be demonstrated by a critique of astrology.

Problems in the Stars

Astrology is probably the most popular pseudo-psychology. **Astrology** holds that the positions of the stars and planets at the time of one's birth determine personality traits and affect behaviour. Like other pseudo-psychologies, astrology has repeatedly been shown to have no scientific validity (Kelly, 1998, 1999; Stewart, 1996). The objections to astrology are numerous and devastating:

1. The zodiac has shifted in the sky by one full constellation since astrology was first set up. However, most astrologers simply ignore this shift. (In other words, if astrology calls you a Scorpio you are really a Libra, and so forth.)
2. There is no connection between the "compatibility" of couples' astrological signs and their marriage and divorce rates.
3. Studies have found no connection between astrological signs and leadership, physical characteristics, career choices, or personality traits.
4. The force of gravity exerted by the obstetrician's body at the moment of birth is greater than that exerted by the stars. Also, astrologers have failed to explain why the moment of birth should be more important than the moment of conception.

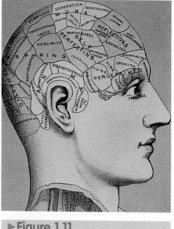

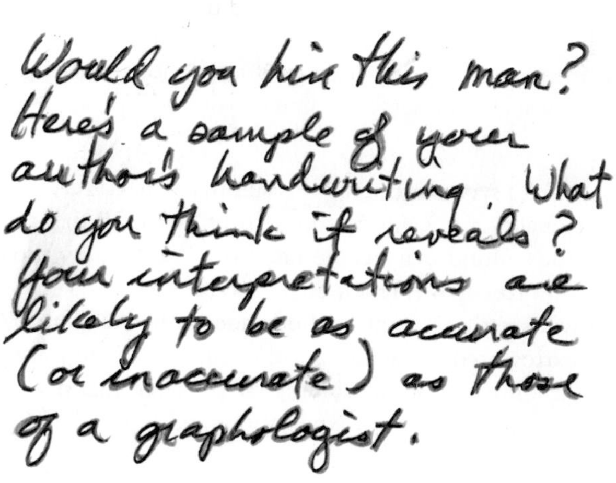

▶Figure 1.11

Phrenology was an attempt to assess personality characteristics by examining various areas of the skull. Phrenologists used charts such as the one shown here as guides. Like other pseudo-psychologists, phrenologists made no attempt to empirically verify their concepts.

Would you hire this man? Here's a sample of your author's handwriting. What do you think it reveals? Your interpretations are likely to be as accurate (or inaccurate) as those of a graphologist.

▶Figure 1.12

Handwriting sample. What can you tell about the person who wrote this?

5. A study of more than 3000 predictions by famous astrologers found that only a small percentage were fulfilled. These "successful" predictions tended to be vague ("There will be a tragedy somewhere in the east in the spring") or easily guessed from current events.

6. If astrologers are asked to match people with their horoscopes, they do not perform better than would be expected by chance (Kelly, 1999).

7. A few astrologers have tried to test astrology. Their results have been just as negative as those obtained by critics. (Sources: Kelly, 1998, 1999; Martens & Trachet, 1998; Stewart, 1996.)

In short, astrology doesn't work.

Then why does astrology often seem to work? The following discussion tells why.

UNCRITICAL ACCEPTANCE   If you have ever had your astrological chart done, you may have been impressed with its apparent accuracy. However, such perceptions are typically based on **uncritical acceptance** (the tendency to believe positive or flattering descriptions of yourself). Many astrological charts are made up of mostly flattering traits. Naturally, when your personality is described in desirable terms, it is hard to deny that the description has the "ring of truth." How much acceptance would astrology receive if a birth sign read like this:

> **Virgo:** You are the logical type and hate disorder. Your nitpicking is unbearable to your friends. You are cold, unemotional, and usually fall asleep while making love. Virgos make good doorstops.

POSITIVE INSTANCES   Even when an astrological description contains a mixture of good and bad traits, it may seem accurate. To find out why, read the following personality description.

Your Personality Profile

> You have a strong need for other people to like you and for them to admire you. You have a tendency to be critical of yourself. You have a great deal of unused energy which you have not turned to your advantage. While you have some personality weaknesses, you are generally able to compensate for them. Your sexual adjustment has presented some problems for you. Disciplined and controlled on the outside, you tend to be worrisome and insecure inside. At times you have serious doubts as to whether you have made the right decision or done the right thing. You prefer a certain amount of change and variety and become dissatisfied when hemmed in by restrictions and limitations. You pride yourself on being an independent thinker and do not accept other opinions without satisfactory proof. You have found it unwise to be too frank in revealing yourself to others. At times you are extroverted, affable, sociable, while at other times you are introverted, wary, and reserved. Some of your aspirations tend to be pretty unrealistic.★

Does this describe your personality? A psychologist read this summary individually to college students who had taken a personality test. Only 5 students out of 79 felt that the description was inaccurate. Another study found that people rated this "personality profile" as more accurate than their actual horoscopes (French et al., 1991).

Reread the description and you will see that it contains both sides of several personality dimensions ("At times you are extroverted . . . while at other times you are introverted"). Its apparent accuracy is an illusion based on the **fallacy of positive instances,** in which we remember or notice things that confirm our expectations and forget the rest.

★Reprinted with permission of author and publisher from: R. E. Ulrich, T. J. Stachnik, and N. R. Stainton, "Student acceptance of generalized personality interpretations," *Psychological Reports, 13,* 1963, 831–834.

Uncritical acceptance The tendency to believe generally positive or flattering descriptions of oneself.

Fallacy of positive instances The tendency to remember or notice information that fits one's expectations, while forgetting discrepancies.

Barnum effect The tendency to consider a personal description accurate if it is stated in very general terms.

The pseudo-psychologies thrive on this effect. For example, you can always find "Leo characteristics" in a Leo. If you looked, however, you could also find "Gemini characteristics," "Scorpio characteristics," or whatever.

THE BARNUM EFFECT   Pseudo-psychologies also take advantage of the **Barnum effect,** which is a tendency to consider personal descriptions accurate if they are stated in general terms. P. T. Barnum, the famed circus showman, had a formula for success: "Always have a little something for everybody." Like the all-purpose personality profile, palm readings, fortunes, horoscopes, and other products of pseudo-psychology are stated in such general terms that they can hardly miss.

Cathy Fichten and Betty Sunerton, two psychology teachers at Dawson College in Montreal, devised a classroom exercise to teach research methodology to students in their introductory psychology classes. Students were asked to validate horoscopes that appeared in a Montreal newspaper using a 10-point rating scale of personal usefulness ("How personally useful would this forecast have been for you if you had read it yesterday?"). Some students were told that the forecasts were for their own zodiac signs, while others rated the same forecasts without knowing the signs. Although students who thought they were rating their own horoscopes rated them as more personally useful than those who did not, the results were not replicated when the procedure was repeated using the same day's horoscopes from a Toronto newspaper. In other words, daily forecasts were not valid (Fichten & Sunerton, 1983). When students who said they read their own horoscopes at least three times a week were asked to match daily horoscopes with their appropriate astrological signs, they did no better than chance. Fichten and Sunerton repeated the exercise several times in their classes and eventually published the results.

A few months after their research was reported in a peer-reviewed psychology journal, one of Cathy Fichten's students came to her waving a copy of a widely circulated tabloid. Under a screaming bold headline ("Horoscopes really true, says psychologist") was an article that summarized the research methodology accurately but conveniently omitted the word "not" when describing the results. In addition, the phrase "Dr. Fichten said" was used repeatedly throughout the article (*The Star*, October 11, 1983, p. 32). However, Fichten was never interviewed by anyone from the tabloid. The tabloid article was later quoted as a source of "scientific" information on the validity of horoscope predictions by a horoscope magazine.

It didn't stop there. For months after, Fichten received phone calls and letters from people looking for "expert" information about their horoscopes, including one woman who wanted advice on who to marry and an 80-year-old woman looking for guidance from the stars about her will (Fichten, 2002).

Astrology's popularity shows that many people have difficulty separating valid psychology from systems that seem valid but are not. The goal of this discussion, then, has been to make you a more critical observer of human behaviour and to clarify what is, and what is not, psychology. Here is what the "stars" say about your future:

> Emphasis now on education and personal improvement. A learning experience of lasting value awaits you. Take care of scholastic responsibilities before engaging in recreation. The word *psychology* figures prominently in your future.

Pseudo-psychologies may seem like no more than a nuisance, but they can do harm. For instance, people seeking treatment for psychological disorders may become the victims of self-appointed "experts" who offer ineffective, pseudo-scientific "therapies" (Kalal, 1999). Valid psychological principles are based on observation and evidence, not fads, opinions, or wishful thinking.

A Look Ahead

To help you get the most out of psychology, each chapter of this text includes a Psychology in Action section like the one that follows. There you will find ideas you can actually use, now or in the future. To complete our discussion, let's take a critical look at information reported in the popular press. You should find this an interesting way to conclude our first tour of psychology and its methods.

Survey Question:
■ How good is psychological information found in the popular media?

Knowledge builder

CLINICAL AND SURVEY METHODS / CRITICAL THINKING

Relate

It is unusual to get through a day without encountering people who believe in pseudo-psychologies or who make unscientific or unfounded statements. How stringently do you evaluate your own beliefs and the claims made by others? Critical thinking requires effort and discipline, but high-quality information is the reward.

Learning Check

1. Case studies can often be thought of as natural tests and are frequently used by clinical psychologists. T or F?
2. For the survey method to be valid, a representative sample of people must be polled. T or F?
3. Amnesia would most likely be investigated by use of
   a. a representative sample *b.* field experiments *c.* the double-blind procedure *d.* case studies
4. _____ is the outdated theory that personality is revealed by the skull. It was popularized by Franz _____.

5. The fallacy of positive instances refers to graphology's accepted value for the detection of forgeries. T or F?
6. Personality descriptions provided by pseudo-psychologies are stated in general terms that provide "a little something for everybody." This fact is the basis of the
   a. palmist's fallacy *b.* uncritical acceptance pattern *c.* fallacy of positive instances *d.* Barnum effect

Critical Thinking

7. A psychologist conducting a survey at a shopping mall (The Gallery of Wretched Excess) flips a coin before stopping passersby. If the coin shows heads, he interviews the person; if it shows tails, he skips that person. Has the psychologist obtained a random sample?

Answers:

1. T 2. T 3. *d* 4. Phrenology, Gall 5. F 6. *d* 7. The psychologist's coin flips might produce a reasonably good sample of people at the mall. The real problem is that people who go to the mall may be mostly from one part of town, from upper-income groups, or from some other non-representative group. The psychologist's sample is likely to be seriously flawed.

PSYCHOLOGY IN THE NEWS—SEPARATING FACT FROM FICTION

Psychology is a popular topic in magazines and newspapers. Unfortunately, much of what you will read is based on wishful thinking rather than science. Here are some suggestions for separating high-quality information from misleading fiction.

Suggestion 1: Be skeptical.

Reports in the popular press tend to be made uncritically and with a definite bias toward reporting "astonishing" findings. Remember, saying, "That's incredible" means, "That's not believable"—which is often true.

EXAMPLE 1: Some years ago, news articles described an amazing new "sixth sense" called "dermo-optical perception." A few gifted people, the articles claimed, could use their fingertips to identify colours and read print while blindfolded.

In reality, such "abilities" are based on what stage magicians call a "nose peek." It is impossible to prepare a blindfold (without damaging the eyes) that does not leave a tiny space on each side of the nose. Were the people who claimed to have "X-ray eyes" taking nose peeks? Apparently they were, because "dermo-optical abilities" disappeared as soon as the opportunity to peek was controlled.

EXAMPLE 2: In 1994, the *National Enquirer* reported that "Top University Researchers Reveal . . . 8 million Americans may have been abducted by UFOs." However, one of the researchers cited in the article actually concluded, "the public can rest assured that there is no evidence that millions of Americans are being abducted." In other words, the *Enquirer* story completely reversed the real findings. You'll find similar misinformation and sensationalism throughout the popular media. Be on guard.

Suggestion 2: Consider the source of information.

It should come as no surprise that information used to sell a product often reflects a desire for profit rather than the objective truth. Here is a typical advertising claim: "Independent laboratory tests prove that no pain reliever is stronger or more effective than Brand X aspirin." A statement like this usually means that there was no difference between the products tested. No other pain reliever was stronger or more effective. But none was weaker either.

Keep the source in mind when reading the claims of makers of home biofeedback machines, sleep-learning devices, subliminal tapes, and the like. Remember that psychological services may be merchandised as well. Be wary of expensive courses that promise instant mental health and happiness, increased efficiency, memory, ESP or psychic ability, control of the unconscious mind, an end to smoking, and so on. Usually they are promoted with a few testimonials and many unsupported claims (Lilienfeld, 1998).

Psychic claims should be viewed with special caution. Stage mentalists make a living by deceiving the public. Understandably, they are highly interested in promoting belief in their non-existent powers. Psychic phenomena, when (and if) they do occur, are quite unpredictable. It would be impossible for a mentalist to do three shows a night, six nights a week without consistently using deception. The same is true of the so-called "psychic advisers" promoted in TV commercials. These charlatans make use of the Barnum effect (described earlier) to create an illusion that they know private information about people who call them.

Suggestion 3: Ask yourself if there was a control group.

The key importance of a control group in any experiment is frequently overlooked by the unsophisticated—an error to which you are no longer susceptible! The popular press is full of reports of "experiments" performed without control groups: "Talking to Plants

Firewalking is based on simple physics, not on any form of supernatural psychological control. The temperature of the coals may be as high as 650°C (1200°F). However, coals are like the air in a hot oven: They are very inefficient at transferring heat during brief contact.

Speeds Growth"; "Special Diet Controls Hyperactivity in Children"; "Food Shows Less Spoilage in Pyramid Chamber"; "Graduates of Firewalking Seminar Risk Their Soles."

Consider the last example for a moment. In recent years, expensive commercial courses have been promoted to teach people to walk barefoot on hot coals. (Why anyone would want to do this is itself an interesting question.) Firewalkers supposedly protect their feet with a technique called "neurolinguistic programming." Many people have paid good money to learn the technique, and most do manage a quick walk on the coals. But is the technique necessary? And is anything remarkable happening? We need a comparison group!

Fortunately, physicist Bernard Leikind has provided one. Leikind showed with volunteers that anyone (with reasonably callused feet) can walk over a bed of coals without being burned. The reason is that the coals, which are light, fluffy carbon, transmit little heat when touched. The principle involved is similar to briefly putting your hand in a hot oven. If you touch a pan, you will be burned because metal transfers heat efficiently. But if your hand stays in the heated air you'll be fine because air transmits little heat (Mitchell, 1987). Mystery solved.

Suggestion 4: Look for errors in distinguishing between correlation and causation.

As you now know, it is dangerous to presume that one thing caused another just because they are correlated. In spite of this, you will see many claims based on questionable correlations. Here's an example of mistaking correlation for causation: Jeanne Dixon, an astrologer, once answered a group of prominent scientists—who had declared that there is no scientific foundation for astrology—by saying, "They would do well to check the records at their local police stations, where they will learn that the rate of violent crime rises and falls with lunar cycles." Dixon, of course, believes that the moon affects human behaviour.

If it is true that violent crime is more frequent at certain times of the month, doesn't that prove her point? Far from it. Increased crime could be due to darker nights, the fact that many people expect others to act crazier, or any number of similar factors. More importantly, direct studies of the alleged "lunar effect" have shown that it doesn't occur (Simon, 1998; Wilkinson et al., 1997). Moonstruck criminals, along with "moon madness," are a fiction (Raison, Klein, & Steckler, 1999).

Suggestion 5: Be sure to distinguish between observation and inference.

If you see a person crying, is it correct to assume that she or he is sad? Although it seems reasonable to make this assumption, it is actually quite risky. We can observe objectively that the person is crying, but to infer sadness may be in error. It could be that the individual has just peeled 10 onions. Or maybe he or she just won a million-dollar lottery or is trying contact lenses for the first time.

Psychologists, politicians, physicians, scientists, and other experts often go far beyond the available facts in their claims. This does not mean that their inferences, opinions, and interpretations have no value; the opinion of an expert on the causes of mental illness, criminal behaviour, learning problems, or whatever can be revealing. But be careful to distinguish between fact and opinion.

Suggestion 6: Beware of oversimplifications, especially those motivated by monetary gain.

Courses or programs that offer a "new personality in three sessions," "six steps to love and fulfillment in marriage," or newly discovered "secrets of unlocking the powers of the mind" should be immediately suspect.

An excellent example of oversimplification is provided by a brochure entitled "Dr. Joyce Brothers Asks: How Do You Rate as a 'Superwoman'?" Dr. Brothers, a "media" psychologist who has no private practice and is not known for research, wrote the brochure as a consultant for the Aerosol Packaging Council of the Chemical Specialties Manufacturers Association. A typical suggestion in this brochure tells how to enhance a marriage: "Sweep him off to a weekend hideaway. Tip: When he's not looking spray a touch of your favorite *aerosol* cologne mist on the bed sheets and pillows" (italics added). Sure, Joyce.

Suggestion 7: Remember, "for example" is not proof.

After reading this chapter, you should be sensitive to the danger of selecting single examples. If you read, "Law student passes bar exam using sleep-learning device," don't rush out to buy one. Systematic research has shown that these devices are of little or no value (Druckman & Bjork, 1994; Wood et al., 1992). A corollary to this suggestion is to ask, Are the reported observations important or widely applicable?

Examples, anecdotes, single cases, and testimonials are all potentially deceptive. Unfortunately, individual cases tell nothing about what is true in general (Stanovich, 1996). For instance, studies of large groups of people show that smoking increases the likelihood of lung cancer. It doesn't matter if you know a lifelong heavy smoker who is 94 years old. The general finding is the one to remember.

Summary

We are all bombarded daily with such a mass of new information that it is difficult to absorb it. The available knowledge, even in a limited area like psychology, biology, medicine, or contemporary rock music, is so vast that no single person can completely know and comprehend it. With this situation in mind, it becomes increasingly important that you become a critical, selective, and informed consumer of information.

Knowledge builder

PSYCHOLOGY IN THE MEDIA

Relate

 Do you tend to assume that a statement must be true if it is in print, on television, or made by an authority? How actively do you evaluate and question claims found in the media? Could you be a more critical consumer of information? Should you be a more critical consumer of information?

Learning Check

1. Newspaper accounts of dermo-optical perception have generally reported only the results of carefully designed psychological experiments. T or F?
2. Stage mentalists and psychics often use deception in their acts. T or F?

3. Blaming the lunar cycle for variations in the rate of violent crime is an example of mistaking correlation for causation. T or F?
4. If a law student uses a sleep learning device to pass the bar exam, it proves that the device works. T or F?

Critical Thinking

5. Many parents believe that children become "hyperactive" when they eat too much sugar, and some early studies seemed to confirm this connection. However, we now know that eating sugar rarely has any effect on children. Why do you think that sugar appears to cause hyperactivity?

Answers:

1. F 2. T 3. T 4. F 5. This is another case of mistaking correlation for causation. Children who are hyperactive may eat more sugar (and other foods) to fuel their frenetic activity levels.

Psychologist's Journal

EPILOGUE

Now that you have an overview of psychology, let's have Gary VandenBos and Brenda Bryant summarize:

> Psychologists are explorers and discoverers. They explore the reactions of human beings to small frustrations and great successes, to pleasing colors and the aftermath of disaster, always looking for answers to how and why people think, feel, and behave as they do. . . . The psychologist, regardless of where she or he may work, is always applying what is known in an effort to resolve the unknown. The psychologist, no matter how small the question being asked may appear to be, is looking for the larger answer (VandenBos & Bryant, 1987).

Bravo! Brava! Yes, that's it exactly.

CHAPTER IN REVIEW

Major Points

▶ Psychology is the science of behaviour and mental processes. Psychology provides objective answers to questions about human behaviour.

▶ Psychologists gather scientific data in order to describe, understand, predict, and control behaviour.

▶ The scientific method consists of highly refined procedures for observing the natural world, testing hypotheses, and drawing valid conclusions.

▶ Psychologists use several specialized research methods. Each has strengths and weaknesses, so all are needed to fully investigate human behaviour.

▶ Experimentation is the most powerful way to identify cause-and-effect relationships.

▶ Critical thinking is central to the scientific method, to psychology, and to effective behaviour in general.

▶ The popular media are rife with inaccurate information. It is essential to critically evaluate information, no matter what its source may be.

Summary

What Is Psychology? What Are Its Goals?

• Psychology is the scientific study of behaviour.

• Some major areas of research in psychology are comparative, learning, sensation, perception, personality, biopsychology, motivation and emotion, social, cognitive, developmental, the psychology of gender, and cultural psychology.

• Psychologists may be directly interested in animal behaviour, or they may study animals as models of human behaviour.

• As a science, psychology's goals are to describe, understand, predict, and control behaviour.

How Did Psychology Emerge as a Field of Knowledge?

• Historically, psychology is an outgrowth of philosophy.

• The first psychological laboratory was established in Germany by Wilhelm Wundt, who tried to study conscious experience.

• The first school of thought in psychology was structuralism, a kind of "mental chemistry" based on introspection and analysis.

• Structuralism was followed by functionalism, behaviourism, and Gestalt psychology.

• Psychodynamic approaches, such as Freud's psychoanalytic theory, emphasize the unconscious origins of behaviour.

• Humanistic psychology accentuates subjective experience, human potentials, and personal growth.

What Are the Major Trends and Specialties in Psychology?

• Five main streams of thought in modern psychology are behaviourism, humanism, the psychodynamic approach, biopsychology, and cognitive psychology.

- Although psychologists, psychiatrists, psychoanalysts, and counsellors all work in the field of mental health, their training and methods differ considerably.
- Clinical and counselling psychologists, who do psychotherapy, represent only two of dozens of specialties in psychology.
- Psychological research may be basic or applied.

Why Is the Scientific Method Important to Psychologists?

- Important elements of a scientific investigation include observing, defining a problem, proposing a hypothesis, gathering evidence/testing the hypothesis, publishing results, and forming a theory.
- Before they can be investigated, psychological concepts must be given operational definitions.

How Do Psychologists Collect Information?

- Naturalistic observation is a starting place in many investigations.
- Three problems with naturalistic observation are the effects of the observer on the observed, observer bias, and an inability to explain observed behaviour.
- In the correlational method, relationships between two traits, responses, or events are measured.
- A correlation coefficient is computed to gauge the strength of the relationship. Correlations allow prediction, but they do not demonstrate cause-and-effect connections.
- Cause-and-effect relationships are best identified by controlled experiments.

How Is an Experiment Performed?

- In an experiment, two or more groups of subjects are formed. These groups differ only with regard to the independent variable (condition of interest as a cause in the experiment).
- Effects on the dependent variable are then measured. All other conditions (extraneous variables) are held constant.
- In experiments that involve drugs, a placebo must be given to control for the effects of expectations. If a double-blind procedure is used, neither subjects nor experimenters know who received a drug.
- A related problem is the experimenter effect (a tendency for experimenters to unconsciously influence the outcome of an experiment). Expectations can create a self-fulfilling prophecy, in which a person changes in the direction of the expectation.

What Other Research Methods Do Psychologists Use?

- The clinical method employs case studies, which are in-depth records of a single subject. Case studies provide important information on topics that cannot be studied any other way.
- In the survey method, people in a representative sample are asked a series of carefully worded questions.

What Is Critical Thinking?

- Critical thinking is the ability to evaluate, compare, analyze, critique, and synthesize information.
- To judge the validity of a claim, it is important to gather evidence for and against the claim and to evaluate the quality of the evidence.

How Does Psychology Differ from False Explanations of Behaviour?

- Numerous pseudo-psychologies exist. These false systems are frequently confused with valid psychology. Belief in pseudo-psychologies is based in part on uncritical acceptance, the fallacy of positive instances, and the Barnum effect.

How Good Is Psychological Information Found in the Popular Media?

- Information in the mass media varies greatly in quality and accuracy.
- It is wise to approach such information with skepticism and caution. This is especially true with regard to the source of information, uncontrolled observation, correlation and causation, inferences, oversimplification, single examples, and unrepeatable results.

PSYCHOLOGY ON THE NET

If you have difficulty finding any of the sites listed here, visit http://psychologyjourney.nelson.com for an updated list of Internet addresses and direct links to relevant sites.

American Psychological Association Home page of the APA, with links to PsychNET, student information, member information, and more. http://www.apa.org/

American Psychological Society Home page of the APS, with links to information, services, and Internet resources. http://www.psychologicalscience.org

The Canadian Counselling Association This site provides information on professional requirements and training. http://www.ccacc.ca/ccacc.htm

Canadian Psychological Association Home page of the CPA, with links to their journals, provincial and territorial associations, and many other Canadian psychology resource websites. http://www.cpa.ca

Ethical Principles of Psychologists and Code of Conduct The full text of the ethical principles that guide professional psychologists. http://www.apa.org/ethics/code.html

The Jane Goodall Institute Information about Goodall's work at Gombe, in Tanzania, where she has studied and protected wild chimpanzees for over 40 years. http://www.janegoodall.org/

Psychweb This award-winning page provides a multitude of services and links. http://www.psychweb.com/

Psycoloquy An online journal with short articles on all areas of psychology. http://www.princeton.edu/~harnad/psyc.html

PsycPORT This site is a large database of psychological information, including daily updates on news related to psychology. http://www.psycport.com

Social Sciences and Humanities Research Council of Canada This government site provides information on research, including how to apply for research grants. http://www.sshrc.ca

Today in the History of Psychology Events in the history of psychology by the date. http://www.cwu.edu/~warren/today.html

InfoTrac College Edition For recent articles related to the pseudo-psychologies discussed in this chapter, use Key Words search for PHRENOLOGY and ASTROLOGY. You can also use a Key Words search for PSYCHOLOGICAL RESEARCH.

INTERACTIVE LEARNING

Psychology: An Interactive Journey Remember that Chapter 1 of the CD-ROM that came with this text has practice tests, flashcards, interactive exercises, a crossword puzzle, and other valuable materials to enhance your learning experience.

PsychNow! 1b. Psychology and Its History, 1c. Research Methods, 1d. Critical Thinking in Psychology.

Psyk.trek 1. History and Methods.

Chart Your Progress

The questions that follow are only a sample of what you need to know. If you miss any of the items, you should review the entire chapter, do the exercises on the CD, and review the Knowledge Builders. Another way to prepare for tests is to get more practice with *WebTutor*, the *Study Guide*, or the *Practice Quizzes* that are available with this text.

1. Psychology is the _____ of _____ and mental processes.
   a. study, the mind
   b. knowledge, philosophy
   c. study, personality
   d. science, behaviour

2. Who among the following is most interested in the growth of young children?
   a. learning theorist
   b. personality theorist
   c. comparative psychologist
   d. developmental psychologist

3. Research that can explain why people remember better if they relate new information to familiar ideas meets which of psychology's goals?
   a. describe
   b. understand
   c. predict
   d. control

4. Which two schools of thought have largely disappeared from contemporary psychology?
   a. behaviourism, Gestalt
   b. humanism, cognitive behaviourism
   c. functionalism, structuralism
   d. structuralism, humanism

5. Who among the following is LEAST likely to treat serious behavioural and emotional disturbances?
   a. psychologist
   b. counsellor
   c. psychiatrist
   d. psychoanalyst

6. A psychologist does a study to see if having control over difficult tasks reduces stress. In the study, he will be testing an
   a. experimental hypothesis
   b. operational definition
   c. empirical definition
   d. anthropomorphic theory

7. Because correlation does not demonstrate causation, psychologists often use _____ to answer questions about behaviour.
   a. experimentation
   b. naturalistic observation
   c. the survey method
   d. the clinical method

8. The outcome of a psychology experiment is revealed by measuring changes in behaviour. Such measures are the _____ variable of the experiment.
   a. independent
   b. correlational
   c. dependent
   d. extraneous

9. Double-blind experiments are designed to control for the
   a. placebo effect
   b. anthropomorphic fallacy
   c. unintended influence of operational definitions
   d. courtesy bias

10. Belief in astrology is based on the fallacy of positive instances, which is a failure to
    a. collect relevant correlations
    b. make use of introspection
    c. distinguish between observation and inference
    d. engage in critical thinking

Answers: 1. d 2. d 3. b 4. c 5. b 6. a 7. a 8. c 9. a 10. d

Chapter 2

Psychologist's Journal

FINDING MUSIC IN TOFU

It's hard to watch and hear a gifted musician without thinking about the brain. Listening to a recording of Bach's *Goldberg Variations* made by the famous Canadian pianist Glenn Gould makes you wonder whether his brain really was that different from those of the rest of his fellow humans that made it possible for him to play music so exquisitely? If Gould had been an athlete, you would definitely say he was "in the zone." His performance of Bach is unforgettable. Of course, in everything from rock to rap, musicians regularly make music that no machine could duplicate. A virtual Bryan Adams? A mechanical Eric Clapton? A synthetic Shania Twain? Certainly not. That's why music is a good example of the central role the brain plays in all that is human.

Your brain is about the size of a grapefruit. It weighs around 1.5 kilograms and looks a lot like tofu. The next time you are in a market that sells beef brains, stop and have a look. What you will see is similar to your own brain, only smaller. How could such a squishy little blob of tissue allow us to make music of exquisite beauty? To seek a cure for cancer? To fall in love? Or to read a book like this one?

Each nerve cell in your brain is linked to as many as 15 000 others. This network makes it possible to process immense amounts of information. In fact, there may be more possible pathways between the neurons in your brain than there are atoms in the entire universe! Undeniably, the human brain is the most amazing of all computers.

Scientists use the power of the brain to study the brain. Yet, even now we must wonder if the brain will ever completely understand itself. Nevertheless, it is clear that answers to many age-old questions about the mind, consciousness, and knowledge lie buried within the brain, waiting to be discovered. Let's visit this fascinating realm.

▶ Neurons—Building a "Biocomputer"

Survey Question:
■ How do nerve cells operate and communicate?

The brain consists of some 100 billion **neurons** (NEW-rons: individual nerve cells). Neurons carry and process information. They also activate muscles and glands. Thus, everything you do, think, or feel can be traced back to these tiny cells. A single neuron is not very smart—it would take at least several just to make you blink. Yet, when neurons form vast networks, they produce intelligence and consciousness. Neurons link to one another in tight clumps and long "chains." Each neuron receives messages from many others and sends its own message on. Millions of neurons must send messages at the same time to produce even the most fleeting thought (Carter, 1998). When Carlos Santana plays one of his signature guitar riffs, literally billions of neurons may be involved.

Parts of a Neuron

What does a neuron look like? What are its main parts? No two neurons are exactly alike, but most have four basic parts (see ▶Figure 2.1). The **dendrites** (DEN-drytes), which look like tree roots, receive messages from other neurons. The **soma** (SOH-mah: cell body) does the same. In addition, the soma sends messages of its own (nerve impulses) down a thin fibre called the **axon** (AK-sahn).

Most axons end in **axon terminals.** These "branches" link up with the dendrites and somas of other neurons. This allows information to pass from neuron to neuron. Some axons are only 0.1 millimetre long. (That's about the width of a pencil line.) Others stretch up to a metre through the nervous system. (From the base of your spine to your big toe, for instance.) Like miniature cables, axons carry messages through the brain and nervous system. Altogether, your brain has about 4.6 million kilometres of axons in it (Hyman, 1999).

Now let's summarize with a metaphor. Imagine that you are standing in a long line of people who are holding hands. A person on the far right end of the line wants to silently send a message to the person on the left end. She does this by pressing the hand of the person to her left, who presses the hand of the person to his left, and so on. The message arrives at your right hand (your dendrites). You decide whether to pass it on (you are the soma). The message goes out through your left arm (the axon). With your left hand (the axon terminals), you squeeze the hand of the person to your left, and the message moves on.

The Nerve Impulse

Each neuron in your brain acts like a tiny biological battery. That is, electrically charged molecules called *ions* (EYE-ons) are found in and around nerve cells (▶Figure 2.2). Some ions have a positive electrical charge. Others have a negative charge. Different numbers of "plus" and "minus" charges are found inside and outside of nerve cells. As a result, the inside of each neuron in your brain will have an electrical charge of about minus 70 millivolts. (A millivolt is one thousandth of a volt.)

Neuron An individual nerve cell.

Dendrites Neuron fibres that receive incoming messages.

Soma The main body of a neuron or other cell.

Axon Fibre that carries information away from the cell body of a neuron.

Axon terminals Branching fibres at the ends of axons.

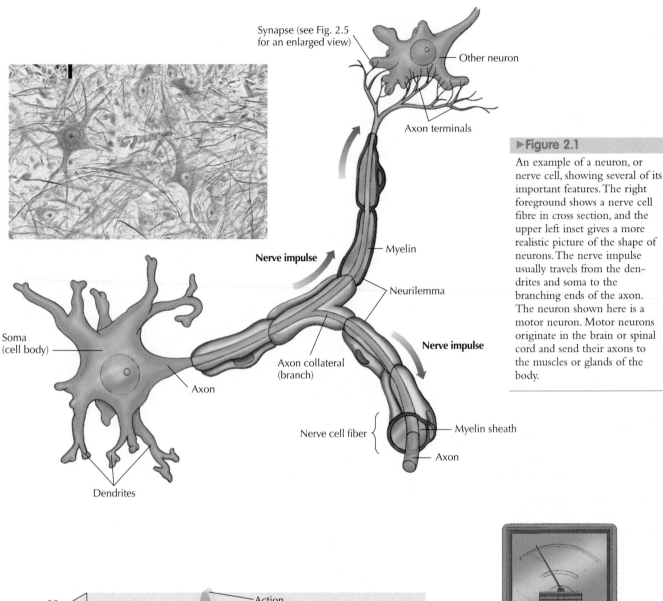

Synapse (see Fig. 2.5 for an enlarged view)

Other neuron

Axon terminals

Figure 2.1

An example of a neuron, or nerve cell, showing several of its important features. The right foreground shows a nerve cell fibre in cross section, and the upper left inset gives a more realistic picture of the shape of neurons. The nerve impulse usually travels from the dendrites and soma to the branching ends of the axon. The neuron shown here is a motor neuron. Motor neurons originate in the brain or spinal cord and send their axons to the muscles or glands of the body.

Nerve impulse

Myelin

Neurilemma

Nerve impulse

Soma (cell body)

Axon

Axon collateral (branch)

Nerve cell fiber

Myelin sheath

Axon

Dendrites

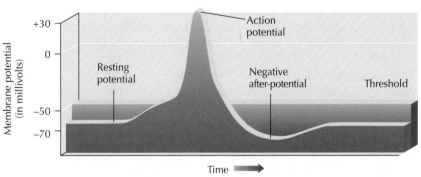

+30

0

−50

−70

Membrane potential (in millivolts)

Action potential

Resting potential

Negative after-potential

Threshold

Time

+ + + + + + + +
− − − − − − − −
− − − − − − − −
+ + + + + + + +

Axon

Figure 2.2

Activity in an axon can be measured by placing electrical probes inside and outside the axon. (The scale is exaggerated here. Such measurements require ultra-small electrodes, as described later in this chapter.) At rest, the inside of an axon is about −60 to −70 millivolts, compared with the outside. Electrochemical changes in a nerve cell generate an action potential. When positively charged sodium ions (Na^+) rush into the cell, its interior briefly becomes positive. This is the action potential. After the action potential, an outward flow of positive potassium ions (K^+) restores the negative charge inside the axon. (See Figure 2.3 for further explanation.)

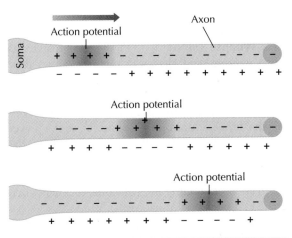

▶Figure 2.3

The inside of an axon normally has a negative electrical charge. The fluid surrounding an axon is normally positive. As an action potential passes along the axon, these charges reverse, so that the interior of the axon briefly becomes positive.

Resting potential
The electrical charge of a neuron at rest.
Action potential
The nerve impulse.
Ion channels
Gaps through the axon membrane.
Negative after-potential
A drop in electrical charge below the resting potential.

The electrical charge of an inactive neuron is called its **resting potential.** But neurons seldom get much rest: Messages arriving from other neurons keep changing the resting potential to higher or lower amounts. If the electrical charge changes to about −50 millivolts, the neuron will reach its *threshold,* or trigger point for firing (see Figure 2.2). It's as if the neuron says, "Ah-ha! It's time to send a message to my neighbours." When a neuron reaches −50 millivolts, an **action potential,** or nerve impulse, sweeps down the axon at up to 320 kilometres per hour (▶Figure 2.3). That may seem fast, but it still takes at least a split second to react. That's one reason why hitting a major league fastball is one of the most difficult feats in all of sports.

What happens during an action potential? The axon membrane is pierced by tiny tunnels called **ion channels.** Normally, these channels are blocked by molecules that act like "gates" or "doors." During an action potential, the gates pop open. This allows sodium ions (Na^+) to rush into the axon (Carlson, 1998). The channels open up first near the soma. Then, gate after gate opens down the axon as the action potential zips along (▶Figure 2.4).

Each action potential is an all-or-nothing event (a nerve impulse occurs completely or not at all). You might find it helpful to picture the axon as a row of dominoes set on end. Tipping over the dominoes is an all-or-nothing act. Once the first domino drops, a wave of falling blocks will zip rapidly to the end of the line. Similarly, when a nerve impulse is triggered near the soma, a wave of activity (the action potential) travels down the length of the axon. This is what happens in long chains of neurons as Glenn Gould's brain told his hands what to do next, note after note.

After each nerve impulse, the cell briefly drops below its resting level, and it becomes less willing to fire. This **negative after-potential** occurs because potassium ions (K^+) flow out of the neuron while the membrane gates are open (see Figure 2.4). After a nerve impulse, ions flow both into and out of the axon, recharging it for more action. In our model, the row of dominoes is quickly set up again. Soon, the axon is ready for another wave of activity.

Synapses and Neurotransmitters

How does information move from one neuron to another? The nerve impulse is primarily electrical. That's why electrically stimulating the brain affects behaviour. To prove the point, researcher José Delgado once entered a bullring with a cape and a radio transmitter. The bull charged. Delgado retreated. At the last instant the speeding bull stopped short. Why? Because Delgado's radio activated electrodes (metal wires) placed deep within the bull's brain. These, in turn, stimulated "control centres" that brought the bull to a halt.

▶Figure 2.4

Cross-sectional views of an axon. The right end of the top axon is at rest, with a negatively charged interior. An action potential begins when the ion channels open and sodium ions (Na^+) enter the axon. In this drawing, the action potential would travel rapidly along the axon, from left to right. In the lower axon, the action potential has moved to the right. After it passes, potassium ions (K^+) flow out of the axon. This quickly renews the negative charge inside the axon, so it can fire again. Sodium ions that enter the axon during an action potential are pumped back out more slowly. Their removal restores the original resting potential.

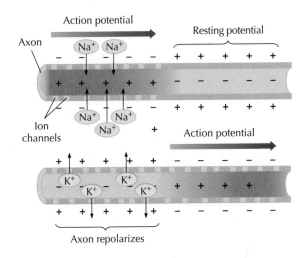

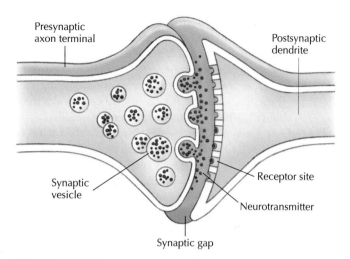

Presynaptic axon terminal

Postsynaptic dendrite

Synaptic vesicle

Receptor site

Neurotransmitter

Synaptic gap

▶Figure 2.5

A highly magnified view of the synapse shown in Figure 2.1. Neurotransmitters are stored in tiny sacs called synaptic vesicles. When a nerve impulse arrives at an axon terminal, the vesicles move to the surface and release neurotransmitters. These transmitter molecules cross the synaptic gap to affect the next neuron. The size of the gap is exaggerated here; it is actually only about one millionth of an inch. Transmitter molecules vary in their effects: Some excite the next neuron and some inhibit its activity.

Synapse The microscopic space between two neurons, over which messages pass.

Neurotransmitter Any chemical released by a neuron that alters activity in other neurons.

Receptor sites Areas on the surface of neurons and other cells that are sensitive to neurotransmitters or hormones.

Acetylcholine The neurotransmitter released by neurons to activate muscles.

Neuropeptides Brain chemicals, such as enkephalins and endorphins, that regulate the activity of neurons.

The nerve impulse is not what relays a message from one neuron to another. This is because there is a microscopic gap called a **synapse** (SIN-aps) (▶Figure 2.5) that exists between two neurons, and electrical impulses cannot flow through physical gaps. You can think about this problem in the following way: You receive electricity from your local power corporation, which generates power many kilometres away from your home. Your home is connected to the power plant through a complex network of wires. A cut in the system of wires anywhere along the intricate maze will disrupt your electrical supply. If we think of neurons as pieces of wires, then an electrical impulse will come to a halt when it reaches the end of the neuronal path.

So if a neuron cannot communicate with its neighbours by sending an electrical impulse, how does it manage to send its message across? When an action potential reaches the tips of the axon terminals, chemical substances called **neurotransmitters** (NUE-roh-TRANS-mit-ers) are released. After crossing the synaptic gap, these chemicals affect the activity of the next neuron.

Let's return to the people standing in a line. To be the example, you and the others shouldn't be holding hands. Instead, each person should have a toy squirt gun in his or her left hand. To pass along a message, you would squirt the right hand of the person to your left. When that person notices this "message," he or she would squirt the right hand of the person to the left, and so on.

When chemical molecules cross over a synapse, they attach to special receiving areas on the next neuron (Figure 2.5). These tiny **receptor sites** on the cell membrane are sensitive to neurotransmitters. The sites are found in large numbers on nerve cell bodies and dendrites. Muscles and glands have receptor sites, too.

Do neurotransmitters always trigger an action potential in the next neuron? No. Some transmitters excite the next neuron (move it closer to firing). Others inhibit it (make firing less likely). At any instant, a single neuron may receive hundreds or thousands of messages. Does it fire an impulse? It depends: If several "exciting" messages arrive close in time, the neuron will fire—but only if it doesn't get too many "inhibiting" messages that push it away from its trigger point. In this way, messages are combined before a neuron "decides" to fire its all-or-nothing action potential. Multiply these events by 100 billion neurons and 100 trillion synapses and you have an amazing computer—one that fits into a space smaller than a shoe box.

More than 100 transmitter chemicals are found in the brain. Some examples are acetylcholine, epinephrine, norepinephrine, serotonin, dopamine, histamine, and various amino acids. Many drugs imitate, duplicate, or block these transmitters. For example, **acetylcholine** (ah-SEET-ul-KOH-leen) normally activates muscles. Without acetylcholine, our musical genius Glenn Gould couldn't even move, much less play Bach. That's exactly why the drug *curare* (cue-RAH-ree) causes paralysis. By attaching to receptor sites on muscles, curare competes with acetylcholine. This prevents acetylcholine from activating muscle cells. As a result, a person or animal given curare cannot move—a fact known to South American Indians of the Amazon River Basin, who use curare as an arrow poison for hunting.

NEURAL REGULATORS More subtle brain activities are affected by chemicals called **neuropeptides** (NEW-row-PEP-tides). Neuropeptides do not carry messages directly. Instead, they regulate the activity of other neurotransmitters. By doing so, they affect memory, pain, emotion, pleasure, mood, hunger, sexual behaviour, and other basic processes. For example, when you touch something hot, you jerk your hand away. The messages for this action are carried by neurotransmitters. At the same time, pain may cause

Enkephalins Opiate-like brain chemicals that regulate reactions to pain and stress.

Endorphins Chemicals that are similar in structure and painkilling effect to opiate drugs such as morphine.

the brain to release **enkephalins** (en-KEF-ah-lins). These opiate-like neural regulators relieve pain and stress. Related chemicals called **endorphins** (en-DORF-ins) are released by the pituitary gland. Together, these chemicals reduce the pain so that it is not too disabling.

Such discoveries help to explain the painkilling effect of placebos (fake pills or injections), which raise endorphin levels (Lipman et al., 1990). A release of endorphins also seems to underlie "runner's high," masochism, acupuncture, and the euphoria sometimes associated with childbirth and painful initiation rites (Sternberg et al., 1998). In each case, pain and stress cause the release of endorphins. These in turn induce feelings of pleasure or euphoria similar to being "high" on morphine (Ulett, 1992). People who say they are "addicted" to running or other sports may be closer to the truth than they realize. And more important, we may at last know why some hardy souls take hot saunas followed by cold showers! Ultimately, brain regulators may help to explain depression, schizophrenia, drug addiction, and other puzzling problems.

▶ The Nervous System—Wired for Action

Survey Question:
■ What are the functions of major parts of the nervous system?

Jamal and Vicki are playing catch with a Frisbee. This may look fairly simple. However, to merely toss the Frisbee or catch it, a huge amount of information must be sensed, interpreted, and directed to countless muscle fibres. As they entertain themselves, Jamal and Vicki's neural circuits are ablaze with activity. Let's explore the "wiring diagram" that makes their Frisbee game possible.

Neurons and Nerves

Are neurons the same as nerves? No. Neurons are tiny cells. You would need a microscope to see one. **Nerves** are large bundles of axons and dendrites. You can easily see nerves without magnification.

Nerve A bundle of neuron fibres.

Myelin A fatty layer coating some axons.

Neurilemma A layer of cells that encases many axons.

Neurogenesis The production of new brain cells.

Many nerves are white because they contain axons coated with a fatty layer, or sheath of tissue, called **myelin** (MY-eh-lin). Small gaps in the myelin help nerve impulses move faster. Instead of passing down the entire length of the axon, the action potential leaps from gap to gap. Without the added speed this allows, it would probably be impossible to brake in time to avoid many automobile accidents. When the myelin layer is damaged, a person may suffer from numbness, weakness, or paralysis. That, in fact, is what happens in multiple sclerosis, a disease that occurs when the immune system attacks and destroys the myelin in a person's body.

A thin layer of cells called the **neurilemma** (NEW-rih-LEM-ah) is also wrapped around most axons outside the brain and spinal cord. (Return to Figure 2.1.) The neurilemma forms a "tunnel" that damaged fibres can follow as they repair themselves.

Until only a few years ago, it was widely believed that we are born with all the brain cells we will ever have. This led to the depressing idea that we all slowly go downhill, as the brain loses thousands of neurons each day. Although it is true that the brain loses cells every day, it grows new neurons to replace at least some of them. This process is called **neurogenesis** (nue-roh-JEN-uh-sis: the production of new brain cells) (Gould et al., 1999). Each day, thousands of new cells originate deep within the brain, move to the surface, and link up with other neurons to become part of the brain's circuitry. This is stunning news to brain scientists, who must now figure out what the new cells do. Most likely they are involved in learning, memory, and our ability to adapt to changing circumstances. In fact, Liisa Galea of the University of British Columbia has observed new neurons in an important region of the brain that is responsible for spatial learning and memory. Experimenting with meadow voles (a type of rodent), Galea's research found that the brains of these small animals increase the production of new neurons under certain circumstances. For example, when they roam quite freely in their natural habitat, the voles need to learn detailed information about their surroundings. Under these circumstances, the brains of these little creatures increase the production of neurons. The new neurons probably help the voles with the acquisition of important information about their behaviour. It seems that the brain is capable of generating new cells in response to environmental changes and learning opportunities (Ormerod & Galea, 2001). These findings are intriguing, but only further research will tell us whether human memory is also aided by the production of new neurons.

BRAIN REPAIR   The discovery of neurogenesis in adult brains has raised new hopes that some types of brain damage can be repaired. For example, doctors are testing a new method to treat strokes. Their attempts involve injecting immature cells called stem cells into damaged areas of the brain. If the technique is successful, the new cells should link up with existing neurons and repair some of the stroke damage (Borlongan, Sanberg, & Freeman, 1999). In a promising experiment, some scientists have recently reported success in reversing paralysis in rats whose spinal cords had been injured. This reversal was achieved by injecting **stem cells** into the affected areas. Their paralysis was not cured completely, but rats who could barely walk before the treatment improved dramatically. This type of research has potential for helping those who suffer from degenerative conditions such as Lou Gehrig's disease (Vastag, 2001). (See the discussion below for another approach to restoring spinal cord functions.)

Neural Networks

As you can see in ▶ Figures 2.6 and 2.7, the **central nervous system (CNS)** consists of the brain and spinal cord. The brain is the central "computer" of the nervous system. Jamal must use this "computer" to anticipate when and where the Frisbee will arrive. Jamal's brain communicates with the rest of his body through a large "cable" called the spinal cord. From there, messages flow through the **peripheral nervous system (PNS).** This intricate network of nerves carries information to and from the CNS.

Stem cells Immature cells that differentiate into various types of mature cells in the body, including neurons.

Central nervous system The brain and spinal cord.

Peripheral nervous system All parts of the nervous system outside the brain and spinal cord.

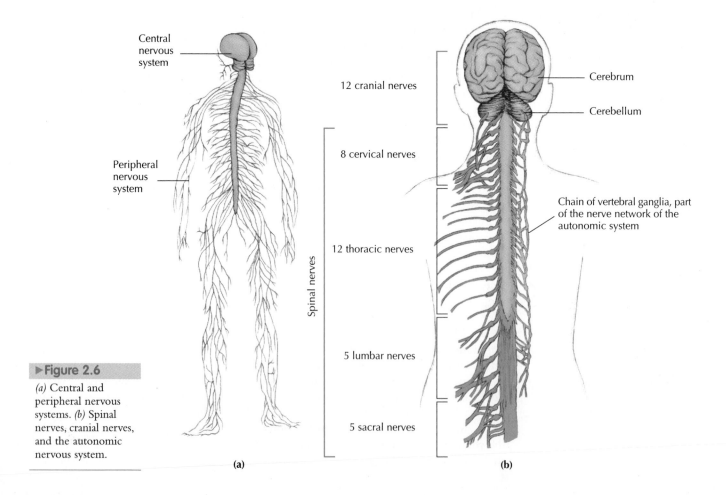

Central nervous system

Peripheral nervous system

12 cranial nerves

8 cervical nerves

Spinal nerves

12 thoracic nerves

5 lumbar nerves

5 sacral nerves

Cerebrum

Cerebellum

Chain of vertebral ganglia, part of the nerve network of the autonomic system

▶**Figure 2.6**

(a) Central and peripheral nervous systems. *(b)* Spinal nerves, cranial nerves, and the autonomic nervous system.

(a)

(b)

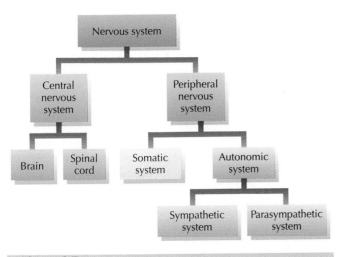

▶Figure 2.7

Subparts of the nervous system.

A serious injury to the brain or spinal cord is usually permanent. However, scientists are starting to make progress in repairing damaged neurons in the CNS. For instance, they were recently able to partially repair cut spinal cords in rats. First they closed the gap with nerve fibres from outside the spinal cord. Then they biochemically coaxed the severed spinal nerve fibres to grow through the "tunnels" provided by the implanted fibres. Within two months, the rats had regained some use of their hind legs (Cheng, Cao, & Olson, 1996). Imagine what that could mean to a person confined to a wheelchair. Although it is unwise to raise false hopes, solutions to such problems are beginning to emerge (Baisden, 1995). For instance, medical researchers recently began the first human trials in which nerve grafts will be used to repair damaged spinal cords (Levesque & Neuman, 1999). Just the same, it is wise to take good care of your own CNS. That means using seatbelts when you drive, a helmet if you ride a motorcycle, wearing protective gear for sports, and avoiding activities that pose a risk to the head or spinal cord.

Somatic system Nerves linking the spinal cord with the body and sense organs.
Autonomic system Nerves carrying information to and from the internal organs and glands.
Sympathetic system A branch of the ANS that arouses the body.
Parasympathetic system A branch of the ANS that quiets the body.

THE PERIPHERAL NERVOUS SYSTEM The peripheral system can be divided into two major parts. The **somatic system** carries messages to and from the sense organs and skeletal muscles. In general, it controls voluntary behaviour, such as when Vicki tosses the Frisbee or B. B. King plays the blues. In contrast, the **autonomic system** serves the internal organs and glands of the body. The word *autonomic* means "self-governing." Activities governed by the autonomic nervous system (ANS) are mostly "vegetative" or automatic, such as heart rate, digestion, or perspiration. Thus, messages carried by the somatic system can make your hand move, but they cannot cause your eyes to dilate. Likewise, messages carried by the ANS can stimulate digestion, but they cannot help you write a letter. If Jamal feels a flash of anger when he misses a catch, a brief burst of activity will spread through his autonomic system.

The autonomic nervous system can be divided into the sympathetic and parasympathetic branches. Both are related to responses involved in emotions, such as sweating, heart rate, and other involuntary behaviour (▶Figure 2.8). The ANS and the somatic system work together to coordinate the body's internal reactions with events in the world outside. For example, if a snarling dog lunges at you, the somatic system will control your leg muscles so you can run. At the same time, the autonomic system will raise your blood pressure, quicken your heart, and so forth.

How do the branches of the autonomic system differ? The **sympathetic syndrome** is an "emergency" system. It prepares the body for "fight or flight" during times of danger or high emotion. In essence, it arouses the body for action. Imagine someone who has a winning lottery ticket for $5 million and ends up misplacing it. No doubt that person's sympathetic nervous system would become quite active when he or she first notices that the lottery ticket is not where it should be.

The **parasympathetic syndrome** quiets the body and returns it to a lower level of arousal. It is most active soon

Parasympathetic

Constricts pupil
Stimulates tears
Stimulates salivation

Inhibits heart rate
Constricts respiration
Constricts blood vessels
Stimulates digestion

Contracts bladder
Stimulates elimination
Stimulates genitals

Sympathetic

Dilates pupil
Inhibits tears
Inhibits salivation
Activates sweat glands
Increases heart rate
Increases respiration
Inhibits digestion
Release of adrenaline
Release of sugar from liver
Relaxes bladder
Inhibits elimination
Inhibits genitals
Ejaculation in males

▶Figure 2.8

Sympathetic and parasympathetic branches of the autonomic nervous system. Both branches control involuntary actions. The sympathetic system generally activates the body. The parasympathetic system generally quiets it. The sympathetic branch relays through clusters of cell bodies outside the spinal cord.

Each year spinal cord injuries rob many thousands of people, like actor Christopher Reeve, of the ability to move. Yet, there is growing hope that nerve-grafting techniques may someday make it possible for some of these people to walk again.

Spinal nerves Major nerves that carry sensory and motor messages in and out of the spinal cord.

Cranial nerves Major nerves that leave the brain without passing through the spinal cord.

Reflex arc The simplest behaviour, in which a stimulus provokes an automatic response.

Sensory neuron A nerve cell that carries information from the senses toward the CNS.

Connector neuron A nerve cell that serves as a link between two others.

Motor neuron A nerve cell that carries motor commands from the CNS to muscles and glands.

Effector cells Cells in muscles and glands that are capable of producing some type of response.

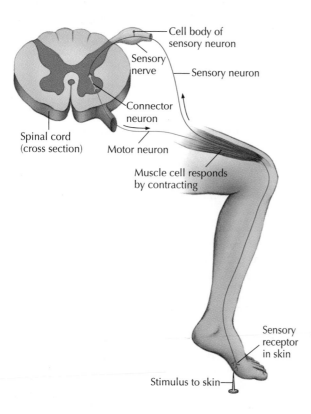

after an emotional event. The parasympathetic branch also helps to keep vital functions such as heart rate, breathing, and digestion at moderate levels.

Of course, both branches of the ANS are always active. At any given moment, their combined activity determines if your body is relaxed or aroused.

THE SPINAL CORD   As mentioned earlier, the spinal cord acts like a cable connecting the brain to other parts of the body. If you were to cut through this "cable," you would see columns of white matter in areas that have lots of myelin. This tissue is made up of axons that eventually leave the spinal cord. Outside the cord, they are bundled together into nerves. Return to Figure 2.6b and you will see that 30 pairs of spinal nerves leave the sides of the spinal cord. Another pair (not shown) leaves the tip. The 31 **spinal nerves** carry sensory and motor messages to and from the spinal cord. In addition, 12 pairs of **cranial nerves** leave the brain directly. Together, these nerves keep your entire body in communication with your brain.

How is the spinal cord related to behaviour? The simplest behaviour pattern is a **reflex arc,** which occurs when a stimulus provokes an automatic response. Such reflexes occur within the spinal cord, without any help from the brain (see ▶Figure 2.9). Imagine that Vicki steps on a thorn. (Yes, they're still playing catch.) Pain is detected in her foot by a **sensory neuron** (a nerve cell that carries messages from the senses toward the CNS). Instantly, the sensory neuron fires off a message to Vicki's spinal cord.

Inside the spinal cord, the sensory neuron synapses with a **connector neuron** (a nerve cell that links two others). The connector neuron activates a **motor neuron** (a cell that carries commands from the CNS to muscles and glands). The muscle fibres are made up of **effector cells** (cells capable of producing a response). The muscle cells contract and cause Vicki's foot to withdraw. Note that no brain activity is required for a reflex arc to occur. Vicki's body will react automatically to protect itself.

In reality, even a simple reflex usually triggers more complex activity. For example, muscles of Vicki's other leg must contract to support her as she shifts her weight. Even this can be done by the spinal cord, but it involves many more cells and several spinal nerves. Also, the spinal cord normally informs the brain of the actions it has taken. As her foot pulls away from the thorn, Vicki will feel the pain and think, "Ouch, what was that?"

Perhaps you have realized how adaptive it is to have a spinal cord capable of responding on its own. Such automatic responses

▶**Figure 2.9**

A simple sensory-motor (reflex) arc. A simple reflex is set in motion by a stimulus to the skin (or other part of the body). The nerve impulse travels to the spinal cord and then back out to a muscle, which contracts. Reflexes provide an "automatic" protective device for the body.

leave the brains of our Frisbee aces free to deal with more important information—such as the location of trees, lampposts, and attractive onlookers—as they take turns making grandstand catches.

In a few moments, we will probe more deeply into the brain. Before we do, it might be wise to explore some of the research tools biopsychologists use. Uncovering the brain's mysteries has not been easy. Let's consider some of the basics.

▶ Research Methods—Charting the Brain's Inner Realms

Survey Question:
■ How do we know how the brain works?

Clinical study An intensive investigation of a single person, especially one suffering from some injury or disease.

Ablation Surgical removal of tissue.

Electrode Any device (such as a wire, needle, or metal plate) used to electrically stimulate nerve tissue or to record its activity.

Deep lesioning Removal of tissue within the brain by use of an electrode.

Electrical stimulation of the brain (ESB) Direct electrical stimulation and activation of brain tissue.

Micro-electrode An electrode small enough to record the activity of a single neuron.

Biopsychology is the study of how biological processes, the brain, and the nervous system relate to behaviour. Many of the functions of the brain have been identified by **clinical studies.** Such studies examine changes in personality, behaviour, or sensory capacity caused by brain diseases or injuries. A related experimental technique is based on **ablation** (ab-LAY-shun: surgical removal) of parts of the brain (see ▶Figure 2.10). When ablation causes changes in behaviour or sensory capacity, we gain insight into the purpose of the missing "part." An alternative approach is to use electrical stimulation to "turn on" brain structures. For example, the surface of the brain can be activated by touching it with a small electrified wire called an **electrode.** When this is done during brain surgery, the patient can tell what effect the stimulation had. (The brain has no pain receptors, so surgery can be done while a patient is awake. Only local painkillers are used for the scalp and skull.) (Any volunteers?) In fact, such experiments were carried out in Montreal by a famous neurosurgeon, Wilder Penfield. While performing surgery on people with epilepsy, Penfield stimulated certain brain areas. Patients heard sounds, parts of their bodies moved automatically, or they were reminded of certain events from their past, depending on what area of the brain was stimulated (Penfield & Perot, 1963).

Even structures below the surface of the brain can be activated or removed. In **deep lesioning** (LEE-zhun-ing), a thin wire electrode, insulated except at the tip, is lowered into a target area inside the brain (see Figure 2.10). An electric current is then used to destroy a small amount of brain tissue. Again, changes in behaviour give clues about the function of the affected area. Using a weaker current, it is also possible to activate target areas rather than remove them. This is called **electrical stimulation of the brain (ESB).** ESB can call forth behaviour with astonishing power. Instantly, it can bring about aggression, alertness, escape, eating, drinking, sleeping, movement, euphoria, memories, speech, tears, and more. By using ESB, researchers are creating a three-dimensional brain map. This "atlas" shows the sensory, motor, and emotional responses that can be elicited from various parts of the brain. It promises to be a valuable guide for medical treatment, as well as for exploring the brain (Carter, 1998; Yoshida, 1993).

Could ESB be used to control a person against his or her will? It might seem that ESB could be used to control a person like a robot. But the details of emotions and behaviours elicited by ESB are modified by personality and circumstances. Sci-fi movies to the contrary, it would be impossible for a ruthless dictator to enslave people by "radio controlling" their brains.

To find out what individual neurons are doing, we need to do a micro-electrode recording. A **micro-electrode** is an extremely thin glass tube filled with a salty fluid. The tip of a micro-electrode is small enough to detect the electrical activity of a single neuron. Watching the action potentials of just one neuron provides a fascinating glimpse into the true origins of behaviour. (The action potential shown in Figure 2.2 was recorded with a micro-electrode.)

What about the bigger picture? Is it possible to record what the brain is doing as a whole? Yes, it is, with electroencephalography (ee-LEK-tro-in-SEF-ah-LOG-ruh-fee). This technique measures the waves of electrical activity produced by the brain. Small disk-shaped metal plates are placed on a person's scalp. Electrical impulses from

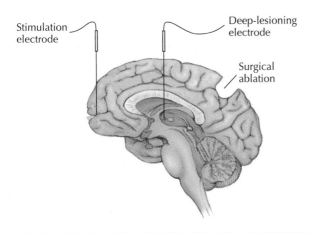

Stimulation electrode

Deep-lesioning electrode

Surgical ablation

▶Figure 2.10

The functions of brain structures are explored by selectively activating or removing them. Brain research is often based on electrical stimulation, but chemical stimulation is also used at times.

Electroencephalograph (EEG) A device that records electrical activity in the brain.

CT scan Computed tomography scan; a computer-enhanced X-ray image of the brain or body.

MRI scan Magnetic resonance imaging; a three-dimensional image of the body, based on its response to a magnetic field.

fMRI scan Functional magnetic resonance imaging that records brain activity.

PET scan Positron emission tomography; a computer-generated image of brain activity, based on glucose consumption in the brain.

the brain are detected by these electrodes and sent to an **electroencephalograph (EEG).** The EEG amplifies these very weak signals (brain waves) and records them on a moving sheet of paper or a computer screen. Various brain-wave patterns can identify the presence of tumours, epilepsy, and other diseases. The EEG also reveals changes in brain activity during sleep, daydreaming, and other mental states.

New Images of the Living Brain

Many of the brain's riddles have been solved with the methods just described, plus others based on drugs and brain chemistry. Yet, each technique lets us see only a part of the whole picture. What if we could "peek" inside an intact brain while a person is thinking, perceiving, and reacting? Rather than seeing individual musical notes, or small musical phrases, what if we could see the brain's entire ongoing symphony? Computer-enhanced images are now making this age-old dream possible. Let's look through some of these newly opened "windows" into the human biocomputer.

CT SCAN Computerized scanning equipment has virtually revolutionized the study of brain diseases and injuries. At best, conventional X-rays produce only shadowy images of the brain. **Computed tomographic (CT) scanning** is a specialized type of X-ray that does a much better job of making the brain visible. In a CT scan, X-ray information is collected by a computer and formed into an image of the brain. A CT scan can reveal the effects of strokes, injuries, tumours, and other brain disorders. These, in turn, can be related to a person's behaviour.

MRI SCAN **Magnetic resonance imaging (MRI)** uses a very strong magnetic field, rather than X-rays, to produce an image of the body's interior. During an MRI scan, the body is placed inside a magnetic field. Processing by a computer then creates a three-dimensional model of the brain or body. Any two-dimensional plane, or slice, of the body can be selected and displayed as an image on a computer screen. This allows us to peer into the living brain almost as if it were transparent (see ▶Figure 2.11).

A **functional MRI (fMRI)** goes one step further by making brain activity visible. For example, the motor areas on the surface of the brain would be highlighted in an fMRI image as Glenn Gould moved his fingers on the piano. Such images are allowing scientists to pinpoint areas in the brain responsible for thoughts, feelings, and actions.

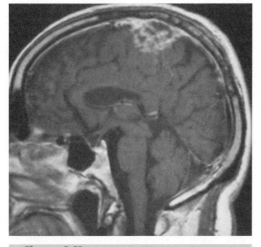

▶Figure 2.11

An MRI scan reveals a brain tumour (see arrow). Notice how it is possible to display a precise "slice" from the middle of the three-dimensional MRI data.

Is it true that most people use only 10 percent of their brain capacity? This is one of the lasting myths about the brain. Brain scans show that all parts of the brain are active during waking hours. Obviously, some people make better use of their innate brain power than others do. Another way to conceptualize this issue is by noting that we use 100 percent of both our hands, but we use them to accomplish different tasks. Glenn Gould used his to create exceptional music, Wilder Penfield used his to perform intricate brain surgery, and Paul Bernardo used his to commit unspeakable crimes. Similarly, all of our brain is put to use but in very different ways for different purposes. In summary, there are no great hidden or untapped reserves of mental capacity in a normally functioning brain.

PET SCAN Positron emission tomography (PET) images of the brain are perhaps the most remarkable of all. A **PET scan** detects positrons (subatomic particles) emitted by weakly radioactive glucose (sugar) as it is consumed by the brain. Since the brain runs on glucose, a PET scan shows which areas are using more energy. Higher energy use corresponds with higher activity. Thus, by placing positron detectors around the head and sending data to a computer, it is possible to create a moving, colour picture of changes in brain activity. As you can see in ▶Figure 2.12, PET scans reveal that very specific brain areas are active when you are reading a word, hearing a word, saying a word, or thinking about the meaning of a word. It is just a matter of time until even brighter beacons are flashed into the shadowy inner world of thought. (See ▶Figure 2.13.)

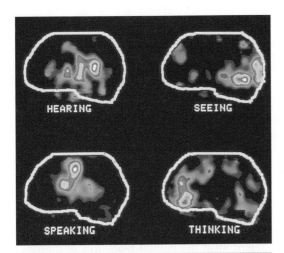

▶Figure 2.12

These PET images show scans of the left side of the brain made while a person heard a word, saw a word, repeated a word aloud, and said a word related to the one that was seen (Petersen et al., 1988).

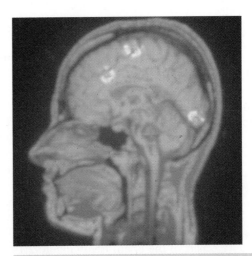

▶Figure 2.13

The bright spots you see here were created by a PET scan. They are similar to the spots in Figure 2.12. However, here they have been placed over an MRI scan so that the brain's anatomy is visible. The three bright spots are areas in the left brain related to language. The spot on the right is active during reading. The top-middle area is connected with speech. The area to the left, in the frontal lobe, is linked with thinking about a word's meaning (Montgomery, 1989).

Knowledge builder

NEURONS, THE NERVOUS SYSTEM, AND BRAIN RESEARCH

Relate

To cope with all of the technical terms in this chapter, it might help to think of neurons as strange little creatures. How do they act? What excites them? How do they communicate? To remember the functions of major branches of the nervous system, think about what you couldn't do if each part were missing.

You suspect that a certain part of the brain is related to memory. How could you use clinical studies, ablation, deep lesioning, and ESB to study the structure? You are interested in finding out how single neurons in the optic nerve respond when the eye is exposed to light. What technique will you use? You want to know which areas of the brain's surface are most active when a person sees a face. What methods will you use?

Learning Check

1. The _____ and _____ are receiving areas where information from other neurons is accepted.
2. Nerve impulses are carried down the _____ to the _____ _____.
3. The _____ potential becomes an _____ potential when a neuron passes the threshold for firing.
4. Neuropeptides are transmitter substances that help to regulate the activity of neurons. T or F?

5. The somatic and autonomic systems are part of the _____ nervous system.
6. Sodium and potassium ions flow through ion channels in the synapse to trigger a nerve impulse in the receiving neuron. T or F?
7. The simplest behaviour sequence is a _____ _____.
8. The parasympathetic nervous system is most active during times of high emotion. T or F?
9. Which of the following research techniques has the most in common with clinical studies of the effects of brain injuries?
   a. EEG recording
   b. deep lesioning
   c. micro-electrode recording
   d. PET scan

Critical Thinking

10. What effect would you expect a drug to have if it blocked passage of neurotransmitters across the synapse?
11. Deep lesioning is used to ablate an area in the hypothalamus of a rat. After the operation, the rat seems to lose interest in food and eating. Why would it be a mistake to conclude that the ablated area is a "hunger centre"?

Answers:

1. dendrites, soma 2. axon, axon terminals 3. resting, action 4. T 5. peripheral 6. F 7. reflex arc 8. F 9. b 10. Such a drug could have wide-ranging effects. If the drug blocked excitatory synapses, it would depress brain activity. If it blocked inhibitory messages, it would act as a powerful stimulant. 11. Because other factors might explain the apparent loss of appetite, the taste or smell of food might be affected, or the rat might simply have difficulty swallowing. It is also possible that hunger originates elsewhere in the brain and the ablated area merely relays messages that cause the rat to eat.

► The Cerebral Cortex—My, What a Big Brain You Have!

Survey Question:
■ How is the brain organized and what do its higher structures do?

Cerebrum The two large hemispheres that cover the upper part of the brain.

Cerebral cortex The outer layer of the cerebrum.

Corticalization An increase in the relative size of the cerebral cortex.

In many ways, we are pretty unimpressive creatures. Animals surpass humans in almost every category of strength, speed, and sensory sensitivity. The one area in which we excel is intelligence.

Do humans have the largest brains? Surprisingly, no. Elephant brains weigh about 6 kilograms, and whale brains 9 kilograms. At about 1.5 kilograms, the human brain seems puny—until we compare brain weight to body weight. We then find that an elephant's brain is 1/1000 of its weight; the ratio for sperm whales is 1 to 10 000. The ratio for humans is 1 to 60. If someone tells you that you have a "whale of a brain," be sure to find out if he or she means size or ratio!

So, relatively speaking, humans have highly developed brains. More importantly, as we move from less complex to more complex animals, more of the brain is devoted to the **cerebrum** (SER-eh-brum or ser-REE-brum: two large hemispheres that cover the upper part of the brain) (see ►Figure 2.14). The cerebrum is the highest brain area in humans. Its outer layer is known as the **cerebral cortex** (seh-REE-brel or ser-EH-brel). Although the cortex is only 3 millimetres thick (one tenth of an inch), it contains 70 percent of the neurons in the central nervous system. Without the cortex, humans wouldn't be much smarter than lizards.

CORTICALIZATION The cerebral cortex looks a little like a giant, wrinkled walnut. It covers most of the brain with a mantle of grey matter (spongy tissue made up mostly of cell bodies). The cortex in many animals is small and smooth. In humans it is twisted, folded, and the largest brain structure. The fact that humans are more intelligent than other animals is related to this **corticalization** (KORE-tih-kal-ih-ZAY-shun), or increase in the size and wrinkling of the cortex. (See "The Brain at Work" for more information.)

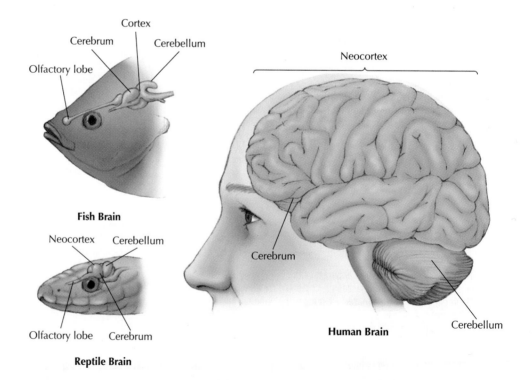

Cortex

Cerebrum Cerebellum

Olfactory lobe

Neocortex

Fish Brain

Neocortex Cerebellum

Cerebrum

Cerebellum

Olfactory lobe Cerebrum

Human Brain

Reptile Brain

►Figure 2.14

An illustration showing the increased relative size of the human cerebrum and cerebral cortex, a significant factor in human adaptability and intelligence.

FOCUS ON RESEARCH The Brain at Work

According to folklore, a person with a large head and a high forehead is likely to be intelligent. But brain efficiency has as much to do with intelligence as brain size does (Gazzaniga, 1995).

Psychologist Richard J. Haier and his colleagues found that the brains of people who perform well on mental tests consume less energy than those of poor performers (Haier et al., 1988). Haier measured brain activity with a PET scan. Recall that a PET scan records the amount of glucose (sugar) used by brain cells. The harder neurons work, the more sugar they use. By using harmless, radioactively labelled glucose, it is possible to record an image of how hard the brain is working (see ▶Figure 2.15).

What did PET scans reveal when subjects took a difficult reasoning test? Surprisingly, the brains of those who scored lowest on the test used the most glucose. Although we might assume that smart brains are hard-working brains, the reverse appears to be true. Brighter subjects actually used less energy than poor performers did. Haier believes this shows that intelligence is related to brain efficiency: Less efficient brains work harder and still accomplish less. We've all had days like that!

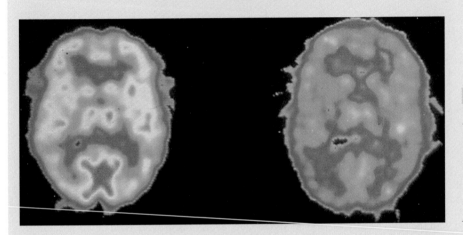

▶Figure 2.15

In the images you see here, red, orange, and yellow indicate high consumption of glucose; green, blue, and pink show areas of low glucose use. The PET scan of the brain on the left shows that a man who solved 11 out of 36 reasoning problems burned more glucose than the man on the right, who solved 33.

Cerebral Hemispheres

Cerebral hemispheres The right and left halves of the cerebrum.

Corpus callosum The bundle of fibres connecting the cerebral hemispheres.

The cortex is composed of two sides, or **cerebral hemispheres** (half-globes). The two hemispheres are connected by a thick band of fibres called the **corpus callosum** (KORE-pus kah-LOH-sum) (see ▶Figure 2.16). The left side of the brain mainly controls the right side of the body. Likewise, the right brain mainly controls left body areas. When our friend Marge had a stroke, her right hemisphere suffered damage. (A stroke occurs when an artery carrying blood to the brain becomes blocked, causing some brain tissue to die.) In Marge's case, the stroke caused some paralysis and loss of sensation on the left side of her body. Damage to the right hemisphere may also cause a curious problem called *spatial neglect*. Affected patients pay no attention to the left side of visual space (see ▶Figure 2.17). Often, the patient will not eat food on the left side of a plate. Some even refuse to acknowledge a paralyzed left arm as their own (Springer & Deutsch, 1998). If you point to the "alien" arm, the patient is likely to say, "Oh, that's not my arm. It must belong to someone else."

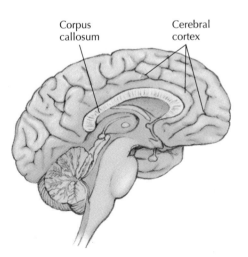

Corpus callosum

Cerebral cortex

▶Figure 2.16

The corpus callosum is the major "cable system" through which the right and left cerebral hemispheres communicate. A recent study found that the corpus callosum is larger in classical musicians than it is in non-musicians. When a person plays a violin or piano, the two hemispheres must communicate rapidly as they coordinate the movements of both hands. Presumably, the size of the corpus callosum can be altered by early experience, such as musical training.

Model   **Patient's copy**

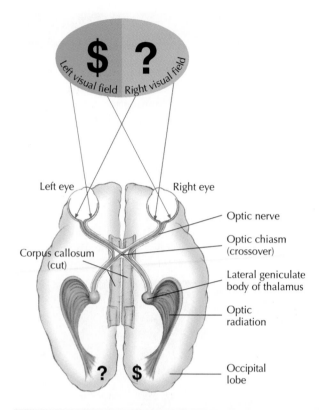

▶**Figure 2.17**

Spatial neglect. A patient with right-hemisphere damage was asked to copy three model drawings. Notice the obvious neglect of the left side in his drawings. (From *Left Brain, Right Brain*, Revised Edition, by S. P. Springer and G. Deutsch, copyright 1981, 1985, 1989, 1993, 1998. Reprinted with the permission of W. H. Freeman and Company.)

▶**Figure 2.18**

Basic nerve pathways of vision. Notice that the left portion of each eye connects only to the left half of the brain; likewise, the right portion of each eye connects to the right brain. When the corpus callosum is cut, a "split brain" results. Then visual information can be directed to one hemisphere or the other by flashing it in the right or left visual field as the person stares straight ahead.

Hemispheric Specialization

In 1981, Roger Sperry (1914–1994) won a Nobel Prize for his remarkable discovery that the right and left brain hemispheres perform differently on tests of language, perception, music, and other capabilities.

How is it possible to test only one side of the brain? One way is to work with people who've had a **"split-brain" operation.** In this rare type of surgery, the corpus callosum is cut to control severe epilepsy. The result is essentially a person with two brains in one body. After the surgery, it is a simple matter to send information to one hemisphere or the other (see ▶Figure 2.18).

"SPLIT BRAINS"   After the right and left brain are separated, each hemisphere will have its own separate perceptions, concepts, and impulses to act.

How does a split-brain person function after the operation? Having two "brains" in one body can create some interesting dilemmas. When one split-brain patient dressed himself, he sometimes pulled his pants down with one hand and up with the other. Once, he grabbed his wife with his left hand and shook her violently. Gallantly, his right hand came to her aid and grabbed the aggressive left hand (Gazzaniga, 1970). However, such conflicts are actually rare. That's because both halves of the brain normally have about the same experience at the same time. Also, if a conflict arises, one hemisphere usually overrides the other.

Split-brain effects are easiest to see in specialized testing. For example, we could flash a dollar sign to the right brain and a question mark to the left brain of a patient named

"Split-brain" operation
Cutting the corpus callosum.

Left Brain

- Language
- Speech
- Writing
- Calculation
- Time sense
- Rhythm
- Ordering of complex movements

Right Brain

- Non-verbal
- Perceptual skills
- Visualization
- Recognition of patterns, faces, melodies
- Recognition and expression of emotion
- Spatial skills
- Simple language comprehension

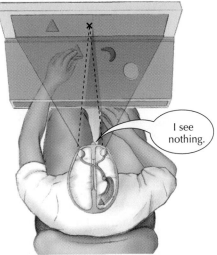

I see a circle.

I see nothing.

Left Hemisphere

Right Hemisphere

▶**Figure 2.19**

If a circle is flashed to the left brain and a split-brain patient is asked to say what she or he saw, the circle is easily named. The person can also pick out the circle by touching shapes with the right hand, out of sight under a tabletop (shown semi-transparent in the drawing). However, the left hand will be unable to identify the shape. If a triangle is flashed to the right brain, the person cannot say what was seen (speech is controlled by the left hemisphere). The person will also be unable to identify the correct shape by touch with the right hand. Now, however, the left hand will have no difficulty picking out the hidden triangle. Separate testing of each hemisphere reveals distinct specializations, as listed above. (Figure adapted from an illustration by Edward Kasper in McKean, 1985.)

Tom. (Figure 2.18 shows how this is possible.) Next, Tom is asked to draw what he saw, using his left hand, out of sight. Tom's left hand draws a dollar sign. If Tom is then asked to point with his right hand to a picture of what his hidden left hand drew, he will point to a question mark (Sperry, 1968). In short, for the split-brain person, one hemisphere may not know what is happening in the other. This has to be the ultimate case of the "right hand not knowing what the left hand is doing"! ▶Figure 2.19 provides another example of split-brain testing.

So far we have described patients whose corpus callosum has been cut for a reason. Let's now turn to a unique group of people who have what could be called a natural split-brain. In some babies, the corpus callosum fails to develop, either partially or completely. We usually do not know that someone lacks a corpus callosum until a problem is suspected and the person is sent for a test with one of the brain imaging methods described earlier. Maryse Lassonde at the University of Montreal has studied this group of people extensively. She has found that, in contrast to surgically created split-brain individuals, those who lack a corpus callosum (known as *acallosals*) do not show as many sensory deficits (Lassonde, 1994). For example, people born without a corpus callosum do much better at identifying objects presented to either hemisphere. You may wonder why acallosal persons perform better than surgical split-brain individuals, *even though* their hemispheres do not appear to be linked. It may be that other brain structures have partly taken over the functions that are normally performed by the corpus callosum. One hemisphere may be able to share information with its counterpart through other pathways in the brain. Callosal surgery is typically performed in adulthood, and by the time we reach this stage, our brains may not be as flexible as the brains of children, who may compensate for a missing corpus callosum by giving some of its functions over to other brain structures.

This is not to say that there are no deficits present when the corpus callosum fails to develop. To illustrate, Lassonde and colleagues taught patients with and without a corpus callosum a task in which they had to aim at a target with one hand only while keeping their gaze fixed at a central point. Presumably, only one hemisphere was involved in the learning process. Both groups of participants mastered this task without difficulty. But when people were asked to aim at the target with the other hand that was not involved in the original learning, the two groups were not equal. Those with an intact corpus callosum were able to perform the task with the untrained hand with relative ease, but acallosal individuals had a hard time of it. In other words, acallosal persons could carry out the aiming task with the help of one brain hemisphere, as in the original learning with one hand, but the learning could not be shared with the other hemisphere, as when the aiming was done with the untrained hand, because they did not possess a corpus callosum to send the necessary information from one hemisphere to the other (Chicoine, Proteau, & Lassonde, 2000). So it seems that the cerebral hemispheres of acallosal individuals are able to share some sensory information, but when it comes to more complex tasks, a lack of this important cable connection becomes more apparent.

There is a related condition in which a corpus callosum is present but its fibres are very thin. Researchers have proposed that this thinning of the corpus callosum may be linked to a variety of learning disabilities. The resulting problems may involve deficits in language, reading, and thinking efficiently. It is only a hypothesis at the moment, but the idea is worth exploring (Jeeves, 1994).

Studying people whose corpus callosum is either fully or partially absent as well as those whose corpus callosum is cut to control epilepsy is giving us useful insights into how the two hemispheres work and how information is shared between them.

RIGHT BRAIN/LEFT BRAIN　*Earlier it was stated that the hemispheres differ in abilities; in what ways are they different?* The brain divides its work in interesting ways. Roughly 94 percent of us use our left brain for language (speaking, writing, and understanding). In addition, the left hemisphere is superior at math, judging time and rhythm, and coordinating the order of complex movements, such as those needed for speech.

In contrast, the right hemisphere can produce only the simplest language and numbers. Working with the right brain is like talking to a child who can say only a dozen words or so. To answer questions, the right hemisphere must use non-verbal responses, such as pointing at objects (see Figure 2.19).

Although it is poor at producing language, the right brain has it own talents. The right brain is especially good at perceptual skills, such as recognizing patterns, faces, and melodies, putting together a puzzle, or drawing a picture. It also helps you express emotions and detect the emotions that other people are feeling (Borod et al., 1998; Christianson, Saisa, & Silvenius, 1995).

ONE BRAIN, TWO STYLES　In general, the left hemisphere is mainly involved with analysis (breaking information into parts). It also processes information *sequentially* (in order, one item after the next). The right hemisphere appears to process information *simultaneously* and *holistically* (all at once) (Springer & Deutsch, 1998).

To summarize further, you could say that the right hemisphere is better at assembling pieces of the world into a coherent picture; it sees overall patterns and general connections. The left brain focuses on small details (see ▶ Figure 2.20). The right brain sees the wide-angle view; the left zooms in on specifics. The focus of the left brain is local; the focus of the right is global (Heinze et al., 1998; Hellige, 1993; Huebner, 1998).

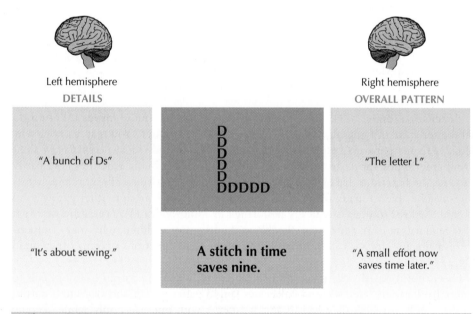

Left hemisphere
DETAILS

Right hemisphere
OVERALL PATTERN

"A bunch of Ds"

D
D
D
D
DDDDD

"The letter L"

"It's about sewing."

A stitch in time saves nine.

"A small effort now saves time later."

▶**Figure 2.20**

The left and right brain have different information-processing styles. The right brain gets the big pattern; the left focuses on small details.

Do people normally do puzzles or draw pictures with just the right hemisphere? Do they do other things with only the left? Numerous books have been written about how to use the right brain to manage, teach, draw, ride horses, learn, cook, and even make love (Carter, 1998). But such books drastically oversimplify right- and left-brain differences. People normally use both sides of the brain at all times. It's true that some tasks may make more use of one hemisphere or the other. But in most "real world" activities, the hemispheres share the work. Each does the parts it does best and shares information with the other side. Popular books and courses that claim to teach "right-brain thinking" ignore the fact that everyone already uses the right brain for thinking (Hellige, 1990; Ornstein, 1997). To do anything well requires the talents and processing abilities of both hemispheres. A smart brain is one that grasps both the details and the overall picture at the same time (Ornstein, 1997). Notice, for instance, that during a concert Glenn Gould would have used his left brain to judge time and rhythm and coordinate the order of his hand movements. At the same time, he would have used his right brain to recognize and organize melodies.

Lobes of the Cerebral Cortex

In addition to the two big hemispheres, the cerebral cortex can be divided into several smaller **lobes** (areas bordered by major grooves or fissures or defined by their functions) (see ▶Figure 2.21).

THE OCCIPITAL LOBES   At the back of the brain, we find the **occipital lobes** (awk-SIP-ih-tal), the primary visual area of the cortex. Patients with tumours (cell growths that interfere with brain activity) in the occipital lobes experience blind spots in their vision.

Do the visual areas of the cortex correspond directly to what is seen? Images are mapped onto the cortex, but the map is greatly stretched and distorted (Carlson, 1998). It is important to avoid thinking of the visual area as being like a little TV screen in the brain. Visual information creates complex patterns of activity in nerve cells; it does not make a TV-like image.

THE PARIETAL LOBES   Bodily sensations register in the **parietal lobes** (puh-RYE-ih-tal), located just above the occipital lobes. Touch, temperature, pressure, and other somatic sensations flow into the **somatosensory area** (SO-mat-oh-SEN-so-ree) on the parietal lobes. Again, we find that the map of bodily sensations is distorted. The drawing in ▶Figure 2.22 shows that the cortex reflects the *sensitivity* of body areas, not their size. For example, the lips are large in the drawing because of their great sensitivity, while the back and trunk, which are less sensitive, are much smaller. Notice that the hands are also large in the map of body sensitivity—which is obviously an aid to musicians, typists, watchmakers, massage therapists, lovers, and brain surgeons.

THE TEMPORAL LOBES   The temporal lobes are located on each side of the brain, above the ears. Auditory information projects directly to the **temporal lobes,** making them the main site where hearing registers. If we did a PET scan of your brain, and then started your favourite musical CD, your temporal lobes would light up. Likewise, if we could stimulate the auditory area of your temporal lobe, you would "hear" a series of sound sensations.

For most people, the left temporal lobe also contains a language "centre." (For 5 to 6 percent of all people, the area is on the right temporal lobe.) Damage to the temporal lobe can severely limit ability to use language. (More on this later.)

THE FRONTAL LOBES   The **frontal lobes** are associated with higher mental abilities. This area is also responsible for the control of movement. Specifically, an arch of tissue over the top of the brain, called the **motor cortex,** directs the body's muscles. If this area is stimulated with an electrical current, various parts of the body will twitch or move. Like the somatosensory area, the motor cortex corresponds to the importance of bodily areas, not

Lobes of the cerebral cortex Areas on the cortex bordered by major fissures or defined by their functions.

Frontal lobe

Parietal lobe

Occipital lobe

Temporal lobe

Cerebellum

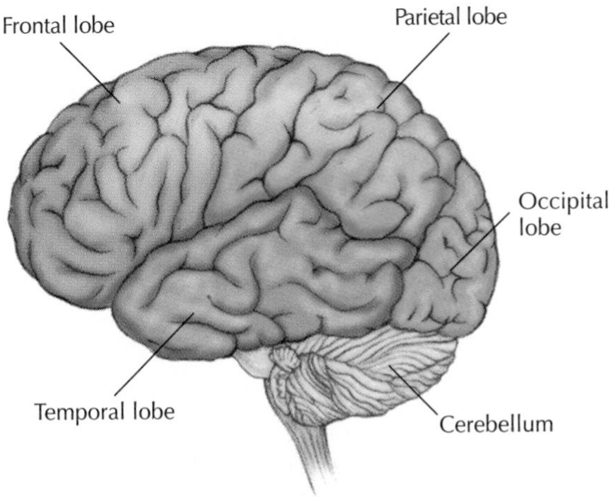

▶**Figure 2.21**

Many of the lobes of the cerebral cortex are defined by larger fissures on the surface of the cerebrum. Others are regarded as separate areas because their functions are quite different.

Occipital lobes Portion of the cerebral cortex where vision registers in the brain.

Parietal lobes Area of the brain where bodily sensations register.

Somatosensory area A receiving area for bodily sensations.

Temporal lobes Areas that include the sites where hearing registers in the brain.

Frontal lobes A brain area associated with movement, the sense of smell, and higher mental functions.

Motor cortex A brain area associated with control of movement.

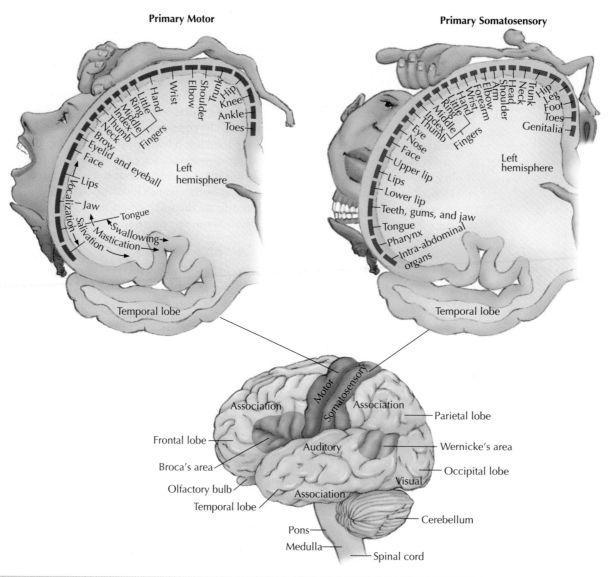

Primary Motor

Primary Somatosensory

Left hemisphere

Temporal lobe

Temporal lobe

Association

Motor

Somatosensory

Association

Parietal lobe

Frontal lobe

Auditory

Wernicke's area

Broca's area

Occipital lobe

Olfactory bulb

Visual

Temporal lobe

Association

Cerebellum

Pons

Medulla

Spinal cord

▶**Figure 2.22**

The lobes of the cerebral cortex and the primary sensory, motor, and association areas on each. The top diagrams show (in cross section) the relative amounts of cortex "assigned" to the sensory and motor control of various parts of the body. (Each cross section, or "slice," of the cortex has been turned 90 degrees so that you see it as it would appear from the back of the brain.)

Association cortex All areas of the cerebral cortex that are not primarily sensory or motor in function.

Survey Question:
■ Why are the brain's association areas important? What happens when they are injured?

to their size. The hands, for example, get more area than the feet (see Figure 2.22). If you've ever wondered why your hands are more dextrous than your feet, it's partly because more motor cortex is devoted to the hands.

The frontal lobes are also related to more complex behaviours. If the frontal lobes are damaged, a person's personality and emotional life may change dramatically. (Remember Phineas Gage, the railroad foreman described in Chapter 1?) Reasoning or planning may also be affected. Patients with frontal lobe damage often get "stuck" on mental tasks and repeat the same wrong answers over and over (Goel & Grafman, 1995). Sadly, drug abuse is one way in which this important area of the brain may be damaged (Liu et al., 1998).

ASSOCIATION AREAS   Only a small part of the cerebral cortex directly controls the body and receives information from the senses. All the surrounding areas, which are called the **association cortex,** combine and process information from the senses. If you see a rose, the association areas will help you recognize it and name it. The association cortex also contributes to higher mental abilities. For example, a person with damage to association

Aphasia A speech disturbance resulting from brain damage.

Broca's area A language area related to grammar and pronunciation.

Wernicke's area An area related to language comprehension.

areas on the left hemisphere may suffer an **aphasia** (ah-FAZE-yah: impaired ability to use language).

One type of aphasia is related to **Broca's area,** a "speech centre" on the left frontal lobe (Leonard, 1997). Damage to Broca's area causes great difficulty in speaking or writing. Typically, a patient's grammar and pronunciation are poor and speech is slow and laboured. For example, the person may say "bife" for bike, "seep" for sleep, or "zokaid" for zodiac. Generally, the person knows what she or he wants to say but can't seem to utter the words (Geschwind, 1979).

If Broca's area is damaged, the amount of language loss a person suffers may relate to his or her sex. "His and Her Brains?" explains why.

A second language site, called **Wernicke's area** (VER-nick-ees; see Figure 2.23), lies on the left temporal lobe. If it is damaged, the person has problems with the meaning of words, not their pronunciation. Someone with Broca's aphasia might say "tssair" when shown a picture of a chair. In contrast, a Wernicke's patient might say "stool" (Leonard, 1997).

In summary, the bulk of our daily experience and all of our understanding of the world can be traced to the sensory, motor, and association areas of the cortex. The human brain is among the most advanced and sophisticated of the brain-bearing species on earth. This, of course, is no guarantee that this marvellous "biocomputer" will be put to good use. Still, we must stand in awe of the potential it represents.

HUMAN DIVERSITY His and Her Brains?

A patient has had a stroke. It looks like Broca's (BRO-cahs) area was damaged. As expected, the patient's speech is impaired. Will the patient recover any language skills? It may depend on his or her sex.

When Broca's area is damaged, women typically regain more of their lost abilities than men do. Why should this be so? Let's look at some male and female brains for an answer.

Researchers used brain imaging to observe brain activity while people did language tasks. As they worked, both men and women showed increased activity in Broca's area, on the left side of the brain. This is exactly

what we would expect. However, to the scientists' surprise, both the left and the right brain were activated in more than half the women tested. Apparently, male and female brains tend to differ in ways that can affect speech and language (Jaeger et al., 1998; Shaywitz & Gore, 1995; Skrandies, Reik, & Kunze, 1999). (▶See Figure 2.23.)

Using both sides of the brain for language may be a big advantage. When Broca's area is damaged, some women can use the right side of their brains to compensate for the loss (Hochstenbach et al., 1998). Men with similar damage have little chance of improving. Thus, when a man says, "I have half a mind to tell you what I think," he may be stating a curious truth.

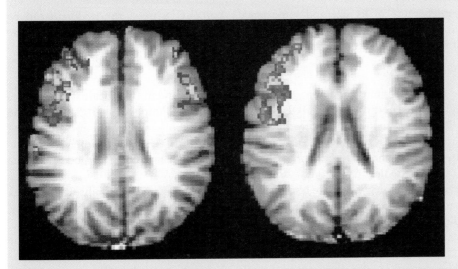

▶**Figure 2.23**

Language tasks activate the left side of the brain in men and both sides in many women.

Knowledge builder

CEREBRAL CORTEX AND LOBES OF THE BRAIN

Relate

Learning the functions of the brain lobes is like learning areas on a map. Try drawing a map of the cortex. Can you label all of the different "countries" (lobes)? Can you name their functions? Where is the motor cortex? The somatosensory area? Broca's area? Keep redrawing the map until it becomes more detailed and you can do it easily.

Learning Check

See if you can match the following.

_____	**1.** Corpus callosum	**A.**	Visual area
_____	**2.** Occipital lobes	**B.**	Language, speech, writing
_____	**3.** Parietal lobes	**C.**	Motor cortex and abstract thinking
_____	**4.** Temporal lobes	**D.**	Spatial skills, visualization, pattern recognition
_____	**5.** Frontal lobes	**E.**	Speech disturbances
_____	**6.** Association cortex	**F.**	Causes sleep
_____	**7.** Aphasias	**G.**	Increased ratio of cortex in brain
_____	**8.** Corticalization		

_____ **9.** Left hemisphere
_____ **10.** Right hemisphere
_____ **11.** "Split brain"

H. Bodily sensations
I. Treatment for severe epilepsy
J. Hearing
K. Fibres connecting the cerebral hemispheres
L. Cortex that is not sensory or motor in function

Critical Thinking

12. If you wanted to increase the surface area of the cerebrum so that more cerebral cortex would fit within the skull, how would you do it?

13. What would be some of the possible advantages and disadvantages of having a "split brain"?

14. If your brain were removed, replaced by another, and moved to a new body, which would you consider to be yourself, your old body with the new brain, or your new body with the old brain?

Answers:

1. K 2. A 3. H 4. J 5. C 6. L 7. E 8. G 9. B 10. D 11. I **12.** One solution would be to gather the surface of the cortex into folds, just as you might if you were trying to fit a large piece of cloth into a small box. This, in fact, is probably why the cortex is more convoluted (folded or wrinkled) in primates. **13.** If information were properly routed to each brain hemisphere, it would be possible to have both hands working simultaneously on conflicting tasks. However, such possible benefits would apply only under highly controlled conditions. **14.** While there is no "correct" answer to this question, your personality, knowledge, personal memories, and self-concept all derive from brain activity—which makes a strong case for your old brain in a new body being more nearly the "real you."

▶ The Subcortex—At the Core of the (Brain) Matter

Survey Question:
■ What kinds of behaviours are controlled by the subcortex?

Subcortex All brain structures below the cerebral cortex.

Brainstem The lower brain, including the cerebellum, medulla, pons, and reticular formation.

Medulla The structure that connects the brain with the spinal cord and controls vital life functions.

Pons An area on the brainstem that acts as a bridge between the medulla and other structures.

Cerebellum A brain structure that controls posture and coordination.

A person can lose large portions of the cerebrum and still survive. Not so with the brain areas below the cortex. Any damage at all could endanger a person's life.

Why are the lower brain areas so important? The **subcortex** lies immediately below the cerebral hemispheres. This area can be divided into the brainstem (or hindbrain), the midbrain, and the forebrain. (The forebrain also includes the cerebral cortex, which we have already discussed because of its size and importance.) For our purposes the midbrain can be viewed as a link between the forebrain and the brainstem. Therefore, let us focus on the rest of the subcortex (see ▶ Figure 2.24).

The Hindbrain

As the spinal cord joins the brain, it widens into the brainstem. The **brainstem** consists mainly of the **medulla** (meh-DUL-ah) and the cerebellum (ser-ah-BEL-uhm). The medulla contains centres important for the reflex control of vital life functions, including heart rate, breathing, swallowing, and the like. Various drugs, diseases, or injuries can disrupt the medulla and end or endanger life. That's why a karate chop to the back of the neck can be extremely dangerous.

The **pons,** which looks like a small bump on the brainstem, acts as a bridge between the medulla and other brain areas. In addition to connecting with many other locations, including the cerebellum, the pons influences sleep and arousal.

The cerebellum, which looks like a miniature cerebral cortex, lies at the base of the brain. The **cerebellum** primarily regulates posture, muscle tone, and muscular coordination. The cerebellum also stores memories related to skills and habits (Thompson, 1991).

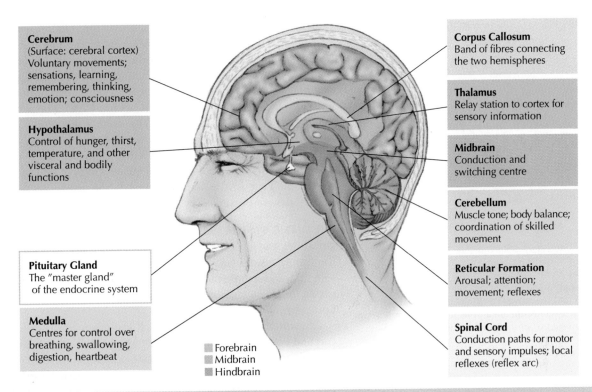

Cerebrum
(Surface: cerebral cortex)
Voluntary movements;
sensations, learning,
remembering, thinking,
emotion; consciousness

Hypothalamus
Control of hunger, thirst,
temperature, and other
visceral and bodily
functions

Pituitary Gland
The "master gland"
of the endocrine system

Medulla
Centres for control over
breathing, swallowing,
digestion, heartbeat

Corpus Callosum
Band of fibres connecting
the two hemispheres

Thalamus
Relay station to cortex for
sensory information

Midbrain
Conduction and
switching centre

Cerebellum
Muscle tone; body balance;
coordination of skilled
movement

Reticular Formation
Arousal; attention;
movement; reflexes

Spinal Cord
Conduction paths for motor
and sensory impulses; local
reflexes (reflex arc)

■ Forebrain
■ Midbrain
■ Hindbrain

▶**Figure 2.24**

This simplified drawing shows the main structures of the human brain and describes some of their most important features. (You can use the
colour code in the foreground to identify which areas are part of the forebrain, midbrain, and hindbrain.)

What happens if the cerebellum is injured? Without the cerebellum, tasks like walking,
running, or playing catch would be impossible. The first symptoms of a crippling disease
called *spinocerebellar degeneration* are tremor, dizziness, and muscular weakness. Eventually,
victims have difficulty merely standing, walking, or feeding themselves.

RETICULAR FORMATION   A network of fibres and cell bodies called the **reticular** (reh-
TICK-you-ler) **formation** (RF) lies inside the medulla and brainstem. As messages flow
into the brain, the RF gives priority to some, while turning others aside. By doing so, the
RF influences attention. It also modifies outgoing commands to the body. In this way the
RF affects muscle tone, posture, and movements of the eyes, face, head, body, and limbs.
At the same time, the RF controls reflexes involved in breathing, sneezing, coughing, and
vomiting (Stalheim-Smith & Fitch, 1993).

Keeping us vigilant, alert, and awake is another important task of the reticular formation. Incoming messages from the sense organs branch into a part of the RF called the
reticular activating system (RAS). The RAS bombards the cortex with stimulation,
keeping it active and alert. For instance, let's say a sleepy driver rounds a bend and sees a
deer standing in the road. The driver snaps to attention and applies the brakes. She can
thank her RAS for arousing the rest of her brain and averting an accident. If you're getting sleepy while reading this chapter, try pinching your ear—a little pain will cause the
RAS to momentarily arouse your cortex.

The Forebrain

Like hidden gemstones, two of the most important parts of your body lie buried deep
within your brain. The *thalamus* (THAL-uh-mus) and an area just below it called the *hypothalamus* (HI-po-THAL-uh-mus) are key parts of the forebrain (see ▶Figure 2.25).

How could these be any more important than other areas already described? The **thalamus**
acts as a final "switching station" for sensory messages on their way to the cortex. Vision,

Reticular formation A
network of neurons in the
brainstem, associated with
attention, alertness, and
some reflexes.
**Reticular activating
system (RAS)** A part of the
reticular formation that
activates the cerebral cortex.
Thalamus A brain structure
that relays sensory
information to the cerebral
cortex.

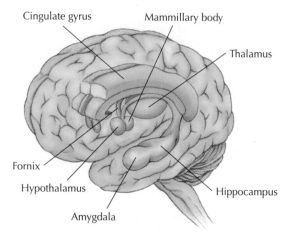

▶Figure 2.25

Parts of the limbic system are shown in this highly simplified drawing. Although only one side is shown, the hippocampus and the amygdala extend out into the temporal lobes at each side of the brain. The limbic system is a sort of "primitive core" of the brain strongly associated with emotion.

Hypothalamus A small area of the brain that regulates emotional behaviours and motives.

Limbic system A system in the forebrain that is closely linked with emotional response.

Amygdala A part of the limbic system associated with fear responses.

Hippocampus A part of the limbic system associated with storing memories.

hearing, taste, and touch all pass through this small, football-shaped structure. Thus, injury to even small areas of the thalamus can cause deafness, blindness, or loss of any other sense, except smell.

The human hypothalamus is about the size of a small grape. Small as it may be, the **hypothalamus** is a kind of master control centre for emotion and many basic motives (Carlson, 1998). The hypothalamus affects behaviours as diverse as sex, rage, temperature control, hormone release, eating and drinking, sleep, waking, and emotion. The hypothalamus is basically a "crossroads" that connects many areas of the brain. It is also the "final path" for many kinds of behaviour leaving the brain. That is, the hypothalamus is the last place where many behaviours are organized or "decided on" before the body reacts.

THE LIMBIC SYSTEM As a group, the hypothalamus, parts of the thalamus, the amygdala, the hippocampus, and other structures make up the limbic system (see Figure 2.25). The **limbic system** has a major role in producing emotion and motivating behaviour. Rage, fear, sexual response, and intense arousal can be obtained from various points in the limbic system.

Scientists used to think that all emotions are processed by the cerebral cortex. However, this is not always the case. Imagine this test of willpower: Go to a zoo and place your face close to the glass in front of a rattlesnake display. Suddenly, the rattlesnake strikes at your face. Do you flinch? Even though you know you are safe, researcher Joseph LeDoux predicts that you will recoil from the snake's attack (LeDoux, 1999).

LeDoux and other researchers have found that an area of the brain called the **amygdala** (ah-MIG-duh-la) specializes in triggering fear. The amygdala receives sensory information very directly and quickly, bypassing the cortex. As a result, it allows us to respond to potentially dangerous stimuli before we really know what's happening. This primitive fear response is not under the control of higher brain centres. The role of the amygdala in emotion may explain why people who suffer from phobias and disabling anxiety often feel afraid without knowing why (LeDoux, 1999).

People who suffer damage to the amygdala become insensitive to emotion. An armed robber could hold a gun to the person's head and the person wouldn't feel fear. Such people are also unable to "read" or understand other people's emotions. Many lose their ability to relate normally to friends, family, and co-workers (Goleman, 1995).

Some parts of the limbic system have taken on additional, higher-level functions. A part called the **hippocampus** (HIP-oh-CAMP-us) is important for forming lasting memories (Bigler et al., 1996). The hippocampus lies inside the temporal lobes, which is why stimulating the temporal lobes can produce memory-like or dream-like experiences. The hippocampus also helps us navigate through space. Your right hippocampus will become more active, for instance, if you mentally plan a drive across town (Maguire, Frackowiak, & Frith, 1997).

In the 1950s, Canadian psychologists at McGill University discovered that animals will learn to press a lever to deliver a rewarding dose of electrical stimulation to the limbic system. The animals act like the stimulation is satisfying or pleasurable. Indeed, several areas of the limbic system act as reward, or "pleasure," pathways. Many are found in the hypothalamus, where they overlap with areas that control thirst, sex, and hunger. Commonly abused drugs, such as cocaine, amphetamines, heroin, nicotine, marijuana, and alcohol, activate many of the same pleasure pathways. According to Roy Wise of Concordia University, this appears to explain, in part, why these drugs are so powerfully rewarding (Wise & Rompre, 1989).

Punishment, or "aversive," areas have also been found in the limbic system. When these locations are activated, animals show discomfort and will work hard to turn off the stimulation. Since much of our behaviour is based on seeking pleasure and avoiding pain, these discoveries continue to fascinate psychologists.

The Magnificent Brain

We have seen that the human brain is an impressive assembly of billions of sensitive cells and nerve fibres. It controls vital bodily functions, keeps track of the external world, issues commands to the muscles and glands, responds to current needs, creates the magic of consciousness, and regulates its own behaviour—all at the same time.

A final note of caution is now in order. For the sake of simplicity, we have assigned functions to each "part" of the brain as if it were a computer. This is only a half-truth. In reality, the brain is a vast information-processing system. Incoming information scatters all over the brain and converges again as it goes out through the spinal cord to muscles and glands. The overall system is much, much more complicated than our discussion of separate "parts" implies.

▶ The Endocrine System—Hormones and Behaviour

Survey Question:
■ Does the glandular system affect behaviour?

Endocrine system Glands whose secretions pass directly into the bloodstream or lymph system.

Hormone A glandular secretion that affects bodily functions or behaviour.

Growth hormone A hormone, secreted by the pituitary gland, that promotes bodily growth.

Our behaviour is not solely a product of the nervous system. The endocrine (EN-duh-krin) glands serve as a second great communication system in the body. The **endocrine system** is made up of glands that pour chemicals directly into the bloodstream or lymph system (see ▶ Figure 2.26). These chemicals, called **hormones,** are carried throughout the body, where they affect both internal activities and visible behaviour. Hormones are related to neurotransmitters. Like other such chemicals, hormones activate cells in the body. To respond, the cells must have receptor sites for the hormone.

How do hormones affect behaviour? Although we are seldom aware of them, hormones affect us in many ways. Here is a brief sample: Hormone output from the adrenal glands rises during stressful situations; androgens ("male" hormones) are related to the sex drive in both males and females; hormones secreted during times of high emotion intensify memory formation; at least some of the emotional turmoil of adolescence is due to elevated hormone levels; different hormones prevail when you are angry, rather than fearful. Since these are just samples, let's consider some additional effects hormones have on the body and behaviour.

The pituitary is a pea-sized globe hanging from the base of the brain (return to Figure 2.26). One of the pituitary's more important roles is to regulate growth. During childhood, the pituitary secretes a hormone that speeds body development. If too little **growth hormone** is released, a person may remain far smaller than average. If this condition is not treated, a child may be 15 to 30 centimetres shorter than age-mates. As adults, some will

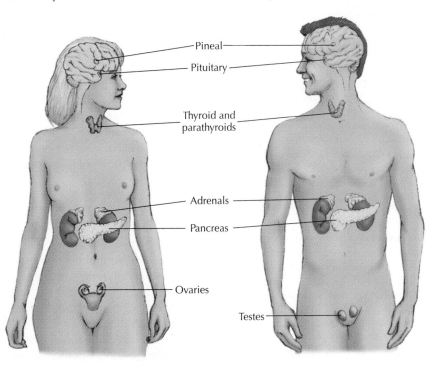

Pineal
Pituitary
Thyroid and parathyroids
Adrenals
Pancreas
Ovaries
Testes

▶Figure 2.26
Location of the endocrine glands in the male and female.

Underactivity of the pituitary gland may produce a dwarf, overactivity a giant.

Hypopituitary dwarfism Shortness and smallness caused by too little growth hormone.

Giantism Excessive bodily growth caused by too much growth hormone.

Acromegaly Enlargement of the arms, hands, feet, and face caused by excess growth hormone late in the human growth period.

Pituitary gland The "master gland" whose hormones influence other endocrine glands.

Pineal gland Gland in the brain that helps regulate body rhythms and sleep.

Melatonin Hormone released by the pineal gland in response to daily cycles of light and dark.

Thyroid gland Endocrine gland that helps regulate the rate of metabolism.

Hyperthyroidism Faster metabolism and excitability caused by an overactive thyroid gland.

Hypothyroidism Slower metabolism and sluggishness caused by an underactive thyroid gland.

Epinephrine An adrenal hormone that tends to arouse the body; epinephrine is associated with fear. (Also known as adrenaline.)

Norepinephrine An adrenal hormone that tends to arouse the body; norepinephrine is associated with anger. (Also known as noradrenaline.)

be **hypopituitary dwarfs** (HI-po-pih-TU-ih-ter-ee). Such individuals are perfectly proportioned, but tiny. Regular injections of growth hormone can raise a hypopituitary child's height by quite a few centimetres, usually to the short side of average. Treatment, however, can last from three to seven years and is very expansive.

Too much growth hormone produces **giantism** (excessive bodily growth). Secretion of too much growth hormone late in the growth period causes **acromegaly** (AK-row-MEG-uh-lee) a condition in which the arms, hands, feet, and facial bones become enlarged. Acromegaly produces prominent facial features, which some people have used as a basis for careers as character actors, wrestlers, and the like. One person who took advantage of his drastically changed appearance resulting from acromegaly was Rondo Hatton. Hatton's unusual condition made it possible for him to enjoy a flourishing acting career. He was featured in many horror films during the 1940s.

The pituitary also governs the functioning of other glands (especially the thyroid, adrenal glands, ovaries and testes). These glands in turn regulate such bodily processes as metabolism, responses to stress, and reproduction. In women, the pituitary controls milk output during pregnancy.

The **pituitary gland** is often called the "master gland" because it influences other endocrine glands. But the master has a master: The pituitary is directed by the hypothalamus, which lies directly above it. In this way, the hypothalamus can affect glands throughout the body. This, then, is the major link between the brain and hormones (Carlson, 1998).

The **pineal gland** (pin-EE-ul) releases a hormone called **melatonin** (mel-ah-TONE-in) in response to daily variations in light. Melatonin levels in the bloodstream rise at dusk and peak around midnight. They fall again as morning approaches. This light-driven cycle helps control body rhythms and sleep cycles. As far as the brain is concerned, it's bedtime when melatonin levels rise (Attenburrow, Cowen, & Sharpley, 1996).

Flight crews often suffer severe disruptions in their sleep cycles. For example, a crew that leaves Vancouver at 4 p.m., bound for London, will arrive in about nine hours. Crew members' bodies, which are on Vancouver time, will act as if it is 1 a.m. Yet in London, it will be 9 a.m.

Studies show that melatonin can be used to minimize jet lag. To reset the body's clock in a new time zone, a small amount of melatonin can be taken about an hour before bedtime. This dose is continued for as many days as necessary to ease jet lag. The same treatment can be used for rotating work shifts (Arendt, 1994; Brown, 1994; Comperatore et al., 1996).

The **thyroid gland,** located in the neck, regulates metabolism. As you may remember from a biology course, metabolism is the rate at which energy is produced and expended in the body. By altering metabolism, the thyroid can have a sizable effect on personality. A person suffering from **hyperthyroidism** (an overactive thyroid) tends to be thin, tense, excitable, and nervous. An underactive thyroid (**hypothyroidism**) in an adult can cause inactivity, sleepiness, slowness, and obesity. In infancy, hypothyroidism limits development of the nervous system, leading to severe mental retardation.

When you are frightened or angry, some important reactions prepare your body for action: Your heart rate and blood pressure rise; stored sugar is released into the bloodstream for quick energy; your muscles tense and receive more blood; and your blood is prepared to clot more quickly in case of injury. As we discussed earlier, these changes are controlled by the autonomic nervous system. Specifically, the sympathetic branch of the ANS causes the hormones *epinephrine* and *norepinephrine* to be released by the adrenal glands. (Epinephrine is also known as adrenaline, which may be more familiar to you.) **Epinephrine** (ep-eh-NEF-rin), which is associated with fear, tends to arouse the body. **Norepinephrine** also tends to arouse the body, but it is linked with anger.

Adrenal glands Endocrine glands that arouse the body, regulate salt balance, adjust the body to stress, and affect sexual functioning.

Adrenal medulla The inner core of the adrenal glands; a source of epinephrine and norepinephrine.

Adrenal cortex The outer layer of the adrenal glands; produces hormones that affect salt intake, reactions to stress, and sexual development.

The **adrenal glands** are located just under the back of the rib cage, atop the kidneys. The **adrenal medulla,** or inner core of the adrenal glands, is the source of epinephrine and norepinephrine. The **adrenal cortex,** or outer "bark" of the adrenal glands, produces a set of hormones called *corticoids* (KOR–tih–coids). One of their jobs is to regulate salt balance in the body. A deficiency of certain corticoids in humans can evoke a powerful craving for the taste of salt. The corticoids also help the body adjust to stress, and they are a secondary source of sex hormones.

An oversecretion of the adrenal sex hormones can cause *virilism* (exaggerated male characteristics). For instance, a woman may grow a beard or a man's voice may become so low it is difficult to understand. Oversecretion early in life can cause premature puberty (full sexual development during childhood). One of the most remarkable cases on record is that of a five-year-old Peruvian girl who gave birth to a son (Strange, 1965).

While we are on the topic of sex hormones, there is a related issue worth mentioning. One of the principal androgens, or "male" hormones, is testosterone, which is supplied in small amounts by the adrenal glands. (The testes are the main source of testosterone in males.) Perhaps you have heard about the use of anabolic steroids by athletes who want to "bulk up" or promote muscle growth. Most of these drugs are synthetic versions of testosterone.

Steroid use may cause serious side effects, including voice deepening or baldness in women and shrinkage of the testicles, sexual impotence, or breast enlargement in men. Also common when steroids are used by younger adolescents are an increased risk of heart attack and stroke, liver damage, or stunted growth (Bahrke, Yesalis, & Brower, 1998). Understandably, all major sports organizations ban the use of anabolic steroids.

Do hormones produce differences in men and women's behaviour? According to a well-respected Canadian psychologist, Doreen Kimura, the answer is yes. In general, research shows that men and women excel at different tasks. For example, on average, men perform better on mathematical reasoning, spatial tasks (e.g., being able to rotate three-dimensional objects in one's head, learning new routes based on geometric information), and gross motor skills (e.g., guiding an object to a target and intercepting an object). Women, on the other hand, are better at verbal skills (e.g., solving word puzzles), arithmetical calculations, fine motor tasks (e.g., inserting pegs into certain holes on a board), and remembering landmarks along a route. Kimura argues that these sex differences are due to different hormones male and female fetuses are exposed to. The male fetus receives higher levels of androgens and the female fetus gets more estrogen. As a result, the brains of the two sexes develop somewhat differently. After birth, the environment interacts with these differently created brains to produce the type of behavioural differences we just mentioned.

Kimura also reports that women's hormone levels during the menstrual cycle affect their performance on a variety of tasks. When estrogen levels are high, as around the middle of the cycle, they tend not to do as well on spatial tasks, but their verbal and fine motor abilities are at their peak. Spatial ability improves when estrogen levels are lower, as during the menstrual phase. In males, testosterone is higher in the morning and declines during the day, higher in the fall than in the spring, and their performance on tasks of spatial ability is better when testosterone levels are lower.

The strongest evidence for Kimura's position comes from research on rats. Female rats tend to learn a route by relying on various landmarks located along a particular route, whereas male rats appear to use geometric cues. This parallels the differences between men and women. If a male rat is castrated after birth, his androgen levels decrease, and his ability to learn a maze is subsequently diminished. On the other hand, if a female rat is administered the male androgens, her spatial performance improves as a result. Hormonal manipulations during adulthood have no detrimental or beneficial effects (Kimura, 1996, 1999). Although animal data are intriguing, it is a huge leap from rodents to humans. We must take into account the strong influence of social and cultural factors on men and women's behaviour.

What then can we conclude about the relationship of hormone levels and the behavioural differences between men and women? Could men and women's performance on various tasks not be explained by the different ways in which they are socialized? After all, women have not received the same opportunities men have enjoyed for so long. Women traditionally have not received much encouragement to pursue scientific careers. It is little wonder, then, that their performance on tasks of mathematical reasoning and spatial ability does not equal that of men. This is exactly what Kimura's critics argue. Finally, it should be remembered that the evidence Kimura puts forward is correlational. No one has convincingly demonstrated in humans a direct causal link between sex hormones and mental ability. Nevertheless, Kimura's ideas have provoked a debate about an age-old issue from an interesting angle. Exactly how hormones and socialization shape our behaviour is a complicated issue, and both are probably important. At this time, however, it would be imprudent to emphasize one over the other.

But if Kimura is right, men should not take their physics and engineering exams early in the morning or during the autumn months, and women should avoid them during the middle of their menstrual cycle. Any chance of convincing your professors?

In our brief discussion of the endocrine system, we have considered only a few of the more important glands. Nevertheless, this should give you an appreciation of how completely behaviour and personality are tied to the ebb and flow of hormones in the body.

A LOOK AHEAD   In the upcoming Psychology in Action section, we will return to the brain to see how hand preference relates to brain organization. You'll also find out if being right- or left-handed affects your chances of living to a ripe old age.

Knowledge builder

SUBCORTEX AND ENDOCRINE SYSTEM

Relate

 If Mr. Medulla met Ms. Cerebellum at a party, what would they say their roles are in the brain? Would a marching band in a "reticular formation" look like a network? Would it get your attention? If you were standing in the final path for behaviour leaving the brain, would you be in the thalamus? Or in the hy-**path**-alamus (please forgive the misspelling)? When you are emotional do you wave your limbs around (and does your limbic system become more active)?

Name as many of the endocrine glands as you can. Which did you leave out? Can you summarize the functions of each of the glands?

Learning Check

1. Three major divisions of the brain are the brainstem or _____, the _____, and the _____.

2. Reflex centres for heartbeat and respiration are found in the
   a. cerebellum b. thalamus c. medulla d. reticular formation

3. A portion of the reticular formation, known as the RAS, serves as an _____ system in the brain.
   a. activating b. adrenal c. adjustment d. aversive

4. The _____ is a final relay, or "switching station," for sensory information on its way to the cortex.

5. "Reward" and "punishment" areas are found throughout the _____ system, which is also related to emotion.

6. Undersecretion from the thyroid can cause
   a. dwarfism b. giantism c. overweight d. mental retardation

7. The body's ability to resist stress is related to the action of the adrenal _____.

Critical Thinking

8. Subcortical structures in humans are quite similar to corresponding lower brain areas in other animals. Why would knowing this allow you to predict, in general terms, what functions are controlled by the subcortex?

9. Where in all the brain's "hardware" do you think the mind is found? What is the relationship between mind and brain?

Answers:

1. hindbrain, midbrain, forebrain 2. c 3. a 4. thalamus 5. limbic 6. d (in infancy) 7. cortex 8. Because the subcortex must be related to basic functions common to all complex animals: motives, emotions, sleep, attention, and vegetative functions, such as heartbeat, breathing, and temperature regulation. The subcortex also routes and processes incoming information from the senses and outgoing commands to the muscles. 9. This question, known as the mind-body problem, has challenged thinkers for centuries. One recent view is that mental states are "emergent properties" of brain activity. That is, brain activity forms complex patterns that are, in a sense, more than the sum of their parts. Or, to use a rough analogy, if the brain were a musical instrument, then mental life would be like music played on that instrument.

HANDEDNESS——IF YOUR BRAIN IS RIGHT, WHAT'S LEFT?

Survey Question:
■ How do right- and left-handed individuals differ?

Handedness A preference for the right or left hand in most activities.

In the English language, "what's right is right," but what's left may be wrong. We have left-handed compliments, people with "two left feet," those who are left out, and the left-handed. On the other hand (so to speak), we have the right way, the right angle, the "right-hand man" (or woman), righteousness, and the right-handed.

The Sinister Hand

Left-handedness has a long and undeserved bad reputation. Southpaws have been accused of being clumsy, stubborn (for refusing to use their right hand), and maladjusted. But as any lefty will tell you, and psychology has confirmed, none of this is true. The supposed clumsiness of lefties is merely a result of living in a right-handed world: If it can be gripped, turned, folded, held, or pulled, it's probably designed for the right hand. Even toilet handles are on the right side.

What causes **handedness** (a preference for the right or left hand)? Why are there more right-handed than left-handed people? How do left-handed and right-handed people differ? Does being left-handed create any problems—or benefits? The answers to these questions lead us back to the brain, where handedness begins. Let's see what research has revealed about handedness, the brain, and you.

Hand Dominance

Take a moment and write your name on a sheet of paper, first using your right hand and then your left. You were probably much more comfortable writing with your dominant hand. This is interesting because there's no real difference in the strength or dexterity of the hands themselves. The agility of your dominant hand is an outward expression of superior motor control on one side of the brain. If you are right-handed, there is literally more area on the left side of your brain devoted to controlling your right hand. If you are left-handed, the reverse applies (Volkmann et al., 1998).

The preceding exercise implies that you are either entirely right- or left-handed. But handedness is a matter of degree, asserts Stanley Coren (1992), a psychologist at the University of British Columbia. To better assess your handedness, circle an answer for each of the questions that follow.

Are You Right- or Left-Handed?
1. Which hand do you normally use to write? Right Left Either
2. Which hand would you use to throw a ball at a target? Right Left Either
3. Which hand do you use to hold your toothbrush? Right Left Either
4. Which hand do you use to hold a knife when cutting food? Right Left Either
5. With which hand do you hold a hammer when hitting a nail? Right Left Either
6. When you thread a needle, which hand holds the thread? Right Left Either

To find your score, count the number of "Rights" you circled and multiply by 3. Then multiply the number of "Eithers" by 2. Next count the number of "Lefts" you circled. Now add all three totals and compare the result with the following scale (adapted from Coren, 1992).

17–18:	Strongly right-handed
15–16:	Moderately right-handed (mixed)
13–14:	Mildly right-handed (mixed)
12:	Ambidextrous
10–11:	Mildly left-handed (mixed)
8–9:	Moderately left-handed (mixed)
6–7:	Strongly left-handed

Table 2.1
Sports and
Handedness

SPORT	HANDEDNESS ADVANTAGE
Boxing	Left
Fencing	Left
Basketball	Mixed and ambidextrous
Ice hockey	Mixed and ambidextrous
Field hockey	Mixed and ambidextrous
Tennis	Strong left or strong right
Squash	Strong left or strong right
Badminton	Strong left or strong right

(Coren, 1992.)

Dominant hemisphere A term usually applied to the side of a person's brain that produces language.

Left-handers have an advantage in sports such as fencing and boxing. Most likely, their movements are less familiar to opponents, who usually face right-handers (Coren, 1992).

A majority of people (about 77 percent) are strongly right- or left-handed. The rest show some inconsistency in hand preference. As Table 2.1 indicates, such differences can affect performance in some sports.

If a person is strongly left-handed, does that mean the right hemisphere is dominant? Not necessarily. It's true that the right hemisphere controls the left hand, but a left-handed person's language-producing, **dominant hemisphere** may be on the opposite side of the brain.

BRAIN DOMINANCE About 97 percent of right-handers process speech in the left hemisphere and are left-brain dominant (see ▶Figure 2.27). A good 68 percent of left-handers produce speech from the left hemisphere, just as right-handed people do. About 19 percent of all lefties and 3 percent of righties use their right brain for language. Some left-handers (approximately 12 percent) use both sides of the brain for language processing. All totalled, 94 percent of the population uses the left brain for language (Coren, 1992).

Is there any way for a person to tell which of his or her hemispheres is dominant? One interesting clue is based on the way you write. Right-handed individuals who write with a straight hand, and lefties who write with a hooked hand, are usually left-brain dominant for language. Left-handed people who write with their hand below the line, and righties who use a hooked position, are usually right-brain dominant (Levy & Reid, 1976). Another hint is provided by the hand gestures. If you gesture mostly with your right hand as you talk, you probably process language in your left hemisphere. Gesturing with your left hand is associated with right-brain language processing (Hellige, 1993). Are your friends right brained or left brained? (See ▶Figure 2.28.)

Before you leap to any conclusions, be aware that writing position is not foolproof. The only sure way to check brain dominance is to do a medical test that involves briefly anesthetizing one cerebral hemisphere at a time (Springer & Deutsch, 1998).

HANDEDNESS How common is left-handedness, and what causes it? Ninety percent of all humans are right-handed; 10 percent are left-handed. The prevalence of right-handedness

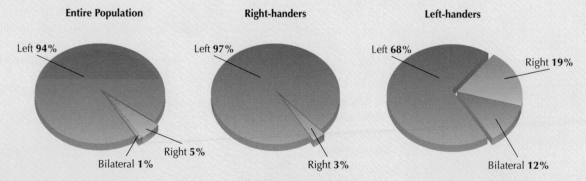

Entire Population **Right-handers** **Left-handers**

Left **94%** Left **97%** Left **68%**

Right **19%**

Right **5%** Right **3%**

Bilateral **1%** Bilateral **12%**

▶**Figure 2.27**

Language is controlled by the left side of the brain in the majority of right- and left-handers.

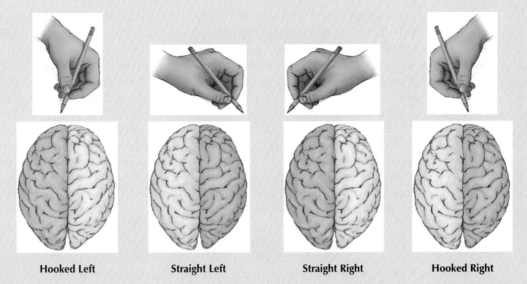

Hooked Left   **Straight Left**   **Straight Right**   **Hooked Right**

▶Figure 2.28

Research suggests that the hand position used in writing may indicate which brain hemisphere is used for language. (Redrawn from an illustration by M. E. Challinor.)

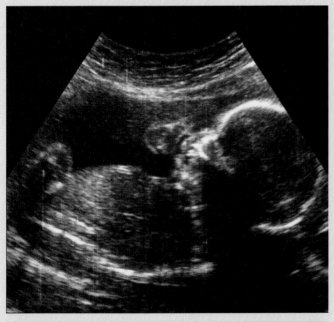

▶Figure 2.29

In this ultrasound image, a four-month-old fetus sucks her right thumb. A study by psychologist Peter Hepper suggests that she will continue to prefer her right hand after she is born and that she will be right-handed as an adult.

probably reflects the left brain's specialization for producing language (Coren, 1992).

In the past, many left-handed children were forced to use their right hand for writing, eating, and other skills. But as fetal ultrasound images show, hand preferences are sometimes apparent even before birth (Hepper, McCartney, & Shannon, 1998). (See ▶Figure 2.29.) This suggests that handedness cannot be dictated. Parents should never try to force a left-handed child to use the right hand. To do so may create speech or reading problems.

Is handedness inherited from parents? Studies of twins show that hand preferences are not directly inherited like eye colour or skin colour (Reiss et al., 1999; Ross et al., 1999). What is inherited is the degree of handedness. If your parents are strongly handed, you probably have a strong hand preference, too—even though your dominant hand may not match theirs. If your parents are ambidextrous or mixed handed, you probably are, too (Coren, 1992).

Are there any drawbacks to being left-handed? A minority of lefties owe their hand preference to birth traumas (such as prematurity, low birth weight, and breech birth). These individuals have a higher incidence of allergies, learning disorders, and other problems (Betancur et al., 1990). But in most instances, left-handedness is unrelated to intelligence or the overall rate of illness and accidental injury, according to a study by Clare Porac and her colleagues at the University of Victoria (Porac et al., 1998; see also McManus et al., 1988).

Many people have been alarmed by news reports that lefties tend to die younger than right-handed persons (Coren & Halpern, 1991). However, three rather decisive studies found that there is no difference in the age at which left- and right-handed persons die (Harris, 1993a, 1993b; Salive, Guralnick, & Glynn, 1993). More importantly, there are some clear advantages to being left-handed.

ADVANTAGE LEFT   Throughout history a notable number of artists have been lefties, from Leonardo da Vinci and Michelangelo to Pablo Picasso and M. C. Escher. Conceivably, since the right hemisphere is superior at imagery and visual abilities, there is some advantage to using the left hand for drawing or painting (Springer & Deutsch, 1998). At the least, lefties are definitely better at visualizing three-dimensional objects. This may be why there are more left-handed architects, artists, and chess players than would be expected (Coren, 1992).

> **Lateralization** Differences between the two sides of the body—especially differences in the abilities of the brain hemispheres.

Lateralization refers to specialization in the abilities of the brain hemispheres. One striking feature of lefties is that they are generally less lateralized than the right-handed (Hellige, 1990). In fact, even the physical size and shape of their cerebral hemispheres are more alike. If you are a lefty, you can take pride in the fact that your brain is less lopsided than most! In general, left-handers are more symmetrical on almost everything, including eye dominance, fingerprints, and even foot size.

In some situations less lateralization may be a real advantage. For instance, individuals who are moderately left-handed or ambidextrous seem to have better than average pitch memory, which is a basic musical skill. Correspondingly, more musicians are ambidextrous than would normally be expected (Springer & Deutsch, 1998).

Math abilities may also benefit from fuller use of the right hemisphere. Students who are extremely gifted in math are much more likely to be left-handed or ambidextrous (Benbow, 1986). Even where ordinary arithmetic skills are concerned, lefties seem to excel (Annett & Manning, 1990).

The clearest advantage of being left-handed shows up when there is a brain injury. Because of their milder lateralization, left-handed individuals typically experience less language loss after damage to either brain hemisphere, and they recover more easily (Geschwind, 1979). Maybe having "two left feet" isn't so bad after all.

Knowledge builder

HANDEDNESS AND BRAIN LATERALIZATION

Relate

Think for a moment about what you "knew" about handedness and left-handed people before you read this section. Which of your beliefs were correct? How has your knowledge about handedness changed?

Learning Check

1. About 97 percent of left-handed people process language on the left side of the brain, the same as right-handed people do. T or F?
2. Left-handed individuals who write with their hand below the line are likely to be right-brain dominant. T or F?

3. Most animals, like most humans, show a preference for the right limb. T or F?
4. In general, left-handed individuals show less lateralization in the brain and throughout the body. T or F?
5. A recent study demonstrated that left-handed individuals have a shorter life expectancy than right-handed persons. T or F?

Critical Thinking

6. Reports that left-handed people tend to die younger were flawed in an important way: The average age of people in the left-handed group was younger than that of subjects in the right-handed group. Why would this make a difference in the conclusions drawn?

Answers:

1. F 2. T 3. F 4. T 5. F 6. Because we can't tell if handedness or average age accounts for the difference in death rates. For example, if we start with a group of 20- to 30-year-old people, in which some die, the average age of death has to be between 20 and 30. If we start with a group of 30- to 40-year-old people, in which some die, the average age of death has to be between 30 and 40. Thus, the left-handed group might have an earlier average age at death simply because members of the group were younger to start with.

Psychologist's Journal

EPILOGUE

We began our exploration of the brain with a brilliant musician. Imagine the other extreme of being completely unable to move or speak. Even though you would remain alert and intelligent, you would be unable to communicate your simplest thoughts and feelings to others. Each year, this is the fate of thousands of people who are paralyzed by stroke, disease, or injury. In a very real sense, these people become prisoners in their own bodies (Christensen, 1999). What if they could "will" a computer to speak for them?

In pioneering studies, doctors Roy Bakay and Philip Kennedy have inserted special electrodes into the motor cortex of paralyzed patients. When the patient thinks certain thoughts, bursts of activity in the brain are detected by the implanted wires. Instantly, these signals are transmitted to a computer, where they control the movements of a cursor on the screen. Patients are now learning to select icons on the screen that tell the computer to say phrases such as "Please turn the light on" or "See you later, nice talking to you" (Kennedy & Bakay, 1998).

Neuroscientists realize that they have taken only baby steps toward freeing "locked-in" patients. Nevertheless, what was merely science fiction a few years ago is starting to become reality. The human brain is just beginning to understand itself. What an adventure the next decade of brain research will be.

CHAPTER IN REVIEW

Major Points

▶ Biopsychologists study how processes in the body, brain, and nervous system relate to behaviour.

▶ Ultimately, all behaviour can be traced to the activity of nerve cells.

▶ To map the brain, researchers activate or disable specific areas and observe changes in behaviour.

▶ Bioelectrical recordings and computer-generated images of brain activity provide additional insights into how the brain works.

▶ Sensations, thoughts, feelings, motives, actions, memories, and all other human capacities are associated with brain activities and structures.

▶ Endocrine glands serve as a chemical communication system within the body. Behaviour is greatly influenced by the ebb and flow of hormones in the bloodstream.

▶ Brain dominance and brain activity determine if you are right-handed, left-handed, or ambidextrous.

Summary

How Do Nerve Cells Operate and Communicate?

• The nervous system is made up of linked neurons that pass information from one to another through synapses.

• The neuronal axons, axon terminals, dendrites, and the soma facilitate the sending and receiving of messages in the nervous system.

• The firing of an action potential (nerve impulse) is basically electrical. Communication between neurons is chemical.

• Neurotransmitters cross the synapse, attach to receptor sites, and excite or inhibit the receiving cell.

• Chemicals called neuropeptides also appear to regulate activity in the brain.

• Nerves are made of axons and associated tissues. Neurons and nerves in the peripheral nervous system can often regenerate. At present, damage in the central nervous system is usually permanent, although scientists are working on ways to repair damaged neural tissue.

What Are the Functions of Major Parts of the Nervous System?

• The nervous system can be divided into the central nervous system and the peripheral nervous system, which includes the somatic (bodily) and autonomic (involuntary) nervous systems.

• The autonomic system has a sympathetic branch and a parasympathetic branch.

How Do We Know How the Brain Works?

• Brain research relies on clinical studies, electrical stimulation, ablation, deep lesioning, electrical recording, micro-electrode recording, and EEG recording.

• Computer-enhanced images are providing three-dimensional pictures of the living human brain and its activity. Examples of such techniques are CT scans, MRI scans, and PET scans.

How Is the Brain Organized, and What Do Its Various Areas Do?

- The human brain is marked by advanced corticalization, or enlargement of the cerebral cortex.
- The left cerebral hemisphere contains speech or language "centres" in most people. It also specializes in writing, calculating, judging time and rhythm, and ordering complex movements.
- The right hemisphere is largely non-verbal. It excels at spatial and perceptual skills, visualization, and recognition of patterns, faces, and melodies.
- "Split brains" have been created in animals and humans by cutting the corpus callosum. The split-brain individual shows a remarkable degree of independence between the right and left hemispheres.
- Some individuals are born with a partial or complete absence of the corpus callosum. In such cases, one hemisphere is able to share some sensory information with its counterpart.
- The most basic functions of the lobes of the cerebral cortex are as follows: occipital lobes—vision; parietal lobes—bodily sensation; temporal lobes—hearing and language; frontal lobes—motor control, speech, and abstract thought. Damage to any of these areas will impair the named functions.

Why Are the Brain's Association Areas Important? What Happens When They Are Injured?

- Association areas on the cortex are neither sensory nor motor in function. They are related to more complex skills such as language, memory, recognition, and problem solving.
- Damage to either Broca's area or Wernicke's area causes speech and language problems known as aphasias.

What Kinds of Behaviours Are Controlled by the Subcortex?

- The brain can be subdivided into the forebrain, midbrain, and hindbrain. The subcortex includes several crucial brain structures found at all three levels, below the cortex.

- The medulla contains centres essential for reflex control of heart rate, breathing, and other "vegetative" functions.
- The cerebellum maintains coordination, posture, and muscle tone.
- The reticular formation directs sensory and motor messages, and part of it, known as the RAS, acts as an activating system for the cerebral cortex.
- The thalamus carries sensory information to the cortex. The hypothalamus exerts powerful control over eating, drinking, sleep cycles, body temperature, and other basic motives and behaviours.
- The limbic system is strongly related to emotion. It also contains distinct reward and punishment areas and an area known as the hippocampus that is important for forming memories.

Does the Glandular System Affect Behaviour?

- The endocrine system provides chemical communication in the body by releasing hormones into the bloodstream. Endocrine glands influence moods, behaviour, and personality.
- Many of the endocrine glands are influenced by the pituitary (the "master gland"), which is in turn influenced by the hypothalamus. Thus, the brain controls the body through the fast nervous system and the slower endocrine system.
- Sex hormones may affect the behaviour of men and women differently, but studies on this issue are not conclusive at present.

How Do Right- and Left-Handed Individuals Differ?

- Hand dominance ranges from strongly left- to strongly right-handed, with mixed handedness and ambidexterity in between. Ninety percent of the population is basically right-handed, and 10 percent is left-handed.
- The vast majority of people are right-handed and therefore left-brain dominant for motor skills. Ninety-seven percent of right-handed persons and 68 percent of the left-handed also produce speech from the left hemisphere.
- In general, the left-handed are less strongly lateralized in brain function than are right-handed persons.

PSYCHOLOGY ON THE NET

If you have difficulty finding any of the sites listed here, visit http://psychologyjourney.nelson.com *for an updated list of Internet addresses and direct links to relevant sites.*

Brain Briefings Articles on a variety of topics in neuroscience. http://www.sfn.org/briefings/

Brain Connection Explains brain research to the public, including common myths about the brain, the effects of various chemicals, how brain research applies to education, and more. http://www.brainconnection.com

The Endocrine System This site describes the endocrine system and hormones. http://kidshealth.org/parent/general/body_basics/endocrine.html

The Human Brain: Dissections of the Real Brain Detailed photographs and drawings of the human brain. http://www.vh.org/Providers/Textbooks/BrainAnatomy/BrainAnatomy.html

Lorin's Left-Handedness Site Answers to common questions about left-handedness. http://duke.usask.ca/~elias/left/

The Montreal Neurological Institute Established by Wilder Penfield, this renowned affiliate of McGill University carries out important research into various aspects of the brain. http://www.mcgill.ca/mni

Probe the Brain Explore the motor homunculus of the brain interactively. http://www.pbs.org/wgbh/aso/tryit/brain/

InfoTrac College Edition For recent articles related to brain mapping, use Key Words search for MAGNETIC RESONANCE IMAGING and ELECTROENCEPHALOGRAPHY.

INTERACTIVE LEARNING

Psychology: An Interactive Journey Remember that Chapter 2 of the CD-ROM that came with this text has practice tests, flashcards, interactive exercises, a crossword puzzle, and other valuable materials to enhance your learning experience.

PsychNow! 2a. Neurons and Synaptic Transmission, 2b. Brain and Behaviour.

Psyk.trek 2. Biological Bases of Behaviour, Psyk.trek Simulations: 2. Hemispheric Specialization.

Chart Your Progress

The questions that follow are only a sample of what you need to know. If you miss any of the items, you should review the entire chapter, do the exercises on the CD, and review the Knowledge Builders. Another way to prepare for tests is to get more practice with *WebTutor*, the *Study Guide*, or the *Practice Quizzes* that are available with this text.

1. The point at which information is passed from one neuron to another links the
   a. neurilemma and myelin
   b. soma and ion channels
   c. axon terminals and dendrites
   d. enkephalin and myelin

2. Muscles are activated by a transmitter substance called
   a. neuropeptide
   b. acetylcholine
   c. enkephalin
   d. endorphin

3. The brain grows new neurons to replace those that are lost. This process is known as
   a. neurogenesis
   b. neuileminal regeneration
   c. autonomic regeneration
   d. neuropeptosis

4. Quieting the body and returning it to a lower level of arousal after an emotional event is a specialty of the
   a. parasympathetic system
   b. peripheral nervous system
   c. spinal nerves
   d. effector cells

5. Which research technique provides an image of ongoing brain activity?
   a. ESB
   b. deep lesioning
   c. PET
   d. surface ablation

6. The left hemisphere of the brain processes information sequentially, and it is superior at
   a. recognizing patterns
   b. holistic thinking
   c. expressing and detecting emotions
   d. analysis

7. Impaired hearing could result from damage to the _____ lobes of the brain.
   a. frontal
   b. temporal
   c. occipital
   d. parietal

8. Damage to Broca's area causes
   a. a loss of coordination
   b. disturbed sleep patterns
   c. aphasia
   d. an inability to remember recent events

9. The endocrine gland that most influences the activities of other glands is the
   a. pituitary
   b. adrenal
   c. pineal
   d. thyroid

10. A majority of both right-handed and left-handed people produce speech from the
    a. right brain hemisphere
    b. corpus callosum
    c. left brain hemisphere
    d. hippocampus

Answers: 1. c 2. b 3. a 4. a 5. c 6. d 7. b 8. c 9. a 10. c

Chapter 3

Psychologist's Journal

A STAR IS BORN—HERE'S AMY!

Olivia has just given birth to her first child, Amy. Frankly, at the moment Amy looks something like a prune, with pudgy arms, stubby legs, and lots of wrinkles. She also has the face of an angel—at least in her parents' eyes. As Olivia and her husband Tom look at Amy, they wonder how her life will unfold. What kind of a person will she be?

What if we could skip ahead through Amy's childhood and observe her at various ages? What could we learn? Seeing the world through her eyes would be both instructive and fascinating. Children are newcomers to the societies in which they live. Because of this, their attempts to figure out how the world works can make us more acutely aware of things that we take for granted. For example, younger children are very literal in their use of language. That's why one three-year-old who thought her bath was too hot asked her father to "Make it warmer, daddy." At first, her father was confused. The bath was already pretty hot. But then he realized that what she really meant was, "Bring the water closer to the temperature we call warm." It makes perfectly good sense if you look at it that way.

Today we can merely guess about Amy's future. However, psychologists have studied many thousands of children. Their findings tell a fascinating story about human growth and development. Let's let Olivia, Tom, and Amy represent parents and children everywhere, as we see what psychology can tell us about the challenges of growing up. Tracing Amy's development might even help answer the question, How did I become the person I am today?

Survey Questions

- How do heredity and environment affect development?
- What can newborn babies do?
- What influence does maturation have on early development?
- Of what significance is a child's emotional bond with parents?
- How important are parenting styles?
- How do children acquire language?
- How do children learn to think?
- What are the typical tasks and dilemmas through the life span?
- How do effective parents discipline their children?

▶ Heredity and Environment—The Nurture of Nature

Survey Question:
- How do heredity and environment affect development?

Children are the heart of **developmental psychology** (the study of progressive changes in behaviour and abilities). However, you should be aware that human development involves every stage of life from conception to death (or "the womb to the tomb"). So do the effects of heredity and environment. Some events in a person's life, such as achieving sexual maturity, are mostly governed by heredity. Others, such as learning to swim or use a computer, are primarily a matter of environment. But which is more important, heredity or environment? Let's consider some arguments on both sides of the nature–nurture debate.

Heredity

Heredity ("nature") refers to the genetic transmission of physical and psychological characteristics from parents to their children. An incredible number of personal features are set at **conception,** when a sperm and an ovum (egg) unite.

How does heredity operate? The nucleus of every human cell contains 46 **chromosomes.** (The word chromosome means "coloured body.") These thread-like structures hold the coded instructions of heredity (see ▶ Figure 3.1). Notable exceptions are sperm cells and ova, which contain only 23 chromosomes. Thus, Amy received 23 chromosomes from Olivia and 23 from Tom. This is her genetic heritage.

Chromosomes are made up of **DNA,** deoxyribonucleic acid (dee-OX-see-RYE-bo-new-KLEE-ik). DNA is a long, ladder-like chain of chemical molecules (see ▶ Figure 3.2). The order of these molecules, or organic bases, acts as a code for genetic information. The DNA in each cell contains 3 billion base pairs. That's enough to record all the instructions needed to make a human—with room left over to spare.

Genes are small areas of the DNA code. Each of the 25 000 genes in your cells affects a particular process or personal characteristic. Sometimes, a single gene is responsible for an inherited feature, such as Amy's eye colour. Most characteristics, however, are **polygenic** (pol-ih-JEN-ik), or controlled by many genes working in combination.

Genes may be dominant or recessive. When a gene is **dominant,** the feature it controls will appear every time the gene is present. When a gene is

Developmental psychology The study of progressive changes in behaviour and abilities from conception to death.

Heredity ("nature") The transmission of physical and psychological characteristics from parents to offspring through genes.

Conception The union of an ovum and a sperm cell.

Chromosomes Thread-like "coloured bodies" in the nucleus of each cell that are made up of DNA.

DNA Deoxyribonucleic acid, a molecular structure that contains coded genetic information.

Genes Specific areas on a strand of DNA that carry hereditary information.

Polygenic characteristics Personal traits or physical properties that are influenced by many genes working in combination.

Dominant gene A gene whose influence will be expressed each time the gene is present.

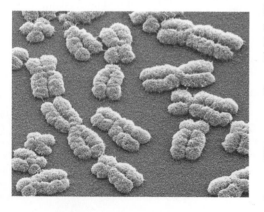

▶Figure 3.1

This image, made with a scanning electron microscope, shows several pairs of human chromosomes. (Colours are artificial.)

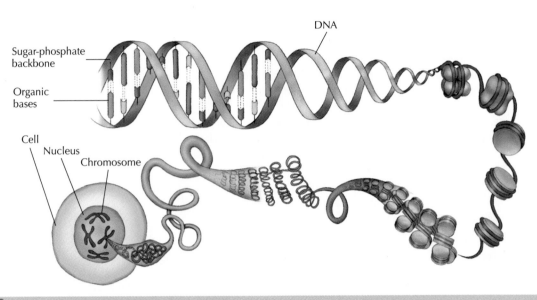

DNA

Sugar-phosphate backbone

Organic bases

Cell
Nucleus
Chromosome

▶Figure 3.2

(Top left) Linked molecules (organic bases) make up the "rungs" on DNA's twisted "molecular ladder." The order of these molecules serves as a code for genetic information. The code provides a genetic blueprint that is unique for each individual (except identical twins). The drawing shows only a small section of a DNA strand. An entire strand of DNA is composed of billions of smaller molecules. *(Bottom left)* The nucleus of each cell in the body contains chromosomes made up of tightly wound coils of DNA. (Don't be misled by the drawing: Chromosomes are microscopic in size and the chemical molecules that make up DNA are even smaller.)

Recessive gene A gene whose influence will be expressed only when it is paired with a second recessive gene.

Senescence Aging; the latter years of life.

Human growth sequence The pattern of physical development from conception to death.

recessive, it must be paired with a second recessive gene before its effect will be expressed. For example, if Amy got a blue-eye gene from Tom and a brown-eye gene from Olivia, Amy will be brown-eyed, because brown-eye genes are dominant.

If brown-eye genes are dominant, why do two brown-eyed parents sometimes have a blue-eyed child? If each parent has two brown-eye genes, the couple's children can only be brown-eyed. But what if each parent has one brown-eye gene and one blue-eye gene? In that case the parents would both have brown eyes. Yet, there is one chance in four that any child will get two blue-eye genes and have blue eyes (see ▶Figure 3.3). Along the same lines, genetics can sometimes be used to predict the chances that a child will be born with various inherited problems.

Genetic Programming

Heredity influences events from conception to **senescence** (seh-NESS-ens: aging) and death (see Table 3.1). That's why the **human growth sequence,** or overall pattern of physical development, is universal. Heredity also determines eye colour, skin colour, and susceptibility to some diseases. To a degree, genetic instructions affect body size and shape, height, intelligence, athletic potential, personality traits, sexual orientation, and a host of other details (Hamer & Copeland, 1998). Score 1 for those who favour heredity as the more important factor in development!

Brown-eyed mother

Mother's genes

Brown-eyed child

Brown-eyed child

Brown-eyed father

Father's genes

Blue-eyed child

Brown-eyed child

▶Figure 3.3

Gene patterns for children of brown-eyed parents, where each parent has one brown-eye gene and one blue-eye gene. Since the brown-eye gene is dominant, one child in four will be blue-eyed. Thus, there is a significant chance that two brown-eyed parents will have a blue-eyed child.

Table 3.1
Human Growth Sequence

PERIOD	DURATION	DESCRIPTIVE NAME
Prenatal period	From conception to birth	
Germinal period	First 2 weeks after conception	Zygote
Embryonic period	2–8 weeks after conception	Embryo
Fetal period	From 8 weeks after conception to birth	Fetus
Neonatal period	From birth to a few weeks after birth	Neonate
Infancy	From a few weeks after birth until child is walking securely; some children walk securely at less than a year, while others may not be able to until age 17–18 months	Infant
Early childhood	From about 15–18 months until about 2–2½ years	Toddler
	From age 2–3 to about age 6	Preschool child
Middle childhood	From about age 6 to age 12	School-age child
Pubescence	Period of about 2 years before puberty	
Puberty	Point of development at which biological changes of pubescence reach a climax marked by sexual maturity	
Adolescence	From the beginning of pubescence until full social maturity is reached (difficult to fix duration of this period)	Adolescent
Adulthood	From adolescence to death; sometimes subdivided into other periods as shown at left	Adult
Young adulthood (19–25)		
Adulthood (26–40)		
Maturity (41 plus)		
Senescence	No defined limit that would apply to all people; extremely variable; characterized by marked physiological and psychological deterioration	Adult (senile), "old age"

*Note: There is no exact beginning or ending point for various growth periods. The ages are approximate, and each period may be thought of as blending into the next. (Table courtesy of Tom Bond.)

Temperament The physical core of personality, including emotional and perceptual sensitivity, energy levels, typical mood, and so forth.

Easy child A child who is temperamentally relaxed and agreeable.

Difficult child A child who is temperamentally moody, intense, and easily angered.

Slow-to-warm-up child A child who is temperamentally restrained and unexpressive.

Environment ("nurture") The sum of all external conditions affecting development, especially the effects of learning.

TEMPERAMENT *How soon do hereditary differences appear?* Some appear right away. For instance, newborn babies differ noticeably in **temperament.** This is the physical core of personality. It includes sensitivity, irritability, distractibility, and typical mood (Braungart et al., 1992). About 40 percent of all newborns are **easy children** who are relaxed and agreeable. Ten percent are **difficult children** who are moody, intense, and easily angered. **Slow-to-warm-up** children (about 15 percent) are restrained, unexpressive, or shy. The remaining children do not fit neatly into a single category (Chess & Thomas, 1986). (Perhaps we should call them "generic" children?)

Imagine that we start with some infants who are very shy and some who are very bold. By the time they are four or five years old, most of these children will be only moderately shy or bold. This suggests that inherited temperaments are modified by learning (Kagan, 1999). In other words, nurture immediately enters the picture.

ENVIRONMENT **Environment ("nurture")** refers to the sum of all external conditions that affect a person. The environments in which a child grows up can have a powerful impact on development. Humans today are genetically very similar to cave dwellers who lived 30 000 years

Identical twins. Twins who share identical genes (identical twins) demonstrate the powerful influence of heredity. Even when they are reared apart, identical twins are strikingly alike in motor skills, physical development, and appearance. At the same time, twins are less alike as adults than they were as children, which shows environmental influences are at work (McCartney, Bernieri, & Harris, 1990).

Critical period During development, a period of increased sensitivity to environmental influences. Also, a time during which certain events must take place for normal development to occur.

Intrauterine environment The physical and chemical environment within the uterus during prenatal development.

Congenital problems Problems or defects that originate during prenatal development in the womb.

Genetic disorders Problems caused by defects in the genes or by inherited characteristics.

Teratogen Radiation, a drug, or other substance capable of altering fetal development in ways that cause birth defects.

ago. Nevertheless, a bright baby born today could learn to become almost anything—a ballet dancer, an engineer, a rapper, or a biochemist who likes to paint in watercolours. But an Upper Paleolithic baby could have become only a hunter or food gatherer. Score 1 for the environmentalists!

Early experiences can have very lasting effects. For example, children who are abused may suffer lifelong emotional problems (Rutter, 1995). At the same time, extra care can sometimes reverse the effects of a poor start in life (Bornstein, 1995). In short, environmental forces guide human development, for better or worse, throughout life.

CRITICAL PERIODS *Why do some experiences have more lasting effects than others?* Part of the answer lies in **critical periods.** These are times when children are more sensitive to environmental influences. Events that occur during a critical period can permanently alter the course of development (Cynader, 1994). For instance, if a woman has German measles during early pregnancy, her child may be born with heart defects, cataracts, or hearing loss. Later in pregnancy, the child would escape without damage.

Often, certain events must occur during a critical period for a person to develop normally. As we will see later, for instance, forming a loving bond with a caregiver early in life seems to be crucial for optimal development.

Prenatal Influences

The impact of nurture actually starts before birth. Although the **intrauterine environment** (interior of the womb) is highly protected, environmental conditions can affect the developing child. For example, when Olivia was pregnant, Amy's fetal heart rate and movements increased when loud sounds or vibrations penetrated the womb (Kisilevsky & Low, 1998).

If Olivia's health or nutrition had been poor, or if she contracted German measles, syphilis, or HIV, or used drugs, or was exposed to X-rays or atomic radiation, Amy might have been harmed. In such cases babies can suffer from **congenital problems** or "birth defects." These problems affect the developing fetus and become apparent at birth. In contrast, **genetic disorders** are inherited from parents. Examples are sickle-cell anemia, hemophilia, cystic fibrosis, muscular dystrophy, albinism, and some forms of mental retardation.

How is it possible for the embryo or the fetus to be harmed? No direct intermixing of blood takes place between a mother and her unborn child. Yet some substances—especially drugs—do reach the fetus. If the mother is addicted to morphine, heroin, or methadone, the baby may be born with an addiction. Repeated heavy drinking during pregnancy causes *fetal alcohol syndrome (FAS).* Affected infants have low birth weight, a small head, bodily defects, and facial malformations. Many also suffer from emotional, behavioural, and mental handicaps (Williams, Odaibo, & McGee, 1999).

Tobacco is also harmful. Pregnant women who smoke greatly reduce the oxygen supply to the fetus. Heavy smokers risk miscarrying or having premature, underweight babies who are more likely to die soon after birth (Slotkin, 1998). Children of smoking mothers score lower on tests of language and mental ability (Fried, O'Connell, & Watkinson, 1992). In other words, an unborn child's future can go "up in smoke."

TERATOGENS Anything capable of causing birth defects is called a **teratogen** (teh-RAT-uh-jen). Sometimes women are exposed to powerful teratogens, such as radiation, lead, pesticides, or

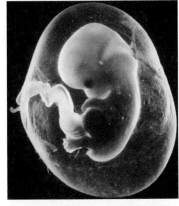

Due to the rapid growth of basic structures, the developing fetus is sensitive to a variety of diseases, drugs, and sources of radiation. This is especially true during the first trimester (three months) of gestation (pregnancy).

Some of the typical features of children suffering from fetal alcohol syndrome include a small non-symmetrical head, a short nose, a flattened area between the eyes, oddly shaped eyes, and a thin upper lip. Many of these features become less noticeable by adolescence. However, mental retardation and other problems commonly follow the FAS child into adulthood. The child shown here represents a moderate example of FAS.

PCBs, without knowing it (Eliot, 1999). But pregnant women do have direct control over many teratogens. For example, a woman who takes cocaine runs a serious risk of injuring her fetus (Arendt et al., 1998; Espy, Kaufmann, & Glisky, 1999; Singer et al., 1999; Swanson et al., 1999). In short, when a pregnant woman takes drugs, her unborn child does too.

Deprivation and Enrichment

Deprivation In development, the loss or withholding of normal stimulation, nutrition, comfort, love, and so forth; a condition of lacking.

Enrichment Deliberately making an environment more novel, complex, and perceptually or intellectually stimulating.

After a child is born, the effects of environment can be clearly seen when conditions of deprivation or enrichment exist. **Deprivation** refers to a lack of normal stimulation, nutrition, comfort, or love. **Enrichment** exists when an environment is deliberately made more complex and intellectually stimulating.

What happens when children suffer severe deprivation? Tragically, a few mistreated children have spent their first years in closets, attics, and other restricted environments. When first discovered, these children are usually mute, retarded, and emotionally damaged. Fortunately, such extreme deprivation is unusual. Nevertheless, milder levels of perceptual, intellectual, or emotional deprivation occur in many families, especially those that must cope with poverty. By the age of five, children who grow up in poor homes tend to have lower IQs. They are also more fearful, unhappy, and prone to hostile or aggressive behaviour (Carnegie Corporation, 1994; McLoyd, 1998). Later in childhood, damage may result from a lack of intellectual stimulation, or parents who are cold, neglectful, or rejecting. In light of this, it is wise to view all of childhood is a *relatively critical period* (Barnet & Barnet, 1998; Nelson, 1999).

Can an improved environment enhance development? To answer this question, psychologists have created enriched environments that are unusually novel, complex, and stimulating. Enriched environments may be the "soil" from which brighter children grow. To illustrate, let us begin with an experiment in which rats were raised in a sort of "rat wonderland." The walls of their cages were decorated with coloured patterns and each cage was filled with platforms, ladders, and cubbyholes. When the rats reached adulthood, they were superior at learning mazes. In addition, they had larger, heavier brains, with a thicker cortex (Benloucif, Bennett, & Rosenzweig, 1995). Of course, it's a long leap from rats to people, but an actual increase in brain size is impressive. If stimulation can enhance the "intelligence" of a lowly rat, it seems reasonable to assume that human infants also benefit from enrichment.

FOCUS ON RESEARCH   The Mozart Effect—Smart Music?

Frances Rauscher and Gordon Shaw reported that after college students listened to a Mozart piano sonata, they scored higher on a spatial reasoning test (Rauscher & Shaw, 1998; Shaw, 1999). Soon after this observation made the news, doting parents were playing Mozart for their babies around the clock. Obviously, they hoped that, like the college students, their babies would become smarter. However, parents should be suspicious of any practice that claims to offer such "magical" benefits.

A major problem with the "Mozart effect" is that the original experiment was done with adults; it tells us nothing about infants. Also, the study didn't test other styles of music. Why not use the music of Bach, Schubert, or MTV, for that matter? An even more important question is, Does the Mozart effect actually exist?

What does the evidence suggest? A few studies have found small increases in spatial intelligence following exposure to Mozart's music (Rideout, Dougherty, & Wernert, 1998; Rideout & Taylor, 1997). However, most researchers have been unable to duplicate the effect (Chabris et al., 1999; Steele, Bass, & Crook, 1999; Steele, Brown, & Stoecker, 1999; Wilson & Brown, 1997).

Why do some studies support the effect and others disconfirm it? Most studies have compared students who heard music to students who rested in silence. However, Canadian psychologists Kristin Nantais and Glenn Schellenberg found that listening to a narrated story also improves test scores. This is especially true for students who like listening to stories. Thus, students who scored higher after listening to Mozart might have just been more alert or in a better mood (Nantais & Schellenberg, 1999).

As wonderful as Mozart's music may be, it appears that there is nothing magical about it, at least as far as infant intelligence is concerned.

Is there any evidence that this is actually the case? Yes, many studies have shown that enriched environments improve abilities or enhance development. Tom and Olivia will be wise to nourish Amy's mind, as well as her body (Dieter & Emory, 1997). (However, see "The Mozart Effect" for another perspective on enrichment.)

What can parents do to enrich a child's environment? Parents can encourage exploration through stimulating play and by paying attention to what holds a baby's interest. Parental attitudes toward investigation also affect intellectual growth. Children who repeatedly hear "Don't touch that" or "I told you not to" may become passive and intellectually dulled. Placing virtually all common objects off-limits is a serious mistake. It is better to "child-proof" a house than to strictly list what a child can and cannot touch. One of the simplest and most effective things a parent can do is to read to a child. Results from a long-term Canadian study (the National Longitudinal Study of Children and Youth) suggest that children whose parents read to them several times a day when they are two and three years old do better in kindergarten and grade 1 than children who are not read to (Lipps & Yiptong-Avila, 1999).

There is also value in actively enriching sensory experiences. Babies should be surrounded by colours, music, people, and things to see, taste, smell, and touch. Infants are not vegetables. It makes perfect sense to take them outside, to hang mobiles over their cribs, to place mirrors nearby, to play music for them, or to rearrange their rooms now and then. The presence of stimulating play materials in the home, together with responsive parents, is strongly related to how quickly children progress (Bradley et al., 1989; Luster & Dubow, 1992).

Nature–Nurture Interactions

As Amy passes through life she will have to learn countless bits of information: how to eat with a fork; the names of animals; proper etiquette at a wedding; how to reboot a computer. This knowledge reflects billions of connections in the brain. No conceivable amount of genetic programming could make it possible. With this fact in mind, the outcome of the nature–nurture debate is clear: Heredity and environment are both important. Heredity gives each of us a variety of potentials and limitations. These, in turn, are affected by environmental influences, such as learning, nutrition, disease, and culture. Thus,

Knowledge builder

HEREDITY AND ENVIRONMENT

Relate

Do you think that heredity or environment best explains who you are today? Can you think of clear examples of the ways in which heredity and environmental forces have affected your development?

What kind of temperament did you have as an infant? How did it affect your relationship with your parents or caregivers?

What advice would you give a friend who has just become pregnant? Be sure to consider the prenatal environment and critical periods.

Learning Check

1. Areas of the DNA molecule called genes are made up of dominant and recessive chromosomes. T or F?
2. Most inherited characteristics can be described as polygenic. T or F?

3. Which of the following represents a correct sequence?
   a. zygote, fetus, embryo, neonate, infant
   b. zygote, embryo, neonate, fetus, infant
   c. embryo, zygote, fetus, neonate, infant
   d. zygote, embryo, fetus, neonate, infant
4. "Slow-to-warm-up" children can be described as restrained, unexpressive, or shy. T or F?
5. A _____ is a time of increased sensitivity to environmental influences.
6. As a child develops, there is a continuous _____ between the forces of heredity and environment.

Critical Thinking

7. Environmental influences can interact with hereditary programming in an exceedingly direct way. Can you guess what it is?

Answers:

1. F 2. T 3. d 4. T 5. critical period 6. interaction 7. Environmental conditions sometimes turn specific genes on or off, thus directly affecting the expression of genetic tendencies (Gottlieb, 1998).

the person you are today reflects a constant interaction, or interplay, between the forces of nature and nurture (Gopnik, Meltzoff, & Kuhl, 1999).

Because of differences in temperament, some babies are more likely than others to smile, cry, vocalize, reach out, or pay attention. This means that babies rapidly become active participants in their own development. Growing infants alter their parents' behaviour at the same time they are changed by it. For example, Amy is an easy baby who smiles frequently and is easily fed. This encourages Olivia to touch, feed, and sing to Amy. Olivia's affection rewards Amy, causing her to smile more. Soon, a dynamic relationship blossoms between mother and child. If Amy were a difficult baby who cried a lot and didn't like to be held, do you think a different dynamic relationship would blossom between mother and child?

A person's **developmental level** is his or her current state of physical, emotional, and intellectual development. To summarize, three factors combine to determine your developmental level at any stage of life. These are heredity, environment, and your own behaviour, each tightly interwoven with the others.

> **Developmental level** An individual's current state of physical, emotional, and intellectual development.

▶ The Newborn Baby—The Basic Model Comes with Options

Survey Question:
■ What can newborn babies do?

At birth the human **neonate** (NEE-oh-NATE: newborn infant) will die if not cared for by adults. Newborn babies cannot lift their heads, turn over, or feed themselves. Does this mean they are inert and unfeeling? Definitely not! Neonates like Amy can see, hear, smell, taste, and respond to pain and touch. Although their senses are less acute, babies are very responsive. Amy will follow a moving object with her eyes and will turn in the direction of sounds.

Babies also have a number of adaptive reflexes. To elicit the **grasping reflex,** press an object in the neonate's palm and she will grasp it with surprising strength. Many infants, in fact, can hang from a raised bar, like little trapeze artists. The grasping reflex aids survival by helping infants avoid falling. You can observe the **rooting reflex** (reflexive head turning and nursing) by touching Amy's cheek. Immediately, she will turn toward your finger, as if searching for something.

How is such turning adaptive? The rooting reflex helps infants find a breast. Then, when a nipple touches the infant's mouth, the **sucking reflex** (rhythmic nursing) helps her obtain needed food. Like other reflexes, this is a genetically programmed action (Koepke & Bigelow, 1997). At the same time, food rewards nursing. As a result, babies quickly learn to nurse more actively. Again, we see how nature–nurture interactions alter a baby's behaviour.

The **Moro reflex** is also interesting. If Amy's position is changed abruptly or if she is startled by a loud noise, she will make a hugging motion. This reaction has been compared to the movements baby monkeys use to cling to their mothers. (It is left to the reader's imagination to decide if there is any connection.)

> **Neonate** A term used for newborn infants during the first weeks following birth.
> **Grasping reflex** A neonatal reflex consisting of grasping objects placed in the palms.
> **Rooting reflex** Neonatal reflex elicited by a light touch to the cheek, causing the infant to turn toward the object and attempt to nurse.
> **Sucking reflex** Neonatal reflex elicited by touching the mouth, whereupon the infant makes rhythmic sucking movements.
> **Moro reflex** Neonatal reflex evoked by sudden loss of support or the sounding of a loud noise; in response, the arms are extended and then brought toward each other.

The World of the Neonate

Thirty years ago, many people thought of newborn babies as mere bundles of reflexes, like the ones just described. But infants are capable of much more. For example, Andrew Meltzoff and Keith Moore (1983) found that babies are born mimics. ▶Figure 3.4 shows Meltzoff as he sticks out his tongue, opens his mouth, and purses his lips at a 20-day-old girl. Will she imitate him? Videotapes of babies confirm that they imitate adult facial gestures. As early as nine months of age, infants can imitate actions a day after seeing them (Heimann & Meltzoff, 1996). Such mimicry obviously aids rapid learning in infancy.

How intelligent are neonates? Babies are smarter than many people think. From the earliest days of life, babies seem to be trying to learn how the world works. They immediately begin to look, touch, taste, and otherwise explore their surroundings. From an evolutionary perspective, a baby's mind is designed to soak up information, which it does at an amazing pace (Gopnik, Meltzoff, & Kuhl, 1999).

In the first weeks and months of life, babies are increasingly able to think, to learn from what they see, to make predictions, and to search for explanations. For example,

▶Figure 3.4

Infant imitation. In the top row of photos, Andrew Meltzoff makes facial gestures at an infant. The bottom row records the infant's responses. Video-tapes of Meltzoff and of tested infants helped ensure objectivity. (Photos courtesy of Andrew N. Meltzoff.)

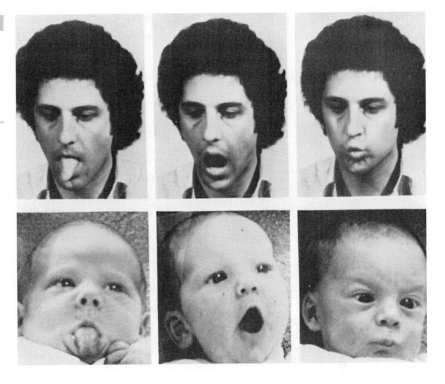

Newborn babies display a special interest in the human face. A preference for seeing their mother's face develops rapidly and encourages social interactions between mother and baby.

Looking chamber An experimental apparatus used to test infant perception by presenting visual stimuli and observing infant responses.

Jerome Bruner (1983) observed that three- to eight-week-old babies seem to understand that a person's voice and body should be connected. If a baby hears his mother's voice coming from where she is standing, the baby will remain calm. If her voice comes from a loudspeaker several feet away, the baby will become agitated and begin to cry.

Another look into the private world of infants can be drawn from testing their vision. However, such testing is a challenge because infants cannot talk.

How is it possible to test a baby's vision? Robert Fantz invented a device called a **looking chamber** to find out what infants can see and what holds their attention (see ▶Figure 3.5a). Imagine that Amy is placed on her back inside the chamber, facing a lighted area above. Next, two objects are placed in the chamber. By observing the movements of Amy's eyes and the images they reflect, we can tell what she is looking at. Such tests show that adult vision is about 30 times sharper, but babies can see large patterns, shapes, and edges.

Fantz found that three-day-old babies prefer complex patterns, such as checkerboards and bull's-eyes, to simpler coloured rectangles. Other researchers have learned that infants are excited by circles, curves, and bright lights (see Figure 3.5b) (Brown, 1990). Immediately after birth, Amy will be aware of changes in the position of objects (Slater et al., 1991). When she is six months old, she will be able to recognize categories of objects that differ in shape or colour. By nine months of age she will be able to tell the difference between dogs and birds or other groups of animals (Mandler & McDonough, 1998). So, there really is a person inside that little body!

Neonates can most clearly see objects about 30 cm away from them. It is as if they are best prepared to see the people who love and care for them (Gopnik, Meltzoff, & Kuhl, 1999). Perhaps that's why babies have a special fascination with human faces. Just hours after they are born, babies begin to prefer seeing their mother's face, rather than a stranger's (Walton, Bower, & Bower, 1992).

In a looking chamber, most infants will spend more time looking at a human face pattern than a scrambled face or a coloured oval (Figure 3.5c). When real human faces are used, infants prefer familiar faces to unfamiliar faces. However, this reverses at about age

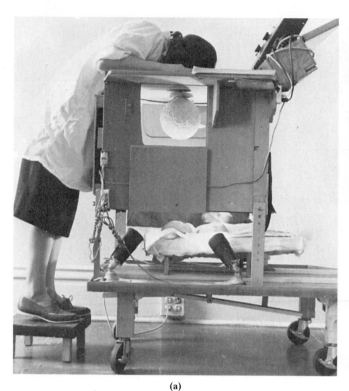

(a)

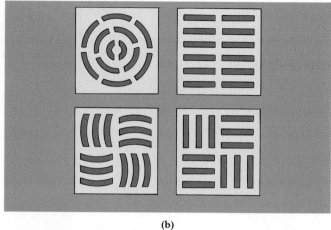

(b)

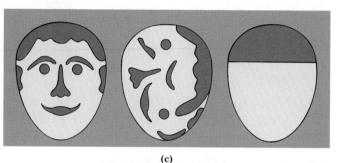

(c)

▶Figure 3.5

(a) Eye movements and fixation points of infants are observed in Fantz's "looking chamber." *(b)* Thirteen-week-old infants prefer concentric and curved patterns, like those on the left, to non-concentric and straight-line patterns like those on the right. *(c)* Infants tested in a looking chamber look at the normal face longer than at the scrambled face and at both faces longer than at the design on the right. (Photo courtesy of David Linton. Drawing from "The Origin of Form Perception" by Robert L. Fantz, Copyright © 1961 by Scientific American, Inc. All rights reserved.)

two. At that time, unusual objects begin to interest the child. For instance, Jerome Kagan (1971) showed face masks to two-year-olds. Kagan found that the toddlers were fascinated by a face with eyes on the chin and a nose in the middle of the forehead. He believes the babies' interest came from a need to understand why the scrambled face differed from what they had come to expect. Such behaviour is further evidence that babies actively try to make sense of their surroundings (Gopnik, Meltzoff, & Kuhl, 1999).

Maturation

The emergence of many basic abilities is closely tied to **maturation** (physical growth and development of the body, brain, and nervous system). Maturation will be especially evident as Amy learns motor skills, such as crawling and walking. Of course, the rate of maturation varies from child to child. Nevertheless, the order of maturation is almost universal. For instance, Amy will be able to sit without support before she has matured enough to crawl. Indeed, infants around the world typically sit before they crawl, crawl before they stand, and stand before they walk (see ▶Figure 3.6).

What about my weird cousin Emo who never crawled? Like cousin Emo, a few children substitute rolling, creeping, or shuffling for crawling. A very few move directly from sitting to standing and walking (Robson, 1984). Even so, an orderly sequence of motor development remains evident. In general, increased muscular control spreads in a pattern that is **cephalocaudal** (SEF-eh-lo-KOD-ul: from head to toe) and **proximodistal** (PROK-seh-moe-DIS-tul: from the centre of the body to the extremities). Even if cousin Emo flunked Elementary Crawling, his motor development followed the standard top-down, centre-outward pattern.

Maturation The physical growth and development of the body and nervous system.

Cephalocaudal From head to toe.

Proximodistal From the centre of the body to the extremities.

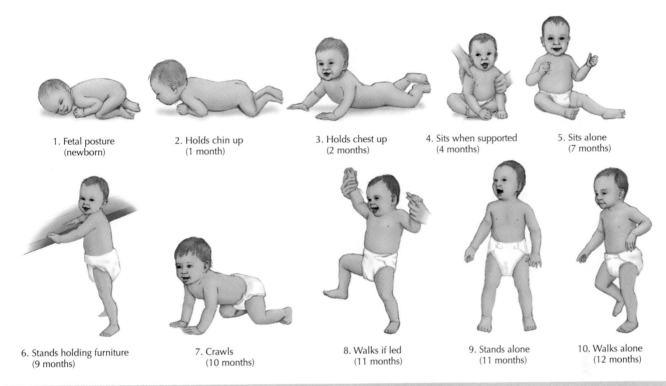

1. Fetal posture (newborn)
2. Holds chin up (1 month)
3. Holds chest up (2 months)
4. Sits when supported (4 months)
5. Sits alone (7 months)

6. Stands holding furniture (9 months)
7. Crawls (10 months)
8. Walks if led (11 months)
9. Stands alone (11 months)
10. Walks alone (12 months)

▶**Figure 3.6**

Motor development. Most infants follow an orderly pattern of motor development. Although the order in which children progress is similar, there are large individual differences in the ages at which each ability appears. The ages listed are averages for American children. It is not unusual for many of the skills to appear one or two months earlier than average or several months later (Frankenburg & Dodds, 1967; Harris & Liebert, 1991). Parents should not be alarmed if a child's behaviour differs some from the average.

Readiness A condition that exists when maturation has advanced enough to allow the rapid acquisition of a particular skill.

Motor Development

While maturation has a big impact, motor skills don't simply "emerge." Amy must learn to control her actions. Babies who are trying to crawl or walk actively try out new movements and select those that work. Amy's first efforts may be flawed—a wobbly crawl or some shaky first steps. However, with practice, babies "tune" their movements to be smoother and more effective. Such learning is evident from the very first months of life (Adolph, 1997; Thelen, 1995). (See ▶Figure 3.7.)

READINESS At what ages will Amy be ready to feed herself, walk alone, or say goodbye to diapers? Such milestones tend to be governed by a child's **readiness** for rapid learning. That is, minimum levels of maturation must occur before some skills can be learned. It is impossible, for instance, to teach children to walk or use a toilet before they have matured enough to control their bodies. Parents are asking for failure when they try to force a child to learn skills too early.

Much needless grief can be avoided by respecting a child's personal rate of growth. Consider the eager parents who toilet trained an

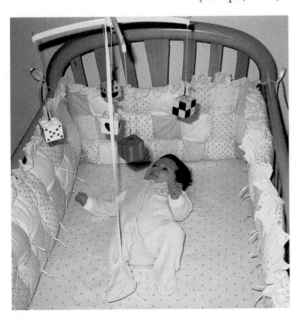

▶**Figure 3.7**

Psychologist Carolyn Rovee-Collier has shown that babies as young as three months old can learn to control their movements. In her experiments, babies lie on their backs under a colourful crib mobile. A ribbon is tied around the baby's ankle and connected to the mobile. Whenever babies spontaneously kick their legs, the mobile jiggles and rattles. Within a few minutes, infants learn to kick faster. Their reward for kicking is a chance to see the mobile move (Hayne & Rovee-Collier, 1995).

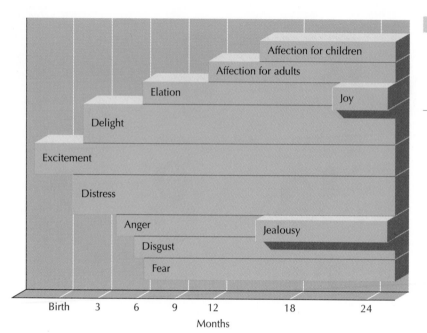

▶ **Figure 3.8**

The traditional view of infancy holds that emotions are rapidly differentiated from an initial capacity for excitement. (After K. M. B. Bridges, 1932. Reprinted by permission of the Society for Research in Child Development, Inc.)

Basic emotions The first distinct emotions to emerge in infancy.
Social smile Smiling elicited by social stimuli, such as seeing a parent's face.

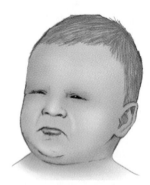

▶ **Figure 3.9**

Infants display many of the same emotional expressions as adults do. Carroll Izard believes such expressions show that distinct emotions appear within the first months of life. Other theorists argue that specific emotions come into focus more gradually, as an infant's nervous system matures. Either way, parents can expect to see a full range of basic emotions by the end of a baby's first year. Over the first two years, children become increasingly active in initiating emotional exchanges with parents (Grolnick, Cosgrove, & Bridges, 1996).

18-month-old child in 10 trying weeks of false alarms and "accidents." If they had waited until the child was 24 months old, they might have succeeded in just three weeks. Parents may control when toilet training starts, but maturation tends to dictate when it will be completed (Luxem & Christophersen, 1994). Around 30 months is average for completion.

Emotional Development

Early emotional development also follows a pattern closely tied to maturation. Even the **basic emotions** of anger, fear, and joy—which appear to be unlearned—take time to develop. General excitement is the only emotion newborn infants clearly express. However, as Tom and Olivia can tell you, a baby's emotional life blossoms rapidly. One researcher (Bridges, 1932) observed that all the basic human emotions appear before age two. Bridges found that emotions appear in a consistent order and that the first basic split is between pleasant and unpleasant emotions (see ▶ Figure 3.8).

Many experts continue to believe that emotions unfold slowly, as the nervous system matures (Camras, Sullivan, & Michel, 1993; Matias & Cohn, 1993). However, psychologist Carroll Izard thinks that infants can express several basic emotions as early as 10 weeks of age. When Izard looks carefully at the faces of babies, he sees abundant signs of emotion (see ▶ Figure 3.9). The most common infant expression, he found, is not excitement, but *interest*—followed by *joy*, *anger*, and *sadness* (Izard et al., 1995).

If Izard is right, then emotions are "hard-wired" by heredity and related to evolution. Perhaps that's why smiling is one of a baby's most common reactions. Smiling probably helps babies survive by inviting parents to care for them (Izard et al., 1995).

At first, a baby's smiling is haphazard. By the age of 10 months, however, infants smile more frequently when another person is nearby (Jones, Collins, & Hong, 1991). This **social smile** is especially rewarding to parents. On the other hand,

Knowledge builder

THE NEONATE AND MATURATION

Relate

What infant reflexes have you observed? How would maturation affect the chances of teaching an infant to eat with a spoon? Can you give an example of how heredity and environment interact during motor development?

To know what a baby is feeling would it be more helpful to be able to detect delight and distress (Bridges) or joy, anger, and sadness (Izard)?

Learning Check

1. If an infant is startled, it will make movements similar to an embrace. This is known as the
   a. grasping reflex *b.* rooting reflex *c.* Moro reflex
   d. adaptive reflex
2. During infancy, a capacity for imitating others first becomes evident at about nine months of age. T or F?

3. After age two, infants tested in a looking chamber show a marked preference for familiar faces and simpler designs. T or F?
4. The orderly sequence observed in the unfolding of many basic responses can be attributed to _____.
5. General excitement or interest is the clearest emotional response present in newborn infants, but meaningful expressions of delight and distress appear soon after. T or F?
6. Neonates display a social smile as early as 10 days after birth. T or F?

Critical Thinking

7. If you were going to test newborn infants to see if they prefer their own mother's face to that of a stranger, what precautions would you take?

Answers:

1. *c* 2. F 3. F 4. maturation 5. T 6. F 7. In one study of the preferences of newborns, the hair colour and complexion of strangers was matched to that of the mothers. Also, only the mother's or stranger's face was visible during testing. And finally, a scent was used to mask olfactory (smell) cues so that an infant's preference could not be based on the mother's familiar odour (Bushnell, Sai, & Mullin, 1989).

Survey Question:
■ Of what significance is a child's emotional bond with parents?

when new parents see and hear a crying baby, they feel annoyed, irritated, disturbed, or unhappy. Babies the world over, it seems, rapidly become capable of letting others know what they like and dislike.

Human infants are transformed from helpless babies to independent persons with dazzling speed. Early growth is extremely rapid. By her third year, Amy will have a unique personality and she will be able to stand, walk, talk, and explore. At no other time after birth does development proceed more rapidly. During the same period, Amy's relationships with other people will expand as well. Before we explore that topic, here's a chance to rehearse what you've learned.

▶ Social Development—Baby, I'm Stuck on You

Social development
The development of self-awareness, attachment to parents or caregivers, and relationships with other children and adults.

Self-awareness
Consciousness of oneself as a person.

Emotional attachment
An especially close emotional bond that infants form with their parents, caregivers, or others.

Primary caregiver A person primarily responsible for the care of an infant; usually the infant's mother or father.

Like all humans, babies are social creatures. Their early **social development** lays a foundation for relationships with parents, siblings, friends, and relatives. A first basic step into the social world involves becoming aware of oneself as a separate person. When you look in a mirror, you recognize the image staring back as your own—except, perhaps, early on Monday mornings. Would Amy recognize herself at age one? At age two? Like many such events, initial **self-awareness** depends on maturation of the nervous system. In a typical test of self-recognition, infants are shown images of themselves on a TV. Most infants have to be 15 months old before they recognize themselves (Lewis & Brooks-Gunn, 1979).

Attachment

The real core of social development is found in the **emotional attachment,** or close emotional bond, that human babies form with their **primary caregivers.** There is a critical period (roughly the first year of life) during which this must occur for optimal development. Returning to Amy's story, we find that attachment keeps her close to Olivia, who provides safety, stimulation, and a secure "home base" from which Amy can go exploring.

Mothers usually begin to cultivate a parent–child bond within hours of giving birth. For example, they touch their own infants more and hold them closer than they do other

A sense of self, or self-awareness, develops at about age 15 months. Before children develop self-awareness, they do not recognize their own image in a mirror. Typically, they think they are looking at another child. Some children hug the child in the mirror or go behind it looking for the child they see there (Lewis, 1995).

Separation anxiety
Distress displayed by infants when they are separated from their parents or principal caregivers.

Secure attachment A stable and positive emotional bond.

Insecure-avoidant attachment An anxious emotional bond marked by a tendency to avoid reunion with a parent or caregiver.

Insecure-ambivalent attachment An anxious emotional bond marked by both a desire to be with a parent or caregiver and some resistance to being reunited.

babies (Kaitz et al., 1995). A direct sign that an emotional bond has formed appears around 8 to 12 months of age. At that time Amy will display **separation anxiety** (crying and signs of fear) when she is left alone or left with a stranger. You may have heard that bonding is especially powerful during the first few hours after birth (Klaus & Kennell, 1982). However, careful studies have generally failed to support a "super-glue" version of the bonding concept. While long-term infant attachments are a reality, "instant bonding" appears to be a myth (Eyer, 1994). Ultimately, it is more important that secure attachment occurs than *when* it occurs.

ATTACHMENT QUALITY Canadian psychologist Mary Ainsworth believed the quality of attachment is revealed by how babies act when their mothers return after a brief separation. Infants who are **securely attached** have a stable and positive emotional bond. They are upset by the mother's absence and seek to be near her when she returns. **Insecure-avoidant** infants have an anxious emotional bond. They tend to turn away from the mother when she returns. **Insecure-ambivalent** attachment is also an anxious emotional bond. In this case, babies are ambivalent: They both seek to be near the returning mother, and angrily resist contact with her. (See ▶ Figure 3.10.)

Attachment can have lasting effects. Infants who are securely attached at the age of one year show more resiliency, curiosity, problem-solving ability, and social competence in preschool (Collins & Gunnar, 1990). In contrast, attachment failures can be quite damaging. Consider, for example, the plight of children raised in severely overcrowded Romanian orphanages and later adopted by Canadian families. These children got almost no attention from adults for at least the first eight months of their lives. St. Francis Xavier University psychologist Kim Chisholm and her colleagues have followed many of these children for several years. Many are poorly attached to their new parents. Some, for instance, will readily wander off with strangers (Chisholm et al., 1995). She also found that parents reported more behaviour problems in their adopted children (Chisholm, 1998).

The key to secure attachment is a mother who is accepting and sensitive to her baby's signals and rhythms (Isabella, 1993; Susman-Stillman et al., 1996). Poor attachment occurs when a mother's actions are inappropriate, inadequate, intrusive, over-stimulating, or rejecting. An example is the mother who tries to play with a drowsy infant or who ignores a baby who is looking at her and vocalizing (Isabella & Belsky, 1991).

What about attachment to fathers? Fathers of securely attached infants tend to be outgoing, agreeable, and happy in their marriage. In general, a warm family atmosphere tends to produce secure children (Belsky, 1996).

Mary D. Salter Ainsworth (1913–1999). One of the most influential developmental psychologists of the 20th century, Mary Ainsworth earned a Ph.D. from the University of Toronto in 1939. A major in the Canadian Army during World War II, she spent two years as the Superintendent of Women's Rehabilitation for the Department of Veterans Affairs. After the war, she returned to the University of Toronto as an assistant professor. In 1950, she went to England to work with John Bowlby, and then to Uganda in 1954 where she studied infant–mother attachment. She received the G. Stanley Hall Award for her contributions to developmental psychology in 1984.

Attachment Category

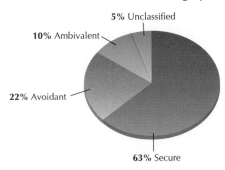

5% Unclassified

10% Ambivalent

22% Avoidant

63% Secure

▶ **Figure 13.10**

About two-thirds of children from middle-class families are securely attached. About one child in three is insecurely attached. (Percentages are approximate. From Kaplan, 1998.)

Affectional needs
Emotional needs for love and affection.
Play Any activity done for sheer enjoyment.
Solitary play Playing alone.
Cooperative play Play in which two or more children must coordinate their actions; if children don't cooperate, the game ends.

As you can see, a baby's **affectional needs** (needs for love and affection) are every bit as important as more obvious needs for food, water, and physical care. Parents are sometimes afraid of "spoiling" babies with too much attention or affection. However, for the first year or two this is nearly impossible (Konner, 1991). As a matter of fact, a later capacity to experience warm and loving relationships may depend on it.

DAY CARE *Does commercial child care interfere with the quality of attachment?* A study by Margaret McKim of the University of Saskatchewan looked at the effects of day care on attachment in 189 infants and toddlers. High-quality day care did not adversely affect attachment to parents. In fact, attachment seems to be more dependent on the child's temperament and the mother's sensitivity than on the kind of care the child receives (McKim et al., 1999). Children receiving high-quality day care also have better cognitive skills and language abilities (Burchinal et al., 2000). A long-term study Canadian study (the National Longitudinal Survey of Children and Youth) found that 40 percent of kindergarten children who attended early childhood programs or day-care centres were judged by their teachers to be near the top of their class, compared to 24 percent of children who stayed at home with a parent (Lipps & Yiptong-Avila, 1999).

Thus, high-quality day care can actually improve children's social and mental skills (Scarr, 1998). However, all of the positive effects just noted are reversed for low-quality day care. One study of 155 four- and five-year-old children attending day-care centres in Montreal found that, while children in high-quality centres showed positive effects, those in low-quality centres showed increased anger and defiance (Hausfather et al., 1997). Parents are wise to carefully evaluate and monitor the quality of day care their children are receiving (Barnet & Barnet, 1998).

What should parents look for when they evaluate the quality of child care? Low-quality day care is risky and it may weaken attachment. Parents seeking quality should insist on at least: (1) a small number of children per caregiver, (2) small overall group size (12–15), (3) trained caregivers, (4) minimal staff turnover, and (5) a stable day-care experience (Howes, 1997). (Also, avoid any child-care centre with the words *zoo, menagerie,* or *stockade* in its name.)

PLAY AND SOCIAL SKILLS A chance to **play** with other children is one of the side benefits of day care. For instance, in one corner, a two-year-old stacks coloured blocks, pounds on them with a toy truck, and then chews on the truck. On the other side of the room some five-year-olds have built a "store" out of cardboard boxes. For the next half hour, one child is the "owner" and the others are "customers." With just three years' difference in age, we see a dramatic change in how children play.

Naturally, play is fun for children. However, it's also serious business. Children use play to explore the world and to practise skills—especially social skills. By the time children are four or five, they will have progressed from **solitary play** (playing alone) to **cooperative play** (in which two or more children must coordinate their actions). Children engaged in cooperative play take parts or play roles, follow rules, and lead or follow others. Playing this way helps them learn to handle cooperation and competition, conflicts, power, role taking, and communication.

Cooperative play is a big step toward participating in social life. It's easy for adults to dismiss play as silly or trivial. In fact, play is one of the most important activities of childhood (Kaplan, 1998).

Knowledge builder

SOCIAL DEVELOPMENT

Relate

Think of a child you know who seems to be securely attached and one who seems to be insecurely attached. How do the children differ? Do their parents treat them differently?

Do you think you were securely or insecurely attached as a child? Are there any parallels in your relationships today?

Learning Check

1. Clear signs of self-awareness or self-recognition are evident in most infants by the time they reach eight months of age. T or F?
2. The development of separation anxiety in an infant corresponds to the formation of an attachment to parents. T or F?

3. In Mary Ainsworth's system for rating the quality of attachment, secure attachment is revealed by a lack of distress when an infant is left alone with a stranger. T or F?
4. Children usually play in small groups before they have developed enough confidence to play alone (solitary play). T or F?

Critical Thinking

5. Can you think of another way to tell if infants have self-awareness?
6. Can emotional bonding begin before birth?
7. Attachment quality is usually attributed to the behaviour of parents or caregivers. How might infants contribute to the quality of attachment?

Answers:

1. F 2. T 3. F 4. F 5. Another successful method is to secretly rub a spot of rouge on an infant's nose. The child is then placed in front of a mirror. The question is, Will the child touch the red spot, showing recognition of the mirror image as his or her own? The probability that a child will do so jumps dramatically during the second year. 6. It certainly can for parents. When a pregnant woman begins to feel fetal movements, she becomes aware that a baby is coming to life inside of her. Likewise, prospective parents who hear a fetal heartbeat at the doctor's office or see an ultrasound image of the fetus begin to become emotionally attached to the unborn child (Konner, 1991). 7. An infant's behaviour patterns, temperament, and emotional style may greatly influence parents' behaviour. As a result, infants can affect attachment as much as parents do (Oatley & Jenkins, 1992).

▶ Maternal and Paternal Influences— Life with Mom and Dad

Survey Question:
■ How important are parenting styles?

Maternal influences The aggregate of all psychological effects mothers have on their children.

Caregiving styles Identifiable patterns of parental caretaking and interaction with children.

Proactive maternal involvement Sensitive caregiving in which the mother actively seeks to interact with her child and to provide educational experiences.

Goodness of fit With respect to caregiving, the degree to which parents and children have compatible temperaments.

For the first few years of life, caregivers are the centre of a child's world. This makes the quality of mothering and fathering very important. For example, one classic study focused on **maternal influences** (all the effects a mother has on her child).

Researchers began by selecting children who were very competent (A children) or low in competence (C children). As they observed younger and younger children, it soon became apparent that A and C patterns were already set by age three. To learn how this was possible, psychologists visited homes and observed **caregiving styles** (White & Watts, 1973). What they saw ranged from the "super mother" to the "zoo-keeper mother." Super mothers went out of their way to provide educational experiences for children and let them initiate activities. This style produced A children, who were competent in most areas of development. At the other end of the scale, zoo-keeper mothers gave their children good physical care, but interacted with them very little. Their child-care routines were rigid and highly structured. The result was C children who were inflexible in their approach to problems.

Optimal Caregiving

More recent studies mirror the earlier findings: Optimal caregiving is marked by **proactive maternal involvement** (warm, educational interactions with a child) (Olson, Bates, & Kaskie, 1992). For example, Olivia is a proactive mother who talks to Amy and helps her explore her surroundings. This approach speeds Amy's mental growth and minimizes behaviour problems.

Optimal caregiving also depends on the **goodness of fit,** or compatibility, of parent and child temperaments (Chess & Thomas, 1986). For instance, Damion is a slow-to-warm-up child who has impatient parents. Damion will probably have more problems than he would with easygoing parents.

Fathering typically makes a contribution to early development that differs in emphasis from mothering.

A third ingredient of caregiving is **parental responsiveness** to a child's feelings, needs, rhythms, and signals. When Amy is a month old, Olivia should focus on touching, holding, feeding, and stimulating her. When Amy is a year old, give-and-take interactions that promote Amy's social skills will be more important. Thus, effective mothers adjust their behaviour to meet children's changing needs (Heermann, Jones, & Wikoff, 1994).

Aren't you overlooking the effects of fathering? Yes. In fact, fathers make a unique contribution to parenting. Studies of **paternal influences** (the sum of all effects a father has on his child) reveal that fathers typically act as playmates for infants (Parke, 1995). In many homes, fathers spend four or five times more hours playing with infants than they do in caregiving. It's true that fathers are beginning to get more involved in child care. Just the same, mothers spend much more time feeding, dressing, grooming, disciplining, teaching, and caring for children (de Luccie & Davis, 1991).

It might seem that the father's role as a playmate makes him less important. Not so. From birth onward, fathers pay more visual attention to children than mothers do. Fathers are much more tactile (lifting, tickling, and handling the baby), more physically arousing (engaging in rough-and-tumble play), and more likely to engage in unusual play (imitating the baby, for example) (Crawley & Sherrod, 1984). In comparison, mothers speak to infants more, play more conventional games (such as peek-a-boo), and, as noted, spend much more time in caregiving. Amy's playtime with Tom is actually very valuable. Young children who spend a lot of time playing with their fathers tend to be more competent in many ways (Pettit et al., 1998).

Overall, fathers can be as affectionate, sensitive, and responsive as mothers are. Nevertheless, infants tend to get very different views of males and females. Females, who offer comfort, nurturance, and verbal stimulation, tend to be close at hand. Males come and go, and when they are present, action, exploration, and risk taking prevail. It's no wonder, then, that the caregiving styles of mothers and fathers have a major impact on children's sex role development (Lindsay, Mize, & Pettit, 1997).

As children mature and become more independent, parents must find ways to control the child's behaviour. ("No, you may not smear pudding on daddy's face.") Such attempts can have a variety of effects, as described next.

Parenting Styles

Psychologist Diana Baumrind (1991) has studied the effects of three major styles of parenting. See if you recognize the styles she describes.

Authoritarian parents enforce rigid rules and demand strict obedience to authority. Typically, they view children as having few rights but adult-like responsibilities. The child is expected to stay out of trouble and to accept, without question, what parents regard as right or wrong. ("Do it because I say so.") The children of authoritarian parents are usually obedient and self-controlled. But they also tend to be emotionally stiff, withdrawn, apprehensive, and lacking in curiosity. One 22-year-long study found that children whose parents are critical, harsh, or authoritarian often become self-absorbed adults. They also have higher rates of violence and drug abuse (Dubow, Huesmann, & Eron, 1987; Weiss et al., 1992).

Overly permissive parents give little guidance, allow too much freedom, or don't hold children accountable for their actions. Typically, the child has rights similar to an adult's but few responsibilities. Rules are not enforced, and the child usually gets his or her way. ("Do whatever you want.") Permissive parents tend to produce dependent, immature children who misbehave frequently. Such children are aimless and likely to "run amok."

Baumrind describes **authoritative parents** as those who supply firm and consistent guidance, combined with love and affection. Such parents balance their own rights with

Parental responsiveness Caregiving that is based on sensitivity to a child's feelings, needs, rhythms, and signals.

Paternal influences The aggregate of all psychological effects fathers have on their children.

Authoritarian parents Parents who enforce rigid rules and demand strict obedience to authority.

Overly permissive parents Parents who give little guidance, allow too much freedom, or do not require the child to take responsibility.

Authoritative parents Parents who supply firm and consistent guidance combined with love and affection.

those of their children. They control their children's behaviour in a caring, responsive, non-authoritarian way. ("Do it for this reason.") Effective parents are firm and consistent, not harsh or rigid. In general, they encourage the child to act responsibly, to think, and to make good decisions. This style produces children who are competent, self-controlled, independent, assertive, and inquiring (Baumrind, 1991).

CULTURE Diana Baumrind's work provides a good overall summary of the effects of parenting. However, her conclusions are probably most valid for families of European descent. Child-rearing in other ethnic groups often reflects different customs and belief systems. This is especially true with respect to the meaning attached to a child's behaviour. Is a particular behaviour "good" or "bad"? Should it be encouraged or discouraged? The answer will depend greatly on parents' cultural values and beliefs (Rubin, 1998).

Effects of Child Discipline

When parents fail to provide **discipline** (guidance regarding acceptable behaviour), children become antisocial, aggressive, and insecure. Effective discipline is fair but loving, authoritative yet sensitive. It socializes a child without destroying the bond of love and trust between parent and child.

TYPES OF DISCIPLINE Parents typically discipline children in one of three ways. **Power assertion** refers to physical punishment or a show of force, such as taking away toys or privileges. As an alternative, some parents use **withdrawal of love** (withholding affection) by refusing to speak to a child, by threatening to leave, by rejecting the child, or by otherwise acting as if the child is temporarily unlovable. **Management techniques** combine praise, recognition, approval, rules, reasoning, and the like to encourage desirable behaviour. Each of these approaches can control a child's behaviour, but their side effects differ considerably.

What are the side effects? Power-oriented techniques—particularly harsh or severe physical punishment—are associated with fear, hatred of parents, and a lack of spontaneity and warmth. Severely punished children also tend to be defiant, rebellious, and aggressive (Patterson, 1982). Despite its drawbacks, power assertion is the most popular mode of discipline (Papps et al., 1995).

Withdrawal of love produces children who tend to be self-disciplined. You could say that such children have developed a good conscience. Often, they are described as "model" children or as unusually "good." But as a side effect, they are also frequently anxious, insecure, and dependent on adults for approval.

Management techniques also have limitations. Most important is the need to carefully adjust to a child's level of understanding. Younger children don't always see the connection between rules, explanations, and their own behaviour. Nevertheless, management techniques receive a big plus in another area. Psychologist Stanley Coopersmith (1968) found a direct connection between discipline and a child's self-esteem.

SELF-ESTEEM If you regard yourself as a worthwhile person, you have **self-esteem.** High self-esteem is essential for emotional health. Individuals with low self-esteem don't think much of themselves as people. In elementary school, children with high self-esteem tend to be more popular, cooperative, and successful in class. Children with low self-esteem are more withdrawn and tend to perform below average (Hay, Ashman, & Van Kraayenoord, 1998).

How does discipline affect self-esteem? Coopersmith found that low self-esteem is related to physical punishment and the withholding of love. And why not? What message do children receive if a parent beats them or tells them they are not worthy of love?

High self-esteem is promoted by management techniques. Thus, it is best to minimize physical punishment and avoid unnecessary withdrawal of love. Children who feel that their parents support them emotionally tend to have high self-esteem (Hay, Ashman, & Van Kraayenoord, 1998; Nielsen & Metha, 1994).

Discipline A framework of guidelines for acceptable behaviour.

Power assertion The use of physical punishment or coercion to enforce child discipline.

Withdrawal of love Withholding affection to enforce child discipline.

Management techniques Combining praise, recognition, approval, rules, and reasoning to enforce child discipline.

Self-esteem Regarding oneself as a worthwhile person; a positive evaluation of oneself.

Knowledge builder

PARENTAL INFLUENCES

Relate

Picture a mother you know who seems to be a good caregiver. Which of the optimal caregiving behaviours does she engage in?

Do you know any parents who have young children and who are authoritarian, permissive, or authoritative? What are their children like?

What do you think are the best ways to discipline children? How would your approach be classified? What are its advantages and disadvantages?

Learning Check

1. Three important elements of effective mothering are _____ maternal involvement, parental _____ to a child's feelings, needs, rhythms, and signals, and compatibility between parent and child _____.

2. Fathers are more likely to act as playmates for their children, rather than caregivers. T or F?
3. According to Diana Baumrind's research, effective parents are authoritarian in their approach to their children's behaviour. T or F?
4. Authoritarian parents view children as having few rights but many responsibilities. T or F?
5. Coopersmith found that high self-esteem in childhood is related to discipline based on either management techniques or withdrawal of love. T or F?

Critical Thinking

6. If power assertion is a poor way to discipline children, why do so many parents use it?

Answers:

1. proactive, responsiveness, temperaments **2.** T **3.** F **4.** T **5.** F **6.** Most parents discipline their children in the same ways that they themselves were disciplined. Parenting is a responsibility of tremendous importance, for which most people receive almost no training.

▶ Language Development—Fast-Talking Babies

Survey Question:
■ How do children acquire language?

There's something almost miraculous about a baby's first words. As infants, how did we manage to leap into the world of language? As will soon be apparent, social development provides a foundation for language learning. But before we probe that connection, let's begin with a quick survey of language development.

Language Acquisition

Cooing Spontaneous repetition of vowel sounds by infants.

Babbling The repetition by infants of meaningless language sounds (including both vowel and consonant sounds).

Single-word stage In language development, the period during which a child first begins to use single words.

Telegraphic speech In language development, the formation of simple two-word sentences that "telegraph" (communicate) a simple idea.

Language development is closely tied to maturation. As every parent knows, babies can cry from birth on. By one month of age, they use crying to gain attention. Typically, parents can tell if an infant is hungry, angry, or in pain from the tone of the crying (Kaplan, 1998). Around six to eight weeks of age, babies begin **cooing** (the repetition of vowel sounds like "oo" and "ah").

By seven months of age, Amy's nervous system will mature enough to allow her to grasp objects, smile, laugh, sit up, and **babble.** In the babbling stage, the consonants *b*, *d*, *m*, and *g* are combined with the vowel sounds to produce meaningless language sounds: *dadadadada* or *bababa*. At first, babbling is the same around the world. But soon, the language spoken by parents begins to have an influence. That is, Chinese babies start to babble in a way that sounds like Chinese, Mexican babies babble in Spanish-like sounds, and so forth (Gopnik, Meltzoff, & Kuhl, 1999). Babbling is not limited to hearing babies making sounds. Laura Petitto of McGill University studied two deaf infants of deaf parents who were learning sign language as their first language. These infants made hand gestures that were the manual equivalent of babbling (Petitto & Marentette, 1991).

At about one year of age, children can stand alone for a short time and respond to real words such as *no* or *hi*. Soon afterward, the first connection between words and objects forms, and children may address their parents as "Mama" or "Dada." By age 18 months to two years, Amy will have learned to stand and walk alone; her vocabulary may include from 24 to 200 words. At first, there is a **single-word stage,** during which children use one word at a time, such as "go," "juice," or "up." Soon after, words are arranged in simple two-word sentences called **telegraphic speech:** "Want-Teddy," "Mama-gone."

LANGUAGE AND THE TERRIBLE TWOS   At about the same time that children begin to put two or three words together, they become much more independent. Two-year-olds understand some of the commands parents make, but they are not always willing to carry them out. A child like Amy may assert her independence by saying "No drink," "Me do it," "My cup, my cup," and the like. It can be worse, of course. A two-year-old may look at you intently, make eye contact, listen as you shout "No, no," and still pour her juice on the cat.

During their second year, children become increasingly capable of mischief and temper tantrums (Kaplan, 1998). Thus, calling this time "the terrible twos" is not entirely inappropriate. One-year-olds can do plenty of things parents don't want them to do. However, it's usually two-year-olds who do things because you don't want them to (Gopnik, Meltzoff, & Kuhl, 1999).

Perhaps parents can take some comfort in knowing that a stubborn, negative two-year-old is simply becoming more independent. When Amy is two, Olivia and Tom would be wise to remember that "This, too, shall pass." After age two, the child's comprehension and use of words takes a dramatic leap forward (Reznick & Goldfield, 1992). From this point on, vocabulary and language skills grow at a phenomenal rate. By first grade, Amy will be able to understand around 8000 words and use about 4000. She will have truly entered the world of language.

The Roots of Language

In a fascinating study, researchers William Condon and Louis Sander (1974) filmed newborn infants as the babies listened to various sounds. A frame-by-frame analysis of the films showed something astonishing: Infants move their arms and legs to the rhythms of human speech. Random noise, rhythmic tapping, or disconnected vowel sounds will not produce a "language dance." Only natural speech has this effect.

Why do day-old infants "dance" to speech but not other sounds? One possibility is that language recognition is innate. Linguist Noam Chomsky (1975, 1986) has long claimed that humans have a **biological predisposition** or hereditary readiness to develop language. According to Chomsky, language patterns are inborn, much like a child's ability to coordinate walking. If such inborn language recognition does exist, it may explain why children around the world use a limited number of patterns in their first sentences. Typical patterns include (Mussen et al., 1979):

Identification:	"See kitty."
Non-existence:	"Allgone milk."
Possession:	"My doll."
Agent-Action:	"Mama give."
Negation:	"Not ball."
Question:	"Where doggie?"

Does Chomsky's theory explain why language develops so rapidly? Perhaps. But many psychologists feel that Chomsky underestimates the importance of learning. **Psycholinguists** (specialists in the psychology of language) have shown that language is not magically "switched on" by adult speech. Imitation of adults and rewards for correctly using words (as when a child asks for a cookie) are an important part of language learning. Also, babies actively participate in language learning by asking questions, such as "What dis?" (Domingo & Goldstein-Alpern, 1999).

When a child makes a language error, parents typically repeat the child's sentence, with needed corrections (Bohannon & Stanowicz, 1988). More important, still, is the fact that parents and children begin to communicate long before the child can speak. Months of shared effort precede a child's first word. From this point of view, an infant's "language dance" reflects a readiness to interact socially with parents, not innate language recognition. The next section explains why.

EARLY COMMUNICATION   How do parents communicate with infants before they can talk? Parents go to a great deal of trouble to get babies to smile and vocalize (▶ Figure 3.11). In doing so, they quickly learn to change their actions to keep the infant's attention, arousal, and activity at optimal levels. A familiar example is the "I'm-Going-to-Get-You Game." In

Biological predisposition The presumed hereditary readiness of humans to learn certain skills, such as how to use language, or a readiness to behave in particular ways.

Psycholinguist A specialist in the psychology of language and language development.

  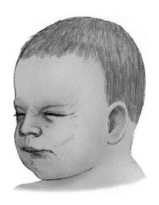

▶**Figure 3.11**

Infant engagement scale. These samples from a 90-point scale show various levels of infant engagement, or attention. Babies participate in prelanguage "conversations" with parents by giving and withholding attention and by smiling, gazing, or vocalizing. (From Beebe et al., 1982.)

85
Medium high positive

50
Neutral attention

20
Avert

Signal In early language development, any behaviour, such as touching, vocalizing, gazing, or smiling, that allows non-verbal interaction and turn-taking between parent and child.

Turn-taking In early language development, the tendency of parent and child to alternate in the sending and receiving of signals or messages.

Motherese (or parentese) A pattern of speech used when talking to infants, marked by a higher-pitched voice, short, simple sentences, repetition, slower speech, and exaggerated voice inflections.

it, the adult says, "I'm gonna getcha. . . . I'm gonna getcha. . . . I'm gonna getcha. . . . Gotcha!" Through such games, adults and babies come to share similar rhythms and expectations (Stern, 1982). Soon a system of shared **signals** is created, including touching, vocalizing, gazing, and smiling. These help lay a foundation for later language use. Specifically, signals establish a pattern of "conversational" **turn-taking** (alternate sending and receiving of messages).

Olivia	*Amy*
	(smiles)
"Oh what a nice little smile!"	
"Yes, isn't that nice?"	
"There."	
"There's a nice little smile."	(burps)
"Well, pardon you!"	
"Yes, that's better, isn't it?"	
"Yes."	(vocalizes)
"Yes."	(smiles)
"What's so funny?"	

From the outside, such exchanges may look meaningless. In reality, they represent real communication. Amy's vocalizations and attention enable her to interact emotionally with Olivia and Tom. Even infants as young as three months make more speech-like sounds when an adult engages them in turn-taking (see ▶Figure 3.12) (Bloom, Russell, & Wassenberg, 1987). The more children interact with parents, the faster they learn to talk and develop thinking abilities (Hart & Risley, 1999; Tamis-LeMonvda & Bornstein, 1994). Unmistakably, social relationships contribute to early language learning.

PARENTESE When they talk to infants, parents use an exaggerated pattern of speaking called **motherese** or **parentese.** Typically, they raise their tone of voice, use short, simple sentences, and repeat themselves more. They also slow their rate of speaking, and use exaggerated voice inflections: "Did Amy eat it A-L-L UP?"

What is the purpose of such changes? Parents are apparently trying to help their children learn language. When a baby is still babbling, parents tend to use long, adult-style sentences. But as soon as the baby says its first word they switch to parentese. By the time babies are four months old, they prefer parentese over normal speech (Cooper et al., 1997).

In addition to being simpler, parentese has a distinct "musical" quality (Fernald & Mazzie, 1991). No matter what language mothers

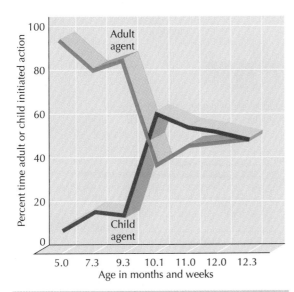

▶**Figure 3.12**

This graph shows the development of turn-taking in games played by an infant and his mother. For several months Richard responded to games such as peek-a-boo and "hand-the-toy-back" only when his mother initiated action. At about nine months, however, he rapidly began to initiate action in the games. Soon, he was the one to take the lead about one half of the time. Learning to take turns and to direct actions toward another person underlie basic language skills. (From Bruner, 1983.)

As with motherese, parents use a distinctive style when singing to an infant, according to University of Toronto psychologist Sandra Trehub. Even people who speak another language can tell if a tape-recorded song was sung to an infant or an adult, or if the person was just pretending to sing to an infant. Likewise, lullabies remain recognizable when electronic filtering removes words (Trehub, Unyk, & Trainor, 1993a, 1993b, 1997).

speak, the melodies, pauses, and inflections they use to comfort, praise, or give warning are universal. Psychologist Anne Fernald has found that mothers of all nations talk to their babies with similar changes in pitch. For instance, we praise babies with a rising, then falling pitch ("BRA-vo!" "GOOD girl!"). Warnings are delivered in a short, sharp rhythm ("Non, non!" "Basta! Basta!" "Not! Dude!"). To give comfort, parents use low, smooth, drawn-out tones ("Oooh poor baaa-by." "Oooh pauvre petit.") A high-pitched, rising melody is used to call attention to objects ("See the pretty BIRDIE?") (Fernald, 1989).

Note that parentese is not literally "baby talk." Many parents can't seem to resist imitating a baby's "cute" mispronunciations of words, like "wa-wa" (water) or "pah-getty" (spaghetti). This is harmless enough for a short time. However, continued use of baby talk may slow language learning. Unless parents help their children pronounce words correctly, a child can easily reach school age still using baby talk. ("Teacher, can I go wee-wee.")

Motherese helps parents get babies' attention, communicate with them, and teach them language (Kaplan et al., 1995). Later, as a child's speaking improves, parents tend to adjust their speech to the child's language ability. Especially from 18 months to four years of age, parents seek to clarify what a child says and prompt the child to say more. Two typical strategies are (Newman & Newman, 1987):

Expansion:	*Child:*	Doggie bite.
	Parent:	Yes, the dog bit the toy.
Prompting:	*Child:*	Doggie briggle.
	Parent:	What did the doggie do?

In summary, some elements of language are innate. Nevertheless, our inherited tendency to learn language does not determine if we will speak English or Vietnamese, French or Russian. Environmental forces also influence whether a person develops simple or sophisticated language skills. The first seven years of life are a critical period in language learning (Eliot, 1999). Clearly, a full flowering of speech requires careful cultivation.

Knowledge builder

LANGUAGE DEVELOPMENT

Relate

In order, see if you can name and imitate the language abilities you had as you progressed from birth to age two years. Now see if you can label and imitate some basic elements of parentese.

In your own words, state at least one argument for and against Chomsky's view of language acquisition.

You are going to spend a day with a person who speaks a different language than you do. Do you think you would be able to communicate with the other person? How does this relate to language acquisition?

Learning Check

1. The development of speech and language usually occurs in which order?
   a. crying, cooing, babbling, telegraphic speech
   b. cooing, crying, babbling, telegraphic speech
   c. babbling, crying, cooing, telegraphic speech
   d. crying, babbling, cooing, identification
2. Simple two-word sentences are characteristic of _____ speech.
3. Noam _____ has advanced the idea that language acquisition is built on innate patterns.
4. Prelanguage turn-taking and social interactions would be of special interest to a psycholinguist. T or F?
5. The style of speaking known as _____ is higher in pitch and has a musical quality.

Critical Thinking

6. The children of professional parents hear more words per hour than the children of welfare parents, and they also tend to score higher on tests of mental abilities. How else could their higher scores be explained?

Answers:

1. *a* 2. telegraphic 3. Chomsky 4. T 5. parentese 6. Children in professional homes receive many educational benefits that are less common in welfare homes. Yet, even when such differences are taken into account, brighter children tend to come from richer language environments (Hart & Risley, 1999).

▶ Cognitive Development—How Do Children Learn to Think?

Survey Question:
■ How do children learn to think?

Now that we have Amy talking, let's move on to a broader view of intellectual development.

How different is a child's understanding of the world from that of an adult? Generally speaking, their thinking is less abstract. Children use fewer generalizations, categories, and principles. They also tend to base their understanding on particular examples and objects they can see or touch.

Before children reach the age of six or seven, their thinking is very concrete. Younger children cannot make **transformations** in which they must mentally change the shape or form of a substance (such as clay or water). Let's visit Amy at age five: If you show her a short, wide glass full of milk and a tall, narrow glass (also full), she will tell you that the taller glass contains more milk. Amy will tell you this even if she watches you pour milk from the short glass into an empty, tall glass. She is not bothered by the fact that the milk appears to be transformed from a smaller to a larger amount. Instead, she responds only to the fact that taller seems to mean more. (See ▶ Figure 3.13.) After about age seven, children are no longer fooled by this situation. Perhaps that's why seven has been called the "age of reason." From age seven on, we see a definite trend toward more logical, adult-like thought (Flavell, 1992).

Is there any pattern to the growth of intellect in childhood? According to the Swiss psychologist and philosopher Jean Piaget (1951, 1952), there is.

▶**Figure 3.13**

Children under age seven intuitively assume that a volume of liquid increases when it is poured from a short, wide container into a taller, thinner one. This boy thinks the tall container holds more than the short one. Actually, each holds the same amount of liquid. Children make such judgments based on the height of the liquid, not its volume.

Piaget's Theory of Cognitive Development

Jean Piaget (Jahn pea-ah-JAY) believed that all children pass through a series of distinct stages in intellectual development. Many of his ideas came from observing his own children as they solved various thought problems. (It is tempting to imagine that Piaget's illustrious career was launched one day when his wife said to him, "Watch the children for a while, will you, Jean?")

MENTAL ADAPTATIONS Piaget was convinced that intellect grows through processes he called assimilation and accommodation. **Assimilation** refers to using existing mental patterns in new situations. Let's say that a plastic hammer is the favourite toy of a boy named Benjamin. Benjamin holds the hammer properly and loves to pound on blocks with it. For his birthday Benjamin gets an oversized toy wrench. If he uses the wrench for pounding, it has been assimilated to an existing knowledge structure.

In **accommodation,** existing ideas are modified to fit new requirements. For instance, a younger child might think that a dime is worth less than a (larger) nickel. However, as children begin to spend money, they must alter their ideas about what "more" and "less" mean. Thus, new situations are assimilated to existing ideas, and new ideas are created to accommodate new experiences.

Piaget's ideas have deeply affected our view of children (Beilin, 1992). The following is a brief summary of what he found.

THE SENSORIMOTOR STAGE (0–2 YEARS) In the first two years of life, known as the **sensorimotor stage**, Amy's intellectual development will be largely non-verbal. She will be mainly concerned

Transformation The mental ability to change the shape or form of a substance (such as clay or water) and to perceive that its volume remains the same.

Assimilation In Piaget's theory, the application of existing mental patterns to new situations (that is, the new situation is assimilated to existing mental schemes).

Accommodation In Piaget's theory, the modification of existing mental patterns to fit new demands (that is, mental schemes are changed to accommodate new information or experiences).

Sensorimotor stage Stage of intellectual development during which sensory input and motor responses become coordinated.

Jean Piaget—philosopher, psychologist, and keen observer of children.

Object permanence
Concept, gained in infancy, that objects continue to exist even when they are hidden from view.

Preoperational stage
Period of intellectual development during which children begin to use language and think symbolically, yet remain intuitive and egocentric in their thought.

Intuitive thought Thinking that makes little or no use of reasoning and logic.

Egocentric thought
Thought that is self-centred and fails to consider the viewpoints of others.

Theory of mind A child's current state of knowledge about the mind, including his or her understanding of desires, beliefs, thoughts, intentions, feelings, and so forth.

with learning to coordinate her movements with information from her senses. Also, **object permanence** (an understanding that objects continue to exist when they are out of sight) emerges at this time. By about 18 months of age, children begin to actively pursue disappearing objects. By age two, they can anticipate the movement of an object behind a screen. For example, when watching an electric train, Amy will look ahead to the end of a tunnel, rather than staring at the spot where the train disappeared.

In general, developments in this stage indicate that the child's ideas about the world are becoming more stable. Objects cease to appear and disappear magically, and a more orderly and predictable world replaces the confusing and disconnected sensations of infancy.

THE PREOPERATIONAL STAGE (2–7 YEARS) During the **preoperational stage,** children begin to think symbolically and use language. But children's thinking is still very **intuitive** (they make little use of reasoning and logic). (Do you remember thinking as a child that the sun and the moon followed you when you took a walk?) In addition, the child's use of language is not as sophisticated as it might seem. Children have a tendency to confuse words with the objects they represent. If Benjamin calls a toy block a "car" and you use it to make a "house," he may be upset. To children, the name of an object is as much a part of the object as its size, shape, and colour. This seems to underlie a preoccupation with name-calling. To the preoperational child, insulting words may really hurt. Consider one rather protected youngster who was angered by her older brother. Searching for a way to retaliate against her larger and stronger foe, she settled on, "You panty-girdle!" It was the worst thing she could think of saying.

During the preoperational stage, the child is also quite **egocentric** (unable to take the viewpoint of other people). The child's ego seems to stand at the centre of his or her world. To illustrate, show Amy a two-sided mirror. Then hold it between you and her, so she can see herself in it. If you ask her what she thinks you can see, she imagines that you see her face reflected in the mirror, instead of your own. Such egocentrism explains why children can seem exasperatingly selfish or uncooperative at times. If Benjamin blocks your view by standing in front of the TV, he assumes that you can see it if he can. If you ask him to move so you can see better, he may move so that he can see better! Benjamin is not being selfish, in the ordinary sense. He just doesn't realize that your view differs from his. (See "A Child's Theory of Mind.")

FOCUS ON RESEARCH   A Child's Theory of Mind—Other People, Other Minds

Why are young children so egocentric? In many instances, it's because they have a limited understanding of mental states, such as desires, beliefs, thoughts, intentions, and feelings. In other words, it could be said that they have a very simplified **theory of mind** (Flavell, 1999).

The following example is based on theory-of-mind research. Imagine that you show five-year-old Nicky a candy box. "What do you think is inside?" you ask. "Candy," Nicky replies. Then you let Nicky look inside, where he finds a surprise: The box contains crayons, not candy. "Nicky," you ask, "what will your friend Max think is inside the box if I show it to him?" "Candy!" Nicky replies, amused at the thought that Max is going to get fooled, too.

Now imagine that we try the procedure again, this time with Shelia, who is only three years old. Like Nicky, Shelia thinks she will find candy in the box. She opens the box and sees the crayons. Now we ask Shelia what she thinks Max will expect to find in the box. "Crayons," she replies. Because Shelia knows that there are crayons in the box, she assumes that everyone else does, too. It's as if only one reality exists for Shelia. She doesn't seem to understand that the minds of other people contain different information, beliefs, thoughts, and so forth (Gopnik, Meltzoff, & Kuhl, 1999).

Between the ages of three and four, children normally gain a richer understanding of mental life. As their "theory of mind" becomes more accurate, they are able to participate more fully in the complex psychological world in which we all live.

Concrete operational stage Period of intellectual development during which children become able to use the concepts of time, space, volume, and number, but in ways that remain simplified and concrete, rather than abstract.

Conservation In Piaget's theory, mastery of the concept that the weight, mass, and volume of matter remains unchanged (is conserved) even when the shape or appearance of objects changes.

Reversibility of thought Recognition that relationships involving equality or identity can be reversed (for example, if A = B, then B = A).

Abstract principles Concepts and ideas removed from specific examples and concrete situations.

Hypothetical possibilities Suppositions, guesses, or projections.

Formal operations stage Period of intellectual development characterized by thinking that includes abstract, theoretical, and hypothetical ideas.

THE CONCRETE OPERATIONAL STAGE (7–11 YEARS) An important development during the **concrete operational stage** is mastery of **conservation** (the concept that mass, weight, and volume remain unchanged when the shape of objects changes). Children have learned conservation when they understand that rolling a ball of clay into a "snake" does not increase the amount of clay. Likewise, pouring liquid from a tall, narrow glass into a shallow dish does not reduce the amount of liquid. In each case, the volume remains the same despite changes in shape or appearance. The original amount is conserved (see Figure 3.13).

During the concrete operational stage, children begin to use concepts of time, space, and number. The child can think logically about very concrete objects or situations, categories, and principles. Such abilities explain why children stop believing in Santa Claus when they reach this stage. Because they can conserve volume, they realize that Santa's sack couldn't possibly hold enough toys for millions of girls and boys.

Another important development at this time is the ability to reverse thoughts or mental operations. A conversation with a four-year-old boy in the preoperational stage shows what happens when a child's thinking lacks reversibility (Phillips, 1969).

> "Do you have a brother?"
> "Yes."
> "What's his name?"
> "Jim."
> "Does Jim have a brother?"
> "No."

Reversibility of thought allows children in the concrete operational stage to recognize that if 4 × 2 = 8, then 2 × 4 does, too. Younger children must memorize each relationship separately. Thus, a preoperational child may know that 4 × 9 = 36, without being able to tell you what 9 × 4 equals.

THE FORMAL OPERATIONS STAGE (11 YEARS AND UP) Sometime after about the age of 11, children begin to break away from concrete objects and specific examples. Thinking is based more on **abstract principles,** such as "democracy," "honour," or "correlation." Children who reach this stage can think about their thoughts, and they become less egocentric. Older children and young adolescents also gradually become able to consider **hypothetical possibilities** (suppositions, guesses, or projections). For example, if you ask a younger child, "What do you think would happen if it suddenly became possible for people to fly?" the child might respond, "People can't fly." Older children are able to consider such possibilities.

Full adult intellectual ability is attained during the **formal operations stage.** Older adolescents are capable of inductive and deductive reasoning, and they can comprehend math, physics, philosophy, psychology, and other abstract systems. They can learn to test hypotheses in a scientific manner. Of course, not everyone reaches this level of thinking. Also, many adults can think formally about some topics, but their thinking becomes concrete when the topic is unfamiliar. This implies that formal thinking may be more a result of culture and learning than maturation. In any case, after late adolescence, improvements in intellect are based on gaining knowledge, experience, and wisdom, rather than on any leaps in basic thinking capacity.

How can parents apply Piaget's ideas? Piaget's theory suggests that the ideal way to guide intellectual development is to provide experiences that are only slightly novel, unusual, or challenging. Remember, a child's intellect develops mainly through accommodation. It is usually best to follow a one-step-ahead strategy, in which your teaching efforts are aimed just beyond a child's current level of comprehension (Heckhausen, 1987).

For your convenience, Table 3.2 briefly summarizes each Piagetian stage. To help you remember Piaget's theory, the table describes what would happen at each stage if we

Table 3.2
Piaget—A
Guide for
Parents

PIAGET	MONOPOLY GAME	GUIDELINES FOR PARENTS
Sensorimotor Stage The stage during which sensory input and motor responses become coordinated.	The child puts houses, hotels, and dice in her mouth and plays with "Chance" cards.	Active play with a child is most effective in this stage. Encourage explorations in touching, smelling, and manipulating objects. Peek-a-boo is a good way to establish the permanence of objects.
Preoperational Stage The period of cognitive development when children begin to use language and think symbolically, yet remain intuitive and egocentric.	The child plays *Monopoly*, but makes up her own rules and cannot understand instructions.	Specific examples and touching or seeing things continue to be more useful than verbal explanations. Learning the concept of conservation may be aided by demonstrations with liquids, beads, clay, and other substances.
Concrete Operational Stage The period of cognitive development during which children begin to use concepts of time, space, volume, and number, but in ways that remain simplified and concrete.	The child understands basic instructions and will play by the rules, but is not capable of hypothetical transactions dealing with mortgages, loans, and special pacts with other players.	Children are beginning to use generalizations, but they still require specific examples to grasp many ideas. Expect a degree of inconsistency in the child's ability to apply concepts of time, space, quantity, and volume to new situations.
Formal Operations Stage The period of intellectual development marked by a capacity for abstract, theoretical, and hypothetical thinking.	The child no longer plays the game mechanically; complex and hypothetical transactions unique to each game are now possible.	It is now more effective to explain things verbally or symbolically and to help children master general rules and principles. Encourage the child to create hypotheses and to imagine how things could be.

played a game of *Monopoly* with the child. You'll also find brief suggestions about how to relate to children in each stage.

Piaget Today

Piaget's theory is a valuable "road map" for understanding how children think. However, many psychologists are convinced that Piaget gave too little credit to the effects of learning. For example, children of pottery-making parents can correctly answer questions about the conservation of clay at an earlier age than Piaget would have predicted (Bransford et al., 1986). According to learning theorists, children continuously gain specific knowledge; they do not undergo stage-like leaps in general mental ability. Thus, the truth may lie somewhere between Piaget's stage theory and modern learning theory.

On a broad scale, many of Piaget's observations have held up well. However, his explanations for the growth of thinking abilities in childhood continue to be debated. Where early infancy is concerned, even Piaget's observations may need revision. It looks like Piaget greatly underestimated the thinking abilities of infants during the sensorimotor stage.

INFANT COGNITION *What evidence is there that Piaget underestimated infant abilities?* Piaget believed that infants under the age of one year cannot think. Babies, he said, have no memory of people and objects that are out of sight. Yet, we now know that infants begin forming representations of the world very early in life. For example, babies as young as three months of age appear to know that objects are solid and do not disappear when out of view (Baillargeon & DeVos, 1992; Johnson & Nanez, 1995).

Why did Piaget fail to detect the thinking skills of infants? Most likely, he mistook babies' limited *physical skills* for mental incompetence. Piaget's tests required babies to search for objects or reach out and touch them. Newer, more sensitive methods are uncovering abilities Piaget missed. One such method takes advantage of the fact that babies, like adults, act surprised when they see something "impossible" or unexpected occur. To make use of this effect, psychologist Renee Baillargeon (1991) puts on little "magic shows" for infants. In her "theatre" babies watch as possible and impossible events occur with toys or other objects. Some three-month-old infants act surprised and gaze longer at impossible events. An example is seeing two solid objects appear to pass through each other. By the time they are eight months old, babies can remember where objects are (or should be) for at least one minute (see ▶Figure 3.14).

Piaget believed that abilities like those described in Figure 3.14 emerge only after a long sensorimotor period of development. However, evidence continues to mount that babies are born with the capacity to form concepts about the world, or acquire this ability early in life, according to University of Waterloo developmental psychologist Andréa Aguiar (Aguiar & Baillargeon, 1998, 1999). It looks as if further study is likely to refine and amend the ideas that grew from Piaget's fateful decision to "watch the children for a while."

Another criticism of Piaget is that he underestimated the impact of culture on mental development. The next section tells how Amy will go about mastering the intellectual tools valued by her culture.

Vygotsky's Sociocultural Theory

Recently, psychologists have become interested in the sociocultural theory of Russian scholar Lev Vygotsky (1896–1934). Vygotsky's key insight is that children's thinking develops through dialogues with more capable persons (Vygotsky, 1962, 1978).

How does that relate to intellectual growth? So far, no one has ever published *A Child's Guide to Life on Earth*. Instead, children must learn about life from various "tutors," such as parents, teachers, and older siblings. Even if *A Child's Guide to Life on Earth* did exist, we would need a separate version for every culture. It is not enough for children to learn how to think. They must also learn specific intellectual skills valued by their culture.

Like Piaget, Vygotsky believed that children actively seek to discover new principles. However, Vygotsky emphasized that many of a child's most important "discoveries" are

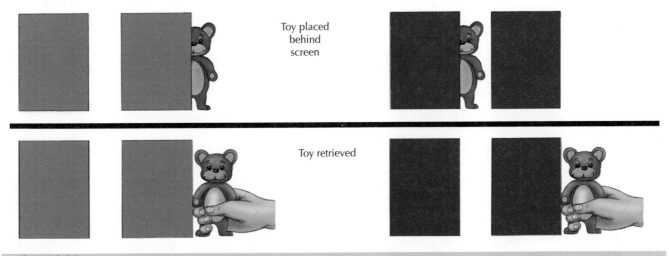

▶Figure 3.14

The panels on the left show a possible event, in which an infant watches as a toy is placed behind the right of two screens. After a delay of 70 seconds, the toy is brought into view from behind the right screen. In the two panels on the right, an impossible event occurs. The toy is placed behind the left screen and retrieved from behind the right. (A duplicate toy was hidden there before testing.) Eight-month-old infants react with surprise when they see the impossible event staged for them. Their reaction implies that they remember where the toy was hidden. Infants appear to have a capacity for memory and thinking that greatly exceeds what Piaget claimed is possible during the sensorimotor period. (Adapted from Baillargeon, DeVos, & Graber, 1989.)

guided by skillful tutors. Developmental psychologist David Shaffer (1999) offers the following example:

> Annie, a 4-year-old, has just received her first jigsaw puzzle as a birthday present. She attempts to work the puzzle but gets nowhere until her father comes along, sits down beside her, and gives her some tips. He suggests that it would be a good idea to put together the corners first, points to the pink area at the edge of one corner piece and says, "Let's look for another pink piece." When Annie seems frustrated, he places two interlocking pieces near each other so that she will notice them, and when Annie succeeds, he offers words of encouragement. As Annie gradually gets the hang of it, he steps back and lets her work more and more independently. (p. 260)

Interactions like this are most helpful when they take place within a child's **zone of proximal development.**

What did Vygotsky mean by that? The word *proximal* means close or nearby. Vygotsky realized that, at any given time, some tasks are just beyond a child's reach. The child is close to having the mental skills needed to do the task, but it is a little too complex to be mastered alone. However, children working within this zone can make rapid progress if they receive sensitive guidance from a skilled partner.

Vygotsky also emphasized a process he called **scaffolding.** A scaffold is a framework or temporary support. Vygotsky believed that adults help children learn how to think by "scaffolding," or supporting, their attempts to solve problems or discover principles. To be most effective, scaffolding must be responsive to a child's needs. For example, as Annie's father helped her with the puzzle, he tailored his hints and guidance to match her evolving abilities. The two of them worked together, step by step, so that Annie could better understand how to assemble a puzzle. In a sense, Annie's father set up a series of temporary bridges that helped her move into new mental territory.

During their collaborations with others, children learn important cultural beliefs and values. For example, imagine that a boy wants to know how many Pokémon cards he has. His mother helps him stack and count the cards, moving each card to a new stack as they count it. She then shows him how to write the number on a slip of paper so he can remember it. This teaches the child not only about counting, but also that writing is valued in our culture. In other parts of the world, a child learning to count might be shown how to make notches on a stick or tie knots in a cord.

SUMMARY   Vygotsky saw that grown-ups play a crucial role in what children know. As they try to decipher the world, children rely on adults to help them understand how things work. Vygotsky further noticed that adults unconsciously adjust their behaviour to give children the information they need to solve problems that interest the child. In this way, children use adults to learn about their culture and society (Gopnik, Meltzoff, & Kuhl, 1999).

▶ The Story of a Lifetime—Rocky Road or Garden Path?

At the beginning of this chapter we noted that developmental psychologists are interested in every phase of life from the womb to the tomb. Thus far, we have concentrated on Amy's first few years because the development during childhood can have such a large impact on a person's life. It is not possible here to satisfy Olivia and Tom's curiosity about what Amy's life will be like. Nevertheless, we can at least sketch the general outlines of her life to come. Every life is marked by a number of **developmental milestones.** These are notable events, markers, or turning points in personal development. Some examples include graduating from school, voting for the first time, getting married, watching a child leave home (or move back!), the death of a parent, becoming a grandparent, retirement, and one's own death (Kimmel, 1990).

Perhaps the best way to get a preview of Amy's life is to consider some of the major psychological challenges she is likely to encounter. Each of us can take pride in being "one of a kind." There really is no such thing as a "typical person" or a "typical life." Neverthe-

Zone of proximal development Refers to the range of tasks a child cannot yet master alone, but that she or he can accomplish with the guidance of a more capable partner.

Scaffolding The process of adjusting instruction so that it is responsive to a beginner's behaviour and supports the beginner's efforts to understand a problem or gain a mental skill.

Survey Question:
■ What are the typical tasks and dilemmas through the life span?

Developmental milestone A significant turning point or marker in personal development.

Knowledge builder

COGNITIVE DEVELOPMENT

Relate

You are going to make cookies with children of various ages. See if you can name each of Piaget's stages and give an example of what a child in that stage might be expected to do.

You have been asked to help a child learn to use a pocket calculator to do simple addition. How would you go about identifying the child's zone of proximal development for this task? How would you scaffold the child's learning?

Learning Check

Match each item with one of the following stages.
A. Sensorimotor B. Preoperational C. Concrete operational D. Formal operations

_____ **1.** egocentric thought
_____ **2.** abstract or hypothetical thought
_____ **3.** purposeful movement
_____ **4.** intuitive thought

_____ **5.** conservation   _____ **6.** reversibility of thought
_____ **7.** object permanence   _____ **8.** non-verbal development

9. Assimilation refers to applying existing thought patterns or knowledge to new situations. T or F?
10. Newer methods for testing infant thinking abilities frequently make note of whether an infant is _____ by seemingly _____ events.
11. Vygotsky called the process of providing a temporary framework of supports for learning new mental abilities _____.

Critical Thinking

12. Using Piaget's theory as a guide, at what age would you expect a child to recognize that a Styrofoam cup has weight?

Answers:

1. B 2. D 3. A 4. B 5. C 6. C 7. A 8. A 9. T 10. surprised, impossible 11. scaffolding 12. Seventy-five percent of four- to six-year-olds say that a Styrofoam cup has no weight after lifting it! Most children judge weight intuitively (by the way an object feels) until they begin to move into the concrete operational stage (Smith, Carey, & Wiser, 1985).

Life stages Widely recognized periods of life corresponding to broad phases of development.

Developmental task Any personal change that must take place for optimal development.

Psychosocial dilemma A conflict between personal impulses and the social world.

less, broad similarities can be found in the **life stages** of infancy, childhood, adolescence, young adulthood, middle adulthood, and old age. Each stage confronts a person with new **developmental tasks** that must be mastered for optimal development. Examples are learning to read in childhood, adjusting to sexual maturity in adolescence, and establishing a vocation as an adult.

In an influential book entitled *Childhood and Society* (1963), personality theorist Erik Erikson (1903–1994) suggests that we face a specific psychosocial dilemma, or "crisis," at each stage of life. A **psychosocial dilemma** is a conflict between personal impulses and the social world. Resolving each dilemma creates a new balance between a person and society. A string of "successes" produces healthy development and a satisfying life. Unfavourable outcomes throw us off balance, making it harder to deal with later crises. Life becomes a "rocky road" and personal growth is stunted. Table 3.3 lists Erikson's dilemmas.

Personality theorist Erik Erikson (1903–1994) is best known for his life stage theory of human development. His last book, *Vital Involvement in Old Age*, published in 1986, described his ideas about successful aging.

Table 3.3
Erikson's Psychosocial Dilemmas

AGE	CHARACTERISTIC DILEMMA
Birth to 1 year	Trust versus mistrust
1 to 3 years	Autonomy versus shame and doubt
3 to 5 years	Initiative versus guilt
6 to 12 years	Industry versus inferiority
Adolescence	Identity versus role confusion
Young adulthood	Intimacy versus isolation
Middle adulthood	Generativity versus stagnation
Late adulthood	Integrity versus despair

What are the major developmental tasks and life crises? A brief description of each psychosocial dilemma follows.

STAGE ONE, FIRST YEAR OF LIFE: TRUST VERSUS MISTRUST   During the first year of life, children are completely dependent on others. Erikson believes that a basic attitude of trust or mistrust is formed at this time. **Trust** is established when babies are given adequate warmth, touching, love, and physical care. **Mistrust** is caused by inadequate or unpredictable care and by parents who are cold, indifferent, or rejecting. Basic mistrust may later cause insecurity, suspiciousness, or an inability to relate to others. Notice that trust comes from the same conditions that help babies become securely attached to their parents.

STAGE TWO, 1–3 YEARS: AUTONOMY VERSUS SHAME AND DOUBT   In stage two, children express their growing self-control by climbing, touching, exploring, and trying to do things for themselves. Tom and Olivia can foster Amy's sense of **autonomy** by encouraging her to try new skills. However, her first efforts may be crude, involving spilling, falling, wetting, and other "accidents." If Tom and Olivia ridicule or overprotect Amy, they may cause her to **doubt** her abilities and feel **shameful** about her actions.

STAGE THREE, 3–5 YEARS: INITIATIVE VERSUS GUILT   In stage three, children move beyond simple self-control and begin to take initiative. Through play, children learn to make plans and carry out tasks. Parents reinforce **initiative** by giving children freedom to play, ask questions, use imagination, and choose activities. Feelings of **guilt** about initiating activities are formed if parents criticize severely, prevent play, or discourage a child's questions.

STAGE FOUR, 6–12 YEARS: INDUSTRY VERSUS INFERIORITY   Many events of middle childhood are symbolized by that fateful day when you first entered school. With dizzying speed your world expanded beyond your family, and you faced a whole series of new challenges.

Erikson describes the elementary school years as the child's "entrance into life." In school, children begin to learn skills valued by society, and success or failure can affect a child's feelings of adequacy. Children learn a sense of **industry** if they win praise for productive activities, such as building, painting, cooking, reading, and studying. If a child's efforts are regarded as messy, childish, or inadequate, feelings of **inferiority** result. For the first time, teachers, classmates, and adults outside the home become as important as parents in shaping attitudes toward oneself.

STAGE FIVE, ADOLESCENCE: IDENTITY VERSUS ROLE CONFUSION   Adolescence is often a turbulent time. Caught between childhood and adulthood, the adolescent faces some unique problems. Erikson considers a need to answer the question "Who am I?" the primary task during this stage of life. As Amy matures mentally and physically, she will have new feelings, a new body, and new attitudes. Like other adolescents, she will need to build a consistent **identity** out of her talents, values, life history, relationships, and the demands of her culture (Douvan, 1997). Her conflicting experiences as a student, friend, athlete, worker, daughter, lover, and so forth must be integrated into a unified sense of self (more on this later). Persons who fail to develop a sense of identity suffer from **role confusion,** an uncertainty about who they are and where they are going.

STAGE SIX, YOUNG ADULTHOOD: INTIMACY VERSUS ISOLATION   *What does Erikson believe is the major conflict in early adulthood?* In stage six, the individual feels a need for intimacy in his or her life. After establishing a stable identity, a person is prepared to share meaningful love or deep friendship with others. By **intimacy,** Erikson means an ability to care about others and to share experiences with them. In line with Erikson's view, 75 percent of college-age men and women rank a good marriage and family life as important adult goals (Bachman & Johnson, 1979). And yet, marriage or sexual involvement is no guarantee of intimacy: Many adult relationships remain superficial and unfulfilling. Failure to establish intimacy with others leads to a deep sense of **isolation** (feeling alone and uncared for in life). This often sets the stage for later difficulties.

Trust versus mistrust A conflict about learning to trust others and the world.

Autonomy versus shame and doubt A conflict between growing self-control and feelings of shame or doubt.

Initiative versus guilt A conflict between learning to take initiative and overcoming feelings of guilt about doing so.

Industry versus inferiority A conflict in middle childhood centred on lack of support for industrious behaviour, which can result in feelings of inferiority.

Identity versus role confusion A conflict concerning the need to establish a personal identity.

Intimacy versus isolation The challenge of establishing intimacy with others, versus feeling a sense of isolation.

STAGE SEVEN, MIDDLE ADULTHOOD: GENERATIVITY VERSUS STAGNATION   According to Erikson, an interest in guiding the next generation is the main source of balance in mature adulthood. Erikson called this quality **generativity.** It is expressed by caring about oneself, one's children, and future generations. Generativity may be achieved by guiding one's own children or by helping other children (as a teacher, clergyman, or coach, for example). Productive or creative work can also express generativity. In any case, a person's concerns and energies must broaden to include the welfare of others and society as a whole. Failure to do this is marked by a **stagnant** concern with one's own needs and comforts. Life loses meaning, and the person feels bitter, dreary, and trapped (Peterson & Klohnen, 1995).

STAGE EIGHT, LATE ADULTHOOD: INTEGRITY VERSUS DESPAIR   *What does Erikson see as the conflicts of old age?* Old age is a time of reflection. According to Erikson, when Amy grows old she must be able to look back over her life with acceptance and satisfaction. People who have lived richly and responsibly develop a sense of **integrity** (self-respect). This allows them to face aging and death with dignity. If previous life events are viewed with regret, the elderly person experiences **despair** (heartache and remorse). In this case, life seems like a series of missed opportunities. The person feels like a failure and knows it's too late to reverse what has been done. Aging and the threat of death then become sources of fear and depression.

To squeeze a lifetime into a few pages, we had to ignore countless details. Although much is lost, the net effect is a clearer picture of an entire life cycle. Is Erikson's description an exact map of Amy's future—or your own? Probably not. Still, the dilemmas we have discussed reflect major psychological events in the lives of many. Knowing about them may allow you to anticipate typical trouble spots in life. You may also be better prepared to understand the problems and feelings of friends and relatives at various stages in the life cycle.

Generativity versus stagnation A conflict in which stagnant self-interest is countered by interest in guiding the next generation.

Integrity versus despair A conflict in old age between feelings of integrity and the despair of viewing previous life events with regret.

Knowledge builder

PSYCHOSOCIAL DILEMMAS

Relate

See if you can think of a person you know who is facing one of Erikson's psychosocial dilemmas. Now see if you can think of specific people who seem to be coping with each of the other dilemmas.

Learning Check

As a way to improve your memory, you might find it helpful to summarize Erikson's eight life stages. Complete this do-it-yourself summary and compare your answers to those given below.

Stage	Crisis	Favourable Outcome
First year of life	**1.** _____ vs. **2.** _____	Faith in the environment and in others
Ages 1–3	Autonomy vs. **3.** _____	Feelings of self-control and adequacy
Ages 3–5	**4.** _____ vs. guilt	Ability to begin one's own activities
Ages 6–12	Industry vs. **5.** _____	Confidence in productive skills, learning how to work

Adolescence	**6.** _____ role confusion	vs.	An integrated image of oneself as a unique person
Young adulthood	Intimacy vs. **7.** _____		Ability to form bonds of love and friendship with others
Middle adulthood	Generativity vs. **8.** _____		Concern for family, society, and future generations
Late adulthood	**9.** _____ **10.** _____	vs.	Sense of dignity, fulfillment, willingness to face death

Critical Thinking

11. Trying to make generalizations about development throughout life is complicated by at least one major factor. What do you think it is?

Answers:

1. Trust 2. mistrust 3. shame or doubt 4. Initiative 5. inferiority 6. Identity 7. isolation 8. stagnation 9. Integrity 10. despair 11. Different cohorts (groups of people born in the same year) live in different historical times. People born in various decades may have very different life experiences. This makes it difficult to identify universal patterns (Stewart & Ostrove, 1998).

PSYCHOLOGY IN ACTION

EFFECTIVE PARENTING—RAISING HEALTHY CHILDREN

Survey Question:
■ How do effective parents discipline their children?

Consistency With respect to child discipline, the maintenance of stable rules of conduct.

When parents fail to give children a good start in life, everybody suffers—the child, the parents, and society as a whole. Children need to grow up with a capacity for love, joy, fulfillment, responsibility, and self-control. Most people discipline their children in the same way they were disciplined. Unfortunately, this means many parents make the same mistakes their parents did (Covell, Grusec, & King, 1995).

Two key ingredients of effective parenting are communication and discipline. In each area, parents must strike a balance between freedom and guidance.

Consistency

How can parents strike a healthy balance? Children should feel free to express their deepest feelings through speech and actions. However, this does not mean they can do whatever they please. Rather, the child is allowed to move freely within well-defined boundaries for acceptable behaviour. Of course, individual parents may choose limits that are more "strict" or less "strict." But this choice is less important than **consistency** (maintaining stable rules of conduct). Consistent discipline gives a child a sense of security and stability. Inconsistency makes the child's world seem insecure and unpredictable.

What does consistent discipline mean in practice? To illustrate the errors parents often make, let's consider some examples of inconsistency (Fontenelle, 1989). The following are mistakes to avoid.

- Saying one thing and doing something else. You tell the child, "Bart, if you don't eat your brussels sprouts you can't have any dessert." Then you feel guilty and offer him some dessert.
- Making statements you don't mean. "If you don't quiet down, I'm going to stop the car and make you walk home."
- Overstating consequences. "Look what you did to the flower bed. You can't ever ride your bike again."
- Changing *no* to *yes*, especially to quiet a nagging child. A good example is the parent who first refuses to buy the child a toy and later gives in and buys it.
- Not checking to see if the child has actually done something you requested, such as picking up clothes or making a bed.
- Contradicting the rules your spouse has set for the child. Parents need to agree on guidelines for child discipline and not undermine each other's efforts.
- Not meaning what you say the first time. Children quickly learn how many times they can be warned before they are actually about to be punished.
- Responding differently to the same misbehaviour. One day a child is sent to his room for fighting with his sister. The next day the fighting is overlooked.

Random discipline makes children feel angry and confused because they cannot control the consequences of their own behaviour. Inconsistency also gives children the message: "Don't believe what I say because I usually don't mean it."

CONSTRUCTIVE DISCIPLINE At one time or another, most parents use power assertion, withdrawal of love, or management techniques to control their children. Each mode of discipline has its place. However, physical punishment and withdrawal of love should always be used with caution. Here are some guidelines.

1. Parents should separate disapproval of the act from disapproval of the child. Instead of saying, "I'm going to punish you because you are bad," say, "I'm upset about what you did."
2. State specifically what misbehaviour you are punishing. Explain why you have set limits on this kind of conduct.
3. Punishment should never be harsh or injurious. Don't physically punish a child while you are angry. Also remember that the message "I

don't love you right now" can be more painful and damaging than any spanking.
4. Punishment is most effective when it is administered immediately. This statement is especially true for younger children.
5. Spanking and other forms of physical punishment are not particularly effective for children under age two. The child will only be confused and frightened. Spankings also become less effective after age five because they tend to humiliate the child and breed resentment.
6. Many psychologists believe that children should never be spanked. If you do use physical punishment, reserve it for situations that pose an immediate danger to younger children; for example, when a child runs into the street.
7. Remember, too, that it is usually more effective to reward children when they are being good than it is to punish them for misbehaviour.

After age five, management techniques are the most effective form of discipline, especially techniques that emphasize communication and the relationship between parent and child.

The Parent–Child Relationship

The heart of child management is the relationship between parents and their children. Parenting experts Don Dinkmeyer and Gary McKay (1997) believe that there are four basic ingredients of positive parent–child interactions.

- *Mutual respect.* Effective parents try to avoid nagging, hitting, debating, and talking down to their children. They also avoid doing things for their children that children can do for themselves. (Constantly stripping children of opportunities to learn and take responsibility prevents them from becoming independent and developing self-esteem.)
- *Shared enjoyment.* Effective parents spend some time each day with their children, doing something that both the parent and child enjoy.
- *Love.* This goes almost without saying, but many parents assume their children know that they are loved. It is important to show them you care—in words and by actions such as hugging.
- *Encouragement.* Children who get frequent encouragement come to believe in themselves. Effective parents don't just praise their children for success, winning, or good behaviour. They also recognize a child's progress and attempts to improve. Show you have faith in children by letting them try things on their own and by encouraging their efforts.

Effective Communication

Creative communication is another important ingredient of successful child management (Bath, 1996). Child expert Haim Ginott (1965) believed that making a distinction between feelings and behaviour is the key to clear communication. Since children (and parents, too) do not choose how they feel, it is important to allow free expression of feelings.

ACCEPTING FEELINGS   The child who learns to regard some feelings as "bad," or unacceptable, is being asked to deny a very real part of his or her experience. Ginott encouraged parents to teach their children that all feelings are appropriate; it is only actions that are subject to disapproval. Many parents are unaware of just how often they block communication and the expression of feelings in their children. Consider this typical conversation excerpted from Ginott's book (1965):

> *Son:* I am stupid, and I know it. Look at my grades in school.
> *Father:* You just have to work harder.
> *Son:* I already work harder and it doesn't help. I have no brains.
> *Father:* You are smart, I know.
> *Son:* I am stupid, I know.

Father: (loudly) You are not stupid!

Son: Yes, I am!

Father: You are not stupid. Stupid!

By debating with the child, the father misses the point that his son feels stupid. It would be far more helpful for the father to encourage the boy to talk about his feelings.

How could he do that? He might say, "You really feel that you are not as smart as others, don't you? Do you feel this way often? Are you feeling bad at school?" In this way, the child is given a chance to express his emotions and to feel understood. The father might conclude by saying, "Look, son, in my eyes you are a fine person. But I understand how you feel. Everyone feels stupid at times."

ENCOURAGEMENT   Again, it is valuable to remember that supportive parents encourage their children. In terms of communication, encouragement sounds like this (Dinkmeyer, McKay, & Dinkmeyer, 1997):

"It looks like you enjoyed that."

"I have confidence in you; you'll make it."

"It was thoughtful of you to _____."

"Thanks. That helped a lot."

"You really worked hard on that."

"You're improving. Look at the progress you've made."

I-MESSAGES   Communication with a child can also be the basis of effective discipline. Thomas Gordon (1970), a child psychologist who developed a program called Parent Effectiveness Training (PET), offers a useful suggestion. Gordon believes that parents should send *I-messages* to their children, rather than *you-messages*.

What's the difference? **You-messages** take the form of threats, name-calling, accusing, bossing, lecturing, or criticizing. Generally, you-messages tell children what's "wrong" with them. An **I-message** tells children what effect their behaviour had on you. To illustrate the difference, consider this example. After a hard day's work, Susan wants to sit down and rest awhile. She begins to relax with a newspaper when her five-year-old daughter starts banging loudly on a toy drum. Most parents would respond with a you-message:

> **You-message**
> Threatening, accusing, bossing, lecturing, or criticizing another person.
>
> **I-message** A message that states the effect someone else's behaviour had on you.

"You go play outside this instant." (bossing)

"Don't ever make such a racket when someone is reading." (lecturing)

"You're really pushing it today, aren't you?" (accusing)

"You're a spoiled brat." (name-calling)

"You're going to get a spanking!" (threatening)

Gordon suggests sending an I-message such as "I am very tired, and I would like to read. I feel upset and can't read with so much noise." This forces the child to accept responsibility for the effects of her actions.

To summarize, an I-message states the behaviour to which you object. It then clearly tells the child the consequence of his or her behaviour and how that makes you feel. Here's a "fill-in-the-blanks" I-message: "When you (state the child's behaviour), I feel (state your feelings) because (state the consequences of the child's behaviour)." For example, "When you go to Jenny's without telling me, I worry that something might have happened to you because I don't know where you are" (Dinkmeyer, McKay, & Dinkmeyer, 1997).

Natural and Logical Consequences

Sometimes events automatically discourage misbehaviour. For example, a child who refuses to eat dinner will get uncomfortably hungry. A child who throws a temper

Natural consequences
The effects that naturally tend to follow a particular behaviour.

Logical consequences
Reasonable consequences that are defined by parents.

tantrum may gain nothing but a sore throat and a headache if the tantrum is ignored (Fontenelle, 1989). In such instances, the child's actions have **natural consequences** (intrinsic effects). In situations that don't produce natural consequences, parents can set up **logical consequences** (rational and reasonable effects). For example, a parent might say, "We'll go to the zoo when you've picked up all these toys," or "You can play with your dolls as soon as you've taken your bath," or "You two can stop arguing or leave the table until you're ready to join us."

The concept of logical, parent-defined consequences can be combined with I-messages to handle many day-to-day instances of misbehaviour. The key idea is to use an I-message to set up consequences and then give the child a choice to make: "Michelle, we're trying to watch TV. You may settle down and watch with us or go play elsewhere. You decide which you'd rather do" (Dinkmeyer, McKay, & Dinkmeyer, 1997).

How could Susan have dealt with her five-year-old—the one who was banging on a drum? A response that combines an I-message with logical consequences would be, "I would like for you to stop banging on that drum; otherwise, please take it outside." If the child continues to bang on the drum inside the house, then she has caused the toy to be put away. If she takes it outside, she has made a decision to play with the drum in a way that respects her mother's wishes. In this way, both parent and child have been allowed to maintain a sense of self-respect and a needless clash has been averted.

After you have stated consequences and let the child decide, be sure to respect the child's choice. If the child repeats the misbehaviour, you can let the consequences remain in effect longer. But later, give the child another chance to cooperate.

With all child management techniques, remember to be firm, kind, consistent, respectful, and encouraging. And most of all, try every day to live the message you wish to communicate.

Knowledge builder

PARENTING AND CHILD DISCIPLINE

Relate

What do you think are the best ways to balance freedom and restraint in child discipline? Parents can probably never be completely consistent. Think of a time when your parents were inconsistent in disciplining you. How did it affect you?

To what extent do the four basic ingredients of positive parent–child interactions apply to any healthy relationship?

Think of a you-message you have recently given a child, family member, roommate, or spouse. Can you change it into an I-message?

Learning Check

1. Effective discipline gives children freedom within a structure of consistent and well-defined limits. T or F?
2. One good way to maintain consistency in child management is to overstate the consequences for misbehaviour. T or F?
3. Spankings and other physical punishments are most effective for children under the age of two. T or F?
4. Giving recognition for progress and attempts to improve is an example of parental _____.
5. I-messages are a gentle way of accusing a child of misbehaviour. T or F?
6. In situations where natural consequences are unavailable or do not discourage misbehaviour, parents should define logical consequences for a child. T or F?

Critical Thinking

7. Several Scandinavian countries have made it illegal for parents to spank their own children. Does this infringe on the rights of parents?

Answers:

1. T 2. F 3. F 4. encouragement 5. F 6. T 7. Such laws are based on the view that it should be illegal to physically assault any person, regardless of their age. While parents may believe they have a "right" to spank their children, it can be argued that children need special protection because they are small, powerless, and dependent.

Psychologist's Journal

EPILOGUE

Here's some final advice for Tom and Olivia: As mentioned earlier, spoiling very young infants is nearly impossible. From about age two on, however, parents are asking for trouble if they do everything and buy everything they can for a child, no matter what. For example, every morning, Derek's mother drills him with flashcards in hopes that he will learn to read before any of the neighbour children. In the afternoon, Derek watches educational videotapes about premath skills. Every evening, a Mozart sonata fills Derek's room, which is knee-deep in toys. Derek is taking dancing lessons and learning sign language. His favourite toy is a fake cellphone. Is this enrichment? It depends. Derek is two-and-a-half. His parents obviously mean well. But by the time he is five, if Derek's parents ask him to change a light bulb, he is likely to hold it in the socket and wait for the world to revolve around him. As this example suggests, "enrichment" that does not match a child's needs is of little value.

Psychologists are highly critical of misguided attempts to produce "super babies" by pushing the pace of development. Overloading a toddler with a barrage of stimuli, flash cards, and exercises is not enriching. True enrichment does not make the child feel pressured to perform. Instead, it should foster interest, enthusiasm, and a desire to learn (Eliot, 1999). Here is a final summary of many of the points we have discussed in this chapter, in the words of child experts Ann Barnet and Richard Barnet (1998):

Babies need closeness, nurture, communication, play, and engagement; they need quiet, stability, and predictability. They need challenge, the stimulation of new experiences, and the opportunity to explore their surroundings in safety. All children need to feel that they are treasured, that their developmental accomplishments are celebrated, and that their parents' devotion is rock solid.

CHAPTER IN REVIEW

Major Points

▶ You are a product of both your genetic heritage and the environments in which you have lived.

▶ Infant development is strongly influenced by heredity. However, environmental factors such as nutrition, parenting, and learning are also important.

▶ Forming an emotional bond with a caregiver is a crucial event during infancy.

▶ Learning to use language is a cornerstone of early intellectual development.

▶ Piaget's stage theory provides a valuable map of how thinking abilities unfold.

▶ Vygotsky's theory reminds us that a child's mind is shaped by human relationships.

▶ Erik Erikson identified a series of challenges that occur across the life span. These range from a need to gain trust in infancy to the need to live with integrity in old age.

▶ Effective child discipline is consistent, humane, encouraging, and based on respectful communication.

Summary

How Do Heredity and Environment Affect Development?

• The nature–nurture controversy concerns the relative contributions to development of heredity (nature) and environment (nurture).

• Hereditary instructions are carried by the chromosomes and genes in each cell of the body. Most characteristics are polygenic and reflect the combined effects of dominant and recessive genes.

• Heredity is also involved in differences in temperament. Most infants fall into one of three temperament categories: easy children, difficult children, and slow-to-warm-up children.

• During critical periods in development, infants experience an increased sensitivity to specific environmental influences.

• Prenatal development is subject to environmental influences in the form of diseases, drugs, radiation, and the mother's diet, health, and emotions. Various teratogens

can cause prenatal damage to the fetus, resulting in congenital problems.
- Early perceptual, intellectual, and emotional deprivation seriously retards development.
- Deliberate enrichment of the environment has a beneficial effect on development in infancy.
- Heredity and environment are inseparable and interacting forces. Therefore, a child's developmental level reflects heredity, environment, and the effects of the child's own behaviour.

What Can Newborn Babies Do?
- The human neonate has a number of adaptive reflexes, including the grasping, rooting, sucking, and Moro reflexes. Neonates show immediate evidence of learning and of appreciating the consequences of their actions.
- Tests in a looking chamber reveal a number of visual preferences in the newborn. The neonate is drawn to bright lights and circular or curved designs.
- Infants prefer human face patterns, especially familiar faces. In later infancy, interest in the unfamiliar emerges.

What Influence Does Maturation Have on Early Development?
- Maturation of the body and nervous system underlies the orderly sequence of motor, cognitive, emotional, and language development.
- The rate of maturation, however, varies from person to person. Also, learning contributes greatly to the development of basic motor skills.
- Emotions develop in a consistent order from the generalized excitement observed in newborn babies. Three of the basic emotions—fear, anger, and joy—may be unlearned.
- Many early skills are subject to the principle of readiness.

Of What Significance Is a Child's Emotional Bond with Parents?
- Emotional attachment of human infants is a critical early event.
- Infant attachment is reflected by separation anxiety. The quality of attachment can be classified as secure, insecure-avoidant, or insecure-ambivalent.
- High-quality day care does not appear to harm children. Low-quality care can be risky.
- Meeting a baby's affectional needs is as important as meeting needs for physical care.

How Important Are Parenting Styles?
- Studies suggest that caregiving styles have a substantial impact on emotional and intellectual development.
- Whereas mothers typically emphasize caregiving, fathers tend to function as playmates for infants.
- Optimal caregiving includes proactive maternal involvement, responsiveness to a child's needs and signals, and a good fit between the temperaments of parents and their children.

- Three major parental styles are authoritarian, permissive, and authoritative (effective). When judged by its effects on children, authoritative parenting appears to benefit children the most.
- Effective parental discipline tends to emphasize child management techniques (especially communication), rather than power assertion or withdrawal of love.

How Do Children Acquire Language?
- Language development proceeds from control of crying, to cooing, to babbling, to the use of single words, to telegraphic speech.
- The underlying patterns of telegraphic speech suggest a biological predisposition to acquire language. This innate predisposition is augmented by learning.
- Prelanguage communication between parent and child involves shared rhythms, non-verbal signals, and turn-taking.
- Motherese or parentese is a simplified, musical style of speaking used by parents to help their children learn language.

How Do Children Learn to Think?
- The intellect of a child is less abstract than that of an adult. Jean Piaget theorized that intellectual growth occurs through a combination of assimilation and accommodation.
- Piaget also held that children go through a fixed series of cognitive stages. The stages and their approximate age ranges are: sensorimotor (0–2), preoperational (2–7), concrete operational (7–11), and formal operations (11 to adult).
- Learning principles provide an alternative explanation that assumes cognitive development is continuous; it does not occur in stages.
- Recent studies of infants under the age of one year suggest that they are capable of thought well beyond that observed by Piaget.
- Lev Vygotsky's sociocultural theory emphasizes that a child's mental abilities are advanced by interactions with more competent partners. Mental growth takes place in a child's zone of proximal development, where a more skillful person may scaffold the child's progress.

What Are the Typical Tasks and Dilemmas Through the Life Span?
- According to Erikson, each life stage provokes a specific psychosocial dilemma.
- In addition to the dilemmas identified by Erikson, we recognize that each life stage requires successful mastery of certain developmental tasks.

How Do Effective Parents Discipline Their Children?
- Responsibility, mutual respect, consistency, love, encouragement, and clear communication are features of effective parenting.
- Much misbehaviour can be managed by use of I-messages and the application of natural and logical consequences.

PSYCHOLOGY ON THE NET

If you have difficulty finding any of the sites listed here, visit http://psychologyjourney.nelson.com for an updated list of Internet addresses and direct links to relevant sites.

Canadian Health Network This accessible site provides a great deal of information for parents and includes a searchable database.
http://www.canadian-health-network.ca/

Diving into the Gene Pool From the Exploratorium, this site teaches about modern genetics. http://www.exploratorium.edu/genepool/genepool_home.html

Human Relations Publications Covers over 50 topics spanning the entire range of human development.
http://muextension.missouri.edu/xplor/hesguide/humanrel/

I Am Your Child Information for parents of children up to three years of age. http://www.iamyourchild.org/

Invest in Kids This national non-profit organization is devoted to helping parents make the most of their children's first five years. http://www.investinkids.ca

Nanny's Place for Parents Comprehensive site full of links for expectant couples and new parents.
http://www.moonlily.com/parents

The NICHD Study of Early Child Care A summary of the findings of a major study on the effects of day care.
http://www.nichd.nih.gov/publications/pubs/early_child_care.htm

Parenthood Web A comprehensive site for parents.
http://www.parenthoodweb.com/

Sesame Street Parents An expert description of physical development from birth to age 11.
http://www.sesameworkshop.com/parents/

 InfoTrac College Edition For recent articles related to Piaget and Vygotsky, use Key Words search for COGNITION IN INFANTS.

INTERACTIVE LEARNING

Psychology: An Interactive Journey Remember that Chapter 3 of the CD-ROM that came with this text has practice tests, flashcards, interactive exercises, a crossword puzzle, and other valuable materials to enhance your learning experience.

PsychNow! 6a. Infant Development, 6b. Child Development, 6c. Adolescent Development, 6d. Adult Development, Aging, and Death

Psyk.trek 9. Human Development

Chart Your Progress

The questions that follow are only a sample of what you need to know. If you miss any of the items, you should review the entire chapter, do the exercises on the CD, and review the Knowledge Builders. Another way to prepare for tests is to get more practice with *WebTutor*, the *Study Guide*, or the *Practice Quizzes* that are available with this text.

1. If a personal trait is controlled by a single dominant gene, the trait cannot be
   a. hereditary
   b. related to DNA sequences
   c. influenced by chromosomes
   d. polygenic

2. The influence of heredity on early child development is most clearly shown by
   a. differences in temperament
   b. the existence of critical periods
   c. congenital problems
   d. the effects of teratogens

3. Cephalocaudal and proximodistal patterns show the effects of _____ on motor development.
   a. enriched environments
   b. maturation
   c. scaffolding
   d. critical periods

4. A baby who turns away from his mother when she returns after a brief separation shows signs of having which type of attachment?
   a. insecure-avoidant
   b. insecure-ambivalent
   c. solitary-ambivalent
   d. maternal-disaffectional

5. Psychologist Diana Baumrind describes parents who enforce rigid rules and demand strict obedience as
   a. authoritative
   b. permissive-repressive
   c. proactive-reactive
   d. authoritarian

6. Turn-taking with non-verbal signals is a first step toward
   a. secure attachment
   b. verbal expansion
   c. using language
   d. gaining an ability to make transformations

7. According to Piaget, a child's mastery of conservation occurs during the
   a. formal operations stage
   b. preoperational stage
   c. concrete operational stage
   d. sensorimotor stage

8. Vygotsky believed that adults help children learn how to think by using a process he called
   a. reversible thinking
   b. scaffolding
   c. accommodation
   d. egocentric reasoning

9. According to Erikson, the dilemma faced by most three- to five-year-olds is
   a. autonomy versus shame and doubt
   b. initiative versus guilt
   c. trust versus mistrust
   d. industry versus inferiority

10. Which type of child discipline takes the form of threats, name-calling, accusing, bossing, lecturing, or criticizing?
    a. I-messages
    b. you-messages
    c. logical consequences
    d. natural consequences

Answers: 1. d 2. a 3. b 4. a 5. d 6. c 7. c 8. b 9. b 10. b

Chapter 4

Psychologist's Journal

CIRCLING THE TRUTH

The truth is out there, we're told. So are automobiles, power tools, chipmunks, and millions of other things that we can recognize—by sight, sound, smell, or with some other sense. How do we do it? How, for example, do we know what any visual object looks like?

One of the ways we investigate this issue is by studying illusions, such as the Ebbinghaus illusion shown in the illustration below. The two central circles are actually the same size, but most people perceive the one surrounded by larger circles as being smaller than the other one. Why do we do that? University of Western Ontario psychologists Mel Goodale and Angela Haffenden asked people to estimate the size of central circles in displays made from real circular objects like pucks. As expected, the resulting estimates showed the Ebbinghaus illusion. Then Haffenden and Goodale asked the same people to reach out and pick up the central circles. As the subjects did this, their grasp aperture (the distance between thumb and fingers) was measured—and no Ebbinghaus illusion appeared. Grasp aperture was the same for both central circles, regardless of the size of the surrounding circles (Haffenden & Goodale, 1998, 2000). They argued that this was evidence for two visual systems—a seeing system and an action system.

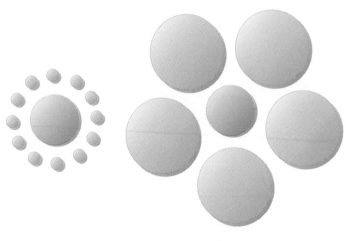

What this result means is that accurate information about the target circle sizes was available in these participants' brains, but did not make it up to their awareness. Why not? To understand this, it may help to think about how some non-human animals perceive the world. Most animals have a very different visual experience of the world than we do. Horses, for example, distinguish red from blue quite well, but have trouble telling yellow from green. Bats "see" by something like radar, bouncing high-pitched squeaks off objects in front of them and reading the returning sound waves. These simpler systems work because animals don't need to see "everything." They need to see only the things that matter—things they might eat or that might eat them, for example. Humans are different. We have a much larger repertoire of possible behaviours, so we need to see the world in more detail. To do that fast enough, we take information provided by the senses and combine it with expectations about what is probably out there, producing our elaborate perception of the world around us. Computing what is out there is faster than actually analyzing the sensory input in minute detail. Most of the time, this operation works well, but sometimes it produces illusions. The seeing system computes what is out there and can make the odd mistake without compromising responses guided by the independent action system.

Without the senses, we would live in a void of darkness and silence. The next time you drink in the beauty of a sunset, a flower, or a friend, remember this: Sensation makes it all possible. Yet, sensing the world is not enough. As the Ebbinghaus circles and other illusions show, sensory information can be interpreted in various ways. In this chapter, we will begin with a look at how the senses operate. Then we will discuss how we assemble sensations into a meaningful "picture" or model of the world. Our perceptions create faces, melodies, works of art, and on occasion, illusions. Let's see how this takes place.

Survey Questions

- In general, how do sensory systems function?
- How is vision accomplished?
- What are the mechanisms of hearing?
- How do the chemical senses operate?
- What are the somesthetic senses and why are they important?
- Why are we more aware of some sensations than others?
- How do perceptual constancies affect our perceptions?
- What basic principles do we use to group sensations into meaningful patterns?
- How is it possible to see depth and judge distance?
- How is perception altered by learning, expectations, and motives?
- Is extrasensory perception possible?
- What can be done to enhance perceptual accuracy?

▶ Sensory Systems—What You See Is What You Get

Survey Question:
■ In general, how do sensory systems function?

Data reduction system
Any system that selects, analyzes, or condenses information.

Transducer A device that converts energy from one system into energy in another.

Sensory analysis
Separation of sensory information into important elements.

Perceptual features Basic elements of a stimulus, such as lines, shapes, edges, or colours.

Feature detector A sensory system highly attuned to a specific stimulus pattern.

Sensory coding Codes used by the sense organs to transmit information to the brain.

Sensory localization The principle that the type of sensation experienced is related to the area of the brain activated.

Vision gives us amazingly wide access to the world. In one instant you can view a star light-years away, and in the next, you can peer into the microscopic universe of a dewdrop. Yet, vision also narrows what we observe. Like the other senses, vision acts as a **data reduction system.** It selects, analyzes, and filters information until only the most important data remain.

How does data reduction take place? Some selection occurs because sensory receptors are biological transducers. A **transducer** is a device that converts one kind of energy into another. For example, an electric guitar converts string vibrations into electrical signals, which are amplified and fed to a speaker. Pluck a string and the speaker will blast out sound. However, if you shine a light on the string, or pour cold water on it, the speaker will remain silent. (The owner of the guitar, however, might get quite loud at this point!) Similarly, each sensory organ is most sensitive to a select type and range of energy that it converts to nerve impulses. For instance, visible light is just a small slice of the electromagnetic spectrum (entire spread of electromagnetic wavelengths). The spectrum also includes infrared and ultraviolet light, radio waves, television broadcasts, gamma rays, and other energies (see Figure 4.3 on page 118). If your eyes weren't limited in sensitivity, you would be able to "see" a disorienting jumble of different energies.

What we experience is also influenced by **sensory analysis,** which divides the world into important **perceptual features** (basic stimulus patterns). For vision, examples are lines, shapes, edges, spots, and colours (see ▶Figure 4.1). Reading the letters on this page is a direct result of sensory analysis (Hubel, 1979b; Hubel & Wiesel, 1979). In some instances, the senses act as **feature detectors** to pick up very specific patterns. Frog eyes, for example, are especially sensitive to small, dark, moving spots. They are basically "wired" to detect bugs flying nearby (Lettvin, 1961). But the insect (spot) must be moving, or the frog's "bug detectors" won't work. A frog could starve to death surrounded by dead flies.

After they have selected and analyzed information, sensory systems must code it. **Sensory coding** refers to converting important features of the world into neural messages understood by the brain (Hubel & Wiesel, 1979). To see coding at work, try closing your eyes for a moment. Then take your fingertips and press firmly on your eyelids. Apply enough pressure to "squash" your eyes slightly. Do this for about 30 seconds and observe what happens. (Readers with eye problems or contact lenses should not try this.)

Did you "see" stars, checkerboards, and flashes of colour? These are called _phosphenes_ (FOSS-feens: visual sensations caused by mechanical excitation of the retina). They occur because the eye's receptor cells, which normally respond to light, are also somewhat sensitive to pressure. Notice though, that the eye is only prepared to code stimulation—including pressure—into visual features. As a result, you experience light sensations, not pressure. Also important in producing this effect is sensory localization in the brain.

What does that mean? **Sensory localization** means that the type of sensation you experience depends on which area of the brain is activated. Some brain areas receive visual

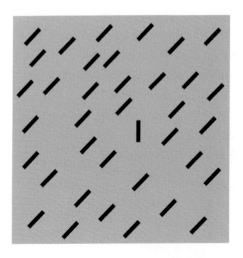

▶Figure 4.1

Notice how eye-catching the single vertical line is among a group of slanted lines. This visual effect is known as pop-out. Pop-out occurs because the visual system is highly sensitive to elementary visual features, such as colours, shapes, and lines. Identification of such features appears to take place very early in the processing of visual information. (Adapted from Ramachandran, 1992b.) Pop-out is so basic that babies as young as three months respond to it (Quinn & Bhatt, 1998).

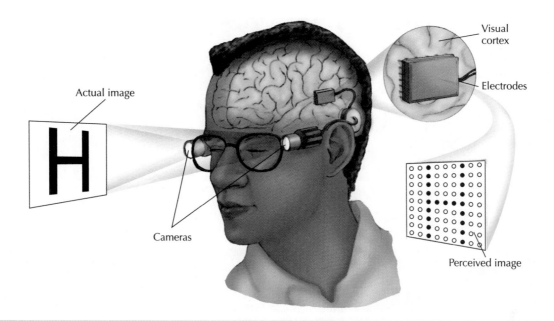

Actual image

Visual cortex

Electrodes

Cameras

Perceived image

▶**Figure 4.2**

In this artificial visual system, TV cameras mounted on a pair of glasses transmit electrical signals to a grid of tiny electrodes placed in the visual areas of the brain (shown in cutaway view). One man who has an experimental implant of this type can "see" 100 dots of light. Like a sports scoreboard, these lights can be used to form crude letters. Researchers are also working on software that alters the TV image so that the edges of objects are accentuated (Dobelle, 2000). This, plus a larger number of dots, could make reading and the perception of large objects, such as furniture and doorways, possible (Normann et al., 1999). A major barrier to such systems is the brain's tendency to reject implanted electrodes.

Sensation A sensory impression; also, the process of detecting physical energies with the sensory organs.

Perception The mental process of organizing sensations into meaningful patterns.

information; others receive auditory information; still others receive taste or touch (see Chapter 2). Knowing which brain areas are active tells us, in general, what kinds of sensations you are feeling. Sensory localization may someday make it possible to artificially stimulate the brain to restore sight, hearing, or other senses. Researchers have already used a miniature television camera to send electrical signals to the visual cortex of the brain (Dobelle, 2000; Normann et al., 1999). (See ▶Figure 4.2.) Unfortunately, artificial vision still faces major hurdles. However, artificial hearing is proving more workable—as we will see later.

It is fascinating to realize that "seeing" and "hearing" take place in the brain, not in the eye or ear. Information arriving from the sense organs creates **sensations.** When the brain organizes sensations into meaningful patterns, we speak of **perception,** which will be covered later. For now, it's time to explore the senses in more detail. Let's begin with vision, the most magnificent sensory system of all.

▶ Vision—Catching Some Rays

Survey Question:
■ How is vision accomplished?

Recently, researchers at the University of Ottawa found that certain fish use electric fields to see: these fish produce an electrical field that surrounds their body. Any object that moves into the field distorts it, and that distortion is registered by the fish's nervous system, giving the distance and size of the object (Lewis & Maler, 2001). Can you imagine what it would be like to see in such a way? There would be very little detail and no colour. Human vision is quite different.

Visible spectrum That part of the electromagnetic spectrum to which the eyes are sensitive.

Hue Classification of colours into basic categories of red, orange, yellow, green, blue, indigo, and violet.

As we have noted, various wavelengths of light make up the **visible spectrum** (electromagnetic energies to which the eyes respond). Visible light starts at "short" wavelengths of 400 *nanometres* (nan-OM-et-er: one billionth of a metre), which produce sensations of purple or violet. Longer waves of light produce blue, green, yellow, and orange, until we reach red, with a wavelength of 700 nanometres (see ▶Figure 4.3).

The term **hue** refers to the basic colour categories of red, orange, yellow, green, blue, indigo, and violet. As we have seen, various hues (or colour sensations) correspond to

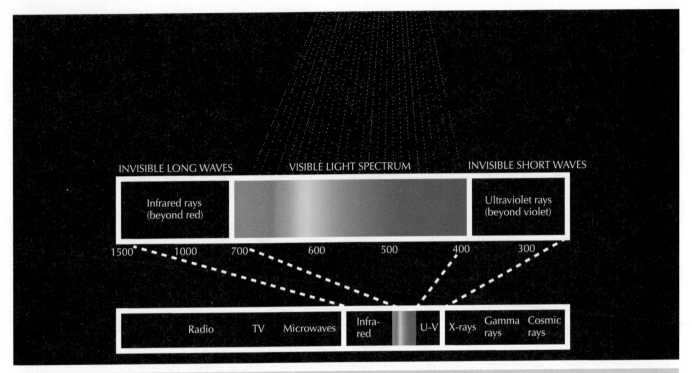

▶Figure 4.3

The visible spectrum.

Saturation The degree of a colour's purity.

Brightness The intensity of lights or colours.

Lens Structure in the eye that focuses light rays.

Photoreceptor A sensory receptor for light.

Retina The light-sensitive layer of cells at the back of the eye.

Cornea Transparent membrane covering the front of the eye.

Accommodation Changes in the shape of the lens of the eye.

Hyperopia Difficulty focusing nearby objects (farsightedness).

Myopia Difficulty focusing distant objects (nearsightedness).

Astigmatism Defects in the cornea, lens, or eye that cause some areas of vision to be out of focus.

light's wavelength. White light, in contrast, is a mixture of many wavelengths. Hues (colours) from a narrow band of wavelengths are very **saturated,** or "pure." (An intense "fire-engine" red is more saturated than a muddy "brick" red.) A third dimension of vision, **brightness,** corresponds roughly to the amplitude, or height, of light waves. Waves of greater amplitude are "taller," carry more energy, and cause colours to appear brighter or more intense. For example, the same "brick" red would look bright under intense, high-energy illumination and drab under dim light.

Structure of the Eye

Is it true that the eye is like a camera? In some ways, it is. Both cameras and eyes have a **lens** to focus images on a light-sensitive layer at the back of a closed space. In a camera, this layer is the film. In the eye, it is a layer of **photoreceptors** (light-sensitive cells). These cells are part of the **retina,** a receiving area for images that is about the size and thickness of a postage stamp (see ▶Figure 4.4).

How does the eye focus? Most focusing is done at the front of the eye by the **cornea,** a clear membrane that bends light inward. Smaller adjustments are made by the lens. The shape of the lens is altered by attached muscles, in a process called **accommodation.** In cameras, focusing is done more simply—by changing the distance between the lens and the film.

VISUAL PROBLEMS   The shape of the eye also affects focusing. If your eye is too short, you won't be able to focus nearby objects, but distant objects will be sharp. This is called **hyperopia** (HI-per-OPE-ee-ah: farsightedness). If your eyeball is too long, the image will fall short of the retina, and distant objects cannot be focused. This results in **myopia** (my-OPE-ee-ah: nearsightedness). When the cornea or the lens is misshapen, part of vision will be focused and part will be fuzzy. In this case, the eye has more than one focal point, a problem called **astigmatism** (ah-STIG-mah-tiz-em). All three visual defects can be corrected by placing glasses (or contact lenses) in front of the eye to change the path of light (see ▶Figure 4.5).

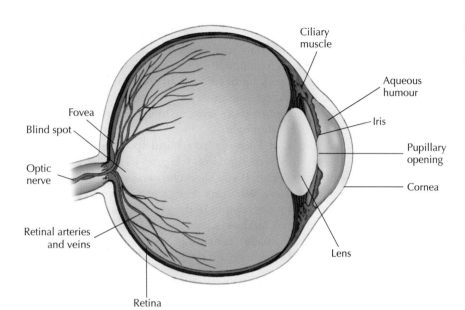

The human eye—a simplified view.

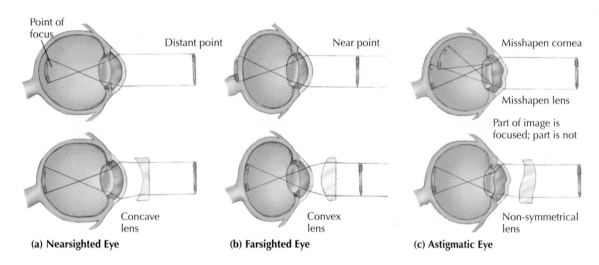

(a) **Nearsighted Eye**　　(b) **Farsighted Eye**　　(c) **Astigmatic Eye**

▶**Figure 4.5**

Visual defects and corrective lenses: *(a)* A myopic (longer than usual) eye. The concave lens spreads light rays just enough to increase the eye's focal length. *(b)* A hyperopic (shorter than usual) eye. The convex lens increases refraction (bending), returning the point of focus to the retina. *(c)* An astigmatic (lens or cornea not symmetrical) eye. In astigmatism, parts of vision are sharp and parts are unfocused. Lenses to correct astigmatism are non-symmetrical.

Presbyopia Farsightedness caused by aging.

As people age, the lens becomes less flexible and less able to accommodate. The result is **presbyopia** (prez-bee-OPE-ee-ah: old vision, or farsightedness due to aging). Perhaps you have seen a grandparent or older friend reading a newspaper at arm's length because of presbyopia. If you now wear glasses for nearsightedness, you may need bifocals as you age. (Unless your arms grow longer in the meantime.) Bifocal lenses correct near vision and distance vision.

As an interesting footnote to this discussion, some evidence suggests that there are cross-cultural differences in willingness to report visual problems. Researchers at the Municipal Institute of Medical Research in Spain studied more than 1400 patients who were about to have cataract surgery. These patients came from Canada, the United States, Spain, and Denmark. Among other findings, Canadian and Spanish patients were *less* likely to report a great deal of visual trouble than Danish and U.S. patients matched with them in terms of the severity of their clinical symptoms (Alonso et al., 1998).

Rods and Cones

Unlike a camera, the eye has two types of "film" consisting of receptor cells called rods and cones. The **cones,** numbering about 6.5 million in each eye, work best in bright light. They also produce colour sensations and pick up fine details. In contrast, the **rods,** numbering about 100 million, are unable to detect colours (see ▶Figure 4.6). Pure rod vision is black and white. However, the rods are much more sensitive to light than the cones are. The rods therefore allow us to see in very dim light.

Surprisingly, the retina has a "hole" in it: Each eye has a **blind spot** because there are no receptors where the optic nerve leaves the eye (see ▶Figure 4.7a). The blind spot shows that vision depends greatly on the brain. If you close one eye, part of what you see will fall on the blind spot of your open eye. Why isn't there a gap in your vision? The answer is that the visual cortex of the brain actively fills in the gap with patterns from surrounding areas (Figure 4.7b). According to folklore, King Charles II of England used to amuse himself by closing one eye and visually "beheading" members of his court by placing their images on his blind spot (Ramachandran, 1992a, 1992b). (Just a hint.)

VISUAL ACUITY　The rods and cones also affect **visual acuity,** or sharpness. The cones lie mainly at the centre of the eye. In fact, the **fovea** (FOE-vee-ah: a small cup-shaped area in the middle of the retina) contains only cones—about 50 000 of them. If you look at your thumbnail at arm's length, its image just about covers the fovea. Like a newspaper photograph made of many small dots, the tightly packed cones in the fovea produce the sharpest images. ▶Figure 4.8 describes a widely used rating system for acuity. If vision can be corrected to no better than 20/200 acuity, a person is considered legally blind. With 20/200 vision, the world is seen as nothing but a blur.

While acuity is determined by basic characteristics of the eye, it can have profound consequences on higher thought processes. As an example, Renata Harland and Stanley Coren of the University of British Columbia recently found that people with poor visual acuity scored poorly on tests of divergent thinking (in this case, thinking up alternative uses for familiar objects). They suggested that poor acuity might compromise use of visual imagery in this task (Harland & Coren, 2001). In other words, impoverished visual expe-

Cones　Visual receptors for colours and daylight visual acuity.

Rods　Visual receptors for dim light that produce only black-and-white sensations.

Blind spot　An area of the retina lacking visual receptors.

Visual acuity　The sharpness of visual perception.

Fovea　An area at the centre of the retina containing only cones.

▶Figure 4.6

Anatomy of the retina, the light-sensitive element of the eye. The retina lies behind the vitreous humour, which is the jelly-like substance that fills the eyeball. Note that light does not fall directly on the rods and cones. It must first pass through the outer layers of the retina, made up of additional nerve cells. Only about one half of the light falling on the front of the eye reaches the rods and cones—testimony to the eye's amazing light sensitivity. The rods and cones are much smaller than implied here. The smallest receptors are 1 micron (one millionth of a metre) wide.

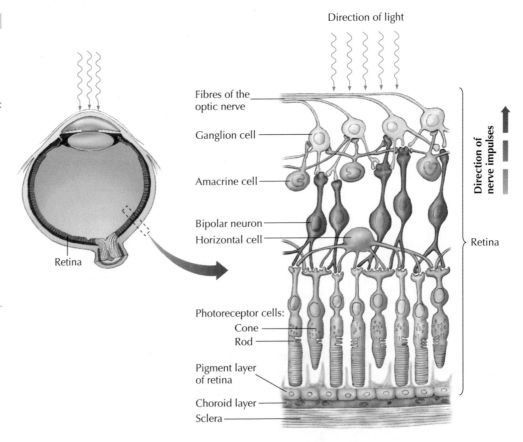

Experiencing the blind spot. *(a)* With your right eye closed, stare at the upper right cross. Hold the book about 30 centimetres from your eye and slowly move it back and forth. You should be able to locate a position that causes the black spot to disappear. When it does, it has fallen on the blind spot. With a little practice you can learn to make people or objects you dislike disappear too! *(b)* Repeat the procedure described, but stare at the lower cross. When the white space falls on the blind spot, the black lines will appear to be continuous. This may help you understand why you do not usually experience a blind spot in your visual field.

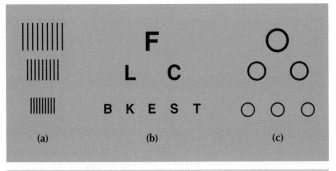

▶**Figure 4.8**

Tests of visual acuity. Here are some common tests of visual acuity. In *(a)*, sharpness is indicated by the smallest grating still seen as individual lines. The Snellen chart *(b)* requires that you read rows of letters of diminishing size until you can no longer distinguish them. The Landolt rings *(c)* require no familiarity with letters. All that is required is a report of which side has a break in it. Normal acuity is designated as 20/20 vision: At 20 feet (6 metres) in distance, you can distinguish what the average person can see at 20 feet. If your vision is 20/40, you can see at 20 feet only what the average person can see at 40 feet (12 metres). If your vision is 20/200, you need glasses! Vision that is 20/12 would mean that you can see at 20 feet what the average person must be 8 feet (2.4 metres) nearer to see, indicating better than average acuity. American astronaut Gordon Cooper, who claimed to see railroad lines in northern India from 100 miles (160 kilometres) above, had 20/12 acuity.

rience due to poor acuity impairs the ability to imagine a solution to a problem.

PERIPHERAL VISION   *What is the purpose of the rest of the retina?* Areas outside the fovea also get light, creating a large region of **peripheral** (side) **vision.** The rods are most numerous about 20 degrees from the centre of the retina, so much of our peripheral vision is rod vision. Although rod vision is not very sharp, the rods maintain a radar-like scan for movement in peripheral vision. The rods are also highly responsive to dim light. Because most rods are 20 degrees to each side of the fovea, the best night vision is obtained by looking next to an object you wish to see. Test this yourself some night by looking at, and next to, a very dim star.

Two Visual Systems

About 15 years ago, a young Scottish woman suffered carbon monoxide intoxication—she breathed enough *CO* to damage her brain. The damage left her unable to see any objects in the world—she is completely unable to tell the shape of any object, or whether it is upside-down, right-side up, or leaning. But, surprisingly, she is able to *do* things with objects, in spite of being unaware of them. For example, she can reach out and pick up an object she could not identify. Her grasp aperture is appropriate, and she reaches to the right point in space.

According to the neuropsychologists who have studied her, Mel Goodale at the University of Western Ontario and David Milner at St. Andrews University, this patient's pattern of spared and lost abilities reflects the separation between vision-for-action and vision-for-perception (Goodale, 1996; Goodale & Milner, 1992; Milner & Goodale, 1995). One system delivers information about what is out there in the world; the other guides our physical movements—reaching, grasping, aiming, walking around, and so on.

In one test, the Scottish patient was shown a device with a slot in it, like the slot in a mailbox. The slot could be rotated to any angle. The patient was completely unable to verbally report the angle the slot was at on any trial. She was also unable to report the angle by holding up a card set to the same angle. But when she was asked to "post" a card (put it

Peripheral vision Vision at the edges of the visual field.

Trichromatic theory Theory of colour vision based on three cone types: red, green, and blue.

Opponent-process theory Theory of colour vision based on three coding systems (red or green, yellow or blue, black or white).

Afterimage Visual sensation that persists after a stimulus is removed.

Visual pigments Light-sensitive chemicals found in the rods and cones.

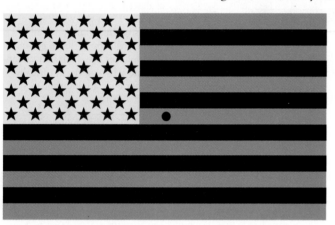

▶**Figure 4.9**

Negative afterimages. Stare at the dot near the middle of the flag for at least 30 seconds. Then look immediately at a plain sheet of white paper or a white wall. You will see the American flag in its normal colours. Reduced sensitivity to yellow, green, and black in the visual system, caused by prolonged staring, results in the appearance of complementary colours. Project the afterimage of the flag on other coloured surfaces to get additional effects.

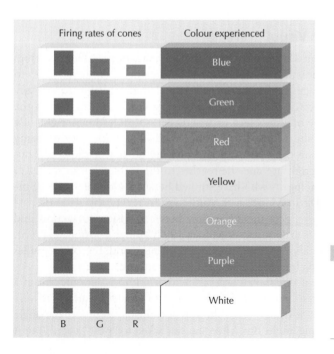

▶**Figure 4.10**

Firing rates of blue, green, and red cones in response to different colours. The taller the coloured bar, the higher the firing rates for that type of cone. As you can see, colours are coded by differences in the activity of all three types of cones in the normal eye. (Adapted from Goldstein, 1999.)

in the slot as if she was posting a letter), she did so as efficiently as a sighted control subject (Goodale et al., 1991). Goodale and his colleagues argued that this patient's brain damage affected her visual perception system, but left her visually guided action system intact.

Colour Vision

How do the cones produce colour sensations? No short answer can do justice to colour vision, but briefly, here is the best current explanation. The **trichromatic theory** (TRY-kro-MAT-ik) holds that there are three types of cones, each most sensitive to red, green, or blue. Other colours result from combinations of these three. Black-and-white sensations are produced by the rods.

A basic problem with the trichromatic theory is that four colours of light—red, green, blue, and yellow—seem to be primary (you can't get them by mixing other colours). Also, why is it impossible to have a reddish green or a yellowish blue? A second view, known as the **opponent-process theory,** states that vision analyzes colours into "either-or" messages. That is, the visual system can produce messages for red or green, yellow or blue, black or white. Coding one colour in a pair (red, for instance) seems to block the opposite message (green) from coming through. As a result, a reddish green is impossible, but a yellowish red (orange) can occur.

According to opponent-process theory, fatigue caused by making one response produces an afterimage of the opposite colour as the system recovers. **Afterimages** are visual sensations that persist after a stimulus is removed—like seeing a spot after a flashbulb goes off. To see an afterimage of the type predicted by opponent-process theory, look at ▶Figure 4.9 and follow the instructions there.

Which colour theory is correct? Both! The three-colour theory applies to the retina, where three types of **visual pigments** (light-sensitive chemicals) have been found. As predicted, each pigment is most sensitive to light in roughly the red, green, or blue region. As a result, the three types of cones fire nerve impulses at different rates when various colours are viewed (see ▶Figure 4.10).

In contrast, the opponent-process theory seems to explain what happens in optic pathways and the brain after information leaves the eye. For example, nerve cells can be found in the brain that are excited by the colour red and inhibited by the colour green. So both theories are "correct." One explains what happens in the eye itself. The other explains how colours are analyzed after messages leave the eye.

Colour blindness A total inability to perceive colours.

Colour weakness An inability to distinguish some colours.

Dark adaptation Increased retinal sensitivity to light.

COLOUR BLINDNESS Do you know anyone who regularly draws hoots of laughter by wearing clothes of wildly clashing colours? Or someone who sheepishly tries to avoid saying what colour an object is? If so, you probably know someone who is colour-blind.

What is it like to be colour-blind? What causes colour blindness? A person who is **colour-blind** cannot perceive colours. It is as if the world is a black-and-white movie. The colour-blind person either lacks cones or has cones that do not function normally (Hsia & Graham, 1997). Such total colour blindness is rare. In **colour weakness,** or partial colour blindness, a person can't see certain colours. Approximately 8 percent of all males (but less than 1 percent of women) are red-green colour-blind. These people see both reds and greens as the same colour, usually a yellowish brown (see ▶Figure 4.11). Another form of colour weakness, involving yellow and blue, is extremely rare (Hsia & Graham, 1997).

You may be surprised to learn that *you* used to be colour-blind. We have all been colour-blind, though none of us remember it, because we were infants at the time. According to Russell Adams and Mary Courage, of Memorial University in Newfoundland, newborns have essentially no colour vision (Adams & Courage, 1998; Adams, Courage, & Mercer, 1995). They found that neonates (one to seven days old) are very poor at distinguishing green, red, and yellow from white. At one month, infants in their studies were able to distinguish a red patch from a colourless background, but had trouble distinguishing other colours. Infant colour perception is not fully developed until about six months of age.

How can colour-blind individuals drive? Don't they have trouble with traffic lights? Red-green colour-blind individuals have normal vision for yellow and blue, so their main problem is telling red lights from green. In practice, that's not difficult. The red light is always on top, and the green light is brighter than the red. Also, "red" traffic signals have yellow light mixed in with the red and a "green" light that is really blue-green.

How can a person tell if she or he is colour-blind? The *Ishihara* test is a common measure of colour blindness and weakness. In the test, numbers and other designs made of dots are placed on a background also made of dots (see ▶Figure 4.12). The background and the numbers are of different colours (red and green, for example). A person who is colour-blind sees only a jumble of dots. The person with normal colour vision can detect the presence of the numbers or designs (Birch & McKeever, 1993).

Dark Adaptation

What happens when the eyes adjust to a dark room? **Dark adaptation** is the dramatic increase in retinal sensitivity to light that occurs after a person enters the dark. Consider walking into a theatre. If you enter from a brightly lighted lobby, you practically need to be led to your seat. After a short time, however, you can see the entire room in detail (including the

▶Figure 4.11

Colour blindness and colour weakness. *(a)* Photograph illustrates normal colour vision. *(b)* Photograph is printed in blue and yellow and gives an impression of what a red-green colour-blind person sees. *(c)* Photograph simulates total colour blindness. If you are totally colour-blind, all three photos will look nearly identical.

▶Figure 4.12

A replica of the *Ishihara* test for colour blindness.

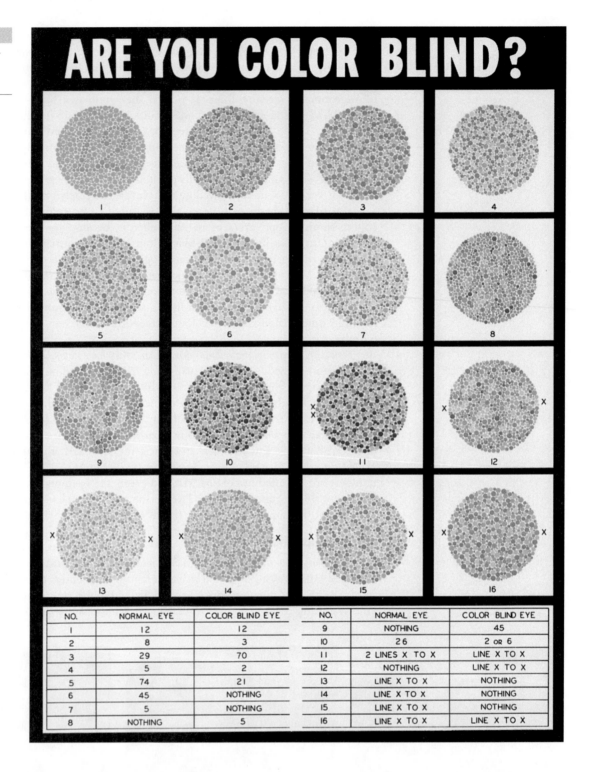

ARE YOU COLOR BLIND?

NO.	NORMAL EYE	COLOR BLIND EYE
1	12	12
2	8	3
3	29	70
4	5	2
5	74	21
6	45	NOTHING
7	5	NOTHING
8	NOTHING	5

NO.	NORMAL EYE	COLOR BLIND EYE
9	NOTHING	45
10	26	2 OR 6
11	2 LINES X TO X	LINE X TO X
12	NOTHING	LINE X TO X
13	LINE X TO X	NOTHING
14	LINE X TO X	NOTHING
15	LINE X TO X	NOTHING
16	LINE X TO X	LINE X TO X

couple kissing over in the corner). It takes about 30 to 35 minutes of complete darkness to reach maximum visual sensitivity (see ▶Figure 4.13). At that point, your eye will be 100 000 times more sensitive to light (Goldstein, 1999).

What causes dark adaptation? Like the cones, the rods contain a light-sensitive visual pigment. When struck by light, visual pigments bleach, or break down chemically. (The afterimages you have seen after looking at a flashbulb are a result of this bleaching.) Visual pigments must recombine to restore light sensitivity, which takes time. Night vision is due mainly to an increase in **rhodopsin** (row-DOP-sin), the rod pigment.

Is there any way to speed up dark adaptation? The rods are insensitive to extremely red light. That's why submarines, airplane cockpits, and ready rooms for fighter pilots are illu-

Rhodopsin The light-sensitive pigment in the rods.

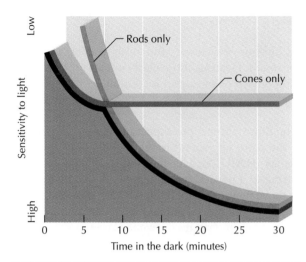

▶Figure 4.13

Typical course of dark adaptation. The black line shows how the threshold for vision lowers as a person spends time in the dark. (A lower threshold means that less light is needed for vision.) The green line shows that the cones adapt first, but they soon cease adding to light sensitivity. Rods, shown by the red line, adapt more slowly. However, they continue to add to improved night vision long after the cones are fully adapted.

minated with red light. In each case, people can move quickly into the dark without having to adapt. Because the red light doesn't stimulate the rods, it is as if they had already spent time in the dark. In contrast, a few seconds of exposure to bright white light can completely wipe out dark adaptation. That's why you should be sure to avoid looking at oncoming headlights when you are driving at night—especially the new bluish-white zenon lights.

Red light allows dark adaptation to occur because it provides little or no stimulation to the rods.

Knowledge builder

SENSORY SYSTEMS AND VISION

Relate

 How does sensation affect what you are experiencing right now? What if data reduction didn't occur? What if you could transduce other energies? What if your senses were tuned to detect different perceptual features? How would the sensory world you live in change?

Pretend you are a beam of light. What will happen to you at each step as you pass into the eye and land on the retina? What will happen if the eye is not perfectly shaped? How will the retina know you've arrived? How will it tell what colour of light you are? What will it tell the brain about you?

Learning Check

1. Sensory receptors are biological _____, or devices for converting one type of energy to another.
2. Lettvin found that a frog's eyes are especially sensitive to phosphenes. T or F?
3. Important features of the environment are transmitted to the brain through a process known as
   a. phosphenation *b.* coding *c.* detection *d.* programming

4. Match:
   _____ Myopia   A. Farsightedness
   _____ Hyperopia   B. Elongated eye
   _____ Presbyopia   C. Farsightedness due to aging
   _____ Astigmatism   D. Lack of cones in fovea
                             E. Misshapen cornea or lens
5. In dim light, vision depends mainly on the _____. In brighter light, colour and fine detail are produced by the _____.
6. The fovea has the greatest visual acuity due to the large concentration of rods found there. T or F?
7. The eyes become more sensitive to light at night because of a process known as _____ _____.

Critical Thinking

8. William James once said, "If a master surgeon were to cross the auditory and optic nerves, we would hear lightning and see thunder." Can you explain what James meant?
9. Sensory transduction in the eye takes place first in the cornea, then in the lens, then in the retina. T or F?

Answers:

1. transducers 2. F 3. b 4. B, A, C, E 5. rods, cones 6. F 7. dark adaptation 8. The explanation is based on sensory localization: If a lightning flash caused rerouted messages from the eyes to activate auditory areas of the brain, we would experience a sound sensation. Likewise, if the ears transduced a thunderclap and sent impulses to the visual area, a sensation of light would occur. 9. False. The cornea and lens bend and focus light rays, but they do not change light from one form of energy. No change in the type of energy takes place until the retina converts light to nerve impulses.

▶ Hearing—Good Vibrations

Survey Question:
■ What are the mechanisms of hearing?

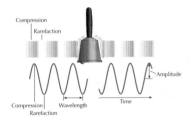

▶**Figure 4.14**

Waves of compression in the air, or vibrations, are the stimulus for hearing. The frequency of sound waves determines their pitch. The amplitude determines loudness.

Sound wave Cyclic, wave-like movement of air molecules.

Loudness The intensity of a sound; determined by the amplitude of sound waves.

Pitch Higher or lower tones; related to the frequency of sound waves.

Pinna The visible, external part of the ear.

Tympanic membrane The eardrum.

Auditory ossicles The three small bones that link the eardrum to the cochlea.

Cochlea The snail-shaped organ that makes up the inner ear.

Oval window
A membrane on the cochlea connected to the third auditory ossicle.

Hair cells Receptor cells within the cochlea that transduce vibrations into nerve impulses.

Organ of Corti Centre part of the cochlea, containing hair cells, canals, and membranes.

Stereocilia Bristle-like structures on hair cells.

Frequency theory Holds that tones up to 4000 hertz are converted to nerve impulses that match the frequency of each tone.

Place theory Theory that higher and lower tones excite specific areas of the cochlea.

Rock, classical, jazz, R & B, country, hip-hop—whatever your musical taste, you have probably been moved by the riches of sound. Hearing also collects information from all around the body, such as detecting the approach of an unseen car. Vision, in all its glory, is limited to stimuli in front of the eyes (unless, of course, your "shades" have rear-view mirrors attached).

What is the stimulus for hearing? If you throw a stone into a quiet pond, a circle of waves will spread in all directions. In much the same way, sound travels as a series of invisible waves of *compression* (peaks) and *rarefaction* (RARE-eh-fak-shun: valleys) in the air. Any vibrating object—a tuning fork, the string of a musical instrument, or the vocal cords—will produce **sound waves** (rhythmic movement of air molecules). Other materials, such as fluids or solids, can also carry sound. But sound does not travel in a vacuum. Movies that show characters reacting to the "roar" of alien starships or titanic battles in deep space are in error.

The amplitude, or physical "height," of a sound wave tells how much energy it contains. Psychologically, amplitude corresponds to sensed **loudness** (sound intensity) (see ▶ Figure 4.14). The *frequency* of sound waves (the number of waves per second) corresponds to the perceived **pitch** (higher or lower tone) of a sound.

Although we'll talk about various forms of deafness below, note that pitch perception can be impaired in people with otherwise normal hearing. Isabell Peretz and her colleagues at the University of Montreal studied *amusia,* or "tone deafness," in hearing subjects (Ayotte, Peretz, & Hyde, 2002). They found a set of people who had never suffered brain damage, had no general learning disability, had taken music lessons during childhood, but had a history of musical failure. There was no simple reason why these people could not perform. Nonetheless, they were unable to tell which of two examples of a melody had a wrong note, and were unable to distinguish a dissonant melody from a harmonious one. Remarkably, these people were just as good as controls at making pitch judgments with speech—they could distinguish a question (e.g., "He speaks French?") from a statement ("He speaks French.") by pitch alone. They had a music-specific disorder of pitch perception.

Mechanisms of Hearing

How are sounds converted to nerve impulses? Hearing involves an elaborate chain of events. These begin with the **pinna** (PIN-ah: the visible, external part of the ear). In addition to being a good place to hang earrings or balance pencils, the pinna acts like a funnel to concentrate sounds. After they are guided into the ear canal, sound waves collide with the **tympanic membrane** (eardrum), setting it in motion. This, in turn, causes three small bones (the **auditory ossicles**) (OSS-ih-kuls) to vibrate (see ▶ Figure 4.15). The ossicles are the *malleus* (MAL-ee-us), *incus,* and *stapes* (STAY-peas). Their common names are the *hammer, anvil,* and *stirrup.* The ossicles link the eardrum with the **cochlea** (KOCK-lee-ah: a snail-shaped organ that makes up the inner ear). The stapes is attached to a membrane on the cochlea called the **oval window.** As the oval window moves back and forth, it makes waves in a fluid inside the cochlea.

The cochlea is really the organ of hearing, because it is here that tiny **hair cells** detect waves in the fluid. The hair cells are part of the **organ of Corti** (KOR-tee), which makes up the centre part of the cochlea. A set of **stereocilia** (STER-ee-oh-SIL-ih-ah) or "bristles" atop each hair cell brush against the tectorial membrane when waves ripple through the fluid surrounding the organ of Corti. As the stereocilia are bent, nerve impulses are triggered, which then flow to the brain. (Are your ears "bristling" with sound?)

How are higher and lower sounds detected? The **frequency theory** of hearing states that as pitch rises, nerve impulses of the same frequency are fed into the auditory nerve. That is, an 800 hertz tone produces 800 nerve impulses per second. (Hertz refers to the number of vibrations per second.) This explains how sounds up to about 4000 hertz reach the brain. But what about higher tones? **Place theory** states that

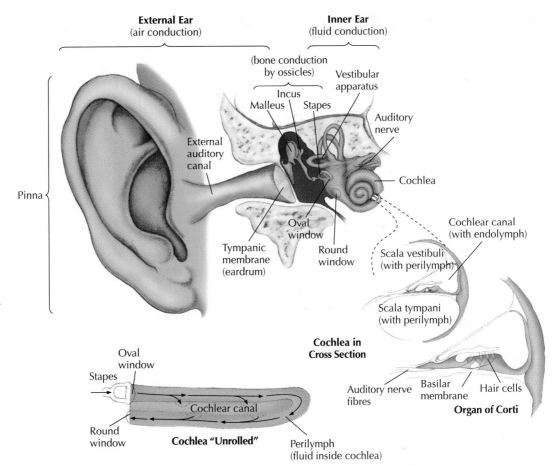

▶**Figure 4.15**

Anatomy of the ear. The entire ear is a mechanism for changing waves of air pressure into nerve impulses. The inset in the foreground shows that as the stapes moves the oval window, the round window bulges outward, allowing waves to ripple through fluid in the cochlea. The waves move membranes near the hair cells, causing cilia or "bristles" on the tips of the cells to bend. The hair cells then generate nerve impulses carried to the brain.

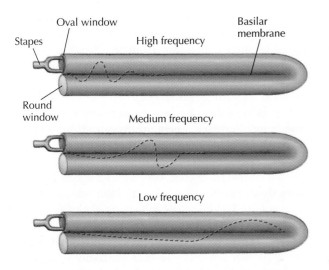

▶**Figure 4.16**

Here we see a simplified side view of the cochlea "unrolled." Remember that the basilar membrane is the elastic "roof" of the lower chamber of the cochlea. The organ of Corti, with its sensitive hair cells, rests atop the basilar membrane. The coloured line shows where waves in the cochlear fluid cause the greatest deflection of the basilar membrane. (The amount of movement is exaggerated in the drawing.) Hair cells respond most in the area of greatest movement, which helps identify sound frequency.

higher and lower tones excite specific areas of the cochlea. High tones register most strongly at the base of the cochlea (near the oval window). Lower tones, on the other hand, mostly move hair cells near the outer tip of the cochlea (see ▶ Figure 4.16). Pitch is therefore signalled by the area of the cochlea most strongly activated. Place theory also explains why hunters sometimes lose hearing in a narrow pitch range. "Hunter's notch," as it is called, occurs when hair cells are damaged in the area affected by the pitch of gunfire.

Recent evidence suggests that, in addition to pitch and loudness, the auditory system can detect the *movement* of a sound source. Researchers at the University of British Columbia studying the "auditory motion after effect" found that, after listening to a sound source that moved repeatedly to the right, subjects perceived a stationary sound source as moving to the left (Dong et al., 2000). A possible explanation is that we have neurons that increase their rate of firing in response to a sound source moving to the right, and decrease the rate for a source moving to the left (analogous to the opponent-process system for colour perception). After repeated exposure to sources moving to the right, these neurons reduce their rate of firing because they are fatigued—and that gives us the impression that we're listening to a sound source that is moving to the left. This reminds us that what we perceive is a conclusion our brain draws about the world.

USING PSYCHOLOGY — Artificial Hearing

In many cases of "nerve" deafness, the nerve is actually intact. This finding has spurred development of cochlear implants that bypass hair cells and stimulate the auditory nerves directly (see ▶Figure 4.17).

As you can see, wires from a microphone carry electrical signals to an external coil. A matching coil under the skin picks up the signals and carries them to one or more areas of the cochlea. The latest implants make use of place theory to separate higher and lower tones. This has allowed some formerly deaf persons to hear human voices and other higher-frequency sounds. About 60 percent of all multi-channel implant patients can understand some spoken words, and some children learn to speak (Cohen, Waltzman, & Fisher, 1993; Tye-Murray, Spencer, & Woodworth, 1995).

At present, artificial hearing remains crude. All but the most successful implant patients describe the sound as "like a radio that isn't quite tuned in." In fact, 30 percent of all adults who have tried implants have given up on them. But the implants are improving. And even now it is hard to argue with enthusiasts like Kristen Cloud. Shortly after Kristen received an implant, she was able to hear a

siren and avoid being struck by a speeding car (Williams, 1984). She says simply, "The implant saved my life."

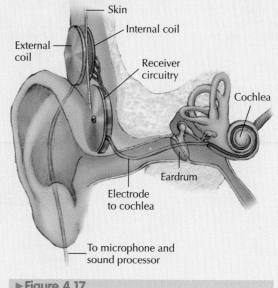

▶ **Figure 4.17**

A cochlear implant, or "artificial ear."

Conduction deafness Poor transfer of sounds from the eardrum to the inner ear.
Nerve deafness Deafness caused by damage to the hair cells or auditory nerve.
Stimulation deafness Damage caused by exposing the hair cells to excessively loud sounds.

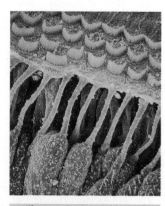

▶ **Figure 4.18**

A highly magnified electron microscope photo of the cilia (orange bristles) on the top of human hair cells. (Colours are artificial.)

DEAFNESS *What causes other types of deafness?* There are two main types of deafness. **Conduction deafness** occurs when sounds are poorly transferred from the eardrum to the inner ear. For example, the eardrums or ossicles may be damaged or immobilized by disease or injury. In many cases, conduction deafness can be overcome by a hearing aid, which makes sounds louder and clearer.

Nerve deafness results from damage to the hair cells or the auditory nerve. Hearing aids are of no help in this case, because auditory messages are blocked from reaching the brain. However, a new artificial hearing system is making it possible for some persons with nerve deafness to break through the wall of silence. (See "Artificial Hearing.")

A particular type of nerve deafness is of special interest, because many jobs, hobbies, and pastimes can cause it. **Stimulation deafness** occurs when very loud sounds damage hair cells in the cochlea (as in hunter's notch). The hair cells, which are about as thick as a cobweb, are very fragile (see ▶Figure 4.18). By the time you are 65, more than 40 percent of them will be gone. If you work in a noisy environment or enjoy loud music, motorcycling, snowmobiling, hunting, or similar pursuits, you may be risking stimulation deafness. Dead hair cells are never replaced: When you abuse them, you lose them.

How loud must a sound be to be hazardous? Daily exposure to 85 decibels or more may cause permanent hearing loss. Even short periods at 120 decibels (a rock concert) may cause temporary deafness. Brief exposure to 150 decibels (a jet airplane nearby) can cause permanent deafness. You might find it interesting to check the decibel ratings of some of your activities in ▶Figure 4.19. Be aware that highly amplified musical concerts, Walkman-style stereo headphones, and "boom-box" car stereos can also damage your hearing.

▶Figure 4.19

▶Figure 4.19

The loudness of sound is measured in decibels. Zero decibels is the faintest sound most people can hear. Sound in the range of 110 decibels is uncomfortably loud. Prolonged exposure to sounds above 85 decibels may damage the inner ear. Rock music, which may rate 120 decibels, is known to have caused hearing loss in musicians and may affect audiences as well. Sounds of 130 decibels pose an immediate danger to hearing.

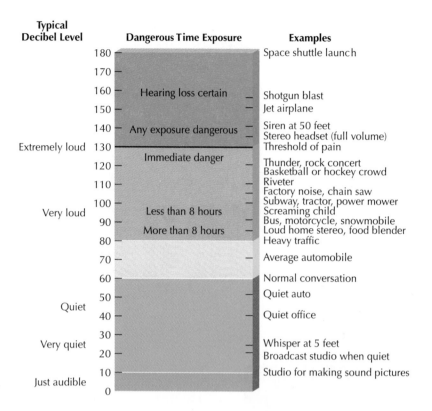

Typical Decibel Level	Dangerous Time Exposure	Examples
180		Space shuttle launch
170		
160	Hearing loss certain	Shotgun blast
150		Jet airplane
140	Any exposure dangerous	Siren at 50 feet / Stereo headset (full volume)
Extremely loud 130		Threshold of pain
120	Immediate danger	Thunder, rock concert / Basketball or hockey crowd
110		Riveter
100		Factory noise, chain saw / Subway, tractor, power mower / Screaming child
Very loud 90	Less than 8 hours	Bus, motorcycle, snowmobile / Loud home stereo, food blender
80	More than 8 hours	Heavy traffic
70		Average automobile
60		Normal conversation
Quiet 50		Quiet auto
40		Quiet office
Very quiet 30		
20		Whisper at 5 feet / Broadcast studio when quiet
10		Studio for making sound pictures
Just audible 0		

▶ Smell and Taste—The Nose Knows When the Tongue Can't Tell

Survey Question:
■ How do the chemical senses operate?

Unless you are a wine taster, a perfume blender, a chef, or a gourmet, you may think of **olfaction** (smell) and **gustation** (taste) as minor senses. Certainly you could survive without these two **chemical senses** (receptors that respond to chemical molecules). Just the same, smell and taste occasionally prevent poisonings and they add pleasure to our lives. Let's see how they operate.

The Sense of Smell

Smell receptors respond primarily to airborne molecules. As air enters the nose, it passes over roughly 5 million nerve fibres embedded in the lining of the upper nasal passages. Molecules passing over the exposed fibres trigger nerve signals that are sent to the brain (see ▶Figure 4.20).

How are different odours produced? This is still an unfolding mystery. One hint comes from a problem called **anosmia** (an–OZE–me–ah: defective smell), a sort of "smell blindness" for a single odour. Anosmia suggests there are receptors for specific odours. Indeed, molecules having a particular odour are quite similar in shape. Specific shapes produce the following types of odours: floral (flower-like), camphoric (camphor-like), musky (Have you ever smelled a sweaty musk ox?), minty (mint-like), and etherish (like ether or cleaning fluid). This does not mean, however, that there are just five different olfactory receptors. At least 1000 types of receptors for smell exist.

Does the existence of 1000 different types of receptors mean that we can sense only 1000 different odours? No, researchers recently discovered that various molecules trigger activity in different combinations of odour receptors. Thus, humans can detect at least 10 000 different odours. Just as you can make many thousands of words from the 26 letters of the alphabet, many combinations of receptors are possible, resulting in many different odours. The brain uses the distinctive patterns of messages it gets from the olfactory receptors to recognize particular scents (Malnic, Hirono, & Buck, 1999; Mombaerts, 1999). (See ▶Figure 4.21.)

Olfaction The sense of smell.

Gustation The sense of taste.

Chemical senses Senses, such as smell and taste, that respond to chemical molecules.

Anosmia Loss or impairment of the sense of smell.

▶ **Figure 4.20**

Receptors for the sense of smell (olfaction). Olfactory nerve fibres respond to gaseous molecules. Receptor cells are shown in cross section at left of part (a).

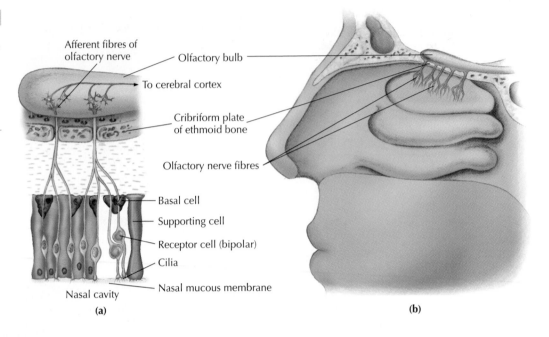

Afferent fibres of olfactory nerve

Olfactory bulb

To cerebral cortex

Cribriform plate of ethmoid bone

Olfactory nerve fibres

Basal cell

Supporting cell

Receptor cell (bipolar)

Cilia

Nasal mucous membrane

Nasal cavity

(a)

(b)

▶ **Figure 4.21**

This extreme close-up of an olfactory receptor cell shows the thread-like fibres that project into the air flow inside the nose. Receptor proteins on the surface of the fibres are sensitive to different airborne molecules. Nerve impulses are triggered when gaseous molecules match the structure of specific proteins in a lock-and-key fashion.

Lock-and-key theory
Holds that odours are related to the shapes of chemical molecules.

Taste bud The receptor organ for taste.

It appears that different-shaped "holes," or "pockets," exist on the surface of olfactory receptors. Like a piece fits in a puzzle, chemicals produce odours when part of a molecule matches a hole of the same shape. This is called the **lock-and-key theory.** Scents are also identified, in part, by the location of receptors in the nose activated by an odour. And finally, the number of activated receptors tells the brain how strong an odour is (Freeman, 1991).

What causes anosmia? Risks include infections, allergies, and blows to the head (which may tear the olfactory nerves). Exposure to chemicals such as ammonia, photo-developing chemicals, and hairdressing potions can also cause anosmia. If you value your sense of smell, be careful what you breathe.

Taste

There are at least four basic taste sensations: *sweet, salt, sour,* and *bitter.* We are most sensitive to bitter, less sensitive to sour, even less sensitive to salt, and least sensitive to sweet. This order may have helped prevent poisonings when most humans foraged for food, because bitter and sour foods are more likely to be inedible (McLaughlin & Margolskee, 1994).

Many experts now believe that a fifth taste quality exists. The Japanese word *umami* describes a pleasant "brothy" taste associated with certain amino acids in chicken soup, some meat extracts, kelp, tuna, human milk, cheese, and soy products (Lindemann, 1996). The receptors for *umami* are sensitive to glutamate, a substance found in MSG. Perhaps MSG's reputation as a "flavour enhancer" is based on the pleasant *umami* taste (Bellisle, 1999). At the very least, we may at last know why chicken soup is such a "comfort food."

If there are only four or five tastes, how can there be so many different flavours? Flavours seem more varied because we tend to include sensations of texture, temperature, smell, and even pain ("hot" chili peppers) along with taste. Smell is particularly important in determining flavour. Small bits of apple, potato, and onion "taste" almost exactly alike when the nose is plugged. So do gourmet jelly beans! It is probably fair to say that subjective flavour is one-half smell. This is why food loses its "taste" when you have a cold.

Taste buds (taste-receptor cells) are mainly located on the top side of the tongue, especially around the edges (see ▶ Figure 4.22). As food is chewed, it dissolves and enters the taste buds, where it sets off nerve impulses to the brain. Much like smell, sweet and bitter tastes appear to be based on a lock-and-key match between molecules and intricately shaped receptors. Saltiness and sourness, however, are triggered by a direct flow of charged atoms into the tips of taste cells.

▶Figure 4.22

Receptors for taste: *(a)* Most taste buds are found around the edges of the tongue. Stimulation of the central part of the tongue causes no taste sensations. Receptors for the four primary taste sensations can be found in all of the shaded areas, as well as under the tongue. That is, anywhere that taste buds are found all taste sensations occur. Textbooks that show specific "taste zones" for sweet, salt, sour, and bitter are in error. *(b)* Detail of a taste bud within the tongue. The buds also occur in other parts of the digestive system, such as the lining of the mouth.

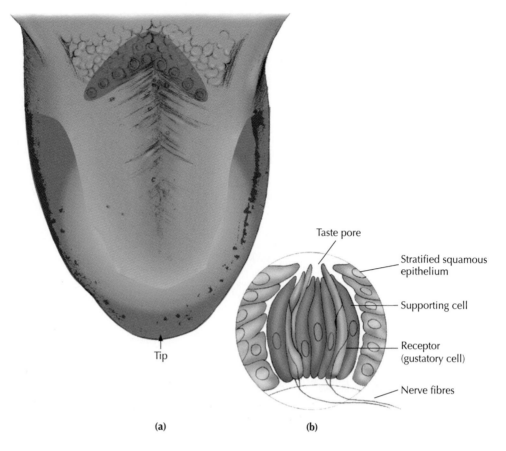

(a)   **(b)**

Somesthetic senses Sensations produced by the skin, muscles, joints, viscera, and organs of balance.

Skin senses The senses of touch, pressure, pain, heat, and cold.

Kinesthetic senses The senses of body movement and positioning.

Vestibular senses The senses of balance, position in space, and acceleration.

How can you get young children to try a novel food? This is a question that perplexed parents often ask when their children refuse to try something new. According to Patricia Pliner of the University of Toronto, older children may be more willing to try a novel food if they have just tried a good-tasting novel food. Older children and adults may also be more willing to try a novel food if it is accompanied by a familiar flavour, such as a sauce or dip (Pliner & Stallberg-White, 2000; Stallberg-White & Pliner, 1999). But for younger children (under 10), even exposure to a good-tasting novel food can decrease willingness to try another novel food immediately afterward. Pliner suggests that the novelty can make younger children anxious. Even when a first result is positive, trying another novel food can increase their anxiety even more, so they don't do it (Loewen & Pliner, 1999).

▶ The Somesthetic Senses—Flying by the Seat of Your Pants

A gymnast "flying" through a routine on the uneven bars may rely as much on the **somesthetic senses** as on vision (*soma* means "body," *esthetic* means "feel"). Even the most routine activities, such as walking, running, or passing a sobriety test, would be impossible without the **skin senses** (touch), the **kinesthetic senses** (receptors in muscles and joints that detect body position and movement), and the **vestibular senses** (receptors in the inner ear for balance, gravity, and acceleration). Because of their importance, let's begin with the skin senses.

Skin Senses

It's difficult to imagine what life would be like without the sense of touch, but the plights of Ian Waterman of England and Ginette Lizotte of Quebec give a hint. Waterman has permanently lost all feeling below his neck, and Lizotte has no feeling below her nose (Cole, 1995; Gallagher & Cole, 1995; Cole & Paillard, 1995; Teasdale et al., 1994). Vision

Survey Question:

■ What are the somesthetic senses and why are they important?

Knowledge builder

HEARING, SMELL, AND TASTE

Relate

Close your eyes and listen to the sounds around you. As you do, try to mentally trace the events necessary to convert vibrations in the air into the sounds you are hearing. Review the discussion of hearing if you leave out any steps.

What is your favourite food odour? What is your favourite taste? Can you explain how you are able to sense the aroma and taste of foods?

Learning Check

1. The frequency of a sound wave corresponds to how loud it is. T or F?
2. Which of the following is not a part of the cochlea?
   a. ossicles *b.* pinna *c.* tympanic membrane *d.* all of the above
3. According to the place theory of hearing, higher tones register most strongly near the base of the cochlea. T or F?
4. Nerve deafness occurs when the auditory ossicles are damaged. T or F?

5. Daily exposure to sounds with a loudness of _____ decibels may cause permanent hearing loss.
6. Cochlear implants have been used primarily to overcome
   a. conduction deafness *b.* stimulation deafness *c.* nerve deafness *d.* hunter's notch
7. Olfaction appears to be at least partially explained by the _____ _____ _____ theory of molecule shapes and receptor sites.
8. *Umami* is a type of "smell blindness" for a particular odour. T or F?

Critical Thinking

9. Why do you think your voice sounds so different when you hear a tape recording of your speech?
10. Smell and hearing differ from vision in a way that may aid survival. What is it?

Answers:

1. F 2. *d* 3. T 4. F 5. 85 6. *c* 7. lock-and-key 8. F 9. The answer lies in another question: How else might vibrations from the voice reach the cochlea? Other people hear your voice only as it is carried through the air. You hear not only that sound, but also vibrations conducted by the bones of your skull. 10. Both smell and hearing can detect stimuli (including signals of approaching danger) around corners, behind objects, and behind the head.

---

is their only source of feedback about their movements—if they cannot see their limbs, they do not know how or whether they are moving them.

Skin receptors produce at least five different sensations: *light touch, pressure, pain, cold,* and *warmth*. Receptors with particular shapes appear to specialize somewhat in various sensations (see ▶ Figure 4.23). However, free nerve endings alone can produce all five sensations (Carlson, 1994). Altogether, the skin has about 200 000 nerve endings for temperature, 500 000 for touch and pressure, and 3 million for pain.

Skin receptors Sensory organs for touch, pressure, pain, cold, and warmth.

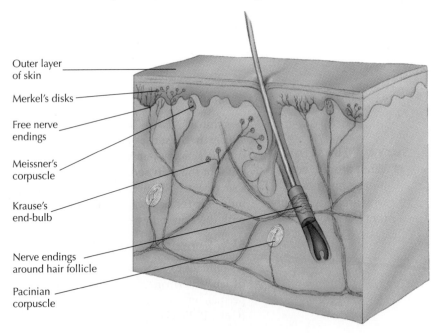

▶Figure 4.23

The skin senses include touch, pressure, pain, cold, and warmth. This drawing shows different forms the skin receptors can take. Other shapes were once recognized, but most turned out to be variations of the shapes shown here. The only clearly specialized receptor is the Pacinian corpuscle, which is highly sensitive to pressure. Free nerve endings are receptors for pain and any of the other sensations. For reasons that are not clear, cold is sensed near the surface of the skin, and warmth is sensed deeper (Carlson, 1994).

Outer layer of skin

Merkel's disks

Free nerve endings

Meissner's corpuscle

Krause's end-bulb

Nerve endings around hair follicle

Pacinian corpuscle

Does the number of receptors in an area of skin relate to its sensitivity? Yes. We could "map" your skin by applying heat, cold, touch, pressure, or pain to points all over your body. This would show that the number of skin receptors varies, and that sensitivity generally matches the number of receptors in a given area. Generally speaking, important areas such as the lips, tongue, face, hands, and genitals have a higher density of receptors.

PAIN   *Does the concentration of pain receptors also vary?* Yes, like the other skin senses, pain receptors vary in their distribution. About 230 pain points per square centimetre are found behind the knee, 180 per centimetre on the buttocks, 60 on the pad of the thumb, and 40 on the tip of the nose. (Is it better, then, to be pinched on the nose than behind the knee? It depends on what you like!)

Pain carried by *large nerve fibres* is sharp, bright, fast, and seems to come from specific body areas. This is the body's **warning system.** Give yourself a small jab with a pin and you will feel this type of pain. As you do, notice that warning pain quickly disappears. Much as we may dislike warning pain, it is usually a signal that the body has been, or is about to be, damaged. Without warning pain, we would be unable to detect or prevent injury. Children who are born with a rare insensitivity to pain repeatedly burn themselves, break bones, bite their tongues, and become ill without knowing it (Larner et al., 1994).

A second type of somatic pain is carried by *small nerve fibres.* This type is slower, nagging, aching, widespread, and very unpleasant. It gets worse if the pain stimulus is repeated. This is the body's **reminding system.** It reminds the brain that the body has been injured. Sadly, the reminding system can cause agony long after an injury has healed or, in terminal illnesses, when the reminder is useless. (If you got carried away with the earlier pin demonstration, maybe you should look at "How to Control Pain" now!)

The Vestibular System

Space flight might look like fun. But if you ever get a ride into space, it is about 70 percent likely that your first experience in orbit will be throwing up (Davis et al., 1988). Weightlessness and space flight affect the vestibular system, often causing severe motion

Warning system Pain based on large nerve fibres; warns that bodily damage may be occurring.

Reminding system Pain based on small nerve fibres; reminds the brain that the body has been injured.

USING PSYCHOLOGY   How to Control Pain

In some cultures, people endure tattooing, stretching, cutting, and burning with little apparent pain. How is such insensitivity achieved? Very likely the answer lies in three factors that anyone can use to reduce pain. These are: (1) anxiety, (2) control, and (3) attention.

Fear or high levels of anxiety almost always increase pain. Anytime you can anticipate pain (such as a trip to the doctor, dentist, or tattoo parlour), you can lower anxiety by making sure you are fully informed. Be sure everything that will happen is explained. Also, be sure to fully discuss any fears you have.

People who are allowed to regulate, avoid, or control painful stimuli suffer less. In general, the more control you feel you have over a painful stimulus, the less pain you will experience (Kruger & Liebeskind, 1984; Wells, 1994). To apply this principle, you should arrange a signal so your doctor, dentist, or body piercer will know when to start and stop a painful procedure.

Distraction also reduces pain. Subjects in one experiment who were exposed to intense pain got significant

relief when they were distracted by watching for signal lights to come on (Johnson et al., 1998). Concentrating on pleasant, soothing images can be especially helpful. Instead of listening to the whirr of a dentist's drill, for example, you might imagine that you are lying in the sun at a beach, listening to the roar of the surf. Or take a Walkman along and crank up your favourite band. At home, music can be a good distraction from chronic pain (Good, 1995; Michel & Chesky, 1995).

An interesting way of combining these techniques is to mask one pain with a second painful stimulus that is under your control. The pain won't seem too bad because you can control it and it is predictable. For instance, if you are having a tooth filled, try pinching yourself or digging a fingernail into a knuckle while the dentist is working. Focus your attention on the pain you are creating, and increase it anytime the dentist's work becomes more painful. This strategy may seem strange, but it works. Generations of children have used it to take the edge off a spanking.

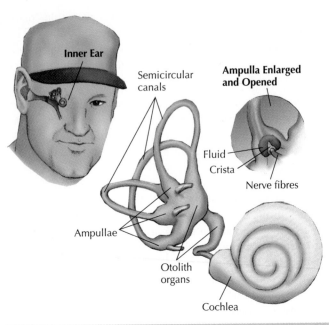

Inner Ear

Semicircular canals

Ampulla Enlarged and Opened

Fluid

Crista

Nerve fibres

Ampullae

Otolith organs

Cochlea

▶Figure 4.24

The vestibular system. (See text for explanation.)

Otolith organs Vestibular structures sensitive to movement, acceleration, and gravity.

Semicircular canals Fluid-filled canals containing the sensory organs for balance.

Crista A floating structure that responds to fluid movement within the semicircular canals.

Ampulla An enlarged area in a semicircular canal containing a crista.

Sensory conflict theory Explains motion sickness as the result of a mismatch between information from vision, the vestibular system, and kinesthesis.

sickness. Within the vestibular system (▶Figure 4.24), fluid-filled sacs called **otolith organs** (OH-toe-lith) are sensitive to movement, acceleration, and gravity. The otolith organs contain tiny crystals in a soft, gelatin–like mass. The tug of gravity or rapid head movements can cause the mass to shift. This, in turn, stimulates hair-like receptor cells, allowing us to sense gravity, acceleration, and movement through space.

Three fluid-filled tubes called the **semicircular canals** are the sensory organs for balance. If you could climb inside these tubes, you would find that head movements cause the fluid to swirl about. As the fluid moves, it bends a small "flap," or "float," called the **crista,** that detects movement in the semicircular canals. A crista can be found within each **ampulla** (am-PULL-ah), a wider part of the canal. The bending of each crista again stimulates hair cells and signals head rotation.

Although movements are severely constrained during sleep, the vestibular system is still active. Working at the University of Waterloo, Kenneth Leslie and Robert Ogilvie studied students who were sleeping in hammocks in a laboratory. During periods of REM sleep (see Chapter 5), Leslie and Ogilvie either rocked the hammocks or left them still. They found that when hammocks were rocked, subjects reported more vestibular (movement) imagery in their dreams and more bizarre dreams than when hammocks were still (Leslie & Ogilvie, 1996).

What causes motion sickness? The most widely accepted explanation is **sensory conflict theory.** According to this theory, dizziness and nausea occur when sensations from the vestibular system don't match sensations from the eyes and body (Warwick-Evans et al., 1998). On solid ground, information from the vestibular system, vision, and kinesthesis usually matches. However, in a heaving, pitching boat, car, or airplane, a serious mismatch can occur—causing disorientation and heaving of another kind.

Why would sensory conflict cause nausea? You can probably blame (or thank) evolution. Many poisons disturb the vestibular system, vision, and the body. Therefore, we may have evolved so that we react to sensory conflict by vomiting to expel poison. The value of this reaction, however, may be of little comfort to anyone who has ever been "green" and miserable with motion sickness. To minimize such conflicts, try to keep your head still, fix your vision on a distant immobile object, and lie down if you can.

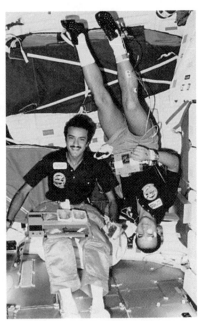

Weightlessness presents astronauts with a real challenge in sensory adaptation.

▶ Adaptation, Attention, and Gating— Tuning In and Tuning Out

Survey Question:
■ Why are we more aware of some sensations than others?

You are surrounded by sights, sounds, odours, tastes, and touch sensations. Which are you aware of? Each of the senses we have described is continuously active. Even so, many sensory events never reach awareness because of *sensory adaptation, selective attention,* and *sensory gating.* Let's see how information is filtered by these processes.

Sensory Adaptation

Think about walking into a house where fried fish, sauerkraut, and headcheese were prepared for dinner. (Some dinner!) You would probably pass out at the door, yet people who had been in the house for some time wouldn't be aware of the food odours. Why? Because sensory receptors respond less to unchanging stimuli, a process called **sensory adaptation.**

Fortunately, the olfactory (smell) receptors adapt quickly. When exposed to a constant odour, they send fewer and fewer nerve impulses to the brain until the odour is no longer noticed. Adaptation to pressure from a wristwatch, waistband, ring, or glasses is based on the same principle. Sensory receptors generally respond best to changes in stimulation. No one wants or needs to be reminded 16 hours a day that his shoes are on (Hubel, 1979a).

Selective Attention

As you sit reading this page, receptors for touch and pressure in the seat of your pants are sending nerve impulses to your brain. Although these sensations have been present all along, you were probably not aware of them until just now. This "seat-of-the-pants phenomenon" is an example of **selective attention** (voluntarily focusing on a specific sensory input). We are able to "tune in on" a single sensory message while excluding others. For example, if you are listening to someone talk, another person nearby can talk *backward* and you will not notice it (Wood & Cowan, 1995).

How is that possible? Selective attention is based on the brain's ability to give some messages priority while putting others on hold (Mangun, 1995). You might find it helpful to think of selective attention as a bottleneck, or narrowing in the information channel linking the senses to perception. When one message enters the bottleneck, it seems to prevent others from passing through (see ▶ Figure 4.25). Imagine, for instance, that you are a pilot preparing to land a jumbo jet. You need to be sure the flaps are down. Just as you are about to check them, your co-pilot says something to you. If you then fail to notice the flaps are still up, an air disaster is just seconds away.

Are some stimuli more attention getting than others? Yes. Very intense stimuli usually command attention. Stimuli that are brighter, louder, or larger tend to capture attention: A gunshot in a library would be hard to ignore. Colours may also be attention demanding—such as what might be called "look-at-me yellow," a colour some people favour for their cars.

Recently, researchers at McMaster University in Hamilton, Ontario, studied people's ability to ignore stimuli based on colour (MacQueen et al., 2000). Ignoring stimuli allows us to focus on what is most important at any given moment, so it is an important process. MacQueen and colleagues were particularly interested in what happens if subjects had to ignore a stimulus of a given colour on one trial of an experimental task, and then attend to a stimulus of that colour on the next trial. They found that normal controls showed the *negative priming effect* (Tipper & Cranston, 1985)—that is, they responded more slowly to a given colour when they had ignored that colour on the previous trial. Yet, in the same study, non-medicated depressed people did not show the negative priming effect, which suggests that depression may involve some impairment of the ability to ignore things.

ATTENTION IS ALSO **FREQUENTLY** RELATED TO contrast OR *change* IN STIMULATION. The contrasting type styles in the preceding sentence draw attention because they are unexpected. Geoffrey Loftus and Norman Mackworth (1978) found that people who look at drawings like ▶ Figure 4.26 focus first and longest on unexpected objects (the octopus, in this case).

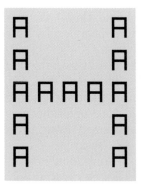

Sensory adaptation A decrease in sensory response to an unchanging stimulus.

Selective attention Giving priority to a particular incoming sensory message.

▶**Figure 4.25**

The attentional "spotlight" can be widened or narrowed. If you focus on local details in this drawing, you will see the letter A repeated 13 times. If you broaden your field of attention to encompass the overall pattern, you will see the letter H. (After Lamb & Yund, 1996.)

▶**Figure 4.26**

One of the drawings used by Loftus and Mackworth (1978) to investigate attention. Observers attend to unexpected objects longer than they do to expected objects. In this drawing, observers looked longer at the octopus than they did at a tractor placed in the same spot. What do you think would happen if a tractor were shown upside down or on the roof of the barn?

Sensory Gating

Sensory gating Alteration of sensory messages in the spinal cord.

Gate control theory Proposes that pain messages pass through neural "gates" in the spinal cord.

Counterirritation Using mild pain to block more intense or long-lasting pain.

Are sensory messages ever blocked before they reach the brain? Yes, a process called **sensory gating** blocks some incoming nerve impulses while allowing others to pass through (Melzack, 1993; Melzack & Wall, 1996). A fascinating example of sensory gating is provided by Ronald Melzack (of McGill University) and Patrick Wall (of St. Thomas's Hospital Medical School in London, England), who studied "pain gates" in the spinal cord (Melzack & Wall, 1996). Melzack and Wall noticed (as described earlier) that one type of pain will sometimes cancel another. Their **gate control theory** suggests that pain messages from different nerve fibres pass through the same neural "gate" in the spinal cord. If the gate is "closed" by one pain message, other messages may not be able to pass through (Humphries, Johnson, & Long, 1996).

How is the gate closed? Messages carried by large, fast nerve fibres seem to close the spinal pain gate directly. Doing so can prevent slower, "reminding system" pain from reaching the brain. As a pain control technique, this is called **counterirritation.** Pain clinics use it by applying a mild electrical current to the skin. This causes only a mild tingling that can greatly reduce more agonizing pain (Long, 1991). Counterirritation is also evident in some of the oldest pain control methods, such as applying ice packs, hot-water bottles, or massage to the body (Kakigi, Matsuda, & Kuroda, 1993; Melzack, 1974).

Messages from small, slow fibres seem to take a different route. After going through the pain gate, they pass on to a "central biasing system" in the brain. Under some circumstances, the brain then sends a message back down the spinal cord, closing the pain gates. (See ▶Figure 4.27.) Melzack and Wall believe that gate control theory explains the painkilling effects of acupuncture.

Acupuncture is the Chinese medical art of relieving pain and illness by inserting thin needles into the body. As the acupuncturist's needles are twirled, heated, or electrified, they activate small pain fibres. These relay through the biasing system to close the gates to intense or chronic pain (Melzack & Wall, 1996). Studies have shown that acupuncture produces short-term pain relief for 50 percent to 80 percent of patients tested (Ernst, 1994; Murray, 1995). (However, it's ability to cure illness is much more debatable.)

The senses supply raw data to the brain, but the information remains mostly meaningless until it is interpreted. It's as if the senses provide only the jumbled pieces of a complex puzzle. In the remainder of this chapter, we will explore how we put the puzzle together.

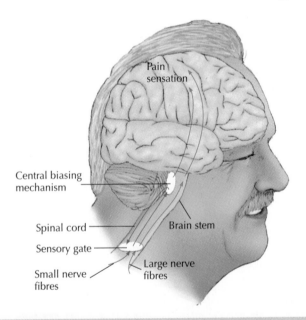

▶**Figure 4.27**

Diagram of a sensory gate for pain. A series of pain impulses going through the gate may prevent other pain messages from passing through. Or pain messages may relay through a "central biasing mechanism" that exerts control over the gate, closing it to other impulses.

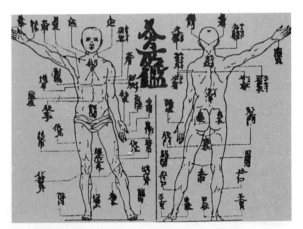

An acupuncturist's chart. Modern research has begun to explain the painkilling effects of acupuncture (see text). Acupuncture's claimed ability to cure diseases is more debatable.

Knowledge builder

SOMESTHETIC SENSES, ADAPTATION, ATTENTION, AND GATING

Relate

 Stand on one foot with your eyes closed. Now touch the tip of your nose with your index finger. Which of the somesthetic senses did you use to perform this feat?

Imagine you are on a boat ride with a friend who starts to feel queasy. Can you explain to your friend what causes motion sickness and what she or he can do to prevent it?

As you sit reading this book, which sensory inputs have undergone adaptation? What new inputs can you become aware of by shifting your focus of attention?

Think about a strategy you have used for reducing pain at the doctor, dentist, or some other painful situation. Did you alter anxiety, control, or attention? Can you think of any ways in which you have used counterirritation to lessen pain?

Learning Check

1. Which of the following is a somesthetic sense?
   a. gustation *b.* olfaction *c.* rarefaction *d.* kinesthesis
2. Warning pain is carried by _____ nerve fibres.
3. Head movements are detected primarily in the semicircular canals, and gravity by the otolith organs. T or F?

4. Sensory conflicts appear to explain nausea caused by poisoning, but not the nausea associated with motion sickness. T or F?
5. Sensory adaptation refers to an increase in sensory response that accompanies a constant or unchanging stimulus. T or F?
6. The brain-centred ability to influence what sensations we will receive is called
   a. sensory gating *b.* central adaptation *c.* selective attention *d.* sensory biasing
7. The painkilling effects of acupuncture appear to result from _____ _____.
8. Like heightened anxiety, increased control tends to increase subjective pain. T or F?

Critical Thinking

9. Drivers are less likely to become car-sick than passengers are. Why do you think drivers and passengers differ in susceptibility to motion sickness?
10. What special precautions would you have to take to test the ability of acupuncture to reduce pain?
11. What measures would you take to ensure that an experiment involving pain is ethical?

Answers:

1. *d* **2.** large **3.** T **4.** F **5.** T **6.** *c* **7.** sensory gating **8.** F **9.** Drivers experience less sensory conflict because they control the car's motion. This allows them to anticipate the car's movements and to coordinate their head and eye movements with those of the car. **10.** At the very least, you would have to control for the placebo effect by giving fake acupuncture to control group members. However, a true double-blind study would be difficult to do. Acupuncturists would always know if they were giving a placebo treatment or the real thing, which means they might unconsciously influence subjects. **11.** Experiments that cause pain must be handled with care and sensitivity. Participation must be voluntary; the source of pain must be non-injurious; and subjects must be allowed to quit at any time.

▶ Perceptual Constancies—Taming an Unruly World

Survey Question:
■ How do perceptual constancies affect our perceptions?

Size constancy The perceived size of an object remains constant, despite changes in its retinal image.

Native perception A perceptual experience based on innate processes.

What would it be like to have your vision restored after a lifetime of blindness? Actually, a first look at the world can be disappointing. Newly sighted persons must learn to identify objects, to read clocks, numbers, and letters, and to judge sizes and distances (Senden, 1960). Learning to "see" can be quite frustrating. Richard Gregory (1990) describes a cataract patient named Mr. S. B. who had been blind since birth. After an operation restored his sight at age 52, Mr. S. B. struggled to use his vision. At first, he could judge distance only in familiar situations. One day he was found crawling out of a hospital window to get a closer look at traffic on the street. It's easy to understand his curiosity, but he had to be restrained. His room was on the fourth floor!

Why would Mr. S. B. try to crawl out of a fourth-storey window? Couldn't he at least tell distance from the size of the cars? No, because you must be familiar with objects to use their size to judge distance. Try holding your left hand a few centimetres in front of your nose and your right hand at arm's length. Your right hand should appear to be about half the size of your left hand. Still, you know your right hand did not suddenly shrink, because you have seen it many times at various distances. We call this **size constancy:** The perceived size of an object remains the same, even though the size of its image on the retina changes.

To perceive your hand accurately, you had to draw on past experience. Some perceptions are so basic they seem to be **native** (inborn). An example is the ability to see a line

Visual perception involves finding meaningful patterns in complex stimuli. If you look closely at this painting by the artist Yvaral, you will see that it is made up entirely of small, featureless squares. An infant or newly sighted person would see only a jumble of meaningless colours. But because the squares form a familiar pattern, you should easily see Marilyn Monroe's face. (Or is that Madonna?) ("Marilyn Numerisée," 1990, courtesy Circle Gallery.)

Empirical perception
A perception strongly influenced by prior experience.

Shape constancy The perceived shape of an object is unaffected by changes in its retinal image.

Brightness constancy The apparent (or relative) brightness of objects remains the same as long as they are illuminated by the same amount of light.

on a piece of paper. Likewise, even newborn babies show some evidence of size constancy (Slater et al., 1991). However, many of our perceptions are **empirical,** or based on prior experience. For instance, cars, houses, and people look like toys when viewed from an unfamiliar perspective, such as from the top of a skyscraper. This suggests that while some size constancy is innate, it is also moulded by experience.

In **shape constancy,** the shape of an object remains stable, even though the shape of its retinal image changes. You can demonstrate shape constancy by looking at this page from directly overhead and then from an angle. Obviously, the page is rectangular, but most of the time the images that reach your eyes are distorted. Yet, while the book's image changes, your perception of its shape remains constant. (For an additional example, see ▶Figure 4.28.) On the highway, alcohol intoxication impairs size and shape constancy, adding to the accident rate among drunk drivers (Farrimond, 1990).

Let's say that you are outside in bright sunlight. Beside you, a friend is wearing a grey skirt and a white blouse. Suddenly a cloud shades the sun. It might seem that the blouse would grow dimmer, but it still appears to be bright white. This happens because the blouse continues to reflect a larger proportion of light than nearby objects. **Brightness constancy** refers to the fact that the brightness of objects appears to stay the same as lighting conditions change. However, this holds true only if the blouse and surrounding objects are all illuminated by the same amount of light. You could make an area on your friend's grey skirt look whiter than the shaded blouse by shining a bright spotlight on the skirt.

To summarize, the energy patterns reaching our senses are constantly changing, even when they come from the same object. Size, shape, and brightness constancy rescue us from a confusing world in which objects would seem to shrink and grow, change shape as if made of rubber, and light up or fade like neon lamps. Gaining these constancies was only one of the hurdles Mr. S. B. faced in learning to see. In the next section, we will consider some others.

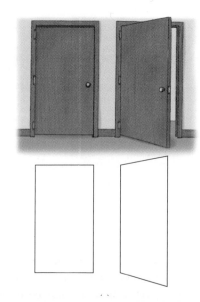

▶Figure 4.28

Shape constancy. When a door is open, its image actually forms a trapezoid. Shape constancy is indicated by the fact that it is still perceived as a rectangle.

Almost everyone's family album has at least one photo like this. Extreme viewing angles can make maintaining size constancy difficult, even for familiar objects.

▶ Perceptual Grouping—Getting It All Together

Survey Question:
■ What basic principles do we use to group sensations into meaningful patterns?

We have seen that Mr. S. B. had to learn to understand his visual sensations. He was soon able to tell time from a large clock and to read block letters he had known only from touch. At a zoo, he recognized an elephant from descriptions he had heard. However, handwriting meant nothing to him for more than a year after he regained sight, and many objects were meaningless until he touched them. Thus, while Mr. S. B. had visual sensations, his ability to perceive remained limited.

How are sensations organized into meaningful perceptions? The simplest organization involves grouping some sensations into an object, or figure, that stands out on a plainer background. **Figure-ground organization** is probably inborn, since it is the first perceptual ability to appear after cataract patients regain sight. In normal figure-ground perception, only one figure is seen. In **reversible figures,** however, figure and ground can be switched. In ▶Figure 4.29, it is equally possible to see either a wineglass figure on a dark background or two face profiles on a light background. As you shift from one pattern to the other, you should get a clear sense of what figure-ground organization means.

Gestalt Principles

How do we separate a figure from its background? The Gestalt psychologists (see Chapter 1) studied this question in detail. Even if you were seeing for the first time, they concluded, several factors would bring some order to your perceptions (see ▶Figure 4.30).

1. *Nearness.* All other things being equal, stimuli that are near each other tend to be grouped together (Kubovy & Holcombe, 1998). Thus, if three people stand near each other and a fourth person stands 3 metres away, the adjacent three will be seen as a group and the distant person as an outsider (see Figure 4.30a).
2. *Similarity.* "Birds of a feather flock together," and stimuli that are similar in size, shape, colour, or form tend to be grouped together (see Figure 4.30b). Picture two bands marching side by side. If their uniforms are different colours, the bands will be seen as two separate groups, not as one large group.
3. *Continuation, or continuity.* Perceptions tend toward simplicity and continuity. In Figure 4.30c, it is easier to visualize a wavy line on a squared-off line than it is to see a complex row of shapes.
4. *Closure.* Closure refers to the tendency to complete a figure, so that it has a consistent overall form. Each of the drawings in Figure 4.30d has one or more gaps, yet each is perceived as a recognizable figure. Our tendency to form shapes—even with minimal cues—is powerful.
5. *Contiguity.* A principle that can't be shown in Figure 4.30 is contiguity, or nearness in time and space. Contiguity is often responsible for the perception that one thing has caused another (Michotte, 1963). A psychologist friend of one of the authors demonstrates this principle in class by knocking on his head with one hand while knocking on a wooden table (out of sight) with the other. The knocking sound is perfectly timed with the movements of his visible hand. This leads to the irresistible perception that his head is made of wood.
6. *Common region.* As you can see in Figure 4.30e, stimuli that are found within a common area tend to be seen as a group (Palmer, 1992). On the basis of similarity and nearness, the stars in Figure 4.30e should be one group and the dots another. However, the coloured backgrounds define regions that create three groups of objects (four stars, two stars plus two dots, and four dots). Perhaps the principle of common region explains why we tend to mentally group together people from a particular country, province, or geographic region.

Clearly, the Gestalt principles shape our day-to-day perceptions. But again it is important to remember that learning and past experience do, too. Take a moment and look for the camouflaged animal pictured in ▶Figure 4.31. (**Camouflage** patterns break up figure-ground organization). If you had never seen similar animals before, could you have

Figure-ground organization Part of a stimulus appears to stand out as an object (figure) against a less prominent background (ground).
Reversible figure A stimulus pattern in which figure-ground organization can be reversed.
Camouflage Designs that break up figure-ground organization.

▶**Figure 4.29**
A reversible figure-ground design. Do you see two faces in profile or a wineglass?

▶Figure 4.30

Perceptual grouping illustrations.

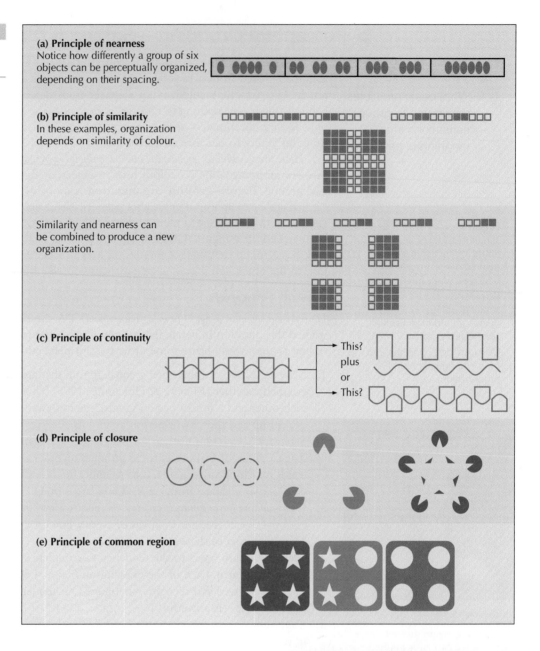

(a) Principle of nearness
Notice how differently a group of six objects can be perceptually organized, depending on their spacing.

(b) Principle of similarity
In these examples, organization depends on similarity of colour.

Similarity and nearness can be combined to produce a new organization.

(c) Principle of continuity

This?
plus
or
This?

(d) Principle of closure

(e) Principle of common region

Perceptual hypothesis
An initial guess regarding how to organize (perceive) a stimulus pattern.

Ambiguous stimuli
Patterns that allow more than one perceptual organization.

located this one? Mr. S. B. would have been at a total loss to find meaning in such a picture.

In a way, we are all detectives, seeking patterns in what we see. In this sense, a meaningful pattern represents a **perceptual hypothesis,** or initial guess about how to organize sensations. Have you ever seen a "friend" in the distance, only to have the person turn into a stranger as you drew closer? Pre-existing ideas and expectations actively guide our interpretation of sensations (Coren, Ward, & Enns, 1994).

The active nature of perception is perhaps most apparent for **ambiguous stimuli** (patterns allowing more than one interpretation). If you look at a cloud, you

▶Figure 4.31

A challenging example of perceptual organization. Once the camouflaged insect (a spiny stick insect) becomes visible, it is almost impossible to view the picture again without seeing the insect.

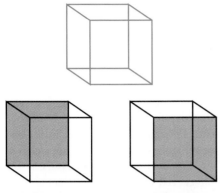

▶Figure 4.32

Necker's cube. Visualize the top cube as a wire box. If you stare at the cube, its organization will change. Sometimes it will seem to project upward, like the lower left cube; other times it will project downward. The difference lies in how the brain interprets the same information.

Impossible figure A stimulus pattern that cannot be organized into a stable perception.

may discover dozens of ways to organize its contours into fanciful shapes and scenes. Even clearly defined stimuli may permit more than one interpretation. Stare at the design in ▶Figure 4.32 if you doubt that perception is an active process. In short, we actively construct meaningful perceptions; we do not passively record the events and stimuli around us (Hoffman, 1999).

In some instances, a stimulus may offer such conflicting information that perceptual organization becomes impossible. For example, the tendency to make a three-dimensional object out of a drawing is frustrated by the "three-pronged widget" (▶Figure 4.33), an **impossible figure.** Such patterns cannot be organized into stable, consistent, or meaningful perceptions.

One of the most amazing perceptual feats is our capacity to create three-dimensional space from flat retinal images. We'll explore that topic in a moment, but first here's a chance to rehearse what you've learned.

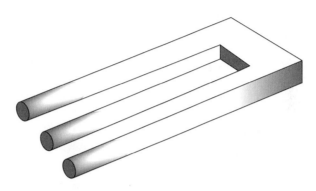

▶Figure 4.33

An impossible figure—the "three-pronged widget." If you cover either end of the drawing, it makes sense perceptually. However, a problem arises when you try to organize the entire drawing. Then, the conflicting information it contains prevents you from forming a stable perception.

Knowledge builder

PERCEPTUAL CONSTANCIES AND GESTALT PRINCIPLES

Relate

If you needed to explain the perceptual constancies to a friend, what would you say? Why are the constancies important for maintaining a stable perceptual world?

As you look around the area in which you are now, how are the Gestalt principles helping to organize your perceptions? Try to find a specific example for each principle.

Learning Check

1. Which among the following are subject to basic perceptual constancy?
   a. figure-ground organization b. size c. ambiguity d. brightness e. continuity f. closure g. shape h. nearness
2. The first and most basic perceptual organization to emerge when sight is restored to a blind person is:

a. continuity b. nearness constancy c. recognition of numbers and letters d. figure-ground
3. At times, meaningful perceptual organization represents a _____, or "guess," held until the evidence contradicts it.
4. The design known as Necker's cube is a good example of an impossible figure. T or F?

Critical Thinking

5. People who have taken psychedelic drugs, such as LSD or mescaline, often report that the objects and people they see appear to be changing in size, shape, and brightness. This suggests that such drugs disrupt what perceptual process?

Answers:

1. b, d, g 2. d 3. hypothesis 4. F 5. Perceptual constancies (size, shape, and brightness).

▶ Depth Perception—What If the World Were Flat?

Survey Question:
■ How is it possible to see depth and judge distance?

Depth perception is the ability to see three-dimensional space and to accurately judge distances. Without depth perception, you would be unable to drive a car or ride a bicycle, play catch, shoot baskets, thread a needle, or simply navigate around a room. The world would look like a flat surface.

Mr. S. B. had trouble with depth perception after his sight was restored. Is depth perception learned? Studies done with a **visual cliff** suggest that depth perception is partly learned and partly innate. Basically, a visual cliff is a glass-topped table (see ▶Figure 4.34). On one side a checkered surface lies directly beneath the glass. On the other side, the checkered surface is more than a metre below. This makes the glass look like a tabletop on one side and a cliff, or drop-off, on the other.

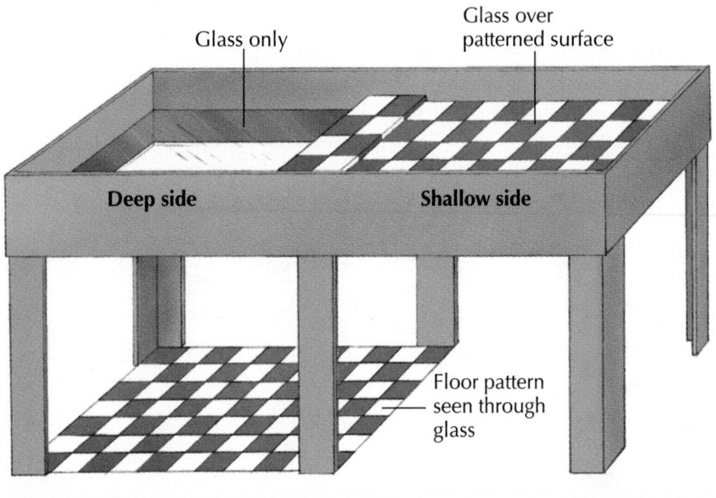

To test for depth perception, 6- to 14-month-old infants were placed in the middle of the visual cliff. This gave them a choice of crawling to the shallow side or the deep side. (The glass prevented them from doing any "skydiving" if they chose the deep side.) Most infants chose the shallow side. In fact, most refused the deep side even when their mothers tried to call them toward it (Gibson & Walk, 1960).

If the infants were at least six months old when they were tested, isn't it possible that they learned to perceive depth? Yes, it is, so let's consider another test. Psychologist Jane Gwiazda fitted infants with goggles that make some designs stand out three-dimensionally while others remain flat. By watching head movements, Gwiazda could tell when babies first became aware of the "3-D" designs. As in other tests, this occurred at age four months. The nearly universal emergence of depth perception at this time suggests that it depends more on brain maturation than on individual learning (Aslin & Smith, 1988). It is very likely that at least a basic level of depth perception is innate.

We also learn to use a variety of depth cues as aids to perceiving three-dimensional space. **Depth cues** are features of the environment and messages from the body that supply information about distance and space. Some cues will work with just one eye (**monocular cues**), while others require two eyes (**binocular cues**).

Glass only

Glass over patterned surface

Deep side

Shallow side

Floor pattern seen through glass

▶Figure 4.34

Human infants and newborn animals refuse to go over the edge of the visual cliff.

Depth perception The ability to see three-dimensional space and to accurately judge distances.
Visual cliff An apparatus that looks like the edge of an elevated platform or cliff.
Depth cues Perceptual features that impart information about distance and three-dimensional space.
Monocular depth cue A depth cue that can be sensed with one eye.
Binocular depth cue A depth cue that requires two eyes.
Accommodation Changes in the shape of the lens of the eye.
Convergence The simultaneous turning inward of the two eyes.

Muscular Cues

As their name implies, muscular cues come from the body. One such cue is **accommodation**, the bending of the lens to focus on nearby objects. Sensations from muscles attached to each lens are channelled back to the brain. Changes in these sensations help us judge distances within about 1.2 metres of the eyes. This information is available even if you are just using one eye, so accommodation is a monocular cue. Beyond 1.2 metres, accommodation has limited value. Obviously, it is more important to a watchmaker or a person trying to thread a needle than it is to a basketball player or someone driving an automobile.

A second bodily source of information about depth is **convergence**, a binocular cue. When you look at a distant object, the lines of vision from your eyes are parallel. However, when you look at something 15 metres or less in distance, your eyes must converge (turn in) to focus the object.

You are probably not aware of it, but whenever you estimate a distance under 15 metres (as when you play catch or zap flies with your personal laser), you are using convergence. How? Convergence is controlled by muscles attached to the eyeball. These muscles feed information on eye position to the brain to help it judge distance. You can feel convergence by exaggerating it: Focus on your fingertip and bring it toward your eyes until they almost cross. At that point you can feel the sensations from the muscles that control eye movement.

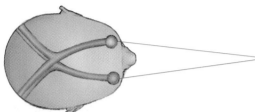

Retinal disparity Small discrepancies in images on the right and left retinas.

Stereoscopic vision Perception of space and depth caused chiefly by the fact that the eyes receive different images.

Stereoscopic Vision

The most basic source of depth perception is **retinal disparity** (a discrepancy in the images that reach the right and left eyes). Retinal disparity, which is a binocular cue, is based on the fact that the eyes are about 6 centimetres apart. Because of this, each eye receives a slightly different view of the world. When the two images are fused into one overall image, **stereoscopic vision** (three-dimensional sight) occurs. The result is a powerful sensation of depth (see ▶Figures 4.35 and 4.36).

Stereoscopic: optic nerve transmissions from each eye are relayed to both sides of brain

Binocular: both eyes have overlapping fields of vision

Allows depth perception with accurate distance estimation

▶**Figure 4.35**

Stereoscopic vision.

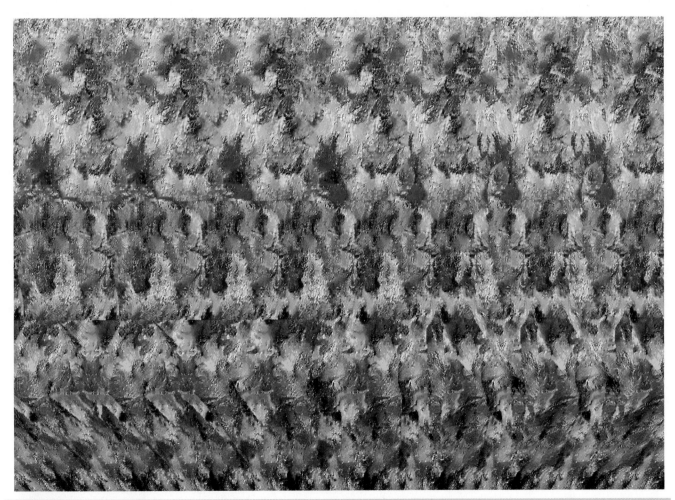

▶**Figure 4.36**

This popular style of computer-generated art creates a 3-D illusion by superimposing two patterns. There are mismatches between some areas of the two patterns. This simulates retinal disparity and creates a sensation of depth. To get the 3-D effect, hold the stereogram about 20 centimetres from the end of your nose. Relax your eyes and look through the art, as if you were focusing on something in the distance. If you're patient, you may see a 3-D fawn. (Copyright © 1994 by N. E. Thing Enterprises. All rights reserved. Reprinted by permission of Andrews McMeel Universal Press Syndicate.)

If disparity is so important, can a person with one eye perceive depth? A one-eyed person lacks convergence and retinal disparity, and accommodation helps us judge only short distances. That means a person with only one eye will have limited depth perception. Try driving a car or riding a bicycle with one eye closed. You will find yourself braking too soon or too late, and you will have difficulty estimating your speed. ("But officer, my psychology text said to . . .") Despite this, you will be able to drive, although it will be more difficult than usual. A person with one eye can even successfully land an airplane—a task that depends strongly on depth perception. Overall, stereoscopic vision is 10 times better for judging depth than perception based on just one eye (Rosenberg, 1994).

Pictorial Cues for Depth

A good movie, painting, or photograph can create a convincing sense of depth where none exists. And, as noted, a one-eyed person can learn to gauge depth.

How is the illusion of depth created on a two-dimensional surface, and how is it possible to judge depth with one eye? The answers lie in the pictorial depth cues, all of which are monocular (they will work with just one eye). **Pictorial depth cues** are features found in paintings, drawings, and photographs that supply information about space, depth, and distance. To understand these cues, imagine that you are looking outdoors through a window. If you trace everything you see onto the glass, you will have an excellent drawing, with convincing depth. Then, if we analyze what is on the glass, we will find the following features.

1. *Linear perspective.* This cue is based on the apparent convergence of parallel lines in the environment. If you stand between two railroad tracks, they appear to meet near the horizon. Because you know they are parallel, their convergence implies great distance (see ▶Figure 4.37a and ▶Figure 4.38).
2. *Relative size.* If an artist wishes to depict two objects of the same size at different distances, the artist makes the more distant object smaller (Figure 4.37b). Films in the *Star Wars* series created sensational illusions of depth by rapidly changing the image size of planets, space stations, and starships. (See ▶Figure 4.39.)
3. *Height in the picture plane.* Objects that are placed higher (closer to the horizon line) in a drawing tend to be perceived as more distant. In the upper frame of Figure 4.37b, the black columns look like they are receding into the distance partly because they become smaller, but also because they move higher in the drawing.

> **Pictorial depth cues**
> Features found in painting, drawings, and photographs that impart information about space, depth, and distance.

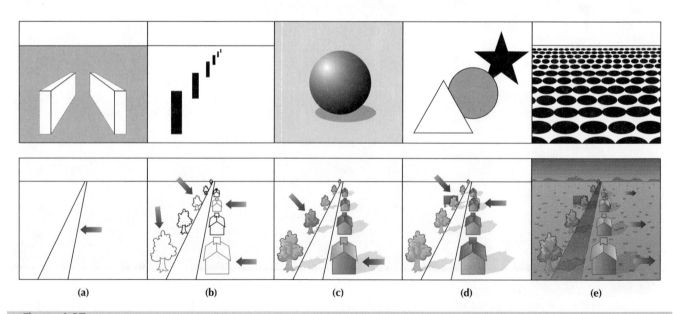

| (a) | (b) | (c) | (d) | (e) |

▶**Figure 4.37**

(a) Linear perspective. *(b)* Relative size. *(c)* Light and shadow. *(d)* Overlap. *(e)* Texture gradients. Drawings in the top row show fairly "pure" examples of each of the pictorial depth cues. In the bottom row, the pictorial depth cues are used to assemble a more realistic scene.

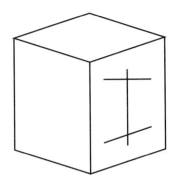

▶**Figure 4.39**

On a dry lake bed, relative size is just about the only depth cue available for judging the camera's distance from this vintage aircraft. What do you estimate the distance to be? For the answer, look ahead to ▶Figure 4.42.

▶**Figure 4.38**

Linear perspective is a very powerful cue for depth. Because of the depth cues implied in this drawing, the upper cross on the vertical line appears to be diagonal. It is actually a right angle. The lower cross, which appears to be a right angle, is actually diagonal to the vertical line. (After Enns & Coren, 1995.)

4. *Light and shadow.* Most objects are lighted in ways that create clear patterns of light and shadow. Copying such patterns of light and shadow can give a two-dimensional design a three-dimensional appearance (see Figure 4.37c). (See ▶Figure 4.40 for more information on light and shadow.)

5. *Overlap.* Overlap (also known as *interposition*) occurs when one object partially blocks another object. Hold your hands up and ask a friend across the room which is nearer. Relative size will give the answer if one hand is much nearer to your friend than the other. But if one hand is only slightly closer than the other, your friend may not be able to see it—until you slide one hand in front of the other. Overlap then removes any doubt (see Figure 4.37d).

6. *Texture gradients.* Changes in texture also contribute to depth perception. If you stand in the middle of a cobblestone street, the street will look coarse near your feet. However, its texture will get smaller and finer if you look into the distance (see Figure 4.37e).

7. *Aerial perspective.* Smog, fog, dust, and haze add to the apparent distance of an object. Because of aerial perspective, distant objects tend to be hazy, washed out in colour, and lacking in detail. Aerial haze is often most noticeable when it is missing. If you have travelled the wide-open spaces of Canada or the United States, you may have seen mountain ranges that seemed to be only a few kilometres away. In reality, you could have been viewing them through 100 kilometres of crystal-clear air.

▶**Figure 4.40**

(Left) We typically make two assumptions when using light and shadow to judge depth in a picture or drawing. First, we usually assume that light comes mainly from one direction. Second, we tend to assume that the source of light is above pictured objects. Squint a little to blur the image you see here. You should perceive a collection of globes projecting outward. If you turn this page upside down, the globes should become cavities. (After Ramachandran, 1995.) *(Right)* The famed Dutch artist M. C. Escher violated both assumptions about light to create the dramatic illusions of depth found in his 1955 lithograph *Convex and Concave.* In this print, light appears to come from all sides of the scene.

Table 4.1
Summary of Visual Depth Cues

BINOCULAR CUES
• *Convergence*
• *Retinal disparity*

MONOCULAR CUES
• *Accommodation*
• *Pictorial depth cues (listed below)*
Linear perspective
Relative size
Height in the picture plane
Light and shadow
Overlap
Texture gradients
Aerial perspective
Relative motion (motion parallax)

Moon illusion The apparent change in size that occurs as the moon moves from the horizon (large moon) to overhead (small moon).

Apparent-distance hypothesis An explanation of the moon illusion stating that the horizon seems more distant than the night sky.

8. *Relative motion.* Relative motion, also known as *motion parallax* (PAIR-ah-lax), can be seen by looking out a window and moving your head from side to side. Notice that nearby objects appear to move a sizable distance as your head moves. Trees, houses, and telephone poles that are farther away appear to move slightly in relation to the background. Distant objects like hills, mountains, or clouds don't seem to move at all.

When combined, pictorial cues can create a powerful illusion of depth. (See Table 4.1 for a summary of all the depth cues we have discussed.)

Is motion parallax really a pictorial cue? Strictly speaking, it is not, except in movies, television, or animated cartoons. However, when parallax is present, we almost always perceive depth. Much of the apparent depth of a good movie comes from relative motion captured by the camera. Imagine that you are in a bus and watching the passing scenery (with your gaze at a right angle to the road). Under these conditions, nearby objects will appear to rush backward. Those farther away, such as distant mountains, will seem to move very little or not at all. Objects that are more remote, such as the sun or moon, will appear to move in the same direction you are travelling. (That's why the moon appears to "follow" you when you take a stroll at night.)

THE MOON ILLUSION *How do the depth perception cues relate to daily experience?* We constantly use both pictorial cues and bodily cues to sense depth and judge distances. Depth cues also produce an intriguing effect called the **moon illusion** (perceiving the moon as larger when it is low in the sky). When the moon is on the horizon, it tends to look like a silver dollar. When it is directly overhead, it looks more like a dime. Contrary to what some people believe, the moon is not magnified by the atmosphere. But the moon looks nearly twice as large when it's low in the sky (Plug & Ross, 1994). This occurs, in part, because the moon's apparent distance is greater when it is near the horizon than when it is overhead (Kaufman & Kaufman, 2000).

But if it seems farther away, shouldn't it look smaller? No. When the moon is overhead, few depth cues surround it. In contrast, when you see the moon on the horizon, it is behind houses, trees, telephone poles, and mountains. These objects add numerous depth cues, which cause the horizon to seem more distant than the sky overhead. Picture two balloons, one 3 metres away and the second 6 metres away. Suppose the more distant balloon is inflated until its image matches the image of the nearer balloon. How do we know the more distant balloon is larger? Because its image is the same size as a balloon that is closer. Similarly, the moon makes the same-size image on the horizon as it does overhead. However, the horizon seems more distant because more depth cues are present. As a result, the horizon moon must be perceived as larger (Kaufman & Kaufman, 2000). (See ▶ Figure 4.41.)

This explanation is known as the **apparent-distance hypothesis** (the horizon seems more distant than the night sky). You can test it by removing depth cues while

▶**Figure 4.41**

The Ponzo illusion may help you understand the moon illusion. Picture the two white bars as resting on the railroad tracks. In the drawing, the upper bar is the same length as the lower bar. However, because the upper bar appears to be farther away than the lower bar, we perceive it as longer. The same logic applies to the moon illusion.

▶**Figure 4.42**

Before you can use familiar size to judge distance, objects must actually be the size you assume they are. Either these men are giants, or the model airplane was closer than you may have thought when you looked at Figure 4.39.

Knowledge builder

DEPTH PERCEPTION

Relate

Part of the rush of excitement produced by action movies and video games is based on the sense of depth they create. Return to the list of pictorial depth cues. What cues have you seen used to portray depth? Try to think of specific examples in a movie or game you have seen recently.

Learning Check

If you have difficulty with any of these questions, skim back over the previous material.

1. The visual cliff is used to test for infant sensitivity to linear perspective. T or F?
2. Write an M or a B after each of the following to indicate if it is a monocular or binocular depth cue.

accommodation _____ convergence _____
retinal disparity _____ linear perspective _____
motion parallax _____ overlap _____ relative size _____

3. Which of the depth cues listed in question 2 are based on muscular feedback? _____.
4. Interpretation of pictorial depth cues requires no prior experience. T or F?
5. The moon's image is greatly magnified by the atmosphere near the horizon. T or F?

Critical Thinking

6. What hearing ability would you say is most closely related to stereoscopic vision?

Answers:

1. F 2. accommodation (M), convergence (M), retinal disparity (B), linear perspective (B), motion parallax (M), overlap (M), relative size (M)
3. accommodation or convergence 4. F 5. F 6. If you close your eyes, you can usually tell the direction and perhaps the location of a sound source, such as a hand-clap. Locating sounds in space is heavily dependent on having two ears, just as stereoscopic vision depends on having two eyes.

looking at a horizon moon. Try looking at the moon through a rolled-up paper tube, or make your hands into a "telescope" and look at the next large moon you see. It will immediately appear to shrink when viewed without depth cues (Plug & Ross, 1994).

▶ Perception and Objectivity—Believing Is Seeing

Survey Question:
■ How is perception altered by learning, expectations, and motives?

Perceptual reconstruction A mental model of external events.

Perceptual learning Changes in perception that can be attributed to prior experience; a result of changes in how the brain processes sensory information.

At the beginning of this chapter we looked at an illusion involving the sizes of circles surrounded by either smaller or larger circles. Observations such as this show that our experiences are **perceptual reconstructions** or mental models of external events. Perceptions are filtered through our needs, expectations, attitudes, values, and beliefs (see ▶ Figure 4.43). Clearly, we don't just believe what we see. We also see what we believe. Let's review some factors that alter or distort our perceptions.

Perceptual Learning

England is one of the few countries in the world where people drive on the left side of the road. In view of this reversal, it is not unusual for visitors to step off curbs in front of cars—after carefully looking for traffic in the *wrong* direction. As this example suggests, learning has a powerful impact on perception.

How does learning affect perception? The term **perceptual learning** refers to changes in the brain that alter how we process sensory information (Ahissar, 1999). For example, to use a computer, you must learn

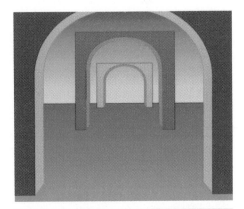

▶**Figure 4.43**

It is difficult to look at this simple drawing without perceiving depth. Yet, the drawing is nothing more than a collection of flat shapes. Turn this page counterclockwise 90 degrees and you will see three Cs, one within another. When the drawing is turned sideways, it seems nearly flat. However, if you turn the page upright again, a sense of depth will reappear. Clearly, you have used your knowledge and expectations to construct an illusion of depth. The drawing itself would be only a flat design if you didn't invest it with meaning.

to pay attention to specific stimuli, such as icons, commands, and signals. We also learn to tell the difference between stimuli that seemed identical at first. An example is the novice chef who discovers how to tell the difference between dried basil, oregano, and tarragon. In other situations, we learn to focus on just one part of a group of stimuli. This saves us from having to process all of the stimuli in the group. For instance, a linebacker in football may be able to tell if the next play will be a run or a pass by watching one or two key players, rather than the entire opposing team (Goldstone, 1998).

PERCEPTUAL HABITS   In general, learning creates **perceptual habits** (ingrained patterns of organization and attention) that affect our daily experience. Stop for a moment and look at ▶ Figure 4.44. The right face looks somewhat unusual, to be sure. But the distortion seems mild—until you turn the page upside down. Viewed normally, the face looks quite grotesque. Why is there a difference? Apparently, most people have little experience with upside-down faces. Perceptual learning, therefore, has less impact on our perceptions of an upside-down face. With a face in the normal position, you know what to expect and where to look. Also, you tend to see the entire face as a recognizable pattern. When a face is inverted, we are forced to perceive its individual features separately (Bartlett & Searcy, 1993).

Magicians rely on perceptual habits when they use sleight of hand to distract observers while performing tricks. Another kind of "magic" is related to consistency. It is usually safe to assume that a room is shaped roughly like a box. This need not be true,

Perceptual habits Well-established patterns of perceptual organization and attention.

▶**Figure 4.44**

The effects of prior experience on perception. The doctored face looks far worse when viewed right side up because it can be related to past experience.

▶**Figure 4.45**

The Ames room. From the front, the room looks normal; actually, the right-hand corner is very short and the left-hand corner is very tall. In addition, the left side of the room slants away from viewers. The diagram shows the shape of the room and reveals why people appear to get bigger as they cross the room toward the nearer, shorter right corner.

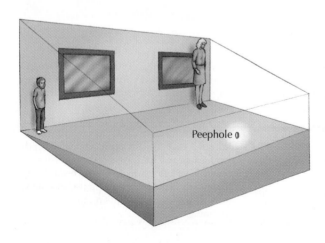

Peephole ◖

however. An *Ames room* (named for the man who designed it) is a lopsided space that appears square when viewed from a certain point (see ▶Figure 4.45). This illusion is achieved by carefully distorting the proportions of the walls, floor, ceiling, and windows. Because the left corner of the Ames room is farther from a viewer than the right, a person standing in that corner looks very small; one standing in the nearer, shorter right corner looks very large. A person who walks from the left to the right corner will seem to "magically" grow larger.

As mentioned earlier, the brain is especially sensitive to **perceptual features** such as lines, shapes, edges, spots, and colours. At least some of this sensitivity appears to be learned. Colin Blakemore and Graham Cooper of Cambridge University raised kittens in a room with only vertical stripes on the walls. Another set of kittens saw only horizontal stripes. When returned to normal environments, the "horizontal" cats could easily jump onto a chair, but when walking on the floor, they bumped into chair legs. "Vertical" cats, on the other hand, easily avoided chair legs, but they missed when trying to jump to horizontal surfaces. The cats raised with vertical stripes were "blind" to horizontal lines, and the "horizontal" cats acted as if vertical lines were invisible. Other experiments show that there is an actual decrease in brain cells tuned to the missing features (Grobstein & Chow, 1975).

ILLUSIONS   Perceptual learning is responsible for a number of illusions. In an **illusion,** length, position, motion, curvature, or direction is consistently misjudged (Gillam, 1980). Note that illusions distort stimuli that actually exist. In a **hallucination,** people perceive objects or events that have no external reality. For example, they hear voices that are not there. If you think you see a 1-metre-tall butterfly, you can confirm you are hallucinating by trying to touch its wings. To detect an illusion, it is often necessary to measure a drawing or apply a straight-edge to it. It can even be necessary to use a computer simulation to detect an illusion, as Donald Redelmeier of the University of Toronto and Robert Tibshirani of Stanford did in their study of why cars in the next lane seem to go faster (Redelmeier & Tibshirani, 1999). Their simulation showed that, with two lanes of traffic moving at the same speed but varying randomly in congestion, any given driver will spend more time being overtaken than overtaking other cars. This is because cars doing the overtaking are going faster; cars going faster are usually spread out more; and it takes you less time to overtake 10 closely packed cars than to be overtaken by 10 distantly spaced cars. Compounding this effect, cars that pass you remain in sight for some time, while cars you pass disappear from view quickly. And the slower you're going, the less busy you are, and the more time you have to look at the next lane to see what's happening. All these differences, according to Redelmeier and Tibshirani, lead drivers to *conclude* that their lane is going more slowly than the next one, even when that isn't true. So, the next time you're in congested traffic, don't bother switching lanes!

Can illusions be explained? Not in all cases, or to everyone's satisfaction. Generally speaking, size and shape constancy, habitual eye movements, continuity, and perceptual habits combine in various ways to produce the illusions in ▶Figure 4.46. Rather than attempt to explain all of the pictured illusions, let's focus on one deceptively simple example.

Figure 4.46a shows the familiar **Müller-Lyer illusion** (MUE-ler-LIE-er). Note that the horizontal line with arrowheads appears shorter than the line with V's. A quick measurement will show that they are the same length. How can we explain this illusion? Evidence suggests it is based on a lifetime of experience with the edges and corners of rooms and buildings. Richard Gregory (1990) believes you see the horizontal line with the V's as if it were the corner of a room viewed from inside (see ▶Figure 4.47). The line with arrowheads, on the other hand, suggests the corner of a room or building seen from outside. In other words, cues that suggest a 3-D space alter our perception of a two-dimensional design (Enns & Coren, 1995).

Earlier, to explain the moon illusion, we said that if two objects make images of the same size, the more distant object must be larger. This is known formally as **size–distance invariance** (the size of an object's image is precisely related to its distance from the eyes). Gregory believes the same concept explains the Müller-Lyer illusion. If the V-tipped line looks farther away than the arrowhead-tipped line, you must compensate by seeing the

---

Perceptual features Important elements of a stimulus pattern, such as lines, shapes, edges, spots, colours.

Illusion A misleading or distorted perception.

Hallucination An imaginary sensation, such as seeing, hearing, or smelling something that does not exist in the external world.

Müller-Lyer illusion Two equal-length lines tipped with inward or outward pointing V's appear to be of different lengths.

Size-distance invariance The strict relationship between the distance an object lies from the eyes and the size of its image.

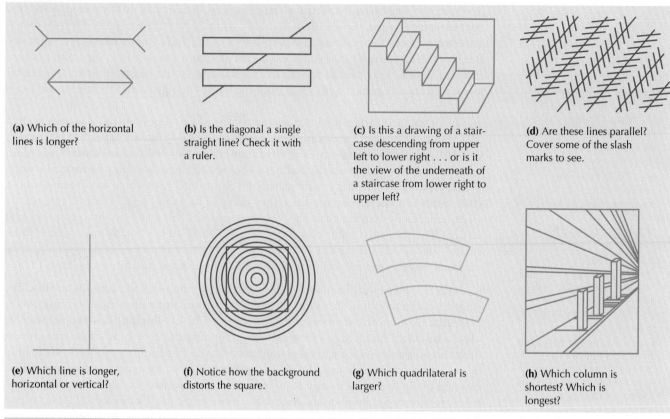

(a) Which of the horizontal lines is longer?

(b) Is the diagonal a single straight line? Check it with a ruler.

(c) Is this a drawing of a staircase descending from upper left to lower right . . . or is it the view of the underneath of a staircase from lower right to upper left?

(d) Are these lines parallel? Cover some of the slash marks to see.

(e) Which line is longer, horizontal or vertical?

(f) Notice how the background distorts the square.

(g) Which quadrilateral is larger?

(h) Which column is shortest? Which is longest?

▶**Figure 4.46**

Some interesting perceptual illusions.

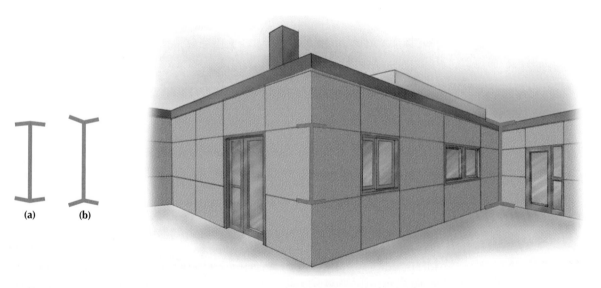

(a)   **(b)**

▶**Figure 4.47**

Why does line *(b)* in the Müller-Lyer illusion look longer than line *(a)*? Probably because it looks more like a distant corner than a nearer one. Because the vertical lines form images of the same length, the more "distant" line must be perceived as larger. As you can see in the drawing on the right, additional depth cues accentuate the Müller-Lyer illusion. (After Enns & Coren, 1995.)

Multistable figure A visual figure that oscillates between alternative subjective forms even though the figure itself does not change.

V-tipped line as longer. This explanation presumes that you have had years of experience with straight lines, sharp edges, and corners—a pretty safe assumption in our culture.

Is there any way to show that past experience causes the illusion? If we could test someone who saw only curves and wavy lines as a child, we would know if experience with a "square" culture is important. Fortunately, a group of people in South Africa, the Zulus, live in a "round" culture. In their daily lives, Zulus rarely encounter a straight line: Their houses are shaped like rounded mounds and arranged in a circle, tools and toys are curved, and there are no straight roads or square buildings.

What happens if a Zulu looks at the Müller-Lyer design? The typical Zulu villager does not experience the illusion. At most, she or he sees the V-shaped line as slightly longer than the other (Gregory, 1990). This seems to confirm the importance of past experience and perceptual habits in determining our view of the world.

MULTISTABLE FIGURES   A separate type of unusual perceptual effect involves **multistable figures,** such as figure-ground reversals and illusory contours (see ▶Figure 4.48). The role of learning in the perception of multistable figures was shown dramatically in a recent study by Maureen Dennis at the University of Toronto (Dennis, Rogers, & Barnes, 2001). Dennis and her colleagues showed 32 children with spina bifida (aged 6 to 16) and 32 age-matched controls two sets of illusory figures. One set involved visual attribute illusions such as those in Figure 4.46. The other set involved items similar to those in Figure 4.48. The spina bifida subjects were much less likely than the controls to perceive both aspects of the multistable figures, but were equivalent to the controls in seeing the visual attribute illusions. Dennis and her colleagues suggest that we perceive multistable figures because of top-down control of processes in the visual cortex—that is, knowledge of the world makes us draw out both possible interpretations of a multistable figure. In people with spina bifida, however, these top-down influences are prevented because of damage to the visual cortex caused by their disorder. Older spina bifida subjects were more likely to see both aspects of multistable figures, suggesting that top-down control of the visual cortex may develop with age.

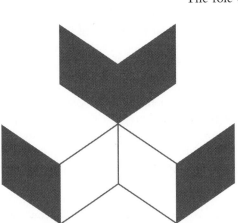

▶Figure 4.48

A multistable figure. What you see in this image varies over time.

MOTIVES   Motives also play a role in perception. For example, if you are hungry, food-related words are more likely to gain your attention than non-food words (Mogg et al., 1998). Advertisers, of course, know that their pitch will be more effective if it gets your attention. That's why ads are loud, repetitious, and often intentionally irritating. They also take advantage of two motives that are widespread in our society: anxiety and sex. Everything from mouthwash to automobile tires is merchandised by using sex to gain attention. Other ads combine sex with anxiety. Deodorant, soaps, toothpaste, and countless other articles are pushed in ads that play on desires to be attractive, to have "sex appeal," or to avoid embarrassment.

In addition to directing attention, motives may alter what is perceived. As part of a supposed study of "the dating practices of college students," male volunteers were shown a picture of a female student and asked to give a first impression of how attractive she was. Before making these ratings, each person read one of two short written passages: One was sexually arousing and the other was not. The men who read the arousing passage rated the female as more attractive (Stephan, Berscheid, & Walster, 1971). This result may come as no surprise if you have ever been infatuated with someone and then fallen out of love. A person who once seemed highly attractive may look quite different when your feelings change.

▶Figure 4.49

Emotionally significant stimuli influence attention (Erdelyi & Appelbaum, 1973), p. 60. Reprinted by permission.

An emotional stimulus can shift attention away from other information. In an experiment, members of a Jewish organization watched as pictures like ▶Figure 4.49 were flashed on a screen for a split second. People were less likely to recognize symbols around the drawing's edge when the centre item was an emotional symbol like the swastika (Erdelyi & Appelbaum, 1973). This effect probably explains why fans of opposing sports teams often act as if they had seen two completely different games.

Perceptual Expectancies

On a piece of paper, draw a circle about 7 centimetres in diameter. Inside the circle, above and to the left of centre, make a large black dot, about 1 centimetre in diameter. Make another dot inside the circle above and to the right of centre. Now, still inside the circle, draw an arc, curved upward and about 5 centimetres long just below the centre of the circle. If you followed these instructions, your reaction might now be, "Oh! Why didn't you just say to draw a happy face?"

Like the happy face drawing, perception seems to proceed in two major ways. In **bottom-up processing,** we analyze information starting at the "bottom" with small sensory units (features) and build upward to a complete perception. The reverse also seems to occur. In **top-down processing,** pre-existing knowledge is used to rapidly organize features into a meaningful whole. Bottom-up processing is like putting together a picture puzzle you've never seen before: You must assemble small pieces until a recognizable pattern appears. Top-down processing is like putting together a puzzle you have solved many times: After only a few pieces are in place, you begin to see outlines of the final picture.

Return to Figure 4.31, the camouflaged insect, on page 140. The first time you saw the photo you probably processed it bottom-up, picking out features until the insect was recognizable. This time, because of top-down processing, you should see the insect instantly. Another good example of top-down processing is found in perceptual expectancies.

PERCEPTUAL SET *What is a perceptual expectancy?* A runner in the starting blocks at a track meet is set to respond in a certain way. Likewise, past experience, motives, context, or suggestions may create a **perceptual expectancy (or set)** that prepares you to perceive in a certain way. If a car backfires, runners at a track meet may jump the gun. As a matter of fact, we all frequently jump the gun when perceiving. In essence, an expectancy is a perceptual hypothesis we are *very likely* to apply to a stimulus—even if applying it is inappropriate.

Perceptual sets often lead us to see what we expect to see. Here's a familiar example: Let's say you are driving across the desert and you're very low on gas. Finally, you see a sign approaching. On it are the words FUEL AHEAD. You relax, knowing you will not be stranded. But as you draw nearer, the words on the sign become FOOD AHEAD. Most people have had similar experiences in which expectations altered their perceptions. To observe perceptual expectancies firsthand, perform the demonstration described in ▶Figure 4.50.

Bottom-up processing Organizing perceptions by beginning with low-level features.

Top-down processing Applying higher-level knowledge to rapidly organize sensory information into a meaningful perception.

Perceptual expectancy (or set) A readiness to perceive in a particular manner, induced by strong expectations.

View I

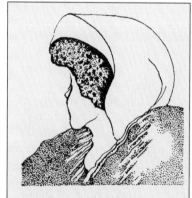

View II

View III

▶**Figure 4.50**

"Young woman/old woman" illustrations. As an interesting demonstration of perceptual expectancy, show some of your friends view I and some view II (cover all other views). Next show your friends view III and ask them what they see. Those who saw view I should see the old woman in view III; those who saw view II should see the young woman in view III. Can you see both? (After Leeper, 1935.)

Perceptual expectancies are frequently created by suggestion. This is especially true of perceiving other people. In one classic experiment, a psychology professor arranged for a guest lecturer to teach his class. Half the students in the class were given a page of notes that described the lecturer as a "rather *cold* person, industrious, critical, practical, and determined." The other students got notes describing him as a "rather *warm* person, industrious, critical, practical, and determined" (Kelley, 1950; italics added). Students who received the "cold" description perceived the lecturer as unhappy and irritable and didn't volunteer in class discussion. Those who got the "warm" description saw the lecturer as happy and good-natured, and they actively took part in discussion with him. In the same way, labels such as "punk," "mental patient," "queer," "illegal immigrant," "bitch," and so on are very likely to distort perceptions.

Those are extremes. Does it really make that much difference what you call someone or something? Perceptual categories, especially those defined by labels, do make a difference. This is especially true in perceiving people, where even trained observers may be influenced. For example, in one study, psychotherapists were shown a videotaped interview. Half of the therapists were told that the man being interviewed was applying for a job. The rest were told that the man was a mental patient. Therapists who thought the man was a job applicant perceived him as "realistic," "sincere," and "pleasant." Those who thought he was a patient perceived him as "defensive," "dependent," and "impulsive" (Langer & Abelson, 1974).

In the next section, we will go beyond normal perception to ask, Is extrasensory perception possible? Before we do that, here's a chance to answer the question, Is remembering the preceding discussion possible?

Knowledge builder

PERCEPTION AND OBJECTIVITY

Relate

How has perceptual learning affected your ability to safely drive a car? For example, what do you pay attention to at intersections? Where do you habitually look as you are driving?

If you spent a year hiking the Amazon River Basin, what effect might it have on your perception of the Müller-Lyer illusion?

You have almost certainly misperceived a situation at some time because of a perceptual expectancy or the influence of motives. How were your perceptions influenced?

Learning Check

1. Perceptual habits may become so ingrained that they lead us to misperceive a stimulus. T or F?
2. Perceptual learning seems to program the brain for sensitivity to important _____ of the environment.
3. The Ames room is used to test infants for depth perception. T or F?

4. Size-distance relationships appear to underlie which two illusions? _____ and _____
5. Research shows that heightened sexual arousal can cause a person to perceive members of the opposite sex as more physically attractive. T or F?
6. In top-down processing of information, individual features are analyzed and assembled into a meaningful whole. T or F?
7. When a person is prepared to perceive events in a particular way, it is said that a perceptual expectancy or _____ exists.

Critical Thinking

8. What size object do you think you would have to hold at arm's length to cover up a full moon?
9. Alcoholic beverage advertisements carry the message "Please enjoy responsibly," a message these companies are not anxious for you to see, since it may make you think about problems associated with alcohol consumption. How is this message made less visible in advertisements?

Answers:

1. T 2. features 3. F 4. moon illusion, Müller-Lyer illusion 5. T 6. F 7. set 8. The most popular answers range from a quarter to a softball. Actually, a pea held in the outstretched hand will cover a full moon (Kunkel, 1993). If you listed an object larger than a pea, be aware that perceptions, no matter how accurate they seem, may distort reality. 9. Advertisers typically put the responsible drinking message in a very small type font near the bottom of the ad, where it will attract the least possible attention. Also, the message is often placed on "busy" backgrounds so that it is partially camouflaged. Finally, the main images in ads are designed to strongly attract attention. This further distracts readers from seeing the responsible drinking message.

▶ Extrasensory Perception—Do You Believe in Magic?

Uri Geller, a self-proclaimed "psychic," once agreed to demonstrate his claimed paranormal abilities. During testing, it seemed that Geller could sense which of 10 film canisters contained a hidden object, correctly guess the number that would come up on a die shaken in a closed box, and reproduce drawings sealed in envelopes.

Was Geller cheating, or was he using some ability beyond normal perception? There is little doubt that Geller was cheating (Randi, 1980). But how? The answer lies in a discussion of **extrasensory perception (ESP)**—the purported ability to perceive events in ways that cannot be explained by known sensory capacities.

Parapsychology is the study of ESP and other **psi phenomena** (events that seem to defy accepted scientific laws). (Psi is pronounced like "sigh.") Parapsychologists seek answers to the questions raised by three basic forms that ESP could take. These are:

1. **Clairvoyance.** The purported ability to perceive events or gain information in ways that appear unaffected by distance or normal physical barriers.
2. **Telepathy.** Extrasensory perception of another person's thoughts, or more simply, the purported ability to read someone else's mind.
3. **Precognition.** The purported ability to perceive or accurately predict future events. Precognition may take the form of prophetic dreams that foretell the future.

While we are at it, we might as well toss in another purported psi ability:

4. **Psychokinesis.** The purported ability to exert influence over inanimate objects by willpower ("mind over matter"). (Psychokinesis cannot be classed as a type of ESP, but it is frequently studied by parapsychologists.)

An Appraisal of ESP

Psychologists as a group are highly skeptical about psi abilities. If you've ever had an apparent clairvoyant or telepathic experience, you might be convinced that ESP exists. However, the difficulty of excluding coincidence makes such experiences less conclusive than they might seem. Consider a typical "psychic" experience: During the middle of the night, a woman away for a weekend visit suddenly had a strong impulse to return home. When she arrived she found the house on fire with her husband asleep inside (Rhine, 1953). An experience like this is striking, but it does not confirm the reality of ESP. If, by coincidence, a hunch turns out to be correct, it may be reinterpreted as precognition or clairvoyance (Marks & Kammann, 1979). If it is not confirmed, it will simply be forgotten. Most people don't realize it, but such coincidences occur quite often.

Formal investigation of psi events owes much to the late J. B. Rhine, who tried to study ESP objectively. Many of Rhine's experiments made use of the Zener cards (a deck of 25 cards, each bearing one of five symbols) (see ▶ Figure 4.51). In a typical clairvoyance test, people tried to guess the symbols on the cards as they were turned up from a shuffled deck. Pure guessing in this test will produce an average score of five "hits" out of 25 cards.

FRAUD AND SKEPTICISM Unfortunately, some of Rhine's most dramatic early experiments used badly printed Zener cards that allowed the symbols to show faintly on the back. It is also very easy to cheat by marking cards with a fingernail or by noting marks on the cards caused by normal use. Even if this were not the case, there is evidence that early experimenters sometimes unconsciously gave people cues about cards with their eyes, facial gestures, or lip movements. In short, none of the early studies in parapsychology were done in a way that eliminated the possibility of fraud or "leakage" of helpful information (Alcock, 1990).

Modern parapsychologists are now well aware of the need for double-blind experiments, security and accuracy in record keeping, meticulous control, and repeatability of experiments (Milton & Wiseman, 1997). In the last 10 years, hundreds of experiments have

---

Extrasensory perception (ESP) The purported ability to perceive events in ways that cannot be explained by known capacities of the sensory organs.

Parapsychology The study of extranormal psychological events, such as extrasensory perception.

Psi phenomena Events that seem to lie outside the realm of accepted scientific laws.

Clairvoyance The purported ability to perceive events at a distance or through physical barriers.

Telepathy The purported ability to directly know another person's thoughts.

Precognition The purported ability to accurately predict future events.

Psychokinesis The purported ability to mentally alter or influence objects or events.

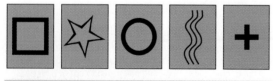

▶**Figure 4.51**

Zener cards used by J. B. Rhine, an early experimenter in parapsychology.

been reported in parapsychological journals. Many of them seem to support the existence of psi abilities.

Then why do most psychologists remain skeptical about psi abilities? For one thing, fraud continues to plague the field. It is remarkable, for instance, that many parapsychologists chose to ignore a famous "psychic's" habit of peeking at ESP cards during testing (Cox, 1994). As one critic put it, positive ESP results usually mean "Error Some Place" (Marks, 1990). The more closely psi experiments are examined, the more likely it is that claimed successes will evaporate (Alcock, 1990; Hyman, 1996b; for a contrary view, see Bem & Honorton, 1994, or Utts, 1996).

STATISTICS AND CHANCE   Inconsistency is a major problem in psi research. For every study with positive results, there are others that fail (Hansel, 1980; Hyman, 1996b). It is rare—in fact, almost unheard of—for a person to maintain psi ability over any sustained period of time (Jahn, 1982). ESP researchers believe this "decline effect" shows that parapsychological skills are very fragile. But critics argue that a person who only temporarily scores above chance has just received credit for a **run of luck** (a statistically unusual outcome that could occur by chance alone). When the run is over, it is not fair to assume that ESP is temporarily gone. We must count all attempts.

To understand the run-of-luck criticism, imagine that you flip a coin 100 times and record the results. You then flip another coin 100 times, again recording the results. The two lists are compared. For any 10 pairs of flips, we would expect heads or tails to match five times. Let's say that you go through the list and find a set of 10 pairs where 9 out of 10 matched. This is far above chance expectation. But does it mean that the first coin "knew" what was going to come up on the second coin? The idea is obviously silly.

Now, what if a person guesses 100 times what will come up on a coin. Again, we might find a set of 10 guesses that matches the results of flipping the coin. Does this mean that the person, for a time, had precognition—then lost it? Parapsychologists tend to believe the answer is yes. Skeptics assume that nothing more than random matching occurred, as in the two-coin example.

INCONCLUSIVE RESEARCH   Unfortunately, many of the most spectacular findings in parapsychology simply cannot be **replicated** (reproduced or repeated) (Hyman, 1996a). Even the same researchers using the same experimental subjects typically can't get similar results every time (Schick & Vaughn, 1995). More importantly, improved research methods usually result in fewer positive results (Hyman, 1996b).

Reinterpretation is also a problem in psi experiments. For example, ex-astronaut Edgar Mitchell claimed he did a successful telepathy experiment from space. Yet news accounts never mentioned that on some trials Mitchell's "receivers" scored above chance, while on others they scored *below* chance. The second outcome, Mitchell decided, was also a "success" because it represented intentional "psi missing." But, as skeptics have noted, if both high scores and low scores count as successes, how can you lose?

Of course, in many ESP tests the outcome is beyond debate. A good example is provided by recent ESP experiments done through newspapers, radio, and television. In these mass media studies, people attempted to identify ESP targets from a distance. Such studies allow large numbers of people to be tested. The results of over 1.5 million ESP trials recently done through the mass media are easy to summarize: There was no significant ESP effect (Milton & Wiseman, 1999). Zero. Zip. Nada. Clearly, lottery organizers have nothing to fear!

Stage ESP

If psychic phenomena do occur, they certainly can't be controlled well enough to be used by entertainers. **Stage ESP** simulates ESP for the purpose of entertainment. Like stage magic, it is based on sleight of hand, deception, and patented gadgets. A case in point is Uri Geller, a former nightclub magician who "astounded" audiences—and some scientists—with apparent telepathy, psychokinesis, and precognition.

It's now clear that tests of Geller's performance were incredibly sloppy. For instance, Geller reproduced sealed drawings in a room next to the one where the drawings were

Run of luck A statistically unusual outcome (as in getting five heads in a row when flipping a coin) that could still occur by chance alone.

Replicate To reproduce or repeat.

Stage ESP The simulation of ESP for the purpose of entertainment.

made. Original reports failed to mention that there was a hole in the wall between the rooms, through which Geller could have heard descriptions of the pictures as they were being drawn. Likewise, in the "die in the box" tests Geller was allowed to hold the box, shake it, and have the honour of opening it (Randi, 1980; Wilhelm, 1976).

Why weren't such details reported? Sensational and uncritical reporting of apparent paranormal events is widespread. Hundreds of books, articles, and television programs are produced each year by people who are getting rich by promoting unsupported claims. If a person did have psychic powers, he or she would not have to make a living by entertaining others. A quick trip to a casino would allow the person to retire for life.

IMPLICATIONS   After 130 years of investigation, it is still impossible to say conclusively whether psi events occur. As we have seen, a close look at psi experiments often reveals serious problems of evidence, procedure, and scientific rigour (Alcock, 1990; Hyman, 1996b; Marks & Kammann, 1979; Swets et al., 1988).

What would it take to scientifically demonstrate the existence of ESP? Quite simply, a set of instructions that would allow any competent, unbiased observer to produce a psi event under standardized conditions that rule out any possibility of fraud (Schick & Vaughn, 1995). Undoubtedly, some intrepid researchers will continue trying to supply just that. Others think it's time to abandon the concept of ESP (Marks, 1990; Swets et al., 1988). At the very least, it seems wise to question the uncritical acceptance of psi events that is rampant in the media. (But then, you already knew we were going to say that, didn't you!)

A LOOK AHEAD   In this chapter, we have moved from basic sensations to the complexities of perceiving people and events. We have also probed some of the controversies concerning ESP. In the Psychology in Action section, we will return to "everyday" perception in our discussion of perceptual awareness.

Knowledge builder

EXTRASENSORY PERCEPTION

Relate

Let's say that a friend of yours is an avid fan of TV shows that feature paranormal themes. See if you can summarize for her or him what is known about ESP. Be sure to include evidence for and against the existence of ESP and some of the thinking errors associated with non-skeptical belief in the paranormal.

Learning Check

1. Four purported psi events investigated by parapsychologists are clairvoyance, telepathy, precognition, and
   _____

2. The _____ cards were used by J. B. Rhine in early tests of ESP.

3. Natural, or "real life," occurrences are regarded as the best evidence for the existence of ESP. T or F?
4. Skeptics attribute positive results in psi experiments to statistical runs of luck. T or F?
5. Replication rates are very high for ESP experiments. T or F?

Critical Thinking

6. What would you estimate is the chance that two people will have the same birthday (day and month, but not year) in a group of 30 people?
7. A "psychic" on television offers to fix broken watches for viewers. Moments later, dozens of viewers call the station to say that their watches miraculously started running again. What have they overlooked?

Answers:

1. psychokinesis 2. Zener 3. F 4. T 5. F 6. Most people assume that this would be a relatively rare event. Actually, there is a 71 percent chance that two people will share a birthday in a group of 30. Most people probably underestimate the natural rate of occurrence of many seemingly mysterious coincidences (Alcock, 1990). 7. When psychologists handled watches awaiting repair at a store, 57 percent began running again, with no help from a "psychic." Believing the "psychic's" claim also overlooks the impact of big numbers: If the show reached a large audience, at least a few "broken" watches would start working merely by chance.

PSYCHOLOGY IN ACTION

BECOMING A BETTER

EYEWITNESS

TO LIFE

? **Survey Question:**

■ What can be done to enhance perceptual accuracy?

Weapon focus The tendency of crime victims to fix their attention on an attacker's weapon.

In courtrooms, the claim "I saw it with my own eyes" carries a lot of weight. Most jurors tend to assume that eyewitness testimony is nearly infallible (Durham & Dane, 1999). But to put it bluntly, eyewitness testimony is frequently wrong. Remember that what an eyewitness sees is a conclusion his or her seeing system draws on the basis of sometimes incomplete evidence and expectation. If you see someone dressed as a pirate at a Halloween party, the next day you might remember that the person had an earring, even if she or he didn't, because we think of pirates as wearing earrings.

What about witnesses who are certain that their perceptions were accurate? Should juries believe them? Actually, having confidence in your testimony has almost no bearing on its accuracy (Wells, 1993)! Psychologists are gradually convincing lawyers, judges, and the police that eyewitness errors are common. Even so, thousands of people have been wrongfully convicted (Loftus, 1993). In one typical court case, a police officer testified that he saw the defendant shoot the victim as both stood in a dimly lit doorway. When a psychologist arranged for a juror to stand in the doorway under identical lighting conditions, none of the other jurors could identify him. The defendant was acquitted (Buckhout, 1974).

Unfortunately, perception rarely provides an "instant replay" of events. Impressions formed when a person is surprised, threatened, or under stress are especially prone to distortion. A recent study of eyewitness cases found that the wrong person was chosen from police lineups 25 percent of the time (Levi, 1998).

Wouldn't the victim of a crime remember more than a mere witness? Not necessarily. A revealing study found that eyewitness accuracy is virtually the same for witnessing a crime (seeing a pocket calculator stolen) as it is for being a victim (seeing one's own watch stolen) (Hosch & Cooper, 1982). Placing more weight on the testimony of victims may be a serious mistake. In many crimes, victims fall prey to **weapon focus.** Understandably, they fix their entire attention on the knife, gun, or other weapon used by an attacker. In doing so, they fail to notice details of appearance, dress, or other clues to identity (Steblay, 1992). Additional factors affecting eyewitnesses are summarized in Table 4.2.

Table 4.2
Factors Affecting the Accuracy of Eyewitness Perceptions

SOURCES OF ERROR	SUMMARY OF FINDINGS
1. Stress	Very high levels of stress impair the accuracy of eyewitness perceptions.
2. Weapon focus	The presence of a weapon impairs an eyewitness's ability to accurately identify the culprit's face.
3. Exposure time	The less time an eyewitness has to observe an event, the less well she or he will perceive and remember it.
4. Accuracy-confidence	An eyewitness's confidence is not a good predictor of his or her accuracy.
5. Cross-racial perceptions	Eyewitnesses are better at identifying members of their own race than they are at identifying people of other races.
6. Post-event information	Eyewitness testimony about an event often reflects not only what was actually seen but also information obtained later on.
7. Colour perception	Judgments of colour made under monochromatic light (such as an orange street light) are highly unreliable.
8. Wording of questions	An eyewitness's testimony about an event can be affected by how the questions put to that witness are worded.
9. Unconscious transference	Eyewitnesses sometimes identify as a culprit someone they have seen in another situation or context.
10. Trained observers	Police officers and other trained observers are no more accurate as eyewitnesses than the average person.
11. Time estimation	Eyewitnesses tend to overestimate the duration of events.
12. Attitudes, expectations	An eyewitness's perception and memory of an event may be affected by his or her attitudes and expectations.

(Adapted from Kassin, Ellsworth, & Smith, 1989.)

▶Figure 4.52

The limits of pure perception. Even simple designs are easily misperceived. Fraser's spiral is actually a series of concentric circles. The illusion is so powerful that people who try to trace one of the circles sometimes follow the illusory spiral and jump from one circle to the next. (After Seckel, 2000.)

Reality testing Obtaining additional information to check on the accuracy of perceptions.
Habituation A decrease in perceptual response to a repeated stimulus.

IMPLICATIONS Now that DNA testing is available, more than 100 North Americans (including seven Canadians) who were convicted of murder, rape, and other crimes have been exonerated on the basis of DNA testing. Each of these innocent people was convicted mainly on the basis of eyewitness testimony. Each also spent years in prison before being cleared (Foxhall, 2000). How often are everyday perceptions as inaccurate or distorted as those of an emotional eyewitness? The answer we have been moving toward is *very frequently*. Bearing this in mind may help you be more tolerant of the views of others and more cautious about your own objectivity. It may also encourage more frequent reality testing on your part.

What do you mean by reality testing? In any situation having an element of doubt or uncertainty, **reality testing** involves obtaining additional information to check your perceptions. ▶ Figure 4.52 shows a powerful illusion called Fraser's spiral. What appears to be a spiral is actually made up of a series of closed circles. Most people cannot spontaneously see this reality. Instead, they must carefully trace one of the circles to confirm what is "real" in the design.

Psychologist Sidney Jourard once offered a prime example of reality testing. One of Jourard's students believed her roommate was stealing from her. The student gradually became convinced of her roommate's guilt, but said nothing. As her distrust and anger grew, their relationship turned cold and distant. Finally, at Jourard's urging, she confronted her roommate. The roommate cleared herself immediately and expressed relief when the puzzling change in their relationship was explained (Jourard, 1974). With their friendship re-established, the true culprit was soon caught. (The cleaning woman did it!)

If you have ever concluded that someone was angry, upset, or unfriendly without checking the accuracy of your perceptions, you have fallen into a subtle trap. Personal objectivity is an elusive quality, requiring frequent reality testing to maintain. At the very least, it pays to ask a person what she or he is feeling when you are in doubt. Clearly, most of us could learn to be better "eyewitnesses" to daily events.

Perceptual Awareness

Do some people perceive things more accurately than others? Humanistic psychologist Abraham Maslow (1969) believed that some people perceive themselves and others with unusual accuracy. Maslow characterized these people as especially alive, open, aware, and mentally healthy. He found that their perceptual styles were marked by immersion in the present, a lack of self-consciousness, freedom from selecting, criticizing, or evaluating, and a general "surrender" to experience. The kind of perception Maslow described is like that of a mother with her newborn infant, a child at Christmas, or two people in love.

In daily life, we quickly **habituate** (respond less) to predictable and unchanging stimuli. Habituation is a type of learning—basically, we learn to cease paying attention to familiar stimuli. For instance, when you buy a new CD, the music initially holds your attention all the way through. But when the CD becomes "old," all the songs may play without your really attending to them. When a stimulus is repeated without change, our response to it habituates, or decreases. Interestingly, creative people habituate more slowly than average. We might expect that they would rapidly become bored with a repeated stimulus. Instead, it seems that creative people actively attend to stimuli, even those that are repeated (Colin, Moore, & West, 1996).

ATTENTION Whereas the average person has not reached perceptual restriction of the "if you've seen one tree, you've seen them all" variety, the fact remains that most of us tend to look at a tree and classify it into the perceptual category of "trees in general" without

Dishabituation A reversal of habituation.

really appreciating the miracle standing before us. How, then, can we bring about **dishabituation** (a reversal of habituation) on a day-to-day basis? Does perceptual clarity require years of effort? Fortunately, a more immediate avenue is available. The deceptively simple key to dishabituation is: Pay attention. The following quote summarizes the importance of attention:

> One day a man of the people said to Zen Master Ikkyu: "Master, will you please write for me some maxims of the highest wisdom?"
>
> Ikkyu immediately took his brush and wrote the word "Attention."
>
> "Is that all?" asked the man. "Will you not add something more?"
>
> Ikkyu then wrote twice running: "Attention. Attention."
>
> "Well," remarked the man rather irritably, "I really don't see much depth or subtlety in what you have just written."
>
> Then Ikkyu wrote the same word three times running: "Attention. Attention. Attention." Half angered, the man demanded, "What does that word 'Attention' mean anyway?"
>
> And Ikkyu answered gently: "Attention means attention." (Kapleau, 1966)

To this we can add only one thought, provided by the words of poet William Blake: "If the doors of perception were cleansed, man would see everything as it is, infinite."

Becoming a Better "Eyewitness" to Life

Here's a summary of ideas from this chapter to help you maintain and enhance perceptual awareness and accuracy.

1. *Remember that perceptions are reconstructions of reality.* Learn to regularly question your own perceptions. Are they accurate? Could another interpretation fit the facts? What assumptions are you making? Could they be false? How might your assumptions be distorting your perceptions?
2. *Break perceptual habits and interrupt habituation.* Each day, try to do some activities in new ways. For example, take different routes when you travel to work or school. Do routines, such as brushing your teeth or combing your hair, with your non-preferred hand. Try to look at friends and family members as if they were persons you just met for the first time.
3. *Shift adaptation levels and broaden frames of reference by seeking out-of-the-ordinary experiences.* The possibilities here range from trying foods you don't normally eat, to reading opinions very different from your own. Experiences ranging from a quiet walk in the woods to a trip to an amusement park may be perceptually refreshing.
4. *Beware of perceptual sets.* Anytime you pigeonhole people, objects, or events, there is a danger that your perceptions will be distorted by expectations or pre-existing categories. Be especially wary of labels and stereotypes. Try to see people as individuals and events as unique, one-time occurrences.
5. *Be aware of the ways in which motives and emotions influence perceptions.* It is difficult to avoid being swayed by your own interests, needs, desires, and emotions. But be aware of this trap and actively try to see the world through the eyes of others. Taking the other person's perspective is especially valuable in disputes or arguments. Ask yourself, "How does this look to her or him?"
6. *Make a habit of engaging in reality testing.* Actively look for additional evidence to check the accuracy of your perceptions. Ask questions, seek clarifications, and find alternative channels of information. Remember that perception is not automatically accurate. You could be wrong—we all are frequently.
7. *Pay attention.* Make a conscious effort to pay attention to other people and your surroundings. Don't drift through life in a haze. Listen to others with full concentration. Watch their facial expressions. Make eye contact. Try to get in the habit of

approaching perception as if you were going to have to testify later about what you saw and heard.

Knowledge builder

PERCEPTUAL AWARENESS AND ACCURACY

Relate

Because perceptions are reconstructions or models of external events, we should all engage in more frequent reality testing. Can you think of a recent event when a little reality testing would have saved you from misjudging a situation?

In order to improve your own perceptual awareness and accuracy, which strategies would you emphasize first?

Learning Check

1. Most perceptions can be described as active reconstructions of external reality. T or F?

2. Inaccuracies in eyewitness perceptions obviously occur in "real life," but they cannot be reproduced in psychology experiments. T or F?

3. Accuracy scores for facts provided by witnesses to staged crimes may be as low as 25 percent correct. T or F?

4. Victims of crimes are more accurate eyewitnesses than are impartial observers. T or F?

5. Reality testing is another term for dishabituation. T or F?

Critical Thinking

6. One of the leading critics of parapsychology research is magician James Randi (known professionally as The Amazing Randi). Why would a magician be a good person to investigate claims of parapsychological performance?

Answers:

1. T 2. F 3. T 4. F 5. F 6. To the extent that parapsychological performance involves deliberate attempts to mislead, it shares common ground with magic. A skilled magician would know what tricks to look for. For example, a magician wanting to carry out an operation using one hand—without the movement being noticed—will create a distraction with the other hand to draw the audience's attention. Randi argues that parapsychologists such as Uri Geller use magician's tricks for the same reason magicians do—to bamboozle you.

Psychologist's Journal

EPILOGUE

Until something surprising happens, like a FUEL AHEAD sign that turns out to read FOOD AHEAD, we tend to take perception for granted. But make no mistake, the world as we know it is created from sensory impressions. In fact, it takes about 50 milliseconds for a visual signal to move from the retina to the brain. Therefore, our perceptions always lag slightly behind events in the "real world." An event that happens quickly, like the pop of a flashbulb, may be over by the time we perceive it.

On the other end of the time scale, perception can blind us to very slow events and gradual changes. Humans evolved to detect sharp changes, such as the sudden appearance of a lion, a potential mate, or sources of food. However, many of the issues we discuss today involve phenomena that develop very slowly. Examples include the stockpiling of nuclear warheads, degradation of the environment, global deforestation, global warming, erosion of the ozone layer, and rapid human population growth. If we want to detect and respond to phenomena that unfold over years, even decades, what do we look for? How can we tell when we've found it? Can individual experts be relied upon to detect such phenomena, or should we try to recruit the combined perceptual power of large numbers of people operating together in something like a market?

CHAPTER IN REVIEW

Major Points

▶ Sensory systems select, analyze, and transduce information from the surrounding world.

▶ All of the senses rely on a complex series of mechanical, chemical, and neural events to generate messages understood by the brain.

▶ Sensory adaptation, selective attention, and sensory gating significantly modify our experiences.

▶ Perception is an active process of assembling sensations into meaningful patterns.

▶ We unconsciously use Gestalt principles to organize sensations into meaningful patterns.

▶ Our wondrous ability to perceive three-dimensional space is based on retinal disparity, bodily cues, and pictorial cues.

▶ Perception is greatly affected by learning, expectations, and motives.

▶ Perceptual accuracy and objectivity can be improved by conscious effort and an awareness of factors that contribute to erroneous perceptions.

Summary

In General, How Do Sensory Systems Function?

• Because of transduction, selectivity, limited sensitivity, feature detection, and coding patterns, the senses act as data reduction systems.

• Sensation can be partially understood in terms of sensory localization in the brain.

How Is Vision Accomplished?

• The eye is a visual system, not a photographic one. The visual system is designed to analyze visual information.

• Four common visual defects are myopia, hyperopia, presbyopia, and astigmatism.

• The rods and cones are photoreceptors in the retina.

• The rods specialize in peripheral vision, night vision, seeing black and white, and motion detection. The cones specialize in colour vision, acuity, and daylight vision.

• Colour vision is explained by the trichromatic theory in the retina and by the opponent-process theory in the visual system beyond the eyes.

• Total colour blindness is rare, but 8 percent of males and 1 percent of females are red-green colour-blind.

- Dark adaptation is caused mainly by an increase in the amount of rhodopsin in the rods.

What Are the Mechanisms of Hearing?

- Sound waves are the stimulus for hearing. They are transduced by the eardrum, auditory ossicles, oval window, cochlea, and ultimately, the hair cells.
- The frequency theory and place theory of hearing together explain how pitch is sensed.
- Three basic types of deafness are nerve deafness, conduction deafness, and stimulation deafness.

How Do the Chemical Senses Operate?

- Olfaction (smell) and gustation (taste) are chemical senses responsive to airborne or liquefied molecules.
- The lock-and-key theory partially explains smell. In addition, the location of the olfactory receptors in the nose helps identify various scents.
- Sweet and bitter tastes are based on a lock-and-key coding of molecule shapes. Salty and sour tastes are triggered by a direct flow of ions into taste receptors.

What Are the Somesthetic Senses and Why Are They Important?

- The somesthetic senses include the skin senses, vestibular senses, and kinesthetic senses (receptors that detect muscle and joint positioning).
- The skin senses are touch, pressure, pain, cold, and warmth. Sensitivity to each is related to the number of receptors found in an area of skin.
- Distinctions can be made between warning pain and reminding pain.
- Pain is greatly affected by anxiety, attention, and control over a stimulus. Pain can be reduced by controlling these factors.
- Various forms of motion sickness are related to messages received from the vestibular system, which detects gravity and movement.

Why Are We More Aware of Some Sensations than Others?

- Incoming sensations are affected by sensory adaptation, selective attention, and sensory gating.
- Selective gating of pain messages takes place in the spinal cord, as explained by gate control theory.

How Do Perceptual Constancies Affect Our Perceptions?

- Perception is the process of assembling sensations into a usable mental representation of the world.
- In vision, the image projected on the retina is constantly changing, but the external world appears stable because of size, shape, and brightness constancy.

What Basic Principles Do We Use to Group Sensations into Meaningful Patterns?

- Separating figure and ground is the most basic perceptual organization.

- The following factors help organize sensations: nearness, similarity, continuity, closure, contiguity, and common region.
- A perceptual organization may be thought of as a hypothesis held until evidence contradicts it.

How Is It Possible to See Depth and Judge Distance?

- A basic capacity for depth perception is present soon after birth.
- Depth perception depends on the muscular cues of accommodation and convergence. Stereoscopic vision is created mainly by retinal disparity.
- Pictorial cues also underlie depth perception. These include linear perspective, relative size, height in the picture plane, light and shadow, overlap, texture gradients, aerial haze, and motion parallax.
- The moon illusion can be explained by the apparent distance hypothesis, which emphasizes that many depth cues are present when the moon is on the horizon.

How Is Perception Altered by Learning, Expectations, and Motives?

- Perception is an active reconstruction of events.
- Perceptual learning influences the ways in which we organize and interpret sensations.
- One of the most familiar of all illusions, the Müller-Lyer illusion, seems to be related to perceptual learning, linear perspective, and size-distance invariance relationships.
- Personal motives and values often alter perceptions by changing the evaluation of what is seen or by altering attention to specific details.
- Perceptions may be based on top-down or bottom-up processing of information.
- Attention, prior experience, suggestion, and motives combine to create perceptual sets, or expectancies.

Is Extrasensory Perception Possible?

- Parapsychology is the study of purported psi phenomena, including clairvoyance, telepathy, precognition, and psychokinesis.
- Research in parapsychology remains controversial because of a variety of problems and shortcomings. The bulk of the evidence to date is against the existence of ESP.
- Stage ESP is based on deception and tricks.

What Can Be Done to Enhance Perceptual Accuracy?

- Eyewitness testimony is surprisingly unreliable. Eyewitness accuracy is further damaged by weapon focus and a number of similar factors.
- When a stimulus is repeated without change, our response to it undergoes habituation.
- Perceptual accuracy is enhanced by reality testing, dishabituation, and conscious efforts to pay attention.
- It is also valuable to break perceptual habits, to broaden frames of reference, to be aware of perceptual sets, and to be aware of the ways in which motives and emotions influence perceptions.

PSYCHOLOGY ON THE NET

If you have difficulty finding any of the sites listed here, visit http://psychologyjourney.nelson.com for an updated list of Internet addresses and direct links to relevant sites.

Grand Illusions This site provides optical illusions and visual effects. http://www.grand-illusions.com/

HEARNET A page that promotes ear protection for rock musicians. http://www.hearnet.com/index.shtml

The Joy of Visual Perception An online book about visual perception. http://www.yorku.ca/eye/

Mayday Pain Project A very wide-ranging and up-to-date site on pain information. http://www.painandhealth.org/index.html

Pain Control An especially interesting website on the use of virtual reality techniques to control pain in burn patients at the University of Washington Harborview Burn Center. http://www.hitl.washington.edu/projects/burn/

The Principles of Artistic Illusions Discusses visual illusions of artistic interest. http://www.lhup.edu/~dsimanek/3d/illus1.htm

Smell and Taste Disorders FAQ A wide range of questions and answers about smell and taste disorders. http://www.nlm.nih.gov/medlineplus/tasteandsmelldisorders.html

Somesthetic Senses An APA Monitor article about Ian Waterman, the man who has lost all sense of touch below the neck and of limb position can be found at http://www.apa.org/monitor/jun98/touch.html

Stereogram Links Provides links to stereograms and information about stereograms, including how to create your own. http://skal.planet-d.net/sis/sis.ang.html

Vestibular Disorders Association Provides links to sites concerned with vestibular problems. http://www.vestibular.org/

Vision Test An on-screen vision test. http://www.milfordeye.com/vision_test.html

Visual Illusions Large collections of visual illusions can be found at Professor Donald Hoffman's University of California, Irvine, website. http://aris.ss.uci.edu/cogsci/personnel/hoffman/illusions.html

InfoTrac College Edition For recent articles related to pain control, use Key Words search for ANXIETY and COUNTERIRRITATION. You can also use a Key Words search for EXTRASENSORY PERCEPTION.

INTERACTIVE LEARNING

Psychology: An Interactive Journey Remember that Chapter 4 of the CD-ROM that came with this text has practice tests, flashcards, interactive exercises, a crossword puzzle, and other valuable materials to enhance your learning experience.

PsychNow! 3a. Vision and Hearing, 3b. Chemical and Somesthetic Senses, 3c. Perception.

Psyk.trek 3. Sensation and Perception, Psyk.trek Simulations: 3. The Poggendorff Illusion.

Chart Your Progress

The questions that follow are only a sample of what you need to know. If you miss any of the items, you should review the entire chapter, do the exercises on the CD, and review the Knowledge Builders. Another way to prepare for tests is to get more practice with *WebTutor*, the *Study Guide*, or the *Practice Quizzes* that are available with this text.

1. The senses divide the world into basic perceptual features and sensory patterns, a process known as
   a. sensory localization
   b. sensory analysis
   c. accommodation
   d. phosphenation

2. Black-and-white vision and a high degree of sensitivity to movement are characteristic of
   a. rod vision
   b. cone vision
   c. the blind spot
   d. the fovea

3. Coloured afterimages are best explained by
   a. trichromatic theory
   b. the effects of astigmatism
   c. sensory localization
   d. opponent-process theory

4. Sounds are ultimately transduced by movements of the
   a. pinna
   b. malleus
   c. cochlea
   d. hair cells

5. The lock-and-key model appears to partly explain
   a. motion sickness
   b. olfaction and gustation
   c. dark adaptation
   d. colour blindness

6. The fact that a mild surface pain can greatly reduce more agonizing pain is consistent with
   a. gate control theory
   b. the concept of sensory adaptation
   c. sensory conflict theory
   d. perceptual constancy theory

7. Which of the following is LEAST likely to contribute to the formation of a perceptual figure?
   a. continuity
   b. closure
   c. similarity
   d. separation

8. The clearest example of a binocular depth cue is
   a. linear perspective
   b. retinal disparity
   c. aerial perspective
   d. motion parallax

9. Top-down perceptual processing is closely related to
   a. perceptual expectancies
   b. the Müller-Lyer illusion
   c. size-distance invariances
   d. precognition

10. A good antidote to perceptual habituation can be found in conscious efforts to
    a. reverse sensory gating
    b. pay attention
    c. achieve visual accommodation
    d. counteract shape constancy

Answers: 1. b 2. a 3. d 4. d 5. b 6. a 7. d 8. b 9. a 10. b

Chapter 5

Psychologist's Journal

A VISIT TO SEVERAL STATES (OF CONSCIOUSNESS)

In New Zealand, a Maori tohunga (priest) performs a night-long ritual to talk to the spirits who created the world during the mythical period the Aborigines call Dreamtime.

In Toronto, three businessmen head for a popular tavern after a particularly stressful day.

In the American Southwest, a Navajo elder gives his congregation peyote tea, a sacrament in the Native American Church, as a drumbeat resounds in the darkness.

In New Delhi, India, a man sits cross-legged in a deep trance in order to experience a state of oneness with the universe.

In Northern Ireland, a nun living in a convent spends an entire week in silent prayer and contemplation.

In Los Angeles, an aspiring actor consults a hypnotist for help in reducing her stage fright.

In Vancouver, an artist spends two hours in a flotation chamber, trying to clear her head before she returns to work on a large painting.

At a park in Amsterdam, a group of street musicians smoke a joint and sing for spare change.

In Montreal, one of your authors pours himself another cup of tea in an attempt to stay alert.

What do all these people have in common? Each person seeks to alter consciousness—in different ways, to different degrees, and for different reasons. As these examples suggest, consciousness can take many forms. In the discussion that follows, we will begin with the familiar realms of sleep and dreaming and then move to more exotic states of consciousness.

Survey Questions

- What is an altered state of consciousness?
- What are the effects of sleep loss or changes in sleep patterns?
- Are there different stages of sleep?
- What are the causes of sleep disorders and unusual sleep events?
- Do dreams have meaning?
- How is hypnosis done, and what are its limitations?
- What is meditation? Does it have any benefits?
- What are the effects of the more commonly used psychoactive drugs?
- How are dreams used to promote personal understanding?

▶ States of Consciousness—The Many Faces of Awareness

Survey Question:
- What is an altered state of consciousness?

To be conscious means to be aware. **Consciousness** consists of all the sensations, perceptions, memories, and feelings you are aware of at any instant (Farthing, 1992). We spend most of our lives in **waking consciousness,** a state of clear, organized alertness. In waking consciousness we perceive time, places, and events as real, meaningful, and familiar. But states of consciousness related to fatigue, delirium, hypnosis, drugs, and ecstasy may differ markedly from "normal" awareness. Everyone experiences at least some altered states, such as sleep, dreaming, and daydreaming. In everyday life, changes in consciousness may also accompany long-distance running, listening to music, making love, or other circumstances.

ALTERED STATES OF CONSCIOUSNESS _How are altered states distinguished from normal awareness?_ During an **altered state of consciousness (ASC),** changes occur in the quality and pattern of mental activity. Typically, there are distinct shifts in perceptions, emotions, memory, time sense, thinking, feelings of self-control, and suggestibility (Tart, 1986). Definitions aside, most people know when they have experienced an ASC.

Are there other causes of ASCs? In addition to those already mentioned, we could add: sensory overload (for example, a rave, Mardi Gras crowd, or mosh pit), monotonous stimulation (such as "highway hypnotism" on long drives), unusual physical conditions (high fever, hyperventilation, dehydration, sleep loss, near-death experiences), restricted sensory input, and many other possibilities. In some instances, altered states of awareness have important cultural significance. (See "Consciousness and Culture" for more information.) In this chapter, we will focus on sleep, dreaming, hypnosis, meditation, and the effects of drugs. Let's begin with questions about sleep, the most familiar ASC.

Consciousness Mental awareness of sensations, perceptions, memories, and feelings.
Waking consciousness A state of normal, alert awareness.
Altered state of consciousness (ASC) A condition of awareness distinctly different in quality or pattern from waking consciousness.

▶ Sleep—A Nice Place to Visit

Survey Question:
- What are the effects of sleep loss or changes in sleep patterns?

Many of us will spend some 25 years of life asleep. Contrary to common belief, you are not totally unresponsive during sleep. For instance, you are more likely to awaken if you hear your own name spoken, instead of another. Likewise, a sleeping mother may ignore a jet thundering overhead, but wake at the slightest whimper of her child. It's even possible to do simple tasks while asleep. In one experiment, people learned to avoid an electric shock by touching a switch each time a tone sounded. Eventually, they could do it without waking. (This is much like the basic survival skill of turning off your alarm clock without waking.) Of course, sleep does impose limitations. Don't expect to learn math, a foreign language, or other complex skills while asleep—especially if the snooze takes place in class (Druckman & Bjork, 1994; Wood et al., 1992).

Because sleep is familiar, many people think they know all about it. Before reading more, test your knowledge with the Sleep Quiz that follows. Were you surprised by any of the answers? Let's see what we know about our "daily retreat from the world."

HUMAN DIVERSITY   Consciousness and Culture

Throughout history, people have found ways to alter consciousness. A dramatic example is the sweat lodge ceremony of the Sioux Indians. During the ritual, several men sit in total darkness inside a small chamber heated by coals. Cedar smoke, bursts of steam, and sage fill the air. The men chant rhythmically. The heat builds. At last they can stand it no more. The door is thrown open. Cooling night breezes rush in. And then? The cycle begins again—often to be repeated four or five times more.

The ritual "sweats" of the Sioux are meant to cleanse the mind and body. When they are especially intense, they bring altered awareness and personal revelation.

People seek some altered states for pleasure, as is often true of drug intoxication. Yet, as the Sioux illustrate, many cultures regard altered consciousness as a pathway to personal enlightenment. Indeed, all cultures and most religions recognize and accept some alterations of consciousness. However, the meaning given to these

In many cultures, rituals of healing, prayer, purification, or personal transformation are accompanied by altered states of consciousness. Many First Nation groups in Canada practise similar sweat ceremonies.

states varies greatly—from signs of "madness" and "possession" by spirits to life-enhancing breakthroughs. Thus, cultural conditioning greatly affects what altered states each of us recognizes, seeks, considers normal, and attains (Metzner, 1998; Ward, 1989).

Sleep Quiz

1. People can learn to sleep for just a few hours a night and still function well. T or F?
2. Everyone dreams every night. T or F?
3. The brain rests during sleep. T or F?
4. Resting during the day can replace lost sleep. T or F?
5. As people get older, they sleep more. T or F?
6. Alcohol may help a person get to sleep, but it disturbs sleep later during the night. T or F?
7. If a person goes without sleep long enough, death will occur. T or F?
8. Dreams mostly occur during deep sleep. T or F?
9. A person prevented from dreaming would soon go crazy. T or F?
10. Sleepwalking occurs when a person acts out a dream. T or F?

Answers: 1. F 2. T 3. F 4. F 5. F 6. T 7. T 8. F 9. F 10. F

Biological rhythm Any repeating cycle of biological activity, such as sleep and waking cycles or changes in body temperature.

Circadian rhythms Cyclical changes in bodily functions and arousal levels that recur on a schedule of about 24 hours. These cycles are governed by internal biological clocks. One such clock regulates sleep and wakefulness.

Microsleep A brief shift in brain-wave patterns to those of sleep.

The Need for Sleep

How strong is the need for sleep? Sleep is an innate **biological rhythm** or **circadian rhythm** (sur-KAY-dee-un) that can never be entirely ignored (Webb, 1994). Of course, sleep will give way temporarily, especially at times of great danger. As one comic put it, "The lion and the lamb shall lie down together, but the lamb will not be very sleepy." However, there are limits to how long humans can go without sleep. A rare disease that prevents sleep always ends the same way: The patient falls into a stupor, followed by coma, followed by death (Oliwenstein, 1993). (See ▶ Figure 5.1.)

Imagine placing an animal on a moving treadmill suspended over a pool of water. This is not a very good way to sleep! Even so, sleep will always win. Under these conditions, animals soon drift into repeated microsleeps (Goleman, 1982). A **microsleep** is a brief shift in brain activity to the pattern normally recorded during sleep. When you drive,

▶**Figure 5.1**

Not all animals sleep, but like humans, those that do have powerful sleep needs. For example, dolphins must voluntarily breathe air, which means they face the choice of staying awake or drowning. The dolphins solve this problem by sleeping on just one side of their brains at a time! The other half of the brain, which remains awake, controls breathing (Jouvet, 1999).

Sleep deprivation Being prevented from getting desired or needed amounts of sleep.

Sleep-deprivation psychosis A major disruption of mental and emotional functioning brought about by sleep loss.

Sleep patterns The order and timing of daily sleep and waking periods.

Short sleeper A person averaging five hours of sleep or less per night.

Long sleeper A person who averages nine hours of sleep or more per night.

remember that microsleeps can lead to macro-accidents. Even if your eyes are open, you can fall asleep for a few seconds. Roughly two out of every 100 highway crashes are caused by sleepiness (Lyznicki et al., 1998). By the way, if you are struggling to stay awake while driving, you should stop, quit fighting it, and take a short nap. Coffee helps too, but briefly giving in to sleep helps more (Horne & Reyner, 1996).

SLEEP DEPRIVATION *How long could a person go without sleep?* With few exceptions, four days or more without sleep becomes hell for everyone. For example, a disc jockey named Peter Tripp once stayed awake for about 200 hours in order to raise money for charity. After 100 hours, he began to hallucinate: He saw cobwebs in his shoes and watched in terror as a tweed coat became a suit of "furry worms." By the end of his ordeal, Tripp was unable to distinguish between his waking nightmares, hallucinations, and reality (Luce, 1965). Despite Tripp's breakdown, longer sleepless periods are possible. The world record is held by Randy Gardner—who at age 17 went 268 hours (11 days) without sleep. Surprisingly, Randy needed only 14 hours of sleep to recover. It is not necessary to completely replace lost sleep. As Randy found, most symptoms of **sleep deprivation** (sleep loss) are reversed by a single night's rest.

What are the costs of sleep loss? Age and personality make a big difference. Although Tripp's behaviour became quite bizarre, Randy was less impaired. However, make no mistake: Sleep is a necessity. At various times, Randy's speech was slurred, and he couldn't concentrate, remember clearly, or name common objects (Coren, 1996). Sleep loss also causes trembling hands, drooping eyelids, inattention, irritability, staring, increased pain sensitivity, and general discomfort (Naitoh, Kelly, & Englund, 1989).

Most people who have not slept for two or three days can still do interesting or complex mental tasks (Binks, Waters, & Hurry, 1999). But they have trouble paying attention, staying alert, and following simple or boring routines. For a driver, pilot, or machine operator, this can spell disaster (Fairclough & Graham, 1999). If a task is monotonous (such as factory work or air traffic control), no amount of sleep loss is safe (Gillberg & Akerstedt, 1998). In fact, if you lose just one hour of sleep a night, it can affect your mood, memory, ability to pay attention, and even your health (Everson, 1998; Maas, 1999).

How can you tell how much sleep you really need? Pick a day when you feel well rested. Then sleep that night until you wake without an alarm clock. If you feel rested when you wake up, that's your natural sleep need. If you're sleeping fewer hours than you need, you're building up a sleep debt every day (Maas, 1999).

Severe sleep loss can cause a temporary **sleep-deprivation psychosis** (loss of contact with reality) like Peter Tripp suffered. Confusion, disorientation, delusions, and hallucinations are typical of this reaction. Hallucinations and delusions rarely appear before 60 hours of wakefulness (Naitoh, Kelly, & Englund, 1989).

Sleep Patterns

Sleep was described as an innate biological rhythm. What does that mean? **Sleep patterns** (daily rhythms of sleep and waking) are very stable. Usually they will continue for many days, even when clocks and light-dark cycles are removed, such as in a cave or a submarine (Palinkas, Suedfeld, & Steel, 1995). However, under such conditions humans eventually shift to a sleep-waking cycle that averages 25 hours, not 24. This suggests that external time markers, especially light and dark, help tie our sleep rhythms to a normal 24-hour day (▶Figure 5.2). Otherwise, many of us would drift into our own unusual sleep cycles.

What is the normal range of sleep? A few individuals can get by on only an hour or two of sleep a night—and feel perfectly fine. However, this is rare. Eight percent of the population are considered **short sleepers,** getting five hours of sleep or less. Fifteen percent of Canadians average less than 6.5 hours of sleep per night (Statistics Canada, 2001). On the other end of the scale we find **long sleepers,** who doze nine hours or more (and tend to be daytime worriers, according to two Cape Breton University researchers [McCann & Stewin, 1988]). The majority of us sleep on a familiar seven- to eight-hour-

Time of Day

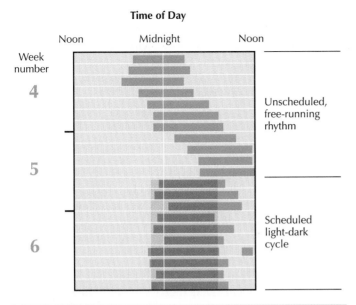

► **Figure 5.2**

Sleep rhythms. Bars show periods of sleep during the fourth, fifth, and sixth weeks of an experiment with a human subject. During unscheduled periods, the subject was allowed to select times of sleep and lighting. The result was a sleep rhythm of about 25 hours. Notice how this free-running rhythm began to advance around the clock. When periods of darkness were scheduled (coloured area), the rhythm quickly resynchronized with 24-hour days. (Adapted from Czeisler et al., 1981.)

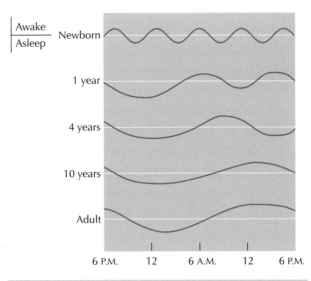

► **Figure 5.3**

Development of sleep patterns. Short cycles of sleep and waking gradually become the night-day cycle of an adult. While most adults don't take naps, mid-afternoon sleepiness is a natural part of the sleep cycle. (After Williams et al., 1964.)

per-night schedule. For a few people, however, it is quite normal to sleep as much as 11 hours a night. Urging everyone to sleep eight hours would be like advising everyone to wear medium-size shoes.

Do elderly people need more sleep? Sleep needs actually remain fairly constant as people age. However, older people rarely get the sleep they need. Total sleep time declines throughout life. Those over the age of 50 average only six hours of sleep a night. In contrast, infants spend about 16 to 18 hours a day sleeping, usually in two- to four-hour cycles.

As they mature, most children go through a "nap" stage and eventually settle into a steady cycle of sleeping once a day (see ► Figure 5.3). Some people, of course, maintain the afternoon "siesta" as an adult pattern. Perhaps we all should: Mid-afternoon sleepiness is a natural part of the sleep cycle. Brief, well-timed naps can help maintain alertness in people like truck drivers and hospital interns, who often must fight drowsiness (Batejat & Lagarde, 1999).

It is very tempting to try to reduce sleep time. However, people on *shortened* cycles— for example, three hours of sleep to six hours awake—often can't get to sleep when the cycle calls for it. That's why astronauts continue to sleep on their normal earth schedule while in space. Adapting to longer than normal days is more promising. Such days can be tailored to match natural sleep patterns, which have a ratio of 2 to 1 between time awake and time asleep. For instance, one study showed that 28-hour "days" work for some people. Overall, however, sleep is a "gentle tyrant." Sleep patterns may be bent and stretched, but they rarely yield entirely to human whims (Akerstedt et al., 1993).

> **Sleep hormone** A sleep-promoting substance found in the brain and spinal cord.

► Stages of Sleep—The Nightly Roller-Coaster Ride

Survey Question:
■ Are there different stages of sleep?

What causes sleep? Early sleep experts thought that something in the bloodstream must cause sleep. But conjoined twins, whose bodies are joined at birth, show that this is false. It's not unusual for one twin to be asleep while the second is awake. During waking hours, a **sleep hormone** (sleep-promoting chemical) collects in the brain and spinal cord, not in the blood. If this substance is extracted from one animal and injected into another, the second animal will sleep deeply for many hours (Cravatt et al., 1995).

Electroencephalograph (EEG) A device designed to detect, amplify, and record electrical activity in the brain.

Beta waves Small, fast brain waves associated with being awake and alert.

Alpha waves Large, slow brain waves associated with relaxation and falling asleep.

Sleep stages Levels of sleep identified by brain-wave patterns and behavioural changes.

Light sleep Stage 1 sleep, marked by small irregular brain waves and some alpha waves.

Hypnic jerk A reflex muscle twitch throughout the body that often occurs as one is falling asleep.

Sleep spindles Distinctive bursts of brain-wave activity that indicate a person is asleep.

Delta waves Large, slow brain waves that occur in deeper sleep (stages 3 and 4).

Whether you are awake or asleep right now depends on the balance between separate sleep and waking systems. Brain circuits and chemicals in one of the systems promote sleep. A network of brain cells in the other system responds to chemicals that inhibit sleep. The two systems see-saw back and forth, switching the brain between sleep and wakefulness. Note that the brain does not "shut down" during sleep. Rather, the pattern of activity changes. The total amount of activity remains fairly constant (Steriade & McCarley, 1990).

Stages of Sleep

What happens when you fall asleep? The changes that come with sleep can be measured with an **electroencephalograph** (eh-LEK-tro-en-SEF-uh-lo-graf), or **EEG.** The brain generates tiny electrical signals (brain waves) that can be amplified and recorded. When you are awake and alert, the EEG reveals a pattern of small, fast waves called **beta** (see ▶Figure 5.4). Immediately before sleep, the pattern shifts to larger and slower waves called **alpha.** (Alpha waves also occur when you are relaxed and allow your thoughts to drift.) As the eyes close, breathing becomes slow and regular, the pulse rate slows, and body temperature drops. Soon after, four separate **sleep stages** occur.

STAGE 1   As you lose consciousness and enter **light sleep** (stage 1 sleep), your heart rate slows even more. Breathing becomes more irregular. The muscles of your body relax. This may trigger a reflex muscle contraction throughout the body called a **hypnic jerk** (HIP-nik: sleep). (This is quite normal, so have no fear about admitting to your friends that you fell asleep with a hypnic jerk.) In stage 1 sleep, the EEG is made up mainly of small, irregular waves with some alpha. Persons awakened at this time may or may not say they were asleep.

STAGE 2   As sleep deepens, body temperature drops further. Also, the EEG begins to include **sleep spindles,** which are short bursts of distinctive brain-wave activity. Spindles seem to mark the true boundary of sleep. Within four minutes after spindles appear, most people will say they were asleep.

STAGE 3   In stage 3, a new brain wave called delta begins to appear. **Delta waves** are very large and slow. They signal a move to deeper sleep and a further loss of consciousness (Shafton, 1995).

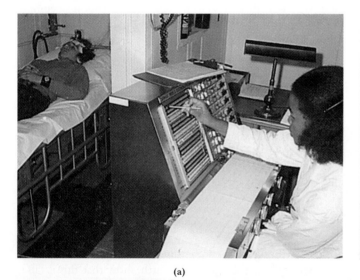

(a)

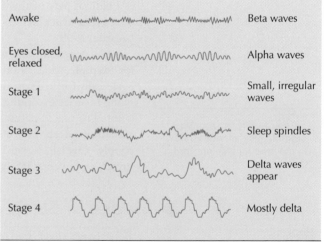

(b)

▶Figure 5.4

(a) Photograph of an EEG recording session. The man in the background is asleep. *(b)* Changes in brain-wave patterns associated with various stages of sleep. Actually, most types of waves are present at all times, but they occur more or less frequently in various sleep stages.

Deep sleep Stage 4 sleep; the deepest form of normal sleep.

Rapid eye movements (REMs) Swift eye movements during sleep.

REM sleep Sleep marked by rapid eye movements and a return to stage 1 EEG patterns.

NREM sleep Non-rapid eye movement sleep characteristic of stages 2, 3, and 4.

STAGE 4   Most people reach **deep sleep** (the deepest level of normal sleep) in about an hour. Stage 4 brain waves are almost pure delta and the sleeper is in a state of oblivion. If you make a loud noise during stage 4, the sleeper will awake up in a state of confusion and may not remember the noise. After spending some time in stage 4, the sleeper returns (through stages 3 and 2) to stage 1. Further shifts between deeper and lighter sleep occur throughout the night (see ▶Figure 5.5).

Two Basic Kinds of Sleep

If you watch a person sleep, you will soon notice that the sleeper's eyes occasionally move under the eyelids. These **rapid eye movements (or REMs)** are associated with dreaming (Figure 5.5). Roughly 85 percent of the time, people awakened during REMs report vivid dreams. In addition to rapid eye movements, **REM sleep** is marked by a return to fast, irregular EEG patterns similar to stage 1 sleep. In fact, the brain is so active during REM sleep that it looks as if the person is awake (Hobson et al., 1998). REM sleep is easy to observe in pets, such as dogs and cats. Watch for eye and face movements and irregular breathing. (You can forget about your pet iguana, though. Reptiles show no signs of REM sleep.)

REM AND NREM SLEEP   The two most basic states of sleep are REM sleep with its associated dreaming and **non-REM (NREM) sleep,** which occurs during stages 1, 2, 3, and 4 (Jouvet, 1999). NREM sleep is dream-free about 90 percent of the time. Your first period of stage 1 sleep is usually free of REMs and dreams. Later returns to stage 1 are usually accompanied by rapid eye movements. Dreams during REM sleep tend to be longer, clearer, more detailed, more bizarre, and more "dream-like" than thoughts and images that occur in NREM sleep (Shafton, 1995). Recent studies have shown that brain areas associated with imagery and emotion become more active during REM sleep. This may explain why REM dreams tend to be more vivid than those that occur during NREM sleep (Braun, Balkin, & Herscovitch, 1998).

What is the function of NREM sleep? NREM sleep increases after physical exertion. This suggests that it helps us recover from bodily fatigue. In comparison, daytime stress tends to increase REM sleep. REM sleep totals only about 90 minutes per night (about the same as a feature movie). Yet, its link with dreaming makes it as important as NREM sleep. REM sleep may rise dramatically when there is a death in the family, trouble at work, a marital conflict, or other emotionally charged events.

REM sleep patterns can be affected in some diseases involving the brain. One example is Alzheimer's disease. At the Sacre-Coeur Hospital in Montreal, Jacques Montplaisir and his colleagues have demonstrated that patients with early signs of Alzheimer's disease spend less time in REM sleep, and their REM EEG activity also slows down in

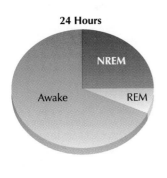

(a)

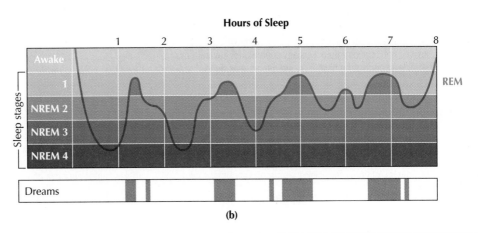

(b)

▶Figure 5.5

(a) Average proportion of time adults spend daily in REM sleep and NREM sleep. REM periods add up to about 20 percent of total sleep time. *(b)* Typical changes in stages of sleep during the night. Notice that dreams mostly coincide with REM periods.

comparison to those who don't have Alzheimer's (Montplaisir et al., 1995). Identifying abnormal patterns of brain-wave activity that occur as Alzheimer's gets progressively worse may eventually help doctors predict which patients are likely to develop more severe forms of Alzheimer's. At the same time, this type of research may also tell us a great deal about how the brain operates during REM sleep in general.

DREAMING   What *happens to the body when a person dreams?* REM sleep is a time of high emotion. The heart beats irregularly. Blood pressure and breathing waver. Both males and females appear to be sexually aroused: Males usually have an erection, and genital blood flow increases in women. This occurs for all REM sleep, so it is not strictly related to erotic dreams (Jouvet, 1999).

During REM sleep your body becomes quite still, as if you were paralyzed. Imagine acting out some of your recent dreams. Very likely, REM-sleep paralysis prevents some hilarious—and even dangerous—nighttime escapades. A lack of muscle paralysis during REM sleep is called **REM behaviour disorder.** People with this problem may thrash violently, leap out of bed, or attack their bed partners. One patient tied himself to his bed every night. That way, he couldn't jump up and crash into furniture or walls (Shafton, 1995).

In a moment we will survey some additional sleep problems—if you are still awake. First, here are a few questions to check your memory of our discussion so far.

> **REM behaviour disorder**
> A failure of normal muscle paralysis, leading to violent actions during REM sleep.

Knowledge builder

ALTERED STATES AND SLEEP

Relate

Make a quick list of some altered states of consciousness you have experienced. What do they have in common? How are they different? What conditions caused them?

Imagine that you are a counsellor at a sleep clinic. You must explain the basics of sleep and dreaming to a new client who knows little about these topics. Can you do it?

Learning Check

1. Altered states of consciousness are defined mainly by changes in patterns of alertness. T or F?
2. A momentary shift in brain activity to a pattern characteristic of sleep is referred to as
   a. delta sleep b. light sleep c. microsleep d. deprivation sleep
3. Delusions and hallucinations typically continue for several days after a sleep-deprived individual returns to normal sleep. T or F?

4. Older adults, and particularly the elderly, sleep more than children do because the elderly are more easily fatigued. T or F?
5. Most studies of sleep patterns show a consistent ratio of 2 to 1 between time awake and time asleep. T or F?
6. Rapid eye movements (REMs) indicate that a person is in deep sleep. T or F?
7. Alpha waves are to presleep drowsiness as _____ _____ are to stage 4 sleep.

Critical Thinking

8. Why might it be better for the unscheduled human sleep-waking cycle to average more than 24 hours, instead of less?
9. Biologically, what advantages might sleeping provide?

Answers:

1. F 2. c 3. F 4. F 5. T 6. F 7. delta waves 8. Sleep experts hypothesize that the 25-hour average leaves a little "slack" in the cycle. External time markers can then retard the bodily cycle slightly to synchronize it with light-dark cycles. If the bodily cycle were shorter than 24 hours, we all might have to "stretch" every day to adjust. 9. Lowering bodily activity and metabolism during sleep may help conserve energy and lengthen life. Also, natural selection may have favoured sleep because animals that remained active at night probably had a higher chance of being killed. (We bet they had more fun, though.)

▶ Sleep Disturbances—Showing Nightly: Sleep Wars!

Survey Question:
■ What are the causes of sleep disorders and unusual sleep events?

Insomnia Difficulty in getting to sleep or staying asleep.

Drug-dependency insomnia Insomnia that follows withdrawal from sleeping pills.

Sleep clinics treat thousands of people each year who suffer from sleep disorders or complaints. Let's explore some of the more interesting problems these people face, starting with insomnia.

Insomnia

Staring at the ceiling at 2 a.m. is pretty low on most people's list of favourite pastimes. In 1992, 20 percent of Canadian adults reported frequent problems getting to sleep or staying asleep. This number had risen sharply to 25 percent by 1998 (Statistics Canada, 2001). About 9 percent of people suffer from serious or chronic insomnia. **Insomnia** includes difficulty in going to sleep, frequent nighttime awakenings, waking too early, or a combination of these problems (Bond & Wooten, 1996). Insomnia lowers people's ability to work, and it damages their health and relationships (Walsh & Uestuen, 1999). (Table 5.1 lists other damaging sleep disturbances.)

North Americans will spend well over half a billion dollars this year on sleeping pills. There is real irony in this expense. Non-prescription sleeping pills such as *Sominex, Nytol,* and *Sleep-eze* have little or no sleep-inducing effect. Even worse are barbiturates. These prescription sedatives decrease both stage 4 sleep and REM sleep, drastically lowering sleep quality. In addition, many users become "sleeping-pill junkies" who need an ever-greater number of pills to get to sleep. The end result is **drug–dependency insomnia** (sleeplessness caused by withdrawal from sleeping pills). Victims must be painstakingly weaned from their sleep medicines. Otherwise, terrible nightmares and "rebound insomnia" may drive them back to drug use.

If sleeping pills are a poor way to treat insomnia, what can be done? Sleep specialists now prefer to treat insomnia with lifestyle changes and behavioural techniques like those described in "Behavioural Remedies for Insomnia" on page 174 (Walsh & Scweitzer, 1999).

**Table 5.1
Sleep Disturbances— Things That Go Wrong in the Night**

Hypersomnia Excessive daytime sleepiness. This can result from depression, insomnia, narcolepsy, sleep apnea, sleep drunkenness, periodic limb movements, drug abuse, and other problems.
Insomnia Difficulty in getting to sleep or staying asleep; also, not feeling rested after sleeping.
Narcolepsy Sudden, irresistible, daytime sleep attacks that may last anywhere from a few minutes to half an hour. Victims may fall asleep while standing, talking, or even driving.
Nightmare disorder Vivid, recurrent nightmares that significantly disturb sleep.
Periodic limb movement syndrome Muscle twitches (primarily affecting the legs) that occur every 20 to 40 seconds and severely disturb sleep.
REM behaviour disorder A failure of normal muscle paralysis, leading to violent actions during REM sleep.
Restless legs syndrome An irresistible urge to move the legs in order to relieve sensations of creeping, tingling, prickling, aching, or tension.
Sleep apnea During sleep, breathing stops for 20 seconds or more until the person wakes a little, gulps in air, and settles back to sleep; this cycle may be repeated hundreds of times per night.
Sleep drunkenness A slow transition to clear consciousness after awakening; sometimes associated with irritable or aggressive behaviour.
Sleep terror disorder The repeated occurrence of night terrors that significantly disturb sleep.
Sleep-wake schedule disorder A mismatch between the sleep-wake schedule demanded by a person's bodily rhythm and that demanded by the environment.
Sleepwalking disorder Repeated incidents of leaving bed and walking about while asleep.

(Bond & Wooten, 1996; DSM-IV, 1994; Hauri & Linde, 1990.)

USING PSYCHOLOGY   Behavioural Remedies for Insomnia

All of the approaches you see here are helpful for treating insomnia (Hopson, 1986). Experiment a little and find out what works for you. According to University of Laval researchers, sleep restriction and stimulus control are the most effective among the methods listed here (Lacks & Morin, 1992).

Stimulants Avoid stimulants such as coffee and cigarettes. Also remember that alcohol, while not a stimulant, impairs sleep quality.

Worries Schedule time in the early evening to write down worries or concerns. Plan what you will do about them the next day. Then put them out of mind until morning.

Relaxation Learn a physical or mental strategy for relaxing, such as progressive muscle relaxation (see Chapter 13), meditation, or blotting out worries with calming images. Strenuous exercise during the day promotes sleep. It is best if done about six hours before bedtime (Maas, 1999). Exercise in the evening is helpful only if it is very light.

Sleep Restriction Even if you miss an entire night's sleep, do not sleep late in the morning, nap more than an hour, sleep during the evening, or go to bed early the following night. Try to restrict sleep to your normal bedtime hours. That way, you will avoid fragmenting your sleep rhythms (Lacks & Morin, 1992).

Stimulus Control Link only sleep with your bedroom so that it does not trigger worrying: (1) Go to bed only when you are feeling sleepy. (2) Awaken at the same time each morning. (3) Avoid non-sleep activities in bed. (4) Always leave the bedroom if sleep has not occurred within 10 minutes. (5) Do something else when you are upset about not being able to sleep (Lacks & Morin, 1992).

Paradoxical Intention To remove the pressures of trying to get to sleep, try instead to keep your eyes open (in the dark) and stay awake as long as possible (Horvath & Goheen, 1990). This allows sleep to overtake you unexpectedly and lowers performance anxiety. Never try to go to sleep. Arrange to let it happen.

Temporary insomnia A brief episode of insomnia.

Tryptophan A sleep-promoting amino acid.

Chronic insomnia Insomnia that persists for more than three weeks.

Stimulus control Linking a particular response with specific stimuli.

TYPES AND CAUSES OF INSOMNIA   Worry, stress, and excitement often cause **temporary insomnia** (a brief period of sleeplessness) and a self-defeating cycle. First, heightened arousal blocks sleep. Then, frustration and anger cause more arousal, which further delays sleep. Delayed sleep causes more frustration, and so on. A good way to beat this cycle is to avoid fighting it. It is usually best to get up and do something useful or satisfying when you have difficulty sleeping. (Reading a textbook might be a good choice of useful activities.) Return to bed only when you begin to feel that you are struggling to stay awake.

What you eat can also affect how easily you get to sleep. Eating starchy foods increases the amount of **tryptophan** (TRIP-tuh-fan: an amino acid) reaching the brain. More tryptophan, in turn, increases the amount of serotonin in the brain. Serotonin is associated with relaxation, a positive mood, and sleepiness. Thus, to promote sleep, try eating a snack that is nearly all starch. Good sleep-inducing snacks are cookies, bread, pasta, oatmeal, pretzels, bagels, and dry cereal. If you really want to drop the bomb on insomnia, try eating a baked potato (which may be the world's largest sleeping pill!) (Sahelian, 1998).

What about more serious cases of insomnia? **Chronic insomnia** exists if sleeping problems last for more than three weeks. Treatment for chronic insomnia usually begins with a careful analysis of a patient's sleep habits, lifestyle, stress levels, and medical problems (Bond & Wooten, 1996). The first thing anyone suffering from insomnia should do is to consume less caffeine, alcohol, and tobacco. Some insomniacs benefit from relaxation training to lower arousal before sleep. **Stimulus control** strategies also help. Stimulus control refers to linking a response with specific stimuli. For example, patients are told to strictly avoid doing anything but sleeping when they are in bed. They are not to study, eat, watch TV, read, pay the bills, or even think in bed. In this way, only sleeping becomes associated with retiring (Hauri & Linde, 1990).

One of the best ways to combat insomnia is also the simplest. Many insomniacs have scattered sleep habits. For these people, adopting a regular schedule helps establish a firm body rhythm, greatly improving sleep. Patients are told to get up and go to sleep at the same time each day, including weekends. (Many people disturb their sleep rhythms by staying up late on weekends.) (Again, see "Behavioural Remedies for Insomnia.")

Sleepwalking and Sleeptalking

Sleepwalking is eerie and fascinating. **Somnambulists** (som-NAM-bue-lists: those who sleepwalk) avoid obstacles, descend stairways, and on rare occasions may step out of windows or in front of automobiles. The sleepwalker's eyes are usually open, but a blank face and shuffling feet reveal that the person is still asleep. A parent who finds a child sleepwalking should gently guide the child back to bed. Awakening a sleepwalker does no harm, but it is not necessary.

People can behave in a highly unusual manner while sleepwalking. In one tragic case, a young Canadian man drove about 23 kilometres to the home of his in-laws, where he took up a kitchen knife, stabbed his mother-in-law to death, viciously beat up his father-in-law, and was injured himself in the scuffle. The young man was subjected to an intense medical and psychological examination, and evidence was sought to determine whether he had carried out these acts consciously. His defence lawyers argued that the savage attacks were not premeditated and that they occurred during an episode of nocturnal somnambulism, in a state of unawareness. The evidence included the following points: (1) the young man had good relations with his parents-in-law; (2) he and his family had a history of sleep-related problems, including sleepwalking; (3) he had no history of aggression against anyone; and (4) his sleep EEG patterns were somewhat unusual and similar to those who engage in sleepwalking. The jury was convinced, and the man was acquitted of all criminal charges. The case reached as far as the Supreme Court, but the verdict of not guilty was upheld throughout the appeal process (Broughton et al. 1994).

Violent acts during sleepwalking, however, are extremely rare. Most somnambulists engage in very innocuous activities such as sitting up in bed, ambling about the room, turning on the lights in the house, or going to the refrigerator for a snack.

Does sleepwalking occur during dreaming? No. Remember that people are normally immobilized during REM sleep. EEG studies have shown that somnambulism occurs during NREM stages 3 and 4. **Sleeptalking** also occurs mostly in NREM stages of sleep. The link with deep sleep explains why sleeptalking makes little sense and why sleepwalkers are confused and remember little when awakened (DSM-IV, 1994).

Nightmares and Night Terrors

Stage 4 sleep is also the realm of night terrors. These frightening episodes are quite different from ordinary nightmares. A **nightmare** is simply a bad dream that takes place during REM sleep. Nightmares, which occur about twice a month, are usually brief and easily remembered (Wood & Bootzin, 1990). During stage 4 **night terrors,** a person suffers total panic and may hallucinate frightening dream images into the bedroom. An attack may last 15 or 20 minutes. When it is over, the person awakens drenched in sweat, but only vaguely remembers the terror. Since night terrors occur during NREM sleep (when the body is not immobilized), victims may sit up, scream, get out of bed, or run around the room. Victims remember little afterward. (Other family members, however, may have a story to tell.) Night terrors are most common in childhood, but they continue to plague about two out of every 100 adults (Ohayon, Guilleminault, & Priest, 1999).

HOW TO ELIMINATE A NIGHTMARE *Is there any way to stop a recurring nightmare?* A bad nightmare can be worse than any horror movie. You can leave a theatre, but we often remain trapped in terrifying dreams. Nevertheless, most nightmares can be banished by following three simple steps. First, write down your nightmare, describing it in detail. Next, change the dream any way you wish, being sure to spell out the details of the new dream. The third step is **imagery rehearsal,** in which you mentally rehearse the changed dream before you fall asleep again (Krakow & Neidhardt, 1992). Imagery rehearsal may work because it makes upsetting dreams familiar while a person is awake and feeling safe. Or perhaps it mentally "reprograms" future dream content. In any case, the technique has helped many people (Krakow et al., 1996). Lucid dreaming is another technique that can

---

Somnambulism
Sleepwalking; occurs during NREM sleep.

Sleeptalking Speaking that occurs during NREM sleep.

Nightmare A bad dream that occurs during REM sleep.

Night terror A state of panic that occurs during NREM sleep.

Imagery rehearsal Mentally rehearsing and changing a nightmare in order to prevent it from reoccurring.

reduce the severity of nightmares (see the Psychology in Action section at the end of the chapter).

Sleep Apnea

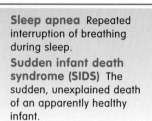

Sleep apnea Repeated interruption of breathing during sleep.

Sudden infant death syndrome (SIDS) The sudden, unexplained death of an apparently healthy infant.

Some sage once said, "Laugh and the whole world laughs with you; snore and you sleep alone." Nightly "wood sawing" is often harmless, but it can signal a serious problem. A person who snores loudly, with short silences and loud gasps or snorts, may suffer from apnea (AP-nee-ah: interrupted breathing). In **sleep apnea,** breathing stops for periods of 20 seconds to two minutes. As the need for oxygen becomes intense, the person wakes a little and gulps in air. She or he then settles back to sleep. But soon, breathing stops again. This cycle is repeated hundreds of times a night. As you might guess, apnea victims complain of hypersomnia (hi-per-SOM-nee-ah: excessive daytime sleepiness) (DSM-IV, 1994).

What causes sleep apnea? Some cases occur because the brain stops sending signals to the diaphragm to maintain breathing. Another cause is blockage of the upper air passages. Anyone who snores loudly should seek treatment at a sleep clinic (Koenig, 1996).

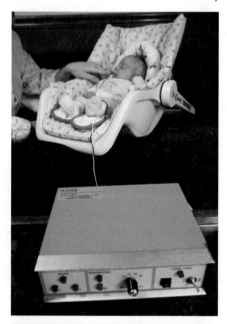

►Figure 5.6

Infants at risk for SIDS are often attached to devices that monitor breathing and heart rate during sleep. An alarm sounds to alert parents if either pulse or respiration falters. SIDS rarely occurs after an infant is one year old. To reduce the risk of SIDS, babies should be placed on their sides or on their backs. (Photo © David H. Wells/Corbis/Magma.)

SIDS Sleep apnea is suspected as one cause of **sudden infant death syndrome (SIDS),** or "crib death." SIDS is the most frequent cause of death for infants under one year of age in North America. In the "typical" crib death, a slightly premature or small baby with some signs of a cold or cough is bundled up and put to bed. A short time later, parents return and find the child is dead.

Babies at risk for SIDS must be carefully watched for the first six months of life. To aid parents in this task, a special monitor may be used that sounds an alarm when breathing or pulse becomes weak (see ►Figure 5.6). Here are some danger signals for SIDS:

- The mother is a teenager.
- The baby is premature.
- The baby has a shrill, high-pitched cry.
- The baby engages in "snoring," breath-holding, or frequent awakening at night.
- The baby breathes mainly through an open mouth.
- The baby remains passive when her or his face rolls into a pillow or blanket and moves little during sleep.
- Parents or other adults in the home are smokers.

"BACK TO SLEEP" Pop quiz: Should babies be placed face down or face up in bed? Another major risk factor for SIDS is the position in which babies sleep. Experts believe that healthy infants are better off sleeping on their backs or sides (Meyers et al., 1998). (Premature babies, those with respiratory problems, and those who often vomit may need to sleep face down. Ask a pediatrician for guidance.) Since this advice was first publicized, there has been a substantial drop in SIDS deaths. To illustrate, in Canada during the year 1990, 332 babies were victims of SIDS, but the number of deaths had dropped sharply to 88 deaths in 2000. In other words, there has been a fourfold decrease in the rate of SIDS over one decade (Canadian Foundation for the Study of Infant Deaths, 2001). Remember, "back to sleep" is the safest position for most infants (Willinger, Hoffman, & Hartford, 1994).

► Dreams—A Separate Reality?

Survey Question:
■ Do dreams have meaning?

The discovery of REM sleep ushered in a "Golden Era" of dream inquiry. To conclude our discussion, let's consider some age-old questions about dreaming.

Does everyone dream? Do dreams occur in an instant? Most people dream four or five times a night, but not all people remember their dreams. "Non-dreamers" are often surprised by their dreams when first awakened during REM sleep. Dreams are usually spaced about 90 minutes apart. The first dream lasts only about 10 minutes; the last averages

30 minutes and may run as long as 50. Dreams, therefore, occur in real time, not as a "flash" (Shafton, 1995).

REM Sleep Revisited

How important is REM sleep? Is it essential for normal functioning? To answer these questions, sleep expert William Dement awakened volunteers each time they entered REM sleep. Soon, their need for "dream time" grew more urgent. By the fifth night, many had to be awakened 20 or 30 times to prevent REM sleep. When the volunteers were finally allowed to sleep undisturbed, they dreamed extra amounts. This effect, called a **REM rebound,** explains why alcoholics have horrible nightmares after they quit drinking. Alcohol suppresses REM sleep and sets up a powerful rebound when it is withdrawn. It's worth remembering that while alcohol and other depressant drugs may help a person get to sleep, they greatly reduce sleep quality (Lobo & Tufik, 1997).

Dement's volunteers complained of memory lapses, poor concentration, and daytime anxiety. For a while, it was thought that people deprived of REM sleep might go crazy. But this is now known as the "REM myth." Later experiments showed that missing any sleep stage can cause a rebound for that stage. In general, daytime disturbances are related to the total amount of sleep lost, not to the type of sleep lost (Devoto et al., 1999).

FUNCTIONS OF REM SLEEP   What, then, is the purpose of REM sleep? Early in life, REM sleep may stimulate the developing brain. Newborn babies spend a hearty eight or nine hours a day in REM sleep. That's about 50 percent of their total sleep time. In adulthood, REM sleep may prevent sensory deprivation during sleep and it may help us process emotional events. REM sleep also seems to help us sort and integrate memories that help us cope with the world (Maquet et al., 2000; Smith, 1995). Speaking very loosely, it's as if the dreaming brain were reviewing messages left on a telephone answering machine, in order to decide which are worth keeping. During the day, when information is streaming in, the brain may be too busy to efficiently select useful memories. Although we still have much to figure out, it's clear that REM sleep and dreaming are valuable for keeping the brain in good working order (Hobson, 1999; Shafton, 1995).

DREAM WORLDS   Calvin Hall, a noted dream expert, collected and analyzed over 10 000 dreams (Hall, 1966; Hall et al., 1982). Hall found that most dreams reflect everyday events. The favourite dream setting is a familiar room in a house. Action usually takes place between the dreamer and two or three other emotionally important people—friends, enemies, parents, or employers. Dream actions are also mostly familiar: running, jumping, riding, sitting, talking, and watching. About half of all dreams have sexual elements, at least among young college students. Dreams of flying, floating, and falling occur less frequently. Hall also found that if you're dreaming more now, you may be enjoying it less. Unpleasant emotions such as fear, anger, and sadness are more common in dreams than pleasant emotions (Merritt et al., 1994).

Dream Theories

How meaningful are dreams? Most theorists agree that dreams reflect our waking thoughts, fantasies, and emotions (Cartwright & Lamberg, 1992; Domhoff, 1999). Thus, the real question might be, How deep should we dig in interpreting dreams? Some theorists believe that dreams have deeply hidden meanings. Others regard dreams as no more meaningful than ordinary thinking. Let's examine both views.

PSYCHOANALYTIC DREAM THEORY   Sigmund Freud's landmark book *The Interpretation of Dreams* (1900) first advanced the idea that many dreams are based on **wish fulfillment** (an expression of unconscious desires). Thus, a student who is angry with a teacher might dream of embarrassing the teacher in class; a lonely person may dream of romance; or a hungry child may dream of food.

Freud's **psychoanalytic theory** of dreaming emphasizes internal conflicts and unconscious forces. While many of his ideas may seem persuasive, there is evidence against them. For example, volunteers in a study of starvation showed no particular increase in

---

REM rebound The occurrence of extra rapid eye movement sleep following REM sleep deprivation.

Wish fulfillment Freudian belief that many dreams express unconscious desires.

Psychoanalytic dream theory A theory that emphasizes internal conflicts, motives, and unconscious forces.

dreams about food and eating. People who have been victimized by traumatic experiences such as rape or wartime brutalities relive their experiences in dreams. In general, dreams show few signs of directly expressing hidden wishes (Fischer & Greenberg, 1996).

Freud's response to critics, no doubt, would have been that dreams rarely express needs so directly. Freud believed that dreams express unconscious desires and conflicts as disguised **dream symbols** (images that have deeper symbolic meaning) (Globus, 1987). For instance, death might be symbolized by a journey, children by small animals, or sexual intercourse by horseback riding or dancing. Similarly, a woman sexually attracted to her best friend's husband might dream of taking her friend's wedding ring and placing it on her own hand, an indirect symbol of her true desires.

Do all dreams have hidden meanings? Probably not. Even Freud realized that some dreams are trivial "day residues" or carryovers from ordinary waking events. On the other hand, dreams do tend to reflect a person's current concerns, so Freud wasn't entirely wrong (Nikles et al., 1998).

THE ACTIVATION-SYNTHESIS HYPOTHESIS Psychiatrists Allan Hobson and Robert McCarley have a radically different view of dreaming. Hobson and McCarley believe that dreams are made in this way: During REM sleep, brain cells are activated that normally control eye movements, balance, and actions. However, messages from the cells are blocked from reaching the body, so no movement occurs. Nevertheless, the cells continue to tell higher brain areas of their activities. Struggling to interpret this information, the brain searches through stored memories and manufactures a dream (Hobson, 1999).

How does that help explain dream content? Let's use the classic chase dream as an example. In such dreams we feel we are running but not going anywhere. This occurs because the brain is told the body is running, but it gets no feedback from the motionless legs. To make sense of this information, the brain creates a chase drama. A similar process probably explains dreams of floating or flying.

Hobson and McCarley call their view of dreaming the **activation-synthesis hypothesis.** Hobson explains that several parts of the brain are "turned on" (activated) during REM sleep. This triggers sensations, motor commands, and memories. The cortex of the brain, which also becomes more active during REM sleep, synthesizes this activity into stories and visual images. However, frontal areas of the cortex, which control higher mental abilities, are mostly shut down during REM sleep. This explains why dreams are more primitive and more bizarre than daytime thoughts (Hobson, 1999). Viewed this way, dreams are merely a different type of thinking that occurs during sleep (McCarley, 1998).

Does the activation-synthesis hypothesis rule out the idea that dreams have meaning? No. Because dreams are created from memories and past experiences, they can tell us quite a lot about each person's mental life, emotions, and concerns (Hobson, 1999). However, many psychologists continue to believe that dreams have deeper meaning (Cartwright & Lamberg, 1992; Globus, 1987; Shafton, 1995).

There seems to be little doubt that dreams can make a difference in our lives: Veteran sleep researcher William Dement once dreamed that he had lung cancer. In the dream a doctor told Dement he would die soon. At the time, Dement was smoking two packs of cigarettes a day. He says, "I will never forget the surprise, joy, and exquisite relief of waking up. I felt reborn." Dement quit smoking the following day.

▶ Hypnosis—Look into My Eyes

Dream symbols Images in dreams that serve as visible signs of hidden ideas, desires, impulses, emotions, relationships, and so forth.

Activation-synthesis hypothesis An attempt to explain how dream content is affected by motor commands in the brain that occur during sleep, but are not carried out.

Hypnosis An altered state of consciousness characterized by narrowed attention and increased suggestibility.

Survey Question:
■ How is hypnosis done, and what are its limitations?

"Your body is becoming heavy. You can barely keep your eyes open. You are so tired you can't move. Relax. Let go. Relax. Close your eyes and relax." These are the last words a textbook should ever say to you, and the first a hypnotist might say.

Hypnosis is an altered state of consciousness characterized by narrowed attention and an increased openness to suggestion (Kosslyn et al., 2000). Not all psychologists accept this definition. To them, hypnosis is merely a blend of conformity, relaxation, imagination, obedience, suggestion, and role-playing (Braffman & Kirsch, 1999). Either way, hypnosis can be explained by normal psychological principles. It is not mysterious or "magical."

Knowledge builder

SLEEP DISTURBANCES AND DREAMING

Relate

Almost everyone suffers from insomnia at least occasionally. Are any of the techniques for combating insomnia similar to strategies you have discovered on your own?

How many sleep disturbances can you name (including those listed in Table 5.1)? Are there any that you have experienced? Which do you think would be most disruptive?

Do you think the activation-synthesis hypothesis provides an adequate explanation of your own dreams? Have you had dreams that seem to reflect Freudian wish fulfillment? Do you think your dreams have symbolic meaning?

Learning Check

1. Night terrors, sleepwalking, and sleeptalking all occur during stage 1, NREM sleep. T or F?
2. Sleep _____ is suspected as one cause of SIDS.
3. Which of the following is not a behavioural remedy for insomnia?

a. daily hypersomnia *b.* stimulus control *c.* progressive relaxation *d.* paradoxical intention

4. The favoured setting for dreams is
   a. work *b.* school *c.* outdoors or unfamiliar places *d.* familiar rooms
5. Unpleasant emotions such as fear, anger, and sadness are more frequent in dreams than pleasant emotions. T or F?
6. According to the activation-synthesis hypothesis of dreaming, dreams are constructed from _____ to explain messages received from nerve cells controlling eye movement, balance, and bodily activity.
7. REM sleep seems to contribute to the formation of _____ that aid survival or coping.

Critical Thinking

8. Even without being told that somnambulism is an NREM event, you could have predicted that sleepwalking doesn't occur during dreaming. Why?

Answers:

1. F 2. apnea 3. a 4. d 5. T 6. memories 7. memories 8. Because people are immobilized during REM sleep and REM sleep is strongly associated with dreaming. This makes it unlikely that sleepwalkers are acting out dreams.

Mesmerize To hypnotize.
Hypnotic susceptibility One's capacity for becoming hypnotized.

Interest in hypnosis began in the 1700s with Franz Mesmer, whose name gave us the term **mesmerize** (to hypnotize). Mesmer, an Austrian physician, believed he could cure various diseases with magnets. Mesmer's strange "treatments" are related to hypnosis because they were actually based on the power of suggestion, not "animal magnetism." For a time, Mesmer enjoyed quite a following. In the end, however, his theories of "animal magnetism" were rejected and he was recognized as a fraud.

The term *hypnosis* was coined by an English surgeon named James Braid. The Greek word *hypnos* means "sleep," and Braid used it to describe the hypnotic state. Today we know that hypnosis is not sleep. Confusion about this point remains because some hypnotists give the suggestion, "Sleep, sleep." However, EEG records made during hypnosis differ from those seen when a person is asleep (Graffin, Ray, & Lundy, 1995).

Hypnotic Susceptibility

Can everyone be hypnotized? About eight people out of ten can be hypnotized, but only one or two out of ten will be good hypnotic subjects. People who are imaginative and prone to fantasy tend to respond well to hypnosis (Silva & Kirsch, 1992). But people who lack these traits may also be hypnotized to some degree. If you are willing to be hypnotized, chances are good that you could be. Hypnosis depends more on the efforts and abilities of the hypnotized person than the skills of the hypnotist (Kirsch & Lynn, 1995).

Hypnotic susceptibility refers to how easily a person can become hypnotized. It can be measured by giving a series of suggestions and counting the number to which a person responds. A typical hypnotic test is the *Stanford Hypnotic Susceptibility Scale* shown in Table 5.2. (See also ▶Figure 5.7.) If you were to score high on the scale today, you probably would do the same years from now. Hypnotizability is very stable over time (Piccione, Hilgard, & Zimbardo, 1989).

Table 5.2
Stanford Hypnotic Susceptibility Scale

SUGGESTED BEHAVIOUR	CRITERION OF PASSING
1. Postural sway	Falls without forcing
2. Eye closure	Closes eyes without forcing
3. Hand lowering (left)	Lowers at least 6 inches (15 cm) by end of 10 seconds
4. Immobilization	Arm (right arm) rises less than 1 inch (2.5 cm) in 10 seconds
5. Finger lock	Incomplete separation of fingers at end of 10 seconds
6. Arm rigidity (left arm)	Less than 2 inches (5 cm) of arm bending in 10 seconds
7. Hands moving together	Hands at least as close as 6 inches (15 cm) after 10 seconds
8. Verbal inhibition (name)	Name unspoken in 10 seconds
9. Hallucination (fly)	Any movement, grimacing, acknowledgment of effect
10. Eye catalepsy	Eyes remain closed at end of 10 seconds
11. Posthypnotic (changes chairs)	Any partial movement response
12. Amnesia test	Three or fewer items recalled

(Adapted from Weitzenhoffer & Hilgard, 1959.)

▶Figure 5.7

In one test of hypnotizability, subjects attempt to pull their hands apart after hearing suggestions that their fingers are "locked" together.

Self-hypnosis A state of hypnosis attained without the aid of a hypnotist; autosuggestion.

Basic suggestion effect The tendency of hypnotized persons to carry out suggested actions as if they were involuntary.

INDUCING HYPNOSIS *How is hypnosis done? Could I be hypnotized against my will?* Hypnotists use many different methods. Still, all techniques encourage a person (1) to focus attention on what is being said, (2) to relax and feel tired, (3) to "let go" and accept suggestions easily, and (4) to use vivid imagination (Druckman & Bjork, 1994). Basically, you must cooperate to become hypnotized. Many theorists believe that all hypnosis is really **self-hypnosis** (autosuggestion). From this perspective, a hypnotist merely helps another person to follow a series of suggestions. These suggestions, in turn, alter sensations, perceptions, thoughts, feelings, and behaviours (Druckman & Bjork, 1994; Kirsch & Lynn, 1995).

What does it feel like to be hypnotized? You might be surprised at some of your actions during hypnosis. Bear in mind that personal experiences vary widely. You might have mild feelings of floating, sinking, anesthesia, or separation from your body. A key element in hypnosis is the **basic suggestion effect** (a tendency of hypnotized persons to carry out suggested actions as if they were involuntary). Hypnotized persons feel like their actions and experiences are automatic—they seem to happen without effort (Kihlstrom, 1985). Here is how one person described his hypnotic session:

I felt lethargic, my eyes going out of focus and wanting to close. My hands felt real light. . . . I felt I was sinking deeper into the chair. . . . I felt like I wanted to relax more and more. . . . My responses were more automatic. I didn't have to wish to do things so much or want to do them. . . . I just did them. . . . I felt floating . . . very close to sleep. (Hilgard, 1968)

Contrary to the way hypnosis is portrayed in movies, hypnotized people generally remain in control of their behaviour and aware of what is going on. For instance, most people will not act out hypnotic suggestions that they consider immoral or repulsive (such as disrobing in public or harming someone) (Kirsch & Lynn, 1995).

Effects of Hypnosis

What can (and cannot) be achieved with hypnosis? Many abilities have been tested during hypnosis, leading to the following conclusions (Burgess & Kirsch, 1999; Kihlstrom, 1985; Kirsch & Lynn, 1995):

1. *Superhuman acts of strength.* Hypnosis has no more effect on physical strength than instructions that encourage a person to make his or her best effort.
2. *Memory.* There is some evidence that hypnosis can enhance memory. However, it frequently increases the number of false memories as well. For this reason, many jurisdictions now bar persons from testifying in court if they were hypnotized to improve their memory of a crime they witnessed.
3. *Amnesia.* A person told not to remember something heard during hypnosis may claim not to remember. In some instances, this may be nothing more than a deliberate attempt to avoid thinking about specific ideas. However, brief memory loss of this type actually does seem to occur, as has been pointed out by the University of Waterloo psychologists (Bowers & Woody, 1996).
4. *Pain relief.* Hypnosis can relieve pain (Mauer et al., 1999). Therefore, it can be especially useful in situations where chemical painkillers cannot be used or are ineffective. One such situation is control of phantom limb pain. (Phantom limb pain is a recurring pain that amputees sometimes feel coming from the missing limb.)
5. *Age regression.* Given the proper suggestions, some hypnotized people appear to "regress" to childhood. However, most theorists now believe that "age-regressed" subjects are only acting out a suggested role.
6. *Sensory changes.* Hypnotic suggestions concerning sensations are among the most effective. Given the proper instructions, a person can be made to smell a small bottle of ammonia and respond as if it were a wonderful perfume. It is also possible to alter colour vision, hearing sensitivity, time sense, perception of illusions, and many other sensory responses.

Hypnosis is a valuable tool. It can help people relax, feel less pain, and make better progress in therapy (Kirsch, Montgomery, & Sapirstein, 1995). Generally, hypnosis is more successful at changing subjective experience than it is at modifying behaviours such as smoking or overeating. In short, hypnotic effects are useful, but seldom amazing (Druckman & Bjork, 1994; Gibson & Heap, 1991).

Stage Hypnosis

On stage the hypnotist intones, "When I count to three, you will imagine that you are on a train to Disneyland and growing younger and younger as the train approaches." Responding to these suggestions, grown men and women begin to giggle and squirm like children on their way to a circus.

How do stage entertainers use hypnosis to get people to do strange things? They don't. Little or no hypnosis is needed to do a good hypnosis act. **Stage hypnosis** is often merely a simulation of hypnotic effects. T. X. Barber, an authority on hypnosis, said that stage hypnotists make use of several features of the stage setting to perform their act (Barber, 1970).

Stage hypnosis Use of hypnosis to entertain; often, merely a simulation of hypnosis for that purpose.

1. *Waking suggestibility.* We are all more or less open to suggestion, but on stage people are unusually cooperative because they don't want to "spoil the act." As a result, they will readily follow almost any instruction given by the entertainer.
2. *Selection of responsive subjects.* Participants in stage hypnotism (all volunteers) are first "hypnotized" as a group. Thus, anyone who doesn't yield to instructions is eliminated.
3. *The hypnosis label disinhibits.* Once a person has been labelled "hypnotized," she or he can sing, dance, act silly, or whatever, without fear or embarrassment. On stage, being "hypnotized" takes away personal responsibility for one's actions.
4. *The hypnotist as a "director."* After volunteers loosen up and respond to a few suggestions, they find that they are suddenly the stars of the show. Audience response to the antics on stage brings out the "ham" in many people. All the "hypnotist" needs to do is direct the action.
5. *The stage hypnotist uses tricks.* Stage hypnosis is about 50 percent taking advantage of the situation and 50 percent deception. One of the more impressive stage tricks is to rigidly suspend a person between two chairs. This is astounding only because the

▶Figure 5.8

Arrange three chairs as shown. Have someone recline as shown. Ask him or her to lift slightly while you remove the middle chair. Accept the applause gracefully! (Concerning hypnosis and similar phenomena, the moral, of course, is "Suspend judgment until you have something solid to stand on.")

audience does not question it. Anyone can do it, as is shown in the photographs and instructions in ▶Figure 5.8. Try it!

To summarize, hypnosis is real, and it can significantly alter private experience. Hypnosis is a useful tool that has been applied in a variety of settings. The TV or night-club stage, however, is not one of these settings. Stage "hypnotists" entertain; they rarely hypnotize.

▶ Meditation—The 20-Minute Vacation

Survey Question:
■ What is meditation? Does it have any benefits?

Meditation refers to mental exercises that are used to alter consciousness. In general, these exercises focus attention and interrupt the typical flow of thoughts, worries, and analysis (Druckman & Bjork, 1994). People who use meditation to reduce stress often report less daily physical arousal and anxiety (Wilson, 1986).

Meditation takes two major forms. In **concentrative meditation,** attention is given to a single focal point, such as an object, a thought, or one's own breathing. In contrast, **receptive meditation** is "open," or expansive. In this case, attention is widened to embrace a total, non-judgmental awareness of the world (Walsh, 1984). An example is losing all self-consciousness while walking in the wilderness with a quiet and receptive mind. Although it may not seem so, receptive meditation is more difficult to attain than concentrative meditation (Smith, 1986). For this reason, we will discuss concentrative meditation as a practical self-control method.

Performing Concentrative Meditation

How is concentrative meditation done? The basic idea is to sit still and quietly focus on some external object or on a repetitive internal stimulus, such as your own breathing (Wilson, 1986). As an alternative, you can silently repeat a **mantra** (a word used as the focus of attention in concentrative meditation). Typical mantras are smooth, flowing sounds that are easily repeated. A widely used mantra is the word "om." A mantra could also be a phrase from a familiar prayer. If other thoughts arise as you repeat a mantra, just return attention to it as often as necessary to maintain meditation.

THE RELAXATION RESPONSE   Many commercial meditation courses claim to offer mantras tailored to each individual. But medical researcher Herbert Benson found that the physical benefits of meditation are the same no matter what word is used. They include lowered heart rate, blood pressure, muscle tension, and other signs of stress.

Benson believes that the core of meditation is the **relaxation response**—an innate physiological pattern that opposes the body's fight-or-flight mechanisms. Benson feels, quite simply, that most of us have forgotten how to relax deeply. People in his experiments have learned to produce the relaxation response by following these instructions:

Meditation A mental exercise for producing relaxation or heightened awareness.

Concentrative meditation Mental exercise based on attending to a single object or thought.

Receptive meditation Mental exercise based on widening attention to become aware of everything experienced at any given moment.

Mantra A flowing word or sound repeated silently during concentrative meditation.

Relaxation response The pattern of internal bodily changes that occurs at times of relaxation.

FOCUS ON RESEARCH   **Sensory Deprivation—Getting a Little REST**

Throughout history, sensory deprivation has been one of the most widely used means of altering consciousness. **Sensory deprivation (SD)** refers to any major reduction in the amount or variety of sensory stimulation.

What happens when stimulation is greatly reduced? A hint comes from reports by prisoners in solitary confinement, Arctic explorers, high-altitude pilots, long-distance truck drivers, and radar operators. When faced with limited or monotonous stimulation, people sometimes have bizarre sensations, dangerous lapses in attention, and distorted perceptions. Initial experiments involving sensory deprivation were conducted at McGill University in the 1950s. Subjects were offered a high monetary reward to spend as many days as they could in small cubicles with a severe reduction in sensory input. Under these confining conditions, subjects could not last very long, and the experiment was over within two or three days. It was quite common for subjects to be confused and restless, and to experience hallucinations; their performance on intellectual tasks was severely hampered (Bexton, Heron, & Scott, 1954).

Not surprisingly, the effects of this experiment were quite devastating for the people involved. Psychologists have also explored the possible benefits of mild sensory

restriction. Much of this work has involved small isolation tanks like the one pictured in ▶Figure 5.9.

Oddly enough, brief periods of sensory restriction can be very relaxing (Forgays & Belinson, 1986). An hour or two spent in a flotation tank, for instance, causes a large drop in blood pressure, muscle tension, and other signs of stress. Of course, it could be argued that a warm bath has the same effect. Nevertheless, brief sensory deprivation appears to be one of the surest ways to induce deep relaxation (Suedfeld & Borrie, 1999).

Psychologists have also found that mild sensory deprivation can help people quit smoking, lose weight, and reduce their use of alcohol and drugs (Borrie, 1990–91; Cooper, Adams, & Scott, 1988; Suedfeld, 1990). Psychologist Peter Suedfeld calls such benefits Restricted Environmental Stimulation Therapy, or **REST.** REST also shows promise as a way to stimulate creative thinking (Norlander, Anonymous, & Archer, 1998). Other researchers have reported that REST sessions can enhance performance in skilled sports, such as gymnastics, tennis, basketball, darts, and marksmanship (Druckman & Bjork, 1994; Norlander, Bergman, & Archer, 1999). There is also evidence that REST can improve memory, relieve pain, and reduce stress. Clearly, there is much yet to be learned from studying "nothingness" (Suedfeld & Borrie, 1999).

Sensory deprivation Any major reduction in the amount or variety of sensory stimulation.
REST Restricted Environmental Stimulation Therapy.

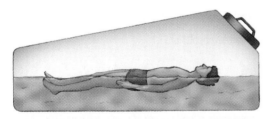

▶**Figure 5.9**

A sensory isolation chamber. Small flotation tanks like the one pictured have been used by psychologists to study the effects of mild sensory deprivation. Subjects float in darkness and silence. The shallow body-temperature water contains hundreds of pounds of Epsom salts, so that subjects float near the surface. Mild sensory deprivation produces deep relaxation.

Sit quietly in a comfortable position. Close your eyes. Deeply relax all your muscles, beginning at your feet and progressing up to your face. Keep them deeply relaxed.

Breathe through your nose. Become aware of your breathing. As you breathe out, say the word "one" silently to yourself.

Do not worry about whether you are successful in achieving a deep level of relaxation. Maintain a passive attitude and permit relaxation to occur at its own pace. Expect distracting thoughts. When these distracting thoughts occur, ignore them and continue repeating "one." (Adapted from Benson, 1977)

EFFECTS OF MEDITATION   *What effects does meditation have other than producing relaxation?* Many extravagant claims have been made about meditation. For example, members of the Transcendental Meditation (TM) movement have stated that 20 minutes of meditation is as restful as a full night's sleep. This, however, is simply not true. In fact, one study found that merely "resting" for 20 minutes produces the same bodily effects as meditation (Holmes, 1984; Holmes et al., 1983). (The relaxation response can also be produced by brief sensory restriction—see "Sensory Deprivation.")

Long-term meditators have claimed that the practice improves memory, alertness, creativity, and intuition. Again, such claims must be regarded as unproven. Most are based on personal testimonials or poorly controlled studies. A major problem with most studies of TM is that they use devoted meditators. It is quite likely that the beliefs and lifestyles of these people influence the results of the studies as much as meditation does (Druckman & Bjork, 1994). It is perhaps for this reason one study found that the Quebec government had a decrease in the cost of medical expenses for a group of TM practitioners over a seven-year period (Herron et al., 1996).

While many of the claimed benefits of meditation appear to be overstated, meditation does reliably elicit the relaxation response (Janowiak & Hackman, 1994). In defence of meditation, it is important to remember that relaxation can be mental as well as physical. Meditation may be beneficial for people who find it difficult to "turn off" upsetting thoughts when they need to relax. For example, college students who tried meditation as part of a study felt happier, less anxious, and less depressed after just two weeks of twice-a-day meditation (Smith, Compton, & West, 1995). More promising and encouraging results were obtained in one recent study conducted in Alberta, which showed meditation to be effective in the reduction of emotional problems among cancer patients. Compared to a control group, those who meditated for seven weeks experienced a substantial decrease in stress, depression, anger, and irritability, as well as a variety of physical symptoms, and were consequently found to be in a better mood (Speca et al., 2000).

SUMMARY   To summarize, research suggests that concentrative meditation is only one of several ways to elicit the relaxation response. For many people, sitting quietly and "resting" can be as effective. Similar stress reduction occurs when people set aside time daily to engage in other restful activities, such as muscle relaxation, positive daydreaming, and even leisure reading. However, if you are the type of person who finds it difficult to ignore upsetting thoughts, then concentrative meditation might be a good way to promote relaxation. Meditation and similar techniques provide a valuable, stress-lowering "time-out" from the normal clamour of thoughts and worries—something almost everyone could use in our fast-paced society.

Knowledge builder

HYPNOSIS, MEDITATION, AND SENSORY DEPRIVATION

Relate

How have your beliefs about hypnosis changed after reading the preceding section? Can you think of specific examples in which hypnosis was misrepresented? For example, in high-school assemblies, stage acts, movies, or TV dramas?

Various activities can produce the relaxation response. When do you experience states of deep relaxation, coupled with a sense of serene awareness? What similarities do these occurrences have to meditation?

Have you experienced any form of sensory restriction or sensory deprivation? How did you react? Would you be willing to try REST in order to break a bad habit?

Learning Check

1. The term *hypnotism* was coined by a British surgeon named *a.* Franz Mesmer *b.* James Stanford *c.* T. A. Kreskin *d.* James Braid
2. Only two out of ten people can be hypnotized. T or F?
3. Which of the following can most definitely be achieved with hypnosis?

a. unusual strength *b.* pain relief *c.* improved memory *d.* sleep-like brain waves
4. The focus of attention in concentrative meditation is "open," or expansive. T or F?
5. Mantras are words said silently to oneself to end a session of meditation. T or F?
6. Research conducted by Herbert Benson indicates that careful selection of a mantra is necessary to obtain the physical benefits of meditation. T or F?
7. The most immediate benefit of meditation appears to be its capacity for producing the relaxation response. T or F?
8. Prolonged periods of extreme sensory deprivation lower anxiety and induce deep relaxation. T or F?

Critical Thinking

9. What kind of control group would you need in order to identify the true effects of hypnosis?
10. Regular meditators report lower levels of stress and a greater sense of well-being. What other explanations must we eliminate before this effect can be regarded as genuine?

Answers:

1. *d* 2. F 3. *b* 4. F 5. F 6. F 7. T 8. F 9. Most experiments on hypnosis include a control group in which people are asked to simulate being hypnotized. Without such controls, the tendency of subjects to cooperate with experimenters makes it difficult to identify true hypnotic effects. 10. Studies on the effects of meditation must control for the placebo effect and the fact that those who meditate may not be a representative sample of the general population. Studies controlling for such factors still show that meditation is beneficial (Pagano & Warrenburg, 1983).

▶ Drug-Altered Consciousness—The High and Low of It

Survey Question:

■ What are the effects of the more commonly used psychoactive drugs?

Alcohol, heroin, amphetamines, barbiturates, marijuana, cocaine, LSD, caffeine, nicotine ... The list of mind-altering drugs—legal and illegal—is extensive. The surest way to alter human consciousness is to administer a **psychoactive drug** (a substance capable of altering attention, judgment, memory, time sense, self-control, emotion, or perception) (Julien, 1998).

Facts about Drugs

Psychoactive drug A substance capable of altering attention, memory, judgment, time sense, self-control, mood, or perception.

Stimulant A substance that increases activity in the body and nervous system.

Depressant A substance that decreases activity in the body and nervous system.

Physical dependence Physical addiction, as indicated by the presence of drug tolerance and withdrawal symptoms.

Withdrawal symptoms Physical illness and discomfort following the withdrawal of a drug.

Drug tolerance A reduction in the body's response to a drug.

Psychological dependence Drug dependence that is based primarily on emotional or psychological needs.

Most psychoactive drugs can be placed on a scale ranging from stimulation to depression. A **stimulant** increases activity in the body and nervous system. A **depressant** does the reverse. ▶Figure 5.10 shows various drugs and their approximate effects. A more complete summary of frequently abused psychoactive drugs is given in Table 5.3.

DEPENDENCE   Drug dependence falls into two broad categories. When a person compulsively uses a drug to maintain bodily comfort, a **physical dependence** (addiction) exists. Physical dependence occurs most often with drugs that cause **withdrawal symptoms** (physical illness that follows removal of a drug) (Julien, 1998). Withdrawal from drugs such as alcohol, barbiturates, and opiates can be extremely unpleasant. Quitting opiates, for example, causes violent flu-like symptoms of nausea, vomiting, diarrhea, chills, sweating, and cramps (Feldman & Meyer, 1996). Addiction is often accompanied by a **drug tolerance** (reduced response to a drug). This leads users to take larger and larger doses to get the desired effect.

It's fascinating to note that withdrawal from alcohol, nicotine, caffeine, food, gambling, and even a love relationship can all produce similar symptoms. This may occur because a variety of rewards activate the same pleasure pathways in the brain. In this sense, a person may be "addicted" to food, sex, or love, as well as to drugs (Gilbert, Gilbert, & Schultz, 1998).

When a person develops a **psychological dependence,** he or she feels that a drug is necessary to maintain feelings of comfort or well-being. Usually, the person intensely craves the drug and its rewarding qualities (Feldman & Meyer, 1996). Psychological dependence can be just as powerful as physical addiction. That's why some psychologists define addiction as any compulsive habit pattern. By this definition, a person who has lost control over drug use, for whatever reason, is addicted (Marlatt et al., 1988). In fact, most people who answer yes to both of the following questions have an alcohol or drug problem and should seek professional help (Brown et al., 1997):

- In the last year, did you ever drink or use drugs more than you meant to?
- Have you felt you wanted or needed to cut down on your drinking or drug use in the last year?

DRUGS OF ABUSE   Note in Table 5.3 that the drugs most likely to lead to physical dependence are alcohol, amphetamines, barbiturates, cocaine, codeine, heroin, methadone, morphine, and tobacco (nicotine). Using any of the drugs listed in

Drug Effects	STIMULATION	Drug Groups
Death		
		Strychnine
Convulsions		
Extreme nervousness, tremors		Amphetamines
Anxiety, palpitations		Cocaine (large dose)
		Antidepressants
Feeling of well-being, euphoria		Cocaine (small dose)
Distortion of time and space		Hallucinogens (LSD, mescaline, marijuana)
		Nicotine
Increased alertness		Caffeine
	NEUTRAL AREA	
Anxiety relief		Tranquillizers
Feeling of well-being, euphoria		Narcotics, barbiturates, alcohol (small dose)
Loss of pain		Narcotics (medium dose)
Drowsiness		Barbiturates, alcohol (medium dose)
Sleep		Hypnotics
Loss of consciousness		Narcotics, barbiturates, alcohol (large dose)
Convulsions		Anesthetics
Death	DEPRESSION	

▶Figure 5.10

Spectrum and continuum of drug action. Many drugs can be rated on a stimulation-depression scale according to their effects on the central nervous system. Although LSD, mescaline, and marijuana are listed here, the stimulation-depression scale is less relevant to these drugs. The principal characteristic of such hallucinogens is their mind-altering quality.

Table 5.3
Comparison of Psychoactive Drugs

NAME	CLASSIFICATION	MEDICAL USE	USUAL DOSE	DURATION OF EFFECT
Alcohol	Sedative-hypnotic	Solvent, antiseptic	Varies	1–4 hours
Amphetamines	Stimulant	Relief of mild depression, control of appetite and narcolepsy	2.5–5 milligrams	4 hours
Barbiturates	Sedative-hypnotic	Sedation, relief of high blood pressure, hyper-thyroidism	50–100 milligrams	4 hours
Benzodiazepines	Anxiolytic	Tranquillizer	2–100 milligrams	1–8 hours
Caffeine	Stimulant	Counteract depressant drugs, treatment of migraine headaches	Varies	Varies
Cocaine	Stimulant, local anesthetic	Local anesthesia	Varies	Varied, brief periods
Codeine	Narcotic	Ease pain and coughing	30 milligrams	4 hours
Heroin	Narcotic	Pain relief	Varies	4 hours
LSD	Hallucinogen	Experimental study of mental function, alco-holism	100–500 milligrams	10 hours
Marijuana (THC)	Relaxant, euphoriant; in high doses, hallucinogen	Treatment of glaucoma and side effects of chemotherapy	1–2 cigarettes	4 hours
MDMA	Stimulant/ hallucinogen	None	1–6 milligrams or more	4–6 hours
Mescaline	Hallucinogen	None	350 micrograms	12 hours
Methadone	Narcotic	Pain relief	10 milligrams	4–6 hours
Morphine	Narcotic	Pain relief	15 milligrams	6 hours
PCP	Anesthetic	None	2–10 milligrams	4–6 hours, plus 12-hour recovery
Psilocybin	Hallucinogen	None	25 milligrams	6–8 hours
Tobacco (nicotine)	Stimulant	Emetic (nicotine)	Varies	Varies

Question marks indicate conflict of opinion. It should be noted that illicit drugs are frequently adulterated and thus pose unknown hazards to the user.

EFFECTS SOUGHT	LONG-TERM SYMPTOMS	PHYSICAL DEPENDENCE POTENTIAL	PSYCHOLOGICAL DEPENDENCE POTENTIAL	ORGANIC DAMAGE POTENTIAL
Sense alteration, anxiety reduction, sociability	Cirrhosis, toxic psychosis, neurologic damage, addiction	Yes	Yes	Yes
Alertness, activeness	Loss of appetite, delusions, hallucinations, toxic psychosis	Yes	Yes	Yes
Anxiety reduction, euphoria	Addiction with severe withdrawal symptoms, possible convulsions, toxic psychosis	Yes	Yes	Yes
Anxiety relief	Irritability, confusion, depression, sleep disorders	Probably	Yes	No
Wakefulness, alertness	Insomnia, heart arrhythmias, high blood pressure	No?	Yes	Yes
Excitation, talkativeness	Depression, convulsions	Yes	Yes	Yes
Euphoria, prevent withdrawal discomfort	Addiction, constipation, loss of appetite	Yes	Yes	No
Euphoria, prevent withdrawal discomfort	Addiction, constipation, loss of appetite	Yes	Yes	No*
Insightful experiences, exhilaration, distortion of senses	May intensify existing psychosis, panic reactions	No	No?	No?
Relaxation; increased euphoria, perceptions, sociability	Possible lung cancer, other health risks	No	Yes	Yes
Excitation, euphoria	Personality change, hyperthermia, liver damage	No	Yes	Yes
Insightful experiences, exhilaration, distortion of senses	May intensify existing psychosis, panic reactions	No	No?	No?
Prevent withdrawal discomfort	Addiction, constipation, loss of appetite	Yes	Yes	No
Euphoria, prevent withdrawal discomfort	Addiction, constipation, loss of appetite	Yes	Yes	No*
Euphoria	Unpredictable behaviour, suspicion, hostility, psychosis	Debated	Yes	Yes
Insightful experiences, exhilaration, distortion of senses	May intensify existing psychosis, panic reactions	No	No?	No?
Alertness, calmness, sociability	Emphysema, lung cancer, mouth and throat cancer, cardiovascular damage, loss of appetite	Yes	Yes	Yes

*Persons who inject drugs under non-sterile conditions run a high risk of contracting AIDS, hepatitis, abscesses, or circulatory disorders.

Table 5.3 can result in psychological dependence. Note, too, that people who take drugs intravenously are at high risk for developing hepatitis and AIDS (see Chapter 11). The discussion that follows focuses on the drugs most often abused by students.

▶ Uppers—Amphetamines, Cocaine, Caffeine, Nicotine

Amphetamines

Amphetamines A class of synthetic drugs having stimulant effects on the nervous system.

Amphetamine psychosis A severe disruption of psychological functioning caused by abuse of amphetamines.

Amphetamines form a large group of synthetic stimulants. These drugs were once widely prescribed for weight loss and depression. But too many patients became dependent on the legal amphetamines. Today, the only fully legitimate medical use of amphetamines is to treat certain medical conditions such as narcolepsy and overdose of depressant drugs. Illicit use of amphetamines is widespread, especially by people seeking to stay awake and by those who think drugs can improve mental or physical performance.

Amphetamines rapidly produce a drug tolerance. Most abusers begin with one or two pills a day and end up taking dozens to get the same effect. Eventually, some users switch to injecting Methedrine ("speed") directly into the bloodstream. True speed freaks typically go on binges lasting several days, after which they "crash" from lack of sleep and food.

ABUSE *How dangerous are amphetamines?* Amphetamines pose many dangers. To stay high, the abuser must take more and more of the drug as the body's tolerance grows. Higher doses can cause nausea, vomiting, dangerously high blood pressure, fatal heart arrhythmias, and crippling strokes. Also, it is important to realize that amphetamines speed up the use of bodily resources; they do not magically supply energy. Hence, the after-effects of an amphetamine binge can include crippling fatigue, depression, terrifying nightmares, confusion, uncontrolled irritability, and aggression. Repeatedly overextending the body with stimulants may lead to self-starvation, sores and ulcers, chronic chest infections, liver disease, and brain hemorrhage. Amphetamines can also cause a loss of contact with reality known as **amphetamine psychosis.** Affected users suffer from paranoid delusions that someone is out to get them. Acting on these delusions, they may become violent, resulting in self-injury or injury to others (Kratofil, Baberg, & Dimsdale, 1996).

A potent new smokable form of crystal methamphetamine has recently added to the risks of stimulant abuse. This drug, known as "ice" on the street, is highly addictive. Like "crack," the smokable form of cocaine, it produces an intense high. But also like crack (discussed in a moment), crystal methamphetamine leads very rapidly to compulsive abuse and severe drug dependence.

DESIGNER DRUGS Small variations in the structure of a drug can change its effects. For example, the drug MDMA ("ecstasy") is chemically similar to amphetamine. But in addition to producing a rush of energy, users say it makes them feel closer to others and heightens their sensory experiences.

MDMA is a "designer drug," a chemically engineered variation of an existing drug, created to get around drug laws. Because designer drugs are not tested for safety, some have extremely toxic effects. One notorious drug damaged the brain in a way that left hundreds of users suffering from severe Parkinson's disease. The risk posed by MDMA remains unclear. In England, a number of deaths have been traced to the use of MDMA at "rave" parties. However, these deaths were caused by heat exhaustion, not by drug poisoning. MDMA raises body temperature, which can be fatal when combined with all-night dancing in an overheated club.

MDMA sometimes causes severe liver damage, which can also be fatal. Aside from these documented risks, the long-term effects of MDMA are unknown. It may take another 10 to 20 years before MDMA's impact on the health of users emerges. Of more immediate concern is the fact that many of the street drugs sold as "ecstasy" are impure and adulterated with other substances. Like other designer drugs, MDMA may ultimately prove to be a costly trip into the unknown (Abbott & Concar, 1992; McKim, 1997).

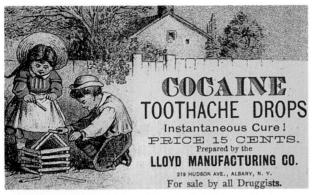

Cocaine was the main ingredient in many non-prescription elixirs before the turn of the 20th century. Today cocaine is recognized as a powerful and dangerous drug. Its high potential for abuse has damaged the lives of countless users.

Cocaine A crystalline drug derived from coca leaves; used as a central nervous system stimulant and local anesthetic.

Anhedonia An inability to feel pleasure.

Caffeine A natural drug with stimulant properties; found in coffee and tea and added to artificial beverages and medicines.

Cocaine

Cocaine is a powerful central nervous system stimulant extracted from the leaves of the coca plant. Cocaine produces feelings of alertness, euphoria, well-being, power, boundless energy, and pleasure (Julien, 1998).

Cocaine has a long history of use and misuse. At the turn of the 20th century, dozens of non-prescription potions and cure-alls contained cocaine. It was during this time that Coca-Cola was indeed the "real thing." From 1886 until 1906, when the United States Pure Food and Drug Act was passed, Coca-Cola contained cocaine (which has since been replaced with caffeine). Statistics collected in 1994 showed that approximately 3.8 percent of Canadians had used cocaine at least once in their lives, and 0.7 percent had used the drug during 1993 (Canadian Centre on Substance Abuse, 1999).

How does cocaine differ from amphetamines? The two are very much alike in their effects on the central nervous system. The main difference is that amphetamine lasts several hours; cocaine is quickly metabolized, so its effects last only about 15 to 30 minutes.

ABUSE   *How dangerous is cocaine?* Cocaine is one of the most dangerous drugs of abuse. Even casual or first-time users run a risk because cocaine can cause convulsions, heart attack, or a stroke (Cregler & Mark, 1985; Lacayo, 1995). The highly publicized death of American basketball star Len Bias is a case in point.

A person who stops using cocaine does not experience heroin-like withdrawal symptoms. But cocaine can be highly addictive. The brain adapts to cocaine abuse in ways that upset its chemical balance, causing depression when cocaine is withdrawn. First, there is a jarring "crash" of mood and energy. Within a few days, the person enters a long period of fatigue, anxiety, paranoia, boredom, and **anhedonia** (an-he-DAWN-ee-ah: an inability to feel pleasure). Before long, the urge to use cocaine grows overwhelming. So, while cocaine does not fit the classic pattern of physical addiction, there is little doubt about its potential for compulsive abuse. Even a person who gets through withdrawal may crave cocaine months or years later (Withers et al., 1995). Many authorities estimate that if cocaine were cheaper, nine out of ten users would progress to compulsive abuse. In fact, rock cocaine (or "crack"), which is cheaper, produces very high abuse rates. Here are some signs of cocaine abuse (Pursch, 1983).

- *Compulsive use.* If cocaine is available—say, at a party—you will undoubtedly use it. You can't say no to it.
- *Loss of control.* Once you have had some cocaine, you will keep using it until you are exhausted or the cocaine is gone.
- *Disregarding consequences.* You don't care if the rent gets paid, your job is endangered, your lover disapproves, or your health is affected—you'll use cocaine anyway.

Clearly, cocaine's capacity for abuse and social damage rivals that of heroin. Anyone who thinks she or he has a cocaine problem should seek advice at a drug clinic or a Cocaine Anonymous meeting. Quitting cocaine is extremely difficult. Nevertheless, three out of four cocaine abusers who remain in treatment do succeed in breaking their coke dependence (Simpson et al., 1999).

Caffeine

Caffeine is the most frequently used psychoactive drug in North America. **Caffeine** stimulates the brain by blocking chemicals that normally inhibit or slow nerve activity (Julien, 1998). Its effects become apparent with doses as small as 50 milligrams, the amount found in about one-half cup of brewed coffee. Physically, caffeine causes sweating, talkativeness, tinnitus (ringing in the ears), and hand tremors. Psychologically, caffeine suppresses fatigue or drowsiness and increases feelings of alertness (Smith, Clark, & Gallagher, 1999). Some people have a hard time starting a day (or writing another paragraph) without it.

Table 5.4
Average Caffeine Content of Various Foods

Instant coffee (150 mL), 64 milligrams
Percolated coffee (150 mL), 108 milligrams
Drip coffee (150 mL), 145 milligrams
Decaf. coffee (150 mL), 3 milligrams
Black tea (150 mL), 42 milligrams
Canned ice tea (500 mL), 30 milligrams
Cocoa drink (175 mL), 8 milligrams
Chocolate drink (235 mL), 14 milligrams
Sweet chocolate (30 g), 20 milligrams
Colas (355 mL), 50 milligrams

Caffeinism Excessive consumption of caffeine, leading to dependence and a variety of physical and psychological complaints.
Nicotine A potent stimulant drug found primarily in tobacco; nicotine is a known carcinogen.
Carcinogen A substance capable of causing cancer.

How much caffeine did you consume today? Although it is common to think of coffee as the major source of caffeine, there are many others. Caffeine is found in tea, many soft drinks (especially colas), chocolate, and cocoa (see Table 5.4). Over 2000 non-prescription drugs also contain caffeine, including stay-awake pills, cold remedies, and many name-brand aspirin products.

ABUSE *Are there any serious drawbacks to using caffeine?* Serious abuse may result in an unhealthy dependence on caffeine known as **caffeinism.** Insomnia, irritability, loss of appetite, chills, racing heart, and elevated body temperature are all signs of caffeinism. Many people with these symptoms drink 15 or 20 cups of coffee a day. However, even at lower doses, caffeine can intensify anxiety and other psychological problems (Larson & Carey, 1998).

Caffeine has a variety of health risks. Caffeine encourages the growth of breast cysts in women, and it may contribute to bladder cancer, heart problems, and high blood pressure. Pregnant women should consider giving up caffeine entirely because of a suspected link between caffeine and birth defects. Pregnant women who consume six or more cups of coffee a day double the risk of having a miscarriage (Klebanoff et al., 1999).

It is customary to think of caffeine as a non-drug. But as few as 2.5 cups of coffee a day (or the equivalent) can be a problem. People who consume even such modest amounts may experience anxiety, depression, fatigue, headaches, and flu-like symptoms during withdrawal (Silverman et al., 1992). About half of all caffeine users show some signs of dependence (Hughes et al., 1998). It is wise to remember that caffeine is a drug and use it in moderation.

Nicotine

Nicotine is a natural stimulant found mainly in tobacco. Next to caffeine, it is the most widely used psychoactive drug (Julien, 1998).

How does nicotine compare with other stimulants? Nicotine is a potent drug. It is so toxic that it is sometimes used to kill insects! In large doses it causes stomach pain, vomiting and diarrhea, cold sweats, dizziness, confusion, and muscle tremors. In very large doses, nicotine may cause convulsions, respiratory failure, and death. For a non-smoker, 50 to 75 milligrams of nicotine taken in a single dose could be lethal. (Chain-smoking about 17 to 25 cigarettes will produce this dosage.) Most first-time smokers get sick on one or two cigarettes. In contrast, a heavy smoker may inhale 40 cigarettes a day without feeling ill. This indicates that regular smokers build a tolerance for nicotine (Perkins, 1995; Stolerman & Jarvis, 1995).

ABUSE *Is it true that nicotine can be addicting?* A vast array of evidence confirms that nicotine is addictive (Henningfield & Heishman, 1995). For many smokers, withdrawal from nicotine causes headaches, sweating, cramps, insomnia, digestive upset, irritability, and a sharp craving for cigarettes (Killen & Fortmann, 1997). These symptoms may last from two to six weeks and may be worse than heroin withdrawal. Indeed, relapse patterns are nearly identical for alcoholics, heroin addicts, cocaine abusers, and smokers who try to quit (Stolerman & Jarvis, 1995). A staggering eight out of ten people who quit smoking relapse within a year (Jarvik, 1995).

IMPACT ON HEALTH *How serious are the health risks of smoking?* A burning cigarette releases a large variety of potent **carcinogens** (car-SIN-oh-jins: cancer-causing substances). Lung cancer and other cancers caused by smoking are now considered the single most preventable cause of death in Canada and the United States. Among men, 97 percent of lung cancer deaths are caused by smoking. For women, 74 percent of all lung cancers are due to smoking. Here are some sobering facts about smoking:

Actress Lily Tomlin took up smoking for a role in the movie *Shadows and Fog* and developed a four-pack-a-day habit. As Tomlin's experience shows, the best way to avoid developing a nicotine addiction is to not begin smoking in the first place.

Smoking Facts

- Every cigarette reduces a smoker's life expectancy by seven minutes.
- Smoking is the number one cause of deaths in Canada and the United States—more than the number of deaths from alcohol, drugs, car accidents, and AIDS combined.
- In Canada, one in six deaths is caused by smoking. In 1995, there were 34 728 deaths, which is estimated to have led to a total of 500 345 years of potential life lost (Canadian Centre on Substance Abuse, 1999).
- Tobacco cost the Canadian economy a staggering $9.6 billion in 1992 (Canadian Centre on Substance Abuse, 1999).
- Forty percent of all smokers who develop throat cancer try smoking again.
- Each year, only one out of five smokers who tries to quit smoking succeeds.
- Some tobacco companies manipulate nicotine levels in their cigarettes to keep smokers addicted.
- Daily exposure to second-hand smoke at home or work causes a 24 to 39 percent increase in cancer risk to non-smokers.

If you think smoking is harmless, or that there's no connection between smoking and cancer, you're kidding yourself. The scientific link between tobacco smoking and cancer is undeniable. Skeptics please note: Wayne McLaren, who portrayed the rugged "Marlboro Man" in cigarette ads, died of lung cancer at age 51.

Smokers don't just risk their own health, they also endanger those who live and work nearby. Secondary smoke causes 20 percent of all lung cancers. Non-smoking women who are married to smokers suffer a 30 percent increase in their risk of developing lung cancer. It is particularly irresponsible of smokers to expose young children to second-hand smoke (Abramson, 1993).

QUITTING SMOKING   *Is it better for a person to quit smoking abruptly or taper down gradually?* For many years, smokers were advised to quit cold turkey. The current view is that quitting all at once isn't as effective as tapering off. Going cold turkey makes quitting an all-or-nothing proposition. Smokers who smoke even one cigarette after "quitting forever" tend to feel they've failed. Many figure they might just as well resume smoking. Those who quit gradually accept that success may take many attempts, spread over several months. However, switching to "light" cigarettes is not a good way to quit gradually. Heavy smokers tend to adjust their smoking to keep bodily levels of nicotine constant. Thus, when they smoke lighter cigarettes, they smoke more. This can do extra damage, because light cigarettes have as much tar as regular cigarettes (Kozlowski et al., 1998).

"New Strategies to Stop Smoking" on page 192 summarizes several ways to quit smoking. Whatever approach is taken, quitting smoking is not easy. It does help, though, if you get a spouse or partner to support your efforts (Cohen & Lichtenstein, 1990). Also, as we have noted, anyone trying to quit should be prepared to make several attempts before succeeding. But the good news is millions of people have quit.

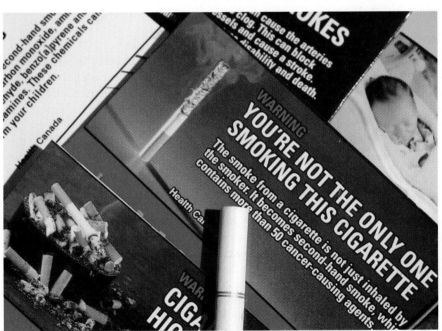

A study of 5th–12th graders found that those who smoke are less likely than non-smokers to believe the health warning labels on cigarette packs (Cecil, Evans, & Stanley, 1996). Smokers in general are less likely to believe that smoking poses a serious risk to health.

USING PSYCHOLOGY New Strategies to Stop Smoking

If you smoke and would like to quit, here are some basic steps you can take: (1) Delay having a first cigarette in the morning. Then try to delay a little longer each day. (2) Gradually reduce the total number of cigarettes you smoke each day. (3) Quit completely, but for just one week. Then quit again, a week at a time, for as many times as necessary to make it stick (Pierce, 1991).

You will probably be most successful at strategy number 2 if you schedule a gradual reduction in smoking. To begin, count the number of cigarettes you smoke per day. For the first week your goal will be to smoke only two thirds of that "baseline" number each day. In addition, you should divide the 16 waking hours in each day by the number of cigarettes you will smoke that day. For example, if you plan to smoke 16 cigarettes per day, then you only get to smoke one per hour. When

a scheduled "smoking time" arrives, smoke only for five minutes, whether you finish the cigarette or not. Don't smoke any "missed" cigarettes later.

During the second week, you should smoke only one third as many cigarettes as you did during your baseline. Again, divide each 16-hour day by the number of cigarettes, so you can plan how much time to allow between smoking periods.

During week three, reduce your cigarette allowance to 20 percent of the original baseline number.

In the fourth week, stop smoking entirely.

Gradually stretching the time periods between cigarettes is a key part of this program. Scheduled smoking apparently helps people learn to cope with the urge to smoke. As a result, people using this method are more likely to succeed. Also, they more often remain permanent non-smokers than people using other approaches (Cinciripini, Wetter, & McClure, 1997).

▶ Downers—Sedatives, Tranquillizers, and Alcohol

How do downers differ from the stimulant drugs? The most widely used downers, or depressant drugs, are alcohol, barbiturates, and benzodiazepine (ben-zoe-die-AZ-eh-peen) tranquillizers. These drugs are much alike in their effects. In fact, barbiturates and tranquillizers are sometimes referred to as "solid alcohol." Let's examine the properties of each.

Barbiturates

Barbiturate One of a large group of sedative drugs that depress activity in the nervous system.

Tranquillizer A drug that lowers anxiety and reduces tension.

Barbiturates are sedative drugs that depress brain activity. Medically, they are used to calm patients or to induce sleep. In mild doses, barbiturates have an effect similar to alcohol intoxication. Higher doses can cause severe mental confusion or even psychotic symptoms (a loss of contact with reality). Overdoses can easily cause coma or death. Barbiturates are often taken in excess amounts because a first dose may be followed by others, as the user becomes uninhibited or forgetful. Overdoses first cause unconsciousness. Then they severely depress brain centres that control heartbeat and breathing. The result is death (McKim, 1997).

Tranquillizers

A **tranquillizer** is a drug that lowers anxiety and reduces tension. Doctors prescribe benzodiazepine tranquillizers to alleviate nervousness and stress. Valium is the best-known drug in this family; others are Xanax, Halcion, and Librium. Even at normal doses these drugs can cause drowsiness, shakiness, and confusion. When used at too high a dose or for too long a time, benzodiazepines have strong addictive potential (McKim, 1997).

Recently, a drug sold under the trade name Rohypnol (ro-HIP-nol) has added to the problem of tranquillizer abuse. This drug, which is related to Valium, is cheap and potent. It lowers inhibitions and produces relaxation or intoxication. Large doses induce short-term amnesia and sleep. "Roofies," as they are known on the street, are odourless and tasteless. They have been used to spike drinks, which are given to the unwary. Drugged victims are then sexually assaulted or raped while they are unconscious (Navarro, 1995). (Be aware, however, that drinking too much alcohol is by far the most common prelude to rape.)

Drug interaction
A combined effect of two drugs that exceeds the addition of one drug's effects to the other.

Alcohol Common name for ethyl alcohol, the intoxicating element in fermented and distilled liquors.

Binge drinking
Consuming five or more drinks in a short time.

ABUSE   Repeated use of any barbiturate can cause physical dependence. Some abusers suffer severe emotional depression that may end in suicide. Similarly, when tranquillizers are used at too high a dose or for too long a time, addiction may occur. Many people have learned the hard way that their legally prescribed tranquillizers are as dangerous as many illicit drugs (McKim, 1997).

Combining barbiturates or tranquillizers with alcohol is extremely risky. When mixed, the effects of both drugs are multiplied by a **drug interaction** (one drug enhances the effect of another). Drug interactions are responsible for many hundreds of fatal drug overdoses every year. All too often, depressants are gulped down with alcohol or added to a spiked punch bowl. This is the lethal brew that left a young woman named Karen Ann Quinlan in a coma that lasted 10 years, ending with her death. It is no exaggeration to restate that mixing depressants with alcohol can be deadly.

Alcohol

Alcohol is the common name for ethyl alcohol, the intoxicating element in fermented and distilled liquors. Contrary to popular belief, alcohol is not a stimulant. The noisy animation at drinking parties is due to alcohol's effect as a *depressant*. As ▶Figure 5.11 shows, small amounts of alcohol reduce inhibitions and produce feelings of relaxation and euphoria. Larger amounts cause ever-greater impairment of the brain until the drinker loses consciousness. Alcohol is also not an aphrodisiac. Rather than enhancing sexual arousal, it usually impairs performance, especially in males. As William Shakespeare observed long ago, drink "provokes the desire, but it takes away the performance."

ABUSE   Alcohol, the world's favourite depressant, breeds our biggest drug problem. Over 200 million people in Canada and the United States use alcohol. An estimated 25 million have serious drinking problems. An alarming trend is the high level of alcohol abuse among adolescents and young adults. Fifty percent of male college students and 40 percent of college women have engaged in binge drinking. For fraternity and sorority members, the figure jumps to 84 percent. **Binge drinking** is defined as downing five or more drinks in a short time. Apparently, many students think it's entertaining to get completely wasted and throw up on their friends. However, binge drinking is a serious sign of alcohol abuse (Wechsler et al., 1999). Approximately 6500 Canadians lost their lives as a consequence of alcohol consumption in 1995, and nearly 81 000 were hospitalized (Canadian Centre on Substance Abuse, 1999).

Positive reinforcement—drinking for pleasure—motivates most people who consume alcohol. What sets alcohol abusers apart is that they also drink to cope with negative emotions, such as anxiety and depression. That's why alcohol abuse increases with the level of stress in people's lives. People who drink to cope with bad feelings run a great risk of becoming alcoholics (Kenneth, Carpenter, & Hasin, 1998).

RECOGNIZING PROBLEM DRINKING   *What are the signs of alcohol abuse?* Because alcohol abuse is such a common problem, it is important to recognize the danger signals of growing dependency. The path from a social drinker to an alcohol abuser to an alcoholic is often subtle. Jellinek (1960) gives these typical steps in the development of a drinking problem.

1. *Initial phase.* At first, the social drinker begins to turn more often to alcohol to relieve tension or to feel good. Four danger signals in this period that signal excessive dependence on alcohol are:
   - *Increasing consumption.* The individual drinks more and more and may begin to worry about his or her drinking.
   - *Morning drinking.* Morning drinking is a dangerous sign, particularly when it is used to combat a hangover or to "get through the day."
   - *Regretted behaviour.* The person engages in extreme behaviour while drunk that leaves her or him feeling guilty or embarrassed.
   - *Blackouts.* Abusive drinking may be revealed by an inability to remember what happened during intoxication.

▶Figure 5.11

The behavioural effects of alcohol are related to blood alcohol content and the resulting suppression of higher mental function. The legal blood alcohol limit for drivers in Canada is .08 (80 milligrams of alcohol in 100 millilitres of blood).

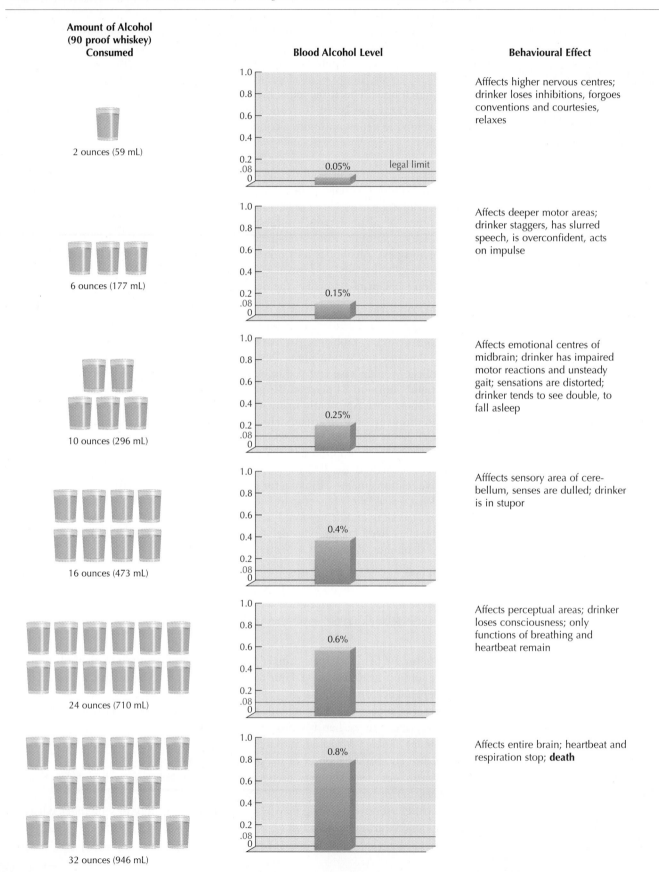

Amount of Alcohol (90 proof whiskey) Consumed

2 ounces (59 mL)

6 ounces (177 mL)

10 ounces (296 mL)

16 ounces (473 mL)

24 ounces (710 mL)

32 ounces (946 mL)

Blood Alcohol Level

0.05%   legal limit

0.15%

0.25%

0.4%

0.6%

0.8%

Behavioural Effect

Afffects higher nervous centres; drinker loses inhibitions, forgoes conventions and courtesies, relaxes

Affects deeper motor areas; drinker staggers, has slurred speech, is overconfident, acts on impulse

Affects emotional centres of midbrain; drinker has impaired motor reactions and unsteady gait; sensations are distorted; drinker tends to see double, to fall asleep

Afffects sensory area of cerebellum, senses are dulled; drinker is in stupor

Affects perceptual areas; drinker loses consciousness; only functions of breathing and heartbeat remain

Affects entire brain; heartbeat and respiration stop; **death**

2. *Crucial phase.* A crucial turning point comes as the person begins to lose control over drinking. At this stage, there is still some control over when and where a first drink is taken. But one drink starts a chain reaction leading to a second and a third, and so on.

3. *Chronic phase.* At this point, the person is alcohol dependent. Victims drink compulsively and continuously. They rarely eat, they become intoxicated from far less alcohol than before, and they crave alcohol when deprived of it. Work, family ties, and social life all deteriorate. The person's self-drugging is usually so compulsive that when given a choice, the bottle comes before friends, relatives, employment, and self-esteem. The person is an addict.

THE DEVELOPMENT OF A DRINKING PROBLEM   To add to this summary, the following lists will help you form a more detailed picture of how alcohol abuse develops.

Early Warnings

- You are beginning to feel guilty about your drinking.
- You drink more than you used to and tend to gulp your drinks.
- You try to have a few extra drinks before or after drinking with others.
- You have begun to drink at certain times or to get through certain situations.
- You drink to relieve feelings of boredom, depression, anxiety, or inadequacy.
- You are sensitive when others mention your drinking.
- You have had memory blackouts or have passed out while drinking.

Signals Not to Be Ignored

- There are times when you need a drink.
- You drink in the morning to overcome a hangover.
- You promise to drink less and are lying about your drinking.
- You often regret what you have said or done while drinking.
- You have begun to drink alone.
- You have weekend drinking bouts and Monday hangovers.
- You have lost time at work or school because of drinking.
- You are noticeably drunk on important occasions.
- Your relationship to family and friends has changed because of your drinking.

MODERATED DRINKING   Many social-recreational drinkers could do a far better job of managing their use of alcohol. Almost everyone has been to a party spoiled by someone who drank too much too fast. Those who avoid overdrinking have a better time, and so do their friends. But how do you avoid drinking too much? After all, as one wit once observed, "The conscience dissolves in alcohol." Psychologists Roger Vogler and Wayne Bartz (1982, 1992) have observed that it takes skill to regulate drinking in social situations, where the temptation to drink can be strong. If you choose to drink, here are some guidelines that may be helpful (adapted from Vogler & Bartz, 1992).

Paced Drinking

1. Think about your drinking beforehand and plan how you will manage it.
2. Drink slowly, eat while drinking, and make every other drink (or more) a non-alcoholic beverage.
3. Limit drinking primarily to the first hour of a social event or party.
4. Practise how you will politely but firmly refuse drinks.
5. Learn how to relax, meet people, and socialize without relying on alcohol.

Detoxification In the treatment of alcoholism, the withdrawal of the patient from alcohol.

TREATMENT   Treatment for alcohol dependence begins with sobering up the person and cutting off the supply. This phase is referred to as **detoxification** (literally, "to remove poison"). It frequently produces all the symptoms of drug withdrawal and can be extremely unpleasant. The next step is to try to restore the person's health. Heavy abuse of alcohol usually causes severe damage to body organs and the nervous system. After alcoholics have "dried out," and some degree of health has been restored, they may be treated with tranquillizers, antidepressants, or psychotherapy. Unfortunately, the success of these procedures has been limited.

One mutual-help approach that has been fairly successful is Alcoholics Anonymous (AA). AA acts on the premise that it takes a former alcoholic to understand and help a current alcoholic. The organization emphasizes a sense of spirituality and community. Participants at AA meetings admit that they have a problem, share feelings, and resolve to stay "dry" one day at a time. Other group members provide support for those struggling to end dependency. (Cocaine Anonymous and Narcotics Anonymous use the same approach.)

Eighty-one percent of those who remain in AA over one year get through the following year without a drink. However, AA's success rate may simply reflect the fact that members join voluntarily, meaning they have admitted they have a serious problem (Morgenstern et al., 1997). Sadly, it seems that alcohol abusers will often not face their problems until they have "hit rock bottom." If they are willing, though, AA presents a practical approach to the problem.

Two newer groups offer a rational, non-spiritual approach to alcohol abuse that better fits the needs of some people. These are Rational Recovery and Secular Organizations for Sobriety (SOS). Other alternatives to AA include medical treatment, group therapy, and individual psychotherapy (Institute of Medicine, 1990). There is a strong tendency for abusive drinkers to deny they have a problem. The sooner they seek help, the better.

▶ Marijuana—What's in the Pot?

Marijuana The leaves and flowers of the hemp plant *Cannabis sativa*.

Hashish Resinous material scraped from the leaves of the hemp plant; hashish has a high concentration of THC.

THC Tetrahydrocannabinol, the main active chemical in marijuana.

Hallucinogen A substance that alters or distorts sensory impressions.

Marijuana and hashish are derived from the hemp plant *Cannabis sativa*. **Marijuana** consists of the leaves and flowers of the hemp plant. **Hashish** is a resinous material scraped from Cannabis leaves. The main active chemical in marijuana is **tetrahydrocannabinol** (tet-rah-hydro-cah-NAB-ih-nol), or **THC.** THC is a mild **hallucinogen** (hal-LU-sin-oh-jin: a substance that alters sensory impressions).

Hallucinogens

The drug LSD (lysergic acid diethylamide) is perhaps the best-known hallucinogen. Even when taken in tiny amounts, LSD can produce hallucinations and psychosis-like disturbances in thinking and perception. Two other common hallucinogens are mescaline (peyote) and psilocybin ("magic mushrooms"). Incidentally, the drug PCP (phencyclidine) can have hallucinogenic effects. However, PCP, which is an anesthetic, also has stimulant and depressant effects. This potent combination can cause extreme agitation, disorientation, violence—and too often, tragedy. All of the hallucinogens, including marijuana, typically affect neurotransmitter systems that carry messages between neurons (Julien, 1998).

MARIJUANA   Marijuana's psychological effects include a sense of euphoria or well-being, relaxation, altered time sense, and perceptual distortions. At high dosages, however, paranoia, hallucinations, and delusions can occur (Palfai & Jankiewicz, 1991). All considered, marijuana intoxication is relatively subtle by comparison to drugs such as LSD or alcohol (Kelly et al., 1990). Despite this, driving a car while high on marijuana can be extremely hazardous. As a matter of fact, driving under the influence of any intoxicating drug is dangerous.

No overdose deaths have been reported from marijuana. However, marijuana cannot be considered harmless. Particularly worrisome is the fact that THC accumulates in the body's fatty tissues, especially in the brain and reproductive organs. Even if a person smokes marijuana just once a week, the body is never entirely free of THC. Scientists have located a specific receptor site on the surface of brain cells where THC binds to produce its effects (see ▶ Figure 5.12). These receptor sites are found in large numbers in the cerebral cortex, which is the seat of human consciousness (Matsuda et al., 1990).

Does marijuana produce physical dependence? Studies of long-term heavy users of marijuana in Jamaica, Greece, and Costa Rica failed to find any physical dependence (Carter,

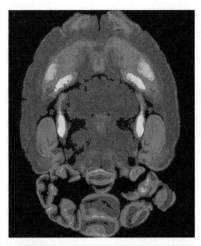

▶ Figure 5.12

This thin slice of a rat's brain has been washed with a radioactive THC-like drug. Yellowish areas show where the brain is rich in THC receptors. In addition to the cortex, or outer layer of the brain, THC receptors are found in abundance in areas involved in the control of coordinated movement. Naturally occurring chemicals similar to THC may help the brain cope with pain and stress. However, when THC is used as a drug, high doses can cause paranoia, hallucinations, and dizziness (Julien, 1998).

1980; Rubin & Comitas, 1975; Stefanis, Dornbush, & Fink, 1977). Marijuana's potential for abuse lies primarily in the realm of psychological dependence, not physical. Nevertheless, frequent users of marijuana find it very difficult to quit, so dependence is a risk (Budney, Novy, & Hughes, 1999; Haney et al., 1999).

Dangers of Marijuana Use

There have been very alarming reports in the press about the dangers of marijuana. Are they accurate? As one pharmacologist put it, "Those reading only *Good Housekeeping* would have to believe that marijuana is considerably more dangerous than the black plague." Unfortunately, an evaluation of marijuana's risks has been clouded by emotional debate. Let's see if we can make a realistic appraisal.

In the past it was widely reported that marijuana causes brain damage, genetic damage, and a loss of motivation. Each of these charges can be criticized for being based on poorly done or inconclusive research. However, that doesn't mean that marijuana gets a clean bill of health. For about a day after a person smokes marijuana, his or her attention, coordination, and short-term memory are affected (Pope, Gruber, & Yurgelun-Todd, 1995). Long-term marijuana users tend to show small but persistent impairments of learning, memory, attention, and thinking abilities. These changes, while subtle, can be a serious problem for frequent users (Pope & Yurgelun-Todd, 1996; Solowij, Michie, & Fox, 1995).

Does marijuana affect overall intelligence? To answer this question, Peter Fried and his colleagues at Carleton University followed 77 people for about a decade. They noted the amount of marijuana use and administered an IQ test on different occasions over the study period. IQ tests measure a number of cognitive abilities (see Chapter 8). Heavy users (smoking at least five joints weekly) had significant declines in IQ scores compared to when they were non-users. Interestingly, however, heavy users who had quit the drug did not show intellectual deficits. Finally, current light smokers also showed no declines in IQ scores (Fried et al., 2002). Before you jump to the conclusion that only current heavy marijuana users are negatively affected by the drug and former heavy users and current light users are unaffected, you must keep in mind two important points: First, this study assessed global or overall IQ levels, and global IQ scores may not be sensitive enough to pick up deficits in individual cognitive abilities, such as attention, memory, and so on. Second, this was one small study, and scientific consensus comes about through many studies that find similar results, so we need more research on this issue. What we can say for now is that the final truth about the impact of marijuana on intelligence is still to be unearthed.

HEALTH RISKS   After many years of conflicting information, some of marijuana's health hazards are also being clarified. Marijuana's long-term effects include the following health risks.

1. In regular users, marijuana causes pre-cancerous changes in lung cells. At present no direct link between marijuana and lung cancer has been established, but it is suspected. Marijuana smoke contains 50 percent more cancer-causing hydrocarbons than tobacco smoke does. One marijuana cigarette has 16 times more tar than one tobacco cigarette. Thus, smoking several "joints" a week may be the equivalent of smoking a dozen cigarettes a day (Barsky et al., 1998).

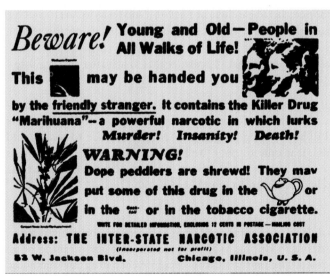

An outdated anti-marijuana poster demonstrates the kind of misinformation that has long been attached to this drug. Research has finally begun to sort out the risks associated with the use of marijuana.

2. Marijuana temporarily lowers sperm production in males, and users produce more abnormal sperm. This could be a problem for a man who is marginally fertile and wants to have a family (Palfai & Jankiewicz, 1991).

3. In experiments with female monkeys, THC causes abnormal menstrual cycles and disrupts ovulation. Other animal studies show that THC causes a higher rate of miscarriages and that it can reach the developing fetus. As is true for so many other drugs, it appears that marijuana should be avoided during pregnancy.

4. THC can suppress the body's immune system, possibly increasing the risk of disease (Turkington, 1986).

5. In animals, marijuana causes genetic damage within cells of the body. It is not known to what extent this happens in humans, but it does suggest that marijuana can be detrimental to health (Zimmerman & Zimmerman, 1990).

6. Activity levels in the cerebellum are lower than normal in marijuana abusers. This may explain why chronic marijuana users tend to show some loss of coordination (Volkow et al., 1996).

7. There is some evidence that THC damages parts of the brain important for memory (Chan et al., 1998).

Does marijuana have any medical benefits? It is claimed that smoking marijuana can relieve the excruciating pain experienced by glaucoma sufferers, can help increase the appetite of those suffering from AIDS (and thus combat weight-loss problems linked with the illness), and can reduce the nausea associated with chemotherapy in the treatment of cancer. There are many anecdotal reports about the alleged medical benefits of marijuana, but controlled scientific research on this issue is still to be performed. Recently, the government of Canada has made some policy decisions concerning the controlled medical use of marijuana, and the following four important developments are noteworthy:

1. The government has passed legislation that allows people with certain conditions, including multiple sclerosis, spinal cord injury, cancer, HIV infection/AIDS, severe arthritis, and epilepsy, to smoke marijuana as a therapeutic agent. They must, however, obtain permission from the government before using the drug.

2. Under the new law, people suffering from serious illnesses can apply to either grow their own marijuana or to have someone else cultivate the plant for them (Health Canada, 2001).

3. The government has sanctioned the researchers at McGill University to carry out a year-long study to determine the possible effects of smoked marijuana on the reduction of pain.

4. A Senate committee has recommended that Canada legalize marijuana and regulate its sale.

There have been plenty of emotional arguments on marijuana's potential health benefits. Some believe that the drug is a panacea for all sorts of medical problems, while others insist that marijuana is devoid of any healing properties, is a great menace to society, and therefore should remain banned. It is only through well-designed scientific investigations that we can ever hope to learn the genuine facts about this drug. All we can do at the moment is wait and let researchers reveal to us what's really in the pot.

Summary

Why is drug abuse such a common problem? People seek drug experiences for many reasons, ranging from curiosity and a desire to belong to a group, to a search for meaning or an escape from feelings of inadequacy. The best predictors of adolescent drug use and abuse are drug use by peers, parental drug use, delinquency, parental maladjustment, poor self-esteem, social nonconformity, and stressful life changes. A recent study conducted by Richard Tremblay and his colleagues at the University of Montreal found that adolescents who abuse drugs tend to be maladjusted, alienated, impulsive, and emotionally distressed (Masse & Tremblay, 1997). Antisocial behaviour, school failure, and risky sexual behaviour are also commonly associated with drug abuse (Ary et al., 1999). Such patterns make it clear that taking drugs is a symptom, rather than a cause, of personal and social maladjustment (Derzon & Lipsey, 1999; Welte et al., 1999).

Many abusers turn to drugs in a self-defeating attempt to cope with life. All of the frequently abused drugs produce immediate feelings of pleasure. The negative consequences follow much later. This combination of immediate pleasure and delayed punishment allows abusers to feel good on demand. In time, of course, most of the pleasure goes out of drug abuse, and the abuser's problems get worse. But if an abuser merely feels better (however briefly) after taking a drug, drug taking can become compulsive (Barrett, 1985). In contrast, people who stop using drugs often say that they quit because the drawbacks had come to exceed the benefits (Toneatto et al., 1999).

Although a large sum of money has been spent on drug enforcement in recent years, there has been an increase in the overall level of drug use in North America. Most drug use begins in early adolescence (Chen & Kandel, 1995). Given this fact, some experts believe that prevention through education and early intervention is the answer to drug problems (Julien,1998). What do you think?

A LOOK AHEAD   Of the many states of consciousness we have discussed, dreaming remains one of the most familiar—and the most surprising. Are there lessons to be learned from dreams? What personal insights lie hidden in the ebb and flow of your dream images? Let's find out.

Knowledge builder

PSYCHOACTIVE DRUGS

Relate

 What legal drugs did you use in the last year? Did any have psychoactive properties? How do psychoactive drugs differ from other substances in their potential for abuse?

Learning Check

1. Which of the drugs listed below are known to cause a physical dependence?
   a. heroin *b.* morphine *c.* codeine *d.* methadone *e.* barbiturates *f.* alcohol *g.* LSD *h.* amphetamines *i.* nicotine *j.* cocaine
2. Amphetamine psychosis is similar to extreme _____, in which the individual feels threatened and suffers from delusions.
3. Cocaine is very similar to which of the following in its effects on the central nervous system?
   a. alcohol *b.* codeine *c. Cannabis d.* amphetamine

4. The combination of _____ or _____ and alcohol can be fatal.
5. One drink starts a chain reaction leading to a second and a third in the crucial phase of problem drinking. T or F?
6. This country's biggest drug problem centres on abuse of
   a. marijuana *b.* alcohol *c.* LSD *d.* cocaine
7. Most experts now acknowledge that marijuana is physically addicting. T or F?

Critical Thinking

8. Many governments around the world continue to fund anti-smoking campaigns and smoking-related health research at the same time as subsidizing tobacco growers. Can you explain this contradiction?
9. Why do you think there is such a contrast between the laws regulating marijuana and those regulating alcohol and tobacco?

Answers:

1. All but *g* 2. paranoia 3. *d* 4. barbiturates, tranquillizers 5. T 6. *b* 7. F 8. Neither can we. 9. Drug laws in Western societies reflect cultural values and historical patterns of use. Inconsistencies in the law often cannot be justified on the basis of pharmacology, health risks, or abuse potential.

EXPLORING AND USING DREAMS

Dream processes Mental filters that hide the true meanings of dreams.

Condensation Combining several people, objects, or events into a single dream image.

Displacement Directing emotions or actions toward safe or unimportant dream images.

Symbolization The non-literal expression of dream content.

Secondary elaboration Making a dream more logical and complete while remembering it.

At one time or another, almost everyone has had a dream that seemed to have deep meaning. What strategies do psychologists use to interpret dreams? Let's start with Sigmund Freud's approach.

To unlock dreams, Freud identified four **dream processes,** or mental filters, that disguise the meanings of dreams. The first is **condensation,** in which several people, objects, or events are combined into a single dream image. A dream character that looks like a teacher, acts like your father, talks like your mother, and is dressed like your employer might be a condensation of authority figures in your life.

Displacement is a second way of disguising dream content. Displacement may cause important emotions or actions of a dream to be redirected toward safe or seemingly unimportant images. Thus, a student angry with his parents might dream of accidentally wrecking their car instead of directly attacking them.

A third dream process is **symbolization.** As mentioned earlier, Freud believed that dreams are often expressed in images that are symbolic rather than literal. That's why it helps to ask what feelings or ideas a dream image might symbolize. Let's say, for example, that a student dreams of coming to class naked. A literal interpretation would be that the student is an exhibitionist! A more likely symbolic meaning is that the student feels vulnerable or unprepared in the class.

Secondary elaboration is the fourth method by which dream meanings are disguised. **Secondary elaboration** is the tendency to make a dream more logical and to add details when remembering it. The fresher a dream memory is, the more useful it is likely to be.

Looking for condensation, displacement, symbolization, and secondary elaboration may help you unlock your dreams. But there are other ways to proceed that may be more effective. Dream theorist Calvin Hall (1974) preferred to think of dreams as plays and the dreamer as a playwright. Hall admitted that dream images and ideas tend to be more primitive than waking thoughts. Nevertheless, much can be learned by simply considering the *setting, cast of characters, plot,* and *emotions* portrayed in a dream.

Another dream theorist, Rosalind Cartwright, suggests that dreams are primarily "feeling statements." According to her, the overall emotional tone (underlying mood) of a dream is a major clue to its meaning. Is the dream comical, threatening, joyous, or depressing? Were you lonely, jealous, frightened, in love, or angry? Cartwright believes that exploring everyday dream life can be a source of personal enrichment and personal growth (Cartwright & Lamberg, 1992).

In many ways, dreams can be thought of as a message from yourself to yourself. Thus, the way to understand dreams is to remember them, write them down, look for the messages they contain, and become deeply acquainted with your own symbol system. Here's how.

How would you try to find the meaning of a dream? A traditional approach is to look for symbolic messages as well as literal meanings. If you find yourself wearing a mask in a dream, for instance, it could relate to important roles that you play at school, work, or home. It could also mean that you want to hide or that you are looking forward to a costume party. However, to accurately interpret a dream you need to learn your own "vocabulary" of dream images and meanings. Keeping a dream diary is the first step toward gaining valuable insights.

How to Catch a Dream

1. Before retiring, plan to remember your dreams. Keep a pen and paper or a tape recorder beside your bed.
2. If possible, arrange to awaken gradually without an alarm. Natural awakening almost always follows soon after a REM period.
3. If you rarely remember your dreams, you may want to set an alarm clock to go off an hour before you

Table 5.5
Effects of Selected Drugs on Dreaming

DRUG	EFFECT ON REM SLEEP
Alcohol	Decrease
Amphetamines	Decrease
Barbiturates	Decrease
Caffeine	None
Cocaine	Decrease
LSD	Slight increase
Marijuana	Slight decrease or no effect
Opiates	Decrease
Valium	Decrease

usually awaken. Although less desirable than awakening naturally, this may let you catch a dream.

4. Upon awakening, lie still and review the dream images with your eyes closed. Try to recall as many details as possible.
5. If you can, make your first dream record (whether by writing or by tape) with your eyes closed. Opening your eyes will disrupt dream recall.
6. Review the dream again and record as many additional details as you can remember. Dream memories disappear quickly. Be sure to describe feelings as well as the plot, characters, and actions of the dream.
7. Put your dreams into a permanent dream diary. Keep dreams in chronological order and review them periodically. This procedure will reveal recurrent themes, conflicts, and emotions. It almost always produces valuable insights.
8. Remember, a number of drugs suppress dreaming (see Table 5.5).

DREAM WORK   Because each dream has several possible meanings or levels of meaning, there is no fixed way to work with it. Telling the dream to others and discussing its meaning can be a good start. Describing it may help you relive some of the feelings in the dream. Also, family members or friends may be able to offer interpretations of which you may be unaware. Watch for verbal or visual puns and other playful elements in dreams. For example, if you dream that you are in a wrestling match and your arm is pinned behind your back, it may mean that you feel someone is "twisting your arm" in real life.

The meaning of most dreams will yield to a little detective work. Rosalind Cartwright suggests asking a series of questions about dreams you would like to understand (Cartwright and Lamberg, 1992).

Probing Dreams

1. Who was in the dream? Do you recognize any of the characters?
2. What was happening? Were you active in the dream or watching it transpire? Did someone else do something to you?
3. Where did the action of the dream take place? Have you seen the setting or any part of it in real life, or was it a fantasy scene?
4. What was the time frame? What was your age in the dream?
5. Who is responsible for what happened in the dream?
6. Who are you in your dreams? Are you someone you would like to be or someone you'd rather not be?

If you still have trouble seeing the meaning of a dream, you may find it helpful to use a technique developed by Fritz Perls. Perls, the originator of Gestalt therapy, considered most dreams a special message about what's missing in our lives, what we avoid doing, or feelings that need to be "re-owned." Perls felt that dreams are a way of filling in gaps in personal experience (Perls, 1969).

An approach that Perls found helpful is to "take the part of" or "speak for" each of the characters and objects in the dream. In other words, if you dream about a strange man standing behind a doorway, you would speak aloud to the man, and then answer for him. To use Perls's method, you would even speak for the door, perhaps saying something like, "I am a barrier. I keep you safe, but I also keep you locked inside. The stranger has something to tell you. You must risk opening me to learn it."

A particularly interesting dream exercise is to continue a dream as waking fantasy so that it may be concluded or carried on to a more meaningful ending. As the world of dreams and your personal dream language become more familiar, you will doubtless find many answers, paradoxes, intuitions, and insights into your own behaviour.

Using Your Dreams

Creative people tend to remember more dreams (Schredl, 1995). It could be that such people just pay more attention to their dreams. But dream theorist Gordon Globus (1987) believes that dreams make a major contribution to creativity. Globus points out that some of our most creative moments take place during dreaming. Even unimaginative people may create amazing worlds each night in their dreams. For many of us, this rich ability to create is lost in the daily rush of sensory input. How might we tap the creative power of dreams that is so easily lost during waking?

DREAMS AND CREATIVITY   History is full of cases where dreams have been a pathway to creativity and discovery. A striking example is provided by Dr. Otto Loewi, a pharmacologist and recipient of a Nobel prize. Loewi had spent years studying the chemical transmission of nerve impulses. A tremendous breakthrough in his research came when he dreamed of an experiment three nights in a row. The first two nights he woke up and scribbled the experiment on a pad. But the next morning, he couldn't tell what the notes meant. On the third night, he got up after having the dream. This time, instead of making notes he went straight to his laboratory and performed the crucial experiment. Loewi later said that if the experiment had occurred to him while awake he would have rejected it.

Loewi's experience gives some insight into using dreams to produce creative solutions. Inhibitions are reduced during dreaming, which may be especially useful in solving problems that require a fresh point of view.

Being able to take advantage of dreams for problem solving is improved if you "set" yourself before retiring. Before you go to bed, try to think intently about a problem you wish to solve. Steep yourself in the problem by stating it clearly and reviewing all relevant information. Then use the suggestions listed in the previous section to catch your dreams. While this method is not guaranteed to produce a novel solution or a new insight, it is certain to be an adventure. About half of a group of college students using the method for one week recalled a dream that helped them solve a personal problem (Barrett, 1993).

LUCID DREAMING   If you would like to press further into the territory of dreams, you may want to learn lucid dreaming, a relatively rare but fascinating experience. Have you ever been aware in your dream that you were dreaming? If you answered yes to the above question, you are what psychologists call a lucid dreamer. Many people have had at least one **lucid dream** in their lives, but only about 20 percent have them regularly (Blackmore, 1991).

Lucid dream A dream in which the dreamer feels awake and capable of normal thought and action.

Stephen La Berge and his colleagues at the Stanford University Sleep Research Center have used a unique approach to show that lucid dreams are real and that they occur during REM sleep. In the sleep lab, lucid dreamers agree to make prearranged signals when they become aware they are dreaming. One such signal is to look up abruptly in a dream, causing a distinct upward eye movement. Another signal is to clench the right and left fists (in the dream) in a prearranged pattern. In other words, lucid dreamers can partially overcome REM sleep paralysis. Such signals show very clearly that lucid dreaming and voluntary action in dreams is possible (La Berge, 1981, 1985; Moss, 1989).

How would a person go about learning to have lucid dreams? Dream researcher Stephen La Berge found he could greatly increase lucid dreaming by following this simple routine: When you awaken spontaneously from a dream, take a few minutes to try to memorize it. Next, engage in 10 to 15 minutes of reading or any other activity requiring full wakefulness. Then, while lying in bed and returning to sleep, say to yourself, "Next time I'm dreaming, I want to remember I'm dreaming." Finally, visualize yourself lying in bed asleep while in the dream you just rehearsed. At the same time, picture yourself realizing that you are dreaming. Follow this routine each time you awaken (substitute a dream memory from another occasion if you don't awaken from a dream). Researchers have also found that stimulation from the vestibular system tends to increase lucidity. Thus, sleeping in a hammock, a boat, or on a waterbed might increase the number of lucid dreams you have (Leslie & Ogilvie, 1996).

Why would anyone want to have more lucid dreams? Researchers are interested in lucid dreams because they provide a tool for understanding dreaming. Using subjects who can signal while they are dreaming makes it possible to explore dreams with firsthand data from the dreamer's world itself.

One interesting application of lucid dreaming is in the treatment of nightmares. Researchers at the Sacre-Coeur Hospital in Montreal have taught people with serious nightmares how to create lucid dreams; that is, to become aware that they are having a dream or, perhaps, a nightmare. After realizing that they were having a recurrent nightmare, clients were encouraged to change the direction of their terrifying dream to something that was not so unpleasant. Once people had succeeded in recognizing that they were dreaming and were able to alter the course of the unwanted dreams, the frequency and severity of their nightmares decreased substantially (Zadra & Pihl, 1997).

Consider yet another example of how lucid dreams can lead to emotional growth. A recently divorced woman kept dreaming that she was being swallowed by a giant wave. Rosalind Cartwright asked the woman to try swimming the next time the wave engulfed her. She did, with great determination, and the nightmare lost its terror. More importantly, her revised dream made her feel that she could cope with life again. For reasons such as this, people who have lucid dreams tend to feel a sense of emotional well-being (Wolpin et al., 1992).

The phenomenon of lucid dreaming raises intriguing questions about the nature of consciousness. To what extent do the rules that operate under waking consciousness—the ability to use logic, to have a coherent sense of oneself and one's surroundings—also operate during the nightly drama? If we can control the content of our dreams, should we still call dreams "dreams"? Is dreaming not just an extension of our waking consciousness, or vice versa? We do not have enough information to be able to answer these questions precisely, but we can certainly dream!

Knowledge builder

EXPLORING AND USING DREAMS

Relate

 Some people are very interested in remembering and interpreting their dreams. Others pay little attention to dreaming. What importance do you place on dreams? Do you think dreams and dream interpretation can increase self-awareness?

Learning Check

1. In secondary elaboration, one dream character stands for several others. T or F?
2. Calvin Hall's approach to dream interpretation emphasizes the setting, cast, plot, and emotions portrayed in a dream. T or F?

3. Rosalind Cartwright stresses that dreaming is a relatively mechanical process having little personal meaning. T or F?
4. Both alcohol and LSD cause a slight increase in dreaming. T or F?
5. "Taking the part of" or "speaking for" dream elements is a dream interpretation technique originated by Fritz Perls. T or F?
6. Recent research shows that lucid dreaming occurs primarily during NREM sleep or micro-awakenings. T or F?

Critical Thinking

7. The possibility of having a lucid dream raises an interesting question: If you were dreaming right now, how could you prove it?

Answers:

1. F 2. T 3. F 4. F 5. T 6. F 7. In waking consciousness, our actions have consequences that produce immediate sensory feedback. Dreams lack such external feedback. Thus, trying to walk through a wall or doing similar tests would reveal if you were dreaming.

Psychologist's Journal

EPILOGUE

Now that we have nearly reached the end of consciousness, let's see what we can learn from people who have nearly reached the end of consciousness. What happens when a person "dies" and returns to tell about it?

The emergency room doctors work feverishly over a heart attack victim. The patient, who appears to have died, hears a buzzing sound. From somewhere above, he sees his own lifeless body on the table. Then he enters a dark tunnel and passes into an area of bright light. There he is met by a "being of light" who shows him a rapid playback of his entire life. At some point he reaches a barrier. He is completely at peace and feels engulfed by love, but he knows he must go back. Suddenly, he is in his body again. The patient recovers. For the rest of his life, he is profoundly affected by his journey to the threshold of death and back.

Unmistakably, our patient had a near-death experience (NDE), an altered state that may occur when a person is clinically dead and then resuscitated. During an NDE, people typically experience all or most of the following: a feeling of separation from their body, entering darkness or a tunnel, seeing a light, entering the light, a life review, and feeling at peace.

Many people regard NDEs as spiritual experiences that seem to verify the existence of an afterlife. In contrast, medical explanations attribute NDEs to the physiological reactions of an oxygen-starved brain. Indeed, many elements of NDEs can be produced by hallucinogenic drugs, migraine headaches, general anesthetics, extreme fatigue, high fever, or just falling asleep.

While the debate continues, one thing is certain: Near-death experiences can profoundly change personality and life goals. Many near-death survivors say that they are no longer motivated by greed, competition, or material success. Instead, they become more concerned about the needs of other people. As we have noted, many religions recognize that altered states can help people see their lives from a higher perspective. That's certainly true of close encounters with death, which have proved to be an excellent way to learn what's really important in life. (Sources: Blackmore, 1991, 1993; Kellehear, 1993; MacHovec, 1994; Moody, 1975; Ring, 1980.)

CHAPTER IN REVIEW

Major Points

▶ Consciousness and altered states of awareness are core features of mental life.
▶ Sleep is necessary for survival; dreaming appears to contribute to memory consolidation and perhaps to general mental and emotional health.
▶ Sleep loss and sleep disorders are serious health problems that should be corrected when they persist.
▶ Dreams are at least as meaningful as waking thoughts. Whether they have deeper meaning is still debated.
▶ Hypnosis is useful but not "magical." Hypnosis can change private experiences more readily than habits.
▶ Meditation can be used to alter consciousness, as well as to reliably produce deep relaxation.
▶ Psychoactive drugs, which alter consciousness, are highly prone to abuse.
▶ Collecting and interpreting your dreams can promote self-awareness.

Summary

What Is an Altered State of Consciousness?

• States of awareness that differ from normal, alert, waking consciousness are called altered states of consciousness (ASCs). Altered states are especially associated with sleep and dreaming, hypnosis, sensory deprivation, and psychoactive drugs.
• Cultural conditioning greatly affects what altered states a person recognizes, seeks, considers normal, and attains.

What Are the Effects of Sleep Loss and Changes in Sleep Patterns?

• Sleep is an innate biological rhythm essential for survival. Higher animals and people deprived of sleep experience involuntary microsleeps.
• Moderate sleep loss mainly affects vigilance and performance on routine or boring tasks. Extended sleep loss can produce a temporary sleep-deprivation psychosis.

- Sleep patterns show some flexibility, but seven to eight hours remains average. The amount of daily sleep decreases steadily from birth to old age. Once-a-day sleep patterns, with a 2-to-1 ratio of waking and sleep, are most efficient for most people.

Are There Different Stages of Sleep?

- Sleep occurs in four stages. Stage 1 is light sleep, and stage 4 is deep sleep. The sleeper alternates between stages 1 and 4 (passing through stages 2 and 3) several times each night.
- There are two basic sleep states, rapid eye movement (REM) sleep and non-REM (NREM) sleep. REM sleep is much more strongly associated with dreaming than non-REM sleep is.
- Dreaming and REMs occur mainly during light sleep, similar to stage 1. Dreaming is accompanied by emotional arousal but relaxation of the skeletal muscles.
- People deprived of dream sleep show a REM rebound when allowed to sleep without interruption. However, total sleep loss seems to be more important than loss of a single stage.
- In addition to several other possible functions, REM sleep appears to aid the processing of memories.

What Are the Causes of Sleep Disorders and Unusual Sleep Events?

- Sleepwalking and sleeptalking occur during NREM sleep. Night terrors occur in NREM sleep, whereas nightmares occur in REM sleep.
- Sleep apnea (interrupted breathing) is one source of insomnia and daytime hypersomnia (sleepiness).
- Apnea is suspected as one cause of sudden infant death syndrome (SIDS). Healthy infants should sleep face up or on their sides.
- Insomnia may be temporary or chronic. When it is treated through the use of drugs, sleep quality is often lowered and drug-dependency insomnia may develop.
- Behavioural approaches to managing insomnia, such as sleep restriction and stimulus control, are quite effective.

Do Dreams Have Meaning?

- Most dream content is about familiar settings, people, and actions. Dreams involve negative emotions more often than positive emotions.
- The Freudian, or psychoanalytic, view is that dreams express unconscious wishes, frequently hidden by dream symbols.
- Many theorists have questioned Freud's view of dreams. For example, the activation-synthesis hypothesis portrays dreaming as a physiological process.

How Is Hypnosis Done, and What Are Its Limitations?

- Hypnosis is an altered state characterized by narrowed attention and increased suggestibility.
- Hypnosis appears capable of producing relaxation, controlling pain, and altering perceptions. Stage hypnotism uses deception to simulate hypnosis.

What Is Meditation? Does It Have Any Benefits?

- Concentrative meditation can be used to focus attention, alter consciousness, and reduce stress. Major benefits of meditation are its ability to interrupt anxious thoughts and to elicit the relaxation response.
- Brief exposure to sensory deprivation can also elicit the relaxation response. Under proper conditions, sensory deprivation may help break longstanding habits.

What Are the Effects of the More Commonly Used Psychoactive Drugs?

- A psychoactive drug is a substance that affects the brain in ways that alter consciousness. Most psychoactive drugs can be placed on a scale ranging from stimulation to depression.
- Drugs may cause a physical dependence (addiction) or a psychological dependence, or both. All psychoactive drugs can lead to psychological dependence.
- Stimulant drugs are readily abused because of the period of depression that often follows stimulation. The greatest risks are associated with amphetamines, cocaine, and nicotine, but even caffeine can be a problem. Nicotine includes the added risk of lung cancer, heart disease, and other health problems.
- Barbiturates and tranquillizers are depressant drugs whose action is similar to that of alcohol. Mixing barbiturates or tranquillizers and alcohol may result in a fatal drug interaction.
- Alcohol is the most heavily abused drug in common use today. The development of a drinking problem is usually marked by an initial phase of increasing consumption, a crucial phase, in which a single drink can set off a chain reaction, and a chronic phase, in which a person lives to drink and drinks to live.
- Marijuana is subject to an abuse pattern similar to alcohol. Studies have linked chronic marijuana use with lung cancer, various mental impairments, and other health problems.
- Drug abuse is related to a variety of factors, especially personal and social maladjustment, attempts to cope, the immediate reinforcing qualities of psychoactive drugs, peer group influences, and expectations about the value and effects of drugs.
- Proposed remedies for drug abuse have ranged from severe punishment to legalization. The search for a solution continues.

How Can Dreams Be Used to Promote Personal Understanding?

- Dreams may be used to promote self-understanding. Freud held that the meaning of dreams is hidden by condensation, displacement, symbolization, and secondary elaboration.
- Hall emphasized the setting, cast, plot, and emotions of a dream. Cartwright's view of dreams as feeling statements and Perls's technique of speaking for dream elements are also helpful.

- Dreams may be used for creative problem solving, especially when dream awareness is achieved through lucid dreaming.

PSYCHOLOGY ON THE NET

If you have difficulty finding any of the sites listed here, visit http://psychologyjourney.nelson.com for an updated list of Internet addresses and direct links to relevant sites.

Alcoholics Anonymous (AA)   Home page of Alcoholics Anonymous.
http://www.alcoholics-anonymous.org/index.html

The Antidrug.com   Advice to parents and other adults about how to help children resist drug use.
http://theantidrug.com

CAMH   The Centre for Addiction and Mental Health presents a short quiz to identify drinking problems.
http://notes.camh.net/efeed.nsf/feedback

The Canadian Sleep Society   Offers plenty of useful information about sleep and sleep disorders. You can also post questions for experts on any aspect of sleep.
http://www.css.to/about/index.htm

Cocaine Anonymous   Offers advice and information on how to quit cocaine addiction. http://www.ca.org/

Disorders of the Sleep/Wake Cycle   Basic information about circadian rhythms and jet lag.
http://www.stanford.edu/~dement/circadian.html

Dream and Nightmare Laboratory   Useful information about dreaming and dreaming-related problems can be found at a site hosted at the University of Montreal. You can even participate in their research on dreams.
http://www.crhsc.umontreal.ca/dreams/index.html

Key Concepts in Hypnosis   An informative paper by a Canadian researcher discusses various aspects of the hypnotic phenomenon.
http://www.fmsonline.org/hypnosis.html#watmheoh

Marijuana Anonymous   Offers advice and information on how to quit smoking marijuana.
http://www.marijuana-anonymous.org/

Recreational Drugs Information Home Page   A comprehensive list of psychoactive drugs and useful information about their behavioural effects.
http://www.a1b2c3.com/drugs/

 InfoTrac College Edition   For recent articles related to the "Psychology in Action" feature, use Key Words search for DREAMS.

INTERACTIVE LEARNING

Psychology: An Interactive Journey Remember that Chapter 5 of the CD-ROM that came with this text has practice tests, flashcards, interactive exercises, a crossword puzzle, and other valuable materials to enhance your learning experience.

PsychNow! 2c. Sleep and Dreaming, 2d. Psychoactive Drugs.

Psyk.trek 4. Consciousness.

Chart Your Progress

The questions that follow are only a sample of what you need to know. If you miss any of the items, you should review the entire chapter, do the exercises on the CD, and review the Knowledge Builders. Another way to prepare for tests is to get more practice with *WebTutor*, the *Study Guide*, or the *Practice Quizze*s that are available with this text.

1. Alyssa experiences a microsleep while driving. Most likely, this indicates that she
   a. was producing mostly beta waves
   b. had high levels of sleep hormones in her blood- stream
   c. switched from delta waves to alpha waves
   d. was sleep deprived

2. Which of the following would normally be most incompatible with moving your arms and legs while asleep?
   a. REM sleep
   b. sleep spindles
   c. delta waves
   d. NREM sleep

3. Eating a snack that is nearly all starch can promote sleep because it increases _____ in the brain.
   a. beta waves
   b. tryptophan
   c. EEG activity
   d. hypnic cycling

4. Sorting and integrating memories is one function of
   a. activation-synthesis cycles
   b. REM sleep
   c. deep sleep
   d. NREM sleep

5. Research has shown that hypnosis cannot produce
   a. unusual strength
   b. improved memory
   c. pain relief
   d. sensory changes

6. Which terms do not belong together?
   a. concentrative meditation—relaxation response
   b. sensory deprivation—relaxation response
   c. receptive meditation—mantra
   d. sensory deprivation—REST

7. Drug tolerance is most closely associated with
   a. psychological dependence
   b. marijuana
   c. withdrawal symptoms
   d. anhedonia

8. Cocaine is most similar to _____ in its effects on the nervous system.
   a. marijuana
   b. benzodiazepine
   c. serotonin
   d. amphetamine

9. Drug interactions are a special danger when a person combines
   a. marijuana and amphetamine
   b. barbiturates and alcohol
   c. alcohol and cocaine
   d. marijuana and THC

10. Which is NOT one of the four dream processes identified by Freud?
    a. condensation
    b. lucidity
    c. displacement
    d. symbolization

Answers: 1. d. 2. a. 3. b. 4. b. 5. a. 6. c. 7. c. 8. d. 9. b. 10. b.

Chapter 6

Psychologist's Journal

WHAT DID YOU LEARN TODAY?

Imagine that one night you and a friend go out for dinner—there's a great new restaurant that everyone's talking about. Feeling adventurous, or maybe amorous, you order raw oysters for the first time. It takes a little getting used to, but you quickly learn to appreciate them, and happily scarf down three orders. Later that night, you awaken from a sound sleep only to find that you are horribly nauseated. You make it to the bathroom just in time. For a while, you alternate between running to the bathroom and staggering back to bed. Finally, you give up and, taking your blanket, curl up in a miserable heap on the bathroom floor. Although for a while you think you are going to die, in a day or two you're back to normal—at least until the next time someone offers you a raw oyster. To your surprise, you suddenly feel sick. You can't even *look* at oysters.

Your reaction to oysters is a result of classical conditioning, one of the topics of this chapter.

Now, let's say that you are at school and you feel like you are "starving to death." You locate a vending machine and deposit your last loonie to buy a candy bar. Then you press the button, and . . . nothing happens. Being civilized and in complete control, you press the other buttons and try the coin return. Still nothing. Impulsively, you give the machine a little kick (just to let it know who's the boss). Then, as you turn away, out pops a candy bar plus 25 cents change. Once this happens, chances are good that you will repeat the "kicking response" in the future. If it pays off several times more, kicking vending machines may become a regular feature of your behaviour. In this case, learning is based on operant conditioning (also called instrumental learning).

Classical and operant conditioning reach into every corner of our lives. Are you ready to learn more about learning? If so, read on!

Survey Questions

- What is learning?
- How does classical conditioning occur?
- Does conditioning affect emotions?
- How does operant conditioning occur?
- Are there different kinds of operant reinforcement?
- How are we influenced by patterns of reward?
- What does punishment do to behaviour?
- What is cognitive learning?
- Does learning occur by imitation?
- How does conditioning apply to practical problems?

▶ ## What Is Learning—Does Practice Make Perfect?

Survey Question:
- What is learning?

Learning Any relatively permanent change in behaviour that can be attributed to experience.

Reinforcement Any event that increases the probability that a particular response will occur.

Response Any identifiable behaviour.

Antecedents Events that precede a response.

Consequences Effects that follow a response.

Reflex An innate, automatic response to a stimulus (for example, an eye-blink).

Most behaviour is learned. Imagine if you suddenly lost all you had ever learned. What could you do? You would be unable to read, write, or speak. You couldn't feed yourself, find your way home, drive a car, play the bassoon, or "party." Needless to say, you would be totally incapacitated.

Learning is obviously important. What's a formal definition of learning? **Learning** is a relatively permanent change in behaviour due to experience. Notice that this definition excludes changes caused by motivation, fatigue, maturation, disease, injury, or drugs. Each of these can alter behaviour, but none qualifies as learning.

Isn't learning the result of practice? It depends on what you mean by practice. Merely repeating a response will not necessarily produce learning. You could close your eyes and swing a tennis racket hundreds of times without learning anything about tennis. Reinforcement is the key to most learning. **Reinforcement** refers to any event that increases the probability that a response will occur again. A **response** is any identifiable behaviour. Responses may be observable actions, such as blinking, eating a piece of candy, or turning a doorknob. They can also be internal, such as having a faster heartbeat.

To teach a dog a trick, you could reinforce correct responses by giving the dog some food each time it sits up. Similarly, you could teach a child to be neat by praising her for picking up her toys. Learning can also occur in other ways. For instance, if a girl gets stung by a bee, she may learn to fear bees. In this case, the girl's fear is reinforced by the pain she feels immediately after seeing the bee. Later, you'll discover how such varied experiences lead to learning.

ANTECEDENTS AND CONSEQUENCES   Unlocking the secrets of learning begins with noting what happens before and after a response. Events that precede a response are called **antecedents.** Effects that follow a response are **consequences.** Paying careful attention to the "before and after" of learning is a key to understanding it.

Classical Conditioning

Classical conditioning is based on what happens before a response. We begin with a stimulus that reliably triggers a response. Imagine, for example, that a puff of air (the stimulus) is aimed at your eye. The air puff will make you blink (a response) every time. The eye-blink is a **reflex** (automatic, non-learned response). Other examples of reflex responses include salivation, contraction of the pupil in response to bright light, and flexion of the leg when the area just below the knee is tapped. Babies have several reflexes, which are described in Chapter 3, and the reflex arc is explained in Chapter 2.

Now, assume that we sound a horn (another stimulus) just before each puff of air hits your eye. If the horn and the air puff occur together many times, what happens? Soon the horn alone will make you blink. Clearly, you've learned something. Before, the horn didn't

►Figure 6.1

In classical conditioning, a stimulus that does not produce a response is paired with a stimulus that does elicit a response. After many such pairings, the stimulus that previously had no effect begins to produce a response on its own. In the example shown, a horn precedes a puff of air to the eye. Eventually, the horn alone will produce an eye-blink. In operant conditioning, a response that is followed by a reinforcing consequence becomes more likely to occur on future occasions. In the example shown, a dog learns to sit up when it hears a whistle.

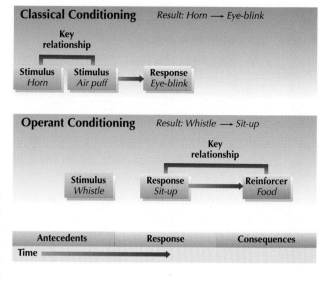

Classical conditioning A form of learning in which reflex responses are associated with new stimuli.

Operant conditioning Learning based on the consequences of responding.

make you blink. Now it does. Similarly, if your mouth waters each time you eat a cookie, you may learn to salivate when you merely see a cookie, a picture of cookies, a cookie jar, or other stimuli that preceded salivation.

In **classical conditioning,** antecedent events become associated with one another: A stimulus that does not produce a response is linked with one that does (a horn is associated with a puff of air to the eye, for example). Learning is evident when the new stimulus will also elicit (bring forth) responses (see ►Figure 6.1).

Operant Conditioning

In **operant conditioning,** learning is based on the consequences of responding. A response may be followed by a reinforcer (such as food). Or by punishment. Or by nothing. These results determine whether a response is likely to be made again (see Figure 6.1). For example, if you wear a particular hat and get lots of compliments (reinforcement), you are likely to wear it more often. If people snicker or laugh at you (punishment), you will probably wear it less often.

Now that you have an idea of what happens in the two basic kinds of learning, let's look at each one in more detail.

► Classical Conditioning—Does the Name Pavlov Ring a Bell?

Survey Question:
■ How does classical conditioning occur?

How was classical conditioning discovered? At the beginning of the 20th century, something happened in the lab of Russian physiologist Ivan Pavlov that brought him lasting fame. The event now seems so trivial that a lesser man might have ignored it: Pavlov's subjects drooled at him.

Actually, Pavlov was studying digestion. To observe salivation, he placed meat powder or some tidbit on a dog's tongue. After doing this many times, Pavlov noticed that his dogs were salivating before the food reached their mouths. Later, the dogs began to salivate even when they saw Pavlov enter the room. Was this misplaced affection? Pavlov knew better. Salivation is normally a reflex. For the animals to salivate at the mere sight of food, some type of learning had to have occurred. Pavlov called it conditioning (see ►Figure 6.2). Because of its impor-

►Figure 6.2

An apparatus for Pavlovian conditioning. A tube carries saliva from the dog's mouth to a lever that activates a recording device *(far left)*. During conditioning, various stimuli can be paired with a dish of food placed in front of the dog. The device pictured here is more elaborate than the one Pavlov used in his early experiments.

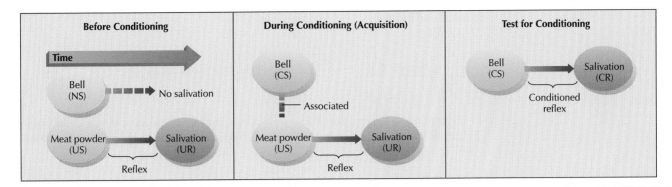

►Figure 6.3

The classical conditioning procedure.

---

tance in psychology's history, it is now called *classical conditioning* (also known as *Pavlovian conditioning* or *respondent conditioning*).

PAVLOV'S EXPERIMENT *How did Pavlov study conditioning?* After Pavlov observed that meat powder made his dogs salivate, he began his classic experiments (Figure 6.2). To begin, he rang a bell. At first, the bell was a neutral stimulus (it did not evoke a response). Immediately after Pavlov rang the bell, he placed meat powder on the dog's tongue, which caused reflex salivation. This sequence was repeated many times: bell, meat powder, salivation; bell, meat powder, salivation. Eventually (as conditioning took place), the dogs began to salivate when they heard the bell (see ►Figure 6.3). By association, the bell, which before had no effect, began to evoke the same response as food. To show this, Pavlov sometimes rang the bell alone. The dog would salivate, even when no food was present.

Psychologists use several terms to describe these events. The bell in Pavlov's experiment starts out as a **neutral stimulus (NS).** In time, the bell becomes a **conditioned stimulus (CS)** (a stimulus that, because of learning, will evoke a response). The meat powder is an **unconditioned stimulus** (**US**) (a stimulus innately capable of eliciting a response). Notice that the dog did not have to learn to respond to the US. Such stimuli naturally elicit reflexes or emotional reactions.

Since a reflex is innate, or "built in," it is called an **unconditioned** (non-learned) **response (UR).** Reflex salivation was the UR in Pavlov's experiment. When Pavlov's bell also produced salivation, the dog was making a new response. Thus, salivation had become a **conditioned** (learned) **response (CR)** (see Figure 6.3). Table 6.1 summarizes the important elements of classical conditioning.

Are all these terms really necessary? Yes, because they help us recognize similarities in various instances of learning. Let's summarize the terms using an earlier example:

Before Conditioning	Example
US → UR	Puff of air → eye-blink
NS → no effect	Horn → no effect

Neutral stimulus
A stimulus that does not evoke a response.
Conditioned stimulus
A stimulus that evokes a response because it has been repeatedly paired with an unconditioned stimulus.
Unconditioned stimulus
A stimulus innately capable of eliciting a response.
Unconditioned response
An innate reflex response elicited by an unconditioned stimulus.
Conditioned response
A learned response elicited by a conditioned stimulus.

Table 6.1
Elements of Classical Conditioning

Element	Symbol	Description	Example
Neutral stimulus	NS	A stimulus that does not evoke a response	Bell
Unconditioned stimulus	US	A stimulus innately capable of eliciting a response	Meat powder
Conditioned stimulus	CS	A stimulus that evokes a response because it has been repeatedly paired with an unconditioned stimulus	Bell
Unconditioned response	UR	An innate reflex response elicited by an unconditioned stimulus	Reflex salivation
Conditioned response	CR	A learned response elicited by a conditioned stimulus	Salivation

After Conditioning	Example
CS → CR	Horn → eye-blink

▶ Principles of Classical Conditioning—Teach Your Little Brother to Salivate

To observe conditioning, you could ring a bell, squirt lemon juice into a child's mouth, and condition salivation to the bell. The child's reactions might then be used to explore other aspects of classical conditioning. Let's see how this occurs.

Acquisition

During **acquisition,** or training, a conditioned response must be **reinforced** (strengthened) (see ▶ Figure 6.4). Classical conditioning is reinforced when the CS is followed by, or paired with, an unconditioned stimulus. For our child, the bell is the CS; salivating is the UR; and the sour lemon juice is an unconditioned stimulus. To reinforce salivating to the bell, we must link the bell with the lemon juice. Conditioning will be most rapid if the US (lemon juice) follows immediately after the CS (the bell). With most reflexes, the optimal delay between CS and US is from one-half second to about five seconds (Schwartz & Robbins, 1995).

HIGHER-ORDER CONDITIONING Once a response is learned, it can bring about **higher-order conditioning.** In this case, a well-learned CS is used to reinforce further learning. That is, the CS has become strong enough to be used like an unconditioned stimulus. Let's illustrate again with our salivating child.

As a result of earlier learning, the bell now makes the boy salivate. (No lemon juice is needed.) To go a step further, you could clap your hands and then ring the bell. (Again, no lemon juice would be used.) Through higher-order conditioning, the child would soon learn to salivate when you clapped your hands (▶ Figure 6.5). (This little trick could be a real hit with friends and neighbours.)

Higher-order conditioning extends learning one or more steps beyond the original conditioned stimulus. Many advertisers use this effect by pairing images that evoke good feelings (such as people smiling and having fun) with pictures of their products. Obviously, they hope that you will learn, by association, to feel good when you see their products (Johnsrude et al., 1999).

Expectancies

Many psychologists believe that classical conditioning is related to information that might aid our survival. According to this **informational view,** we look for associations among events. Doing so creates new mental **expectancies,** or expectations about how events are interconnected.

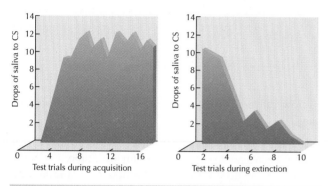

▶ **Figure 6.4**

Acquisition and extinction of a conditioned response. (After Pavlov, 1927.)

Acquisition The period in conditioning during which a response is reinforced.

Respondent reinforcement Reinforcement that occurs when an unconditioned stimulus closely follows a conditioned stimulus.

Higher-order conditioning Classical conditioning in which a conditioned stimulus is used to reinforce further learning; that is, a CS is used as if it were a US.

Informational view Perspective that explains learning in terms of information imparted by events in the environment.

Expectancy An anticipation concerning future events or relationships.

▶ **Figure 6.5**

Higher-order conditioning takes place when a well-learned conditioned stimulus is used as if it were an unconditioned stimulus. In this example, a child is first conditioned to salivate to the sound of a bell. In time, the bell will elicit salivation. At that point, you could clap your hands and then ring the bell. Soon, after repeating the procedure, the child would learn to salivate when you clapped your hands.

Before Conditioning			
		US ➡	**UR**
		Lemon juice	*Salivation*
During Conditioning			
CS —	**US** ➡		**UR**
Bell	*Lemon juice*		*Salivation*
Test for Conditioning			
	CS ➡		**CR**
	Bell		*Salivation*
Higher-Order Conditioning			
CS₂ —	**CS₁** ➡		**CR**
Clap	*Bell*		*Salivation*
Test for Conditioning			
	CS₂ ➡		**CR**
	Clap		*Salivation*

How does classical conditioning alter expectancies? Notice that the conditioned stimulus reliably precedes the unconditioned stimulus. Because it does, the CS predicts the US (Rescorla, 1987). During conditioning, the brain learns to expect that the US will follow the CS. As a result, the brain prepares the body to respond to the US. Here's an example: When you are about to get a shot with a hypodermic needle, your muscles tighten and there is a catch in your breathing. Why? Because your body is preparing for pain. You have learned to expect that getting poked with a needle will hurt. This expectancy, which was acquired during classical conditioning, changes your behaviour.

Extinction and Spontaneous Recovery

After conditioning has occurred, what would happen if the US no longer followed the CS? If the US never again follows the CS, conditioning will fade away. Let's return to the boy and the bell. If you ring the bell many times and do not follow it with lemon juice, the boy's expectancy that "bell precedes lemon juice" will weaken. As it does, he will lose his tendency to salivate when he hears the bell. Thus, we see that a classically conditioned response can be weakened by removing the unconditioned stimulus (see Figure 6.4). This is called **extinction.**

If conditioning takes a while to build up, shouldn't it take time to reverse? Yes. In fact, it may take several extinction sessions to completely reverse conditioning. Let's say that we ring the bell until the child quits responding. It might seem that extinction is complete. However, the boy will probably respond to the bell again on the following day, at least at first. The reappearance of a response following its apparent extinction is called **spontaneous recovery.** It explains why people who have had terrifying automobile accidents may need many slow, calm rides before their fears extinguish.

Generalization

After conditioning, other stimuli that are similar to the CS may also trigger a response. This is called **stimulus generalization.** For example, we might find that our child salivates to the sound of a ringing telephone or doorbell, even though they were never used as conditioning stimuli.

It is easy to see the value of stimulus generalization. Consider the child who burns her finger while playing with matches. Most likely, lighted matches will become conditioned fear stimuli for her. But will she fear only matches? Because of stimulus generalization, she should also have a healthy fear of flames from lighters, fireplaces, stoves, and so forth. It's fortunate that generalization extends learning to related situations. Otherwise, we would be far less adaptable.

As you may have guessed, stimulus generalization has limits. As stimuli become less like the original CS, responding decreases. If you condition a person to blink each time you play a particular note on a piano, blinking will decline as you play higher or lower notes. If the notes are much higher or lower, the person will not respond at all (see ▶Figure 6.6). Stimulus generalization explains why some stores carry imitations of nationally known products. For many customers, positive attitudes conditioned to real products tend to generalize to cheaper knockoffs (Till & Priluck, 2000).

Discrimination

Let's consider one more idea with our salivating child (who by now must be ready to hide in the closet). Suppose the child is again conditioned with a bell as the CS. As an experiment, we occasionally sound a buzzer instead of the bell, but never follow it with the US (lemon juice). At first, the buzzer produces salivation (because of generalization). But after hearing the buzzer several times more, the child will stop responding to it. The child has now learned to discriminate, or respond differently, to the bell and the buzzer. In essence, the child's generalized response to the buzzer has extinguished.

Extinction The weakening of a conditioned response through removal of reinforcement.

Spontaneous recovery The reappearance of a learned response after its apparent extinction.

Stimulus generalization The tendency to respond to stimuli similar but not identical to a conditioned stimulus.

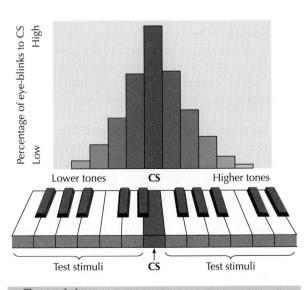

▶ **Figure 6.6**

Stimulus generalization. Stimuli similar to the CS also elicit a response.

Stimulus discrimination
The learned ability to respond differently to similar stimuli.

Stimulus discrimination is the ability to respond differently to various stimuli. As an example, you might remember the feelings of anxiety or fear you had as a child when your mother's or father's voice changed to its you're-about-to-get-swatted tone. (Or the dreaded give-me-that-Game-Boy tone.) Most children quickly learn to discriminate voice tones associated with pain from those associated with praise or affection.

▶ Classical Conditioning in Humans

Survey Question:
■ Does conditioning affect emotions?

How much human learning is based on classical conditioning? At its simplest, classical conditioning depends on reflex responses. As mentioned earlier, a reflex is a dependable, inborn stimulus-and-response connection. For example, your hand reflexively draws back from pain. Bright light causes the pupil of the eye to narrow. Various foods elicit salivation. Any of these reflexes, and others as well, can be associated with a new stimulus. At the very least, you have probably noticed how your mouth waters when you see or smell a bakery. Even pictures of food may make you salivate (a photo of a sliced lemon is great for this).

Conditioned Emotional Responses

Of larger importance, perhaps, are the more subtle ways that conditioning affects us. In addition to simple reflexes, more complex emotional, or "gut," responses may be linked to new stimuli. For instance, if your face reddened when you were punished as a child, you may blush now when you are embarrassed or ashamed. Or think about the effects of associating pain with a dentist's office during your first visit. On later visits, did your heart pound and your palms sweat before the dentist even began to drill?

Many *involuntary,* autonomic nervous system responses ("fight-or-flight" reflexes) are linked with new stimuli and situations by classical conditioning. For example, learned reactions aggravate many cases of hypertension (high blood pressure). Traffic jams, arguments with a spouse, and similar situations can become conditioned stimuli that trigger a dangerous rise in blood pressure (Reiff, Katkin, & Friedman, 1999).

Of course, emotional conditioning also applies to animals. One of the most common mistakes people make with pets (especially dogs) is hitting them if they do not come when called. Calling the animal then becomes a conditioned stimulus for fear and withdrawal. No wonder the pet disobeys when called on future occasions. Parents who belittle, scream at, or physically abuse their children make the same mistake.

Phobia An intense and unrealistic fear of some specific object or situation.

Conditioned emotional response An emotional response that has been linked to a previously non-emotional stimulus by classical conditioning.

Desensitization Reducing fear or anxiety by repeatedly exposing a person to emotional stimuli while the person is deeply relaxed.

LEARNED FEARS   Some phobias (FOE-bee-ahs) are also based on emotional conditioning. A **phobia** is a fear that persists even when no realistic danger exists. Fears of animals, water, heights, thunder, fire, bugs, elevators, and the like are common. Psychologists believe that many phobias begin as **conditioned emotional responses (CERs).** (A CER is a learned emotional reaction to a previously neutral stimulus.) People who have phobias can often trace their fears to a time when they were frightened, injured, or upset by a particular stimulus. Many spider phobias, for example, start in childhood. Just one bad experience with a spider may condition fears that last for years (Merckelbach & Muris, 1997).

Stimulus generalization and higher-order conditioning can broaden CERs to other stimuli (Gewirtz & Davis, 1998). As a result, what began as a limited fear may become a disabling phobia. However, a therapy called **desensitization** is now widely used to extinguish fears, anxieties, and phobias. This is done by gradually exposing the phobic person to feared stimuli while she or he remains calm and relaxed (see Chapter 13). Incidentally, desensitization works on animals, too. For example, dogs have been desensitized for fears of fireworks, thunder, airplanes, bees, hot-air balloons, and other frightening stimuli (Rogerson, 1997).

Undoubtedly, we acquire many of our likes, dislikes, and fears as conditioned emotional responses. For example, in one study, college students developed CERs when coloured geometric shapes were paired with the theme music from the movie *Star Wars.* The coloured shapes were the CS, and the music, which made the students feel good, was the US. When tested later, the students gave higher ratings to shapes paired with the pleasant music than to shapes associated with silence (Bierley, McSweeney, &

Vannieuwkerk, 1985). As noted before, advertisers try to achieve the same effect by pairing products with pleasant images and music. So do many students on a first date.

Vicarious, or Secondhand, Conditioning

Conditioning also occurs indirectly, which adds to its impact on us. Let's say, for example, that you watch another person get an electric shock. Each time, a signal light comes on before the shock is delivered. Even if you don't receive a shock yourself, you will soon develop a CER to the light (Bandura & Rosenthal, 1966). Children who learn to fear thunder by watching their parents react to it have undergone similar conditioning.

Vicarious classical conditioning occurs when we learn to respond emotionally to a stimulus by observing another person's emotional reactions. Such "secondhand" learning affects feelings in many situations. For example, "horror" movies filled with screaming actors probably add to fears of snakes, caves, spiders, heights, and other terrors. If movies can affect us, we might expect the emotions of parents, friends, and relatives to have even more impact. How, for instance, does a city child learn to fear snakes and respond emotionally to mere pictures of them? Being told that "snakes are dangerous" may not explain the child's emotional response. More likely, the child has observed others reacting fearfully to the word *snake* or to snake images on television (Ollendick & King, 1991).

The emotional attitudes we develop toward foods, political parties, ethnic groups, escalators—whatever—are probably conditioned not only by direct experiences, but vicariously as well. No one is born prejudiced—all attitudes are learned. Parents may do well to look in a mirror if they wonder how or where a child "picked up" a particular fear or emotional attitude (Mineka & Hamida, 1998).

Conditioned Taste Aversions

Remember the student described at the beginning of this chapter who became ill after eating oysters and afterward felt sick at the sight of them? This is an example of a **conditioned taste aversion,** an aversive response to a specific food. The response is also due to classical conditioning. Let's see how this might have happened. Conditioned taste aversions develop when a novel or unfamiliar food is associated with an unpleasant reaction (in this case, nausea and vomiting). It doesn't matter whether the food actually caused the illness or not. The unfamiliar food, like oysters in this example, is the conditioned stimulus. The unconditioned stimulus is whatever caused the illness in the first place—a virus, too much alcohol, a bad oyster, whatever. The vomiting is the unconditioned response, and the nausea you feel when you now see or smell oysters is the conditioned response. The association is made specifically to the food—its taste and smell—and not to other aspects of the situation, such as the pattern on the china or the person you were with (fortunately). And it is usually unfamiliar foods, or those you eat infrequently, rather than familiar ones, that develop taste aversions.

Fine, I won't eat oysters any more. So what? Actually, there is a serious aspect to this discussion. In situations where people are given drugs that cause frequent, severe nausea and vomiting, they can develop taste aversions to many different foods, making it difficult for them to maintain good nutrition. This is especially problematic for people receiving chemotherapy. Research has demonstrated that a taste aversion can be established by giving a novel-tasting food prior to the administration of the drugs. Children undergoing chemotherapy, for example, were fed a novel flavour of ice cream prior to their treatment. When offered the ice cream again a week later, they turned it down. Children undergoing medical treatments that did not cause nausea did not show the same distaste for the ice cream (Bernstein, 1978).

Classical Conditioning and Tolerance to Drugs

Shephard Siegel and his colleagues at McMaster University have done extensive research on the role of classical conditioning in the development of tolerance to drugs. When a person uses drugs, certain physiological responses compensate for the effects of the drug. For example, if the drug causes the heart to beat more slowly, physiological changes in the body speed up the heart rate to compensate. Because these physiological responses occur at the same time as the drug use, they become classically conditioned to injection of the drug. That is, the drug is an unconditioned stimulus for these responses. Since these changes compensate to some extent for the effects of the drug, the person will need more of the drug to experience the same effects. Environmental cues, such as the location and the paraphernalia used to prepare the drugs for injection, also become associated with these compensatory responses by classical conditioning. When people use drugs in unfamiliar settings, the compensatory responses normally elicited by these environmental cues do not occur, and the drug user may suffer a fatal overdose even though the amount of drug taken is within their tolerance level. Classical conditioning can also explain why people may experience drug cravings after they are released from detoxification programs and return to their old haunts. Previously conditioned environmental cues can elicit compensatory physiological responses, which are interpreted as withdrawal symptoms and trigger the cravings (Siegel, 1999; Siegel et al., 2000).

Knowledge builder

CLASSICAL CONDITIONING

Relate

US, CS, UR, CR—How will you remember these terms? First, you should note that we are interested in either a stimulus (S) or a response (R). What else do we need to know? Each S or R can be either conditioned (C) or unconditioned (U).

Can a stimulus provoke a response before any learning has occurred? If it can, then it's a US. Do you have to learn to respond to the stimulus? If you do, then it's a CS.

Does a response occur without being learned? If it does, then it's a UR. If it has to be learned, then it's a CR.

Learning Check

1. In learning, antecedents are the effects that follow the making of a response. T or F?
2. Classical conditioning, studied by the Russian physiologist _____, is also referred to as _____ conditioning.

3. Classical conditioning is strengthened or reinforced when the _____ follows the _____.
   a. CS, US b. US, CS c. UR, CR d. CS, CR
4. The informational view says that classical conditioning is based on changes in mental _____ about the CS and US.
5. Training that inhibits (or weakens) a conditioned response is called _____.
6. Psychologists theorize that many phobias begin when a CER generalizes to other, similar situations. T or F?
7. Conditioning brought about by observing pain, joy, or fear in others is called _____ conditioning.

Critical Thinking

8. Lately you have been getting a shock of static electricity every time you touch a door handle. Now there is a hesitation in your door-opening movements. Can you analyze this situation in terms of classical conditioning?

Answers:

1. F 2. Pavlov, respondent 3. b 4. expectancies 5. extinction 6. T 7. vicarious 8. Door handles have become conditioned stimuli that elicit the reflex withdrawal and muscle tensing that normally follows getting a shock. This conditioned response has also generalized to other handles.

▶ Operant Conditioning—Can Pigeons Play Ping-Pong?

Survey Question:
■ How does operant conditioning occur?

Operant conditioning Learning based on the consequences of responding.

Law of effect Responses that lead to desirable effects are repeated; those that produce undesirable results are not.

As stated earlier, in **operant conditioning** (or instrumental learning) we associate responses with their consequences. The basic principle is simple: Acts that are reinforced tend to be repeated. Pioneer learning theorist Edward L. Thorndike called this the **law of effect** (the probability of a response is altered by the effect it has). Learning is strengthened each time a response is followed by a satisfying state of affairs. Think of the earlier example of the vending machine. Because kicking the machine had the effect of producing food and money, the odds of repeating the "kicking response" increased.

Classical conditioning is passive. It simply "happens to" the learner when a US follows a CS. In operant conditioning, the learner actively "operates on" the environment. Thus, operant conditioning refers mainly to learning voluntary responses. For example, waving your hand in class to get a teacher's attention is a learned operant response. It is reinforced by gaining the teacher's attention. (See Table 6.2 for a further comparison of classical and operant conditioning.)

Table 6.2
Comparison of Classical and Operant Conditioning

	CLASSICAL CONDITIONING	OPERANT CONDITIONING
Nature of response	Involuntary, reflex	Spontaneous, voluntary
Reinforcement	Occurs before response (conditioned stimulus paired with unconditioned stimulus)	Occurs after response (response is followed by reinforcing stimulus or event)
Role of learner	Passive (response is elicited by US)	Active (response is emitted)
Nature of learning	Neutral stimulus becomes a CS through association with a US	Probability of making a response is altered by consequences that follow it
Learned expectancy	US will follow CS	Response will have a specific effect

Operant reinforcer Any event that reliably increases the probability or frequency of responses it follows.

Conditioning chamber An apparatus designed to study operant conditioning in animals; a Skinner box.

Positive Reinforcement

The idea that reward affects learning is certainly nothing new to parents (and other trainers of small animals). However, parents, as well as teachers, politicians, supervisors, and even you, may use reward in ways that are inexact or misguided. A case in point is the term *reward.* To be correct, it is better to say *reinforcer.* Why? Because rewards do not always increase responding. If you try to give licorice candy to a child as a "reward" for good behaviour, it will work only if the child likes licorice. What is reinforcing for one person may not be for another. As a practical rule of thumb, psychologists define an **operant reinforcer** as any event that follows a response and increases the probability that the response will recur (see ▶Figure 6.7).

Acquiring an Operant Response

Most studies of instrumental learning take place in a **conditioning chamber,** an apparatus designed for the study of operant conditioning in animals. This device is also sometimes called a Skinner box, after B. F. Skinner, who invented it (see ▶Figure 6.8). A look into a typical Skinner box will clarify the process of operant conditioning.

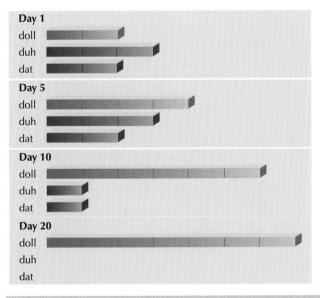

▶Figure 6.7

Assume that a child who is learning to talk points to her favourite doll and says either "doll," "duh," or "dat" when she wants it. Day 1 shows the number of times the child uses each word to ask for the doll (each block represents one request). At first, she uses all three words interchangeably. To hasten learning, her parents decide to give her the doll only when she names it correctly. Notice how the child's behaviour shifts as operant reinforcement is applied. By Day 20, saying "doll" has become the most probable response.

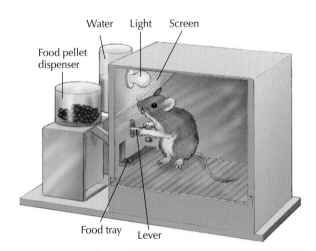

▶Figure 6.8

The Skinner box. This simple device, invented by B. F. Skinner, allows careful study of operant conditioning. When the rat presses the bar, a pellet of food or a drop of water is automatically released. (A photograph of a Skinner box appears in Chapter 1 on page 8.)

The Adventures of Mickey Rat

A hungry rat is placed in a small cage-like chamber. The walls are bare except for a metal lever and a tray into which food pellets can be dispensed (see Figure 6.8).

Frankly, there's not much to do in a Skinner box. This increases the chances that our rat will make the response we want to reinforce, which is pressing the bar. Also, hunger keeps the animal motivated to seek food and actively *emit,* or freely give off, a variety of responses. Now let's see what happens.

Further Adventures of Mickey Rat

For a while our rat walks around, grooms, sniffs at the corners, or stands on his hind legs—all typical rat behaviours. Then it happens. He places his paw on the lever. Click! The lever depresses, and a food pellet drops into the tray. The rat walks to the tray, eats the pellet, and then grooms himself. Up and exploring the cage again, he leans on the lever. Click! After a trip to the food tray, he returns to the bar and sniffs it, then puts his foot on it. Click! Soon the rat settles into a smooth pattern of frequent bar pressing.

Notice that the rat did not acquire a new skill in this situation. He was already able to depress the bar. Reward alters only how frequently he presses the bar. In operant conditioning, reinforcement is used to alter the frequency of responses, or to mould them into new patterns.

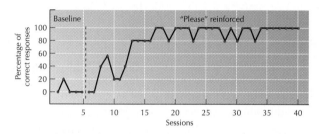

▶ Figure 6.9

Reinforcement and human behaviour. The percentage of times that a severely disturbed child said "Please" when he wanted an object was increased dramatically by reinforcing him for making a polite request. Reinforcement produced similar improvements in saying "Thank you" and "You're welcome," and the boy applied these terms in new situations as well. (Adapted from Matson et al., 1990.)

Response-contingent reinforcement
Reinforcement given only when a particular response is made.

INFORMATION   Like classical conditioning, operant learning is based on information and expectancies. In operant conditioning, *we learn to expect that a certain response will have a certain effect at certain times* (Bolles, 1979). That is, we learn that a particular stimulus is associated with a particular response that is associated with reinforcement (Dragoi & Staddon, 1999). From this point of view, a reinforcer tells a person or an animal that a response was "right" and worth repeating.

▶ Figure 6.9 shows how operant reinforcement can change behaviour. The results are from an effort to teach a severely disturbed nine-year-old child to say "Please," "Thank you," and "You're welcome." As you can see, during the initial, baseline period, the child rarely used the word *please.* Typically, he just grabbed objects and became angry if he couldn't have them. However, when he was reinforced for saying "Please," he soon learned to use the word nearly every time he wanted something. When the child said "Please," he was reinforced in three ways: He received the object he asked for (a crayon, for example); he was given a small food treat, such as a piece of candy, popcorn, or a grape; and he was praised for his good behaviour (Matson et al., 1990).

CONTINGENT REINFORCEMENT   Operant reinforcement works best when it is **response contingent** (kon-TIN-jent). That is, it must be given only after a desired response has occurred. If the disturbed child received reinforcers haphazardly, his behaviour wouldn't have changed at all. In situations ranging from studying to working hard on the job, contingent reinforcement also affects the performance of responses. "Life in an Operant Community" discusses an interesting application of this principle.

The Timing of Reinforcement

Operant reinforcement is most effective when it rapidly follows a correct response. For rats in a Skinner box, very little learning occurs when the delay between bar pressing and receiving food reaches 50 seconds. If the food reward is delayed more than a minute and a half, no learning occurs (Perin, 1943) (see ▶ Figure 6.10). In general, you will be most successful if you present a reinforcer immediately after a response you wish to change.

USING PSYCHOLOGY   **Life in an Operant Community**

B. F. Skinner's utopian novel, *Walden Two,* describes a model community based on behavioural engineering. Would such a community work? On a small scale, the answer appears to be yes. At the University of Kansas, college students took part in an Experimental Living Project that was quite successful (Miller, 1976). Thirty men and women shared a large house where work, leadership, and self-government were tied to behavioural principles.

Work sharing illustrates the project's operant approach. Basic jobs such as preparing food and cleaning were divided into approximately 100 tasks. Residents did all of the tasks themselves, and one community member checked daily to see that each job was completed. (This role was rotated.) To maintain job performance, credits were assigned for each task. At the end of the month, residents who had collected 400 credits got a sizable rent reduction.

This system was very effective in maintaining day-to-day work habits. As anyone who has shared living quarters knows, good intentions are no guarantee that the chores will get done. More importantly, most residents were highly satisfied with the system (Miller, 1976). The Experimental Living Project is a good example of the possibilities of applying conditioning principles to human behaviour. While no major "operant communities" exist today, the fact remains that operant principles greatly affect behaviour in homes, schools, and businesses. It is always worthwhile to try to arrange reinforcers so that productive and responsible behaviour is encouraged.

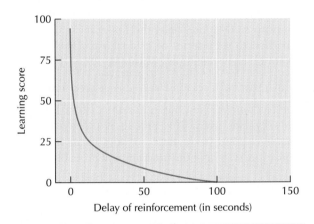

▶ Figure 6.10

The effect of delay of reinforcement. Notice how rapidly the learning score drops when the reward is delayed. Animals learning to press a bar in a Skinner box showed no signs of learning if the delay between the bar press and the food reward was more than 100 seconds (Perin, 1943).

Thus, a child who is helpful or courteous should be praised immediately for her good behaviour.

Let's say I work hard all semester in a class to get an A grade. Wouldn't the delay in reinforcement keep me from learning anything? No, for several reasons. First, as a human you can anticipate future reward. Second, you get reinforced by quiz and test grades all through the semester. Third, a single reinforcer can often maintain a long **response chain** (a linked series of actions that lead to reinforcement). For instance, the long series of events necessary to prepare a meal is rewarded by the final eating. A violin maker may carry out thousands of steps for the final reward of hearing a first musical note. Tying a shoe is a short but familiar response chain.

SUPERSTITIOUS BEHAVIOUR   Reinforcers affect not only the response they follow, but also other responses that occur shortly before. This helps explain many human superstitions. If a golfer taps her club on the ground three times and then hits an unusually fine shot, what happens? The successful shot reinforces not only the correct swing but also the three taps. During operant training, animals often develop similar unnecessary responses. If a rat scratches its ear just before its first bar press, it may continue to scratch before every bar press. Pressing the bar is all that is required to produce food, but the animal may continue to "superstitiously" scratch its ear, as if this were necessary.

Superstitious behaviours are repeated because they appear to produce reinforcement, even though they are actually unnecessary (Pisacreta, 1998). If you get the large half of a wishbone and have good fortune soon after, you may credit your luck to the wishbone. If you walk under a ladder and then break a leg, you may avoid ladders in the future. Each time you avoid a ladder and nothing bad happens, your superstitious action is reinforced. Belief in magic can also be explained along such lines. Rituals to bring rain, ward off illness, or produce abundant crops very likely earn the faith of participants because they occasionally appear to succeed. Besides, better safe than sorry!

Shaping

How is it possible to reinforce responses that rarely occur? Even in a barren Skinner box, it could take a long time for a rat to accidentally press the bar and get a food pellet. We

Response chain A linked series of separate actions that lead to reinforcement.

Superstitious behaviour A behaviour repeated because it seems to produce reinforcement, even though it is actually unnecessary.

might wait forever for more complicated responses to occur. For example, you would have to wait a long time for a duck to accidentally walk out of its cage, turn on a light, play a toy piano, turn off the light, and walk back to its cage. If this is what you wanted to reward, you would never get the chance. And if your duck was waiting to get fed, it might starve first.

Then how are the animals on TV and at amusement parks taught to perform complicated tricks? The answer lies in **shaping**, which is the gradual moulding of responses to a desired pattern. Let's look again at our friend, Mickey Rat.

Mickey Rat Shapes Up

Assume that the rat has not yet learned to press the bar. He also shows no signs of interest in the bar. Instead of waiting for the first accidental bar press, we can shape his behaviour. At first, we settle for just getting him to face the bar. Any time he turns toward the bar, he is reinforced with a bit of food. Soon Mickey spends much of his time facing the bar. Next, we reinforce him every time he takes a step toward the bar. If he turns toward the bar and walks away, nothing happens. But when he faces the bar and takes a step forward, click! His responses are being shaped.

By changing the rules about what makes a successful response, we can gradually train the rat to approach the bar and press it. In other words, **successive approximations** (ever-closer matches) to a desired response are reinforced during shaping. B. F. Skinner once taught two pigeons to play Ping-Pong in this way (see ▶Figure 6.11). Shaping applies to humans, too. Let's say you want to study more, clean the house more often, or exercise more. In each case, it would be best to set a series of gradual, daily goals. Then you can reward yourself for small steps in the right direction (Watson & Tharp, 1996).

Operant Extinction

Would a rat stop bar pressing if no more food arrived? Yes, but not immediately. Learned responses that are not reinforced gradually fade away. This process is called **operant extinction.** Just as acquiring an operant response takes time, so does extinction. For example, if a TV program repeatedly bores you, watching the program will probably extinguish over time.

Even after extinction seems complete, the previously reinforced response may return. If a rat is removed from a Skinner box after extinction and given a short rest, the rat will press the bar again when returned to the box. Similarly, a few weeks after they give up on buying lottery tickets, many people are tempted to try again.

Does extinction take as long the second time? If reinforcement is still withheld, a rat's bar pressing will extinguish again, usually more quickly. The brief return of an operant response after extinction is another example of spontaneous recovery (mentioned earlier regarding classical conditioning). Spontaneous recovery is very adaptive. After a rest period, the rat responds again in a situation that produced food in the past: "Just checking to see if the rules have changed!"

Marked changes in behaviour occur when reinforcement and extinction are combined. For example, parents often unknowingly reinforce children for **negative attention seeking** (using misbehaviour to gain attention). Children are generally ignored when they are playing quietly. They get attention when they become louder and louder, yell "Hey, Mom!" at the top of their lungs, throw tantrums, show off, or break something. Granted, the attention they get is often a scolding, but attention is a powerful reinforcer, nevertheless. Parents report dramatic improvements when they ignore their children's disruptive behaviour and praise or attend to a child who is quiet or playing constructively.

Negative Reinforcement

Until now, we have stressed **positive reinforcement,** which occurs when a pleasant or desirable event follows a response. How else could operant learning be reinforced? The time has come to consider **negative reinforcement,** which occurs when making a

▶Figure 6.11
Operant conditioning principles were used to train these pigeons to play Ping-Pong.

Shaping Gradually moulding responses to a final desired pattern.

Successive approximations A series of steps or ever-closer matches to a desired response pattern.

Operant extinction The weakening or disappearance of a non-reinforced operant response.

Negative attention seeking Using misbehaviour to gain attention.

Positive reinforcement Occurs when a response is followed by a reward or other positive event.

Negative reinforcement Occurs when a response is followed by an end to discomfort or by the removal of an unpleasant event.

response removes an unpleasant event. Don't be fooled by the word *negative*. Negative reinforcement also increases responding. However, it does so by ending discomfort.

Let's say that you have a headache and take an aspirin. Your aspirin taking will be negatively reinforced if the headache stops. That is, the next time you have a headache, you will most likely reach for the aspirin bottle. Likewise, a rat could be taught to press a bar to get food (positive reinforcement), or the rat could be given a continuous mild shock (through the floor of its cage) that is turned off by a bar press (negative reinforcement). Either way, bar pressing would increase. Why? Because it leads to a desired state of affairs (food or an end to pain). Often, positive and negative reinforcement combine. If you are uncomfortably hungry, eating a meal is reinforced by the good-tasting food (positive reinforcement) and by an end to nagging hunger (negative reinforcement).

Punishment

Many people mistake negative reinforcement for punishment. However, **punishment** is any event following a response that *decreases* its likelihood of occurring again. As noted, negative reinforcement, like positive reinforcement, increases responding. The difference can be seen in a hypothetical example. Let's say you live in an apartment and your neighbour's stereo is blasting so loudly that your ears hurt. If you pound on the wall and the volume suddenly drops (negative reinforcement), future wall pounding will be more likely. But if you pound on the wall and the volume increases (punishment), or if the neighbour comes over and pounds on you (more punishment), wall pounding becomes less likely.

As another example, consider a drug addict undergoing withdrawal. Taking the drug will temporarily end painful withdrawal symptoms. Drug taking is therefore negatively reinforced. If the drug made the pain worse (punishment), the addict would quickly stop taking it.

Isn't it also punishing to have privileges, money, or other positive things taken away for making a particular response? Yes. Punishment also occurs when a reinforcer or positive state of affairs is removed, such as losing privileges. This second type of punishment is called **response cost.** Parents who "ground" their teenage children for misbehaviour are applying response cost. Parking tickets and other fines are also based on response cost. For your convenience, Table 6.3 summarizes four basic consequences of making a response.

If the terms are still unclear, remember first that both types of reinforcement increase responding and both types of punishment decrease responding. Positive reinforcement occurs when you add something. For example, food is given (added) after a response. In negative reinforcement, something is subtracted. For example, a response causes an electric shock to end (pain is subtracted or taken away). Punishment can also be positive or negative. Responding will decrease if it is followed by a negative event (for example, pain is added) or if a positive event is subtracted (for example, food is removed).

Punishment Any event that follows a response and decreases its likelihood of occurring again.
Response cost Removal of a positive reinforcer after a response is made.

Table 6.3
Behavioural Effects of Various Consequences

	CONSEQUENCE OF MAKING A RESPONSE	EXAMPLE	EFFECT ON RESPONSE PROBABILITY
Positive reinforcement	Positive event begins	Food given	Increase
Negative reinforcement	Negative event ends	Pain stops	Increase
Punishment	Negative event begins	Pain begins	Decrease
Punishment (response cost)	Positive event ends	Food removed	Decrease
Non-reinforcement	Nothing	————	Decrease

▶ Operant Reinforcers—What's Your Pleasure?

For humans, an effective operant reinforcer may be anything from an M&M candy to a pat on the back. In categorizing such reinforcers, useful distinctions can be made between primary reinforcers, secondary reinforcers, and feedback. Operant reinforcers of all types have a large impact on our lives. Let's examine them in more detail.

Primary Reinforcers

Primary reinforcers are natural, non-learned, and rooted in biology: They produce comfort, end discomfort, or fill an immediate physical need. Food, water, and sex are obvious examples. Every time you open the refrigerator, walk to a drinking fountain, turn up the heat, or order a double latte, your actions reflect primary reinforcement.

In addition to obvious examples, there are other less natural primary reinforcers. One of the most powerful is **intra-cranial stimulation (ICS).** ICS involves direct activation of "pleasure centres" in the brain (Olds & Fobes, 1981) (see ▶Figure 6.12). Much of the early research on the brain's mechanisms of reward was carried out at McGill University by James Olds and Peter Milner.

Wiring a Rat for Pleasure

Use of brain stimulation for reward requires the permanent implantation of tiny electrodes in specific areas of the brain. A rat "wired for pleasure" can be trained to press the bar in a Skinner box to deliver electrical stimulation to its own brain. Some rats will press the bar thousands of times per hour to obtain brain stimulation. After 15 or 20 hours of constant pressing, animals sometimes collapse from exhaustion. When they revive, they begin pressing again. If the reward circuit is not turned off, an animal will ignore food, water, and sex in favour of bar pressing.

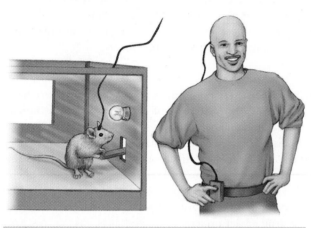

▶Figure 6.12

In the apparatus shown in *(a)*, the rat can press a bar to deliver mild electric stimulation to a "pleasure centre" in the brain. Humans also have been "wired" for brain stimulation, as shown in *(b)*. However, in humans, this has been done only as an experimental way to restrain uncontrollable outbursts of violence. Implants have not been done merely to produce pleasure.

Many natural primary reinforcers activate the same pleasure pathways in the brain that make ICS so powerful (McBride, Murphy, & Ikemoto, 1999).

One shudders to think what might happen if brain implants were easy and practical to do. (Fortunately, they are not.)

Secondary Reinforcers

In some traditional societies, learning is still strongly tied to food, water, and other primary reinforcers. Most of us, however, respond to a much broader range of rewards and reinforcers. Money, praise, attention, approval, success, affection, grades, and the like all serve as learned or **secondary reinforcers.**

How does a secondary reinforcer gain its ability to promote learning? Some secondary reinforcers are simply associated with a primary reinforcer. For example, if you would like to train a dog to follow you ("heel") when you take a walk, you could reward the dog with small food treats for staying close by your side. If you praise the dog each time you give it a treat, praise will become a secondary reinforcer. In time, you will be able to skip giving treats and simply praise your pup for doing the right thing. The same principle applies to children. One reason that parents' praise becomes a secondary reinforcer is because it is frequently associated with food, candy, hugs, and other primary reinforcers.

TOKENS Secondary reinforcers that can be exchanged for primary reinforcers gain their value more directly. Printed money obviously has little or no value of its own. You can't eat it, drink it, or sleep with it. However, it can be exchanged for food, water, lodging, and other necessities.

Primary reinforcers Non-learned reinforcers; usually those that satisfy physiological needs.

Intra-cranial stimulation Direct electrical stimulation and activation of brain tissue.

Secondary reinforcer A learned reinforcer; often one that gains reinforcing properties by association with a primary reinforcer.

Token reinforcer
A tangible secondary reinforcer such as money, gold stars, poker chips, and the like.

Social reinforcers
Reinforcers, such as attention and approval, provided by other people.

A **token reinforcer** is a tangible secondary reinforcer, such as money, gold stars, poker chips, and the like. In a series of classic experiments, chimpanzees were taught to work for tokens. The chimps were first trained to put poker chips into a "Chimp-O-Mat" vending machine. Each chip dispensed a few grapes or raisins. Once the animals had learned to exchange tokens for food, they would learn new tasks to earn the chips (Cowles, 1937; Wolfe, 1936).

A major advantage of tokens is that they don't lose reinforcing value as quickly as primary reinforcers do. For instance, if you use candy to reinforce a child for correctly naming things, the child might lose interest once he is satiated (fully satisfied) or no longer hungry. It would be better to use tokens as immediate rewards for learning. Later, the child could exchange his tokens for food, toys, or a trip to the movies.

Tokens have been used in similar ways with troubled children and adults in special programs, and even in ordinary elementary school classrooms (Spiegler & Guevremont, 1998). (See ▶Figure 6.13.) In each case, the goal is to provide an immediate reward for learning. Typically, tokens may be exchanged for food, desired goods, special privileges, or trips to movies, amusement parks, and so forth. Many parents find that tokens greatly reduce discipline problems with younger children. For example, children can earn points or gold stars during the week for good behaviour. If they earn enough tokens, they are allowed on Sunday to choose one item out of a "grab bag" of small treats.

SOCIAL REINFORCERS   As we have noted, learned desires for attention and approval, which are called **social reinforcers,** often influence human behaviour. This fact can be used in a classic, if somewhat mischievous, demonstration. If you try this, and your teacher catches on, you didn't learn it here!

Shaping a Teacher

For this activity, about one half (or more) of the students in a classroom must participate. First, select a target behaviour. This should be something like "lecturing from the right side of the room." (Keep it simple, in case your teacher is a slow learner.) Begin training in this way: Each time the instructor turns toward the right or takes a step in that direction, participating students should look really interested. Also, smile, ask questions, lean forward, and make eye contact. If the teacher turns to the left or takes a step in that direction, participating students should lean back, yawn, check out their split ends, close their eyes, or generally look bored. Soon, without being aware of why, the instructor should be spending most of his or her time each class period lecturing from the right side of the classroom.

This trick has been a favourite of psychology students for decades. In one case, a professor delivered all of his lectures from the right side of the room while toying with the cords from the venetian blinds. (The students added the cords the second week!) The point to remember from this example is that attention and approval can change the behaviour of children, family members, friends, roommates, and co-workers. Be aware of what you are reinforcing.

Feedback

His eyes, driven and blazing, dart from side to side. His left hand twitches, dances, rises, and strikes, hitting its target again and again. At the same time, his right hand furiously spins in circular motions. Does this describe some strange neurological disorder? Actually, it depicts 10-year-old Mark as he plays his favourite video game, an animated skateboarding adventure!

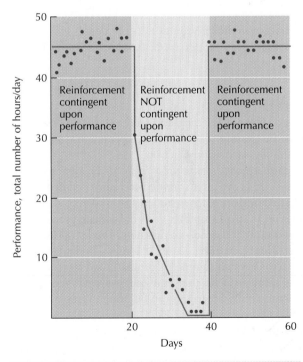

▶ Figure 6.13

Reinforcement in a token economy. This graph shows the effects of using tokens to reward socially desirable behaviour in a mental hospital ward. Desirable behaviour was defined as cleaning, bed making, attending therapy sessions, and so forth. Tokens earned could be exchanged for basic amenities such as meals, snacks, coffee, game-room privileges, or weekend passes. The graph shows more than 24 hours per day because it represents the total number of hours of desirable behaviour performed by all patients in the ward. (Adapted from Ayllon & Azrin, 1965.)

Feedback Information returned to a person about the effects a response has had; also known as knowledge of results.

Knowledge of results (KR) Informational feedback.

Programmed instruction Any learning format that presents information in small amounts, gives immediate practice, and provides continuous feedback to learners.

Computer-assisted instruction (CAI) Learning aided by computer-presented information, exercises, and feedback.

Branching program A computer program that gives learners corrective information and exercises based on the nature of their errors.

How did Mark learn the complex movements needed to excel at virtual skateboarding? After all, he was not rewarded with food or money. The answer lies in the fact that Mark's favourite video game provides two key elements that underlie learning: *a responsive environment* and *information*.

Every time a player moves, a video game responds instantly with sounds, animated actions, and a higher or lower score. The machine's responsiveness and the information flow it provides can be very motivating if you want to win. The same principle applies to many other learning situations: If you are trying to learn to use a computer, to play a musical instrument, to cook, or to solve math problems, reinforcement comes from knowing that you achieved a desired result.

The adaptive value of information helps explain why much human learning occurs without obvious reinforcement by food, water, and the like. Humans readily learn responses that merely have a desired effect or that bring a goal closer. Let's explore this idea further.

KNOWLEDGE OF RESULTS   Imagine that you are asked to throw darts at a target. Each dart must pass over a screen that prevents you from telling if you hit the target. Even if you threw 1000 darts, we would expect little improvement in your performance, because no feedback is provided. **Feedback** (information about the effect a response had) is particularly important in human learning. Mark's video game did not explicitly reward him for correct responses. Yet, because it provided feedback, rapid learning took place.

How can feedback be applied? Increased feedback (also called **knowledge of results,** or **KR**) almost always improves learning and performance (Lee & Carnahan, 1990). If you want to learn to play a musical instrument, to sing, to speak a second language, or to deliver a speech, tape-recorded feedback can be very helpful. In sports, videotapes are used to improve everything from tennis serves to pick-off moves in baseball. (Taped replays of this kind are most helpful when a skilled coach directs attention to key details.) Whenever you are trying to learn a complex skill, it pays to get more feedback (Wulf, Shea, & Matschiner, 1998).

Types of Conditioning

classical reflex voluntary — Much _____ conditioning involves involuntary _____ responses. In contrast, operant conditioning affects spontaneous, or _____ , responses.

response CS — Reinforcement occurs before the _____ in classical conditioning as the _____ is paired with the US.

reinforcement after reinforcer — In operant conditioning, _____ occurs _____ the response. In this case, the response is followed by a _____ .

passive elicited — In classical conditioning, the learner is _____ because responses are _____ by the US.

learner emits — In operant conditioning, the _____ actively _____ responses that are affected by reinforcement.

▶ **Figure 6.14**

To sample a programmed instruction format, try covering the terms on the left with a piece of paper. As you fill in the blanks, uncover one new term for each response. In this way, your correct (or incorrect) responses will be followed by immediate feedback. (Actually, this is a somewhat simplified example. In true programmed instruction, new ideas are presented along with opportunities to practise them.)

Learning Aids

In recent years, operant learning and feedback have been combined in two interesting ways. These are programmed instruction and computer–assisted instruction.

How do these techniques make use of feedback? Feedback is most effective when it is frequent, immediate, and detailed. **Programmed instruction** teaches students in a format that presents information in small amounts, gives immediate practice, and provides continuous feedback to learners. Frequent feedback keeps learners from practising errors. It also lets students work at their own pace. (A small sample of programmed instruction is shown in ▶ Figure 6.14 so that you can see what the format looks like.) Programmed learning can be done in book form or presented by a computer (Mabry, 1998).

In **computer-assisted instruction (CAI),** learning is aided by computer-presented information and exercises. In addition to giving immediate feedback, the computer can analyze the answers that learners give. This allows use of a **branching program** that supplies extra information and asks extra questions based on the errors made by the learner. CAI programs that use artificial intelligence (see Chapter 8) can even give hints about why an answer was wrong and what is needed to correct it (Light, 1997).

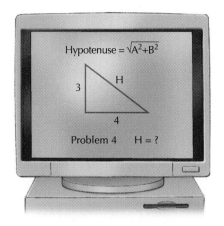  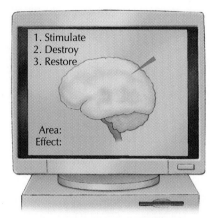

▶**Figure 6.15**

Computer-assisted instruction. The screen on the left shows a typical drill-and-practice math problem, in which students must find the hypotenuse of a triangle. The centre screen presents the same problem as an instructional game to increase interest and motivation. In the game, a child is asked to set the proper distance on a ray gun in the hovering space ship to "vaporize" an attacker. The screen on the right depicts an educational simulation. Here, students place a "probe" at various spots in a human brain. They then "stimulate," "destroy," or "restore" areas. As each area is altered, it is named on the screen, and the effects on behaviour are described. This allows students to explore basic brain functions on their own.

Drill and practice A basic CAI format, typically consisting of questions and answers.

Instructional games Educational computer programs designed to resemble games in order to motivate learning.

Educational simulations Computer programs that simulate real-world settings or situations to promote learning.

Interactive CD-ROM instruction Computerized multimedia instruction.

Although the final level of skill or knowledge is not necessarily higher than that gained by conventional methods, CAI can save much time and effort. In addition, people often do better with feedback from a computer because they don't feel they are being watched and evaluated (Schneider & Shugar, 1990). This allows students to freely make mistakes and learn from them. For example, CAI can give medical students unlimited practice at diagnosing diseases from symptoms, such as "acute chest pain" (Papa, Aldrich, & Schumacker, 1999).

The simplest computerized instruction consists of self-paced **drill and practice.** In this format, students answer questions similar to those in printed workbooks, but they instantly get correct answers. In addition, the computer can give extra KR, such as how fast you worked, your percentage correct, or how your work compared with previous scores.

Higher-level CAI programs include instructional games and educational simulations. **Instructional games** use stories, competition with a partner, sound effects, and game-like graphics to increase interest and motivation (see ▶Figure 6.15). The best instructional games show that it is possible to have fun and improve skills at same time (Stoney & Wild, 1998).

In **educational simulations,** students explore an imaginary situation or "microworld" that simulates real-world problems. By seeing the effects of their choices, students discover basic principles of physics, biology, psychology, or other subjects (Cordova & Lepper, 1996).

Recently, interactive CD-ROMs have added a new dimension to CAI. **Interactive CD-ROM instruction** (multimedia-based learning) provides a stimulating mixture of text, still photos, motion video, and sound, as well as built-in feedback and coaching (Tannenbaum & Yukl, 1992).

Psychologists are only now beginning to fully explore the value and limits of computer-assisted instruction. Nevertheless, it seems likely that their efforts will improve not only education, but our understanding of human learning as well.

Let's pause now for some learning exercises so you can get some feedback about your mastery of the preceding ideas.

Knowledge builder

OPERANT CONDITIONING

Relate

How have your thoughts about the effects of "rewards" changed now that you've read about operant conditioning? Can you explain the difference between positive reinforcement, negative reinforcement, and punishment? Can you give an example of each concept from your own experience?

A friend of yours punishes his dog all the time. What advice would you give him about how to use reinforcement, extinction, and shaping instead of punishment?

Learning Check

1. Responses in operant conditioning are _____, whereas those in classical conditioning are passive, _____ responses.
2. Changing the rules in small steps, so that an animal (or person) is gradually trained to respond as desired, is called _____.

3. Positive reinforcers increase the rate of responding and negative reinforcers decrease it. T or F?
4. Primary reinforcers are those learned through classical conditioning. T or F?
5. Superstitious responses are those that are
   a. shaped by secondary reinforcement b. extinguished c. prepotent d. unnecessary to obtain reinforcement
6. Knowledge of results, or KR, is also known as _____
7. Branching programs are a basic feature of CAI. T or F?

Critical Thinking

8. How might operant conditioning principles be used to encourage people to pick up litter? (What rewards could be offered, and how might the cost of rewards be kept low?)

Answers:

1. voluntary or emitted, involuntary or elicited 2. shaping 3. F 4. F 5. d 6. feedback 7. T 8. A strategy that has been used with some success is to hold drawings for various prizes, such as movie or concert passes. Each time a person turns in a specific amount of litter, he or she receives one chance (a token) to enter in the drawing. Giving refunds for cans and bottles is another way to reinforce recycling of litter.

► Partial Reinforcement—The Montreal Casino, a Human Skinner Box?

Survey Question:
- How are we influenced by patterns of reward?

Schedule of reinforcement A rule or plan for determining which responses will be reinforced.

Continuous reinforcement A schedule in which every correct response is followed by a reinforcer.

Partial reinforcement A pattern in which only a portion of all responses are reinforced.

Partial reinforcement effect Responses acquired with partial reinforcement are more resistant to extinction.

SERENDIPITY *(n):* to discover one thing while looking for another.

B. F. Skinner, so the story goes, was studying operant conditioning when he ran short of food pellets. In order to continue, he arranged for a pellet to reward every other response. Thus began the formal study of **schedules of reinforcement** (plans for determining which responses will be reinforced). Until now, we have treated operant reinforcement as if it were continuous. **Continuous reinforcement** means that a reinforcer follows every correct response. This is fine for the lab, but it has little to do with the real world. Most of our responses are more inconsistently rewarded. In daily life, learning is usually based on **partial reinforcement,** in which reinforcers do not follow every response.

Partial reinforcement can be given in several patterns. Each has a distinct effect on behaviour. In addition to these (which will be explored in a moment), there is a general effect: Responses acquired by partial reinforcement are highly resistant to extinction. For some obscure reason, lost in the lore of psychology, this is called the **partial reinforcement effect.**

How does getting reinforced part of the time make a habit stronger? If you have ever visited a casino, you have probably seen row after row of people playing slot machines. To gain insight into partial reinforcement, imagine that you are visiting the Montreal Casino for the first time. You put a loonie in a slot machine and pull the handle. Ten dollars spills into the tray. Using one of your newly won coins, you pull the handle again. Another payoff! Let's say this continues for 15 minutes. Every pull is followed by a payoff. Suddenly each pull is followed by nothing. Obviously, you would respond several times more before giving up. However, when continuous reinforcement is followed by extinction, the message soon becomes clear: No more payoffs.

The one-armed bandit (slot machine) is a dispenser of partial reinforcement.

Fixed ratio schedule
A set number of correct responses must be made to get a reinforcer. For example, a reinforcer is given for every four correct responses.

Variable ratio schedule
A varied number of correct responses must be made to get a reinforcer. For example, a reinforcer is given after three to seven correct responses; the actual number changes randomly.

Contrast this with partial reinforcement. Again, imagine that this is your first encounter with a slot machine. You put a loonie in the machine five times without a payoff. You are just about to quit, but decide to play once more. Bingo! The machine returns $20. After this, payoffs continue on a partial schedule; some are large, and some are small. All are unpredictable. Sometimes you hit two in a row, and sometimes 20 or 30 pulls go unrewarded.

Now let's say the payoff mechanism is turned off again. How many times do you think you would respond this time before your handle-pulling behaviour extinguished? Since you have developed the expectation that any play may be "the one," it will be hard to resist just one more play . . . and one more . . . and one more. Also, since partial reinforcement includes long periods of non-reward, it will be harder to discriminate between periods of reinforcement and extinction. It is no exaggeration to say that the partial reinforcement effect has left many people penniless. Even psychologists visiting casinos may get "cleaned out"—and they should know better!

Schedules of Partial Reinforcement

Partial reinforcement could be given in many different patterns. Let's consider the four most basic, which have some interesting effects on the way we behave.

FIXED RATIO (FR)   What would happen if a reinforcer followed only every other response? Or what if we followed every third, fourth, fifth, or some other number of responses with reinforcement? Each of these patterns is a **fixed ratio (FR) schedule** (a set number of correct responses must be made to obtain a reinforcer). Notice that in an FR schedule the ratio of reinforcers to responses is fixed: FR-2 means that every other response is rewarded; FR-3 means that every third response is reinforced; in an FR-10 schedule, exactly 10 responses must be made to obtain a reinforcer.

Fixed ratio schedules produce *very high response rates* (see ▶Figure 6.16). A hungry rat on an FR-10 schedule will quickly run off 10 responses, pause to eat, and will then run off 10 more. A similar situation occurs when factory or farm workers are paid on a piece-work basis. When a fixed number of items must be produced for a set amount of pay, work output is high.

VARIABLE RATIO (VR)   In a **variable ratio (VR) schedule,** a varied number of correct responses must be made to get a reinforcer. Instead of reinforcing, for example, every fourth response (FR-4), a person or animal on a VR-4 schedule gets rewarded on the average every fourth response. Sometimes two responses must be made to obtain a reinforcer; sometimes it's five, sometimes four, and so on. The actual number varies, but it averages out to four (in this example). Variable ratio schedules also produce high response rates.

VR schedules seem less predictable than FR. Does that have any effect on extinction? Yes. Since reinforcement is less predictable, VR schedules tend to produce greater resistance to extinction than fixed ratio schedules. Playing a slot machine is an example of behaviour maintained by a variable ratio schedule. Another would be a child asking for a "treat" at the supermarket. The number of times the child must ask before getting reinforced varies, so the child becomes quite persistent. Golf, tennis, and many other sports are also reinforced on a variable ratio basis: An average of perhaps one good shot in five or ten may be all that's needed to create a sports fanatic.

▶Figure 6.16

Typical response patterns for reinforcement schedules. Results such as these are obtained when a cumulative recorder is connected to a Skinner box. The device consists of a moving strip of paper and a mechanical pen that jumps upward each time a response is made. Rapid responding causes the pen to draw a steep line; a horizontal line indicates no response. Small tick marks on the lines show when a reinforcer was given.

Fixed interval schedule
A reinforcer is given only when a correct response is made after a set amount of time has passed since the last reinforced response. Responses made during the time interval are not reinforced.

Variable interval schedule A reinforcer is given for the first correct response made after a varied amount of time has passed since the last reinforced response. Responses made during the time interval are not reinforced.

FIXED INTERVAL (FI)   In another pattern, reinforcement is given only when a correct response is made after a fixed amount of time has passed. This time interval is measured from the last reinforced response. Responses made during the time interval are not reinforced. In a **fixed interval (FI) schedule,** the first correct response made after the time period has passed is reinforced. Thus, a rat on an FI-30-second schedule has to wait 30 seconds after the last reinforced response before a bar press will pay off again. The rat can press the bar as often as it wants during the interval, but it will not be rewarded.

Fixed interval schedules produce moderate response rates. These are marked by spurts of activity mixed with periods of inactivity. Animals working on an FI schedule seem to develop a keen sense of the passage of time (Eckerman, 1999). For example:

Mickey Rat Takes a Break

Mickey Rat, trained on an FI-60-second schedule, has just been reinforced for a bar press. What does he do? He saunters around the cage, grooms himself, hums, whistles, reads magazines, and polishes his nails. After 50 seconds, he walks to the bar and gives it a press—just testing. After 55 seconds, he gives it two or three presses, but there's still no payoff. Fifty-eight seconds, and he settles down to rapid pressing, 59 seconds, 60 seconds, and he hits the reinforced press. After one or two more presses (unrewarded), he wanders off again for the next interval.

Is getting paid every two weeks an FI schedule? Pure examples of fixed interval schedules are rare, but getting paid biweekly at work does come close. Notice, however, that most people do not work faster just before payday, as an FI schedule predicts. A closer parallel would be having a test every five weeks in your psychology class. Right after a test, your work would probably drop to zero for a week or more. Then, as the next test draws near, a work frenzy occurs as you try to catch up on your reading.

VARIABLE INTERVAL (VI)   **Variable interval (VI) schedules** are a variation on fixed intervals. Here, reinforcement is given for the first correct response made after a varied amount of time. On a VI-30-second schedule, reinforcement is available after an interval that averages 30 seconds.

VI schedules produce slow, steady rates of response and tremendous resistance to extinction (Lattal, Reilly, & Kohn, 1998). When you dial a phone number and get a busy signal, reward (getting through) is on a VI schedule. You may have to wait 30 seconds or 30 minutes. If you are like most people, you will doggedly dial over and over again until you get a connection. Success in fishing is also on a VI schedule—which may explain the bulldog tenacity of many anglers (Schwartz & Robbins, 1995).

▶ Stimulus Control—Red Light, Green Light

When you are driving, your behaviour at intersections is controlled by traffic lights. In a similar fashion, many of the stimuli we encounter each day act like stop or go signals that guide our behaviour. To state the idea more formally, stimuli that consistently precede a rewarded response tend to influence when and where the response will occur. This effect is called **stimulus control.** Notice how it works with our friend Mickey Rat.

Stimulus control Stimuli present when an operant response is acquired tend to control when and where the response is made.

Lights Out for Mickey Rat

While learning the bar-pressing response, Mickey has been in a Skinner box illuminated by a bright light. During several training sessions, the light is alternately turned on and off. When the light is on, a bar press will produce food. When the light is off, bar pressing goes unrewarded. We soon observe that the rat presses vigorously when the light is on and ignores the bar when the light is off.

In this example, the light signals what consequences will follow if a response is made. Evidence for stimulus control could be shown by turning the food delivery on when the light is off. A well-trained animal might never discover that the rules had changed. A sim-

Operant stimulus generalization The tendency to respond to stimuli similar to those that preceded operant reinforcement.

Operant stimulus discrimination The tendency to make an operant response when stimuli previously associated with reward are present and to withhold the response when stimuli associated with non-reward are present.

Discriminative stimuli Stimuli that precede rewarded and non-rewarded responses in operant conditioning.

ilar example of stimulus control would be a child learning to ask for candy when her mother is in a good mood, but not asking at other times.

GENERALIZATION   Two important aspects of stimulus control are generalization and discrimination. Let's return to the example of the vending machine (from the Psychologist's Journal) to illustrate these concepts. First, generalization.

Is generalization the same in operant conditioning as it is in classical conditioning? Basically, yes. **Operant stimulus generalization** is the tendency to respond to stimuli similar to those that preceded operant reinforcement. That is, a reinforced response tends to be made again when similar antecedents are present. Assume, for instance, that you have been reliably rewarded for kicking one particular vending machine. Your kicking response tends to occur in the presence of that machine. It has come under stimulus control. Now let's say that there are three other machines on campus identical to the one that pays off. Because they are similar, your kicking response will very likely transfer to them. If each of these machines also pays off when kicked, your kicking response may generalize to other machines only mildly similar to the original. Similarly, generalization explains why children may temporarily call all men *daddy*—much to the embarrassment of their parents.

DISCRIMINATION   Meanwhile, back at the vending machine ... As stated earlier, to discriminate means to respond differently to varied stimuli. Because one vending machine reinforced your kicking response, you began kicking other identical machines (generalization). Because these also paid off, you began kicking similar machines (more generalization). If kicking these new machines has no effect, the kicking response that generalized to them will extinguish because of non-reinforcement. Thus, your response to machines of a particular size and colour is consistently rewarded, whereas the same response to different machines is extinguished. Through **operant stimulus discrimination** you have learned to differentiate between antecedent stimuli that signal reward and non-reward. As a result, your response pattern will shift to match these **discriminative stimuli** (stimuli that precede rewarded and non-rewarded responses).

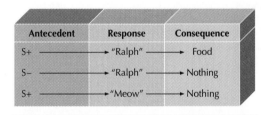

Antecedent	Response	Consequence
S+	"Ralph"	Food
S–	"Ralph"	Nothing
S+	"Meow"	Nothing

▶**Figure 6.17**

A diagram of Ralph the cat's discrimination training.

A discriminative stimulus that many drivers are familiar with is an Ontario Provincial Police car on the 401. This stimulus is a clear signal that a specific set of reinforcement contingencies applies. As you have probably observed, the presence of a police car brings about rapid reductions in driving speed, lane changes, tailgating, and other kinds of bad driving.

The role of discriminative stimuli may be clarified by an interesting feat achieved by a psychologist we'll call Jack. Jack decided to teach his cat to say its name. Here is how he proceeded. First he gave the cat a pat on the back. If the cat meowed in a way that sounded anything like its name, Jack immediately gave the cat a small amount of food. If the cat made this unusual meow at other times, it received nothing. This process was repeated many times each day.

By gradual shaping, the cat's meow was made to sound very much like its name. Also, this peculiar meow came under stimulus control: When it received a pat on the back, the cat said its name; without the pat, it remained silent or meowed normally. Psychologists symbolize a stimulus that precedes reinforced responses as an S1. Discriminative stimuli that precede unrewarded responses are symbolized as S2 (Schwartz & Robbins, 1995). Thus, ▶Figure 6.17 summarizes the cat's training.

Jack's friend, whom we'll call Bob (and who's also a psychologist), was unaware that Jack had a new cat or that he had trained it. Bob went to visit Jack one night and met the cat on the front steps. Bob gave the cat a pat on the back and said, "Hi kitty, what's your name?" Imagine his surprise when the cat immediately replied, "Ralph"!

Stimulus control. Operant shaping was used to teach this whale to "bow" to an audience. Fish were used as reinforcers. Notice the trainer's hand signal, which serves as a discriminative stimulus to control the performance.

Stimulus discrimination is also aptly illustrated by the "sniffer" dogs who locate drugs and explosives at airports and border crossings. Operant discrimination is used to teach these dogs to recognize contraband. During training, they are reinforced only for approaching containers baited with drugs or explosives.

Stimulus discrimination clearly has an impact on human behaviour. Learning to recognize different automobile brands, birds, animals, wines, types of music, and even the answers on psychology tests all depends, in part, on operant discrimination learning.

Knowledge builder

PARTIAL REINFORCEMENT AND STIMULUS CONTROL

Relate

Think of something you do that is reinforced only part of the time. Do you pursue this activity persistently? How have you been affected by partial reinforcement? See if you can think of at least one everyday example of the four basic schedules of reinforcement.

Doors that are meant to be pushed outward have metal plates on them. Those that are meant to be pulled inward have handles. Do these discriminative stimuli affect your behaviour? (If they don't, how's your nose doing?)

Learning Check

1. Two aspects of stimulus control are _____ and _____.
2. Responding tends to occur in the presence of discriminative stimuli associated with reinforcement and tends not to occur in the presence of discriminative stimuli associated with non-reinforcement. T or F?
3. Stimulus generalization refers to making an operant response in the presence of stimuli similar to those that preceded reinforcement. T or F?

4. When a reward follows every response, it is called
   a. continuous reinforcement b. fixed reinforcement c. ratio reinforcement d. controlled reinforcement
5. Partial reinforcement tends to produce slower responding and reduced resistance to extinction. T or F?
6. The schedule of reinforcement associated with playing slot machines and other types of gambling is
   a. fixed ratio b. variable ratio c. fixed interval d. variable interval

Critical Thinking

7. A business owner who pays employees an hourly wage wants to increase productivity. How could the owner make more effective use of reinforcement?
8. How could you use conditioning principles to teach a dog or a cat to come when called?
9. Is the beep on telephone message recorders a discriminative stimulus?

Answers:

1. generalization, discrimination 2. T 3. T 4. a 5. F 6. b 7. Continuing to use fixed interval rewards (hourly wage or salary) would guarantee a basic level of income for employees. To reward extra effort, the owner could add some fixed ratio reinforcement (such as incentives, bonuses, commissions, or profit sharing) to employees' pay. 8. An excellent way to train a pet to come when you call is to give a distinctive call or whistle each time you feed the animal. This makes the signal a secondary reinforcer and a discriminative stimulus for reward (food). Of course, it also helps to directly reinforce an animal with praise, petting, or food for coming when called. 9. Yes, it is. The beep is a signal that speaking will pay off (your message will be recorded). Most of us are well conditioned to "wait for the beep" before talking.

▶ Punishment—Putting the Brakes on Behaviour

Survey Question:
■ What does punishment do to behaviour?

Punishment The process of suppressing a response.
Punisher Any event that decreases the probability or frequency of responses it follows.

Spankings, reprimands, fines, jail sentences, firings, failing grades, and the like are commonly used to control behaviour. Clearly, the story of learning is unfinished without a return to the topic of punishment. Recall that **punishment** lowers the probability that a response will occur again. To be most effective, punishment must be given contingently (only after an undesired response occurs).

Punishers, like reinforcers, are best defined by observing their effects on behaviour. A **punisher** is any consequence that reduces the frequency of a target behaviour. It is not always possible to know ahead of time what will act as a punisher for a particular person. For example, when Jason's mother reprimanded him for throwing toys, he stopped doing it. In this instance, the reprimand was a punisher. However, Chris is starved for attention of any kind from his parents. For Chris, a reprimand, or even a spanking, might actually reinforce toy throwing. Remember, too, that a punisher can be either the onset of an unpleasant event or the removal of a positive state of affairs (response cost).

Severe punishment
Intense punishment; punishment capable of suppressing a response for long periods.

Mild punishment
Punishment that has a relatively weak effect— especially punishment that only temporarily slows responding.

Variables Affecting Punishment

How effective is punishment? Many people assume that punishment stops unacceptable behaviour. Is this always true? Actually, the effectiveness of punishers depends greatly on their *timing, consistency,* and *intensity.* Punishment works best when it occurs as the response is being made, or *immediately* afterward (timing), and when it is given each time a response occurs (consistency). Thus, you could effectively (and humanely) punish a dog that barks incessantly by spraying water on its nose each time it barks. Usually 10 to 15 such treatments are enough to greatly reduce barking. This would not be the case if you applied punishment haphazardly or long after the barking stopped. If you discover that your dog dug up a tree and ate it while you were gone, punishing the dog hours later will do little good. Likewise, the commonly heard childhood threat, "Wait 'til your father comes home, then you'll be sorry," just makes the father a feared brute; it doesn't effectively punish an undesirable response.

Severe punishment (an intensely aversive or unpleasant stimulus) can be extremely effective in stopping behaviour. If three-year-old Beavis sticks his finger in a light socket and gets a shock, that may be the last time he ever tries it. More often, however, punishment only temporarily suppresses a response. If the response is still reinforced, punishment may be particularly ineffective. Responses suppressed by **mild punishment** usually reappear later. If seven-year-old Alissa sneaks a snack from the refrigerator before dinner and is punished for it, she may pass up snacks for a short time. But since snack sneaking was also rewarded by the sneaked snack, she will probably try sneaky snacking again, sometime later (the sneaky little devil).

This fact was demonstrated by slapping rats on the paw as they were bar pressing in a Skinner box. Two groups of well-trained rats were placed on extinction. One group was punished with a slap for each bar press, while the other group was not. It might seem that the slap would cause bar pressing to extinguish more quickly. Yet, this was not the case, as you can see in ▶ Figure 6.18. Punishment temporarily slowed responding, but it did not cause more rapid extinction. Slapping the paws of rats or children has little permanent effect on a reinforced response. It is worth stating again, however, that intense punishment may permanently suppress responding, even for actions as basic as eating. Animals severely punished while eating may never eat again (Bertsch, 1976).

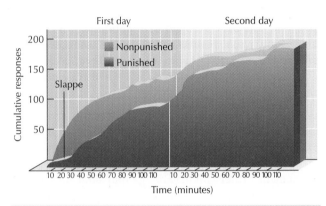

▶**Figure 6.18**

The effect of punishment on extinction. Immediately after punishment, the rate of bar pressing is suppressed, but by the end of the second day, the effects of punishment have disappeared. (After B. F. Skinner, *The Behavior of Organisms.* © 1938. D. Appleton-Century Co., Inc. Reprinted by permission of Prentice-Hall, Inc.)

Using Punishment Wisely

In light of its drawbacks, should punishment be used to control behaviour? Parents, teachers, animal trainers, and the like have three basic tools to control simple learning: (1) Reinforcement strengthens responses; (2) non-reinforcement causes responses to extinguish; (3) punishment suppresses responses. (Consult ▶ Figure 6.19 if you need to refresh your memory about the different types of reinforcement and punishment.) These tools work best in combination.

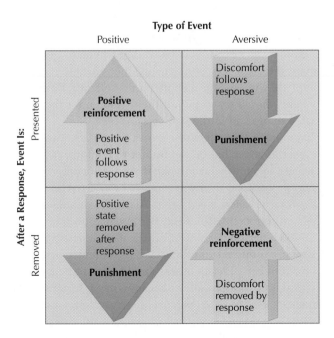

▶**Figure 6.19**

Types of reinforcement and punishment. The impact of an event depends on whether it is presented or removed after a response is made. Each square defines one possibility: Arrows pointing upward indicate that responding is increased; downward-pointing arrows indicate that responding is decreased. (Adapted from Kazdin, 1975.)

If punishment is used at all, it should always be mild. But remember that mild punishment will be ineffective if reinforcers are still available in the situation. That's why it is best to also reward an alternative, desired response. For example, a child who has a habit of taking toys from her sister should not just be reprimanded for it. She should also be praised for cooperative play and sharing her toys with others. Punishment tells a person or an animal that a response was "wrong." However, it does not say what the "right" response is, so it does not teach new behaviours. If reinforcement is missing from the formula, punishment becomes less effective.

In a situation that poses immediate danger, such as when a child reaches for something hot or a dog runs into the street, mild punishment may prevent disaster. Punishment in such cases works best when it produces actions incompatible with the response you want to suppress. Let's say a child reaches toward a stove burner. Would a swat on the bottom serve as an effective punisher? Probably so. It would be better, however, to slap the child's outstretched hand so it will be *withdrawn* from the source of danger. See "If You Must Punish, Here's How" for some additional tips on using punishment.

Side Effects of Punishment

What are the drawbacks of using punishment? The basic problem with punishment is that it is **aversive** (painful or uncomfortable). As a result, people and situations associated with punishment tend, through classical conditioning, to become feared, resented, or disliked. The aversive nature of punishment makes it especially poor to use when teaching children to eat politely or in toilet training.

ESCAPE AND AVOIDANCE   A second major problem is that aversive stimuli encourage escape and avoidance learning. In **escape learning** we learn to make a response in order to end an aversive stimulus. For example, if you work with a loud and obnoxious person, you may at first escape from conversations with him to obtain relief. (Notice that escape learning is based on negative reinforcement.) Later you may dodge him altogether. This is

Aversive stimulus
A stimulus that is painful or uncomfortable.

Escape learning Learning to make a response in order to end an aversive stimulus.

USING PSYCHOLOGY   If You Must Punish, Here's How

There are times when punishment may be necessary to manage the behaviour of an animal, child, or even another adult. If you feel that you must punish, here are some tips to keep in mind.

1. *Don't use punishment at all if you can discourage misbehaviour in other ways.* Make liberal use of positive reinforcement, especially praise, to encourage good behaviour. Also, try extinction first: See what happens if you ignore a problem behaviour; or shift attention to a desirable activity and then reinforce it with praise.

2. *Apply punishment during, or immediately after, misbehaviour.* Of course, immediate punishment is not always possible. With older children and adults, you can bridge the delay by clearly stating what act you are punishing. If you cannot punish an animal immediately, wait for the next instance of misbehaviour.

3. *Use the minimum punishment necessary to suppress misbehaviour.* Often, a verbal rebuke or a scolding is enough. Never use harsh physical punishment. Taking away privileges or other positive reinforcers (response cost) is usually best for older children and adults. Fre-

quent punishment may lose its effectiveness, and harsh or excessive punishment has serious negative side effects (discussed in a moment).

4. *Be consistent.* Be very clear about what you regard as misbehaviour. Punish every time the misbehaviour occurs. Don't punish for something one day and ignore it the next. If you are usually willing to give a child three chances, don't change the rule and explode without warning after a first offence. Both parents should try to punish their children for the same things and in the same way.

5. *Expect anger from a punished person.* Briefly acknowledge this anger, but be careful not to reinforce it. Be willing to admit your mistake if you wrongfully punish someone or if you punished too severely.

6. *Punish with kindness and respect.* Allow the punished person to retain self-respect. For instance, do not punish a person in front of others, if at all possible. A strong, trusting relationship tends to minimize behaviour problems. Ideally, others should want to behave well to get your praise, not because they fear punishment.

Avoidance learning
Learning to make a response in order to postpone or prevent discomfort.

an example of **avoidance learning** (making a response in order to postpone or prevent discomfort). Each time you sidestep him, your avoidance is again reinforced by a sense of relief. In many situations involving frequent punishment, similar desires to escape and avoid are activated. For example, children who run away from punishing parents (escape) may soon learn to lie about their behaviour (avoidance) or to spend as much time away from home as possible (also an avoidance response).

AGGRESSION   A third problem with punishment is that it can greatly increase aggression. Animals react to pain by attacking whomever or whatever else is around (Azrin, Hutchinson, & McLaughlin, 1965). A common example is the faithful dog that nips its owner during a painful procedure at the veterinarian's office. Likewise, humans who are in pain have a tendency to lash out at others.

We also know that one of the most common responses to frustration is aggression. Generally speaking, punishment is painful, frustrating, or both. Punishment, therefore, sets up a powerful environment for learning aggression. When a child is spanked, the child may feel angry, frustrated, and hostile. What if the child then goes outside and hits a brother, a sister, or a neighbour? The danger is that aggressive acts may feel good because they release anger and frustration. If so, aggression has been rewarded and will tend to occur again in other frustrating situations.

A recent study found that children who are physically punished are more likely to engage in aggressive, impulsive, antisocial behaviour (Straus & Mouradian, 1998). Another study of angry adolescent boys found that they were severely punished at home. This suppressed their misbehaviour at home, but made them more aggressive elsewhere. Parents were often surprised to learn that their "good boys" were in trouble for fighting at school (Bandura & Walters, 1959). Yet another study of classroom discipline problems found that physical punishment, yelling, and humiliation are generally ineffective. Positive reinforcement, in the form of praise, approval, and reward, is much more likely to quell classroom disruptions, defiance, and inattention (Tulley & Chiu, 1995).

SHOULD YOU PUNISH OR NOT?   To summarize, the most common error in using punishment is to rely on it alone for training or discipline. The overall emotional adjustment of a child or pet disciplined mainly by reward is usually superior to one disciplined mainly by punishment. Frequent punishment makes a person or an animal unhappy, confused, anxious, aggressive, and fearful.

Parents and teachers should be aware that using punishment can be "habit forming." When children are being noisy, messy, disrespectful, or otherwise misbehaving, the temptation to punish them can be strong. The danger is that punishment often works. When it does, a sudden end to the adult's irritation acts as a negative reinforcer. This encourages the adult to use punishment more often in the future (Alberto & Troutman, 1998). Immediate silence may be "golden," but its cost can be very high in terms of a child's emotional health. "Sparing the rod" will not spoil a child. In fact the reverse is true: Two recent studies found that many young children with behaviour problems were harshly punished at home (Brenner & Fox, 1998; DeKlyen et al., 1998).

Knowledge builder

PUNISHMENT

Relate

Think of how you were punished as a child. Was the punishment immediate? Was it consistent? What effect did these factors have on your behaviour? Was the punishment effective? Which of the side effects of punishment have you witnessed or experienced?

Learning Check

1. Negative reinforcement increases responding; punishment suppresses responding. T or F?
2. Three factors that greatly influence the effects of punishment are timing, consistency, and _____.

continued

3. Mild punishment tends to only temporarily _____ a response that is also reinforced.
   a. enhance b. aggravate c. replace d. suppress
4. Three undesired side effects of punishment are: (1) conditioning of fear and resentment, (2) encouragement of aggression, and (3) the learning of escape or _____ responses.
5. Using punishment can be "habit forming" because putting a stop to someone else's irritating behaviour can _____ the person who applies the punishment.

Critical Thinking

6. Using the concept of partial reinforcement, can you explain why inconsistent punishment is especially ineffective?
7. Escape and avoidance learning have been applied to encourage automobile seat belt use. Can you explain how?

Answers:

1. T 2. T 3. intensity 4. *d* 5. negatively reinforce 6. An inconsistently punished response will continue to be reinforced on a partial schedule, which makes it even more resistant to extinction. 7. Many automobiles have an unpleasant buzzer that sounds if the ignition key is turned before the driver's seat belt is fastened. Most drivers quickly learn to fasten the belt to stop the annoying sound. This is an example of escape conditioning. Avoidance conditioning is evident when a driver learns to buckle up before the buzzer sounds.

▶ Cognitive Learning—Beyond Conditioning

Survey Question:
■ What is cognitive learning?

Cognitive learning
Higher-level learning involving thinking, knowing, understanding, and anticipation.

Cognitive map Internal images or other mental representations of an area (maze, city, campus, and so forth) that underlie an ability to choose alternative paths to the same goal.

Latent learning Learning that occurs without obvious reinforcement and that remains unexpressed until reinforcement is provided.

Is all learning just a connection between stimuli and responses? Some learning can be thought of this way. But, as we have seen, even basic conditioning has "mental" elements. As a human, you can anticipate future reward or punishment and react accordingly. Here's why: There is no doubt that human learning includes a large cognitive, or mental, dimension. As humans, we are greatly affected by information, expectations, perceptions, mental images, and the like.

Loosely speaking, **cognitive learning** refers to understanding, knowing, anticipating, or otherwise making use of information-rich higher mental processes. Cognitive learning extends beyond basic conditioning into the realms of memory, thinking, problem solving, and language. Since these topics are covered in later chapters, our discussion here is limited to a first look at learning beyond conditioning.

COGNITIVE MAPS How do you navigate around the town you live in? Is it fair to assume that you have simply learned to make a series of right and left turns to get from one point to another? It is far more likely that you have an overall mental picture of how the town is laid out. This cognitive map acts as a guide even when you must detour or take a new route. A **cognitive map** is an internal representation of an area, such as a maze, city, or campus. Even the lowly rat—not exactly a mental giant—learns *where* food is found in a maze, not just which turns to make to reach the food (Tolman, Ritchie, & Kalish, 1946). Research by Anneke Olthof and her colleagues at the University of Western Ontario, however, suggests that rats' cognitive maps are specific to the original maze, and do not transfer to a new situation (Olthof et al., 1999). In a sense, cognitive maps also apply to other kinds of knowledge. For instance, it could be said that you have been developing a "map" of psychology while reading this book. This may be why students sometimes find it helpful to draw pictures or diagrams of how they envision concepts fitting together.

LATENT LEARNING Cognitive learning is also revealed by latent (hidden) learning. **Latent learning** occurs without obvious reinforcement and remains hidden until reinforcement is provided. Here's an example from a classic animal study: Two groups of rats were allowed to explore a maze. The animals in one group found food at the far end of the maze. Soon they learned to rapidly make their way through the maze when released. Rats in the second group were unrewarded and showed no signs of learning. But later, when the "uneducated" rats were given food in the maze, they ran the maze as quickly as the rewarded group (Tolman & Honzik, 1930). Although there was no outward sign of it, the unrewarded animals had learned their way around the maze. Their learning, therefore,

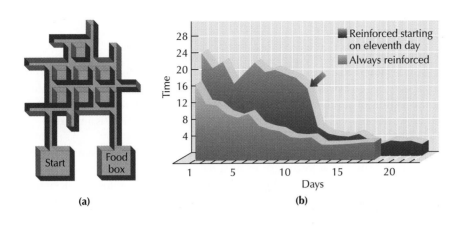

(a)   **(b)**

▶**Figure 6.20**

Latent learning. *(a)* The maze used by Tolman and Honzik to demonstrate latent learning by rats. *(b)* Results of the experiment. Notice the rapid improvement in performance that occurred when food was made available to the previously unreinforced animals. This indicates that learning had occurred, but that it remained hidden or unexpressed. (Adapted from Tolman & Honzik, 1930.)

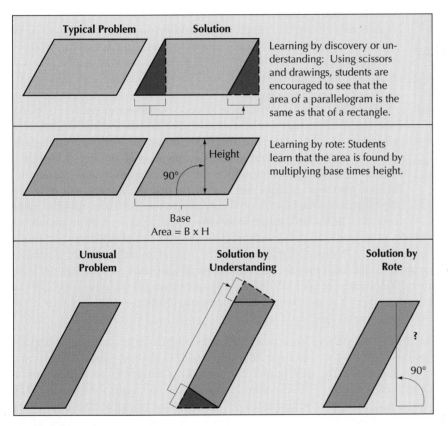

▶Figure 6.21

Learning by understanding and by rote. For some types of learning, understanding may be superior, although both types of learning are useful. (After Wertheimer, 1959.)

Rote learning Learning that takes place mechanically, through repetition and memorization, or by learning rules.

Discovery learning Learning based on insight and understanding.

remained latent at first (see ▶ Figure 6.20).

How did they learn if there was no reinforcement? Just satisfying curiosity can be enough to reward learning (Harlow & Harlow, 1962). In humans, latent learning is related to higher-level abilities, such as anticipating future reward. For example, if you give an attractive classmate a ride home, you may make mental notes about how to get to his or her house, even if a date is only a remote future possibility.

DISCOVERY LEARNING   Much of what is meant by cognitive learning is summarized by the word *understanding*. Each of us has, at times, learned ideas by **rote** (repetition and memorization). Although rote learning is efficient, many psychologists believe that learning is more lasting and flexible when people discover facts and principles on their own. In **discovery learning**, skills are gained by insight and understanding instead of by rote. Discovery learning is an important element of computerized educational simulations and instructional games, as mentioned earlier (de Jong & van Joolingen, 1998).

As long as learning occurs, what difference does it make if it is by discovery or by rote? ▶ Figure 6.21 illustrates the difference. Two groups of students were taught to calculate the area of a parallelogram. Some were encouraged to see that a "piece" of a parallelogram could be "moved" to create a rectangle. Later, they were better able to solve unusual problems. Students who simply memorized a rule were confused by the same problems (Wertheimer, 1959). As this implies, discovery leads to a better understanding of new or unusual problems. Whenever possible, people should try new strategies and discover new solutions during learning (McDaniel & Schlager, 1990).

▶ Modelling—Do as I Do, Not as I Say

Survey Question:
■ Does learning occur by imitation?

The class watches intently as a skilled potter pulls a spinning ball of clay into the form of a vase. There is little doubt that many skills are learned by what Albert Bandura (1971) calls *observational learning,* or *modelling.* **Observational learning** is achieved by watching and imitating the actions of another person or by noting the consequences of the person's actions. In other words, modelling is any process in which information is imparted by example, before direct practice is allowed (Rosenthal & Steffek, 1991).

The value of learning by observation is obvious: Imagine trying to tell someone how to tie a shoe, do a dance step, crochet, or play a guitar. Bandura believes that anything that can be learned from direct experience can be learned by observation. Often, this allows a person to skip the tedious trial-and-error stage of learning.

OBSERVATIONAL LEARNING *It seems obvious that we learn by observation, but how does it occur?* By observing a **model** (someone who serves as an example), a person may (1) learn new responses, (2) learn to carry out or avoid previously learned responses (depending on what happens to the model for doing the same thing), or (3) learn a general rule that can be applied to various situations.

For observational learning to occur, several things must take place. First, the learner must pay attention to the model and remember what was done. (A beginning auto mechanic might be interested enough to watch an entire tune-up, but unable to remember all the steps.) Next, the learner must be able to reproduce the modelled behaviour. (Sometimes this is a matter of practice, but it may be that the learner will never be able to perform the behaviour. We all admire the feats of world-class gymnasts, but there aren't many of us who could reproduce those moves, no

Observational learning often imparts much information that would be difficult to obtain by reading instructions or memorizing rules.

Observational learning Learning achieved by watching and imitating the actions of another or noting the consequences of those actions.

Model A person who serves as an example in observational learning.

matter how much we practise.) If a model is successful at a task or rewarded for a response, the learner is more likely to imitate the behaviour. In general, models who are attractive, trustworthy, capable, admired, powerful, or high in status also tend to be imitated (Bandura & Walters, 1963; Brewer & Wann, 1998). Finally, once a new response is tried, normal reinforcement determines if it will be repeated thereafter. (Notice the similarity to latent learning, described earlier.)

IMITATING MODELS Modelling has a powerful effect on behaviour. In a classic experiment, children watched an adult attack a large blowup "Bo-Bo the Clown" doll. Some children saw an adult sit on the doll, punch it, hit it with a hammer, and kick it around the room. Others saw a movie of these actions. A third group saw a cartoon version of the aggression. Later, the children were frustrated by having some attractive toys taken away from them. Then, they were allowed to play with the Bo-Bo doll. Most imitated the adult's attack (▶Figure 6.22). Some even added new aggressive acts of their own! Interestingly, the cartoon was only slightly less effective in encouraging aggression than the live adult model and the filmed model (Bandura, Ross, & Ross, 1963).

▶Figure 6.22

A nursery school child imitates the aggressive behaviour of an adult model he has just seen in a movie. (Photos courtesy of Albert Bandura.)

Then do children blindly imitate adults? No. Remember that observational learning only prepares a person to duplicate a response. Whether it is actually imitated depends on whether the model was rewarded or punished for what was done. Nevertheless, when parents tell a child to do one thing, but model a completely different response, children tend to imitate what the parents do, and not what they say (Bryan & Walbek, 1970). Thus, through modelling, children learn not only attitudes, gestures, emotions, and personality traits, but fears, anxieties, and bad habits as well. A good example is the children of smokers, who are much more likely to try smoking than children from smoke-free homes (Rowe et al., 1996).

Now, consider a typical situation: Little Shawn Jones has just been interrupted at play by his younger brother, Mildew. Angry and frustrated, he screams at Mildew. This behaviour interrupts his father's TV watching. Father promptly spanks little Shawn, saying, "This will teach you to hit your little brother." And it will. Because of modelling effects, it is unrealistic to expect a child to "Do as I say, not as I do." The message the father has given the child is clear: "You have frustrated me; therefore, I will hit you." The next time little Shawn is frustrated, it won't be surprising if he imitates his father and hits his brother.

Modelling and Television

Does television promote observational learning? The impact of TV can be found in these figures: By the time the average person has graduated from high school, she or he will have viewed some 15 000 hours of TV, compared with only 11 000 hours spent in the classroom. In that time, such viewers will have seen some 18 000 murders and countless acts of robbery, arson, bombing, torture, and beatings (Pogatchnik, 1990). It's true that TV programming has improved somewhat during the last decade. Overall, however, violent acts, dynamite blasts, gun battles, high-speed car wrecks, stereotypes, and sexism still prevail.

Life after TV

What effect does the North American penchant for TV watching have on behaviour? To answer this question, a team of researchers found a town in northwestern Canada that did not receive TV broadcasts. Discovering that the town was about to get TV, the team seized a rare opportunity. Tannis Williams and her colleagues carefully tested residents of the town just before TV arrived and again two years later. This natural experiment revealed that after the tube came to town:

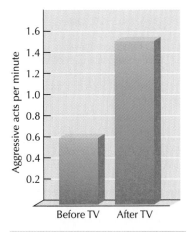

▶ **Figure 6.23**

This graph shows the average number of aggressive acts per minute before and after television broadcasts were introduced into a Canadian town. The increase in aggression after television watching began was significant. Two other towns that already had television were used for comparison. Neither showed significant increases in aggression during the same time period. (Data compiled from Joy, Kimball, & Zabrack, 1986.)

- Reading development among children declined (Corteen & Williams, 1986).
- Children's scores on tests of creativity dropped (Harrison & Williams, 1986).
- Children's perceptions of sex roles became more stereotyped (Kimball, 1986).
- There was a significant increase in both verbal and physical aggression (see ▶ Figure 6.23). This occurred for both boys and girls, and it applied equally to children who were high or low in aggression before they began watching TV (Joy, Kimball, & Zabrack, 1986).

TELEVISED AGGRESSION   The last finding comes as no surprise. Studies show conclusively that if large groups of children watch a great deal of televised violence, they will be more prone to behave aggressively (Hogben, 1998; Hughes & Hasbrouck, 1996). In other words, not all children will become more aggressive, but many will. Incidentally, playing violent video games also tends to encourage greater hostility (Ballard & West, 1996; Dietz, 1998; Kirsh, 1998).

Is it fair to say, then, that televised violence causes aggression in viewers (especially children)? Fortunately, that would be an exaggeration. Televised violence can make aggression more likely, but it does not invariably "cause" it to occur (Freedman, 1984; Levinger, 1986). Many other factors affect the chances that hostile thoughts will be turned into actions (Berkowitz, 1984). Among children, one such factor is the extent to which a child identifies with aggressive characters (Huesmann et al., 1983).

A case in point is the popular *Power Rangers* TV programs for children. In each episode, the Power Rangers "morph" into superheroes who use karate and other violent actions to conquer monsters. After watching an episode of the *Power Rangers*, a group of

TV heroes can act as powerful models for observational learning of aggression.

seven-year-old children committed seven times more aggressive acts than a control group that didn't watch. The aggressive children hit, kicked, and karate-chopped their peers, often directly imitating the Power Rangers (Boyatzis, Matillo, & Nesbitt, 1995). Younger children, in particular, are more likely to be influenced by such programs because they don't fully recognize that the characters and stories are fantasies (McKenna & Ossoff, 1998).

Youngsters who believe that aggression is an acceptable way to solve problems, who believe that TV violence is realistic, and who identify with TV characters are most likely to copy televised aggression (Huesmann, Moise, & Podolski, 1997). In view of such findings, it is understandable that Canada, Norway, and Switzerland have restricted the amount of permissible violence on television. Should all countries do the same?

A LOOK AHEAD   Conditioning principles are often derived from animal experiments. However, it should be apparent that the same principles apply to human behaviour. Perhaps the best way to appreciate this fact is to observe how reinforcement affects your own behaviour. With this in mind, the upcoming Psychology in Action section proposes a personal experiment in operant conditioning. We'll also consider steps you can take to better manage your learning at school. Don't miss these coming attractions!

Knowledge builder

COGNITIVE LEARNING AND IMITATION

Relate

Try to think of at least one personal example of each of these concepts: cognitive map, latent learning, discovery learning.

Describe a skill you have learned primarily through observational learning. How did modelling help you learn?

What entertainment or sports personalities did you identify with when you were a child? How did it affect your behaviour?

Learning Check

1. An internal representation of relationships is referred to as a _____ _____.

2. Learning that suddenly appears when a reward or incentive for performance is given is called
   a. discovery learning b. latent learning c. rote learning d. reminiscence

3. Psychologists use the term _____ to describe observational learning.

4. If a model is successful, rewarded, attractive, or high in status, his or her behaviour is
   a. difficult to reproduce b. less likely to be attended to c. more likely to be imitated d. subject to positive transfer

5. Children who observed a live adult behave aggressively became more aggressive; those who observed movie and cartoon aggression did not. T or F?

6. Children are most likely to imitate TV characters with whom they identify, but this applies primarily to characters who are non-violent. T or F?

7. Psychological research indicates that televised violence causes aggressive behaviour in children. T or F?

Critical Thinking

8. Draw a map of your school's campus as you picture it now. Draw a map of the campus as you pictured it after your first visit. Why do the maps differ?

9. Children who watch many aggressive programs on television tend to be more aggressive than average. Why doesn't this observation prove that televised aggression causes aggressive behaviour?

Answers:

1. cognitive map 2. b 3. modelling 4. c 5. F 6. F 7. F 8. Your cognitive map of the campus has undoubtedly become more accurate and intricate over time as you have added details to it. Your drawings should reflect this change. 9. Because the observation is based on a correlation. Children who are already aggressive may choose to watch more aggressive programs, rather than being made aggressive by them. It took experimental studies to verify that televised aggression promotes aggression by viewers.

BEHAVIOURAL SELF-MANAGEMENT

This discussion could be the start of one of the most personal applications of psychology in this book. Many people have learned to use reinforcement to manage their own behaviour (Watson & Tharp, 1996). This, then, is an invitation to carry out a self-management project of your own. Would you like to increase the number of hours you spend studying each week? Would you like to exercise more, attend more classes, concentrate longer, stop smoking, or read more books? All these activities and many others can be improved by following the rules described here.

Self-Managed Behaviour—A Rewarding Project

The principles of operant conditioning can be adapted to manage your own behaviour. Here's how:

1. *Choose a target behaviour.* Identify the activity you want to change.
2. *Record a baseline.* Record how much time you currently spend performing the target activity, or count the number of desired or undesired responses you make each day.
3. *Establish goals.* Remember the principle of shaping, and set realistic goals for gradual improvement on each successive week. Also, set daily goals that add up to the weekly goal.
4. *Choose reinforcers.* If you meet your daily goal, what reward will you allow yourself? Daily rewards might be watching television, eating a candy bar, socializing with friends, playing a musical instrument, or whatever you enjoy. Also establish a weekly reward. If you reach your weekly goal, what reward will you allow yourself? A movie? A dinner out? A weekend hike?
5. *Record your progress.* Keep accurate records of the amount of time spent each day on the desired activity or the number of times you make the desired response.
6. *Reward successes.* If you meet your daily goal, collect your reward. If you fall short, be honest with yourself and skip the reward. Do the same for your weekly goal.
7. *Adjust your plan as you learn more about your behaviour.* Overall progress will reinforce your attempts at self-management.

If you have trouble finding rewards, or if you don't want to use the entire system, remember that anything done often can serve as reinforcement. This is known as the **Premack principle.** It is named after David Premack, a psychologist who popularized its use. For example, if you watch television every night and want to study more, make it a rule not to turn on the set until you have studied for an hour (or whatever length of time you choose). Then lengthen the requirement each week. Here is a sample of one student's plan:

1. *Target behaviour:* number of hours spent studying for school.
2. *Recorded baseline*: an average of 25 minutes per day for a weekly total of three hours.
3. *Goal for the first week*: an increase in study time to 40 minutes per day; weekly goal of five hours total study time. Goal for second week: 50 minutes per day and six hours per week. Goal for third week: one hour per day and seven hours per week. Ultimate goal: to reach and maintain 14 hours per week study time.
4. *Daily reward for reaching goal:* one hour of guitar playing in the evening; no playing if the goal is not met. *Weekly reward for reaching goal:* going to a movie or buying a compact disc.

Self-Recording Even if you find it difficult to give and withhold rewards, you are likely to succeed. Simply knowing that you are reaching a desired goal can be reward enough. The key to any self-management program, therefore, is **self-recording** (keeping records of response frequencies). The concept is demonstrated by students in a psychology course. Some of the students recorded their study time and graphed their daily and weekly study behaviour. Even though no extra rewards were offered, these students

Premack principle Any high-frequency response can be used to reinforce a low-frequency response.

Self-recording Self-management based on keeping records of response frequencies.

earned better grades than others who were not required to keep records (Johnson & White, 1971).

As discussed earlier, feedback is also valuable for changing personal behaviour. Feedback can help you decrease bad habits as well as increase desirable responses. Keep track of the number of times daily that you arrive late to class, smoke a cigarette, watch an hour of TV, drink a cup of coffee, bite your fingernails, swear, or whatever you are interested in changing. A simple tally on a piece of paper will do, or you can get a small mechanical counter like those used to keep golf scores or count calories. Record keeping helps break patterns, and the feedback can be motivating as you begin to make progress.

GOOD WAYS TO BREAK BAD HABITS *How can I use learning principles to break a bad habit?* By using the methods we have discussed, you can reinforce yourself for decreasing unwanted behaviours, such as swearing, nail biting, criticizing others, smoking, drinking coffee, excess TV watching, or any other behaviour you choose to target. However, breaking bad habits may require some additional techniques. Here are four strategies to help you change bad habits.

Alternative Responses A good strategy for change is to try to get the same reinforcement with a new response.

Example: Marta often tells jokes at the expense of others. Her friends sometimes feel hurt by her sharp-edged humour. Marta senses this and wants to change. What can she do? Usually, Marta's joke telling is reinforced by attention and approval. She could just as easily get the same reinforcement by giving other people praise or compliments. Making a change in her behaviour should be easy because she will continue to receive the reinforcement she seeks.

Extinction Try to discover what is reinforcing an unwanted response and remove, avoid, or delay the reinforcement (Ferster, Nurnberger, & Levitt, 1962).

Example: Tiffany has developed a habit of taking longer and longer "breaks" to watch TV when she should be studying. Obviously, TV watching is reinforcing her break taking. To improve her study habits, Tiffany could delay reinforcement by studying at the library or some other location a good distance from her TV.

Response Chains Break up response chains that precede an undesired behaviour. The key idea is to scramble the chain of events that leads to an undesired response (Watson & Tharp, 1996).

Example: Almost every night Steve comes home from work, turns on the TV, and eats a whole bag of cookies or chips. He then takes a shower and changes clothes. By dinnertime he has lost his appetite. Steve realizes he is substituting junk food for dinner. Steve could solve the problem by breaking the response chain that precedes dinner. For instance, he could shower immediately when he gets home or he could avoid turning on the television until after dinner.

Cues and Antecedents Try to avoid, narrow down, or remove stimuli that elicit the bad habit.

Example: Saul wants to cut down on smoking. He has taken many smoking cues out of his surroundings by removing ashtrays, matches, and extra cigarettes from his house, car, and office. Saul should try narrowing antecedent stimuli even more. He could begin by smoking only in the lounge at work, never in his office or in his car. He could then limit his smoking to home. Then to only one room at home. Then to one chair at home. If he succeeds in getting this far, he may want to limit his smoking to only one unpleasant place, such as a bathroom, basement, or garage (Goldiamond, 1971).

Behavioural contract
A formal agreement stating behaviours to be changed and consequences that apply.

Contracting If you try the techniques described here and have difficulty sticking with them, you may want to try **behavioural contracting.** In a behavioural contract, you state a specific problem behaviour you want to control, or a goal you want to achieve. Also state the rewards you will receive, privileges you will forfeit, or punishments you must accept. The contract should be typed and signed by you and a person you trust.

A behavioural contract can be quite motivating, especially when mild punishment is part of the agreement. Here's an example reported by Nurnberger and Zimmerman (1970): A student working on his Ph.D. had completed all requirements but his dissertation, yet for two years had not written a single page. A contract was drawn up for him in which he agreed to meet weekly deadlines on the number of pages he would complete. To make sure he would meet the deadlines, he wrote post-dated cheques. These were to be forfeited if he failed to reach his goal for the week. The cheques were made out to organizations he despised. From the time he signed the contract until he finished his degree, the student's work output was greatly improved.

Effective learning at school poses a special set of challenges. The next section describes some steps you can take to increase your chances of success.

Self-Regulated Learning—Academic All-Stars

Think for a moment about a topic that you are highly interested in, such as music, sports, fashion, automobiles, cooking, politics, or movies. Whatever the topic may be, you have probably learned a large amount of information about it—painlessly. How could you make your school work more like voluntary learning? An approach known as self-regulated learning might be a good start. **Self-regulated learning** is *active, self-guided study*. You can use the strategies described here to change passive studying into more active, goal-oriented learning (Zimmerman, 1996a).

> **Self-regulated learning**
> Active, self-guided learning.

1. *Set specific, objective learning goals.* Try to begin each learning session with specific goals in mind. What knowledge or skills are you trying to master? What do you hope to accomplish? (Schunk, 1990).
2. *Plan a learning strategy.* How will you accomplish your goals? Make daily, weekly, and monthly plans for learning. Then put them into action.
3. *Be your own teacher.* Effective learners silently give themselves guidance and ask themselves questions. For example, when you are reading, you might ask yourself at the end of each paragraph, "What is the main idea here? What do I remember? What don't I understand? What do I need to review? What should I do next?"
4. *Monitor your progress.* Self-regulated learning depends on feedback. Exceptional learners keep records of their progress toward learning goals (pages read, hours of studying, assignments completed, and so forth). They quiz themselves, use study guides, and find other ways to check their understanding while learning.
5. *Use self-reinforcement.* When you meet your daily, weekly, or monthly performance standards, reward your efforts in some way. Be aware that self-praise also rewards learning. Being able to say "Hey, I did it!" or "Good work!" and know that you deserve it can be very reinforcing. In the long run, success, feelings of accomplishment, and personal satisfaction provide the real payoffs for self-regulated learning.
6. *Evaluate your progress and goals.* It is a good idea to frequently evaluate your performance records and goals. Are there specific areas of your work that need improvement? If you are not making good progress toward long-range goals, do you need to revise your short-term targets?
7. *Take corrective action.* If you fall short of your goals, you may need to adjust how you budget your time. You may also need to change your learning environment, to deal with distractions such as watching TV, daydreaming, talking to friends, or testing the structural integrity of the walls with your stereo system.
8. *Boost your motivation.* One way to keep yourself motivated is to work for self-selected rewards, such as taking a nap, watching TV, eating ice cream, or socializing with friends. Some students also find it helpful to remind themselves that what they are learning is valuable. For example, think of a time in the future when knowing the material will be important (Wolters, 1998).

If you discover that you lack necessary knowledge or skills, ask for help, take advantage of tutoring programs, or look for sources of information beyond your courses and textbooks. Knowing how to regulate and control learning can be a key to lifelong enrichment and personal empowerment.

GETTING HELP Attempting to manage or alter your own behaviour may be more difficult than it sounds. If you feel you need more information, consult either of the books listed below. You will also find helpful advice in the Psychology in Action section of Chapter 13. If you do try a self-modification project or self-regulated learning, but find it impossible to reach your goals, be aware that professional advice is available.

WHERE TO OBTAIN MORE INFORMATION:

- Watson, D. L. and Tharp, R. G. *Self-directed behavior*. Pacific Grove, CA: Wadsworth-Brooks/Cole, 1996.
- Williams, R. L. and Long, J. D. *Toward a self-managed life style*. Boston, MA: Houghton Mifflin, 1991.

Knowledge builder

BEHAVIOURAL SELF-MANAGEMENT

Relate

Even if you don't expect to carry out a self-management project right now, outline a plan for changing your own behaviour. Be sure to describe the behaviour you want to change, set goals, and identify reinforcers.

To what extent do you already engage in self-regulated learning? What additional steps could you take to become a more active, goal-oriented learner?

Learning Check

1. After a target behaviour has been selected for reinforcement, it's a good idea to record a baseline so you can set realistic goals for change. T or F?
2. Self-recording, even without the use of extra rewards, can bring about desired changes in target behaviours. T or F?

3. The Premack principle states that behavioural contracting can be used to reinforce changes in behaviour. T or F?
4. A self-management plan should make use of the principle of shaping by setting a graduated series of goals. T or F?
5. A key aspect of self-_____ learning is feedback, which means you should find ways to _____ your progress.
6. Self-instruction refers to the process of comparing short-term performance to long-term goals. T or F?

Critical Thinking

7. How does setting daily goals in a behavioural self-management program help maximize the effects of reinforcement?

Answers:

1. T 2. T 3. F 4. T 5. regulated, monitor 6. F 7. Daily performance goals and rewards reduce the delay of reinforcement, which maximizes its impact.

Psychologist's Journal

EPILOGUE

Most psychologists enjoy seeing behavioural principles used to solve practical problems. One area of behaviour very much in need of attention is our "throwaway" society. We burn fossil fuels, destroy forests, use chemical products, strip, clear, and farm the land. In doing so, we alter the very face of the Earth. What can be done? One approach involves changing the consequences of wasteful energy use, polluting, and the like. For example, energy taxes can be used to increase the cost of using fossil fuels (response cost). On the reinforcement side of the equation, rebates can be offered for installing insulation and buying energy-efficient appliances or cars, and tax breaks can be given to companies that take steps to preserve the environment.

On a daily level, people can help recycle materials such as paper, steel, glass, aluminum, and plastic. Again, behavioural principles come into play. For instance, people who set their own goals for recycling tend to meet them. (This is much like self-regulated learning.) Likewise, when families, work groups, factories, and dorms receive feedback, on a weekly basis, about how much they recycled, they typically recycle more. We also know that people are most likely to continue recycling if they feel a sense of satisfaction from helping to protect the environment (Werner & Makela, 1998). Is such satisfaction sufficiently reinforcing to encourage more people to reduce, reuse, and recycle? Let's hope so.

CHAPTER IN REVIEW

Major Points

▶ Conditioning is a fundamental type of learning that affects many aspects of daily life.
▶ In classical conditioning, a neutral stimulus is repeatedly paired with a stimulus that reliably provokes a response. By association, the neutral stimulus also begins to elicit a response.
▶ In operant conditioning, responses that are followed by reinforcement occur more frequently.
▶ Cognitive learning involves acquiring higher-level information, rather than just linking stimuli and responses.
▶ We also learn by observing and imitating the actions of others.
▶ Behavioural principles can be used to manage one's own behaviour.
▶ Effective performance in school is based on self-regulated learning, an active, self-guided approach to studying.

Summary

What Is Learning?

• Learning is a relatively permanent change in behaviour due to experience. Learning resulting from conditioning depends on reinforcement. Reinforcement increases the probability that a particular response will occur.

• Classical, or respondent, conditioning and instrumental, or operant, conditioning are two basic types of learning.
• In classical conditioning, a previously neutral stimulus begins to elicit a response through association with another stimulus.
• In operant conditioning, the frequency and pattern of voluntary responses are altered by their consequences.

How Does Classical Conditioning Occur?

• In classical conditioning, a neutral stimulus (NS) is associated with an unconditioned stimulus (US).
• The US causes a reflex called the unconditioned response (UR). If the NS is consistently paired with the US, it becomes a conditioned stimulus (CS) capable of producing a conditioned (learned) response (CR).
• When the CS is followed by the US, conditioning is reinforced (strengthened).
• From an informational view, conditioning creates expectancies, which alter response patterns. That is, the CS creates an expectancy that the US will follow.
• Higher-order conditioning occurs when a well-learned conditioned stimulus is used as if it were an unconditioned stimulus, bringing about further learning.
• When the CS is repeatedly presented alone, conditioning is extinguished (weakened or inhibited). After extinction seems to be complete, a rest period may lead to the temporary reappearance of a conditioned response. This is called spontaneous recovery.

- Through stimulus generalization, stimuli similar to the conditioned stimulus will also produce a response. Generalization gives way to stimulus discrimination when an organism learns to respond to one stimulus, but not to similar stimuli.

Does Conditioning Affect Emotions?

- Conditioning applies to visceral or emotional responses as well as simple reflexes. As a result, conditioned emotional responses (CERs) also occur.
- Irrational fears called phobias may be CERs. Conditioning of emotional responses can occur vicariously (secondhand) as well as directly.

How Does Operant Conditioning Occur?

- Operant conditioning occurs when a voluntary action is followed by a reinforcer. Reinforcement in operant conditioning increases the frequency or probability of a response. This result is based on the law of effect.
- Complex operant responses can be taught by reinforcing successive approximations to a final desired response. This is called shaping. It is particularly useful in training animals.
- If an operant response is not reinforced, it may extinguish (disappear). But after extinction seems complete, it may temporarily reappear (spontaneous recovery).

Are There Different Kinds of Operant Reinforcement?

- In positive reinforcement, a reward or a pleasant event follows a response. In negative reinforcement, a response that ends discomfort becomes more likely.
- Primary reinforcers are "natural," physiologically based rewards.
- Secondary reinforcers are learned. They typically gain their reinforcing value by direct association with primary reinforcers or because they can be exchanged for primary reinforcers. Tokens and money gain their reinforcing value in this way.
- Feedback, or knowledge of results, aids learning and improves performance. It is most effective when it is immediate, detailed, and frequent.
- Programmed instruction breaks learning into a series of small steps and provides immediate feedback. Computer-assisted instruction (CAI) does the same, and also provides added information when needed.

How Are We Influenced by Patterns of Reward?

- Delayed reinforcement is less effective, but long chains of responses may be built up so that a single reinforcer maintains many responses.
- Superstitious behaviours often become part of response chains because they appear to produce reinforcement.
- Reward or reinforcement may be given continuously (after every response), or on a schedule of partial reinforcement. Partial reinforcement produces greater resistance to extinction.
- The four most basic schedules of reinforcement are fixed ratio, variable ratio, fixed interval, and variable interval. Each produces a distinct pattern of responding.

- Stimuli that precede a reinforced response tend to control the response on future occasions (stimulus control). Two aspects of stimulus control are generalization and discrimination.
- In generalization, an operant response tends to occur when stimuli similar to those preceding reinforcement are present.
- In discrimination, responses are given in the presence of discriminative stimuli associated with reinforcement (S+) and withheld in the presence of stimuli associated with non-reinforcement (S−).

What Does Punishment Do to Behaviour?

- Punishment decreases responding. Punishment occurs when a response is followed by the onset of an aversive event or by the removal of a positive event (response cost).
- Punishment is most effective when it is immediate, consistent, and intense.
- The undesirable side effects of punishment include the conditioning of fear to punishing agents and situations associated with punishment; the learning of escape and avoidance responses; and the encouragement of aggression.

What Is Cognitive Learning?

- Cognitive learning involves higher mental processes, such as understanding, knowing, or anticipating. Even in relatively simple learning situations, animals and people seem to form cognitive maps (internal representations of relationships).
- In latent learning, learning remains hidden or unseen until a reward or incentive for performance is offered.
- Discovery learning emphasizes insight and understanding, in contrast to rote learning.

Does Learning Occur by Imitation?

- Much human learning is achieved through observation, or modelling. Observational learning is influenced by the personal characteristics of the model and the success or failure of the model's behaviour.
- Television characters can act as powerful models for observational learning. Televised violence increases the likelihood of aggression by viewers.

How Does Conditioning Apply to Practical Problems?

- When managing your own behaviour, self-reinforcement, self-recording, feedback, and behavioural contracting are all helpful.
- Four strategies that can help change bad habits are reinforcing alternative responses, promoting extinction, breaking response chains, and avoiding antecedent cues.
- In school, self-regulated learners typically do all of the following: They set learning goals, plan learning strategies, use self-instruction, monitor their progress, evaluate themselves, reinforce successes, and take corrective action when required.

PSYCHOLOGY ON THE NET

If you have difficulty finding any of the sites listed here, visit http://psychologyjourney.nelson.com for an updated list of Internet addresses and direct links to relevant sites.

Memory A short tutorial on classical conditioning, operant conditioning, and cognitive learning. http://www.science.wayne.edu/~wpoff/memory.html

Observational Learning Presents Bandura's original work on modelling, with graphs. http://www.valdosta.peachnet.edu/~whuitt/psy702/behsys/social.html

OppaToons Cartoons of rats undergoing conditioning. http://www.thecroft.com/psy/toons/OppaToons.html

● **InfoTrac College Edition** For recent articles related to the impact of television, use Key Words search for VIOLENCE ON TELEVISION.

INTERACTIVE LEARNING

Psychology: An Interactive Journey

Remember that Chapter 6 of the CD-ROM that came with this text has practice tests, flashcards, interactive exercises, a crossword puzzle, and other valuable materials to enhance your learning experience.

● *PsychNow!* 5a. Classical Conditioning, 5b. Operant Conditioning, 5c. Observational Learning.

● *Psyk.trek* 5. Learning, Psyk.trek Simulations: 4. Shaping in Operant Conditioning.

Chart Your Progress

The questions that follow are only a sample of what you need to know. If you miss any of the items, you should review the entire chapter, do the exercises on the CD, and review the Knowledge Builders. Another way to prepare for tests is to get more practice with *WebTutor*, the *Study Guide*, or the *Practice Quizzes* that are available with this text.

1. The concept of reinforcement applies to both
   a. antecedents and consequences
   b. neutral stimuli and rewards
   c. classical and operant conditioning
   d. acquisition and spontaneous recovery

2. According to the informational view, classical conditioning creates new
   a. expectancies
   b. unconditioned responses
   c. unconditioned stimuli
   d. generalizations

3. At least some phobias can be thought of as
   a. NS-CR connections
   b. desensitization gradients
   c. extinction responses
   d. CERs

4. The law of effect defines the role of _____ in learning.
   a. antecedent stimuli
   b. stimulus generalization
   c. operant reinforcers
   d. stimulus approximations

5. Negative reinforcement _____ responding.
   a. increases
   b. decreases
   c. reverses
   d. extinguishes

6. Response cost is one form of
   a. discrimination conditioning
   b. generalization
   c. higher-order conditioning
   d. punishment

7. Which is a correct match?
   a. social reinforcer—primary reinforcement
   b. token reinforcer—secondary reinforcement
   c. ICS—secondary reinforcement
   d. negative reinforcer—punishment

8. Moderate response rates that are marked by spurts of activity and periods of inactivity are characteristic of
   a. FR schedules
   b. VR schedules
   c. FI schedules
   d. VI schedules

9. Children who watch a great deal of televised violence are more prone to be aggressive, an effect that is best explained by
   a. negative reinforcement
   b. shaping and successive approximations
   c. observational learning
   d. vicarious classical conditioning

10. As a behavioural management strategy, self-recording applies _____ to personal habits.
    a. vicarious conditioning
    b. feedback
    c. behavioural contracting
    d. the Premack principle

MEMORY

Chapter 7

Psychologist's Journal

HAS ANYONE SEEN MY MEMSAVE?

Cef-Wol is a typical inhabitant of the planet Gex. For many hundreds of years, the Gex endured high levels of industrial pollution. They've cleaned up now, but many Gex suffer from a serious loss of memory, caused by their exposure to toxic chemicals. Being a technologically advanced society, the Gex issued small, hand-held memory devices to all affected individuals. Cef-Wol, like many other Gex, now relies on her MemSave to get through the day. But she hates the endless chore of entering information into her MemSave, hour by hour, day after day. Cef-Wol also has another problem—when she needs information she has stored in her MemSave, Cef-Wol sometimes forgets that she has a MemSave.

Cef-Wol may be a fictional character, but her plight is not entirely fanciful. Consider K.C., who suffered a head injury in a motorcycle accident in Toronto in 1981. Since that injury, K.C. has been unable to form new memories of the events of his life. Although he still has knowledge about the world, and has even added to that knowledge since his accident (for example, he knows what the Internet is), he can't create any new memories of his experiences, nor retrieve old ones. He remembers the rules of chess, but cannot remember a single game he has played (Tulving et al., 1988).

Other types of memory loss can be even more devastating. For instance, when victims of total amnesia look in a mirror, a stranger stares back at them. Imagine the terror of having all of your own memories wiped out. You would have no identity, no knowledge, and no life history. You wouldn't recognize friends or family members. Clearly, a life without memory would be emotionally empty.

Recently, Cef-Wol visited Earth to find out how human memory works. Perhaps reading this chapter will help you do the same.

▶ Stages of Memory—Do You Have a Mind Like a Steel Trap? Or a Sieve?

Survey Question:
- ■ Is there more than one type of memory?

Many people think memory is "a dusty storehouse of facts." In reality, **memory** is an active system that stores, organizes, alters, and recovers information (Baddeley, 1996). In some ways, memory acts like a computer (see ▶Figure 7.1). Incoming information is first **encoded,** or changed into a usable form. This step is like typing data into a computer (or Cef-Wol's MemSave). Next, information is **stored,** or held in the system. (As we will see in a moment, human memory can be pictured as three separate storage systems.) Finally, memories must be **retrieved,** or taken out of storage, to be useful. If you're going to remember all of the 9856 new terms on your next psychology exam, you must successfully encode, store, and retrieve them.

What are the three separate memory systems just mentioned? Psychologists have identified three stages of memory. To be stored for a long time, information must pass through all three (see ▶Figure 7.2).

Sensory Memory

Let's say a friend asks you to pick up several things at a market. How will you remember them? New information first enters **sensory memory,** which can hold an exact copy of what is seen or heard, for a few seconds or less. For instance, look at a flower and then close your eyes. An **icon** (EYE-kon), or fleeting mental image, of the flower will persist for about half a second. Similarly, when you hear information, it is held in sensory memory as an echo for up to two seconds (Schweickert, 1993). (An **echo** is a brief continuation of activity in the auditory system.) In general, sensory memory holds information just long enough to move it to the second memory system (Neath, 1998).

Short-Term Memory

Not everything we see or hear is kept in memory. Imagine that a radio is playing in the background as your friend reads her shopping list to you. Will you remember what the announcer on the radio says, too? Will you remember your friend asking you if you are going to the store? Probably not, because **selective attention** (focusing on a selected portion of sensory input) controls what information moves on to short-term memory. You can think of this as a skill—some of us are better at it than others. For example, Katharine Arbuthnott, of the University of Regina, and Jamie Campbell, of the University of Saskatchewan, drew three conclusions about selective attention: (1) we can all exclude irrelevant information through selective attention (e.g., the voice on the radio); (2) we can all eliminate no longer relevant

Retrieval

Storage

Encoding

▶**Figure 7.1**

In some ways, a computer acts like a mechanical memory system. Both computer and human memory process information, and both allow encoding, storage, and retrieval of data.

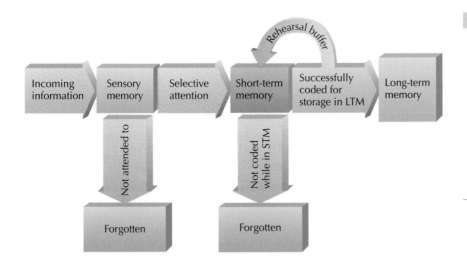

►Figure 7.2

Remembering is thought to involve at least three steps. Incoming information is first held for a second or two by sensory memory. Information selected by attention is then transferred to temporary storage in short-term memory. If new information is not rapidly encoded, or rehearsed, it is forgotten. If it is transferred to long-term memory, it becomes relatively permanent, although retrieving it may be a problem. The preceding is a useful *model* of memory; it may not be literally true of what happens in the brain (Eysenck & Keane, 1995).

Memory The mental system for receiving, encoding, storing, organizing, altering, and retrieving information.

Encoding Converting information into a form in which it will be retained in memory.

Storage Holding information in memory for later use.

Retrieval Recovering information from storage in memory.

Sensory memory The first stage of memory, which holds an exact record of incoming information for a few seconds or less.

Icon A mental image or visual representation.

Echo A brief continuation of sensory activity in the auditory system after a sound is heard.

Selective attention Voluntarily focusing on a selected portion of sensory input.

Short-term memory (STM) The memory system used to hold small amounts of information for relatively brief time periods.

Phonological storage Storing a word in memory on the basis of its sound.

Working memory Another name for short-term memory, especially as it is used for thinking and problem solving.

information (e.g., your friend asking if you are going to the store); and (3) some of us are definitely better at both processes than others (Arbuthnott & Campbell, 2000). **Short-term memory (STM)** holds small amounts of information for relatively brief periods. By paying attention to your friend, you will place the shopping list in short-term memory (while you ignore the voice on the radio saying, "Buy Burpo Butter").

How are short-term memories encoded? Short-term memories can be stored as images. But more often they are stored **phonologically** (by sound), especially in recalling words and letters (Neath, 1998). If you are introduced to Tim at a party and you forget his name, you are more likely to call him by a name that sounds like Tim (Jim, Kim, or Slim, for instance) than a name that sounds different, such as Bob or Mike. Your friend with the shopping list may be lucky if you don't bring home jam instead of ham and soap instead of soup!

Short-term memory is a *temporary* storehouse for small amounts of information. When you dial a phone number or remember a shopping list, you are using STM. Notice that unimportant information is quickly "dumped" from STM and forever lost. Short-term memory prevents our minds from storing useless names, dates, telephone numbers, and other trivia. At the same time, it provides an area of **working memory** where we do much of our thinking. Working memory acts as a sort of "mental scratchpad." It holds information for short periods of time while other mental activities are taking place, such as when you do mental arithmetic (Becker & Morris, 1999).

As you may have noticed when dialling a telephone, STM is very sensitive to *interruption,* or *interference.* You've probably had something like this happen with STM: Someone leaves a phone number on your answering machine. You listen to the number and repeat it to yourself. As you are about to make the call, the doorbell rings and you rush to see who is there. When you return to the phone a few minutes later, you have completely forgotten the number. You listen to the message again and memorize the number. This time as you begin to place the call, someone asks you a question. You answer, turn to the phone, and find that you have forgotten the number. Notice again that human working memory can handle only small amounts of information. It is very difficult to do more than one task at a time in STM (Anderson, Reder, & Lebiere, 1996).

Two researchers at the University of Waterloo, Ontario, Pierre Jolicoeur and Roberto Dell'Acqua, created a situation very similar to that phone-call-and-doorbell scenario in their laboratory. They gave people letters and symbols to remember, and then presented an auditory tone to which the people responded by pressing a button, after which the letters and symbols were recalled. Jolicoeur and Dell'Acqua found that the more closely the tone followed the letters and symbols, the longer it took to press the button, and this effect was stronger when the memory load was increased. They concluded that actually inserting information into STM ("encoding") is an effortful process. When a second process (here, auditory tone detection) has to be carried out at the same time, one or both of the two processes will suffer (Jolicoeur & Dell'Acqua, 1999).

Long-Term Memory

If short-term memory is brief, easily interrupted, and limited in "size," how do we remember for greater lengths of time? Information that is important or meaningful is transferred to **long-term memory (LTM),** which acts as a lasting storehouse for information. LTM contains everything you know about the world—from aardvark to zucchini, math to Myst, facts to fantasy. And yet, there appears to be no danger of running out of room. LTM can hold nearly limitless amounts of information. In fact, the more you know, the easier it becomes to add new information to memory. This is the reverse of what we would expect if LTM could be "filled up" (Eysenck & Keane, 1995). It is also one of many reasons for getting an education.

Are long-term memories also encoded as sounds? They can be. But as University of Toronto psychologists Fergus Craik and Robert S. Lockhart have demonstrated, new memories can be encoded in a variety of ways, of which the most useful is encoding on the basis of meaning and importance (Craik & Lockhart, 1972). If information in STM can be linked to knowledge already stored in LTM, it gains meaning. This makes it easier to remember.

DUAL MEMORY   Most of our daily memory chores are handled by STM and LTM. To summarize their connection, picture short-term memory as a small desk at the front of a huge warehouse full of filing cabinets (LTM). As information enters the warehouse, it is first placed on the desk. Since the desk is small, it must be quickly cleared off to make room for new information. Unimportant items are simply tossed away. Meaningful or important information is placed in the files (long-term memory).

When we want to use knowledge from LTM to answer a question, the information is returned to STM. Or, in our analogy, a folder is taken out of the files (LTM) and moved to the desk (STM), where it can be used. (Computer users may prefer to think of STM as being like RAM and LTM as being like a hard drive.) However, it is unlikely that short- and long-term memories are simply stored at different locations in the human brain. STM and LTM appear to be different stages in the storage of information (Best, 1999).

Now that you have a general picture of STM and LTM, it is time to explore both in more detail. The discussion that follows should add to your understanding. But first, here's a chance to rehearse what you've learned.

> **Long-term memory (LTM)**
> The memory system used for relatively permanent storage of meaningful information.

Knowledge builder

MEMORY SYSTEMS

Relate

Wave a pencil back and forth in front of your eyes while focusing on something in the distance. The pencil's image looks transparent. Why? (Because sensory memory briefly holds an image of the pencil. This image persists after the pencil passes by.)

Think of a time today when you used short-term memory (such as briefly remembering a phone number, an Internet address, or someone's name). How long did you retain the information? How did you encode it? How much do you remember now?

How is long-term memory helping you read this sentence? If the words weren't already stored in LTM, could you read at all? How else have you used LTM today?

Learning Check

Match: **A.** Sensory memory **B.** STM **C.** LTM

_____ **1.** Working memory
_____ **2.** Holds information for a few seconds or less
_____ **3.** Stores an icon or echo
_____ **4.** Permanent, unlimited capacity
_____ **5.** Temporarily holds small amounts of information
_____ **6.** Selective attention determines its contents
_____ **7.** STM is improved by interruption, or interference, because attention is more focused at such times. T or F?

Critical Thinking

8. Why is sensory memory important to filmmakers?

Answers:

1. B 2. A 3. A 4. C 5. B 6. B 7. F 8. Without sensory memory, a movie would look like a series of still pictures. The split-second persistence of visual images helps blend one motion-picture frame into the next.

▶ Short-Term Memory—Do You Know the Magic Number?

Survey Question:
■ What are the features of each type of memory?

Digit-span test A test of attention and short-term memory in which a string of numbers is recalled.
Information bits Meaningful units of information, such as numbers, letters, words, or phrases.
Information chunks Information bits grouped into larger units.
Recoding Reorganizing or modifying information to assist storage in memory.
Maintenance rehearsal Silently repeating or mentally reviewing information to hold it in short-term memory.

How much information can be held in short-term memory? For an answer, read the following numbers once. Then close the book and write as many as you can in the correct order.

8 5 1 7 4 9 3

This is called a **digit-span test.** It is a measure of attention and short-term memory. If you were able to correctly repeat seven digits, you have an average short-term memory. Now try to memorize the following list, reading it only once.

7 1 8 3 5 4 2 9 1 6 3

This series was probably beyond your short-term memory capacity. Psychologist George Miller found that short-term memory is limited to the "magic number" seven (plus or minus two) **information bits** (Miller, 1956). A bit is a single meaningful "piece" of information, such as a digit. It is as if short-term memory has seven "slots" or "bins" into which separate items can be placed. Actually, a few people can remember up to nine bits, and for some types of information five bits is the limit. Thus, an *average* of seven information bits can be stored in short-term memory (Neath, 1998).

When all of the "slots" in STM are filled, there is no room for new information. Picture how this works at a party: Let's say your hostess begins introducing everyone who is there, "Ted, Barbara, Donna, Roseanna, Wayne, Shawn, Linda . . ." Stop, you think to yourself. But she continues, "Eddie, Jay, Gordon, Frank, Marietta, Dan, Patty, Glen, Ricky." The hostess leaves, satisfied that you have met everyone. And you spend the evening talking with Ted, Barbara, and Ricky, the only people whose names you remember!

Recoding

Before we continue, try your short-term memory again, this time on letters. Read the following letters once, then look away and try to write them in the proper order.

T V I   B M E S   P Y   M C A

Notice that there are 12 letters, or "bits" of information. This should be beyond the seven-item limit of STM. However, since the letters are in four groups, or chunks of information, many students are able to memorize them. **Information chunks** are made up of bits of information grouped into larger units.

How does chunking help? Chunking **recodes** (reorganizes) information into units that are already in LTM. In an experiment that used lists like this one, people remembered best when the letters were read as familiar meaningful chunks: TV, IBM, ESP, YMCA (Bower & Springston, 1970). If you recoded the letters this way, you probably remembered the entire list. (By the way, despite her memory impairment, Cef-Wol had no difficulty remembering the entire list, because back home on Gex, Tvibmespymca is the name of her favourite band.)

Chunking suggests that STM holds about five to seven of whatever units we are using. A single chunk could be made up of numbers, letters, words, phrases, or familiar sentences (Barsalou, 1992). Picture STM as a small desk again. Through chunking, we combine several items into one "stack" of information. This allows us to place seven stacks on the desk, where before there was room for only seven separate items.

Rehearsal

How long do short-term memories last? Short-term memories disappear very rapidly. However, you can prolong a short-term memory by a process called rehearsal. Actually, as first pointed out by Craik and Lockhart at the University of Toronto, there are two kinds of rehearsal (Craik & Lockhart, 1972). The first type they called **maintenance rehearsal.** This involves silently repeating the memory. You have probably remembered an address or telephone number this way. The more times a short-term memory is rehearsed, the greater its chances of being stored in LTM (Barsalou, 1992).

What if rehearsal is prevented, so a memory cannot be recycled or moved to LTM? Without maintenance rehearsal, STM is incredibly short. In one experiment, subjects heard meaningless syllables like XAR followed by a number like 67. As soon as subjects heard the number, they began counting backward by threes (to prevent them from repeating the syllable). After only 18 seconds of delay, memory scores fell to zero (Peterson & Peterson, 1959).

After *18 seconds* without rehearsal, the short-term memories were gone forever! Keep this in mind when you get only one chance to hear information you want to remember. If you are introduced to someone, and the name slips out of STM, it is gone forever. To escape this awkward situation, you might try saying something like, "I'm curious, how do you spell your name?" Unfortunately, the response is often an icy reply like, "B-O-B S-M-I-T-H, it's really not too difficult." To avoid embarrassment, pay careful attention to the name, repeat it to yourself several times, and try to use it in the next sentence or two before you lose it (Neath, 1998).

Maintenance rehearsal is not a very good way to transfer information to long-term memory. A better way involves what Craik and Lockhart called **elaborative rehearsal.** This process, which makes information more meaningful, is far more effective. In other words, it's best to link new information to existing memories and knowledge. That's why passively reading a textbook is a poor way to study. If you don't elaborate, digest, extend, and think about information, you won't remember much later. As you read, try to frequently ask yourself "why" questions, such as "Why would that be true?" (Willoughby et al., 1997). Also, try to relate new ideas to your own experiences. In doing so, you'll be taking advantage of what Tim Rogers at the University of Calgary calls the **self-reference effect.** We remember best when we encode new information on the basis of meaning rather than superficial features. And this effect is strongest if the meaning is personally relevant. If you see a dog in the park, you'll remember it better if you think of it chasing a cat than if you focus on the colour of its fur. But you'll do better still if you remember it chasing *your* cat. That's the self-reference effect (Rogers, Kuiper, & Kirker, 1977).

Elaborative rehearsal
Rehearsal that links new information with existing memories and knowledge.

Self-reference effect
Memory works better when you encode for meaning and emphasize personal relevance of the material.

▶ Long-Term Memory—Where the Past Lives

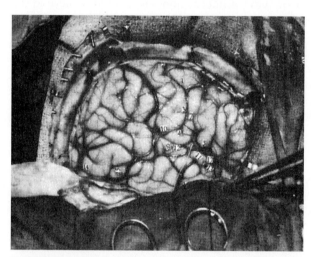

▶Figure 7.3

Exposed cerebral cortex of a patient undergoing brain surgery. Numbers represent points that reportedly produced "memories" when electrically stimulated. A critical evaluation of such reports suggests that they are more like dreams than memories. This fact raises questions about claims that long-term memories are permanent. (From Wilder Penfield, *The Excitable Cortex in Conscious Man*, 1958. Courtesy of the author and Charles C. Thomas, Publisher, Springfield, Illinois.)

An electrode was placed at location number 11 on the patient's brain. She immediately said, "Yes, sir, I think I heard a mother calling her little boy somewhere. It seemed to be something happening years ago. It was somebody in the neighbourhood where I live." A short time later the electrode was applied to the same spot. Again the patient said, "Yes, I hear the same familiar sounds, it seems to be a woman calling, the same lady" (Penfield, 1958). These statements were made by a woman undergoing brain surgery. Only local anesthetics were used (there are no pain receptors in the brain), so the patient was awake as her brain was electrically stimulated (see ▶Figure 7.3). When activated, some brain areas seemed to produce vivid memories of long-forgotten events.

PERMANENCE *Is every experience permanently recorded in memory?* Results like those described led Montreal neurosurgeon Wilder Penfield to claim that the brain records the past like a "continuous strip of movie film, complete with sound track" (Penfield, 1957). But as you know, this is an exaggeration. Many events never get past short-term memory. Also, brain stimulation produces memory-like experiences in only about 3 percent of cases. Most reports resemble dreams more than memories, and many are clearly imaginary. Memory experts now believe that long-term memories are only relatively permanent (Barsalou, 1992; Loftus & Loftus, 1980). Perfect, indelible, eternal memories are a myth.

Try It Yourself: How's Your Memory?

In order to better appreciate the next topic, pause for a moment and read the words you see here. Read through the list once. Then continue reading the next section of this chapter.

bed dream blanket doze pillow nap snore

mattress alarm clock rest slumber nod

sheet bunk cot cradle groggy

Constructing Memories

Instead of storing the past in great detail, the brain takes a more efficient approach: constructing memories by combining partial memories of an event and knowledge of the world ("what must have happened"). As new long-term memories are formed, older memories are often updated, changed, lost, or revised (Baddeley, 1990, 1996). To illustrate this point, Elizabeth Loftus and John Palmer (1974) showed people a filmed automobile accident. Afterward, some participants were asked to estimate how fast the cars were going when they "smashed" into each other. For others the words "bumped," "contacted," or "hit" replaced "smashed." One week later, each person was asked, "Did you see any broken glass?" Those asked earlier about the cars that "smashed" into each other were more likely to say yes. (No broken glass was shown in the film.) The new information ("smashed") was included in memories and altered them.

Try It Yourself: Old or New?

Now, without looking back to the list of words you read a moment ago, see if you can tell which of the following are "old" words (items from the list you read) and which are "new" words (items that weren't on the list). Mark each of the following words as old or new:

sofa sleep lamp kitchen

> **Constructive processing** Reorganizing or updating memories on the basis of logic, reasoning, or the addition of new information.
> **Pseudo-memory** A false memory that a person believes is real or accurate.

Updating our memories is called **constructive processing.** Gaps in memory, which are common, may be filled in by logic, guessing, or new information (Schacter, Norman, & Koutstaal, 1998). Indeed, it is possible to have "memories" for things that never happened (such as remembering broken glass at an accident when there was none). People in Elizabeth Loftus's experiments who had these **pseudo-memories** (false memories) were often quite upset to learn they had given false "testimony" (Loftus & Ketcham, 1991).

Try It Yourself: And Now, the Results

Return now and look at the labels you wrote on the "old or new" word list. If you answered as most people do, this exercise may help you appreciate how often we have false memories. All of the listed words are "new." None was on the original list! If you thought you "remembered" that sleep was on the original list, you had a false memory. The word *sleep* is associated with most of the words on the original list, which creates a strong impression that you saw it before (Roediger & McDermott, 1995).

False long-term memories are a common problem in police work. For example, a witness may select a photo of a suspect from police files or see a photo in the news. Later, the witness identifies the suspect in a line-up or in court. Did the witness really remember the suspect from the scene of the crime? Or was the memory from the more recently seen photograph? Under some circumstances, an innocent person may be "remembered" as the criminal.

Does the new information "overwrite" the original memory? No, the real problem is that we often can't remember the source of a memory. This can lead witnesses to "remember" a

FOCUS ON RESEARCH Hypnosis, Imagination, and Memory

In 1976, near Chowchilla, California, 26 children were abducted from a school bus and held captive for ransom. Under hypnosis, the bus driver recalled the licence plate number of the kidnappers' van. This memory helped break the case and led to the children's rescue. Such successes seem to imply that hypnosis can improve memory. But does it? Read on, and judge for yourself.

Research has shown that a hypnotized person is more likely than normal to use imagination to fill in gaps in memory. Also, when hypnotized persons are given false information, they tend to weave it into their memories (Sheehan & Statham, 1989). Even when a memory is completely false, the hypnotized person's confidence in it can be unshakable (Burgess & Kirsch, 1999).

Most telling of all is the fact that hypnosis increases false memories more than it does true ones. Jane Dywan of Brock University in St. Catharines, Ontario, found that 80 percent of the additional memories produced after hypnosis by subjects in one experiment were incorrect (Dywan & Bowers, 1983). Overall, it can be concluded that hypnosis does not greatly improve memory (Burgess & Kirsch, 1999).

Then why did it help in the Chowchilla case? It is true that hypnosis sometimes uncovers more information, as it did in Chowchilla (Schreiber & Schreiber, 1999). However, when it does, there is no sure way to tell which memories are true and which are false (Perry et al., 1996). Clearly, hypnosis is not the "magic bullet" against forgetting that some police investigators hoped it would be (Kebbell & Wagstaff, 1998).

face that they actually saw somewhere other than the crime scene (Schacter, Norman, & Koutstaal, 1998). Many tragic cases of mistaken identity occur this way.

Couldn't hypnosis be used to avoid such problems? News stories often give the impression that it can. Is this true? "Hypnosis, Imagination, and Memory" examines research done on this intriguing question.

To summarize, forming and using memories is an active, creative, highly personal process. Our memories are coloured by emotions, judgments, and quirks of personality. If you and a friend were lashed together, and you went through life side by side, you would still have different memories. What we remember depends on what we pay attention to, what we regard as meaningful or important, and what we feel strongly about (Schacter, 1996). But there is a built-in safeguard in this system. Memory is not entirely constructed—remember Tim Rogers's finding that the more self-relevant information is, the more likely it is to be remembered correctly.

Organization

Survey Question:
- Is there more than one type of long-term memory?

Long-term memory stores a seemingly limitless amount of information in a lifetime. How is it possible to quickly find specific memories? The answer is that each person's "memory index" is highly organized.

Do you mean that information is arranged alphabetically, as in a dictionary? Not a chance! If someone asks you to name a black-and-white animal that lives on ice, is related to a chicken, and cannot fly, you don't have to go from aardvark to zebra to find the answer. You will probably only think of black-and-white birds living in the Antarctic. Which of these cannot fly? Voila, the answer is penguin.

Information in LTM may be arranged according to rules, images, categories, symbols, similarity, formal meaning, or personal meaning (Baddeley, 1990, 1996). In recent years, psychologists have begun to develop a picture of the *structure,* or organization, of memories. **Memory structure** refers to the pattern of associations among items of information. For example, assume that you are given two statements, to which you must answer yes or no: *A canary is an animal. A canary is a bird.* Which do you answer more quickly? For most people, *A canary is a bird* produces a faster yes than *A canary is an animal* (Collins & Quillian, 1969). Why should this be so? Psychologists believe that a **network model** of memory explains why. According to this view, LTM is organized as a network of linked ideas (see ▶Figure 7.4). When ideas are "farther" apart, it takes a longer chain of associations to connect them. The more two items are separated, the longer it takes to answer. In terms of information links, *canary* is probably "close" to *bird* in your "memory files." *Animal*

Memory structure Patterns of associations among bits of information stored in memory.

Network model A model of memory that views it as an organized system of linked information.

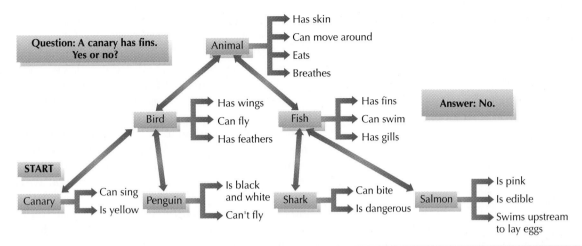

> ▶Figure 7.4

A hypothetical network of facts about animals shows what is meant by the structure of memory. Small networks of ideas such as this are probably organized into larger and larger units and higher levels of meaning. (Adapted from Collins & Quillian, 1969.)

Procedural memory
Long-term memories of conditioned responses and learned skills.

Declarative memory That part of long-term memory containing specific factual information.

Semantic memory A subpart of declarative memory that records impersonal knowledge about the world.

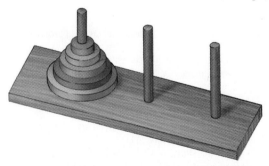

> ▶Figure 7.5

The tower puzzle. In this puzzle, all the coloured disks must be moved to another post, without ever placing a larger disk on a smaller one. Only one disk may be moved at a time, and a disk must always be moved from one post to another (it cannot be held aside). An amnesic patient learned to solve the puzzle in 31 moves, the minimum possible. Even so, each time he began, he protested that he did not remember ever solving the puzzle before and that he did not know how to begin. Evidence like this suggests that skill memory is distinct from fact memory.

and *canary* are farther apart. Remember though, this has nothing to do with alphabetical order. We are talking about organization based on linked meanings.

Types of Long-Term Memory

How many types of long-term memory are there? It is becoming clear that more than one type of long-term memory exists. Let's probe a little further into the mysteries of memory.

SKILL MEMORY AND FACT MEMORY A curious thing happens to many people who develop amnesia. Amnesic patients may be unable to learn a telephone number, an address, or a person's name. And yet, the same patients can learn to solve complex puzzles in the same amount of time as normal subjects (Squire & Zola-Morgan, 1988) (see ▶Figure 7.5). These and other observations have led many psychologists, notably Paul Kolers at the University of Toronto, to conclude that long-term memories fall into at least two categories (Kolers, 1975). One is called *procedural memory* (or skill memory). The other is *declarative memory* (also sometimes called fact memory).

Procedural memory includes basic conditioned responses and learned actions like those involved in typing, solving a puzzle, or swinging a golf club. Memories such as these can be fully expressed only as actions (or "know-how"). It is likely that skill memories register in "lower" brain areas, especially the cerebellum. They represent the more basic "automatic" elements of conditioning, learning, and memory (Gabrieli, 1998).

Declarative memory stores specific factual information, such as names, faces, words, dates, and ideas. Declarative memories are expressed as words or symbols. For example, knowing that Steven Spielberg directed both *Close Encounters of the Third Kind* and *Jurassic Park* is a declarative memory. This is the type of memory that a person with amnesia lacks and that most of us take for granted. In 1972, Endel Tulving of the University of Toronto, perhaps the most influential Canadian memory researcher ever, argued that declarative memory can be further divided into *semantic memory* and *episodic memory* (Nyberg & Tulving, 1996; Tulving, 1972).

SEMANTIC MEMORY Most of our basic factual knowledge about the world is almost totally immune to forgetting. The names of objects, the days of the week or months of the year, simple math skills, the seasons, words and language, and other general facts are all quite lasting. Such impersonal facts make up a part of LTM called **semantic memory.** Semantic memory serves as a mental dictionary or encyclopedia of basic knowledge.

> **Episodic memory** A subpart of declarative memory that records personal experiences that are linked with specific times and places.

Sensory memory

↓

Short-term memory

↓

Long-term memory

Procedural memory | **Declarative memory**

Semantic memory | **Episodic memory**

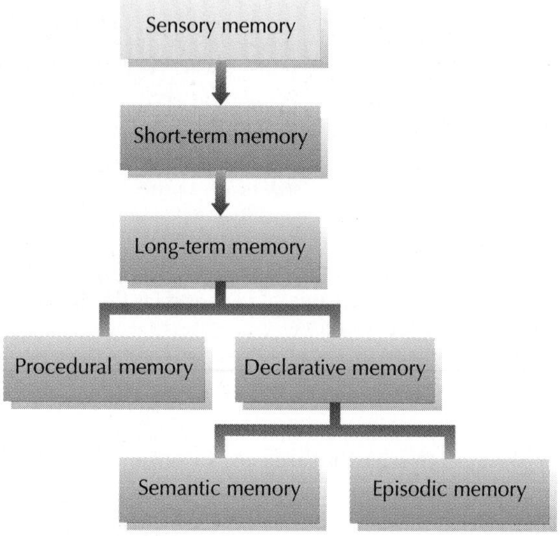

▶ **Figure 7.6**

In the model shown here, long-term memory is divided into procedural memory (learned actions and skills) and declarative memory (stored facts). Declarative memories can be either semantic (impersonal knowledge) or episodic (personal experiences associated with specific times and places).

EPISODIC MEMORY   Semantic memory has no connection to times or places. It would be rare, for instance, to remember when and where you first learned the names of the seasons. In contrast, **episodic memory** (ep-ih-SOD-ik) is an "autobiographical" record of personal experiences. It stores life events (or "episodes") day after day, year after year. Can you remember your seventh birthday? Your first date? An accident you witnessed? The first day of college? What you had for breakfast three days ago? All are episodic memories.

Are episodic memories as lasting as semantic memories? In general, episodic memories are more easily forgotten than semantic memories. This is because new information constantly pours into episodic memory. Stop for a moment and remember what you did last summer. That was an episodic memory. Notice that you now remember that you just remembered something. You have a new episodic memory in which you remember that you remembered while reading this text! It's easy to see how much we ask of our memory.

Do you remember K. C. who was described at the beginning of this chapter? Endel Tulving reported that, while K.C. could remember lots of facts about family and friends, such as names and addresses, he couldn't recall any of the events of his life; high-school graduation, a brother's wedding, and even the death of another brother in a boating accident were all lost to him (Tulving et al., 1988).

HOW MANY TYPES OF MEMORY?   In summary, it is very likely that three kinds of long-term memories exist: procedural, semantic, and episodic (Mitchell, 1989; Squire, Knowlton, & Musen, 1993) (see ▶ Figure 7.6). While other types of memory may be discovered, it appears that some pieces of the puzzle are falling into place.

Knowledge builder

STM AND LTM

Relate

Telephone numbers are divided into an area code (three digits) and a seven-digit number that is divided into three digits, plus four more. Can you relate this practice to STM? How about to chunking and recoding?

Think about how you've used your memory in the last hour. See if you can identify an example of each of the following: a procedural memory, a declarative memory, a semantic memory, and an episodic memory.

Learning Check

1. There is evidence that STM lasts about 18 seconds without rehearsal. T or F?
2. Information is best transferred from STM to LTM when a person engages in
   a. maintenance chunking *b.* maintenance recoding *c.* elaborative networking *d.* elaborative rehearsal

3. Constructive processing is often responsible for creating pseudo-memories. T or F?
4. Electrical stimulation of the brain has shown conclusively that all memories are stored permanently, but not all memories can be retrieved. T or F?
5. Memories elicited under hypnosis are more vivid, complete, and reliable than normal. T or F?
6. _____ of related information are an example of the structure or organization found in LTM.
7. Procedural memories are stored in STM, whereas declarative memories are stored in LTM. T or F?

Critical Thinking

8. Parents sometimes warn children not to read comic books, fearing that they will learn less in school if they "fill their heads up with junk." Why is this warning unnecessary?

Answers:

1. T 2. *d* 3. T 4. F 5. F 6. Networks 7. F 8. Because the more information you have in long-term memory, the greater the possibilities for linking new information to it. Generally, the more you know, the more you can learn—even if some of what you know is "junk."

▶ Measuring Memory—The Answer Is on the Tip of My Tongue

Survey Question:
■ How is memory measured?

Tip-of-the-tongue state The feeling that a memory is available but not quite retrievable.

Feeling of knowing A feeling that allows people to predict beforehand whether they will be able to remember something.

Memory task Any task designed to test or assess memory.

Recall To supply or reproduce memorized information with a minimum of external cues.

Serial position effect The tendency to make the most errors in remembering the middle items of an ordered list.

Recognition memory An ability to correctly identify previously learned information.

You either remember something or you don't, right? Wrong. Partial memories are common. For instance, imagine that a clerk helps you at a clothing store. Will you remember her six months later? Probably not—unless you happen to see her again at the mall. If you remember her then, you will have used a form of partial memory called *recognition*.

Partial memory is also demonstrated by the **tip-of-the-tongue (TOT) state.** This is the feeling that a memory is available, but not quite retrievable. It is as if an answer or a memory is just out of reach—on the "tip of your tongue." For instance, in one study, university students read the definitions of words such as *sextant, sampan,* and *ambergris.* Students who "drew a blank" and couldn't name a defined word were asked to give whatever other information they could. Often, they could accurately guess the first and last letter and even the number of syllables of the word they were seeking. They also gave words that sounded like or meant the same thing as the defined word (Brown & McNeill, 1966).

Closely related to the TOT state is the fact that people can often tell beforehand if they are likely to remember something. This is called the **feeling of knowing** (Nelson, 1987). Feeling-of-knowing reactions are easy to observe on television game shows, where they occur just before contestants are allowed to answer.

Because memory is not an all-or-nothing event, there are several ways of measuring it. Three commonly used **memory tasks** (tests of memory) are *recall, recognition,* and *relearning.* Let's see how they differ.

Recall

What is the name of the first song on your favourite compact disc? Who won the World Series last year? Who wrote *Hamlet*? If you can answer these questions, you are using **recall,** a direct retrieval of facts or information. Tests of recall often require *verbatim* (word-for-word) memory. If you study a poem until you can recite it without looking, you are recalling it. If you complete a fill-in-the-blank question, you are using recall. When you answer an essay question by providing facts and ideas, you are also using recall, even though you didn't learn your essay verbatim.

The order in which information is memorized has an interesting effect on recall. To experience it, try to memorize the following list, reading it only once:

bread, apples, soda, ham, cookies, rice, lettuce, beets,

mustard, cheese, oranges, ice cream, crackers, flour, eggs

If you are like most people, it will be hardest for you to recall items from the middle of the list. ▶Figure 7.7 shows the results of a similar test. Notice that most errors occur with middle items of an ordered list. This is the **serial position effect.** You can remember the last items on a list because they are still in STM. The first items are also remembered well because they entered an "empty" short-term memory. This allows you to rehearse the items so they move into long-term memory (Medin & Ross, 1992). The middle items are neither held in short-term memory nor moved to long-term memory, so they are often lost.

Recognition

Try to write down everything you can remember from a class you took last year. (You have three minutes, which should be more than enough time!) If you actually did this, you might conclude that you had learned very little. However, a more sensitive test based on recognition could be used. In **recognition memory,** previously learned material is correctly identified. For instance, you could take

▶Figure 7.7

The serial position effect. The graph shows the percentage of subjects correctly recalling each item in a 15-item list. Recall is best for the first and last items. (Data from Craik, 1970)

a multiple-choice test on facts and ideas from the course. Since you would only have to recognize correct answers, we would probably find that you had learned a lot.

Recognition memory can be amazingly accurate for pictures, photographs, or other visual input. One investigator showed people 2560 photographs at a rate of one every 10 seconds. Each person was then shown 280 pairs of photographs. Each pair included an "old" picture (from the first set of photos) and a similar "new" image. Subjects could tell 85 to 95 percent of the time which photograph they had seen before (Haber, 1970). This finding may explain why people so often say, "I may forget a name, but I never forget a face." (It's also why we rarely need to see our friends' vacation photos more than once.)

Recognition is usually superior to recall. That's why police departments use photographs or a line-up to identify criminal suspects. Witnesses who disagree when they try to recall a suspect's height, weight, age, or eye colour often agree completely when recognition is all that is required.

Is recognition always superior? It depends greatly on the kind of **distractors** used. These are false items included with an item to be recognized. If distractors are very similar to the correct item, memory may be poor. A reverse problem occurs when only one choice looks like it could be correct. This can produce a **false positive,** or false sense of recognition, like the false memory you had earlier when you thought you remembered seeing the word *sleep.*

Many variables influence the accuracy of both recall and recognition. For example, Daniel Yarmey, at the University of Guelph, had a female assistant approach people on the street and speak to them briefly before walking away. Minutes later, Yarmey asked these people to identify the woman and to describe her. Identifications were more likely to be wrong when people looked at photographs of just one woman, and had to say yes or no, than when they looked at a photograph of six women and had to choose one. Descriptions of the woman were more accurate when people were allowed to recall freely than when they were asked specific questions (Yarmey, Yarmey, & Yarmey, 1996).

Relearning

In a classic experiment, a psychologist read a short passage in Greek to his son. He did this each day when the boy was between 15 months and three years of age. At age eight, the boy was asked if he remembered the Greek passage. He showed no evidence of recall. He was then shown selections from the passage he heard and selections from other Greek passages. Could he recognize the one he heard as an infant? "It's all Greek to me!" he said, indicating a lack of recognition (and drawing a frown from everyone in the room).

Had the psychologist stopped, he might have concluded that no memory of the Greek remained. However, the child was then asked to memorize the original quotation and others of equal difficulty. This time his earlier learning became evident. The boy memorized the passage he had heard in childhood 25 percent faster than the others (Burtt, 1941). As this experiment suggests, **relearning** is typically the most sensitive measure of memory.

When a person is tested by relearning, how do we know a memory still exists? As with the boy described, relearning is measured by a **savings score** (the amount of time saved when relearning information). Let's say it takes you one hour to memorize all the names in a telephone book. (It's a small town.) Two years later you relearn them in 45 minutes. Because you "saved" 15 minutes, your savings score would be 25 percent (15 divided by 60 times 100). Savings of this type are a good reason for studying a wide range of subjects. It may seem that learning algebra, history, or a foreign language is wasted if you don't use the knowledge immediately. But when you do need such information, you will be able to relearn it quickly.

Implicit and Explicit Memory

Many memories remain outside of conscious awareness. For example, if you know how to type, it is apparent that you know where the letters

Distractors False items included with a correct item to form a test of recognition memory (for example, the wrong answers on a multiple-choice test).

False positive A false sense of recognition.

Relearning Learning again something that was previously learned. Used to measure memory of prior learning.

Savings score The amount of time saved (expressed as a percentage) when relearning information.

Police line-ups make use of the sensitivity of recognition memory. However, unless great care is taken, false identifications are still possible (Naka, 1998).

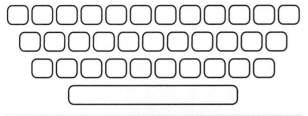

▶Figure 7.8

Can you label the letter keys on this blank keyboard? If you can, you probably used implicit memory to do it.

are on the keyboard. But how many typists could correctly label blank keys in a drawing of a keyboard? (See ▶Figure 7.8.) Many people find that they cannot directly remember such information, even though they "know" it.

Who were the last three prime ministers of Canada? What did you have for breakfast today? What is the title of Alanis Morissette's best-selling album? Explicit memory is used in answering each of these questions. **Explicit memories** are past experiences that are consciously brought to mind. Recall, recognition, and the tests you take in school rely on explicit memories. In contrast, **implicit memories** lie outside of awareness (Roediger, 1990). That is, we are not aware that a memory exists. Nevertheless, implicit memories—such as unconsciously knowing where the letters are on a keyboard—greatly influence our behaviour (Neath, 1998).

Explicit memory
A memory that a person is aware of having; a memory that is consciously retrieved.

Implicit memory
A memory that a person does not know exists; a memory that is retrieved unconsciously.

Priming Facilitating the retrieval of an implicit memory by using cues to activate hidden memories.

Internal images Mental images or visual depictions used in memory and thinking.

Eidetic imagery The ability to retain a "projected" mental image long enough to use it as a source of information.

PRIMING   *How is it possible to show that a memory exists if it lies outside of awareness?* Psychologists first noticed implicit memory while studying memory loss caused by brain injuries. Let's say, for example, that a patient is shown a list of common words, such as *chair, tree, lamp, table,* and so on. A few minutes later, the patient is asked to recall words from the list. Sadly, he has no memory of the words.

Now, instead of asking the patient to explicitly recall the list, we could "prime" his memory by giving him the first two letters of each word. "We'd like you to say a word that begins with these letters," we tell him. "Just say whatever comes to mind." Of course, many words could be made from each pair of letters. For example, the first item (from chair) would be the letters CH. The patient could say "child," "chalk," "chain," "check," or many other words. Instead, he says "chair," a word from the original list. The patient is not aware that he is remembering the list, but as he gives a word for each letter pair, almost all are from the list. Apparently, the letters **primed** (activated) hidden memories, which then influenced his answers.

Similar effects have been found for people with normal memories. As the preceding example implies, implicit memories are often revealed by giving a person limited cues, such as the first letter of words or partial drawings of objects. Typically, the person believes that he or she is just saying whatever comes to mind. Nevertheless, information previously seen or heard affects the person's answers (Tulving & Schacter 1990). Some nutritionists like to say, "You are what you eat." In the realm of memory, it appears that we are what we experience—to a far greater degree than once realized.

▶ Exceptional Memory—Wizards of Recall

Survey Question:
■ What are "photographic" memories?

Can you remember how many doors there are in your house or apartment? To answer a question like this, many people form **internal images** (mental pictures) of each room and count the doorways they visualize. As this example implies, many memories are stored as mental images (Dewhurst & Conway, 1994).

Stephen Kosslyn, Thomas Ball, and Brian Reiser (1978) found an interesting way to show that memories do exist as images. People first memorized a sort of treasure map similar to the one shown in ▶Figure 7.9a. They were then asked to picture a black dot moving from one object, such as one of the trees, to another, such as the hut at the top of the island. Did participants really form an image to do this task? It seems they did. As shown in Figure 7.9b, the time it took to "move" the dot was directly related to actual distances on the map.

Is the "treasure map" task an example of photographic memory? In some ways, internal memory images do have "photographic" qualities. However, the term *photographic memory* is more often used to describe eidetic imagery.

Eidetic Imagery

Eidetic (eye-DET-ik) **imagery** occurs when a person has visual images clear enough to be "scanned" or retained for at least 30 seconds. Internal memory images can be "viewed"

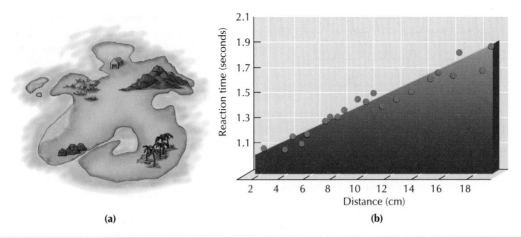

(a)   (b)

▶Figure 7.9

(a) "Treasure map" similar to the one used by Kosslyn, Ball, and Reiser (1978) to study images in memory. (b) This graph shows how long it took subjects to move a visualized spot various distances on their mental images of the map. (See text for explanation.)

▶Figure 7.10

Test picture like that used to identify children with eidetic imagery. To test your eidetic imagery, look at the picture for 30 seconds. Then look at a blank surface and try to "project" the picture on it. If you have good eidetic imagery, you will be able to see the picture in detail. Return now to the text and try to answer the questions there. (Redrawn from an illustration in *Alice in Wonderland,* by Lewis Carroll.)

mentally with the eyes closed. In contrast, eidetic images are "projected" out in front of a person. That is, they are best "seen" on a plain surface, such as a blank piece of paper. In this respect, eidetic images are somewhat like the after-images you might have after looking at a flashbulb or a brightly lit neon sign (Kunzendorf, 1989).

Eidetic memory occurs most often in childhood, with about eight children out of 100 having eidetic images. In one series of tests, children were shown a picture from *Alice's Adventures in Wonderland* (▶Figure 7.10). To test your eidetic imagery, look at the picture and read the instructions there.

Now, let's see how much you remember. Can you say (without looking again) which of Alice's apron strings is longer? Are the cat's front paws crossed? How many stripes are on the cat's tail? Don't be disappointed if you didn't do too well when you tried your eidetic skills. Most eidetic imagery disappears during adolescence and becomes rare by adulthood (Kunzendorf, 1989). Actually, this may not be much of a loss. The majority of eidetic memorizers have no better long-term memory than average.

Exceptional Memory

Let's return now to the concept of internal memory images. In rare instances, such images may be so vivid that it is reasonable to say that a person has "photographic memory." A notable example was reported by Aleksandr Luria (1968) in his book *The Mind of a Mnemonist.* Luria studied a man he called Mr. S, who had practically unlimited memory for visual images. Mr. S could remember almost everything that ever happened to him with incredible accuracy. Luria tried to test Mr. S's memory by using longer and longer lists of words or numbers. However, he soon discovered that no matter how long the list, Mr. S was able to recall it without error. Mr. S could memorize, with equal ease, strings of digits, meaningless consonants, mathematical formulas, and poems in foreign languages. His memory was so powerful that he had to devise ways to *forget*—such as writing information on a piece of paper and then burning it.

Mr. S's abilities seemed fantastic to Cef-Wol, just as they might to any student of memory. However, Mr. S remembered so much that he couldn't separate important facts from trivia or facts from fantasy (Neath, 1998). For instance, if you asked him to read this chapter he might remember every word. Yet, he might also recall all the images each word made him think of and all the sights, sounds, and feelings that occurred as he was reading. Therefore, finding the answer to a specific question, writing a logical essay, or even understanding a single sentence was very difficult for him.

Few people in history have had memories like Mr. S.'s. Just the same, you probably know at least one person who has an especially good memory. Is superior memory a biological gift? Or do excellent memorizers merely make better-than-average use of normal memory capacities? Let's investigate further.

LEARNED STRATEGIES   At first, a student volunteer named Steve could remember seven digits—a typical score for a college student. Could he improve with practice? For 20 months Steve practised memorizing ever-longer lists of digits. Ultimately, he was able to memorize around 80 digits, like this sample:

92842048050842268953990190252912807999970

660657471731060108058526972602635733332135

How did Steve reach such lofty heights of memory? Basically, he worked by chunking digits into meaningful groups containing three or four digits each. Steve's avid interest in long-distance running helped greatly. For instance, to him the first three digits above represented 9 minutes and 28 seconds, a good time for a two-mile run. When running times wouldn't work, Steve used other associations, such as ages or dates, to chunk digits (Ericsson & Chase, 1982). It seems apparent that Steve's success was based on learned strategies. Indeed, by using similar memory systems, other people have trained themselves to equal Steve's feat (Bellezza, Six, & Phillips, 1992).

Psychologist Anders Ericsson believes that exceptional memory is merely a learned extension of normal memory. As evidence, he notes that Steve's short-term memory did not improve during months of practice. For example, Steve could still memorize only seven consonants. Steve's phenomenal memory for numbers grew as he figured out new ways to encode digits and store them in LTM. Steve began with a normal memory for digits. He extended his memory by diligent practice.

Compelling evidence of the importance of learning was provided by Laurent Mottron at the University of Montreal. Mottron and his colleagues have studied N. M., an autistic man in his thirties who has an amazing memory for proper names, but not for anything else. Mottron and his colleagues (1996) noted that N. M. compulsively memorizes obituary columns and phone books. He addresses people the way they are listed in the phone book, last name first. He can name all the people buried in his local cemetery in the order of plots, and all the people he shared a hospital ward with in the early 1990s. His extraordinary memory for proper names—but nothing else—reflects learning of a special kind: his obsession with people's names. Clearly, exceptional memory can be learned (Neath, 1998). However, we still have to wonder, do some people have naturally superior memories?

Memory Champions

In 1991, the first World Memory Championship was held in London, England. There, a variety of mental athletes competed to see who had the best memory. To remain in the running, each contestant had to rapidly memorize daunting amounts of information, such as long lists of unrelated words and numbers. Psychologists John Wilding and Elizabeth Valentine saw an opportunity to study exceptional memory and persuaded the contestants to take some additional memory tests. These ranged from ordinary (recall a story), to challenging (recall the telephone numbers of six different people), to diabolical (recall 48 numerals arranged in rows and columns [see ▶Figure 7.11]; recognize 14 previously seen pictures of snowflakes among 70 new photos) (Wilding & Valentine, 1994a).

Wilding and Valentine found that exceptional memorizers:

*   Use memory strategies and techniques
*   Have specialized interests and knowledge that make certain types of information easier to encode and recall
*   Have naturally superior memory abilities, often including vivid mental images

8 7 3 7 9 2 6 8
2 0 1 1 7 4 9 5
0 1 7 5 8 7 8 3
1 9 4 7 6 0 6 9
3 6 1 6 8 1 5 4
4 5 2 4 0 2 9 7

▶**Figure 7.11**

This number matrix is similar to the ones contestants in the World Memory Championship had to memorize. To be scored as correct, digits had to be recalled in their proper positions (Wilding & Valentine, 1994a).

The first two points confirm what we learned from Steve's acquired memory ability. Many of the contestants, for example, actively used memory strategies called *mnemonics* (nee-MON-iks). Specialized interests and knowledge also helped for some tasks. For example, one contestant, who is a mathematician, was exceedingly good at memorizing numbers (Wilding & Valentine, 1994a).

Several of the memory contestants were able to excel on tasks that prevented the use of learned strategies and techniques. This observation implies that superior memory ability can be a "gift" as well as a learned skill. Wilding and Valentine conclude that exceptional memory may be based on either natural ability or learned strategies. Usually, it requires both. In fact, most exceptional memorizers use strategies to augment their natural talents, whenever possible. Some of their strategies are described in this chapter's Psychology in Action section. Please do remember to read it.

Knowledge builder

MEASURING MEMORY AND EXCEPTIONAL MEMORY

Relate

Have you experienced the TOT state recently? Were you able to retrieve the word you were searching for? If not, what could you remember about it?

Do you prefer tests based primarily on recall or recognition? Have you observed a savings effect while relearning information you studied in the past (such as in high school)?

Can you think of things you do that are based on implicit memories? For instance, how do you know which way to turn various handles in your house, apartment, or dorm? Do you have to explicitly think, "Turn it to the right," before you act?

What kinds of information are you good at remembering? Why do you think your memory is better for those topics?

Learning Check

Unless you have a memory like Mr. S's, it might be a good idea to see if you can answer these questions before reading on.

1. Four techniques for measuring or demonstrating memory are_____ _____ _____ _____
2. Essay tests require _____ of facts or ideas.
3. As a measure of memory, a savings score is associated with
   a. recognition *b.* eidetic images *c.* relearning *d.* reconstruction
4. Tests of _____ memory are designed to reveal the influences of information that is stored but remains unconscious.
5. Children with eidetic imagery typically have no better than average long-term memory. T or F?
6. In order to perform well on tests of memory, one must be born with naturally superior memory abilities. T or F?

Critical Thinking

7. Mr. S had great difficulty remembering faces. Can you guess why?

Answers:

1. recall, recognition, relearning, priming 2. recall 3. c 4. implicit 5. T 6. F 7. Mr. S's memory was so specific that faces seemed different and unfamiliar if he saw them from a new angle or if a face had a different expression on it than when Mr. S last saw it.

▶ Forgetting—Why We, Uh, Let's See; Why We, Uh . . . Forget!

? Survey Question:
■ What causes forgetting?

Nonsense syllables
Invented three-letter words used to test learning and memory.

Curve of forgetting
A graph that shows the amount of memorized information remembered after varying lengths of time.

Why are some memories lost so quickly? For example, why is it hard to remember information a week or two after taking a test in class? Most forgetting tends to occur immediately after memorization. In a famous set of experiments, Herman Ebbinghaus (1885) tested his own memory at various times after learning. Ebbinghaus wanted to be sure he would not be swayed by prior learning, so he memorized **nonsense syllables.** These are meaningless three-letter words such as CEF, WOL, and GEX. The importance of using meaningless words is shown by the fact that, in the United States, VEL, FAB, and DUZ are no longer used on memory tests. Subjects who recognize these words as names of detergents used in the U.S. find them very easy to remember. This is another reminder that memory is improved by relating new information what you already know.

By waiting various lengths of time before testing himself, Ebbinghaus plotted a **curve of forgetting.** This graph shows the amount of information remembered after varying

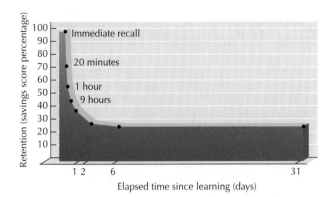

▶Figure 7.12

The curve of forgetting. This graph shows the amount remembered (measured by relearning) after varying lengths of time. Notice how rapidly forgetting occurs. The material learned was nonsense syllables. Forgetting curves for meaningful information also show early losses followed by a long gradual decline, but overall, forgetting occurs much more slowly. (After Ebbinghaus, 1885.)

Encoding failure Failure to store sufficient information to form a useful memory.

Memory traces Physical changes in nerve cells or brain activity that take place when memories are stored.

Memory decay The fading or weakening of memories assumed to occur when memory traces become weaker.

---

lengths of time (see ▶Figure 7.12). Because Ebbinghaus took great care in his work, his findings remain valid today. Notice that forgetting is rapid at first and is then followed by a slow decline.

As a student, you should note that forgetting is minimized by a short delay between studying and taking a test. However, this is no reason for cramming. If you cram, you don't have to remember for very long, but you may not learn enough in the first place. If you use short, daily study sessions and review intensely before a test, you will get the benefit of good preparation and a minimum time lapse.

The Ebbinghaus curve shows less than 30 percent remembered only two days after learning. Is forgetting really that rapid? No, not always. Meaningful information is not lost nearly as quickly as nonsense syllables. For example, it took students who completed a university psychology course about three years to forget 30 percent of the facts they had learned. After that, little more forgetting occurred (Conway, Cohen, & Stanhope, 1992). In fact, as learning grows stronger, some knowledge may become nearly permanent. Semantic memories and implicit memories (both mentioned earlier) appear to be very lasting (Bower, 1990).

"I'll never forget old, old . . . oh, what's his name?" Forgetting is both frustrating and embarrassing. Why do we forget? The Ebbinghaus curve gives a general picture of forgetting, but it doesn't explain it. To understand forgetting, we must search further.

Encoding Failure

The Queen's head appears on one side of all Canadian coins, but what appears on the other side? Which animal appears on a quarter? What is written at the top of a penny? A picture of a penny appears on the next page (▶Figure 7.13). Before you look at it, try to draw one and label it correctly. In an interesting experiment, Ray Nickerson and Marilyn Adams (1979) asked a large group of students to draw a penny. Few could. Well then, could the students at least recognize a drawing of a real penny among fakes? Again, few could. Twenty years later, Mike Rinck of the Technical University of Dresden in Germany asked students to remember the layout of numbers on calculators and push-button telephones, and found both recall and recognition were very poor (Rinck, 1999).

The most obvious reason for forgetting is also the most commonly overlooked. In many cases, we "forget" because of **encoding failure.** That is, a memory was never formed in the first place. Obviously, few of us ever encode the details of a penny. If you are bothered by frequent forgetting, it is wise to ask yourself, "Have I been storing the information in the first place?" If you tend to be absent-minded, encoding failure is probably to blame (Schachter, 1999). (Encoding failures also affect our memories of people. See "College Students—They're All Alike!" on page 264.)

When 140 college professors were asked what strategies they use to improve their memory, the favourite technique was to *write things down* (Park, Smith, & Cavanaugh, 1990). Making notes or using a hand-held personal organizer ensures that information will not be lost from short-term memory before you can review it and store it more permanently.

Decay

One view of forgetting holds that **memory traces** (changes in nerve cells or brain activity) **decay** (fade or weaken) over time. Decay appears to be a factor in the loss of sensory memories. Such fading also applies to short-term memory. Information stored in STM seems to initiate a brief flurry of activity in the brain that quickly dies out. Short-term memory therefore operates like a "leaky bucket": New information constantly pours in, but it rapidly fades away and is replaced by still newer information. Let's say that you

HUMAN DIVERSITY   College Students—They're All Alike!

Imagine yourself in this situation: As you are walking on campus, a young man who looks like a college student approaches you and asks for directions. While you are talking, two workers carrying a door pass between you and the young man. While your view is blocked by the door, another man takes the place of the first. Now you are facing a different person than the one who was there just seconds earlier. If this happened to you, do you think you would notice the change? Remarkably, only half of the people tested in this way noticed the switch (Simons & Levin, 1998)!

How could anyone fail to notice that one stranger had been replaced by another? The people who didn't remember the first man were all older adults. College students weren't fooled by the switch. The authors of this study, Daniel Simons and Daniel Levin, believe that older adults encoded the first man in very general terms as a "college student." As a result, that's all they remembered about

him. Because his replacement also looked like a college student, they thought he was the same person (Simons & Levin, 1998).

Actually, such memory failures are not as surprising as they might seem. We all tend to categorize strangers according to the groups they belong to: Is the person young or old, male or female, a member of my ethnic group or another? This tendency to encode only general information about strangers is one reason why eyewitnesses are better at identifying members of their own ethnic group than they are at identifying people from other groups (Kassin, Ellsworth, & Smith, 1989). It may seem harsh to say so, but when social contacts are brief or superficial, people really do act like members of other ethnic groups "all look alike." Of course, this bias disappears when we get to know specific members of other groups. Then, we encode more details about each person, which allows us to recognize and appreciate them as individuals.

▶ **Figure 7.13**

A Canadian penny. Most people would not be able to draw it accurately, because we identify it by size and colour rather than by the images and the print.

Disuse Theory that memory traces weaken when memories are not periodically used or retrieved.

Memory cue Any stimulus associated with a particular memory. Memory cues usually enhance retrieval.

are trying to remember a short list of letters, numbers, or words after seeing or hearing them once. If it takes you more than four to six seconds to repeat the list, you will forget some of the items (Dosher & Ma, 1998).

DISUSE   Is it possible that the decay of memory traces also explains long-term forgetting? That is, could long-term memory traces fade from **disuse** (infrequent retrieval) and eventually become too weak to retrieve? There is evidence that memories not retrieved and "used" or rehearsed become weaker over time (Schachter, 1999). However, disuse alone cannot fully explain forgetting.

Disuse doesn't seem to account for our ability to recover seemingly forgotten memories through relearning and priming. It also fails to explain why some unused memories fade, while others are carried for life. A third contradiction will be recognized by anyone who has spent time with the elderly. People growing senile may become so forgetful that they can't remember what happened a week ago. Yet at the same time your Uncle Oscar's recent memories are fading, he may have vivid memories of trivial and long-forgotten events from the past. "Why, I remember it as clearly as if it were yesterday," he will say, forgetting that the story he is about to tell is one he told earlier the same day. In short, disuse offers no more than a partial explanation of long-term forgetting.

If decay and disuse don't fully explain forgetting, what does? Let's briefly consider some additional possibilities.

Cue-Dependent Forgetting

Often, memories appear to be *available,* but not *accessible.* An example is having an answer on the "tip of your tongue." You know the answer is there, but it remains just "out of reach." This suggests that many memories are "forgotten" because **memory cues** (stimuli associated with a memory) are missing when the time comes to retrieve information. For example, if you were asked, "What were you doing on Monday afternoon of the third week in September two years ago?" your reply might be, "Come on. How should I know?" However, if you were reminded, "That was the day the courthouse burned" or "That was the day Stacy had her automobile accident," you might remember immediately.

The presence of appropriate cues almost always enhances memory. In theory, for instance, memory will be best if you study in the same room where you will be tested.

External cues like those found in a photograph, a scrapbook, or during a walk through an old neighbourhood often aid recall of seemingly lost memories. For many U.S. veterans, finding a familiar name engraved in the Vietnam Veterans Memorial unleashes a flood of memories.

Since this is often impossible, try to visualize the room where you will be tested, while you are studying. Doing so can enhance memory later (Jerabek & Standing, 1992).

STATE-DEPENDENT LEARNING   Have you heard the story about the drunk who misplaced his wallet and had to get drunk again to find it? Although this tale is often told as a joke, it is not too farfetched. The bodily state that exists during learning can be a strong cue for later memory, an effect known as **state-dependent learning** (Neath, 1998). Being very thirsty, for instance, might prompt you to remember events that took place on another occasion when you were thirsty. Because of such effects, information learned under the influence of a drug is best remembered when the drugged state occurs again (Bruins Slot & Colpaert, 1999).

A similar effect applies to emotional states (Eich, 1995). For instance, Gordon Bower (1981) found that people who learned a list of words while in a happy mood recalled them better when they were again happy. People who learned while they felt sad remembered best when they were sad (see ▶ Figure 7.14). Similarly, if you are in a happy mood you are more likely to remember recent happy events (Salovey & Singer, 1989). If you are in a bad mood you will tend to have unpleasant memories (Eich, Rachman, & Lopatka, 1990). Such links between emotional cues and memory could explain why couples who quarrel often end up remembering—and rehashing—old arguments.

Interference

Further insight into forgetting comes from a classic experiment in which college students learned lists of nonsense syllables. After studying, students in one group slept for eight hours and were then tested for memory of the lists. A second group remained awake for eight hours and went about business as usual. When members of the second group were tested, they remembered less than the group that slept (see ▶ Figure 7.15). This difference is based on the fact that new learning can interfere with previous learning. **Interference** refers to the tendency for new memories to impair retrieval of older memories (and the reverse). It seems to apply to both short-term and long-term memory.

It is not completely clear if new memories alter existing memory traces or if they make it harder to "locate" (retrieve) earlier memories. In any case, there is no doubt that interference is a major cause of forgetting (Neath, 1998). College students who memorized 20 lists of words (one list each day) were able to recall only 15 percent of the last

State-dependent learning Memory influenced by one's bodily state at the time of learning and at the time of retrieval. Improved memory occurs when the bodily states match.

Interference The tendency for new memories to impair retrieval of older memories, and the reverse.

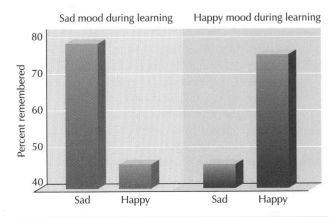

▶Figure 7.14

The effect of mood on memory. Subjects best remembered a list of words when their mood during testing was the same as their mood was when they learned the list. (Adapted from Bower, 1981.)

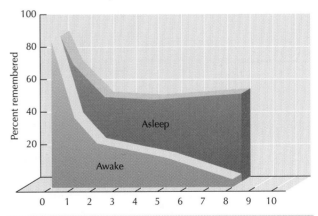

▶Figure 7.15

The amount of forgetting after a period of sleep or of being awake. Notice that sleep causes less memory loss than activity that occurs while one is awake. (After Jenkins & Dallenbach, 1924.)

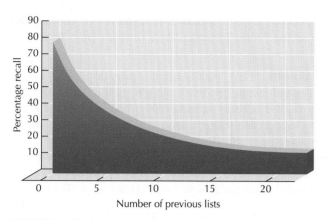

▶**Figure 7.16**

Effects of interference on memory. A graph of the approximate relationship between number of different word lists memorized and percentage of words recalled. (Adapted from Underwood, 1957.)

Retroactive interference
The tendency for new memories to interfere with the retrieval of old memories.

Proactive interference
The tendency for old memories to interfere with the retrieval of newer memories.

list. Students who learned only one list remembered 80 percent (Underwood, 1957) (see ▶Figure 7.16).

ORDER EFFECTS The sleeping college students remembered more because retroactive (RET-ro-AK-tiv) interference was held to a minimum. **Retroactive interference** refers to the tendency for new learning to impair retrieval of old learning. Avoiding new learning prevents retroactive interference. Of course, this doesn't mean you need to hide in a closet after you study for a test. However, you should avoid studying other subjects until after the exam. Sleeping after studying can help you retain memories, and reading, writing, or even watching TV may cause interference.

Retroactive interference is easily demonstrated in the laboratory by this arrangement:

Experimental group:	Learn A	Learn B	Test A
Control group:	Learn A	Rest	Test A

Imagine yourself as a member of the experimental group. In task A, you learn a list of telephone numbers. In task B, you learn a list of social insurance numbers. How do you score on a test of task A (the telephone numbers)? If you do not remember as much as the control group that learns only task A, then retroactive interference has occurred. The second thing learned has interfered with memory of the first thing learned; the interference went "backward," or was "retroactive" (see ▶Figure 7.17).

Proactive (pro-AK-tiv) interference is a second basic source of forgetting. **Proactive interference** occurs when prior learning impairs the retrieval of later learning. A test for proactive interference would take this form:

Experimental group:	Learn A	Learn B	Test B
Control group:	Rest	Learn B	Test B

If the experimental group remembers less than the control group on a test of task B, then learning task A has interfered with memory of task B.

Then proactive interference goes "forward"? Yes. For instance, if you cram for a psychology exam and then later the same night cram for a history exam, your memory for the second subject studied (history) will be less accurate than if you had studied only history. (Because of retroactive interference, your memory for psychology would probably also suffer.) The greater the similarity in the two subjects studied, the more interference takes place. The moral, of course, is don't procrastinate in preparing for exams.

Interestingly, N. M., the autistic man who remembers proper names, was completely immune to retroactive interference when asked to remember lists of names, and showed only very slight proactive interference (Mottron et al., 1998). But that may not be a good thing. Mottron and his colleagues suggest that N. M. may be immune to interference effects because his memory is not organized in the usual way, with

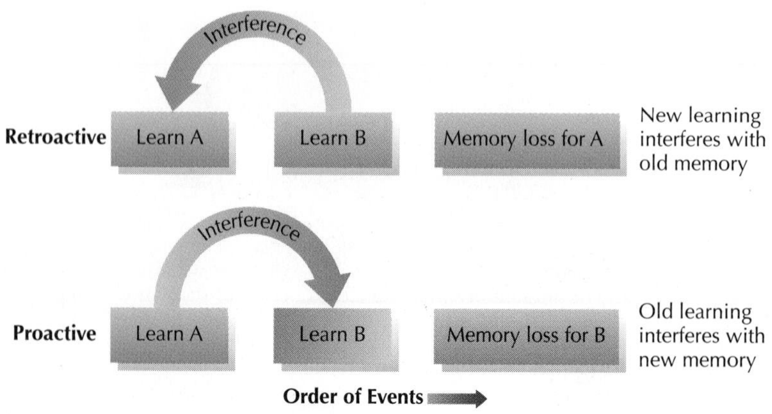

▶**Figure 7.17**

Retroactive and proactive interference. Retroactive interference works backward (new material interferes with retrieval of old). Proactive interference works forward (old material interferes with retrieval of new).

connections among related ideas. That would make understanding the world much more difficult—a high price to pay for avoiding interference.

Repression and Suppression

Survey Question:
■ How accurate are everyday memories?

Repression Unconsciously pushing unwanted memories out of awareness.

Suppression A conscious effort to put something out of mind or to keep it from awareness.

Take a moment and scan over the events of the last few years of your life. What kinds of things most easily come to mind? Many people remember happy, positive events better than disappointments and irritations (Linton, 1979). A clinical psychologist would call this tendency **repression,** or motivated forgetting. Through repression, painful, threatening, or embarrassing memories are held out of consciousness. An example is provided by soldiers who have repressed some of the horrors they saw during combat (Karon & Widener, 1997, 1998).

The forgetting of past failures, upsetting childhood events, the names of people you dislike, or appointments you don't want to keep may reveal repression. People prone to repression tend to be hypersensitive to emotional events. As a result, they use repression to protect themselves from threatening thoughts (Mendolia, Moore, & Tesser, 1996).

It's possible that some adults who were sexually abused as children have repressed memories of their mistreatment. It's also possible that such memories may surface during psychotherapy or other circumstances. However, as discussed in ▶Figure 7.18, caution is required anytime accusations are made on the basis of seemingly "recovered" memories. See "The Recovered Memory/False Memory Debate" on page 268 for further cautions.

If I try to forget a test I failed, am I repressing it? No. Repression can be distinguished from **suppression,** an active, conscious attempt to put something out of mind. By not thinking about the test, you have merely suppressed a memory. If you choose to, you can remember the test. Clinicians consider true repression an unconscious event. When a memory is repressed we are unaware that forgetting has even occurred. (See Chapter 11 for more information on repression.)

▶Figure 7.18

In what appeared to be an extreme case of repression, Eileen Franklin testified in court in 1990 that her father, George Franklin, abducted, raped, and killed eight-year-old Susan Nason in 1969. Eileen testified that the memory surfaced one day as she looked into the eyes of her own young daughter. Her father was convicted solely on the basis of her "repressed" memory. However, in 1996, the conviction was overturned when DNA tests cleared her father of a second murder she also accused him of committing. As the Franklin case illustrates, trying to separate true memories from fantasies has become a major headache for psychologists and the courts.

People who survive traumatic events, such as the attack on the World Trade Center buildings on September 11, 2001, in New York City, almost always have flashbulb memories of the event. Typically, people vividly remember where they were when the event started, what they thought as it was occurring, and how they reacted to it.

FOCUS ON RESEARCH   The Recovered Memory/False Memory Debate

Many sexually abused children develop problems that persist into adulthood. In some instances, they repress all memory of the abuse. According to some psychologists, uncovering these hidden memories can be an important step toward regaining emotional health.

While the preceding may be true, the search for repressed memories of sexual abuse has itself proved to be a problem. Cases have surfaced in which families were torn apart by accusations of sexual abuse that later turned out to be completely false.

Certainly, some memories of abuse that return to awareness are genuine and must be dealt with. However, in the absence of firm supporting evidence, there is no way to tell if a memory is real or not. No matter how real a recovered memory may seem, it could be false unless it can be verified by others, or by court or medical records.

Why would anyone have false memories about such disturbing events? Several popular books and a few misguided therapists have actively encouraged people to find repressed memories of abuse. Hypnosis, guided visualization, suggestion, age regression, and similar techniques can elicit fantasies that are mistaken for real memories. False allegations of sexual abuse create a living nightmare for the accused. There is almost no way they can prove their innocence.

Canadian researchers have been very active in this area, offering a variety of perspectives. At the University of Victoria, Stephen Lindsay and his colleagues have argued that children are not especially susceptible to suggestion. In particular, when events are experienced several times, children in lab studies resist false suggestions about stable aspects of those events (Connolly & Lindsay, 2001). If a child was repeatedly sexually abused, this finding would suggest that the child's recall would be less susceptible to manipulation.

On the other side of the country, and the debate, Maggie Bruck of McGill University and Stephen Ceci of Cornell have shown that children, particularly preschoolers, are susceptible to suggestion under some circumstances. They are more likely to accept as real, and to subsequently report, a false suggestion when the interviewer is biased (Ceci & Bruck, 1995), when asked specific rather than open-ended questions (Ceci & Bruck, 1993), and when false events are suggested repeatedly (Bruck, Hembrooke, & Ceci, 1997).

To summarize, some memories of abuse that return to awareness appear to be genuine. However, there is little doubt that some "recovered" memories are pure fantasy. Researchers have identified many instances in which "recovered" traumatic memories were absolutely false.

A few years ago, an "epidemic" of recovered memories took place. It subsided as psychologists developed new guidelines for therapists to minimize the risk of influencing clients' memories. Today, both recovered memories and false accusations are relatively uncommon. Nevertheless, false claims about childhood abuse still occasionally make the news. The saddest thing about such claims is that they deaden public sensitivity to actual abuse. Childhood sexual abuse is widespread. Awareness of its existence must not be repressed.

(Sources: Byrd, 1994; Courtois, 1999; Goldstein, 1997; Lindsay, 1998; Loftus, 1994; Palm & Gibson, 1998; Pendergast, 1995; Reisner, 1996; Schacter, 1999.)

Psychologists Kenneth Bowers and Peter Farvolden believe that repression is a form of avoidance. If you have experienced a painful emotional event, you will probably avoid all thoughts associated with it. This tends to keep cues out of mind that could trigger a painful memory (Bowers & Farvolden, 1996).

Flashbulb Memories

Flashbulb memories
Memories created at times of high emotion that seem especially vivid.

Why are some traumatic events vividly remembered while others are repressed? Psychologists use the term **flashbulb memories** to describe images that seem to be frozen in memory at times of personal tragedy, accident, or other emotionally significant events (Finkenauer et al., 1998).

Depending on your age, you may have a "flashbulb" memory of the World Trade Center attack, the death of Princess Diana, the Montreal massacre, or the *Challenger* space shuttle disaster. Flashbulb memories are most often formed when an event is surprising, important, or emotional (Rubin, 1985). They are frequently associated with public tragedies, but memories of positive events may also have "flashbulb" clarity—such as Team

An *Aplysia*. The relatively simple nervous system of this sea animal allows scientists to study memory as it occurs in single nerve cells.

To summarize (and simplify greatly), the hippocampus handles memory consolidation. Once long-term memories are formed, they appear to be stored in the cortex of the brain (Gabrieli, 1998; Teng & Squire, 1999).

How are memories recorded in the cortex? Scientists are beginning to identify the exact ways in which nerve cells record information. For example, Eric Kandel and his colleagues have studied learning in the marine snail *Aplysia* (ah-PLEEZ-yah). Kandel found that learning in *Aplysia* occurs when certain nerve cells in a circuit alter the amount of transmitter chemicals they release (Kandel, 1999). According to Bryan Kolb and Ian Whishaw of Lethbridge University in Alberta, learning also alters the activity, structure, and chemistry of brain cells. Such changes determine which circuits get stronger and which become weaker. This results in a "reprogramming" of the brain that records information (Kolb & Whishaw, 1998).

Knowledge builder

FORGETTING

Relate

Which of the following concepts best explain why you have missed some answers on psychology tests: encoding failure, decay, disuse, memory cues, interference?

Do you know someone whose name you have a hard time remembering? Do you like or dislike that person? Do you think your difficulty is an instance of repression? Suppression? Interference? Encoding failure?

Have you had a flashbulb memory? How vivid is the memory today? How accurate do you think it is?

Here's a mnemonic tip: Elephants are supposed to have good memories, but a *hippo campus* is the place to go if you want to learn to consolidate memories.

Learning Check

1. According to the Ebbinghaus curve of forgetting, we forget slowly at first and then a rapid decline occurs. T or F?
2. Which explanation seems to account for the loss of short-term memories?
   a. decay *b.* disuse *c.* repression *d.* interference

3. When memories are available but not accessible, forgetting may be cue dependent. T or F?
4. When learning one thing makes it more difficult to recall another, forgetting may be caused by _____.
5. You are asked to memorize long lists of telephone numbers. You learn a new list each day for 10 days. When tested on the third list, you remember less than a person who learned only the first three lists. Your larger memory loss is probably caused by
   a. disuse *b.* retroactive interference *c.* regression *d.* proactive interference
6. Repression is thought of as a type of motivated forgetting. T or F?
7. Retrograde amnesia results when consolidation is speeded up. T or F?

Critical Thinking

8. Based on state-dependent learning, why do you think that music often strongly evokes memories?
9. You must study French, Spanish, psychology, and biology in one evening. What do you think would be the best order in which to study these subjects so as to minimize interference?
10. There may be another way to explain why flashbulb memories are so long lasting. Can you think of one?

Answers:

1. F **2.** *a* and 3. T **4.** interference **5.** *b* **6.** T **7.** F **8.** Music tends to affect the mood that a person is in, and moods tend to affect memory (Balch & Lewis, 1996). **9.** Any order that separates French from Spanish and psychology from biology would work (for instance: French, psychology, Spanish, biology). **10.** Memories of emotionally significant events may be unusually strong because such memories are rehearsed more frequently. People usually mentally review emotionally charged events many times.

► Improving Memory—Keys to the Memory Bank

While we're waiting around for the development of a memory pill, let's focus on some ways of improving your memory skills right now.

KNOWLEDGE OF RESULTS Learning proceeds best when feedback, or **knowledge of results,** allows you to check your progress. Feedback can help you identify ideas that need extra practice. In addition, knowing that you have remembered or answered correctly is rewarding. A prime way to provide feedback for yourself while studying is *recitation.*

Knowledge of results
During learning, feedback about the correctness of responses or other aspects of performance.

Recitation As a memory aid, repeating aloud information one wishes to retain.

Rehearsal Silently repeating or mentally reviewing information to improve memory.

Whole learning Studying an entire package of information (such as a complete poem) at once.

Part learning Separately studying subparts of a larger body of information (such as sections of a textbook chapter).

Progressive part method Breaking information into a series of short units and then learning increasingly longer groups of units.

Serial position effect The tendency for the greatest number of memory errors to occur in the middle portion of a list.

RECITATION If you are going to remember something, eventually you will have to retrieve it. **Recitation** refers to summarizing aloud while you are learning. Recitation forces you to practise retrieving information. When you are reading a text, you should stop frequently and try to remember what you have just read by restating it in your own words. In one experiment, the best memory score was earned by a group of students who spent 80 percent of their time reciting and only 20 percent reading (Gates, 1958). Maybe students who talk to themselves aren't crazy after all.

REHEARSAL The more you **rehearse** (mentally review) information as you read, the better you will remember it. But remember that maintenance rehearsal alone is not very effective. Elaborative rehearsal, in which you look for connections to existing knowledge, is far better. Thinking about facts helps link them together in memory. To learn college-level information, you must make active use of rehearsal strategies (Nist, Sharman, & Holschuh, 1996).

SELECTION The Dutch scholar Erasmus said that a good memory should be like a fish net: It should keep all the big fish and let the little ones escape. If you boil down the paragraphs in most textbooks to one or two important terms or ideas, your memory chores will be more manageable. Practise very selective marking in your texts and use marginal notes to further summarize ideas. Most students mark their texts too much instead of too little. If everything is underlined, you haven't been selective. And, very likely, you didn't pay much attention in the first place (Peterson, 1992).

ORGANIZATION Assume that you must memorize the following list of words: north, man, red, spring, woman, east, autumn, yellow, summer, boy, blue, west, winter, girl, green, south. This rather difficult list could be reorganized into chunks as follows: north-east-south-west, spring-summer-autumn-winter, red-yellow-green-blue, man-woman-boy-girl. This simple reordering made the second list much easier to learn when college students were tested on both lists (Deese & Hulse, 1967). Organizing class notes and summarizing chapters can be quite helpful (Dickinson & O'Connell, 1990). You may even want to summarize your summaries, so that the overall network of ideas becomes clearer and simpler. Summaries improve memory by encouraging better encoding of information (Hadwin, Kirby, & Woodhouse, 1999).

WHOLE VERSUS PART LEARNING If you have to memorize a speech, is it better to try to learn it from beginning to end? Or in smaller parts like paragraphs? Generally it is better to practise whole packages of information rather than smaller parts (**whole learning**). This is especially true for fairly short, organized information. An exception is that learning parts may be better for extremely long, complicated information. In **part learning,** subparts of a larger body of information are studied (such as sections of a textbook chapter). To decide which approach to use, remember to study the *largest meaningful amount of information* you can at one time.

For very long or complex material, try the **progressive part method,** by breaking a learning task into a series of short sections. At first, you study part A until it is mastered. Next, you study parts A and B; then A, B, and C; and so forth. This is a good way to learn the lines of a play, a long piece of music, or a poem (Ash & Holding, 1990). After the material is learned, you should also practise by starting at points other than A (at C, D, or B, for example). This will help you avoid getting "lost" or going blank in the middle of a performance.

SERIAL POSITION Whenever you must learn something in *order,* be aware of the **serial position effect.** As you will recall, this is the tendency to make the most errors in remembering the middle of a list. If you are introduced to a long line of people, the names you are likely to forget will be those in the middle, so you should make an extra effort to attend to them. You should also give extra practice to the middle of a list, poem, or speech. Try to break long lists of information into short sublists, and make the middle sublists the shortest of all.

Memory cue Any stimulus associated with a particular memory. Memory cues usually enhance retrieval.

Overlearning Study or learning that continues after initial mastery of skills or information.

Spaced practice A practice schedule that alternates study periods with brief rests.

Massed practice A practice schedule in which studying continues for long periods, without interruption.

CUES The best **memory cues** (stimuli that aid retrieval) are those that were present during encoding (Reed, 1996). For example, students in one study had the daunting task of trying to recall a list of 600 words. As they read the list (which they did not know they would be tested on), the students gave three other words closely related in meaning to each listed word. In a test given later, the words each student supplied were used as cues to jog memory. The students recalled an astounding 90 percent of the original word list (Mantyla, 1986).

The preceding example shows, once again, that it often helps to *elaborate* information as you learn. When you study, try to use new names, ideas, or terms in several sentences. Also, form images that include the new information, and relate it to knowledge you already have (Pressley et al., 1988). Your goal should be to knit meaningful cues into your memory code to help you retrieve information when you need it. Actors can remember large amounts of complex information for many months, even when learning new roles in between. During testing, they remember their lines best when they are allowed to move and gesture as they would when performing. Apparently their movements supply cues that aid recall (Noice & Noice, 1999).

OVERLEARNING Numerous studies have shown that memory is greatly improved when you **overlearn.** That is, when study is continued beyond bare mastery. After you have learned material well enough to remember it once without error, you should continue studying. Overlearning is your best insurance against going blank on a test because of being nervous.

SPACED PRACTICE To keep boredom and fatigue to a minimum, try alternating short study sessions with brief rest periods. This pattern, called **spaced practice,** is generally superior to **massed practice,** in which little or no rest is given between learning sessions. By improving attention and consolidation, three 20-minute study sessions can produce more learning than one hour of continuous study. There's an old joke that goes, "How do you get to Carnegie Hall?" The answer is, "Practise, practise, practise." A better answer would be "Practise, wait awhile, practise, wait awhile, practise" (Neath, 1998).

Perhaps the best way to make use of spaced practice is to *schedule* your time. To make an effective schedule, designate times during the week before, after, and between classes when you will study particular subjects. Then treat these times just as if they were classes you had to attend.

SLEEP Remember that sleeping after study reduces interference. However, unless you are a "night person," late evening may not be a very efficient time for you to study. Also, you obviously can't sleep after every study session or study everything just before you sleep. That's why your study schedule (see the "Spaced Practice" section above) should include ample breaks between subjects. Using your breaks and free time in a schedule is as important as living up to your study periods.

HUNGER People who are hungry almost always score lower on memory tests. So mother was right, it's a good idea to make sure you've had a good breakfast or lunch before you take tests at school (Martin & Benton, 1999; Smith, Clark, & Gallagher, 1999).

EXTEND HOW LONG YOU REMEMBER When you are learning new information, test yourself repeatedly. As you do, gradually lengthen the amount of time that passes before you test yourself again. For example, if you are studying German words on flashcards, look at the first card and then move it a few cards back in the stack. Do the same with the next few cards. When you get to the first "old" card, test yourself on it and check the answer. Then move it farther back in the stack. Do the same with other "old" cards as they come up. When "old" cards come up for the third time, put them clear to the back of the stack (Cull, Shaughnessy, & Zechmeister, 1996).

REVIEW If you have spaced your practice and overlearned, review will be like icing on your study cake. Reviewing shortly before an exam cuts down the time during which you must remember details that may be important for the test. When reviewing, hold the amount of new information you try to memorize to a minimum. It may be realistic to take what you have actually learned and add a little more to it at the last minute by cramming. But remember that more than a little new learning may interfere with what you already know.

USING A STRATEGY TO AID RECALL   Successful recall is usually the result of a planned search of memory (Reed, 1996). For example, one study found that students were most likely to recall names that eluded them if they made use of partial information (Reed & Bruce, 1982). The students were trying to answer questions such as, "He is best remembered as the scarecrow in the Judy Garland movie *The Wizard of Oz.*" (The answer is Ray Bolger.) Partial information that helped students remember included impressions about the length of the name, letter sounds within the name, similar names, and related information (such as the names of other characters in the movie). A similar helpful strategy is to go through the alphabet, trying each letter as the first sound of a name or word you are seeking.

Using a variety of cues, even partial ones, opens more paths to a memory. "Memory Detectives" gives further hints for recapturing context and jogging memories. After that, the Psychology in Action section covers some of the most powerful memory techniques of all.

Cognitive interview
Use of various cues and strategies to improve the memory of eyewitnesses.

USING PSYCHOLOGY   Memory Detectives

You may not think of yourself as a "memory detective," but active probing often helps improve recall. A case in point is the **cognitive interview,** a technique used to jog the memory of eyewitnesses. The cognitive interview was created by R. Edward Geiselman and Ron Fisher to help police detectives. When used properly, it produces 35 percent more correct information than standard questioning (Geiselman et al., 1986). This improvement comes without adding to the number of false memories elicited, as occurs with hypnosis (Kebbell & Wagstaff, 1998).

By following four simple steps, you can apply cognitive principles to your own memory. The next time you are searching for a "lost" memory—one that you know is in there somewhere—try the following search strategies.

1. Say or write down everything you can remember that relates to the information you are seeking. Don't worry about how trivial any of it seems; each bit of information you remember can serve as a cue to bring back others.

2. Try to recall events or information in different orders. Let your memories flow out backward or out of order, or start with whatever impressed you the most.

3. Recall from different viewpoints. Review events by mentally standing in a different place. Or try to view information as another person would remember it. When taking a test, for instance, ask yourself what other students or your professor would remember about the topic.

4. Mentally put yourself back in the situation where you learned the information. Try to mentally re-create the learning environment or relive the event. As you do, include sounds, smells, details of weather, nearby objects, other people present, what you said or thought, and how you felt as you learned the information (Fisher & Geiselman, 1987).

These strategies help re-create the context in which information was learned, and they provide multiple memory cues. If you think of remembering as a sort of "treasure hunt," you might even learn to enjoy the detective work.

Some police detectives, following the advice of psychologists, re-create crime scenes to help witnesses remember what they saw. Typically, people return to the scene at the time of day the crime occurred. They are also asked to wear the same clothing they wore and go through the same motions as they did before the crime. With so many memory cues available, witnesses sometimes remember key items of information they hadn't recalled before.

A LOOK AHEAD Psychologists still have much to learn about the nature of memory and how to improve it. For now, one thing stands out clearly: People who have good memories excel at organizing information and making it meaningful. With this in mind, the Psychology in Action discussion for this chapter tells how you can combine organization and meaning into a powerful method for improving memory.

Knowledge builder

IMPROVING MEMORY

Relate

 Return to the topic headings in the preceding pages that list techniques for improving memory. Place a check mark next to those that you have used recently. Review any you didn't mark and think of a specific example of how you could use each technique at school, at home, or at work.

Learning Check

1. To improve memory, it is reasonable to spend as much or more time reciting as reading. T or F?
2. Organizing information while studying has little effect on memory because long-term memory is already highly organized. T or F?

3. The progressive part method of study is best suited to long and complex learning tasks. T or F?
4. Sleeping immediately after studying is highly disruptive to the consolidation of memories. T or F?
5. As new information is encoded and rehearsed, it is helpful to elaborate on its meaning and connect it to other information. T or F?

Critical Thinking

6. What advantages would there be to taking notes as you read a textbook, as opposed to underlining words in the text?

Answers:

1. T 2. F 3. T 4. F 5. T 6. Note-taking is a form of recitation; it encourages elaborative rehearsal and facilitates the organization and selection of important ideas. In addition, your notes can be used for review.

MNEMONICS—

MEMORY MAGIC

Survey Question:
- How can memory be improved?

Mnemonic Any kind of memory system or aid.

Some stage performers use memory as part of their acts. Do they have eidetic imagery? Various "memory experts" entertain by memorizing the names of everyone at a banquet, the order of all the cards in a deck, long lists of words, or other seemingly impossible amounts of information. Such feats may seem like magic, but if they are, you can have a magic memory too. These tricks are performed through the use of *mnemonics* (Wilding & Valentine, 1994b). A **mnemonic** is any kind of memory system or aid. In some cases, mnemonic strategies increase recall 10-fold (Patten, 1990).

Some mnemonic systems are so common that almost everyone knows them. If you are trying to remember how many days there are in a month, you may find the answer by reciting, "Thirty days hath September . . ." Physics teachers often help students remember the colours of the spectrum by giving them the mnemonic "Roy G. Biv": **R**ed, **O**range, **Y**ellow, **G**reen, **B**lue, **I**ndigo, **V**iolet. The budding sailor who has trouble telling port from starboard may remember that port and left both have four letters or may remind herself, "I *left* port." And what beginning musician hasn't remembered the notes represented by the lines and spaces of the musical staff by learning "F–A–C–E" and "**E**very **G**ood **B**oy **D**oes **F**ine"?

Mnemonic techniques are ways to avoid rote learning (learning by simple repetition). The superiority of mnemonic learning as opposed to rote learning has been demonstrated many times. For example, Bower (1973) asked college students to study five different lists of 20 unrelated words. At the end of a short study session, subjects tried to recall all 100 items. People using mnemonics remembered an average of 72 items, whereas members of a control group using rote learning remembered an average of 28.

Stage performers rarely have naturally superior memories. Instead, they make extensive use of memory systems to perform their feats (Wilding & Valentine, 1994b). Few of these systems are of practical value to you as a student, but the principles underlying mnemonics are. By practising mnemonics you should be able to greatly improve your memory with little effort (Dretzke & Levin, 1996).

Here, then, are the basic principles of mnemonics.

1. *Use mental pictures.* Visual pictures, or images, are generally easier to remember than words. Turning information into mental pictures is therefore very helpful. Make these images as vivid as possible (Campos & Perez, 1997).
2. *Make things meaningful.* Transferring information from short-term to long-term memory is aided by making it meaningful. If you encounter technical terms that have little or no immediate meaning for you, give them meaning, even if you have to stretch the term to do so. (This point is clarified by the examples following this list.)
3. *Make information familiar.* Connect it to what you already know. Another way to get information into long-term memory is to connect it to information already stored there. If some facts or ideas in a chapter seem to stay in your memory easily, associate other more difficult facts with them.
4. *Form bizarre, unusual, or exaggerated mental associations.* Forming images that make sense is better in most situations. However, when associating two ideas, terms, or especially mental images, you may find that the more outrageous and exaggerated the association, the more likely you are to remember. Bizarre images make stored information more distinctive and therefore easier to retrieve (Worthen & Marshall, 1996). Imagine, for example, that you have just been introduced to Mr. Rehkop. To remember his name, you could picture him wearing a police uniform. Then replace his nose with a ray gun. This bizarre image will provide two hints when you want to remember Mr. Rehkop's name: *ray* and *cop* (Carney, Levin, & Stackhouse, 1997).

Bizarre images mainly help improve immediate memory, and they work best for fairly simple information (Robinson-Riegler & McDaniel, 1994). Nevertheless, they can be a first step toward learning.

Keyword method As an aid to memory, using a familiar word or image to link two items.

▶**Figure 7.20**

Exaggerated mental images can link two words or ideas in ways that aid memory. Here, the keyword method is used to link the English word *letter* with the Spanish word *carta*.

A sampling of typical applications of mnemonics should make these four points clear to you.

Example 1 Let's say you have 30 new vocabulary words to memorize in Spanish. You can proceed by rote memorization (repeat them over and over until you begin to get them), or you can learn them with little effort by using the **keyword method** (Pressley, 1987). In the keyword method, a familiar word or image is used to link two other words or items. To remember that the word *pájaro* (pronounced PAH-hah-ro) means bird, you can link it to a "key" word in English: *Pájaro* sounds kind of like "parked car-o." Therefore, to remember that *pájaro* means bird, you might visualize a parked car jam-packed full of birds. Try to make this image as vivid and exaggerated as possible, with birds flapping and chirping and feathers flying everywhere. Similarly, for the word *carta* (which means "letter"), you could imagine a shopping cart filled with postal letters (see ▶Figure 7.20).

If you link similar keywords and images for the rest of the list, you may not remember them all, but you will get most without any more practice. As a matter of fact, if you have formed the *pájaro* and *carta* images just now, it is going to be almost impossible for you to see these words anytime during the next few days without remembering what they mean.

What about a year from now? How long do keyword memories last? Mnemonic memories work best in the short run. Later, they may be more fragile than conventional memories. That's why it's usually best to use mnemonics during the initial stages of learning (Carney & Levin, 1998). To create more lasting memories, you'll need to use the techniques discussed earlier in this chapter.

Example 2 Let's say you have to learn the names of all the bones and muscles in the human body for biology. You are trying to remember that the jawbone is the *mandible*. This one is easy because you can associate it to a *man nibbling,* or maybe you can picture a *man dribbling* a basketball with his jaw (make this image as ridiculous as possible). If the muscle name *latissimus dorsi* gives you trouble, familiarize it by turning it into "*the ladder misses the door, sigh.*" Then picture a ladder glued to your back where the muscle is found. Picture the ladder leading up to a small door at your shoulder. Picture the ladder missing the door. Picture the ladder sighing like an animated character in a cartoon.

This seems like more to remember, not less; and it seems like it would cause you to misspell things. Mnemonics are not a complete substitute for normal memory; they are an aid to normal memory. Mnemonics are not likely to be helpful unless you make extensive use of images (Willoughby et al., 1997). Your mental pictures will come back to you easily. As for misspellings, mnemonics can be thought of as a built-in hint in your memory. Often, when taking a test, you will find that the slightest hint is all you need to remember correctly. A mnemonic image is like having someone leaning over your shoulder who says, "Psst, the name of that muscle sounds like 'ladder misses the door, sigh.'" If misspelling continues to be a problem, try to create memory aids for spelling, too.

Here are two more examples to help you appreciate the flexibility of a mnemonic approach to studying.

Example 3 Your art history teacher expects you to be able to name the artist when you are shown slides as part of exams. You have seen many of the slides only once before in class. How will you remember them? As the slides are shown in class, make each artist's name into an object or image. Then picture the object in the paintings done by the artist. For example, you can picture van Gogh as a *van* (automobile) *going* through the middle of each van Gogh painting. Picture the van running over things and knocking things over. Or, if you remember that van Gogh cut off his ear, picture a giant bloody ear in each of his paintings.

Example 4 If you have trouble remembering history, try to avoid thinking of it as something from the dim past. Picture each historical

Mnemonics can be an aid in preparing for tests. However, because mnemonics help most in the initial stages of storing information, it is important to follow through with other elaborative learning strategies.

personality as a person you know right now (a friend, teacher, parent, and so on). Then picture these people doing whatever the historical figures did. Also, try visualizing battles or other events as if they were happening in your town or make parks and schools into countries. Use your imagination.

How can mnemonics help you remember things in order? Here are three techniques that are useful.

1. *Form a chain.* To remember lists of ideas, objects, or words in order, try forming an exaggerated association (mental image) connecting the first item to the second, then the second to the third, and so on. To remember the following short list in order—elephant, doorknob, string, watch, rifle, oranges—picture a full-sized *elephant* balanced on a *doorknob* playing with a *string* tied to him. Picture a *watch* tied to the string, and a *rifle* shooting *oranges* at the watch. This technique can be used quite successfully for lists of 20 or more items. In a test, people who used a linking mnemonic did much better at remembering lists of 15 and 22 errands (Higbee et al., 1990). Try it next time you go shopping and leave your list at home.

2. *Take a mental walk.* Ancient Greek orators had an interesting way to remember ideas in order when giving a speech. Their method was to take a mental walk along a familiar path. As they did, they associated topics with the images of statues found along the walk. You can do the same thing by "placing" objects or ideas along the way as you mentally take a familiar walk (Neath, 1998).

3. *Use a system.* Many times, the first letters or syllables of words or ideas can be formed into another word that will serve as a reminder of order. "Roy G. Biv" is an example. As an alternative, learn the following: 1 is a bun, 2 is a shoe, 3 is a tree, 4 is a door, 5 is a hive, 6 is sticks, 7 is heaven, 8 is a gate, 9 is a line, 10 is a hen. To remember a list in order, form an image associating bun with the first item on your list. For example, if the first item is *frog*, picture a "frog-burger" on a bun to remember it. Then, associate shoe with the second item, and so on.

If you have never used mnemonics, you may still be skeptical, but give this approach a fair trial. Most people find they can greatly extend their memory through the use of mnemonics. But remember, like most things worthwhile, remembering takes effort.

Knowledge builder

MNEMONICS

Relate

 As an exercise, see if you can create mnemonics for the words *icon, implicit memory,* and *mnemonic.* The best mnemonics are your own, but here are some examples to help you get started. An icon is a visual image: Picture an *eye* in a *can* to remember that icons store visual information. Implicit memories are "hidden": Picture an *imp* hiding in memory. A mnemonic is a memory aid: Imagine writing a phone number on your knee to remember it. Imagine your *knee moaning,* "*Ick,* you shouldn't write on me."

Now, go through the glossary items in this chapter and make up mnemonics for any terms you have difficulty remembering.

Learning Check

1. Memory systems and aids are referred to as

_____.

2. Which of the following is least likely to improve memory?
   a. using exaggerated mental images
   b. forming a chain of associations
   c. turning visual information into verbal information
   d. associating new information to information that is already known or familiar

3. Bizarre images make stored information more distinctive and therefore easier to retrieve. T or F?

4. Bower's 1973 study showed that, in general, mnemonics improve memory only for related words or ideas. T or F?

Critical Thinking

5. How are elaborative rehearsal and mnemonics alike?

Answers:
1. mnemonics 2. c 3. T 4. F 5. Both attempt to relate new information to information stored in LTM that is familiar or already easy to retrieve.

Psychologist's Journal

EPILOGUE

Tatiana Cooley recently won a national memory contest held in New York. To win, she had to memorize long lists of words and numbers, the order of the cards in a shuffled deck, a 54-line poem, and 100 names and faces. Tatiana thinks that memorization is fun. You might expect that she would also be good at everyday memory chores. On the contrary, Tatiana describes herself as "incredibly absent-minded." When asked how many brothers and sisters she has, she replies, "Six—er, seven—er, six." The year she graduated from high school? She pauses for a several seconds: "1990." The elementary school grade she was in when she won a regional spelling bee? She can't remember. Ever fearful of forgetting, Tatiana keeps a daily to-do list and surrounds herself with a thicket of Post-it notes (Levinson, 1999).

What can we learn about memory from Tatiana? First, we should all be more tolerant of occasional memory lapses. Even memory champions have less than perfect memories! As we have seen throughout this chapter, memory is not like a tape recorder or a video camera. Information is frequently lost, and memories change as they are stored and retrieved. This can be frustrating at times, but it's also a good thing. The flexibility of human memory allows us to focus on what's important and meaningful, even though it also contributes to some inaccuracies. A person with total recall would probably be very literal, like a computer. If you type the name of a computer file and leave out one letter, a computer will essentially say, "I'm sorry, I've never heard of that file." A person would say, "That's misspelled, but I think I remember where it is."

Tatiana's success as a "memory athlete" also suggests that making full use of memory requires effort and practice. With that in mind, here are some parting words from our fictional companion, Cef-Wol, spoken just before she departed for Gex: "I didn't appreciate memories until I began to lose them. In a very real sense, we are our memories. You must remember this!"

CHAPTER IN REVIEW

Major Points

▶ Remembering is an active process. Our memories are frequently lost, altered, revised, or distorted.

▶ The best way to remember depends, to an extent, on which memory system you are using.

▶ Remembering is not an all-or-nothing process. Even when you think you can't recall anything, some information may continue to exist in memory.

▶ Understanding how and why forgetting occurs will allow you to make better use of your memory.

▶ Some people have naturally superior memories, but everyone can learn to improve his or her memory.

▶ Memory systems (mnemonics) greatly improve immediate memory. However, conventional learning tends to create the most lasting memories.

Summary

Is There More than One Type of Memory?

• Memory is an active, computer-like system that encodes, stores, and retrieves information.

• Humans appear to have three interrelated memory systems. These are sensory memory, short-term memory (STM, also called working memory), and long-term memory (LTM).

What Are the Features of Each Type of Memory?

• Sensory memory is exact but very brief. Through selective attention, some information is transferred to STM.

• STM has a capacity of about five to seven bits of information, but this can be extended by chunking, or recoding. Short-term memories are brief and very sensitive to interruption, or interference; however, they can be prolonged by maintenance rehearsal.

• LTM functions as a general storehouse of information, especially meaningful information. Elaborative rehearsal helps transfer information from STM to LTM. Long-term memories are relatively permanent, or lasting. LTM seems to have an almost unlimited storage capacity.

• LTM is subject to constructive processing, or ongoing revision and updating. LTM is highly organized to allow retrieval of needed information. The pattern, or structure, of memory networks is the subject of current memory research.

Is There More than One Type of Long-Term Memory?

- Within long-term memory, declarative memories for facts differ from procedural memories for skills.
- Declarative memories may be further categorized as semantic memories or episodic memories.

How Is Memory Measured?

- The tip-of-the-tongue state shows that memory is not an all-or-nothing event. Memories may therefore be revealed by recall, recognition, relearning, or priming.
- In recall, memory proceeds without explicit cues, as in an essay exam. Recall of listed information often reveals a serial position effect (middle items on the list are most subject to errors).
- A common test of recognition is the multiple-choice question.
- In relearning, "forgotten" material is learned again, and memory is indicated by a savings score.
- Recall, recognition, and relearning mainly measure explicit memories. Other techniques, such as priming, are necessary to reveal implicit memories.

What Are "Photographic" Memories?

- Eidetic imagery (photographic memory) occurs when a person is able to project an image onto a blank surface.
- Eidetic imagery is rarely found in adults. However, many adults have internal memory images, which can be very vivid.
- Exceptional memory can be learned by finding ways to directly store information in LTM.
- Learning has no effect on the limits of STM. Some people may have exceptional memories that exceed what can be achieved through learning.

What Causes Forgetting?

- Forgetting and memory were extensively studied by Herman Ebbinghaus. His work shows that forgetting is most rapid immediately after learning (the curve of forgetting).
- Failure to encode information is a common cause of "forgetting."
- Forgetting in sensory memory and STM probably reflects decay of memory traces in the nervous system.

Decay or disuse of memories may also account for some LTM loss.

- Often, forgetting is cue dependent. The power of cues to trigger memories is revealed by state-dependent learning and the link between moods and memory.
- Much forgetting in both STM and LTM can be attributed to interference.
- When recent learning interferes with retrieval of prior learning, retroactive interference has occurred.
- If old learning interferes with new learning, proactive interference has occurred.

How Accurate Are Everyday Memories?

- Repression is the forgetting of painful, embarrassing, or traumatic memories.
- Repression is thought to be unconscious, in contrast to suppression, which is a conscious attempt to avoid thinking about something.

What Happens in the Brain When Memories Are Formed?

- Retrograde amnesia and the effects of electroconvulsive shock (ECS) may be explained by the concept of consolidation.
- Consolidation theory holds that engrams (permanent memory traces) are formed during a critical period after learning. Until they are consolidated, long-term memories are easily destroyed.
- The hippocampus is a brain area that has been linked with consolidation of memories. Once memories are consolidated, they appear to be stored in the cortex of the brain.
- The search within the brain for engrams has now settled on changes in nerve cells and how they interconnect.

How Can Memory Be Improved?

- Memory can be improved by using feedback, recitation, and rehearsal; by selecting and organizing information; and by using the progressive part method, spaced practice, overlearning, and active search strategies. Effects of serial position, sleep, review, cues, and elaboration should also be kept in mind when studying or memorizing.
- Mnemonic systems use mental images and unusual associations to link new information with familiar memories already stored in LTM. Such strategies give information personal meaning and make it easier to recall.

PSYCHOLOGY ON THE NET

If you have difficulty finding any of the sites listed here, visit http://psychologyjourney.nelson.com for an updated list of Internet addresses and direct links to relevant sites.

Active Brain Areas in Working Memory A three-dimensional MRI reconstruction of a person's brain while holding letters in working memory. http://www.nimh.nih.gov/events/prfmri2.cfm

Brain: The World Inside Your Head Pfizer's website has an excellent virtual tour of the brain. http://www.pfizer.com/brain/etour1.html

Exploratorium: Memory Demonstrations and articles related to memory from an exceptional science museum. http://www.exploratorium.org/memory

False Memory Reading Group You will find lots of reading resources at the False Memory Reading Group

page run by Dr. James Lampinen of the University of Arkansas. http://comp.uark.edu/~lampinen/read.html

The Magical Number Seven, Plus or Minus Two Full text of George Miller's original article. http://www.well.com/user/smalin/miller.html

Memory Techniques and Mnemonics Links to information on mnemonics. http://www.demon.co.uk/mindtool/memory.html

Questions and Answers about Memories of Childhood Abuse From the APA, a summary of the repressed memory issue. http://www.apa.org/pubinfo/mem.html

InfoTrac College Edition For recent articles on the Psychology in Action feature, use Key Words search for MNEMONICS.

INTERACTIVE LEARNING

Psychology: An Interactive Journey Remember that Chapter 7 of the CD-ROM that came with this text has practice tests, flashcards, interactive exercises, a crossword puzzle, and other valuable materials to enhance your learning experience.

PsychNow! 5d. Memory Systems, 5e. Forgetting.

Psyk.trek 6. Memory and Thought, Psyk.trek Simulations: 5. Memory processes.

Chart Your Progress

The questions that follow are only a sample of what you need to know. If you miss any of the items, you should review the entire chapter, do the exercises on the CD, and review the Knowledge Builders. Another way to prepare for tests is to get more practice with *WebTutor*, the *Study Guide*, or the *Practice Quizzes* that are available with this text.

1. Selective attention controls which information moves from sensory memory to
   a. phonetic memory
   b. iconic memory
   c. STM
   d. LTM

2. Information in LTM is stored mainly on the basis of
   a. meaning
   b. sounds and phonetics
   c. icons and echoes
   d. how it will be retrieved

3. The digit-span test is primarily a measure of
   a. LTM
   b. elaborative rehearsal
   c. recoding
   d. STM

4. Which of the following is a type of skill memory?
   a. semantic memory
   b. declarative memory
   c. episodic memory
   d. procedural memory

5. Which type of memory test would be most likely to reveal a serial position effect?
   a. recall
   b. recognition
   c. relearning
   d. implicit

6. For most people, having an especially good memory is based on
   a. maintenance rehearsal
   b. constructive processing
   c. phonetic imagery
   d. learned strategies

7. A saxophone player learns three new pieces of music, one after the other, in a single afternoon. The next day he is least able to remember the third piece because of
   a. state-dependent learning
   b. the time decay of memory traces
   c. proactive interference
   d. disuse of memory cues

8. Flashbulb memories could be thought of as the reverse of
   a. repressed memories
   b. proactive memories
   c. retroactive memories
   d. episodic memories

9. Memory consolidation would most likely be disrupted by
   a. rehearsal
   b. ECS
   c. overlearning
   d. sleep

10. The keyword method is a commonly used
    a. cognitive interviewing technique
    b. massed practice strategy
    c. mnemonic technique
    d. first step in the progressive part method

Chapter 8

Psychologist's Journal

MAPS AND IMAGES

Psychologist Irwin Silverman and his colleagues took some undergraduate volunteers into a densely wooded area on the York University campus and asked them to find their way back to the starting point. Silverman made two striking observations. First, male students were significantly better than female students at finding their way back. Second, there was a strong connection between skill at finding the way back and mental rotation ability (the ability to alter the position and orientation of an object in mental space) (Silverman et al., 2000).

Silverman believes that men evolved better spatial skills than women because men spent more time tracking prey animals and finding their way home. But why the connection to mental rotation? According to Silverman, both tasks require the capacity to maintain a "bird's-eye view"—whether of an imagined object being rotated or of a route one is walking in the woods. Men who had this ability were more likely to survive than men who didn't. That wasn't true for women.

There is a wider application of the idea of *wayfinding* that is central to this chapter. Wayfinding is not just knowing how to go home. More generally, it is knowing how to get from where you are to any goal. This is reflected in our everyday language—we speak of searching for a solution, being off-track, finding a path in life, and getting somewhere.

Wayfinding usually involves knowledge. The goal might be diagnosing a patient's medical disorder, predicting whether a violent offender will reoffend if paroled, or, as a new employee, figuring out who in the organization has the knowledge you need in order to do your job. In each case, the task can be thought of as moving through a space defined by information. This chapter is about how we use knowledge or, to put it most simply, how we find our way. In the pages that follow, we will investigate thinking, problem solving, intelligence, and creativity.

Survey Questions

- What is the nature of thought?
- In what ways are images related to thinking?
- How are concepts learned? Are there different kinds of concepts?
- What is the role of language in thinking?
- Can animals be taught to use language?
- What do we know about problem solving?
- What is artificial intelligence?
- How is human intelligence defined and measured?
- How do IQ scores relate to achievement and thinking ability?
- What is the nature of creative thinking?
- How accurate is intuition?
- What can be done to improve thinking and promote creativity?

▶ What Is Thinking?—It's All in Your Head!

Survey Question:
- What is the nature of thought?

Cognition The process of thinking or mentally processing information (images, concepts, words, rules, and symbols).

Cognitive psychology The study of thinking, knowing, understanding, problem solving, creativity, and information processing.

Internal representation Any image, concept, precept, symbol, or process used to mentally represent information during thought.

Image Most often, a mental representation that has picture-like qualities; an icon.

Concept A generalized idea representing a class of related objects or events.

Language Words or symbols, and rules for combining them, that are used for thinking and communication.

Cognition refers to mentally processing information. Our thoughts take many forms, including daydreaming, problem solving, and reasoning (to name but a few). Although thinking is not limited to humans, imagine trying to teach an animal to match the feats of Shakuntala Devi, who holds the "world record" for mental calculation. Devi once multiplied two 13-digit numbers (7 686 369 774 870 times 2 465 099 745 779) in her head, giving the answer in 28 seconds. (That's 18 947 668 104 042 434 089 403 730, if you haven't already figured it out.)

Doing research on thinking is similar to figuring out how a computer works by asking, "I wonder what would happen if I did this?" But in **cognitive psychology** (the study of human information processing), the "computer" is the brain and thinking is the "programming" we seek to understand.

Some Basic Units of Thought

At its most basic, thinking is an **internal representation** (mental expression) of a problem or situation. (Picture a chess player who mentally tries out several moves before actually touching a chess piece.) The power of being able to mentally represent problems is dramatically illustrated by chess grand master Miguel Najdorf, who once simultaneously played 45 chess games while blindfolded. How did Najdorf do it? Like most people, he used the following basic units of thought: (1) images, (2) concepts, and (3) language, or symbols. **Images** are most often mental representations with picture-like qualities. **Concepts** are generalized ideas representing a class of related objects or events. **Language** consists of words or symbols, and rules for combining them. Thinking often involves all three units. For example, blindfolded chess players rely on visual images, concepts ("Game 2 is an English opening"), and the special notational system, or "language," of chess.

In a moment we will delve further into imagery, concepts, and language. Be aware, however, that thinking involves attention, pattern recognition, memory, decision making, intuition, knowledge, and more. This chapter is only a sample of what cognitive psychology is about.

▶ Mental Imagery—Does a Frog Have Lips?

Survey Question:
- In what ways are images related to thinking?

Ninety-seven percent of us have visual images and 92 percent have auditory images. Over 50 percent have imagery for movement, touch, taste, smell, and pain. Thus, mental images can be more than just "pictures." For example, your image of a bakery may also include its delicious odour. Despite such variations, it is generally accepted that most people use images to think, remember, and solve problems. Here are some ways in which we use mental images (Kosslyn et al., 1990):

The Church of the Sacred Family in Barcelona, Spain, was designed by Antonio Gaudi. Could a person lacking mental imagery design such a masterpiece? Three people out of 100 find it impossible to produce mental images, and three out of 100 have very strong imagery. Most artists, architects, designers, sculptors, and filmmakers have excellent visual imagery.

Mental rotation The ability to change the position of an image in mental space.

- To make a decision or solve a problem (choosing what clothes to wear; figuring out how to arrange furniture in a room).
- To change feelings (thinking of pleasant images to get out of a bad mood; imagining oneself as thin to help stay on a diet).
- To improve a skill or to prepare for some action (using images to improve a swimming stroke; mentally rehearsing how you will ask for a raise).
- To aid memory (picturing Mr. Cook wearing a chef's hat, so you can remember his name).

The Nature of Mental Images

Mental images are not flat, like photographs. Researcher Stephen Kosslyn demonstrated this by asking people, "Does a frog have lips and a stubby tail?" Unless you often kiss frogs, you will probably tackle this question by using mental images. Most people picture a frog, "look" at its mouth, and then mentally rotate the frog to check its tail (Kosslyn, 1983). **Mental rotation** alters the position and orientation of an image in mental space. This ability is at least partly based on making imagined movements (see ▶Figure 8.1). That is, we mentally pick up an object and turn it around (Wexler, Kosslyn, & Berthoz, 1998). This task is often used to study mental images because, according to Vandenberg & Kuse (1978), mental rotation problems are among the least likely to be solved verbally. Giving someone directions, for example, can be done verbally (go to the corner, turn left…). But mental rotation can really only be done using mental images.

What happens in the brain when a person has visual images? Seeing something in your "mind's eye" is similar to seeing real objects. Information from the eyes normally activates the brain's primary visual area, creating an image (see ▶Figure 8.2). Other brain areas then help us recognize the image by relating it to stored knowledge. When you form a mental image, the system works in reverse. Brain areas where memories are stored send signals back to the visual cortex, where once again, an image is created (Farah, 1988; Farah et al., 1989; Kosslyn, Thompson, & Alpert, 1995).

It's worth noting some recent Canadian evidence that much simpler animals appear to have mental images—they seem to be capable of mental rotation. Catherine Plowright and her colleagues at the University of Ottawa trained bees to discriminate between a pattern they would be reinforced for choosing and a pattern they would not be reinforced for. Later, the bees reliably chose the reinforcing pattern even when it was rotated away from the orientation they were familiar with. For several reasons, Plowright and her colleagues have suggested that this means the bees are capable of mental rotation (Plowright et al., 2001).

Researchers at Dalhousie University in Halifax have found evidence that pigeons may also be capable of mental rotation. Using an approach similar to that adopted by Plowright, Jeff Hamm and his colleagues trained pigeons to discriminate among line drawings of objects, and then tested them with rotated objects. The pigeons' response time and accuracy in discriminating the objects both depended upon how far the objects

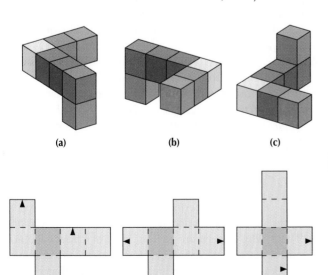

(a)   (b)   (c)

(d)   (e)   (f)

▶Figure 8.1

Imagery in thinking. *(Top)* Subjects were shown a drawing similar to *(a)* and drawings of how *(a)* would look in other positions, such as *(b)* and *(c)*. Subjects could recognize *(a)* after it had been "rotated" from its original position. However, the more *(a)* was rotated in space, the longer it took to recognize it. This result suggests that subjects actually formed a three-dimensional image of *(a)* and rotated the image to see if it matched. (Shepard, 1975.) *(Bottom)* Try your ability to manipulate mental images: Each of these shapes can be folded to make a cube; in which do the arrows meet? (After Kosslyn, 1985.)

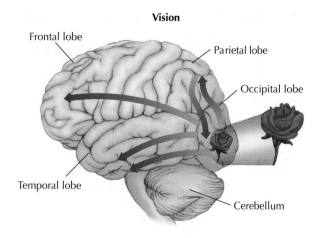

Vision

Frontal lobe

Parietal lobe

Occipital lobe

Temporal lobe

Cerebellum

Visual Image

Frontal lobe

Parietal lobe

Occipital lobe

Temporal lobe

Cerebellum

▶**Figure 8.2**

When you see a flower, its image is represented by activity in the primary visual area of the cortex, at the back of the brain. Information about the flower is also relayed to other brain areas. If you form a mental image of a flower, information follows a reverse path. The result, once again, is activation of the primary visual area.

Kinesthetic image Any mental representation based on produced, remembered, or imagined muscular sensations.

---

were rotated—the classic index that mental rotation is occurring (Hamm, Matheson, & Honig, 1997).

Why might bees, pigeons, and humans be capable of mental rotation? Can you think of ways that being able to rotate a mental image might improve the chances of survival of individuals in each of these species?

USING MENTAL IMAGES *Are some people better than others at using mental images?* As suggested in the Psychologist's Journal at the beginning of the chapter, some people are better at using mental images than others. In fact, Albert Einstein, Thomas Edison, Lewis Carroll, and many of history's most original intellects relied heavily on imagery (West, 1991). There is also variation among ordinary people. In particular, men are on average better at imagery tasks than women. For example, Daniel Voyer, of St. Francis Xavier University in Antigonish, Nova Scotia, reported that men performed better than women on a mental rotation task, and showed more improvement with practice (Voyer, 1995).

Does the "size" of a mental image affect thinking? To find out, first picture a cat sitting beside a housefly. Now try to "zoom in" on the cat's ears so you see them clearly. Next, picture a rabbit sitting beside an elephant. How quickly can you "see" the rabbit's front feet? Did it take longer than picturing the cat's ears?

When a rabbit is pictured with an elephant, the rabbit's image must be small because the elephant is large. Using such tasks, Stephen Kosslyn found that the smaller an image is, the harder it is to "see" its details. To put this finding to use, try forming oversized images of things you want to think about. For example, to understand electricity, picture the wires as large pipes with electrons the size of golf balls moving through them; to understand the human ear, explore it (in your mind's eye) like a large cave; and so forth.

KINESTHETIC IMAGERY *How do muscular responses relate to thinking?* In a sense, we think with our bodies as well as our heads. **Kinesthetic images** are created from produced, remembered, or imagined muscular sensations (Oyama & Ichikawa, 1990). Such images help us think about movements and actions.

Kinesthetic imagery arises from kinesthetic sensations (feelings from the muscles and joints). As you think and talk, these sensations tend to guide the flow of ideas. For example, if you try to tell a friend how to make bread, you may move your hands as if kneading the dough. Or, try answering this question: Which direction do you turn the hot-water handle in your kitchen to shut off the water? Most people haven't simply memorized the words "Turn it clockwise" or "Turn it counterclockwise." Instead you will probably "turn" the faucet in your imagination before answering. You may even make a turning motion with your hand before answering.

Kinesthetic images are especially important in music, sports, dance, martial arts, and other movement-oriented skills. People with good kinesthetic imagery learn such skills faster than those with poor imagery (Glisky, Williams, & Kihlstrom, 1996).

▶ Concepts—I'm Positive, It's a Whatchamacallit

Survey Question:
■ How are concepts learned? Are there different kinds of concepts?

A concept is an idea that represents a class of objects or events. Concepts are powerful tools because they allow us to think more abstractly. Concepts also help us identify important features of objects or events. That's why experts in various areas of knowledge are good at classifying objects. Bird watchers, tropical fish fanciers, five-year-old dinosaur enthusiasts, and other experts have all learned to look for identifying details that beginners tend to miss. If you are knowledgeable about a topic, such as horses, flowers, or football, you literally see things differently from the way less well-informed people do (Johnson & Mervis, 1997).

Concept Formation

How are concepts learned? **Concept formation** is the process of classifying information into meaningful categories. At its most basic, concept formation is based on experience with positive and negative instances (examples that belong, or do not belong, to the concept class). Concept formation is not as simple as it might seem. Imagine a child learning the concept of *dog*.

Dog Daze

A child and her father go for a walk. At a neighbour's house, they see a medium-sized dog. The father says, "See the dog." As they pass the next yard, the child sees a cat and says, "Dog!" Her father corrects her, "No, that's a cat." The child now thinks, "Aha, dogs are large and cats are small." In the next yard, she sees a Pekingese and says, "Cat!" "No, that's a dog," replies her father.

The child's confusion is understandable. At first she might even mistake a Pekingese for a dust mop. However, with more positive and negative instances, the child will eventually recognize everything from Great Danes to Chihuahuas as members of the same category—dogs.

As adults, we often acquire concepts by learning or forming rules. A **conceptual rule** is a guideline for deciding if objects or events belong to a concept class. For example, a triangle must be a closed shape with three sides made of straight lines. Rules are an efficient way to learn concepts, but examples remain important. It's unlikely that memorizing rules would allow a new listener to accurately categorize *punk, hip-hop, fusion, salsa, heavy metal, grunge rock,* and *rap* music.

Types of Concepts

Are there different kinds of concepts? Yes, **conjunctive concepts** or "and concepts" are defined by the presence of two or more features. In other words, an item must have "this feature and this feature and this feature." For example, a *motorcycle* must have two wheels *and* an engine *and* handlebars.

Relational concepts are based on how an object relates to something else, or how its features relate to one another. All of the following are relational concepts: *larger, above, left, north,* and *upside down.* Another example is *sister,* which is defined as "a female considered in her relation to another person having the same parents."

Disjunctive concepts have at *least* one of several possible features. These are "either/or" concepts. To belong to the category, an item must have "this feature or that feature or another feature." For example, in baseball, a *strike* is *either* a swing and a miss *or* a pitch down the middle *or* a foul ball. The either/or quality of disjunctive concepts makes them hard to learn.

EXEMPLARS   A group of Canadian psychologists at McMaster University in Hamilton, Ontario, have argued for the role of **exemplars** (stored representations of individual experiences) in our ability to identify concepts. Lee Brooks (1987) suggested that individual experiences with a stimulus are not blended into an abstract "prototype" representation, but stored in their own right. These individual experiences can then support categorization decisions.

Imagine, for example, that you are responsible for deciding whether a particular person has a mental disorder. How would you do this? Brooks and his colleague Geoffrey Norman believe that clinical diagnosis often involves matching of the current patient to a previously treated patient who was similar. That is, instead of analyzing a case in terms of concepts, experienced clinicians search memory for a similar case. They do this because that is how they store information about the various disorders they can identify—in terms of exemplars (Norman & Brooks, 1997). In terms of our wayfinding theme, suppose you found yourself in a strange city and needed to get downtown. You might remember that

Concept formation The process of classifying information into meaningful categories.

Conceptual rule A formal rule for deciding if an object or event is an example of a particular concept.

Conjunctive concept A class of objects that have two or more features in common. (For example, to qualify as an example of the concept an object must be both red and triangular.)

Relational concept A concept defined by the relationship between features of an object or between an object and its surroundings (for example, "greater than," "lopsided").

Disjunctive concept A concept defined by the presence of at least one of several possible features. (For example, to qualify an object must be either blue *or* circular.)

Exemplars Stored representations of individual experiences.

When does a cup become a bowl or a vase? Deciding if an object belongs to a conceptual class is aided by relating it to a prototype, or ideal example. Subjects in one experiment chose number 5 as the "best" cup. (After Labov, 1973.)

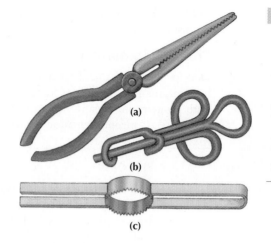

▶**Figure 8.4**

Use of prototypes in concept identification. Even though its shape is unusual, item *(a)* can be related to a model (an ordinary set of pliers) and thus recognized. But what are items *(b)* and *(c)*? If you don't recognize them, look ahead to ▶Figure 8.6. (After Bransford & McCarrell, 1977.)

Prototype An ideal model used as a prime example of a particular concept.
Denotative meaning The exact, dictionary definition of a word or concept; its objective meaning.
Connotative meaning The subjective, personal, or emotional meaning of a word or concept.
Semantic differential A measure of connotative meaning obtained by rating words or concepts on several dimensions.

the last time you were in a city, the downtown area was full of tall buildings. Then you could look for some tall buildings and head for those. We'll come across this wayfinding technique again below.

PROTOTYPES   When you think of the concept *bird*, do you mentally list the features that birds have? Probably not. In addition to rules features, and exemplars, we may use **prototypes,** or ideal models, to identify concepts (Rosch, 1977; Smith, 1989). A robin, for example, is a model bird; an ostrich is not. In other words, some items are better examples of a concept than others are. Which of the drawings in ▶ Figure 8.3 best represents a cup? At some point, as a cup grows taller or wider it becomes a vase or a bowl. How do we know when the line is crossed? Probably, we mentally compare objects to an "ideal" cup, like number 5. That's why it's hard to identify concepts when we can't come up with relevant prototypes. What, for example, are the objects shown in ▶Figure 8.4?

CONNOTATIVE MEANING   Generally speaking, concepts have two types of meaning. The **denotative meaning** of a word or concept is its exact definition. The **connotative meaning** is its emotional or personal meaning. The word *naked* denotes the same thing (having no clothes) for a nudist or a movie censor. However, we could expect their connotations to be quite different. Such differences can influence how we think about important issues. For example, the term *enhanced radiation device* has a more positive connotation than *neutron bomb* does (Gruner & Tighe, 1995).

Can you clarify what a connotative meaning is? Connotative meaning can be measured with the **semantic differential,** as shown in ▶Figure 8.5. When words or concepts are rated on various scales, most of their connotative meaning boils down to the dimensions good/bad, strong/weak, and

Rate this word: **JAZZ**

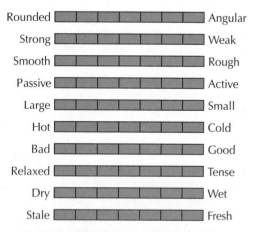

Rounded	Angular
Strong	Weak
Smooth	Rough
Passive	Active
Large	Small
Hot	Cold
Bad	Good
Relaxed	Tense
Dry	Wet
Stale	Fresh

▶**Figure 8.5**

This is an example of Osgood's semantic differential. The connotative meaning of the word *jazz* can be established by rating it on the scales. To create your own rating, put a mark on each red line in the position that expresses your choice (e.g., more round? more angular?). Connect the marks with a line from top to bottom; then have a friend rate the word and compare your responses. It might be interesting to do the same for *rock and roll, classical,* and *rap.* You also might want to try the word *psychology.* (From C. E. Osgood, 1952.)

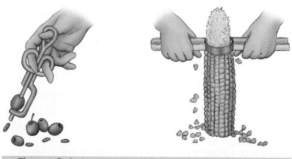

▶**Figure 8.6**

Context can substitute for a lack of appropriate prototypes in concept identification.

active/passive. (Sounds like a good movie title, doesn't it: *The Good, the Bad, the Strong, the Weak, the Active, and the Passive.*) Words that vary in just these three dimensions can have very different connotations, even when their denotative means are similar. For example, you might consider yourself *conscientious,* someone else *careful,* and still another *nit-picky!*

▶ Language—Don't Leave Home without It

Encoding Changing information into a form that allows it to be manipulated in thought.
Semantics The study of meanings in language.
Phonemes The basic speech sounds of a language.
Morphemes The smallest meaningful units in a language, such as syllables or words.

As we have seen, thinking may occur without language. Everyone has searched for a word to express an idea that exists as a vague image or feeling. Nevertheless, most thinking relies heavily on language, because words **encode** (translate) the world into symbols that are easy to manipulate (see ▶ Figure 8.7).

The study of meaning in language is known as **semantics.** It is here that the link between words and thinking becomes most evident. Suppose, on an intelligence test, you were asked to circle the word that does not belong in this series:

SKYSCRAPER   CATHEDRAL   TEMPLE   PRAYER

If you circled *prayer,* you answered as most people do. Now try another problem, again circling the odd item:

CATHEDRAL   PRAYER   TEMPLE   SKYSCRAPER

Did you circle *skyscraper* this time? The new order subtly alters the meaning of the last word (Mayer, 1995). This occurs because words get much of their meaning from context. For example, the word *shot* means different things when we are thinking of marksmanship, bartending, medicine, photography, or golf (Miller, 1999).

Semantics affect thinking when the words we choose alter meaning: Has one country's army "invaded" another? Or "effected a protective incursion"? Is the city reservoir "half full" or "half empty"? Would you rather eat "prime beef" or "dead cow"? Translating languages may also cause semantic problems. Perhaps the San Jose, California, public library can be excused for displaying a large banner that was supposed to say, "You are welcome" in a native Philippine language. The banner actually said, "You are circumcised."

Likewise, we may forgive Pepsi for translating "Come alive, you Pepsi generation" into Thai as "Pepsi brings your ancestors back from the dead." However, in more important situations, such as in international diplomacy, avoiding semantic confusion may be vital.

The Structure of Language

What does it take to make a language? First of all, a language must provide *symbols* that can stand for objects and ideas. The symbols we call words are built out of **phonemes** (FOE-neems: basic speech sounds) and **morphemes** (MOR-feems: speech sounds collected into individual units of meaning, such as *pre-* [meaning "before"] or *cat*). Note that a collection of phonemes does not always produce a morpheme. In English, *cat* by itself is a morpheme, but as the first three letters of *catch,* it is not, because no meaning is attached to that part of the word by itself. (See also ▶ Figure 8.8.)

▶ Figure 8.7

Wine tasting illustrates the encoding function of language. To communicate their experiences to others, wine connoisseurs must put taste sensations into words. The wine you see here is "Marked by deeply concentrated nuances of plum, blackberry, and currant, with a nice balance of tannins and acid, building to a spicy oak finish." (Don't try this with a Pop-tart!)

Albanian	mak, mak
Chinese	gua, gua
Dutch	rap, rap
English	quack, quack
French	coin, coin
Italian	qua, qua
Spanish	cuá, cuá
Swedish	kvack, kvack
Turkish	vak, vak

▶ Figure 8.8

Animals around the world make pretty much the same sounds. Notice, however, how various languages use slightly different phonemes to express these sounds.

Grammar A set of rules for combining language units into meaningful speech or writing.

Syntax Rules for ordering words when forming sentences.

Transformation rules Rules by which a simple declarative sentence may be changed to other voices or forms (past tense, passive voice, and so forth).

Productivity The capacity of language to generate new ideas and possibilities.

Next, a language must have a **grammar,** or set of rules for making sounds into words and words into sentences. One part of grammar, known as **syntax,** concerns rules for word order. Syntax is important because rearranging words almost always changes the meaning of a sentence: "Dog bites man" versus "Man bites dog."

Traditional grammar is concerned with "surface" language—the sentences we actually speak. Linguist Noam Chomsky has focused instead on the unspoken rules we use to change core ideas into various sentences. Chomsky (1986) believes that we do not learn all the sentences we might ever say. Rather, we actively create them by applying **transformation rules** to universal, core patterns. This allows us to change a simple declarative sentence into other voices or forms. For example, the core sentence "Dog bites man" can be transformed to the pattern you see below (and others as well):

Past: The dog bit the man.
Passive: The man was bitten by the dog.
Negative: The dog did not bite the man.
Question: Did the dog bite the man?

Children seem to be using transformation rules when they say things such as "I runned home." That is, the child applied the normal past tense rule to the irregular verb *to run.*

A true language is also **productive**—it can generate new thoughts or ideas. In fact, words can be rearranged to produce a nearly infinite number of meaningful sentences. Some are silly: "Please don't feed me to the goldfish." Some are profound: "If you cut me, do I not bleed?" In either case, the productive quality of language makes it a powerful tool for thinking.

It is common to think of language in terms of speaking and writing. However, as "Gestural Languages—A Voice for the Deaf" explains, language is not limited to speech.

The Animal Language Debate

Survey Question:
■ Can animals be taught to use language?

Do animals use language? Animals do communicate. They react immediately to cries, gestures, and mating calls made by other members of their species (Premack, 1983). For the most part, however, natural animal communication is quite limited. Even apes and monkeys make only a few dozen distinct cries, which carry messages such as "attack," "flee," or "food here." More important, animal communication is not productive. When a monkey gives an "eagle distress call," it means something like, "I see an eagle." The monkey has no way of saying, "I don't see an eagle," or "Thank heavens that wasn't an eagle," or "That sucker I saw yesterday was some huge eagle" (Glass, Holyoak, & Santa, 1979). Let's explore some successes and failures in trying to teach animals to use language.

TALKING CHIMPS   Early attempts to teach chimps to talk were a dismal failure. The world record was held by Viki, a chimp who could say only four words (*mama, papa, cup,* and *up*) after six years of intensive training (Fleming, 1974; Hayes, 1951). (Actually, all four words sounded something like a belch.) Then there was a breakthrough. Beatrix Gardner and Allen Gardner used operant conditioning and imitation to teach a chimp named Washoe to use American Sign Language.

Washoe's communication skills blossomed rapidly as her "vocabulary" grew. Soon she began to put together primitive sentences like "Come-gimme sweet," "Out please," "Gimme tickle," and "Open food drink." Washoe's peak vocabulary was about 240 signs, and she could construct six-word sentences (Gardner & Gardner, 1989).

A chimp named Sarah was another well-known pupil of human language. David Premack taught Sarah to use 130 "words" consisting of plastic chips arranged on a magnetized board (see ▶Figure 8.9). From the beginning, Sarah was required to use proper word order. She learned to answer questions, to label things "same" or "different," to classify objects by colour, shape, and size, and to form compound sentences (Premack & Premack, 1983). Sarah's greatest achievement was the use of conditional sentences. A conditional statement contains a qualification, often in the if–then form: "If Sarah take apple, then Mary give Sarah chocolate." "If Sarah take banana, then Mary no give Sarah chocolate."

HUMAN DIVERSITY   Gestural Language—A Voice for the Deaf

Suppose you were a judge in a court, and an accused person was brought before you. Perhaps your most important task would be to make sure the accused understood the court proceedings. If that person were deaf, you would arrange for a sign language interpreter, probably one who used American Sign Language (ASL). But what if the accused person did not understand ASL or any widely known sign language—what would you do? Authorities in Nunavut turned to James Macdougall of the Canadian Deafness Research and Training Institute in Montreal.

In 1997, Macdougall was asked to determine whether a deaf Inuk living in Baker Lake, Nunavut, was able to stand trial. Macdougall concluded that a trial would not be possible, for two reasons. First, although the Inuk communicated in sign, it was not ASL, but something created locally. The only translators available would be members of the accused person's family, who could be expected to have some bias. Second, the sign language used had no terms for the specialized legal vocabulary of the court—terms such as *plea, evidence, guilty,* and *sentence.*

Macdougall subsequently investigated indigenous northern sign languages for the Canadian government. Visiting Baker Lake, Pangnirtung, and Rankin Inlet, he found a number of deaf Inuit who, having never been south for education nor learned ASL, communicated in a local sign language. He also discovered that a significant number of people outside each deaf person's family also used this "Inuit Sign Language" (ISL) and were able to

communicate with the deaf people, and that users of ISL are able to discuss a variety of topics and express emotions verbally. Macdougall observed that ISL was used by hearing Inuit when they meet another Inuit who speaks a different dialect, and he suggested that this is not unusual for nomadic hunters and others living in isolated places. Similar locally based sign languages have been reported in Martha's Vineyard (Groce, 1985), the Yucatan, Mexico (Macdougall, 1999), and the Caribbean (Washabaugh, 1980, 1981).

Readers interested in ISL will enjoy Macdougall's account of how he first came across it during a failed hunting expedition that nearly ended in disaster—he and his party quite literally had trouble with wayfinding in a featureless subarctic landscape (Macdougall, 2000). He also raises a series of important questions about how deaf people in remote communities can interact with the wider population. How can an accused person whose only form of communication is ISL be tried? In the case of a deaf person who experiences violence in the family, but who can be understood by only a very few people, primarily *in* the family, how is he or she to be identified and helped?

Sign languages naturally arise out of a need to communicate visually. But they also embody a personal identity and define a distinct community. Sign is the true voice of the deaf and hearing impaired. Those who "speak" sign share not just a language, but a rich culture as well (Kemp, 1998; Meier, 1991; Sacks, 1990; Schaller, 1991).

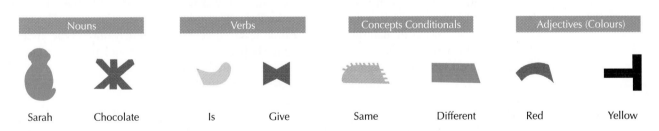

Nouns		Verbs		Concepts Conditionals		Adjectives (Colours)	
Sarah	Chocolate	Is	Give	Same	Different	Red	Yellow

▶Figure 8.9

Here is a sample of some of the symbols that Sarah the chimpanzee used to communicate with humans. In our minds, these symbols are associated with words, but are they words for Sarah? (After Premack & Premack, 1972).

CRITICISMS   Such interchanges are impressive. But communication and real language usage are different things. Even untrained chimps use simple gestures to communicate with humans. For example, a chimp will point at a banana that is out of reach, while glancing back and forth between the banana and a person standing nearby (Leavens & Hopkins, 1998). (The meaning of the gesture is clear. The meaning of the exasperated look on the chimp's face is less certain, but it probably means, "Yes, give me the banana, you idiot.")

Some psychologists doubt that apes can really use language. For one thing, the chimps rarely "speak" without prompting from humans. Also, it appears that the apes may be simply performing chains of operant responses to get food, play, or other "goodies" (Hixon, 1998). By using such responses, the apes then manipulate their trainers to get what they want.

You might say the critics believe the apes have made monkeys out of their trainers. However, psychologists Roger and Debbi Fouts studied some 6000 conversations between chimps. Only 5 percent had anything to do with food (Fouts, Fouts, & Schoenfield, 1984). Another study found that chimps hold real conversations, even when people are not around to cue them (Greenfield & Savage-Rumbaugh, 1993). So, maybe the chimps will make monkeys out of the critics.

PROBLEMS WITH SYNTAX   At this point, numerous chimps, a gorilla named Koko, and an assortment of dolphins and sea lions have learned to communicate with word symbols of various kinds. Yet, even if some criticisms can be answered, linguists such as Noam Chomsky remain unconvinced that animals can truly use language. The core issue is that problems with syntax (word order) have plagued almost all animal language experiments. For example, when a chimp named Nim Chimpsky (no relation to Chomsky) wanted an orange, he would typically signal a grammarless string of words: "Give orange me give eat orange me eat orange give me eat orange give me you." This might be communication, but it is not language.

LEXIGRAMS   More recently, the flames of controversy were fanned again by Kanzi, a pygmy chimpanzee studied by Duane Rumbaugh and Sue Savage-Rumbaugh. Kanzi communicates using gestures and push buttons on a computer keyboard. Each of the 250 buttons is marked with a **lexigram,** or geometric word-symbol. Using the lexigrams, Kanzi can create primitive sentences several words long. He can also understand about 650 spoken sentences. During testing, Kanzi hears spoken words over headphones, so his caretakers cannot visually prompt him (Savage-Rumbaugh et al., 1990; Savage-Rumbaugh & Lewin, 1996).

Kanzi's sentences consistently follow correct word order. Like a child learning language, Kanzi picked up some rules from his caregivers (Savage-Rumbaugh & Lewin, 1996). However, he has developed other patterns on his own. For example, Kanzi usually places action symbols in the order he wants to carry them out, such as "chase tickle" or "chase hide." Psycholinguist Patricia Marks Greenfield says that Kanzi's use of grammar is on a par with that of a two-year-old child (Savage-Rumbaugh et al., 1993).

Kanzi's ability to invent a simple grammar may help us better understand the roots of human language. It is certainly the strongest answer yet to the critics. On the other hand, Chomsky insists that if chimps were biologically capable of language they would use it on their own. Although the issue is far from resolved, such research may unravel the mysteries of language learning. In fact, it has already been helpful for teaching language to children with serious language impairments (Savage-Rumbaugh et al., 1990).

Lexigram A geometric shape used as a symbol for a word.

▶ Problem Solving—Getting an Answer in Sight

A good way to start a discussion of problem solving is to solve a problem. Give this one a try.

Survey Question:
■ What do we know about problem solving?

A famous ocean liner (the *Queen Ralph*) is steaming toward port at 20 kilometres per hour. It is 50 kilometres from shore when a seagull takes off from its deck and flies toward port. At the same instant, a speedboat leaves port at 30 kilometres per hour. The bird flies back and forth between the speedboat and the *Queen Ralph* at a speed of 40 kilometres per hour. How far will the bird have flown when the two boats pass?

If you don't immediately see the answer to this problem, read it again. (The answer is revealed in the "Insightful Solutions" section on page 295.)

Knowledge builder

IMAGERY, CONCEPTS, AND LANGUAGE

Relate

Name some ways in which you have used imagery in the thinking you have done today.

Write a conceptual rule for the following idea: *unicycle*. Were you able to define the concept with a rule? Would positive and negative instances help make the concept clearer for others?

A true sports car has two seats, a powerful engine, good brakes, and excellent handling. What kind of a concept is the term *sports car*? What do you think of as a prototypical sports car?

Here's some mnemonic help: You use a *phone* to send *phonemes*. To *morph* them into words, you have to hit them with a *grammar*. What wrong is with sentence this? (The answer is not a *sin tax*, but it still may tax you.)

You must learn to communicate with an alien life form whose language cannot be reproduced by the human voice. Do you think it would it be better to use a gestural language or lexigrams? Why?

Learning Check

1. List three primary units of thought:

   _____

   _____

   _____

2. Our reliance on imagery in thinking means that problem solving is impaired by the use of language or symbols. T or F?
3. Humans appear capable of forming three-dimensional images that can be moved or rotated in mental space. T or F?
4. A *mup* is defined as anything that is small, blue, and hairy. *Mup* is a _____ concept.
5. The connotative meaning of the word *naked* is "having no clothes." T or F?
6. True languages are _____ because they can be used to generate new possibilities.
7. The basic speech sounds are called _____; the smallest meaningful units of speech are called

   _____.

Critical Thinking

8. A Liberal and a Progressive Conservative are asked to rate the word *liberal* on the semantic differential. Under what conditions would their ratings be most alike?
9. Chimpanzees and other apes are intelligent and entertaining animals. If you were doing language research with a chimp, what major problem would you have to guard against?

Answers:

1. images, concepts, language or symbols (others could be listed) **2.** F **3.** T **4.** conjunctive **5.** F **6.** productive **7.** phonemes, morphemes **8.** If they both assume the word refers to an attitude, not a political party or a candidate. **9.** The problem of anthropomorphizing (ascribing human characteristics to animals) is especially difficult to avoid when researchers spend many hours "conversing" with chimps.

We all solve many problems every day. Problem solving can be as commonplace as figuring out how to make a non-poisonous meal out of leftovers or as significant as developing a cure for cancer. How do we find solutions to such problems?

Mechanical Solutions

Mechanical solution A problem solution achieved by trial and error or by a fixed procedure based on learned rules.

Understanding In problem solving, a deeper comprehension of the nature of the problem.

For routine problems, a **mechanical solution** may be adequate. Mechanical solutions are achieved by trial and error or by rote. If you forget the combination to your bike lock, you may be able to discover it by trial and error. In an era of high-speed computers, many trial-and-error solutions are best left to machines. A computer could generate all possible combinations of the five numbers on the lock in a split second. (Of course, it would take you a long time to try them all.) When a problem is solved by rote, thinking is guided by a learned set of rules. If you have a good background in math, you may have solved the problem of the bird and the boats by rote. (We hope you did not. There is an easier solution.)

Solutions by Understanding

Many problems cannot be solved mechanically. In that case, **understanding** (deeper comprehension of a problem) is necessary. Try this problem:

A person has an inoperable stomach tumour. A device is available that produces rays that at high intensity will destroy tissue (both healthy and diseased). How can the tumour be destroyed without damaging surrounding tissue? (See the sketch in ▶Figure 8.10.)

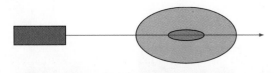

▶**Figure 8.10**

A schematic representation of Duncker's tumour problem. The dark spot represents a tumour surrounded by healthy tissue. How can the tumour be destroyed without injuring surrounding tissue? (After Duncker, 1945.)

Close analogy
A comparison of a target concept and a very similar concept that improves understanding of the target concept.

Distant analogy A comparison emphasizing the similarity on some dimension between a target concept and a very different concept.

Random search strategy Trying possible solutions to a problem in a more or less random order.

Heuristic Any strategy or technique that aids problem solving, especially by limiting the number of possible solutions to be tried.

What does this problem show about problem solving? German psychologist Karl Duncker did a classic series of studies in which he gave college students this problem. Duncker asked them to think aloud as they worked. Very few of the students solved the problem. (One solution is to focus weak rays on the tumour from several angles.) Many years later, Mary Gick, now at Carleton University in Ottawa, and her UCLA colleague Keith Holyoak found a way to increase the chance of someone solving this problem—by giving them an analogy. The analogy involved an attack on a fortress that could succeed only if the attacking force split up and approached from several angles. When Gick and Holyoak instructed students to use the story as an analogy, more than half of them solved Duncker's problem. In contrast, only 8 percent of those who did not read the story solved the problem.

Studies like this suggest that, although analogy can be very helpful, people won't spontaneously use it—they have to be pressed to do so. But is that really true? Recall that Norman & Brooks (1997) found that clinicians use similar cases in diagnosing disorders. In fact, it turns out that people are far more likely to use analogical reasoning outside the lab than inside, a phenomenon documented by Kevin Dunbar of McGill University. Dunbar has found that scientists, journalists, and politicians depend heavily upon analogical reasoning. For example, when scientists are wayfinding—searching for a solution to a problem—use of analogies saves time, whether in forming a theory, developing an experimental method, or interpreting data (Dunbar, 2000). Further, he distinguished between close and distant analogies. A **close analogy** would be if you explained the behaviour of a dog by referring to a wolf. A **distant analogy** would be if you explained the dog's behaviour by referring to a tornado. Dunbar found that scientists use close analogies when talking among themselves, and distant analogies when talking to those less familiar with their work.

The same distinction was found with journalists and politicians in a study of analogy use during the 1995 Quebec referendum campaign (Blanchette & Dunbar, 2001). Surveying three Montreal newspapers in the days immediately before and after the October 1995 vote on Quebec's separation from Canada, Blanchette and Dunbar found that both politicians and journalists made frequent use of analogies. Three-quarters of the analogies used were distant—that is, from outside politics. This means that the analogies involved concepts that were similar structurally rather than superficially (e.g., *separating from Canada* and *starting a new business*). The most common analogies involved magic/religion, sports, and family relationships. Further, politicians and journalists on both the "Yes" and the "No" sides chose positive analogies when supporting their own arguments, and negative analogies when attacking opposing positions.

The critical point is that scientists, politicians, and journalists all use analogies frequently to solve problems and build arguments. Thus it is often worth asking whether results found in the lab will also be true in the outside world. To put it another way: Is the lab a good analogy for the real world? When it comes to analogies, the answer appears to be no!

Heuristics

"You can't get there from here." Or so it may seem when we face a problem. Solving problems often requires a strategy. If the number of alternatives is small, a **random search strategy** might work. This is another example of trial-and-error thinking in which all possibilities are tried, more or less randomly. Imagine, for example, that you are travelling and decide to look up an old friend, J. Smith, in a city you are visiting. You open the phone book and find 47 J. Smiths listed. Of course, you could dial each number until you find the right one. "Forget it," you say to yourself. "Is there any way I can narrow the search?" "Oh, yeah! I remember hearing that Janet lives by the beach." Then you take out a map and call only the numbers with addresses near the waterfront (Ellis & Hunt, 1992).

The approach used in this example is a **heuristic** (hew-RIS-tik: a strategy for identifying and evaluating problem solutions). Typically, a heuristic is a "rule of thumb" that reduces the number of alternatives thinkers must consider. This raises the odds of success, although it does not guarantee a solution. McGill's Kevin Dunbar, whose work on analogy we reviewed above, has offered some heuristics that he thinks should be part of science education: follow up on surprising results; reason by analogy; talk to other scientists; and think about your goals (Dunbar, 2000). Here are some other heuristic strategies that often work in a variety of situations:

- Try to identify how the current state of affairs differs from the desired goal. Then find steps that will reduce the difference.
- Try working backward from the desired goal to the starting point or current state.
- If you can't reach the goal directly, try to identify an intermediate goal or sub-problem that at least gets you closer.
- Represent the problem in other ways, with graphs, diagrams, or analogies, for instance.
- Generate a possible solution and test it. Doing so may eliminate many alternatives, or it may clarify what is needed for a solution.

Insightful Solutions

A thinker who suddenly solves a problem has usually experienced **insight.** Most insights are so *rapid* and *clear* that we wonder why we didn't see the solution sooner. Insight is usually based on reorganizing a problem. This allows us to see problems in new ways and makes their solutions seem obvious (Durso, Rea, & Dayton, 1994).

One type of insight that is especially important to psychologists is the clinical patient's recognition that they have a mental illness. Some therapies require even deeper insight. Psychoanalysis, for example, works by helping patients develop insight into their internal conflicts. For many approaches, clinical outcome is correlated with level of insight—patients with more insight have better outcomes. So, insight is good, isn't it? Not always, unfortunately. Toronto researchers Charmaine Williams and April Collins have discussed the phenomenon of *engulfment*—identifying oneself with the role of patient. That identification is good if it leads a person who needs help to seek it, but it is not so good if it leads that person to believe that he or she is "damaged goods." Williams and Collins have found that higher levels of insight are associated with higher levels of engulfment. They point out that any intervention intended to increase the patient's insight may also increase the patient's sense of being different in a bad way. The challenge is to promote help-seeking without promoting "destructive role constriction" (Williams & Collins, 2002).

Let's return now to the problem of the boats and the bird. The best way to solve it is by insight. Because the boats will cover the 50-kilometre distance in exactly one hour, and the bird flies 40 kilometres per hour, the bird will have flown 40 kilometres when the boats meet. No math is necessary if you have insight into this problem. ▶ Figure 8.11 lists some additional insight problems you may want to try.

In an interesting experiment, college students rated how "warm" (close to an answer) they felt while solving insight problems. Those who had insights usually jumped directly from "cold" to the correct answer. Students who only got "warmer" usually produced wrong answers (Metcalfe, 1986). Thus, you may be headed for a mistake if an insight is not rapid. Real insight tends to be an all-or-nothing event (Smith & Kounios, 1996).

THE NATURE OF INSIGHT Psychologists Robert Sternberg and Janet Davidson (1982) believe that insight involves three abilities. These are **selective encoding,** which refers to selecting information that is relevant to a problem, while ignoring distractions; **selective combination,** or bringing together seemingly unrelated bits of useful information; and **selective comparison,** the ability to compare new problems with old information or with problems already solved.

FIXATIONS One of the most important barriers to problem solving is **fixation,** the tendency to get "hung up" on wrong solutions or to become blind to alternatives. This

Insight A sudden mental reorganization of a problem that makes the solution obvious.

Selective encoding The ability to select information relevant to a problem while ignoring useless or distracting information.

Selective combination In problem solving, the ability to connect seemingly unrelated items of information.

Selective comparison The ability to relate a present problem to similar problems solved in the past or to prior experience.

Fixation The tendency to repeat wrong solutions or faulty responses, especially as a result of becoming blind to alternatives.

Water lilies

Problem: Water lilies growing in a pond double in area every 24 hours. On the first day of spring, only one lily pad is on the surface of the pond. Sixty days later, the pond is entirely covered. On what day is the pond half-covered?

Twenty dollars

Problem: Jessica and Blair both have the same amount of money. How much must Jessica give Blair so that Blair has $20 more than Jessica?

How many pets?

Problem: How many pets do you have if all of them are birds except two, all of them are cats except two, and all of them are dogs except two?

Between 2 and 3

Problem: What one mathematical symbol can you place between 2 and 3 that results in a number greater than 2 and less than 3?

One word

Problem: Rearrange the letters NEWDOOR to make one word.

Solutions to these problems are listed in ◆*Table 8.1, on page 297.*

▶**Figure 8.11**

Functional fixedness A rigidity in problem solving caused by an inability to see new uses for familiar objects.

▶**Figure 8.12**

Four trees can be placed equidistant from one another by piling dirt into a mound. Three of the trees are planted equal distances apart around the base of the mound. The fourth tree is planted on the top of the mound. If you were fixated on arrangements that involve level ground, you may have been blind to this three-dimensional solution.

usually occurs when we place unnecessary restrictions on our thinking (Isaak & Just, 1995). How, for example, could you plant four small trees so that each is an equal distance from all the others? (The answer is shown in ▶Figure 8.12.)

A prime example of restricted thinking is **functional fixedness.** This is an inability to see new uses (functions) for familiar objects or for things that were used in a particular way. If you have ever used a dime as a screwdriver, you've overcome functional fixedness.

How does functional fixedness affect problem solving? Karl Duncker illustrated the effects of functional fixedness by asking students to mount a candle on a vertical board so the candle could burn normally. Duncker gave each student three candles, some matches, some cardboard boxes, some thumbtacks, and other items. Half of Duncker's subjects received these items inside the cardboard boxes. The others were given all the items, including the boxes, spread out on a tabletop.

Duncker found that when the items were in the boxes, solving the problem was very difficult. Why? If students saw the boxes as containers, they didn't realize the boxes might be part of the solution. (If you haven't guessed the solution, check ▶Figure 8.13.) Undoubtedly, we could avoid many fixations by being more flexible in categorizing the world (Langer & Piper, 1987). For instance, creative thinking could be facilitated in the container problem by saying, "This could be a box," instead of "This is a box."

Common Barriers to Problem Solving

Functional fixedness is just one of the mental blocks that prevent insight. The list that follows identifies other common mental blocks and fixations that can hinder problem solving.

1. *Emotional barriers:* Inhibition and fear of making a fool of oneself, fear of making a mistake, inability to tolerate ambiguity, excessive self-criticism.

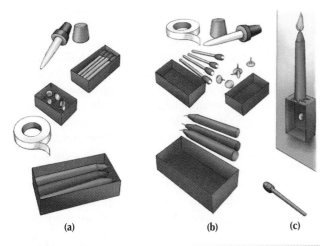

▶Figure 8.13

Materials for solving the candle problem were given to subjects in boxes *(a)* or separately *(b)*. Functional fixedness caused by condition *(a)* interfered with solving the problem. The solution to the problem is shown in *(c)*.

Table 8.1 Solutions to Insight Problems	**Water lilies:** Day 59 **Twenty dollars:** $10 **How many pets?** Three (one bird, one cat, and one dog) **Between 2 and 3:** A decimal point **One word:** ONE WORD (You may object that the answer is two words, but the problem called for the answer to be "one word," and it is.)

Example: An architect is afraid to try an unconventional design because she fears that other architects will think it is frivolous.

2. *Cultural barriers:* Values which hold that fantasy is a waste of time; that playfulness is for children only; that reason, logic, and numbers are good; that feelings, intuitions, pleasure, and humour are bad or have no value in the serious business of problem solving.

   Example: A corporate manager wants to solve a business problem, but becomes stern and angry when members of his marketing team joke playfully about possible solutions.

3. *Learned barriers:* Conventions about uses (functional fixedness), meanings, possibilities, taboos.

   Example: A cook doesn't have any clean mixing bowls and fails to see that he could use a frying pan as a bowl.

4. *Perceptual barriers:* Habits leading to a failure to identify important elements of a problem.

   Example: A beginning artist concentrates on drawing a vase of flowers without seeing that the "empty" spaces around the vase are part of the composition, too.

Much of what we know about thinking comes from direct studies of how people solve problems. Yet, surprisingly, much can also be learned from machines. As the next section explains, computerized problem solving provides a fascinating "laboratory" for testing ideas about how we think.

▶ Artificial Intelligence—I Compute, Therefore I Am

Survey Question:
■ What is artificial intelligence?

It's been a long time since Johann Sebastian Bach, the 18th-century German composer, last wrote any music. But listeners sometimes mistake music created by Kemal Ebcioglu for Bach's work. Ebcioglu wrote a computer program that creates harmonies remarkably similar to Bach's. By analyzing Bach's music, Ebcioglu came up with 350 rules that govern harmonization. The result is a program that displays *artificial intelligence*.

Artificial intelligence (AI) refers to computer programs capable of doing things that require intelligence when done by people (Best, 1999). Artificial intelligence is based on the fact that many tasks—from harmonizing music to medical diagnosis—can be reduced to a set of rules applied to a body of information. AI is valuable in situations where speed, vast memory, and persistence are required. In fact, AI programs are better at some tasks than humans are. An example is world chess champion Garry Kasparov's loss, in 1997, to a computer called Deep Blue.

Artificial intelligence Any artificial system (often a computer program) that is capable of human-like problem solving or intelligent responding.

AI and Cognition

Artificial intelligence provides a way to probe how we comprehend language, make decisions, and solve problems. Increasingly, AI is being used as a research tool in *computer simulations* and *expert systems*.

Computer simulations
Computer programs that mimic some aspect of human thinking, decision making, or problem solving.

Expert systems Computer programs designed to respond as a human expert would; programs based on the knowledge and rules that underlie human expertise in specific topics.

Organized knowledge Orderly and highly refined information about a particular topic or skill.

Acquired strategies Learned tactics for swiftly solving the problems encountered in one's area of expertise.

Computer simulations are programs that attempt to duplicate human behaviour, especially thinking, decision making, or problem solving. Here, the computer acts as a "laboratory" for testing models of cognition. If a computer program behaves as humans do (including making the same errors), then the program may be a good model of how we think (Mayer, 1995). For example, Roger Hall at the University of Manitoba developed an AI model of the process by which companies and other organizations develop policies (Hall, 1999). The program is given information about the organization system—its divisions, their goals, and how information flows between them. This information captures variables such as influences on revenue, costs, and retention of customers. It then works out how manipulating any of these variables affects the others, thus creating a "cognitive map" of such effects. Hall (1999) used the program to simulate the rise and fall of a real magazine publishing company. Among other things, he found that more accurate cognitive maps resulted in more conflict among divisions within the organization. In other words, when everyone has a good idea of what a change will mean, they are more likely to have different views about it.

Expert systems are computer programs that respond as a human expert would. They have demystified some human abilities by converting complex skills into clearly stated rules a computer can follow. Expert systems can predict the weather, analyze geological formations, diagnose disease, play chess, read, tell when to buy or sell stocks, and do many other tasks. But as Raymond Carlson (1993) of Dalhousie University has pointed out, to the extent that expert clinicians rely on memory rather than analysis (which Lee Brooks and many others have shown is true), rule-based expert systems may not be as effective as human experts at diagnosis.

EXPERTS AND NOVICES Working with artificial intelligence has helped especially to clarify how novices differ from experts. Research on chess masters, for example, shows that their skills are based on specific **organized knowledge** (systematic information) and **acquired strategies** (learned tactics). In other words, becoming a star performer does not come from some general strengthening of the mind. Master chess players don't necessarily have better memories than beginners (except for realistic chess positions) (Gobet & Simon, 1996). And, typically, they don't explore more moves ahead than lesser players.

What does set master players apart is their ability to recognize *patterns* that suggest what lines of play should be explored next (Best, 1999). This helps eliminate a large number of possible moves. The chess master, therefore, does not waste time exploring unproductive pathways. Experts are better able to see the true nature of problems and to define them in terms of general principles (Anderson, 1995).

THE FUTURE OF AI AI may lead to robots that recognize voices and that speak and act "intelligently." But cognitive scientists are becoming aware that machine "intelligence" is ultimately "blind" outside its underlying set of rules. In contrast, human cognition is much more flexible. For example, u cann understnd wrds thet ar mizpeld. Computers are very literal and easily stymied by such errors.

Clearly, artificial intelligence will play a major role in cognitive research and in our lives. However, it is not likely to soon replace the human touch in many areas. Although Bach might have been fascinated by AI, it is doubtful that his musical magic will be eclipsed by a machine. The next two sections, therefore, are devoted to a discussion of human intelligence and creativity.

▶ Human Intelligence—The IQ and You

Survey Question:
■ How is human intelligence defined and measured?

Thinking and problem solving are closely related to intelligence. Like so many important concepts in psychology, intelligence cannot be observed directly. Nevertheless, we feel certain it exists. So did French psychologist Alfred Binet when, in 1904, the minister of education in Paris asked him to find a way to distinguish slower students from the more capable (or the capable but lazy). In a flash of brilliance, Binet and an associate created a test made up of "intellectual" questions and problems. Next, they learned which questions

Knowledge builder

PROBLEM SOLVING AND ARTIFICIAL INTELLIGENCE

Relate

Identify at least one problem you have solved mechanically or by rote. Now identify a problem you solved by understanding. Did the second problem involve finding a general solution or a functional solution? Or both? What heuristics did you use to solve the problem?

What is the best insightful solution you've ever come up with? Did it involve selective encoding, combination, or comparison?

Can you think of a time when you overcame functional fixedness to solve a problem?

Learning Check

1. Insight refers to rote, or trial-and-error, problem solving. T or F?
2. The first phase in problem solving by understanding is to discover the general properties of a correct solution. T or F?
3. Problem-solving strategies that guide the search for solutions are called _____.

4. A common element underlying insight is that information is encoded, combined, and compared
   a. mechanically b. by rote c. functionally d. selectively
5. The term *fixation* refers to the point at which a helpful insight becomes fixed in one's thinking. T or F?
6. Two aspects of artificial intelligence are computer simulations and automated creativity. T or F?

Critical Thinking

7. Do you think that it is true that "a problem clearly defined is a problem half solved"?
8. Sea otters select suitably sized rocks and use them to hammer shellfish loose for eating. They then use the rock to open the shell. Does this qualify as thinking?
9. Is it ever accurate to describe a machine as "intelligent"?

Answers:
1. F 2. T 3. heuristics 4. d 5. F 6. F 7. Although this might be an overstatement, it is true that clearly defining a starting point and the desired goal can serve as a heuristic in problem solving. 8. Psychologist Donald Griffin (1984) believes it does because thinking is implied by actions that appear to be planned with an awareness of likely results. 9. Rule-driven expert systems may appear "intelligent" within a narrow range of problem solving. However, they are "stone stupid" at everything else. This is usually not what we have in mind when discussing human intelligence.

---

an average child could answer at each age. By giving children the test, they could tell if a child was performing up to his or her potential (Kaufman, 2000).

Defining Intelligence

Is there an accepted definition of intelligence? University of British Columbia psychologists Delroy Paulhus and Monical Landolt recently studied ordinary people's implicit theories of intelligence by asking students for examples of intelligent people. Over 16 years, many different people were nominated, but the most frequent nominees tended to be consistent, with Albert Einstein winning the most votes. The Canadian and British prime ministers and U.S. presidents were also frequently named. Beyond these obvious candidates—obvious because they are famous—nominations reflected some basic motives. Students nominated people who were similar to them in attitudes, occupations, and sex, as well as people they liked (Paulhus & Landolt, 2000).

Most psychologists would probably agree that **intelligence** is the global capacity to act purposefully, to think rationally, and to deal effectively with the environment. A survey of experts suggests that we should also add the following to our definition: abstract thinking or reasoning, problem-solving ability, capacity to acquire knowledge, memory, and adaptation to one's environment (Snyderman & Rothman, 1987).

Beyond this, there is so much disagreement that many psychologists simply accept an **operational definition** of intelligence. (We define a concept operationally by specifying what procedures will be used to measure it.) By selecting test items, a psychologist is saying in a very direct way, "This is what I mean by intelligence." A test that measures memory, reasoning, and verbal fluency offers a very different definition of intelligence than one that measures strength of grip, shoe size, length of the nose, or the person's best Duke Nukem score.

Intelligence An overall capacity to think rationally, act purposefully, and deal effectively with the environment.

Operational definition A definition that states the operations (actions or procedures) used to measure a concept.

Intelligence Tests

Stanford-Binet Intelligence Scale
A widely used individual test of intelligence; a direct descendant of Alfred Binet's first intelligence test.

American psychologists quickly saw the value of Alfred Binet's test. In 1916, Lewis Terman and others at Stanford University revised it for use in the United States. After more updates, the **Stanford-Binet Intelligence Scale, Fourth Edition,** is still a widely used individual test of intelligence. The original Stanford-Binet assumed that mental ability improves each year during childhood. That's why the Stanford-Binet (or Binet-4) is still primarily made up of age-ranked questions of increasing difficulty. Table 8.2 lists the subtests of the Binet-4.

Table 8.2
Stanford-Binet 4: Ability Areas and Subtests

VERBAL REASONING	
Vocabulary	Name a pictured object or define a word.
Comprehension	Answer questions requiring logic or common sense.
Absurdities	Tell what is wrong with pictures (for example, a bicycle has square wheels).
Verbal relations	Given four words, tell how three are similar.
QUANTITATIVE REASONING	
Quantitative	Use numbered blocks to add and count; solve word problems.
Number series	Given a series of numbers, tell what two numbers would come next. For example, 3, 6, 9 would be followed by 12 and 15.
Equation building	Given a set of numbers and mathematical signs, arrange them to make a true equation. For example, 3, 4, 7, + = would be arranged as 3 + 4 = 7.
ABSTRACT/VISUAL REASONING	
Pattern analysis	Put picture puzzles together; reproduce patterns with blocks.
Copying	Copy arrangements of blocks or draw copies of designs.
Matrices	Complete a matrix of shapes that has one part missing.
Paper folding and cutting	Choose pictures that show how a piece of paper would look if folded or cut.
SHORT-TERM MEMORY	
Bead memory	Correctly remember the order of beads placed on a stick.
Memory for sentences	Repeat sentences exactly after hearing them once.
Memory for digits	Repeat a series of digits (forward or backward) after hearing them once.
Memory for objects	After seeing several objects, point to the objects in the same order as they were shown.

Modern intelligence tests are widely used to measure intellectual abilities. When properly administered, such tests provide an operational definition of intelligence.

Chronological age
A person's age in years.
Mental age The average mental ability people display at a given age.

Intelligence Quotients

Imagine that a child named Yuan can answer intelligence test questions that an average seven-year-old can answer. How smart is she? Actually, we can't say yet, because we don't know how old Yuan is. If she is 10, she's not very smart. If she's five, she is very bright. Thus, to estimate a child's intelligence we need to know both her **chronological age** (age in years) and her **mental age** (average intellectual performance).

A person's mental age is based on the level of age-ranked questions she or he can answer. For example, at ages eight or nine, very few children can define the word *connection*. At age 10, 10 percent can. At age 13, 60 percent can. In other words, the ability to define *connection* indicates mental ability equal to that of an average 13-year-old. If we had only this one item to test children with, those who answered correctly would be given a mental age of 13. When scores from many items are combined, a child's overall mental age can be found. Table 8.3 is a sample of items that persons of average intelligence can answer at various ages.

Mental age is a good measure of actual ability. But mental age says nothing about whether overall intelligence is high or low, compared with that of other people of the same age. To find out what a particular mental age means, we must also consider a person's chronological age. Then we can relate mental age to actual age. This yields an **IQ,** or

Table 8.3
Sample Items from the Stanford-Binet Intelligence Scale

2 years old	On a large paper doll, points out the hair, mouth, feet, ears, nose, hands, and eyes.
	When shown a tower built of four blocks, builds one like it.
3 years old	When shown a bridge built of three blocks, builds one like it.
	When shown a drawing of a circle, copies it with a pencil.
4 years old	Fills in the missing word when asked, "Brother is a boy; sister is a _____."
	"In daytime it is light; at night it is _____."
	Answers correctly when asked, "Why do we have houses?" "Why do we have books?"
5 years old	Defines *ball, hat,* and *stove.*
	When shown a drawing of a square, copies it with a pencil.
9 years old	Answers correctly when examiner says, "In an old graveyard in Spain they have discovered a small skull which they believe to be that of Christopher Columbus when he was about 10 years old. What is foolish about that?"
	Answers correctly when asked, "Tell me the name of a colour that rhymes with head." "Tell me a number that rhymes with tree."
Adult	Can describe the difference between laziness and idleness, poverty and misery, character and reputation.
	Answers correctly when asked, "Which direction would you have to face so your right hand would be toward the north?"

(Terman & Merrill, 1960.)

Intelligence quotient (IQ)
An index of intelligence defined as a person's mental age divided by his or her chronological age and multiplied by 100.

Deviation IQ An IQ obtained statistically from a person's relative standing in his or her age group; that is, how far above or below average the person's score was relative to other scores.

intelligence quotient. A quotient results from dividing one number by another. When the Stanford-Binet was first used, IQ was defined as mental age (MA) divided by chronological age (CA) and multiplied by 100. (Multiplying by 100 changes the IQ to a whole number, rather than a decimal.)

$$\frac{MA}{CA} \times 100 = IQ$$

An advantage of the original IQ is that intelligence could be compared among children with different chronological and mental ages. For instance, 10-year-old Justin has a mental age of 12. Thus, his IQ is 120:

$$\frac{(MA)\ 12}{(CA)\ 10} \times 100 = 120\ (IQ)$$

Justin's friend Suke also has a mental age of 12. However, Suke's chronological age is 12, so his IQ is 100:

$$\frac{(MA)\ 12}{(CA)\ 12} \times 100 = 100\ (IQ)$$

The IQ shows that 10-year-old Justin is brighter than his 12-year-old friend Suke, even though their intellectual skills are about the same. Notice that a person's IQ will be 100 when mental age equals chronological age. An IQ score of 100 is therefore defined as average intelligence.

Then does a person with an IQ score below 100 have below average intelligence? Not unless the IQ is well below 100. An IQ of 100 is the *mathematical* average (or mean) for such scores. However, average intelligence is usually defined as any score from 90 to 109. The important point is that IQ scores will be over 100 when mental age is higher than age in years. IQ scores below 100 occur when a person's age in years exceeds his or her mental age. An example of the second situation would be a 15-year-old with an MA of 12:

$$\frac{12}{15} \times 100 = 80\ (IQ)$$

DEVIATION IQS   The preceding examples may give you insight into the meaning of IQ scores. However, it's no longer necessary to directly calculate IQs. Instead, modern tests use **deviation IQs.** These scores are based on a person's relative standing in his or her age group. That is, they tell how far above or below average the person's score falls. Tables

Wechsler Adult Intelligence Scale-Third Edition (WAIS-III) An adult intelligence test that rates both verbal and performance intelligence.

Wechsler Intelligence Scale for Children-Third Edition (WISC-III) An intelligence test for children that rates both verbal and performance intelligence.

Performance intelligence Intelligence measured by solving puzzles, assembling objects, completing pictures, and other non-verbal tasks.

Verbal intelligence Intelligence measured by answering questions involving vocabulary, general information, arithmetic, and other language- or symbol-oriented tasks.

Culture-fair test A test (such as an intelligence test) designed to minimize the importance of skills and knowledge that may be more common in some cultures than in others.

supplied with the test are then used to convert a person's relative standing in the group to an IQ score (Neisser et al., 1996).

The Wechsler Tests

Is the Stanford-Binet the only intelligence test? A widely used alternative is the **Wechsler Adult Intelligence Scale—Third Edition,** or **WAIS-III.** A version for children is called the **Wechsler Intelligence Scale for Children—Third Edition (WISC-III).**

The Wechsler tests are similar to the Stanford-Binet test but different in important ways. For one thing, the WAIS-III was specifically designed to test adult intelligence. Of course, the Stanford-Binet may be used to test adults, but it tends to be better suited for children and adolescents. The Wechsler tests yield a single overall IQ, just as the Stanford-Binet does. However, the WAIS and WISC also give separate scores for **performance** (non-verbal) **intelligence** and **verbal** (language- or symbol-oriented) **intelligence.** The abilities measured by the Wechsler tests and some sample test items are listed in Table 8.4.

Culture-Fair Tests

It is important to realize that intelligence tests may not be equally valid for all groups. As Jerome Kagan says, "If the Wechsler and Binet scales were translated into Spanish, Swahili, and Chinese and given to every 10-year-old in Latin America, East Africa, or China, the majority would obtain IQ scores in the mentally retarded range."

Certainly we cannot believe that children of different cultures are all retarded. The fault must lie in the test. Cultural values, traditions, and experiences can greatly affect performance on tests designed for Western cultures (Neisser et al., 1996; Nixon, 1990). To avoid this problem, **culture-fair tests** attempt to measure intelligence without being affected by a person's verbal skills, cultural background, and educational level. (For a sample of culture-fair test items, see ▶Figure 8.14.) Culture-fair tests are also useful for

Table 8.4
Sample Items Similar to Those Used on the WAIS-III

VERBAL SUBTESTS	SAMPLE ITEMS
Information	How many wings does a bird have?
	Who wrote *Paradise Lost*?
Digit span	Repeat from memory a series of digits, such as 3 1 0 6 7 4 2 5, after hearing it once.
General comprehension	What is the advantage of keeping money in the bank?
	Why is copper often used in electrical wires?
Arithmetic	Three men divided 18 golf balls equally among themselves. How many golf balls did each man receive?
	If 2 apples cost 15¢ what will be the cost of a dozen apples?
Similarities	In what way are a lion and a tiger alike?
	In what way are a saw and a hammer alike?
Vocabulary	The test consists simply of asking, "What is a _____?" or "What does _____ mean?" The words cover a wide range of difficulty or familiarity.

PERFORMANCE SUBTESTS	DESCRIPTION OF ITEM
Picture arrangement	Arrange a series of cartoon panels to make a meaningful story.
Picture completion	What is missing from these pictures?
Block design	Copy designs with blocks (as shown at right).
Object assembly	Put together a jigsaw puzzle.
Digit symbol	Fill in the symbols:

1	2	3	4
X	III	I	0

3	4	1	3	4	2	1	2

(Courtesy of The Psychological Corporation.)

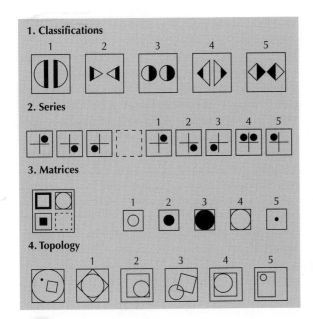

1. Classifications

2. Series

3. Matrices

4. Topology

▶Figure 8.14

Sample items from a culture-fair test. 1. Which pattern is different from the remaining four? (Number 3.) 2. Which of the five figures on the right would properly continue the three on the left—that is, fill the blank? (Number 5.) 3. Which of the figures on the right should go in the square on the left to make it look right? (Number 2.) 4. At left, the dot is outside the square and inside the circle. In which of the figures on the right could you put a dot outside the square and inside the circle? (Number 3.) (Courtesy of R. B. Cattell.)

testing children who come from poor communities, rural areas, or ethnic minority families (Stephens et al., 1999).

Group Tests

The Binet-4 and the Wechsler scales are **individual intelligence tests,** which must be given to a single person by a trained specialist. In contrast, **group intelligence tests** can be taken by large groups of people with minimal supervision. Group tests usually require people to read, to follow instructions, and to solve problems of logic, reasoning, mathematics, or spatial skills. There are group tests not only of intelligence but also of other abilities. For example, many students who come from another country to study in Canada take a group test to determine their language skills. The well-known Test of English as a Foreign Language (TOEFL) measures the proficiency of non-Native speakers in both comprehension and expression in English.

Variations in Intelligence

IQ scores are classified as shown in Table 8.5. Notice that the distribution (or scattering) of IQ scores approximates a **normal** (bell-shaped) **curve.** That is, most scores fall close to the average and very few are found at the extremes. ▶Figure 8.15 shows this characteristic of measured intelligence.

IQ AND ACHIEVEMENT   *How do IQ scores relate to success in school, jobs, and other endeavours?* If we look at a broad range of scores, the correlation between IQ and school grades is .50. This is a sizable association. It would be even higher, but motivation, special talents, off-campus educational opportunities, and many other factors also influence grades. The same is true of "real world" success outside of school. Where art, music, writing, dramatics, science, and leadership are concerned, IQ is not at all good at predicting success. Tests of creativity are much more strongly related to achievement in these areas (Neisser et al., 1996; Wallach, 1985).

SEX AND INTELLIGENCE   *On the average, do males and females differ in intelligence?* IQ scores cannot answer this question because test items were selected to be equally difficult for both sexes. On the one hand, the consensus among

Survey Question:
■ How do IQ scores relate to achievement and thinking ability?

Individual intelligence test A test of intelligence designed to be given to a single individual by a trained specialist.

Group intelligence test Any intelligence test that can be administered to a group of people with minimal supervision.

Normal curve A bell-shaped curve characterized by a large number of scores in a middle area, tapering to very few extremely high and low scores.

Average
Bright normal
Dull normal
Superior
Borderline
Very superior
Retarded

Percent
24
20
16
12
8
4

40   60   80   100   120   140   160   180

Mean = 101.8   IQ

▶Figure 8.15

Distribution of Stanford-Binet Intelligence Test scores for 3184 children. (After Terman & Merrill, 1960.)

Table 8.5
Distribution of Adult IQ Scores on WAIS-III

IQ	DESCRIPTION	PERCENT
Above 130	Very superior	2.2
120–129	Superior	6.7
110–119	Bright normal	16.1
90–109	Average	50.0
80–89	Dull normal	16.1
70–79	Borderline	6.7
Below 70	Mentally retarded	2.2

psychologists is that men and women do not differ in overall intelligence (Halpern, 1997; Neisser et al., 1996) On the other hand, tests like the WAIS-III used to show that women, as a group, performed best on items that require verbal ability, vocabulary, and rote learning. Men, in contrast, were best at items that require spatial visualization and arithmetic reasoning. Today, there is debate about whether such male–female differences still exist. For example, Tavris (1992) suggests that any differences that remain appear to be related to a tendency for parents and teachers to encourage males to learn math and spatial skills. If Tavris is right, most male–female performance gaps can be traced to social differences in the opportunities given to men and women. But as we have already noted, Daniel Voyer of St. Francis Xavier University has reported better performance for men than for women on mental rotation tests. More recently, Susan Levine and her colleagues at the University of Chicago found robust sex differences in several spatial skills in children as young as four years, six months (Levine et al., 1999). Further, some biological influences on spatial test performance suggest sex differences are not learned. Beth Casey, Ronald Nuttall, and Elizabeth Pezaris reported that spatial ability measures predicted math achievement for all boys and for girls who were non-right-handed, but not for right-handed girls (Casey et al., 1992). If spatial skill reflects learning, why are right-handed and non-right-handed girls different?

When IQs are extreme—below 70 or above 140—differences in a person's potential for success become unmistakable. Only about 3 percent of all people are found in these ranges. Nevertheless, millions of people have exceptionally high or low IQs. Discussions of the mentally gifted and mentally retarded follow.

The Mentally Gifted

How high is the IQ of a genius? Only two people out of 100 score above 130 on IQ tests. These bright individuals are usually described as "gifted." Less than .5 percent of the population scores above 140. These people are certainly gifted or perhaps even "geniuses." However, some psychologists reserve the term *genius* for people with even higher IQs or those who are exceptionally creative (Kamphaus, 1993).

GIFTED CHILDREN *Do high IQ scores in childhood predict later ability?* To directly answer this question, Lewis Terman selected 1500 children with IQs of 140 or more. Starting in the 1920s, Terman followed this gifted group (the "Termites" as he called them) into adulthood and found that most were quite successful. A large percentage of them completed college, earned advanced degrees, held professional positions, and had written books or scientific articles (Terman & Oden, 1959). As noted earlier, IQ scores are not generally good predictors of real-world success. However, when people score in the gifted range, their chances for high achievement do seem to be higher (Shurkin, 1992).

IDENTIFYING GIFTED CHILDREN *How might a parent spot an unusually bright child?* Early signs of giftedness are not always purely "intellectual." **Giftedness** can be either a high IQ or having special talents or aptitudes. The following signs may reveal that a child is gifted: a tendency to seek out older children and adults; an early fascination with explanations and problem solving; talking in complete sentences as early as two or three years of age; an unusually good memory; precocious talent in art, music, or number skills; an early interest in books, early reading (often by age three); showing of kindness, understanding, and cooperation toward others (Alvino, 1996).

Notice that this list goes beyond straight "academic" intelligence. In fact, if artistic talent, mechanical aptitude, musical aptitude, athletic potential, and so on were considered, 19 out of 20 children could be labelled as having a special "gift" of some sort. Limiting giftedness to high IQ can shortchange children with special talents or potentials (see "Frames of Mind—Eight Intelligences?"). This is especially true of ethnic minority children, who may be the victims of subtle biases in standardized intelligence tests. These children, as well as children with physical disabilities, are less likely to be recognized as gifted (Robinson & Clinkenbeard, 1998). Indeed, as University of Alberta psychologist Lorraine Wilgosh has pointed out, the picture with ethnic minorities can sometimes be complicated by the need to identify gifted but underachieving children. How do we find our

Giftedness The possession of either a high IQ or special talents or aptitudes.

USING PSYCHOLOGY · Frames of Mind—Eight Intelligences?

At an elementary school, a student who is two grades behind in reading shows his teacher how to solve a difficult computer software problem. In a nearby room, one of his classmates, who is poor in math, plays intricate music on a piano. Both of these children show clear signs of intelligence. And yet, each might score below average on a traditional IQ test. Such observations have convinced many psychologists that it is time to define intelligence more broadly. Their basic goal is to better predict real-world success—not just the likelihood of success in school (Sternberg, 1996).

One such psychologist is Howard Gardner of Harvard University. Gardner (1993) theorizes that there are actually eight different kinds of intelligence. These are different mental "languages" that people use for thinking. Each is listed below, with examples of pursuits that make use of them.

1. *Language*—writer, lawyer, comedian
2. *Logic and math*—scientist, accountant, programmer
3. *Visual and spatial thinking*—engineer, inventor, artist
4. *Music*—composer, musician, music critic
5. *Bodily-kinesthetic skills*—dancer, athlete, surgeon
6. *Intrapersonal skills* (self-knowledge)—poet, actor, minister
7. *Interpersonal skills* (social abilities)—psychologist, teacher, politician
8. *Naturalist skills* (an ability to classify plants and animals and understand the natural environment)—biologist, medicine man, organic farmer

Most of us are probably strong in only a few types of intelligence. In contrast, geniuses like Albert Einstein seem to be able to use all of the intelligences, as needed, to solve problems.

If Gardner's theory of *multiple intelligences* is correct, traditional IQ tests measure only a part of real-world intelligence—namely, linguistic, logical-mathematical, and spatial abilities. A further implication is that our schools may be wasting a lot of human potential. For example, some children might find it easier to learn math or reading if these topics were tied into art, music, dance, drama, and so on.

Not all psychologists agree with Gardner's broader definition of intelligence. But whether or not he is right, it seems likely that in the future intelligence will not be so strongly equated with IQ. Already, many schools are using Gardner's theory to cultivate a wider range of skills and talents (Woo, 1995).

Mental retardation The presence of a developmental disability, a formal IQ score below 70, or a significant impairment of adaptive behaviour.

Adaptive behaviours Basic skills and actions considered necessary for self-care and for dealing successfully with the environment.

way here? IQ tests are inappropriate, and for various reasons minority children may have trouble demonstrating their ability. Wilgosh has used creative work by Inuit children to assess their ability, and recommended development of particular cognitive strategies in response to underachievement (Wilgosh, 1991).

Mental Retardation

A person with mental abilities far below average is termed **mentally retarded** or **developmentally disabled.** An IQ of about 70 or below is regarded as the dividing line for retardation. However, a person's ability to perform **adaptive behaviours** (basic skills such as dressing, eating, communicating, shopping, and working) also figures into evaluating retardation (DSM-IV, 1994; Kamphaus, 1993). (See Table 8.6.)

It is important to realize that the developmentally disabled have no handicap where feelings are concerned. They are sensitive to rejection and easily hurt by teasing or ridicule. Likewise, they respond warmly to love and acceptance. Professionals working

Table 8.6
Levels of Mental Retardation

IQ RANGE	DEGREE OF RETARDATION	EDUCATIONAL CLASSIFICATION	REQUIRED LEVEL OF SUPPORT
50–55 to 70	Mild	Educable	Intermittent
35–40 to 50–55	Moderate	Trainable	Limited
20–25 to 35–40	Severe	Dependent	Extensive
Below 20–25	Profound	Life support	Pervasive

(DSM-IV, 1994; Hodapp, 1994.)

These youngsters are participants in the Special Olympics—an athletic event for the mentally retarded. It is often said of the Special Olympics that "everyone is a winner—participants, coaches, and spectators."

Birth injury Any injury or damage that occurs to an infant during delivery.

Fetal damage A congenital problem; that is, damage or injury that occurs to the fetus during prenatal development.

Metabolic disorder Any disorder in metabolism (the rate of energy production and use in the body).

Genetic abnormality Any abnormality in the genes, including missing genes, extra genes, or defective genes.

Familial retardation Mild retardation associated with homes that are intellectually, nutritionally, and emotionally impoverished.

Fraternal twins Twins conceived from two separate eggs. Fraternal twins are no more alike genetically than other siblings.

Identical twins Twins who develop from a single egg and therefore have identical genes.

with the retarded emphasize their rights to self-respect and to a place in the community. This is especially important during childhood, when the support of others adds greatly to the person's chances of becoming a well-adjusted member of society.

CAUSES OF RETARDATION *What causes mental retardation?* About 50 percent of all cases of mental retardation are *organic,* or related to physical disorders. Typical problems include **birth injuries** (such as a lack of oxygen) and **fetal damage** (from disease, infection, or the mother's abuse of drugs or alcohol). **Metabolic disorders** also cause retardation. These are problems with the rate of energy production and use in the body. Some forms of retardation are linked to **genetic abnormalities,** including missing genes, extra genes, or defective genes. Malnutrition and exposure to lead, PCBs, and other toxins early in childhood can also cause organic retardation (Bryant & Maxwell, 1999).

In 30 to 40 percent of cases, no known biological problem can be identified. In many such cases, retardation is mild, in the 50 to 70 IQ range. Quite often, other family members are also mildly retarded. *Familial retardation,* as this is called, occurs mostly in very poor households. In some such homes, nutrition, early stimulation, medical care, the intellectual climate, and emotional support are inadequate. This suggests that **familial retardation** is based largely on an impoverished environment. Thus, many cases of retardation might be prevented by better nutrition, education, and early childhood enrichment programs (Hunt, 1995; Zigler, 1995).

Heredity, Environment, and Intelligence

Is intelligence inherited? Most people are aware that there is a moderate similarity in the intelligence of parents and their children, or between brothers and sisters. As ▶ Figure 8.16 shows, the similarity in IQ scores among relatives grows in proportion to their closeness on the family tree.

Does that indicate that intelligence is hereditary? Not necessarily. Brothers, sisters, and parents share similar environments as well as similar heredity. To separate heredity and environment, we need to make some selected comparisons.

TWIN STUDIES Notice in Figure 8.16 that the IQ scores of fraternal twins are more alike than those of ordinary siblings. **Fraternal twins** come from two separate eggs fertilized at the same time. They are no more genetically alike than ordinary siblings. Why, then, should the twins' IQ scores be more similar? The reason is environmental: Parents treat twins more alike than ordinary siblings, resulting in a closer match in IQs.

More striking similarities are observed with **identical twins,** who develop from a single egg and have identical genes. At the top of Figure 8.16 you can see that identical twins who grow up in the same family have highly correlated IQs. This is what we would expect with identical heredity and very similar environments. Now, let's consider what happens when identical twins are reared apart. As you

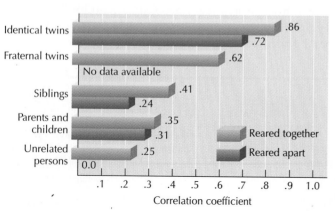

▶Figure 8.16

Approximate correlations between IQ scores for persons with varying degrees of genetic and environmental similarity. Notice that the correlations grow smaller as the degree of genetic similarity declines. Also note that a shared environment increases the correlation in all cases. (Estimates from Bouchard, 1983; Henderson, 1982.)

Fluid intelligence The ability to reason and to solve problems, especially unfamiliar ones.

Crystal intelligence The extent to which a person has acquired his or her culture's accumulated knowledge.

can see, the correlation drops, but only from .86 to .72. Psychologists who emphasize genetics believe figures like these show that differences in adult intelligence are roughly 50 percent hereditary (Casto, DeFries, & Fulker, 1995; Neisser et al., 1996; Plomin & Rende, 1991).

University of Western Ontario psychologist Philip Vernon and his colleagues have carried out both twin studies and studies of biological correlates of intelligence such as brain volume, cerebral glucose metabolic rate, and neural processing speed. One interesting observation is that brain volume is correlated with measures of **fluid intelligence** but not of **crystallized intelligence** (Wickett, Vernon, & Lee, 2000). This distinction is roughly the difference between forming new concepts and associations (fluid) and using existing ones (crystallized). In other words, having a big brain may help you acquire new concepts but won't make you more likely to use what you've already learned.

How do environmentalists interpret the figures? Environmentalists point out that some separated twins differ by as much as 20 IQ points. In every case where this occurs, there are large educational and environmental differences between the twins. Also, separated twins are almost always placed in homes socially and educationally similar to their biological parents. This fact would tend to inflate apparent genetic effects by making the separated twins' IQs more alike.

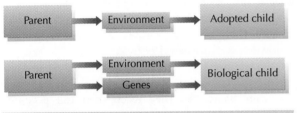

▶ **Figure 8.17**

Comparison of an adopted child and a biological child reared in the same family. (After Kamin, 1981.)

ENVIRONMENTAL INFLUENCES   Strong evidence for an environmental view of intelligence comes from families having one adopted child and one biological child. As ▶ Figure 8.17 shows, parents contribute genes and environment to their biological child. With an adopted child they contribute only environment. If intelligence is highly genetic, the IQs of biological children should be more like their parents' IQs than are the IQs of adopted children. However, children reared by the same mother tend to resemble her IQ to the same degree. It does not matter whether or not they share her genes (Horn, Loehlin, & Willerman, 1979; Kamin, 1981; Weinberg, 1989). (See also "The Bell Curve—Race, Culture, and IQ.")

HUMAN DIVERSITY   The Bell Curve—Race, Culture, and IQ

African-American children in the United States score an average of about 15 points lower on standardized IQ tests than white children. As a group, Japanese-American children score above average in IQ. Could such differences be genetic?

In 1994, Richard Herrnstein and Charles Murray, in a highly controversial book titled *The Bell Curve*, proclaimed that IQ is largely dictated by heredity (Herrnstein & Murray, 1994).

Were they right? Are ethnic group differences in IQ based on genetics? No. Herrnstein and Murray misused statistics and ignored the effects of culture and environment. For example, as a group, African Americans in the United States are more likely to live in environments that are educationally disadvantaged. Japanese-American culture, on the other hand, tends to place a high value on educational achievement. Such differences can significantly affect how people score on IQ tests. When unequal edu-

cation is part of the equation, IQs tell us little about how heredity affects intelligence (Neisser et al., 1996).

Recently, a distinguished group of psychologists evaluated the claims made in *The Bell Curve*. There is no scientific evidence, they concluded, that group differences in average IQ are based on genetics. In fact, studies that used actual blood-group testing found no significant correlations between ethnic ancestry and IQ scores. Group differences in IQ scores are based on cultural and environmental differences, not on heredity (Alva, 1993; Caplan, Choy, & Whitmore, 1992; Neisser et al., 1996; Yee et al., 1993).

This controversy provides students a good opportunity to practise their own critical-thinking skills. Suppose someone made the claim to you personally that IQ differences between groups are produced by heredity. Based on the knowledge of IQ testing you have gleaned from this chapter, what critical questions would you ask the person about his or her evidence?

IQ AND ENVIRONMENT   *How much can environment alter intelligence?* In one study, striking increases in IQ occurred in 25 children who were moved from an orphanage to more stimulating environments. The children, all considered mentally retarded, were moved to an institution where they received personal attention from adults. Later, these supposedly retarded children were adopted by parents who gave them love, a family, and a stimulating environment. The IQs of the children showed an average gain of 29 points. For one child, the increase was an amazing 58 points. A second group of initially less "retarded" children who remained in the orphanage lost an average of 26 IQ points (Skeels, 1966)! Another study found average IQ gains of 15 points in 14 nations during the last 30 years (Flynn, 1987; Horgan, 1995). These IQ boosts seem to reflect the effects of improved education or other advantages. Support for this interpretation comes from the fact that the longer children stay in school, the more their IQ scores rise. This is another encouraging indication that intelligence can be raised by an improved environment (Perkins, 1995).

SUMMARY   To sum up, few psychologists seriously believe that heredity is not a factor in intelligence, and all acknowledge that environment affects it. Estimates of the impact of each factor continue to vary. But ultimately, most experts agree that improving social conditions and education can raise intelligence.

There is probably no limit to how far down intelligence can go in an extremely poor environment. On the other hand, heredity does seem to impose upper limits on IQ, even under ideal conditions. It is telling, nevertheless, that gifted children tend to come from homes where parents spend time with their children, answer their questions, and encourage intellectual exploration (Snowden & Christian, 1999).

The fact that intelligence is partly determined by heredity tells us little of any real value. Genes are fixed at birth. Improving the environments in which children learn and grow is the main way in which we can assure that they reach their full potential (Turkheimer, 1998).

As a final summary, it might help to think of inherited intellectual potential as a rubber band that is stretched by outside forces. A long rubber band may be stretched more

Knowledge builder

INTELLIGENCE

Relate

If you were going to write an intelligence test, what kinds of questions would you include? How much would they resemble the questions found on the Binet-4, the WAIS-III, or culture-fair tests?

How has your understanding of the following concepts changed: IQ, giftedness, mental retardation?

A friend says to you, "I think intelligence is entirely inherited from parents." What could you tell your friend to make sure she or he is better informed?

Learning Check

1. The first successful intelligence test was developed by _____.
2. If we define intelligence by writing a test, we are using an _____ definition.
3. IQ was originally defined as _____ 3 100.

4. The WAIS-III is a group intelligence test. T or F?
5. The distribution of IQs approximates a _____ (bell-shaped) curve.
6. Only about 6 percent of the population scores above 140 on IQ tests. T or F?
7. Many cases of mental retardation without known organic causes appear to be _____.
8. Most psychologists believe that intelligence is 90 percent hereditary. T or F?

Critical Thinking

9. How rare are high IQ scores? If you were to meet 50 people at random, how many would you expect to have an IQ score above 130 (based on Table 8.5)?
10. Some people treat IQ as if it were a fixed number, permanently stamped on the forehead of each child. Why is this view in error?

Answers:

1. Alfred Binet 2. operational 3. MA/CA 4. F 5. normal 6. F 7. familial 8. F 9. Approximately 1 person in 50 or 2 out of 100. 10. Because one's IQ depends on the intelligence test used to measure it: Change the test and you will change the score. Also, heredity establishes a range of possibilities; it does not automatically preordain a person's intellectual capacities.

easily, but a shorter one can be stretched to the same length if enough force is applied. Of course, a superior genetic gift may allow for a higher maximum IQ. In the final analysis, intelligence reflects development as well as potential, nurture as well as nature (Rose, 1995; Weinberg, 1989).

▶ Creative Thinking—Down Roads Less Travelled

Survey Question:
■ What is the nature of creative thinking?

Inductive thought
Thinking in which a general rule or principle is gathered from a series of specific examples; for instance, inferring the laws of gravity by observing many falling objects.

Deductive thought
Thought that applies a general set of rules to specific situations; for example, using the laws of gravity to predict the behaviour of a single falling object.

Logical thought Drawing conclusions on the basis of formal principles of reasoning.

Illogical thought Thought that is intuitive, haphazard, or irrational.

Fluency In tests of creativity, fluency refers to the total number of solutions produced.

Flexibility In tests of creativity, flexibility is indicated by the number of different types of solutions produced.

Originality In tests of creativity, originality refers to how novel or unusual solutions are.

Convergent thinking
Thinking directed toward discovery of a single established correct answer; conventional thinking.

Divergent thinking
Thinking that produces many ideas or alternatives; a major element in original or creative thought.

We have seen that problem solving may be mechanical, insightful, or based on understanding. To this we can add that thinking may be **inductive** (going from specific facts or observations to general principles) or **deductive** (going from general principles to specific situations). Thinking may also be **logical** (proceeding from given information to new conclusions on the basis of explicit rules) or **illogical** (intuitive, associative, or personal).

What distinguishes creative thinking from more routine problem solving? Creative thinking involves all of these thinking styles, plus *fluency, flexibility,* and *originality.* Let's say that you would like to find some creative uses for the millions of automobile tires discarded each year. The creativity of your suggestions could be rated in this way: **Fluency** is defined as the total number of suggestions you are able to make. **Flexibility** is the number of times you shift from one class of possible uses to another. **Originality** refers to how novel or unusual your suggestions are. By counting the number of times you showed fluency, flexibility, and originality, we could rate the creativity of your suggestions. Speaking more generally, we would be rating your capacity for *divergent thinking* (Baer, 1993).

Divergent thinking is widely used to measure creativity. In routine problem solving or thinking, there is one correct answer, and the problem is to find it. This leads to **convergent thinking** (lines of thought converge on the answer). **Divergent thinking** (see ▶Figure 8.18) is the reverse, in which many possibilities are developed from one starting point (Baer, 1993). (See Table 8.7 for some examples.) Rather than repeating learned solutions, creative thinking produces new answers, ideas, or patterns (Michalko, 1998).

Fluency is an important part of creative thinking. Mozart produced more than 600 pieces of music. Picasso (shown here) created more than 20 000 artworks. Shakespeare wrote 154 sonnets. Not all of these works were masterpieces. However, a fluent outpouring of ideas fed the creative efforts of each of these geniuses.

▶Figure 8.18

The first paper clip was patented in 1899. Competition for sales, combined with divergent thinking, has resulted in a remarkable array of alternative designs. These are drawings of just a few of the variations that have appeared over the years. (After Kim, 2000.)

Table 8.7
Convergent and Divergent Problems

CONVERGENT PROBLEMS
• What is the area of a triangle that is 3 metres wide at the base and 2 metres tall?
• Erica is shorter than Zoey but taller than Carlo, and Carlo is taller than Jared. Who is the second tallest?
• If you simultaneously drop a baseball and a bowling ball from a tall building, which will hit the ground first?

DIVERGENT PROBLEMS
• What objects can you think of that begin with the letters BR?
• How could discarded aluminum cans be put to use?
• Write a poem about fire and ice.

Tests of Creativity

Unusual Uses Test A test of creativity in which subjects try to think of new uses for a common object.

Consequences Test A test of creativity in which subjects try to list as many consequences as possible that would follow if some basic change were made in the world.

Anagrams Test A test of creativity in which subjects try to make as many new words as possible from the letters in a given word.

There are several ways to measure divergent thinking. In the **Unusual Uses Test** a person is asked to think of as many uses as possible for some object, such as the tires mentioned earlier. In the **Consequences Test** the goal is to list the consequences that would follow a basic change in the world. For example, you might be asked, "What would happen if everyone suddenly lost the sense of balance and could no longer stay in an upright position?" People try to list as many reactions as possible. If you were to take the **Anagrams Test,** you would be given a word such as *creativity* and asked to make as many new words as possible by rearranging the letters. Each of these tests can be scored for fluency, flexibility, and originality. (For an example of other tests of divergent thinking, see ▶ Figure 8.19.) Tests of divergent thinking seem to tap something quite different from intelligence. Generally, there is little correlation between such tests and IQ test scores (Wallach, 1985).

Creativity tests have been useful, but they are not the whole story. If you want to predict whether a person will be creative in the future, it helps to look at two more kinds of information (Feldhusen & Goh, 1995):

- The *products* of creative thinking (such as essays, poems, drawings, or constructed objects) are often more informative than test results. When creative people are asked to actually produce something, others tend to judge their work as creative.
- A simple listing of a person's *past creative activities and achievements* is an excellent guide to the likelihood that she or he will be creative in the future.

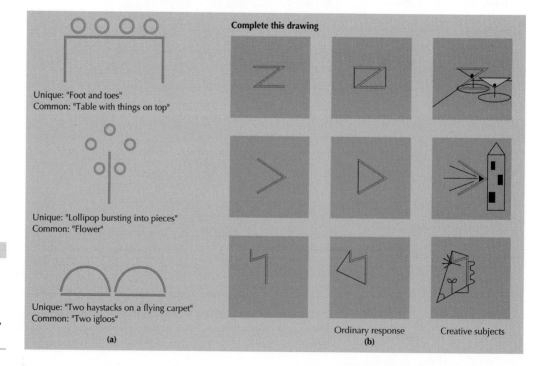

Complete this drawing

Unique: "Foot and toes"
Common: "Table with things on top"

Unique: "Lollipop bursting into pieces"
Common: "Flower"

Unique: "Two haystacks on a flying carpet"
Common: "Two igloos"

Ordinary response   Creative subjects
(a)   **(b)**

▶**Figure 8.19**

Some tests of divergent thinking. Creative responses are more original and more complex. (a) after Wallach & Kogan, 1965; (b) after Barron, 1958.

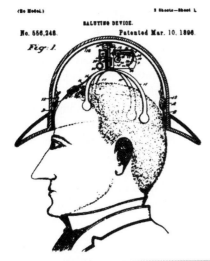

▶ **Figure 8.20**

Hat-tipping device. According to the patent, it is for "automatically effecting polite salutations by the elevation and rotation of the hat on the head of the saluting party when said person bows to the person or persons saluted." In addition to being original or novel, a creative solution must fit the demands of the problem. Is this a creative solution to the "problem" of hat tipping?

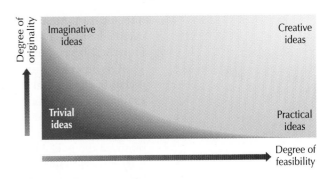

▶ **Figure 8.21**

Creative ideas combine originality with feasibility. (Adapted from McMullan & Stocking, 1978.)

Isn't creativity more than divergent thought? What if a person comes up with a large number of useless answers to a problem? A good question. Divergent thinking is definitely an important part of creativity, but there is more to it. To be creative, the solution to a problem must be more than novel, unusual, or original (see ▶Figure 8.20). It must also be practical if it is an invention and sensible if it is an idea (Finke, 1990). This is the dividing line between a "harebrained scheme" and a "stroke of genius" (see ▶Figure 8.21). In other words, the creative person brings reasoning and critical thinking to bear on new ideas once they are produced (Feldhusen, 1995).

Stages of Creative Thought

Is there any pattern to creative thinking? Typically, five stages occur during creative problem solving:

1. *Orientation.* As a first step, the problem must be defined and important dimensions identified.
2. *Preparation.* In the second stage, creative thinkers saturate themselves with as much information pertaining to the problem as possible.
3. *Incubation.* Most major problems produce a period during which all attempted solutions will have proved futile. At this point, problem solving may proceed on a subconscious level: While the problem seems to have been set aside, it is still "cooking" in the background.
4. *Illumination.* The stage of incubation is often ended by a rapid insight or series of insights. These produce the "Aha!" experience, often depicted in cartoons as a light bulb appearing over the thinker's head.
5. *Verification.* The final step is to test and critically evaluate the solution obtained during the stage of illumination. If the solution proves faulty, the thinker reverts to the stage of incubation.

Of course, creative thought is not always so neat. Nevertheless, the stages listed are a good summary of the most typical sequence of events.

You may find it helpful to relate the stages to the following more or less true story. Legend has it that the king of Syracuse (a city in ancient Greece) once suspected that his goldsmith had substituted cheaper metals for some of the gold in a crown and kept the extra gold. Archimedes, a famous mathematician and thinker, was given the problem of discovering whether the king had been cheated.

Archimedes began by defining the problem (*orientation*): "How can I determine what metals have been used in the crown without damaging it?" He then checked all known methods of analyzing metals (*preparation*). All involved cutting or melting the crown, so he was forced to temporarily set the problem aside (*incubation*). Then one day as he stepped into his bath, Archimedes suddenly knew he had the solution (*illumination*). He was so excited he is said to have run naked through the streets shouting, "Eureka, eureka!" (I have found it, I have found it!).

On observing his own body floating in the bath, Archimedes realized that different metals of equal weight would displace different amounts of water. A kilogram of brass, for example, occupies more space than a kilogram of gold, which is denser. All that remained was to test the solution (*verification*). Archimedes placed an amount of gold (equal in weight to that given the goldsmith) in a tub of water. He marked the water level and removed the gold. He then placed the crown in the water. Was the crown pure gold? If it was, it would raise the water to exactly the same level. Unfortunately, the purity of the crown and the fate of the goldsmith are to this day unknown!

The preceding account is a good general description of creative thinking. However, creative thinking can be highly complex. Some authors believe that truly exceptional creativity requires a rare combination of thinking skills, personality, and a supportive social environment. This mix, they believe, accounts for creative giants such as Edison, Freud, Mozart, Picasso, Tolstoy, and others (Tardif & Sternberg, 1988).

The Creative Personality

What makes a person creative? According to the popular stereotype, highly creative people are eccentric, introverted, neurotic, socially inept, unbalanced in their interests, and on the edge of madness. Some artists and musicians cultivate this public image, but is there any truth in it? York University researcher Elizabeth Ralevski asked exactly this question in her recent doctoral dissertation. She measured aspects of personality, creativity of word associations, and emotional tone (for example, tendency to moodiness, irritability, or depression) in 80 successful European and North American artists, and 34 control subjects. She found that success among the artists was related to narcissism and isolation. In addition, more depressed artists gave more original responses on the word association test, but this was not true for the controls (Ralevski, 2001).

Here are some other things we know about creative individuals:

1. For people of normal intelligence, there is a small positive correlation between creativity and IQ. In other words, smarter people have a slight tendency to be more creative. However, IQs above 120 do not seem to add anything more to creative ability. For the most part, at any given level of IQ, some people are creative and some are not (Sternberg & Lubart, 1995).

2. Creative people usually have a greater than average range of knowledge and interests, and they are more fluent in combining ideas from various sources. They are also good at using mental images and metaphors in thinking.

3. Creative people have an openness to experience. They accept irrational thoughts and are uninhibited about their feelings and fantasies (McCrae, 1987). They tend to use broad categories, challenge assumptions, break mental sets, and find order in chaos. They also experience more unusual states of consciousness, such as vivid dreams and mystical experiences (Ayers, Beaton, & Hunt, 1999).

4. Creative people enjoy symbolic thought, ideas, concepts, and possibilities. They tend to be interested in truth, form, and beauty, rather than in recognition or success. Their creative work is an end in itself (Sternberg & Lubart, 1995).

5. Highly creative people value independence and have a preference for complexity. However, they are unconventional and non-conforming primarily in their work; otherwise they do not have particularly unusual, outlandish, or bizarre personalities.

It is widely accepted that people are often creative only in particular areas of skill or knowledge. For example, a person who is a creative writer might be an uncreative artist or businessperson. Perhaps this is because creativity favours a prepared mind. Those who are creative in a particular field often are building on a large store of existing knowledge (Sternberg & Lubart, 1995).

Can creativity be learned? It is beginning to look as if some creative thinking skills can be taught. In particular, creativity can be increased by practice in divergent thinking (Baer, 1993). You'll find some helpful strategies later, in the Psychology in Action section of this chapter.

▶ Intuitive Thought—Mental Shortcut? Or Dangerous Detour?

Survey Question:
■ How accurate is intuition?

At the same time that irrational, intuitive thought may contribute to creative problem solving, it can also lead to thinking errors. To see how this can happen, try the following problems.

Problem 1 An epidemic breaks out, and 600 people are about to die. Doctors have two choices. If they give drug A, 200 lives will be saved. If they give drug B, there is a one-third chance that 600 people will be saved, and a two-thirds chance that none will be saved. Which drug should they choose?

Problem 2 Again, 600 people are about to die, and doctors must make a choice. If they give drug A, 400 people will die. If they give drug B, there is a one-third chance that no one will die, and a two-thirds chance that 600 will die. Which drug should they choose?

Most people choose drug A for the first problem and drug B for the second. This is fascinating because the two problems are identical. The only difference is that the first is stated in terms of lives saved, the second in terms of lives lost. Yet, even people who realize that their answers are contradictory find it difficult to change them (Kahneman & Tversky, 1972, 1973).

Intuition

Intuition Quick, impulsive thought that does not make use of formal logic or clear reasoning.

As the example shows, we often make decisions intuitively, rather than logically. **Intuition** is quick, impulsive thought that does not make use of clear reasoning. It can provide fast answers, but may also be misleading and sometimes disastrous. University of Alberta researcher Carolyn Yewchuk (1999) has defined intuition as "the apprehension of knowledge without conscious analysis." This means, roughly, knowing something without knowing how you know, a state often true of experts in many areas. Yewchuk points out that it is also often true of people with intellectual disabilities, such as savants. Yet, as Yewchuk reminds us, we often distinguish between the inability of great artists to verbalize how they do what they do and the inability of individuals with a disability to do the same thing. Yewchuk's cogent question is: Why do we do this?

Two noted psychologists, Daniel Kahneman (KON–eh–man) and Amos Tversky (tuh–VER–ski) (1937–1996), have studied how we make decisions in the face of uncertainty. They have found that human judgment is sometimes seriously flawed (Kahneman, Slovic, & Tversky, 1982). Kahneman won the 2002 Nobel Prize in Economic Sciences for the work described below. Let's explore some common intuitive thinking errors, so you will be better prepared to avoid them. Keep in mind our experience with the use of analogy in problem solving—unusual in the laboratory, common in the outside world. Whether something similar is true with the research described below is an open question.

REPRESENTATIVENESS One very common pitfall in judgment is illustrated by the question: Which is more probable?

A. Venus Williams will lose the first set of a tennis match but win the match.

B. Venus Williams will lose the first set.

Tversky and Kahneman (1982) found that most people regard statements like A as more probable than B. However, this intuitive answer overlooks an important fact: The likelihood of two events occurring together is lower than the probability of either one alone. (For example, the probability of getting one head when flipping a coin is one-half, or .5. The probability of getting two heads when flipping two coins is one-fourth, or .25.) Therefore, A is less likely to be true than B.

According to Tversky and Kahneman, such faulty conclusions are based on the **representativeness heuristic.** That is, we tend to give a choice greater weight if it seems to be representative of what we already know. Thus, the information about Venus Williams is compared to your mental model of what a tennis pro's behaviour should be like. Answer A seems to better represent the model. Therefore, it seems more likely than answer B, even though it isn't.

UNDERLYING ODDS   A second common error involves ignoring the **base rate,** or underlying probability of an event. In one experiment, subjects were told they would receive descriptions of 100 people—70 lawyers and 30 engineers. Subjects were then asked to guess, without knowing anything about a person, whether she or he was an engineer or a lawyer. All correctly stated the probabilities as 70 percent for lawyer and 30 percent for engineer. Participants were then given this description:

> Dick is a 30-year-old man. He is married with no children. A man of high ability and high motivation, he promises to be quite successful in his field. He is well liked by his colleagues.

Notice that the description gives no new information about Dick's occupation. He could still be either an engineer or a lawyer. Therefore, the odds should again be estimated as 70-30. However, most people changed the odds to 50-50. Intuitively it seems that Dick has an equal chance of being either an engineer or a lawyer. But this guess completely ignores the underlying odds.

Working at Queen's University in Kingston, Joelle Mamuza asked whether base rate neglect would be found in actuarial prediction of future criminal behaviour. Mamuza found that when subjects based their decisions on fictional case histories, they ignored base rate information. However, when decisions were based on actual risk assessments, subjects used the base rates (Mamuza, 2001). This is one more piece of evidence that human decision making is better than we might think if all we knew about it came from the psychology laboratory!

Perhaps it is fortunate that we do at times ignore underlying odds. Were this not the case, how many people would get married when the divorce rate is 50 percent? Or how many would start high-risk businesses? On the other hand, people who smoke, drink and then drive, or skip wearing auto seat belts ignore rather high odds of injury or illness. In many high-risk situations, ignoring base rates is the same as thinking you are an exception to the rule.

FRAMING   The most general conclusion from Kahneman and Tversky's work is that the way a problem is stated, or **framed,** affects decisions (Tversky & Kahneman, 1981). As the first example in this discussion revealed, people often give different answers to the same problem if it is stated in slightly different ways. To gain some added insight into framing, try another thinking problem:

> A couple are divorcing. Both parents seek custody of their only child, but custody can be granted to just one parent. If you had to make a decision based on the following information, to which parent would you award custody of the child?
>
> *Parent A:* average income, average health, average working hours, reasonable rapport with the child, relatively stable social life.
>
> *Parent B:* above-average income, minor health problems, lots of work-related travel, very close relationship with the child, extremely active social life.

Most people choose to award custody to Parent B, the parent who has some drawbacks but also several advantages (such as above-average income). That's because people tend to look for *positive qualities* that can be *awarded* to the child. However, how would you choose if you were asked this question: Which parent should be denied custody? In this case, most people choose to deny custody to Parent B. Why is Parent B a good choice one moment and a poor choice the next? It's because the second question asked who should be *denied* custody. To answer this question, people tend to look for *negative qualities* that would *disqualify* a parent. As you can see, the way a question is framed can channel people down a narrow path where they attend to only part of the information provided, rather than weighing all the pros and cons (Shafir, 1993).

Usually, the *broadest* way of framing or stating a problem produces the best decisions. However, people often state problems in increasingly narrow terms until a single, seemingly "obvious" answer emerges. For example, to select a career, it would be wise to consider pay, working conditions, job satisfaction, needed skills, future employment outlook, and many other factors. Instead, such decisions are often narrowed to thoughts such as, "I like to write, so I'll be a journalist," "I want to make good money and law pays well," or "I can be creative in photography." Framing decisions so narrowly greatly increases the risk of making a poor choice. If you would like to think more critically and analytically, it is important to pay attention to how you are defining problems before you try to solve them. Remember, shortcuts to answers often short-circuit clear thinking.

A LOOK AHEAD   We have discussed only some of the intuitive errors made in the face of uncertainty. In the upcoming Psychology in Action section, we will return to the topic of creative thinking for a look at ways to promote creativity.

Knowledge builder

CREATIVE THINKING AND INTUITION

Relate

Make up a question that would require convergent thinking to answer. Now do the same for divergent thinking.

Which of the tests of creativity described in the text do you think you would do best on? (Look back if you can't remember them all.)

To better remember the stages of creative thinking, make up a short story that includes these words: *orient, prepare, in Cuba, illuminate, verify.*

Explain in your own words how representativeness and base rates contribute to thinking errors.

Learning Check

1. Fluency, flexibility, and originality are characteristics of
   a. convergent thought *b.* deductive thinking *c.* creative thought *d.* trial-and-error solutions
2. List the typical stages of creative thinking in the correct order.

   _____   _____

   _____   _____

   _____

3. Reasoning and critical thinking tend to block creativity; these are non-creative qualities. T or F?
4. To be creative, an original idea must also be practical or feasible. T or F?
5. Intelligence and creativity are highly correlated; the higher a person's IQ, the more likely he or she is to be creative. T or F?
6. Kate is single, outspoken, and very bright. As a college student, she was deeply concerned with discrimination and other social issues and participated in several protests. Which statement is more likely to be true?
   a. Kate is a bank teller. *b.* Kate is a bank teller and a feminist.

Critical Thinking

7. A coin is flipped four times with one of the following results: *(a)* H T T H, *(b)* T T T T, *(c)* H H H H, *(d)* H H T H. Which sequence would most likely precede getting a head on the fifth coin flip?

Answers:

1. *c* 2. orientation, preparation, incubation, illumination, verification 3. F 4. T 5. F 6. *a* 7. The chance of getting a head on the fifth flip is the same in each case. Each time you flip a coin, the chance of getting a head is 50 percent, no matter what happened before. However, many people intuitively think that *b* is the answer because a head is "overdue," or that *c* is correct because the coin is "on a roll" for heads.

ENHANCING
CREATIVE
BRAINSTORMS

Survey Question:
What can be done to improve thinking and promote creativity?

Thomas Edison once wrote that "Genius is 1 percent inspiration and 99 percent perspiration." Indeed, many studies show that "genius" and "eminence" owe as much to persistence and dedication as they do to inspiration (Ericsson & Charness 1994). Once it is recognized that creativity can be hard work, then something can be done to enhance it. Here are some suggestions on how to begin.

1. Break mental sets and challenge assumptions. A *mental set* is the tendency to perceive a problem in a way that blinds us to possible solutions. Mental sets are a major barrier to creative thinking. Usually, they lead us to see a problem in preconceived terms that impede our problem-solving attempts. (Fixations and functional fixedness, which were described earlier, are specific types of mental sets.)

Try the problems pictured in ▶Figure 8.22. If you have difficulty, try asking yourself what assumptions you are making. The problems are designed to demonstrate the limiting effects of a mental set. (The answers to these problems, along with an explanation of the sets that prevent their solution, are found in ▶Figure 8.24.)

Now that you have been forewarned about the danger of faulty assumptions, see if you can correctly answer the following questions.

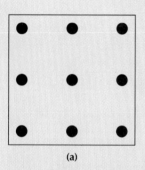
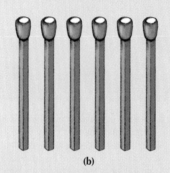

1. A farmer had 19 sheep. All but 9 died. How many sheep did the farmer have left?
2. It is not unlawful for a man living in Winston-Salem, North Carolina, to be buried west of the Mississippi River. T or F?
3. Some months have 30 days, some have 31. How many months have 28 days?
4. Jimmy has two coins that together total 30 cents. One of the coins is not a nickel. What are the two coins?
5. If there are 12 one-cent candies in a dozen, how many two-cent candies are there in a dozen?

(a)   (b)

▶**Figure 8.22**

(a) Nine dots are arranged in a square. Can you connect them by drawing four continuous straight lines without lifting your pencil from the paper? *(b)* Six matches must be arranged to make four triangles. The triangles must be the same size, with each side equal to the length of one match. (The solutions to these problems appear in Figure 8.24.)

These questions are designed to cause thinking errors. Here are the answers:

1. Nineteen—9 alive and 10 dead. **2.** F. It is against the law to bury a living person anywhere. **3.** All of them. **4.** A quarter and a nickel. One of the coins is not a nickel, but the other one is! **5.** Twelve.

If you got caught on any of the questions, consider it an additional reminder of the value of actively challenging the assumptions you are making in any instance of problem solving.

2. Define problems broadly. An effective way to break mental sets is to enlarge the definition of a problem. For instance, assume your problem is: Design a better doorway. This is likely to lead to ordinary solutions. Why not change the problem to: Design a better way to get through a wall? Now your solutions will be more original. Best of all might be to state the problem as: Find a better way to define separate areas for living and working. This could lead to truly creative solutions (Adams, 1988).

Let's say you are leading a group that's designing a new can opener. Wisely, you ask the group to think about opening in general, rather than about can openers. This was just the approach that led to the pop-top can (▶Figure 8.23). As the design group discussed the concept of opening, one member suggested that nature has its own openers, like the soft seam on a pea pod. Instead of a new can-opening tool, the group invented the self-opening can (Stein, 1974).

▶**Figure 8.23**

Thinking about *opening* in general, rather than about can openers, led designers to the concept of the self-opening can.

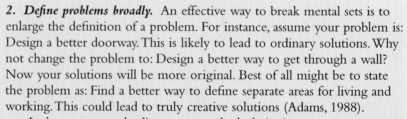

3. Restate the problem in different ways. Stating problems in novel ways also tends to produce more creative solutions. See if you can cross out six letters to make a single word out of the following:

C S R I E X L E A T T T E R E S

If you're having difficulty, it may be that you need to restate the problem. Were you trying to cross out six letters? The real solution is to cross out the letters in the words "six letters," which yields the word CREATE.

One way to restate a problem is to imagine how another person would view it. What would a child, engineer, professor, mechanic, artist, psychologist, judge, or minister ask about the problem? Also, you should almost always ask the following questions:

- What information do I have?
- What don't I know?
- What can I extract from the known information?
- Have I used all of the information?
- What additional information do I need?
- What are the parts of the problem?
- How are the parts related?
- How could the parts be related?
- Is this in any way like a problem I've solved before?

Remember, to think more creatively you must find ways to jog yourself out of mental sets and habitual modes of thought (Michalko, 1998).

4. Allow time for incubation. Trying to hurry or to force a solution may simply encourage fixation on a dead end. Creativity takes time. You need to be able to revise or embellish initial solutions, even those based on rapid insight (Tardif & Sternberg, 1988). Incubation is especially fruitful when you are exposed to external cues that relate to the problem (remember Archimedes' bath?). For example, Johannes Gutenberg, creator of the printing press, realized while at a wine harvest that the mechanical pressure used to crush grapes could also be used to imprint letters on paper (Dorfman, Shames, & Kihlstrom, 1996).

5. Seek varied input. Remember, creativity requires divergent thinking. Rather than digging deeper with logic, you are attempting to shift your mental "prospecting" to new areas. As an example of this strategy, Edward de Bono (1970, 1992) recommends that you randomly look up words in the dictionary and relate them to the problem. Often the words will trigger a fresh perspective or open a new avenue. For instance, let's say you are asked to come up with new ways to clean oil off a beach. Following de Bono's suggestion, you would read the following randomly selected words, relate each to the problem, and see what thoughts are triggered: *weed, rust, poor, magnify, foam, gold, frame, hole, diagonal, vacuum, tribe, puppet, nose, link, drift, portrait, cheese, coal.* You may get similar benefits from relating various objects to a problem. Or, take a walk, skim through a newspaper, or look through a stack of photographs to see what thoughts they trigger (Michalko, 1998).

6. Look for analogies. Many "new" problems are really old problems in new clothing (Siegler, 1989). Representing a problem in a variety of ways is often the key to solution. Most problems become easier to solve when they are effectively represented. For example, consider this problem:

Two backpackers start up a steep trail at 6 a.m. They hike all day, resting occasionally, and arrive at the top at 6 p.m. The next day they start back down the trail at 6 a.m. On the way down they stop several times and vary their pace. They arrive back at 6 p.m. On the way down, one of the hikers, who is a mathematician, tells the other that she has realized that they will pass a point on the trail at exactly the same time as they did the day before. Her non-mathematical friend finds this hard to believe, because on both days they have stopped and started many times and changed their pace. The problem: Is the mathematician right?

Perhaps you will see the answer to this problem immediately. If not, think of it this way: What if there were two pairs of backpackers, one going up the trail, the second coming down, and both hiking on the same day? It becomes obvious that the two pairs of hikers will pass each other at some point on the trail. Therefore, they will be at the same place at the same time. The mathematician was right.

7. *Take sensible risks.* A willingness to go against the crowd is a key element in doing creative work. Unusual and original ideas may be rejected at first by conventional thinkers. Often, creative individuals must persevere and take some risks before their ideas are widely accepted. For example, Post-it notes were invented by an engineer who accidentally created a weak glue. Rather than throw the mixture out, the engineer put it to a highly creative new use. However, it took him some time to convince others that a "bad" adhesive could be a useful product. Today, stick-on notepapers are one of the 3M Company's most successful products (Sternberg & Lubart, 1995).

8. *Delay evaluation.* Various studies suggest that people are most likely to be creative when they are given the freedom to play with ideas and solutions without having to worry about whether they will be evaluated. In the first stages of creative thinking, it is important to avoid criticizing your efforts. Worrying about the correctness of solutions tends to inhibit creativity (Amabile, 1983). This idea is expanded in the discussion that follows.

An alternative approach to enhancing creativity is called brainstorming. Although brainstorming is a group technique, it can be applied to individual problem solving as well.

BRAINSTORMING   The essence of **brainstorming** is that producing and evaluating ideas are kept separate. In group problem solving, each person is encouraged to produce as many ideas as possible without fear of criticism (Buyer, 1988). This encourages divergent thinking. Some of the most successful brainstorming takes place on computer networks, where each person's fears of being evaluated are minimized (Siau, 1996).

Only at the end of a brainstorming session are ideas reconsidered and evaluated. As ideas are freely generated, an interesting **cross–stimulation effect** takes place in which one participant's ideas trigger ideas from others (Brown et al., 1998).

The basic rules for successful brainstorming are:

1. Criticism of ideas is absolutely barred. Defer evaluation until later in the session.
2. Modification or combination with other ideas is encouraged. Don't worry about giving credit for ideas or keeping them neat. Mix them up!
3. Quantity of ideas is sought. In the early stages of brainstorming, quantity is more important than quality. Try to generate lots of ideas.
4. Unusual, remote, or wild ideas are sought. Let your imagination run amok!
5. Record ideas as they occur.
6. Elaborate or improve on the most promising ideas. (Michalko, 1998)

It is important to be persistent when you are brainstorming. Most groups give up too soon, usually when the flow of new ideas begins to slow (Nijstad, Stroebe, & Lodewijkx, 1999).

How is brainstorming applied to individual problem solving? The essential point to remember is to suspend judgment. Ideas should first be produced without regard for logic, organiza-

Brainstorming Method of creative thinking that separates the production and evaluation of ideas.

Cross-stimulation effect In group problem solving, the tendency of one person's ideas to trigger ideas from others.

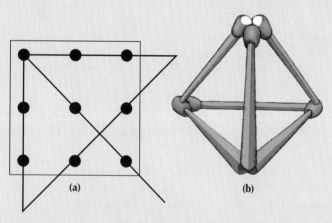

▶**Figure 8.24**

Problem solutions. *(a)* The dot problem can be solved by extending the lines beyond the square formed by the dots. Most people assume incorrectly that they may not do this. *(b)* The match problem can be solved by building a three-dimensional pyramid. Most people assume that the matches must be arranged on a flat surface. If you remembered the four-tree problem from earlier in the chapter, the match problem may have been easy to solve.

tion, accuracy, practicality, or any other evaluation. In writing an essay, for instance, you would begin by writing ideas in any order, the more the better, just as they occur to you. Later you would go back and reorganize, rewrite, and criticize your efforts.

As an aid to following rules 2, 3, and 4 of the brainstorming method, you might find this checklist helpful for encouraging original thought. It can be used to see if you have overlooked a possible solution.

Creativity Checklist

1. *Redefine.* Consider other uses for all elements of the problem. (This is designed to alert you to fixations that may be blocking creativity.)
2. *Adapt.* How could other objects, ideas, procedures, or solutions be adapted to this particular problem?
3. *Modify.* Imagine changing anything and everything that could be changed.
4. *Magnify.* Exaggerate everything you can think of. Think on a grand scale.
5. *Minify.* What if everything were scaled down? What if all differences were reduced to zero? "Shrink" the problem down to size.
6. *Substitute.* How could one object, idea, or procedure be substituted for another?
7. *Rearrange.* Break the problem into pieces and shuffle them.
8. *Reverse.* Consider reverse orders and opposites, and turn things inside out.
9. *Combine.* This one speaks for itself.

By making a habit of subjecting a problem to each of these procedures, you should be able to greatly reduce the chances that you will overlook a useful, original, or creative solution.

Knowledge builder

ENHANCING CREATIVITY

Relate

 Review the preceding pages and note which methods you could use more often to improve the quality of your thinking. Now mentally summarize the points you especially want to remember.

Learning Check

1. Fixations and functional fixedness are specific types of mental sets. T or F?
2. The incubation period in creative problem solving usually lasts just a matter of minutes. T or F?

3. Exposure to creative models has been shown to enhance creativity. T or F?
4. In brainstorming, each idea is critically evaluated as it is generated. T or F?
5. Defining a problem broadly produces a cross-stimulation effect that can inhibit creative thinking. T or F?

Critical Thinking

6. What mode of thinking does the "Creativity Checklist" (redefine, adapt, modify, magnify, and so forth) encourage?

Answers:

1. T 2. F 3. T 4. F 5. F 6. Divergent thinking.

Psychologist's Journal

EPILOGUE

Many people who think in conventional ways live intelligent, successful, and fulfilling lives. Just the same, creative thinking can add spice to life and lead to exciting personal insights. Psychologist Mihalyi Csikszentmihalyi (sik-sent-me-HALE-yee) (1997) makes these recommendations about how to become more creative:

- Find something that surprises you every day.
- Try to surprise at least one person every day.
- If something sparks your interest, follow it.
- Make a commitment to doing things well.
- Seek challenges.
- Take time for thinking and relaxing.
- Start doing more of what you really enjoy, less of what you dislike.
- Try to look at problems from as many viewpoints as you can.

Even if you don't become more creative by following these suggestions, they are still good advice. Life is not a standardized test with a single set of correct answers. It is much more like a blank canvas on which you can create designs that uniquely express your talents and interests. To live more creatively, you must be ready to seek new ways of doing things. Try to surprise at least one person today—yourself, if no one else.

CHAPTER IN REVIEW

Major Points

▶ Thinking, problem solving, language, and creativity are the origins of intelligent behaviour.

▶ Thinking is influenced by the form in which information is represented—as images, concepts, or symbols.

▶ Language is an especially powerful way to encode information and manipulate ideas.

▶ Understanding problem solving can make you more effective at finding solutions.

▶ Expert problem solving is based on acquired knowledge and strategies.

▶ Intelligence tests only estimate real-world intelligence. A high IQ does not automatically lead to high achievement.

▶ Creative thinking is novel, divergent, and tempered with a dash of practicality.

▶ Some thinking errors can be avoided if you know the pitfalls of intuitive thought.

▶ Creativity can be enhanced by strategies that promote divergent thinking.

Summary

What Is the Nature of Thought?

- Thinking is an internal representation of external stimuli or situations.
- Three basic units of thought are images, concepts, and language (or symbols).

In What Ways Are Images Related to Thinking?

- Images may be stored in memory or created to solve problems.
- Images can be three-dimensional, they can be rotated in space, and their size may change.
- Kinesthetic images are used to represent movements and actions.

How Are Concepts Learned? Are There Different Kinds of Concepts?

- A concept is a generalized idea of a class of objects or events.
- Concept formation may be based on positive and negative instances or rule learning.

- In practice, concept identification frequently makes use of prototypes, or ideal models.
- Concepts may be conjunctive ("and" concepts), disjunctive ("either/or" concepts), or relational.
- The denotative meaning of a word or concept is its dictionary definition. Connotative meaning is personal or emotional.

What Is the Role of Language in Thinking?
- Language allows events to be encoded into symbols for easy mental manipulation. The study of meaning in language is called semantics.
- Language carries meaning by combining a set of symbols according to a set of rules (grammar), which includes rules about word order (syntax).
- True languages are productive and can be used to generate new ideas or possibilities.
- Complex gestural systems, such as American Sign Language, are true languages.

Can Animals Be Taught to Use Language?
- Animal communication is relatively limited because it lacks symbols that can be rearranged easily.
- Chimpanzees and other primates have been taught American Sign Language and similar systems. Studies that make use of lexigrams provide the best evidence to date of animal language use.

What Do We Know about Problem Solving?
- The solution to a problem may be arrived at mechanically (by trial and error or by rote application of rules), but mechanical solutions are often inefficient.
- Solutions by understanding usually begin with discovery of the general properties of an answer. Next comes the proposal of a functional solution.
- Problem solving is frequently aided by heuristics, which narrow the search for solutions.
- When understanding leads to a rapid solution, insight has occurred. Three elements of insight are selective encoding, selective combination, and selective comparison.
- Insight and other problem solving can be blocked by fixations, such as functional fixedness.

What Is Artificial Intelligence?
- Artificial intelligence refers to any system that can perform tasks that require intelligence when done by people.
- Two principal areas of artificial intelligence research are computer simulations and expert systems.
- Expert human problem solving is based on organized knowledge and acquired strategies, rather than some general improvement in thinking ability.

How Is Human Intelligence Defined and Measured?
- Intelligence refers to the general capacity to act purposefully, think rationally, and deal effectively with the environment. In practice, intelligence is operationally defined by intelligence tests.
- The first practical intelligence test was assembled by Alfred Binet. A modern version of Binet's test is the Stanford-Binet Intelligence Scale.
- A second major intelligence test is the Wechsler Adult Intelligence Scale (WAIS). The WAIS measures both verbal and performance intelligence. Culture-fair and group intelligence tests are also available.
- Intelligence is expressed as an intelligence quotient (IQ), defined as mental age divided by chronological age and then multiplied by 100. The distribution of IQ scores approximates a normal curve.

How Do IQ Scores Relate to Achievement and Thinking Ability?
- IQ is related to achievement in school, but many other factors are also important. Outside school, the connection between IQ and achievement is even weaker.
- As a group, males and females do not differ in overall IQ. Also, their intellectual strengths and educational goals are becoming more alike.
- People with IQs in the gifted or "genius" range of above 140 tend to be superior in many respects. However, by criteria other than IQ, many children can be considered gifted or talented in one way or another.
- The terms *mentally retarded* and *developmentally disabled* are applied to those whose IQ falls below 70 or who lack various adaptive behaviours.
- About 50 percent of the cases of mental retardation are organic. The remaining cases are of undetermined cause. Many of these cases are thought to reflect familial retardation.
- Intelligence is partially determined by heredity. However, environment is also important, as revealed by IQ increases induced by education and stimulating environments.

What Is the Nature of Creative Thinking?
- To be creative, a solution must be practical and sensible as well as original. Creative thinking requires divergent thought, characterized by fluency, flexibility, and originality. Tests of creativity measure these qualities.
- Five stages often seen in creative problem solving are orientation, preparation, incubation, illumination, and verification. Not all creative thinking fits this pattern.
- Studies suggest that the creative personality has a number of characteristics, most of which contradict popular stereotypes. There is only a very small correlation between IQ and creativity.

How Accurate Is Intuition?
- Intuitive thinking often leads to errors. Wrong conclusions may be drawn when an answer seems highly representative of what we already believe is true.
- A second problem is ignoring the base rate (or underlying probability) of an event.

- Clear thinking is usually aided by stating or framing a problem in broad terms.

What Can Be Done to Improve Thinking and Promote Creativity?

- Various strategies that promote divergent thinking tend to enhance creative problem solving.

- In group situations, brainstorming may lead to creative solutions. The principles of brainstorming can also be applied to individual problem solving.

PSYCHOLOGY ON THE NET

If you have difficulty finding any of the sites listed here, visit http://psychologyjourney.nelson.com for an updated list of Internet addresses and direct links to relevant sites.

The Bell Curve Flattened An article that summarizes objections to *The Bell Curve*. http://slate.msn.com/default.aspx?id=2416

Creativity Web Multiple links to resources on creativity. http://www.ozemail.com.au/~caveman/Creative/

Helping Your Highly Gifted Child Advice for parents of gifted children. http://www.kidsource.com/kidsource/content/help.gift.html

Introduction to Mental Retardation Answers to basic questions about mental retardation. http://TheArc.org/faqs/mrqa.html

IQ Tests Provides links to a number of IQ tests. http://www.stud.ntnu.no/studorg/mensa/iq.html

The Knowns and Unknowns of Intelligence From the APA, what is known about intelligence and intelligence tests. http://www.apa.org/releases/intell.html

The Language Research Center This site from Georgia State University discusses language research in primates. http://www.gsu.edu/~wwwlrc

Primate Use of Language This MIT page contains information about primate language and related links. http://www.pigeon.psy.tufts.edu/psych26/language.htm

InfoTrac College Edition For recent articles on "talking" chimps, use Key Words search for ANIMAL LANGUAGE. For more information on the controversy concerning the book *The Bell Curve*, use Key Words search for BELL CURVE.

INTERACTIVE LEARNING

Psychology: An Interactive Journey Remember that Chapter 8 of the CD-ROM that came with this text has practice tests, flashcards, interactive exercises, a crossword puzzle, and other valuable materials to enhance your learning experience.

PsychNow! 5f. Cognition and Language, 5g. Problem Solving and Creativity.

Psyk.trek 6. Memory and Thought, 7. Testing and Intelligence, Psyk.trek Simulations: 1. Experimenting with the Stroop Test, 6. Problem Solving—The Hobbits and Orcs Problem, 7. Measuring Creativity—The Remote Associates Test.

Chart Your Progress

The questions that follow are only a sample of what you need to know. If you miss any of the items, you should review the entire chapter, do the exercises on the CD, and review the Knowledge Builders. Another way to prepare for tests is to get more practice with *WebTutor*, the *Study Guide*, or the *Practice Quizzes* that are available with this text.

1. A person doing mental rotation would need to use which basic unit of thought?
   a. concepts
   b. language
   c. images
   d. symbols

2. A triangle must be a closed shape and have three sides and the sides must be straight lines. Triangle is a
   a. conjunctive concept
   b. relational concept
   c. disjunctive concept
   d. connotative concept

3. Which of the following is NOT an element of spoken language?
   a. grammar
   b. syntax
   c. phonemes
   d. lexigrams

4. Functional fixedness is a major barrier to
   a. insightful problem solving
   b. using random search strategies
   c. mechanical problem solving
   d. achieving fixations through problem solving

5. Computer simulations and expert systems are primary research tools in
   a. psycholinguistics
   b. the field of AI
   c. studies of divergent thinking
   d. studies of the semantic differential

6. By definition, a person has average intelligence when
   a. MA = CA
   b. CA = 100
   c. MA = 100
   d. MA × CA = 100

7. One thing that the mentally gifted and the developmentally disabled have in common is that both have
   a. a tendency to suffer from metabolic disorders
   b. to be tested with the WAIS, rather than the Binet-4
   c. MAs that are higher than their CAs
   d. extreme IQ scores

8. Which is NOT one of the eight types of intelligence identified by Howard Gardner?
   a. cyber skills
   b. music skills
   c. visual and spatial skills
   d. naturalist skills

9. A test scored for fluency and flexibility is obviously designed to measure
   a. intuitive thinking
   b. convergent thinking
   c. divergent thinking
   d. base rates and framing

10. By seeking varied information, delaying evaluation, and looking for analogies, you should be able to increase
    a. intuitive thinking
    b. convergent thinking
    c. divergent thinking
    d. functional fixedness

Answers: 1. c. 2. a. 3. d. 4. a. 5. b. 6. a. 7. d. 8. a. 9. c. 10. c.

Chapter 9

Psychologist's Journal

RISKY BUSINESS

In 1983, Quebec made driver training mandatory for all new drivers. Until that year, it had been mandatory only for 16- and 17-year-olds. Five years later, University of Montreal researcher Louise Potvin and her colleagues reported that accident rates went up after the change, with the largest increases among 16- and 17-year-olds—not what the government had expected (Potvin, Champagne, & Laberge-Nadeau, 1988).

In Finland, authorities installed light reflectors on posts along a 548 km stretch of highway to improve night visibility. They compared accident rates for that stretch and another stretch that got no reflectors. If anything, the accident rate increased slightly on the "improved" stretch, as drivers responded by going faster (Kallberg, 1992).

In fact, according to Gerald Wilde of Queen's University in Kingston, all efforts between 1927 and 1987 to improve car safety, driver training, roads, lighting, and traffic laws in the United States had no effect on the death rate per capita from car accidents (Simonet & Wilde, 1997). And airbags, the latest safety innovation, are only making things worse (Paterson & Hoffer, 1994). How can this be? Why don't any of these eminently sensible interventions produce the desired decrease in the number of people killed in car accidents each year?

According to Gerald Wilde and his colleague Sebastian Simonet, the answer is that accident rates reflect the amount of risk drivers are prepared to accept. When carmakers produce cars with better brakes, drivers can either drive at the same speed and reduce their risk or increase speed and maintain the same risk as before. Most of us choose the latter. Wilde explains this in terms of his "homeostatic theory of risk"—people will act to maintain their preferred level of risk. In order to change accident rates, then, you have to change people's preferred level of risk.

This chapter is about the motives and emotions that underlie human behaviour. As the data on traffic accidents suggest, before you can change human behaviour, you need to understand the motivation that produces it. Let's begin with basic motives, such as hunger and thirst, and then explore how emotions affect us. While emotions can be the spice of life, they are sometimes the spice of death as well. Read on to find out why.

▶ Motivation—Forces That Push and Pull

Survey Question:

- ■ What is motivation? Are there different types of motives?

What are your goals? Why do you pursue them? How vigorously do you try to reach them? When are you satisfied? When do you give up? **Motivation** refers to these dynamics of behaviour—the ways in which our actions are initiated, sustained, directed, and terminated (Petri, 1996).

Can you clarify that? Yes. Imagine that a student named Marcy is studying psychology in the library. She begins to feel hungry and can't concentrate. Her stomach growls. She grows restless and decides to buy an apple from a vending machine. The machine is empty, so she goes to the cafeteria. Closed. Marcy drives home, where she cooks a meal and eats it. At last her hunger is satisfied, and she resumes studying. Notice how Marcy's food seeking was *initiated* by a bodily need. Her search was *sustained* because her need was not immediately met, and her actions were *directed* by possible sources of food. Finally, her food seeking was *terminated* by achieving her goal.

A Model of Motivation

Many motivated activities begin with a **need,** or internal deficiency. The need that initiated Marcy's search was a depletion of key substances in her body. Needs cause a **drive** (an energized motivational state) to develop. The drive was hunger, in Marcy's case. Drives activate a **response** (an action or series of actions) designed to attain a **goal** (the "target" of motivated behaviour). Reaching a goal that satisfies the need will end the chain of events. Thus, a simple model of motivation can be shown in this way:

$$\text{NEED} \longrightarrow \text{DRIVE} \longrightarrow \text{RESPONSE} \longrightarrow \text{GOAL}$$
$$\text{(NEED REDUCTION)}$$

Motivation Internal processes that initiate, sustain, and direct activities.

Need An internal deficiency that may energize behaviour.

Drive The psychological expression of internal needs or valued goals (for example, hunger, thirst, or a drive for success).

Response Any action, glandular activity, or other identifiable behaviour.

Goal The target or objective of motivated behaviour.

It's important to note the distinction between a physical state ("need") and the psychological state ("drive") it produces. The need–drive relation can be complex. For example, University of British Columbia psychologist John Pinel recently pointed out that animals, including humans, who live in food-rich environments tend to eat too much, which has negative consequences for health (Pinel, Assanand, & Lehman, 2000). Why would we evolve a need-drive system that leads us to eat too much? It would make sense in an environment in which food was both scarce and unpredictable. On rare occasions when lots of food was available, "pigging out" was more adaptive than eating more modestly. Being able to store energy in the body and draw on it later, when food was scarce, outweighed possible long-term health consequences of overeating.

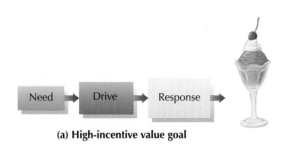

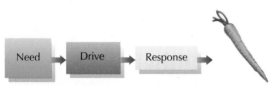

(a) High-incentive value goal

(b) Low-incentive value goal

▶**Figure 9.1**

Needs and incentives interact to determine drive strength *(above)*. *(a)* Moderate need combined with a high-incentive goal produces a strong drive. *(b)* Even when a strong need exists, drive strength may be moderate if a goal's incentive value is low. It is important to remember, however, that incentive value lies "in the eye of the beholder." No matter how hungry, few people would be able to eat the pictured caterpillars in coconut cream sauce.

> **Incentive value** The value of a goal above and beyond its ability to fill a need.
> **Primary motives** Innate motives based on biological needs.
> **Stimulus motives** Innate needs for stimulation and information.
> **Secondary motives** Motives based on learned needs, drives, and goals.

Aren't needs and drives the same thing? No, because the strength of needs and drives can differ. If you begin fasting today, your bodily need for food will increase every day. However, you would probably feel less "hungry" on the seventh day of fasting than you did on the first. While your need for food steadily increases, the hunger drive comes and goes.

Now let's observe Marcy again. It's Saturday night: For dinner, Marcy has soup, salad, a large steak, a baked potato, four pieces of bread, two pieces of cheesecake, and three cups of coffee. After dinner, she complains that she is "too full to move." Soon after, Marcy's roommate arrives with a strawberry pie. Marcy exclaims that strawberry pie is her favourite dessert and eats three large pieces! Is this hunger? Certainly, Marcy's dinner satisfied her biological needs for food.

How does that change the model of motivation? Marcy's "pie lust" illustrates that motivated behaviour can be energized by the "pull" of external stimuli, as well as by the "push" of internal needs.

INCENTIVES The "pull" of a goal is called its **incentive value** (the goal's appeal beyond its ability to fill a need). Some goals are so desirable (strawberry pie, for example) that they can motivate behaviour in the absence of an internal need. Other goals are so low in incentive value that they may be rejected even if they meet the internal need (see ▶Figure 9.1). Fresh, live grubworms, for instance, are highly nutritious. However, it is doubtful that you would eat one no matter how hungry you might be.

Usually, our actions are energized by a mixture of internal needs and external incentives. That's why a strong need may change an unpleasant incentive into a desired goal. Perhaps you've never eaten a grubworm, but I'll bet you've eaten some pretty horrible leftovers when the refrigerator was bare. Similarly, a strong incentive can change both behaviour and expectations about behaviour, as demonstrated by Roger Buehler and his colleagues at Wilfrid Laurier University. Buehler, Griffin, and MacDonald (1997) reported that people offered an incentive for speed overestimated how fast they would respond in a simple task. The lesson in that result is that, when there's a lot at stake, you may overestimate your ability to do a certain task. Keep that in mind when organizing your study schedule before exams!

TYPES OF MOTIVES For our purposes, motives can be divided into three major categories:

1. **Primary motives** are based on biological needs that must be met for survival. The most important primary motives are hunger, thirst, pain avoidance, and needs for air, sleep, elimination of wastes, and regulation of body temperature. Primary motives are innate.

2. **Stimulus motives** express our needs for stimulation and information. Examples include activity, curiosity, exploration, manipula-tion, and physical contact. While such motives also appear to be innate, they are not strictly necessary for survival.

3. **Secondary motives** are based on learned needs, drives, and goals. Learned motives help explain many human activities, such as making music, creating a website, or trying to win the skateboarding finals in the X Games. Many secondary motives are related to learned needs for power, affiliation (the need to be with others), approval, status, security, and achievement. Fear and aggression also appear to be greatly affected by learning.

Primary Motives and Homeostasis

How important is food in your life? Water? Sleep? Air? Temperature regulation? Finding a public rest room? For most of us, satisfying biological needs is so routine that we tend to overlook how much of our behaviour they direct. But exaggerate any of these needs through famine, shipwreck, poverty, near-drowning, bitter cold, or drinking 10 cups of coffee, and their powerful grip on behaviour becomes evident. We are, after all, still animals in many ways.

Biological drives are essential because they maintain *homeostasis* (HOE-me-oh-STAY-sis), or bodily equilibrium (Cannon, 1932).

What is homeostasis? The term **homeostasis** means "standing steady," or "steady state." Optimal levels exist for body temperature, for chemicals in the blood, for blood pressure, and so forth. When the body deviates from these "ideal" levels, automatic reactions begin to restore equilibrium. Thus, it might help to think of homeostasis as being similar to a thermostat set at a particular temperature. (As we'll see in the section on pain below, McGill University psychologist Ronald Melzack suggests that pain is a neural response to disruption of equilibrium by injury.)

> **Homeostasis** A steady state of bodily equilibrium.

A (Very) Short Course on Thermostats

When room temperature falls below the level set on a thermostat, the heat is automatically turned on to warm the room. When the heat equals or slightly exceeds the ideal temperature, it is automatically turned off. In this way room temperature is kept in a state of equilibrium hovering around the ideal level.

The first reactions to disequilibrium in the human body are also automatic. For example, if you become too hot, more blood will flow through your skin and you will begin to perspire, thus lowering body temperature. Usually, we are not aware of such changes, unless continued disequilibrium drives us to seek shade, warmth, food, or water.

However, people actively seek homeostasis at higher levels, too, as suggested by Gerald Wilde, who was mentioned in Psychologist's Journal at the beginning of this chapter. Wilde argues that people set a target risk rate for various activities such as driving. The target allows certain rewards (going places) for certain costs (risk of traffic accident). Wilde argues that we get information about the risk from various sources—seeing accidents, hearing about them on the news, and seeing what proportion of cars on the street have dents in them. If the cost goes down (because cars become safer), people go for more reward—they driver further—bringing the risk back up to the desired level. If the risk goes up (say, in bad weather), people reduce their reward (drive less), bringing the risk back down.

As Simonet and Wilde (1997) pointed out, if we don't influence the target risk drivers choose, we will not influence road safety. For example, lowering speed limits will result in drivers paying less attention to their driving, because at slower speeds they can maintain their preferred risk rate while being less attentive.

Knowledge builder

OVERVIEW OF MOTIVATION

Relate

Motives help explain why we do what we do. See if you can think of something you do that illustrates the concepts of need, drive, response, and goal. Does the goal in your example vary in incentive value? What effects do high- and low-incentive-value goals have on your behaviour?

Mentally list some primary motives you have satisfied today. Some stimulus motives. Some secondary motives. How did each influence your behaviour?

Learning Check

1. Motives _____, sustain, _____, and terminate activities.

continued

2. Needs provide the _____ of motivation, whereas incentives provide the _____.

Classify the following needs or motives by placing the correct letter in the blank.

A. Primary motive   **B.** Stimulus motive   **C.** Secondary motive

3. _____ curiosity
4. _____ status
5. _____ sleep
6. _____ thirst
7. _____ achievement
8. _____ physical contact
9. Maintaining bodily equilibrium is called thermostasis. T or F?

10. A goal high in incentive value may create a drive in the absence of any internal need. T or F?

Critical Thinking

11. There's an old saying that "You can lead a horse to water, but you can't make him drink." Can you restate this in motivational terms?

12. Many people mistakenly believe that they suffer from "hypoglycemia" (low blood sugar), which is often blamed for fatigue, difficulty concentrating, irritability, and other symptoms. Why is it unlikely that many people actually have hypoglycemia?

Answers:

1. initiate, direct 2. push, pull 3. B 4. C 5. A 6. B 7. C 8. C 9. F 10. T 11. Providing an incentive (water) will not automatically lead to drinking in the absence of an internal need for water. 12. Because of homeostasis: Blood sugar is normally maintained within narrow bounds. While blood sugar levels fluctuate enough to affect hunger, true hypoglycemia is an infrequent medical problem.

▶ Hunger—Pardon Me, That's Just My Hypothalamus Growling

Survey Question:
■ What causes hunger? Overeating? Eating disorders?

Hypothalamus An area in the brain that regulates motivation and emotion.

What causes hunger? When you feel hungry, you probably think of your stomach. That's why Walter Cannon and A. L. Washburn decided to see if stomach contractions cause hunger. In an early study, Washburn trained himself to swallow a balloon, which could be inflated through an attached tube. This allowed Cannon to record the movements of Washburn's stomach (see ▶Figure 9.2). When Washburn's stomach contracted, he reported that he felt "hunger pangs." In view of this, the two scientists concluded that hunger is nothing more than the contractions of an empty stomach (Cannon & Washburn, 1912). (Unfortunately, this proved to be an inflated conclusion.)

For many people, hunger produces an overall feeling of weakness or shakiness, rather than a "growling" stomach. Of course, eating is limited when the stomach is stretched or distended (full). (Remember last Thanksgiving?) However, we now know that the stomach is not essential for feeling hunger. For medical reasons, many people have had their stomachs removed. Despite this, they continue to feel hungry and eat regularly (Woods et al., 2000).

Then what does cause hunger? One important signal for hunger is lowered levels of glucose (sugar) in the blood (Campfield et al., 1996). Strange as it may seem, the liver also affects hunger.

The liver? Yes, the liver responds to a lack of bodily "fuel" by sending nerve impulses to the brain. These "messages" contribute to a desire to eat (Woods et al., 2000).

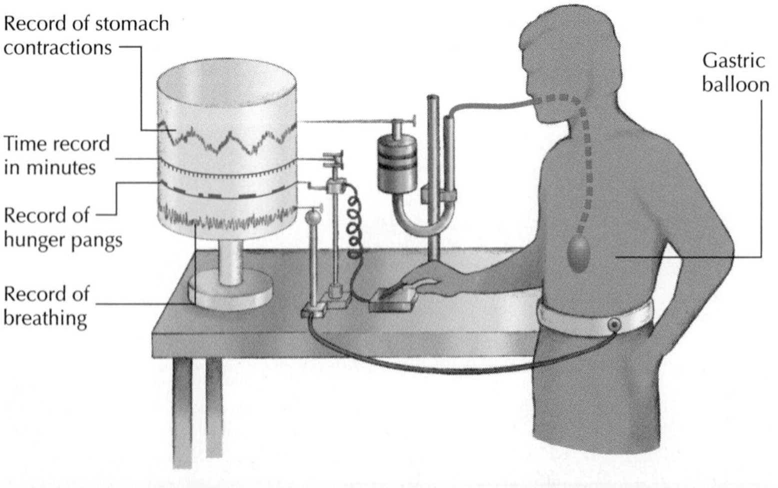

Brain Mechanisms

What part of the brain controls hunger? When you are hungry, many parts of the brain are affected, so no single "hunger centre" exists. However, a small area called the **hypothalamus** (HI-po-THAL-ah-mus) regulates many motives, including hunger, thirst, and the sex drive (see ▶Figure 9.3).

The hypothalamus is sensitive to levels of sugar in the blood (and other substances

▶Figure 9.2

Record of stomach contractions

Time record in minutes

Record of hunger pangs

Record of breathing

Gastric balloon

In Walter Cannon's early study of hunger, a simple apparatus was used to simultaneously record hunger pangs and stomach contractions. (After Cannon, 1934.)

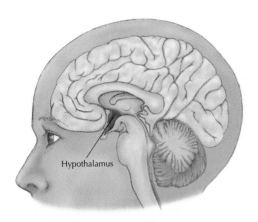

▶**Figure 9.3**

Location of the hypothalamus in the human brain.

Feeding system Areas in the hypothalamus that initiate eating when stimulated.

Satiety system Areas in the hypothalamus that terminate eating.

Neuropeptide Y A substance in the brain that initiates eating.

Glucagon-like peptide 1 A substance in the brain that terminates eating.

Set point The proportion of body fat that tends to be maintained by changes in hunger and eating.

Leptin A substance released by fat cells that inhibits eating.

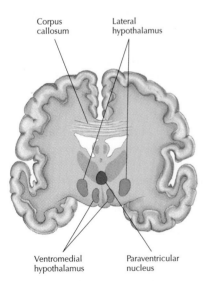

Corpus callosum
Lateral hypothalamus
Ventromedial hypothalamus
Paraventricular nucleus

▶**Figure 9.4**

This is a cross section through the middle of the brain (viewed from the front of the brain). Indicated areas of the hypothalamus are associated with hunger and the regulation of body weight.

described in a moment). It also receives neural messages from the liver and the stomach. When combined, these signals regulate hunger (Woods et al., 2000).

One part of the hypothalamus acts as a **feeding system** that initiates eating. If the *lateral hypothalamus* is "turned on" with an electrified probe, even a well-fed animal will immediately begin eating. (The term *lateral* simply means the sides of the hypothalamus. See ▶Figure 9.4.) If the same area is destroyed, an animal will never eat again.

A second area in the hypothalamus is part of a **satiety system,** or "stop mechanism" for eating. If the *ventromedial hypothalamus* (VENT-ro-MEE-dee-al) is destroyed, dramatic overeating results. (*Ventromedial* refers to the bottom middle of the hypothalamus.) Rats with such damage will eat until they balloon up to weights of 1000 grams or more (▶Figure 9.5). A normal rat weighs about 180 grams. To put this weight gain in human terms, picture someone you know who weighs 90 kilograms growing to a weight of 500 kilograms.

The *paraventricular nucleus* (PAIR-uh-ven-TRICK-you-ler) of the hypothalamus also affects hunger (see Figure 9.4). This area helps keep blood sugar levels steady. As a result, it is involved in both starting and stopping eating. The paraventricular nucleus is very sensitive to a substance called **neuropeptide Y** (NPY). If NPY is present in large amounts, an animal will eat until it cannot hold another bite (Woods et al., 2000).

How do we know when to stop eating? A chemical called **glucagon-like peptide 1 (GLP-1)** causes eating to cease. GLP-1 is released by the intestines after you eat a meal. From there, it travels in the bloodstream to the brain. When enough GLP-1 arrives, your desire to eat ends (Nori, 1998; Turton et al., 1996). It takes about 10 minutes for the hypothalamus to respond after you begin eating. That's why you are less likely to overeat if you eat slowly, which gives your brain time to get the message that you've had enough (Liu et al., 2000).

SET POINT   In addition to knowing when to start eating, and when a meal is over, your body needs to regulate weight over longer periods of time. This is done by monitoring the amount of fat stored in the body (Woods, Seeley, & Porte, 1998). Basically, your body has a **set point** for the proportion of fat it maintains. The set point acts like a "thermostat" for fat levels. Your own set point is the weight you maintain when you are making no effort to gain or lose weight. When your body goes below its set point, you will feel hungry most of the time. On the other hand, fat cells release a substance called leptin when your "spare tire" is well inflated. **Leptin** is carried in the bloodstream to the brain, where it tells us to eat less (Considine et al., 1996; Mercer et al., 1998).

Set points are only one piece in a complex puzzle that's worth solving. Obesity is a major health risk and, for many, a source of social stigma and low self-esteem.

▶**Figure 9.5**

Damage to the hunger satiety system in the hypothalamus can produce a very fat rat, a condition called hypothalamic *hyperphagia*. (Hi-per-FAGE-Hah: overeating). This rat weighs 1080 grams. (The pointer has gone completely around the dial and beyond.) (Photo courtesy of Neal Miller.)

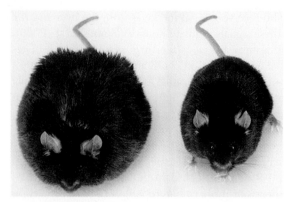

The mouse on the left has a genetic defect that prevents its fat cells from producing normal amounts of leptin. Without this chemical signal, the mouse's body acts as if its set point for fat storage is, shall we say, rather high.

Plentiful, eye-catching foods provide powerful incentives for overeating. In North America, numerous external eating cues and diets high in sweetness, fat, and variety have contributed to excessive weight gains in one adult out of every three.

External eating cue Any external stimulus that tends to encourage hunger or to elicit eating.
Diet The types and amounts of food and drink regularly consumed over a period of time.
Metabolic rate The rate at which energy is consumed by bodily activity.

Obesity

Why do people overeat? If internal needs alone controlled eating, fewer people would overeat. However, most of us are also sensitive to **external eating cues.** These are signs and signals linked with food. Do you tend to eat more when food is attractive, highly visible, and easy to get? If so, then external cues affect your food intake. In cultures like ours, where food is plentiful, eating cues add greatly to the risk of overeating (Woods et al., 2000).

Which Canadian city has the highest proportion of overweight adults? According to Statistics Canada data from the 2000 Community Health Survey, St. John's, Newfoundland, is Canada's fattest city, with 56.6 percent of adults being overweight. (Overweight means that at least 25 percent of their body weight is made up of fat; obese means that at least 30 percent of weight is fat.) In contrast, 37 percent of adults in Vancouver are overweight. Other cities with a weight problem include Thunder Bay (55.3 percent) and Sudbury (55.2 percent), while the thin towns included Chicoutimi (39 percent overweight) and Sherbrooke (39.2 percent). The survey of 130 000 people over the age of 12 suggests that Canadians are getting fatter—in 2000, 2.8 million Canadians were classified as obese—partly as a result of the aging of the baby boomer generation. Another 6.1 million Canadians were classified as overweight.

Clearly, obesity is increasing in North America, which is a particular problem because it is a risk factor for several health problems, including type 2 diabetes. Of special concern is that obesity and diabetes are more common among Native Canadians. The Canadian government reported the prevalence of type 2 diabetes to be almost three times higher in a representative Native sample than in the general population. Ojistoh Horn of the Kahnawake Schools Diabetes Prevention Project in Kahnawake, Quebec, and colleagues at McGill and the University of Montreal looked for correlates of obesity among Mohawk children in two Native communities: Kahnawake, and Tyendinaga, Ontario (Horn et al., 2001). This study, part of a long-term diabetes prevention project, found that change in skinfold thickness (a measure of obesity) from a baseline to two years later was predicted by the amount of physical activity and television viewing for girls, but not for boys. For boys, only the baseline skinfold thickness predicted change over two years. That other variables (activity, television-watching) did not predict change for boys may suggest a genetic contribution to obesity.

DIET A diet is not just a way to lose weight. Your current **diet** is defined by the types and amounts of food you regularly eat. Some diets actually encourage overeating. For instance, placing animals on a "supermarket" diet leads to gross obesity. In one experiment, rats were given meals of chocolate chip cookies, salami, cheese, bananas, marshmallows, milk chocolate, peanut butter, and fat. These pampered rodents gained almost three times as much weight as rats that ate only laboratory chow (Sclafani & Springer, 1976). (Rat chow is a dry mixture of several bland grains. If you were a rat, you'd probably eat more cookies than rat chow, too.)

THE PARADOX OF YO-YO DIETING If dieting works, why are hundreds of "new" diets published each year? The answer is that while dieters do lose weight, most regain it soon after they stop dieting. In fact, many people end up weighing even more than before. Why should this be so? Dieting (starving) slows the body's **rate of metabolism** (the rate at which energy is used up). In effect, a dieter's body becomes highly efficient at *conserving* calories and storing them as fat (Leibel, Rosenbaum, & Hirsch, 1995). And it may not matter how the weight loss occurs. Patricia Wainwright and her colleagues at the Univer-

Numerous studies show that you can lose weight on almost any diet. However, you will almost certainly gain it back in a few years. Only through regular exercise and revised eating habits can you stabilize your weight.

Weight cycling Repeated swings between losing and gaining weight.
Cultural values The importance and desirability of various objects and activities as defined by people in a given culture.
Taste aversion An active dislike for a particular food.
Behavioural dieting Weight reduction based on changing exercise and eating habits, rather than temporary self-starvation.
Anorexia nervosa Active self-starvation or a sustained loss of appetite that has psychological origins.

sity of Waterloo found that mice that lost weight either through food restriction or through exercise on a treadmill increased body fat relative to a control group of mice that did neither (Randall-Simpson et al., 1994).

"Yo-yo dieting," or repeated weight loss and gain, may be dangerous. Frequent **weight cycling** (losing and gaining weight) can dramatically slow the body's metabolic rate. This may make it harder to lose weight each time a person diets and easier to regain weight when the diet ends. However, the U.S. National Institute of Health's official position is that the risks associated with yo-yo dieting are still unclear, while the risks associated with obesity are well known. For this reason, NIH argues that obese adults should continue to try to lose weight (see the Weight-Control Information Network website listed in Psychology on the Net, at the end of this chapter).

To summarize, overeating is related to internal and external influences, diet, emotions, genetics, exercise, and many other factors. To answer the question we began with, people become obese in different ways and for different reasons. Clearly, scientists are still a long way from winning the "battle of the bulge." Nevertheless, many people have learned to take control of eating by applying psychological principles. See "Behavioural Dieting" on page 332 for more information.

Other Factors in Hunger

As research on overeating suggests, "hunger" is affected by more than just bodily needs for food. Let's consider some additional factors.

CULTURAL FACTORS   Learning to think of some foods as desirable and others as revolting has a large impact on what we eat. In North America we would never consider eating the eyes out of the steamed head of a monkey, but in some parts of the world they are considered a delicacy. By the same token, vegans and vegetarians think it is barbaric to eat any kind of meat. In short, cultural values greatly affect the *incentive value* of foods. (**Cultural values** are widely held beliefs about the desirability of various objects and activities.)

TASTE   Even tastes for "normal" foods vary considerably. For example, the hungrier you are, the more pleasant sweet foods taste (Cabanac & Duclaux, 1970). On the other hand, if you eat too much of a particular food, it will become less appealing. This probably helps us maintain variety in our diets. However, it also encourages obesity in societies where tasty foods are plentiful. If you overdose on fried chicken or French fries, moving on to some cookies or chocolate cheesecake certainly won't do your body much good (Pinel, Assanand, & Lehman, 2000).

As you may have noticed, it is easy to acquire a longer-lasting **taste aversion,** or active dislike, for a particular food. This can happen if a food causes sickness or is merely associated with nausea (Jacobsen et al., 1993). Not only do we learn to avoid such foods, they too can become nauseating. A friend who once became ill after eating a cheese Danish (well, actually, several) has never again been able to come face to face with this delightful pastry.

If getting sick occurs long after eating, how does it become associated with a particular food? A good question. Taste aversions are a type of classical conditioning. As stated in Chapter 6, a long delay between the CS and US usually prevents conditioning. However, psychologists theorize that we have a biological tendency to associate an upset stomach with foods eaten earlier. Such learning is usually protective. Yet, sadly, many cancer patients suffer taste aversions long after the nausea of their drug treatments has passed (Stockhorst, Klosterhalfen, & Steingrueber, 1998).

Eating Disorders

Under the sheets of her hospital bed Krystal looks like a skeleton. If her **anorexia nervosa** (AN-uh-REK-see-yah ner-VOH-sah: self-starvation) cannot be stopped, Krystal may die of malnutrition. Victims of anorexia, who are mostly adolescent females (5 to 10 percent are male), suffer devastating weight losses from severe, self-inflicted dieting (Wakeling, 1996).

USING PSYCHOLOGY   Behavioural Dieting

As we have noted, dieting is usually followed by rapid weight gains (Walsh & Flynn, 1995). If you really want to permanently lose weight, you must overhaul your eating habits, an approach called **behavioural dieting.** Here are some helpful behavioural techniques.

1. *Get yourself committed to weight loss.* Involve other people in your efforts. Programs such as Overeaters Anonymous or Take Off Pounds Sensibly can be a good source of social support (Foreyt, 1987).

2. *Exercise.* No diet can succeed for long without an increase in exercise, because exercise lowers the body's set point. Stop saving steps and riding elevators. Add activity to your routine in every way you can think of. Burning just 200 extra calories a day can help prevent weight gains (Wadden et al., 1998).

3. *Learn your eating habits by observing yourself and keeping a "diet diary."* Begin by making a complete, two-week record of when and where you eat, what you eat, and the feelings and events that occur just before and after eating. Is a roommate, relative, or spouse encouraging you to overeat? What are your most "dangerous" times and places for overeating?

4. *Learn to weaken your personal eating cues.* When you have learned when and where you do most of your eating, avoid these situations. Try to restrict your eating to one room, and do not read, watch TV, study, or talk on the phone while eating. Require yourself to interrupt what you are doing in order to eat.

5. *Count calories, but don't starve yourself.* To lose, you must eat less, and calories allow you to keep a record of your food intake. If you have trouble eating less every day, try dieting four days a week. People who diet intensely every other day lose as much as those who diet moderately every day (Viegener et al., 1990).

6. *Develop techniques to control the act of eating.* Begin by taking smaller portions. Carry to the table only what you plan to eat. Put all other food away before leaving the kitchen. Eat slowly, sip water between bites of food, leave food on your plate, and stop eating before you are completely full.

7. *Avoid snacks.* It is generally better to eat several small meals a day than three large ones (Assanand, Pinel, & Lehman, 1998). However, high-calorie snacks tend to be eaten in addition to meals. If you have an impulse to snack, set a timer for 20 minutes and see if you are still hungry then. Delay the impulse to snack several times if possible. Dull your appetite by filling up on raw carrots, bouillon, water, coffee, or tea.

8. *Chart your progress daily.* Record your weight, the number of calories eaten, and whether you met your daily goal. Set realistic goals by cutting down calories gradually. Losing about a half a kilogram per week is realistic, but remember, you are changing habits, not just dieting. Diets don't work!

9. *Set a "threshold" for weight control.* A study found that people who successfully maintained weight losses had a regain limit of under 2 kilograms. In other words, if they gained more than 1 or 2 kilograms, they immediately began to make corrections in their eating habits and amount of exercise (Brownell et al., 1986).

Be patient with this program. It takes years to develop eating habits. You can expect it to take at least several months to change them. If you are unsuccessful at losing weight with these techniques, you might find it helpful to seek the aid of a psychologist familiar with behavioural weight-loss techniques.

Do anorexics lose their appetite? No, many continue to feel hungry, yet struggle to starve themselves to excessive thinness. Often, anorexia starts with "normal" dieting that slowly begins to dominate the person's life. In time, anorexics suffer debilitating weakness, an absence of menstrual cycles, and various infections. Five to 8 percent (more than one in 20) die of malnutrition or related problems. Table 9.1 lists the symptoms of anorexia nervosa.

You may be surprised to learn that these excessively thin, physically weak women share their distorted perception with what seems like an unlikely group of men—bodybuilders, some of whom appear to have what has been called "reverse anorexia" (Pope, Katz, & Hudson, 1993). Reverse anorexia is the belief on the part of large, well-muscled bodybuilders that they are too small. At York University in Toronto, Caroline Davis and Lori Scott-Robertson recently compared anorexic women to competitive male bodybuilders on a variety of psychological tests. Compared to the normal population, both groups were significantly more obsessional, perfectionistic, narcissistic, and anhedonic

Anorexia nervosa can be far more dangerous than many people realize. This haunting photo shows popular singer Karen Carpenter shortly before her death. Carpenter died of heart failure induced by starvation. Many more victims of eating disorders die each year (Witherspoon, 1994).

Bulimia nervosa Excessive eating (gorging) usually followed by self-induced vomiting and/or taking laxatives.

Table 9.1
Recognizing Eating Disorders

ANOREXIA NERVOSA

- ☐ Body weight below 85 percent of normal for one's height and age.
- ☐ Refusal to maintain body weight in normal range.
- ☐ Intense fear of becoming fat or gaining weight, even though underweight.
- ☐ Disturbance in one's body image or perceived weight.
- ☐ Self-evaluation is unduly influenced by body weight.
- ☐ Denial of seriousness of abnormally low body weight.
- ☐ Absence of menstrual periods.
- ☐ Purging behaviour (vomiting or misuse of laxatives or diuretics).

BULIMIA NERVOSA

- ☐ Normal or above-normal weight.
- ☐ Recurring binge eating.
- ☐ Eating within an hour or two an amount of food that is much larger than most people would consume.
- ☐ Feeling a lack of control over eating.
- ☐ Purging behaviour (vomiting or misuse of laxatives or diuretics).
- ☐ Excessive exercise to prevent weight gain.
- ☐ Fasting to prevent weight gain.
- ☐ Self-evaluation is unduly influenced by body weight.

(DSM-IV, 1994.)

(deriving little pleasure from physical sensations such as touch, smell, and movement). However, the two groups differed in their feelings of self-worth, with the anorexic women, but not the bodybuilders, having much lower self-esteem than normal (Davis & Scott-Robertson, 2000).

Bulimia nervosa (bue–LIHM-ee-yah) is a second major eating disorder. Bulimic persons gorge on food, and then vomit or take laxatives to avoid gaining weight (see Table 9.1). Like anorexics, most victims of bulimia are girls or women. Approximately 5 percent of college women are bulimic, and as many as 61 percent have milder eating problems. Binging and purging can seriously damage health. Typical risks include sore throat, hair loss, muscle spasms, kidney damage, dehydration, tooth erosion, swollen salivary glands, menstrual irregularities, loss of sex drive, and even heart attack.

Recently, a connection between bulimia and seasonal affective disorder (SAD) has been noted. University of British Columbia psychiatrist Raymond Lam reported that many bulimia patients show winter worsening of mood (Lam, Goldner, & Grewal, 1996). In a separate study, Lam gave light therapy every day for four weeks to 22 female SAD patients who also suffered bulimia with the seasonal pattern. The patients' depression was alleviated, and their binge and purge scores significantly reduced, although only two of the 22 abstained from binge/purge episodes completely (Lam et al., 2001).

CAUSES   *What causes anorexia and bulimia?* Anorexic and bulimic persons have distorted views of themselves and exaggerated fears of becoming fat (Gardner & Bokenkamp, 1996). Many overestimate their body size by 25 percent or more. As a result, they think they are "fat" when they are actually wasting away (see ▶Figure 9.6) (Wichstrom, 1995).

Anorexic teens are usually described as "perfect" daughters—helpful, considerate, conforming, and obedient. Many seem to be seeking perfect control in their lives by being perfectly slim (Pliner & Haddock, 1996). People suffering from bulimia are also concerned with control. Typically, they are obsessed with thoughts of weight, food, eating, and ridding themselves of food. As a result, they feel guilt, shame, self-contempt, and anxiety after a binge. Vomiting reduces their anxiety, which makes purging highly reinforcing (Powell & Thelen, 1996).

▶Figure 9.6

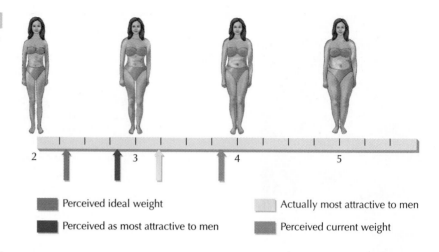

▶Figure 9.6
Women with abnormal eating habits were asked to rate their body shape on a scale similar to the one you see here. The images above the scale give an impression of body types at various points on the scale. As a group, they chose ideal figures much thinner than what they thought their current weights were. (Most women say they want to be thinner than they currently are, but to a lesser degree than women with eating problems.) Notice that the women with eating problems chose an ideal weight that was even thinner than what they thought men prefer. This is not typical of most women. In this study, only women with eating problems wanted to be thinner than what they thought men find attractive (Zellner, Harner, & Adler, 1989).

■ Perceived ideal weight
■ Perceived as most attractive to men
■ Actually most attractive to men
■ Perceived current weight

TREATMENT   People suffering from eating disorders need professional help. Treatment for anorexia usually begins with a medical diet to restore weight and health. Next, a counsellor may help patients work on the emotional conflicts that led to weight loss. For bulimia, behavioural counselling may include self-monitoring of food intake. The urge to vomit can be treated with extinction training. A related cognitive-behavioural approach focuses on changing the thinking patterns and beliefs about weight and body shape that perpetuate eating disorders (Whittal, Agras, & Gould, 1999).

Most people suffering from eating disorders will not seek help on their own. Typically, it takes strong urging by family or friends to get victims into treatment.

▶ Primary Motives Revisited—Thirst, Sex, and Pain

Survey Question:
■ Is there more than one type of thirst? In what ways are pain avoidance and the sex drive unusual?

Most biological motives work in ways that are similar to hunger. For example, thirst is only partially controlled by dryness of the mouth. If you were to take a drug that made your mouth constantly wet or dry, your water intake would remain normal. Like hunger, thirst is regulated by separate *thirst* and *thirst satiety* systems in the hypothalamus. Also like hunger, thirst is strongly affected by learning and cultural values.

Thirst

Extracellular thirst Thirst caused by a reduction in the volume of fluids found between body cells.
Intracellular thirst Thirst triggered when fluid is drawn out of cells due to an increased concentration of salts and minerals outside the cell.

You may not have noticed, but there are actually two kinds of thirst. **Extracellular thirst** occurs when fluids surrounding the cells of your body lose water. Bleeding, vomiting, diarrhea, sweating, and drinking alcohol cause this type of thirst (Petri, 1996). If a person loses water and minerals in any of these ways—especially by perspiration—a slightly salty liquid may be more satisfying than plain water.

Why would a thirsty person want to drink salty water? Before the body can retain water, it must replace minerals lost through perspiration (mainly salt). In lab tests, animals greatly prefer drinking saltwater after salt levels in their bodies are lowered (Strickler & Verbalis, 1988). Similarly, some nomadic peoples of the Sahara Desert prize blood as a beverage, probably because of its saltiness. (Maybe they should try Gatorade?)

A second type of thirst occurs when you eat a salty meal. In this instance your body does not lose fluid. Instead, excess salt causes fluid to be drawn out of cells. As the cells "shrink," **intracellular thirst** is triggered. Thirst of this type is best quenched by plain water. Intracellular thirst, if not remedied, can have significant effects, particularly on the brain. As Robert Lalonde of Hotel Dieu Hospital in Montreal has noted, elderly people may not respond adaptively to thirst—causing cell-shrinkage in the brain. On the basis of studies with aging mice, Lalonde suggested that dehydration might be related to apathy and neophobia (fear of new things) in the elderly (Lalonde & Badescu, 1995).

The drives for food, water, air, sleep, and elimination are all similar in that they are generated by a combination of activities in the body and the brain, and they are influ-

Tolerance for pain and the strength of a person's motivation to avoid discomfort are greatly affected by cultural practices and beliefs.

enced by various external factors. However, the sex drive and the drive to avoid pain are more unusual.

Pain

How is the drive to avoid pain different? Hunger, thirst, and sleepiness come and go in a fairly regular cycle each day. Pain avoidance, by contrast, is an **episodic drive** (ep-ih-SOD-ik). That is, it occurs in distinct episodes when bodily damage takes place or is about to occur. Most drives prompt us to actively seek a desired goal (food, drink, warmth, and so forth). Pain prompts us to avoid or eliminate sources of discomfort.

A leading pain researcher, McGill's Ronald Melzack argues for a significant psychological component of pain. That is, he suggests that it is not simply a matter of damaged tissue in the body—a burned finger, a scraped knee—sending a "pain signal" to the brain. Rather, Melzack claims that we must understand pain in terms of a system in the brain (a "neuromatrix") responsible for regulating the body's physical state (homeostasis again). This system, given somatosensory information about an injury to the body, plus other information (such as what the wound looks like, memory, and a stress-coping mechanism), produces the experience of pain as part of its response to the wound (Melzack, 1999; Melzack et al., 2001).

Given the strong psychological component of pain, it's not surprising that some people feel they must be "tough" and not show any distress. Others complain loudly at the smallest ache or pain. The first attitude raises pain tolerance, and the second lowers it. As this suggests, the drive to avoid pain is partly learned. That's why members of some societies endure cutting, burning, whipping, tattooing, and piercing of the skin that would agonize most people (but apparently not devotees of piercing and "body art"). As University of Western Ontario psychologist Gary Rollman has observed, we learn how to react to pain by observing family members, friends, and other role models (Rollman, 1998).

The Sex Drive

Many psychologists do not think of sex as a primary motive, because sex (contrary to anything your personal experience might suggest) is not necessary for *individual* survival. It is necessary, of course, for *group* survival.

The term **sex drive** refers to the strength of one's motivation to engage in sexual behaviour. In lower animals the sex drive is directly related to hormones. Female mammals (other than humans) are interested in mating only when their fertility cycles are in the stage of **estrus,** or "heat." Estrus is caused by a release of **estrogen** (a female sex hormone) into the bloodstream. Hormones are important in males as well. In most animals, castration will abolish the sex drive. But in contrast to females, the normal male animal is almost always ready to mate. His sex drive is primarily aroused by the behaviour of a receptive female. Therefore, in many species mating is closely tied to female fertility cycles.

How much do hormones affect human sex drives? Hormones affect the human sex drive, but not as directly as in animals. The sex drive in men is related to the amount of **androgens** (male hormones) provided by the testes. When the supply of androgens dramatically increases at puberty, so does the male sex drive. Likewise, the sex drive in women is related to their estrogen levels (Graziottin, 1998). However, "male" hormones also affect the female sex drive. In addition to estrogen, a woman's body produces small amounts of androgens. When their androgen levels increase, many women experience a corresponding increase in sex drive (Van Goozen et al., 1995).

Does alcohol increase the sex drive? In general, no. Alcohol is a *depressant.* As such, it may, in small doses, stimulate erotic desire by lowering inhibitions. This effect no doubt accounts for alcohol's reputation as an aid to seduction. (Humorist Ogden Nash once summarized this bit of folklore by saying, "Candy is dandy, but liquor is quicker.") However,

---

Episodic drive A drive that occurs in distinct episodes.

Sex drive The strength of one's motivation to engage in sexual behaviour.

Estrus Changes in the sexual drives of animals that create a desire for mating; particularly used to refer to females in heat.

Estrogen A female sex hormone.

Androgen Any of a number of male sex hormones.

Non-homeostatic drive
A drive that is relatively independent of physical deprivation cycles or bodily need states.

in larger doses alcohol suppresses orgasm in women and erection in men. Getting drunk decreases sexual desire, arousal, pleasure, and performance (Crowe & George, 1989).

Perhaps the most interesting fact about the sex drive is that it is largely **non-homeostatic** (relatively independent of bodily need states). In humans, the sex drive can be aroused at virtually any time by almost anything. It therefore shows no clear relationship to deprivation (the amount of time since the drive was last satisfied). Certainly, an increase in desire may occur as time passes. But recent sexual activity does not prevent sexual desire from occurring again. Notice, too, that people may seek to arouse the sex drive as well as to reduce it. This unusual quality may explain why sex is used to sell almost everything imaginable.

Sex is an important motive that affects the lives of most people. Let's explore human sexuality in a little more detail.

▶ Sexual Behaviour—Mapping the Erogenous Zone

Survey Question:
- What are the typical patterns of human sexual response?

Human sexual arousal is complex. It may, of course, be produced by direct stimulation of the body's **erogenous zones** (eh-ROJ-eh-nus: productive of pleasure or erotic desire). Human erogenous zones include the genitals, mouth, breasts, ears, anus, and to a lesser degree, the entire surface of the body. It is clear, however, that more than physical contact is involved: A urological or gynecological exam rarely results in any sexual arousal. Likewise, an unwanted sexual advance may produce only revulsion. Human sexual arousal obviously includes a large mental element.

Are men more easily sexually aroused than women? Overall, women and men have equal potential for sexual arousal and women are no less physically responsive than men. However, women tend to place more emphasis on emotional closeness with a lover than men do (Laan et al., 1995).

Based on the frequency of orgasm (from masturbation or intercourse), the peak of male sexual activity is at age 18. The peak rate of female sexual activity appears to occur a little later (Janus & Janus, 1993). However, male and female sexual patterns are rapidly becoming more alike (Oliver & Hyde, 1993). ▶Figure 9.7 shows the results of a major survey of sexual behaviour among American adults. As you can see, the frequency of sexual intercourse is very similar for men and women (Laumann et al., 1994).

Sexual Orientation

Erogenous zones Areas of the body that produce pleasure and/or provoke erotic desire.

Sexual orientation One's degree of emotional and erotic attraction to members of the same sex, opposite sex, or both sexes.

Heterosexual A person romantically and erotically attracted to members of the opposite sex.

Homosexual A person romantically and erotically attracted to same-sex persons.

Bisexual A person romantically and erotically attracted to both men and women.

Sexual behaviour and romantic relationships are strongly influenced by a person's sexual orientation. **Sexual orientation** refers to your degree of emotional and erotic attraction to members of the same sex, opposite sex, or both sexes. **Heterosexual** people are romantically and erotically attracted to members of the opposite sex. Those who are **homosexual** are attracted to people whose sex matches their own. A person who is **bisexual** is attracted to both men and women. In short, sexual orientation answers these questions:

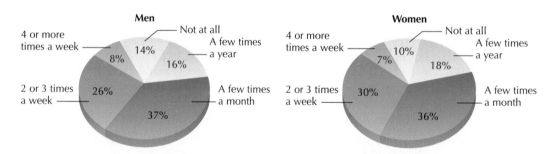

▶Figure 9.7

These graphs show the frequency of sexual intercourse for American adults. To generalize, about one third of the people surveyed have sex twice a week or more, one third a few times a month, and one third a few times a year or not at all. The overall average is about once a week (Laumann et al., 1994).

Who are you attracted to? Who do you have erotic fantasies about? Do you love men, or women, or both? (Garnets & Kimmel, 1991; Seligman, 1994).

Sexual orientation is a very deep part of personal identity. Starting with their earliest erotic feelings, most people remember being attracted to either the opposite sex or the same sex. The chances are practically nil of an exclusively heterosexual or homosexual person being "converted" from one orientation to the other. If you are heterosexual, you are probably certain that nothing could ever make you have homoerotic feelings. If so, then you know how homosexual persons feel about the prospects for changing their sexual orientation (Seligman, 1994).

What determines a person's sexual orientation? Research suggests that biological, social, cultural, and psychological influences combine to produce one's sexual orientation (Money, 1987; Van Wyk & Geist, 1995). New evidence also suggests that sexual orientation is at least partly hereditary. Some researchers now estimate that sexual orientation is from 30 to 70 percent genetic (Bailey et al., 1993; Bailey & Pillard, 1991).

We should not forget that the label "genetic" includes influences in the womb. A recent development relates sexual orientation to birth weight and birth order. Ray Blanchard of the Toronto Centre for Addiction and Mental Health reported that, in a sample of over 3000 men and women, homosexual males with older brothers weighed on average 170 grams less at birth than heterosexual males with older brothers (Blanchard & Ellis, 2001). He suggested that the older brothers caused an immune response in the mothers, which led to lower birth weight for subsequent male babies. A strong enough immune response may increase the probability of homosexuality. Anthony Bogaert of Brock University also reported a connection between birth order and homosexuality, and provided evidence that the relation cannot be attributed to sibling sexual activity (Bogaert, 2000).

How could genes affect sexual orientation? Possibly, heredity affects areas of the brain that orchestrate sexual behaviour. In support of this idea, scientists have shown that various brain structures differ in heterosexuals and homosexuals (LeVay, 1993).

Many people mistakenly believe that homosexuality is caused by a hormone imbalance. However, the hormone levels of most homosexual men and women are within the normal range (Banks & Gartrell, 1995). It is also a mistake to think that parenting makes children homosexual. There is little difference in the development of children with gay or lesbian parents and those who have heterosexual parents (Chan, Raboy, & Patterson, 1998; Parks, 1998). It appears that nature strongly prepares people to be either homosexual or heterosexual (LeVay, 1993). In view of this, discriminating against homosexuals is much like rejecting a person for being blue-eyed or left-handed (Hamill, 1995).

Human Sexual Response

In a pioneering series of studies, William Masters and Virginia Johnson directly studied sexual intercourse in nearly 700 males and females. The objective information they gained has given us a much clearer picture of human sexuality (Masters & Johnson, 1966, 1970). According to Masters and Johnson, sexual response can be divided into four phases: (1) excitement, (2) plateau, (3) orgasm, and (4) resolution (see ▶Figures 9.8 and 9.9). These four phases can be described as follows:

- **Excitement phase.** The first level of sexual response, indicated by initial signs of sexual arousal.
- **Plateau phase.** The second level of sexual response, during which physical arousal intensifies.
- **Orgasm.** A climax and release of sexual excitement.
- **Resolution.** The final phase of sexual response, involving a return to lower levels of sexual tension and arousal.

The four phases are the same for people of all sexual orientations (Garnets & Kimmel, 1991).

FEMALE RESPONSE   In women, the excitement phase is marked by a complex pattern of changes that prepare the vagina for intercourse. At the same time, the nipples become

Excitement phase
The first phase of sexual response, indicated by initial signs of sexual arousal.

Plateau phase The second phase of sexual response during which physical arousal is further heightened.

Orgasm A climax and release of sexual excitement.

Resolution The fourth phase of sexual response, involving a return to lower levels of sexual tension and arousal.

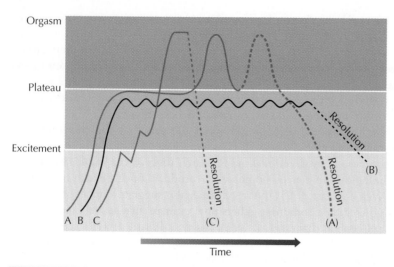

▶ Figure 9.8

Female sexual response cycle. The green line shows that sexual arousal rises through the excitement phase and levels off for a time during the plateau phase. Arousal peaks during orgasm and then returns to pre-excitement levels. In pattern A, arousal rises from excitement, through the plateau phase, and peaks in orgasm. Resolution may be immediate, or it may first include a return to the plateau phase and a second orgasm (dotted line). In pattern B, arousal is sustained at the plateau phase and slowly resolved without sexual climax. Pattern C shows a fairly rapid rise in arousal to orgasm. Little time is spent in the plateau phase and resolution is fairly rapid. (Reproduced by permission from Frank A. Beach [ed.], *Sex and Behavior*, NY: John Wiley & Sons, Inc., 1965.)

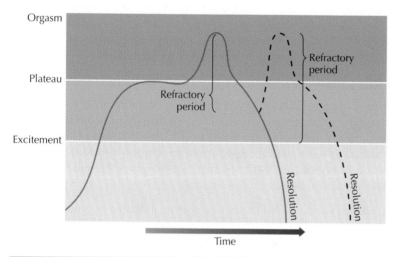

▶ Figure 9.9

Male sexual response cycle. The green line shows that sexual arousal rises through the excitement phase and levels off for a time during the plateau phase. Arousal peaks during orgasm and then returns to pre-excitement levels. During the refractory period, immediately after orgasm, a second sexual climax is typically impossible. However, after the refractory period has passed, there may be a return to the plateau phase, followed by a second orgasm (dotted line). (Reproduced by permission from Frank A. Beach [ed.], *Sex and Behavior*, NY: John Wiley & Sons, Inc., 1965.)

erect, pulse rate rises, and the skin may become flushed or reddened. If sexual stimulation ends, the excitement phase will gradually subside. If the person moves into the plateau phase, physical changes and subjective feelings of arousal become more intense. Sexual arousal that ends during this phase tends to ebb more slowly, which may produce considerable frustration. Occasionally, women skip the plateau phase (see Figure 9.8). For some women, this is almost always the case. Orgasm is usually followed by resolution, a return to lower levels of sexual tension and arousal. After orgasm, about 15 percent of all women return to the plateau phase and may have one or more additional orgasms.

MALE RESPONSE Sexual arousal in the male is signalled by erection of the penis during the excitement phase. There is also a rise in heart rate, increased blood flow to the genitals, enlargement of the testicles, erection of the nipples, and numerous other bodily changes. As is true of female sexual response, continued stimulation moves the male into the plateau phase. Again, physical changes and subjective feelings of arousal become more intense. Further stimulation during the plateau phase brings about a reflex release of sexual tension, resulting in orgasm.

In the mature male, orgasm is usually accompanied by ejaculation (release of sperm and seminal fluid). Afterward, it is followed by a short refractory period during which a second orgasm is impossible. Only rarely is the male refractory period immediately followed by a second orgasm. Both orgasm and resolution in the male usually do not last as long as they do for females.

Comparing Male and Female Responses

Male and female sexual responses are generally quite similar. However, the differences that do exist can affect sexual adjustment. For example, women typically go through the sexual phases more slowly than men do. However, during masturbation, 70 percent of females reach orgasm in four minutes or less. This is quite comparable to male response times. It suggests again that women are no less physically responsive than men.

In one regard, women are clearly more responsive. Only about 5 percent of males are capable of multiple orgasm (and then only after an unavoidable refractory period). Most men are limited to a second orgasm at best. In contrast, Masters and Johnson's findings suggest that most women who regularly experience orgasm are capable of multiple orgasm. According to one survey, 48 percent of all women have had multiple orgasms (Darling et al., 1992). Remember though, that only about 15 percent regularly have multiple orgasms. A woman should not automatically assume that something is wrong if she isn't orgasmic or multiorgasmic. Many women have satisfying sexual experiences even when orgasm is not involved.

Sexual Scripts

> **Sexual script** An unspoken mental plan that defines a "plot," dialogue, and actions expected to take place in a sexual encounter.

In a restaurant we commonly expect certain things to occur. It could even be said that each of us has a restaurant "script" that defines a plot, dialogue, and actions that should take place. Researcher John Gagnon (1977) has pointed out that, similarly, we learn a variety of **sexual scripts,** or unspoken mental plans that guide our sexual behaviour. Such scripts determine when and where we are likely to express sexual feelings, and with whom. They provide a "plot" for the order of events in lovemaking and they outline "approved" actions, motives, and outcomes.

One thing that many students have a sexual script for is surely spring break. Everyone knows what happens when young men and women meet on the beaches and in the bars, don't they? Perhaps not. Researchers Eleanor Maticka-Tyndale of the University of Windsor and Edward Herold and Dawn Mewhinney of the University of Guelph interviewed students on spring break (they went to Florida to do this) and after the students' return to Canada. They found that many students think casual sex is common on spring break, part of the sexual script (Mewhinney, Herold, & Maticka-Tyndale, 1995). But a survey of almost 700 students during or immediately after the break showed that 75 percent of respondents engaged in either no sex at all or limited "fooling around." Only 6 percent reported having intercourse with someone they met on spring break (Maticka-Tyndale & Herold, 1997). Perhaps the script needs revision.

Knowledge builder

HUNGER, THIRST, PAIN, AND SEX

Relate

 Think of the last meal you ate. What caused you to feel hungry? What internal signals told your body to stop eating? How sensitive are you to external eating cues? Have you developed any taste aversions?

A friend of yours seems to be engaging in yo-yo dieting. Can you explain to her or him why such dieting is ineffective?

Even if you're not overweight, reread each of the weight control techniques listed in the Using Psychology box on page 332 and visualize how you would carry out the suggested behaviours.

If you wanted to provoke extracellular thirst in yourself, what would you do? How could you make intracellular thirst occur?

In what ways are sexual responses of members of the opposite sex similar to your own? In what ways are they different?

Learning Check

1. The hunger satiety system in the hypothalamus signals the body to start eating when it receives signals from the liver or detects changes in blood sugar. T or F?
2. People who diet frequently tend to benefit from practice: They lose weight more quickly each time they diet. T or F?
3. Anorexia nervosa is also known as the binge-purge syndrome. T or F?
4. In addition to burning calories, physical exercise can lower the body's set point. T or F?
5. Thirst may be either intracellular or _____.
6. Pain avoidance is an _____ drive.
7. Sexual behaviour in animals is largely controlled by estrogen levels in the female and the occurrence of estrus in the male. T or F?
8. List the four phases of sexual response identified by Masters and Johnson: _____ _____ _____ _____

Critical Thinking

9. Kim, who is overweight, is highly sensitive to external eating cues. How might her wristwatch contribute to her overeating?
10. Charting weight loss makes use of a behavioural principle discussed in Chapter 6, "Conditioning and Learning." Can you name it?

Answers:

1. F 2. F 3. F 4. T 5. extracellular 6. episodic 7. F 8. excitement, plateau, orgasm, resolution 9. The time of day can influence eating, especially for externally cued eaters, who tend to get hungry at mealtimes, irrespective of their internal needs for food. 10. Feedback.

▶ Stimulus Drives—Skydiving, Horror Movies, and the Fun Zone

Survey Question:
■ How does arousal relate to motivation?

Stimulus drives Drives based on needs for exploration, manipulation, curiosity, and stimulation.

Arousal theory Assumes that people prefer to maintain ideal, or comfortable, levels of arousal.

Arousal The overall level of activation in the body and nervous system of a person or animal.

Sensation seeking A personality characteristic of persons who prefer high levels of stimulation.

Most people enjoy a steady "diet" of new movies, novels, tunes, fashions, games, news, websites, and adventures. Yet **stimulus drives,** which reflect needs for information, exploration, manipulation, and sensory input, go beyond mere entertainment. Stimulus drives also help us survive. As we scan our surroundings, we constantly identify sources of food, danger, shelter, and other key details. Stimulus drives are readily apparent in animals as well as humans. For example, monkeys will quickly learn to solve a mechanical puzzle made up of interlocking metal pins, hooks, and hasps (Butler & Harlow, 1954) (see ▶Figure 9.10). No food treats or other external rewards are needed to get them to explore and manipulate their surroundings. The monkeys seem to work for the sheer fun of it.

Arousal Theory

Are stimulus drives homeostatic? Yes. According to a perspective called **arousal theory,** ideal levels of activation exist for various activities. Additionally, we try to keep arousal near these optimal levels (Hebb, 1966). In other words, when your level of arousal is too low, stimulus seeking helps to raise it.

What do you mean by arousal? **Arousal** refers to activation of the body and the nervous system. Arousal is zero at death; it is low during sleep; it is moderate during normal daily activities; and it is high at times of excitement, emotion, or panic. Arousal theory assumes that we become uncomfortable when arousal is too low ("I'm bored") or when it is too high, as in fear, anxiety, or panic ("The dentist will see you now").

SENSATION SEEKERS *Do people vary in their needs for stimulation?* Picture a city dweller who is visiting the country. Very soon, she complains that it is "too quiet," and seeks some "action." Now imagine a country dweller who is visiting the city. Very soon, she finds the city "overwhelming" and seeks peace and quiet. These examples are extremes, but arousal theory also suggests that people learn to seek particular levels of arousal. Marvin Zuckerman (1990) has devised a test to measure such differences. The *Sensation-Seeking Scale* (SSS), as he calls it, includes statements like the samples shown here (from Zuckerman, 1996; Zuckerman, Eysenck, & Eysenck, 1978):

Thrill and Adventure Seeking
- I would like to try parachute jumping.
- I think I would enjoy the sensations of skiing very fast down a high mountain slope.

Experience Seeking
- I like to explore a strange city or section of town myself, even if it means getting lost.
- I like to try new foods that I have never tasted before.

Disinhibition
- I like wild, "uninhibited" parties.
- I often like to get high (drinking liquor or smoking marijuana).

Boredom Susceptibility
- I can't stand watching a movie that I've seen before.
- I like people who are sharp and witty, even if they do sometimes insult others.

Sensation seeking is a trait of people who prefer high levels of stimulation. Whether you are high or low in sensation seeking is prob-

▶Figure 9.10

Monkeys happily open locks that are placed in their cage. Since no reward is given for this activity, it provides evidence for the existence of stimulus needs. (Photo courtesy of Harry F. Harlow.)

ably based on how your body responds to new, unusual, or intense stimulation (Zuckerman, 1990). People who score high on the SSS tend to be bold, independent individuals who value change. They also report more sexual partners than low scorers; they are more likely to smoke, and they prefer spicy, sour, and crunchy foods over bland foods. Low sensation seekers are orderly, nurturant, giving, and they enjoy the company of others. Which are you? (Most people fall somewhere between the extremes.)

Levels of Arousal

Is there an ideal level of arousal for peak performance? If we set aside individual differences, most people perform best when their arousal level is *moderate*. Let's say that you have to take an essay exam. If you are sleepy or feeling lazy (arousal level too low), your performance will suffer. If you are in a state of anxiety or panic about the test (arousal level too high), you will also perform below par. Thus, the relationship between arousal and performance forms an **inverted U function** (a curve in the shape of an upside-down U) (see ▶Figure 9.11) (Anderson, 1990).

The inverted U tells us that at very low levels of arousal your body is not sufficiently energized to perform well. With increased arousal, performance continues to improve up to the middle regions of the curve. Then it begins to drop off as a person becomes emotional, frenzied, or disorganized. Imagine trying to start a car stalled on a railroad track, with a speeding train bearing down on you. Apparently, the same thing happens in professional baseball, where batting averages drop dramatically near the end of close games (Davis & Harvey, 1992).

Is performance always best at moderate levels of arousal? No, the ideal level of arousal depends on the complexity of a task. If a task is relatively simple, it is best for arousal to be high. When a task is more complex, the best performance occurs at lower levels of arousal. This relationship is called the **Yerkes-Dodson law** (see Figure 9.11). It applies to a wide variety of tasks and to measures of motivation other than arousal.

Then is it true that by learning to calm down, a person would do better on tests? Usually, but not always. Studies show that students are most anxious when they don't know the material. If this is the case, calming down simply means you will remain calm while failing. (See "Coping with Test Anxiety" on page 342 to learn how to avoid excessive arousal.)

Circadian Rhythms

We have seen that moment-to-moment changes in activation can have a major impact on us. What about larger cycles of arousal? Do they affect energy levels, motivation, and performance? Scientists have long known that the bodily activity is guided by internal "biological clocks." Every 24 hours, your body undergoes a cycle of changes called **circadian** (SUR-kay-dee-AN) **rhythms** (*circa*: about; *diem*: a day) (Orlock, 1993). Throughout the

> **Inverted U function** A curve, roughly in the shape of an upside-down U, that relates performance to levels of arousal.
>
> **Yerkes-Dodson law** A summary of the relationships among arousal, task complexity, and performance.
>
> **Circadian rhythms** Cyclical changes in bodily functions and arousal levels that vary on a schedule approximating a 24-hour day.

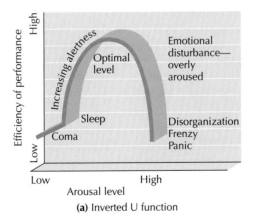
(a) Inverted U function

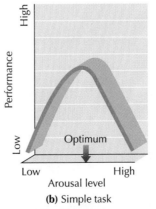
(b) Simple task

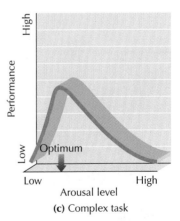
(c) Complex task

▶Figure 9.11

(a) The general relationship between arousal and efficiency can be described by an inverted U curve. The optimal level of arousal or motivation is higher for a simple task *(b)* than for a complex task *(c)*.

USING PSYCHOLOGY   Coping with Test Anxiety

Would you like to win a million dollars on a game show? Or would you merely like to do well on classroom tests? In either case, your ability to answer questions will be impaired if you are too nervous. **Test anxiety** is a combination of *heightened physiological arousal* (nervousness, sweating, pounding heart) and *excessive worry*. This combination—worry plus arousal—tends to distract students with a rush of upsetting thoughts and feelings (Gierl & Rogers, 1996). Let's see what you can do to alleviate test anxiety.

Preparation

The most direct antidote for test anxiety is *hard work*. Many test-anxious students simply study too little, too late. That's why improving your study skills is a good way to reduce test anxiety (Jones & Petruzzi, 1995). Test anxiety is highest before exams on which students expect to do poorly. The best solution is to *overprepare* by studying long before the "big day." Students who are well prepared score higher, worry less, and are less likely to panic (Zohar, 1998).

Relaxation

Learning to relax is another way to lower test anxiety (Ricketts & Galloway, 1984). You can learn self-relaxation skills by looking at Chapter 13, where a relaxation technique is described. Emotional support from others can also help you relax (Sarason, 1981). If you are test anx-

ious, discuss the problem with your professors or study for tests with a supportive classmate.

Rehearsal

To reduce your nervousness during tests, rehearse how you will cope with upsetting events. Before taking a test, imagine yourself going blank, running out of time, or feeling panicked. Then calmly plan how you will handle each situation—by keeping your attention on the task, by focusing on one question at a time, and so forth (Watson & Tharp, 1996).

Restructuring Thoughts

Many test-anxious students benefit from listing the distracting and upsetting thoughts they typically have during exams. They then learn to combat their worries with calming, rational replies (Jones & Petruzzi, 1995). (These are called *coping statements;* see Chapter 11 for more information.)

Let's say that a student thinks, "I'm going to fail this test and everybody will think I'm stupid." A good reply to this upsetting thought would be to say, "If I prepare well and control my worries, I will probably pass the test. Even if I don't, it won't be the end of the world. I can try to improve on the next test."

Students who cope well with exams usually try to do the best they can, even under trying circumstances. With practice, most people can learn to be less testy at test-taking time (Zeidner, 1995).

Test anxiety High levels of arousal and worry that seriously impair test performance.

day, activities in the liver, kidneys, and endocrine glands undergo large changes. Body temperature, blood pressure, and amino acid levels also shift from hour to hour. These activities, and many others, peak once a day (see ▶Figure 9.12). People are usually more energetic and alert at the high point of their circadian rhythms (Natale & Cicogna, 1996).

There is a related variation in mood. In most healthy people, subjective mood declines with body temperature to the bottom of the daily cycle around 7 a.m., then improves with increasing temperature, peaking at about 10 p.m. As noted by McGill University psychiatrist Diane Boivin (2000), this connection between mood and circadian rhythm may have therapeutic value. Although we don't know why, sleep dep-

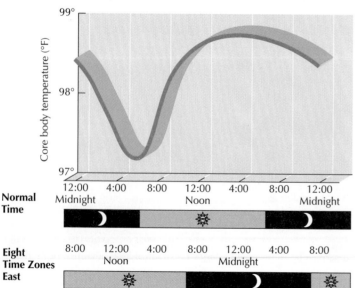

▶Figure 9.12

Core body temperature is a good indicator of a person's circadian rhythm. Most people reach a low point two to three hours before their normal waking time. It's no wonder that both the Chernobyl and Three Mile Island nuclear power plant accidents occurred around 4 a.m. Rapid travel to a different time zone, shift work, depression, and illness can throw sleep and waking patterns out of synchronization with the body's core rhythm. Mismatches of this kind are very disruptive (Hauri & Linde, 1990).

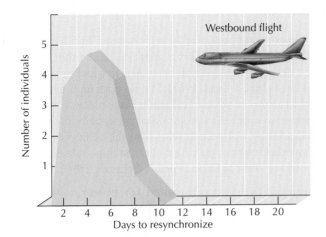

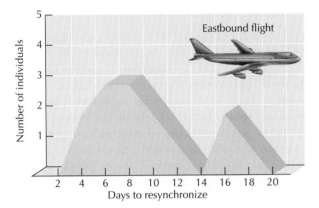

▶Figure 9.13

Time required to adjust to air travel across six time zones. The average time to resynchronize was shorter for westbound travel than for eastbound flights. (Data from Beljan et al., 1972; cited by Moore-Ede, Sulzman, & Fuller, 1982.)

Preadaptation Gradual matching of sleep-waking cycles to a new time schedule.

Social motives Learned motives acquired as part of growing up in a particular society or culture.

rivation can relieve symptoms of depression, and subsequent sleep recovery can cause a return of the symptoms.

SHIFT WORK AND JET LAG   Circadian rhythms are most noticeable after a major change in time schedules. Businesspersons, athletes, and other time zone travellers tend to perform poorly when their body rhythms are disturbed (Rader & Hicks, 1987). If you travel great distances east or west, the peaks and valleys of your circadian rhythms will be out of phase with the sun and clocks. For example, you might be wide awake at midnight and feel like you're sleepwalking during the day (return to Figure 9.12). Shift work has the same effect, causing fatigue, irritability, upset stomach, and depression (Akerstedt, 1990).

How fast do people adapt to rhythm changes? For major time zone shifts (five hours or more) it can take from several days to two weeks to resynchronize. Adjusting to jet lag is slowest when you stay indoors, where you can sleep and eat on "home time." Getting outdoors, where you must sleep, eat, and socialize on the new schedule, speeds adaptation. A five-hour dose of bright sunlight early each day is particularly helpful for resetting your circadian rhythm (Czeisler et al., 1989). The direction of travel also affects adaptation (Harma et al., 1994). If you fly west, adapting is relatively easy, taking an average of four to five days. If you fly east, adapting takes 50 percent longer or more (see ▶Figure 9.13).

Why is there a difference? When you fly east, the sun comes up earlier relative to your "home" time. Let's say that you live in Vancouver and fly to Toronto. If you get up at 7 a.m. in Toronto, it's only 4 a.m. back in Vancouver—and your body knows it. If you fly west, the sun comes up later. In this case, it is easier for people to "advance" (stay up later and sleep in) than it is to shift backward.

The difference may be important for people taking medication to control mental disorders. Queen's University psychiatrist Kola Oyewumi reported on a patient whose psychosis was controlled by the drug Clozapine. This patient suffered a relapse on an eastward trans-Atlantic flight. A dosage increase got his psychosis under control again, but the increased dose was found to be excessive on the return (westward) flight (Oyewumi, 1998).

How does this affect those of us who are not world travellers? Most college students have "pulled an all-nighter," especially for final exams. At such times it is wise to remember that departing from your regular schedule usually costs more than it's worth. Often, you can do as much during one hour in the morning as you could have done in three hours of work after midnight. You might just as well go to sleep two hours earlier.

In general, if you can anticipate an upcoming body rhythm change, it is best to *preadapt* to your new schedule. **Preadaptation** refers to gradually matching your sleep-waking cycle to a new time schedule. Before travelling, for instance, you should go to sleep one hour later (or earlier) each day until your sleep cycle matches the time at your destination. If you are unable to do that, it helps to fly early in the day when you fly east. When you fly west, it is better to fly late. (Remember, the *E* in *east* matches the *E* in *early*.)

▶ Learned Motives—In Pursuit of Excellence

Survey Question:
■ What are social motives? Why are they important?

Competition and achievement are highly valued in Western culture. Some of your friends are more interested than others in success, money, possessions, status, love, approval, grades, dominance, power, or belonging to groups—all of which are **social motives** or goals. We acquire social motives in complex ways, through socialization and cultural conditioning. The behaviour of outstanding artists, scientists, athletes, educators, and leaders is best understood in terms of such learned needs, particularly the need for achievement.

The Need for Achievement

To many people, being "motivated" means being interested in achievement. In Chapter 14 we will investigate aggression, helping, affiliation, seeking approval, and other social motives. For now, let us focus on the **need for achievement (nAch),** which is a desire to meet an internal standard of excellence (McClelland, 1961). People with high needs for achievement strive to do well in any situation in which evaluation takes place.

Is that like the aggressive businessperson who strives for success? Not necessarily. Needs for achievement may lead to wealth and prestige, but people who are high achievers in art, music, science, or amateur sports may excel without seeking riches. Such people typically enjoy challenges and relish a chance to test their abilities (Puca & Schmalt, 1999).

POWER   The need for achievement is not the same as the **need for power,** which is a desire to have impact or control over others (McClelland, 1975). People with strong needs for power want their importance to be visible: They buy expensive possessions, wear prestigious clothes, and exploit other people. People whose main goal in life is to make lots of money tend to be poorly adjusted and unhappy (Kasser & Ryan, 1996).

CHARACTERISTICS OF ACHIEVERS   David McClelland (1917–1998) and others have probed the need for achievement. Using a simple measure, McClelland found that he could predict the behaviour of high and low achievers in many situations. For instance, McClelland compared people's occupations with scores on an achievement test they took in their second year of college. Fourteen years later, those who scored high in nAch tended to have jobs that involved risk and responsibility (McClelland, 1965).

Here's a test: In front of you are five targets. Each is placed at an increasing distance from where you are standing. You are given a beanbag to toss at the target of your choice. Target A, anyone can hit; target B, most people can hit; target C, some people can hit; target D, very few people can hit; target E is rarely if ever hit. If you hit A, you will receive $2; B, $4; C, $8; D, $16; and E, $32. You get only one toss. Which one would you choose? McClelland's research suggests that if you have a high need for achievement, you will select C or perhaps D. Those high in nAch are moderate risk takers. When faced with a problem or a challenge, persons high in nAch avoid goals that are too easy.

Why do they pass up sure success? They do it because easy goals offer no sense of satisfaction. They also avoid long shots because there is either no hope of success, or "winning" will be due to luck rather than skill. Persons low in nAch select sure things or impossible goals. Either way, they don't have to take any responsibility for failure.

Desires for achievement and calculated risk taking lead to success in many situations. People high in nAch complete difficult tasks, they earn better grades, and they tend to excel in their occupations. College students high in nAch attribute success to their own ability, and failure to insufficient effort. Thus, high-nAch students are more likely to renew their efforts when they perform poorly. When the going gets tough, high achievers get going.

In college and university, a great deal of importance is placed on academic achievement. In light of this, it is understandable that students are sometimes tempted to buy self-help tapes that promise to improve their motivation to study. Such tapes are aggressively advertised and available in many campus bookstores. However, if you're ever tempted to buy one of these tapes, you should ask a crucial question: Do they work? Read "Mail-Order Motivation?" for an answer.

The Key to Success?

What does it take to achieve extraordinary success? Psychologist Benjamin Bloom did an interesting study of top concert pianists, Olympic swimmers, sculptors, tennis players, mathematicians, and research neurologists. Bloom (1985) found that drive and determination, not great natural talent, led to exceptional success.

The upshot of Bloom's work is that talent is nurtured by dedication and hard work. It is most likely to blossom when parents actively support a child's special interests and emphasize doing your best at all times. Studies of child prodigies and eminent adults also show that intensive practice and expert coaching are common ingredients of high

---

Need for achievement The desire to excel or meet some internalized standard of excellence.

Need for power The desire to have social impact and control over others.

FOCUS ON RESEARCH   Mail-Order Motivation?

Each year, consumers spend millions of dollars on so-called subliminal self-help audiotapes. These tapes supposedly contain messages presented below the level of conscious awareness. Usually, "subliminal messages" are embedded in relaxing music or the soothing sounds of ocean waves. The tapes are purported to "subconsciously" influence motivation to help listeners lose weight, relieve pain, gain intimacy, succeed financially, improve grades, and so forth. Do the tapes work?

Russell, Rowe, and Smouse (1991) obtained the tapes "Improve Study Habits" and "Passing Exams" from the largest U.S. manufacturer of subliminal audiotapes. Three groups of university students took part in a 10-week evaluation. An "active treatment group" listened to tapes containing subliminal suggestions. An "inactive treatment group" listened to placebo tapes with ocean wave sounds but no subliminal messages. Students in a control group did not listen to any tapes.

The results of the experiment were certainly not subliminal. The message came through loud and clear: Average final exam grades and semester grade point averages for all three groups revealed no effects or benefits from listening to the tapes (Russell, Rowe, & Smouse, 1991).

Philip Merikle and Heather Skanes (1992) of the University of Waterloo found similar results when comparing weight loss among women who listened to a subliminal tape from a manufacturer, a placebo tape, or no tape at all. The three groups all lost the same amount of weight. Merikle and Skanes concluded that the weight loss occurred because during the study the women thought more about their weight (see also Benoit & Thomas, 1992; Greenwald et al., 1991; Moore, 1995; Staum & Brotons, 1992).

---

achievement. Elite performance typically requires at least 10 years of dedicated practice (Ericsson & Charness, 1994). The old belief that talent will emerge on its own is largely a myth.

SELF-CONFIDENCE   Achieving elite performance may be reserved for the dedicated few. Nevertheless, you may be able to improve everyday motivation by increasing your self-confidence. People with **self-confidence** believe they can successfully carry out an activity or reach a goal. To enhance self-confidence, it is wise to do the following (Druckman & Bjork, 1994):

> **Self-confidence** Belief that one can successfully carry out an activity or reach a goal.
>
> **Hierarchy of human needs** Abraham Maslow's ordering of needs, based on their presumed strength or potency.

- Set goals that are specific and challenging, but attainable.
- Advance in small steps.
- When you first acquire a skill, your goal should be to make progress in learning. Later, you can concentrate on improving your performance, compared with other people.
- Get expert instruction that helps you master the skill.
- Find a skilled model (someone good at the skill) to emulate.
- Get support and encouragement from an observer.
- If you fail, regard it as a sign that you need to try harder, not that you lack ability.

Self-confidence affects motivation by influencing the challenges you will undertake, the effort you will make, and how long you will persist when things don't go well. You can be confident that self-confidence is worth cultivating.

▶ Motives in Perspective—A View from the Pyramid

> **Survey Question:**
> ■ Are some motives more basic than others?

What motivates people who live fully and richly? As you may recall from Chapter 1, Abraham Maslow called the full use of personal potential *self-actualization*. As a sidelight to his work on self-actualization, Maslow also described a **hierarchy of human needs.** By this he meant that some needs are more basic or powerful than others. Think for a moment about the needs that influence your own behaviour. Which seem strongest? Which do you spend

▶**Figure 9.14**

Maslow believed that lower needs in the hierarchy are dominant. Basic needs must be satisfied before growth motives are fully expressed. Desires for self-actualization are reflected in various meta-needs (see text).

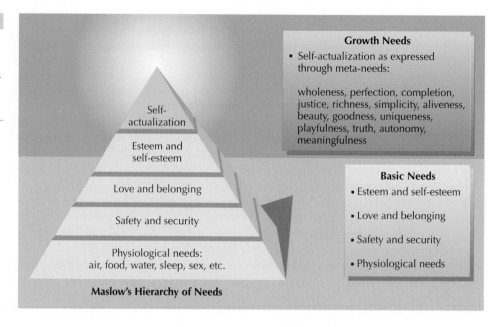

Growth Needs
- Self-actualization as expressed through meta-needs:

  wholeness, perfection, completion, justice, richness, simplicity, aliveness, beauty, goodness, uniqueness, playfulness, truth, autonomy, meaningfulness

Self-actualization

Esteem and self-esteem

Love and belonging

Safety and security

Physiological needs: air, food, water, sleep, sex, etc.

Basic Needs
- Esteem and self-esteem
- Love and belonging
- Safety and security
- Physiological needs

Maslow's Hierarchy of Needs

Basic needs The first four levels of needs in Maslow's hierarchy; lower needs tend to be more potent than higher needs.

Growth needs In Maslow's hierarchy, the higher-level needs associated with self-actualization.

Meta-needs In Maslow's hierarchy, needs associated with impulses for self-actualization.

the most time and energy satisfying? Now look at Maslow's hierarchy (▶Figure 9.14). Note that physiological needs are at the base of the pyramid. Since these are necessary for survival, they tend to be *prepotent,* or dominant over the higher needs. It could be said, for example, that "to a starving person, food is god."

Maslow believed that our higher, more fragile needs are expressed only after we satisfy our physiological needs. This is also true of needs for safety and security. Until such needs are met, a person may have little interest in higher pursuits. A person who is extremely thirsty, for instance, might have little interest in writing poetry or even talking with friends. For this reason, Maslow described the first four levels of the hierarchy as **basic needs.** Other basic needs include love and belonging (family, friendship, caring), and needs for esteem and self-esteem (recognition and self-respect).

All of the basic needs are *deficiency* motives. That is, they are activated by a lack of food, water, security, love, esteem, or other basic needs. At the top of the hierarchy we find **growth needs,** represented by the need for self-actualization. The need for self-actualization is not based on deficiencies. Rather, it is a positive, life-enhancing force for personal growth. Like other humanistic psychologists, Maslow believed that people are basically good. If our basic needs are met, he said, we will tend to move on to actualizing our potentials.

How are needs for self-actualization expressed? Maslow called the less powerful but humanly important actualization motives **meta-needs** (Maslow, 1970). They are listed in Table 9.2. According to Maslow, we have a tendency to move up the hierarchy to the meta-needs. A person whose survival needs are met, but whose meta-needs are unfulfilled, falls into a "syndrome of decay." The lives of such people are marked by despair, apathy, and alienation.

Maslow's hierarchy is not well documented by research, and many questions can be raised about it. How, for instance, do we explain the actions of people who fast as a means of social protest? How can the meta-need for justice overcome the more basic need for food? (Perhaps the answer is that fasting is temporary and self-imposed.) Despite such objections, Maslow's views are a good way to understand and appreciate the rich interplay of human motives.

Did Maslow believe that many people are motivated by meta-needs? Maslow estimated that few people are primarily motivated by self-actualization needs. Most of us are more concerned with esteem, love, or security. Perhaps this is because incentives and

Wheelchair athletes engage in vigorous competition. Maslow considered such behaviour an expression of the need for self-actualization.

Table 9.2
Maslow's List of Meta-Needs

Meta-needs are seen as an expression of tendencies for self-actualization, the full development of personal potential.

1. Wholeness (unity)
2. Perfection (balance and harmony)
3. Completion (ending)
4. Justice (fairness)
5. Richness (complexity)
6. Simplicity (essence)
7. Aliveness (spontaneity)
8. Beauty (rightness of form)
9. Goodness (benevolence)
10. Uniqueness (individuality)
11. Playfulness (ease)
12. Truth (reality)
13. Autonomy (self-sufficiency)
14. Meaningfulness (values)

Intrinsic motivation
Motivation that comes from within, rather than from external rewards; motivation based on personal enjoyment of a task or activity.

Extrinsic motivation
Motivation based on obvious external rewards, obligations, or similar factors.

rewards in our society are slanted to encourage conformity, uniformity, and security in schools, jobs, and relationships. When was the last time you met a meta-need?

Intrinsic and Extrinsic Motivation

Some people cook for a living and consider it hard work. Others cook for pleasure and dream of opening a restaurant. For some people, carpentry, gardening, writing, photography, or making jewellery is fun. For others the same activities are drudgery they must be paid to do. How can the same activity be "work" for one person and "play" for another?

When you do something for enjoyment, to show your ability, or to gain skill, your motivation is usually *intrinsic*. **Intrinsic motivation** occurs when we act without any obvious external rewards. We simply enjoy an activity, see it as a challenge, want to enhance our abilities, or seek a chance to explore and learn. In contrast, **extrinsic motivation** stems from obvious external factors, such as pay, grades, rewards, obligations, and approval. Most of the activities we think of as "work" are extrinsically rewarded (Ryan & Deci, 2000).

Turning Play into Work

It might seem that extrinsic incentives would strengthen motivation, but this is not always the case (Lepper, Keavney, & Drake, 1996). In fact, excessive rewards can decrease intrinsic motivation and spontaneous interest (Tang & Hall, 1995). For instance, children who were lavishly rewarded for drawing with felt-tip pens later showed little interest in playing with the pens again (Greene & Lepper, 1974). Apparently, "play" can be turned into "work" by *requiring* people to do something they would otherwise enjoy. When we are coerced or "bribed" to act, we tend to feel as if we are "faking it." Employees who lack initiative and teenagers who reject school and learning are good examples of such reactions (Ryan & Deci, 2000).

CREATIVITY People are more likely to be creative when they are intrinsically motivated. On the job, salaries and bonuses may increase how much work people do. However, work *quality* is tied more to intrinsic factors, such as interest, freedom to choose, and useful feedback (Kohn, 1987). Intrinsic motivation also tends to lead to greater creativity (Ruscio, Whitney, & Amabile, 1998). When a person is intrinsically motivated, a dash of challenge, surprise, and complexity makes a task rewarding. When extrinsic motivation is stressed, complexity, surprise, and challenge just become barriers to reaching a goal (Sternberg & Lubart, 1995).

How can the concept of intrinsic motivation be applied? Both types of motivation are necessary. But extrinsic motivation shouldn't be overused, especially with children. Greene and Lepper (1974) summarize: (1) If there's no intrinsic interest in an activity to begin with, you have nothing to lose by using extrinsic rewards; (2) if basic skills are lacking, extrinsic rewards may be necessary at first; (3) extrinsic rewards can focus attention on an activity so real interest will develop; (4) if extrinsic rewards are used, they should be small and phased out as soon as possible. It also helps to tell children they seem to be *really interested* in drawing, playing the piano, learning a language, or whatever activity you are rewarding (Cialdini et al., 1998).

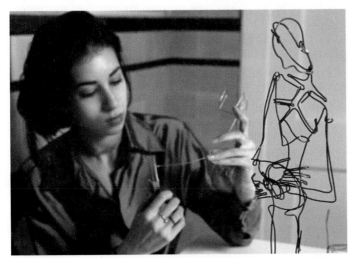

People who are intrinsically motivated feel free to explore creative solutions to problems.

Knowledge builder

STIMULUS MOTIVES, LEARNED MOTIVES, MASLOW, AND INTRINSIC MOTIVATION

Relate

Does arousal theory seem to explain any of your own behaviour? Think of at least one time when your performance was impaired by arousal that was too low or too high. Now think of some personal examples that illustrate the Yerkes-Dodson law.

In situations involving risk and skill, do you like to "go for broke"? Or do you prefer sure things? Do you think you are high, medium, or low in nAch?

Which levels of Maslow's hierarchy of needs occupy most of your time and energy?

Name an activity you do that is intrinsically motivated and one that is extrinsically motivated. How do they differ?

Learning Check

1. Exploration, manipulation, and curiosity provide evidence for the existence of _____ drives.
2. People who score high on the SSS tend to be extroverted, independent, and individuals who value change. T or F?

3. When a task is complex, the ideal level of arousal is _____; when a task is simple, the optimal level of arousal is _____.
4. Two key elements of test anxiety that must be controlled are _____ and excessive _____.
5. People with high nAch are attracted to "long shots" and "sure things." T or F?
6. According to Maslow, meta-needs are the most basic and prepotent sources of human motivation. T or F?
7. Intrinsic motivation is often undermined in situations in which obvious external rewards are applied to a naturally enjoyable activity. T or F?

Critical Thinking

8. Over 75 percent of all first-year college students say that "being well-off financially" is an essential life goal. Seventy-three percent indicate that "making more money" was a very important factor in their decision to attend college. Which meta-needs are fulfilled by "making more money"?

Answers:

1. stimulus 2. T 3. low, high 4. arousal, worry 5. F 6. F 7. T 8. None of them.

▶ Inside an Emotion—How Do You Feel?

Survey Question:

■ What happens during emotion? Can lie detectors really detect lies?

Emotion A state characterized by physiological arousal, and changes in facial expression, gestures, posture, and subjective feelings.

Adaptive behaviours Actions that aid attempts to survive and adapt to changing conditions.

Physiological changes (in emotion) Alterations in heart rate, blood pressure, perspiration, and other involuntary responses.

Adrenaline A hormone produced by the adrenal glands that tends to arouse the body.

Emotional expression Outward signs that an emotion is occurring.

If a mad scientist replaced your best friend's brain with a computer, how would you know that something was wrong? An absence of emotion might be one of the first telltale signs. **Emotion** is characterized by physiological arousal, and changes in facial expressions, gestures, posture, and subjective feelings.

The word *emotion* means "to move," and emotions do indeed move us. First, the body is physically aroused during emotion. Such bodily stirrings are what cause us to say we were "moved" by a play, a funeral, or an act of kindness. Second, we are often motivated, or moved to take action, by emotions such as fear, anger, or joy. Many of the goals we seek make us feel good. Many of the activities we avoid make us feel bad. We feel happy when we succeed and sad when we fail (Oatley & Jenkins, 1992).

Emotions are linked to many basic **adaptive behaviours,** such as attacking, fleeing, seeking comfort, helping others, reproducing, and the like. Such behaviours help us survive and adjust to changing conditions (Plutchik, 1990, 1994). However, it is also apparent that emotions can have negative effects. Stage fright or "choking up" in sports can spoil performances. Hate, anger, contempt, disgust, and fear disrupt behaviour and relationships. But more often, emotions aid survival.

A pounding heart, sweating palms, "butterflies" in the stomach, and other bodily reactions are a major element of fear, anger, joy, and other emotions. These **physiological changes** include alterations in heart rate, blood pressure, perspiration, and other bodily stirrings. Most of these changes are caused by **adrenaline,** a hormone produced by the adrenal glands. Activity in the sympathetic nervous system causes adrenaline to be released into the bloodstream.

Emotional expressions, or outward signs of what a person is feeling, are another major ingredient of emotion. For example, when you are intensely afraid, your hands tremble, your face contorts, your posture becomes tense and defensive, and your voice

▶Figure 9.15
How accurately do facial expressions reveal emotion? After you have guessed what emotion these people are feeling, turn to Figure 9.20 on page 355.

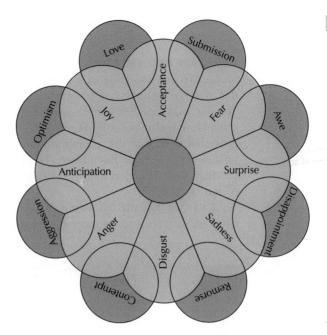

▶Figure 9.16
Primary and mixed emotions. In Robert Plutchik's model there are eight primary emotions, as listed in the inner areas. Adjacent emotions may combine to give the emotions listed around the perimeter. Mixtures involving more widely separated emotions are also possible. For example, fear plus anticipation produces anxiety. (Adapted from Plutchik, 1980.)

Emotional feelings
The private, subjective experience of having an emotion.

Primary emotions
According to Robert Plutchik's theory, the most basic emotions are fear, surprise, sadness, disgust, anger, anticipation, joy, and acceptance.

Mood A low-intensity, long-lasting emotional state.

changes. In general, these expressions tell others what emotions we are experiencing (see ▶Figure 9.15). **Emotional feelings** (a person's private emotional experience) are the third element of emotion. This is the part of emotion with which we are usually most familiar.

Primary Emotions

Are some emotions more basic than others? Robert Plutchik (1990, 1994) has identified eight **primary emotions.** These are fear, surprise, sadness, disgust, anger, anticipation, joy, and acceptance (receptivity). If the list seems too short, it's because each emotion can vary in *intensity*. Anger, for instance, may vary from rage to simple annoyance.

One of Plutchik's most interesting ideas concerns the mixing of primary emotions. As shown in ▶Figure 9.16, each pair of adjacent emotions can be mixed to yield a third, more complex emotion. Other mixtures are also possible. For example, five-year-old Shannon feels both joy and fear as she eats a stolen cookie. The result? Guilt—as you may recall from your own childhood. Likewise, jealousy could be a mixture of love, anger, and fear.

A *mood* is the mildest form of emotion (see ▶Figure 9.17). **Moods** are low-intensity emotional states that can last for many hours or even days. Moods often affect day-to-day behaviour by preparing us to act in certain ways. For example, when your neighbour Roseanne is in an irritable mood she may react angrily to almost anything you say. When she is in a happy mood, she can easily laugh off an insult (Oatley & Jenkins, 1992). Our moods are closely tied to circadian rhythms. When body temperature is at its daily low point, people tend to feel "down,"

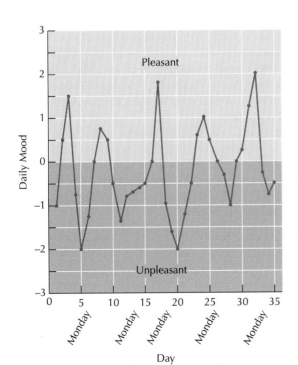

▶Figure 9.17
Folklore holds that people who work or attend school on a weekly schedule experience their lowest moods on "Blue Monday." Actually, moods tend to be generally lower for most weekdays than they are on weekends. The graph shown here plots the average daily mood ratings made by a group of college students over a five-week period. As you can see, many people find that their moods rise and fall on a seven-day cycle. For most students, a low point tends to occur around Monday or Tuesday and a peak on Friday or Saturday. (Adapted from Larsen & Kasimatis, 1990.) In other words, moods are often entrained (pulled along) by weekly schedules.

emotionally. When body temperature is at its peak, your mood is likely to be positive—even if you missed a night of sleep (Boivin, Czeisler, & Waterhouse, 1997).

THE BRAIN AND EMOTION   The primary emotions we have discussed can be further reduced to just two categories: positive and negative emotions. Ordinarily, we might think that positive and negative emotions are opposites. But this is not the case. As Shannon's "cookie guilt" implies, people can experience positive and negative emotions at the same time. How is that possible? Recordings of brain activity show that positive emotions are processed mainly in the left hemisphere of the brain. In contrast, negative emotions are processed in the right hemisphere. The fact that positive and negative emotions are based on different brain areas helps explain why we can feel happy and sad at the same time (Canli et al., 1998).

Later we will attempt to put the elements of emotion together into a single picture. But first, we need to look more closely at physiological arousal and emotional expressions.

▶ Physiology and Emotion—Arousal, Sudden Death, and Lying

An African Bushman frightened by a lion and a city dweller frightened by a prowler will react in much the same way (Mesquita & Frijda, 1992). Such encounters usually produce muscle tension, a pounding heart, irritability, dryness of the throat and mouth, sweating, butterflies in the stomach, frequent urination, trembling, restlessness, sensitivity to loud noises, and numerous other bodily changes. These reactions are nearly universal because they are innate. Specifically, they are caused by the **autonomic nervous system (ANS)** (the neural system that connects the brain with internal organs and glands). As you may recall from Chapter 2, activity of the ANS is automatic rather than voluntary.

Fight or Flight

There are two divisions of the ANS, one called the sympathetic branch and the other the parasympathetic branch. The two branches are active at all times. Whether you are relaxed or aroused at any moment depends on the combined activity of both branches.

What does the ANS do during emotion? In general, the **sympathetic branch** activates the body for emergency action—for "fighting or fleeing." It does this by arousing some bodily systems and inhibiting others (see Table 9.3.) These changes have a purpose. Sugar is released into the bloodstream for quick energy, the heart beats faster to supply blood to the muscles, digestion is temporarily slowed, blood flow in the skin is restricted to reduce bleeding, and so forth. Such reactions improve the chances of surviving an emergency.

The **parasympathetic branch** reverses emotional arousal. This calms and relaxes the body. After a period of high emotion, the heart is slowed, the pupils return to normal size, blood pressure drops, and so forth. In addition to restoring balance, the parasympathetic system helps build up and conserve bodily energy.

The parasympathetic system responds much more slowly than the sympathetic system does. That's why a pounding heart, muscle tension, and other signs of arousal do not fade for 20 or 30 minutes after you feel an intense emotion, such as fear. Moreover, after a strong emotional shock, the parasympathetic system may overreact and lower blood pressure too much. This can cause people to become dizzy or faint after seeing something shocking, such as a horrifying accident (Kleinknecht, 1986).

SUDDEN DEATH   An overreaction to intense emotion is called a **parasympathetic rebound.** If the rebound is severe, it can sometimes cause death. In times of war, for instance, combat can be so savage that some soldiers literally die of fear (Moritz & Zamchech, 1946). Apparently, such deaths occur because the parasympathetic nervous system slows the heart to a stop. Even in civilian life this is possible. In one case, a terrified young woman was admitted to a hospital because she felt she was going to die. A backwoods midwife had predicted that the woman's two sisters would die before their 16th and 21st birthdays. Both died as predicted. The midwife also predicted that this woman would die before her 23rd birthday. She was found dead in her hospital bed the day after she was

Autonomic nervous system (ANS) The system of nerves that connects the brain with the internal organs and glands.

Sympathetic branch A part of the ANS that activates the body at times of stress.

Parasympathetic branch A part of the autonomic system that quiets the body and conserves energy.

Parasympathetic rebound Excess activity in the parasympathetic nervous system following a period of intense emotion.

Table 9.3
Autonomic
Nervous
System
Effects

ORGAN	PARASYMPATHETIC SYSTEM	SYMPATHETIC SYSTEM
Pupils of eyes	Constricts to diminish light	Dilates to increase light
Tear glands Mucous membranes of nose and throat Salivary glands	Stimulates secretion	Inhibits secretion, causes dryness
Heart Blood vessels	Slowing of heart, constriction of blood vessels	Acceleration of heart; dilation of blood vessels to increase blood flow
Lungs, windpipe	Constricts bronchi of lungs to relax breathing	Dilates bronchi to increase breathing
Esophagus Stomach Abdominal blood vessels	Stimulates secretion and movement	Inhibits secretion and movement, diverts blood flow
Liver	Releases bile	Retains bile, releases blood sugar
Pancreas	Stimulates secretion	Inhibits secretion
Intestines Rectum Kidney Bladder	Excitation, expulsion of feces and urine	Inhibition, retention of feces and urine
Skin blood vessels	Dilate, increase blood flow	Constrict; skin becomes cold and clammy
Sweat glands	Inhibited	Stimulated to increase perspiration
Hair follicles	Relaxed	Tensed to make hair stand on end

Polygraph A device for recording heart rate, blood pressure, respiration, and galvanic skin response; commonly called a "lie detector."

Galvanic skin response (GSR) A change in the electrical resistance (or inversely, the conductance) of the skin, due to sweating.

admitted. It was two days before her 23rd birthday (Seligman, 1989). The woman was an apparent victim of her own terror.

Is the parasympathetic nervous system always responsible for such deaths? Probably not. In the case of older persons or those with heart problems, the direct effects of sympathetic activation may be enough to bring about heart attack and collapse. For example, five times more people than usual died of heart attacks on the day of a major 1994 earthquake in Los Angeles (Leor, Poole, & Kloner, 1996).

Lie Detectors

Did O.J. do it? Did Monica tell the whole truth? Has a trusted employee been stealing from the business? There are many situations in which we would like to be able to detect lying. The most popular method for revealing lies measures bodily changes that accompany emotion. However, the accuracy of "lie detector" tests is doubtful, and they can be a serious invasion of privacy (Iacono & Lykken, 1997; Lykken, 1998; Saxe, 1994).

What is a lie detector? Do lie detectors really detect lies? The lie detector (see ▶ Figure 9.18) is more accurately called a *polygraph,* a word that means "many writings." A typical **polygraph** records changes in heart rate, blood pressure, breathing rate, and the galvanic skin response. The **galvanic skin response (GSR)** is recorded from the surface of the hand by electrodes that measure skin

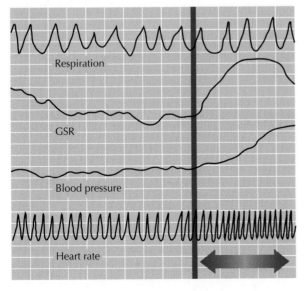

Respiration

GSR

Blood pressure

Heart rate

▶Figure 9.18

A typical polygraph includes devices for measuring heart rate, blood pressure, respiration, and galvanic skin response. Changes in the area marked by the arrow indicate emotional arousal. If such responses appear when a person answers a question, he or she may be lying, but other causes of arousal are also possible.

Irrelevant questions In a polygraph exam, neutral, non-threatening, or non-emotional questions.

Relevant questions In a polygraph exam, questions to which only a guilty person should react.

Control questions In a polygraph exam, questions that almost always provoke anxiety.

conductance or, more simply, sweating. The polygraph is popularly known as a lie detector because it is used by the police. In reality, the polygraph is not a lie detector at all. The device only records *general emotional arousal*—it can't tell the difference between lying and fear, anxiety, or excitement (Lykken, 1998).

When trying to detect a lie, the polygraph operator begins by asking **irrelevant** (neutral, non-emotional) **questions,** such as, "Is your name [person's name]?" "Did you eat lunch today?" and so forth. This establishes a "baseline" for normal emotional responsiveness. Then the examiner asks relevant questions: "Did you murder Hensley?" **Relevant questions** are those to which only a guilty person should react. A person who lies will presumably become anxious or emotional when answering relevant questions.

Wouldn't a person be nervous just from being questioned? Yes, but to minimize this problem, skilled polygraph examiners ask a series of questions with critical items mixed among them. An innocent person may respond emotionally to the whole procedure, but only a guilty person is supposed to react to key questions. For example, a suspected bank robber might be shown several pictures and asked, "Was the teller who was robbed this person? Was it this person?"

As an alternative, subjects may be asked **control questions,** which are designed to make almost anyone anxious: "Have you ever stolen anything from your place of work?" Typically, such questions are very difficult to answer truthfully with an unqualified no. In theory they allow the examiner to see how a person reacts to doubt or misgivings. The person's reaction to critical questions can then be compared with responses to control questions.

Even when questioning is done properly, lie detection may be inaccurate (Dawson, 1990). For example, a man named Floyd Fay was convicted of murdering his friend Fred Ery. To prove his innocence, Fay volunteered to take a lie detector test, which he failed. Fay spent two years in prison before the real killer confessed to the crime. Psychologist David Lykken (1998) has documented many such cases in which innocent people were jailed after being convicted on the basis of polygraph evidence.

If Floyd Fay was innocent, why did he fail the test? Put yourself in his place, and it's easy to see why. Imagine the examiner asking, "Did you kill Fred?" Since you knew Fred, and you are a suspect, it's no secret that this is a critical question. What would happen to your heart rate, blood pressure, breathing, and perspiration under such circumstances?

Proponents of lie detection claim from 90 to 95 percent accuracy. But in one laboratory experiment, accuracy was dramatically lowered when people thought about past emotional situations as they answered irrelevant questions (Ben-Shakhar & Dolev, 1996). Similarly, the polygraph may be thrown off by self-inflicted pain, by tranquillizing drugs, or by people who can lie without anxiety (Waid & Orne, 1982). Worst of all, the test's most common error is to label an innocent person guilty, rather than a guilty person innocent. In studies involving real crimes and criminal suspects, an average of approximately one innocent person in five was rated as guilty by the lie detector (Lykken, 1998; Patrick & Iacono, 1989; Saxe, Dougherty, & Cross, 1985).

Despite the lie detector's unreliability, you may be tested for employment or for other reasons. Should this occur, the best advice is to remain calm; then actively challenge the results if the machine wrongly questions your honesty.

▶ Expressing Emotions—Making Faces and Talking Bodies

Survey Question:
■ How accurately are emotions expressed by "body language" and the face?

Are emotional expressions a carryover from earlier stages of human evolution? Charles Darwin thought so. Darwin (1872) observed that angry tigers, monkeys, dogs, and humans all bare their teeth in the same way. Darwin believed that emotional expressions evolved to communicate our feelings to others, which aids survival. Indeed, such messages give us valuable hints about what other people are likely to do next (Ekman & Rosenberg, 1997).

It's not surprising, then, that emotional expressions can be perceived outside the focus of attention, and can draw attention to a point in the visual world. Those are the conclusions reached by researchers at the University of Waterloo. Eastwood, Smilek, and Merikle

Knowledge builder

EMOTION AND PHYSIOLOGICAL AROUSAL

Relate

How did your most emotional moment of the past week affect your behaviour, expressions, feelings, and bodily state? Could you detect both sympathetic and parasympathetic effects?

Make a list of the emotions you consider to be most basic. To what extent do they agree with Plutchik's list?

What did you think about the lie detector test before reading this chapter? What do you think now?

Learning Check

1. Many of the physiological changes associated with emotion are caused by secretion of which hormone?
   a. atropine b. adrenaline c. attributine d. amoduline
2. Emotional _____ often serve to communicate a person's emotional state to others.

3. Awe, remorse, and disappointment are among the primary emotions listed by Robert Plutchik. T or F?
4. Emotions are closely related to activity of the _____ nervous system.
5. The sympathetic system prepares the body for "fight or flight" by activating the parasympathetic system. T or F?
6. The parasympathetic system inhibits digestion and raises blood pressure and heart rate. T or F?
7. What bodily changes are measured by a polygraph?

_____

_____

Critical Thinking

8. Can you explain why people "cursed" by shamans or "witch doctors" sometimes actually die?

Answers:

1. b 2. expressions 3. F 4. autonomic 5. F 6. F 7. heart rate, blood pressure, breathing rate, galvanic skin response 8. In cultures where there is deep belief in magic or voodoo, a person who thinks that she or he has been cursed may become uncontrollably emotional. After several days of intense terror, a parasympathetic rebound is likely. If the rebound is severe enough, it can lead to physical collapse and death.

(2001) found that when subjects searched arrays of simple face stimuli (a circle with dot-eyes and a line-mouth), they were better at finding the one negatively toned (frowning) face among a lot of neutral faces than at finding the one positively toned (smiling) face among neutral faces. Eastwood and colleagues argue that this is consistent with other evidence that threatening stimuli are perceived efficiently (without attention).

Facial Expressions

Are emotional expressions the same for all people? The most basic expressions are fairly universal (see ▶ Figure 9.19). Children who are born blind can't learn emotional expressions from others. Even so, they display joy, sadness, fear, anger, and disgust in the same way as sighted people do (Galati, Scherer, & Ricci-Bitti, 1997).

Many facial expressions are shaped by learning. As a result, some are found only in specific cultures. Among the Chinese, for example, sticking out the tongue is a gesture of surprise, not of disrespect or teasing. If a person comes from another culture, it is wise to remember that you may easily misunderstand his or her expressions. At such times, knowing the social context in which an expression occurs helps clarify its meaning (Carroll & Russell, 1996; Ekman, 1993). (See also "Cultural Differences in Emotion" on page 354.)

▶ **Figure 9.19**

Facial expressions of anger often act as a warning of threat or impending attack. Is anger expressed the same way in different cultures? A study of masks from 18 cultures found that those meant to be frightening or threatening were strikingly similar. Shared features included angular, diagonal, or triangular eyes, eyebrows, nose, cheeks, and chin, together with an open, downward-curved mouth. (Keep this list in mind next Halloween.) Obviously, the pictured mask is not meant to be warm and cuddly. Your ability to "read" its emotional message suggests that basic emotional expressions have universal biological roots (Aronoff, Barclay, & Stevenson, 1988).

HUMAN DIVERSITY   Cultural Differences in Emotion

How many times have you been angry this week? Once? Twice? Several times? If it was more than once, you're not unusual. Anger is a very common emotion in Western cultures. Very likely this is because our culture emphasizes personal independence and a free expression of individual rights and needs. In North America, anger is widely viewed as a "natural" reaction to feeling that you have been treated unfairly.

On the opposite side of the globe, many Asian cultures place a high value on group harmony. In Asia, expressing anger in public is less common and anger is regarded as less "natural." The reason for this is that anger tends to separate people. Thus, being angry is at odds with a culture that values cooperation.

It is common to think of emotion as an individual event. However, as you can see, emotion is shaped by cultural ideas, values, and practices (Markus, Kitayama, & VandenBos, 1996).

Gender and Emotion

Women have a reputation for being "more emotional" than men. Are they? There is little reason to think that men and women differ in their private experiences of emotion. However, in Western cultures women do tend to be more emotionally expressive (Kring & Gordon, 1998). Why should this be so? The answer again lies in learning: As they are growing up, boys learn to suppress their emotional expressions; girls tend to increase theirs (Polce-Lynch et al., 1998). For many men, an inability to express feelings is a major barrier to having close, satisfying relationships with others (Bruch, Berko, & Haase, 1998). It may even contribute to tragedies like the mass murders at Columbine High School in Littleton, Colorado. For many young males, anger is the only emotion they can freely express.

Kinesics Study of the meaning of body movements, posture, hand gestures, and facial expressions; commonly called body language.

Emotional tone The underlying emotional state an individual is experiencing at any given moment.

Facial blend A mix of two or more basic facial expressions.

Despite cultural differences, facial expressions of fear, anger, disgust, sadness, and happiness (enjoyment) are recognized around the world. Contempt, surprise, and interest may also be universal, but researchers are less certain of these expressions (Ekman, 1993). Notice that this list covers most of the primary emotions described earlier. It's also nice to note that a smile is the most universal and easily recognized facial expression of emotion.

Body Language

If a friend walked up to you and said, "Hey, ugly, what are you doing?" would you be offended? Probably not, because such remarks are usually delivered with a big grin. The facial and bodily gestures of emotion speak a language all their own and add to what a person says.

Kinesics (kih-NEEZ-iks) is the study of communication through body movement, posture, gestures, and facial expressions. Informally, we call it body language. To see a masterful use of body language, turn off the sound on a television and watch a popular entertainer or politician at work.

What kinds of messages are sent with body language? Again, it is important to realize that cultural learning affects the meaning of gestures. What, for instance, does it mean if you touch your thumb and first finger together to form a circle? In North America it means "Everything is fine" or "A-okay." In France and Belgium it means "You're worth zero." In southern Italy it means "You're an ass!" (Ekman et al., 1984). Thus, when the layer of culturally defined meanings is removed, it is more realistic to say that body language reveals an overall **emotional tone** (underlying emotional state).

Your face can produce some 20 000 different expressions, which makes it the most expressive part of your body. Most of these are **facial blends** (a mixture of two or more basic expressions). Imagine, for example, that you just received an F on an unfair test. Quite likely, your eyes, eyebrows, and forehead would reveal anger, while your mouth would be turned downward in a sad frown.

Emotions are often unconsciously revealed by gestures and body positioning.

Most of us believe we can fairly accurately tell what others are feeling by observing their facial expressions. If thousands of facial blends occur, how do we make such judgments? The answer is that facial expressions can be boiled down to basic dimensions of **pleasantness–unpleasantness, attention–rejection,** and **activation** (or arousal) (Schlosberg, 1954). By smiling when you give a friend a hard time, you add an emotional message of pleasantness and acceptance to the verbal insult, which changes its meaning. As they say in movie Westerns, it makes a big difference to "Smile when you say that, partner."

▶ Theories of Emotion—Several Ways to Fear a Bear

Survey Question:
■ How do psychologists explain emotions?

Is it possible to explain what takes place during emotion? How are arousal, behaviour, cognition, expressions, and feelings interrelated? Theories of emotion offer different answers to these questions. Let's explore four views. Each appears to have a part of the truth, so we will try to put them all together in the end.

The James-Lange Theory (1884–1885)

You're hiking in the woods when a bear suddenly steps out onto the trail. What will happen next? Common sense tells us that we see a bear, feel fear, become aroused, and run (and sweat and yell). But is this the correct order of events? In the 1880s, William James and Carl Lange proposed that common sense had it backward. According to James and Lange, bodily arousal (such as a rapidly beating heart) does not follow a feeling such as fear. Instead, they argued, emotional feelings follow bodily arousal. Thus, we see a bear, run, are aroused, and then feel fear as we become aware of our bodily reactions (see ▶ Figure 9.20).

To support this line of thought, James pointed out that we often do not experience an emotion until after reacting. For example, imagine that you are driving. Suddenly a car pulls out in front of you. You swerve and skid to an abrupt halt at the side of the road. Only after you have come to a stop do you notice your pounding heart, rapid breathing, and tense muscles—and recognize your fear.

The Cannon-Bard Theory (1927)

Walter Cannon (1932) and Phillip Bard disagreed with the James-Lange theory. According to them, emotional feelings and bodily arousal *occur at the same time*. Cannon and Bard believed that seeing a bear activates the thalamus in the brain. The thalamus, in turn, alerts the cortex and the hypothalamus for action. The cortex produces our emotional feelings and emotional behaviour. The hypothalamus triggers a chain of events that arouses the body. Thus, if you see a dangerous-looking bear, brain activity will simultaneously produce bodily arousal, running, and a feeling of fear (see ▶ Figure 9.21).

Schachter's Cognitive Theory of Emotion (1971)

The previous theories are mostly concerned with our physical responses. Stanley Schachter realized that cognitive (mental) factors also enter into emotion. According to Schachter, emotion occurs when we apply a particular label to general physical *arousal*. Schachter believed that when we are aroused, we have a need to interpret our feelings. Assume, for instance, that someone sneaks up behind you on a dark street and says, "Boo!" No matter who the person is, your body will be aroused (pounding heart, sweating palms, and so on). If the person is a total stranger, you might interpret this arousal as fear; if the person is a close friend, the arousal may be labelled as surprise or delight. The label (such as anger, fear, or happiness) that you apply to bodily arousal is influenced by your past

Pleasantness–unpleasantness As reflected by facial expressions, the degree to which a person is experiencing pleasure or displeasure.

Attention–rejection As reflected by facial expressions, the degree of attention given to a person or object.

Activation As reflected by facial expressions, the degree of arousal a person is experiencing.

James-Lange theory States that emotional feelings follow bodily arousal and come from awareness of such arousal.

Cannon-Bard theory States that activity in the thalamus causes emotional feelings and bodily arousal to occur simultaneously.

Schachter's cognitive theory States that emotions occur when physical arousal is labelled or interpreted on the basis of experience and situational cues.

▶Figure 9.20

Facial displays and gestures that express complex emotions can be difficult to judge accurately. The agonized expression on the face of Frank De Vito is deceptive. When this photograph was taken, Mr. De Vito and his wife had just learned that he won $1 million in a lottery.

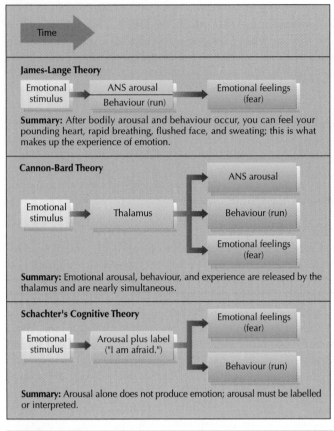

▶ Figure 9.21

Theories of emotion.

Which theory of emotion best describes the reactions of these people? Given the complexity of emotion, each theory appears to possess an element of truth.

experiences, the situation, and the reactions of others (see Figure 9.21).

Support for the cognitive theory of emotion comes from an experiment in which people watched a slapstick movie (Schachter & Wheeler, 1962). Before viewing the movie, one third of the people received an injection of adrenaline, one third got a placebo (salt water) injection, and everyone else was given a tranquillizer. People who received the adrenaline rated the movie funniest and laughed the most while watching it. In contrast, those given the tranquillizer were least amused. The placebo group fell in between.

According to the cognitive theory of emotion, individuals who received adrenaline had a stirred-up body, but no explanation for what they were feeling. Consequently, they became happy when the movie implied that their arousal was due to amusement. This and similar experiments make it clear that emotion is much more than just an agitated body. Perception, experience, attitudes, judgment, and many other mental factors also affect the emotions we feel. Schachter's theory would predict, then, that if you met a bear, you would be aroused. If the bear seemed unfriendly, you would interpret your arousal as fear, and if the bear offered to shake your "paw," you would be happy, amazed, and relieved!

ATTRIBUTION   We now move from slapstick movies and fear of bear bodies to an appreciation of bare bodies. Researcher Stuart Valins (1967) added an interesting wrinkle to Schachter's theory of emotion. According to Valins, arousal can be attributed to various sources, a process that alters our perceptions of emotion. To demonstrate **attribution,** Valins (1966) showed male college students slides of nude females. While viewing the photographs, each subject heard an amplified heartbeat that he believed was his own. In reality, students were listening to a recorded heartbeat carefully designed to beat *louder* and *stronger* when some (but not all) of the slides were shown.

After watching the slides, each student was asked to say which was most attractive. Students who heard the false heartbeat consistently rated slides paired with a "pounding heart" as the most attractive. In other words, when a student saw a slide and heard his heart beat louder, he attributed his "emotion" to the slide. His interpretation seems to have been, "Now that one I like!" His next reaction, perhaps, was "But why?" Later research suggests that subjects persuaded themselves that the slide really was more attractive in order to explain their apparent arousal (Truax, 1983).

Attribution The mental process of assigning causes to events. In emotion, the process of attributing arousal to a particular source.

That seems somewhat artificial. Does it really make any difference what arousal is attributed to? Yes. To illustrate attribution in the "real world," consider what happens when parents interfere with the budding romance of a son or daughter. Often, trying to separate a young couple intensifies their feelings. Meddling parents add frustration, anger, and fear or excitement (as in seeing each other "on the sly") to the couple's feelings. Since they already care for each other, they are likely to attribute all this added emotion to "true love" (Walster, 1971).

Attribution theory predicts that you are most likely to "love" someone who gets you stirred up emotionally (Foster et al., 1998). This is true even when fear, anger, frustration, or rejection is part of the formula. Thus, if you want to successfully propose marriage, take your intended to the middle of a narrow, windswept suspension bridge over a deep chasm and look deeply into his or her eyes. As your beloved's heart pounds wildly (from being on the bridge, not from your irresistible charms), say, "I love you." Attribution theory predicts that your companion will conclude, "Oh wow, I must love you too."

The preceding is not as far-fetched as it may seem. In a famous study by psychologists Don Dutton and Arthur Aron at the University of British Columbia, an attractive female interviewer spoke to men in a park in Vancouver. Some were on a swaying suspension bridge more than 70 metres above a river. The rest were on a solid wooden bridge just 3 metres above the ground. After the interview, the psychologist gave each man her telephone number, so he could "find out about the results" of the study. Men interviewed on the suspension bridge were much more likely to give the "lady from the park" a call (Dutton & Aron, 1974). Apparently, these men experienced heightened arousal, which they interpreted as attraction to the experimenter—a clear case of love at first fright!

The Facial Feedback Hypothesis

Schachter added thinking and interpretation (cognition) to our view of emotion, but the picture still seems incomplete. What about expressions? How do they influence emotion? As Charles Darwin observed, the face is very central to emotion—certainly it must be more than just an "emotional billboard."

Psychologist Carrol Izard (1977, 1990) was among the first to suggest that the face does, indeed, affect emotion. According to Izard and others, emotions cause innately programmed changes in our facial expressions. Sensations from the face then provide cues to the brain that help us tell what emotion we are feeling. This idea is known as the **facial feedback hypothesis** (Adelmann & Zajonc, 1989). Stated another way, it says that having facial expressions and becoming aware of them is what produces our private emotional experiences. Exercise, for instance, arouses the body, but this arousal is not experienced as emotion because it does not trigger emotional expressions.

Let's take this idea one step further. Paul Ekman believes that "making faces" can actually cause emotion (Ekman, 1993). In one study, people were guided as they arranged their faces, muscle by muscle, into expressions of surprise, disgust, sadness, anger, fear, and happiness (see ▶Figure 9.22). At the same time, each person's bodily reactions were monitored.

Contrary to what you might expect, "making faces" affected the autonomic nervous system, as shown by changes in heart rate and skin temperature. In addition, each facial expression produced a different pattern of activity. An angry face, for instance, raised heart rate and skin temperature, whereas disgust lowered both (Ekman, Levenson, & Friesen, 1983). In a related experiment, people rated how funny they thought cartoons were while holding a pen crosswise in their mouths. Those who held the pen in their teeth thought the cartoons were funnier than did people who held the pen in their lips. Can you guess why? The answer is that if you hold a pen with your teeth, you are forced to form a smile. Holding it with the lips makes a frown. As predicted by the facial feedback hypothesis, emotional experiences were influenced by the facial expressions that people made (Strack, Martin, & Stepper, 1988). Next time you're feeling sad, bite a pen!

It appears, then, that not only do emotions influence expressions, but expressions also influence emotions (McIntosh, 1996). (See Table 9.4.) This may explain why forcing

Facial feedback hypothesis States that sensations from facial expressions help define what emotion a person feels.

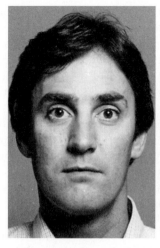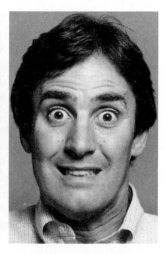

▶Figure 9.22

Facial feedback and emotion. Participants in Ekman's study formed facial expressions like those normally observed during emotion. When they did this, emotion-like changes took place in their bodily activity. (After Ekman, Levenson, & Friesen, 1983.)

Table 9.4
Facial
Muscles
and Felt
Emotion

CONTRACTED FACIAL MUSCLES	FELT EMOTION
Forehead	Surprise
Brow	Anger
Mouth (down)	Sadness
Mouth (smile)	Joy

(Adelmann & Zajonc, 1989.)

Emotional appraisal
Evaluating the personal meaning of a stimulus or situation.

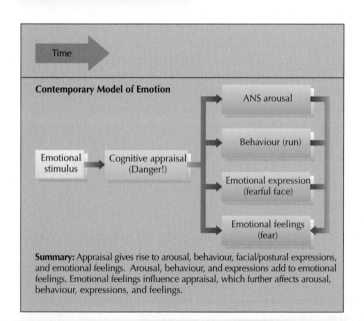

Summary: Appraisal gives rise to arousal, behaviour, facial/postural expressions, and emotional feelings. Arousal, behaviour, and expressions add to emotional feelings. Emotional feelings influence appraisal, which further affects arousal, behaviour, expressions, and feelings.

▶Figure 9.23

A contemporary model of emotion.

yourself to smile when you are "down" can actually improve your mood (Kleinke, Peterson, & Rutledge, 1998).

A Contemporary Model of Emotion

To summarize, James and Lange were right that feedback from arousal and behaviour adds to our emotional experiences. Cannon and Bard were right about the timing of events. Schachter showed us that cognition is important. In fact, psychologists are increasingly aware that how you appraise a situation greatly affects your emotions (Strongman, 1996). **Emotional appraisal** refers to evaluating the personal meaning of a stimulus: Is it good/bad, threatening/supportive, relevant/irrelevant, and so on.

In recent years many new theories of emotion have appeared. Rather than pick one theory, let's put the best points of several together in a single model of emotion (see ▶ Figure 9.23). Imagine that a large snarling dog lunges at you with its teeth bared. A modern view of your emotional reactions goes something like this: An *emotional stimulus* (the dog) is *appraised* (judged) as a threat or other cause for emotion (see Table 9.5). (You think to yourself, "Uh oh, big trouble!") Your appraisal gives rise to *ANS arousal* (your heart pounds and your body becomes stirred up). The appraisal also releases *innate emotional expressions* (your face twists into a mask of fear and your posture becomes tense). At the same time, your appraisal leads to *adaptive behaviour* (you run from the dog). It also causes a change in consciousness that you recognize as the subjective experience of fear. (The intensity of this *emotional feeling* is directly related to the amount of ANS arousal taking place in your body.)

Each element of emotion—ANS arousal, adaptive behaviour, subjective experience, and your emotional expressions—may further alter your appraisal of the situation, as well as your thoughts, judgments, and perceptions. Such changes affect each of the other reactions, which again alter your appraisal and interpretation of events. Thus, emotion may blossom, change course, or diminish as it proceeds. Note too that the original emotional stimulus

Table 9.5
Appraisals and Corresponding Emotions

APPRAISAL	EMOTION
You have been slighted or demeaned	Anger
You feel threatened	Anxiety
You have experienced a loss	Sadness
You have broken a moral rule	Guilt
You have not lived up to your ideals	Shame
You desire something another has	Envy
You are near something repulsive	Disgust
You fear the worst but yearn for better	Hope
You are moving toward a desired goal	Happiness
You are linked with a valued object or accomplishment	Pride
You have been treated well by another	Gratitude
You desire affection from another person	Love
You are moved by someone's suffering	Compassion

(Paraphrased from Lazarus, 1991a.)

can be external, like the attacking dog, or internal, such as a memory of being chased by a dog, rejected by a lover, or praised by a friend. That's why mere thoughts and memories can make us fearful, sad, or happy (Strongman, 1996).

Our discussion suggests that emotion is greatly influenced by how you think about an event. For example, as psychologists Gilles Kirouac of Laval and Ursula Hess of the University of Quebec have argued, information about social groups will be factored into your assessment of an emotional display. In other words, what you believe about how men or women, or members of other groups, typically express emotion will influence your perception of an emotional expression on the part of a member of such a group. Is there anything you can do about this? Perhaps you can catch yourself doing it (Kirouac & Hess, 1999). Before making an assumption about someone's emotional expression based on their group membership, try asking them how they feel.

Kirouac & Hess's suggestion that you try to alter your perception of another person's emotion brings up an important issue: how good are we at perceiving and deliberately altering our perception of other people's mental states and motives? For example, if another driver "cuts you off" on the highway, you could become very angry. But if you do, you will add five or ten minutes of emotional upset to your day. (If you give the other driver the universal signal of disrespect, the consequences could be even more dire.) By changing your appraisal, you could just as easily choose to laugh at the other driver's childish behaviour—and minimize the emotional wear-and-tear. Such self-control would be one example of what psychologists call *emotional intelligence,* our next subject.

Emotional Intelligence

Many psychologists believe that there is some kind of skill that has little to do with formal or academic intelligence, especially verbal intelligence. E. L. Thorndike, a pioneer in the development of intelligence testing, called this "social intelligence" (Thorndike, 1920). Over the years, a number of people tried to define and measure this concept without much success. Some focused on social perception as critical (Chapin, 1939; Walker & Foley, 1973). Others considered social intelligence to be multidimensional (e.g., Cantor & Kihlstrom, 1987). Because social intelligence was difficult to measure, and because some researchers focused on understanding and others on behaviour (Ford & Tisak, 1983), many psychologists looked for an alternative way of thinking about non-academic intelligence.

An important development was Howard Gardner's Multiple Intelligences Theory (see "Frames of Mind—Eight Intelligences?" on page 305 in Chapter 8). One of the types of intelligence Gardner argued for was *personal intelligence,* consisting of *intrapersonal* intelligence (understanding your own internal processes and states) and *interpersonal* intelligence (reading other people's needs, emotions, and intentions). In Gardner's formulation, this was just one of eight different intelligences. In 1990, Salovey and Mayer argued for the central importance of interpersonal skill, and introduced the term *emotional intelligence (EI).* A best-selling book by Daniel Goleman (1995) popularized the concept, which is now written about frequently.

Emotional intelligence
Emotional competence, including empathy, self-control, self-awareness, and other skills.

Emotional intelligence refers to a combination of skills. These are empathy, self-control, self-awareness, sensitivity to the feelings of others, persistence, and self-motivation, among others (Salovey & Mayer, 1997). Daniel Goleman believes that people who excel in life tend to be emotionally intelligent. Indeed, the costs of poor emotional skills can be high. They range from problems in marriage and parenting to poor physical health. A lack of emotional intelligence can ruin careers and sabotage achievement. Perhaps the greatest toll falls on children and teenagers. For them, having poor emotional skills can contribute to depression, eating disorders, unwanted pregnancy, aggression, and violent crime.

Of course, in a multiethnic society such as Canada's, things may be more complex than this. University of Waterloo psychologist Dov Cohen has drawn attention to a basic East–West difference in reading emotional expressions (Cohen & Gunz, 2002). Western people tend to project their own emotions onto others, whereas Eastern people tend to project the emotion a generalized other person could be expected to feel in a given situation. At the University of British Columbia, psychologist Daniel Zhang offered a Chinese perspective on depression (Zhang, 1995). Zhang suggested that emotional expression is a sensitive issue in China, and that affective problems such as depression are less acceptable there. As a result, depression is not diagnosed as frequently in China as it is in the West. Depressed people may in fact complain of more acceptable somatic problems. When we assess emotional intelligence, we need to take these cultural variations into account.

Understandably, many psychologists believe that schools should promote emotional competence as well as intellectual skills. The result, they feel, would be greater self-control, altruism, and compassion—all basic capacities needed if our society is to thrive (Goleman, 1995).

Knowledge builder

EMOTIONAL EXPRESSION AND THEORIES OF EMOTION

Relate

Write a list of emotions that you think you can accurately detect from facial expressions. Does your list match Paul Ekman's? Would you be more confident in rating pleasantness–unpleasantness, attention–rejection, and activation? Why?

Which theory seems to best explain your own emotional experiences? Try frowning or smiling for five minutes. Did facial feedback have any effect on your mood? Cover the left column of Table 9.5 on page 359. Read each emotional label in the right column. What appraisal do you think would lead to the listed emotion? Do the appraisals in the table match your predictions?

Learning Check

1. Charles Darwin held that emotional expressions aid survival for animals. T or F?
2. A formal term for "body language" is _____.
3. Which three dimensions of emotion are communicated by facial expressions?
   a. pleasantness–unpleasantness *b.* complexity
   c. attention–rejection *d.* anger *e.* curiosity–disinterest
   f. activation

4. According to the James-Lange theory, emotional experience precedes physical arousal and emotional behaviour. (We see a bear, are frightened, and run.) T or F?
5. The Cannon-Bard theory of emotion says that bodily arousal and emotional experience occur _____.
6. According to Schachter's cognitive theory, bodily arousal must be labelled or interpreted for an emotional experience to occur. T or F?
7. Subjects in Valins's false heart rate study attributed increases in their heart rate to the action of a placebo. T or F?
8. As you try to wiggle your ears, you keep pulling the corners of your mouth back into a smile. Each time you do, you find yourself giggling. Which of the following provides the best explanation for this reaction?
   a. attribution *b.* the Cannon-Bard theory *c.* appraisal *d.* facial feedback

Critical Thinking

9. People with high spinal injuries may feel almost no signs of physiological arousal from their bodies. Nevertheless they still feel emotion, which can be intense at times. What theory of emotion does this observation contradict?

Answers:

1. T 2. kinesics 3. *a, c, f* 4. F 5. simultaneously 6. T 7. F 8. *d* 9. The James-Lange theory and Schachter's cognitive theory. The facial feedback hypothesis also helps explain the observation.

WELL-BEING AND HAPPINESS—WHAT MAKES A GOOD LIFE?

Survey Question:
■ What factors contribute most to a happy and fulfilling life?

Subjective well-being
General life satisfaction combined with frequent positive emotions and relatively few negative emotions.

What makes you happy? Love? Money? Music? Sports? Partying? Religion? Clearly, there is no simple, universal formula for happiness. And what does it mean to have a good life? Is it a matter of health? Achievement? Friendship? Leisure? Personal growth? Again, there is no simple answer. Both happiness and living a "good life" depend greatly on individual needs, goals, and values. Nevertheless, psychologists are beginning to understand some aspects of what it means to be happy and live well.

Happiness

To study happiness, psychologist Ed Diener and his associates have focused on what they call **subjective well-being** (SWB). According to them, feelings of well-being, or happiness, occur when people are satisfied with their lives, have frequent positive emotions, and have relatively few negative emotions (Diener et al., 1999).

What does life satisfaction refer to? You are high in life satisfaction if you strongly agree that "The conditions of my life are excellent" (Pavot & Diener, 1993). This statement covers a lot of what it means to be happy. However, day-to-day emotional experiences are also important. We all have good days and bad days, but even the best days involve a mixture of positive and negative emotions. That's why happiness is not just a matter of having good feelings. The happiest people are those who have many positive emotional experiences and relatively few negative experiences (Diener et al., 1999).

Life Events

Then do good and bad events in life dictate if a person is happy? Happiness is related to good and bad life events, but the impact is smaller than you might imagine. The reason for this is that happiness tends to come from within a person. Subjective well-being is affected by our goals, choices, emotions, values, and personality. The way you appraise, interpret, and manage events is as important as the nature of the events themselves. People who are good at dodging life's hard knocks tend to create their own "luck." As a result, they are happier and seem to negotiate life's demands more smoothly (Eronen & Nurmi, 1999).

Personal Factors

What about factors such as income, age, or marital status? Are they related to happiness? Personal characteristics have only a small connection with overall happiness. Let's see why.

WEALTH It is tempting to think that wealth brings happiness. But does it? To a small degree wealthier people are happier than poorer people. However, the overall association between money and happiness is weak. Basically, money can't buy happiness (King and Napa, 1998).

EDUCATION Well-educated people tend to be a little happier than the less educated. However, this is most likely just another way of saying that there is a small connection between wealth and happiness. Higher education generally results in higher income and more social status.

MARRIAGE Married people report greater happiness than people who are divorced, separated, or single. It could be that happier people are simply more likely to get married. But a better explanation for this association is that marriage partners can act as emotional and economic buffers against the hardships of life.

RELIGION There is a small but positive association between happiness and holding spiritual beliefs. Religious beliefs may add to feelings of purpose and meaning in life, resulting in greater happiness. Another possibility is that church membership may simply provide social support that softens the impact of life's negative events.

AGE The stereotype of the crotchety old person who is dissatisfied with everything is inaccurate. Life satisfaction and happiness generally *do not* decline with age. People are living longer and staying healthier, which has greatly delayed age-related declines. When declines do occur, older people today seem better able to cope with them.

SEX　Overall, men and women do not differ in happiness. However, women do have a tendency to experience higher emotional highs and lower lows than men do. Thus, more women are found among those rare individuals who are extremely happy or unhappy.

WORK　People who are satisfied with their jobs tend to be happier, but the association is weak. If fact, it probably just reflects the fact that job satisfaction is a large part of greater life satisfaction.

PERSONALITY　With respect to happiness and personality, it may be fair to paraphrase the movie character Forest Gump and say that "Happy is as happy does." To a degree, some people are more temperamentally disposed to be happy, regardless of life events. In general, happier people also tend to be extraverted (outgoing), optimistic, and worry-free. This combination probably influences the balance of positive and negative emotions that people feel (Diener et al., 1999).

Goals and Happiness

The preceding account gives some insight into who is happy, but we can learn more by examining people's goals. To know if someone is happy, it is helpful to ask, "What is this person trying to do in life? How well is she or he succeeding at it?"

Do you want to be healthy and physically fit? To do well in school? To be liked by friends? To own a shopping mall? A Ferrari? The goals people choose vary widely. Nevertheless, people tend to be happy if they are meeting their personal goals. This is especially true if you feel you are making progress, on a day-to-day basis, on smaller goals that relate to long-term, life goals (King, Richards, & Stemmerich, 1998; McGregor & Little, 1998).

It seems that people who attain their goals are sometimes no happier than before. If making progress toward one's goals brings happiness, how could that be?

MEANING AND INTEGRITY　Canadian psychologists Ian McGregor and Brian Little believe they can explain why achieving one's goals doesn't always lead to happiness. Picture a highly successful person who is absorbed in her accomplishments. All it may take is a crisis, like a child's illness or the death of a friend, to make life seem meaningless. But if the person begins to act with integrity, her life will regain meaning and the crisis will subside. Thus, McGregor and Little believe that the best lives involve *integrity* as well as an ability to reach goals. "Doing well," they say, brings happiness. "Being yourself" makes life meaningful. The goals we pursue must express our true interests. This is crucial, because overall well-being is a combination of happiness and meaning. Pursuing goals that are inconsistent with personal interests and values can leave people feeling uneasy, bothered, and uncomfortable (McGregor & Little, 1998).

Conclusion

In summary, happier persons tend to be married, comfortable with their work, extraverted, religious, optimistic, and generally satisfied with their lives. They are also making progress toward their goals (Diener et al., 1999). However, attaining goals that do not match your deeper interests and values may add little to happiness (Sheldon & Elliot, 1999).

What, then, makes a good life? As we have seen, a good life is one that is happy and meaningful (McGregor & Little, 1998). "To thine own self be true" may seem like a cliché, but it's actually not a bad place to begin a search for happiness.

Knowledge builder

WELL-BEING AND HAPPINESS

Relate

How do you think you would rate in SWB? What other factors discussed in this section are related to your own level of happiness?

It is common for students to pursue goals and personal projects that are imposed on them. Which of your activities do you regard as most meaningful? How do they relate to your personal beliefs and values?

Learning Check

1. Subjective well-being consists of a mixture of _____ _____, positive emotions, and negative emotions.

2. People who experience many positive emotions are, by definition, very happy. T or F?

3. Happiness has only a small positive correlation with wealth. T or F?

4. Single persons are generally happier than those who are married. T or F?

5. Making day-by-day progress toward important _____ _____ is a major source of happiness.

Critical Thinking

6. Under what circumstances would you expect having money to be more strongly associated with happiness?

_____

Answers:

1. life satisfaction 2. F 3. T 4. F 5. life goals 6. In poorer countries where life can be harsh, the association between material wealth and happiness is stronger than it is in North America.

Psychologist's Journal

EPILOGUE

Playwright Oscar Wilde wrote that "In this world there are only two tragedies. One is not getting what one wants, and the other is getting it. The last is the real tragedy."

The frustration of not getting what you want is easy to understand. But how could it be a tragedy to actually get what you want? Wilde probably was thinking about the disappointment that can come from getting something you have dreamed about for a long time.

What are your most treasured goals? Do you think you have idealized them? Would attaining your goals really make you happy? When expectations are high, reality can be a letdown. Many lottery winners, for instance, are no happier after they become rich than they were before.

Psychologists would interpret Wilde's statement in a different way. Seeking valued goals is what keeps us going, and happiness is associated with making progress toward our goals. Thus, if you achieve a long-sought goal, the question may become "What next?" For instance, what will your main goal be after you graduate from college or university? Where will your motivation come from? What will you do next to give structure and direction to your life? Whatever the answers may be, it is clear that it pays to be aware of your goals. The goals you pursue in coming years will have a major impact on how you spend your time and energy. Be sure to choose wisely—and make sure your goals truly reflect your interests and values.

CHAPTER IN REVIEW

Major Points

▶ Motives and goals greatly influence what we do and how we expend our energies.

▶ The brain monitors various internal signals to control basic motives, such as hunger and thirst.

▶ Motivated behaviour is also influenced by learned habits, external cues, and cultural values.

▶ Many activities are related to needs for stimulation and our efforts to maintain desired levels of arousal.

▶ Many needs, goals, and drives are learned.

▶ Emotions can be disruptive, but overall they help us to adapt and survive.

▶ Personal well-being is a combination of happiness and meaning in life.

Summary

What Is Motivation? Are There Different Types of Motives?

• Motives initiate, sustain, and direct activities. Motivation typically involves the sequence need, drive, goal, and goal attainment (need reduction).

• Behaviour can be activated either by needs (push) or by goals (pull).

• The attractiveness of a goal and its ability to initiate action are related to its incentive value.

• Three principal types of motives are primary motives, stimulus motives, and secondary motives.

• Most primary motives operate to maintain homeostasis.

What Causes Hunger? Overeating? Eating Disorders?

• Hunger is influenced by a complex interplay between fullness of the stomach, blood sugar levels, metabolism in the liver, and fat stores in the body.

• The most direct control of eating comes from the hypothalamus, which is sensitive to both neural and chemical messages that affect eating.

• Other factors influencing hunger are the body's set point, external eating cues, the attractiveness and variety of diet, emotions, learned taste preferences and aversions, and cultural values.

• Obesity is the result of internal and external influences, diet, emotions, genetics, and exercise.

• Behavioural dieting is based on techniques that change eating patterns and exercise habits.

• Anorexia nervosa and bulimia nervosa are two prominent eating disorders. Both tend to involve conflicts about self-image, self-control, and anxiety.

Is There More than One Type of Thirst? In What Ways Are Pain Avoidance and the Sex Drive Unusual?

- Like hunger, thirst and other basic motives are primarily under the central control of the hypothalamus. Thirst may be either intracellular or extracellular.
- Pain avoidance is episodic as opposed to cyclic. Pain avoidance and pain tolerance are partially learned.
- The sex drive is unusual because it is non-homeostatic.

What Are the Typical Patterns of Human Sexual Response?

- Sexual arousal is related to the body's erogenous zones, but mental and emotional reactions are the ultimate source of sexual responsiveness.
- Sexual orientation refers to one's degree of emotional and erotic attraction to members of the same sex, opposite sex, or both sexes.
- A combination of hereditary, biological, social, and psychological influences combine to produce one's sexual orientation.
- Human sexual response can be divided into four phases: excitement, plateau, orgasm, and resolution.
- Overall, male and female sexual responses are similar. However, males experience a refractory period after orgasm, and only 5 percent of men are multi-orgasmic. Fifteen percent of women are multi-orgasmic.

How Does Arousal Relate to Motivation?

- The stimulus drives reflect needs for information, exploration, manipulation, and sensory input.
- Arousal theory states that an ideal level of bodily arousal will be maintained if possible.
- Optimal performance usually occurs at moderate levels of arousal, as described by an inverted U function. The Yerkes-Dodson law further states that for simple tasks the ideal arousal level is higher, and for complex tasks it is lower.
- Circadian rhythms are closely tied to sleep, activity, and energy cycles. Time zone travel and shift work can seriously disrupt sleep and bodily rhythms.

What Are Social Motives? Why Are They Important?

- Social motives are learned through socialization and cultural conditioning. Such motives account for much of the diversity of human motivation.
- A high need for achievement (nAch) is correlated with success in many situations, with career choice, and with moderate risk taking.
- Self-confidence greatly affects motivation in everyday life.

Are Some Motives More Basic than Others?

- Maslow's hierarchy of motives categorizes needs as either basic or growth oriented. Lower needs are assumed to be prepotent (dominant) over higher needs. Self-actualization, the highest and most fragile need, is reflected in meta-needs.

- Meta-needs are closely related to intrinsic motivation. In some situations, external rewards can undermine intrinsic motivation, enjoyment, and creativity.

What Happens During Emotion? Can "Lie Detectors" Really Detect Lies?

- Emotions are linked to many basic adaptive behaviours. Three major elements of emotion are physiological changes in the body, emotional expressions, and emotional feelings.
- The primary emotions are fear, surprise, sadness, disgust, anger, anticipation, joy, and acceptance. Other emotions are mixtures of these primaries.
- Physical changes associated with emotion are caused by the hormone adrenaline, and by activity in the autonomic nervous system (ANS).
- The sympathetic branch of the ANS is primarily responsible for arousing the body, the parasympathetic branch for quieting it.
- The polygraph, or "lie detector," measures emotional arousal by monitoring heart rate, blood pressure, breathing rate, and the galvanic skin response (GSR).
- The accuracy of the lie detector can be disturbingly low.

How Accurately Are Emotions Expressed by "Body Language" and the Face?

- Basic emotional expressions appear to be unlearned. Facial expressions are a central feature of emotion.
- Body gestures and movements (body language) also express feelings, mainly by communicating emotional tone.
- Three dimensions of facial expressions are pleasantness–unpleasantness, attention–rejection, and activation.

How Do Psychologists Explain Emotions?

- The James-Lange theory says that emotional experience follows bodily reactions. In contrast, the Cannon-Bard theory says that bodily reactions and emotional experiences occur simultaneously.
- Schachter's cognitive theory emphasizes the labels we apply to feelings of bodily arousal. In addition, emotions are affected by attribution (ascribing bodily arousal to a particular source).
- The facial feedback hypothesis holds that facial expressions help define the emotions we feel.
- Contemporary views of emotion emphasize the effects of cognitive appraisals. Also, all of the elements of emotion are seen as interrelated and interacting.

What Factors Contribute Most to a Happy and Fulfilling Life?

- Subjective well-being (happiness) is related to general life satisfaction and to having more positive emotions than negative ones.
- Life events and various demographic factors have relatively little influence on happiness.

- People with extraverted (outgoing), optimistic, and worry-free personalities tend to be happier.
- Making progress toward one's goals is associated with happiness.

- Overall well-being is a combination of happiness and meaning in life.

PSYCHOLOGY ON THE NET

If you have difficulty finding any of the sites listed here, visit http://www.psychologyjourney.nelson.com for an updated list of Internet addresses and direct links to relevant sites.

College Student Diet   For a Canadian site aimed at students, try the University of British Columbia's Wellness site. http://students.ubc.ca/health/wellness/guide.cfm?page=eating

Controlling Anger   Discusses anger and some strategies for its control. http://www.apa.org/pubinfo/anger.html

Eating Disorders Website   Home page of a self-help group for those afflicted with eating disorders. http://www.something-fishy.org

Emotional Intelligence   This site discusses emotional intelligence. http://trochim.human.cornell.edu/gallery/young/emotion.htm

Non-Verbal Communication   You can learn about important differences in Japanese body language and communication at this site. http://www.shinnova.com/part/99-japa/abj17-e.htm

Research on Human Emotions   This is the social neuroscience lab at Laval University. The site offers a tour

of the lab and information about how scientists study emotion. http://www.psy.ulaval.ca/~arvid/Arvid3e.html

The Validity of Polygraph Examinations   Information about the doubtful validity of polygraph examinations. http://www.apa.org/releases/liedetector.html

Weight-Control Information   Get information about the Weight-Control Information Network at http://www.niddk.nih.gov/health/nutrit/win.htm. For information about yo-yo dieting, check http://www.niddk.nih.gov/health/nutrit/pubs/wcycling.htm.

What's Your Emotional Intelligence Quotient?   Visitors may take an online quiz about their E-IQ developed by Daniel Goleman at http://www.utne.com/azEq2.tmpl. Other emotional intelligence tests can be found at http://quiz.ivillage.com/health/tests/eqtest2.htm, http://www.queendom.com/tests/access/emotional_iq.html, and http://www.helpself.com/iq-test.htm.

   InfoTrac College Edition   For recent articles on lie detection, use Key Words search for POLYGRAPH.

INTERACTIVE LEARNING

Psychology: An Interactive Journey   Remember that Chapter 9 of the CD-ROM that came with this text has practice tests, flashcards, interactive exercises, a crossword puzzle, and other valuable materials to enhance your learning experience.

PsychNow!   4a. Motivation, 4b. Emotion.

Psyk.trek   8. Motivation and Emotion.

Chart Your Progress

The questions that follow are only a sample of what you need to know. If you miss any of the items, you should review the entire chapter, do the exercises on the CD, and review the Knowledge Builders. Another way to prepare for tests is to get more practice with *WebTutor*, the *Study Guide*, or the *Practice Quizzes* that are available with this text.

1. Desirable goals are motivating because they are high in
   a. secondary value
   b. stimulus value
   c. homeostatic value
   d. incentive value

2. Maintaining your body's set point for fat is closely linked with the amount of _____ in the bloodstream.
   a. hypothalamic factor-1
   b. ventromedial peptide-1
   c. NPY
   d. leptin

3. Binging and purging are characteristic of people who have
   a. taste aversions
   b. anorexia
   c. bulimia
   d. strong sensitivity to external eating cues

4. One thing that men and women have in common is that their sex drive is
   a. affected by androgens
   b. extracellular
   c. controlled by estrogen
   d. homeostatic and episodic

5. The typical phases of human sexual arousal are
   a. estrus, refractory period, orgasm, resolution
   b. excitement, orgasm, resolution, refractory period
   c. estrus, orgasm, plateau, resolution
   d. excitement, plateau, orgasm, resolution

6. Complex tasks, such as taking a classroom test, tend to be disrupted by high levels of arousal, an effect predicted by
   a. the Sensation-Seeking Scale
   b. the Yerkes-Dodson law
   c. studies of circadian arousal patterns
   d. studies of the need for achievement

7. People high in nAch
   a. prefer long shots
   b. prefer sure things
   c. are moderate risk takers
   d. prefer change and high levels of stimulation

8. The highest level of Maslow's hierarchy of motives involves
   a. meta-needs
   b. needs for safety and security
   c. needs for love and belonging
   d. extrinsic needs

9. Polygraph operators try to use which component of emotion to detect deception?
   a. adaptive behaviours
   b. physiological changes
   c. emotional expressions
   d. the parasympathetic rebound

10. Holding a pen crosswise in your mouth is likely to improve your mood, a result predicted by
   a. The Cannon-Bard theory
   b. attribution theory
   c. the facial-feedback hypothesis
   d. Schachter's cognitive theory

11. People tend to be happy if they are meeting personal goals that
   a. satisfy extrinsic needs
   b. are personally meaningful
   c. lead to celebrity and wealth
   d. satisfy most of a person's deficiency motives

Answers: 1.d 2.d 3.c 4.a 5.d 6.b 7.c 8.a 9.b 10.c 11.b

Chapter 10

Psychologist's Journal

THE HIDDEN ESSENCE

One sunny winter afternoon Genevieve is seen consoling a distraught mother who is holding an infant in her arms. Genevieve helps to run a women's shelter in the working-class Saint-Henri area of Montreal. But she has not always been a social worker. In fact, she attended an exclusive private school in New Brunswick, went on to study at a prestigious European university, and spent many years pleading cases on behalf of a reputable law firm in Vancouver.

Four years ago, Genevieve decided to devote her life to a "higher cause." Against the well-meaning advice of her family, friends, and colleagues, she gave up her job and comfortable life, bicycled across the country, and ended up in Montreal. If Genevieve's old friends were to meet her now, would they recognized the outgoing and ambitious person who once played basketball like a pro and dreamed of a career in politics? Has her personality changed so drastically that they would no longer connect with her? Chances are she's still very much like her "old self." What's really changed in her life are her surroundings and her choice of work.

Perhaps you have had a similar experience. After several years of separation, it is always intriguing to see an old friend. At first you may be struck by how the person has changed. Soon, however, you will probably be delighted to discover that the semi-stranger before you is still the person you once knew. It is exactly this core of consistency that psychologists have in mind when they use the term *personality*.

Without doubt, personality touches our daily lives. Falling in love, choosing friends, getting along with co-workers, voting in elections, or coping with your zaniest relatives—all raise questions about personality.

What is personality? How does it differ from temperament, character, or attitudes? Is it possible to measure personality? These and related questions are the focus of this chapter.

- How do psychologists use the term personality? What core concepts make up the psychology of personality?
- Are some personality traits more basic or important than others?
- How do psychodynamic theories explain personality?
- What do behaviourists emphasize in their approach to personality?
- How do humanistic theories differ from other perspectives?
- How do psychologists measure personality?
- What causes shyness? What can be done about it?

▶ The Psychology of Personality— Do You Have Personality?

Survey Question:
- How do psychologists use the term *personality*? What core concepts make up the psychology of personality?

Personality A person's unique and relatively stable behaviour pattern.

Character Personal characteristics that have been judged or evaluated; a person's desirable or undesirable qualities.

Temperament The hereditary aspects of personality, including sensitivity, activity levels, prevailing mood, irritability, and adaptability.

"Jim's not handsome, but he has a great personality." "Tom's business friends think he's a nice guy. They should see him at home where his real personality comes out." "It's hard to believe Tanya and Nikki are sisters. They have such opposite personalities." "Genevieve has a very optimistic personality."

It's obvious that we all frequently use the term *personality*, but many people seem hard-pressed to define it. Most simply end up saying something about "charm," "charisma," or "style." If you use *personality* in such ways, you are giving it a different meaning than psychologists do.

Then how do psychologists use the term? Most regard **personality** as a person's unique and relatively stable behaviour patterns. In other words, personality refers to the consistency in who you are, have been, and will become. It also refers to the special blend of talents, attitudes, values, hopes, loves, hates, and habits that makes each of us a unique person.

How is that different from the way most people use the term? Many people confuse personality with *character*. The term **character** implies that a person has been evaluated, not just described (Skipton, 1997). If, by saying someone has "personality," you mean the person is friendly, outgoing, and attractive, you are really referring to what we regard as good character in our culture. But in some cultures it is deemed good for people to be fierce, warlike, and cruel. So, while everyone in a particular culture has personality, not everyone has character—or at least not good character. (Do you know any good characters?)

Personality is also distinct from *temperament*. Temperament is the "raw material" from which personality is formed. **Temperament** refers to the hereditary aspects of personality. Temperamental differences are readily apparent in infants, who vary in sensitivity, activity levels, prevailing mood, irritability, and adaptability (Kagan, 1989). Knowing Genevieve's adult personality, we would guess that she was an active, happy baby.

Psychologists use a large number of terms to describe and explain personality. It might be wise, therefore, to start with a few key concepts. These ideas should help you keep your bearings as you read this chapter.

Traits

We use the idea of traits every day to talk about the personalities of others. For instance, Dan is *sociable, orderly,* and *intelligent*. His sister Kayla is *shy, sensitive,* and

Chosen as Canada's top newsmaker of the 20th century, Prime Minister Pierre Elliott Trudeau (1919–2000) had a major impact on his country's social and political life. Trudeau brought in many progressive laws, championed the patriation of the Canadian Constitution, and helped in the adoption of the Charter of Rights and Freedoms. A fashion-conscious man, he dated several well-known, glamorous women of his time. Many people thought he had a very charismatic and charming personality, but some believed he was arrogant and insensitive. What are your own thoughts about Trudeau's personality?

Do these men have personality? Do you?

Psychologists and employers are especially interested in the personality traits of individuals who hold high-risk, high-stress positions involving public safety, such as police officers, air-traffic controllers, and nuclear power plant employees.

Personality trait A stable, enduring quality that a person shows in most situations.

Personality type A style of personality defined by a group of related traits.

Introvert A person whose attention is focused inward; a shy, reserved, timid person.

Extrovert A person whose attention is directed outward; a bold, outgoing person.

Self-concept A person's perception of his or her own personality traits.

creative. In general, **personality traits** are stable qualities that a person shows in most situations. Typically, traits are inferred from behaviour. If you see Dan talking to strangers—first at a supermarket and later at a party—you might deduce that he is "sociable." Identifying this trait might then lead you to predict that Dan will be sociable at school or at work.

As you can see, traits tend to predict future behaviour. Another example is provided by a study of students who are extroverted, agreeable, and conscientious. Predictably, such students usually make more friends and have less conflict with other students. They are also more likely to fall in love (Asendorpf & Wilpers, 1998).

WHEN IS THE PLASTER SET?   As we observed with Genevieve, personality traits are usually quite stable (Gustavsson et al., 1997). Think about how little the traits of your best friends have changed in the last five years. It would be strange indeed to feel like you were talking with a different person every time you met a friend or acquaintance.

At what age are the major outlines of personality firmly established? It is rare for personality to change dramatically. During the 20s, personality slowly begins to harden. By age 30, personality is usually quite stable. The person you are at age 30 is, for the most part, the person you will be at age 60 (Costa & McCrae, 1992; Roan, 1992).

Types

Have you ever asked the question, "What type of person is she (or he)?" A **personality type** refers to people who have *several traits in common* (Potkay & Allen, 1986). Informally, your own thinking might include categories such as the executive type, the athletic type, the motherly type, the hip-hop type, the techno geek, and so forth. If we asked you to define these informal types, you would probably list a different collection of traits for each one.

How valid is it to speak of personality "types"? Over the years, psychologists have proposed many ways to categorize personalities into types. For example, Swiss psychiatrist Carl Jung (yoong) proposed that people are either *introverts* or *extroverts*. An **introvert** is a shy, self-centred person whose attention is focused inward. An **extrovert** is a bold, outgoing person whose attention is directed outward. These terms are so widely used that you may think of yourself and your friends as being one type or the other. However, the wildest, wittiest, most party-loving "extrovert" you know is introverted at times. Likewise, extremely introverted persons are assertive and sociable in some situations. In short, two categories (or even several) are often inadequate to fully capture differences in personality. That's why rating people on a list of traits tends to be more informative than classifying them into two or three types.

Even though types tend to oversimplify personality, they do have value. Most often, types are a shorthand way of labelling people who have several key traits in common. For example, in the next chapter we will discuss Type A personality. These are people whose personality traits increase their chance of suffering a heart attack (see ▶ Figure 10.1). Similarly, you will read in Chapter 12 about unhealthy personality types such as the paranoid personality, the dependent personality, and the antisocial personality. Each is defined by a specific collection of maladaptive traits.

Self-Concept

Another way of understanding personality is to focus on a person's self-concept. The rough outlines of your self-concept would be revealed by this request: "Please tell us about yourself." In other words, your **self-concept** consists of all your ideas, perceptions, and feelings about who you are.

Self-concepts have a major impact on behaviour. We creatively build our self-concepts out of daily experiences. Then we slowly revise them as we have new experiences. Once a stable self-concept exists, it tends to guide what we pay attention to, remember, and think about (Markus & Nurius, 1986).

Traits

Personality Type

Agreeable

Ambitious

Cautious

Competitive

Honest

Hostile

Striving

Type A

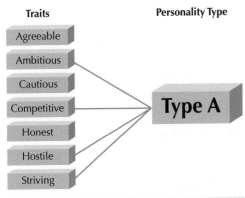

▶**Figure 10.1**

Personality types are defined by the presence of several specific traits. For example, several possible personality traits are shown in the left column. A person who has a Type A personality typically possesses all or most of the highlighted traits. Type A persons are especially prone to heart disease (see Chapter 11).

Self-concepts can be remarkably consistent. In an interesting study, very old people were asked how they had changed over the years. Almost all thought they were essentially the same person they were when they were young (Troll & Skaff, 1997).

Self-concepts can greatly affect personal adjustment—especially when they are *inaccurate* or *inadequate* (Potkay & Allen, 1986). For example, Maryanne thinks she is stupid, worthless, and a failure, despite getting good grades in college. With such a negative self-concept, Maryanne will probably be depressed or anxious no matter how well she does as a student.

SELF-ESTEEM   Note that Maryanne also suffers from low **self-esteem** (how she evaluates herself). A person with high self-esteem is confident, proud, and self-respecting. One who is insecure, lacking in confidence, and self-critical has low self-esteem. Like Maryanne, people with low self-esteem are usually anxious and unhappy.

Self-esteem tends to rise when we experience success. It is also enhanced by praise from others. Thus, a person who is competent and effective and who is loved, admired, and respected by others will almost always have high self-esteem (Baumeister, 1994).

The reasons for having high self-esteem can vary in different cultures. (See "Self-Esteem and Culture.") For example, researchers have found that the Japanese tend to have a lower self-esteem than do Canadians. Living in Canada boosts the self-esteem of Japanese persons, and if Canadians make Japan their home for a while, their self-esteem

Self-esteem Regarding oneself as a worthwhile person; a positive evaluation of oneself.

HUMAN DIVERSITY   Self-Esteem and Culture—Hotshot or Team Player?

You and some friends are playing an informal game of volleyball. Your team wins, in part because you make some good plays. After the game, you bask in the glow of having performed well. You don't want to brag about being a hotshot, but your self-esteem does get a boost from your personal success.

In Japan, Shinobu is playing volleyball with some friends. His team wins, in part because he makes some good plays. After the game, Shinobu is happy because his team did well. However, Shinobu also dwells on the ways in which he let his team down. He thinks about how he could improve in the future and he resolves to be a better team player.

These sketches illustrate a basic difference in Eastern and Western psychology. In individualistic cultures such as Canada and the United States, self-esteem is based on success, competence, and outstanding performance; the path to higher self-esteem lies in self-enhancement. We are pumped up by our successes and tend to ignore our faults and failures.

Japan and many other Asian cultures place a greater emphasis on collectivism or mutual interdependence among people. In such cultures, self-esteem is related to group success. It is also based on identifying personal failures and correcting them. Doing so contributes to the welfare of the group. As a result, Japanese people tend to be more self-critical than we are in North America. For them, self-esteem is based on a secure sense of belonging to social groups. This makes self-criticism a way of contributing to the success and well-being of the entire group.

Perhaps self-esteem is still based on success in both Eastern and Western cultures, and it is fascinating that cultures define success in such different ways. The North American emphasis on winning is not the only way to feel good about oneself.

(Sources: Heine & Lehman, 1999; Kitayama et al., 1997; Lay & Verkuyten, 1999; Markus & Kitayama, 1998.)

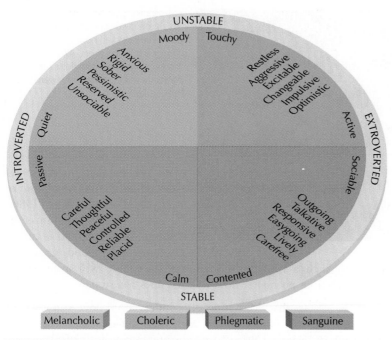

▶Figure 10.2

English psychologist Hans Eysenck (1916–1997) believed that many personality traits are related to whether you are mainly introverted or extroverted, whether you tend to be emotionally stable or unstable (highly emotional), and whether you show signs of concern for others or lack empathy. Some of these characteristics are related to four basic types of temperament first recognized by the early Greeks. The types are: *melancholic* (sad, gloomy), *choleric* (hot-tempered, irritable), *phlegmatic* (sluggish, calm), and *sanguine* (cheerful, hopeful). (Adapted from Eysenck, 1981.)

tends to decline. Does this mean that the Japanese culture has a negative impact on people's perception of themselves? The answer is no. It is likely that the meaning of what it is to be a person depends on where you live and whether you accept the values and beliefs of another culture (Heine et al., 1999).

Personality Theories

It would be easy to get lost without a framework for understanding personality. How do our thoughts, actions, and feelings relate to one another? How does personality develop? Why do some people suffer from psychological problems? How can they be helped? To answer such questions, psychologists have created a dazzling array of theories. A **personality theory** is a system of concepts, assumptions, ideas, and principles proposed to explain personality (see ▶Figure 10.2).

Many personality theories exist, so it is possible to introduce only a few here. The four major perspectives we will consider are these:

1. *Trait theories* attempt to learn what traits make up personality and how they relate to actual behaviour.
2. *Psychodynamic theories* focus on the inner workings of personality, especially internal conflicts and struggles.
3. *Behaviouristic theories* place importance on the external environment and on the effects of conditioning and learning.
4. *Humanistic theories* stress private, subjective experience and personal growth.

Now that you are oriented, let's take a deeper look at personality.

▶ The Trait Approach—Describe Yourself in 18 000 Words or Less

Survey Question:
■ Are some personality traits more basic or important than others?

How many words can you think of to describe the personality of a close friend? Your list might be long: Over 18 000 English words refer to personal characteristics. As you know, traits are stable and enduring qualities that a person shows in most situations. For example, if you are usually optimistic, reserved, and friendly, these qualities could be traits of your personality.

What if you are sometimes pessimistic, uninhibited, or shy? The original three qualities are still traits as long as they are most typical of your behaviour. Let's say our friend Genevieve approaches most situations with optimism, but tends to expect the worst each time she applies for a job. If her pessimism is limited to this situation or a few others, it is still accurate and useful to describe her as an optimistic person.

Predicting Behaviour

Personality theory
A system of concepts, assumptions, ideas, and principles used to understand and explain personality.

As we have noted, separating people into broad types, such as "introvert" or "extrovert," may oversimplify personality. However, introversion/extroversion can also be thought of as a trait. Knowing how you rate on this single dimension would allow us to predict how you will behave in a variety of settings. Where, for example, do you prefer to study in the library? Researchers have found that students high in the trait of extroversion study in noisy locations where there's a good chance of talking with others (Campbell & Hawley,

Table 10.1
Adjective
Checklist

Check the traits you feel are characteristic of your personality. Are some more basic than others?

aggressive	organized	ambitious	clever
confident	loyal	generous	calm
warm	bold	cautious	reliable
sensitive	mature	talented	jealous
sociable	honest	funny	religious
dominant	dull	accurate	nervous
humble	uninhibited	visionary	cheerful
thoughtful	serious	helpful	emotional
orderly	anxious	conforming	good-natured
liberal	curious	optimistic	kind
meek	neighbourly	passionate	compulsive

1982). In the library at Colgate University (where the study was done), you can find extroverted students in the second-floor lounge. Or, if you prefer, more introverted students can be found in the carrels on the first and third floors!

Describing People

In general, psychologists try to identify traits that best describe a person. Take a moment to check the traits in Table 10.1 that describe your personality. Are the traits you checked of equal importance? Are some stronger or more basic than others? Do any overlap? For example, if you checked "dominant," did you also check "confident" and "bold"? Answers to these questions would interest a trait theorist. To better understand personality, **trait theorists** attempt to analyze, classify, and interrelate traits.

Classifying Traits

Are there different types of traits? Yes, psychologist Gordon Allport (1961) identified several kinds. **Common traits** are characteristics shared by most members of a culture. Common traits tell us how people from a particular nation or culture are similar, or which traits a culture emphasizes. In Western cultures, for example, competitiveness is a fairly common trait. Among the Hopi of Northern Arizona, it is relatively rare. Newfoundlanders are described as hospitable, generous, and friendly, so we could say that the culture of Newfoundland is marked by these common traits.

Of course, common traits tell us little about individuals. While many people are competitive in our culture, each person may rate high, medium, or low in this trait. Usually we are also interested in these **individual traits**, which define a person's unique personal qualities.

Here's an analogy to help you separate common traits from individual traits: If you decide to buy a pet dog, you will want to know the general characteristics of the dog's breed (its common traits). In addition, you will want to know about the "personality" of a specific dog (its individual traits) before you decide to take it home.

Allport also made distinctions between *cardinal traits, central traits,* and *secondary traits.* A **cardinal trait** is so basic that all of a person's activities can be traced to the trait. For instance, an overriding factor in the life of Mother Teresa was compassion for the poor. Likewise, the personality of Terry Fox was dominated by the cardinal traits of courage and determination. According to Allport, few people have cardinal traits.

CENTRAL TRAITS *How do central and secondary traits differ from cardinal traits?* **Central traits** are the core qualities or basic building blocks of personality. A surprisingly small number of central traits can capture the essence of a person. For instance, just six traits would provide a good description of Genevieve's personality: dominant, sociable, honest, cheerful, intelligent, and optimistic. When college students were asked to describe someone they knew well, they mentioned an average of seven central traits (Allport, 1961).

Secondary traits are the less consistent, relatively superficial aspects of a person. Any number of secondary traits could be listed in a personality description. Your own

Trait theorist A psychologist interested in classifying, analyzing, and interrelating traits to understand personality.

Common traits Personality traits that are shared by most members of a particular culture.

Individual traits Personality traits that define a person's unique individual qualities.

Cardinal trait A personality trait so basic that all of a person's activities relate to it.

Central traits The core traits that characterize an individual personality.

Secondary traits Traits that are inconsistent or relatively minor.

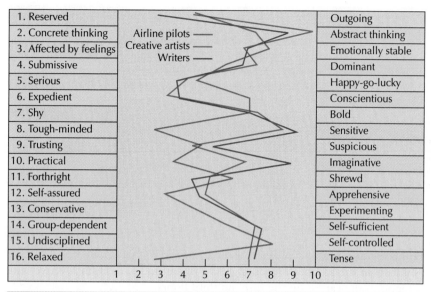

	Airline pilots —— Creative artists —— Writers ——	
1. Reserved		Outgoing
2. Concrete thinking		Abstract thinking
3. Affected by feelings		Emotionally stable
4. Submissive		Dominant
5. Serious		Happy-go-lucky
6. Expedient		Conscientious
7. Shy		Bold
8. Tough-minded		Sensitive
9. Trusting		Suspicious
10. Practical		Imaginative
11. Forthright		Shrewd
12. Self-assured		Apprehensive
13. Conservative		Experimenting
14. Group-dependent		Self-sufficient
15. Undisciplined		Self-controlled
16. Relaxed		Tense
	1 2 3 4 5 6 7 8 9 10	

▶**Figure 10.3**

The 16 source traits measured by Cattell's 16 PF are listed beside the graph. Scores can be plotted as a profile for an individual or a group. The profiles shown here are group averages for airline pilots, creative artists, and writers. Notice the similarity between artists and writers and the difference between these two groups and pilots. (After Cattell, 1973.)

Surface traits The visible or observable traits of one's personality.

Source traits Basic underlying traits of personality; each source trait is reflected in a number of surface traits.

Factor analysis A statistical technique used to correlate multiple measurements and identify general underlying factors.

Trait profile A graph of the scores obtained on several personality traits.

Five-factor model Proposes that there are five universal dimensions of personality.

secondary traits include such things as food preferences, attitudes, political opinions, musical tastes, and so on. In Allport's terms, a personality description might therefore include the following items:

Name: Jane Doe
Age: 22
Cardinal traits: None
Central traits: Possessive, autonomous, artistic, dramatic, self-centred, trusting
Secondary traits: Prefers colourful clothes, likes to work alone, politically liberal, always late

SOURCE TRAITS A second major approach to traits is illustrated by the work of Raymond B. Cattell (1906–1998). Cattell wanted to dig deeper into personality to learn how traits are interlinked. He began by studying features that make up the visible areas of personality. He called these **surface traits.** Through the use of questionnaires, direct observations, and life records, Cattell assembled data on the surface traits of a large number of people. He then noted that surface traits often appear in *clusters,* or groups. In fact, some traits appeared together so often that they seemed to represent a single more basic trait. Cattell called such underlying personality characteristics **source traits** (Cattell, 1965).

How do source traits differ from Allport's central traits? The main difference is that Allport classified traits subjectively, whereas Cattell used a statistical technique called *factor analysis* to reduce surface traits to source traits. In a **factor analysis,** psychologists look at the correlations among several variables. If patterns emerge in these correlations they are assumed to reflect general, underlying factors. Using this approach, Cattell developed a list of 16 source traits. He considered this the basic number necessary to describe a personality.

Cattell's source traits are measured by a test called the *Sixteen Personality Factor Questionnaire* (the 16 PF). Like many tests of its type, the 16 PF can be used to produce a **trait profile,** or graph of a person's score on each trait. Trait profiles draw a "picture" of individual personalities, which makes it easier to compare them (see ▶ Figure 10.3).

The Big Five

Noel is outgoing and friendly, conscientious, emotionally stable, and smart. His brother Joel is introverted, hostile, irresponsible, emotionally unpredictable, and disinterested in ideas (stupid). You will be spending a week in a space capsule with either Noel or Joel. Who would you choose? If the answer seems obvious, it's because Noel and Joel were described with the **five-factor model,** a system that identifies the five most basic dimensions of personality.

The "Big Five" factors listed in ▶ Figure 10.4 attempt to further reduce Cattell's 16 factors to just five universal dimensions (Digman, 1990; Goldberg, 1993). The Big Five may be the best answer of all to the question, What is the essence of human personality? (De Raad, 1998; McCrae & Costa, 1997).

FIVE KEY DIMENSIONS If you would like to compare the personalities of two people, try rating them informally on the five dimensions shown in Figure 10.4. For factor 1, *extroversion,* rate how introverted or extroverted each person is. Factor 2, *agreeableness,* refers to how friendly, nurturing, and caring a person is, as opposed to cold, indifferent, self-centred, or spiteful. A person who is *conscientious* (factor 3) is self-disciplined, responsible, and achieving. People low on this factor are irresponsible, careless, and undepend-

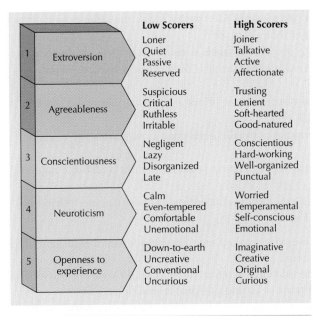

		Low Scorers	High Scorers
1	Extroversion	Loner Quiet Passive Reserved	Joiner Talkative Active Affectionate
2	Agreeableness	Suspicious Critical Ruthless Irritable	Trusting Lenient Soft-hearted Good-natured
3	Conscientiousness	Negligent Lazy Disorganized Late	Conscientious Hard-working Well-organized Punctual
4	Neuroticism	Calm Even-tempered Comfortable Unemotional	Worried Temperamental Self-conscious Emotional
5	Openness to experience	Down-to-earth Uncreative Conventional Uncurious	Imaginative Creative Original Curious

► **Figure 10.4**

The Big Five. According to the five-factor model, basic differences in personality can be "boiled down" to the dimensions shown here. The five-factor model answers these essential questions about a person: Is she or he extroverted or introverted? Agreeable or difficult? Conscientious or irresponsible? Emotionally stable or unstable? Smart or unintelligent? These questions cover a large measure of what we might want to know about someone's personality. (Trait descriptions adapted from McCrae & Costa, 1990.)

Facet traits Personality traits that characterize the Big Five personality dimensions and are part of them as well. Each of the big five factors has its unique set of facet traits.

Knowing where a person stands on the "Big Five" personality factors helps predict his or her behaviour. For example, people who score high on conscientiousness tend to be safe drivers who are unlikely to have automobile accidents (Arthur & Graziano, 1996).

able. Factor 4, *neuroticism,* refers to negative, upsetting emotions. People who are high in neuroticism tend to be anxious, emotionally "sour," irritable, and unhappy. Finally, people who rate high on factor 5, *openness to experience,* are intelligent and open to new ideas (Digman, 1990). The beauty of this model is that almost any trait you can name will be related to one of the five factors. If you were selecting a college roommate, hiring an employee, or answering a singles ad, you would probably like to know all of the personal dimensions covered by the Big Five. But how accurately can we predict behaviour based on our knowledge of where someone fits on the Big Five dimensions?

Some Canadian researchers have attempted to answer just this question. Their conclusions are interesting but not as straightforward as we might think at first. The Big Five factors were reasonably good at predicting everyday behaviour of students, but not as good as when the researchers relied on *facet traits.* Think of the Big Five as major categories of traits and **facet traits** as subclasses of characteristics that are part of those major categories. For instance, the trait of conscientiousness includes the facet-level trait of responsibility. The relationship between the Big Five and the facet traits is similar to Cattell's distinction between source and surface traits. To predict your academic performance, we would do better by knowing how you rate on the variables of need for achievement and need for understanding, than by knowing how you rate on the corresponding Big Five Factors of conscientiousness and openness to experience (Paunonen & Ashton, 2001).

In other words, knowing that your potential roommate is highly conscientious tells you that he is reliable, generally speaking, but it does not say anything about whether he is going to be as neat and organized as you are! To predict whether he is neat and organized, you will have to know how he rates on the facet trait of neatness.

Before you read the next section, take a moment to answer the questions that follow. Doing so will add to your understanding of a long-running controversy in the psychology of personality.

Rate Yourself: How Do You View Personality?

1. My friends' actions are fairly consistent from day to day and in different situations. T or F?

2. Whether a person is honest or dishonest, kind or cruel, a hero or a coward, depends mainly on circumstances. T or F?

3. Most people I have known for several years have pretty much the same personalities now as they did when I first met them. T or F?

4. The reason that people in some professions (such as teachers, lawyers, or doctors) seem so much alike is that their work requires that they act in particular ways. T or F?

5. One of the first things I would want to know about a potential roommate is what the person's personality is like. T or F?

6. I believe that immediate circumstances usually determine how people act at any given time. T or F?

7. To be comfortable in a particular job, a person's personality must match the nature of the work. T or F?

8. Almost anyone would be polite at a wedding reception; it doesn't matter what kind of personality the person has. T or F?

Now count the number of times you marked true for the odd-numbered items. Do the same for the even-numbered items.

If you agreed with most of the odd-numbered items, you tend to view behaviour as strongly influenced by personality traits or lasting personal dispositions.

If you agreed with most of the even-numbered items, you view behaviour as strongly influenced by external situations and circumstances.

If the number of times you answered true is nearly equal for odd and even items, you place equal weight on traits and situations as sources of behaviour. This is the view now held by many personality psychologists (Mischel & Shoda, 1998).

Traits, Consistency, and Situations

To predict how a person will act, is it better to focus on personality traits or external circumstances? Actually, it's best to take both into account. Personality traits are quite consistent (Roan, 1992). Yet, situations also greatly influence our behaviour. For instance, it would be unusual for you to dance at a movie or read a book at a football game. Likewise, few people sleep in roller coasters or tell off-colour jokes at funerals. However, your personality traits may predict whether you choose to read a book, go to a movie, or attend a football game in the first place. Typically, traits interact with situations to determine how we will act (Sheldon et al., 1997).

Trait-situation interactions occur when external circumstances influence the expression of personality traits. For instance, imagine what would happen if you moved from a church to a classroom to a party to a football game. As the setting changed, you would probably become louder and more boisterous. This change would demonstrate situational effects on behaviour. At the same time, your personality traits would also be apparent: If you were quieter than average in class, you would probably be quieter than average in the other settings too. Where do such differences come from? The next section explores one source of personality traits.

Trait-situation interaction The influence that external settings or circumstances have on the expression of personality traits.

Behavioural genetics The study of inherited behavioural traits and tendencies.

Do We Inherit Personality?

How much does heredity affect personality traits? Some breeds of dogs have reputations for being friendly, aggressive, intelligent, calm, or emotional. Such differences fall in the realm of **behavioural genetics**—the study of inherited behavioural traits. We know that facial features, eye colour, body type, and many other physical characteristics are inherited. So too are many behavioural tendencies. For example, selective breeding of animals can lead to striking differences in social behaviour, emotionality, learning ability, aggression, activity, and other behaviours (Steen, 1996; Trut, 1999).

To what extent do such findings apply to humans? Genetic studies of humans must rely on comparisons of identical twins and other close relatives. As a result, they are not as conclusive as animal studies (Rose, 1995). Nonetheless, they show that intelligence, some mental disorders, and temperament are influenced by heredity. In view of findings like these, we also might wonder whether genes affect personality.

Wouldn't comparing the personalities of identical twins help answer the question? It would indeed—especially if the twins were separated at birth or soon after.

TWINS AND TRAITS   For two decades, psychologists at the University of Minnesota have been studying identical twins who grew up in different homes. At the university, reunited twins take a wide range of medical and psychological tests. These tests show that identical twins are very much alike, even when they are reared apart (Bouchard et al., 1990; Lykken et al., 1992).

Reunited twins are astonishingly similar in appearance, voice quality, facial gestures, hand movements, and nervous tics such as nail biting. Separated twins also tend to have similar talents. If one twin excels at art, music, dance, drama, or athletics, the other is likely to as well—despite wide differences in childhood environment. However, as the next section explains, it's wise to be cautious about reports of extraordinary similarities in reunited twins.

THE MINNESOTA TWINS   Many reunited twins in the Minnesota study have displayed similarities far beyond what would be expected on the basis of heredity. A good example is provided by the "Jim twins," James Lewis and James Springer. Both Jims had married and divorced women named Linda. Both had undergone police training. Both had named their firstborn sons James Allan. Both drove Chevrolets and vacationed at the same beach each summer. Both listed carpentry and mechanical drawing among their hobbies. Both had built benches around trees in their yards. And so forth (Holden, 1980).

Does heredity actually control such details of our lives? Are there child-naming genes and bench-building genes? Of course, the idea is preposterous. How, then, do we explain the eerie similarities in separated twins' lives?

The astute reader will realize that completely unrelated persons can also share "amazing" similarities. One study, for instance, compared twins to unrelated pairs of students. The unrelated pairs, who were the same age and sex, were almost as alike as the twins. They had highly similar political beliefs, musical interests, religious preferences, job histories, hobbies, favourite foods, and so on (Wyatt et al., 1984). Why were the unrelated students so similar? Basically, it's because people of the same age and sex live in the same historical times and select from similar societal options.

Imagine that you were separated at birth from a twin brother or sister. If you were reunited with your twin today, what would you do? Quite likely, you would spend the next several days comparing every imaginable detail of your lives. Under such circumstances it is virtually certain that you and your twin would compile a long list of similarities. ("Wow! I use the same brand of toothpaste you do!") Yet, two unrelated persons of the same age, sex, and race could probably rival your list—if they were as motivated to find similarities.

To summarize, many of the seemingly "astounding" coincidences shared by reunited twins may be a special case of the fallacy of positive instances, described in Chapter 1. Similarities blaze brightly in the memories of reunited twins, while differences are ignored.

SUMMARY   Studies of twins make it clear that heredity has a sizable effect on each of us. All told, it seems reasonable to conclude that heredity is responsible for about 25 to 50 percent of the variation in many personality traits (Jang et al., 1998; Loehlin et al., 1998). Notice, however, that the same figures imply personality is shaped as much, or more, by environment as it is by heredity (Gatz, 1990).

Each personality is a unique blend of heredity and environment, biology and culture. We are not—thank goodness—genetically programmed robots whose behaviour and personality traits are "wired in" for life. Where you go in life is the result of the choices you make. To a degree, these choices are influenced by inherited tendencies (Saudino et al., 1997). However, they are not merely a product of your genes (Rose, 1995).

Knowledge builder

PERSONALITY AND TRAIT THEORIES

Relate

See if you can define or describe the following terms in your own words: personality, character, temperament, trait, type, self-concept, self-esteem.

List six or seven traits that best describe your personality. Which system of traits seems to best match your list: Allport's, Cattell's, or the Big Five?

Choose a prominent trait from your list. Does its expression seem to be influenced by specific situations? Do you think that heredity contributed to the trait?

Learning Check

1. _____ refers to the hereditary aspects of a person's emotional nature.
2. The term _____ refers to the presence or absence of desirable personal qualities.
   a. personality *b.* source trait *c.* character *d.* temperament
3. A system that classifies all people as either introverts or extroverts is an example of a _____ approach to personality.

4. An individual's perception of his or her own personality constitutes that person's _____.
5. Central traits are those shared by most members of a culture. T or F?
6. Which of the following is not one of the Big Five personality factors?
   a. submissiveness *b.* agreeableness *c.* extroversion *d.* neuroticism
7. Facet traits are similar to Cattell's _____ traits.
8. To understand personality it is wise to remember that traits and situations _____ to determine our behaviour.

Critical Thinking

9. In what way would memory contribute to the formation of an accurate or inaccurate self-concept?
10. Are situations equally powerful in their impact on behaviour?

Answers:

1. Temperament **2.** *c* **3.** type **4.** self-concept **5.** F **6.** *a* **7.** surface **8.** interact **9.** As discussed in Chapter 7, memory is highly selective, and long-term memories are often distorted by recent information. Such properties add to the mouldability of self-concept. **10.** No. Circumstances can have a strong or weak influence. In some situations, almost everyone will act what their personality traits may be. In other situations, traits may be of greater importance.

▶ Psychoanalytic Theory—Id Came to Me in a Dream

Survey Question:
■ How do psychodynamic theories explain personality?

Psychodynamic theorists are not content with studying traits. Instead, they try to probe under the surface of personality—to learn what drives, conflicts, and energies animate us. **Psychoanalytic theory,** the best-known psychodynamic approach, grew out of the work of Sigmund Freud, a Viennese physician. As a doctor, Freud was fascinated by patients whose problems seemed to be more emotional than physical. From about 1890 until he died in 1939, Freud evolved a theory of personality that deeply influenced modern thought. Let's consider some of its main features.

Psychoanalytic theory
Freudian theory of personality that emphasizes unconscious forces and conflicts.

The Structure of Personality

How did Freud view personality? Freud's model portrays personality as a dynamic system directed by three mental structures: the **id,** the **ego,** and the **superego.** According to Freud, most behaviour involves activity of all three systems. (Freud's theory includes a large number of concepts. For your convenience, they are defined in Table 10.2 rather than in page margins.)

THE ID   The id is made up of innate biological instincts and urges. It is self-serving, irrational, impulsive, and totally unconscious. The id operates on the **pleasure principle.** That is, it seeks to freely express pleasure-seeking urges of all kinds. If we were solely under control of the id, the world would be chaotic beyond belief.

The id acts as a well of energy for the entire **psyche** (sie-KEY), or personality. This energy, called **libido** (lih-BEE-doe), flows from the life instincts (or **Eros**). According to Freud, libido underlies our efforts to survive, as well as our sexual desires and pleasure seeking. Freud also described a **death instinct. Thanatos,** as he called it, produces aggressive and destructive urges. Freud offered humanity's long history of wars and vio-

Table 10.2
Key Freudian Concepts

Anal stage The psychosexual stage corresponding roughly to the period of toilet training (ages one to three years).

Anal-expulsive personality A disorderly, destructive, cruel, or messy person.

Anal-retentive personality A person who is obstinate, stingy, or compulsive, and who generally has difficulty "letting go."

Conscience The part of the superego that causes guilt when its standards are not met.

Conscious Region of the mind that includes all mental contents a person is aware of at any given moment.

Ego The executive part of personality that directs rational behaviour.

Ego ideal The part of the superego representing ideal behaviour; a source of pride when its standards are met.

Electra conflict A girl's sexual attraction to her father and feelings of rivalry with her mother.

Erogenous zone Any body area that produces pleasurable sensations.

Eros Freud's name for the "life instincts."

Fixation A lasting conflict developed as a result of frustration or overindulgence.

Genital stage Period of full psychosexual development, marked by the attainment of mature adult sexuality.

Id The primitive part of personality that remains unconscious, supplies energy, and demands pleasure.

Latency According to Freud, a period in childhood when psychosexual development is more or less interrupted.

Libido In Freudian theory, the force, primarily pleasure oriented, that energizes the personality.

Moral anxiety Apprehension felt when thoughts, impulses, or actions conflict with the superego's standards.

Neurotic anxiety Apprehension felt when the ego struggles to control id impulses.

Oedipus conflict A boy's sexual attraction to his mother, and feelings of rivalry with his father.

Oral stage The psychosexual stage (roughly birth to one year of age) when infants are preoccupied with the mouth as a source of pleasure and means of expression.

Oral-aggressive personality A person who uses the mouth to express hostility by shouting, cursing, biting, and so forth. Also, one who actively exploits others.

Oral-dependent personality A person who wants to passively receive attention, gifts, love, and so forth.

Phallic personality A person who is vain, exhibitionistic, sensitive, and narcissistic.

Phallic stage The psychosexual stage (roughly ages three to six years) when a child is preoccupied with the genitals.

Pleasure principle A desire for immediate satisfaction of wishes, desires, or needs.

Preconscious An area of the mind containing information that can be voluntarily brought to awareness.

Psyche The mind, mental life, and personality as a whole.

Psychosexual stages The oral, anal, phallic, and genital stages, during which various personality traits are formed.

Reality principle Delaying action (or pleasure) until it is appropriate.

Superego A judge or censor for thoughts and actions.

Thanatos The death instinct postulated by Freud.

Unconscious The region of the mind that is beyond awareness—especially impulses and desires not directly known to a person.

lence as evidence of such urges. Most id energies, then, are aimed at discharging tensions related to sex and aggression.

THE EGO The ego is sometimes described as the "executive," because it directs energies supplied by the id. The id is like a tyrannical king or queen whose power is awesome but who must rely on others to carry out orders. The id can only form mental images of things it desires. The ego wins power to direct behaviour by relating the desires of the id to external reality.

The ego is guided by the **reality principle.** That is, it delays action until it is practical or appropriate. The ego is the system of thinking, planning, problem solving, and deciding. It is in conscious control of the personality.

THE SUPEREGO *What is the role of the superego?* The superego acts as a judge or censor for the thoughts and actions of the ego. One part of the superego, called the **conscience,** reflects actions for which a person has been punished. When standards of the conscience are not met, you are punished internally by *guilt* feelings.

Freud considered personality an expression of two conflicting forces, life instinct and the death instinct. Both are symbolized in this drawing by Allan Gilbert. (If you don't immediately see the death symbolism, stand farther from the drawing.)

A second part of the superego is the **ego ideal.** The ego ideal reflects all behaviour one's parents approved of or rewarded. The ego ideal is a source of goals and aspirations. When its standards are met, we feel *pride*.

The superego acts as an "internalized parent" to bring behaviour under control. In Freudian terms, a person with a weak superego will be a delinquent, criminal, or anti-social personality. In contrast, an overly strict or harsh superego may cause inhibition, rigidity, or unbearable guilt.

The Dynamics of Personality

How do the id, ego, and superego interact? Freud didn't strictly picture the id, ego, and superego as parts of the brain or as "little people" running the human psyche. Instead, they are conflicting mental processes. Freud theorized a delicate balance of power among the three. For example, the id's demands for immediate pleasure often clash with the superego's moral restrictions. Perhaps an example will help clarify the role of each part of the personality.

Freud in a Nutshell

Let's say you are sexually attracted to an acquaintance. The id clamours for immediate satisfaction of its sexual desires, but is opposed by the superego (which finds the very thought of sex shocking). The id says, "Go for it!" The superego icily replies, "Never even think that again!" And what does the ego say? The ego says, "I have a plan!"

Of course, this is a drastic simplification, but it does capture the core of Freudian thinking. To reduce tension, the ego could begin actions leading to friendship, romance, courtship, and marriage. If the id is unusually powerful, the ego may give in and attempt a seduction. If the superego prevails, the ego may be forced to displace or sublimate sexual energies to other activities (sports, music, dancing, push-ups, cold showers). According to Freud, much of this activity occurs at the unconscious level.

Is the ego always caught in the middle? Basically yes, and the pressures on it can be intense. In addition to meeting the conflicting demands of the id and superego, the over-worked ego must deal with external reality.

According to Freud, you feel anxiety when your ego is threatened or overwhelmed. Impulses from the id cause **neurotic anxiety** when the ego can barely keep them under control. Threats of punishment from the superego cause **moral anxiety** (guilt). Each person develops habitual ways of calming these anxieties, and many resort to using *ego-defence mechanisms* to lessen internal conflicts. Defence mechanisms are mental processes that deny, distort, or otherwise block out sources of threat and anxiety. The ego defence mechanisms that Freud identified are used as a form of protection against stress, anxiety, and threatening events (see Chapter 11). In addition, Freud argued that it is the repressed unconscious thoughts, wishes, and feelings that can potentially cause maladaptive behaviours or mental disorders (see Chapter 12).

LEVELS OF AWARENESS Like other psychodynamic theorists, Freud believed that our behaviour often expresses unconscious (or hidden) internal forces. The **unconscious** holds repressed memories and emotions, plus the instinctual drives of the id. Interestingly, modern scientists have found that the brain's limbic system does, in fact, seem to trigger unconscious emotions and memories (LeDoux, 1996).

Even though they are beyond awareness, unconscious thoughts, feelings, or urges may slip into behaviour in disguised or symbolic form. For example, if you meet someone you would like to know better, you may unconsciously leave a book or a jacket at that person's house to ensure another meeting.

Earlier you said that the id is completely unconscious. Are the actions of the ego and superego unconscious? At times, yes, but they also operate on two other levels of awareness (see ►Figure 10.5). The **conscious** level includes everything you are aware of at a given moment, including thoughts, perceptions, feelings, and memories. The **preconscious** contains material that can be easily brought to awareness. If you stop to think about a time

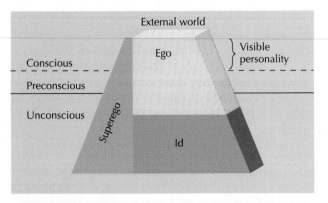

▶Figure 10.5

The approximate relationship between the id, ego, and superego, and the levels of awareness.

when you felt angry or rejected, you will be moving this memory from the preconscious to the conscious level of awareness.

The superego's activities also reveal differing levels of awareness. At times we consciously try to live up to moral codes or standards. Yet, at other times a person may feel guilty without knowing why. Psychoanalytic theory credits such guilt to unconscious workings of the superego. Indeed, Freud believed that the unconscious origins of many feelings cannot be easily brought to awareness.

Personality Development

How does psychoanalytic theory explain personality development? Freud hypothesized that the core of personality is formed by the age of six years in a series of **psychosexual stages.** Freud believed that erotic childhood urges have lasting effects on development. As you might expect, this is a controversial idea. However, Freud used the terms *sex* and *erotic* very broadly to refer to many physical sources of pleasure.

A FREUDIAN FABLE?   Freud identified four psychosexual stages: the **oral, anal, phallic,** and **genital.** (He also described a period of "latency" between the phallic and genital stages. Latency is explained in a moment.) At each stage, a different part of the body becomes a child's primary **erogenous zone** (an area capable of producing pleasure). Each area then serves as the main source of pleasure, frustration, and self-expression. Freud believed that many adult personality traits can be traced to **fixations** in one or more of the stages.

What is a fixation? A fixation is an unresolved conflict or emotional hang-up caused by overindulgence or by frustration. As we describe the psychosexual stages, you'll see why Freud considered fixations important.

THE ORAL STAGE   During the first year of life, most of an infant's pleasure comes from stimulation of the mouth. If a child is overfed or frustrated, oral traits may be created. Adult expressions of oral needs include gum chewing, nail biting, smoking, kissing, overeating, and alcoholism.

What if there is an oral fixation? Fixation early in the oral stage produces an **oral-dependent** personality. Oral-dependent persons are gullible (they swallow things easily!) and passive and need lots of attention (they want to be mothered and showered with gifts). Frustrations later in the oral stage may cause aggression, often in the form of biting. Fixations here create cynical, **oral-aggressive** adults who exploit others. They also like to argue ("biting sarcasm" is their forte!).

THE ANAL STAGE   Between the ages of one and three years, the child's attention shifts to the process of elimination. When parents attempt toilet training, the child can gain approval or express rebellion or aggression by "holding on" or by "letting go." Therefore, harsh or lenient toilet training can cause an anal fixation that may lock such responses into personality. Freud described the **anal-retentive** (holding-on) personality as obstinate, stingy, orderly, and compulsively clean. The **anal-expulsive** (letting-go) personality is disorderly, destructive, cruel, or messy.

THE PHALLIC STAGE   Adult traits of the **phallic personality** are vanity, exhibitionism, sensitive pride, and narcissism (self-love). Freud thought that phallic fixations develop between the ages of three and six years. At this time, increased sexual interest causes the child to be physically attracted to the parent of the opposite sex. In males this attraction leads to an **Oedipus conflict** (ED-eh-pes). In it, the boy feels a rivalry with his father for the affection of his mother. Freud believed that the male child feels threatened by the father (specifically, the boy fears castration). To ease his anxieties, the boy must *identify* with the father. Their rivalry ends when the boy seeks to become more like his father. As he does, he begins to accept the father's values and forms a conscience. His love for his mother is repressed or pushed back into the unconscious.

What about the female child? Girls experience an **Electra conflict.** In this case, the girl loves her father and competes with her mother. However, according to Freud, the girl identifies with the mother more gradually than the boy does with the father.

Freud believed that females already feel castrated. Because of this, they are less driven to identify with their mothers than boys are with their fathers. This, he said, is less effective in creating a conscience. This particular part of Freudian thought has been thoroughly rejected by modern feminists. It is probably best understood as a reflection of the male-dominated times in which Freud lived.

LATENCY   According to Freud, there is a period of **latency** from age six years to puberty. Latency is not actually a stage. Rather, it is a quiet time during which psychosexual development is dormant. Freud's belief that psychosexual development is "on hold" at this time is hard to accept. Nevertheless, Freud saw latency as a relatively quiet time compared to the stormy first six years of life.

THE GENITAL STAGE   At puberty an upswing in sexual energies activates all the unresolved conflicts of earlier years. This upsurge, according to Freud, is the reason adolescence can be filled with emotion and turmoil. The genital stage begins at puberty. It is marked, during adolescence, by a growing capacity for responsible social-sexual relationships. The genital stage ends with a mature capacity for love and the realization of full adult sexuality.

CRITICAL COMMENTS   As bizarre as Freud's theory might seem, it has been influential for several reasons. First, it emphasized the idea that the first years of life help to shape adult personality. Second, it identified feeding, toilet training, and early sexual experiences as critical events in personality formation. Third, Freud was among the first to propose that development proceeds through a series of stages. (Erik Erikson's psychosocial stages, which cover development from birth to old age, are a modern offshoot of Freudian thinking. See Chapter 3.)

Is the Freudian view of development widely accepted? Few psychologists wholeheartedly embrace Freud's theory today. In some cases Freud was clearly wrong. His portrayal of the elementary school years (latency) as free from sexuality and unimportant for personality development is hard to believe. His idea of the role of a stern or threatening father in the development of a strong conscience in males has also been challenged. Studies show that a son is more likely to develop a strong conscience if his father is affectionate and accepting, rather than stern and punishing. Freud also overemphasized sexuality in personality development. Other motives and cognitive factors are of equal importance.

Recently, Freud has been criticized for his views of patients who believed they were sexually molested as children. Freud assumed that such events were merely childhood fantasies. This view led to a longstanding tendency to disbelieve children who have been molested and women who have been raped (Brannon, 1996).

Many more criticisms of Freud could be listed, but the fact remains that his theory contains some grains of truth. At the same time, a major remaining problem with Freud's theory is insurmountable: Whatever value it may have clinically, it has been difficult to verify scientifically. Some go as far as to claim that his ideas have been sufficiently tested but the results of these studies do not confirm Freud's conjectures about personality development (Erwin, 1996).

▶ Learning Theories of Personality— Habit I Seen You Before?

Survey Question:
■ What do behaviourists emphasize in their approach to personality?

How do behaviourists approach personality? According to some critics, as if people are robots like R2D2 of *Star Wars* fame. Actually, the behaviourist position is not nearly that mechanistic, and its value is well established. Behaviourists have shown repeatedly that children can learn things like kindness, hostility, generosity, or destructiveness. What does this have to do with personality? Everything, according to the behavioural viewpoint.

Knowledge builder

PSYCHODYNAMIC THEORY

Relate

Try to think of at least one time when your thoughts, feelings, or actions seemed to reflect the workings of each of the following: the id, the ego, and the superego.

Do you know anyone who seems to have oral, anal, or phallic personality traits? Do you think Freud's concept of fixation explains their characteristics?

Do any of your personal experiences support the existence of an Oedipus conflict or an Electra conflict? If not, is it possible that you have repressed feelings related to these conflicts?

Learning Check

1. List the three divisions of personality postulated by Freud.

2. Which division is totally unconscious?

3. Which division is responsible for moral anxiety?

4. Freud proposed the existence of a life instinct known as Thanatos. T or F?

5. Freud's view of personality development is based on the concept of _____ stages.

6. Arrange these stages in the proper order: phallic, anal, genital, oral. _____

7. Freud considered the anal-retentive personality to be obstinate and stingy. T or F?

Critical Thinking

8. Many adults would find it embarrassing or humiliating to drink from a baby bottle. Can you explain why?

Answers:

1. id, ego, superego 2. id 3. superego 4. F 5. psychosexual 6. oral, anal, phallic, genital 7. T 8. A psychoanalytic theorist would say that it is because the bottle rekindles oral conflicts and feelings of vulnerability and dependence.

Behavioural personality theory Any model of personality that emphasizes learning and observable behaviour.

Learning theorist A psychologist interested in the ways that learning shapes behaviour and explains personality.

Situational determinants External conditions that strongly influence behaviour.

Freud believed that aggressive urges are "instinctual." In contrast, behavioural theories assume that personal characteristics such as aggressiveness are learned. Is this child's aggression the result of observational learning, harsh punishment, or prior reinforcement?

Behavioural personality theories emphasize that personality is no more (or less) than a collection of learned behaviour patterns. Personality, like other learned behaviour, is acquired through classical and operant conditioning, observational learning, reinforcement, extinction, generalization, and discrimination. When Mother says, "It's not nice to make mud pies with Mommy's blender. If we want to grow up to be a big girl, we won't do it again, will we?" she serves as a model and in other ways shapes her daughter's personality.

Strict **learning theorists** reject the idea that personality is made up of traits. They would assert, for instance, that there is no such thing as a trait of "honesty" (Bandura, 1973; Mischel, 1968).

Certainly some people are honest while others are not. How can honesty not be a trait? A learning theorist would agree that some people are honest more often than others. But knowing this does not allow us to predict for certain whether a person will be honest in a specific situation. It would not be unusual, for example, to find that a person honoured for returning a lost wallet had cheated on a test, bought a term paper, or broken the speed limit. If you were to ask a learning theorist, "Are you an honest person?" the reply might be, "In what situation?"

A good example of how situations influence behaviour is shown by a study in which people were intentionally overpaid for doing an assigned task. Under normal circumstances, 80 percent kept the extra money without saying anything about it. But as few as 17 percent were dishonest if the situation was restructured. For instance, if people thought the money was coming out of the pocket of the person doing the study, far fewer were dishonest (Bersoff, 1999).

As you can see, learning theorists are especially interested in the **situational determinants** (external causes) of our actions. However, this does not entirely remove the person from the picture. Situations always interact with a person's prior learning history to activate behaviour.

Situations vary greatly in their impact. Some are powerful. Others are trivial and have little effect on behaviour. The more powerful the situation, the easier it is to see what is meant by situational determinants. For example, each of the following situations would undoubtedly have a strong influence on behaviour: an escaped lion walks into a supermarket; you accidentally sit on a lighted cigarette; you find your lover in bed with your best friend. Yet even these situations could provoke very different reactions from different personalities. That's why behaviour is always a product of both prior learning and the situations in which we find ourselves (Mischel & Shoda, 1998).

As discussed earlier, trait theorists also believe that situations affect behaviour. But in their view, situations interact with traits, rather than a person's learning history. So, in essence, learning theorists favour replacing "traits" with "prior learning" to explain behaviour.

Personality = Behaviour

How do learning theorists view the structure of personality? The behavioural view of personality can be illustrated with an early theory proposed by John Dollard and Neal Miller (1950). In their view, **habits** (learned behaviour patterns) make up the structure of personality. As for the dynamics of personality, habits are governed by four elements of learning: *drive, cue, response,* and *reward*. A **drive** is any stimulus strong enough to goad a person to action (such as hunger, pain, lust, frustration, or fear). **Cues** are signals from the environment. These signals guide **responses** (actions) so that they are most likely to bring about **reward** (positive reinforcement).

How does that relate to personality? Let's say a child named Kindra is frustrated by her older brother Kelvin, who takes a toy from her. Kindra could respond in several ways: She could throw a temper tantrum, hit Kelvin, tell Mother, and so forth. The response she chooses is guided by available cues and the previous effects of each response. If telling Mother has paid off in the past, and the mother is present, telling again may be her immediate response. If a different set of cues exists (if Mother is absent or if Kelvin looks particularly menacing), Kindra may select some other response. To an outside observer, Kindra's actions seem to reflect her personality. To a learning theorist, they simply express the combined effects of drive, cue, response, and reward.

Doesn't this analysis leave out a lot? Yes. Learning theorists first set out to provide a simple, clear model of personality. But in recent years they have had to face a fact that they originally tended to overlook. The fact is: People think. The new breed of behavioural psychologists—who include perception, thinking, expectations, and other mental events in their views—are called social learning theorists. Learning principles, modelling, thought patterns, perceptions, expectations, beliefs, goals, emotions, and social relationships are combined in **social learning theory** to explain personality (Mischel & Shoda, 1998).

Social Learning Theory

The "cognitive behaviourism" of social learning theory can be illustrated by three concepts proposed by Julian Rotter. They are the psychological situation, expectancy, and reinforcement value (Rotter & Hochreich, 1975). Let's examine each.

Someone trips you. How do you respond? Your reaction probably depends on whether you think it was planned or an accident. It is not enough to know the setting in which a person responds. We also need to know the person's **psychological situation** (how the person interprets or defines the situation). As another example, let's say you score low on an exam. Do you consider it a challenge to work harder, a sign that you should drop the class, or an excuse to get drunk? Again, your interpretation is important.

An **expectancy** refers to your anticipation that making a response will lead to reinforcement. To continue the example, if working harder has paid off in the past, it is a likely reaction to a low test score. But to predict your response, we would also have to know if you expect your efforts to pay off in the present situation. In fact, expected reinforcement may be more important than actual past reinforcement. And what about the value you attach to grades, school success, or personal ability? Rotter's third concept, **reinforcement value,** states that humans attach different subjective values to various activities or rewards. This, too, must be taken into account to understand personality.

One more idea deserves mention. At times, we all evaluate our actions and may reward ourselves with special privileges or treats for "good behaviour." With this in mind,

Habit A deeply ingrained, learned pattern of behaviour.

Drive Any stimulus (especially an internal stimulus such as hunger) strong enough to provoke a person to action.

Cue External stimuli that guide responses, especially by signalling the presence or absence of reinforcement.

Response Any behaviour, either observable or internal.

Reward Anything that produces pleasure or satisfaction; a positive reinforcer.

Social learning theory An explanation of personality that combines learning principles, cognition, and the effects of social relationships.

Psychological situation A situation as it is perceived and interpreted by an individual, not as it exists objectively.

Expectancy Anticipation about the effect a response will have, especially regarding reinforcement.

Reinforcement value The subjective value a person attaches to a particular activity or reinforcer.

Self-reinforcement
Praising or rewarding oneself for having made a particular response (such as completing a school assignment).

Social reinforcement
Praise, attention, approval, and/or affection from others.

Critical situations
Situations during childhood that are capable of leaving a lasting imprint on personality.

Identification Feeling emotionally connected to a person and seeing oneself as like him or her.

Imitation An attempt to match one's own behaviour to another person's behaviour.

social learning theory adds the concept of self-reinforcement to the behaviouristic view. **Self-reinforcement** refers to praising or rewarding yourself for having made a particular response (such as completing a school assignment). Thus, habits of self-praise and self-blame become an important part of personality. In fact, self-reinforcement can be thought of as the behaviourist's counterpart to the superego.

Self-reinforcement is closely related to high self-esteem. The reverse is also true: Mildly depressed college students tend to have low rates of self-reinforcement. It is not known if low self-reinforcement leads to depression, or the reverse. In either case, self-reinforcement is associated with less depression and greater life satisfaction (Seybolt & Wagner, 1997; Wilkinson, 1997). From a behavioural viewpoint, there is value in learning to be "good to yourself."

Behaviouristic View of Development

How do learning theorists account for personality development? Many of Freud's ideas can be restated in terms of learning theory. Dollard and Miller (1950) agree with Freud that the first six years are crucial for personality development, but for different reasons. Rather than thinking in terms of psychosexual urges and fixations, they ask, "What makes early learning experiences so lasting in their effects?" Their answer is that childhood is a time of urgent drives, powerful rewards and punishments, and crushing frustrations. Also important is **social reinforcement,** which is based on praise, attention, or approval from others. These forces combine to shape the core of personality.

CRITICAL SITUATIONS   Miller and Dollard believe that during childhood four **critical situations** are capable of leaving a lasting imprint on personality. These are (1) feeding, (2) toilet or cleanliness training, (3) sex training, and (4) learning to express anger or aggression.

Why are these of special importance? Feeding serves as an illustration. If children are fed when they cry, it encourages them to actively manipulate their parents. The child allowed to cry without being fed learns to be passive. Thus, a basic active or passive orientation toward the world may be created by early feeding experiences. Feeding can also affect later social relationships because the child learns to associate people with pleasure or with frustration and discomfort.

Toilet and cleanliness training can be a particularly strong source of emotion for both parents and children. Tom's parents were aghast the day they found him smearing feces about with joy. They reacted with sharp punishment, which frustrated and confused Tom. Many attitudes toward cleanliness, conformity, and bodily functions are formed at such times. Studies also show that severe, punishing, or frustrating toilet training can have undesirable effects on personality development (Sears, Maccoby, & Levin, 1957). Because of this, toilet and cleanliness training demand patience and a sense of humour.

What about sex and anger? When, where, and how a child learns to express anger and sexual feelings can leave an imprint on personality. Specifically, permissiveness for sexual and aggressive behaviour in childhood is linked to adult needs for power (McClelland & Pilon, 1983). This link probably occurs because permitting such behaviours allows children to get pleasure from asserting themselves. Sex training also involves learning socially defined "male" and "female" gender roles—which also affect personality.

BECOMING MALE OR FEMALE   From birth onward, children are labelled as boys or girls and encouraged to learn sex-appropriate behaviour. According to social learning theory, identification and imitation contribute greatly to personality development and to sex training. **Identification** refers to the child's emotional attachment to admired adults, especially those who provide love and care. Identification typically encourages **imitation,** a desire to act like the admired person. Many "male" or "female" traits come from children's attempts to imitate a same-sex parent with whom they identify.

If children are around parents of both sexes, why don't they imitate behaviour typical of the opposite sex as well as of the same sex? Recall from Chapter 6 that

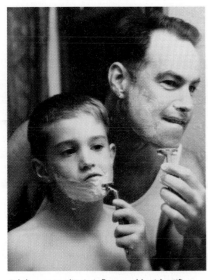
Adult personality is influenced by identification with parents and imitation of their behaviour.

learning takes place vicariously as well as directly. This means that we can learn by observing and remembering the actions of others. But the actions we choose to imitate depend on their outcomes. For example, boys and girls have equal chances to observe adults and other children acting aggressively. However, girls are less likely than boys to imitate aggressive behaviour because they rarely see female aggression rewarded or approved. Thus, many arbitrary "male" and "female" qualities are passed on at the same time that gender identity is learned.

Lisa Serbin and her colleagues at Concordia University in Montreal have found interesting differences in the way teachers perceive and respond to boys and girls in their classrooms. At about the age of three years, when children begin to prefer to play with same-sex playmates, their teachers perceive girls to be socially more sensitive and boys to be more active and disruptive (Moller & Serbin, 1996).

Another study with preschoolers found that teachers were three times more likely to pay attention to aggressive or disruptive boys than to girls acting the same way. Boys who hit other students or who broke things typically got loud scoldings. This made them the centre of attention for the whole class. When teachers responded to disruptive girls, they gave brief, soft rebukes that others couldn't hear (Serbin & O'Leary, 1975). We know that attention of almost any kind reinforces children's behaviour. Therefore, it is clear that the boys were being encouraged to be active and aggressive. Girls got the most attention when they were within arm's reach, more or less clinging to the teacher.

The pattern just described grows stronger throughout elementary school. In all grades, boys are louder, faster, and more boisterous than girls. Day after day, boys receive a disproportionate amount of the teacher's attention (Sadker & Sadker, 1994). It's easy to see that teachers unwittingly encourage girls to be submissive, dependent, and passive. Similar differences in reinforcement probably explain why males are responsible for much more aggression in society than females are. By age 10, boys expect to get less disapproval from parents for aggression than girls do. This is especially true if the aggression is provoked by another boy (Perry, Perry, & Weiss, 1989). Among adults, rates of murder and assault are consistently higher for men than women. The roots of this difference may lie in childhood.

Overall, parents and other adults tend to encourage boys to engage in **instrumental** (goal-directed) **behaviours,** to be aggressive, to hide their emotions, and to prepare for the world of work. Girls, on the other hand, are encouraged in **expressive** (emotion-oriented) **behaviours** and, to a lesser degree, are socialized for motherhood. What effects do such differences have on adult personality? To find out, let's explore what it means to have "masculine" or "feminine" traits.

> ### ► Androgyny—Are You Masculine, Feminine, or Androgynous?

Are you aggressive, ambitious, analytical, assertive, athletic, competitive, decisive, dominant, forceful, independent, individualistic, self-reliant, and willing to take risks? If so, you are quite "masculine." Are you affectionate, cheerful, childlike, compassionate, flatterable, gentle, gullible, loyal, sensitive, shy, soft-spoken, sympathetic, tender, understanding, warm, and yielding? If so, then you are quite "feminine." What if you have traits from both lists? In that case, you may be *androgynous* (an-DROJ-ih-nus).

The two lists you just read are from the work of psychologist Sandra Bem. By combining 20 "masculine" traits (self-reliant, assertive, and so forth), 20 "feminine" traits (affectionate, gentle), and 20 neutral traits (truthful, friendly), Bem created the **Bem Sex Role Inventory (BSRI).** Next, she and her associates gave the BSRI to thousands of people, asking them to say whether each trait applied to them. Of those surveyed, 50 percent fell into traditional feminine or masculine categories; 15 percent scored higher on traits of the opposite sex; and 35 percent were androgynous, getting high scores on both feminine and masculine items.

The word **androgyny** (an-DROJ-ih-nee) literally means "man-woman." Psychologically, it refers to having both feminine and masculine traits. Bem is convinced that our complex society requires flexibility with respect to gender-related traits. It is necessary, she

---

Instrumental behaviours Behaviours directed toward the achievement of some goal; behaviours that are instrumental in producing some effect.

Expressive behaviours Behaviours that express or communicate emotion or personal feelings.

Bem Sex Role Inventory (BSRI) A list of 60 personal traits including "masculine," "feminine," and "neutral" traits; used to rate one's degree of androgyny.

Androgyny The presence of both "masculine" and "feminine" traits in a single person (as masculinity and femininity are defined within one's culture).

Androgynous individuals adapt easily to both traditionally "feminine" and "masculine" situations.

believes, for men to be gentle, compassionate, sensitive, and yielding and for women to be forceful, self-reliant, independent, and ambitious—as the situation requires. In short, Bem feels that more people should be androgynous.

ADAPTABILITY   Bem has shown that androgynous individuals are more adaptable because they are less hindered by images of "feminine" or "masculine" behaviour. For example, in one study people were given the choice of doing either a "masculine" activity (oil a hinge, nail boards together, and so forth) or a "feminine" activity (prepare a baby bottle, wind yarn into a ball, and so on). Masculine men and feminine women consistently chose to do gender-appropriate activities, even when the opposite choice paid more!

It appears that having rigid gender traits can seriously restrict behaviour, especially for men (Bem, 1975, 1981). Masculine males tend to have great difficulty expressing warmth, playfulness, and concern—even when they are appropriate. Masculine men, it seems, view such feelings as too "feminine." Masculine men also find it hard to accept emotional support from others, particularly from women (Ashton & Fuehrer, 1993). Highly feminine women face opposite problems. For them, being independent and assertive is difficult, even when these qualities are desirable.

Androgyny has been hotly debated over the years. Now, as the dust begins to settle, the picture looks like this:

- Having "masculine" traits primarily means that a person is independent and assertive. Scoring high in "masculinity" is related to high self-esteem and to success in many situations (Long, 1989).) Although both men and women who are high in masculinity may feel good about themselves, their understanding of theirs and others' emotions is less sophisticated than that of people who score lower in masculinity, according to Michael Conway (2000), a Concordia University researcher.
- Having "feminine" traits primarily means that a person is nurturing and interpersonally oriented. People who score high in "femininity" tend to experience greater social closeness with others and more happiness in marriage.

In sum, there are advantages to possessing both "feminine" and "masculine" traits (Ickes, 1993; Spence, 1984). In general, androgynous persons are more flexible when it comes to coping with difficult situations (Jurma & Powell, 1994; Spangenberg & Lategan, 1993). (See ▶Figure 10.6.) Androgynous persons also tend to be more satisfied with their lives. Apparently, they can use both instrumental and emotionally expressive capacities to enhance their lives and relationships (Dean-Church & Gilroy, 1993; Ramanaiah, Detwiler, & Byravan, 1995).

►**Figure 10.6**

Another indication of the possible benefits of androgyny is found in a study of reactions to stress. When confronted with an onslaught of negative events, strongly masculine or feminine persons become more depressed than androgynous individuals do (adapted from Roos & Cohen, 1987).

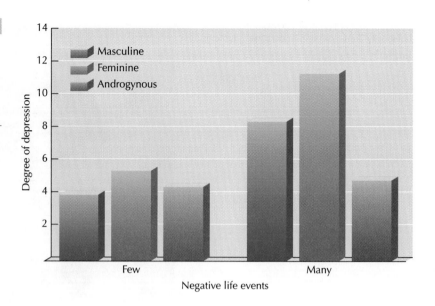

It is worth saying again that many people remain comfortable with traditional views of gender. Nevertheless, "feminine" traits and "masculine" traits can readily exist in the same person, and androgyny can be a highly adaptive balance.

Knowledge builder

BEHAVIOURAL AND SOCIAL LEARNING THEORIES

Relate

What is your favourite style of food? Can you relate Dollard and Miller's concepts of habit, drive, cue, response, and reward to explain your preference?

Some people love to shop. Others hate it. How have the psychological situation, expectancy, and reinforcement value affected your willingness to "shop 'til you drop"?

Who did you identify with as a child? What aspects of that person's behaviour did you imitate?

Think of three people you know, one who is androgynous, one who is traditionally feminine, and one who is traditionally masculine. What advantages and disadvantages do you see in each collection of traits? How do you think you would be classified if you took the BSRI?

Learning Check

1. Learning theorists believe that personality "traits" really are _____ acquired through prior learning. They also emphasize _____ determinants of behaviour.

2. Dollard and Miller consider cues the basic structure of personality. T or F?
3. To explain behaviour, social learning theorists include mental elements, such as _____ (the anticipation that a response will lead to reinforcement).
4. Self-reinforcement is to behaviouristic theory as superego is to psychoanalytic theory. T or F?
5. Which of the following is not a "critical situation" in the behaviourist theory of personality development?
   a. feeding b. sex training c. language training d. anger training
6. In addition to basic rewards and punishments, a child's personality is shaped by _____ reinforcement.
7. Social learning theories of development emphasize the impact of identification and _____.
8. A person who is aggressive, ambitious, analytical, and assertive would be rated as androgynous on the BSRI. T or F?

Critical Thinking

9. Julian Rotter's concept of reinforcement value is closely related to a motivational principle discussed in Chapter 9. Can you name it?

Answers:

1. habits, situational 2. F 3. expectancies 4. T 5. c 6. social 7. imitation 8. F 9. incentive value

▶ Humanistic Theory—Peak Experiences and Personal Growth

Survey Question:
■ How do humanistic theories differ from other perspectives?

Humanism An approach that focuses on human experience, problems, potentials, and ideals.

Human nature Those traits, qualities, potentials, and behaviour patterns most characteristic of the human species.

Free choice The ability to freely make choices that are not controlled by genetics, learning, or unconscious forces.

Subjective experience Reality as it is perceived and interpreted, not as it exists objectively.

Self-actualization The process of fully developing personal potentials.

Self-actualizer One who is living creatively and making full use of his or her potentials.

Humanism focuses on human experience, problems, potentials, and ideals. It is a reaction to the static quality of traits, the pessimism of psychoanalytic theory, and the mechanical nature of learning theory. At its core is a positive image of what it means to be human. Humanists reject the Freudian view of personality as a battleground for instincts and unconscious forces. Instead, they view human nature as inherently good. (**Human nature** consists of the traits, qualities, potentials, and behaviour patterns most characteristic of the human species.) Humanists also oppose the mechanical, "thing-like" overtones of the behaviourist viewpoint. We are not, they say, merely a bundle of mouldable responses. Rather, we are creative beings capable of **free choice** (an ability to choose that is not controlled by genetics, learning, or unconscious forces). In short, humanists seek ways to encourage our potentials to blossom.

To a humanist the person you are today is largely the product of all the choices you have made. The humanistic view also emphasizes immediate **subjective experience** (private perceptions of reality), rather than prior learning. Humanists believe that there are as many "real worlds" as there are people. To understand behaviour, we must comprehend how a person subjectively views the world—what is "real" for her or him.

Who are the major humanistic theorists? Many psychologists have added to the humanistic tradition. Of these, the best known are Carl Rogers (1902–1987) and Abraham Maslow (1908–1970). Since Maslow's idea of self-actualization was introduced in Chapter 1, let's begin with a more detailed look at this facet of his thinking.

Maslow and Self-Actualization

Abraham Maslow became interested in people who were living unusually effective lives. How were they different? To find an answer, Maslow began by studying the lives of great men and women, such as Albert Einstein, William James, Jane Addams, Eleanor Roosevelt, Abraham Lincoln, John Muir, and Walt Whitman. From there he moved on to directly study living artists, writers, poets, and other creative individuals.

Along the way, Maslow's thinking changed radically. At first he studied only people of obvious creativity or high achievement. However, it eventually became clear that a housewife, clerk, student, or someone like Genevieve could live a rich, creative, and satisfying life. Maslow referred to the process of fully developing personal potentials as **self-actualization** (Maslow, 1954). The heart of self-actualization is a continuous search for personal fulfillment (Sumerlin, 1997).

CHARACTERISTICS OF SELF-ACTUALIZERS   A **self-actualizer** is a person who is living creatively and fully using his or her potentials. In his studies, Maslow found that self-actualizers share many similarities. Whether famous or unknown, well-schooled or uneducated, rich or poor, self-actualizers tend to fit the following profile.

1. *Efficient perceptions of reality.* Self-actualizers are able to judge situations correctly and honestly. They are very sensitive to the fake and dishonest.
2. *Comfortable acceptance of self, others, nature.* Self-actualizers accept their own human nature with all its flaws. The shortcomings of others and the contradictions of the human condition are accepted with humour and tolerance.
3. *Spontaneity.* Maslow's subjects extended their creativity into everyday activities. Actualizers tend to be unusually alive, engaged, and spontaneous.
4. *Task centring.* Most of Maslow's subjects had a mission to fulfill in life or some task or problem outside of themselves to pursue. Humanitarians such as Albert Schweitzer and Mother Teresa represent this quality.
5. *Autonomy.* Self-actualizers are free from reliance on external authorities or other people. They tend to be resourceful and independent.
6. *Continued freshness of appreciation.* Self-actualizers seem to constantly renew appreciation of life's basic goods. A sunset or a flower will be experienced as intensely time

after time as it was at first. There is an "innocence of vision," like that of an artist or child.

7. *Fellowship with humanity.* Maslow's subjects felt a deep identification with others and the human situation in general.

8. *Profound interpersonal relationships.* The interpersonal relationships of self-actualizers are marked by deep, loving bonds.

9. *Comfort with solitude.* Despite their satisfying relationships with others, self-actualizing persons value solitude and are comfortable being alone (Sumerlin & Bundrick, 1996).

10. *Non-hostile sense of humour.* This refers to the wonderful capacity to laugh at oneself. It also describes the kind of humour a man like Abraham Lincoln had. Lincoln probably never made a joke that hurt anybody. His wry comments were a gentle prodding of human shortcomings.

11. *Peak experiences.* All of Maslow's subjects reported the frequent occurrence of peak experiences (temporary moments of self-actualization). These occasions were marked by feelings of ecstasy, harmony, and deep meaning. Self-actualizers reported feeling at one with the universe, stronger and calmer than ever before, filled with light, beautiful and good, and so forth.

In summary, self-actualizers feel safe, calm, accepted, loved, loving, and alive. There seems to be good agreement among humanistic psychologists from a number of different countries, including Canada, the United States, Belgium, and France, about the essential features of the concept of self-actualization (Leclerc et al., 1998).

Maslow's choice of self-actualizing people for study seems pretty subjective. Is it really a fair representation of self-actualization? Although Maslow tried to investigate self-actualization empirically, his choice of people for study was subjective. Undoubtedly there are many ways to make full use of personal potential. Maslow's primary contribution was to draw our attention to the possibility of lifelong personal growth.

What steps can be taken to promote self-actualization? Maslow made few specific recommendations about how to proceed. Nevertheless, several helpful ideas can be gleaned from his writings (Maslow, 1954, 1967, 1971). See "Steps toward Self-Actualization" for some specific suggestions.

Fully functioning person
A person living in harmony with her or his deepest feelings, impulses, and intuitions.

Self A continuously evolving conception of one's personal identity.

Self-image Total subjective perception of one's body and personality (another term for self-concept).

Symbolization
The process of bringing an experience into awareness.

Incongruence State that exists when there is a discrepancy between one's experiences and self-image or between one's self-image and ideal self.

Carl Rogers's Self Theory

Carl Rogers, another well-known humanist, based his theory on clinical experience with unhappy people. Nevertheless, he emphasized the human capacity for inner peace and happiness. The **fully functioning person,** he said, lives in harmony with her or his deepest feelings and impulses. Such people are open to their experiences and they trust their inner urges and intuitions (Rogers, 1961). Rogers believed that this attitude is most likely to occur when a person receives ample amounts of love and acceptance from others.

PERSONALITY STRUCTURE AND DYNAMICS   Rogers's theory emphasizes the **self,** a flexible and changing perception of personal identity. Much behaviour can be understood as an attempt to maintain consistency between our *self-image* and our actions. (Your **self-image** is a total subjective perception of your body and personality.) For example, people who think of themselves as kind tend to be considerate in most situations.

Let's say you know a person who thinks she is kind, but she really isn't. How does that fit Rogers's theory? According to Rogers, experiences that match the self-image are **symbolized** (admitted to awareness) and contribute to gradual changes in the self. Information or feelings inconsistent with your self-image are said to be incongruent. Thus, a person who thinks she is kind, but really isn't, is in a psychological state of **incongruence.** That is, there is a discrepancy between her experiences and her self-image. As another example, it would be incongruent to believe that you are a person who "never gets angry," if you spend much of each day seething inside.

Humanists consider self-image a central determinant of behaviour and personal adjustment.

USING PSYCHOLOGY   Steps toward Self-Actualization

There is no magic formula for leading a more creative life. Self-actualization is primarily a *process*, not a goal or an end point. As such, it requires hard work, patience, and commitment. Here are some ways to begin.

1. *Be willing to change.* Begin by asking yourself, "Am I living in a way that is deeply satisfying to me and that truly expresses me?" If not, be prepared to make changes in your life. Indeed, ask yourself this question often and accept the need for continual change.
2. *Take responsibility.* You can become an architect of self by acting as if you are personally responsible for every aspect of your life. Shouldering responsibility in this way helps end the habit of blaming others for your own shortcomings.
3. *Examine your motives.* Self-discovery involves an element of risk. If your behaviour is restricted by a desire for safety or security, it may be time to test some limits. Try to make each life decision a choice for growth, not a response to fear or anxiety.
4. *Experience honestly and directly.* Wishful thinking is another barrier to personal growth. Self-actualizers trust themselves enough to accept all kinds of information without distorting it to fit their fears and desires. Try to see yourself as others do. Be willing to admit, "I was wrong" or "I failed because I was irresponsible."

5. *Make use of positive experiences.* Maslow considered peak experiences temporary moments of self-actualization. Therefore, you might actively repeat activities that have caused feelings of awe, amazement, exaltation, renewal, reverence, humility, fulfillment, or joy.
6. *Be prepared to be different.* Maslow felt that everyone has a potential for "greatness," but most fear becoming what they might. As part of personal growth, be prepared to trust your own impulses and feelings; don't automatically judge yourself by the standards of others. Accept your uniqueness.
7. *Get involved.* With few exceptions, self-actualizers tend to have a mission or "calling" in life. For these people, "work" is not done just to fill deficiency needs, but to satisfy higher yearnings for truth, beauty, community, and meaning. Get personally involved and committed. Turn your attention to problems outside yourself.
8. *Assess your progress.* There is no final point at which one becomes self-actualized. It's important to gauge your progress frequently and to renew your efforts. If you feel bored at school, at a job, or in a relationship, consider it a challenge. Have you been taking responsibility for your own personal growth? Almost any activity can be used as a chance for self-enhancement if it is approached creatively.

Incongruent person
A person who has an inaccurate self-image or whose self-image differs greatly from the ideal self.
Ideal self An idealized image of oneself (the person one would like to be).

Experiences seriously incongruent with the self-image can be threatening. Because of this, we often distort or deny such experiences, which prevents the self from changing. In time, a gulf develops between the self-image and reality. As the self-image grows more inaccurate and unrealistic, the **incongruent person** becomes confused, vulnerable, dissatisfied, or seriously maladjusted (see ▶Figure 10.7). Interestingly, a study of college students confirmed that being authentic is vital for healthy functioning. Basically, to be happy, we need to feel that our behaviour accurately expresses who we are (Sheldon et al., 1997).

When your self-image is consistent with what you really think, feel, do, and experience, you are best able to actualize your potentials. Rogers also considered it essential to have congruence between the self-image and the **ideal self.** The ideal self is similar to Freud's ego ideal. It is an image of the person you would most like to be.

Incongruence

Ideal self

Self-image   True self

Congruence

Ideal self
Self-image
True self

▶**Figure 10.7**

Incongruence occurs when there is a mismatch between any of these three entities: the ideal self (the person you would like to be), your self-image (the person you think you are), and the true self (the person you actually are). Self-esteem suffers when there is a large difference between one's ideal self and self-image. Anxiety and defensiveness are common when the self-image does not match the true self.

Is it really incongruent not to live up to your ideal self? Rogers was aware that we never fully attain our ideals. Nevertheless, the larger the gap between the way you see yourself and the way you would like to be, the more tension and anxiety you will experience.

Rogers emphasized that to maximize our potentials, we must accept information about ourselves as honestly as possible. In accord with this, researchers have found that people with a close match between their self-image and ideal self tend to be socially poised, confident, and resourceful. Those with a poor match tend to be depressed, anxious, and insecure (Alfeld-Liro & Sigelman, 1998; Scott & O'Hara, 1993).

Humanistic View of Development

Why do mirrors, photographs, video cameras, and the reactions of others hold such fascination and threat for many people? Carl Rogers's theory suggests it is because they provide information about one's self. The development of a self-image depends greatly on information from the environment. It begins with a sorting of perceptions and feelings: my body, my toes, my nose, I want, I like, I am, and so on. Soon, it expands to include self-evaluation: I am a good person, I did something bad just now, and so forth.

How does development of the self contribute to later personality functioning? Rogers believed that positive and negative evaluations by others cause children to develop internal standards of evaluation called **conditions of worth.** In other words, we learn that some actions win our parents' love and approval whereas others are rejected. More important, parents may label some feelings as bad or wrong. For example, a child might be told that it is wrong to feel angry toward a brother or sister—even when anger is justified. Likewise, a little boy might be told that he must not cry or show fear, two very normal emotions.

Learning to evaluate some experiences or feelings as "good" and others as "bad" is directly related to a later capacity for self-esteem, positive self-evaluation, or **positive self-regard,** to use Rogers's term. To think of yourself as a good, lovable, worthwhile person, your behaviour and experiences must match your internal conditions of worth. The problem is that this can cause incongruence by leading to the denial of many true feelings and experiences.

To put it simply, Rogers blamed many adult emotional problems on attempts to live by the standards of others. He believed that congruence and self-actualization are encouraged by replacing conditions of worth with **organismic valuing** (a natural, undistorted, full-body reaction to an experience). Organismic valuing is a direct, gut-level response to life that avoids the filtering and distortion of incongruence. It involves trusting one's own feelings and perceptions. Organismic valuing is most likely to develop, Rogers felt, when children (or adults) receive **unconditional positive regard** (unshakable love and approval) from others. That is, when they are "prized" as worthwhile human beings, just for being themselves, without any conditions or strings attached. Although this may be a luxury few people enjoy, a recent study confirmed that we are more likely to move toward our ideal selves if we receive affirmation and support from a close partner (Drigotas et al., 1999).

Conditions of worth
Internal standards used to judge the value of one's thoughts, actions, feelings, or experiences.

Positive self-regard
Thinking of oneself as a good, lovable, worthwhile person.

Organismic valuing
A natural, undistorted, full-body reaction to an experience.

Unconditional positive regard Unshakable love and approval given without qualification.

Knowledge builder

HUMANISTIC THEORY

Relate

How do your views of human nature and free choice compare with those of the humanists?

Do you know anyone who seems to be making especially good use of his or her personal potentials? Does that person fit Maslow's profile of a self-actualizer?

How much difference do you think there is between your self-image, your ideal self, and your true self? Do you think Rogers is right about the effects of applying conditions of worth to your perceptions and feelings?

Learning Check

1. Humanists view human nature as basically good and they emphasize the effects of subjective learning and unconscious choice. T or F?

2. Maslow used the term _____ to describe the tendency of certain individuals to fully use their talents and potentials.

3. According to Rogers, a close match between the self-image and the ideal self creates a condition called incongruence. T or F?

continued

4. Rogers's theory considers acceptance of conditions of _____ a troublesome aspect of development of the self.

5. According to Maslow, a preoccupation with one's own thoughts, feelings, and needs is characteristic of self-actualizing individuals. T or F?

6. Maslow regarded _____ experiences as times of temporary self-actualization.

7. What role has your self-image played in your choice of a college major?

Answers:

1. F 2. self-actualization 3. F 4. worth 5. F 6. peak 7. Career decisions almost always involve, in part, picturing oneself occupying various occupational roles. Such "future selves" play a role in many of the major decisions we make (Markus & Nurius, 1986).

▶ Personality Theories—Overview and Comparison

Which personality theory is right? Each theory has added to our understanding by organizing observations of human behaviour. Theories can never be fully proved or disproved. We can only ask, Does the evidence tend to support this theory or disconfirm it? The best way to judge a theory is in terms of its usefulness. Does the theory adequately explain behaviour? Does it stimulate new research? Does it suggest how to treat psychological disorders? Each theory has fared differently in these areas.

In the final analysis, we need all four major perspectives to explain personality. Each provides a sort of lens through which human behaviour can be viewed. In many instances, a balanced picture emerges only when each theory is considered. Table 10.3 provides a final overview of the four principal approaches to personality.

Table 10.3
Comparison of Four Views of Personality

	TRAIT THEORIES	PSYCHOANALYTIC THEORY	BEHAVIOURISTIC THEORY	HUMANISTIC THEORY
View of human nature	neutral	negative	neutral	positive
Is behaviour free or determined?	determined	determined	determined	free choice
Principle motives	depends on one's traits	sex and aggression	drives of all kinds and the environment	self-actualization
Personality structure	traits	id, ego, superego	habits	self
Role of unconscious	minimized	maximized	practically nonexistent	minimized
Conception of conscience	traits of honesty, etc.	superego	self-reinforcement punishment history	ideal self, valuing process
Developmental emphasis	combined effects of heredity and environment	psychosexual stages	critical learning situations identification and imitation	development of self-image
Barriers to personal growth	unhealthy traits	unconscious conflicts, fixations	maladaptive habits; unhealthy environment	conditions of worth; incongruence

▶ Personality Assessment—Psychological Yardsticks

Survey Question:
■ How do psychologists measure personality?

Studies of personality have greatly improved the quality of personality measurement in industry, education, and clinical work.

How is personality "measured"? Psychologists use interviews, observation, questionnaires, and projective tests to assess personality. Each method has strengths and limitations. For this reason, they are often used in combination.

What is your initial impression of the person wearing the sleeveless blouse? If you think that she looks friendly, attractive, or neat, your subsequent perceptions might be altered by a positive first impression. Interviewers are often influenced by the halo effect (see text).

Formal personality measures are refinements of more casual ways of judging a person. At one time or another, you have probably "sized up" a potential date, friend, or roommate by engaging in conversation (interview). Perhaps you have asked a friend, "When I am delayed I get angry. Do you?" (questionnaire). Maybe you watch your professors when they are angry or embarrassed to learn what they are "really" like (observation). Or possibly you have noticed that when you say, "I think people feel . . . ," you may be expressing your own feelings (projection). Let's see how psychologists apply each of these methods to probe personality.

The Interview

In an **interview,** psychologists use questioning to learn about a person's life history, personality traits, or current mental state. In an **unstructured interview,** conversation is informal and topics are taken up freely as they arise. In a **structured interview,** the interviewer obtains information by asking a planned series of questions.

How are interviews used? Interviews are used to identify personality disturbances; to select people for jobs, colleges, or special programs; and to study the dynamics of personality. Interviews also provide information for counselling or therapy. For instance, a counsellor might ask a depressed person, "Have you ever contemplated suicide? What were the circumstances?" The counsellor might then follow by asking, "How did you feel about it?" or "How is what you are now feeling different from what you felt then?"

In addition to providing information, interviews make it possible to observe a person's tone of voice, hand gestures, posture, and facial expressions. Such "body language" cues are important because they may radically alter the message sent, as when a person claims to be "completely calm" but trembles uncontrollably.

LIMITATIONS Interviews give rapid insight into personality, but they have certain limitations. For one thing, interviewers can be swayed by preconceptions. A person identified as a "housewife," "college student," "high-school athlete," "punk," or "ski bum" may be misjudged because of an interviewer's bias toward a particular lifestyle. Second, an interviewer's own personality or even gender may influence a client's behaviour. When this occurs, it can accentuate or distort the person's apparent traits (Pollner, 1998). A third problem is that people sometimes try to deceive interviewers. For example, a person accused of a crime might pretend to be mentally disabled to avoid punishment.

A fourth problem is the **halo effect,** which is the tendency to generalize a favourable or unfavourable first impression to unrelated details of personality. A person who is likable or physically attractive may be rated more mature, intelligent, or adjusted than she or he actually is. The halo effect is something to keep in mind when interviewing for employment. First impressions do make a difference (Lance, LaPointe, & Stewart, 1994).

Even with their limitations, interviews are a respected method of personality assessment. In many cases, interviews are an essential step to additional personality testing and an essential prelude to beginning counselling or therapy.

Direct Observation and Rating Scales

Are you fascinated by airports, bus depots, parks, taverns, subway stations, or other public places? Many people relish a chance to observe the actions of others. When used as an assessment procedure, **direct observation** (looking at behaviour) is a simple extension of this natural interest in "people watching." For instance, a psychologist might arrange to observe a disturbed child as she plays with other children. Is the child withdrawn? Does she become hostile or aggressive without warning? By careful observation, the psychologist will identify personality traits and clarify the nature of the child's problems.

Wouldn't observation be subject to the same problems of misperception as an interview? Yes. Misperceptions can be a problem. A solution is to use **rating scales** (see ▶ Figure 10.8) to evaluate a person. A rating scale is a list of personality traits or specific aspects of behav-

Interview (personality) A face-to-face meeting held for the purpose of gaining information about an individual's personal history, personality traits, current psychological state, and so forth.

Unstructured interview An interview in which conversation is informal and topics are taken up freely as they arise.

Structured interview An interview that follows a prearranged plan, usually a series of planned questions.

Halo effect The tendency to generalize a favourable or unfavourable first impression to unrelated details of personality.

Direct observation Assessing behaviour through direct surveillance.

Rating scale A list of personality traits or aspects of behaviour on which a person is rated.

► **Figure 10.8**

Sample rating scale items. To understand how the scale works, imagine someone you know well. Where would you place check marks on each of the scales to rate that person's characteristics?

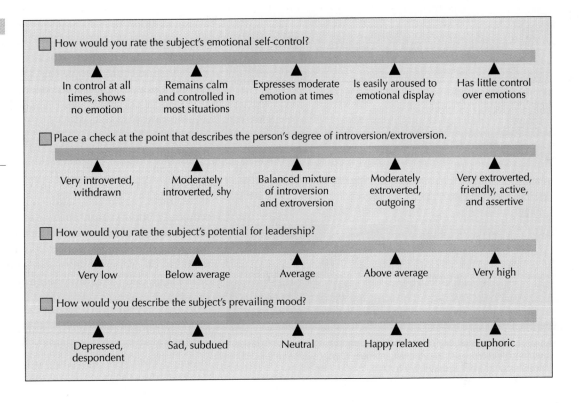

☐ How would you rate the subject's emotional self-control?

| In control at all times, shows no emotion | Remains calm and controlled in most situations | Expresses moderate emotion at times | Is easily aroused to emotional display | Has little control over emotions |

☐ Place a check at the point that describes the person's degree of introversion/extroversion.

| Very introverted, withdrawn | Moderately introverted, shy | Balanced mixture of introversion and extroversion | Moderately extroverted, outgoing | Very extroverted, friendly, active, and assertive |

☐ How would you rate the subject's potential for leadership?

| Very low | Below average | Average | Above average | Very high |

☐ How would you describe the subject's prevailing mood?

| Depressed, despondent | Sad, subdued | Neutral | Happy relaxed | Euphoric |

Behavioural assessment
Recording the frequency of various behaviours.
Situational test Simulating real-life conditions so that a person's reactions may be directly observed.

iour. Rating scales reduce the risk that some traits will be overlooked while others are exaggerated (Merenda, 1996). Perhaps they should be a standard procedure for choosing a roommate, spouse, or lover!

An alternative is to do a **behavioural assessment** by recording the frequency of specific behaviours. In this case, observers record actions, not what traits they think a person has. For example, a psychologist working with hospitalized mentally ill patients might record the frequency of a patient's aggression, self-care, speech, and unusual behaviours. Behavioural assessments are not strictly limited to visible actions. They can also be helpful in probing thought processes. In one study, for example, students high in math anxiety were asked to think aloud while doing math problems. Later, their thoughts were analyzed to pinpoint the cause of their math fears (Blackwell et al., 1985).

SITUATIONAL TESTING In **situational testing,** real-life conditions are simulated so that a person's spontaneous reactions can be observed. Such tests assume that the best way to learn how people react is to put them in realistic situations and watch what happens. Situational tests expose people to frustration, temptation, pressure, boredom, or other conditions capable of revealing personality characteristics (Weekley & Jones, 1997). Some of the recently popular "reality TV" programs, such as *Survivor,* bear some similarity to situational tests—which may account for their ability to attract millions of viewers.

How are situational tests done? An interesting example of situational testing is the judgmental firearms training provided by many police departments. At times, police officers must make split-second decisions about using their weapons. A mistake could be fatal. In a typical shoot–don't shoot test, actors play the part of armed criminals. As various high-risk scenes are acted out live or on videotape, officers must decide to shoot or hold fire. A newspaper reporter who once took the test (and failed it) gives this account (Gersh, 1982):

> I judged wrong. I was killed by a man in a closet, a man with a hostage, a woman interrupted when kissing her lover, and a man I thought was cleaning a shotgun. . . . I shot a drunk who reached for a comb, and a teenager who pulled out a black water pistol. Looked real to me.

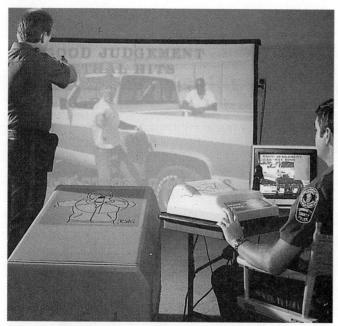

A police officer undergoes judgmental firearms training. Variations on this situational test are used by a growing number of police departments. All officers must score a passing grade.

In-basket test A testing procedure that simulates the individual decision-making challenges that executives face.

Leaderless group discussion A test of leadership that simulates group decision making and problem solving.

Personality questionnaire A paper-and-pencil test consisting of questions that reveal aspects of personality.

Objective test A test that gives the same score when different people correct it.

Reliability The ability of a test to yield nearly the same score each time it is given to the same person.

Validity The ability of a test to measure what it purports to measure.

Minnesota Multiphasic Personality Inventory-2 (MMPI-2) One of the best-known and most widely used objective personality questionnaires.

In addition to the training it provides, situational testing uncovers police cadets who lack the good judgment needed to carry a gun out on the street.

When selecting people for employment, situational tests present difficult but realistic work situations to applicants (Borman et al., 1997). For example, in one exercise applicants are given an **in-basket test** that simulates the decision-making challenges executives face. The test consists of a basket full of memos, requests, and typical business problems. Each applicant is asked to quickly read all of the materials and take appropriate action. In another, more stressful test, applicants take part in a **leaderless group discussion** that requires group decision making and problem solving. While the group grapples with a realistic business problem, "clerks" bring in price changes, notices about delayed supplies, and so forth. By observing applicants, it is possible to evaluate leadership skills and to see how job candidates cope with stress.

Personality Questionnaires

Most **personality questionnaires** are paper-and-pencil tests that reveal personality characteristics. Questionnaires are more objective than interviews or observation. (An **objective test** gives the same score when different people correct it.) Questions, administration, and scoring are all standardized so that scores are unaffected by the opinions or prejudices of the examiner. However, this is not enough to ensure a test's accuracy. A good test must also be reliable and valid. A test is **reliable** if it yields close to the same score each time it is given to the same person. A test has **validity** if it measures what it claims to measure. Unfortunately, many personality tests you will encounter, such as those in magazines or on the Internet, have little or no validity.

Many personality tests have been devised, including the *Jackson Personality Inventory* (developed by University of Western Ontario psychologist Douglas Jackson), the *Guilford-Zimmerman Temperament Survey*, the *California Psychological Inventory*, the *Allport-Vernon Study of Values*, the 16 PF, and many more. One of the best-known and most widely used objective tests is the **Minnesota Multiphasic Personality Inventory-2 (MMPI-2)**. The MMPI-2 is composed of 567 items to which a test taker must respond "true" or "false." Items include statements such as the following:

- Everything tastes the same.
- There is something wrong with my mind.
- I am made nervous by certain animals.
- Whenever possible I avoid being in a crowd.
- I have never indulged in any unusual sex practices.
- Someone has been trying to poison me.
- I daydream very little.★

How can these items show anything about personality? For instance, what if a person has a cold so that "everything tastes the same"? For an answer (and a little bit of fun), read the following items. Answer "Yes," "No," or "Don't bother me, I can't cope!"

- I would enjoy the work of a chicken flicker.
- My eyes are always cold.
- Frantic screaming makes me nervous.
- I believe I smell as good as most people.
- I use shoe polish to excess.

★ Excerpt from *Minnesota Multiphasic Inventory 2* (MMPI-2) reprinted by permission of the University of Minnesota Press. Copyright © 1989 by the University of Minnesota Press.

MMPI-2 profile A graphic representation of an individual's scores on each of the primary scales of the MMPI-2.

Validity scales Scales that tell whether test scores should be invalidated for lying, inconsistency, or "faking good."

- The sight of blood no longer excites me.
- As an infant I had very few hobbies.
- Dirty stories make me think about sex.
- I stay in the bathtub until I look like a raisin.
- I salivate at the sight of mittens.
- I never finish what I

These items were written by humorist Art Buchwald (1965) and psychologist Carol Sommer to satirize personality questionnaires. Such questions may seem ridiculous, but they are not very different from the real thing. How, then, do the items on tests such as the MMPI-2 reveal anything about personality? The answer is that a single item tells little about personality. For example, a person who agrees that "Everything tastes the same" might simply have a cold. It is only through patterns of response that personality dimensions are revealed.

Items on the MMPI-2 were selected for their ability to correctly identify people with particular psychological problems. For instance, if a series of items is consistently answered in a particular way by depressed persons, it is assumed that others who answer the same way are also prone to depression. As silly as the gag items might seem, it is possible that some could actually work in a legitimate test. But before an item could be part of a test, it would have to correlate highly with some trait or dimension of personality.

The MMPI-2 measures 10 major aspects of personality (listed in Table 10.4). After the MMPI-2 is scored, results are charted graphically as an **MMPI-2 profile** (see ▶Figure 10.9). By comparing a person's profile to scores produced by normal adults, a psychologist can identify various personality disorders. Additional scales identify substance abuse, eating disorders, Type A (heart-attack prone) behaviour, repression, anger, cynicism, low self-esteem, family problems, inability to function in a job, and other problems (Hathaway & McKinley, 1989).

How accurate is the MMPI-2? Personality questionnaires are accurate only if people tell the truth about themselves. Because of this, the MMPI-2 has additional **validity scales** that reveal whether a person's scores should be discarded. The validity scales detect attempts by test takers to "fake good" (make themselves look good) or "fake bad" (make it look like they have problems). Other scales uncover defensiveness or tendencies to exaggerate

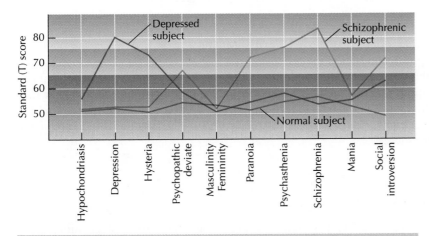

▶ **Figure 10.9**

An MMPI-2 profile showing hypothetical scores indicating normality, depression, and psychosis. High scores begin at 66 and very high scores at 76. An unusually low score (40 and below) may also reveal personality characteristics or problems.

Table 10.4
MMPI-2 Basic Clinical Subscales

1. **Hypochondriasis** (HI-po-kon-DRY-uh-sis). Exaggerated concern about one's physical health.
2. **Depression.** Feelings of worthlessness, hopelessness, and pessimism.
3. **Hysteria.** The presence of physical complaints for which no physical basis can be established.
4. **Psychopathic deviate.** Emotional shallowness in relationships and a disregard for social and moral standards.
5. **Masculinity/femininity.** One's degree of traditional "masculine" aggressiveness or "feminine" sensitivity.
6. **Paranoia.** Extreme suspiciousness and feelings of persecution.
7. **Psychasthenia** (sike-as-THEE-nee-ah). The presence of obsessive worries, irrational fears (phobias), and compulsive (ritualistic) actions.
8. **Schizophrenia.** Emotional withdrawal and unusual or bizarre thinking and actions.
9. **Mania.** Emotional excitability, manic moods or behaviour, and excessive activity.
10. **Social introversion.** One's tendency to be socially withdrawn.

FOCUS ON RESEARCH   Honesty Tests—Do They Tell the Truth?

Each year, millions of anxious job seekers take paper-and-pencil honesty tests given by companies that hope to avoid hiring dishonest workers. **Honesty tests** (also known as integrity tests) assume that poor attitudes toward dishonest acts predispose a person to dishonest behaviour. Examples include attitudes toward taking office supplies home or leaving work early. Most of the tests also ask people how honest they think the average person is and how honest they are in comparison. Surprisingly, many job applicants willingly rate their own honesty as below average (Neuman & Baydoun, 1998). (You have to admire them for being honest about it!) Honesty tests also ask about prior brushes with the law, past acts of theft or deceit, and attitudes toward alcohol and drug use.

Is honesty testing valid? This question is still very much in dispute. Some psychologists believe that the best honesty tests are sufficiently valid to be used for making

hiring decisions (Ones, Viswesvaran, & Schmidt, 1993). Others, however, remain unconvinced. Most studies have failed to demonstrate that honesty tests can accurately predict if a person will be a poor risk on the job (Saxe, 1991). Psychologists are also concerned because honesty tests are often administered by untrained people. Yet another cause for concern is the fact that 96 percent of test takers who fail are *falsely labelled* as dishonest (Camara & Schneider, 1994). In North America alone, that means well over a million workers a year are wrongly accused of being dishonest (Rieke & Guastello, 1995).

In some jurisdictions, the use of honesty tests as the sole basis for deciding whether to hire a person has been banned. Yet, it's easy to understand why employers want to do whatever they can to reduce theft and dishonesty in the workplace. The pressures to use honesty tests are intense. No doubt, the debate about honesty testing will continue. Honest.

Honesty test A paper-and-pencil test designed to detect attitudes, beliefs, and behaviour patterns that predispose a person to dishonest behaviour.

shortcomings and troubles. When taking the MMPI-2, it is best to answer honestly, without trying to second-guess the test.

A clinical psychologist trying to decide if a person has emotional problems would be wise to take more than the MMPI-2 into account. Test scores are informative, but they can incorrectly label some people (Cronbach, 1990). ("Honesty Tests" discusses a related problem.) Fortunately, clinical judgments usually rely on information from interviews, tests, and other sources.

▶ Projective Tests of Personality— Inkblots and Hidden Plots

Projective tests take a different approach to personality. Interviews, observation, rating scales, and inventories try to directly identify overt, observable traits (Vane & Guarnaccia, 1989). By contrast, projective tests seek to uncover deeply hidden or unconscious wishes, thoughts, and needs.

As a child you may have delighted in finding faces and objects in cloud formations. Or perhaps you have learned something about your friends' personalities from their reactions to movies or paintings. If so, you will have some insight into the rationale for projective tests. In a **projective test,** a person is asked to describe ambiguous stimuli or make up stories about them. Describing an unambiguous stimulus (a picture of an automobile, for example) tells little about your personality. But when you are faced with an unstructured stimulus, you must organize what you see in terms of your own life experiences. Everyone sees something different in a projective test, and what is perceived is believed to reveal the inner workings of personality.

Projective tests have no right or wrong answers, making them difficult to fake (Vane & Guarnaccia, 1989). Moreover, projective tests can be a rich source of information, since responses are not restricted to simple true/false or yes/no answers.

Projective tests Psychological tests making use of ambiguous or unstructured stimuli.

Rorschach Technique A projective test composed of 10 standardized inkblots.

The Rorschach Inkblot Test

The inkblot test, or **Rorschach Technique** (ROR-shock), is one of the oldest and most widely used projective tests. Developed by Swiss psychiatrist Hermann Rorschach in the

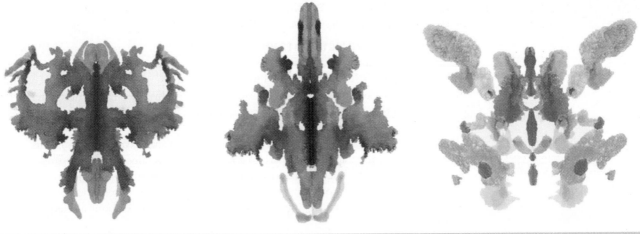

▶**Figure 10.10**

Inkblots similar to those used on the Rorschach. What do you see?

Thematic Apperception Test (TAT) A projective test consisting of 20 different scenes and life situations about which respondents make up stories.

1920s, it consists of 10 standardized inkblots. These vary in colour, shading, form, and complexity.

How does the test work? First, a person is shown each blot and asked to describe what she or he sees in it (see ▶Figure 10.10). Later the psychologist may return to a blot, asking the person to identify specific sections of it, to expand previous descriptions, or to give new impressions about what it contains. Obvious differences in content—such as "blood dripping from a dagger" versus "flowers blooming in a field"—are important for identifying personal conflicts and fantasies. But surprisingly, content is less important than what parts of the inkblot are used to organize images. These factors allow psychologists to detect emotional disturbances by observing how a person perceives the world. The Rorschach is especially good at detecting psychosis, one of the most serious of all mental disorders (Ganellen, 1996).

The Thematic Apperception Test

Another popular projective test is the **Thematic Apperception Test (TAT)** developed by personality theorist Henry Murray (1893–1988).

How does the TAT differ from the Rorschach? The TAT consists of 20 sketches depicting various scenes and life situations (see ▶Figure 10.11). During testing, a person is shown each sketch and asked to make up a story about the people in it. Later, the person looks at each sketch a second or a third time and elaborates on previous stories or creates new stories.

To score the TAT, psychologists analyze the content of the stories. Interpretations focus on how people feel, how they interact, what events led up to the incidents depicted in the sketch, and how the story will end. For example, TAT stories told by bereaved college students typically include themes of death, grief, and coping with loss (Balk et al., 1998).

A psychologist might also count the number of times the central figure in a TAT story is angry, overlooked, apathetic, jealous, or threatened. Here is a story written by a student to describe Figure 10.11:

> The girl has been seeing this guy her mother doesn't like. The mother is telling her that she better not see him again. The mother says, "He's just like your father." The mother and father are divorced. The mother is smiling because she thinks she is right. But she doesn't really know what the girl wants. The girl is going to see the guy again, anyway.

▶**Figure 10.11**

This is a picture like those used for the Thematic Apperception Test. If you wish to simulate the test, tell a story that explains what led up to the pictured situation, what is happening now, and how the action will end.

As this example implies, the TAT is especially good at revealing feelings about a person's social relationships (Alvarado, 1994).

LIMITATIONS OF PROJECTIVE TESTING   Although projective tests have been popular, their validity is considered lowest among tests of personality (Lilienfeld, 1999). Objectivity and reliability (consistency) are also low for different users of the TAT and Rorschach. Note that after a person interprets an ambiguous stimulus, the scorer must interpret the person's (sometimes) ambiguous responses. In a sense, the interpretation of a projective test may be a projective test for the scorer!

Despite their drawbacks, projective tests still have value (Weiner, 1997). This is especially true when they are used as part of a **test battery** (collection of assessment devices and interviews). In the hands of a skilled clinician, projective tests can detect major conflicts and aid in setting goals for therapy (Weiner, 1996). Moreover, since projective tests are unstructured, they can be a good way to get clients to talk about anxiety-provoking topics.

Test battery A group of tests and interviews given to the same individual.

▶ Sudden Murderers—A Research Example

Personality assessments provide us with clues to some of the most perplexing human events. Consider Fred Cowan, a model student in school and described by those who knew him as quiet, gentle, and a man who loved children. Despite his size (he was quite a large man), Fred was described by a co-worker as "someone you could easily push around."

Fred Cowan represents a puzzling phenomenon: We occasionally read in the news about sudden murderers—gentle, quiet, shy, good-natured people who explode without warning into violence (Lee, Zimbardo, & Bertholf, 1977). Two weeks after he was suspended from his job, Fred returned to work determined to get even with his supervisor. Unable to find the man, he killed four co-workers and a policeman before taking his own life.

Isn't such behaviour contrary to the idea of personality traits? It might seem that sudden murderers are newsworthy simply because they are unlikely candidates for violence. On the contrary, research conducted by Melvin Lee, Philip Zimbardo, and Minerva Bertholf suggests that sudden murderers explode into violence because they are shy, restrained, and inexpressive, not in spite of it. These researchers studied prisoners at a California prison. Ten were inmates whose homicide was an unexpected first offence. Nine were criminals with a record of habitual violence prior to murder. Sixteen were inmates convicted of non-violent crimes.

Did the inmates differ in personality makeup? Each of the inmates took a battery of tests, including the MMPI, a measure of shyness, and an adjective checklist. Personal interviews were also done with each inmate. As expected, the sudden murderers were passive, shy, and overcontrolled (restrained) individuals. The habitually violent inmates were "masculine" (aggressive), undercontrolled (impulsive), and less likely to view themselves as shy than the average person (Lee, Zimbardo, & Bertholf, 1977).

Psychologists have learned that quiet, overcontrolled individuals are likely to be especially violent if they ever lose control. Their attacks are usually triggered by a minor irritation or frustration, but the attack reflects years of unexpressed feelings of anger and belittlement. When sudden murderers finally release the strict controls they have maintained on their behaviour, a furious and frenzied attack ensues. Usually it is totally out of proportion to the offence against them, and many have amnesia concerning their violent actions.

In comparison, the previously violent murderers showed very different reactions. Although they killed, their violence was moderate—usually only enough to do the necessary damage. Typically, they felt they had been cheated or betrayed and that they were doing what was necessary to remedy the situation or maintain their manhood (Lee, Zimbardo, & Bertholf, 1977).

A LOOK AHEAD   The preceding example illustrates how some of the concepts and techniques discussed in this chapter can be applied to further our understanding of human personality. The Psychology in Action section that follows should add balance to your view of personality. Don't be shy. Read on!

Knowledge builder

PERSONALITY ASSESSMENT

Relate

How do you assess personality? Do you informally make use of any of the methods described in this chapter?

You are a candidate for a desirable job. Your personality is going to be assessed by a psychologist. What method (or methods) would you prefer that she or he use? Why?

Learning Check

1. The halo effect is the tendency of an interviewer to influence what is said by the interviewee. T or F?
2. Which of the following is considered the most objective measure of personality?
   a. rating scales *b.* personality questionnaires *c.* projective tests *d.* TAT
3. Situational testing allows direct _____ of personality characteristics.
4. A psychotic person would probably score highest on which MMPI-2 scale?
   a. depression *b.* hysteria *c.* schizophrenia *d.* mania

5. The use of ambiguous stimuli is most characteristic of
   a. interviews *b.* projective tests *c.* personality inventories
   d. direct observation
6. The content of one's responses to the MMPI-2 is considered an indication of unconscious wishes, thoughts, and needs. T or F?
7. Doing a behavioural assessment requires direct observation of the person's actions or a direct report of the person's thoughts. T or F?
8. A surprising finding is that sudden murderers are usually under-controlled, very masculine, and more impulsive than average. T or F?
9. A test is considered valid if it consistently yields the same score when the same person takes it on different occasions. T or F?

Critical Thinking

10. Can you think of one more reason why personality traits may not be accurately revealed by interviews?
11. Projective testing would be of greatest interest to which type of personality theorist?

Answers:

1. F 2. *b* 3. observation 4. *c* 5. *b* 6. F 7. T 8. F 9. F 10. Because of trait-situation interactions, a person may not behave in a normal fashion while being evaluated in an interview. 11. Psychodynamic; because projective testing is designed to uncover unconscious thoughts, feelings, and conflicts.

BARRIERS AND
BRIDGES—
UNDERSTANDING SHYNESS

Survey Question:
■ What causes shyness? What can be done about it?

Shyness A tendency to avoid others plus uneasiness and strain when socializing.

Social skills Proficiency at interacting with others.

Social anxiety A feeling of apprehension in the presence of others.

Evaluation fears Fears of being inadequate, embarrassed, ridiculed, or rejected.

Self-defeating bias A distortion of thinking that impairs behaviour.

Private self-consciousness Preoccupation with inner feelings, thoughts, and fantasies.

Public self-consciousness Intense awareness of oneself as a social object.

As a personality trait, **shyness** refers to a tendency to avoid others, as well as feelings of social inhibition (uneasiness and strain when socializing) (Buss, 1980). Shy persons fail to make eye contact, retreat when spoken to, speak too quietly, and display little interest or animation in conversations. Do you:

- Find it hard to talk to strangers?
- Lack confidence with people?
- Feel uncomfortable in social situations?
- Feel nervous with people who are not close friends?

If so, you may be part of the 50 percent of college students who consider themselves shy (Carducci & Stein, 1988). Mild shyness may be no more than a nuisance. However, extreme shyness is often associated with depression, loneliness, fearfulness, social anxiety, inhibition, and low self-esteem (Henderson, 1997; Schmidt & Fox, 1995).

ELEMENTS OF SHYNESS *What causes shyness?* To begin with, shy persons often lack **social skills** (proficiency at interacting with others). Many simply have not learned how to meet people or how to start a conversation and keep it going. **Social anxiety** (a feeling of apprehension in the presence of others) is also a factor in shyness. Almost everyone feels nervous in some social situations (such as meeting an attractive stranger). Typically, this is a reaction to **evaluation fears** (fears of being inadequate, embarrassed, ridiculed, or rejected). Although fears of rejection are common, they are much more frequent or intense for shy persons (Jackson, Towson, & Narduzzi, 1997). A third problem for shy persons is a **self-defeating bias** (distortion) in their thinking. Specifically, shy persons almost always blame themselves when a social encounter doesn't go well.

SITUATIONAL CAUSES OF SHYNESS Shyness is most often triggered by *novel* or *unfamiliar* social situations. A person who does fine with family or close friends may become shy and awkward when meeting a stranger. Shyness is also magnified by formality, by meeting someone of higher status, by being noticeably different from others, or by being the focus of attention (as in giving a speech) (Buss, 1980).

Don't most people become cautious and inhibited in such circumstances? Yes. That's why we need to see how the personalities of shy and non-shy persons differ.

DYNAMICS OF THE SHY PERSONALITY There is a tendency to think that shy persons are wrapped up in their own feelings and thoughts. But surprisingly, researchers Jonathan Cheek and Arnold Buss (1979) found no connection between shyness and **private self-consciousness** (attention to inner feelings, thoughts, and fantasies). Instead, they discovered that shyness is linked to **public self-consciousness** (acute awareness of oneself as a social object).

Persons who rate high in public self-consciousness are intensely concerned about what others think of them (Buss, 1980). They worry about saying the wrong thing or appearing foolish. In public, they may feel "naked" or as if others can "see through them." Such feelings trigger anxiety or outright fear during social encounters, leading to awkwardness and inhibition (Buss, 1986). The shy person's anxiety, in turn, often causes her or him to misperceive others in social situations (Schroeder, 1995).

As mentioned, almost everyone feels anxious in at least some social situations. But there is a key difference in the way shy and non-shy persons label this anxiety. Shy persons tend to consider their social anxiety a lasting personality trait. Shyness, in other words, becomes part of their self-concept. In contrast, non-shy persons believe that external situations cause their occasional feelings of shyness. When non-shy persons feel anxiety or "stage fright," they assume that almost anyone would feel as they do under the same circumstances (Zimbardo, Pilkonis, & Norwood, 1978).

Labelling is important because it affects *self-esteem*. In general, non-shy persons tend to have higher self-esteem than shy persons. This is because non-shy persons give themselves credit for their social successes and they recognize that failures are often due to cir-

cumstances. In contrast, shy people blame themselves for social failures and never give themselves credit for successes (Buss, 1980; Girodo, 1978).

SHY BELIEFS *What can be done to reduce shyness?* While directing a shyness clinic, psychologist Michel Girodo (1978) observed that shyness is often maintained by unrealistic or self-defeating beliefs. Here's a sample of such beliefs.

1. *If you wait around long enough at a social gathering, something will happen.*
   Comment: This is really a cover-up for fear of starting a conversation. For two people to meet, at least one has to make an effort, and it might as well be you.
2. *Other people who are popular are just lucky when it comes to being invited to social events or asked out.*
   Comment: Except for times when a person is formally introduced to someone new, this is false. People who are more active socially typically make an effort to meet and spend time with others. They join clubs, invite others to do things, strike up conversations, and generally leave little to luck.
3. *The odds of meeting someone interested in socializing are always the same, no matter where I am.*
   Comment: This is another excuse for inaction. It pays to seek out situations that have a higher probability of leading to social contact, such as clubs, teams, and school events.
4. *If someone doesn't seem to like you right away, he or she really doesn't like you and never will.*
   Comment: This belief leads to much needless shyness. Even when a person doesn't show immediate interest, it doesn't mean the person dislikes you. Liking takes time and opportunity to develop.

Unproductive beliefs like the preceding can be replaced with statements such as the following.

1. I've got to be active in social situations.
2. I can't wait until I'm completely relaxed or comfortable before taking a social risk.
3. I don't need to pretend to be someone I'm not; it just makes me more anxious.
4. I may think other people are harshly evaluating me, but actually I'm being too hard on myself.
5. I can set reasonable goals for expanding my social experience and skills.
6. Even people who are very socially skillful are never successful 100 percent of the time. I shouldn't get so upset when an encounter goes badly. (Adapted from the work of University of Ottawa psychologist Michel Girodo, 1978.)

SOCIAL SKILLS Learning social skills takes practice. There is nothing "innate" about knowing how to meet people or start a conversation. Social skills can be directly practised in a variety of ways. It can be helpful, for instance, to get a tape recorder and listen to several of your conversations. You may be surprised by the way you pause, interrupt, miss cues, or seem disinterested. Similarly, it can be useful to look at yourself in a mirror and exaggerate facial expressions of surprise, interest, dislike, pleasure, and so forth. By such methods, most people can learn to put more animation and skill into their self-presentation. (For a discussion of related skills, see the section on self-assertion in Chapter 14.)

CONVERSATION One of the simplest ways to make better conversation is by learning to ask questions. A good series of questions shifts attention to the other person and shows you are interested. Nothing fancy is needed. You can do fine with questions such as, "Where do you (work, study, live)? Do you like (dancing, travel, music)? How long have you (been at this school, worked here, lived here)?" After you've broken the ice, the best questions are often those that are open ended (they can't be answered yes or no):

- "What parts of the country have you seen?" (as opposed to: "Have you ever been to Banff National Park?")
- "What's it like living on the west side?" (as opposed to: "Do you like living on the west side?")
- "What kinds of food do you like?" (as opposed to: "Do you like Chinese cooking?")

It's easy to see why open-ended questions are helpful. In replying to open-ended questions, people often give "free information" about themselves. This extra information can be used to ask other questions or to lead into other topics of conversation.

This brief sampling of ideas is no substitute for actual practice. Overcoming shyness requires a real effort to learn new skills and test old beliefs and attitudes. It may even require the help of a counsellor or therapist. At the very least, a shy person must be willing to take social risks. Breaking down the barriers of shyness will always include some awkward or unsuccessful encounters. Nevertheless, the rewards are powerful: human companionship and personal freedom.

Knowledge builder

SHYNESS AND SOCIAL SKILLS

Relate

If you are shy, see if you can summarize how social skills, social anxiety, evaluation fears, self-defeating thoughts, and public self-consciousness contribute to your social inhibition. If you're not shy, imagine how you would explain these concepts to a shy friend.

Learning Check

1. Social anxiety and evaluation fears are seen almost exclusively in shy individuals; the non-shy rarely have such experiences. T or F?

2. Unfamiliar people and situations most often trigger shyness. T or F?
3. Public self-consciousness plus a tendency to label oneself as shy are major characteristics of the shy personality. T or F?
4. Changing personal beliefs and practising social skills can be helpful in overcoming shyness. T or F?

Critical Thinking

5. Shyness is a trait of Vonda's personality. Like most shy people, Vonda is most likely to feel shy in unfamiliar social settings. Vonda's shy behaviour demonstrates that the expression of traits is governed by what concept?

Answers:

1. F 2. T 3. T 4. T 5. Trait-situation interactions (again).

Psychologist's Journal

EPILOGUE

At the beginning of this chapter you met Genevieve, an interesting personality, to say the least. Genevieve is one of those people who seem to have lived many lives in the time that most of us manage only one. For example, Genevieve and some friends climbed Mount Robson in British Columbia and on another occasion worked with indigenous groups in South America in an effort to preserve the rain forests. At the moment, Genevieve is helping victims of violence at a women's shelter and serving as an activist for animal rights. Every summer, she moves to the eastern townships in Quebec and helps in the operation of a cooperative farm.

Like Genevieve, you may have pondered many possible personal identities. Psychologists Hazel Markus and Paula Nurius (1986) believe that each of us harbours images of various possible selves (persons one could become). These selves include the person we would most like to be (the ideal self), as well as other selves we could become or are afraid of becoming.

Possible selves translate our hopes, fears, fantasies, and goals into specific images of who we could be. Thus, a beginning law student might picture herself as a successful lawyer; an enterprising business student might imagine himself as a dot-com entrepreneur; and a person on a diet might imagine both slim and grossly obese possible selves. Such images tend to direct our future behaviour.

Of course, almost everyone over age 30 has probably felt the anguish of realizing that some cherished possible selves will never be realized. Nevertheless, there is value in asking yourself not just "Who am I?" but also "Who would I like to become?" As you do, remember Maslow's advice that everyone has a potential for "greatness," but most fear becoming what they might.

CHAPTER IN REVIEW

Major Points

▶ Each of us displays consistent behaviour patterns that define our own personalities and allow us to predict how other people will act.

▶ Personality can be understood by identifying traits, by probing mental conflicts and dynamics, by noting the effects of prior learning and situations, and by knowing how people perceive themselves.

▶ Psychologists use interviews, direct observation, questionnaires, and projective tests to measure and assess personality.

▶ Shyness is related to public self-consciousness and other psychological factors that can be altered, which makes it possible for some people to overcome shyness.

Summary

How Do Psychologists Use the Term *Personality*?

• Personality is made up of one's unique and enduring behaviour patterns.

• Character is personality evaluated, or the possession of desirable qualities.

• Temperament refers to the hereditary and physiological aspects of one's emotional nature.

What Core Concepts Make Up the Psychology of Personality?

• Personality traits are lasting personal qualities that are inferred from behaviour.

• Personality types group people into categories on the basis of shared traits.

• Behaviour is influenced by self-concept, which is a perception of one's own personality traits.

• A positive self-evaluation leads to high self-esteem. Low self-esteem is associated with stress, unhappiness, and depression.

• Personality theories combine interrelated assumptions, ideas, and principles to explain personality.

Are Some Personality Traits More Basic or Important than Others?

- Trait theories identify qualities that are most lasting or characteristic of a person.
- Allport made useful distinctions between common traits and individual traits and between cardinal, central, and secondary traits.
- Cattell's theory attributes visible surface traits to the existence of 16 underlying source traits.
- Source traits are measured by the *Sixteen Personality Factor Questionnaire* (16 PF).
- The five-factor model identifies five universal dimensions of personality: extroversion, agreeableness, conscientiousness, neuroticism, and openness to experience.
- Facet traits characterize the Big Five personality dimensions and they are better predictors of everyday behaviour than those five factors.
- Traits interact with situations to explain our behaviour.
- Behavioural genetics and studies of identical twins suggest that heredity contributes significantly to adult personality traits.

How Do Psychodynamic Theories Explain Personality?

- Like other psychodynamic approaches, Sigmund Freud's psychoanalytic theory emphasizes unconscious forces and conflicts within the personality.
- In Freud's theory, personality is made up of the id, ego, and superego.
- Libido, derived from the life instincts, is the primary energy running the personality. Conflicts within the personality may cause neurotic anxiety or moral anxiety and motivate us to use ego-defence mechanisms.
- The personality operates on three levels: the conscious, preconscious, and unconscious.
- The Freudian view of personality development is based on a series of psychosexual stages: the oral, anal, phallic, and genital stages. Fixation at any stage can leave a lasting imprint on personality.

What Do Behaviourists Emphasize in Their Approach to Personality?

- Behavioural theories of personality emphasize learning, conditioning, and immediate effects of the environment (situational determinants).
- Learning theorists Miller and Dollard consider habits the basic core of personality. Habits express the combined effects of drive, cue, response, and reward.
- Social learning theory adds cognitive elements to the behavioural view of personality. Examples include the psychological situation, expectancies, and reinforcement value.
- The behaviouristic view of personality development holds that social reinforcement in four situations is critical. The situations are feeding, toilet or cleanliness training, sex training, and anger or aggression training.

- Identification and imitation are of particular importance in learning to be "male" or "female."
- Psychological androgyny is related to greater behavioural adaptability and flexibility.

How Do Humanistic Theories Differ from Other Perspectives?

- Humanistic theory emphasizes subjective experience and needs for self-actualization.
- Abraham Maslow found that self-actualizers share characteristics that range from efficient perceptions of reality to frequent peak experiences.
- Carl Rogers viewed the self as an entity that emerges from personal experience. We tend to become aware of experiences that match our self-image, while excluding those that are incongruent with it.
- The incongruent person has a highly unrealistic self-image and/or a mismatch between the self-image and the ideal self. The congruent or fully functioning person is flexible and open to experiences and feelings.
- As parents apply conditions of worth to children's behaviour, thoughts, and feelings, children begin to do the same. Internalized conditions of worth then contribute to incongruence, which disrupts the organismic valuing process.

How Do Psychologists Measure Personality?

- Techniques typically used for personality assessment are interviews, observation, questionnaires, and projective tests.
- Structured and unstructured interviews provide much information, but they are subject to interviewer bias and misperceptions. The halo effect may also lower the accuracy of an interview.
- Direct observation, sometimes involving situational tests, behavioural assessment, or the use of rating scales, allows evaluation of a person's actual behaviour.
- Personality questionnaires, such as the *Minnesota Multiphasic Personality Inventory-2* (MMPI-2), are objective and reliable, but their validity is open to question.
- Projective tests ask a person to project thoughts or feelings to an ambiguous stimulus or unstructured situation.
- The *Rorschach Technique,* or inkblot test, is a well-known projective technique. A second is the *Thematic Apperception Test (TAT).*
- Projective tests are low in validity and objectivity. Nevertheless, they are considered useful by many clinicians, particularly as part of a test battery.

What Causes Shyness? What Can Be Done About It?

- Shyness is a mixture of social inhibition and social anxiety. It is marked by heightened public self-consciousness and a tendency to regard one's shyness as a lasting trait.
- Shyness can be lessened by changing self-defeating beliefs and by improving social skills.

PSYCHOLOGY ON THE NET

If you have difficulty finding any of the sites listed here, visit http://www.psychologyjourney.nelson.com for an updated list of Internet addresses and direct links to relevant sites.

About Humanistic Psychology   Discusses the history and future of humanistic psychology. http://ahpweb.org/aboutahp/whatis.html

The Canadian Psychoanalytic Society   Offers information about psychoanalysis and its own activities. http://www.psychoanalysis.ca

Christina.net   This site provides a version of the Bem Sex Role Inventory. http://www.christina.net/bsri.html

FAQ about Psychological Tests   Answers to commonly asked questions about tests and testing. http://www.apa.org/science/faq-findtests.html

Personality and IQ Tests   Multiple links to personality tests and IQ tests that are scored online. http://www.davideck.com/online-tests.html

Personality FAQ   Summarizes major models of personality and relevant research. http://www.personalityresearch.org/faq.html

QueenDom.com   Provides many personality and intelligence tests that you can take for fun. http://www.queendom.com

 InfoTrac College Edition   For recent articles related to heritability of personality traits, use Key Words search for TWIN STUDIES.

INTERACTIVE LEARNING

Psychology: An Interactive Journey   Remember that Chapter 10 of the CD-ROM that came with this text has practice tests, flashcards, interactive exercises, a crossword puzzle, and other valuable materials to enhance your learning experience.

PsychNow!   7a. Theories of Personality, 7e. Assessment.

Psyk.trek   10. Personality Theory.

Chart Your Progress

The questions that follow are only a sample of what you need to know. If you miss any of the items, you should review the entire chapter, do the exercises on the CD, and review the Knowledge Builders. Another way to prepare for tests is to get more practice with *WebTutor*, the *Study Guide*, or the *Practice Quizzes* that are available with this text.

1. When someone's personality has been evaluated, we are making a judgment about his or her
   a. temperament
   b. character
   c. extroversion
   d. self-esteem

2. Which of the following is NOT one of the Big Five personality dimensions?
   a. extroversion
   b. agreeableness
   c. neuroticism
   d. androgyny

3. According to Freud, which division of personality is governed by the reality principle?
   a. ego
   b. id
   c. ego ideal
   d. superego

4. Freudian theory states that a person who is passive, dependent, and needs lots of attention has a fixation in the
   a. oral stage
   b. superego
   c. Oedipal stage
   d. genital stage

5. The situational determinants of our actions are of special interest and importance to
   a. psychodynamic theorists
   b. humanistic theorists
   c. learning theorists
   d. behavioural geneticists

6. Maslow thought of peak experiences as temporary moments of
   a. congruence
   b. positive self-regard
   c. self-actualization
   d. self-reinforcement

7. Situational testing is primarily an example of using _____ to assess personality.
   a. direct observation
   b. structured interviewing
   c. the halo effect
   d. projective techniques

8. Which of the following items DOES NOT belong with the others?
   a. Rorschach Technique
   b. TAT
   c. MMPI
   d. projective testing

9. Which MMPI-2 scale is designed to detect phobias and compulsive actions?
   a. Hysteria
   b. Paranoia
   c. Psychasthenia
   d. Mania

10. Contrary to what many people think, shyness is NOT related to
    a. private self-consciousness
    b. social anxiety
    c. self-esteem
    d. blaming oneself for social failures

Answers: 1. b 2. d 3. a 4. a 5. c 6. c 7. a 8. c 9. c 10. a

HEALTH, STRESS, AND COPING

Chapter 11

Psychologist's Journal

TAYLOR'S (NOT SO VERY) FINE ADVENTURE

Somehow, Taylor had managed to survive the rush of make-or-break term papers, projects, and classroom presentations. Then it was on to final exams, where his tests seemed perfectly timed to inflict as much suffering as possible. His two hardest exams fell on the same day! Great.

On the last day of exams, Taylor got caught in traffic on his way to school. Two drivers cut him off, and another gave him the finger. When Taylor finally got to school, the parking lot was swarming with frantic students. Most of them, like him, were within minutes of missing a final exam. At last, Taylor spied an empty space. As he started toward it, a Volkswagen darted around the corner and into "his" place. The driver of the car behind him began to honk impatiently. For a moment, Taylor was seized by a colossal desire to run over anything in sight.

Finally, after a week and a half of stress, pressure, and frustration, Taylor's exams were over. Sleep deprivation, litres of coffee, too much junk food, and equal portions of cramming and complaining had carried him through. He was off for the summer. At last, he could relax and have some fun. Or could he? Just four days later, Taylor got a bad cold, followed by bronchitis that lasted nearly a month.

Was this just more bad luck? Or does Taylor's experience illustrate what happens when stress, emotion, personal habits, and health collide? While the timing of his cold might have been a coincidence, odds are it wasn't. Periods of stress are frequently followed by illness (Biondi & Zannino, 1997).

Stress occurs whenever a challenge or a threat forces a person to *adjust* or *adapt*. Stress is a normal part of life. But when stress is chronic or severe, it can damage health. Stress, in other words, is a *behavioural* factor that directly affects personal well-being.

In the first part of this chapter, we will explore a variety of behavioural health risks. Then we will look more closely at what stress is and how it affects us. After that, we will address ways of coping with stress. In addition, we will look at the work of Hans Selye, who spent most of his career at the University of Montreal and is considered one of the pioneers of stress research.

Survey Questions

■ What is health psychology? How does behaviour affect health?

■ What is stress? What factors determine its severity?

■ What causes frustration and what are typical reactions to it?

■ Are there different types of conflict? How do people react to conflict?

■ What are defence mechanisms?

■ What do we know about coping with feelings of helplessness and depression?

■ How is stress related to health and disease?

■ What are the best strategies for managing stress?

▶ Health Psychology—Here's to Your Good Health

Survey Question:

■ What is health psychology? How does behaviour affect health?

Most people agree that health is important—especially their own. Yet, almost one half of all deaths in North America are primarily due to unhealthy behaviour. **Health psychology** aims to do something about such deaths. Health psychologists use behavioural principles to promote health and prevent illness (Terborg, 1998). Psychologists working in the allied field of **behavioural medicine** apply psychology to manage medical problems, such as diabetes or asthma. Their interests include pain control, helping people cope with chronic illness, stress-related diseases, self-screening for diseases (such as breast cancer), and similar topics (Luiselli, 1994).

Behavioural Risk Factors

Health psychology Study of how behavioural principles can be used to prevent illness and promote health.

Behavioural medicine The study of behavioural factors in medicine, physical illness, and medical treatment.

Lifestyle disease A disease related to health-damaging personal habits.

Around the turn of the 20th century, people died primarily from infectious diseases and accidents. Today, people generally die from **lifestyle diseases**, which are related to health-damaging personal habits. Examples include heart disease, stroke, and lung cancer (McGinnis & Foege, 1993) (see ▶Figure 11.1). Clearly, some lifestyles promote health, whereas others lead to illness and death. As the late Walt Kelly, author of the comic strip "Pogo" put it, "We have met the enemy and he is us."

What kinds of behaviour are you referring to as unhealthy? Some causes of poor health are beyond our control. Nevertheless, a number of behavioural risk factors can be controlled.

▶Figure 11.1

Some of the leading causes of death in Canada are shown in this figure. Many of them, including some cancers, other lung diseases, heart disease, and liver disease, are related to behavioural risk factors such as alcohol use, smoking, lack of exercise, and risky sexual behaviours.

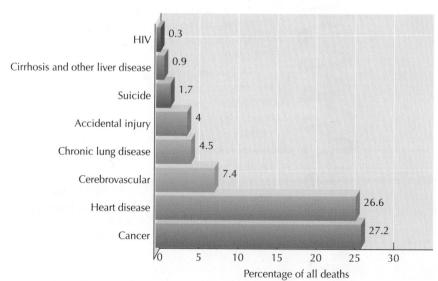

Selected Leading Causes of Death in Canada (1999)

Cause	Percentage of all deaths
HIV	0.3
Cirrhosis and other liver disease	0.9
Suicide	1.7
Accidental injury	4
Chronic lung disease	4.5
Cerebrovascular	7.4
Heart disease	26.6
Cancer	27.2

Behavioural risk factors
Behaviours that increase the chances of disease, injury, or premature death.

Disease-prone personality A personality type associated with poor health, marked by persistent negative emotions.

Behavioural risk factors are behaviours that increase the chances of disease, injury, or early death. For example, just being overweight is enough to double a person's chance of dying from cancer or heart disease. Thus, being fat is not just a matter of fashion—in the long run it could kill you (Calle et al., 1999).

Each of the following is a major behavioural risk factor (Baum & Posluszny, 1999; Groth-Marnat & Schumaker, 1995):

- High levels of stress
- Untreated high blood pressure
- Cigarette smoking
- Abuse of alcohol or other drugs
- Overeating
- Inadequate exercise
- Unsafe sexual behaviour
- Exposure to toxic substances
- Violence
- Excess sun exposure
- Driving at excessive speeds
- Disregarding personal safety

Lifestyle diseases related to just three behaviours—smoking, alcohol, and illicit drug use—accounted for 20 percent of all deaths and nearly 10 percent of hospital admissions in Canada in 1995 (Single et al., 2000).

▶Figure 11.2 gives the percentages of young Canadians who engaged in four common risky behaviours according to a survey done by Nancy Galambos of the University of Victoria. She found that over one-quarter of Canadians between the ages of 15 and 19 were regular or occasional smokers. Binge drinking was even more common than smoking. More than half of the women in the sample reported rarely or never using condoms, compared to 29 percent of the men, thus putting them at serious risk for both unintended pregnancy and sexually transmitted diseases. The data also show that risky behaviours that start in adolescence often continue into adulthood—the percentages for binge drinking, smoking, and sex without condoms were higher in both males and females between 20 and 24. Unfortunately, many people do not stop at one risky behaviour. Nearly one-quarter of the males and 19 percent of the females engaged in two of the four risky behaviours, 9 percent of females and 14 percent of males engaged in three of them, and 5 percent of males and females engaged in all four risky behaviours (Galambos & Tilton-Weaver, 1998).

In addition to specific risk factors, a general **disease-prone personality** type also exists. Such people tend to be chronically depressed, anxious, hostile—and frequently ill (Taylor, 1990). In contrast, people who are intellectually resourceful, compassionate, optimistic, and non-hostile tend to enjoy good health (Lawler et al., 1999; Taylor et al., 2000).

LIFESTYLE In your mind's eye, fast-forward an imaginary film of your life all the way to old age. Do it twice—once with a lifestyle including a large number of behavioural risk factors, and again without them. It should be obvious that countless small risks can add up to dramatically raise the chance of illness. If stress is a frequent part of your life, visualize your body seething with emotion, day after day. If you smoke, picture a lifetime's worth of cigarette smoke blown through your lungs in a week. If you drink, take a lifetime of alcohol's assaults on the brain, stomach, and liver and squeeze them into a month: Your body would be poisoned, ravaged, and soon dead. If you eat a high-fat, high-cholesterol diet, fast-forward a lifetime of heart-killing plaque clogging your arteries.

This discussion is not meant to be a sermon. It is merely a reminder that risk factors do make a difference. To make matters worse, unhealthy lifestyles almost always create multiple risks. That is, people who smoke are also likely to drink excessively. Those who overeat usually do not get enough exercise (Emmons et al., 1998). And so on.

Risky Behaviours in Young Canadians

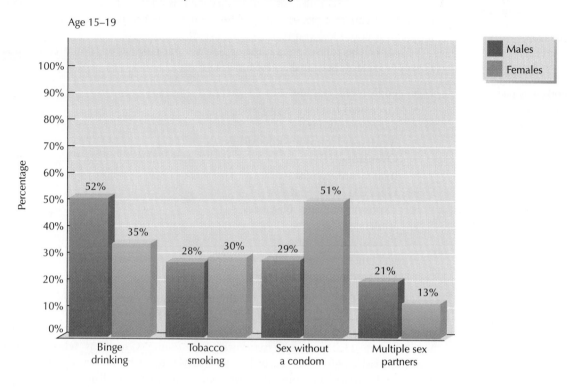

Age 15–19

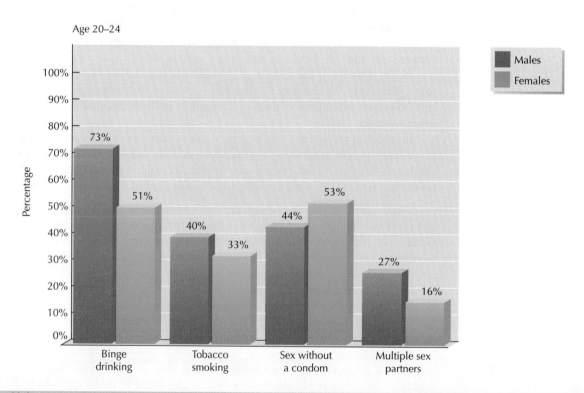

Age 20–24

▶Figure 11.2

Percentages of Canadians ages 15–19 and 20–24 who engage in four major risky behaviours (from Galambos & Tilton-Weaver, 1998).

In the long run, behavioural risk factors and lifestyles do make a difference in health and life expectancy.

Health-Promoting Behaviours

To prevent disease, health psychologists first try to remove behavioural risk factors. All the medicine in the world may not be enough to restore health without changes in behaviour. We all know someone who has had a heart attack or lung disease who couldn't change the habits that led to the illness.

Beyond this, psychologists are also interested in getting people to increase behaviours that promote health. **Health-promoting behaviours** include such obvious practices as getting regular exercise, controlling smoking and alcohol use, maintaining a balanced diet, getting good medical care, and managing stress (Glik, Kronenfeld, & Jackson, 1996). Even something as simple as using seat belts in a car greatly increases life expectancy.

In some cases, diseases can be treated or prevented by making specific changes in behaviour. For example, hypertension (high blood pressure) is often deadly. Yet, for some people simple lifestyle changes will fend off this "silent killer." Here's the recipe for lower blood pressure: lose weight, consume less sodium (salt), use alcohol sparingly, and get more exercise (Dubbert, 1995).

To summarize, a small number of behavioural patterns account for many common health problems (Kolbe, Collins, & Cortese, 1997). Table 11.1 lists several major ways to promote good health.

EARLY PREVENTION   Smoking is the largest preventable cause of death and the single most lethal behavioural risk factor (McGinnis & Foege, 1993). As such, it illustrates the prospect for preventing illness.

What have health psychologists done to lessen the risks? Attempts to "immunize" youths against pressures to start smoking provide a good example. The smoker who says "Quitting is easy, I've done it dozens of times" states a basic truth—only one smoker in ten has long-term success at quitting. Thus, the best way to deal with smoking is to prevent it before it becomes a lifelong habit.

Smoking develops slowly, which gives time to expose young people to prevention efforts. Examples include peer quizzes about the effects of smoking, anti-smoking art contests, poster and T-shirt giveaways, anti-smoking pamphlets for parents, and student quizzes of parents (Biglan et al., 1996). Such efforts persuade kids that smoking is dangerous and "uncool."

Some of the best anti-smoking programs include **refusal skills training.** In this case, youths learn to resist pressures to begin smoking (or using other drugs) (Botvin et al., 1997). For example, students in grades 6, 7, and 8 can role-play ways to resist smoking pressures from peers, adults, and cigarette ads. Similar methods can be applied to other health risks, such as sexually transmitted diseases and unwanted pregnancy (Botvin et al., 1995).

Health-promoting behaviour Any practice that tends to maintain or enhance good health.

Refusal skills training Program that teaches youths how to resist pressures to begin smoking. (Can also be applied to other drugs and health risks.)

Table 11.1
Major Health-Promoting Behaviours

	SOURCE	DESIRABLE BEHAVIOURS
	Nutrition	Eating a balanced, low-fat diet; appropriate caloric intake; maintenance of healthy body weight
	Exercise	At least 30 minutes of aerobic exercise, five days per week
	Blood pressure	Lower blood pressure with diet and exercise, or medicine if necessary
	Alcohol and drugs	No more than two drinks per day; abstain from using drugs
	Tobacco	Do not smoke; do not use smokeless tobacco
	Sleep and relaxation	Avoid sleep deprivation; provide for periods of relaxation every day
	Sex	Practise safer sex; avoid unplanned pregnancy
	Injury	Curb dangerous driving habits, use seat belts; minimize sun exposure; forgo dangerous activities
	Stress	Learn stress management; lower hostility

The latest health programs also teach students general life skills. The idea is to give kids skills that will help them cope with day-to-day stresses. That way, they will be less tempted to escape problems through drug use or other destructive behaviours. **Life skills training** includes practice in stress reduction, self-protection, decision making, self-control, and social skills (Jones et al., 1995).

▶ STDs and Safer Sex—Risk and Responsibility

Unsafe sex is one area in which relatively small changes in behaviour can almost completely eliminate a health hazard. Attempts to change eating or exercise habits or to quit smoking can be very difficult. Avoiding risky sex should be far easier—but is it?

Sexually Transmitted Diseases

A **sexually transmitted disease (STD)** is passed from one person to another by intimate physical contact. Sexually active people run a high risk of getting chlamydia (klah-MID-ee-ah), gonorrhea, hepatitis B, herpes, syphilis, and other STDs. Many people who carry STDs remain **asymptomatic** (a-SIMP-teh-mat-ik: lacking obvious symptoms). It is easy to be infected without knowing it. Nearly 75 percent of women with chlamydia have no noticeable symptoms, and 80 percent of women with gonorrhea have no symptoms in the early stages of infection (Rathus et al., 2001). Because of this, it is often impossible to tell if a sexual partner is infectious. Thus, sexual risk taking poses a serious health hazard (Ramirez-Valles, Zimmerman, & Newcomb, 1998).

For many sexually active people, the **human immunodeficiency virus (HIV)** has added a new threat. HIV is a sexually transmitted virus that disables the immune system. Whereas most other STDs are treatable, HIV infections can be lethal. Check your knowledge about HIV against the following summary.

Life skills training A program that teaches stress reduction, self-protection, decision making, self-control, and social skills.

Sexually transmitted disease (STD) A disease that is typically passed from one person to the next by intimate physical contact. Sometimes known as a venereal disease.

Asymptomatic Refers to having a disease while lacking obvious symptoms of illness.

Human immunodeficiency virus (HIV) A sexually transmitted virus that disables the immune system.

AIDS

Acquired immune deficiency syndrome (AIDS) is caused by an HIV infection. As the immune system weakens, various infections invade the body without resistance. Many people with AIDS eventually die of multiple infections (although a new three-drug therapy has improved the odds of survival). The first symptoms of AIDS may show up two months after infection or they may not appear for more than seven years. Because of this long incubation period, infected persons often pass the AIDS virus on to others without knowing it. For at least the first six months after infection, a negative test result for the HIV virus is no guarantee that a person is a "safe" sex partner.

HIV infections are spread by direct contact with body fluids—especially blood, semen, and vaginal secretions. The AIDS virus cannot be transmitted by casual contact. People do not get AIDS from shaking hands, touching or using objects touched by an AIDS patient, eating food prepared by an infected person, or from social kissing, sweat or tears, sharing drinking glasses, sharing towels, and so forth.

AIDS can be spread by all forms of unprotected sexual intercourse, as well as sharing drug needles, and it has affected persons of all sexual orientations. One in 75 men and one in 700 women in North America are now infected with HIV, and mothers can pass the virus to their unborn children. As a result, people who engage in unsafe sex are gambling with their lives—at very poor odds (see ▶Figure 11.3). In addition, new strains of the HIV virus are appearing. One in particular, which has spread explosively among heterosexuals in Africa, has been detected in North America.

Behavioural Risk Factors

Sexually active people can do much to protect their own health. Because the organisms that cause STDs are "equal opportunity germs," the behaviours listed here are risky when performed with *any* infected person—male or female, young or old, gay or straight.

Risky Behaviours

- Sharing drug needles and syringes
- Anal sex, with or without a condom
- Vaginal or oral sex with someone who injects drugs or engages in anal sex
- Sex with someone you don't know well, or with someone you know has had several partners
- Unprotected sex (without a condom) with an infected partner
- Having two or more sex partners (additional partners further increase the risk)

It's important to remember that you can't tell from appearance if a person is infected. Many people would be surprised to learn that their partners have engaged in behaviour that places them both at risk (Seal & Palmer-Seal, 1996).

The preceding high-risk behaviours can be contrasted with the following list of safer sexual practices. Note, however, that unless a person completely abstains, sex can be made safer, but not risk-free (Hawkins, Gray, & Hawkins, 1995).

Safer Sex Practices

- Not having vaginal or anal sex
- Using a condom
- Sex with one mutually faithful, uninfected partner
- Not injecting drugs
- Discussing contraception and safer sex practices with partner
- Being selective regarding sexual partners
- Reducing the number of sexual partners
- Discussing partner's sexual health prior to engaging in sex
- Not engaging in sex while intoxicated
- Getting tested for HIV and other STDs with a partner

Acquired immune deficiency syndrome (AIDS) A frequently fatal disease caused by HIV infection. In AIDS, the immune system is weakened, allowing other infections to attack the body.

▶Figure 11.3

Popular professional basketball star Earvin "Magic" Johnson stunned fans in 1991 when he announced that he had tested positive for HIV. Johnson, who is heterosexual, emphasized that his infection is a warning that anyone who is sexually active can contract the AIDS virus if they don't follow safe sex practices. Johnson further stressed that abstinence is the surest way to prevent AIDS. Johnson's infection increased public awareness about AIDS. Unfortunately, though, it has resulted in little real change in risky behaviour (Brown et al., 1996).

Table 11.2
Common Excuses for Not Practising Safer Sex

REASONS FOR NOT HAVING SAFER SEX	PERCENTAGE GIVING EXCUSE
Condom not available	20
Didn't want to use a condom	19
"Couldn't stop ourselves"	15
Partner didn't want to use a condom	14
Alcohol or drug use	11
(Kusseling et al., 1996.)	

Sexually active persons should practise safer sex until both partners have been tested for STDs and HIV. In the survey of nearly 2000 Canadians aged 15 to 24 mentioned earlier, 51 percent of women between the ages of 15 and 19 reported that they had had sex without a condom during the past year, compared with 29 percent of the males. These numbers are even higher for people over 20, with 53 percent of the women and 44 percent of the men admitting to engaging in sex without condoms (Galambos & Tilton-Weaver, 1998). Table 11.2 lists some of the excuses people give for engaging in risky sex (Kusseling et al., 1996).

One chilling study of HIV patients—who knew they were infectious—found that 41 percent of those who were sexually active did not always use condoms (Sobel et al., 1996)! Thus, responsibility for "safer sex" rests with each sexually active individual. It is unwise to count on a sexual partner for protection against HIV infection or any STD for that matter.

Isn't it possible that practising safer sex would be interpreted as a sign that you mistrust your lover? Actually, taking precautions could, instead, be defined as a way of showing that you really care about the welfare of your partner (Hammer et al., 1996). As is the case with other behavioural risk factors, it's certainly a way of showing that you care about your own health.

▶ Health and Wellness—Job Number One

Community health campaign A community-wide education program that provides information about how to lessen risk factors and promote health.

Role model A person who serves as a positive example of desirable behaviour.

Wellness A positive state of good health; more than the absence of disease.

In addition to the prevention efforts described earlier, health psychologists have had some success with **community health campaigns.** These are community-wide education projects designed to lessen a combination of major risk factors. Health campaigns inform people of risks such as stress, alcohol abuse, high blood pressure, high cholesterol, smoking, STDs, or excessive sun exposure. This is followed by efforts to motivate people to change their behaviour. Campaigns sometimes provide **role models** (positive examples) who show people how to improve their own health. They also direct people to services for health screening, advice, and treatment (Cheadle et al., 1992–93). Health campaigns may reach people through the mass media, public schools, health fairs, their work, or self-help programs (Calvert & Cocking, 1992; Schooler, Flora, & Farquhar, 1993). The federal government is running a major anti-smoking campaign.

Wellness

Health is not just an absence of disease. People who are truly healthy enjoy a positive state of **wellness** or well-being. Maintaining wellness is a lifelong pursuit and, ideally, a labour of love. People who attain optimal wellness are both physically and psychologically healthy. They are happy, optimistic, self-confident individuals who can bounce back emotionally from adversity (Lightsey, 1996).

People who enjoy a sense of well-being also have supportive relationships with others, they do meaningful work, and they live in a clean environment. Many of these aspects of wellness are addressed in other chapters of this book. In this chapter we will give special attention to the role that stress plays in health and sickness. As stated earlier, stress management is a major activity of health psychologists. Understanding stress, and learning to control it, can improve not only your health, but the quality of your life as well. For these reasons, a discussion of stress and stress management follows.

Health Canada's Second-hand Smoke and Youth campaign aims to raise young people's awareness of the dangers of second-hand smoke.

Knowledge builder

HEALTH PSYCHOLOGY

Relate

If you were to work as a health psychologist would you be more interested in preventing disease or managing it?

Make a list of the major behavioural risk factors that apply to you. Are you laying the foundation for a lifestyle disease?

Which of the health-promoting behaviours listed in Table 11.1 would you like to increase?

If you were designing a community health campaign, who would you use as role models of healthful behaviour?

Learning Check

1. Adjustment to chronic illness and the control of pain are topics that would more likely be of interest to a specialist in

_____

rather than a health psychologist.

2. With respect to health, which of the following is *not* a major behavioural risk factor?
   a. overexercise *b.* cigarette smoking *c.* stress *d.* high blood pressure

3. Health psychologists tend to prefer _____ rather than modifying habits (like smoking) that become difficult to break once they are established.

4. The disease-prone personality is marked by _____, anxiety, and hostility.

Critical Thinking

5. The general public is increasingly well informed about health risks and healthful behaviour. Can you apply the concept of reinforcement to explain why so many people fail to act on this information?

_____

Answers:

1. behavioural medicine 2. *a* 3. prevention 4. depression 5. Many health payoffs are delayed by months or years, greatly lessening the immediate rewards for healthful behaviour.

▶ Stress—Thrill or Threat?

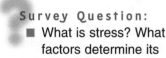

Survey Question:

■ What is stress? What factors determine its severity?

Stress The mental and physical condition that occurs when a person must adjust or adapt to the environment.

Stress reaction The physical response to stress, consisting mainly of bodily changes related to autonomic nervous system arousal.

Stress isn't always bad. Stress researcher Hans Selye (SEL-yay) (1976), who worked at the University of Montreal for over 50 years, once observed, "To be totally without stress is to be dead." As noted earlier, **stress** is the mental and physical condition that occurs when a person must adjust or adapt to the environment. Unpleasant events such as work pressures, marital problems, or financial woes naturally produce stress. But so do travel, sports, a new job, mountain climbing, dating, and other positive activities. Even if you aren't a thrill seeker, a healthy lifestyle may include a fair amount of *eustress* (good stress). Eustress can be energizing. Activities that provoke "good stress" are usually experienced as challenging and rewarding.

A **stress reaction** begins with the same autonomic nervous system arousal that occurs during emotion. Imagine you are standing at the top of a wind–whipped ski jump for the first time. Internally, there would be a rapid surge in your heart rate, blood pressure, respiration, muscle tension, and other ANS responses. Short-term stresses of this kind can be uncomfortable, but they rarely do any damage. (Your landing might be another matter, however.) Later we will describe the long-term physical impact of prolonged stress—which can do harm. For now, Table 11.3 gives an overview of typical signs or symptoms of ongoing stress.

Table 11.3
Warning Signs of Stress

EMOTIONAL SIGNS	BEHAVIOURAL SIGNS	PHYSICAL SIGNS
Anxiety	Avoidance of responsibilities and relationships	Excessive worry about illness
Apathy	Extreme or self-destructive behaviour	Frequent illness
Irritability	Self-neglect	Exhaustion
Mental fatigue	Poor judgment	Overuse of medicines
		Physical aliments and complaints

(Doctor & Doctor, 1994.)

Other than when it is long lasting, why is stress sometimes damaging and sometimes not? Stress reactions are complex. Let's examine some of the chief factors that determine whether or not stress is harmful.

When Is Stress a Strain?

It goes almost without saying that some events are more likely to cause stress than others. A **stressor** is a condition or event that challenges or threatens a person. Police officers, for instance, suffer from a high rate of stress-related diseases. The threat of injury or death, plus occasional confrontations with drunk or belligerent citizens, takes a toll. A major factor here is the unpredictable nature of police work. An officer who stops a car to issue a traffic ticket never knows if a cooperative citizen or an armed gang member is waiting inside.

A study done with rats shows how unpredictable events add to stress. Rats in one group were given shocks preceded by a warning tone. A second group got shocks without warning. The third group received no shocks, but heard the tone. After a few weeks, the animals that received unpredictable shocks had severe stomach ulcers. Those given predictable shocks showed little or no ulceration. The lucky group that received no shocks also had no ulcers (Weiss, 1972).

Pressure is another element in stress, especially job stress. **Pressure** occurs when a person must meet urgent external demands or expectations (Weiten, 1998). For example, we feel pressured when activities must be speeded up, when deadlines must be met, when extra work is added unexpectedly, or when we must work near maximum capacity for long periods. Most students who have survived final exams are familiar with the effects of pressure.

What if I set deadlines for myself? Does it make a difference where the pressure comes from? Yes. People generally feel more stress in situations over which they have little or no control (Taylor et al., 2000). For example, Douglas DeGood (1975) subjected college students to an unpleasant shock-avoidance task. Some students were allowed to select their own rest periods, while others rested at times selected for them. Participants allowed to control their own rest periods showed lower stress levels (as measured by blood pressure) than those given no choice.

To summarize, when emotional "shocks" are *intense* or *repeated, unpredictable, uncontrollable,* and linked to *pressure,* stress will be magnified and damage is likely to result. (See Table 11.4 for a list of jobs that contain these elements.) At work, chronic stress sometimes results in *burnout,* a pattern of emotional exhaustion described in "Burnout—The High Cost of Caring."

Appraising Stressors

External events are not the whole story of stress. As noted in Chapter 9, our emotions are greatly affected by how we appraise situations. That's why some people are distressed by events that others view as a thrill or a challenge (eustress). Ultimately, stress depends on how a situation is perceived. For example, a middle-aged man may find it stressful to listen to five of his son's rap CDs in a row. His son, on the other hand, may find it stressful to listen to one of his father's opera CDs. To know if you are stressed, we must know what meaning you place on events. As we will see in a moment, whenever a stressor is appraised as a **threat** (potentially harmful), a powerful stress reaction follows (Lazarus, 1991a).

"AM I OKAY OR IN TROUBLE?"   Situation: You have been selected to give a speech to 300 people. Or, a doctor tells you that you must undergo a dangerous and painful operation. Or, the one true love of your life walks out the door. What would your emotional response to these events be? How do you cope with an emotional threat?

According to Richard Lazarus (1991a), there are two important steps in managing a threat. The first is a **primary appraisal,** in which you decide if a situation is relevant or irrelevant, positive or threatening. In essence, this step answers the question "Am I okay or in trouble?" Then you make a **secondary appraisal,** in which you assess your resources and choose a way to meet the threat or challenge. ("What can I do about this situation?") Thus, the way a

---

Stressor A specific condition or event in the environment that challenges or threatens a person.

Pressure A stressful condition that occurs when a person must meet urgent external demands or expectations.

Threat An event or situation perceived as potentially harmful.

Primary appraisal Deciding if a situation is relevant to oneself and if it is a threat.

Secondary appraisal Deciding how to cope with a threat or challenge.

Table 11.4
Examples of Highly Stressful Jobs

Firefighter
Senior corporate executive
Indy-class race car driver
Taxi driver
Surgeon
Astronaut
Police officer
Air-traffic controller

(Adapted from Krantz, 1995.)

FOCUS ON RESEARCH | Burnout—The High Cost of Caring

Margo, a young nurse, realizes with dismay that she has "lost all patience with her patients" and wishes they would "go somewhere else to be sick." Margo's feelings are clearly a sign of job **burnout,** a condition in which workers are physically, mentally, and emotionally drained. What does it mean to be "burned out"? The problem has three aspects (Maslach, 1982; Yadama & Drake, 1995).

First of all, burnout involves *emotional exhaustion.* Affected persons are fatigued, tense, apathetic, and suffer from physical ailments. They feel "used up" and have an "I don't give a damn anymore" attitude toward work.

A second problem is *depersonalization,* or detachment from others. Burned-out workers no longer care about their clients and coldly treat them like objects.

The third aspect of burnout is a feeling of *reduced personal accomplishment.* Burned-out workers do poor work and feel helpless, hopeless, or angry. Their self-esteem slumps, and they yearn to change jobs or careers.

Burnout may occur in any job, but it is a special problem in emotionally demanding helping professions, such as nursing, teaching, social work, child care, counselling, caring for AIDS patients, or police work (Bellani et al., 1996; Matthews, 1990; Poulin & Walter, 1993; Yadama & Drake, 1995).

It's ironic that the same work that produces burnout can also be highly rewarding. If our society wishes to keep caring people in the helping professions, some changes may be needed. A good start would be to redesign jobs to create a better balance between demands and satisfactions. As in other stressful situations, people are more likely to burn out if they feel they have little control over their work (McKnight & Glass, 1995).

Building stronger social support systems could also help prevent burnout. A good example is the growing use of support groups for nurses and other caregivers. In a **support group,** workers give and receive emotional encouragement as they talk about feelings, problems, and stresses (Greenglass, Burke, & Konarski, 1998).

Ultimately, the best solution for burnout may be for each of us to better appreciate the stresses felt by people whose work requires caring about the needs of others (Capner & Caltabiano, 1993).

Burnout A job-related condition of mental, physical, and emotional exhaustion.

Support group A group formed to provide emotional support for its members through discussion of stresses and shared concerns.

Problem-focused coping Directly managing or remedying a stressful or threatening situation.

situation is "sized up" greatly affects one's ability to cope with it (see ▶Figure 11.4). Public speaking, for instance, can be appraised as an intense threat or as a chance to perform. Emphasizing the threat—by imagining failure, rejection, or embarrassment—obviously invites disaster (Lazarus, 1993).

THE NATURE OF THREAT   What does it mean to feel threatened by a stressor? Certainly in most day-to-day situations it doesn't mean you think your life is in danger. Threat has more to do with the idea of control. We are particularly prone to feel stressed when we can't—or think we can't—control our immediate environment. In short, a *perceived lack of control* is just as threatening as an actual lack of control (DasGupta, 1992). If your answer to the question "What can I do about this situation?" is "nothing," you will feel emotionally stressed.

A sense of control also comes from believing you can reach desired goals. It is threatening to feel that we lack *competence* to cope with life's demands (Bandura, 1986). Because of this, the intensity of the body's stress reaction often depends on what we think and tell ourselves about stressors. That's why it's valuable to learn to think in ways that ward off the body's stress response. (Some strategies for controlling upsetting thoughts are described in this chapter's Psychology in Action section.)

Coping with Threat

You have appraised a situation as threatening. What will you do next? There are two major choices. **Problem-focused coping**

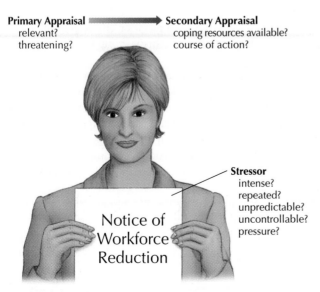

Primary Appraisal ➡ **Secondary Appraisal**
relevant?   coping resources available?
threatening?   course of action?

Stressor
intense?
repeated?
unpredictable?
uncontrollable?
pressure?

Notice of Workforce Reduction

▶**Figure 11.4**

Stress is the product of an interchange between a person and the environment.

Emotion-focused coping
Managing or controlling
one's emotional reaction to a
stressful or threatening
situation.

is aimed at managing or altering the distressing situation itself. In **emotion-focused coping,** people try to control their emotional reactions to the situation (Lazarus, 1993).

Couldn't both types of coping occur together? Yes. Sometimes the two types of coping aid one another. Say, for example, that a woman feels anxious as she steps to the podium to give a speech. If she does some deep breathing to reduce her anxiety (emotion-focused coping), she will be better able to glance over her notes to improve her delivery (problem-focused coping).

It is also possible for coping efforts to clash. For instance, if you have to make a difficult decision, you may suffer intense emotional distress. In such circumstances there is a temptation to make a quick and ill-advised choice, just to end the suffering. Doing so may allow you to cope with your emotions, but it shortchanges problem-focused coping.

In general, problem-focused coping tends to be especially useful when you are facing a controllable stressor—that is, a situation you can actually do something about. Emotion-focused efforts are best suited to managing stressors that you cannot control (Lazarus, 1993; Taylor, 1990). To improve your chances of coping effectively, the stress-fighting strategies described in this chapter include a mixture of both techniques.

We will soon return to another look at stress and its effects. But first, let's examine two major (and all too familiar) causes of stress: frustration and conflict.

▶ Frustration—Blind Alleys and Lead Balloons

Survey Question:
■ What causes frustration and what are typical reactions to it?

Do you remember how frustrated Taylor was when he couldn't find a parking place? **Frustration** is a negative emotional state that occurs when people are prevented from reaching desired goals. In Taylor's case, the goal of finding a parking space was blocked by another car.

Obstacles of many kinds cause frustration. A useful distinction can be made between external and personal sources of frustration. **External frustration** is based on conditions outside the individual that impede progress toward a goal. All of the following are external frustrations: getting stuck with a flat tire; having a marriage proposal rejected; finding the cupboard bare when you go to get your poor dog a bone; finding the refrigerator bare when you go to get your poor tummy a T-bone; finding the refrigerator gone when you return home; being chased out of the house by your starving dog. In other words, external frustrations are based on delays, failure, rejection, loss, and other direct blocking of motivated behaviour.

Frustration A negative
emotional state that occurs
when one is prevented from
reaching a goal.
External frustration
Distress caused by external
conditions that hinder
progress toward a goal.

Notice that external obstacles can be either *social* (slow drivers, tall people in theatres, people who cut into lines) or *non-social* (stuck doors, a dead battery, rain on the day of the game). If you ask 10 of your friends what has frustrated them recently, most will probably mention someone's behaviour ("My sister wore one of my dresses when I wanted to wear it," "My supervisor is unfair," "My history teacher grades too hard"). As social animals, we humans are highly sensitive to social sources of frustration (Peeters, Buunk, & Schaufeli, 1995). That's probably why unfair treatment associated with racial or ethnic prejudice is a major source of frustration and stress in the lives of many minority group members (Clark et al., 1999).

Frustration usually increases as the strength, urgency, or importance of a blocked motive increases. Taylor was especially frustrated in the parking lot because he was late for an exam. Likewise, an escape artist submerged in a tank of water and bound with 100 kilograms of chain would become quite frustrated if a trick lock jammed. Remember, too, that motivation becomes stronger as we near a goal. As a result, frustration is more intense when a person runs into an obstacle very close to a goal. If you've ever missed an A grade by 5 points, you were probably very frustrated. If you've missed an A by 1 point—well, frustration builds character, right?

A final factor affecting frustration is summarized by the old phrase "the straw that broke the camel's back." The effects of repeated frustrations can accumulate until a small irritation sets off an unexpectedly violent response. A case in point is the fact that people with long commutes are more likely to display "road rage" (angry, aggressive driving) (Harding et al., 1998).

Personal frustration Distress caused by personal characteristics that impede progress toward a goal.

Aggression Any response made with the intent of causing harm.

Displaced aggression Redirecting aggression to a target other than the actual source of one's frustration.

Scapegoating Blaming a person or a group of people for conditions not of their making.

Personal frustrations are based on personal characteristics. If you are very short and aspire to be a professional basketball player, you very likely will be frustrated. If you want to sing professionally but are tone deaf, you will likewise be frustrated. In both examples, frustration is actually based on personal limitations. Yet, failure may be perceived as externally caused. We will return to this point in the Psychology in Action section. In the meantime, let's look at some typical reactions to frustration.

Reactions to Frustration

Aggression is any response made with the intent of harming a person or an object. It is one of the most persistent and frequent responses to frustration (Berkowitz, 1988). The frustration–aggression link is so common, in fact, that experiments are hardly necessary to show it. A glance at almost any newspaper will provide examples.

Does frustration always cause aggression? Aren't there other reactions? Although the connection is strong, frustration does not always provoke aggression. More often, frustration is met first with *persistence*. This is characterized by more vigorous efforts and varied responses (see ▶Figure 11.5). For example, if you put your last loonie in a vending machine and pressing the button has no effect, you will probably press harder and faster (vigorous effort). Then you will press all the other buttons (varied response). Persistence may help you get around a barrier in order to reach your goal. However, if the machine still refuses to deliver, or return your loonie, you may become aggressive and kick the machine (or at least tell it what you think of it).

Persistence can be very adaptive. Overcoming a barrier ends the frustration and allows the need or motive to be satisfied. The same is true of aggression that removes or destroys a barrier. Picture a small band of nomadic humans, parched by thirst but separated from a water hole by a menacing animal. It is easy to see that attacking the animal might ensure their survival. In modern society such direct aggression is seldom acceptable. If you find a long line at the drinking fountain, aggression is hardly appropriate. Because direct aggression is discouraged, it is frequently displaced.

How is aggression displaced? Does displaced aggression occur often? Directing aggression toward a source of frustration may be impossible, or it may be too dangerous. If you are frustrated by your boss at work or by a teacher at school, the cost of direct aggression may be too high (losing your job or failing a class). Instead, the aggression may be displaced, or redirected, toward whomever or whatever is available. Targets of **displaced aggression** tend to be perceived as safer, or less likely to retaliate, than the original source of frustration.

Sometimes long *chains* of displacement occur, in which one person displaces aggression to the next. For instance, a businesswoman who is frustrated by high taxes reprimands an employee, who swallows his anger until he reaches home and then yells at his wife, who in turn yells at the children, who then tease the dog. The dog chases the cat, who later eats the goldfish.

Psychologists attribute much hostility and violence to displaced aggression. A disturbing example is the finding that when unemployment increases, so does child abuse (Steinberg, Catalano, & Dooley, 1981). A pattern known as **scapegoating,** in which a person or group of people are blamed for conditions not of their making, is particularly troubling. A *scapegoat* is a person who has become a habitual target of displaced aggression. Despite recent progress, many minority groups continue to suffer from hostility based on scapegoating. Think, for example, about the hostility expressed toward recent immigrants during times of economic hardship. In many communities, layoffs and job losses continue to be associated with increases in violence (Catalano, Novaco, & McConnell, 1997).

I have a friend who dropped out of school to hitchhike around the country. He seemed very frustrated before he quit. What type of response to frustration is

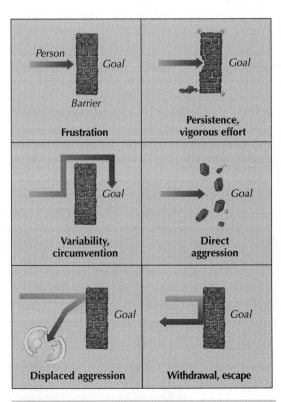

▶ **Figure 11.5**

Frustration and common reactions to it.

Escape Reducing discomfort by leaving frustrating situations or by psychologically withdrawing from them.

that? Another major reaction to frustration is escape, or withdrawal. It is stressful and unpleasant to be frustrated. If other reactions do not reduce feelings of frustration, a person may try to escape. **Escape** may mean actually leaving a source of frustration (dropping out of school, quitting a job, ending an unhappy relationship), or it may mean psychologically escaping. Two common forms of psychological escape are apathy (pretending not to care) and the use of drugs such as cocaine, alcohol, marijuana, or narcotics. (See Figure 11.5 for a summary of common reactions to frustration.)

▶ Conflict—Yes, No, Yes, No, Yes, No, Well, Maybe

Survey Question:
■ Are there different types of conflict? How do people react to conflict?

Conflict occurs whenever a person must choose between contradictory needs, desires, motives, or demands. Choosing between school and work, marriage and single life, or study and failure are common conflicts. There are four general forms of conflict. As we will see, each has its own properties (see ▶Figures 11.6 and 11.7).

APPROACH–APPROACH CONFLICTS A simple **approach–approach conflict** comes from having to choose between two positive, or desirable, alternatives. Choosing between coconut-mocha-champagne ice and orange-marmalade swirl at the ice cream parlour may throw you into a temporary conflict. However, if you really like both choices, your decision will be quickly made. Even when more important decisions are at stake, approach-approach conflicts tend to be the easiest to resolve. The old fable about the mule that died of thirst and starvation while standing between a bucket of water and a bucket of oats is obviously unrealistic. When both options are positive, the scales of decision are easily tipped in one direction or the other.

AVOIDANCE–AVOIDANCE CONFLICTS Being forced to choose between two negative, or undesirable, alternatives creates an **avoidance–avoidance conflict.** A person in an avoidance conflict is caught between "the devil and the deep blue sea" or "between a rock and a hard place." In real life, double-avoidance conflicts involve dilemmas such as choosing between an unplanned pregnancy and an abortion, the dentist and tooth decay, a monotonous job and poverty, or residence food and starvation.

Suppose I don't object to abortion. Or suppose that I consider any pregnancy sacred and not to be tampered with? Like many other stressful situations, these examples can be defined as conflicts only on the basis of personal needs and values. If a woman wants

▶Figure 11.6

The three most basic forms of conflict. For this woman, choosing between pie and ice cream is a minor approach-approach conflict; deciding whether to take a job that will require weekend work is an approach-avoidance conflict; and choosing between paying higher rent and moving is an avoidance-avoidance conflict.

▶Figure 11.7

Conflict diagrams. As shown by the coloured areas in the graphs, desires to approach and to avoid increase near a goal. The effects of these tendencies are depicted below each graph. The "behaviour" of the ball in each example illustrates the nature of the conflict above it. An approach conflict *(left)* is easily decided. Moving toward one goal will increase its attraction *(graph)* and will lead to a rapid resolution. (If the ball moves in either direction, it will go all the way to one of the goals.) In an avoidance conflict *(centre)*, tendencies to avoid are deadlocked, resulting in inaction. In an approach-avoidance conflict *(right)*, approach proceeds to the point where desires to approach and avoid cancel each other. Again, these tendencies are depicted *(below)* by the action of the ball. (Graphs after Miller, 1944.)

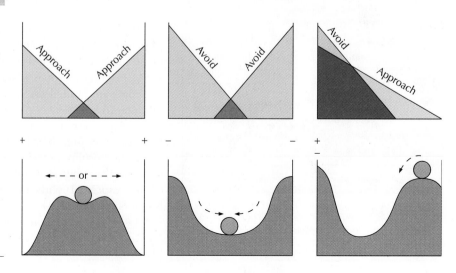

Conflict A stressful condition that occurs when a person must choose between incompatible or contradictory alternatives.

Approach-approach conflict Choosing between two positive, or desirable, alternatives.

Avoidance-avoidance conflict Choosing between two negative, or undesirable, alternatives.

Approach-avoidance conflict Being attracted to and repelled by the same goal or activity.

Ambivalence Mixed positive and negative feelings or simultaneous attraction and repulsion.

Double approach-avoidance conflict Being simultaneously attracted to and repelled by each of two alternatives.

Vacillation Wavering in intention or feelings.

to end a pregnancy and does not object to abortion, she experiences no conflict. If she would not consider abortion under any circumstances, there is no conflict.

Avoidance conflicts often have a "damned if you do, damned if you don't" quality. In other words, both choices are negative, but *not choosing* may be impossible or equally undesirable. To illustrate, imagine the plight of a woman trapped in a hotel fire 20 floors from the ground. Should she jump from the window and almost surely die on the pavement? Or should she try to dash through the flames and almost surely die of smoke inhalation and burns? When faced with a choice such as this, it is easy to see why people often *freeze,* finding it impossible to decide or take action. A trapped individual may first think about the window, approach it, and then back away after looking down 20 stories. Next, she may try the door and again back away as heat and smoke billow in. In actual disasters of this sort, people are often found dead in their rooms, victims of an inability to take action.

Indecision, inaction, and freezing are not the only reactions to double-avoidance conflicts. Since avoidance conflicts are stressful and rarely solved, people sometimes pull out of them entirely. This reaction, called *leaving the field,* is another form of escape. It may explain the behaviour of a student who could not attend school unless he worked. However, if he worked he could not earn passing grades. His solution after much conflict and indecision? He joined the Canadian Armed Forces.

APPROACH-AVOIDANCE CONFLICTS Approach-avoidance conflicts are also difficult to resolve. In some ways they are more troublesome than avoidance conflicts because people seldom escape them. A person in an **approach-avoidance conflict** is "caught" by being attracted to, and repelled by, the same goal or activity. Attraction keeps the person in the situation, but its negative aspects cause turmoil and distress. For example, a high-school student arrives to pick up his date for the first time. He is met at the door by her father, who is a professional wrestler—over 2 metres tall and 150 kilograms (or so it seems to him). The father gives the boy a crushing handshake and growls that he will break him in half if the girl is not home on time. The student considers the girl attractive and has a good time. But does he ask her out again? It depends on the relative strengths of his attraction and his fear. Almost certainly he will feel *ambivalent* about asking her out again, knowing that another encounter with her father awaits him.

Ambivalence (mixed positive and negative feelings) is a central characteristic of approach-avoidance conflicts. Ambivalence is usually translated into partial approach (Miller, 1944). Since our student is still attracted to the girl, he may spend time with her at school and elsewhere. But he may not actually date her again. Some more realistic examples of approach-avoidance conflicts are dating someone your parents strongly disapprove of, wanting to be in a play but suffering stage fright, wanting to buy a car but not wanting to make monthly payments, and wanting to eat when overweight. Many of life's important decisions have approach-avoidance dimensions.

Aren't real-life conflicts more complex than the ones described here? Yes. Conflicts are rarely as clear-cut as those described. People in conflict are usually faced with several dilemmas at once, so several types of conflict may be intermingled. The fourth type of conflict moves us closer to reality.

MULTIPLE CONFLICTS You are offered two jobs: One has good pay but poor hours and dull work; the second has interesting work and excellent hours, but low pay. Which do you select? This situation is more typical of the choices we must usually make. It offers neither completely positive nor completely negative options. It is, in other words, a **double approach-avoidance conflict,** in which each alternative has both positive and negative qualities.

As with single approach-avoidance conflicts, people faced with double approach-avoidance conflicts feel ambivalent about each choice. This causes them to *vacillate,* or waver between the alternatives. Just as you are about to choose one such alternative, its undesirable aspects tend to loom large. So, what do you do? You swing back toward the other choice. If you have ever been romantically attracted to two people at once—each having qualities you like and dislike—then you have probably experienced **vacillation.** Another example that may be familiar is trying to decide between two areas of study, each with advantages and disadvantages.

Multiple approach-avoidance conflict Being simultaneously attracted to and repelled by each of several alternatives.

Anxiety Apprehension, dread, or uneasiness similar to fear but based on an unclear threat.

In real life it is common to face **multiple approach-avoidance conflicts** in which several alternatives each have positive and negative features. An example would be trying to choose which university to attend. On a day-to-day basis, most multiple approach-avoidance conflicts are little more than an annoyance. When they involve major life decisions, such as choosing a career, a school, a mate, or a job, they can add greatly to the amount of stress we experience.

One common multiple approach-avoidance conflict faced by many young people concerns the decision to become sexually active. The perceived advantages—getting closer to the other person, strengthening the relationship, and satisfaction of sexual desires—may be offset by the possible disadvantages, such as the risk of unplanned pregnancy and sexually transmitted diseases, or disappointment at failing to live up to one's religious, family, or moral values. One way to deal with this situation that is common with many younger teens is to avoid making a decision and to "just let it happen." The consequence is an increased risk of pregnancy and STDs, because condoms are not used.

Knowledge builder

STRESS, FRUSTRATION, AND CONFLICT

Relate

What impact did pressure, control, predictability, repetition, and intensity have on your last stress reaction?

What type of coping do you tend to use when you face a stressor such as public speaking or taking an important exam?

Think of a time when you were frustrated. What was your goal? What prevented you from reaching it? Was your frustration external or personal?

Have you ever displaced aggression? Why did you choose another target for your hostility?

Review the major types of conflict and think of a conflict you have faced that illustrates each type. Did your reactions match those described in the text?

Learning Check

1. Emotional exhaustion, depersonalization, and reduced accomplishment are characteristics of job _____.
2. Stress tends to be greatest when a situation is appraised as a _____ and a person does not feel _____ to cope with the situation.
3. According to Lazarus, coping with threatening situations can be both problem-focused and _____ focused.

4. Which of the following is *not* a common reaction to frustration? *a.* ambivalence *b.* aggression *c.* displaced aggression *d.* persistence
5. Sampson Goliath is 2 metres tall and weighs 150 kilograms. He has failed miserably in his aspirations to become a jockey. The source of his frustration is mainly _____.
6. Inaction and freezing are most characteristic of avoidance-avoidance conflicts. T or F?
7. Approach-avoidance conflicts produce mixed feelings called _____.

Critical Thinking

8. Which do you think would produce more stress: (a) appraising a situation as mildly threatening but feeling like you are totally incompetent to cope with it, or (b) appraising a situation as very threatening but feeling that you have the resources and skills to cope with it?
9. Being frustrated is unpleasant. If some action, including aggression, ends frustration, why might we expect the action to be repeated on other occasions?

Answers:

1. burnout **2.** threat, competent **3.** emotion- **4.** a **5.** personal **6.** T **7.** ambivalence **8.** There is no correct answer here because individual stress reactions vary greatly. However, the secondary appraisal of a situation often determines just how stressful it is. Feeling incapable of coping is very threatening. **9.** If a response ends discomfort, the response has been negatively reinforced. This makes it more likely to occur in the future (see Chapter 6).

▶ Psychological Defence—Mental Karate?

Survey Question:
■ What are defence mechanisms?

Threatening situations tend to produce **anxiety.** A person who is anxious feels tense, uneasy, apprehensive, worried, and vulnerable. This can lead to emotion-focused coping that is defensive in nature (Lazarus, 1991b). Since anxiety is unpleasant and uncomfortable, we are usually motivated to avoid it. Psychological defence mechanisms allow us to reduce feelings of anxiety caused by stressful situations or by our shortcomings.

Defence mechanism
A habitual and often unconscious psychological process used to reduce anxiety.

Denial Protecting oneself from an unpleasant reality by refusing to perceive it or believe it.

Repression Unconsciously preventing painful or dangerous thoughts from entering awareness.

Reaction formation Preventing dangerous impulses from being expressed in behaviour by exaggerating opposite behaviour.

What are psychological defence mechanisms and how do they reduce anxiety? A **defence mechanism** is any mental process used to avoid, deny, or distort sources of threat or anxiety, including threats to one's self-image. Many of these defence mechanisms were first identified by Sigmund Freud, who assumed they operate *unconsciously.* Often, defence mechanisms create large blind spots in awareness. For instance, an extremely stingy person might be completely unaware that he is a tightwad.

Everyone has at one time or another used defence mechanisms. Let's consider some of the most common. (A more complete listing is given in Table 11.5.)

DENIAL One of the most basic defences is **denial** (protecting oneself from an unpleasant reality by refusing to accept it or believe it). Denial is closely linked with death, illness, and similar painful and threatening events. For instance, if you were told that you had only three months to live, how would you react? Your first thoughts might be "Aw, come on, someone must have mixed up the X-rays" or "The doctor must be mistaken" or simply "It can't be true!" Similar denial and disbelief are common reactions to the unexpected death of a friend or relative: "It's just not real. I don't believe it. I just don't believe it!" People may also deny or underestimate the real risks posed by a situation—"I can still pass the test even if I didn't study" or "I can have unprotected sex and not get pregnant, or catch an infection."

REPRESSION Freud noticed that his patients had tremendous difficulty recalling shocking or traumatic events from childhood. It seemed that powerful forces were holding these painful memories from awareness. Freud called this **repression.** He believed that we protect ourselves by repressing threatening thoughts and impulses. Feelings of hostility toward a family member, the names of people we dislike, and past failures are common targets of repression.

REACTION FORMATION In a **reaction formation,** impulses are not just repressed; they are also held in check by exaggerating opposite behaviour. For example, a mother who unconsciously resents her children may, through reaction formation, become absurdly overprotective and overindulgent. Her real thoughts of "I hate them" and "I wish they were gone" are replaced by "I love them" and "I don't know what I would do without them." The mother's hostile impulses are traded for "smother" love, so that she won't have to admit she hates her children. Thus, the basic idea in a reaction formation is that the individual acts out an opposite behaviour to block threatening impulses or feelings.

Table 11.5
Psychological Defence Mechanisms

Compensation	Counteracting a real or imagined weakness by emphasizing desirable traits or seeking to excel in the area of weakness or in other areas.
Denial	Protecting oneself from an unpleasant reality by refusing to perceive it.
Fantasy	Fulfilling unmet desires in imagined achievements or activities.
Identification	Taking on some of the characteristics of an admired person, usually as a way of compensating for perceived personal weaknesses or faults.
Intellectualization	Separating emotion from a threatening or anxiety-provoking situation by talking or thinking about it in impersonal, "intellectual" terms.
Isolation	Separating contradictory thoughts or feelings into "logic-tight" mental compartments so that they do not come into conflict.
Projection	Attributing one's own feelings, shortcomings, or unacceptable impulses to others.
Rationalization	Justifying your behaviour by giving reasonable and "rational," but false, reasons for it.
Reaction formation	Preventing dangerous impulses from being expressed in behaviour by exaggerating opposite behaviour.
Regression	Retreating to an earlier level of development or to earlier, less demanding habits or situations.
Repression	Unconsciously preventing painful or dangerous thoughts from entering awareness.
Sublimation	Working off unmet desires, or unacceptable impulses, in activities that are constructive or socially acceptable.

Regression Retreating to an earlier stage of development or to earlier, less demanding habits or situations.

Projection Attributing one's own feelings, shortcomings, or unacceptable impulses to others.

Rationalization Justifying personal behaviour by giving reasonable and "rational" but false reasons for it.

Compensation Counteracting a real or imagined weakness by emphasizing desirable traits or seeking to excel in the area of weakness or in other areas.

Sublimation Working off frustrated desires or unacceptable impulses in substitute activities that are constructive or accepted by society.

REGRESSION   In its broadest meaning, **regression** refers to any return to earlier, less demanding situations or habits. Most parents who have a second child have to put up with at least some regression by the older child. Threatened by a new rival for affection, an older child may regress to childish speech, bed-wetting, or infantile play after the new baby arrives, as well as being more clingy and demanding. If you've ever seen a child get home-sick at summer camp or on a vacation, you've observed regression. An adult who throws a temper tantrum or a married adult who "goes home to mother" is also regressing.

PROJECTION   Projection is an unconscious process that protects us from the anxiety we would feel if we were to discern our faults. A person who is projecting tends to see his or her own feelings, shortcomings, or unacceptable impulses in others. **Projection** lowers anxiety by exaggerating negative traits in others. This justifies one's own actions and directs attention away from personal failings.

RATIONALIZATION   Every teacher is familiar with this strange phenomenon: On the day of an exam, an incredible wave of disasters sweeps through the city. Mothers, fathers, sisters, brothers, aunts, uncles, grandparents, friends, relatives, and pets become ill or die. Motors suddenly fall out of cars. Books are lost or stolen. Alarm clocks go belly-up and ring no more.

The making of excuses comes from a natural tendency to explain our behaviour. **Rationalization** refers to justifying personal actions by giving "rational" but false reasons for them. When the explanation you give for your behaviour is reasonable and convincing—but not the real reason—you are *rationalizing*. For example, Taylor failed to turn in an assignment given at the beginning of the semester in one of his classes. Here's the explanation he gave his professor:

> My car broke down two days ago, and I couldn't get to the library until yesterday. Then I couldn't get all the books I needed because some were checked out, but I wrote what I could. Then last night, as the last straw, the cartridge in my printer ran out, and since all the stores were closed, I couldn't finish the paper on time.

When asked why he left the assignment until the last minute (the real reason it was late), Taylor offered another set of rationalizations. Like many people, Taylor had difficulty seeing himself without the protection of his rationalizations.

All of the defence mechanisms described seem pretty undesirable. Do they have a positive side? People who overuse defence mechanisms become less adaptable, because they consume great amounts of emotional energy to control anxiety and maintain an unrealistic self-image. Defence mechanisms do have value, though. Often, they help keep us from being overwhelmed by immediate threats. This can provide time for a person to learn to cope in a more effective, problem-focused manner. If you recognize some of your own behaviour in the descriptions here, it is hardly a sign that you are hopelessly defensive. As noted earlier, most people occasionally use defence mechanisms.

Two defence mechanisms that have a decidedly more positive quality are compensation and sublimation.

COMPENSATION   Compensatory reactions are defences against feelings of inferiority. A person who has a defect or weakness (real or imagined) may go to unusual lengths to overcome the weakness or to compensate for it by excelling in other areas. Consider the case of André Roussimoff (1946–1993). Not only was he a tall child of tall parents, but he had a hormonal abnormality that caused him to grow to 2.3 metres tall. Some professional wrestlers saw him working out in a gym in Paris and persuaded him to join them on the circuit. He came to Montreal, and became well known as André the Giant. There are dozens of examples of **compensation** at work. A childhood stutterer may excel in debating at university. Ray Charles, Stevie Wonder, Jeff Healey, and a number of other well-known musicians are blind.

SUBLIMATION   The defence called **sublimation** (sub-lih-MAY-shun) is defined as working off frustrated desires (especially sexual desires) through socially acceptable activities. Freud believed that art, music, dance, poetry, scientific investigation, and other creative activities can serve to rechannel sexual energies into productive behaviour. Freud also felt that almost any strong desire can be sublimated. For example, a very aggressive person may find social acceptance as a professional soldier, boxer, or football player. Greed may be refined into a successful business career. Lying may be sublimated into storytelling, creative writing, or politics.

Sexual motives appear to be the most easily and widely sublimated. Freud would have had a field day with such modern pastimes as surfing, motorcycle riding, drag racing, and dancing to or playing rock music, to name but a few. People enjoy each of these activities for a multitude of reasons, but it is hard to overlook the rich sexual symbolism apparent in each.

Learned helplessness A learned inability to overcome obstacles or to avoid punishment; learned passivity and inaction to aversive stimuli.

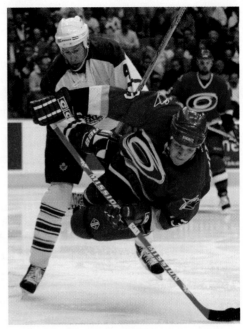

For some players—and fans—hockey probably allows sublimation of aggressive urges. *Mortal Kombat* and similar computer games may serve the same purpose.

▶ Learned Helplessness— Is There Hope?

Survey Question:

■ What do we know about coping with feelings of helplessness and depression?

What would happen if a person's defences failed or if the person appraised a threatening situation as hopeless? Martin Seligman studied the case of a young marine who seem to have adapted to the stresses of being held prisoner in Vietnam. The marine's health was related to a promise made by his captors: If he cooperated, they said, he would be released on a certain date. As the date approached, his spirits soared. Then came a devastating blow. He had been deceived. His captors had no intention of ever releasing him. He immediately lapsed into a deep depression, refused to eat or drink, and died shortly thereafter.

This seems like an extreme example. Does anything similar occur outside of concentration camps? Apparently so. For example, researchers in Finland found that even in everyday life, people who feel a sense of hopelessness die at elevated rates (Everson, Goldberg, & Salonen, 1996).

How can we explain such patterns? Psychologists have focused on the concept of learned helplessness (Seligman, 1989). **Learned helplessness** is an acquired inability to overcome obstacles and avoid aversive stimuli. To observe learned helplessness, let's see what happens when animals are tested in a shuttle box (see ▶ Figure 11.8). If placed in one side of a divided box, dogs will quickly learn to leap to

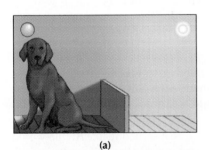
(a)

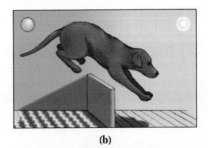
(b)

(c)

(d)

▶Figure 11.8

In the normal course of escape and avoidance learning, a light dims shortly before the floor is electrified *(a)*. Since the light does not yet have meaning for the dog, the dog receives a shock (non-injurious, by the way) and leaps the barrier *(b)*. Dogs soon learn to watch for the dimming of the light *(c)* and to jump before receiving a shock *(d)*. Dogs made to feel "helpless" rarely even learn to escape shock, much less to avoid it.

the other side to escape an electric shock. If they are given a warning before the shock occurs (for example, a light that dims), most dogs learn to avoid the shock by leaping the barrier before the shock arrives. This is true of most dogs, but not those who have learned to feel helpless (Overmier & LoLordo, 1998).

How is a dog made to feel helpless? Before being tested in the shuttle box, a dog can be placed in a harness (from which the dog cannot escape). The dog is then given several painful shocks. The animal is helpless to prevent these shocks. When placed in the shuttle box, dogs prepared this way react to the first shock by crouching, howling, and whining. None of them try to escape. They helplessly resign themselves to their fate. After all, they have already learned that there is nothing they can do about shock.

As the shuttle box experiments suggest, helplessness is a psychological state that occurs when events *appear to be uncontrollable* (Seligman, 1989). Helplessness also afflicts humans. It is a common reaction to repeated failure and to unpredictable or unavoidable punishment. A prime example is students who feel helpless about their school work. Such students tend to procrastinate and give up easily (McKean, 1994).

Where humans are concerned, attributions (discussed in Chapter 9) have a large effect on helplessness. Persons who are made to feel helpless in one situation are more likely to act helpless in other situations if they attribute their failure to *lasting, general* factors. An example would be concluding "I must be stupid" after failing to solve a series of puzzles. In contrast, attributing failure to specific factors in the original situation ("I'm not too good at puzzles" or "I wasn't really interested") tends to prevent learned helplessness from spreading (Alloy et al., 1984; Anderson et al., 1984).

Depression

Depression A state of despondency marked by feelings of powerlessness and hopelessness.

Mastery training Reinforcement of responses that lead to mastery of a threat or control over one's environment.

Seligman and others have pointed out the similarities between learned helplessness and **depression.** Both are marked by feelings of despondency, powerlessness, and hopelessness. "Helpless" animals display decreased activity, lowered aggression, blunted appetite, and a loss of sex drive. Humans suffer from similar effects and also tend to see themselves as failing, even when they're not (Seligman, 1989).

Depression is one of the most widespread emotional problems, and it undoubtedly has many causes. However, learned helplessness seems to explain many cases of depression and hopelessness. For example, Seligman (1972) describes the fate of Archie, a 15-year-old boy. For Archie, school is an unending series of shocks and failures. Other students treat him as if he's stupid; in class he rarely answers questions because he doesn't know some of the words. He feels knocked down everywhere he turns. These may not be electric shocks, but they are certainly emotional "shocks," and Archie has learned to feel helpless to prevent them. When he leaves school, his chances of success will be poor. He has learned to passively endure whatever shocks life has in store for him. Archie is not alone in this regard. Hopelessness is almost always a major element of depression (Alloy & Clements, 1998).

HOPE *Does Seligman's research give any clues about how to "unlearn" helplessness?* With dogs, an effective technique is to forcibly drag them away from shock into the "safe" compartment. After this is done several times, the animals regain "hope" and feelings of control over the environment. Just how this can be done with humans is a question psychologists are exploring. It seems obvious, for instance, that someone like Archie would benefit from an educational program that would allow him to "succeed" repeatedly.

In **mastery training,** responses are reinforced that lead to mastery of a threat or control over one's environment. Animals who undergo such training become more resistant to learned helplessness (Volpicelli et al., 1983). For example, animals that first learn to escape shock become more persistent in trying to flee inescapable shock. In effect, they won't give up, even when the situation really is "hopeless."

Mastery training can occur informally when people learn to cope with challenges. For example, 18- to 21-year-old trainees on a transatlantic sailing voyage showed marked improvements in their ability to cope with stress (Norris & Weinman, 1996).

Such findings suggest that we might be able to "immunize" people against helplessness and depression by allowing them to master difficult

In a recent survey, Canadian college and university students reported elevated levels of psychological distress (Adlaf et al., 2001).

challenges. The Outward Bound schools, in which people pit themselves against the rigours of mountaineering, white-water canoeing, and wilderness survival, might serve as a model for such a program.

The value of hope should not be overlooked. As fragile as this emotion seems to be, it is a powerful antidote to depression and helplessness. As an individual, you may find hope in religion, nature, human companionship, or even technology. Wherever you find it, remember its value: Hope is among the most important of all human emotions. Having positive beliefs, such as optimism, hope, and a sense of meaning and control, is closely related to overall well-being (Lachman & Weaver, 1998; Taylor et al., 2000).

Depression—A Problem for Everyone

During the school year, up to 78 percent of all college students suffer some symptoms of depression. At any given time, from 16 to 30 percent of the student population is depressed (McLennan, 1992; Wong & Whitaker, 1993). A study of 7800 Canadian university students also found that university students were more likely to report higher rates of distress than the general population (Adlaf et al., 2001).

WHY STUDENTS GET THE BLUES   Why should so many students be "blue"? Various problems contribute to depressive feelings. Here are some of the most common:

1. Stresses from college work and pressures to choose a career can leave students feeling that they are missing out on fun or that all their hard work is meaningless.
2. Isolation and loneliness are common when students leave their support groups behind. In the past, family, a circle of high-school friends, and often a boyfriend or girlfriend could be counted on for support and encouragement.
3. Problems with studying and grades frequently trigger depression. Many students start college with high aspirations and little prior experience with failure. At the same time, many lack basic skills necessary for academic success.
4. Another common problem is the breakup of an intimate relationship, either with a former boyfriend or girlfriend or with a newly formed college romance.
5. Students who find it difficult to live up to their idealized images of themselves are especially prone to depression (Scott & O'Hara, 1993).
6. An added danger is that depressed students are more likely to abuse alcohol, which itself is a depressant (Camatta & Nagoshi, 1995).

RECOGNIZING DEPRESSION   Most people know, obviously enough, when they are "down." Aaron Beck, an authority on depression, suggests you should assume that more than a minor fluctuation in mood is involved when five conditions exist:

1. You have a consistently negative opinion of yourself.
2. You engage in frequent self-criticism and self-blame.
3. You place negative interpretations on events that usually wouldn't bother you.
4. The future looks bleak and negative.
5. You feel that your responsibilities are overwhelming.

What can be done to combat depression? Bouts of the college blues are closely related to stressful events. Learning to manage school work and to challenge self-critical thinking can help alleviate mild school-related depression. See "Coping with Depression" on page 430 for some helpful suggestions.

Attacks of the college blues are common and should be distinguished from more serious cases of depression. Severe depression is a serious problem that can lead to suicide or a major impairment of emotional functioning. In such cases it would be wise to seek professional help.

USING PSYCHOLOGY — Coping with Depression

If you don't do well on a test or a class assignment, how do you react? If you see it as a small, isolated setback, you probably won't feel too bad. However, if you feel like you have "blown it" in a big way, depression may follow. Students who strongly link everyday events to long-term goals (such as a successful career or high income) tend to overreact to day-to-day disappointments (McIntosh, Harlow, & Martin, 1995).

What does the preceding tell us about the college blues? The implication is that it's important to take daily tasks one step at a time and chip away at them. That way, you are less likely to feel overwhelmed, helpless, or hopeless. Beck and Greenberg (1974) suggest that when you feel "blue," you should make a daily schedule for yourself. Try to schedule activities to fill up every hour during the day. It is best to start with easy activities and progress to more difficult tasks. Check off each item as it is completed. That way, you will begin to break the self-defeating cycle of feeling helpless and falling further

behind. (Depressed students spend much of their time sleeping.) A series of small accomplishments, successes, or pleasures may be all that you need to get going again. However, if you are lacking skills needed for success in college, ask for help in getting them. Don't remain "helpless."

Feelings of worthlessness and hopelessness are usually supported by self-critical or negative thoughts. Beck and Greenberg recommend writing down such thoughts as they occur, especially those that immediately precede feelings of sadness. After you have collected these thoughts, write a rational answer to each. For example, the thought "No one loves me" should be answered with a list of those who do care. (See Chapter 13 for more information.) One more point to keep in mind is this: When events begin to improve, try to accept it as a sign that better times lie ahead. Positive events are most likely to end depression if you view them as stable and continuing, rather than temporary and fragile (Needles & Abramson, 1990).

Knowledge builder

DEFENSE MECHANISMS, HELPLESSNESS, AND DEPRESSION

Relate

We tend to be blind to our own reliance on defence mechanisms. Return to the definitions in Table 11.5 and see if you can think of one example of each defence that you have observed someone else using.

Have you ever felt helpless in a particular situation? What caused you to feel that way? Does any part of Seligman's description of learned helplessness match your own experience?

Imagine that a friend of yours is suffering from the college blues. What advice would you give your friend?

Learning Check

1. Fulfilling frustrated desires in imaginary achievements or activities defines the defence mechanism of
   a. compensation b. isolation c. fantasy d. sublimation

2. Of the defence mechanisms, two that are considered relatively constructive are
   a. compensation b. denial c. isolation d. projection e. regression
   f. rationalization g. sublimation

3. Depression in humans is similar to _____ _____ observed in animal experiments.

4. At any given time, over one half of the college student population suffers symptoms of depression. T or F?

5. Countering negative, self-critical thoughts only calls attention to them and makes depression worse. T or F?

Critical Thinking

6. Learned helplessness is closely related to which of the factors that determine the severity of stress?

Answers:

1. c 2. a, g 3. learned helplessness 4. F 5. F 6. Feelings of incompetence and lack of control.

▶ Stress and Health—Unmasking a Hidden Killer

Survey Question:
■ How is stress related to health and disease?

Disaster, depression, and sorrow often precede illness. As Taylor (our intrepid student) found after finals week, stressful events reduce the body's natural defences against disease. More surprising is the finding that major life changes—both good and bad—can increase susceptibility to accidents or illness.

Social Readjustment Rating Scale (SRRS) A scale that rates the impact of various life events on the likelihood of illness.

Life change units (LCUs) Numerical values assigned to each life event on the SRRS.

Life Events and Stress

How can I tell if I am subjecting myself to too much stress? Some 30 years ago, Dr. Thomas Holmes and his associates developed a rating scale to estimate the health hazards faced when stresses add up (Holmes & Masuda, 1972). More recently, Mark Miller and Richard Rahe updated the scale for use today. The **Social Readjustment Rating Scale (SRRS)** is reprinted in Table 11.6. Notice that the effect of life events is expressed in **life change units (LCUs)** (numerical values assigned to each life event).

As you read the scale, note again that positive life events may be as costly as disasters. Marriage rates 50 life change units, even though it is usually a happy event. You'll also see

Table 11.6
The Social Readjustment Rating Scale (SRRS)

RANK	LIFE EVENT	LIFE CHANGE UNITS
1	Death of spouse or child	119
2	Divorce	98
3	Death of close family member	92
4	Marital separation	79
5	Fired from work	79
6	Major personal injury or illness	77
7	Jail term	75
8	Death of close friend	70
9	Pregnancy	66
10	Major business readjustment	62
11	Foreclosure on a mortgage or loan	61
12	Gain of new family member	57
13	Marital reconciliation	57
14	Change in health or behaviour of family member	56
15	Change in financial state	56
16	Retirement	54
17	Change to different line of work	51
18	Change in number of arguments with spouse	51
19	Marriage	50
20	Spouse begins or ends work	46
21	Sexual difficulties	45
22	Child leaving home	44
23	Mortgage or loan greater than $10 000	44
24	Change in responsibilities at work	43
25	Change in living conditions	42
26	Change in residence	41
27	Begin or end school	38
28	Trouble with in-laws	38
29	Outstanding personal achievement	37
30	Change in work hours or conditions	36
31	Change in schools	35
32	Christmas	30
33	Trouble with boss	29
34	Change in recreation	29
35	Mortgage or loan less than $10 000	28
36	Change in personal habits	27
37	Change in eating habits	27
38	Change in social activities	27
39	Change in number of family get-togethers	26
40	Change in sleeping habits	26
41	Vacation	25
42	Change in church activities	22
43	Minor violations of the law	22

(From M.A. Miller and R.H. Rahe, "Life changes scaling for the 1990s" in *Journal of Psychosomatic Research*, 43(3), 1997, 279–292, Table II, p. 282. Copyright © 1997 Elsevier Science Ltd. Reprinted by permission.)

many items that read "Change in . . ." This means that an improvement in life conditions can be as costly as a decline. A stressful adjustment may be required in either case.

To use the scale, add up the LCUs for all life events you have experienced during the last year and compare the total to the following standards.

0–150	No significant problems
150–199	Mild life crisis (33 percent chance of illness)
200–299	Moderate life crisis (50 percent chance of illness)
300 or more	Major life crisis (80 percent chance of illness)

According to Holmes, there is a high chance of illness or accident when your LCU total exceeds 300 points. A more conservative rating of stress can be obtained by totalling LCU points for only the previous six months.

Many of the listed life changes don't seem relevant to young adults or college students. Does the SRRS apply to these people? The SRRS tends to be more appropriate for older, more established adults. However, research has shown that the health of college students is also affected by stressful events, such as entering college, changing majors, or the breakup of a steady relationship (Crandall, Preisler, & Aussprung, 1992).

People differ greatly in their reactions to the same event. For such reasons, the SRRS is at best a rough index of stress. Nevertheless, it's hard to ignore a study in which people were deliberately exposed to the virus that causes common colds. The results were nothing to sneeze at: If a person had a high stress score, she or he was much more likely to actually get a cold (Cohen, Tyrrell, & Smith, 1993). In view of such findings, a high LCU score should be taken seriously. If your score goes much over 300, an adjustment in your activities or lifestyle may be needed.

THE HAZARDS OF HASSLES *There must be more to stress than major life changes. Isn't there a link between ongoing stresses and health?* In addition to having a direct impact, major life events spawn countless daily frustrations and irritations (Pillow, Zautra, & Sandler, 1996). Also, many of us face ongoing stresses at work or at home that do not involve major life changes. In view of these facts, psychologist Richard Lazarus and his associates studied the impact of minor but frequent stresses. Lazarus (1981) calls such distressing daily annoyances **hassles,** or **microstressors.** Hassles range from traffic jams to losing classroom notes; from an argument with a roommate to an employer's unrealistic demands (see Table 11.7).

In a year-long study, Lazarus had 100 men and women record the hassles they endured. Participants also reported on their physical and mental health. As Lazarus suspected, frequent and severe hassles turned out to be better predictors of day-to-day health than major life events were. However, major life events did predict changes in health one or two years after the events took place. It appears that daily hassles are closely linked to immediate health and psychological well-being (Johnson & Sherman, 1997; Roberts, 1995). Major life changes have more of a long-term impact.

What can be done about a high LCU score or feeling excessively hassled? A good response is to use stress management skills. For serious problems, stress management should be learned directly from a therapist or a stress clinic. When ordinary stresses are involved, there is much you can do on your own. This chapter's Psychology in Action section will give you a start. In the meantime, take it easy!

Psychosomatic Disorders

As we have seen, chronic or repeated stress can damage physical health, as well as upset emotional well-being. Prolonged stress reactions are closely related to a large number

Marriage is usually considered a positive life event. Nevertheless, the many changes it brings can be stressful.

Microstressor Any distressing, day-to-day annoyance; also called a *hassle*.

Table 11.7
Examples of Daily Hassles

Too many responsibilities or commitments
Problems with work, boss, or co-workers
Unexpected houseguests
Inconsiderate neighbours
Noisy, messy, or quarrelling children
Regrets over past decisions
Having trouble making decisions
Money worries or concerns
Not enough time for family, relaxation, or entertainment
Loneliness, social isolation, separated from family
Physical illness, symptoms, complaints
Concerns about weight, appearance
Frustrations with daily chores
Delays, transportation problems
Paperwork, filling out forms
Misplacing or losing things
Noise, pollution, deteriorating neighbourhoods
Bad weather
Crime, disturbing news events

Psychosomatic disorders
Illnesses in which psychological factors contribute to bodily damage.

Hypochondriac A person who complains about illnesses that appear to be imaginary.

Biofeedback Information given to a person about his or her ongoing bodily activities; aids voluntary regulation of bodily states.

of psychosomatic (SIKE-oh-so-MAT-ik) illnesses. In **psychosomatic disorders** (*psyche*: mind; *soma*: body), psychological factors contribute to actual bodily damage or to damaging changes in bodily functioning. Psychosomatic problems, therefore, are not the same as hypochondria. **Hypochondriacs** (HI-po-KON-dree-aks) imagine that they suffer from diseases. There is nothing imaginary about asthma, a migraine headache, or high blood pressure. Severe psychosomatic disorders can be fatal. The person who says, "Oh, it's just psychosomatic" misunderstands how serious stress-related diseases really are.

The most common psychosomatic problems are gastrointestinal and respiratory (stomach pain and asthma, for example), but many others exist. Typical problems include eczema (skin rash), hives, migraine headaches, rheumatoid arthritis, hypertension (high blood pressure), colitis (ulceration of the colon), and heart disease. Actually, these are only the major problems. Lesser health complaints are also frequently stress related. Typical examples include sore muscles, headaches, neckaches, backaches, indigestion, constipation, chronic diarrhea, fatigue, insomnia, premenstrual problems, and sexual dysfunctions (Brown, 1980; De Benedittis, Lorenzetti, & Pieri, 1990). For some of these problems, biofeedback may be helpful. The next section explains how.

Biofeedback

Psychologists have discovered that people can learn to control bodily activities once thought to be involuntary. This is done by applying informational feedback to bodily control, a process called **biofeedback.** If someone were to say to you, "Raise the temperature of your right hand," you probably couldn't because you wouldn't know if you were succeeding. To make your task easier, we could attach a sensitive thermometer to your hand. The thermometer could be wired so that an increase in temperature would activate a signal light. Then, all you would have to do is try to keep the light on as much as possible. With practice and the help of biofeedback, you could learn to raise your hand temperature at will.

Biofeedback holds promise as a way to treat some psychosomatic problems (see ▶Figure 11.9). For instance, people have been trained to prevent migraine headaches with biofeedback. Sensors are taped to patients' hands and foreheads. Patients then learn to redirect blood flow away from the head to their extremities. Since migraine headaches involve excessive blood flow to the head, biofeedback helps patients reduce the frequency of their headaches (Gauthier, Cote, & French, 1994; Kropp et al., 1997).

Early successes led many to predict that biofeedback would offer a cure for psychosomatic illnesses, anxiety, phobias, drug abuse, and a long list of other problems. In reality, biofeedback has proved helpful, but not an instant cure (Amar, 1993). Biofeedback can help relieve muscle-tension headaches, migraine headaches, and chronic pain (Arena et al., 1995; Buckelew et al., 1998). It shows promise for lowering blood pressure and controlling heart rhythms (Blanchard et al., 1996; Lal et al., 1998). The technique has been used with some success to control epileptic seizures and hyperactivity in children (Potashkin & Beckles, 1990; Sterman, 1996). Insomnia also responds to biofeedback therapy (Barowsky, Moskowitz, & Zweig, 1990).

How does biofeedback help? Some researchers believe that many of its benefits arise from *general relaxation.* Others stress that there is no magic in biofeedback itself. The method simply acts as a "mirror" to help a person perform tasks involving self-regulation. Just as a mirror does not comb your hair, biofeedback does not do anything by itself. It can, however, help people make desired changes in their behaviour (Amar, 1993; Weems, 1998).

The Cardiac Personality

It would be a mistake to assume that stress is the sole cause of psychosomatic diseases. Hereditary differences, organ weaknesses, and learned reactions to stress combine to do damage. Personality also enters the picture. As mentioned earlier, a

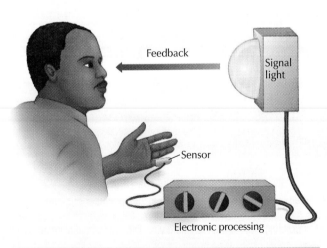

Feedback

Signal light

Sensor

Electronic processing

▶Figure 11.9

In biofeedback training, bodily processes are monitored and processed electronically. A signal is then routed back to the patient through headphones, signal lights, or other means. This information helps the patient alter bodily activities not normally under voluntary control.

Individuals with Type A personalities feel a continuous sense of anger, irritation, and hostility.

Type A personality A personality type with an elevated risk of heart disease; characterized by time urgency, anger, and hostility.

Type B personality All personality types other than Type A; a low cardiac-risk personality.

general disease-prone personality type exists. To a degree, there are also "headache personalities," "asthma personalities," and so on. The best documented of such patterns is the "cardiac personality"—a person at high risk for heart disease.

Two noted cardiologists, Meyer Friedman and Ray Rosenman, offer a glimpse at how some people create stress for themselves. In a landmark study of heart problems, Friedman and Rosenman (1983) classified people as either **Type A personalities** (those who run a high risk of heart attack) or **Type B personalities** (those who are unlikely to have a heart attack). Then they did an eight-year follow-up, finding more than twice the rate of heart disease in Type A individuals than in Type Bs (Rosenman et al., 1975).

TYPE A *What is the Type A personality like?* Type A people are hard driving, ambitious, highly competitive, achievement oriented, and striving. Type A people believe that with enough effort they can overcome any obstacle, and they "push" themselves accordingly.

Perhaps the most telltale signs of a Type A personality are *time urgency* and chronic *anger* or *hostility*. Type A people hurry from one activity to another, racing the clock in self-imposed urgency. As they do, they feel a constant sense of frustration and anger. Feelings of anger and hostility, in particular, are strongly related to increased risk of heart attack (Miller et al., 1996). One study found that 15 percent of a group of 25-year-old doctors and lawyers who scored high on a hostility test were dead by age 50. The most damaging pattern may occur in hostile persons who keep their anger "bottled up." This increases their pulse rate and blood pressure and puts a tremendous strain on the heart (Bongard, al'Absi, & Lovallo, 1998).

To summarize, there is growing evidence that anger or hostility may be the core lethal factor of Type A behaviour (King, 1997). To date, hundreds of studies have supported the validity of the Type A concept. In view of this, Type A individuals would be wise to take their increased health risks seriously (Miller et al., 1991; Sprafka et al., 1990).

How are Type A people identified? Characteristics of Type A people are summarized in the short self-identification test presented in Table 11.8. If most of the list applies to you, you may be a Type A. However, confirmation of your type would require more powerful testing methods. Also, remember that the original definition of Type A behaviour was probably too broad. The key psychological factors that increase heart disease risk appear to be anger, hostility, and mistrust (Suls & Swain, 1994).

Table 11.8 Characteristics of the Type A Person

CHECK THE ITEMS THAT APPLY TO YOU. DO YOU:

_____ Have a habit of explosively accentuating various key words in ordinary speech even when there is no need for such accentuation?

_____ Finish other persons' sentences for them?

_____ *Always* move, walk, and eat rapidly?

_____ Quickly skim reading material and prefer summaries or condensations of books?

_____ Become easily angered by slow-moving lines or traffic?

_____ Feel an impatience with the rate at which most events take place?

_____ Tend to be unaware of the details or beauty of your surroundings?

_____ Frequently strive to think of or do two or more things simultaneously?

_____ Almost always feel vaguely guilty when you relax, vacation, or do absolutely nothing for several days?

_____ Tend to evaluate your worth in quantitative terms (number of A's earned, amount of income, number of games won, and so forth)?

_____ Have nervous gestures or muscle twitches, such as grinding your teeth, clenching your fists, or drumming your fingers?

_____ Attempt to schedule more and more activities into less time and in so doing make fewer allowances for unforeseen problems?

_____ Frequently think about other things while talking to someone?

_____ Repeatedly take on more responsibilities than you can comfortably handle?

Shortened and adapted from Meyer Friedman and Ray H. Rosenman, *Type A Behavior and Your Heart* (New York: Knopf, 1983).

Because our society places a premium on achievement, competition, and mastery, it is not surprising that many people develop Type A personalities. The best way to avoid the self-made stress this causes is to adopt behaviour that is the opposite of that listed in Table 11.8 (Karlberg, Krakau, & Unden, 1998).

It is entirely possible to succeed in life without sacrificing your health or happiness in the process. People who frequently feel angry and hostile toward others may benefit from the advice of Redford Williams, a physician interested in Type A behaviour. "Strategies for Reducing Hostility" summarizes his advice.

The Hardy Personality

Hardy personality
A personality style associated with superior stress resistance.

How do Type A people who do not develop heart disease differ from those who do? Psychologist Salvatore Maddi and others have studied people who have a **hardy personality.** Such people seem to be unusually resistant to stress. The first study of hardiness began with two groups of managers at a large utility company. All of the managers held high-stress positions. Yet, some tended to get sick after stressful events, while others were rarely ill. How did the people who were thriving differ from their "stressed-out" colleagues? Both groups seemed to have traits typical of the Type A personality, so that wasn't the explanation. They were also quite similar in most other respects. The main difference was that the hardy group seemed to hold a world view that consisted of three traits (Maddi, Kahn, & Maddi, 1998):

1. They had a sense of personal *commitment* to self, work, family, and other stabilizing values.
2. They felt that they had *control* over their lives and their work.
3. They had a tendency to see life as a series of *challenges,* rather than as a series of threats or problems.

USING PSYCHOLOGY   Strategies for Reducing Hostility

According to Redford Williams, reducing hostility involves three goals. First, you must stop mistrusting the motives of others. Second, you must find ways to reduce how often you feel anger, indignation, irritation, and rage. Third, you must learn to be kinder and more considerate. Based on his clinical experience, Williams (1989) recommends 12 strategies for reducing hostility and increasing trust.

1. Become aware of your angry, hostile, and cynical thoughts by logging them in a notebook. Record what happened, what you thought and felt, and what actions you took. Review your hostility log at the end of each week.
2. Admit to yourself and to someone you trust that you have a problem with excessive anger and hostility.
3. Interrupt hostile, cynical thoughts whenever they occur. (The Psychology in Action section of Chapter 13 explains a thought-stopping method you can use for this step.)
4. When you have an angry, hostile, or cynical thought about someone, silently look for the ways in which it is irrational or unreasonable.

5. When you are angry, try to mentally put yourself in the other person's shoes.
6. Learn to laugh at yourself and use humour to defuse your anger.
7. Learn reliable ways to relax. Two methods are described in this chapter's Psychology in Action section. Another can be found in the Psychology in Action discussion of Chapter 13.
8. Practise trusting others more. Begin with situations where no great harm will be done if the person lets you down.
9. Make an effort to listen more to others and to really understand what they are saying.
10. Learn to be assertive, rather than aggressive, in upsetting situations. (See Chapter 14 for information about self-assertion skills.)
11. Rise above small irritations by pretending that today is the last day of your life.
12. Rather than blaming people for mistreating you, and becoming angry over it, try to forgive them. We all have shortcomings.

How do such traits protect people from the effects of stress? Persons strong in commitment find ways of turning whatever they are doing into something that seems interesting and important. They tend to get involved rather than feeling alienated.

Persons strong in control believe that they can more often than not influence the course of events around them. This prevents them from passively seeing themselves as victims of circumstance.

Finally, people strong in challenge believe that fulfillment is found in continual growth. They seek to learn from their experiences, rather than accepting easy comfort, security, and routine (Maddi, Kahn, & Maddi, 1998).

HARDINESS AND HAPPINESS   Good and bad events occur in all lives. What separates happy people from those who are unhappy is largely a matter of attitude. Happy people tend to see their lives in more positive terms, even when trouble comes their way. For example, happier people tend to find humour in disappointments. They look at setbacks as challenges. They are strengthened by losses (Lyubomirsky & Tucker, 1998). In short, happiness tends to be related to hardiness. It is a general personal characteristic, not simply a reaction to circumstances (Brebner, 1998).

At this point we have left a very basic issue unexplained: How does stress, and our response to it, translate into disease? The answer seems to lie in the body's defences against stress, a pattern known as the general adaptation syndrome.

The General Adaptation Syndrome

The **general adaptation syndrome (G.A.S.)** is a series of bodily reactions to prolonged stress. University of Montreal physiologist Hans Selye (1976) noticed that the first symptoms of almost any disease or trauma (poisoning, infection, injury, or stress) are almost identical. Selye's studies showed that the body responds in the same way to any stress, be it infection, failure, embarrassment, a new job, trouble at school, or a stormy romance.

What pattern does the body's response to stress take? The G.A.S. consists of three stages: an alarm reaction, a stage of resistance, and a stage of exhaustion (Selye, 1976).

In the **alarm reaction,** the body mobilizes its resources to cope with added stress. The pituitary gland signals the adrenal glands to produce more adrenaline and noradrenaline. As these stress hormones are dumped into the bloodstream, some bodily processes are speeded up and others are slowed. This allows bodily resources to be applied where they are needed.

We should all be thankful that our bodies automatically respond to emergencies. But brilliant as this emergency system is, it can also cause problems. In the first phase of the alarm reaction, people have such symptoms as headache, fever, fatigue, sore muscles, shortness of breath, diarrhea, upset stomach, loss of appetite, and a lack of energy. Notice that these are also the symptoms of being sick, of stressful travel, of high-altitude sickness, of final exams, and (possibly) of falling in love!

During the **stage of resistance**, bodily adjustments to stress stabilize. As the body's defences come into balance, symptoms of the alarm reaction disappear. Outwardly, everything seems normal. However, this appearance of normality comes at a high cost. The body is better able to cope with the original stressor, but its resistance to other stresses is lowered (see ▶ Figure 11.10). For example, animals placed in extreme cold become more resistant to the cold, but more susceptible to infection. It is during the stage of resistance that the first signs of psychosomatic disorders begin to appear.

Continued stress leads to the **stage of exhaustion** in which the body's resources are drained and stress hormones are depleted. Unless a way of relieving stress is found, the result will be a psychosomatic disease, a serious loss of health, or a complete collapse.

The G.A.S. may sound melodramatic if you are young and healthy or if you've never endured prolonged stress. However, stress

General adaptation syndrome (G.A.S.) A series of bodily reactions to prolonged stress; occurs in three stages: alarm, resistance, and exhaustion.

Alarm reaction First stage of the G.A.S., during which bodily resources are mobilized to cope with a stressor.

Stage of resistance Second stage of the G.A.S., during which bodily adjustments to stress stabilize, but at a high physical cost.

Stage of exhaustion Third stage of the G.A.S., at which time the body's resources are exhausted and damage occurs.

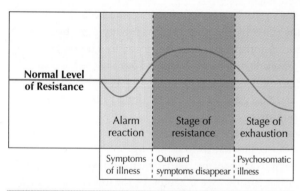

▶ Figure 11.10

The General Adaptation Syndrome. During the initial alarm reaction to stress, resistance falls below normal. It rises again as bodily resources are mobilized, and it remains high during the stage of resistance. Eventually, resistance falls again as the stage of exhaustion is reached. (From *The Stress of Life* by Hans Selye. Copyright © 1976 by Hans Selye. Used by permission of McGraw-Hill Book Company.)

FOCUS ON RESEARCH Stress, Illness, and the Immune System

How else might stress affect health? An answer can be found in the **immune system,** which mobilizes defences (such as white blood cells) against invading microbes and other disease agents (Ader & Cohen, 1993). The immune system is regulated, in part, by the brain. Because of this link, stress and upsetting emotions can affect the immune system in ways that increase susceptibility to disease (Miller, 1998; Pike et al., 1997). (By the way, the study of links among behaviour, stress, disease, and the immune system is called **psychoneuroimmunology.** Try dropping that into a conversation sometime if you want to see a stress reaction!)

Studies show that the immune system is weakened in students during major exam times. Immunity is also lowered by divorce, bereavement, troubled marriage, job loss, depression, and similar stresses (Gilbert et al.,

1996; Herbert & Cohen, 1993; Stein, Miller, & Trestman, 1990). Lowered immunity explains why the "double whammy" of getting sick when you are trying to cope with prolonged or severe stress is so common (Biondi & Zannino, 1997).

Could reducing stress help prevent illness? Yes. Psychological approaches, such as support groups, relaxation exercises, guided imagery, and stress management training, can actually boost immune system functioning (Kiecolt-Glaser & Glaser, 1992). By doing so, they help promote and restore health. There is even evidence that such measures improve the chances of survival following life-threatening diseases, such as cancer (Anderson, Kiecolt-Glaser, & Glaser, 1994).

No one is immune to stress. Nevertheless, it's reassuring to know that managing stress can help protect your immune system and your health.

Immune system System that mobilizes bodily defences against invading microbes and other disease agents.

Psychoneuroimmunology Study of the links among behaviour, stress, disease, and the immune system.

should not be taken lightly. When Selye examined animals in the later stages of the G.A.S., he found that their adrenal glands were enlarged and discoloured. There was intense shrinkage of internal organs such as the thymus, spleen, and lymph nodes, and many animals had stomach ulcers. In addition to such direct effects, stress can disrupt the body's immune system, as described in "Stress, Illness, and the Immune System."

A LOOK AHEAD The work we have reviewed here has drawn new attention to the fact that each of us has a personal responsibility for maintaining and promoting health. In the Psychology in Action section that follows, we will look at what you can do to better cope with stress and the health risks that it entails. But first, the questions in the Knowledge Builder box may help you maintain a healthy grade on your next psychology test.

Knowledge builder

STRESS AND HEALTH

Relate

Pick a year from your life that was unusually stressful. Use the SRRS to find your LCU score for that year. Do you think there was a connection between your LCU score and your health? Or have you observed more of a connection between microstressors and your health?

Mindy complains about her health all the time, but she actually seems to be just fine. An acquaintance of Mindy's dismisses her problems by saying, "Oh, she's not really sick. It's just psychosomatic." What's wrong with this use of the term *psychosomatic?*

Do you think you are basically a Type A or a Type B personality? To what extent do you possess traits of the hardy personality?

Can you say psychoneuroimmunology? Have you impressed anyone with the word yet?

Learning Check

1. Holmes's SRRS appears to predict long-range changes in health, whereas the frequency and severity of daily microstressors is closely related to immediate ratings of health. T or F?
2. Ulcers, migraine headaches, and hypochondria are all frequently psychosomatic disorders. T or F?
3. Which of the following is *not* classified as a psychosomatic disorder?
   a. hypertension *b.* colitis *c.* eczema *d.* thymus
4. Two major elements of biofeedback training appear to be relaxation and self-regulation. T or F?
5. Evidence suggests that the most important feature of the Type A personality is a sense of time urgency rather than feelings of anger and hostility. T or F?
6. A sense of commitment, challenge, and control characterizes the hardy personality. T or F?
7. The first stage of the G.A.S. is called the _____ reaction.
8. Whereas stressful incidents suppress the immune system, stress management techniques have almost no effect on immune system functioning. T or F?

Critical Thinking

9. People with a hardy personality type appear to be especially resistant to which of the problems discussed earlier in this chapter?

Answers:

1. T 2. F 3. *d* 4. T 5. F 6. T 7. alarm 8. F 9. Learned helplessness.

STRESS MANAGEMENT

Stress management is the use of behavioural strategies to reduce stress and improve coping skills. As promised, this section describes strategies for managing stress. Before you continue reading, you may want to assess your level of stress again, this time using a scale developed for undergraduate students (see Table 11.9). Like the SRRS, high scores on the *College Life Stress Inventory* suggest that you have been exposed to health-threatening levels of stress (Renner & Mackin, 1998).

The *College Life Stress Inventory* is scored by adding the ratings for all of the items that have happened to you in the last year. The scale below is an approximate guide to the meaning of your score. But remember, stress is an internal state. If you are good at coping with stressors, a high score may not be a problem for you.

Survey Question:
■ What are the best strategies for managing stress?

2351+	Extremely high
1911–2350	Very high
1471–1910	High
1031–1470	Average
591–1030	Below average
151–590	Low
0–150	Very low

Stress management The application of behavioural strategies to reduce stress and improve coping skills.

Now that you have a picture of your current level of stress, what can you do about it? The simplest way of coping with stress is to modify or remove its source—by leaving a stressful job, for example. Obviously this is often impossible, which is why learning to manage stress is so important.

Table 11.9
College Life Stress Inventory

Circle the "stress rating" number for any event item that has happened to you in the last year, and then add them.

EVENT	STRESS RATING	EVENT	STRESS RATING
Being raped	100	Talking in front of a class	72
Finding out that you are HIV-positive	100	Lack of sleep	69
Being accused of rape	98	Change in housing situation (hassles, moves)	69
Death of a close friend	97	Competing or performing in public	69
Death of a close family member	96	Getting in a physical fight	66
Contracting a sexually transmitted disease (other than AIDS)	94	Difficulties with a roommate	66
Concerns about being pregnant	91	Job changes (applying, new job, work hassles)	65
Final exams	90	Declaring a major or concerns about future plans	65
Concerns about your partner being pregnant	90	A class you hate	62
Oversleeping for an exam	89	Drinking or use of drugs	61
Flunking a class	89	Confrontations with professors	60
Having a boyfriend or girlfriend cheat on you	85	Starting a new semester	58
Ending a steady dating relationship	85	Going on a first date	57
Serious illness in a close friend or family member	85	Registration	55
Financial difficulties	84	Maintaining a steady dating relationship	55
Writing a major term paper	83	Commuting to campus or work, or both	54
Being caught cheating on a test	83	Peer pressures	53
Drunk driving	82	Being away from home for the first time	53
Sense of overload in school or work	82	Getting sick	52
Two exams in one day	80	Concerns about your appearance	52
Cheating on your boyfriend or girlfriend	77	Getting straight A's	51
Getting married	76	A difficult class that you love	48
Negative consequences of drinking or drug use	75	Making new friends; getting along with friends	47
Depression or crisis in your best friend	73	Fraternity or sorority rush	47
Difficulties with parents	73	Falling asleep in class	40
		Attending an athletic event (e.g., football game)	20

(From M.J. Renner and R.S. Mackin in *Teaching of Psychology, 25*(1), p. 47. Copyright © 1998 Lawrence Erlbaum Associates, Inc. Reprinted with permission of author and publisher.)

As shown in ▶Figure 11.11, stress triggers bodily effects, upsetting thoughts, and ineffective behaviour. Also shown is the fact that each element worsens the others in a vicious circle. Indeed, the basic idea of the "Stress Game" is that once it begins, you lose—unless you take action to break the cycle. The information that follows tells how.

Managing Bodily Reactions

Much of the immediate discomfort of stress is caused by fight-or-flight emotional responses. The body is ready to act, with tight muscles and a pounding heart. If action is prevented, we merely remain "uptight." A sensible remedy is to learn a reliable, drug-free way of relaxing.

EXERCISE Stress-based arousal can be dissipated by using the body. Any full-body exercise can be effective. Swimming, dancing, jumping rope, yoga, most sports, and especially walking are valuable outlets (Anshel, 1995). Regular exercise alters hormones, circulation, muscle tone, and a number of other aspects of physical functioning. Together, such changes can lower the risks for disease (Baum & Posluszny, 1999).

Be sure to choose activities that are vigorous enough to relieve tension, yet enjoyable enough to be done repeatedly. Exercising for stress management is most effective when it is done daily (Wheeler & Frank, 1988). Remember, though, that this refers to light exercise, such as walking. If you do more vigorous exercise to maintain aerobic fitness, three to four times a week is about right.

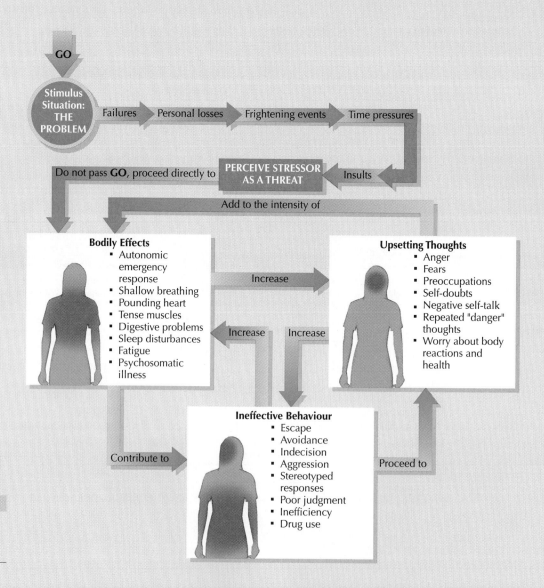

▶**Figure 11.11**

The Stress Game. (Adapted from Rosenthal and Rosenthal, 1980.)

MEDITATION   Many stress counsellors recommend meditation for quieting the body and promoting relaxation. Meditation and its effects were discussed in Chapter 5. Here, it is enough to restate that meditation is easy to learn—taking an expensive commercial course is unnecessary. It is also one of the most effective ways to relax (Eppley, Abrams, & Shear, 1989). But be aware that listening to or playing music, taking nature walks, enjoying hobbies, and the like can be meditations of sorts. Anything that reliably interrupts upsetting thoughts and promotes relaxation can be helpful.

PROGRESSIVE RELAXATION   It is possible to relax systematically, completely, and by choice. To learn the details of how this is done, consult Chapter 13 of this book. The basic idea of **progressive relaxation** is to tighten all the muscles in a given area of your body (the arms, for instance) and then voluntarily relax them. By first tensing and relaxing each area of the body, you can learn what muscle tension feels like. Then when each area is relaxed, the change is more noticeable and more controllable. In this way it is possible, with practice, to greatly reduce tension.

GUIDED IMAGERY   In a technique called **guided imagery,** people visualize images that are calming, relaxing, or beneficial in other ways. Relaxation, for instance, can be promoted by visualizing peaceful scenes. Pick several places where you feel safe, calm, and at ease. Typical locations might be a beach or lake, the woods, floating on an air mattress in a warm pool, or lying in the sun at a quiet park. To relax, vividly imagine yourself in one of these locations. In the visualized scene, you should be alone and in a comfortable position. It is important to visualize the scene as realistically as possible. Try to feel, taste, smell, hear, and see what you would actually experience in the calming scene. Practise forming such images several times a day for about five minutes each time. When your scenes become familiar and detailed, they can be used to reduce anxiety and encourage relaxation (Rosenthal, 1993).

Modifying Ineffective Behaviour

Stress is often made worse by our misguided responses to it. The following suggestions may help you deal with stress more effectively.

SLOW DOWN   Remember that stress can be self-generated. Try to do things at a slower pace, especially if your pace has speeded up over the years. Tell yourself, "What counts most is not if I get there first, but if I get there at all" or "My goal is distance, not speed."

ORGANIZE   Disorganization creates stress. Try to take a fresh look at your situation and get organized. Setting priorities can be a real stress fighter. Ask yourself what's really important and concentrate on the things that count. Learn to let go of trivial but upsetting irritations. And above all, when you are feeling stressed, remember to K.I.S.: **K**eep **I**t **S**imple. (Some people prefer K.I.S.S.: Keep It Simple, Stupid.)

STRIKE A BALANCE   Work, school, family, friends, interests, hobbies, recreation, community, church—there are many important elements in a satisfying life. Damaging stress often comes from letting one element—especially work or school—get blown out of proportion. Your goal should be quality in life, not quantity. Try to strike a balance between challenging "good stress" and relaxation (Wheeler & Frank, 1988). Remember, when you are "doing nothing" you are actually doing something very important: Set aside time for "me acts" such as loafing, browsing, puttering, playing, and napping.

RECOGNIZE AND ACCEPT YOUR LIMITS   Many of us set unrealistic and perfectionistic goals. Given that no one can ever be perfect, this attitude leaves many people feeling inadequate, no matter how well they have performed. Set gradual, achievable goals for yourself. Also, set realistic limits on what you try to do on any given day. Learn to say no to added demands or responsibilities.

SEEK SOCIAL SUPPORT   **Social supports** (close, positive relationships with others) facilitates good health and morale (Greenglass, Burke, & Konarski, 1998). One reason for this is that support from family and friends serves as a buffer to cushion the impact of stressful events (Taylor, 1990). Talking out problems and expressing tensions can be incredibly helpful. If things really get bad, seek help from a therapist, counsellor, or clergyman.

Progressive relaxation A method for producing deep relaxation of all parts of the body.

Guided imagery Intentional visualization of images that are calming, relaxing, or beneficial in other ways.

Social support Close, positive relationships with other people.

WRITE ABOUT YOUR FEELINGS   If you don't have someone you can talk to about stressful events, you might try expressing your thoughts and feelings in writing. Several studies have found that students who write about their upsetting experiences, thoughts, and feelings are better able to cope with stress, experience fewer illnesses, and get better grades (Esterling et al., 1999; Pennebaker & Francis, 1996). For some people, just expressing their feelings is beneficial. For others it also helps to make specific plans for coping with upsetting experiences after writing about them (Cameron & Nicholls, 1998).

Avoiding Upsetting Thoughts

Assume you are taking a test. Suddenly you realize that you are running short of time. If you say to yourself, "Oh no, this is terrible, I've blown it now," your body's response will probably be sweating, tenseness, and a knot in your stomach. On the other hand, if you say, "I should have watched the time, but getting upset won't help, I'll just take one question at a time," your stress level will be much lower.

As stated earlier, stress is greatly affected by the views we take of events. Physical symptoms and a tendency to make poor decisions are increased by negative thoughts or "self-talk." In many cases what you say to yourself can be the difference between coping and collapsing (Matheny et al., 1996).

COPING STATEMENTS   University of Waterloo psychologist Donald Meichenbaum has popularized a technique called **stress inoculation.** In it, clients learn to fight fear and anxiety with an internal monologue of positive coping statements. First, clients learn to identify and monitor **negative self-statements** (self-critical thoughts that increase anxiety). Negative thoughts are a problem because they tend to directly elevate physical arousal. To counter this effect, clients learn to replace negative statements with coping statements from a supplied list. Eventually they are encouraged to make their own lists (Saunders et al., 1996).

How are coping statements applied? **Coping statements** are reassuring and self-enhancing. They are used to block out, or counteract, negative self-talk in stressful situations. Before giving a short speech, for instance, you would replace "I'm scared," "I can't do this," "My mind will go blank and I'll panic," or "I'll sound stupid and boring" with "I'll give my speech on something I like," "I'll breathe deeply before I start my speech," or "My pounding heart just means I'm psyched up to do my best." Additional examples of coping statements follow.

Preparing for Stressful Situation

- I'll just take things one step at a time.
- If I get nervous I'll just pause a moment.
- Tomorrow I'll be through it.
- I've managed to do this before.
- What exactly do I have to do?

Confronting the Stressful Situation

- Relax now, this can't really hurt me.
- Stay organized, focus on the task.
- There's no hurry, take it step by step.
- Nobody's perfect, I'll just do my best.
- It will be over soon, just be calm.

Meichenbaum cautions that saying the "right" things to yourself may not be enough to improve stress tolerance. You must practise this approach in actual stress situations. Also, it is important to develop your own personal list of coping statements by finding what works for you. Ultimately, the value of learning this and other stress management skills ties back into the idea that much stress is self-generated. Knowing that you can manage a demanding situation is in itself a major antidote for stress.

LIGHTEN UP   Humour is worth cultivating as a way to reduce stress. A good sense of humour can lower your distress/stress reaction to difficult events (Lefcourt & Thomas,

Stress inoculation Use of positive coping statements to control fear and anxiety.
Negative self-statements Self-critical thoughts that increase anxiety and lower performance.
Coping statements Reassuring, self-enhancing statements that are used to stop self-critical thinking.

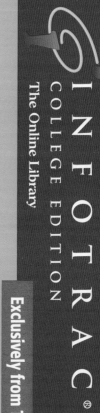

Here's your passcode for your

Free 4-month subscription
to InfoTrac® College Edition

24-hour access

Easy to search

A real time-saver

Log on and get started!

Exclusively from Thomson Learning™!

1998). In addition, an ability to laugh at life's ups and downs is associated with better immunity to disease (McCelland & Cheriff, 1997). Don't be afraid to laugh at yourself and at the many ways in which we humans make things difficult for ourselves. Humour is one of the best antidotes for anxiety and emotional distress (Cann, Holt, & Calhoun, 1999).

Coping with Frustration and Conflict

In a classic experiment, a psychologist studying frustration placed rats on a small platform at the top of a tall pole. Then he forced them to jump off the platform toward two elevated doors, one locked and the other unlocked. If the rat chose the correct door, it swung open and the rat landed safely on another platform. Rats who chose the locked door bounced off it and fell into a net far below.

The problem of choosing the open door was made unsolvable and very frustrating by randomly alternating which door was locked. After a time, most rats chose the same door every time. This door was then locked. All the rats had to do was to jump to the other door to avoid a fall, but they did not (Maier, 1949).

Isn't that an example of persistence? No. Persistence that is inflexible can turn into stereo-typed behaviour like that of the rats. When dealing with frustration, you must know when to change direction. Here are some suggestions to help you avoid needless frustration.

1. Try to identify the source of your frustration. Is it external or personal?
2. Can the source of frustration be changed? How hard would you have to work to change it? Is it under your control at all?
3. If the source of your frustration can be changed or removed, is the effort worth it?

The answers to these questions help determine if persistence will not work. There is value in learning to accept gracefully those things that cannot be changed.

It is also important to distinguish between real and imagined barriers. Too often we create our own imaginary barriers. For example, Anita wants a part-time job to earn extra money. At the first place she applies, she is told that she doesn't have enough "experience." Now she says she is frustrated because she needs "experience" to work, but can't get experience without working. She has quit looking for a job.

Is Anita's need for experience a real barrier? Unless she applies for many jobs we cannot tell if she has overestimated its importance. For her the barrier is real enough to prevent further efforts, but with persistence she might locate an "unlocked door." If a reasonable amount of effort does show that experience is essential, it might be obtained in other ways—through temporary volunteer work, for instance.

How can I handle conflicts more effectively? Most of the suggestions just made also apply to conflicts. However, here are some additional things to remember when you are in conflict or must make a difficult decision.

1. Slow down when making important decisions. Take time to collect information and to weigh pros and cons. Hasty decisions are often regretted. Even if you do make a faulty decision, it will trouble you less if you know that you did everything possible to avoid a mistake.
2. Try out important decisions partially when possible. If you are thinking about moving to a new town, try to spend a few days there first. If you are choosing between schools, do the same. If classes are in progress, sit in on some. If you want to learn to scuba dive, rent equipment for a reasonable length of time before buying.
3. Look for workable compromises. Again it is important to get all available information. If you think that you have only one or two alternatives and they are undesirable or unbearable, seek the aid of a teacher, counsellor, minister, or social service agency. You may be overlooking possible alternatives these people will know about.
4. When all else fails, make a decision and live with it. Indecision and conflict exact a high cost. Sometimes it is best to select a course of action and stick with it unless you find that it is very obviously wrong after you have taken it.

In class you may want to describe some of the frustrations and conflicts you have experienced and how you handled them. Prepare to discuss frustrations and conflicts you have resolved in an unusually effective manner or that you might have handled better. Do you have some additional hints to share with other students?

Knowledge builder

COPING WITH STRESS

Relate

If you were going to put together a "tool kit" for stress management, what items would you include?

Learning Check

1. Exercise, meditation, and progressive relaxation are considered effective ways of countering negative self-statements. T or F?
2. Research shows that social support from family and friends has little effect on the health consequences of stress. T or F?

3. One element of stress inoculation is training in the use of positive coping statements. T or F?
4. Stereotyped responding can be particularly troublesome in coping with frustration. T or F?

Critical Thinking

5. Steve always feels extremely pressured when the due date arrives for his major term papers. How could he reduce stress in such instances?

Answers:

1. F 2. F 3. T 4. T 5. The stress associated with doing term papers can be almost completely eliminated by making a long-term assignment into many small daily or weekly assignments. Students who habitually procrastinate are often amazed at how pleasant college work can be once they renounce "brinkmanship."

Psychologist's Journal

EPILOGUE

Until recently, research on stress has focused on the body's "fight-or-flight" reactions. Physically, both men and women experience fight-or-flight activation when confronted by stressors. However, what men and women do about feeling stressed may differ significantly. Psychologist Shelley Taylor and her colleagues believe that women typically respond to stressful situations by protecting themselves and their children and by connecting with other people, especially other women. Taylor calls this the "tend-and-befriend" pattern. In contrast, men who are stressed tend to become aggressive or to withdraw emotionally. Women are more likely to nurture those around them and to seek support from others (Taylor et al., 2000). (This may be why "manly men" won't ask for help, whereas women in trouble call their friends.)

It remains to be seen if women really do tend-and-befriend more often than men do. Nevertheless, it is well documented that people with strong social networks are healthier, happier, and live longer than isolated people. Seeking support from others, and offering support in return, may be among the most adaptive of all human behaviours.

CHAPTER IN REVIEW

Major Points

▶ A variety of personal habits and behaviour patterns affect health.

▶ Maintaining good health is a personal responsibility, not a matter of luck. Wellness is based on minimizing risk factors and engaging in health-promoting behaviours.

▶ Stress is a normal part of life; however, it is also a major risk factor for illness and disease.

▶ While some events are more stressful than others, stress always represents an interaction between people and the environments in which they live.

▶ Personality characteristics affect the amount of stress a person experiences and the subsequent risk of illness.

▶ The body's reactions to stress can directly damage internal organs, and stress impairs the body's immune system, increasing susceptibility to disease.

▶ The damaging effects of stress can be reduced with stress management techniques.

Summary

What Is Health Psychology? How Does Behaviour Affect Health?

• Health psychologists are interested in behaviour that helps maintain and promote health.

• Studies of health and illness have identified a number of behavioural risk factors and health-promoting behaviours.

• Many sexually active people continue to take unnecessary risks with their health by failing to follow safer sex practices.

• Health psychologists have pioneered efforts to prevent the development of unhealthy habits and to improve well-being through community health campaigns.

What Is Stress? What Factors Determine Its Severity?

• Stress occurs when demands are placed on an organism to adjust or adapt.

• Stress is more damaging in situations involving pressure, a lack of control, unpredictability of the stressor, and intense or repeated emotional shocks.

• Stress is intensified when a situation is perceived as a threat and when a person does not feel competent to cope with it.

• In work settings, prolonged stress can lead to burnout.

• The primary appraisal of a situation greatly affects our emotional response to it.

• During a secondary appraisal, a problem-focused or emotion-focused way of coping is selected.

What Causes Frustration and What Are Typical Reactions to It?

• Frustration is the negative emotional state that occurs when progress toward a goal is blocked.

• External frustrations are based on delay, failure, rejection, loss, and other direct blocking of motives. Personal frustration is related to personal characteristics over which one has little control.

• Frustrations of all types become more intense as the strength, urgency, or importance of the blocked motive increases.

• Major behavioural reactions to frustration include persistence, more vigorous responding, circumvention, direct aggression, displaced aggression (including scapegoating), and escape or withdrawal.

Are There Different Types of Conflict? How Do People React to Conflict?

• Conflict occurs when one must choose between contradictory alternatives.

• Five types of conflict are approach-approach, avoidance-avoidance, approach-avoidance, double approach-avoidance, and multiple approach-avoidance.

• Approach-approach conflicts are usually the easiest to resolve.

• Avoidance conflicts are difficult to resolve and are characterized by inaction, indecision, freezing, and a desire to escape.

• People usually remain in approach-avoidance conflicts, but fail to fully resolve them, which leads to ambivalence and partial approach.

• Vacillation is a common reaction to double approach-avoidance conflicts.

What Are Defence Mechanisms?

• Anxiety, threat, or feelings of inadequacy frequently lead to the use of defence mechanisms that reduce anxiety.

• Many defence mechanisms have been identified, including compensation, denial, fantasy, intellectualization, isolation, projection, rationalization, reaction formation, regression, repression, and sublimation.

What Do We Know about Coping with Feelings of Helplessness and Depression?

• Learned helplessness has been used as a model for understanding depression. Mastery training acts as an antidote to helplessness.

• Depression is a major, and surprisingly common, emotional problem. Actions and thoughts that reverse feelings of helplessness tend to reduce depression.

• The college blues are a relatively mild form of depression. Learning to manage college work and to challenge self-critical thinking can help cure the college blues.

How Is Stress Related to Health and Disease?

• Work with the *Social Readjustment Rating Scale* indicates that multiple life changes tend to increase long-range susceptibility to accident or illness.

- Immediate psychological and mental health is more closely related to the intensity and severity of daily hassles (microstressors).
- Intense or prolonged stress may cause damage in the form of psychosomatic problems.
- During biofeedback training, bodily processes are monitored and converted to a signal that tells what the body is doing. This allows people to control some bodily activities and alleviate some psychosomatic illnesses.
- People with Type A personalities are competitive, striving, hostile, and impatient. These characteristics—especially hostility—double the risk of heart attack.
- People who have traits of the hardy personality seem to be unusually resistant to stress.

- The body reacts to stress in a series of stages called the general adaptation syndrome (G.A.S.).
- The stages of the G.A.S. are alarm, resistance, and exhaustion. The G.A.S. appears to explain how psychosomatic disorders develop.
- Studies of psychoneuroimmunology show that stress also lowers the body's immunity to disease.

What Are the Best Strategies for Managing Stress?

- A sizable number of coping skills can be applied to manage stress. Most of these focus on one of three areas: bodily effects, ineffective behaviour, and upsetting thoughts.

PSYCHOLOGY ON THE NET

If you have difficulty finding any of the sites listed here, visit http://www.psychologyjourney.nelson.com for an updated list of Internet addresses and direct links to relevant sites.

Burnout Test   A short questionnaire on job burnout. http://www.prohealth.com/articles/burnout.htm

The Canadian Cancer Society   This site offers links and information on cancer prevention and treatments. http://www.cancer.ca

Canadian Institute for Health Information   This institute provides health information from Health Canada, Statistics Canada, and other organizations. http://www.cihi.ca

The Canadian Institute of Stress   This organization, founded by Dr. Hans Selye in 1979, endeavours to reduce stress in our daily lives. http://www.stresscanada.org

Focus on Stress   A series of articles about stress. http://helping.apa.org/work/index.html

Health Canada   An excellent source of information on all health issues. http://www.hc-sc.gc.ca/

Planned Parenthood Federation of Canada   A good source of information on issues related to sexuality. http://www.ppfc.ca

Preventive Health Center   A general source of information on how to maintain health and prevent disease. http://www.md-phc.com/index.html

Stress Management: Review of Principles   Links to articles on stress management. http://www.unl.edu/stress/mgmt/

Type A Behaviour   Describes Type A behaviour, with links to an online test and related sites. http://www.msnbc.com/onair/nbc/nightlynews/stress/default.asp

 InfoTrac College Edition   For recent articles related to the college blues and more serious forms of depression, use Key Words search for MENTAL DEPRESSION.

INTERACTIVE LEARNING

Psychology: An Interactive Journey   Remember that Chapter 11 of the CD-ROM that came with this text has practice tests, flashcards, interactive exercises, a crossword puzzle, and other valuable materials to enhance your learning experience.

PsychNow!   4c. Coping with Emotion, 4d. Stress and Health.

Psyk.trek   11f. Types of Stress, 11g. Responding to stress.

Chart Your Progress

The questions that follow are only a sample of what you need to know. If you miss any of the items, you should review the entire chapter, do the exercises on the CD, and review the Knowledge Builders. Another way to prepare for tests is to get more practice with *WebTutor*, the *Study Guide*, or the *Practice Quizzes* that are available with this text.

1. Lifestyle diseases related to just three behaviours account for 20 percent of all deaths in Canada. The behaviours are smoking, alcohol abuse, and
   a. driving too fast
   b. excessive sun exposure
   c. unsafe sex
   d. illicit drug use

2. For the first _____ after infection, a negative test result for HIV is no guarantee that a person is a "safe" sex partner.
   a. 3 weeks
   b. 6 weeks
   c. 6 months
   d. 3 years

3. According to Richard Lazarus, choosing a way to meet a threat or challenge takes place during the
   a. primary stress reaction
   b. secondary stress reaction
   c. primary appraisal
   d. secondary appraisal

4. Aggression is an especially common reaction to
   a. frustration
   b. scapegoating
   c. approach conflicts
   d. ambivalence

5. You would be most likely to experience vacillation if you found yourself in
   a. an approach–approach conflict
   b. an avoidance–avoidance conflict
   c. a double approach–avoidance conflict
   d. the condition called emotion-focused coping

6. Justifying your actions by making excuses that appear to explain your behaviour is called
   a. sublimation
   b. reaction formation
   c. compensation
   d. rationalization

7. Learned helplessness tends to occur when events appear to be
   a. frustrating
   b. in conflict
   c. uncontrollable
   d. problem-focused

8. Ratings on the SRRS are based on the total number of _____ a person has for the preceding year.
   a. hassles
   b. LCUs
   c. STDs
   d. psychosomatic illnesses

9. In many ways, a person who has a hardy personality is the opposite of a person who has
   a. a high STD score
   b. a low LCU score
   c. Type A traits
   d. Type B traits

10. Exercise, meditation, progressive relaxation, and guided imagery would be least likely to help a person who is in the G.A.S. stage of
    a. alarm
    b. resistance
    c. exhaustion
    d. adaptation

Answers: 1. d 2. c 3. d 4. a 5. c 6. d 7. c 8. b 9. c 10. c

Chapter 12

Psychologist's Journal

BEWARE THE HELICOPTERS

"The helicopters. Oh no, not the helicopters. Have come to tear the feathers out of my frontal lobes. Help me, nurse, help me, can't you hear them? Gotta get back into my body to save it. . . . The doctor is thinking I would make good glue."

These are the words of Carol North, a psychiatrist who survived schizophrenia. In addition to the hallucinated helicopters, Carol was plagued by voices that said: "Be good," "Do bad," "Stand up," "Sit down," "Collide with the other world," "Do you want a cigar?" (North, 1987).

North's painful journey into the shadows of madness left her incapacitated for nearly two decades. Her case is but one hint of the magnitude of mental health problems. Here are the facts on psychological disorders:

- About 20 percent of Canada's adult population suffers from a mental disorder or drug abuse in a given year.
- One out of every 100 persons will become so severely disturbed as to require hospitalization at some point in his or her lifetime.
- Some 3 to 6 percent of the aged suffer from organic psychoses.
- Schizophrenia affects over 200 000 Canadians.
- Five percent of Canada's population suffers from either depression or manic depression, and 10 percent of people have an anxiety disorder.
- One out of every eight school-age children is seriously maladjusted.
- Each year in North America, over 2 million people are admitted for psychiatric treatment in general hospitals.
- Twenty-five percent of all hospital days in Canada are spent in the care of patients with a mental illness.

What does it mean to be "crazy"? In the 1800s, doctors and non-professionals alike used terms such as "crazy," "insane," "cracked," and "lunatic" quite freely. The "insane" were thought of as bizarre and definitely different from the rest of the population. Today, our understanding of psychological disorders is more sophisticated. To draw the line between normal and abnormal, we must weigh some complex issues. Let's explore some of those issues, as well as an array of psychological problems.

Survey Questions

- ■ How is normality defined, and what are the major psychological disorders?
- ■ What is a personality disorder?
- ■ What problems result when a person suffers high levels of anxiety?
- ■ How do psychologists explain anxiety-based disorders?
- ■ What are the general characteristics of psychotic disorders?
- ■ How do delusional disorders differ from other psychotic disorders?
- ■ What forms does schizophrenia take? What causes it?
- ■ What are mood disorders? What causes depression?
- ■ Why do people commit suicide? Can suicide be prevented?

▶ Normality—What Is Normal?

Survey Question:
- ■ How is normality defined, and what are the major psychological disorders?

Psychopathology The scientific study of mental, emotional, and behavioural disorders; also refers to abnormal behaviour.

Subjective discomfort Personal, private feelings of discomfort, unhappiness, or emotional distress.

Statistical abnormality Abnormality defined on the basis of an extreme score on some dimension, such as IQ or anxiety.

Normal curve A bell-shaped curve with a large number of scores in the middle, tapering to very few extremely high and low scores.

"That guy is really wacko. His porch lights are dimming." "Yeah, the butter's sliding off his waffle. I think he's ready to go postal." Informally, it's tempting to make snap judgments about mental health. However, to seriously classify people as psychologically unhealthy raises complex and age-old issues. The scientific study of mental, emotional, and behavioural disorders is known as **psychopathology.** The term also refers to mental disorders themselves, such as schizophrenia or depression, and to behaviour patterns that make people unhappy and impair personal growth (Carson, Butcher, & Mineka, 1997).

Defining abnormality can be tricky. We might begin by saying that psychopathology is characterized by **subjective discomfort** (anxiety, depression, or other signs of emotional distress), as Carol North endured.

But couldn't a person be seriously disturbed without feeling discomfort? Yes. Psychopathology doesn't always cause personal anguish. A person suffering from mania might feel "on top of the world." Also, a *lack* of discomfort may reveal a problem. For example, if you showed no signs of grief after the death of a close friend, we might suspect psychopathology. In practice, subjective discomfort explains most instances in which people voluntarily seek professional help.

Some psychologists use statistics to define normality more objectively. **Statistical abnormality** refers to scoring very high or low on some dimension, such as intelligence, anxiety, or depression. Anxiety, for example, is a feature of several psychological disorders. To measure it, we could create a test to learn how many people show low, medium, or high levels of anxiety. Usually, the results of such tests will form a **normal** (bell-shaped) **curve,** as shown in ▶ Figure 12.1. (*Normal* in this case is a statistical concept. It refers only to the shape of the curve.) Notice that most people score in the central region of such curves. A person who deviates from the average by being anxious all the time (high anxiety) might be abnormal. So, too, might a person who never feels anxiety.

Then a statistical definition of abnormality tells us nothing about the meaning of deviations from the norm? Right. It is as statistically "abnormal" (unusual) for a person to score above 145 on

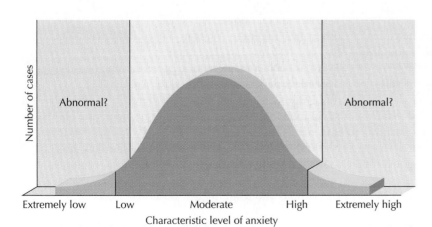

Extremely low   Low   Moderate   High   Extremely high
Characteristic level of anxiety

(y-axis: Number of cases; labels: Abnormal?   Abnormal?)

▶ **Figure 12.1**

The number of people displaying a personal characteristic may help define what is statistically abnormal.

Social non-conformity does not automatically indicate psychopathology.

Social non-conformity
Failure to conform to societal norms or the usual minimum standards for social conduct.
Situational context The social situation, behavioural setting, or general circumstances in which an action takes place.

an IQ test as it is to score below 55. However, only the lower score is regarded as "abnormal" or undesirable (Wakefield, 1992).

Statistical definitions also can't tell us where to draw the line between normality and abnormality. To take a new example, we could obtain the average frequency of sexual intercourse for persons of a particular age, sex, sexual orientation, and marital status. Clearly, a person who feels driven to have sex dozens of times a day has a problem. But as we move back toward the norm we face the statistical problem of drawing lines. How often does a normal behaviour have to occur before it becomes abnormal? As you can see, statistical boundary lines tend to be somewhat arbitrary (Widiger & Trull, 1991).

Non-conformity may also underlie psychological disorders. **Social non-conformity** refers to disobeying social standards for acceptable conduct. Extreme non-conformity can lead to destructive or self-destructive behaviour. (Think, for instance, of a drug abuser or a prostitute.) However, we must be careful to separate unhealthy non-conformity from creative lifestyles. Many eccentric "characters" are charming and emotionally stable. Note, too, that strictly following social norms is no guarantee of mental health. In some cases, psychopathology involves rigid conformity.

Before any behaviour can be defined as abnormal, we must consider the **situational context** (social situation, behavioural setting, or general circumstances) in which it occurs. Is it normal to stand outside and water a lawn with a hose? It depends on whether it is raining. Is it abnormal for a grown man to remove his pants and expose himself to another man or woman in a place of business? It depends on whether the other person is a bank clerk or a doctor! Almost any imaginable behaviour can be considered normal in some contexts. In mid-October 1972, an airplane carrying a rugby team called the Old Christians crashed in the snow-capped Andes of South America. Incredibly, 16 of the 45 people who had been aboard at the time of the crash survived 73 days in deep snow and subfreezing temperatures. They were forced to use extremely grim measures to do so—they ate the bodies of those who had died in the crash.

Culture is one of the most influential contexts in which any behaviour is judged. In some cultures it is considered normal to defecate or urinate in public or to appear naked in public. In our culture such behaviours would be considered unusual or abnormal. In some Muslim cultures, women who remain completely housebound are considered normal or even virtuous. In western cultures they might be diagnosed as suffering from a

HUMAN DIVERSITY   The Politics of Madness

The year is 1840. You are a slave who has tried repeatedly to escape from a cruel and abusive master. An expert is consulted about your "abnormal" behaviour. His conclusion? You are suffering from "drapetomania," a mental "disorder" that causes slaves to run away (Wakefield, 1992).

As this example suggests, psychiatric terms are easily abused. Historically, some have been applied to culturally disapproved behaviours that are not really disorders. For example, all of the following were once considered disorders: drapetomania, childhood masturbation, lack of vaginal orgasm, self-defeating personality (applied mainly to women), and nymphomania (a woman with a healthy sexual appetite) (Wakefield, 1992). Even today, race, gender, and social class continue to affect the diagnosis of various disorders (Nathan & Langenbucher, 1999).

Gender is probably the most common source of bias in judging normality because standards tend to be based on males (Hartung & Widiger, 1998). According to a well-known Canadian psychologist Paula Caplan (1995) and others, women are penalized both for conforming to female stereotypes and for ignoring them. If a woman is independent, aggressive, and unemotional, she may be considered "unhealthy." Yet at the same time, a woman who is vain, emotional, irrational, and dependent on others (all "feminine" traits in our culture) may be classified as a histrionic or dependent personality (Bornstein, 1996). Indeed, a majority of persons classified as having dependent personality disorder are women. In view of this, Paula Caplan asks, Why isn't there a category called "delusional dominating personality disorder" for obnoxious men (Caplan, 1995)?

The differences we have reviewed illustrate the subtle influence that culture can have on perceptions of disorder and normality. Be cautious before you leap to conclusions about the mental health of others.

Cultural relativity
Perceptions and judgments made relative to the values of one's culture.

Maladaptive behaviour
Behaviour that makes it difficult to adapt to the environment and meet the demands of day-to-day life.

Mental disorder
A significant impairment in psychological functioning.

Psychotic disorder
A severe mental disorder characterized by a retreat from reality, hallucinations and delusions, and social withdrawal.

Organic mental disorder
A mental or emotional problem caused by brain diseases or injuries.

disorder called agoraphobia (Widiger & Sankis, 2000). (Agoraphobia is described later in this chapter.)

Thus, **cultural relativity** (the idea that judgments are made relative to the values of one's culture) can affect the diagnosis of psychological disorders (Alarcon, 1995). (See "The Politics of Madness.") Still, all cultures classify people as abnormal if they fail to communicate with others or are consistently unpredictable in their actions.

Core Features of Disordered Behaviour

If abnormality is so hard to define, how are judgments of psychopathology made? It's clear that all of the standards we have discussed are relative. However, abnormal behaviour does have two core features. First, it is **maladaptive.** Rather than helping people cope successfully, abnormal behaviour makes it more difficult for them to meet the demands of day-to-day life. Second, people suffering from psychological disorders have much less control than others over their ability to control thoughts, behaviours, or feelings. For example, gambling is not a problem if people bet for entertainment and can maintain self-control. However, compulsive gambling is a sign of psychopathology. The voices that Carol North kept hearing are a prime example of what it means to lose control of one's thoughts. In the most extreme cases, people become a danger to themselves or others, which is clearly maladaptive (Widiger & Sankis, 2000).

In practice, deciding that a person needs help usually occurs when the person *does something* (hits someone, hallucinates, stares into space, collects rolls of toilet paper, and so forth) that *annoys* or *gains the attention* of a person in a *position of power* in the person's life (an employer, teacher, parent, spouse, or the person himself or herself). That person then *does something* about it. (A police officer may be called, the person may be urged to see a psychologist, a relative may start commitment proceedings, or the person may voluntarily seek help.)

▶ Classifying Mental Disorders—Problems by the Book

In Canada and the United States, psychological problems are classified by using the *Diagnostic and Statistical Manual of Mental Disorders* (DSM-IV-TR, 2000). The DSM helps psychologists and psychiatrists identify mental disorders and select the best therapies to treat them (Nathan & Langenbucher, 1999).

A **mental disorder** is a significant impairment in psychological functioning (Widiger & Trull, 1991). If you were to glance through DSM-IV-TR, you would see many disorders described, including those in Table 12.1 on page 452. It's impossible here to discuss all of these problems. Major disorders are listed in the table so you can see the types of problems found in the DSM. (You don't need to memorize all of them.) The descriptions that follow will give you an overview of some selected problems.

An Overview of Psychological Disorders

People suffering from **psychotic disorders** have hallucinations and delusions, they are socially withdrawn, and they have "retreated from reality." Psychotic disorders tend to be severely disabling and may lead to hospitalization. In addition to having hallucinations, psychotic patients cannot control their thoughts and actions. A young college student who became psychotic told his father:

> It's the strangest thing. I hear voices, hundreds of them, telling me that everyone wants me dead. It's like all the radios of the world blaring all the stations at once, and it doesn't stop. It jams my brain. . . . (Weisburd, 1990)

Psychotic symptoms are found in schizophrenia, delusional disorders, and some mood disorders. Psychosis is also related to medical problems (such as brain diseases), drug abuse, and other conditions (DSM-IV-TR, 2000). (Table 12.2, on page 453, provides a simplified list of major disorders.)

Organic mental disorders are problems caused by brain pathology; that is, by drug damage, diseases of the brain, injuries, poisons, and so forth. A person with an organic

Table 12.1
Major DSM-IV-TR Categories

DISORDERS USUALLY FIRST DIAGNOSED IN INFANCY, CHILDHOOD, OR ADOLESCENCE

Mental retardation
Example: Mild mental retardation
Learning disorders
Example: Reading disorder
Motor skills disorder
Example: Developmental coordination disorder
Pervasive developmental disorders
Example: Autistic disorder
Disruptive behaviour and attention-deficit disorders
Example: Attention-deficit/hyperactivity disorder
Feeding and eating disorders of infancy or early childhood
Example: Pica
Tic disorders
Example: Transient tic disorder
Communication disorders
Example: Stuttering
Elimination disorders
Example: Enuresis (bedwetting)
Other disorders of infancy, childhood, or adolescence
Example: Separation anxiety disorder

DELIRIUM, DEMENTIA, AMNESTIC, AND OTHER COGNITIVE DISORDERS

Delirium
Example: Delirium due to a general medical condition
Dementia
Example: Dementia of the Alzheimer's type
Amnestic disorders (memory loss)
Example: Amnestic disorder due to a general medical condition
Cognitive disorder not otherwise specified

MENTAL DISORDERS DUE TO A GENERAL MEDICAL CONDITION NOT ELSEWHERE CLASSIFIED

Catatonic disorder due to a general medical condition
Personality change due to a general medical condition
Mental disorder not otherwise specified due to a general medical condition

SUBSTANCE-RELATED DISORDERS

Example: Cocaine use disorders

SCHIZOPHRENIA AND OTHER PSYCHOTIC DISORDERS

Schizophrenia
Example: Schizophrenia, paranoid type
Schizophreniform disorder
Schizoaffective disorder
Delusional disorder
Example: Delusional disorder, grandiose type
Brief psychotic disorder
Shared psychotic disorder (folie à deux)
Psychotic disorder due to a general medical condition

Substance-induced psychotic disorder
Psychotic disorder not otherwise specified

MOOD DISORDERS

Depressive disorders
Example: Major depressive disorder
Bipolar disorders
Example: Bipolar I disorder
Mood disorder due to a general medical condition
Substance-induced mood disorder
Mood disorder not otherwise specified

ANXIETY DISORDERS

Example: Panic disorder

SOMATOFORM DISORDERS

Example: Conversion disorder

FACTITIOUS DISORDERS (FAKED DISABILITY OR ILLNESS)

Example: Factitious disorder

DISSOCIATIVE DISORDERS

Example: Dissociative identity disorder

SEXUAL AND GENDER IDENTITY DISORDERS

Sexual dysfunctions
Example: Sexual arousal disorders
Paraphilias
Example: Voyeurism
Sexual disorder not otherwise specified
Gender identity disorders
Example: Gender identity disorder

EATING DISORDERS

Example: Anorexia nervosa

SLEEP DISORDERS

Primary sleep disorders
  Dyssomnias
    Example: Primary insomnia
  Parasomnias
    Example: Sleep terror disorder
Sleep disorders related to another mental disorder
Example: Insomnia related to post-traumatic stress disorder
Other sleep disorders
Example: Substance-induced sleep disorder

IMPULSE CONTROL DISORDERS NOT ELSEWHERE CLASSIFIED

Example: Kleptomania

ADJUSTMENT DISORDERS

Example: Adjustment disorder

PERSONALITY DISORDERS

Example: Antisocial personality disorder

Table 12.2
Some
Selected
Categories of
Psycho-
pathology

PROBLEM	PRIMARY SYMPTOM	TYPICAL SIGNS OF TROUBLE
Psychotic disorders	Loss of contact with reality	You hear or see things that others don't; your mind has been playing tricks on you
Mood disorders	Mania or depression	You feel sad and hopeless; or you talk too loud and too fast and have a rush of ideas and feelings that others think are unreasonable
Anxiety disorders	High anxiety or anxiety-based distortions of behaviour	You have anxiety attacks and feel like you are going to die; or you are afraid to do things that most people can do; or you spend unusual amounts of time doing things like washing your hands or counting your heartbeats
Somatoform disorders	Bodily complaints without an organic (physical) basis	You feel physically sick, but your doctor says nothing is wrong with you; or you suffer from pain that has no physical basis; or you are preoccupied with thoughts about being sick
Dissociative disorders	Amnesia, feelings of unreality, multiple identities	There are major gaps in your memory of events; you feel like you are a robot or a stranger to yourself; others tell you that you have done things that you don't remember doing
Personality disorders	Unhealthy personality patterns	Your behaviour patterns repeatedly cause problems at work, school, and in your relationships with others
Sexual and gender identity disorders	Disturbed gender identity, deviant sexual behaviour, problems in sexual adjustment	You feel that you are a man trapped in a woman's body (or the reverse); or you can gain sexual satisfaction only by engaging in highly atypical sexual behaviour; or you have problems with sexual desire, arousal, or performance
Substance-related disorders	Disturbances related to drug abuse or dependence	You have been drinking too much, using illegal drugs, or taking prescription drugs more often than you should

Substance-related disorder Abuse of or dependence on a mood- or behaviour-altering drug.

Mood disorder A major disturbance in mood or emotion, such as depression or mania.

Anxiety disorder Disruptive feelings of fear, apprehension, or anxiety, or distortions in behaviour that are anxiety related.

disorder may have severe emotional disturbances, impaired thinking, memory loss, personality changes, delirium, or psychotic symptoms (Costello & Costello, 1992).

In reality, almost all mental disorders are partly biological (Widiger & Sankis, 2000). That's why DSM-IV-TR does not list "organic mental disorders" as a separate category. Nevertheless, all of the following problems are closely associated with organic damage: delirium, dementia, amnesia, and other cognitive disorders; mental disorders due to a general medical condition; and substance-related disorders (drug abuse).

Substance–related disorders involve abuse of, or dependence on, mood- or behaviour-altering drugs. Typical culprits include alcohol, barbiturates, opiates, cocaine, amphetamines, hallucinogens, marijuana, and nicotine. Problems of this type damage functioning at home or on the job, because the person cannot stop using the drug. Active drug intoxication or drug withdrawal, delirium, dementia, amnesia, psychosis, emotional problems, sexual problems, and sleep disturbances may also be related to drug abuse (Boutros & Bowers, 1996).

Mood disorders primarily involve disturbances in affect (emotion). Afflicted persons may be manic, meaning agitated, elated, and hyperactive, or they may be depressed. Some people cycle between mania and depression. In each case, their extreme of moods are intense or long lasting. Mood disorders sometimes include psychotic symptoms, and they can be caused by medical conditions or drug abuse (DSM-IV-TR, 2000).

Anxiety disorders are marked by fear, apprehension or anxiety, and distortions of behaviour. Some anxiety disorders involve feelings of panic. Others are expressed as phobias (irrational fears) or just overwhelming anxiety. Two additional anxiety disorders are post-traumatic stress disorder and acute stress disorder. Obsessive-compulsive behaviour patterns are also associated with high levels of anxiety. (These problems are described later in this chapter.)

The self-portraits shown here were painted by Andy Wilf between 1978 and 1981. During that time, Wilf is said to have increasingly abused drugs and alcohol. This dramatic series of images is a record of his self-destructive descent into a private hell. The third painting shows a shrouded skull—and foretells the artist's fate. Wilf died of a drug overdose. Drug abuse is but one of the many psychopathologies, or "problems in living," psychologists seek to alleviate. (Courtesy of Ulrike Kantor, Ulrike Kantor Gallery.)

Somatoform disorder Physical symptoms that mimic disease or injury for which there is no identifiable physical cause.

Dissociative disorder Temporary amnesia, multiple personality, or depersonalization.

Personality disorder A maladaptive personality pattern.

Sexual and gender identity disorders Any of a wide range of difficulties with sexual identity, deviant sexual behaviour, or sexual adjustment.

Neurosis An outdated term once used to refer to anxiety disorders, somatoform disorders, dissociative disorders, and some forms of depression.

Somatoform disorders (so-MAT-oh-form) occur when a person has physical symptoms that mimic disease or injury (paralysis, blindness, illness, or chronic pain, for example), for which there is no identifiable physical cause. In such cases it is assumed that psychological factors underlie the symptoms.

Dissociative disorders include cases of sudden temporary amnesia or multiple identity (multiple personality). Also included in this category are frightening episodes of depersonalization. Depersonalization refers to feeling like you are outside of your body, are behaving like a robot, or are lost in a dream world.

Personality disorders are deeply ingrained, unhealthy personality patterns. Such patterns usually appear by adolescence and they continue through much of adult life. They include paranoid (overly suspicious), narcissistic (self-loving), dependent, borderline, and antisocial personality types, as well as others.

Sexual and gender identity disorders include any of a wide range of difficulties with sexual identity, deviant sexual behaviour, or sexual adjustment. In gender identity disorders, sexual identity does not match a person's physical sex. Deviations in sexual behaviour known as paraphilias include exhibitionism, fetishism, voyeurism, and so on. Also found in this category are a variety of sexual dysfunctions (problems in sexual desire, arousal, or response).

Shouldn't neurosis be listed here? Neurosis was once a recognized mental disorder. However, it is no longer included in the DSM because the term *neurosis* is too imprecise. Behaviour that psychologists used to refer to as "neurotic" is now part of anxiety, somatoform, or dissociative disorders. Even though **neurosis** is an outdated term, you may hear it used to loosely refer to problems involving excessive anxiety.

In addition to the formal mental disorders we have reviewed, many cultures have names for "unofficial" psychological "disorders." See "Running Amok with Cultural Maladies" for some samples.

General Risk Factors

What causes mental and psychological disorders like those listed in Table 12.2? We will soon explore the causes of some specific problems. For now, it is worth noting that a variety of risk factors contribute to psychopathology.

- *Social conditions:* poverty, stressful living conditions, homelessness, social disorganization, overcrowding
- *Family factors:* parents who are immature, mentally disturbed, criminal, or abusive; severe marital strife; extremely poor child discipline; disordered family communication patterns

HUMAN DIVERSITY   Running Amok with Cultural Maladies

Every culture recognizes the existence of psychopathology, and most have at least a few folk names for afflictions. Here are some examples from around the world:

- *Amok.* Men in Malaysia, Laos, the Philippines, and Polynesia who believe they have been insulted are sometimes known to go amok. After a period of brooding they erupt into an outburst of violent, aggressive, or homicidal behaviour randomly directed at people and objects.
- *Ataque de nervios.* Among Latinos from the Caribbean, the symptoms of an *ataque de nervios* (attack of nerves) include shouting, crying, trembling, aggression, threats of suicide, and seizures or fainting. *Ataques de nervios* frequently occur after a stressful event, such as the death of a close relative, divorce, or an accident involving a family member.
- *Ghost sickness.* Among many North American Aboriginal tribes, people who become preoccupied with death and the deceased are said to suffer from ghost sickness. The symptoms of ghost sickness include bad dreams, weakness, loss of appetite, fainting, dizziness, fear, anxiety, hallucinations, loss of consciousness, confusion, feelings of futility, and a sense of suffocation.
- *Koro.* In south and east Asia, a man may experience sudden and intense anxiety that his penis (or, occasionally in females, the vulva and nipples) will recede into the body. In addition to the terror this incites, victims also believe that advanced cases of *koro* can cause death.
- *Locura.* Latinos in Latin America and the United States use the term *locura* to refer to people who suffer from chronic psychotic symptoms such as incoher-

ence, agitation, auditory and visual hallucinations, inability to follow social rules, unpredictability, and violence.
- *Pibloktoq (or Arctic hysteria).* In the Arctic region, an Inuit person may experience mild irritation and isolation, followed by a spell involving highly unusual behaviours. The person may yell obscenities, break objects, tear off clothing, eat feces, or perform other irrational acts. This period of wild excitement is followed by seizures and coma. Interestingly, the affected person typically remembers nothing about the intense episode.
- *Zar.* In North African and Middle Eastern societies, *zar* is said to occur when spirits possess an individual. *Zar* is marked by shouting, laughing, hitting the head against a wall, singing, or weeping. Victims may become apathetic or withdrawn and they may refuse to eat or carry out daily tasks.

The existence of such terms emphasizes that people have a need to label and categorize disturbed behaviour. As you can see, however, folk terminology tends to be vague. Most of the problems listed here include symptoms from more than one of the psychological disorders described in DSM-IV-TR. As a result, like the now-defunct term *neurosis,* they provide little guidance about the true nature of a person's problems or the best ways to treat them. That's why the DSM is based on empirical data and clinical observations. Otherwise, psychologists and psychiatrists would be no better than folk healers or shamans when making diagnoses.

(Sources: "Outline for Cultural," 1994; Regeser López & Guarnaccia, 2000.)

- *Psychological factors:* stress, low intelligence, learning disorders, lack of control or mastery
- *Biological factors:* genetic defects or inherited vulnerabilities, poor prenatal care, very low birth weight, chronic physical illness or disability, exposure to toxic chemicals or drugs, head injuries

Insanity A legal term that refers to a mental inability to manage one's affairs or to be aware of the consequences of one's actions.

Expert witness A person recognized by a court of law as being qualified to give expert testimony on a specific topic.

Insanity

Which of the mental disorders causes insanity? None. **Insanity** is a legal term. It refers to an inability to manage one's affairs or foresee the consequences of one's actions. People who are declared insane are not legally responsible for their actions. If necessary, they can be involuntarily committed to a mental hospital. The Canadian criminal code uses the expression "criminally not responsible on account of mental disorder" instead of insanity.

Legally, insanity is established by testimony from expert witnesses (psychologists and psychiatrists). An **expert witness** is a person recognized by a court of law as being qualified to give opinions on a specific topic. People who are involuntarily committed are usually judged to be a danger to themselves or to others, or they are severely mentally disabled (Turkheimer & Parry, 1992). Involuntary commitments happen most often when people are brought to emergency rooms. Then, if two doctors agree that the person will either commit suicide or hurt someone else, she or he is put into the hospital (Gorman, 1996).

▶ Personality Disorders—Blueprints for Maladjustment

Survey Question:
■ What is a personality disorder?

"Get out of here and leave me alone so I can die in peace," Judy screamed at her nurses in the seclusion room of the psychiatric hospital. On one of her arms, long dark red marks mingled with the scars of previous suicide attempts. Judy once bragged that her record was 67 stitches. Today, the nurses had to strap her into restraints to keep her from gouging her own eyes. She was given a sedative and slept for 12 hours. She woke calmly and asked for her therapist—even though her latest outburst began when he cancelled a morning appointment and changed it to afternoon.

Judy has a borderline personality disorder. Although she is capable of working, Judy has repeatedly lost jobs because of her turbulent relationships with other people. At times she can be friendly and a real charmer. At other times she is extremely unpredictable, moody, and even suicidal. Being a friend to Judy can be a fearsome challenge. Cancelling an appointment, forgetting a special date, a wrong turn of phrase—these and similar small incidents may trigger Judy's anger or, worse yet, a suicide attempt.

Maladaptive Personality Patterns

As stated earlier, a person with a personality disorder has a very maladaptive personality pattern. For example, people who have paranoid personality disorder are suspicious, hypersensitive, and wary of others. Narcissistic persons need constant admiration, and they are lost in fantasies of power, wealth, brilliance, beauty, or love. The dependent personality has an extreme lack of self-confidence. Dependent persons allow others to run their lives and they place everyone else's needs before their own. People with a histrionic personality disorder constantly seek attention by dramatizing their emotions and actions.

Typically, patterns such as the ones just described begin during adolescence or even childhood. The list of personality disorders is long (see Table 12.3), so let us focus on a single frequently misunderstood problem, the antisocial personality.

Antisocial personality
A person who lacks a conscience, is emotionally shallow, impulsive, selfish, and tends to manipulate others.

Antisocial Personality

What are the characteristics of an antisocial personality? A person with an **antisocial personality** lacks a conscience. Such people are impulsive, selfish, dishonest, emotionally shallow,

---

**Table 12.3
Personality
Disorders
and Typical
Degree of
Impairment**

MODERATE IMPAIRMENT

Dependent Unhealthy submissiveness and dependence on others (clinging)
Histrionic Excessive emotion and attention-seeking behaviour
Narcissistic Exaggerated self-importance and desire for constant admiration
Antisocial Irresponsible and antisocial behaviour, such as aggression, deceit, recklessness, and lack of remorse

HIGH IMPAIRMENT

Obsessive-compulsive Traits of orderliness, perfectionism, and rigid routine
Schizoid Limited emotion and a lack of interest in close personal relationships with others
Avoidant Discomfort in social situations, fear of evaluation, timidity

SEVERE IMPAIRMENT

Borderline Extremely unstable self-image, relationships, moods, and impulses
Paranoid A deep distrust and suspiciousness of the motives of others, which are seen as demeaning or threatening
Schizotypal Social isolation, extremely odd behaviour, and disturbed thought patterns, but not actively psychotic

(From DSM-IV-TR, 2000; Millon, 1981.)

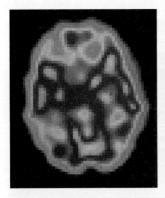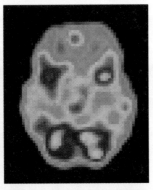

▶Figure 12.2

Using a sophisticated brain scanning technique, Canadian psychologist Robert Hare found that the normally functioning brain *(left)* lights up with activity when a person sees emotion-laden words such as "maggot" or "cancer." But the brain of a person with antisocial personality disorder *(right)* remains inactive, especially in areas associated with feelings and self-control. When Dr. Hare showed the right image to several neurologists, one asked, "Is this person from Mars?" (Images courtesy of Robert Hare.)

and manipulative (Lykken, 1995). Antisocial persons, who are sometimes called *sociopaths* or *psychopaths,* are poorly socialized and seem to be incapable of having deep feelings, such as guilt, shame, fear, loyalty, or love (DSM–IV–TR, 2000).

What causes sociopathy? Typically, people with antisocial personalities were emotionally deprived, neglected, and physically abused as children (Pollock et al., 1990). Adult sociopaths also display subtle neurological problems (see ▶Figure 12.2). For example, they have unusual brain-wave patterns that suggest under-arousal of the brain. This may explain why sociopaths tend to be thrill seekers. Quite likely, they are searching for stimulation strong enough to overcome their chronic under-arousal and feelings of "boredom" (Carson, Butcher, & Mineka, 1997; Hare, 1996).

In a revealing study, psychopaths were shown extremely grisly and unpleasant photographs. The photos were so upsetting that normal people are visibly startled by them. The psychopaths, however, showed no startle response to the photos (Patrick, Bradley, & Lang, 1993). (They didn't "bat an eyelash.") Those with antisocial personalities might therefore be described as *emotionally cold.* They simply do not feel normal pangs of conscience, guilt, or anxiety (Hare, 1996). This coldness seems to account for an unusual ability to calmly lie, cheat, steal, or take advantage of others (Lykken, 1995).

The case of Paul Bernardo fits the definition of antisocial personality disorder perfectly. Known as the Scarborough rapist, Bernardo raped many young women in the late 1980s in the Toronto suburb of Scarborough. Together with his wife Karla Homolka acting as a willing accomplice, Bernardo went on to kidnap, brutally torture, rape, and murder teenaged girls in the Niagara region. Homolka's own sister was one of their victims. The videotapes showing Bernardo's sadistic torture were so horrific that even some lawyers could not bring themselves to watch them. Bernardo has allegedly self-confessed to having no conscience. He planned and carried out gruesome acts without regard for others' feelings or their right to exist. You would not be able to guess any of this if you had met him at a social gathering—he may have appeared very charming and proven to be delightful company.

Are sociopaths always dangerous to society? Bernardo was clearly a very dangerous criminal. Not all individuals with antisocial personality disorder commit rape or murder, however. Some may be successful businesspeople, entertainers, or politicians. They attain success by lying, cheating, and coldly taking advantage of others (Rice, 1997). The defining feature of their personality is that they feel no remorse over their deceitful tendencies.

Can sociopathy be treated? Antisocial personality disorder is rarely treated with success. All too often, sociopaths manipulate therapy, just like any other situation. If it is to their advantage to act "cured," they will do so. However, they return to their former behaviour patterns as soon as possible. On a more positive note, antisocial behaviour does tend to decline somewhat after age 40, even without treatment.

Studies show that more than 65 percent of all persons with antisocial personalities have been arrested, usually for crimes such as robbery, vandalism, or rape. Paul Bernardo, shown here, is one of the most notorious criminals of our recent past. He fits the definition of antisocial personality disorder to the T. (See the text for details.)

Knowledge builder

NORMALITY, PSYCHOPATHOLOGY, AND PERSONALITY DISORDERS

Relate

Think of an instance of abnormal behaviour you have witnessed. By what formal standards would the behaviour be regarded as abnormal? In what way was the behaviour maladaptive?

What disorders would the following sentences help you remember? An anxious psychotic in a bad mood asked for an organic substance. "First you have to fill out a somato form and tell us what sex or gender you are," he was told. "Don't diss my personality," he replied.

Many of the qualities that define personality disorders exist to a minor degree in normal personalities. Try to think of a person you know who has some of the characteristics described for each type of personality disorder.

Learning Check

1. Statistical definitions of abnormality successfully avoid the limitations of other approaches. T or F?
2. One of the most powerful contexts in which judgments of normality and abnormality are made is
   a. the family b. occupational settings c. religious systems d. culture
3. Amnesia, multiple identities, and depersonalization are possible problems in
   a. mood disorders b. somatoform disorders c. psychosis d. dissociative disorders

4. Which one of the following is *not* a major psychological problem listed in DSM-IV-TR?
   a. mood disorders b. personality disorders c. insanity d. anxiety disorders
5. A major difference between psychotic disorders and anxiety disorders (or other milder problems) is that in psychosis the individual has lost contact with reality as shown by the presence of
   _____ or
   _____.
6. Which of the following personality disorders is associated with an inflated sense of self-importance and a constant need for attention and admiration?
   a. narcissistic b. antisocial c. paranoid d. manipulative
7. Antisocial personality disorder is difficult to treat, but there is typically a decline in psychopathic behaviour a year or two after adolescence. T or F?

Critical Thinking

8. Brian, a fan of grunge rock, occasionally wears a skirt in public. Does Brian's cross-dressing indicate that he has a mental disorder?
9. Many U.S. states began to restrict use of the insanity defence after John Hinkley, Jr., who tried to murder former U.S. President Ronald Reagan, was acquitted by reason of insanity. What does this trend reveal about insanity?

Answers:

1. F 2. d 3. d 4. c 5. delusions, hallucinations 6. a 7. F 8. Probably not. Undoubtedly, Brian's cross-dressing is socially disapproved by many people. Nevertheless, to be classified as a mental disorder it must cause him to feel disabling shame, guilt, depression, or anxiety. The cultural relativity of behaviour like Brian's is revealed by the fact that it is fashionable and acceptable for women to wear men's clothing. 9. It emphasizes that insanity is a legal concept, not a psychiatric diagnosis. Laws reflect community standards. When those standards change, lawmakers may seek to alter definitions of legal responsibility.

▶ Anxiety-Based Disorders—When Anxiety Rules

Survey Question:
■ What problems result when a person suffers high levels of anxiety?

Imagine that you are waiting to take an important test for which you are unprepared, waiting to give a speech to a large audience of strangers, or being followed by a police car while you are driving. You've almost certainly felt *anxiety* in one of these situations.

Anxiety refers to feelings of apprehension, dread, or uneasiness. We all feel anxiety, but anxiety that is out of proportion to a situation may reveal a problem. Tim, a college student, became unbearably anxious whenever he took exams. By the time he went to see a counsellor, Tim had skipped several tests and was in danger of dropping out of school. In general, anxiety-related problems like Tim's involve:

Anxiety Apprehension, dread, or uneasiness similar to fear but based on an unclear threat.

- High levels of anxiety and/or restrictive, self-defeating behaviour patterns
- A tendency to use elaborate defence mechanisms or avoidance responses to get through the day
- Pervasive feelings of stress, insecurity, inferiority, unhappiness, and dissatisfaction with life

Typically, people with anxiety-related problems feel threatened, but they don't do anything constructive about it. They struggle to preserve control, but their efforts are ineffective and they remain unhappy (Zinbarg et al., 1992).

If anxiety is a normal emotion, when does it signify a problem? A problem exists when intense anxiety prevents people from doing what they want or need to do. Also, their anxieties are out of control—they simply cannot stop worrying.

Adjustment Disorders

Do such problems cause a "nervous breakdown"? People suffering from anxiety-based problems may be miserable, but they rarely experience a "breakdown." Actually, the term *nervous breakdown* has no formal meaning. Nevertheless, a problem known as an *adjustment disorder* does come close to what many people have in mind when they say someone had a "breakdown."

Adjustment disorders occur when ordinary stresses push people beyond their ability to cope with life. Examples of such stresses are prolonged unemployment, intense marital strife, and chronic physical illness. People suffering from an adjustment disorder may be extremely irritable, anxious, apathetic, or depressed. They also have trouble sleeping, lose their appetite, and suffer from various physical complaints (DSM-IV-TR, 2000). Often, their problems can be relieved by rest, sedation, supportive counselling, and a chance to "talk through" fears and anxieties.

How is an adjustment disorder different from an anxiety disorder? The outward symptoms are similar. However, adjustment disorders disappear when a person's life circumstances improve. People suffering from anxiety disorders experience a sense of misery, regardless of what's happening around them.

Anxiety Disorders

In most anxiety disorders, distress seems greatly out of proportion to a person's circumstances. For example, consider the following description of Ethel B:

> She was never completely relaxed, and complained of vague feelings of restlessness, and a fear that something was "just around the corner." Although she felt that she had to go to work to help pay the family bills, she could not bring herself to start anything new for fear that something terrible would happen on the job. She had experienced a few extreme anxiety attacks during which she felt "like I couldn't breathe, like I was sealed up in a transparent envelope. I thought I was going to have a heart attack. I couldn't stop shaking." (Suinn, 1975)

Distress like Ethel B's is a key ingredient in anxiety disorders. Many psychologists believe it also underlies dissociative and somatoform disorders, where maladaptive behaviour serves to reduce anxiety and discomfort. To deepen your understanding, let's first examine the anxiety disorders themselves (see Table 12.4). Then we will see how anxiety contributes to other problems.

GENERALIZED ANXIETY DISORDER   A person with a **generalized anxiety disorder** has experienced at least six months of excessive anxiety and worry (DSM-IV-TR, 2000; Dugas et al., 1998). Sufferers typically complain of sweating, a racing heart, clammy hands, dizziness, upset stomach, rapid breathing, irritability, and poor concentration. Overall, more women than men have these symptoms (Brawman-Mintzer & Lydiard, 1996).

Was Ethel B's problem a generalized anxiety disorder? No, her anxiety attacks reveal that she suffered from panic disorder.

PANIC DISORDER (WITHOUT AGORAPHOBIA) In a **panic disorder (without agoraphobia),** people are highly anxious and also have moments when they feel sudden, intense, unexpected panic. During a panic attack, victims experience a racing heart, chest pain, choking, dizziness, feelings of unreality, trembling, or fears of losing control. Many believe that they are having a heart attack,

---

Adjustment disorder An emotional disturbance caused by ongoing stressors within the range of common experience.

Generalized anxiety disorder The person is in a chronic state of tension and worries about work, relationships, ability, or impending disaster.

Panic disorder (without agoraphobia) The person is in a chronic state of anxiety and also has brief moments of sudden, intense, unexpected panic.

Table 12.4
Anxiety Disorders

Generalized anxiety disorder
Panic disorder
   Without agoraphobia
   With agoraphobia
Agoraphobia (without a history of panic disorder)
Specific phobia
Social phobia
Obsessive-compulsive disorder
Post-traumatic stress disorder
Acute stress disorder

(DSM-IV-TR, 2000.)

Panic disorder (with agoraphobia) A chronic state of anxiety and brief moments of sudden panic. The person fears that these panic attacks will occur in public places or unfamiliar situations.

Agoraphobia (without panic) The person fears that something extremely embarrassing will happen to him or her if he or she leaves the house or enters unfamiliar situations.

Specific phobia An intense, irrational fear of specific objects, activities, or situations.

Social phobia An intense, irrational fear of being observed, evaluated, embarrassed, or humiliated by others in social situations.

are going insane, or are about to die. This pattern leaves victims unhappy and uncomfortable much of the time. Again, the majority of people who suffer from panic disorder are women (Sansone, Sansone, & Righter, 1998).

To get an idea of how a panic attack feels, imagine that you are trapped in your stateroom on a sinking ocean liner (the *Titanic?*). The room fills with water. When only a small air space remains near the ceiling and you are gasping for air, you'll know what a panic attack feels like.

PANIC DISORDER (WITH AGORAPHOBIA) In a **panic disorder (with agoraphobia),** people suffer from chronic anxiety and brief moments of sudden panic. In addition, they have **agoraphobia** (ah-go-rah-FOBE-ee-ah), which is an intense, irrational *fear that a panic attack will occur* in a public place or unfamiliar situation. That is, agoraphobics intensely fear leaving their home and familiar surroundings. Typically, they find ways of avoiding places that frighten them—such as crowds, open roads, supermarkets, automobiles, and so on. As a result, some people with agoraphobia become prisoners in their own homes (DSM-IV-TR, 2000).

AGORAPHOBIA Agoraphobia can also occur without panic. In this case, people fear that something extremely embarrassing will happen if they leave home or enter an unfamiliar situation. For example, an agoraphobic person may refuse to go outside because he or she fears having a sudden attack of dizziness, diarrhea, or shortness of breath. Going outside the home alone, being in a crowd, standing in line, crossing a bridge, or riding in a car can be impossible for an agoraphobic person (DSM-IV-TR, 2000). About 7 percent of all adults suffer from agoraphobia (with or without panic) during their lifetime (Magee, Eaton, & Wittchen, 1996).

Table 12.5
Common Phobias

Acrophobia—fear of heights
Astraphobia—fear of storms, thunder, lightning
Arachnophobia—fear of spiders
Aviophobia—fear of airplanes
Claustrophobia—fear of closed spaces
Hematophobia—fear of blood
Microphobia—fear of germs
Nyctophobia—fear of darkness
Pathophobia—fear of disease
Pyrophobia—fear of fire
Xenophobia—fear of strangers
Zoophobia—fear of animals

SPECIFIC PHOBIA As we noted earlier, phobias are intense, irrational fears that a person cannot shake off, even when there is no real danger. In a **specific phobia,** the person's fear, anxiety, and avoidance are focused on particular objects, activities, or situations. People affected by phobias recognize that their fears are unreasonable, but they cannot control them. Specific phobias can be linked to nearly any object or situation. Many have been given names, such as those listed in Table 12.5.

By combining the appropriate root word with the word *phobia,* any number of unlikely fears can be named. Some of these include: *acarophobia,* fear of itching; *zemmiphobia,* fear of the great mole rat; *phobosophobia,* fear of fear; *arachibutyrophobia,* fear of peanut butter sticking to the roof of the mouth; and *hippopotomonstrosesquipedaliophobia,* fear of long words!

Almost everyone has a few mild phobias, such as fears of heights, closed spaces, or bugs and crawly things. A phobic disorder differs from such garden-variety fears in that it produces overwhelming anxiety. True phobias may lead to vomiting, wild climbing and running, or fainting. For a phobic disorder to exist, the person's fear must disrupt his or her daily life. Phobic persons are so threatened that they will go to almost any length to avoid the feared object or situation. About 11 percent of all adults have phobic disorders during their lifetime (Magee, Eaton, & Wittchen, 1996).

SOCIAL PHOBIA In a **social phobia,** people fear social situations in which they can be observed, evaluated, embarrassed, or humiliated by others. This leads them to avoid certain social situations, such as eating, writing, using the washroom, or speaking in public. When such situations cannot be avoided, people endure them with intense anxiety or distress. Social phobias greatly impair functioning at work, at school, and in personal relationships (DSM-IV-TR, 2000). About 13 percent of all adults are affected by social phobias at one time or another (Fones et al., 1998).

For a person with a fear of snakes (ophidophobia), merely looking at this picture may be unsettling.

Obsessive-Compulsive Disorder

Obsessive-compulsive disorder An extreme preoccupation with certain thoughts and compulsive performance of certain behaviours.

Obsession Recurring irrational or disturbing thoughts or mental images that a person cannot prevent.

Compulsion An act an individual feels driven to repeat, often against his or her will.

Stress disorder A significant emotional disturbance caused by stresses outside the range of normal human experience.

Acute stress disorder A psychological disturbance lasting up to one month following stresses that would produce anxiety in anyone who experienced them.

Post-traumatic stress disorder A psychological disturbance lasting more than one month following stresses that would produce anxiety in anyone who experienced them.

People who suffer from **obsessive-compulsive disorder** are preoccupied with certain distressing thoughts and they feel compelled to perform certain behaviours. You have probably experienced a mild obsessional thought, such as a song or stupid commercial jingle that repeats over and over in your mind. This may be irritating, but it's usually not terribly disturbing. True **obsessions** are images or thoughts that force their way into awareness against a person's will. They are so disturbing that they cause intense anxiety. The most common obsessions are about violence or harm (such as poisoning one's spouse or being hit by a car), about being "dirty" or "unclean," about whether one has performed some action (such as turning off the stove), and about committing immoral acts. A recent survey determined that 0.6 percent of Canadians had obsessive-compulsive disorder during a one-month period (Stein et al., 1997).

Obsessions usually give rise to **compulsions.** These are irrational acts that people feel driven to repeat. Often, compulsive acts help control or block out anxiety caused by an obsession. For example, a minister who finds profanities popping into her mind might start compulsively counting her heartbeats. Doing this would prevent her from thinking "dirty" words.

Many compulsive people are checkers or cleaners. For instance, people who feel guilty and unclean because they masturbate or "think dirty thoughts" may be driven to wash their hands hundreds of times a day. Typically, such compulsive behaviour will continue even after the person's hands become raw and painful (Tallis, 1996). Likewise, a young mother who repeatedly pictures a knife plunging into her baby might check once an hour to make sure all the knives in her house are locked away. Doing so may reduce her anxieties, but it will probably also take over her life.

Of course, not all obsessive-compulsive behaviours are so dramatic. Many simply involve extreme orderliness and rigid routine. Compulsive attention to detail and rigidly following rules helps keep activities totally under control and makes the highly anxious person feel more secure. (Notice that if such patterns are longstanding, but less intense, they are classified as a personality disorder.)

Stress Disorders

What happens when people endure sudden disasters, such as floods, tornadoes, earthquakes, or horrible accidents? Often, emotional damage follows in the wake of such events.

Stress disorders occur when stresses outside the range of normal human experience cause a major emotional disturbance (DSM-IV-TR, 2000). They also affect many political hostages, combat veterans, prisoners of war, and victims of terrorism, violent crime, child molestation, rape, or people who witness the death or injury of another person (Berman et al., 1996; Coyne & Downey, 1991).

Symptoms of stress disorders include repeatedly reliving the traumatic event, avoiding reminders of the event, and blunted emotions. Also common are insomnia, nightmares, wariness, poor concentration, irritability, and explosive anger or aggression. If such reactions last less than a month after a traumatic event, the problem is called an **acute stress disorder.** If they last more than a month, the person is suffering from **post-traumatic stress disorder (PTSD)** (DSM-IV-TR, 2000).

PTSD may persist for years after the stress has passed—as has happened to many veterans of various wars around the world. Canadians gained firsthand knowledge of PTSD as they became aware of the tragedy affecting one of their heroes, General Romeo Dallaire, who was the commander of U.N. forces in Rwanda in 1994. In just 100 days, nearly 800 000 (mostly Tutsi) were ruthlessly slaughtered by the Hutu, making it one of the worst genocides of our time. The outside help he requested did not materialize, and so Dallaire could do nothing but watch helplessly as the sounds, sights, and the horror of death engulfed the country. Upon his return to Canada, he was praised for his valiant efforts and was given numerous honours. Dallaire, however, was far from being in a celebratory mood. He was tormented by the memories of the horrors he had witnessed, and went on

General Romeo Dallaire was in charge of United Nations forces in Rwanda in 1994. He was totally helpless as 800 000 people were brutally put to death. Haunted by the gruesome nature of the slaughter he witnessed in Rwanda, Dallaire went on to develop post-traumatic stress disorder.

Dissociative amnesia Loss of memory (partial or complete) for important information related to personal identity.

Dissociative fugue Sudden travel away from home, plus confusion about one's personal identity.

Dissociative identity disorder The presence of two or more distinct personalities (multiple personality).

Hypochondriasis A preoccupation with fears of having a serious disease. Ordinary physical signs are interpreted as proof of disease, but no physical abnormality can be found.

Somatization disorder Afflicted persons have numerous physical complaints. Typically, they have consulted many doctors, but no organic problems can be identified.

to develop post-traumatic stress disorder. He experienced terrifying spells of anxiety and nightmares, became suicidal, and was forced to take time off to seek therapy.

The experience of Dallaire is not unique. Estimates are that up to 20 percent of Canadian peacekeepers suffer from the disabling effects of war trauma (CBC, 1999). The Canadian military has set up a special program to help those who have developed PTSD as a result of their overseas duties in the theatre of war.

Another event that has become embedded in the minds of millions of people and has caused many to develop PTSD is the terrorist attacks of September 11, 2001. For many who helped in the rescue operations and those who managed to escape the burning fires and the collapsing World Trade Center buildings, the terrifying images are very intense and disturbing.

Dissociative Disorders

In dissociative reactions we see striking episodes of amnesia, fugue, or multiple identity. **Dissociative amnesia** is an inability to recall one's name, address, or past. **Dissociative fugue** (sounds like "fewg") involves sudden travel away from home and confusion about personal identity. Dissociations are often triggered by highly traumatic events (Lipschitz et al., 1996). In such cases, forgetting personal identity and fleeing unpleasant situations can serve as defences against intolerable anxiety.

A person suffering from a **dissociative identity disorder** has two or more separate identities or personality states (DSM-IV-TR, 2000). (Note that identity disorders are not the same as schizophrenia. Schizophrenia, which is a psychotic disorder, is discussed later in this chapter.) A dramatic example of multiple identity is described in the book *Sybil* (Schreiber, 1973). Sybil reportedly had 16 different personality states. Each identity had a distinct voice, vocabulary, and posture. One personality could play the piano (not Sybil), but the others could not.

When an identity other than Sybil was in control, Sybil experienced a "time lapse," or memory blackout. Sybil's amnesia and separate identities first appeared during childhood. As a girl she was beaten, locked in closets, perversely tortured, sexually abused, and almost killed. Sybil's first dissociations allowed her to escape by creating another person who would suffer torture in her place. Dissociative identity disorder often begins with unbearable childhood experiences, like those Sybil endured. A history of childhood trauma, especially sexual abuse, is found in over 95 percent of persons whose personalities split into multiple identities (Scroppo et al., 1998; Tutkun, Yargic, & Sar, 1995).

Flamboyant cases like Sybil's have led some experts to question the existence of multiple personalities (Rieber, 1999). Based on newly discovered tapes of therapy sessions between Sybil and her psychiatrists, Rieber claims that Sybil's multiple selves were not real; they were the products of her therapists' beliefs in the existence of multiple personality disorder and their use of hypnosis to persuade and encourage Sybil to produce lots of different identities. Nevertheless, many psychologists think that multiple identity is a real, if rare, problem (Cormier & Thelen, 1998).

Therapy for dissociative identity disorder may make use of hypnosis, which allows contact with the various personality states. The goal of therapy is integration and fusion of the identities into a single, balanced personality. Fortunately, multiple identity disorders are far rarer in real life than they are in TV dramas!

Somatoform Disorders

Have you ever known someone who seemed to be obsessed by fears of having a serious disease? These people are preoccupied with bodily functions, such as their heartbeat or breathing or digestion. Minor physical problems—even a small sore or an occasional cough—may convince them that they have cancer or some other dreaded disease. Typically, they can't give up their fears of illness, even if doctors can find no medical basis for their complaints (DSM-IV-TR, 2000).

Are you describing hypochondria? Yes. In **hypochondriasis** (HI-po-kon-DRY-uh-sis), people interpret normal bodily sensations as proof that they have a terrible disease. In a related problem called **somatization disorder** (som-ah-tuh-ZAY-shun), people express their anxieties through various bodily complaints. That is, they suffer from problems such as vomiting or nausea, shortness of breath, difficulty swallowing, or painful menstrual periods. Typically, the person feels ill much of the time and visits doctors repeatedly. Most sufferers take medicines or other treatments, but no physical cause can be found for their distress (Ford, 1995). Similarly, a person with **pain disorder** is disabled by pain that has no identifiable physical basis (DSM-IV-TR, 2000).

A rarer somatoform disorder is called a *conversion reaction*. In a **conversion disorder,** severe emotional conflicts are "converted" into symptoms that actually disturb physical functioning or closely resemble a physical disability. For instance, a soldier might become deaf or lame or develop "glove anesthesia" just before a battle.

What is "glove anesthesia"? "Glove anesthesia" is a loss of sensitivity in the areas of the skin that would normally be covered by a glove. Glove anesthesia shows that conversion symptoms often contradict known medical facts. The system of nerves in the hands does not form a glove-like pattern and could not cause such symptoms (see ▶Figure 12.3).

If symptoms disappear when a victim is asleep, hypnotized, or anesthetized, a conversion reaction must be suspected (Russo et al., 1998). Another sign to watch for is that victims of conversion reactions may be strangely unconcerned about their sudden disability.

> **Pain disorder** Pain that has no identifiable physical cause and appears to be of psychological origin.
>
> **Conversion disorder** A bodily symptom that mimics a physical disability but is actually caused by anxiety or emotional distress.

Uncontrollable sneezing, which may continue for days or weeks, is often a conversion disorder. In such cases, sneezing is atypical in rate and rhythm. In addition, the person's eyes do not close during a sneeze and sneezing does not occur during sleep. (A normal sneeze is shown here.) All of these signs suggest that the cause of the sneezing is psychological, not physical (Fochtmann, 1995).

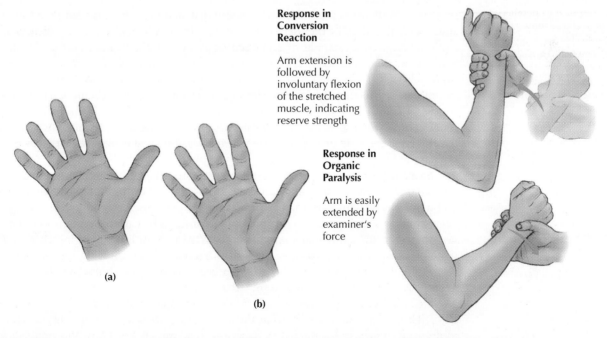

Response in Conversion Reaction

Arm extension is followed by involuntary flexion of the stretched muscle, indicating reserve strength

Response in Organic Paralysis

Arm is easily extended by examiner's force

(a)

(b)

▶**Figure 12.3**

(left) "Glove" anesthesia is a conversion reaction involving loss of feeling in areas of the hand that would be covered by a glove *(a)*. If the anesthesia were physically caused, it would follow the pattern shown in *(b)*. *(right)* To test for organic paralysis of the arm, an examiner can suddenly extend the arm, stretching the muscles. A conversion reaction is indicated if the arm pulls back involuntarily. (Adapted from Weintraub, 1983.)

▶ Anxiety and Disorder—Four Pathways to Trouble

Survey Question:
■ How do psychologists explain anxiety-based disorders?

What causes the problems described in the preceding discussion? Because we are both biological and social creatures, it is not surprising that susceptibility to anxiety-based disorders appears to be partly inherited. Studies of parents suffering from panic disorder, for instance, show that an unusually large number (60 percent) of their children are born with a fearful, inhibited temperament (Rosenbaum et al., 1989). Such children are irritable and wary as infants, shy and fearful as toddlers, and quiet and cautious introverts in elementary school. By the time they reach adulthood, they are at high risk for anxiety problems, such as panic attacks, in adulthood (Rosenbaum et al., 1991).

At least four major perspectives on the causes of dissociative, anxiety, and somatoform disorders exist. These are (1) the psychodynamic approach, (2) the humanistic-existential approach, (3) the behavioural approach, and (4) the cognitive approach.

Psychodynamic Approach

Psychodynamic Pertaining to internal motives, conflicts, unconscious forces, and other dynamics of mental life.

Humanistic Any system of thought focused on subjective experience and human problems and potentials.

Self-image Total subjective perception of oneself; another term for self-concept.

Existentialism A system of thought that focuses on the elemental problems of existence, such as death, meaning, choice, and responsibility.

Behaviouristic Any approach that emphasizes overt, observable behaviour and the effects of learning and conditioning.

The term **psychodynamic** refers to internal motives, conflicts, unconscious forces, and other dynamics of mental life. Freud was the first to propose a psychodynamic explanation for what he called "neurosis." According to Freud, disturbances like those we have described represent a raging conflict among subparts of the personality—the id, ego, and superego.

Freud emphasized that intense anxiety can be caused by forbidden id impulses for sex or aggression that threaten to break through into behaviour. The person constantly fears doing something "crazy" or forbidden. She or he may also be tortured by guilt, which the superego creates in response to forbidden impulses. Caught in the middle, the ego is eventually overwhelmed. This forces the person to use rigid defence mechanisms and misguided, inflexible behaviour to prevent a disastrous loss of control.

Humanistic-Existential Approaches

Humanistic theories emphasize subjective experience, human problems, and personal potentials. Humanistic psychologist Carl Rogers regarded emotional disorders as the end product of a faulty **self-image** (your total perception of yourself; in other words, your self-concept) (Rogers, 1959). Rogers believed that anxious individuals have built up unrealistic mental images of themselves. This leaves them vulnerable to contradictory information. Let's say, for example, that an essential part of Carli's self-image is the idea that she is highly intelligent. If Carli does poorly in school, she may deny or distort her perceptions of herself and her perceptions of the situation. Should Carli's anxiety become severe, she may resort to the rigid use of defence mechanisms. A conversion reaction, anxiety attacks, or similar symptoms could also result from threats to her self-image. These symptoms, in turn, would become new threats that provoke further distortions. We would soon have a classic example of a vicious cycle of maladjustment and anxiety that feeds on itself once started.

Existentialism focuses on the elemental problems of existence, such as death, meaning, choice, and responsibility. Psychologists who take a more existential view stress that unhealthy anxiety reflects a loss of meaning in one's life. According to them, we must show courage and responsibility in our choices if life is to have meaning. Too often, they say, we give in to "existential anxiety" and back away from life-enhancing choices. Existential anxiety is the unavoidable anguish that comes from knowing we are personally responsible for our lives. Hence, we have a crushing need to choose wisely and courageously as we face life's empty and impersonal void.

From the existential view, people who are unhappy and anxious are living in "bad faith." That is, they have collapsed in the face of the awesome responsibility to choose a meaningful existence. In short, they have lost their way in life. From this point of view, making choices that don't reflect what you really value, feel, and believe can make you sick.

Behavioural Approach

Behaviouristic approaches emphasize overt, observable behaviour and the effects of learning and conditioning. Behaviourists assume that the "symptoms" we have discussed are learned, just as other behaviours are. You might recall from Chapter 6, for instance, that phobias can be acquired through classical conditioning. Similarly, anxiety attacks may reflect conditioned emotional responses that generalize to new situations. As another example, the "sickness behaviour" of someone who suffers from hypochondriasis may be reinforced by the sympathy and attention he or she gets.

One point that all theorists agree on is that disordered behaviour is ultimately self-defeating and paradoxical. A paradox is a contradiction. The contradiction in self-defeating behaviour is that it makes the person more miserable in the long run, even though it temporarily lowers anxiety.

But if the person becomes more miserable in the long run, how does the pattern get started? The behavioural explanation is that self-defeating behaviour begins with avoidance learning (described in Chapter 6). **Avoidance learning** occurs when making a particular response delays or prevents the onset of a painful or unpleasant stimulus. Here's a quick review to refresh your memory:

> An animal is placed in a special cage. After a few minutes a light comes on, followed a moment later by a painful shock. Quickly, the animal escapes into a second chamber. After a few minutes, a light comes on in this chamber, and the shock is repeated. Soon the animal learns to avoid pain by moving before the shock occurs. Once an animal learns to avoid the shock, it can be turned off altogether. A well-trained animal may avoid the non-existent shock indefinitely.

The same analysis can be applied to human behaviour. A behaviourist would say that the powerful reward of immediate relief from anxiety keeps self-defeating avoidance behaviour alive. This view, known as the **anxiety reduction hypothesis,** seems to explain why the behaviour patterns we have discussed often look very "stupid" to outside observers.

Cognitive Approach

The **cognitive view** is that distorted thinking causes people to magnify ordinary threats and failures, which leads to distress (Foa et al., 1996). For example, Pierre, who has social phobia, constantly has upsetting thoughts about being evaluated. One reason for this is that people with social phobia tend to be perfectionists. Like others with social phobia, Pierre is excessively concerned about mistakes. He also perceives criticism where none exists (Juster et al., 1996). Pierre tends to focus too much attention on himself, which intensifies his anxiety in social situations (Woody, 1996). Even when persons with social phobia are successful, distorted thinking leads them to think they have failed (Alden & Wallace, 1995). In short, changing the thinking patterns of anxious individuals like Pierre can greatly lessen their fears (Poulton & Andrews, 1996).

SUMMARY There is probably a core of truth to all four psychological explanations. For this reason, understanding anxiety-based disorders may be aided by combining parts of each perspective. Each viewpoint also suggests a different approach to treatment. Because there are many possibilities, therapy is discussed later, in Chapter 13.

Avoidance learning Learning that occurs when making a particular response delays or prevents the onset of a painful or unpleasant stimulus.

Anxiety reduction hypothesis Explains the self-defeating nature of avoidance responses as a result of the reinforcing effects of relief from anxiety.

Cognitive view Holds that distorted thinking causes people to magnify ordinary threats and failures, leading to anxiety and distress.

Knowledge builder

ANXIETY-BASED DISORDERS

Relate

Which of the anxiety disorders would you least want to suffer from? Why?

What minor obsessions or compulsions have you experienced?

What is the key difference between a stress disorder and an adjustment disorder? (Review both discussions if you don't immediately know the answer.)

Which of the four main explanations of anxiety-based disorders do you find most convincing?

Learning Check

1. Excessive anxiety over ordinary life stresses is characteristic of which of the following disorders?
   a. PTSD *b.* agoraphobia *c.* hypochondriasis *d.* adjustment disorder

continued

2. Panic disorder can occur with or without agoraphobia, but agoraphobia cannot occur alone, without the presence of a panic disorder. T or F?

3. Alice has a phobic fear of blood. What is the formal term for her fear?
   a. nyctophobia b. hematophobia c. pathophobia d. pyrophobia

4. A person who intensely fears eating, writing, or speaking in public suffers from _____ _____.

5. "Checkers" and "cleaners" suffer from which disorder?
   a. acarophobia b. panic disorder with agoraphobia c. generalized anxiety disorder d. obsessive-compulsive disorder

6. The symptoms of acute stress disorders last less than one month; post-traumatic stress disorders last more than one month. T or F?

7. Which of the following is not a dissociative disorder?
   a. fugue b. amnesia c. conversion reaction d. multiple identity

8. Freud's original psychodynamic explanation of "neurosis" was based on the avoidance learning hypothesis. T or F?

9. Many of the physical complaints associated with anxiety disorders are closely related to activity of what part of the nervous system?

10. Why would you expect the rate of PTSD to be especially high among Canadian soldiers who witnessed the genocide in Rwanda?

Answers:

1. d 2. F 3. b 4. social phobia 5. d 6. T 7. c 8. F 9. The autonomic nervous system (ANS), especially the sympathetic branch of the ANS. 10. In addition to the unusual stresses they experienced, Canadian soldiers had neither the resources nor the mandate from the U.N. to take any decisive actions to stop the genocide, which further increased their sense of helplessness.

▶ Psychotic Disorders—Life in the Shadow of Madness

Survey Question:
■ What are the general characteristics of psychotic disorders?

Psychotic disorders are among the most serious of all mental problems. A person who is psychotic undergoes a number of striking changes in thinking, behaviour, and emotion. Basic to all of these changes is the fact that **psychosis** (psycho*sis*, singular; psycho*ses*, plural) reflects a loss of contact with shared views of reality. The following comments, made by two patients with psychosis, illustrate what is meant by a "split" from reality (Torrey, 1988).

> Everything is in bits. You put the picture up bit by bit into your head. It's like a photograph that's torn in bits and put together again. If you move it's frightening.

> Last week I was with a girl and suddenly she seemed to get bigger and bigger, like a monster coming nearer and nearer.

What are the major features of psychotic disorders? Delusions and hallucinations are core features, but there are others as well.

People who suffer from **delusions** hold false beliefs that they insist are true, regardless of how much the facts contradict them. An example is a 43-year-old man with schizophrenia who was convinced he was pregnant (Mansouri & Adityanjee, 1995). People with other common delusions may believe that they have committed a sinful deed, that their body is diseased or "rotting away," that they are a famous historical figure, or that others are "out to get" them (DSM-IV-TR, 2000).

Hallucinations are imaginary sensations, such as seeing, hearing, or smelling things that don't exist in the real world. The most common psychotic hallucination is hearing voices, like the voice that told a Toronto man to push a person onto the path of an oncoming subway train. Sometimes these voices command patients to hurt themselves. Unfortunately, many people obey (Kasper, Rogers, & Adams, 1996). More rarely, psychotic people may feel "insects crawling under their skin," taste "poisons" in their food, or smell "gas" their "enemies" are using to "get" them. Sensory changes, such as anesthesia (numbness, or a loss of sensation) or extreme sensitivity to heat, cold, pain, or touch, can also occur.

During a psychotic episode, emotions are often severely disturbed. For instance, a person may be wildly elated, depressed, hyper-emotional, or apathetic. Sometimes patients display **flat affect,** a condition in which the face is frozen in a blank expression. How-

Psychosis A withdrawal from reality marked by hallucinations and delusions, disturbed thought and emotions, and personality disorganization.

Delusion A false belief held against all contrary evidence.

Hallucination An imaginary sensation, such as seeing, hearing, or smelling things that don't exist in the real world.

Flat affect An extreme lack of emotional expressiveness.

Table 12.6 **Warning** **Signs of** **Psychotic** **Disorders** **and Major** **Mood** **Disorders**	—You express bizarre thoughts or beliefs that defy reality —You have withdrawn from family members and other relationships —You hear unreal voices or sees things others don't —You are extremely sad, persistently despondent, or suicidal —You are excessively energetic and have little need for sleep —You lose your appetite, sleep excessively, and have no energy —You exhibit extreme mood swings —You believe someone is trying to get you —You have engaged in antisocial, destructive, or self-destructive behaviour (Sources: Harvey et al., 1996; Sheehy & Cournos, 1992.)

ever, behind their "frozen masks," people continue to feel emotions just as strongly as ever (Sison et al., 1996).

Some psychotic symptoms can be thought of as a primitive type of communication. That is, many patients can only use their actions to say, "I need help" or "I can't handle it any more." **Disturbed verbal communication** is a nearly universal symptom of psychotic disorders. In fact, psychotic speech tends to be so garbled and chaotic that it sometimes sounds like a "word salad."

Major disturbances such as those just described—as well as added problems in thought, memory, and attention—bring about personality disintegration and a break with reality. **Personality disintegration** occurs when a person's thoughts, actions, and emotions are no longer coordinated. Personality disintegration seriously impairs a person's work, social relations, and self-care. When psychotic disturbances and a fragmented personality are evident for weeks or months (often including a period of deterioration, an active phase, and a residual phase), the person has suffered a psychosis (DSM-IV-TR, 2000). (See Table 12.6.)

Are there different types of psychotic disorders? Two major types of psychosis are delusional disorders and schizophrenia. Mood disorders, which primarily involve extremes of emotion, can also have psychotic features. Information on each of these problems is provided in upcoming discussions.

As we will see later, psychotic disorders appear to involve physical changes in the brain. In a sense, then, all psychoses are partly organic. However, the general term **organic psychosis** is usually reserved for problems involving clear-cut brain injuries or diseases. For example, poisoning by lead or mercury can damage the brain and cause hallucinations, delusions, and a loss of emotional control (see ▶ Figure 12.4). A particularly dangerous situation is found in old buildings that contain leaded paints. Lead tastes sweet. Thus, young children may be tempted to eat leaded paint flakes as if they were candy. Children who eat leaded paint can become psychotic or develop mental retardation (Dyer, 1993; Mielke, 1999).

Leaded paints also release powdered lead into the air. Children may breathe the powder or eat it after handling contaminated toys. Other sources of lead are soldered water pipes, old lead-lined drinking fountains, lead-glazed pottery, and lead from automobile exhaust. On a much larger scale, "poisoning" of another type, in the form of drug abuse, can also produce psychotic symptoms (DSM-IV-TR, 2000).

The most common organic problem is **dementia** (duh-MEN-sha), a serious mental impairment in old age caused by deterioration of the brain. In dementia, we see major disturbances in memory, reasoning, judgment, impulse control, and personality. This combination usually leaves people confused, suspicious, apathetic, or withdrawn. Some common causes of dementia are circulatory problems, repeated strokes, or general shrinkage and

Disturbed verbal communication Speech that is disorganized, garbled, or unintelligible.

Personality disintegration A shattering of the coordination among thoughts, actions, and emotions normally found in personality.

Organic psychosis A psychosis caused by brain injury or disease.

Dementia Serious mental impairment in old age caused by physical deterioration of the brain.

▶**Figure 12.4**

The Mad Hatter, from Lewis Carroll's *Alice's Adventures in Wonderland.* History provides numerous examples of psychosis caused by toxic chemicals. Carroll's Mad Hatter character is modelled after an occupational disease of the 18th and 19th centuries. In that era, hat-makers were heavily exposed to mercury used in the preparation of felt. Consequently, many suffered brain damage and became psychotic, or "mad" (Kety, 1979).

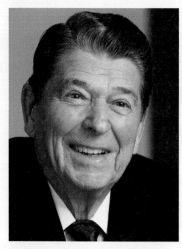

Former U.S. President Ronald Regan was diagnosed with Alzheimer's disease in 1995. Like many Alzheimer's victims, Reagan slipped into a slow mental decline that severely restricted his activities.

atrophy of the brain. The majority of people who suffer from dementia slowly lose their mental abilities without becoming psychotic. However, some do develop delusions and lose contact with reality. The most common cause of dementia is *Alzheimer's disease.*

ALZHEIMER'S DISEASE **Alzheimer's disease** (ALLS-hi-merz) is one of the most fearsome problems of aging. It is a disorder characterized by impaired memory, confusion, and a progressive loss of mental abilities.

Alzheimer's victims at first have difficulty remembering recent events. Then they slowly become more disoriented, suspicious, and confused. In time they lose the ability to work, cook, drive, or use tools. As their condition worsens, victims can no longer read, write, or do arithmetic. Eventually they are mute, bedridden, and unable to walk, sit up, or smile (Larson, 1990).

Researchers suspect that Alzheimer's disease is caused by unusual webs and tangles in brain cells leading to and from the hippocampus (Nagy et al., 1996). (This area, you may recall, is important for learning and memory.) Changes also take place in an area called the nucleus basalis and in chemicals that carry messages within the brain. One out of every 10 adults over age 65 is a victim of Alzheimer's disease. Although the disease tends to progress slowly, it is ultimately fatal. There is no known remedy. Understandably, efforts to find a cure for Alzheimer's disease are expanding. For some of us, such efforts may be a race against time. As the baby boomers get older over the next few decades, the number of Alzheimer's cases is expected to be quite high.

▶ Delusional Disorders—An Enemy behind Every Tree

Survey Question:
■ How do delusional disorders differ from other psychotic disorders?

People with delusional disorders usually do not suffer from hallucinations, emotional excesses, or personality disintegration. Even so, their break with reality is unmistakable. The main feature of **delusional disorders** is the presence of deeply held false beliefs, which may take the following forms (DSM-IV-TR, 2000):

- *Erotomanic type.* In this disorder, people have erotic delusions that they are loved by another person, especially by someone famous or of higher status.
- *Grandiose type.* In this case, people suffer from the delusion that they have some great, unrecognized talent, knowledge, or insight. They may also believe that they have a special relationship with an important person or with God or that they are a famous person. (If the famous person is alive, the deluded person regards her or him as an imposter.)
- *Jealous type.* Typical of this type of delusion is an all-consuming, unfounded belief that one's spouse or lover is unfaithful.
- *Persecutory type.* Delusions of persecution involve the belief that one is being conspired against, cheated, spied on, followed, poisoned, maligned, or harassed.
- *Somatic type.* People suffering from somatic delusions typically believe that their bodies are diseased or rotting, or infested with insects or parasites, or that parts of their bodies are misshapen or defective.

Although they are false, and sometimes far-fetched, all of these delusions are about experiences that could conceivably occur in real life (Manschreck, 1996). In other types of psychosis, delusions tend to be much more bizarre.

Paranoid Psychosis

The most common delusional disorder, often called **paranoid psychosis,** centres on delusions of persecution. Many self-styled reformers, crank letter writers, "Communist hunters," "UFO abductees," and the like suffer paranoid delusions. Paranoid individuals often believe that they are being cheated, spied on, followed, poisoned, harassed, or plotted against. Usually they are intensely suspicious, believing they must be on guard at all times.

The evidence such people find to support their beliefs usually fails to persuade others. Every detail of the paranoid person's existence is woven into a private version of "what's really going on." Buzzing during a telephone conversation may be interpreted as

Alzheimer's disease An age-related disease characterized by memory loss, mental confusion, and (in its later stages) a nearly total loss of mental abilities.

Delusional disorder A psychosis marked by severe delusions of grandeur, jealousy, persecution, or similar preoccupations.

Paranoid psychosis A delusional disorder centred especially on delusions of persecution.

"someone listening"; a stranger who comes to the door asking for directions may be seen as "really trying to get information"; and so forth.

People suffering paranoid delusions are rarely treated. It is almost impossible for them to accept that they need help. Anyone who suggests that they have a problem simply becomes part of the "conspiracy" to "persecute" them.

Paranoid people frequently lead lonely, isolated, and humourless lives dominated by constant suspicion and hostility. While they are not necessarily dangerous to others, they can be. People who believe that the Mafia, the "government agents," "space aliens," or a street gang is slowly closing in on them may be moved to violence by their irrational fears. Imagine that a stranger comes to the door to ask a paranoid person for directions. If the stranger has his hand in his coat pocket, he could become the target of a paranoid attempt at "self-defence."

▶ Schizophrenia—Shattered Reality

Survey Question:
■ What forms does schizophrenia take? What causes it?

Schizophrenia A psychosis characterized by delusions, hallucinations, apathy, and a "split" between thought and emotion.

Disorganized schizophrenia Schizophrenia marked by incoherence, grossly disorganized behaviour, bizarre thinking, and flat or grossly inappropriate emotions.

Catatonic schizophrenia Schizophrenia marked by stupor, rigidity, unresponsiveness, posturing, mutism, and sometimes agitated, purposeless behaviour.

Paranoid schizophrenia Schizophrenia marked by a preoccupation with delusions or by frequent auditory hallucinations related to a single theme, especially grandeur or persecution.

Undifferentiated schizophrenia Schizophrenia lacking the specific features of catatonic, disorganized, or paranoid types.

Schizophrenia (SKIT-soh-FREE-nee-uh) is marked by delusions, hallucinations, apathy, thinking abnormalities, and a "split" between thought and emotion. In schizophrenia, emotions may become blunted or very inappropriate. For example, if a man with schizophrenia is told his mother just died, he might smile, or giggle, or show no emotion at all. Schizophrenic delusions may include the idea that the person's thoughts and actions are being controlled, that thoughts are being broadcast (so others can hear them), that thoughts have been "inserted" into the person's mind, or that thoughts have been removed. In addition, schizophrenia involves withdrawal from contact with others, a loss of interest in external activities, a breakdown of personal habits, and an inability to deal with daily events. One person in 100 will develop schizophrenia, and roughly half of all the people admitted to mental hospitals suffer from this disorder.

Remember the psychotic person who said, "Everything is in bits. . . . It's like a photograph that's torn in bits and put together again"? Many schizophrenic symptoms appear to arise from impaired selective attention (Hirt & Pithers, 1991; Lenzenweger, Cornblatt, & Putnick, 1991; Ward et al., 1991). In other words, it is hard for people with schizophrenia to focus on one item of information at a time. This may be why they are overwhelmed by a jumble of thoughts, sensations, images, and feelings.

Is there more than one type of schizophrenia? Schizophrenia appears to be a group of related disturbances. It has four major subtypes (DSM-IV-TR, 2000):

- **Disorganized schizophrenia** is marked by incoherence, grossly disorganized behaviour, bizarre thinking, and flat or grossly inappropriate emotions.
- **Catatonic schizophrenia** is marked by stupor, rigidity, unresponsiveness, posturing, mutism, and sometimes agitated, purposeless behaviour.
- **Paranoid schizophrenia** is marked by a preoccupation with delusions or by frequent auditory hallucinations related to a single theme, especially grandeur or persecution.
- **Undifferentiated schizophrenia** has prominent psychotic symptoms, but none of the specific features of catatonic, disorganized, or paranoid types.

Disorganized Schizophrenia

The disorder known as disorganized schizophrenia (sometimes called hebephrenic schizophrenia) comes close to matching the stereotyped images of "madness" seen in movies. In disorganized schizophrenia, personality disintegration is almost complete: Emotions, speech, and behaviour are all highly disorganized. The result is silliness, laughter, and bizarre or obscene behaviour, as shown by this intake interview of a patient named Edna:

Doctor: *I am Dr. _____. I would like to know something more about you.*

Patient: *You have a nasty mind. Lord! Lord! Cat's in a cradle.*

Doctor: *Tell me, how do you feel?*

In disorganized schizophrenia, behaviour is marked by silliness, laughter, and bizarre or obscene behaviour.

Can the characteristic catatonic features of rigid postures and stupor be understood in terms of abnormal body chemistry? Environment? Heredity?

Patient: *London's bell is a long, long dock. Hee! Hee! (Giggles uncontrollably.)*

Doctor: *Do you know where you are now?*

Patient: *D_____n! S_____t on you all who rip into my internals! The grudgerometer will take care of you all! (Shouting) I am the Queen, see my magic, I shall turn you all into smidgelings forever!*

Doctor: *Your husband is concerned about you. Do you know his name?*

Patient: *(Stands, walks to and faces the wall) Who am I, who are we, who are you, who are they, (turns) I . . . I . . . I . . . I! (Makes grotesque faces.)*

Edna was placed in the women's ward where she proceeded to masturbate. Occasionally, she would scream or shout obscenities. At other times she giggled to herself. She was known to attack other patients. She began to complain that her uterus was attached to a "pipeline to the Kremlin" and that she was being "infernally invaded" by Communism (Suinn, 1975).

Disorganized schizophrenia typically develops in early adolescence or young adulthood. It is often preceded by serious personality disorganization in earlier years. Chances of improvement are limited, and social impairment is usually extreme (DSM-IV-TR, 2000).

Catatonic Schizophrenia

Catatonic schizophrenia brings about a stuporous condition in which odd positions may be held for hours or even days. These periods of immobility may be similar to the tendency to "freeze" at times of great emergency or panic. Catatonic individuals appear to be struggling desperately to control their inner turmoil. One sign of this is the fact that stupor may occasionally give way to agitated outbursts or violent behaviour. The following excerpt describes a catatonic episode.

> Manuel appeared to be physically healthy upon examination. Yet he did not regain his awareness of his surroundings. He remained motionless, speechless, and seemingly unconscious. One evening an aide turned him on his side to straighten out the sheet, was called away to tend another patient, and forgot to return. Manuel was found the next morning, still on his side, his arm tucked under his body, as he had been left the night before. His arm was turning blue from lack of circulation, but he seemed to be experiencing no discomfort. (Suinn, 1975)

Notice that Manuel did not speak. Mutism, along with a marked decrease in responsiveness to the environment, makes the patient difficult to "reach." Fortunately, this bizarre form of schizophrenia has become rare in Europe and North America (DSM-IV-TR, 2000).

Paranoid Schizophrenia

Paranoid schizophrenia is the most common schizophrenic disorder. Paranoid schizophrenia, like a paranoid delusional disorder, centres on delusions of grandeur and persecution. However, people with paranoid schizophrenia also hallucinate, and their delusions are more bizarre and unconvincing than those in a delusional disorder.

Thinking that their minds are being controlled by God, the government, or "cosmic rays from space," or that someone is trying to poison them, people suffering from paranoid schizophrenia may feel forced into violence to "protect" themselves (see ▶Figure 12.5). An example is James Huberty, who brutally murdered 21 people at a McDonald's restaurant in San Ysidro, California. Huberty suffered from paranoid schizophrenia and felt persecuted and cheated by life. Shortly before he announced to his wife that he was "going hunting humans," Huberty had been hearing hallucinated voices.

How dangerous are the mentally ill? Depictions in the news certainly give the impression that practically everyone who is mentally ill is dangerous. But are they? You might be surprised by the answer, found in "Are the Mentally Ill Prone to Violence?"

▶Figure 12.5

Over a period of years, Theodore Kaczynski mailed bombs to unsuspecting victims, many of whom were maimed or killed. As a young adult, Kaczynski was a brilliant mathematician. At the time of his arrest, he had become the Unabomber—a reclusive "loner" who deeply mistrusted other people and modern technology. After his arrest, Kaczynski was judged to be suffering from paranoid schizophrenia.

The Causes of Schizophrenia

Former British Prime Minister Winston Churchill once described a question that perplexed him as "a riddle wrapped in a mystery inside an enigma." The same words might describe the causes of schizophrenia.

ENVIRONMENT   *What causes schizophrenia?* An increased risk of developing schizophrenia may begin at birth or even before. Women who are exposed to the influenza (flu) virus during the middle of pregnancy have children who are more likely to develop schizophrenia than the children of women exposed to the virus later in pregnancy. Malnutrition during pregnancy and complications at the time of birth can have a similar impact. Possibly, such events disturb brain development, leaving people more vulnerable to a psychotic break with reality (Cannon, 1998; Takei et al., 1994; Woods, 1998).

FOCUS ON RESEARCH   Are the Mentally Ill Prone to Violence?

News reports and television programs tend to greatly exaggerate the connection between mental illness and violence (Diefenbach, 1997). In reality, research on this question leads to these conclusions:

- Only persons who are *actively psychotic* are more violence prone than non-patients. That is, if a person is experiencing delusions and hallucinations, the risk of violence is elevated. Other mental problems are unrelated to violence.
- Only persons *currently* experiencing psychotic symptoms are at increased risk for violence. Violent behaviour is not related to having been a mental patient or having had psychotic symptoms *in the past.*

Thus, most news stories give a false impression. Even when we consider people who are actively psychotic, we find that the vast majority are not violent. The risk of violence from mental patients is actually many times lower than that posed by persons who have the following attributes: young, male, poor, and intoxicated.

Beliefs about mental disorders are important because they affect laws and personal attitudes toward the mentally ill. People who strongly believe that the mentally ill are prone to violence are typically afraid to have former mental patients as neighbours, co-workers, or friends. But as you can see, only a small minority of the actively mentally ill pose an increased risk. Former mental patients, in particular, are no more likely to be violent than people in general. No matter how disturbed a person may have been, she or he merits respect and compassion. Remember, the overwhelming majority of violent crimes are committed by people who are not mentally ill.

(Sources: Monahan, 1992; Noble, 1997; Rice, 1997; Teplin, Abram, & McClelland, 1994.)

Many news stories give the impression that the mentally ill are dangerous. Consider, for example, the ghastly case of Jeffrey Dahmer, who killed, sexually molested, and then ate his victims. Like Dahmer, most of the mentally disordered persons who make the evening news have committed murder or some other horrible crime. This tends to give the impression that the mentally ill are violent and dangerous. Yet in reality, only a tiny percentage of all mentally disordered persons are more violent than average.

Psychological trauma
A psychological injury or shock, such as that caused by violence, abuse, neglect, separation, and so forth.

Disturbed family environment Stressful or unhealthy family relationships, communication patterns, and emotional atmosphere.

Deviant communication Patterns of communication that cause guilt, anxiety, confusion, anger, conflict, and emotional turmoil.

Biochemical abnormality A disturbance of the body's chemical systems, especially in brain chemicals or neurotransmitters.

Dopamine An important transmitter substance found in the brain—especially in the limbic system, an area associated with emotional response.

Early **psychological trauma** (a psychological injury or shock) may also add to the risk. Often, the victims of schizophrenia were exposed to violence, sexual abuse, death, divorce, separation, or other stresses in childhood (Mirsky & Duncan, 1986). Living in a troubled family is a related risk factor. In a **disturbed family environment,** stressful relationships, communication patterns, and negative emotions prevail. For example, a 15-year study found that the chance of developing schizophrenia is related to deviant communication within families (Goldstein, 1985). **Deviant communication patterns** cause anxiety, confusion, anger, conflict, and turmoil. Typically, disturbed families interact in ways that are laden with guilt, prying, criticism, negativity, and emotional attacks (Bressi, Albonetti, & Razzoli, 1998; Docherty et al., 1998).

Although they are attractive, environmental explanations alone are not enough to account for schizophrenia (Fowles, 1992). For example, when the children of parents with schizophrenia are raised away from their chaotic home environment, they are still more likely to become psychotic.

Does that mean that heredity affects the risk of developing schizophrenia?

HEREDITY   Evidence has grown stronger in recent years that heredity is a factor in schizophrenia. It now appears that some individuals inherit a *potential* for developing schizophrenia. They are, in other words, more vulnerable to the disorder than others are (Cannon et al., 1998; Fowles, 1992).

How has that been shown? If one identical twin develops schizophrenia (remember, identical twins have identical genes), then the other twin has a 48 percent chance of also developing the disorder (Lenzenweger & Gottesman, 1994). The figure for twins can be compared to the risk of schizophrenia for the population in general, which is 1 percent. (See ►Figure 12.6 for other relationships.) In general, it is clear that schizophrenia is more common among close relatives and it tends to run in families (Plomin & Rende, 1991). There's even a case on record of four identical quadruplets all developing schizophrenia. In light of such evidence, researchers are beginning to search for specific genes related to schizophrenia (Gershon et al., 1998).

BRAIN CHEMISTRY   *How could someone inherit a susceptibility to schizophrenia?* Amphetamine, LSD, PCP ("angel dust"), and similar drugs produce effects that partially mimic the symptoms of schizophrenia. Also, the same drugs (phenothiazines) used to treat LSD overdoses tend to alleviate psychotic symptoms. Facts such as these suggest that **biochemical abnormalities** (disturbances in brain chemicals or neurotransmitters) may occur in people with schizophrenia. It is possible that the affected brain produces some substance similar to a psychedelic (mind-altering) drug. At present, one likely candidate is **dopamine** (DOPE-ah-meen), an important chemical messenger found in the brain (Abi-Dargham et al., 1998).

Many researchers believe that schizophrenia is related to overactivity in brain dopamine systems (Heinrichs, 1993). Another possibility is that dopamine receptors become super-responsive to normal amounts of dopamine (Port & Seybold, 1995). Dopamine appears to trigger a flood of unrelated thoughts, feelings, and perceptions, which may account for the voices, hallucinations, and delusions of schizophrenia (Gottesman, 1991). The implication is that individuals with schizophrenia may be on a sort of drug trip caused by their own bodies (see

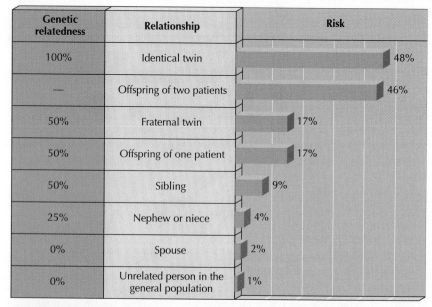

Genetic relatedness	Relationship	Risk
100%	Identical twin	48%
—	Offspring of two patients	46%
50%	Fraternal twin	17%
50%	Offspring of one patient	17%
50%	Sibling	9%
25%	Nephew or niece	4%
0%	Spouse	2%
0%	Unrelated person in the general population	1%

►**Figure 12.6**

Lifetime risk of developing schizophrenia is associated with how closely a person is genetically related to a person with schizophrenia. A shared environment also increases the risk. (Estimates from Lenzenweger & Gottesman, 1994.)

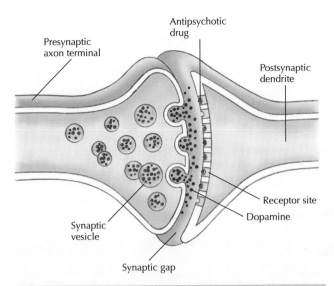

Antipsychotic drug

Presynaptic axon terminal

Postsynaptic dendrite

Receptor site

Dopamine

Synaptic vesicle

Synaptic gap

► **Figure 12.7**

Dopamine normally crosses the synapse between two neurons, activating the second cell. Antipsychotic drugs bind to the same receptor sites as dopamine does, blocking its action. In people suffering from schizophrenia, a reduction in dopamine activity can quiet a person's agitation and psychotic symptoms.

CT scan Computed tomography scan; a computer-enhanced X-ray image of the brain or body.

MRI scan Magnetic resonance imaging; a computer-enhanced three-dimensional representation of the brain or body, based on the body's response to a magnetic field.

PET scan Positron emission tomography; a computer-generated colour image of brain activity, as revealed by the consumption of radioactive sugar.

► Figure 12.7). In short, most evidence suggests that schizophrenia is a brain disease (Heinrichs, 1993).

The Schizophrenic Brain

Medical researchers have long hoped for a way to directly observe the schizophrenic brain. Three medical techniques are now making it possible. One, called a **CT scan,** provides an X-ray picture of the brain. (CT stands for computed tomography, or computer-enhanced X-ray images.) When John Hinkley, Jr. (who shot former U.S. President Ronald Reagan and three other men in 1981) had a CT scan taken of his brain, it showed that his brain differed from the norm. Specifically, it had wider surface fissuring, as is seen in the brains of people with schizophrenia. In his trial, Hinkley was declared insane.

MRI scans (magnetic resonance imaging) are allowing researchers to peer inside the schizophrenic brain. What they find is that people with schizophrenia tend to have enlarged ventricles (fluid-filled spaces within the brain) (Sharma et al., 1998). Other brain regions also appear to be abnormal. It is telling that the affected areas are crucial for regulating motivation, emotion, perception, actions, and attention (Degreef et al., 1992; Frazier et al., 1996; Gur et al., 1998).

A third technique, called a **PET scan** (positron emission tomography), provides an image of brain activity. To make a PET scan, a radioactive sugar solution is injected into a vein. When the sugar reaches the brain, an electronic device measures how much is used in each area. These data are then translated into a colour map, or scan, of brain activity (see ► Figure 12.8). Researchers are finding patterns in such scans that are consistently linked with schizophrenia, affective disorders, and other problems. For instance, activity tends to be abnormally low in the frontal lobes of the brains of people with schizophrenia (Velakoulis & Pantelis, 1996). In the future, PET scans may be used more accurately to diagnose schizophrenia.

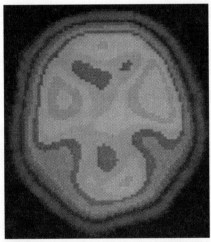

NORMAL

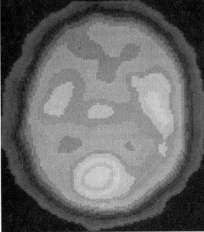

SCHIZOPHRENIC

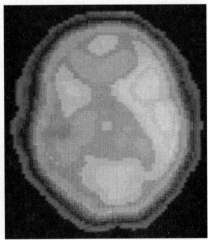

MANIC-DEPRESSIVE

► **Figure 12.8**

Positron emission tomography produces PET scans of the human brain. In the scans shown here, red, pink, and orange indicate lower levels of brain activity; white and blue indicate higher activity levels. Notice that activity in the schizophrenic brain is quite low in the frontal lobes (top area of each scan) (Velakoulis & Pantelis, 1996). Activity in the manic-depressive brain is low in the left brain hemisphere and high in the right brain hemisphere. The reverse is more often true of the schizophrenic brain. Researchers are trying to identify consistent patterns like these to aid diagnosis of mental disorders.

IMPLICATIONS In summary, the emerging picture of psychotic disorders such as schizophrenia takes this form: Anyone subjected to enough stress may be pushed to a psychotic break. (Battlefield psychosis is an example.) However, some people inherit a difference in brain chemistry or brain structure that makes them more susceptible—even to normal life stresses.

Thus, the right mix of inherited potential and environmental stress brings about mind-altering changes in brain chemicals and brain structure. This explanation is called a **stress–vulnerability model.** It attributes psychotic disorders to a blend of environmental stress and inherited susceptibility. The model seems to apply to other forms of psychopathology as well, such as depression (Fowles, 1992; Gottesman, 1991; Yank, Bentley, & Hargrove, 1993) (see ▶Figure 12.9). Just the same, psychosis remains "a riddle wrapped in a mystery inside an enigma." Let us hope the recent advances that we have so briefly explored are as promising as they appear to be.

Stress-vulnerability model Attributes psychosis to a combination of environmental stress and inherited susceptibility.

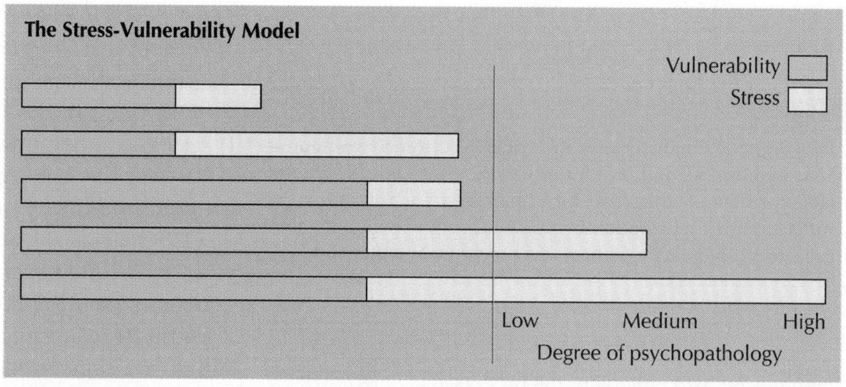

▶**Figure 12.9**

Various combinations of vulnerability and stress may produce psychological problems. The top bar shows low vulnerability and low stress. The result? No problem. The same is true of the next bar down, where low vulnerability is combined with moderate stress. Even high vulnerability (third bar) may not lead to problems if stress levels remain low. However, when high vulnerability combines with moderate or high stress (bottom two bars) the person "crosses the line" and suffers from psychopathology.

The Stress-Vulnerability Model

Vulnerability ☐
Stress ☐

Low   Medium   High
Degree of psychopathology

Knowledge builder

PSYCHOSIS, DELUSIONAL DISORDERS, AND SCHIZOPHRENIA

Relate

What did you think psychosis was like before you read about it? How has your understanding changed? If you were writing a "recipe" for psychosis, what would the main "ingredients" be?

If you were asked to play the role of a paranoid person for a theatre production, what symptoms would you emphasize?

You have been asked to explain the causes of schizophrenia to the parents of a teenager with schizophrenia. What would you tell them?

Learning Check

1. Carol wrongly believes that her body is "rotting away." She is suffering from
a. depressive hallucinations b. a delusion c. flat affect
d. Alzheimer's disease
2. Jean, who has suffered a psychotic break, is hearing voices. This symptom is referred to as
a. flat affect b. hallucination c. a word salad
d. organic delusions
3. A psychosis caused by lead poisoning would be regarded as an organic disorder. T or F?

4. Hallucinations and personality disintegration are the principal features of paranoid psychosis. T or F?
5. Environmental explanations of schizophrenia emphasize emotional trauma and
a. manic parents b. schizoaffective interactions c. psychedelic interactions d. disturbed family relationships
6. The _____ _____ of a person with schizophrenia runs a 48 percent chance of also becoming psychotic.
7. Enlarged surface fissures and ventricles, as revealed by CT scans, are found only in the brains of people with chronic schizophrenia. T or F?

Critical Thinking

8. Researchers have found nearly double the normal number of dopamine receptor sites in the brains of people with schizophrenia. Why might that be important?
9. Enlarged surface fissures and ventricles are frequently found in the brains of people with chronic schizophrenia. Why is it a mistake to conclude that such features cause schizophrenia?

Answers:

1. *b* 2. *b* 3. T 4. F 5. *d* 6. identical twin 7. F 8. Because of the extra receptors, people with schizophrenia may get psychedelic effects from normal levels of dopamine in the brain. 9. Because correlation does not confirm causation. Structural brain abnormalities are merely correlated with schizophrenia. They could be additional symptoms, rather than causes, of the disorder.

▶ Mood Disorders—Peaks and Valleys

Survey Question:
■ What are mood disorders? What causes depression?

Mood disorder Major disturbances in mood or emotion.
Depressive disorders Emotional disorders primarily involving sadness and depression.
Bipolar disorders Emotional disorders involving both depression and mania or hypomania.
Dysthymic disorder Moderate depression that persists for two years or more.
Cyclothymic disorder Moderate manic and depressive behaviour that persists for two years or more.
Major mood disorders Disorders marked by lasting extremes of mood or emotion and sometimes accompanied by psychotic symptoms.
Major depressive disorder A mood disorder in which the person has suffered one or more intense episodes of depression.

Nobody loves you when you're down and out—or so it seems. Psychologists have come to realize that **mood disorders** (major disturbances in emotion) are among the most serious of all. Two general types of mood disorder are *depressive disorders* and *bipolar disorders*. (See Table 12.7.) In **depressive disorders** sadness and despondency are exaggerated, prolonged, or unreasonable. Signs of a depressive disorder are dejection, hopelessness, and an inability to feel pleasure or to take interest in anything. Other common symptoms are fatigue, disturbed sleep and eating patterns, feelings of worthlessness, a very negative self-image, and thoughts of suicide. In **bipolar disorders** people go both "up" and "down" emotionally (DSM-IV-TR, 2000).

Depending on where you happen to live in the world, your chances of becoming depressed can vary markedly. For example, the lifetime rate of major depression is as low as 0.9 percent in urban Taiwan, and as high as 19 percent in Beirut. In the United States, 4.6 percent of people can be expected to develop major depression. In Edmonton 8.6 percent, in Christchurch, New Zealand, 12.6 percent, and in Paris about 16 percent of the population suffers from this disorder (Bland, 1997).

Some mood disorders are long-lasting but relatively moderate problems. If a person is mildly depressed for at least two years, the problem is called a **dysthymic disorder** (dis-THY-mik). If depression alternates with periods when the person's mood is cheerful, expansive, or irritable, the problem is a **cyclothymic disorder** (SIKE-lo-THY-mik) (DSM-IV-TR, 2000). Even at this level, mood disorders can be debilitating. However, major mood disorders are much more damaging.

Major Mood Disorders

Major mood disorders are marked by extreme emotions. About 14 percent of patients admitted to mental hospitals suffer from major mood disorders. The person who only goes "down" emotionally suffers from a **major depressive disorder.** During major depressive episodes people reach an extreme low point emotionally. Everything looks bleak and hopeless and the person's suffering is intense. Feelings of failure, sinfulness, worthlessness, and total despair are dominant. The person becomes extremely subdued or withdrawn and may be intensely suicidal. Depressive reactions pose a serious threat. Suicide attempted during a major depression is rarely a simple "plea for help." Usually, the person intends to succeed and may give no prior warning.

Table 12.7
DSM-IV-TR Classification of Mood Disorders

PROBLEM	PRIMARY SYMPTOM	TYPICAL SIGNS OF TROUBLE
Depressive Disorders Major depressive disorder	Extreme emotional depression for at least two weeks	You feel extremely sad, worthless, fatigued, and empty; you are unable to feel pleasure; you are having thoughts of suicide
Dysthymic disorder	Moderately depressed mood on most days during the last two years	You feel down and depressed more days than not, your self-esteem and energy levels have been low for many months
Bipolar Disorders Bipolar I disorder	Extreme mania and depression	At times you have little need for sleep, can't stop talking, your mind races, and everything you do is of immense importance; at other times you feel extremely sad, worthless, and empty
Bipolar II disorder	Moderate depression and at least one episode of mild mania	Most of the time you feel extremely sad, worthless, fatigued, and empty; however, at times you feel unusually good, cheerful, energetic, or "high"
Cyclothymic disorder	Periods of moderate depression and moderate mania for at least two years	You have been experiencing upsetting emotional ups and downs for many months

Bipolar I disorder A mood disorder in which a person has episodes of mania (excited, hyperactive, energetic, grandiose behaviour) and also periods of deep depression.

Bipolar II disorder A mood disorder in which a person is mostly depressed (sad, despondent, guilt-ridden) but has also had one or more episodes of mild mania (hypomania).

Endogenous depression Depression that appears to be produced from within (perhaps by chemical imbalances in the brain), rather than as a reaction to life events.

In a **bipolar I disorder** people experience both extreme mania and deep depression. During manic episodes, the person is loud, elated, hyperactive, grandiose, and energetic. Manic patients may go bankrupt in a matter of days, get arrested, or go on a binge of promiscuous sex. During periods of depression, the person is deeply despondent and possibly suicidal.

In a **bipolar II disorder** the person is mostly sad and guilt-ridden, but has had one or more mildly manic episodes (called hypomania). That is, in a bipolar II disorder both elation and depression occur, but the person's mania is not as extreme as it is in a bipolar I disorder. Bipolar II patients who are hypomanic usually just manage to irritate everyone around them. They are excessively cheerful, aggressive, or irritable, and they may brag, talk too fast, interrupt conversations, or spend too much money (Gorman, 1996).

In serious cases of depression it is impossible for a person to function at work or at school. Sometimes, depressed individuals cannot even feed or dress themselves. In cases of depression and/or mania that are even more severe, the person may also lose touch with reality and display various psychotic symptoms.

How do major mood disorders differ from dysthymic and cyclothymic disorders? As mentioned, the major mood disorders involve more severe emotional changes. Also, major mood disorders more often appear to be **endogenous** (en-DODGE-eh-nus: produced from within) rather than a reaction to external events.

The Causes of Mood Disorders

How is depression explained? Depression and other mood disorders have resisted adequate explanation and treatment. Some scientists are focusing on the biology of mood changes. They are interested in brain chemicals and transmitter substances, especially serotonin, noradrenaline, and dopamine levels (Ricci & Wellman, 1990). Their findings are incomplete, but progress has been made. For example, the chemical *lithium carbonate* can be effective for treating some cases of bipolar disorder.

Other researchers seek psychological explanations. Psychoanalytic theory, for instance, holds that depression is caused by repressed anger. This rage is displaced and turned inward as self-blame and self-hate (Isenberg & Schatzberg, 1976). As discussed in Chapter 11, behavioural theories of depression emphasize learned helplessness (Seligman, 1989). Cognitive psychologists believe that self-criticism and negative, distorted, or self-defeating thoughts underlie many cases of depression. (This view is discussed in Chapter 13.) Clearly, life stresses trigger many mood disorders (Kessler, 1997). This is especially true for people who have personality traits and thinking patterns that make them vulnerable to depression (Franche & Dobson, 1992; Gatz, 1990; Miranda, 1992).

Overall, women are twice as likely as men to experience depression (Culertson, 1997). Authorities believe that social and environmental conditions are the main reason for this difference. Factors that contribute to women's greater risk of depression include work and parenting, the strain of providing emotional support for others, and conflicts about birth control and pregnancy. Marital strife, sexual and physical abuse, and poverty are also factors. Nationwide, women and children are most likely to live in poverty. As a result, poor women frequently suffer the stresses associated with single parenthood, loss of control over their lives, poor housing, and dangerous neighbourhoods (Russo, 1990).

As you might guess, the fact that major mood disorders appear to be endogenous implies that genetics may be involved, especially in bipolar disorders (Gershon et al., 1998). As a case in point, if one identical twin has bipolar disorder, the other has an 80 percent chance of developing the same disorder, too. For non-twin siblings the probability is 35 percent. As we have noted, psychological causes are important in many cases of depression. But for major mood disorders, biological factors seem to play a larger role. (For an interesting look at another cause of depression, see "Feeling Sad?")

USING PSYCHOLOGY   Feeling Sad? Could Be SAD

Unless you have experienced a winter of "cabin fever" in the Far North, you may be surprised to learn that the rhythms of the seasons underlie some depressions. Researcher Norman Rosenthal has found that some people suffer from **seasonal affective disorder (SAD),** or depression that occurs only during the fall and winter months. Almost anyone can get a little depressed when days are short, dark, and cold. But when a person's symptoms are lasting and disabling, the problem may be SAD. Here are some of the major symptoms of SAD (Rosenthal, 1993):

- *Oversleeping and difficulty staying awake.* Your sleep patterns may be disturbed and waking very early in the morning is common.
- *Fatigue.* You feel too tired to maintain a normal routine.
- *Craving.* You hunger for carbohydrates and sweets, leading to overeating and weight gain.
- *Inability to cope.* You feel irritable and stressed.
- *Social withdrawal.* You become unsocial in the winter but are socially active during other seasons.

Starting in the fall, people with SAD sleep longer but more poorly. During the day they feel tired and drowsy, and they tend to overeat. With each passing day they become more sad, anxious, irritable, and socially withdrawn.

Although their depressions are not severe, many victims of SAD face each winter with a sense of foreboding. SAD is believed to be especially prevalent in northern latitudes, where days are very short during the winter (Booker & Hellekson, 1992). However, the problem may be worse for people who relocate from southern to more northern latitudes. For example, 13 percent of college students living in northern New England were found to have signs of SAD. The students most likely to be affected were those who had moved from the south to attend college (Low & Feissner, 1998). Research conducted in a northern community in Canada found that SAD was more common among people who had moved there from more southern latitudes (Williams & Schmidt, 1993).

Studies also support the idea that some northern people may be genetically protected against SAD. For example, the rate of SAD has been found to be quite low among people of Iceland, as well as among the descendents of Icelandic settlers living in Manitoba (Magnusson & Axelsson, 1993).

Generally speaking, seasonal depression is related to the release of more melatonin during the winter. This hormone, which is secreted by the pineal gland, regulates the body's response to changing light conditions. That's why 80 percent of SAD patients can be helped by extra doses of bright light, a remedy called phototherapy (see ▶ Figure 12.10). **Phototherapy** involves exposing SAD patients to one or more hours of very bright fluorescent light each day (Lewy et al., 1998). For many SAD sufferers, a hearty dose of light appears to be the next best thing to vacationing in the tropics.

▶ **Figure 12.10**

An hour or more of bright light a day can dramatically reduce the symptoms of seasonal affective disorder. This man wears a pith helmet fitted with a battery-powered full-spectrum fluorescent light to treat his SAD. The energy from this light source is equivalent to exposing himself to natural sunlight for several hours a day. Treatment is usually necessary from fall through spring. Light therapy typically works best when it is used early in the morning. (Lewy et al., 1998).

Seasonal affective disorder Depression that occurs only during fall and winter; presumably related to decreased exposure to sunlight.

Phototherapy A treatment for seasonal affective disorder that involves exposure to bright, full-spectrum light.

▶ Mental Hospitalization—Treating Major Mental Disorders

Psychotherapy Any psychological treatment for behavioural or emotional problems.

Medical therapies Any bodily therapy, such as drug therapy, electroshock, or psychosurgery.

Mental hospitalization Placing a person in a protected, therapeutic environment staffed by mental health professionals.

Partial hospitalization An approach in which patients receive treatment at a hospital during the day, but return home at night.

Halfway house A community-based facility for individuals making the transition from an institution (mental hospital, prison, and so forth) to independent living.

What can be done about major mental disorders? Two basic forms of treatment exist for psychological disorders of all types. The first, called **psychotherapy,** is any psychological treatment for behavioural or emotional problems. Psychotherapy is based on a special relationship between a mental health professional and a person in trouble. It typically involves two people talking about one person's problems. **Medical therapies** range from prescribing drugs to performing brain surgery. Because treatment approaches vary greatly, a complete discussion of therapies is found in the next chapter.

Hospitalization

For major mental disorders, therapy is often best done in a controlled setting, such as a psychiatric hospital. **Mental hospitalization** involves placing a person in a protected, therapeutic environment staffed by mental health professionals. This, by itself, can be a form of treatment. Staying in a hospital removes patients from situations that may be provoking or maintaining their problems. For example, people with drug addictions may find it nearly impossible to resist the temptations for drug abuse in their daily lives. Hospitalization can help them make a clean break from their former self-destructive behaviour patterns (Gorman, 1996).

At its best, the hospital is a sanctuary that provides diagnosis, support, refuge, and therapy. This is generally true of psychiatric units in general hospitals. At worst, confinement to an institution can be a brutalizing experience that leaves people less prepared to face the world than they were before they arrived.

In most instances, hospitals are best used as a last resort, after other forms of treatment within the community have been exhausted. Actually, most psychiatric patients do as well with short-term hospitalization as they do with longer periods. For this reason, the average stay in psychiatric hospitals is now just 20 days, rather than three to four months, as it was 20 years ago.

A new trend in psychiatric treatment is **partial hospitalization.** In this approach, patients spend only part of their time at the hospital. Even for the acutely ill, overnight hospital stays are becoming less common. For example, some patients spend their days in the hospital, but go home at night. Others attend therapy sessions during the evening. A major advantage of partial hospitalization is that patients can go home and practise what they've been learning. Gradually, the amount of time patients spend at the hospital is reduced. Eventually, most people return to normal life. Overall, partial hospitalization is comparable to full hospitalization in its effectiveness (Sledge et al., 1996).

Large mental hospitals once served as warehouses for society's unwanted, but many former patients are no better off in bleak nursing homes, single-room hotels, board-and-care homes, jails, or shelters (Isaac & Armat, 1990). Ironically, high-quality care is available in most communities. A simple lack of funding prevents people from getting the help they need (Torrey, 1996).

It would help greatly if better rehabilitation programs were offered after hospital treatment (Anthony, Cohen, & Kennard, 1990). One such approach is the use of *halfway houses,* which can ease a patient's return to the community. **Halfway houses** are short-term group living facilities for individuals making the transition from an institution (mental hospital, prison, and so forth) to independent living. Typically, they offer supervision and support, without being as restrictive and medically slanted as hospitals. They also keep people near their families. Most important, halfway houses can reduce a person's chances of being readmitted to a hospital (Coursey, Ward-Alexander, & Katz, 1990).

PROSPECT Major mental disorders that have organic causes usually cannot be "cured," but their symptoms may be alleviated with drugs and other techniques. With psychoses the outlook is still rather negative, but many people do recover (see ▶Figure 12.11). It is wrong to fear "former mental patients" or to exclude them from work, friendships, and other social situations. A psychotic episode does not inevitably lead to lifelong dysfunc-

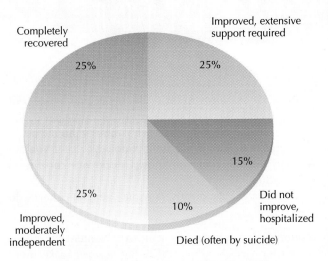

Schizophrenic patients 10 years after diagnosis

Completely recovered 25%

Improved, extensive support required 25%

Did not improve, hospitalized 15%

Died (often by suicide) 10%

Improved, moderately independent 25%

▶ **Figure 12.11**

At least one in four patients with schizophrenia had completely recovered 10 years after being diagnosed. Three out of four had improved. New treatments for schizophrenia and other major mental disorders may improve these odds.

tion. Too often, however, it leads to unnecessary rejection based on groundless fears (Monahan, 1992).

A LOOK AHEAD   By the time you finish reading this page, someone in the world will have attempted suicide. Suicide is a disturbing and widely misunderstood problem. What can be done about it? This chapter's Psychology in Action section will provide some answers.

Knowledge builder

MOOD DISORDERS AND MENTAL HOSPITALIZATION

Relate

On a piece of paper write "Bipolar Disorders" and "Depressive Disorders." How much of Table 12.7 can you fill in under these headings? Keep reviewing until you can recreate the table (in your own words).

To what extent does the stress-vulnerability model relate to mood disorders?

Learning Check

1. Dysthymic disorder is to depression as cyclothymic disorder is to manic-depression. T or F?
2. Major mood disorders, especially bipolar disorders, often appear to be endogenous. T or F?

3. Learned helplessness is emphasized by _____ theories of depression.
   a. humanistic b. biological c. behaviouristic d. psychoanalytic
4. The drug lithium carbonate has been shown to be an effective treatment for anxiety disorders. T or F?
5. The acronym SAD stands for schizotypal affective disorder. T or F?
6. Partial hospitalization refers to the practice of placing mental patients in halfway houses. T or F?

Critical Thinking

7. Many provinces have reduced mental hospital populations as a way to save money and speed the return of patients to their communities. What risks might there be in this practice?

Answers:

1. T 2. T 3. c 4. F 5. F 6. F 7. Many chronic patients have been discharged to a lonely existence in hostile communities without adequate care, where they have joined the ranks of the homeless. Others are repeatedly jailed for minor crimes. All too often, patients who move from hospitalization to unemployment, homelessness, and social isolation just end up rehospitalized or in jail (Goldman, 1998).

PSYCHOLOGY IN ACTION

SUICIDE—LIVES ON

THE BRINK

"Suicide: A permanent solution to a temporary problem."

Suicide ranks as the seventh cause of death in North America. Roughly one person out of 100 attempts suicide during his or her life. We tend to be very concerned about the seemingly high rate of murder. However, for every person who dies by homicide in Canada, seven will kill themselves (Langlois & Morrison, 2002). Sooner or later you are likely to be affected by the suicide attempt of someone you know. Check your knowledge of suicide against the following information.

What factors affect suicide rates? Suicide rates vary greatly, but some general patterns do emerge.

?

Survey Question:

■ Why do people commit suicide? Can suicide be prevented?

Sex Men have the questionable honour of being better at suicide than women. Four times as many men as women complete suicide (see ▶ Figure 12.12), but women make more attempts. Male suicide attempts are more lethal because men typically use a gun or an equally fatal method (Garland & Zigler, 1993). Women most often attempt a drug overdose, so there's a better chance of help arriving before death occurs. Sadly, women are beginning to use more deadly methods and may soon equal men in their risk of death by suicide.

Age Age is also a factor in suicide. Suicide rates gradually rise during adolescence. They then sharply increase during young adulthood (ages 20 to 24) (Statistics Canada, 2000). Generally speaking, from then until old age the rate continues to rise gradually. As a result, about half of all suicide cases are over 44 years of age. Unfortunately, as Figure 12.12 shows, even children are not immune from the risk of suicide.

In recent years there has been a steady increase in the suicide rates for adolescents and young adults (Diekstra & Garnefski, 1995). Among college students, suicide has become the leading cause of death. School is a factor in some suicides, but only in the sense that suicidal students were not living up to their own extremely high standards. Many were good students. Other important factors in student suicide are chronic health problems (real or imagined) and interpersonal difficulties (some suicides are rejected lovers, but others are simply withdrawn and friendless people).

Ethnicity In Canada, the suicide rate among Aboriginal people is about three times the national average; however, there are wide fluctuations across different groups. According to Chandler and Lalonde (1998), some Native groups in British Columbia show extremely elevated suicide rates, especially among the youth, whereas in other bands suicide is a rare phenomenon. Suicide is relatively low among those Aboriginal bands that have taken steps toward self-government and the preservation of cultural heritage.

Place of Residence Newfoundland can claim the honour of being the province with the lowest suicide rate in Canada. Ontario and Prince Edward Island show low rates as well.

▶ **Figure 12.12**

As this bar graph shows, in each age category more males die from suicide than females do. In general, rates tend to increase with an advance in age, reaching a peak between 45 and 59. Even children and adolescents are not immune from the risk of suicide, and many elderly people are also claimed by suicide. (Data for 1998. Adapted from Langlois and Morrison, 2002.)

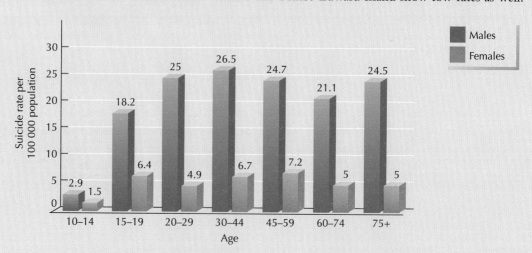

480

NEL

Provinces with the highest rates are Quebec and Alberta. In 1996, about 37 percent of all suicides were recorded in Quebec, even though the province accounts for only about 25 percent of Canada's total population (Statistics Canada, 2000).

Income   Some professions, such as medicine and psychiatry, have higher than average suicide rates. Overall, however, suicide is equally a problem for the rich and the poor.

Marital Status   Marriage (when successful) may be the best natural guard against suicidal impulses. The highest suicide rates are found among the divorced, the next-highest rates occur among the widowed, lower rates are recorded for single persons, and married individuals have the lowest rates of all.

IMMEDIATE CAUSES OF SUICIDE   *Why do people try to kill themselves?* The best explanation for suicide may simply come from a look at the conditions that precede it. The following are all major risk factors for suicide (Gould et al., 1998; Hall, Platt, & Hall, 1999):

- Drug or alcohol abuse
- A prior suicide attempt
- Depression or other mood disorder
- Feelings of hopelessness, worthlessness
- Antisocial, impulsive, or aggressive behaviour
- Severe anxiety, panic attacks
- Family history of suicidal behaviour
- Shame, humiliation, failure, or rejection
- Availability of a firearm

Suicidal people usually have a history of trouble with family, a lover, or a spouse. Often they have drinking or drug abuse problems, sexual adjustment problems, or job difficulties. Depression is a factor in 70 percent of all suicides (Lecomte & Fornes, 1998). Of the 129 persons who committed suicide in the Montreal Metro System between 1986 and 1996, 105 had a serious mental illness and 27 percent were under hospital care at the time of death (Mishara, 1999). Mental problems can lead to a preoccupation with death as a way to end the person's suffering.

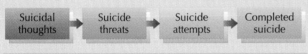

▶**Figure 12.13**

Suicidal behaviour usually progresses from suicidal thoughts, to threats, to attempts. A person is unlikely to make an attempt without first making threats. Thus, suicide threats should be taken seriously (Garland & Zigler, 1993).

Typically, suicidal people isolate themselves from others, feel worthless, helpless, and misunderstood, and want to die. An extremely negative self-image and severe feelings of hopelessness are warnings that the risk of suicide is very high (Beck et al., 1990; Boergers, Spirito, & Donaldson, 1998). A long history of such conditions is not always necessary to produce a desire for suicide. Anyone may temporarily reach a state of depression severe enough to attempt suicide. Most dangerous for the average person are times of divorce, separation, rejection, failure, and bereavement. Each situation can seem intolerable and motivate an intense desire to die, to escape, or to obtain relief (Boergers, Spirito, & Donaldson, 1998).

Table 12.8
Warning Signs of Potential Suicide

—Withdrawal from contact with others
—Sudden swings in mood
—Recent occurrence of life crisis or emotional shock
—Personality change
—Gift giving of prized possessions
—Depression/hopelessness
—Aggression and/or risk taking
—Single-car accident
—Preoccupation with death
—Drug use
—Death imagery in art
—Direct threats to commit suicide

PREVENTING SUICIDE   *Is it true that people who talk about or threaten suicide are rarely the ones who try it?* No, this is a major fallacy. Of every ten potential suicides, eight give warning beforehand. A person who threatens suicide should be taken seriously. (See ▶Figure 12.13.) A suicidal person may say nothing more than "I feel sometimes like I'd be better off dead." Warnings may also come indirectly. If a friend gives you a favourite ring and says, "Here, I won't be needing this anymore," or comments, "I guess I won't get my watch fixed—it doesn't matter anyway," it may be a plea for help. The warning signs listed in Table 12.8—especially if observed in combination—can signal an impending suicide attempt (Leenaars, 1995; Slaby, Garfinkel, & Garfinkel, 1994).

Is it true that suicide can't be prevented, that the person will find a way to do it anyway? No. Suicide attempts usually come when a person is alone, depressed, and unable to view matters objectively. You should intervene if someone seems to be threatening suicide.

It is estimated that about two-thirds of all suicide attempts fall in the "to be" category. That is, they are made by people who do not really want to die. Almost a third more are characterized by a "to be or not to be" attitude. These people are ambivalent or undecided about dying.

Only 3 to 5 percent of suicide cases involve people who really want to die. Most people, therefore, are relieved when someone comes to their aid. Remember that suicide is almost always a cry for help and that you can help. As suicide expert Edwin Shneidman (1987a) puts it, "Suicidal behaviour is often a form of communication, a cry for help born out of pain, with clues and messages of suffering and anguish and pleas for response."

HOW TO HELP   *What is the best thing to do if someone drops hints about suicide?* It helps to know some of the common characteristics of suicidal thoughts and feelings. Edwin Shneidman (1987b) has identified several.

1. *Escape.* Everyone at times feels like running away from an upsetting situation. Running away from home, quitting school, abandoning a marriage—these are all departures. Suicide, of course, is the ultimate escape. It helps when suicidal persons see that the natural wish for escape doesn't have to be expressed by ending it all.
2. *Unbearable psychological pain.* Emotional pain is what the suicidal person is seeking to escape. A goal of anyone hoping to prevent suicide should be to reduce the pain in any way possible. Ask the person, "Where does it hurt?"
3. *Frustrated psychological needs.* Often, suicide can be prevented if a distressed person's frustrated needs can be identified and eased. Is the person deeply frustrated in his or her search for love, achievement, trust, security, or friendship?
4. *Constriction of options.* The suicidal person feels helpless and decides that death is the only solution. The person has narrowed all his or her options solely to death. The rescuer's goal, then, is to help broaden the person's perspective. Even when all the choices are unpleasant, suicidal persons can usually be made to see that their least unpleasant option is better than death.

Knowing these patterns will give some guidance in talking to a suicidal person. In addition, your most important task may be to establish rapport (a harmonious connection) with the person. You should offer support, acceptance, and legitimate caring.

Remember that a suicidal person feels misunderstood. Try to accept and understand the feelings the person is expressing. Acceptance should also extend to the idea of suicide itself. It is completely acceptable to ask, "Are you thinking of suicide?"

Establishing communication with suicidal persons may be enough to carry them through a difficult time. You may also find it helpful to get day-by-day commitments from them to meet for lunch, share a ride, and the like. Let the person know you expect her or him to be there. Such commitments, even though small, can be enough to tip the scales when a person is alone and thinking about suicide.

Don't end your efforts too soon. A dangerous time for suicide is when a person suddenly seems to get better after a severe depression. This often means the person has finally decided to end it all. The improvement in mood is deceptive because it comes from an anticipation that suffering is about to end.

Crisis Intervention   Most cities have mental health crisis intervention teams or centres for suicide prevention. Both have staff members trained to talk with suicidal persons over the phone. Give a person who seems to be suicidal the number of one of these services. Urge the person to call you or the other number if she or he becomes frightened or impulsive. Or better yet, help the person make an appointment to get psychological treatment (Garland & Zigler, 1993).

The preceding applies mainly to persons who are having mild suicidal thoughts. If a person actually threatens suicide, you must act more quickly. Ask how the person plans to carry out the suicide. A person who has a specific, workable plan, and the means to carry it out, should be asked to accompany you to the emergency ward of a hospital.

If a person seems on the verge of attempting suicide, don't worry about overreacting. Call the police, crisis intervention, or a rescue unit. Of course, you should call immediately if a person is in the act of attempting suicide or if a drug has already been taken. The majority of suicide attempts come at temporary low points in a person's life and may never be repeated. Get involved—you may save a life!

Knowledge builder

SUICIDE AND SUICIDE PREVENTION

Relate

You're working a suicide hotline and you take a call from a very distressed young man. What risk factors will you look for as he tells you about his anguish?

What are the common characteristics of suicidal thoughts and feelings identified by Edwin Shneidman? If a friend of yours were to express any of these thoughts or feelings, how would you respond?

Learning Check

1. More women than men use guns in their suicide attempts. T or F?

2. While the overall suicide rate has remained about the same, there has been a decrease in adolescent suicides. T or F?
3. Suicide is equally a problem of the rich and the poor. T or F?
4. The highest suicide rates are found among the divorced. T or F?
5. The majority (two-thirds) of suicide attempts fall in the "to be" category. T or F?

Critical Thinking

6. If you follow popular music, see if you can answer this question: What two major risk factors contributed to the 1994 suicide of Kurt Cobain, lead singer for the rock group Nirvana?

Answers:

1. F 2. F 3. T 4. T 5. T 6. Drug or alcohol abuse and availability of a firearm.

Psychologist's Journal

EPILOGUE

A final note: If used carelessly, the terms discussed in this chapter can hurt people. Everyone has felt or acted "crazy" during brief periods of stress or high emotion. People with psychological disorders have problems that are more severe or longer lasting than most of us experience. Otherwise, they may not be that different from ourselves or our friends. Generally, it is better to label problems than to label people. Think of the difference between saying, "You are experiencing a serious psychological disorder" and saying, "You are a schizophrenic." Which would you prefer to have said about yourself?

When Carol North (described at the beginning of this chapter) became a patient, she learned firsthand that the mentally ill tend to be stigmatized (rejected and disgraced). People who have been labelled mentally ill (at any time in their lives) are less likely to be hired. They also tend to be denied housing and they are more likely to be falsely accused of crimes. Thus, people who are grappling with mental illness may be harmed as much by social stigma as they are by their psychological problems (Corrigan & Penn, 1999). One former patient told one of us the following story:

After I got back from the hospital, my friends tried to act like nothing had changed. But I could tell they weren't being honest. For instance, a friend invited me to dinner and everything went fine until I dropped my fork. Both my friend and his wife jumped up and stared at me like they thought I might explode. I was quite embarrassed.

Fortunately, a growing number of people recognize that individuals with psychological disorders should be treated with respect and kindness. Remember, it's entirely possible that you, or someone you love, will someday be the one who needs compassion.

CHAPTER IN REVIEW

Major Points

▶ Judgments of normality are relative, but psychological disorders clearly exist and need to be classified, explained, and treated.

▶ Psychopathology, which involves identifying, classifying, and explaining psychological disorders, is worthwhile and necessary.

▶ Psychologically unhealthy behaviour is maladaptive and it involves a loss of adequate control over thoughts, feelings, and actions.

▶ Maladaptive behaviour patterns, unhealthy personality types, and excessive levels of anxiety underlie many mental disorders.

▶ The most severe forms of psychopathology involve emotional extremes and/or a break with reality.

▶ Psychological disorders are complex and have multiple causes.

▶ Suicide is a relatively frequent cause of death that can, in many cases, be prevented.

Summary

How Is Normality Defined, and What Are the Major Psychological Disorders?

• Psychopathology refers to maladaptive behaviour and to the scientific study of mental disorders.

• Definitions of normality usually take into account the following: subjective discomfort, statistical abnormality, social non-conformity, and the cultural or situational context of behaviour.

• Two key elements in judgments of disorder are that a person's behaviour must be maladaptive and it must involve a loss of control.

• Major mental disorders include psychotic disorders, dementia, substance-related disorders, mood disorders, anxiety disorders, somatoform disorders, dissociative

disorders, personality disorders, and sexual or gender identity disorders.
* Insanity is a legal term defining whether a person may be held responsible for his or her actions. Sanity is determined in court on the basis of testimony by expert witnesses.

What Is a Personality Disorder?
* Personality disorders are deeply ingrained maladaptive personality patterns.
* Antisocial personality or sociopathy is a common personality disorder. Antisocial persons seem to lack a conscience. They are emotionally unresponsive, manipulative, shallow, and dishonest.

What Problems Result When a Person Suffers High Levels of Anxiety?
* Anxiety disorders, dissociative disorders, and somatoform disorders are characterized by high levels of anxiety, rigid defence mechanisms, and self-defeating behaviour patterns.
* The term *nervous breakdown* has no formal meaning. However, "emotional breakdowns" do correspond somewhat to the occurrence of an adjustment disorder.
* Anxiety disorders include generalized anxiety disorder, panic disorder with or without agoraphobia, agoraphobia (without panic), specific phobias, social phobia, obsessive-compulsive disorders, post-traumatic stress disorder, and acute stress disorder.
* Dissociative disorders may take the form of dissociative amnesia, dissociative fugue, or dissociative identity disorder.
* Somatoform disorders centre on physical complaints that mimic disease or disability. Four examples of somatoform disorders are hypochondriasis, somatization disorder, somatoform pain disorder, and conversion disorder.

How Do Psychologists Explain Anxiety-Based Disorders?
* The psychodynamic approach emphasizes unconscious conflicts as the cause of disabling anxiety.
* The humanistic approach emphasizes the effects of a faulty self-image.
* The behaviourists emphasize the effects of previous learning, particularly avoidance learning.
* Cognitive theories of anxiety focus on distorted thinking, judgment, and attention.

What Are the General Characteristics of Psychotic Disorders?
* Psychosis is a break in contact with reality that is marked by delusions, hallucinations, sensory changes, disturbed emotions, disturbed communication, and personality disintegration.
* An organic psychosis is based on known injuries or diseases of the brain.
* Some common causes of organic psychosis are poisoning, drug abuse, and dementia (especially Alzheimer's disease).

How Do Delusional Disorders Differ from Other Psychotic Disorders?
* Delusional disorders are almost totally based on the presence of delusions of grandeur, persecution, infidelity, romantic attraction, or physical disease.
* The most common delusional disorder is paranoid psychosis. Paranoid persons may be violent if they believe they are threatened.

What Forms Does Schizophrenia Take? What Causes It?
* Schizophrenia involves a split between thought and emotion, delusions, hallucinations, and communication difficulties.
* Disorganized schizophrenia is marked by extreme personality disintegration and silly, bizarre, or obscene behaviour. Social impairment is usually extreme.
* Catatonic schizophrenia is associated with stupor, mutism, and odd postures. Sometimes violent and agitated behaviour also occurs.
* In paranoid schizophrenia (the most common type), outlandish delusions of grandeur and persecution are coupled with psychotic symptoms and personality breakdown.
* Current explanations of schizophrenia emphasize a combination of inherited susceptibility, early trauma, environmental stress, and abnormalities in the brain.
* Environmental factors that increase the risk of schizophrenia include viral infection or malnutrition during the mother's pregnancy, birth complications, early psychological trauma, and a disturbed family environment.
* Heredity is a major factor in schizophrenia.
* Recent biochemical studies have focused on the brain transmitter dopamine and its receptor sites.
* The dominant explanation of schizophrenia, and other problems as well, is the stress–vulnerability model.

What Are Mood Disorders? What Causes Depression?
* Mood disorders primarily involve disturbances of mood or emotion, producing manic or depressive states.
* Depression that is long lasting, though relatively moderate, is called a dysthymic disorder. Chronic, though moderate, swings in mood between depression and elation are called a cyclothymic disorder.
* Bipolar disorders combine mania and depression. In a bipolar I disorder the person swings between mania and depression. In a bipolar II disorder the person is mostly depressed, but has had periods of mild mania.
* A major depressive disorder involves extreme sadness and despondency but no evidence of mania.
* Seasonal affective disorder (SAD), which occurs during the winter months, is another common form of depression. SAD is typically treated with phototherapy.
* Biological, psychoanalytic, cognitive, and behavioural theories of depression have been proposed. Heredity is clearly a factor in susceptibility to mood disorders. Research on the causes and treatment of depression continues.

Why Do People Commit Suicide? Can Suicide Be Prevented?

- Suicide is statistically related to such factors as age, sex, and marital status.
- In individual cases, the potential for suicide is best identified by a desire to escape, unbearable psychological

pain, frustrated psychological needs, and a constriction of options.

- Suicide can often be prevented by the efforts of family, friends, and mental health professionals.

PSYCHOLOGY ON THE NET

If you have difficulty finding any of the sites listed here, visit http://www.psychologyjourney.nelson.com for an updated list of Internet addresses and direct links to relevant sites.

Alzheimer Society of Canada   Provides information on various aspects of Alzheimer's disease. http://www.alzheimer.ca

Canadian Mental Health Association   A national organization that speaks for the rights of people who suffer from mental illness. The site presents a variety of resources on mental health and mental disorders. http://www.cmha.ca/

Canadian Network for Mood and Anxiety Treatments   Includes helpful information on anxiety and mood disorders. http://www.canmat.org

Canadian Psychological Association   Provides important information on a variety of mental disorders, as well as advice on how to look for a psychologist in all provinces and territories. http://www.cpa.ca/

DSM-IV Questions and Answers   Answers to common questions about the DSM-IV. http://www.psych.org/clin_res/dsm/faq81301.cfm

Internet Mental Health   Comprehensive page on mental health, with links to many other sites. http://www.mentalhealth.com/

Schizophrenia Society of Canada   Provides useful information on this disorder. http://www.schizophrenia.ca

Suicide Information and Education Centre   Provides important facts and information about suicide. http://www.suicideinfo.ca

UBC Mood Disorders Centre   Provides comprehensive information on mood disorders, including SAD. http://www.psychiatry.ubc.ca/mood

 InfoTrac College Edition   For recent articles related to the Psychology in Action feature, use Key Words search for SUICIDE PREVENTION.

INTERACTIVE LEARNING

Psychology: An Interactive Journey   Remember that Chapter 12 of the CD-ROM that came with this text has practice tests, flashcards, interactive exercises, a crossword puzzle, and other valuable materials to enhance your learning experience.

PsychNow!   7c. Abnormality and Psychopathology, 7d. Non-psychotic, Psychotic, and Affective Disorders.

Psyk.trek   11. Abnormal Behaviour and Therapy.

Chart Your Progress

The questions that follow are only a sample of what you need to know. If you miss any of the items, you should review the entire chapter, do the exercises on the CD, and review the Knowledge Builders. Another way to prepare for tests is to get more practice with *WebTutor*, the *Study Guide*, or the *Practice Quizzes* that are available with this text.

1. One of the core features of abnormal behaviour is that it is
   a. statistically unusual
   b. maladaptive
   c. socially non-conforming
   d. a source of subjective discomfort

2. A person who has periods of extreme mania suffers from
   a. a somatoform disorder
   b. a mood disorder
   c. an anxiety disorder
   d. a neurosis

3. Pibloktoq occurs among
   a. the people of Brazil
   b. Latinos
   c. the Inuit
   d. the Chinese

4. A person who is impulsive, dishonest, emotionally cold, and manipulative may suffer from
   a. antisocial personality disorder
   b. histrionic personality disorder
   c. dependent personality disorder
   d. obsessive-compulsive personality disorder

5. Agoraphobia is most often a feature of
   a. adjustment disorder
   b. panic disorder
   c. PTSD
   d. obsessive-compulsive disorder

6. According to the _____ view, anxiety disorders are the end result of a faulty self-image.
   a. psychodynamic
   b. humanistic
   c. behaviouristic
   d. cognitive

7. Paranoid psychosis is the most common type of
   a. catatonic schizophrenia
   b. delusional disorder
   c. personality disorder
   d. dementia

8. Biochemical explanations of schizophrenia have focused on excessive amounts of _____ in the brain.
   a. radioactive sugar
   b. webs and tangles
   c. PCP
   d. dopamine

9. Bipolar disorders that are not too severe are called
   a. endogenous disorders
   b. cyclothymic disorders
   c. seasonal affective disorders
   d. dysthymic disorders

10. The risk that a person may attempt suicide is greatest if the person has
    a. a concrete, workable plan
    b. had a recent life crisis
    c. withdrawn from contact with others
    d. frustrated psychological needs

Answers: 1. b 2. b 3. c 4. a 5. b 6. b 7. b 8. d 9. b 10. a

Chapter 13

Psychologist's Journal

COLD TERROR ON A WARM AFTERNOON

(Dennis Coon) The warm spring sun was shining brightly. Outside my office window an assortment of small birds sang sweetly. I could hear them between Susan's frightened sobs.

As a psychologist, I meet many students with personal problems. Still, I was surprised to see Susan at my office door. Her excellent work in class and her healthy, casual appearance left me unprepared for her first words. "I feel like I'm losing my mind," she said. "Can I talk to you?"

In the next hour, Susan described her own personal hell. Her calm appearance hid a world of overwhelming fear, anxiety, and depression. At work, she was deathly afraid of talking to co-workers and customers. Her social phobia led to frequent absenteeism and embarrassing behaviour. At each job she held, it was only a matter of time until she got fired.

At school Susan felt "different" and was sure that other students could tell she was "weird." Several disastrous romances had left her terrified of men. Lately she had been so depressed that she had thought of suicide. Often, she became terrified for no apparent reason. Each time, her heart pounded wildly and she felt she was about to completely lose control.

Susan's visit to my office was an important turning point. Emotional conflicts had made her existence a nightmare. At a time when she was becoming her own worst enemy, Susan realized she needed help from another person. In Susan's case, that person was a talented psychologist to whom I referred her. With psychotherapy, the psychologist was able to help Susan come to grips with her emotions and restore her balance.

This chapter discusses methods used to alleviate problems like Susan's. First, we describe therapies that emphasize the value of gaining insight into personal problems. Then we focus on behaviour therapies and cognitive therapies, which directly change troublesome actions and thoughts. We conclude with medical therapies, which employ psychiatric drugs and other physical treatments.

▶ Psychotherapy—Getting Better by the Hour

Survey Question:

■ How do psychotherapies differ? How did psychotherapy originate?

Fortunately, the odds are that you will not experience an emotional problem like Susan's. But if you did, what help is available? In most cases, it would be some form of **psychotherapy.** For the most part, psychotherapy involves verbal interaction between trained mental health professionals and their clients. Some therapists also use learning principles to directly alter troublesome behaviours. Basically, psychotherapy refers to any psychological technique that can bring about positive changes in personality, behaviour, or adjustment.

Dimensions of Therapy

Psychotherapists have many approaches to choose from: psychoanalysis, desensitization, Gestalt therapy, client-centred therapy, reality therapy, and behaviour therapy—to name but a few. With so many therapies in use, some confusion may exist about how they differ. To begin, it is helpful to recognize that therapies vary widely in emphasis. For this reason, the best approach for a particular person or problem may also vary.

The terms listed below describe basic aspects of various therapies. Notice that more than one term may apply to a particular therapy. For example, it is possible to have a directive, action-oriented group therapy or a non-directive, individual, insight-oriented therapy.

> **Psychotherapy** Any psychological technique used to facilitate positive changes in a person's personality, behaviour, or adjustment.

- *Individual therapy.* A therapy involving only one client and one therapist.
- *Group therapy.* A therapy session in which several clients participate at the same time.
- *Insight therapy.* Any psychotherapy whose goal is to lead clients to a deeper understanding of their thoughts, emotions, and behaviour.
- *Action therapy.* Any therapy designed to bring about direct changes in troublesome thoughts, habits, feelings, or behaviour, without seeking insight into their origins or meanings.
- *Directive therapy.* Any approach in which the therapist provides strong guidance.
- *Non-directive therapy.* A style of therapy in which clients assume responsibility for solving their own problems; the therapist assists, but does not guide or give advice.
- *Supportive therapy.* An approach in which the therapist's goal is to offer support, rather than to promote personal change. A person who is trying to get through

an emotional crisis or who wants to solve day-to-day problems may benefit from supportive therapy.

- *Time-limited therapy.* Any therapy begun with the expectation that it will last only a limited number of sessions.

MYTHS Psychotherapy has been depicted as producing a complete personal transformation—a sort of "major overhaul" of the psyche. But therapy is not equally effective for all problems. Chances of improvement are fairly good for phobias, low self-esteem, some sexual problems, and marital conflicts. More complex problems can be difficult to solve. For many people, the major benefit of therapy is that it provides comfort, support, and a way to make constructive changes (Hellerstein et al., 1998).

In short, it is often unrealistic to expect psychotherapy to undo a person's entire past history. Yet even when problems are severe, therapy may help a person gain a new perspective or learn behaviours to better cope with life. Psychotherapy can be hard work for both clients and therapists. But when it succeeds, there are few activities more worthwhile.

It is also worth noting that psychotherapy is not always undertaken to solve problems or end a crisis. Therapy can promote personal growth for people who are already doing well (Buck, 1990). Table 13.1 lists some of the elements of positive mental health that therapists seek to restore or promote (Bergin, 1991).

Table 13.1 Elements of Positive Mental Health

- Personal autonomy and independence
- A sense of identity
- Feelings of personal worth
- Skills in interpersonal communication
- Sensitivity, nurturance, and trust
- Genuine and honest with self and others
- Self-control and personal responsibility
- Committed and loving in personal relationships
- Capacity to forgive others and oneself
- Personal values and a purpose in life
- Self-awareness and motivation for personal growth
- Adaptive coping strategies for managing stresses and crises
- Fulfillment and satisfaction in work
- Good habits of physical health

(Adapted from Bergin, 1991.)

How often do people turn to psychologists, and who uses their services? In the mid-1990s, 2.15 percent of Canadians over the age of 11 years consulted a psychologist during a 12-month period. This translates to about 515 000 persons. People from all walks of life visit psychologists, but some use their services more than others. For example, two-thirds of the clients seen by psychologists are female. Users also tend to be middle-aged, single, separated, widowed, and have higher education and income (Hunsley, Lee, & Aubry, 1999). The same study also found that a significant proportion of the Canadian population with mental health problems was not receiving any help from psychologists. Reasons for underutilization of services include the following:

- People are often unaware of what psychologists do.
- Many potential clients do not know how to look for a psychologist.
- Many people lack the financial resources to pay for psychological services.
- In recent years, governments have cut funding of publicly funded services.
- Many individuals believe that people ought to be able to solve their own problems (Farberman, 1997; Hunsley, Lee, & Aubrey, 1999).

Whatever the reason, it is unfortunate that many people with serious mental health problems are not receiving proper treatment, especially when effective ways of addressing such problems are available.

▶ Origins of Therapy—Bored Skulls and Hysteria on the Couch

Early treatments for mental problems give ample reason for appreciating modern therapies. Archaeological findings dating to the Stone Age suggest that most ancient approaches were marked by fear and superstitious belief in demons, witchcraft, and magic. One of the more dramatic "cures" practised by ancient "therapists" was a process called *trepanning*

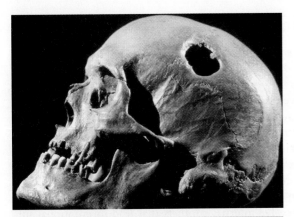

▶ **Figure 13.1**

Ancient "treatment" for mental disorders sometimes took the form of boring a hole in the skull. This example shows signs of healing, which means the patient survived the treatment. Many didn't.

(left) Many early asylums were no more than prisons with inmates held in chains. *(right)* One late 19th-century "treatment" was based on swinging the patient in a harness—presumably to calm the patient's nerves.

Trepanning In modern usage, any surgical procedure in which a hole is bored in the skull; historically, the chipping or boring of holes in the skull to "treat" mental disturbance.

Demonology In medieval Europe, the study of demons and the treatment of persons "possessed" by demons.

Exorcism The practice of driving off an "evil spirit," especially from the body of a person who is "possessed."

Ergotism A pattern of psychosis-like symptoms that accompanies poisoning by ergot fungus.

Philippe Pinel The French physician who initiated humane treatment of mental patients in 1793.

Hysteria Wild emotional excitability sometimes associated with the development of apparent physical disabilities (numbness, blindness, and the like) without known physical cause.

(treh–PAN-ing; also sometimes spelled *trephining*). In modern usage, **trepanning** is any surgical procedure in which a hole is bored in the skull. In the hands of ancient therapists it meant boring, chipping, or bashing holes into a patient's head. Presumably this was done to relieve pressure or release evil spirits (see ▶Figure 13.1).

During the Middle Ages, treatments for mental illness in Europe focused on **demonology,** the study of demons and persons plagued by spirits. Medieval "therapists" commonly blamed abnormal behaviour on supernatural forces, such as possession by the devil, or on curses from witches and wizards. As a cure, they used **exorcism** to "cast out evil spirits." For the fortunate, exorcism was a religious ritual. More often, physical torture was used to make the body an inhospitable place for the devil to reside.

One reason for the rise of demonology may lie in **ergotism** (AIR–got-ism), a psychosis-like condition caused by ergot poisoning. In the Middle Ages, rye fields were often infested with ergot fungus. Ergot, we now know, is a natural source of LSD and other mind-altering chemicals. Eating tainted bread could have caused symptoms that were easily mistaken for possession, bewitchment, or madness. Pinching sensations, muscle twitches, facial spasms, delirium, and hallucinations are all signs of ergot poisoning (Kety, 1979; Matossian, 1982). Thus, many people "treated" with demonology may have been doubly victimized.

It wasn't until 1793 that the emotionally disturbed were regarded as "mentally ill" and given compassionate treatment. That was the year a French doctor named **Philippe Pinel** changed the Bicêtre Asylum in Paris from a squalid "madhouse" into a mental hospital by personally unchaining inmates. Although over 200 years have passed since Pinel began humane treatment, the process of improving psychiatric care continues today.

When was psychotherapy developed? Sigmund Freud was among the pioneers who developed the first true psychotherapy around the late 1800s. As a physician in Vienna, Freud was intrigued by cases of **hysteria,** in which physical symptoms (such as paralysis or numbness) occur without known physical causes. As you may recall, such problems are now called somatoform disorders (see Chapter 12). Slowly, Freud became convinced that hysteria was caused by deeply hidden unconscious conflicts. Based on this insight, Freud developed a therapy called psychoanalysis. Since it is the "granddaddy" of more modern therapies, let us examine psychoanalysis in some detail.

▶ Psychoanalysis—Expedition into the Unconscious

? Survey Question:
■ Is Freudian psycho-analysis still used?

Psychoanalysis A Freudian therapy that emphasizes the use of free association, dream interpretation, resistances, and transference to uncover unconscious conflicts.

Free association In psychoanalysis, the technique of having a client say anything that comes to mind, regardless of how embarrassing or unimportant it may seem.

Latent dream content The hidden or symbolic meaning of a dream, as revealed by dream interpretation and analysis.

Manifest dream content The surface, "visible" content of a dream; dream images as they are remembered by the dreamer.

Dream symbols Images in dreams whose personal or emotional meanings differ from their literal meanings.

Resistance A blockage in the flow of free association; topics the client unconsciously resists thinking or talking about.

Transference The tendency of patients to transfer to a therapist feelings that correspond to those the patient had for important persons in his or her past.

Isn't psychoanalysis the therapy in which the patient lies on a couch? Freud's patients usually reclined on a couch during therapy, while Freud sat out of sight taking notes and offering interpretations. This arrangement was supposed to encourage a free flow of thoughts and images from the unconscious. However, it is the least important characteristic of psychoanalysis and many modern analysts have abandoned it.

How did Freud treat emotional problems? Freud's theory stressed that "neurosis" and "hysteria" are caused by repressed memories, motives, and conflicts—particularly those stemming from instinctual drives for sex and aggression. Although they are hidden, these factors remain active in the personality. This forces the person to develop rigid ego-defence mechanisms and to engage in compulsive and self-defeating behaviour. Thus, the main goal of **psychoanalysis** is to resolve internal conflicts that lead to emotional suffering (Wolitzky, 1995).

Freud relied on four basic techniques to uncover the unconscious roots of neuroses (Freud, 1949). These are free association, dream analysis, analysis of resistance, and analysis of transference.

FREE ASSOCIATION The process of **free association** involves saying whatever comes to mind. Patients must speak without concern for whether ideas are painful, embarrassing, or illogical. Thoughts are simply allowed to move freely from one thought to the next. The purpose of free association is to lower defences so that unconscious material can emerge (Wolitzky, 1995).

DREAM ANALYSIS Freud believed that dreams provide a "royal road to the unconscious" because they express forbidden desires and unconscious feelings. Such feelings are found in the **latent content** (hidden, symbolic meaning) of dreams. A dream's **manifest content** (obvious, visible meaning) tends to disguise information from the unconscious.

Freud was very interested in unconscious messages revealed by **dream symbols** (images that have personal or emotional meanings). Let's say a young man reports a dream in which he pulls a pistol from his waistband and aims at a target while his wife watches. The pistol repeatedly fails to discharge, and the man's wife laughs at him. Freud might have seen this as an indication of repressed feelings of sexual impotence, with the gun serving as a disguised image of the penis.

ANALYSIS OF RESISTANCE When free associating or describing dreams, patients may resist talking about or thinking about certain topics. Such **resistances** (blockages in the flow of ideas) are said to reveal particularly important unconscious conflicts. As analysts become aware of resistances, they bring them to the patient's awareness so the patient can deal with them realistically (Wolitzky, 1995). Rather than being roadblocks in therapy, resistances can be challenges and guides (May, 1996).

ANALYSIS OF TRANSFERENCE **Transference** is the tendency to "transfer" to a therapist feelings that match those the patient had for important persons in his or her past. At times, the patient may act as if the analyst is a rejecting father or an unloving or overprotective mother. As the patient re-experiences repressed emotions, the therapist can help the patient recognize and understand them. Troubled persons often provoke anger, rejection, boredom, criticism, and other negative reactions from others. Effective therapists learn to avoid reacting as others do and playing the patient's habitual "games." This, too, contributes to therapeutic change (Strupp, 1989).

Psychoanalysis Today

What is the status of psychoanalysis today? Traditional psychoanalysis called for three to five therapy sessions a week, often for many years. Today, most patients are seen only once or twice per week, but treatment may still go on for years (Friedman et al., 1998). Because of the huge amounts of time and money this requires, psychoanalysts have become relatively rare.

Many therapists have switched to doing **brief psychodynamic therapy,** which uses direct questioning to reveal unconscious conflicts (Book & Luborsky, 1998). Modern therapists also actively provoke emotional reactions to lower defences and provide insights (Davanloo, 1995). Interestingly, brief therapy seems to accelerate recovery. It is as if patients realize that they need to get to the heart of their problems quickly (Reynolds et al., 1996).

The development of newer, more streamlined dynamic therapies is in part due to questions about the effectiveness of traditional psychoanalysis. One critic, Hans Eysenck (1967, 1994), suggested that psychoanalysis simply takes so long that patients experience a **spontaneous remission** of symptoms (improvement due to the mere passage of time). How could we tell if a particular therapy or the passage of time is responsible for a person's improvement? Typically, some patients are randomly assigned for treatment, while others are placed on a waiting list. If members of this **waiting-list control group,** who receive no treatment, improve at the same rate as those in therapy, the therapy may be of little value.

How seriously should the possibility of spontaneous remission be taken? It is true that problems ranging from hyperactivity to anxiety improve with the passage of time. However, researchers have confirmed that psychoanalysis does, in fact, produce improvement in a majority of patients (Doidge, 1997).

The real value of Eysenck's critique is that it encouraged psychologists to try new ideas and techniques. Researchers began to ask: "When does psychoanalysis work, why does it work? What procedures are essential, and which are unnecessary?" Modern therapists have given surprisingly varied answers to these questions. Upcoming sections will acquaint you with some of the other therapies currently in use.

Knowledge builder

PSYCHOTHERAPY AND PSYCHOANALYSIS

Relate

How has your understanding of psychotherapy changed? How many types of therapy can you name?

Make a list describing what you think it means to be mentally healthy. How well does your list match the items in Table 13.1?

The use of trepanning, demonology, and exorcism all implied that the mentally ill are "cursed." To what extent are the mentally ill rejected and stigmatized today?

Try to free associate (aloud) for 10 minutes. How difficult was it? Did anything interesting surface?

Can you explain, in your own words, the role of dream analysis, resistances, and transference in psychoanalysis?

Learning Check

Match:

_____ **1.** Directive therapies
_____ **2.** Action therapies

_____ **3.** Insight therapies

_____ **4.** Non-directive therapies

A. Change behaviour
B. Place responsibility on the client
C. The client is guided strongly
D. Seek understanding

5. Pinel is famous for his use of exorcism. T or F?
6. In psychoanalysis, what is an emotional attachment to the therapist by the patient called?
   a. free association *b.* manifest association *c.* resistance *d.* transference.

Critical Thinking

7. Waiting-list control groups help separate the effects of therapy from improvement related to the mere passage of time. What other type of control group might be needed to learn if therapy is truly beneficial?

Answers:

1. C 2. A 3. D 4. B 5. F 6. *d* 7. Placebo therapy is sometimes used to assess the benefits of real therapy. Placebo therapy superficially resembles the real thing, but lacks key elements that are thought to be therapeutic.

▶ Humanistic Therapies—Restoring Human Potential

Survey Question:
■ What are the major humanistic therapies?

The goal of traditional psychoanalysis is adjustment. Freud claimed that his patients could expect only to change their "hysterical misery into common unhappiness"! Humanistic therapies are generally more optimistic. Most assume that it is possible for people to use their potentials fully and live rich, rewarding lives. Psychotherapy is seen as a way to give natural tendencies toward mental health a chance to emerge.

Client-Centred Therapy

What is client-centred therapy? How is it different from psychoanalysis? Psychoanalysts delve into the unconscious. Psychologist Carl Rogers (1902–1987) found it more beneficial to explore *conscious* thoughts and feelings. The psychoanalyst tends to take a position of authority, stating what dreams, thoughts, or memories "mean." In contrast, Rogers believed that what is right or valuable for the therapist may be different for the client. (Rogers preferred the term *client* to *patient* because "patient" implies a person is "sick" and needs to be "cured.") Consequently, the client determines what will be discussed during each session. Thus, **client-centred therapy** (also called person-centred therapy) is non-directive and based on insights from conscious thoughts and feelings (Bohart, 1995).

If the client runs things, what does the therapist do? The therapist's job is to create an "atmosphere of growth." The therapist provides opportunities for change, but the client must actively seek to solve his or her problems. The therapist cannot "fix" the client (Bohart & Tallman, 1996).

Psychotherapist Carl Rogers, who originated client-centred therapy.

HEALTH-PROMOTING CONDITIONS   Rogers believed that effective therapists maintain four basic conditions. First, the therapist offers the client **unconditional positive regard** (unshakable personal acceptance). The therapist refuses to react with shock, dismay, or disapproval to anything the client says or feels. Total acceptance by the therapist is the first step to self-acceptance by the client.

Second, the therapist attempts to achieve genuine **empathy** by trying to see the world through the client's eyes and feeling some part of what the client is feeling.

As a third essential condition, the therapist strives to be **authentic** (genuine and honest). The therapist must not hide behind a professional role. Rogers believed that phony fronts destroy the growth atmosphere sought in client-centred therapy.

Fourth, the therapist does not make interpretations, propose solutions, or offer advice. Instead, the therapist **reflects** (rephrases, summarizes, or repeats) the client's thoughts and feelings. This allows the therapist to act as a psychological "mirror" so clients can see themselves more clearly. Rogers hypothesized that a person armed with a realistic self-image and greater self-acceptance will gradually discover solutions to life's problems.

Client-centred therapy A non-directive therapy based on insights gained from conscious thoughts and feelings; emphasizes accepting one's true self.

Unconditional positive regard An unqualified, unshakable acceptance of another person.

Empathy A capacity for taking another's point of view; the ability to feel what another is feeling.

Authenticity In Carl Rogers's terms, the ability of a therapist to be genuine and honest about his or her own feelings.

Reflection In client-centred therapy, the process of rephrasing or repeating thoughts and feelings expressed by clients so they can become aware of what they are saying.

Existential therapy An insight therapy that focuses on the elemental problems of existence, such as death, meaning, choice, and responsibility; emphasizes making courageous life choices.

Free will The presumed ability of humans to freely make choices not determined by heredity, past conditioning, or other concerns.

Existential Therapy

According to the existentialists, "being in the world" (existence) creates deep conflicts. Each of us must deal with the realities of death. We must face the fact that we create our private world by making choices. We must overcome isolation on a vast and indifferent planet. Most of all, we must confront feelings of meaninglessness.

What do these concerns have to do with psychotherapy? **Existential therapy** focuses on the problems of existence, such as meaning, choice, and responsibility. Like client-centred therapy, it promotes self-knowledge and self-actualization. However, there are important differences. Client-centred therapy seeks to uncover a "true self" hidden behind a screen of defences. In contrast, existential therapy emphasizes **free will,** the human ability to make choices. Accordingly, existential therapists believe you can choose to become the person you want to be.

Existential therapists try to give clients the *courage* to make rewarding and socially constructive choices. Typically, therapy focuses on **death, freedom, isolation,** and **meaninglessness,** the "ultimate concerns" of existence (Yalom, 1980). These universal human challenges include an awareness of one's mortality; the

Death, freedom, isolation, meaninglessness The universal challenges of existence, including an awareness that everyone will die; the responsibility that comes with freedom to choose; the fact that each person is ultimately isolated and alone in his or her private world; and the reality that meaning must be created in life.

Confrontation In existential therapy, the process of confronting clients with their own values and with the need to take responsibility for the quality of their existence.

Gestalt therapy An approach that focuses on immediate experience and awareness to help clients rebuild thinking, feeling, and acting into connected wholes; emphasizes the integration of fragmented experiences.

responsibility that comes with freedom to choose; being alone in one's private world; and the reality that meaning must be created in life.

What does the existential therapist do? The therapist helps clients discover self-imposed limitations in personal identity. To be successful, the client must fully accept the challenge of changing his or her life (Bugental & Sterling, 1995). A key aspect of existential therapy is **confrontation,** in which clients are challenged to examine their values and choices and to take responsibility for the quality of their existence (Gerwood, 1998).

An important part of confrontation is the unique, intense, here-and-now encounter between two human beings. When existential therapy is successful, it brings about a renewed sense of purpose and a reappraisal of what's important in life. Some clients even experience an emotional rebirth like that seen after people survive a close brush with death. As Marcel Proust wrote, "The real voyage of discovery consists not in seeing new landscapes but in having new eyes."

Gestalt Therapy

Gestalt therapy, which is most often associated with Frederick (Fritz) Perls (1969), is built around the idea that perception, or *awareness,* is disjointed and incomplete in the maladjusted individual. The German word *Gestalt* means "whole," or "complete." **Gestalt therapy** helps individuals rebuild thinking, feeling, and acting into connected wholes. This is achieved by expanding personal awareness, by accepting responsibility for one's thoughts, feelings, and actions, and by filling in gaps in experience (Yontef, 1995).

What do you mean by gaps in experience? Gestalt therapists believe that we often shy away from expressing or "owning" upsetting feelings. This creates a gap in self-awareness that may become a barrier to personal growth. For example, a person who feels anger after the death of a parent might go for years without fully expressing it. This and similar threatening gaps may impair emotional health.

The Gestalt approach is more directive than client-centred therapy and it emphasizes immediate experience. Working either one-to-one or in a group setting, the Gestalt therapist encourages clients to become more aware of their moment-to-moment thoughts, perceptions, and emotions (Cole, 1998). Rather than discussing why clients feel guilt, anger, fear, or boredom, they are encouraged to have these feelings in the "here and now" and become fully aware of them. The therapist promotes awareness by drawing attention to a client's posture, voice, eye movement, and hand gestures. Clients may also be asked to exaggerate vague feelings until they become clear. Gestalt therapists believe that expressing such feelings allows people to "take care of unfinished business" and break through emotional impasses.

In all his writings, Perls's basic message comes through clearly: Emotional health comes from knowing what you *want* to do, not dwelling on what you *should* do, *ought* to do, or *should want* to do. Another way of stating this idea is that emotional health comes from taking full responsibility for one's feelings and actions. For example, it means changing "I can't" to "I won't" or "I must" to "I choose to."

How does Gestalt therapy help people discover their real wants? Above all else, Gestalt therapy emphasizes present experience. Clients are urged to stop intellectualizing and talking about feelings. Instead, they learn to live now; live here; stop imagining; experience the real; stop unnecessary thinking; taste and see; express rather than explain, justify, or judge; give in to unpleasantness and pain just as to pleasure; and surrender to being as you are (Naranjo, 1970). Gestalt therapists believe that, paradoxically, the best way to change is to become who you really are (Yontef, 1995).

Because of their emphasis on verbal interaction, humanistic therapies may be conducted at a distance, by telephone or e-mail. Let's investigate this possibility.

▶ Psychotherapy at a Distance—Psych Jockeys and Cybertherapy

How valid are psychological services offered over the phone and on the Internet? For better or worse, psychotherapy and counselling are rapidly entering the electronic age. Today, psychological services are available through radio, telephone, videoconferencing, and e-mail. What are the advantages and disadvantages of getting help "online"? What are the risks and possible benefits?

Media Psychologists

By now, you have probably heard a phone-in radio psychologist. On a typical program, callers describe problems arising from child abuse, loneliness, love affairs, phobias, sexual adjustment, or depression. The radio psychologist then offers reassurance, advice, or suggestions for getting help. Talk-radio psychology may seem harmless, but it raises some important questions. For instance, is it reasonable to give advice without knowing anything about a person's background? Might the advice do harm? What good can a psychologist do in three minutes?

In defence of themselves, radio psychologists point out that listeners may learn solutions to their problems by hearing others talk. Many also stress that their work is educational, not therapeutic. Nevertheless, the question arises, When does advice become therapy? The American Psychological Association urges media psychologists to discuss problems only of a general nature, instead of actually counselling anyone. For example, if a caller complains about insomnia, the radio psychologist should talk about insomnia in general, not probe the caller's personal life.

By giving information, advice, and social support, radio psychologists probably do help some listeners (Levy, 1989). Even so, a good guide for anyone tempted to call a radio psychologist might be "let the consumer beware."

Telephone Therapists

The same caution applies to telephone therapists. These "counsellors" can be reached through 900-number services for $3 to $5 per minute. To date, there is no evidence that telephone counselling is effective. Successful face-to-face therapy is based on a continuing relationship between two people. Telephone therapy is seriously undermined by a lack of visual cues (such as facial expressions and body language) and by limited personal contact (Haas, Benedict, & Kobos, 1996).

It's important to note that legitimate therapists occasionally use the phone to calm, console, or advise clients between therapy sessions. Others are experimenting with actually doing therapy by telephone (Sanders & Rosenfield, 1998). Also, use of the telephone for suicide hotlines and crisis counselling is well established. However, where commercial telephone therapists are concerned, consumers might well ask themselves, How much confidence would I place in a physician who would make a diagnosis over the phone? Many telephone "therapists" may be nothing more than untrained operators (Newman, 1994).

Cybertherapy

You can find almost anything on the Internet. Recently, "cybertherapy," psychological advice, support groups, and self-help magazines have been added to the list. Some services, such as support groups, are free. Online counselling or advice, in contrast, is typically offered for a fee. Some online therapists will "discuss" problems with you through e-mail messages. Others merely answer questions or give advice concerning specific problems.

Online counselling and advice services do have some advantages. For one thing, clients can remain anonymous. Thus, a person who might hesitate to see a psychologist can seek help privately online. Likewise, the Internet can link people who live in rural areas with professional psychologists residing in large cities. And, compared with traditional office visits, cybertherapy is relatively inexpensive.

As with radio talk shows and telephone counsellors, many objections can be raised about online psychological services. Clearly, brief e-mail messages are no way to make a diagnosis. And forget about facial expressions or body language—not even tone of voice reaches the cybertherapist. Typing little smiley faces or frowns is a poor substitute for real human interaction. Another problem is that e-mail counselling may not be completely confidential. In some cases, highly personal messages could be intercepted and misused.

Of special concern is the fact that "cybershrinks" may or may not be trained professionals (Bloom, 1998). And even if they are, questions have been raised about whether a psychologist licensed in one province can legally conduct therapy in another province via the Internet. Despite these concerns, some therapists have forged ahead with this form of therapy. They have also developed a code of ethics to guide and regulate what therapists can and cannot do.

Telehealth

Many of the limitations and drawbacks we have discussed can be avoided with videoconferencing. In this emerging approach, therapists provide services to people who live too far away to be seen in person on a regular basis. A two-way audio-video link allows the client and therapist to see one another on TV screens and talk via speakerphones. Doing therapy this way still lacks the close, personal contact of face-to-face interaction. However, it does remove many of the objections to doing therapy at a distance. Some experts predict that "telehealth" services will become a major source of mental health care in coming years (Nickelson, 1998; Stamm, 1998).

SUMMARY   As you can see, psychological services that rely on electronic communication may serve some useful purposes. However, the effectiveness of therapy conducted by telephone or over the Internet has not been established. As a result, the very best advice given by media psychologists, telephone counsellors, or cybertherapists may be, "You should consider discussing this problem with a psychologist or counsellor in your own community." But if you happen to live in rural areas of Canada where psychological services are nonexistent, cybertherapy may be better than no therapy at all. (Additional sources: Hannon, 1996; Sleek, 1995; Zgodzinski, 1996.)

Knowledge builder

INSIGHT THERAPIES

Relate

Here's a mnemonic for the elements of client-centred therapy: Picture a therapist saying "I ear u" to a client. The E stands for empathy, A for authenticity, R for reflection, and U for unconditional positive regard.

What would an existential therapist say about the choices you have made so far in your life? Should you be choosing more "courageously"?

You are going to play the role of a therapist for a classroom demonstration. How would you act if you were a client-centred therapist? An existential therapist? A Gestalt therapist?

A neighbour of yours is thinking about getting counselling on the Internet. What would you tell her about the pros and cons of distance therapy?

Learning Check

Match:

_____ **1.** Client-centred therapy   A. Electronic advice
_____ **2.** Gestalt therapy   B. Unconditional positive regard
_____ **3.** Existential therapy   C. Gaps in awareness
_____ **4.** Cybertherapy   D. Choice and becoming

5. The Gestalt therapist tries to reflect a client's thoughts and feelings. T or F?
6. Client-centred therapy is directive. T or F?
7. Confrontation and encounter are concepts of existential therapy. T or F?

Critical Thinking

8. How might using the term *patient* affect the relationship between an individual and a therapist?

Answers:

1. B 2. C 3. D 4. A 5. F 6. F 7. T 8. The terms *doctor* and *patient* imply a large gap in status and authority between the individual and his or her therapist. Client-centred therapy attempts to narrow this gap by making the person the final authority concerning solutions to his or her problems. Also, the word *patient* implies that a person is "sick" and needs to be "cured." Many regard this as an inappropriate way to think about human problems.

▶ Behaviour Therapy—Healing by Learning

Behaviour therapy Any therapy designed to actively change behaviour.

Behaviour modification The application of learning principles to change human behaviour, especially maladaptive behaviour.

Classical conditioning A form of learning in which reflex responses are associated with new stimuli.

Conditioned aversion A learned dislike or conditioned negative emotional response to a particular stimulus.

Aversion therapy Suppressing an undesirable response by associating it with aversive (painful or uncomfortable) stimuli.

Five times a day, for several days, Brooks Workman stopped what she was doing and vividly imagined opening a soft-drink can. She then pictured herself bringing the can to her mouth and placing her lips on it. Just as she was about to drink, hordes of roaches poured out of the can and scurried into her mouth—writhing, twitching, and wiggling their feelers (Williams & Long, 1991).

Why would anyone imagine such a thing? Brooks Workman's behaviour is not as strange as it may seem. Her goal was self-control: Brooks was drinking too many colas and she wanted to cut down. The method she chose (called *covert sensitization*) is a form of behaviour therapy (Cautela & Kearney, 1986). **Behaviour therapy** is the use of learning principles to make constructive changes in behaviour. Behavioural approaches include behaviour modification, aversion therapy, desensitization, token economies, and other techniques.

Behaviour therapists believe that deep insight into one's problems is often unnecessary for improvement. Instead, they try to directly alter troublesome thoughts and actions. Brooks Workman didn't need to probe into her past or her emotions and conflicts; she simply wanted to break her habit of drinking too many colas. Even when more serious problems are at stake, techniques like the one she used have proved valuable.

In general, how does behaviour therapy work? Behaviour therapists assume that people have learned to be the way they are. If they have learned responses that cause problems, then they can change them by relearning more appropriate responses. Broadly speaking, **behaviour modification** refers to any use of classical or operant conditioning to directly alter human behaviour (Spiegler & Guevremont, 1998).

How does classical conditioning work? I'm not sure I remember. **Classical conditioning** is a form of learning in which simple responses (especially reflexes) are associated with new stimuli. Here is a brief review of conditioning principles:

A neutral stimulus is followed by an *unconditioned stimulus* (US) that consistently produces an unlearned reaction, called the *unconditioned response* (UR). Eventually, the previously neutral stimulus begins to produce this response directly. The response is then called a *conditioned response* (CR), and the stimulus becomes a *conditioned stimulus* (CS). Thus, for a child the sight of a hypodermic needle (CS) is followed by an injection (US), which causes anxiety or fear (UR). Eventually the sight of a hypodermic (the conditioned stimulus) may produce anxiety or fear (a conditioned response) *before* the child gets an injection.

What does classical conditioning have to do with behaviour modification? Classical conditioning can be used to associate discomfort with a bad habit, as Brooks Workman did. A more powerful version of this approach is called aversion therapy.

Aversion Therapy

Imagine that you are eating an apple. Suddenly you discover that you just bit a large green worm in half. You vomit. Months pass before you can eat an apple again without feeling ill. You now have a conditioned aversion to apples. (A **conditioned aversion** is a learned dislike or negative emotional response to some stimulus.)

How are conditioned aversions used in therapy? In **aversion therapy,** an individual learns to associate a strong aversion with an undesirable habit such as smoking, drinking, or gambling. Aversion therapy has been used to cure hiccups, sneezing, stuttering, vomiting, nail-biting, bed-wetting, compulsive hair-pulling, alcoholism, and the smoking of tobacco, marijuana, or crack cocaine. (To learn how aversion therapy can help people quit smoking, see "Puffing Up an Aversion.") Actually, aversive conditioning is an everyday occurrence. For example, not many physicians who treat lung cancer are smokers, nor do many emergency room doctors drive without using their seat belts (Rosenthal & Steffek, 1991).

An excellent example of aversion therapy is provided by the work of Roger Vogler and his associates (1977). Vogler works with alcoholics who are unable to stop drinking.

USING PSYCHOLOGY   Puffing Up an Aversion

The fact that nicotine is toxic makes it easy to create an aversion to smoking. Behaviour therapists have found that electric shock, nauseating drugs, and similar aversive stimuli are not required to make smokers uncomfortable. All that is needed is for the smoker to smoke—rapidly and for a long time.

Rapid smoking (prolonged smoking at a forced pace) is the most widely used aversion therapy for smoking (Lichtenstein, 1982). In this method, clients are told to smoke continuously, taking a puff every six to eight seconds. Rapid smoking continues until the smoker is miserable and can stand it no more. By then, most people are thinking, "I never want to see another cigarette for the rest of my life."

Studies suggest that rapid smoking is one of the most effective behaviour therapies for smoking (Tiffany, Martin, & Baker, 1986). Nevertheless, anyone tempted to try rapid smoking should realize that it is very unpleasant. Without the help of a therapist, most people quit too soon for the procedure to succeed. (An alternative method that is more practical is described in the Psychology in Action section of this chapter.)

The most basic problem with rapid smoking—as with other stop-smoking methods—is that about one half of those who quit smoking begin again. During at least the first year after quitting, there is no "safe point" after which relapse becomes less likely (Swan & Denk, 1987).

Because the "evil weed" calls so strongly to former smokers, support from a stop-smoking group or a close, caring person can make a big difference. Former smokers who get encouragement from others are much more likely to stay smoke-free (Gruder et al., 1993). Those whose social groups include many smokers are more likely to begin smoking again (Mermelstein, 1986).

Aversion therapy for drinking. The sights, smells, and tastes of drinking are associated with unpleasant electric shocks applied to the hand.

For many clients, aversion therapy is a last chance. While drinking an alcoholic beverage, clients receive a painful (although non-injurious) electric shock to the hand. Most of the time, these shocks occur as the client is beginning to take a drink of alcohol.

This **response-contingent** (response-connected) shock obviously takes the pleasure out of drinking. Shocks also cause the alcohol abuser to develop a conditioned aversion to drinking. Normally, the misery caused by alcohol abuse comes long after the act of drinking—too late to have much effect. But if alcohol can be linked with immediate discomfort, then drinking will begin to make the individual very uncomfortable.

Is it really acceptable to treat clients this way? People are often disturbed (shocked?) by such methods. However, clients usually volunteer for aversion therapy because it helps them overcome a destructive habit. Indeed, commercial aversion programs for overeating, smoking, and alcohol abuse have attracted many willing customers. And more important, aversion therapy can be justified by its long-term benefits. As behaviourist Donald Baer put it, "A small number of brief, painful experiences is a reasonable exchange for the interminable pain of a lifelong maladjustment."

Rapid smoking Prolonged smoking at a forced pace; used to produce discomfort in aversion therapy for smoking.
Response-contingent consequences Reinforcement, punishment, or other consequences that are applied only when a certain response is made.
Hierarchy A rank-ordered series of higher and lower amounts, levels, degrees, or steps.

Desensitization

Assume that you are a swimming instructor who wants to help a child named Jamie overcome fear of the high diving board. How might you proceed? Directly forcing Jamie off the high board could be a psychological disaster. Obviously, a better approach would be to begin by teaching her to dive off the edge of the pool. Then she could be taught to dive off the low board, followed by a platform 2 metres above the water and then a 3-metre platform. As a last step, Jamie could try the high board.

WHO'S AFRAID OF A HIERARCHY?   This rank-ordered series of steps is called a **hierarchy.** The hierarchy allows Jamie to undergo adaptation. Gradually, she adapts to the high dive and overcomes her fear, much as one adapts to a cool swimming pool on a hot day. When Jamie has conquered her fear, we can say that *desensitization* (dee-SEN-sih-tih-ZAY-shun) has occurred (Spiegler & Guevremont, 1998).

Survey Question:
■ How is behaviour therapy used to treat phobias, fears, and anxieties?

Reciprocal inhibition The presence of one emotional state can inhibit the occurrence of another, such as joy preventing fear or anxiety inhibiting pleasure.

Systematic desensitization A reduction in fear, anxiety, or aversion brought about by planned exposure to aversive stimuli.

Phobia An intense and unrealistic fear of some object or situation.

Model A person (either live or filmed) who serves as an example for observational learning or vicarious conditioning.

Vicarious desensitization A reduction in fear or anxiety that takes place vicariously ("secondhand") when a client watches models perform the feared behaviour.

Desensitization is also based on **reciprocal inhibition** (using one emotional state to block another) (Wolpe & Plaud, 1997). For instance, it is impossible to be anxious and relaxed at the same time. If we can get Jamie onto the high board in a relaxed state, her anxiety and fear will be inhibited. Repeated visits to the high board should cause fear in this situation to disappear. Again we would say that Jamie has been desensitized. Typically, **systematic desensitization** (a guided reduction in fear, anxiety, or aversion) is attained by gradually approaching a feared stimulus while maintaining relaxation.

What is desensitization used for? Desensitization is primarily used to help people unlearn or countercondition **phobias** (intense, unrealistic fears) or strong anxieties. For example, each of these people might be a candidate for desensitization: a teacher with stage fright, a student with test anxiety, a salesperson who fears people, or a newlywed with an aversion to sexual intimacy.

PERFORMING DESENSITIZATION   *How is desensitization done?* First, the client and the therapist construct a hierarchy. This is a list of fear-provoking situations, arranged from least disturbing to most frightening. Second, the client is taught exercises that produce deep relaxation. (These are described in this chapter's Psychology in Action section.) Once the client is relaxed, she or he proceeds to the third step by trying to perform the least disturbing item on the list. For a fear of heights (acrophobia), this might be: "(1) Stand on a chair." The first item is repeated until no anxiety is felt. Any change from complete relaxation is a signal that clients must repeat the relaxation process before continuing. Slowly, clients move up the hierarchy: "(2) Climb to the top of a small stepladder"; "(3) Look down a flight of stairs"; and so on, until the last item is performed without fear: "(20) Fly in an airplane."

For many phobias, desensitization works best when people are directly exposed to the stimuli and situations they fear (Menzies & Clarke, 1993). For something like a simple spider phobia, this exposure can even be done in groups (Ost, 1996). Also, for some fears (such as fear of riding an elevator) desensitization may be completed in a single session (Sturges & Sturges, 1998).

Programs for treating fear of flying combine relaxation, systematic desensitization, group support, and lots of direct exposure to airplanes. Many such programs conclude with a brief flight, so that participants can "test their wings" (Roberts, 1989). Air Canada offers one such program that is given by a pilot and a psychologist. It lasts five sessions and costs about $800. It is available only in Vancouver, Toronto, and Montreal. If you are truly committed to fighting your fear of flying, Air Canada claims a success rate of about 90 percent.

VICARIOUS DESENSITIZATION   *I understand how some fears could be desensitized by gradual approach—as in the case of the child on the high dive. But how would a therapist use desensitization to combat fear of sexual intimacy?* For a person with a fear of heights, the steps of the hierarchy might be acted out. Often, however, this is impractical. In some cases the problem can be handled by having clients observe models who are performing the feared behaviour (see ▶Figure 13.2) (Rosenthal & Steffek, 1991). A **model** is a person who serves as an example for observational learning. If such **vicarious desensitization** (secondhand learning) is not practical, there is yet another option. Fortunately, desensitization works almost as well when a person vividly imag-

▶**Figure 13.2**

Treatment of a snake phobia by vicarious desensitization. The photographs show models interacting with snakes. To overcome their own fears, people with phobias observed the models. (Bandura, Blanchard, & Ritter, 1969. Photos courtesy of Albert Bandura.)

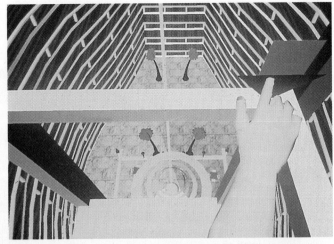

▶Figure 13.3

(Left) Dr. Barbara Rothbaum and Dr. Larry Hodges show how a virtual reality system is used to expose people to feared stimuli. Many patients say that they would rather face exposure to feared stimuli in a virtual environment than in a real physical environment. *(Right)* A computer image from a virtual elevator. Over an eight-week period, patients who suffered from acrophobia "rode" in the elevator. Each session took them to greater heights. (Image courtesy of Larry Hodges, Thomas Meyer, and Rob Kooper.)

Virtual reality exposure Use of computer-generated images to present fear stimuli. The virtual environment responds to a viewer's head movements and other inputs.

Eye movement desensitization and reprocessing (EMDR) A technique for reducing fear or anxiety; based on holding upsetting thoughts in mind while rapidly moving the eyes from side to side.

ines each step in the hierarchy (Deffenbacher & Suinn, 1988). If the steps can be visualized without anxiety, fear in the actual situation is reduced.

VIRTUAL REALITY EXPOSURE   In an important new development, psychologists are beginning to use virtual reality to treat phobias. Virtual reality is a computer-generated, three-dimensional "world" that viewers enter by wearing a head-mounted video display. **Virtual reality exposure** presents computerized fear stimuli to patients in a controlled fashion. It has already been used to treat acrophobia (fear of heights), fear of flying, spider phobia, and claustrophobia (Botella et al., 1998; Rothbaum et al., 1995; Rothbaum et al., 1996; Rothbaum, Hodges, & Kooper, 1997) (see ▶Figure 13.3).

Desensitization has been one of the most successful behaviour therapies. A second new technique may provide yet another way to lower fears, anxieties, and psychological pain. The highlight titled "Eye Movement Desensitization" has the details.

FOCUS ON RESEARCH   Eye Movement Desensitization— Watching Trauma Fade?

Traumatic events produce painful memories. Victims of accidents, disasters, molestations, muggings, rapes, or emotional abuse are often haunted by disturbing flashbacks. Recently, Dr. Francine Shapiro developed **eye movement desensitization and reprocessing (EMDR)** to help ease traumatic memories and post-traumatic stress.

In a typical EMDR session, the client is asked to visualize the images that most upset her or him. At the same time, a pencil (or other object) is moved rapidly from side to side in front of the person's eyes. Watching the moving object causes the person's eyes to dart swiftly back and forth. After about 30 seconds, patients describe any memories, feelings, and thoughts that emerged and discuss them with the therapist. These steps are repeated

until troubling thoughts and emotions no longer surface (Shapiro, 1995).

A number of studies indicate that EMDR lowers anxiety and takes the pain out of traumatic memories (Carlson et al., 1998; Lazgrove et al., 1998; Scheck, Schaeffer, & Gillette, 1998). However, EMDR is highly controversial. Some studies, for example, have found that eye movements add nothing to the treatment. The apparent success of EMDR may simply be based on gradual exposure to upsetting stimuli, as in other forms of desensitization (Cahill, Carrigan, & Frueh, 1999; Davidson & Parker, 2001; Lohr, Tolin, & Lilienfeld, 1998; Muris & Merckelbach, 1999).

Is EMDR a breakthrough? Or will it prove to be a case of wishful thinking? Given the frequency of traumas in modern society, it shouldn't be long before we find out.

Knowledge builder

BEHAVIOUR THERAPY

Relate

Can you describe three problems for which you think behaviour therapy would be an appropriate treatment? A friend of yours has a dog that goes berserk during thunderstorms. You own an audiotape of a thunderstorm. How could you use the tape to desensitize the dog? (Hint: The tape player has a volume control.)

Have you ever become naturally desensitized to a stimulus or situation that at first made you anxious (for instance, heights, public speaking, or driving on freeways)? How would you explain your reduced fear?

Learning Check

1. What two types of conditioning are used in behaviour modification? _____ and _____
2. Shock, pain, and discomfort play what role in conditioning an aversion?
   a. conditioned stimulus b. unconditioned response
   c. unconditioned stimulus d. conditioned response
3. If shock is used to control drinking, it must be _____ contingent.
4. What two principles underlie systematic desensitization? _____ and _____
   _____
5. When desensitization is carried out through the use of live or filmed models, it is called
   a. cognitive therapy b. flooding c. covert desensitization
   d. vicarious desensitization
6. The three basic steps in systematic desensitization are: construct a hierarchy, flood the person with anxiety, and imagine relaxation. T or F?
7. In EMDR therapy, computer-generated virtual reality images are used to expose patients to fear-provoking stimuli. T or F?

Critical Thinking

8. Alcoholics who take a drug called Antabuse become ill after drinking alcohol. Why, then, don't they develop an aversion to drinking?
9. A natural form of desensitization often takes place in hospitals. Can you guess what it is?

Answers:

1. classical (or respondent), operant 2. c 3. response 4. adaptation, reciprocal inhibition 5. d 6. F 7. F 8. Their discomfort is delayed enough to prevent it from being closely associated with drinking; there are safer, better ways to do aversion therapy (Wilson, 1987). 9. Doctors and nurses learn to relax and remain calm at the sight of blood because of their frequent exposure to it.

▶ Operant Therapies—All the World Is a Skinner Box?

Survey Question:
■ What role does reinforcement play in behaviour therapy?

Aversion therapy and desensitization are based on classical conditioning. Where does operant conditioning fit in? As you may recall, **operant conditioning** refers to learning based on the consequences of making a response. The operant principles most often used by behaviour therapists to deal with human behaviour are:

1. *Positive reinforcement.* Responses that are followed by reward tend to occur more frequently. If children whine and get attention, they will whine more frequently. If you get A's in your psychology class, you may become a psychology major.
2. *Non-reinforcement.* A response that is not followed by reward will occur less frequently.
3. *Extinction.* If a response is not followed by reward after it has been repeated many times, it will go away. After winning three times, you pull the handle on a slot machine 30 times more without a payoff. What do you do? You go away. So does the response of handle pulling (for that particular machine, at any rate).
4. *Punishment.* If a response is followed by discomfort or an undesirable effect, the response will be suppressed (but not necessarily extinguished).
5. *Shaping.* Shaping means rewarding actions that are closer and closer approximations to a desired response. For example, if you want to reward an intellectually disabled child for saying "ball," you might begin by rewarding the child for saying anything that starts with a *b* sound.
6. *Stimulus control.* Responses tend to come under the control of the situation in which they occur. If you set your clock 10 minutes fast, you can get to work on time in the morning. Your departure is under the stimulus control of the clock, even though you know it is fast.

Operant conditioning A type of learning that occurs when the behaviour of a person or an animal changes in response to the consequences of actions.

7. *Time out.* A time-out procedure usually involves removing the individual from a situation in which reinforcement occurs. Time out is a variation of non-reinforcement: It prevents reward from following an undesirable response. For example, children who fight with each other can be sent to separate rooms and allowed out only when they are able to behave more calmly (Olson & Roberts, 1987). (For a more thorough review of operant learning, return to Chapter 6.)

As simple as these principles may seem, they have been used very effectively to overcome difficulties in work, home, school, and industrial settings. Let's see how.

Non-Reinforcement and Extinction

An extremely overweight, mentally ill patient had a persistent and disturbing habit: She stole food from other patients. No one could persuade her to stop stealing or to diet. For the sake of her health, a behaviour therapist assigned her a special table in the ward dining room. If she approached any other table, she was immediately removed from the dining room. Since her attempts to steal food went unrewarded, they rapidly disappeared. Additionally, any attempt to steal from others caused the patient to miss her own meal (Ayllon, 1963).

What operant principles did the therapist in this example use? The therapist used non-reward to produce extinction. The most frequently occurring human behaviours lead to some form of reward. An undesirable response can be eliminated by identifying and removing the rewards that maintain it. But people don't always do things for food, money, or other obvious rewards. Most of the rewards maintaining human behaviour are more subtle. Attention, approval, and concern are common yet powerful reinforcers for humans (see ▶Figure 13.4).

Non-reward and extinction can eliminate many problem behaviours, especially in schools, hospitals, and institutions. Often, difficulties centre on a limited number of particularly disturbing responses. Time out is a good way to remove such responses, usually by refusing to pay attention to a person who is misbehaving. For example, 14-year-old Zeke periodically appeared in the nude in the activity room of a training centre for disturbed adolescents. This behaviour always generated a great deal of attention from staff and other patients. Usually Zeke was returned to his room and confined there. During this "confinement," he often missed doing his usual chores. As an experiment he was placed on time out. The next time he appeared nude, counsellors and other staff members greeted him normally and then ignored him. Attention from other patients rapidly subsided. Sheepishly he returned to his room and dressed.

Tokens Symbolic rewards, or secondary reinforcers (such as plastic chips, gold stars, or points) that can be exchanged for real reinforcers.

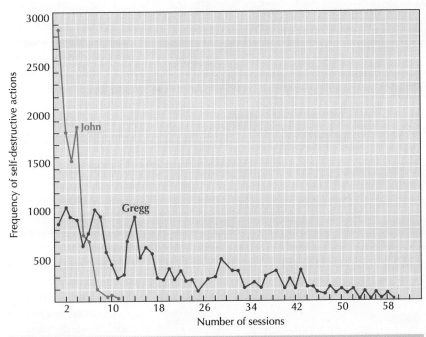

▶**Figure 13.4**

This graph shows extinction of self-destructive behaviour in two autistic boys. Before extinction began, the boys received attention and concern from adults for injuring themselves. During extinction, self-damaging behaviour was ignored. (Adapted from Lovaas & Simmons, 1969.)

Reinforcement and Token Economies

A distressing problem therapists sometimes face is how to break through to severely ill patients who won't talk. Conventional psychotherapy offers little hope of improvement for such patients.

What can be done for them? One widely used approach is based on **tokens** (symbolic rewards, such as plastic chips, that can be exchanged for real rewards). Tokens may be printed slips of paper, check marks, points, or gold stars. Whatever form they take,

Target behaviours
Actions or other behaviours (such as speech) that a therapist selects as the focus for behaviour modification efforts.

Token economy
A therapeutic program in which desirable behaviours are reinforced with tokens that can be exchanged for goods, services, activities, and privileges.

tokens serve as rewards because they may be exchanged for candy, food, cigarettes, recreation, or privileges, such as private time with a therapist, outings, or watching TV. Tokens are used in mental hospitals, halfway houses, schools for people with intellectual disabilities, programs for delinquents, and ordinary classrooms. They usually produce dramatic improvements in behaviour (Foxx, 1998; Mohanty, Pati, & Kumar, 1998; Truchlicka, McLaughlin, & Swain, 1998).

By using tokens, a therapist can *immediately reward* positive responses. For maximum impact, therapists select specific **target behaviours** (actions or other behaviours the therapist seeks to modify). Target behaviours are then reinforced with tokens. For example, a mute mentally ill patient might first be given a token each time he or she says a word. Next, tokens may be given for speaking a complete sentence. Later, the patient could gradually be required to speak more often, then to answer questions, and eventually to carry on a short conversation in order to receive tokens. In this way, deeply withdrawn patients have been returned to the world of normal communication.

Full-scale use of tokens in an institutional setting produces a *token economy*. In a **token economy** patients are rewarded with tokens for a wide range of socially desirable or productive activities (Spiegler & Guevremont, 1998). They must pay tokens for privileges and for engaging in problem behaviours (see ▶Figure 13.5). For example, tokens are given to patients who get out of bed, dress themselves, take required medication, arrive for meals on time, and so on. Constructive activities, such as gardening, cooking, or cleaning, may also earn tokens. Patients can exchange tokens for meals and private rooms, movies, passes, off-ward activities, and other privileges. They are charged tokens for staying in bed, disrobing in public, talking to themselves, fighting, crying, and similar target behaviours (Morisse et al., 1996).

Token economies can radically change a patient's overall adjustment and morale. Patients are given an incentive to change, and they are held responsible for their actions. The use of tokens may seem manipulative, but it actually empowers patients. Many severely retarded, mentally ill, and delinquent people have been returned to productive lives by means of token economies (Corrigan, 1997). By the time they are ready to leave, patients may be earning tokens on a weekly basis for maintaining socially desirable behaviours (Binder, 1976). Typically, the most effective token economies are those that gradually switch from tokens to social rewards such as praise, recognition, and approval. Such rewards are what patients will receive when they return to family, friends, and community.

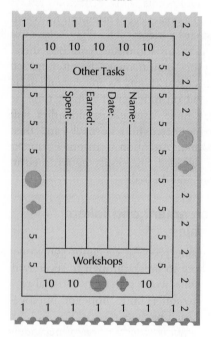

Credit Card

OXNARD DAY TREATMENT CENTER CREDIT INCENTIVE SYSTEM

EARN CREDITS BY		SPEND CREDITS FOR	
MONITOR DAILY	15	COFFEE	5
MENU PLANNING CHAIRMAN	50	LUNCH	10
PARTICIPATE	5	EXCEPT THURSDAY	15
BUY FOOD AT STORE	10	BUS TRIP	5
COOK FOR/PREPARE LUNCH	5	BOWLING	8
WIPE OFF KITCHEN TABLE	3	GROUP THERAPY	5
WASH DISHES	5-10	PRIVATE STAFF TIME	5
DRY AND PUT AWAY DISHES	5	DAY OFF	5-20
MAKE COFFEE AND CLEAN URN	15	WINDOW SHOPPING	5
CLEAN REFRIGERATOR	20	REVIEW WITH DR.	10
ATTEND PLANNING CONFERENCE	1	DOING OWN THING	1
OT PREPARATION	1-5	LATE 1 PER EVERY 10 MIN	
COMPLETE OT PROJECT	5	PRESCRIPTION FROM DR.	10
RETURN OT PROJECT	2		
DUST AND POLISH TABLES	5		
PUT AWAY GROCERIES	3		
CLEAN TABLE	5		
CLEAN 6 ASH TRAYS	2		
CLEAN SINK	5		
CARRY OUT CUPS & BOTTLES	5		
CLEAN CHAIRS	5		
CLEAN KITCHEN CUPBOARDS	5		
ASSIST STAFF	5		
ARRANGE MAGAZINES NEATLY	3		
BEING ON TIME	5		
MONITOR-ANN			

▶**Figure 13.5**

Shown here is a token used in one token economy system; also pictured is a list of credit values for various activities. Tokens may be exchanged for items or for privileges listed on the board. (After photographs by Robert P. Liberman.)

▶ Cognitive Therapy—Think Positive!

Survey Question:
■ Can therapy change thoughts and emotions?

How would a behaviour therapist treat a problem like depression? None of the techniques described seem to apply. As we have discussed, behaviour therapists usually try to change troublesome actions. However, in recent years, therapists have become interested in what people think, believe, and feel, as well as how they act (Meichenbaum, 1993). In general, **cognitive therapy** helps clients change thinking patterns that lead to troublesome emotions or behaviours (Freeman & Reinecke, 1995). For example, compulsive hand-washing can be greatly reduced by changing a client's thoughts and beliefs about dirt and contamination (Jones & Menzies, 1998).

Cognitive Therapy for Depression

Cognitive therapy has been especially effective for treating depression. As you may recall from Chapter 11, Aaron Beck (1991) believes that negative, self-defeating thoughts underlie depression. According to Beck, depressed persons see themselves, the world, and the future in negative terms. Beck believes this occurs because of major distortions in thinking. The first error is **selective perception,** which refers to perceiving only certain stimuli in a larger array. If five good things happen during the day and three bad things, depressed people focus only on the bad. A second thinking error in depression is **overgeneralization,** the tendency to let upsetting events affect unrelated situations. An example would be considering yourself a total failure, or completely worthless, if you were to lose a part-time job or fail a test. To complete the picture, depressed persons tend to magnify the importance of undesirable events by engaging in **all-or-nothing thinking.** That is, they see events as completely good or bad, right or wrong, and themselves as either successful or failing miserably (Beck, 1985).

How do cognitive therapists alter such patterns? Cognitive therapists make a step-by-step effort to correct negative thoughts that lead to depression or similar problems. At first, clients are taught to recognize and keep track of their own thoughts. The client and therapist then look for ideas and beliefs that cause depression, anger, and avoidance. For example, here's how a therapist might challenge all-or-nothing thinking (Burns & Persons, 1982):

Patient: *I'm feeling even more depressed. No one wants to hire me, and I can't even clean up my apartment. I feel completely incompetent!*

Therapist: *I see. The fact that you are unemployed and have a messy apartment proves that you are completely incompetent?*

Patient: *Well . . . I can see that doesn't add up.*

Next, clients are asked to gather information to test their beliefs. For instance, a depressed person might list his or her activities for a week. The list is then used to challenge all-or-nothing thoughts, such as "I had a terrible week" or "I'm a complete failure." With more coaching, clients learn to alter their thoughts in ways that improve their moods, actions, and relationships.

Cognitive therapy is as effective as drugs for treating many cases of depression. More important, people who have adopted new thinking patterns are less likely to become depressed again—a benefit that drugs can't impart (Fava et al., 1998; Gloaguen et al., 1998).

In an alternative approach, cognitive therapists look for an absence of effective coping skills and thinking patterns, not for the presence of self-defeating thoughts (Freeman & Reinecke, 1995). The aim is to teach clients how to cope with anger, depression, shyness, stress, and similar problems. Stress inoculation, which was described in Chapter 11, is a good example of this approach.

Cognitive therapy is a rapidly expanding specialty. Before we leave the topic, let's explore another widely used cognitive therapy.

Cognitive therapy A therapy directed at changing the maladaptive thoughts, beliefs, and feelings that underlie emotional and behavioural problems.

Selective perception Perceiving only certain stimuli among a larger array of possibilities.

Overgeneralization Blowing a single event out of proportion by extending it to a large number of unrelated situations.

All-or-nothing thinking Classifying objects or events as absolutely right or wrong, good or bad, acceptable or unacceptable, and so forth.

Rational-Emotive Behaviour Therapy

Rational-emotive behaviour therapy (REBT) attempts to change irrational beliefs that cause emotional problems. According to Albert Ellis (1973, 1995), the basic idea of rational-emotive behaviour therapy is as easy as A-B-C. Ellis assumes that people become unhappy and develop self-defeating habits because they have unrealistic or faulty *beliefs.*

How are beliefs important? Ellis analyzes problems in this way: The letter A stands for an *activating experience,* which the person assumes to be the cause of C, an *emotional consequence.* For instance, a person who is rejected (the activating experience) feels depressed, threatened, or hurt (the consequence). Rational-emotive behaviour therapy shows the client that the real problem is what comes between A and C: In between is B, the client's irrational and unrealistic *beliefs.* In this example, an unrealistic belief leading to unnecessary suffering is: "I must be loved and approved by almost everyone at all times." REBT holds that events do not cause us to have feelings. We feel as we do because of our beliefs (Kottler & Brown, 1999). (For some examples, see "Ten Irrational Beliefs.")

Ellis (1979, 1987) says that most irrational beliefs come from three core ideas, each of which is unrealistic:

1. I *must* perform well and be approved of by significant others. If I don't, then it is awful, I cannot stand it, and I am a rotten person.
2. You *must* treat me fairly. When you don't, it is horrible, and I cannot bear it.
3. Conditions *must* be the way I want them to be. It is terrible when they are not, and I cannot stand living in such an awful world.

Glossary
Rational-emotive behaviour therapy (REBT) An approach that states that irrational beliefs cause many emotional problems and that such beliefs must be changed or abandoned.

USING PSYCHOLOGY — Ten Irrational Beliefs—Which Do You Hold?

Rational-emotive behaviour therapists have identified numerous beliefs that commonly lead to emotional upsets and conflicts. See if you recognize any of the following irrational beliefs:

1. I must be loved and approved by almost every significant person in my life or it's awful and I'm worthless.
   Example: "One of my roommates doesn't seem to like me. I must be a total zero."
2. I should be completely competent and achieving in all ways to be a worthwhile person.
   Example: "I don't understand my chemistry class. I guess I really am a stupid person."
3. Certain people I must deal with are thoroughly bad and should be severely blamed and punished for it.
   Example: "The old man next door is such a pain. I'm going to play my stereo even louder the next time he complains."
4. It is awful and upsetting when things are not the way I would very much like them to be.
   Example: "I should have gotten an A in that class. The teacher is unfair."
5. My unhappiness is always caused by external events; I cannot control my emotional reactions.

Example: "You make me feel awful. I would be happy if it weren't for you."
6. If something unpleasant might happen, I should keep dwelling on it.
   Example: "I'll never forget the time my boss insulted me. I think about it every day at work."
7. It is easier to avoid difficulties and responsibilities than to face them.
   Example: "I don't know why my wife seems angry. Maybe it will just pass by if I ignore it."
8. I should depend on others who are stronger than I am.
   Example: "I couldn't survive if he left me."
9. Because something once strongly affected my life, it will do so indefinitely.
   Example: "My girlfriend dumped me during my first year in college. I don't know if I can ever trust a woman again."
10. There is always a perfect solution to human problems and it is awful if this solution is not found.
    Example: "I'm so depressed about politics in this country. It all seems hopeless." (Adapted from Rohsenow & Smith, 1982.)

If any of the listed beliefs sound familiar, you may be creating unnecessary emotional distress for yourself by holding on to unrealistic expectations.

Group therapy
Psychotherapy conducted in a group setting to make therapeutic use of group dynamics.

It's easy to see that such beliefs can lead to much grief and needless suffering in a less than perfect world. Rational-emotive behaviour therapists are very directive in their attempts to change clients' irrational beliefs and "self-talk." The therapist may directly attack clients' logic, challenge their thinking, confront them with evidence contrary to their beliefs, and even assign "homework." Here, for instance, are some examples of statements that dispute irrational beliefs (after Kottler & Brown, 1999):

- "Where is the evidence that you are a loser just because you didn't do well this one time?"
- "Who said the world should be fair? That's your rule."
- "What are you telling yourself to make yourself feel so upset?"
- "Is it really terrible that things aren't working out as you would like? Or is it just inconvenient?"

Many of us would probably do well to give up our irrational beliefs. Improved self-acceptance and a better tolerance of daily annoyances are the benefits of doing so.

The value of cognitive approaches is further illustrated by three techniques (*covert sensitization, thought stopping,* and *covert reinforcement*) described in this chapter's Psychology in Action section. A little later you can see what you think of them.

Knowledge builder

OPERANT THERAPIES AND COGNITIVE THERAPIES

Relate

 See if you can give a personal example of how the following principles have affected your behaviour: positive reinforcement, extinction, punishment, shaping, stimulus control, and time out.

You are setting up a token economy for troubled elementary school children. What target behaviours will you attempt to reinforce? For what behaviours will you charge tokens?

We all occasionally engage in negative thinking. Can you remember a time recently when you engaged in selective perception? Overgeneralization? All-or-nothing thinking?

Which of REBT's irrational beliefs have affected your feelings? Which beliefs would you like to change?

Learning Check

1. Behaviour modification programs aimed at extinction of an undesirable behaviour typically make use of what operant principles?

a. punishment and stimulus control b. punishment and shaping c. non-reinforcement and time out d. stimulus control and time out
2. Attention can be a powerful _____ for humans.
3. Token economies depend on the time-out procedure. T or F?
4. Tokens basically allow the operant shaping of desired responses or "target behaviours." T or F?
5. According to Beck, selective perception, overgeneralization, and _____ thinking are cognitive habits that underlie depression.
6. REBT teaches people to change the antecedents of irrational behaviour. T or F?

Critical Thinking

7. In Aaron Beck's terms, a belief such as "I must perform well or I am a rotten person" involves two thinking errors. What are these errors?

Answers:

1. c 2. reinforcer 3. F 4. T 5. all-or-nothing 6. F 7. Overgeneralization and all-or-nothing thinking.

▶ Group Therapy—People Who Need People

Survey Question:
■ Can psychotherapy be done with groups of people?

Group therapy is psychotherapy done with more than one person. Most of the therapies we have discussed can be adapted for use in groups. Psychologists first tried working with groups because there was a shortage of therapists. Surprisingly, group therapy has turned out to be just as effective as individual therapy. In addition, it offers some special advantages (McRoberts, Burlingame, & Hoag, 1998).

What are the advantages of group therapy? In group therapy, a person can act out or directly experience problems. Doing so often produces insights that might not occur from

A group therapy session. Group members offer mutual support while sharing problems and insights.

Psychodrama A therapy in which clients act out personal conflicts and feelings in the presence of others who play supporting roles.

Role-playing The dramatic enactment or re-enactment of significant life events.

Role reversal Taking the role of another person to learn how one's own behaviour appears from the other person's perspective.

Mirror technique Observing another person re-enact one's own behaviour, like a character in a play; designed to help persons see themselves more clearly.

Family therapy Technique in which all family members participate, both individually and as a group, to change destructive relationships and communication patterns.

Sensitivity group A group experience consisting of exercises designed to increase self-awareness and sensitivity to others.

merely talking about a person's difficulties. In addition, other group members with similar problems can offer support and useful input (Corey & Corey, 1996). For reasons such as these, a number of specialized groups have emerged. Because they range from Alcoholics Anonymous to Marriage Encounter, we will look at only a few examples.

Psychodrama

One of the first groups was developed by Jacob L. Moreno (1953), who called his technique psychodrama. In **psychodrama,** clients act out personal conflicts with others who play supporting roles. Through **role-playing** the client re-enacts incidents that cause problems in real life. For example, Don, a troubled teenager, might act out a typical family fight, with the therapist playing his father and with other clients playing his mother, brothers, and sisters. Moreno believed that insights gained in this way transfer to real-life situations.

Therapists using psychodrama often find role reversals especially helpful. A **role reversal** involves taking the part of another person to learn how he or she feels. For instance, Don might role-play his father or mother in order to better understand their feelings. A related method is the **mirror technique,** in which clients observe another person re-enact their behaviour. Thus, Don might briefly join the audience and watch as another group member plays his role. This would allow him to see himself as others do. Later, the group may summarize what happened and reflect on its meaning (Turner, 1997).

Family Therapy

Family relationships are the source of great pleasure, and all too often, of great pain for many people. In **family therapy** husband, wife, and children work as a group to resolve the problems of each family member. Family therapy tends to be brief and focused on specific problems, such as frequent fights or a depressed teenager. For some types of problems, family therapy may be superior to other approaches (Pinsof, Wynne, & Hambright, 1996).

Family therapists believe that a problem experienced by one family member is really the whole family's problem. If the entire pattern of behaviour in a family doesn't change, improvements in any single family member may not last. Thus, family members work together to improve communication, to change destructive patterns, and to see themselves and each other in new ways. This helps them reshape distorted perceptions and interactions directly, with the very persons with whom they have troubled relationships (Goldfried, Greenberg, & Marmar, 1990).

Does the therapist work with the whole family at once? Family therapists treat the family as a unit, but they may not meet with the entire family at each session. If a family crisis is at hand, the therapist may first try to identify the most resourceful family members, who can help solve the immediate problem. The therapist and family members may then work on resolving more basic conflicts and on improving family relationships (Dies, 1995).

Group Awareness Training

During the 1960s and 1970s, the human potential movement led many people to seek personal growth experiences. Often, their interest was expressed by participation in sensitivity training or encounter groups.

What is the difference between sensitivity and encounter groups? Sensitivity groups tend to be less confrontive than encounter groups. Participants in **sensitivity groups** take part in exercises that gently enlarge self-awareness and sensitivity to others. For example, in a "trust walk," participants expand their confidence in others by allowing themselves to be led around while blindfolded.

Encounter group A group experience that emphasizes intensely honest interchanges among participants regarding feelings and reactions to one another.

Large-group awareness training Any of a number of programs (many of them commercialized) that claim to increase self-awareness and facilitate constructive personal change.

Therapy placebo effect Improvement caused not by the actual process of therapy but by a client's expectation that therapy will help.

Encounter groups are based on an honest expression of feelings and intensely personal communication may take place. Typically, the emphasis is on tearing down defences and false fronts. Because there is a danger of hostile confrontation, participation is safest when members are carefully screened and a trained leader guides the group. Encounter group "casualties" are rare, but they do occur (Shaffer & Galinsky, 1989).

In business settings, psychologists still use the basic principles of sensitivity and encounter groups—truth, self-awareness, and self-determination—to improve employee relationships. Specially designed encounter groups for married couples are also widely held.

There also has been much public interest in various forms of large-group awareness training (Finkelstein, Wenegrat, & Yalom, 1982). **Large-group awareness training** refers to programs that claim to increase self-awareness and facilitate constructive personal change. Lifespring, Actualizations, the Forum, and similar commercial programs are well-known examples. Like the smaller groups that preceded them, large-group trainings combine psychological exercises, confrontation, new viewpoints, and group dynamics to promote personal change.

Are sensitivity, encounter, and awareness groups really psychotherapies? These experiences tend to be positive, but they produce only moderate benefits (Faith, Wong, & Carpenter, 1995). Moreover, many of the claimed benefits may result from the **therapy placebo effect,** in which improvement is based on a client's belief that therapy will help. Positive expectations, a break in daily routine, and an excuse to act differently can have quite an impact. Also, less ambitious goals may be easier to attain. For example, one recent program succeeded in teaching stress-management techniques in a large-group setting (Timmerman, Emmelkamp, & Sanderman, 1998). Because of their versatility, groups undoubtedly will continue to be a major tool for solving problems and improving lives.

▶ Psychotherapy—An Overview

Survey Question:
■ What do various therapies have in common?

How effective is psychotherapy? Judging the outcome of therapy is tricky. Nevertheless, there is ample evidence that therapy is beneficial. Hundreds of studies show a strong pattern of positive effects for psychotherapy and counselling (Lambert & Cattani-Thompson, 1996; Lipsey & Wilson, 1993). Even more convincing, perhaps, are the findings of a survey. Nearly nine out of ten people who have sought mental health care say their lives improved as a result of the treatment (Consumer, 1995; Kotkin, Daviet, & Gurin, 1996).

More specific benefits of psychotherapy include the following:

- For certain psychological disorders, psychotherapy provides just as good results as drug treatment, but psychotherapy is 10–50 percent less expensive.
- Fewer people drop out during treatment with psychotherapy than they do with drug therapy.
- Psychotherapy can also help people who suffer from a variety of medical conditions, such as headaches, hypertension, arthritis, diabetes, and chronic low-back pain.
- After successful treatment with psychotherapy, people reduce their use of medical services, which saves the overburdened health-care system a considerable sum of money (Canadian Psychological Association, 2002).

In general, then, psychotherapy works (Kopta et al., 1999). Of course, results vary in individual cases. For some people therapy is immensely helpful; for others it is unsuccessful; overall it is effective for more people than not. Speaking more subjectively, a real success, in which a person's life is changed for the better, can be worth the frustration of several cases in which little progress is made.

It is common to think of therapy as a long, slow process. But this is not always the case. Research shows that about 50 percent of all patients feel better after only eight therapy sessions. After 26 sessions, roughly 75 percent improve (Howard et al., 1986) (see ▶ Figure 13.6). The typical "dose" of therapy is one hourly session per week. This means that the majority of patients improve after six months of therapy, and half feel better in

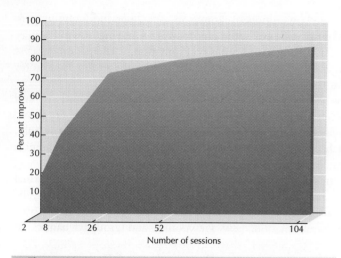

▶**Figure 13.6**

The dose-improvement relationship in psychotherapy. This graph shows the percentage of patients who improved after varying numbers of therapy sessions. Notice that the most rapid improvement took place during the first six months of once-a-week sessions. (From Howard et al., 1986.)

Therapeutic alliance A caring relationship that unites a therapist and a client in working to solve the client's problems.

just two months. Keep in mind, however, that people often suffer for several years before seeking help. In view of this, such rapid improvement is impressive.

Core Features of Psychotherapy

What do psychotherapies have in common? We have sampled only a few of the many therapies in use today. For a summary of major differences among psychotherapies, see Table 13.2. To add to your understanding, let us briefly summarize what all techniques have in common.

All the psychotherapies we have discussed include some combination of the following goals: restoring hope, courage, and optimism; gaining insight; resolving conflicts; improving one's sense of self; changing unacceptable patterns of behaviour; finding purpose; mending interpersonal relations; and learning to approach problems rationally (Seligman, 1998). In order to accomplish these goals, psychotherapies offer the following.

1. Therapy provides a *caring relationship* between the client and therapist, called a therapeutic alliance. Emotional rapport, warmth, friendship, understanding, acceptance, and empathy are the basis for this relationship. The **therapeutic alliance** unites the client and therapist as they work together to solve the client's problems. The strength of this alliance has a major impact on whether therapy succeeds (Gaston et al., 1998; Stiles et al., 1998).

2. Therapy offers a *protective setting* in which emotional catharsis (release) can take place. Therapy is a sanctuary in which the client is free to express fears, anxieties, and personal secrets without fearing rejection or loss of confidentiality (Weiss, 1990).

3. All therapies to some extent offer an *explanation* or *rationale* for the client's suffering. Additionally, they propose a line of action that will end this suffering.

4. Therapy provides clients with a *new perspective* about themselves and their situations and a chance to practise new behaviours (Crencavage & Norcross, 1990; Stiles et al., 1986).

Table 13.2
Comparison of Psychotherapies

	Insight or Action?	Directive or Non-Directive?	Individual or Group?	Therapy's Strength*
Psychoanalysis	Insight	Directive	Individual	Searching honesty
Brief psychodynamic therapy	Insight	Directive	Individual	Productive use of conflict
Client-centred therapy	Insight	Non-directive	Both	Acceptance, empathy
Existential therapy	Insight	Both	Individual	Personal empowerment
Gestalt therapy	Insight	Directive	Both	Focus on immediate awareness
Behaviour therapy	Action	Directive	Both	Observable changes in behaviour
Cognitive therapy	Action	Directive	Individual	Constructive guidance
Rational-emotive behaviour therapy	Action	Directive	Individual	Clarity of thinking and goals
Psychodrama	Insight	Directive	Group	Constructive re-enactments
Family therapy	Both	Directive	Group	Shared responsibility for problems

*This column based in part on Andrews (1989).

Table 13.3
Helping Behaviours

To help another person gain insight into a personal problem it is valuable to keep the following comparison in mind.	
BEHAVIOURS THAT HELP	BEHAVIOURS THAT HINDER
Active listening	Probing painful topics
Acceptance	Judging/moralizing
Reflecting feelings	Criticism
Open-ended questioning	Threats
Supportive statements	Rejection
Respect	Ridicule/sarcasm
Patience	Impatience
Genuineness	Placing blame
Paraphrasing	Opinionated statements

(Adapted from Kottler & Brown, 1999.)

Teams of psychologists and counsellors are often assembled to provide support to victims of major accidents and natural disasters. Because their work is stressful and often heart wrenching, relief workers also benefit from on-site counselling. Expressing emotions and talking about feelings are major elements of disaster counselling. The counsellor shown here is supporting a victim of the tornado that touched down in Pine Lake, Alberta, in July 2000.

If you recall that our discussion began with trepanning and demonology, it is clear that psychotherapy has come a long way. Still, the search for ways to improve psychotherapy remains an urgent challenge for those who devote their lives to helping others.

Basic Counselling Skills

A number of general helping skills can be distilled from the various approaches to therapy. These are points to keep in mind if you would like to comfort a person in distress, such as a troubled friend or relative (see Table 13.3).

ACTIVE LISTENING People frequently talk "at" each other without really listening. A person with problems needs to be heard. Make a sincere effort to listen to and understand the person. Try to accept the person's message without judging it or leaping to conclusions. Let the person know you are listening, through eye contact, posture, your tone of voice, and your replies (Kottler & Brown, 1999).

CLARIFY THE PROBLEM People who have a clear idea of what is wrong in their lives are more likely to discover solutions. Try to understand the problem from the person's point of view. As you do, check your understanding often. For example, you might ask, "Are you saying that you feel depressed just at school? Or in general?" Remember, a problem well defined is often half solved.

FOCUS ON FEELINGS Feelings are neither right nor wrong. By focusing on feelings you can encourage the outpouring of emotion that is the basis for catharsis. Passing judgment on what is said just makes people defensive. For example, a friend confides that he has failed a test. Perhaps you know that he studies very little. If you say, "Just study more and you would do better," he will probably become defensive or hostile. Much more can be accomplished by saying, "You must feel very frustrated" or simply, "How do you feel about it?" (Ivey & Galvin, 1984).

AVOID GIVING ADVICE Many people mistakenly think that they must solve problems for others. Remember that your goal is to provide understanding and support, not solutions. Of course, it is reasonable to give advice when you are asked for it, but beware of the trap of the "Why don't you . . . ? Yes, but . . ." game. According to psychotherapist Eric Berne (1964), this "game" follows a pattern: Someone says, "I have this problem." You say, "Why don't you do thus and so?" The person replies, "Yes, but . . ." and then tells you why your suggestion won't work. If you make a new suggestion the reply will once again be, "Yes, but . . ." Obviously, the person either knows more about his or her personal situation than you do or he or she has reasons for avoiding your advice. The student described earlier knows he needs to study. His problem is to understand why he doesn't want to study.

ACCEPT THE PERSON'S FRAME OF REFERENCE W. I. Thomas said, "Things perceived as real are real in their effects." Try to resist imposing your views on the problems of others. Since we all live in different psychological worlds, there is no "correct" view of a life situation. A person who feels that his or her viewpoint has been understood feels freer to examine it objectively and to question it. (Accepting and understanding the perspective of another person can be especially difficult when cultural differences exist. See "Cultural Issues in Counselling and Psychotherapy" on page 512.)

REFLECT THOUGHTS AND FEELINGS One of the best things you can do when offering support to another person is to give feedback by simply restating what is said. This is also

HUMAN DIVERSITY   Cultural Issues in Counselling and Psychotherapy

When a client and therapist come from different cultural backgrounds, misunderstandings are common (Storck, 1997). For example, in many Native and Asian cultures, one of the ways you show respect is by not making eye contact. Looking a therapist in the eye would be a challenge to his or her authority. But if the therapist doesn't understand this, lack of eye contact looks like a textbook case of poor self-esteem (Heinrich, Corbine, & Thomas, 1990). Misunderstanding such non-verbal communication can lead to serious mistakes by therapists (Singh, McKay, & Singh, 1998).

Culturally skilled therapists are skilled at working with clients from various cultural backgrounds. To be culturally skilled, a counsellor must be able to do all of the following (Lee, 1991):

- Be aware of his or her own cultural values and biases
- Establish rapport with a person from a different cultural background
- Alter and adapt traditional theories and techniques to meet the needs of clients from non-European ethnic or racial groups

- Be sensitive to cultural differences without resorting to stereotypes
- Treat members of racial or ethnic communities as individuals
- Be aware of a client's ethnic identity and degree of acculturation to the majority society
- Use existing helping resources within a cultural group to support efforts to resolve problems

Let's illustrate this with an example. Rod McCormick has looked at how psychotherapy can be best adapted to suit the unique needs and cultural requirements of the First Nations people of British Columbia. He notes that to Native people, healing means having a sense of balance, feeling interconnected, and being spiritual. Therapists should take this particular world view into account if they are to achieve success in therapy (McCormick, 1996). One successful program, designed to treat alcohol and drug abuse problems of First Nations people, fosters a sense of meaning and encourages traditional cultural values (McCormick, 2000).

Culturally skilled therapist A therapist who has the awareness, knowledge, and skills necessary to treat clients from diverse cultural backgrounds.

a good way to encourage a person to talk. If your friend seems to be at a loss for words, restate or paraphrase his or her last sentence. Here's an example:

Friend: *I'm really down about school. I can't get interested in any of my classes. I flunked my French test, and somebody stole my notebook for psychology.*

You: *You're really upset about school, aren't you?*

Friend: *Yeah, and my parents are hassling me about my grades again.*

You: *You're feeling pressured by your parents?*

Friend: *Yeah, damn.*

You: *It must make you angry to be pressured by them.*

As simple as this sounds, it is very helpful to someone trying to sort out feelings. Try it. If nothing else, you'll develop a reputation as a fantastic conversationalist!

SILENCE Studies show that counsellors tend to wait longer before responding than do people in everyday conversations. Pauses of five seconds or more are not unusual, and interrupting is rare. Listening patiently lets the person feel unhurried and encourages her or him to speak freely (Goodman, 1984).

QUESTIONS Because your goal is to encourage free expression, *open questions* tend to be the most helpful (Goodman, 1984). A *closed question* is one that can be answered yes or no. Open questions call for an open-ended reply. Say, for example, that a friend tells you, "I feel like my boss has it in for me at work." A closed question would be, "Oh yeah? So, are you going to quit?" Open questions, such as, "Do you want to tell me about it?" or "How do you feel about it?" are more likely to be helpful.

MAINTAIN CONFIDENTIALITY Your efforts to help will be wasted if you fail to respect the privacy of someone who has confided in you. Put yourself in the person's place. Don't gossip.

These guidelines are not an invitation to play "junior therapist." Professional therapists are trained to approach serious problems with skills far exceeding those described here. However, the points made help define the qualities of a therapeutic relationship. They also emphasize that each of us can supply two of the greatest mental health resources available at any cost: friendship and honest communication.

▶ Medical Therapies—Psychiatric Care

Survey Question:
■ How do psychiatrists treat psychological disorders?

Psychotherapy may be applied to anything from a brief crisis to a full-scale psychosis. However, most psychotherapists do not treat patients with major mood disorders, schizophrenia, or other severe conditions. Major mental disorders are more often treated medically (Knesper, Belcher, & Cross, 1989; Kopta et al., 1999).

Three main types of **somatic** (bodily) **therapy** are *pharmacotherapy, electroconvulsive therapy,* and *psychosurgery.* Somatic therapy is often done in the context of psychiatric hospitalization. All the somatic approaches have a strong medical slant and they are typically administered by psychiatrists.

Drugs

Somatic therapy Any bodily therapy, such as drug therapy, electroconvulsive therapy, or psychosurgery.

Pharmacotherapy The use of drugs to alleviate the symptoms of emotional disturbance.

Minor tranquillizers Drugs (such as Valium) that produce relaxation or reduce anxiety.

Antidepressants Mood-elevating drugs.

Antipsychotics Drugs that, in addition to having tranquillizing effects, tend to reduce hallucinations and delusional thinking. (Also called major tranquillizers.)

The atmosphere in psychiatric wards and mental hospitals changed radically in the mid-1950s with the widespread adoption of *pharmacotherapy* (FAR-meh-koe-THER-eh-pea). **Pharmacotherapy** refers to the use of drugs to treat emotional disturbances. Drugs may relieve the anxiety attacks and other discomforts of milder psychological disorders. More often, however, they are used to combat schizophrenia and major mood disorders.

What sort of drugs are used in pharmacotherapy? Three major types of drugs are used. **Minor tranquillizers** (such as Valium) produce relaxation or reduce anxiety. **Antidepressants** are mood-elevating drugs that combat depression. **Antipsychotics** (also called *major tranquillizers*) have tranquillizing effects and, in addition, reduce hallucinations and delusions. (See Table 13.4 for examples of each class of drugs.)

Are drugs a valid approach to treatment? Drugs have shortened hospital stays and they have greatly improved the chances that people will recover from major psychological disorders. Drug therapy has also made it possible for many people to return to the community, where they can be treated on an outpatient basis.

LIMITATIONS OF DRUG THERAPY Few experts would argue for a return to the conditions that existed before pharmacotherapy became available. However, drugs do have drawbacks. For example, 15 percent of patients taking major tranquillizers for long periods develop a neurological disorder that causes rhythmic facial and mouth movements (Chakos et al., 1996). Newer drugs are often hailed as medical "miracles." However, all drugs involve a trade-off between benefits and risks. For example, the drug Clozaril (clozapine) can relieve the symptoms of schizophrenia in some previously "hopeless" cases (Buchanan et al., 1998). But Clozaril is nearly as dangerous as it is helpful: Two out of 100 patients taking the drug suffer from a potentially fatal blood disease.

Is the risk worth it? Many experts think it is, because chronic schizophrenia robs people of almost everything that makes life worth living. It's possible, of course, that newer drugs will improve the risk-benefit ratio in the treatment of severe problems like schizophrenia. For example, the drug Risperdal (risperidone) appears to be as effective as Clozaril,

Table 13.4 Commonly Prescribed Psychiatric Drugs	CLASS	EXAMPLES (TRADE NAMES)	EFFECTS
	Minor tranquillizers (anti-anxiety drugs)	Ativan, Halcion, Librium, Restoril, Valium, Xanax	Reduce anxiety, tension, fear
	Antidepressants	Anafranil, Elavil, Nardil, Norpramin, Parnate, Paxil, Prozac, Tofranil, Zoloft	Counteract depression
	Antipsychotics (major tranquillizers)	Clozaril, Haldol, Mellaril, Navane, Risperdal, Thorazine	Reduce agitation, delusions, hallucinations, thought disorders

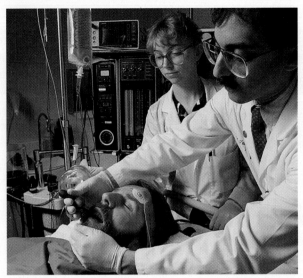

In electroconvulsive therapy, electrodes are attached to the head and a brief electrical current is passed through the brain. ECT is used in the treatment of severe depression.

Electroconvulsive therapy (ECT) A treatment for severe depression, consisting of an electric shock passed directly through the brain, which induces a convulsion.

Psychosurgery Any surgical alteration of the brain designed to bring about desirable behavioural or emotional changes.

Prefrontal lobotomy An antiquated surgery in which portions of the frontal lobes were destroyed or disconnected from other brain areas.

Deep lesioning Use of an electrode (electrified wire) to destroy small areas deep within the brain.

without the lethal risk. But, even the best new drugs are not cure-alls. They help some people and relieve some problems, but not all. It is noteworthy that for serious mental disorders a combination of medication and psychotherapy almost always works better than drugs alone. Nevertheless, where schizophrenia and major mood disorders are concerned, drugs will undoubtedly remain the primary mode of treatment (Thase & Kupfer, 1996).

Shock

In **electroconvulsive therapy (ECT)** a 150-volt electrical current is passed through the brain for slightly less than a second. This rather drastic medical treatment for severe depression triggers a convulsion and causes the patient to lose consciousness for a short time. Muscle relaxants and sedative drugs are given before ECT to soften its impact. Treatments are given in a series of six to eight sessions spread over three to four weeks.

How does shock help? Actually, it is the seizure activity that is believed to be helpful. Proponents of ECT claim that shock-induced seizures alter the biochemical balance in the brain, bringing an end to severe depression and suicidal behaviour (Swartz, 1993). Others have charged that ECT works only by confusing patients so they can't remember why they were depressed (Kohn, 1988).

THE ECT DEBATE Many people consider ECT a distasteful procedure, and not all professionals support its use. However, most experts seem to agree on the following: (1) At best, ECT produces only temporary improvement—it gets the patient out of a bad spot, but it must be combined with other treatments; (2) ECT does cause permanent memory losses in many patients; and (3) ECT should be used only as a last resort after drug therapy has failed (Kohn, 1988). All told, ECT is considered by many to be a valid treatment for selected cases of depression—especially when it rapidly ends wildly self-destructive or suicidal behaviour (Abrams, 1997; Kellner, 1998). It's interesting to note that most ECT patients feel that the treatment helped them. Most, in fact, would have it done again (Bernstein et al., 1998).

Psychosurgery

The most extreme medical treatment is **psychosurgery** (any surgical alteration of the brain). The best-known psychosurgery is the lobotomy. In the **prefrontal lobotomy** the frontal lobes were surgically disconnected from other brain areas. This procedure was supposed to calm persons who didn't respond to any other type of treatment.

When the lobotomy was first introduced in the 1940s, there were enthusiastic claims for its success. But later studies suggested that some patients were calmed, some showed no change, and some became "vegetables." Lobotomies also produced a high rate of undesirable side effects, such as seizures, extreme lack of emotional response, major personality changes, and stupor. At about the same time that such problems became apparent, the first antipsychotic drugs became available. Soon after, the lobotomy was abandoned (Pressman, 1998; Swayze, 1995).

To what extent is psychosurgery used now? Psychosurgery is still considered valid by many neurosurgeons. However, most now use **deep lesioning,** in which small target areas are destroyed in the brain's interior. The appeal of deep lesioning is that it can have fairly specific effects. For instance, patients suffering from a severe type of obsessive-compulsive disorder may be helped by psychosurgery (Cumming et al., 1995).

It is worth remembering that psychosurgery cannot be reversed. A drug can be given or taken away. You can't take back psychosurgery. Many critics argue that psychosurgery should be banned altogether. Others continue to report success with brain surgery. All things considered, it is perhaps most accurate, even after decades of use, to describe psychosurgery as an experimental technique. Nevertheless, it may have value as a remedy for some very specific disorders (Fenton, 1998).

Community Mental Health Programs

Community mental health centres are a bright spot in the area of mental health care. **Community mental health centres** offer a wide range of mental health services, such as prevention, counselling, consultation, and crisis intervention. Such centres try to minimize hospitalization and seek new answers to mental health problems. Typically, they provide short-term treatment, outpatient care, and special crisis or emergency services.

If it is like most, the primary aim of the mental health centre in your community is to directly aid troubled citizens. The second goal of mental health centres is *prevention*. Consultation, education, and **crisis intervention** (skilled management of a psychological emergency) are used to end or prevent problems before they become serious. Also, some centres attempt to raise the general level of mental health in target areas by combating problems such as unemployment, delinquency, and drug abuse (Levine, Toro, & Perkins, 1993).

How have community mental health centres done in meeting their goals? In practice, they have concentrated much more on providing clinical services than they have on prevention. This appears to be primarily the result of wavering government support (translation: money). Overall, community mental health centres have succeeded in making psychological services more accessible than ever before. Many of their programs are made possible by **paraprofessionals** (individuals who work in a near-professional capacity under the supervision of more highly trained staff). Some paraprofessionals are ex-addicts, ex-alcoholics, or ex-patients who have "been there." Many more are persons (paid or volunteer) who have skills in tutoring, crafts, or counselling or who are simply warm, understanding, and skilled at communication.

A LOOK AHEAD   In the Psychology in Action section that follows we will return briefly to behavioural approaches. There you will find a number of useful techniques that you may be able to apply to your own behaviour. You'll also find a discussion of when to seek professional help and how to find it. Here's your authors' professional advice: This is information you won't want to skip.

Community mental health centre A facility offering a wide range of mental health services, such as prevention, counselling, consultation, and crisis intervention.

Crisis intervention Skilled management of a psychological emergency.

Paraprofessional An individual who works in a near-professional capacity under the supervision of a more highly trained person.

Knowledge builder

GROUP THERAPIES, PSYCHOTHERAPY SKILLS, AND MEDICAL THERAPIES

Relate

Would you rather participate in individual therapy or group therapy? What advantages and disadvantages do you think each has?

Based on your own experience, how valid do you think it is to say that within families "a problem for one is a problem for all"?

What lies at the "heart" of psychotherapy? How would you describe it to a friend?

Which of the basic counselling skills do you already use? Which would improve your ability to help a person in distress?

If a family member of yours became severely depressed, what therapies would be available to him or her? What are the pros and cons of each choice?

Learning Check

1. In psychodrama, people attempt to form meaningful wholes out of disjointed thoughts, feelings, and actions. T or F?
2. Most large-group awareness trainings make use of Gestalt therapy. T or F?

3. Which therapy places great emphasis on role-playing? *a.* psychodrama *b.* awareness training *c.* family therapy *d.* encounter
4. Emotional _____ (release) in a protected setting is an element of most psychotherapies.
5. To aid a troubled friend, you should focus on facts rather than feelings, and you should critically evaluate what the person is saying to help him or her grasp reality. T or F?
6. ECT is a modern form of pharmacotherapy. T or F?
7. Currently, the frontal lobotomy is the most widely used form of psychosurgery. T or F?

Critical Thinking

8. In your opinion, do psychologists have a duty to protect others who may be harmed by their clients? For example, if a patient has homicidal fantasies about his ex-wife, should she be informed?
9. In 1982, residents of Berkeley, California, voted on a referendum to ban the use of ECT within city limits. Do you think that the use of certain psychiatric treatments should be controlled by law?

Answers:

1. F 2. F 3. a 4. catharsis 5. F 6. F 7. F 8. According to the law, there is a duty to protect others where a therapist could, with little effort, prevent serious harm. However, this duty can conflict with a client's rights to confidentiality and with client–therapist trust. Therapists often make difficult choices in such situations. 9. The question of who can prescribe drugs, do surgery, and administer ECT is controlled by law. However, psychiatrists strongly object to residents, city councils, or government agencies making medical decisions.

SELF-MANAGEMENT AND SEEKING PROFESSIONAL HELP

Survey Question:
- How are behavioural principles applied to everyday problems?

Covert sensitization Use of aversive imagery to reduce the occurrence of an undesired response.

"Throw out the snake oil, ladies and gentlemen, and throw away your troubles. Doctor B. Haviour Modification is here to put an end to all human suffering."

True? Well, not quite. Behaviour therapy is not a cure-all. Its use is often quite complicated and requires a great deal of expertise. Still, behaviour therapy offers a straightforward solution to many problems.

As mentioned elsewhere in this book, you should seek professional help when a significant problem exists. For lesser difficulties you may want to try applying behavioural principles yourself. Let us see how this might be done.

Covert Reward and Punishment—Boosting Your "Willpower"

"Have you ever decided to quit smoking cigarettes, watching television too much, eating too much, drinking too much, or driving too fast?"

"Well, one of those applies. I have decided several times to quit smoking."

"When have you decided?"

"Usually after I am reminded of how dangerous smoking is—like when I heard that my uncle had died of lung cancer. He smoked constantly."

"If you have decided to quit 'several times' I assume you haven't succeeded."

"No, the usual pattern is for me to become upset about smoking and then to cut down for a day or two."

"You forget the disturbing image of your uncle's death, or whatever, and start smoking again."

"Yes, I suppose if I had an uncle die every day or so, I might actually quit!"

The use of electric shock to condition an aversion seems remote from everyday problems. Even naturally aversive actions are difficult to apply to personal behaviour. As mentioned earlier, for instance, rapid smoking is difficult for most smokers to carry out on their own. And what about a problem like overeating? It would be difficult indeed to eat enough to create a lasting aversion to overeating. (Although it's sometimes tempting to try.)

In view of such limitations, psychologists have developed an alternative procedure that can be used to curb smoking, overeating, and other habits (Cautela & Bennett, 1981; Cautela & Kearney, 1986).

Covert Sensitization   In **covert sensitization** aversive imagery is used to reduce the occurrence of an undesired response. Here's how it's done: Obtain six index cards and on each write a brief description of a scene related to the habit you wish to control. The scene should be so disturbing or disgusting that thinking about it would temporarily make you very uncomfortable about indulging in the habit. For smoking, the cards might read:

- I am in a doctor's office. The doctor looks at some reports and tells me I have lung cancer. He says a lung will have to be removed and sets a date for the operation.
- I am in bed under an oxygen tent. My chest feels caved in. There is a tube in my throat. I can barely breathe.
- I wake up in the morning and smoke a cigarette. I begin coughing up blood.
- Other cards would continue along the same line.
  For overeating the cards might read:
- I am at the beach. I get up to go for a swim and I overhear people whispering to each other, "Isn't that fat disgusting?"
- I am at a store buying clothes. I try on several things that are too small. The only things that fit look like rumpled sacks. Salespeople are staring at me.
- Other cards would continue along the same line.

The trick, of course, is to get yourself to imagine or picture vividly each of these disturbing scenes *several times* a day. Imagining the scenes can be accomplished by placing them under *stimulus control*. Simply choose something you do *frequently* each day (such as getting a cup of coffee or getting up from your chair). Next make a rule: Before you can get a cup of coffee or get up from your chair, or whatever you have selected as a cue, you must take out your cards and vividly picture yourself engaging in the action you wish to curb (overeating or smoking, for example). Then vividly picture the scene described on the top card. Imagine the scene for 30 seconds.

After visualizing the top card, move it to the bottom so the cards are rotated. Make up new cards each week. The scenes can be made much more upsetting than the samples given here. The samples are toned down to keep you from being "grossed out."

Covert sensitization can also be used directly in situations that test your self-control. If you are trying to lose weight, for instance, you might be able to turn down a tempting dessert in this way: As you look at the dessert, visualize maggots crawling all over it. If you make this image as vivid and nauseating as possible, losing your appetite is almost a certainty. If you want to apply this technique to other situations, be aware that vomiting scenes are especially effective. Covert sensitization may sound as if you are "playing games with yourself," but it can be a great help if you want to cut down on a bad habit (Cautela & Kearney, 1986). Try it!

Thought Stopping   As discussed earlier, behaviour therapists accept that thoughts, like visible responses, can also cause trouble. Think of times when you have repeatedly "put yourself down" mentally or when you have been preoccupied by needless worries, fears, or other negative and upsetting thoughts. If you would like to gain control over such thoughts, thought stopping may help you do it.

In **thought stopping** aversive stimuli are used to interrupt or prevent upsetting thoughts. The simplest thought-stopping technique makes use of mild punishment to suppress upsetting mental images and internal "talk." Simply place a large, flat rubber band around your wrist. As you go through the day apply this rule: Each time you catch yourself thinking the upsetting image or thought, pull the rubber band away from your wrist and snap it. You need not make this terribly painful. Its value lies in drawing your attention to how often you form negative thoughts and in interrupting the flow of thoughts. Strong punishment is not required.

It seems like this procedure might be abandoned rapidly. Is there an alternative? A second thought-stopping procedure requires only that you interrupt upsetting thoughts each time they occur. Begin by setting aside time each day during which you will deliberately think the unwanted thought. As you begin to form the thought, shout "Stop!" aloud, with conviction. (Obviously, you should choose a private spot for this part of the procedure!)

Repeat the thought-stopping procedure 10 to 20 times for the first two or three days. Then switch to shouting "Stop!" covertly (to yourself) rather than aloud. Thereafter, thought stopping can be carried out throughout the day, whenever upsetting thoughts occur (Williams & Long, 1991). After several days of practice, you should be able to stop unwanted thoughts whenever they occur.

Covert Reinforcement   Earlier we discussed how punishing images can be used to decrease undesirable responses, such as smoking or overeating. Many people also find it helpful to covertly *reinforce* desired actions. **Covert reinforcement** is the use of positive imagery to reinforce desired behaviour. For example, suppose your target behaviour is, once again, not eating dessert. If this were the case, you could do the following (Cautela & Bennett, 1981; Cautela & Kearney, 1986):

> Imagine that you are standing at the dessert table with your friends. As dessert is passed, you politely refuse and feel good about staying on your diet.

These images would then be followed by imagining a pleasant, reinforcing scene:

Thought stopping Use of aversive stimuli to interrupt or prevent upsetting thoughts.

Covert reinforcement Using positive imagery to reinforce desired behaviour.

Imagine that you are your ideal weight. You look really slim in your favourite colour and style. Someone you like says to you, "Gee, you've lost weight. I've never seen you look so good."

For many people, of course, actual direct reinforcement (as described in the Psychology in Action section of Chapter 6) is the best way to alter behaviour. Nevertheless, covert or "visualized" reinforcement can have similar effects. To make use of covert reinforcement, choose one or more target behaviours and rehearse them mentally. Then follow each rehearsal with a vivid, rewarding image.

Self-Directed Desensitization—Overcoming Common Fears

You have prepared for two weeks to give a speech in a large class. As your turn approaches, your hands begin to tremble. Your heart pounds and you find it difficult to breathe. You say to your body, "Relax!" What happens? Nothing!

> **Tension-release method**
> A procedure for systematically achieving deep relaxation of the body.

Relaxation   The key to desensitization is relaxation. To inhibit fear, one must learn to relax. Here is a description of how the **tension-release method** can be used to achieve deep-muscle relaxation.

> Tense the muscles in your right arm until they tremble. Hold them tight for about five seconds and then let go. Allow your hand and arm to go limp and to relax completely. Repeat the procedure. Releasing tension two or three times will allow you to feel whether or not your arm muscles have relaxed. Repeat the tension-release procedure with your left arm. Compare it with your right arm. Repeat until the left arm is equally relaxed. Apply the tension-release technique to your right leg; to your left leg; to your abdomen; to your chest and shoulders. Clench and release your chin, neck, and throat. Wrinkle and release your forehead and scalp. Tighten and release your mouth and face muscles. As a last step, curl your toes and tense your feet. Then release.

Practise the tension-release method until you can achieve complete relaxation quickly (five to ten minutes).

After you have practised relaxation once a day for a week or two, you will begin to be able to tell when your body (or a group of muscles) is tense. Also, you will begin to be able to relax on command. As an alternative, you might want to try imagining a very safe, pleasant, and relaxing scene. Some people find such images as relaxing as the tension-release method (Rosenthal, 1993). Once you have learned to relax, the next step is to identify the fear you would like to control and construct a hierarchy.

Procedure for Constructing a Hierarchy   Make a list of situations (related to the fear) that make you anxious. Try to list at least 10 situations. Some should be very frightening and others only mildly frightening. Write a short description of each situation on a separate index card. Place the cards in order from the least disturbing situation to the most disturbing. Here is a sample hierarchy for a student afraid of public speaking:

1. Being given an assignment to speak in class
2. Thinking about the topic and the date the speech must be given
3. Writing the speech; thinking about delivering the speech
4. Watching other students speak in class the week before the speech date
5. Rehearsing the speech alone; pretending to give it to the class
6. Delivering the speech to my roommate; pretending my roommate is the teacher
7. Reviewing the speech on the day it is to be presented
8. Entering the classroom; waiting and thinking about the speech
9. Being called; standing up; facing the audience
10. Delivering the speech

Using the Hierarchy   When you have mastered the relaxation exercises and have the hierarchy constructed, set aside time each day to work on reducing your fear. Begin by performing the relaxation exercises. When you are completely relaxed, visualize the scene on the first card (the least frightening scene). If you can *vividly* picture and imagine yourself in the first situation twice *without a noticeable increase in muscle tension,* proceed to the next card. Also, as you progress, relax yourself between cards.

Each day, stop when you reach a card that you cannot visualize without becoming tense in three attempts. Each day, begin one or two cards before the one on which you stopped the previous day. Continue to work with the cards until you can visualize the last situation without experiencing tension (techniques are based on Wolpe, 1974).

By using this approach you should be able to reduce the fear or anxiety associated with things such as public speaking, entering darkened rooms, asking questions in large classes, heights, talking to members of the opposite sex, and taking tests. Even if you are not always able to reduce a fear, you will have learned to place relaxation under voluntary control. This alone is valuable because controlling unnecessary tension can increase energy and efficiency.

Seeking Professional Help—When, Where, and How?

How would I know if I should seek professional help at some point in my life? Although there is no simple answer to this question, the following guidelines may be helpful.

Survey Question:
■ How could a person find professional help?

1. If your level of psychological discomfort (unhappiness, anxiety, or depression, for example) is comparable to a level of physical discomfort that would cause you to see a doctor or dentist, you should consider seeing a psychologist or a psychiatrist.
2. Another signal to watch for is significant changes in behaviour, such as the quality of your work (or schoolwork), your rate of absenteeism, your use of drugs (including alcohol), or your relationships with others.
3. Perhaps you have urged a friend or relative to seek professional help and were dismayed because he or she refused to do so. If you find friends or relatives making a similar suggestion, recognize that they may be seeing things more clearly than you are.
4. If you have persistent or disturbing suicidal thoughts or impulses, you should seek help immediately.

LOCATING A THERAPIST   *How would I go about looking for a right therapist?* Canada has about 13 000 psychologists and 3600 psychiatrists (Goering, Wasylenki, & Durbin, 2000). Here are some suggestions that could help you find the right therapist.

1. *The Yellow Pages.* Some psychologists are listed in the telephone book under "Psychologist" or in some cases under "Counselling Services." Psychiatrists are generally listed as a subheading under "Physicians." Counsellors may be found under the heading "Marriage and Family Counsellors." These listings will usually put you in touch with individuals in private practice.
2. *Community mental health centres.* In many parts of Canada, mental health services may be provided by public mental health facilities. (These may be listed in the phone book.) Public mental health centres usually provide counselling and therapy services directly, and they can refer you to private therapists.
3. *Mental health associations.* Many cities have mental health associations organized by concerned citizens. Groups such as these usually keep listings of qualified therapists and other services and programs in the community. For example, Canada Mental Health Association (CMHA) has offices throughout the country and provides useful information about mental health issues and treatment. You can contact the CMHA branch in your province or territory to obtain a list of therapists in your area.
4. *Colleges and universities.* If you are a student, don't overlook counselling services offered by a student health centre or special student counselling facilities.
5. *Newspaper and radio advertisements.* Some therapists advertise their services in newspapers or on the radio. However, you should carefully inquire into a therapist's training and qualifications. Without the benefit of a referral from a trusted person, it is wise to be cautious.

Table 13.5
Mental
Health
Resources

—Family doctors
—Mental health specialists, such as psychiatrists, psychologists, social workers, or mental health counsellors
—Health maintenance organizations
—Community mental health centres
—Hospital psychiatry departments and outpatient clinics
—University- or medical school-affiliated programs
—Family service/social agencies
—Private clinics and facilities
—Employee assistance programs
—Local medical, psychiatric, or psychological societies

6. *Crisis hotlines.* The typical crisis hotline is a telephone service staffed by community volunteers to provide support to people who may wish to discuss personal issues on the phone. These people are trained to provide information concerning a wide range of mental health problems. They also have lists of organizations, services, and other resources in the community to where you can go for help.

Table 13.5 summarizes all of the sources for psychotherapy, counselling, and referrals we have discussed, as well as some additional possibilities.

Options *How would I know what kind of a therapist to see? How would I pick one?* The choice between a psychiatrist and a psychologist is somewhat arbitrary. Both are trained to do psychotherapy. While a psychiatrist can administer somatic therapy and prescribe drugs, a psychologist can work in conjunction with a physician if such services are needed. Psychologists and psychiatrists are equally effective as therapists (Consumer, 1995; Seligman, 1995).

Visits to psychiatrists are covered under the Medicare program. The average fee charged by psychologists in Canada is about $125 an hour and may roughly range from $60 to $180 (Stephens & Joubert, 2001). Group therapy costs even less because the therapist's fee is divided among several people. If you are covered under a private health insurance plan, chances are good that it covers the cost of psychotherapy with a registered psychologist. This is why you need to be certain that a therapist is a registered psychologist with your provincial or territorial licensing agency. Almost anyone can use the label "therapist" or "psychotherapist," but the designation of "psychologist" can be used only by someone who has a masters or a doctorate degree in psychology and has duly obtained a licence to conduct therapy.

If fees are a problem, keep in mind that many therapists charge on a sliding scale, or ability-to-pay basis, and that community mental health centres almost always charge on a sliding scale.

Some communities and college campuses have counselling services staffed by sympathetic paraprofessionals or peer counsellors. These services are free or very low cost. As mentioned earlier, paraprofessionals are people who work in a near-professional capacity under professional supervision. **Peer counsellors** are non-professional persons who have learned basic counselling skills. There is a natural tendency, perhaps, to doubt the abilities of paraprofessionals. However, many studies have shown that paraprofessional counsellors are often as effective as professionals (Christensen & Jacobson, 1994).

Also, don't overlook self-help groups, which can add valuable support to professional treatment. Members of a self-help group typically share a particular type of problem, such as eating disorders or coping with an alcoholic parent. **Self-help groups** offer members mutual support and a chance to discuss problems. In many instances helping others also serves as therapy for those who give help (Levine, Toro, & Perkins, 1993). For some problems, self-help groups may be the best choice of all (Christensen & Jacobson, 1994; Fobair, 1997).

Qualifications You can usually find out about a therapist's qualifications simply by asking. A reputable therapist will be glad to reveal his or her background. If you have any doubts, credentials may be checked and other helpful information can be obtained from your provincial or territorial licensing agency. You can also contact the following organizations:

- Canadian Psychiatric Association. 260–441 MacLaren Street, Ottawa, ON K2P 2H3 (Phone: 613-234-2815)

Peer counsellor A non-professional person who has learned basic counselling skills.

Self-help group A group of people who share a particular type of problem and provide mutual support to one another.

- Canadian Psychological Association. 151 Slater Street, Suite 205, Ottawa, ON K1P 5H3 (Phone: 1-888-472-0657)
- Canadian Counselling Association. 116 Albert Street, Suite 702, Ottawa, ON K1P 5G3 (Phone: 1-877-765-5565)

The question of how to pick a particular therapist remains. The best way is to start with a short consultation with a respected psychiatrist, psychologist, or counsellor. This will allow the person you consult to evaluate your difficulty and recommend a type of therapy or a therapist who is likely to be helpful. As an alternative, you might ask the person teaching this course for a referral.

Evaluating a Therapist   *How would I know whether or not to quit or ignore a therapist?* A balanced look at psychotherapies suggests that all *techniques* are about equally successful (Wampold et al., 1997). However, all *therapists* are not equally successful. Far more important than the approach used are the therapist's personal qualities (Luborsky et al., 1997). The most consistently successful therapists are those who are willing to use whatever method seems most helpful for a client. They are also marked by personal characteristics of warmth, integrity, sincerity, and empathy (Patterson, 1989; Strupp, 1989).

It is perhaps most accurate to say that at this stage of development, psychotherapy is more of an art than a science. The relationship between a client and therapist is the therapist's most basic tool (Hubble, Duncan, & Miller, 1999). This is why you must trust and easily relate to a therapist for therapy to be effective. Here are some danger signals to watch for in psychotherapy:

- Sexual advances by therapist
- Therapist makes repeated verbal threats or is physically aggressive
- Therapist is excessively blaming, belittling, hostile, or controlling
- Therapist makes excessive small talk; talks repeatedly about his or her own problems
- Therapist encourages prolonged dependence on him or her
- Therapist demands absolute trust or tells client not to discuss therapy with anyone else

Clients who like their therapist are generally more successful in therapy (Talley et al., 1990). An especially important part of the therapeutic alliance is agreement about the goals of therapy. It is therefore a good idea to think about what you would like to accomplish by entering therapy. Write down your goals and discuss them with your therapist during the first session (Goldfried, Greenberg, & Marmar, 1990). Your first meeting with a therapist should also answer all of the following questions (Somberg, Stone, & Claiborn, 1993):

- Will the information I reveal in therapy remain confidential?
- What risks do I face if I begin therapy?
- How long do you expect treatment to last?
- What form of treatment do you expect to use?
- Are there alternatives to therapy that might help me as much or more?

It's always tempting to avoid facing up to personal problems. With this in mind, you should give a therapist a fair chance and not give up too easily. But don't hesitate to change therapists or to terminate therapy if you lose confidence in the therapist or if you don't relate well to the therapist as a person.

Knowledge builder

SELF-MANAGEMENT AND FINDING PROFESSIONAL HELP

Relate

How could you use covert sensitization, thought stopping, and covert reinforcement to change your behaviour? Try to apply each technique to a specific example.

Just for practice, make a fear hierarchy for a situation you find frightening. Does vividly picturing items in the hierarchy make you tense or anxious? If so, can you intentionally relax using the tension-release method?

Assume that you want to seek help from a psychologist or other mental health professional. How would you proceed? Take some time to actually find out what mental health services are available to you.

Learning Check

1. Covert sensitization and thought stopping combine aversion therapy and cognitive therapy. T or F?
2. Like covert aversion conditioning, covert reinforcement of desired responses is also possible. T or F?

3. Exercises that bring about deep-muscle relaxation are an essential element in covert sensitization. T or F?
4. Items in a desensitization hierarchy should be placed in order from the least disturbing to the most disturbing. T or F?
5. The first step in desensitization is to place the visualization of disturbing images under stimulus control. T or F?
6. Persistent emotional discomfort is a clear sign that professional psychological counselling should be sought. T or F?
7. Community mental health centres rarely offer counselling or therapy themselves; they only do referrals. T or F?
8. In many instances, a therapist's personal qualities have more of an effect on the outcome of therapy than does the type of therapy used. T or F?

Critical Thinking

9. Would it be acceptable for a therapist to urge a client to break all ties with a troublesome family member?

Answers:

1. T 2. T 3. F 4. T 5. F 6. T 7. F 8. T 9. Such decisions must be made by clients themselves. Therapists can help clients evaluate important decisions and feelings about significant persons in their lives. However, actively urging a client to sever a relationship borders on unethical behaviour.

Psychologist's Journal

EPILOGUE

Like other humanistic psychologists, Carl Rogers (1980) believed deeply that humans have a natural urge to seek health and self-growth. Rogers's belief is movingly expressed by the following words:

> I remember that in my boyhood the bin in which we stored our winter's supply of potatoes was in the basement, several feet below a small window. The conditions were unfavorable, but pale white sprouts . . . would grow two or three feet in length as they reached toward the light of the distant window. The sprouts were, in their bizarre, futile growth, a sort of desperate expression of the directional tendency I have been describing. . . . In dealing with clients whose lives have been terribly warped, in working with men and women on the back wards of state hospitals, I often think of those potato sprouts. . . . The clue to understanding their behavior is that they are striving, in the only ways that they perceive as available to them, to move toward growth, toward becoming. To healthy persons, the results may seem bizarre and futile but they are life's desperate attempt to become itself. This potent constructive tendency is an underlying basis of the person-centered approach.

Perhaps Susan, the troubled student described at the beginning of this chapter, wouldn't appreciate being compared to a potato! Nevertheless, it seems to us that Rogers has managed to state for clients and therapists alike the reasons for undertaking the often-difficult process of self-examination and personal renewal. Of the many journeys depicted in this book, psychotherapy is one of the most challenging.

CHAPTER IN REVIEW

Major Points

▶ Psychotherapy facilitates positive changes in personality, behaviour, or adjustment.

▶ Before the development of modern therapies, superstition dominated attempts to treat psychological problems.

▶ Five major categories of psychotherapy are psychodynamic, insight, behavioural, cognitive, and group therapies.

▶ Psychotherapy is generally effective, although no single form of therapy is superior to others.

▶ All medical treatments for psychological disorders have pros and cons. Overall, however, their effectiveness is improving.

▶ Some personal problems can be successfully treated using self-management techniques.

▶ Everyone should know how to obtain high-quality mental health care in his or her community.

Summary

How Do Psychotherapies Differ? How Did Psychotherapy Originate?

• Psychotherapies may be classified as insight, action, directive, non-directive, or supportive therapies, and combinations of these.

• Therapies may be conducted either individually or in groups, and they may be time limited.

• Ancient approaches to mental illness were often based on belief in supernatural forces.

• Demonology attributed mental disturbance to demonic possession and prescribed exorcism as the cure.

• In some instances, the actual cause of bizarre behaviour may have been ergot poisoning.

• More humane treatment began in 1793 with the work of Philippe Pinel in Paris.

Is Freudian Psychoanalysis Still Used?

• Freud's psychoanalysis was the first formal psychotherapy. Psychoanalysis seeks to release repressed thoughts and emotions from the unconscious.

- The psychoanalyst uses free association, dream analysis, and analysis of resistance and transference to reveal health-producing insights.
- Some critics argue that traditional psychoanalysis is ineffective and it wrongly receives credit for spontaneous remissions of symptoms.
- Brief psychodynamic therapy (which relies on psychoanalytic theory but is brief and focused) is as effective as other major therapies.

What Are the Major Humanistic Therapies?

- Client-centred (or person-centred) therapy is non-directive and is dedicated to creating an atmosphere of growth.
- Unconditional positive regard, empathy, authenticity, and reflection are combined to give the client a chance to solve his or her own problems.
- Existential therapies focus on the end result of the choices one makes in life. Clients are encouraged through confrontation and encounter to exercise free will and to take responsibility for their choices.
- Gestalt therapy emphasizes immediate awareness of thoughts and feelings. Its goal is to rebuild thinking, feeling, and acting into connected wholes and to help clients break through emotional blockages.
- Media psychologists, telephone counsellors, and cybertherapists may, on occasion, do some good. However, each has serious drawbacks, and the effectiveness of telephone counselling and cybertherapy has not been established.
- Therapy by videoconferencing shows promise as a way to provide mental health services at a distance.

What Is Behaviour Therapy?

- Behaviour therapists use various behaviour modification techniques that apply learning principles to change human behaviour.
- In aversion therapy, classical conditioning is used to associate maladaptive behaviour (such as smoking or drinking) with pain or other aversive events in order to inhibit undesirable responses.

How Is Behaviour Therapy Used to Treat Phobias, Fears, and Anxieties?

- Classical conditioning underlies systematic desensitization, a technique used to overcome fears and anxieties. In desensitization, gradual adaptation and reciprocal inhibition break the link between fear and particular situations.
- Typical steps in desensitization are: construct a fear hierarchy; learn to produce total relaxation; and perform items on the hierarchy (from least to most disturbing).
- Desensitization may be carried out with real settings or it may be done by vividly imagining the fear hierarchy or by watching models perform the feared responses.
- In some cases, virtual reality exposure can be used to present fear stimuli in a controlled manner.

- A new technique called eye movement desensitization and reprocessing (EMDR) shows promise as a treatment for traumatic memories and stress disorders. At present, however, EMDR is highly controversial.

What Role Does Reinforcement Play in Behaviour Therapy?

- Behaviour modification also makes use of operant principles, such as positive reinforcement, non-reinforcement, extinction, punishment, shaping, stimulus control, and time out. These principles are used to extinguish undesirable responses and to promote constructive behaviour.
- Non-reward can extinguish troublesome behaviours. Often this is done by simply identifying and eliminating reinforcers, particularly attention and social approval.
- To apply positive reinforcement and operant shaping, tokens are often used to reinforce selected target behaviours.
- Full-scale use of tokens in an institutional setting produces a token economy. Toward the end of a token economy program, patients are shifted to social rewards such as recognition and approval.

Can Therapy Change Thoughts and Emotions?

- Cognitive therapy emphasizes changing thought patterns that underlie emotional or behavioural problems. Its goals are to correct distorted thinking and/or teach improved coping skills.
- In a variation of cognitive therapy called rational-emotive behaviour therapy (REBT), clients learn to recognize and challenge their own irrational beliefs.

Can Psychotherapy Be Done with Groups of People?

- Group therapy may be a simple extension of individual methods or it may be based on techniques developed specifically for groups.
- In psychodrama, individuals enact roles and incidents resembling their real-life problems. In family therapy, the family group is treated as a unit.
- Although they are not literally psychotherapies, sensitivity and encounter groups attempt to encourage positive personality change. In recent years, commercially offered large-group awareness trainings have become popular. However, the therapeutic benefits of such programs are questionable.

What Do Various Therapies Have in Common?

- To alleviate personal problems, all psychotherapies offer a caring relationship, emotional rapport, a protected setting, catharsis, explanations for the client's problems, a new perspective, and a chance to practise new behaviours.
- Many basic counselling skills underlie a variety of therapies. These include listening actively, helping to clarify the problem, focusing on feelings, avoiding the giving of unwanted advice, accepting the person's perspective, reflecting thoughts and feelings, being patient during

silences, using open questions when possible, and maintaining confidentiality.

- The culturally skilled counsellor must be able to establish rapport with a person from a different cultural background and adapt traditional theories and techniques to meet the needs of clients from non-European ethnic or racial groups.

How Do Psychiatrists Treat Psychological Disorders?

- Three medical, or somatic, approaches to treatment are pharmacotherapy, electroconvulsive therapy (ECT), and psychosurgery. All three techniques are controversial to a degree because of questions about effectiveness and side effects.
- Community mental health centres seek to avoid or minimize mental hospitalization. They also seek to prevent mental health problems through education, consultation, and crisis intervention.

How Are Behavioural Principles Applied to Everyday Problems?

- In covert sensitization, aversive images are used to discourage unwanted behaviour.
- Thought stopping uses mild punishment to prevent upsetting thoughts.
- Covert reinforcement is a way to encourage desired responses by mental rehearsal.
- Desensitization pairs relaxation with a hierarchy of upsetting images in order to lessen fears.

How Could a Person Find Professional Help?

- In most communities, a competent and reputable therapist can be located with public sources of information or through a referral.
- Practical considerations such as cost and qualifications enter into choosing a therapist. However, the therapist's personal characteristics are of equal importance.

PSYCHOLOGY ON THE NET

If you have difficulty finding any of the sites listed here, visit http://www.psychologyjourney.nelson.com for an updated list of Internet addresses and direct links to relevant sites.

Basics of Cognitive Therapy An overview of cognitive therapy, with suggested readings. http://mindstreet.com

Canadian Counselling Association Provides information about the counselling profession in Canada. http://www.ccacc.ca

Canadian Mental Health Association This national organization speaks for the rights of people who suffer from mental illness. The site presents information about mental health and mental disorders. http://www.cmha.ca

Canadian Psychiatric Association Provides useful information about mental health issues and allows access to online articles published in the *Canadian Journal of Psychiatry.* http://www.cpa-apc.org

Canadian Psychological Association Provides important information on mental health and illness, as well as

advice on how to look for a psychologist in all provinces and territories. http://www.cpa.ca

Metanoia Offers useful information about cybertherapy, including advice on how to look for a therapist, and discusses ethical issues surrounding electronic therapy. http://www.metanoia.org

NetPsychology Explores the delivery of psychological services on the Internet. http://netpsych.com/

Science & Pseudoscience Review in Mental Health A review of therapies that are considered to be scientifically dubious. http://www.pseudoscience.org/

Types of Therapies Describes four different approaches to therapy. http://www.grohol.com/therapy.htm

 InfoTrac College Edition For more information about topics in the Psychology in Action feature, use Key Words search for PSYCHOTHERAPY.

INTERACTIVE LEARNING

Psychology: An Interactive Journey Remember that Chapter 13 of the CD-ROM that came with this text has practice tests, flashcards, interactive exercises, a crossword puzzle, and other valuable materials to enhance your learning experience.

PsychNow! 7b. Major Psychological Therapies.

Psyk.trek 11. Abnormal Behaviour and Therapy.

Chart Your Progress

The questions that follow are only a sample of what you need to know. If you miss any of the items, you should review the entire chapter, do the exercises on the CD, and review the Knowledge Builders. Another way to prepare for tests is to get more practice with *WebTutor*, the *Study Guide*, or the *Practice Quizzes* that are available with this text.

1. An approach that is incompatible with insight therapy is
   a. individual therapy
   b. action therapy
   c. non-directive therapy
   d. group therapy

2. Which of the following is NOT a psychoanalytic concept?
   a. free association
   b. resistance
   c. transference
   d. trepanning

3. Carl Rogers did not believe in using _____ in therapy.
   a. empathy
   b. authenticity
   c. reflection
   d. confrontation

4. To date, the most defensible form of "distance therapy" is
   a. media psychology
   b. commercial telephone counselling
   c. Internet-based cybertherapy
   d. telehealth

5. Classical conditioning principles are the basis for
   a. aversion therapy
   b. time out
   c. token economies
   d. EMDR

6. A psychologist interested in overgeneralization and irrational beliefs is obviously a proponent of
   a. exposure therapy
   b. token economies
   c. systematic desensitization
   d. cognitive therapy

7. The mirror technique is frequently used in
   a. exposure therapy
   b. psychodrama
   c. family therapy
   d. EMDR

8. Emotional rapport, warmth, understanding, acceptance, and empathy are the core of
   a. the therapeutic alliance
   b. large-group awareness training
   c. role reversals
   d. action therapies

9. ECT is classified as a type of
   a. somatic therapy
   b. pharmacotherapy
   c. psychosurgery
   d. deep lesioning

10. The tension-release method is an important part of
    a. covert reinforcement
    b. thought stopping
    c. desensitization
    d. peer counselling

Answers:

Chapter 14

Psychologist's Journal

THE SOCIAL ANIMAL

Humans are pack animals—we live in groups, like dogs and zebras. But human behaviour is vastly more complex than dog behaviour. Not surprisingly, the ways that our behaviour is shaped by our group are also more complex. Few demonstrations of that complexity are more compelling than the story of the Jumping Frenchmen of Maine. These are Quebecers living in the Beauce region who show extraordinary startle reactions. When startled, they jump, yell, lash out, and demonstrate "forced obedience"; that is, they do anything they are told to do no matter how silly.

Jumping was first reported by George Beard in 1878, who thought it was a physiological problem. More recently, University of Montreal neurologists Marie-Helene and Jean-Marc Sainte-Hilaire and psychologist Luc Granger have argued for a social origin (Sainte-Hilaire, Sainte-Hilaire, & Granger, 1986). The men of the Beauce have traditionally worked in the lumber camps of Maine. Life in those camps was always difficult, and amusements were scarce. Through long, cold winters, up to 75 men would live in close quarters in a remote camp. Almost the only entertainment they had was to startle jumpers. "An old lumberjack recalls that on the first day of work somebody would yell to discover who was the jumper in the group" (Sainte-Hilaire et al., 1986, p. 1271). Jumpers got something out of the process—attention—which they valued because they were shy. When individual jumpers left the camps and got less attention, their jumping occurred less frequently.

Jumping and related behaviours are examples of startle behaviours, but they are not simply physiological reflexes. The exact details vary with culture. The particular behaviours, the circumstances in which they are elicited, and who may do the teasing differ from culture to culture. Those variations illustrate the themes of this chapter: How do people negotiate influence and status? How do they behave in groups? How does their behaviour change with the social context in which they find themselves?

Social behaviour has been the target of an immense amount of study—too much, in fact, for us to cover in detail. Therefore, this chapter is a social psychology "sampler." We hope that the topics we have selected for this final chapter will prove to be interesting and thought provoking.

Survey Questions

- Why do people affiliate? What factors influence interpersonal attraction?
- How does group membership affect individual behaviour?
- What have social psychologists learned about conformity, obedience, compliance, and self-assertion?
- How are attitudes acquired and changed?
- Under what conditions is persuasion most effective?
- Is brainwashing actually possible? How are people converted to cult membership?
- What causes prejudice and intergroup conflict?
- How do psychologists explain human aggression?
- Why are bystanders so often unwilling to help in an emergency?
- What can be done to lower prejudice and promote social harmony?

▶ Affiliation and Attraction—Come Together

Survey Question:
- Why do people affiliate? What factors influence interpersonal attraction?

Social psychology The scientific study of how individuals behave, think, and feel in social situations.

Need to affiliate The desire to associate with other people.

Social psychology is the scientific study of how people behave, think, and feel in social situations (that is, in the presence, actual or implied, of others) (Baron & Byrne, 1997). Each of us is immersed in a complex and colourful social world. But what brings us together in the first place? The **need to affiliate** (associate with other people) is based on basic human desires for approval, support, friendship, and information. We also seek the company of others to alleviate fear or anxiety. An experiment in which college women were threatened with electric shock illustrates this point.

Zilstein's Shock Shop

A man introduced as Dr. Gregor Zilstein ominously explained to arriving participants, "We would like to give each of you a series of electric shocks . . . these shocks will hurt, they will be painful." In the room was a frightening electrical device that seemed to verify Zilstein's plans. While waiting to be shocked, each woman was given a choice of waiting alone or with other participants. Women frightened in this way more often chose to wait with others; those who expected the shock to be "a mild tickle or tingle" were more willing to wait alone. (Schachter, 1959)

Apparently, the frightened women found it comforting to be with others. Should we conclude that "misery loves company"? Actually, this is not entirely correct. In a later experiment, women expecting to be shocked were given the option of waiting with other shock recipients, with women waiting to see their college advisers, or alone. Most women chose to wait with other future "victims." In short, misery seems to love miserable company! In general, we prefer to be with people in circumstances similar to our own (Gump & Kulik, 1997).

Is there a reason for that? Yes. Other people provide information for evaluating our own reactions. When a situation is threatening or unfamiliar, or when we are in doubt, social comparisons guide our behaviour (Banaji & Prentice, 1994).

Social Comparison Theory

If you want to know how tall you are, you can get out a tape measure. But how do you know if you are a good athlete, guitarist, worker, parent, or friend? How do you know if your views on politics, religion, or grunge rock are unusual or widely shared? When there are no objective standards, the only available yardstick is provided by comparing yourself to others (Festinger, 1954).

Social psychologist Leon Festinger (1919–1989) theorized that group membership fills needs for **social comparison** (comparing your own actions, feelings, opinions, or abilities to those of others). Have you ever "compared notes" with other students after taking an exam? ("How did you do?" "Wasn't that last question hard?") If you have, you were satisfying needs for social comparison.

Social comparisons are not made randomly or on some ultimate scale. To illustrate, let's ask a student named Wendy if she is a good tennis player. If Wendy compares herself to a professional, the answer will be no. But this tells us little about her relative ability. Within her tennis group, Wendy is regarded as an excellent player. Meaningful evaluations are based on comparing yourself with people of similar backgrounds, abilities, and circumstances (Miller, Turnbull, & McFarland, 1988). On a fair scale of comparison, Wendy knows she is good and she takes pride in her tennis skills. In the same way, thinking of yourself as successful, talented, responsible, or fairly paid depends entirely on whom you choose for comparison. In general, social comparison theory holds that desires for self-evaluation provide a motive for associating with others. In doing so, they influence which groups we join.

Don't people also affiliate out of attraction for one another? They do, of course. Let's see why.

Interpersonal Attraction

"Birds of a feather flock together." "Familiarity breeds contempt." "Opposites attract." "Absence makes the heart grow fonder." Are these statements true? Actually, the folklore about friendship is, at best, a mixture of fact and fiction.

What does attract people to each other? **Interpersonal attraction** (affinity to another person) is the basis for most voluntary social relationships. As you might expect, we look for friends and lovers who are kind and understanding, who have attractive personalities, and who like us in return (Sprecher, 1998). In addition, several less obvious factors influence attraction.

ATTRACTION IN CHILDREN   How do children choose their friends? Young children make unsophisticated judgments in many areas, so we might ask, What characteristics draw them to other people? Researchers at McGill University, Frances Aboud and Morton Mendelson, found that for young children similarities in sex, age, race, and preferred activity were more important in determining attraction than attitudes, values, or self-esteem (Aboud & Mendelson, 1998). Does this change with age? William Bukowski of Concordia University in Montreal observed that during the transition to junior high school, children are increasingly drawn to aggressive boys and to peers who "stand out" (Bukowski, Sippola, & Newcomb, 2000). The attraction to children with good classroom behaviour decreases during this period.

Whom children are attracted to has important consequences, as shown by a number of large-scale, longitudinal studies by Frank Vitaro and his colleagues at the University of Montreal. Vitaro has reported links between a child's delinquency and his or her best friend's delinquency (Vitaro, Brendgen, & Tremblay, 2000). Further, children with aggressive friends are more likely to choose aggressive solutions to problems, and children with prosocial friends are more likely to choose prosocial solutions (Brendgen et al., 1999).

PHYSICAL ATTRACTIVENESS   People who are **physically attractive** are regarded as good-looking by other members of their culture. Beautiful people tend to be rated as more appealing than average-looking people. This is due, in part, to the **halo effect,** a tendency to generalize a favourable impression to unrelated personal characteristics. Because of it, we assume that beautiful people are also likable, intelligent, warm, witty, mentally healthy, and socially skilled (Feingold, 1992). However, physical attractiveness actually has almost no connection to intelligence, talents, or abilities (Feingold, 1992). Perhaps that's why beauty mainly affects our initial interest in getting acquainted with others (Keller & Young, 1996). Later, more meaningful personal qualities gain in importance (Berscheid, 1994).

Social comparison Making judgments about ourselves through comparison with others.

Interpersonal attraction Social attraction to another person.

Physical attractiveness A person's degree of physical beauty, as defined by his or her culture.

Halo effect The tendency to generalize a favourable first impression to unrelated personal characteristics.

Physical beauty can be socially advantageous because of the widespread belief that "what is beautiful is good." However, physical beauty is generally unrelated to actual personal traits and talents.

In college dormitories, roommates who are similar in personality and physical attractiveness tend to be more satisfied with their relationship (Carli, Ganley, & Pierce-Otay, 1991).

Competence The degree of general ability or proficiency a person displays.

Similarity The extent to which two people are alike in background, age, interests, attitudes, beliefs, and so forth.

Self-disclosure The process of revealing private thoughts, feelings, and one's personal history to others.

Physical attractiveness is less important in some cultures even for spurring that initial interest. University of Toronto psychologists Kenneth and Karen Dion suggested that in "collectivist" cultures (in which teamwork and the good of the group are more important than the success of the individual) physical attractiveness may not produce the same halo effect. Dion, Pak, and Dion (1990) reported that Chinese students studying at the University of Toronto, when asked to rate the personalities of people shown in pictures, did not rate the physically attractive people more favourably than those who were less physically attractive. They did, however, rate expected life outcome higher for more attractive people—suggesting, perhaps, that they think other people might be biased in favour of physically attractive people.

COMPETENCE   People who are **competent** display a high degree of knowledge, ability, or proficiency. All other things being equal, we are more attracted to people who are talented or competent. However, there's an interesting twist to this. In a revealing study, college students listened to audiotapes of supposed candidates for a "College Quiz Bowl." Two of the candidates seemed to be highly intelligent. The other two were depicted as average in ability. In addition, one "intelligent" candidate and one "average" candidate clumsily spilled coffee on himself. Later, students rated the intelligent candidate who blundered as most attractive. The least attractive person was the candidate who was average and clumsy (Aronson, 1969). Thus, the superior but clumsy person was more attractive than the person who was only superior. The upshot seems to be that we like people who are competent but imperfect—which makes them more "human."

SIMILARITY   Take a moment to make a list of your closest friends. What do they have in common (other than the joy of knowing you)? It is likely that most are similar to you in age and of the same sex and race as you are. There will be exceptions, of course. But similarity on these three dimensions is the general rule for friendships.

Similarity refers to how alike you are to another person in background, age, interests, attitudes, beliefs, and so forth. Social psychologists have repeatedly found that similar people are attracted to each other (Carli, Ganley, & Pierce-Otay, 1991). And why not? It's reinforcing to see our beliefs and attitudes shared by others. It shows we are "right" and reveals that they are clever people as well (Alicke, Yurak, & Vredenburg, 1996)! In fact, according to University of British Columbia psychologist Stanley Coren, some people are so influenced by similarity that they choose dogs that look like them (Coren, 1999). Female college students in Coren's study judged the desirability of four breeds of dogs, two with lop ears (ears that hang down) and two with prick ears (shorter ears that stand up). Long-haired women preferred lop-eared dogs, while short-haired women preferred prick-eared dogs.

Does similarity also influence mate selection? For an answer to this question, read "Selecting a Mate."

Self-Disclosure

How do people who are not yet friends learn if they are similar? To get acquainted you must be willing to talk about more than just the weather, sports, or nuclear physics. At some point you must begin to share private thoughts and feelings and reveal yourself to others. This process, which is called **self-disclosure,** is essential for developing close relationships. Lack of self-disclosure is associated with anxiety, unhappiness, and loneliness (Meleshko & Alden, 1993; Mikulincer & Nachshon, 1991).

We more often reveal ourselves to persons we like than to those we find unattractive. Disclosure also requires a degree of trust. Many people play it safe, or "close to the vest," with people they do not know well. Indeed, self-disclosure is governed by unspoken rules about what's acceptable. We might ask whether jumping (the extreme startle response discussed at the beginning of the chapter) is a form of self-disclosure gone wrong. Like the

FOCUS ON RESEARCH | **Selecting a Mate—Reflections in a Social Mirror**

Ninety percent of all people in Western societies marry at some point. What, beyond attraction, determines how people pair up? The answer is that we tend to marry someone who is like us in almost every way, a pattern called **homogamy** (huh-MOG-ah-me) (Caspi & Herbener, 1990).

Studies show that married couples are highly similar in age, education, race, religion, and ethnic background. In addition, the correlation between their attitudes and opinions is .5. For mental abilities it is .4, and for socioeconomic status, height, weight, and eye colour it is .3. In general, you are far more likely to choose someone similar to yourself as a mate than someone very different. This is probably a good thing. Personality traits tend to be closely matched in the most stable marriages (Kim, Martin, & Martin, 1989). Conversely, the risk of divorce is highest among couples with sizable differences in age

and education (Tzeng, 1992). Most dangerous of all are "fatal attractions," in which qualities that originally made a partner appealing are later disliked. Fatal attractions are likely when an individual is drawn to someone who seems "different," "unique," or "extreme." When two people are similar, disenchantment is less likely to occur (Felmlee, 1998).

Do people look for specific traits in a potential mate? Yes, in North America, both men and women agree that the most important qualities are kindness and understanding, intelligence, exciting personality, good health, adaptability, and physical attractiveness (Buss, 1985). However, women apparently season romance with a dash of practicality. Women regard intelligence, ambition, success, and status as more important in a potential mate than men do (Townsend & Wasserman, 1998). Notice, though, that kindness and understanding are still ranked first by both men and women (Hatfield & Sprecher, 1995).

Homogamy Marriage of two people who are similar to one another.

Reciprocity A reciprocal interchange or return in kind.

Overdisclosure Self-disclosure that exceeds what is appropriate for a particular relationship or social situation.

more familiar version of disclosure, jumping is governed by unspoken rules and reveals something about both the jumper and the person who startles him. But jumping is a counterfeit of disclosure—an attempt to get the benefits (attention, acceptance, connection) without taking the risks.

In the normal case, moderate self-disclosure leads to **reciprocity** (a return in kind). Overdisclosure, however, gives rise to suspicion and it reduces attraction. **Overdisclosure** is self-disclosure that exceeds what is appropriate for a relationship or social situation. What counts as excessive disclosure varies from culture to culture. A dramatic illustration of this point is the fact that the Cree people of northern Quebec have ejected seven out of eight teams of psychological researchers who have come to study them. Among the ways these researchers have offended the Cree are by asking them for self-disclosure, a socially inappropriate activity (Darou, Kurtness, & Hum, 2000). We'll have more to say on this issue when we discuss cohesion among North American Aboriginal groups below.

How is it that we know when it is appropriate to disclose feelings and when it isn't? We learn the standards of our culture as children. Working with children in grades 5 and 6, Nina Howe and colleagues at Concordia University found that both boys' and girls' willingness to disclose thoughts and feelings to a sibling was largely determined by the warmth of the relationship, rather than by the frequency of joint activities. In contrast, Laurie McNelles and Jennifer Connelly of York University reported that intimacy between friends increased between grades 9 and 11. For girls, the increase was fostered by discussion and self-disclosure. For boys, what mattered was shared activities (McNelles & Connelly, 1999). It remains to be seen whether the difference in these two patterns of development reflects the different age groups (grades 5 and 6 versus grades 9 to 11) or situation (with family versus with friends), or both.

Notice that both the Concordia and the York researchers studied the development of intimacy over a period of years. When self-disclosure proceeds at a moderate pace, it is accompanied by growing trust and intimacy. When it is too rapid or inappropriate, we are likely to "back off" and wonder about the person's motives. Thus, as friends talk, they influence each other in ways that gradually deepen the level of liking, trust, and self-disclosure (Miller, 1990).

▶ Loving and Liking—Dating, Rating, Mating

Romantic love Love that is associated with high levels of interpersonal attraction, heightened arousal, mutual absorption, and sexual desire.

Mutual absorption With regard to romantic love, the nearly exclusive attention lovers give to one another.

Liking A relationship based on intimacy, but lacking passion and commitment.

Evolutionary psychology Study of the evolutionary origins of human behaviour patterns.

How does romantic attraction differ from interpersonal attraction? **Romantic love** is based on interpersonal attraction, but it also involves high levels of emotional arousal and/or sexual desire (Regan, 1998) and **mutual absorption** (lovers paying attention almost exclusively to each other). To investigate love, psychologist Zick Rubin (1973) chose to think of it as an attitude held by one person toward another. This allowed him to develop "liking" and "love" scales to measure each "attitude." Next, he asked dating couples to complete the scales twice; once with their date in mind and once for a close friend of the same sex.

What were the results? Love for partners and friends differed more than liking did. (**Liking** is affection without passion or deep commitment.) Basically, dating couples like and love their partners, but mostly they just like their friends. Women, however, were a little more "loving" of their friends than men were. Does this reflect real differences in the strength of male friendships and female friendships? Maybe not, since it is more acceptable in our culture for women to express love for one another than it is for men. Nevertheless, another study confirmed that dating couples feel a mixture of love and friendship for their partners. In fact, 44 percent of a group of dating persons named their romantic partner as their closest friend (Hendrick & Hendrick, 1993).

As is often the case, we must note that these results were obtained in a particular cultural context (North America). Remember the finding that Chinese students at the University of Toronto showed less physical attractiveness bias in personality ratings? Kenneth and Karen Dion argue, too, that romantic love is more likely to be the basis of a long-term relationship in Western societies (which value individualism) than in the "collectivistic" societies (typical in Asia). In China, India, and Japan, for example, marriages have traditionally been arranged, with the welfare of the entire family in mind. After marrying, husbands and wives typically develop their most important relationships not with each other but with a social network. In China and India, the network centres on the husband's extended family. In Japan, it tends to involve associates at work (for the husband) or children and old friends (for the wife) (Dion & Dion, 1993).

Evolution and Mate Selection

Evolutionary psychology is the study of the evolutionary origins of human behaviour patterns. Many psychologists believe that evolution left an imprint on men and women that influences everything from sexual attraction and infidelity to jealousy and divorce.

In a study of 37 cultures on six continents, David Buss found the following patterns: Compared with women, men are more interested in casual sex; they prefer younger, more physically attractive partners; and they get more jealous over real or imagined sexual infidelities than they do over a loss of emotional commitment. Compared with men, women prefer slightly older partners who appear to be industrious, higher in status, or economically successful; women are more upset by a partner who becomes emotionally involved with someone else, rather than one who is sexually unfaithful (Buss, 1994; Buss et al., 1992) (see ▶Figure 14.1).

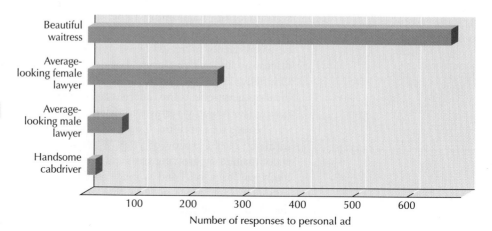

▶Figure 14.1

What do people look for when considering potential dating partners? Here are the results of a study in which personal ads were placed in newspapers. As you can see, men were more influenced by looks, and women by success (Goode, 1996).

Number of responses to personal ad

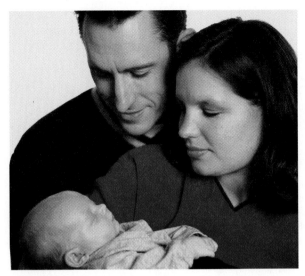

According to evolutionary psychologists, women tend to be concerned with whether mates will devote time and resources to a relationship. Men place more emphasis on physical attractiveness and sexual fidelity.

Why do such differences exist? Buss and others believe that mating preferences evolved in response to the differing reproductive challenges faced by men and women. As a rule, women must invest more time and energy in reproduction and nurturing the young than men do. Consequently, women evolved an interest in whether their partners will stay with them and whether their mates have the resources to provide for their children (Archer, 1996).

In contrast, the reproductive success of men depends on their mates' fertility. Men, therefore, tend to look for health, youth, and beauty in a prospective mate, as signs of suitability for reproduction (Pines, 1998). This preference, perhaps, is why some older men abandon their first wives in favour of young, beautiful "trophy wives." Evolutionary theory further explains that the male emphasis on their mates' sexual fidelity is based on concerns about the paternity of offspring. From a biological perspective, men do not benefit from investing resources in children they did not sire (Schmitt & Buss, 1996).

A sizable body of evidence supports the evolutionary view of mating preferences. However, it is important to remember that evolved mating tendencies are subtle at best and easily overruled by other factors. It is possible, for example, that the differences between women and men will be reduced as women become increasingly self-supporting. A hint of such a change is contained in a study conducted by Thomas Hadjistavropoulos and Myles Genest (1994) at the University of British Columbia in Vancouver. They asked 80 young women to rate the dating desirability of potential male partners for whom they received a personality profile and a picture. Later, the women were asked which characteristics had influenced their ratings. Some of the women were connected to a machine they thought was a lie detector. The others were not. Those connected to the machine reported a stronger influence of physical attractiveness on their ratings than those who didn't think their responses could be checked! As they feel more capable of looking after themselves (and their children), women may adopt different criteria for mate selection. Most important of all, however, remember that when either men or women choose mates, kindness and intelligence still rate highest. They are love's greatest allies.

Needs for affiliation and interpersonal attraction inevitably bring people together in groups. In the next section we will explore several interesting aspects of group membership. But first, here's a chance to review what you have learned.

Knowledge builder

AFFILIATION, FRIENDSHIP, AND LOVE

Relate

How has social comparison affected your behaviour? Has it influenced who you associate with?

Think of three close friends. Which of the attraction factors described earlier apply to your friendships?

To what extent do Rubin's findings about love and liking match your own experiences?

Learning Check

1. Women threatened with electric shock in an experiment generally chose to wait alone or with other women not taking part in the experiment. T or F?
2. Interpersonal attraction is increased by all but one of the following. (Which does not fit?)
   a. competence *b.* similarity *c.* overdisclosure

continued

3. High levels of self-disclosure are reciprocated in most social encounters. T or F?
4. Women rate their friends higher on Rubin's love scale than do men. T or F?
5. The most striking finding about marriage patterns is that most people choose mates whose personalities are quite unlike their own. T or F?

6. Compared with men, women tend to be more upset by sexual infidelity than by a loss of emotional commitment on the part of their mates. T or F?

7. Why might children making the transition to junior high school be drawn to peers who "stand out?"

Answers:

1. F 2. c 3. F 4. T 5. F 6. F 7. Part of the task of children entering their teens is to establish their own identity as independent persons. That can be achieved through deliberate alteration of appearance and behaviour. At the same time, children do not usually want a complete break with their family or their past. Perhaps the two needs—to strike out on your own and to stay in touch—can be met by associating with peers who stand out while not standing out yourself. That is, for some children the solution may be "a foot in both worlds."

▶ Life in Groups—People, People, Everywhere

Survey Question:
■ How does group membership affect individual behaviour?

Each person belongs to many overlapping social groups: families, teams, church groups, work groups, and so on. In each group we occupy a position in the structure of the group. **Social roles** are patterns of behaviour expected of persons in various social positions. For instance, playing the roles of mother, boss, or student involves different sets of behaviours and expectations. Some roles are **ascribed** (they are assigned to a person or are not under personal control): male or female, son, adolescent, inmate. **Achieved roles** are attained voluntarily or by special effort: spouse, teacher, scientist, band leader.

What effect does role-playing have on behaviour? Roles streamline daily interactions by allowing us to anticipate the behaviour of others. When a person is acting as a doctor, mother, clerk, or police officer, we expect certain behaviours. However, roles have a negative side too. Many people experience **role conflicts,** in which two or more roles make conflicting demands on behaviour. Consider, for example, a teacher who must flunk a close friend's daughter. Likewise, the clashing demands of work, family, and school create role conflicts for many students (Hammer, Grigsby, & Woods, 1998).

Group Structure, Cohesion, and Norms

Are there other dimensions of group membership? Two important dimensions of any group are its structure and cohesiveness. **Group structure** consists of the network of roles, communication pathways, and power in a group. Organized groups such as an army or an athletic team have a high degree of structure. Informal friendship groups may or may not be very structured.

Group cohesiveness is basically the degree of attraction among group members or their commitment to remaining in the group. Members of cohesive groups literally stick together: They tend to stand or sit close together, they pay more attention to one another, and they show more signs of mutual affection. Also, their behaviour tends to be closely coordinated (Levine & Moreland, 1990). Cohesiveness is the basis for much of the power that groups exert over their members. Therapy groups, businesses, sports teams, and the like often actively seek to strengthen group cohesion. One reason for this is that members of cohesive groups tend to work better together (Craig & Kelly, 1999).

Clare Brant, a Mohawk psychiatrist from the Bay of Quinte, Ontario, has written about the extent to which values and attitudes that promote group cohesion still influence the behaviour of Aboriginal peoples (Brant, 1990, 1995). Group cohesion was historically important for North American Native people. They could not survive in a harsh environment without being in a group. To live together "cheek by jowl" all their lives, they developed a value system that discouraged conflict. The group-promotion values include non-interference, non-competitiveness, emotional restraint, and sharing. In addition,

Social role Expected behaviour patterns associated with particular social positions (such as daughter, worker, student).

Ascribed role A role that is assigned to a person; a role one has no choice about playing.

Achieved role A role that is assumed voluntarily.

Role conflict Trying to occupy two or more roles that make conflicting demands on behaviour.

Group structure The network of roles, communication pathways, and power in a group.

Group cohesiveness The degree of attraction among group members or their commitment to remaining in the group.

Native culture developed teasing, shaming, and ridiculing as tools to police behaviours that reduced conformity—something Natives share with non-Natives, as we'll see below.

STATUS In addition to defining roles, a person's social position within groups determines his or her **status,** or level of social power and importance. In most groups, higher status bestows special privileges and respect. Given better treatment for people with higher status, we should note a report from the Ivey Business School at the University of Western Ontario. Mitch Rothstein and his colleagues surveyed managers in several large Canadian corporations. Their data suggested that male and female managers get similar amounts of support from their social networks within the company, but that on average, the members of female managers' networks have lower status than the members of male managers' networks (Rothstein, Burke, & Bristor, 2001).

NORMS We are also greatly affected by group norms. A **norm** is an accepted (but often unspoken) standard for appropriate behaviour. If you have the slightest doubt about the power of norms, try this test: Board a crowded bus, find a seat, and begin singing loudly in your fullest voice. Probably only one person in 100 could actually carry out these instructions.

The impact of norms is shown by a recent study at the University of Western Ontario. According to Gammage, Carron, and Estabrooks (2001), students felt that off-season practice was more likely for basketball players on highly cohesive teams with clear, familiar norms that called for high performance levels. Without such clear norms, high cohesion was expected to make off-season practice *less* likely—even than in groups low in cohesion. Thus, if people feel a responsibility to their group, and if the group sets clear goals, greater effort toward the group's goals will be forthcoming.

If you think about it, there's a lot of work involved in being a member of a group—learning the value system, working toward group goals, taking the ridicule if you step out of line. Why do we bother? Because we need the help the group gives us. For a classic example of people without a group, consider the plight of some immigrants to Canada who have left one group behind (in their country of origin) and may have difficulty joining a new one. Researchers at the Royal Ottawa Hospital recently studied the cases of 94 Canadian-born and 23 foreign-born people who committed suicide. The immigrants all lacked significant social support networks. This doesn't mean that anyone without a group will be suicidal, but it does suggest that group membership may help people deal with the stresses of daily life (Chandrasena, Beddage, & Fernando, 1991).

Making Attributions

Every day we must form impressions of people from only the smallest shreds of evidence. How do such impressions affect our behaviour? The answer lies in the process of **attribution.** As we observe others, we tend to make inferences about their actions. Why did Vonda insult Sutchai? Why did Nick change his college major? Why does Kirti talk so fast when she's around men? In answering such questions we *attribute* people's behaviour to various causes. Sometimes we are right about the causes of behaviour and sometimes we are wrong. Either way, it affects how we act in social situations. To learn how we fill in the "person behind the mask," let's explore the making of attributions.

Two people enter a restaurant and order different meals. Nell tastes her food, then salts it. Bert salts his food before he tastes it. How would you explain their behaviour? In Nell's case, you might assume that the food needed salt. If so, you have attributed her actions to an **external cause** (one that lies outside a person). With Bert, you might be more inclined to conclude that he must really like salt. If so, you would be saying that the cause of his behaviour is internal. **Internal causes** of behaviour are assumed to lie within a person. Examples are needs, preferences, and personality traits.

What effects do such interpretations have? It is difficult to fully understand social behaviour without considering the attributions we make. For instance, let's say that at the last five parties you've been to, you've seen a woman named Macy. Based on this, you assume that Macy is very outgoing and likes to socialize. You see Macy at yet another gathering and mention that she seems to like parties. She says, "Actually, I hate these parties, but I

Status An individual's position in a social structure, especially with respect to power, privilege, or importance.

Norm An accepted (but often unspoken) standard of conduct for appropriate behaviour.

Attribution The process of making inferences about the causes of one's own behaviour and that of others.

External cause A cause of behaviour that is assumed to lie outside a person.

Internal cause A cause of behaviour that is assumed to lie within a person—for instance, a need, preference, or personality trait.

get invited to play my tuba at them. My music teacher says I need to practise in front of an audience, so I keep attending these dumb events. Want to hear a Sousa march?"

We seldom know the real reasons for others' actions. That is why we tend to infer causes from circumstances. However, in doing so, we often make mistakes like the one with Macy. The most common error is to attribute the actions of others to internal causes (Jones & Nisbett, 1971). This mistake is called the **fundamental attributional error.** We tend to think the actions of others have internal causes even if they are actually caused by external circumstances.

Where our own behaviour is concerned, we are more likely to think that external causes explain our actions. In other words, there is an **actor-observer bias** in how we explain behaviour. As *observers,* we attribute the behaviour of others to their wants, motives, and personality traits (this is the fundamental attributional error). As *actors,* we tend to find external explanations for our own behaviour (Krueger, Ham, & Linford, 1996). No doubt you chose your major in school because of what it has to offer. Other students choose their majors because of the kind of people they are. Other people who don't leave tips in restaurants are cheapskates. If you don't leave a tip it's because the service was bad. And, of course, other people are always late because they are irresponsible. You are late because you were held up by events beyond your control.

An interesting real-world observation shows an actor-observer bias among physically disabled children. Yvonne Bohr of the University of Toronto assessed friendship quality and social attributions among physically disabled and non-disabled children aged 10 to 14 years (Bohr, 2000). Among other findings, physically disabled children were less likely than non-disabled children to attribute positive social outcomes to other people. They were also less likely to acknowledge their own portion of responsibility for negative social outcomes. Perhaps physically disabled children, as they experience the inability to do certain things other people can do, internalize and extend that inability, and they come to see themselves as less able than other people to have any effect on the world—even a negative effect.

YE OLD DOUBLE STANDARD   Research on attribution has revealed an interesting double standard regarding the abilities of men and women. Lisa Sinclair of the University of Winnipeg analyzed student evaluations of instructors, both in a lab experiment and using actual course evaluations. She found that women instructors were viewed as less competent than men only when they gave students low marks. Women who gave higher marks were considered to be as competent as men giving similar marks (Sinclair & Kunda, 2000).

As early as *kindergarten,* boys tend to take credit for successes. Girls, in contrast, tend to discount their own performances ("put themselves down") (Burgner & Hewstone, 1993). In general, there is a strong tendency to assume "He's skilled, she's lucky" when assessing the performances of men and women (Swim & Sanna, 1996). Throughout life, such attributions no doubt dog the heels of many talented and successful women.

Fundamental attributional error The tendency to attribute the behaviour of others to internal causes (personality, likes, and so forth).

Actor-observer bias The tendency to attribute the behaviour of others to internal causes while attributing one's own behaviour to external causes (situations and circumstances).

Social influence Changes in a person's behaviour induced by the presence or actions of others.

► Social Influence—Follow the Leader

Survey Question:
■ What have social psychologists learned about conformity, obedience, compliance, and self-assertion?

No topic lies nearer the heart of social psychology than **social influence** (changes in behaviour induced by the actions of others). When people interact, they almost always affect one another's behaviour. For example, in a sidewalk experiment, various numbers of people stood on a busy New York City street. On cue they all looked at a sixth-floor window across the street. A camera recorded the number of passersby who also stopped to stare. The larger the influencing group, the more people were swayed to join in staring at the window (Milgram, Bickman, & Berkowitz, 1969).

Are there different kinds of social influence? Social influence ranges from simple suggestion to intensive indoctrination (brainwashing). Our daily behaviour is probably most influenced by group pressures for conformity. Conformity typically occurs when people become aware of differences between themselves and the actions, norms, or values of others (Baron & Byrne, 1997). We all conform to a degree. In fact, some uniformity is a necessity. Imagine being totally unable to anticipate the actions of others. In stores, schools, and homes this would be frustrating and disturbing. On the highways it would be lethal.

Conformity

When John first started working at the Fleegle Flange Factory, he found it easy to process 300 flanges an hour. Others around him averaged only 200. John's co-workers told him to slow down and take it easy. "I get bored," he said and continued to do 300 flanges an hour. At first John was welcomed, but now conversations broke up when he approached. Other workers laughed at him or ignored him when he spoke. Although he never made a conscious decision to conform, in another week John's output had slowed to 200 flanges an hour. Perhaps the most basic of all group norms is, as John discovered, "Thou shalt conform." Like it or not, life is filled with instances of **conformity** (bringing one's own behaviour into agreement with norms or the behaviour of others). And that is not always a bad thing—doing what other people do will often lead to adaptive behaviour, when what those other people did worked. That is, there may be some evolutionary advantage to doing the safe thing (conforming) rather than the risky thing (choosing a new, untried behaviour).

THE ASCH EXPERIMENT *How strong are group pressures for conformity?* One of the better-known experiments on conformity was staged by Solomon Asch (1907–1996). Asch's study is best appreciated by imagining yourself as a subject. Assume that you are seated at a table with six other students. Your task is actually quite simple. On each trial you are shown three lines. Your job is to select the line that matches a "standard" line (see ▶ Figure 14.2).

As the testing begins, each person announces an answer for the first card. When your turn comes, you agree with the others. "This isn't hard at all," you say to yourself. For several more trials your answers agree with those of the group. Then comes a shock. All six people announce that line 1 matches the standard, and you were about to say line 2 matches. Suddenly you feel alone and upset. You nervously look at the lines again. The room falls silent. Everyone seems to be staring at you. The experimenter awaits your answer. Do you yield to the group?

In this experiment the other "students" were all accomplices who gave the wrong answer on about a third of the trials to create group pressure (Asch, 1956). Real students conformed to the group on about one-third of the critical trials. Of those tested, 75 percent yielded at least once. People tested alone erred in less than 1 percent of their judgments. Clearly, those who yielded to group pressures were denying what their eyes told them.

Are some people more susceptible to group pressures than others? People with high needs for structure or certainty are more likely to conform. So are people who are anxious, low in self-confidence, or concerned about the approval of others. People who live in cultures that emphasize group cooperation (such as many Asian cultures) are also more likely to conform (Bond & Smith, 1996). University of Western Ontario psychologists Leslie Janes and James Olson showed that conformity is particularly likely when people want to avoid standing out (Janes & Olson, 2000). They coined the term *jeer pressure* for this phenomenon. In these studies, some subjects observed someone else being ridiculed for a physical characteristic or failure on a task. These subjects subsequently showed more conformity and greater fear of failure in several tasks than other subjects who had not witnessed the ridicule.

In addition to personal characteristics, certain situations tend to encourage conformity—sometimes with disastrous results. "Groupthink—Agreement at Any Cost" on page 538 offers a prime example.

GROUP FACTORS IN CONFORMITY *How do groups enforce norms?* In most groups, we have been rewarded with acceptance and approval for conformity and threatened with rejection or ridicule for non-conformity. These reactions are called **group sanctions.** Negative sanctions range from laughter, staring, or social disapproval to complete rejection or formal

---

Conformity Bringing one's behaviour into agreement or harmony with norms or with the behaviour of others in a group.

Group sanctions Rewards and punishments (such as approval or disapproval) administered by groups to enforce conformity among members.

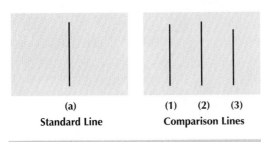

(a)
Standard Line

(1)　(2)　(3)
Comparison Lines

▶**Figure 14.2**

Stimuli used in Solomon Asch's conformity experiments.

USING PSYCHOLOGY   Groupthink—Agreement at Any Cost

What happens when people in positions of power fall prey to pressures for conformity? To find out, Yale psychologist Irving Janis (1918–1990) analyzed a series of disastrous decisions made by government officials. His conclusion? Many such fiascoes are the result of **groupthink**—a compulsion by decision makers to maintain each other's approval, even at the cost of critical thinking (Janis, 1989).

Groupthink has been blamed for many embarrassments, such as John F. Kennedy's backing of the Bay of Pigs invasion in Cuba and Ronald Reagan's Iran-Contra scandal. It also seems to have contributed to the 1986 *Challenger* space shuttle disaster and the loss, in 1999, of the US$165-million *Mars Climate Orbiter*. An analysis of 19 international crises found that groupthink contributed to most (Schafer & Crichlow, 1996).

The core of groupthink is misguided loyalty. Group members are hesitant to "rock the boat" or question sloppy thinking. This self-censorship leads people to believe they agree more than they actually do (Bernthal & Insko, 1993; Esser, 1998).

To prevent groupthink, group leaders should take the following steps:

- Define each group member's role as a "critical evaluator."
- Avoid revealing any personal preferences in the beginning.
- State the problem factually, without bias.
- Invite a group member or outside person to play devil's advocate.
- Make it clear that group members will be held accountable for decisions.
- Encourage open inquiry and a search for alternative solutions (Chen et al., 1996; Kroon, Van Kreveld, & Rabbie, 1992).

In addition, Janis suggested that there should be a "second-chance" meeting to re-evaluate important decisions. That is, each decision should be reached twice.

In an age clouded by the threat of war, meltdowns, and similar disasters, even stronger solutions to the problem of groupthink would be welcome. Perhaps we should form a group to think about it!

Groupthink A compulsion by members of decision-making groups to maintain agreement, even at the cost of critical thinking.

exclusion. If you've ever felt the sudden chill of disapproval by others, you will understand the power of group sanctions.

Wouldn't the effectiveness of group sanctions depend on the importance of the group? Yes. The more important group membership is to a person, the more he or she will be influenced by other group members. That's why the Asch experiments are impressive. Since the groups were only temporary, sanctions were informal and rejection had no lasting importance. Just the same, the power of the group was evident.

If the power of the group is seen with short-term exposure to temporary groups, how much stronger will it be with groups we identify with and spend years as members of? That is the situation many teenagers face. As Darcey Santor and his colleagues at Dalhousie

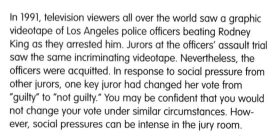

In 1991, television viewers all over the world saw a graphic videotape of Los Angeles police officers beating Rodney King as they arrested him. Jurors at the officers' assault trial saw the same incriminating videotape. Nevertheless, the officers were acquitted. In response to social pressure from other jurors, one key juror had changed her vote from "guilty" to "not guilty." You may be confident that you would not change your vote under similar circumstances. However, social pressures can be intense in the jury room.

University in Halifax have shown, peer pressure is extremely important to teens. In fact, Santor reported that pressure to conform was a better predictor of risky behaviour than the need to be popular. In other words, teens engaged in risky behaviours not to be popular, but in order to avoid standing out.

It's worth noting that psychologists are naturally concerned about conformity promoting risky behaviours. We don't ask whether the desire not to stand out sometimes leads teens to engage in safe behaviours! But remember psychiatrist Clare Brant's ideas about cohesion in Native communities—it evolved for a purpose. In the wilderness, the non-conformist wouldn't live long enough to have children.

Even more important than the size of the majority is its **unanimity** (unanimous agreement). Having at least one person in your corner can greatly reduce pressures to conform. When Asch gave subjects an ally (who also opposed the majority by giving the correct answer), conformity was lessened. In terms of numbers, a unanimous majority of three is more powerful than a majority of eight with one dissenting.

Unanimity Being unanimous or of one mind; agreement.

Knowledge builder

GROUPS, SOCIAL INFLUENCE, AND CONFORMITY

Relate

What are the most prominent roles you play? Which are achieved and which are ascribed? How do they affect your behaviour? What conflicts do they create?

Do you commit the fundamental attributional error? Try to think of a specific example that illustrates the concept.

Identify a recent time when you conformed in some way. How did norms, group pressure, sanctions, and unanimity contribute to your tendency to conform?

Learning Check

1. Status refers to a set of expected behaviours associated with a social position. T or F?
2. The fundamental attributional error is to attribute the actions of others to internal causes. T or F?

3. The effect one person's behaviour has on another is called
   _____.
4. Subjects in Solomon Asch's conformity study yielded on about 75 percent of the critical trials. T or F?
5. Non-conformity is punished by negative group
   _____.
6. Janis used the term _____ to describe a compulsion among decision-making groups to maintain an illusion of unanimity.

Critical Thinking

7. Would it be possible to be completely non-conforming (that is, to not conform to some group norm)?

Answers:

1. F 2. T 3. social influence 4. F 5. sanctions 6. groupthink 7. A person who did not follow at least some norms concerning normal social behaviour would very likely be perceived as extremely bizarre, disturbed, or psychotic.

▶ Obedience—Would You Electrocute a Stranger?

Strength is a quality possessed by individuals. Power is always social—it arises when people come together and disappears when they disperse. A person who has power in one situation may have very little in another. In those situations where a person has power, she or he is described as an *authority*. Let's investigate **obedience,** a special type of conformity to the demands of an authority.

Obedience Conformity to the demands of an authority.

The question is this: If ordered to do so, would you shock a man with a heart condition who is screaming and asking to be released? Certainly we can assume that few people would do so. Or can we? In Nazi Germany, obedient soldiers (once average citizens) helped slaughter over 6 million people in concentration camps. Do such inhumane acts reflect deep character flaws? Are they the acts of heartless psychopaths or crazed killers? Or are they simply the result of obedience to authority? What are the limits of obedience? These are questions that puzzled social psychologist Stanley Milgram (1965) when he began a provocative series of studies on obedience.

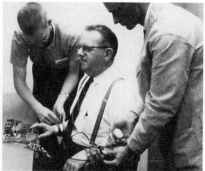

▶Figure 14.3

Scenes from Stanley Milgram's study of obedience: the "shock generator," strapping a "learner" into his chair, and a "teacher" being told to administer a severe shock to the learner.

How did Milgram study obedience? As was true of the Asch experiments, Milgram's research is best appreciated by imagining yourself as a subject. Place yourself in the following situation.

Milgram's Obedience Studies

Imagine answering a newspaper ad to take part in a "learning" experiment at Yale University. When you arrive, a coin is flipped and a second person, a pleasant-looking man in his 50s, is designated the "learner." By chance you have become the "teacher."

Your task is to read a list of word pairs. The learner's task is to memorize them. You are to punish him with an electric shock each time he makes a mistake. The learner is taken to an adjacent room and you watch as he is seated in an "electric chair" apparatus. Electrodes are attached to his wrists. You are then escorted to your position in front of a "shock generator." On this device is a row of 30 switches marked from 15 to 450 volts. Corresponding labels range from "Slight Shock" to "Extreme Intensity Shock" and finally "Danger Severe Shock." Your instructions are to shock the learner each time he makes a mistake. You are to begin with 15 volts and then move one switch (15 volts) higher for each additional mistake (see ▶Figure 14.3).

The experiment begins, and the learner soon makes his first error. You flip a switch. More mistakes. Rapidly you reach the 75-volt level. The learner moans after each shock. At 100 volts he complains that he has a heart condition. At 150 volts he says he no longer wants to continue and demands release. At 300 volts he screams and says he can no longer give answers.

At some point during the experiment, you begin to protest to the experimenter. "That man has a heart condition," you say; "I'm not going to kill that man." The experimenter says, "Please continue." Another shock and another scream from the learner and you say, "You mean I've got to keep going up the scale? No, sir. I'm not going to give him 450 volts!" The experimenter says, "The experiment requires that you continue." For a time the learner refuses to answer any more questions and screams with each shock (Milgram, 1965). Then he falls chillingly silent for the remainder of the experiment.

It's hard to believe many people would do this. What happened? Milgram also doubted that many people would obey his orders. When he polled a group of psychiatrists before the experiment, they predicted that less than 1 percent of those tested would obey. The astounding fact is that 65 percent obeyed completely by going all the way to the 450-volt level. Virtually no one stopped short of 300 volts ("Severe Shock") (see ▶Figure 14.4).

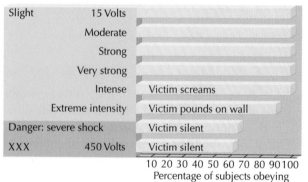

▶Figure 14.4

Results of Milgram's obedience experiment. Only a minority of subjects refused to provide shocks, even at the most extreme intensities. The first substantial drop in obedience occurred at the 300-volt level (Milgram, 1963).

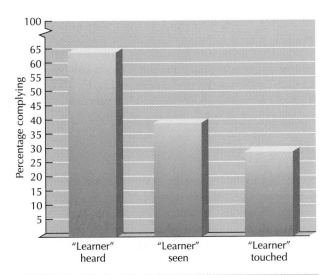

Physical distance from the "learner" had a significant effect on the percentage of subjects obeying orders.

Was the learner injured? The time has come to reveal that the "learner" was actually an actor who turned a tape recorder on and off in the shock room. No shocks were ever administered, but the dilemma for the "teacher" was quite real. Subjects protested, sweated, trembled, stuttered, bit their lips, and laughed nervously. Clearly they were disturbed by what they were doing. Nevertheless, most obeyed the experimenter's orders.

MILGRAM'S FOLLOW-UP *Why did so many people obey?* Some have suggested that the prestige of Yale University contributed to subjects' willingness to obey. Could it be that they assumed the professor running the experiment would not really allow anyone to be hurt? To test this possibility, the experiment was rerun in a shabby office building in nearby Bridgeport, Connecticut. Under these conditions fewer people obeyed (48 percent), but the reduction was minor.

Milgram was disturbed by the willingness of people to knuckle under to authority and senselessly shock someone. In later experiments, he tried to reduce obedience. He found that the distance between the teacher and the learner was important. When subjects were in the *same room* as the learner, only 40 percent obeyed fully. When they were *face to face* with the learner and required to force his hand down on a simulated "shock plate," only 30 percent obeyed (see ▶Figure 14.5). Distance from the authority also had an effect. When the experimenter gave his orders over the phone, only 22 percent obeyed. You may doubt that Milgram's study of obedience applies to you. If so, take a moment to read the following description:

Quack Like a Duck

The demonstration described here has become a favourite of many psychology teachers (Halonen, 1986). Imagine your response to the following events. On the first day of class, your professor begins to establish the basic rules of behaviour for the course. Seats are assigned and you must move to a new location. You are told not to talk during class. Your professor tells you that you must have permission to leave early. You are told to bring your textbook to class at all times. Up to this point you might not have any difficulty obeying your professor's orders. Then the demands become less reasonable. The professor says, "Use only a pencil for taking notes. Borrow one if you must." "Take off your watch." "Keep both hands on your desktop at all times." "All students who are freshmen stand at the back of the class." The demonstration is capped by orders that you cannot follow without looking silly: "Stick two fingers up your nose and quack like a duck."

Where do you think you would draw the line in obeying such orders? In reality, you might find yourself obeying a legitimate authority long after that person's demands had become unreasonable. What would happen, though, if a few students resisted orders early in the sequence? Would that help free others to disobey? For an answer, let's return to some final remarks on Milgram's experiment.

IMPLICATIONS Milgram's research raises nagging questions about our willingness to commit antisocial or inhumane acts commanded by a "legitimate authority." The excuse so often given by war criminals—"I was only following orders"—takes on new meaning in this light. Milgram suggested that when directions come from an authority, people rationalize that they are not personally responsible for their actions. In locales as diverse as Vietnam, Rwanda, Bosnia, South Africa, Nicaragua, Sri Lanka, and Laos the tragic result has been "sanctioned massacres" of chilling proportions (Kelman & Hamilton, 1989). Even in everyday life, crimes of obedience are common. In order to keep their jobs, many people obey orders to do things that they personally regard as dishonest, unethical, or harmful (Hamilton & Sanders, 1995).

Let us end on a more positive note. In one of his experiments, Milgram found that group support can greatly reduce destructive obedience. When real subjects saw two other "teachers" (both actors) resist orders and walk out of the experiment, only 10 percent continued to obey. Thus, a personal act of courage or moral fortitude by one or two members of a group may free others to disobey misguided or unjust authority.

▶ Compliance—A Foot in the Door

In conformity situations the pressure to "get in line" is usually indirect. When an authority commands obedience, the pressure is direct and difficult to resist. There is a third possibility. The term **compliance** refers to situations in which one person bends to the requests of another person who has little or no authority (Deaux, Dane, & Wrightsman, 1993). Pressures to comply are quite common. For example, a stranger might ask you to yield a phone booth so he can make a call; a saleswoman might suggest that you buy a more expensive watch than you had planned on; or a co-worker might ask you for 50 cents to buy a cup of coffee.

What determines whether a person will comply with a request? Many factors could be listed, but three stand out as especially interesting. Let's briefly consider each.

THE FOOT-IN-THE-DOOR EFFECT People who sell door-to-door have long recognized that once they get a foot in the door, a sale is almost a sure thing. To define the **foot-in-the-door effect** more formally, a person who first agrees to a small request is later more likely to comply with a larger demand (Dillard, 1991). For instance, if someone asked you to put a large, ugly sign in your front yard to promote safe driving, you would probably refuse. If, however, you had first agreed to put a small sign in your window, you would later be much more likely to allow the big sign in your yard (Freedman & Fraser, 1966).

Apparently, the foot-in-the-door effect is based on observing one's own behaviour. Seeing yourself agree to a small request helps convince you that you didn't mind doing what was asked. After that, you are more likely to comply with a larger request (Dillard, 1991).

THE DOOR-IN-THE-FACE EFFECT Let's say that a neighbour comes to your door and asks you to feed his dogs, water his plants, and mow his yard while he is out of town for a month. This is quite a major request—one that most people would probably turn down. Feeling only slightly guilty, you tell your neighbour that you're sorry but you can't help him. Now, what if the same neighbour returns the next day and asks if you would at least pick up his mail while he is gone. Chances are very good that you would honour this request, even if you might have resisted it otherwise.

Psychologist Robert Cialdini coined the term **door-in-the-face effect** to describe the tendency for a person who has refused a major request to comply with a smaller request (Cialdini et al., 1975). In other words, after a person has turned down a major request ("slammed the door in your face"), he or she may be more willing to agree to a lesser demand. This strategy works because a person who abandons a large request appears to have given up something. In response, many people feel that they must repay her or him by giving in to the smaller request (Dillard, 1991). In fact, a good way to get another person to comply with a request is to first do a small favour for the person (Whatley et al., 1999).

THE LOW-BALL TECHNIQUE Anyone who has purchased an automobile will recognize a third way of inducing compliance. Automobile dealers are notorious for persuading customers to buy cars by offering "low-ball" prices that undercut the competition. The dealer first gets the customer to agree to buy at an attractively low price. Then, once the customer is committed, various techniques are used to bump the price up before the sale is concluded.

The **low-ball technique** consists of getting a person committed to act and then making the terms of acting less desirable. Here's another example: A fellow student asks to

---

Compliance Bending to the requests of a person who has little or no authority or other form of social power.

Foot-in-the-door effect The tendency for a person who has first complied with a small request to be more likely later to fulfill a larger request.

Door-in-the-face effect The tendency for a person who has refused a major request to subsequently be more likely to comply with a minor request.

Low-ball technique A strategy in which commitment is gained first to reasonable or desirable terms, which are then made less reasonable or desirable.

borrow $25 for a day. This seems reasonable and you agree. However, once you have given your classmate the money, he explains that it would be easier to repay you after payday, in two weeks. If you agree, you've succumbed to the low-ball technique. Here's another example: Let's say you ask someone to give you a ride to school in the morning. Only after the person has agreed do you tell her that you have to be there at 6 a.m.

Passive Compliance

Complying with requests is a normal part of daily social life. At times, however, a willingness to comply can exceed what is reasonable. Researcher Thomas Moriarty (1975) demonstrated excessive, passive compliance under realistic conditions. **Passive compliance** refers to quietly bending to unreasonable demands or unacceptable conditions. Moriarty observed that many people will put up with almost anything to avoid a confrontation. For example, he and his students staged loud conversations behind people in movie theatres or people studying in a library. Very few protested. In other naturalistic experiments, people were accosted in phone booths. The experimenter explained that he had left a ring in the booth and asked if the person had found it. When subjects said no, the experimenter demanded that they empty their pockets. Most did.

In these and similar situations, people passively accepted having their personal rights trampled, even when objecting presented no threat to their safety (see Figure 14.6). Overly passive women, in particular, tend to be ripe targets for exploitation, especially by men (Richards, Rollerson, & Phillips, 1991). Have we become "a nation of willing victims?" We hope not. Let's see how assertive people handle difficult social situations.

ASSERTIVENESS TRAINING   Have you ever done any of the following?

- Hesitated to question an error on a restaurant bill because you were afraid of making a scene?
- Backed out of asking for a raise or a change in working conditions?
- Said yes when you wanted to say no?
- Been afraid to question a grade that seemed unfair?

If you've ever had trouble with similar situations, **assertiveness training** (instruction in how to be self-assertive) may offer a solution. In assertiveness training group exercises, videotapes, mirrors, and staged conflicts are used to teach assertive behaviour. People learn to practise honesty, disagreeing, questioning authority, and assertive postures and gestures. As their self-confidence improves, non-assertive clients are taken on "field trips" to shops and restaurants where they practise what they have learned.

The first step in assertiveness training is to convince yourself of three basic rights: You have the right to refuse, to request, and to right a wrong. **Self-assertion** involves standing up for these rights by speaking out in your own behalf.

Is self-assertion just getting things your own way? Not at all. A basic distinction can be made between *self-assertion* and *aggressive* behaviour. Self-assertion is a direct, honest expression of feelings and desires. It is not exclusively self-serving. People who are non-assertive are usually patient to a fault. Sometimes their pent-up anger explodes with unexpected fury, which can be very destructive to relationships. In contrast to assertive behaviour, **aggression** involves hurting another person or achieving one's goals at the expense of another. Aggression does not take into account the feelings or rights of others. It is an attempt to get one's own way no matter what. Assertion techniques emphasize firmness, not attack (see Table 14.1 on page 544).

Sidebar definitions

Passive compliance Passively bending to unreasonable demands or circumstances.

Assertiveness training Instruction in how to be self-assertive and self-confident.

Self-assertion A direct, honest expression of feelings and desires.

Aggression Hurting another person or achieving one's goals at the expense of another person.

▶ **Figure 14.6**

In an experiment done at an airport, a smoker intentionally sat or stood near non-smokers. Only 9 percent of the non-smokers asked the smoker to stop smoking, even when no-smoking signs were clearly visible nearby (Gibson & Werner, 1994).

Table 14.1
Comparison of Assertive, Aggressive, and Non-Assertive Behaviour

	ACTOR	RECEIVER OF BEHAVIOUR
Non-assertive behaviour	Self-denying, inhibited, hurt, and anxious; lets others make choices; goals not achieved	Feels sympathy, guilt, or contempt for actor; achieves goals at actor's expense
Aggressive behaviour	Achieves goals at others' expense; expresses feelings, but hurts others; chooses for others or puts them down	Feels hurt, defensive, humiliated, or taken advantage of; does not meet own needs
Assertive behaviour	Self-enhancing; acts in own best interests; expresses feelings; respects rights of others; goals usually achieved; self-respect maintained	Needs respected and feelings expressed; may achieve goal; self-worth maintained

Self-assertion does not supply instant poise, confidence, or self-assurance. However, it is a way of combating anxieties associated with life in an impersonal and sometimes intimidating society. That is one reason for interest in reports that girls become less assertive in the presence of boys than when they are not with boys (e.g., Charlesworth & LaFreniere, 1983). McGill University researcher Joyce Benenson has recently pointed out that this reduction in assertiveness occurs only when the girls are among unfamiliar children. In Benenson's studies, girls were equally assertive in all–girl groups, in groups having a majority of girls, and in groups in which girls were the minority—so long as the girls knew all of the children involved (Benenson, Aikins–Ford, & Apostolaris, 1998).

If you are interested in more information on self-assertion, you can consult a book entitled *Your Perfect Right* by Alberti and Emmons (1995).

Knowledge builder

SOCIAL POWER, OBEDIENCE, AND COMPLIANCE

Relate

Are you surprised that so many people obeyed orders in Milgram's experiments? Do you think you would have obeyed? How actively do you question authority?

You would like to persuade people to donate to a deserving charity. How, specifically, could you use compliance techniques to get people to donate?

Pick a specific instance when you could have been more assertive. How would you handle the situation if it occurs again? Think of a specific instance when you were angry and acted aggressively. How could have handled the situation through self-assertion, instead of aggression?

Learning Check

1. The term *compliance* refers to situations in which a person complies with commands made by a person who has authority. T or F?
2. Obedience in Milgram's experiments was related to
   a. distance between learner and teacher *b.* distance between experimenter and teacher *c.* obedience of other teachers *d.* all of these
3. By repeating his obedience experiment in a downtown office building, Milgram demonstrated that the prestige of Yale University was the main reason for subjects' willingness to obey in the original experiment. T or F?
4. The research of Thomas Moriarty and others has highlighted the problem of _____, rather than obedience to authority.
5. In assertiveness training, people learn techniques for getting their way in social situations and angry interchanges. T or F?
6. Non-assertive behaviour causes hurt, anxiety, and self-denial in the actor and sympathy, guilt, or contempt in the receiver. T or F?

Critical Thinking

7. Modern warfare allows killing to take place impersonally and at a distance. How does this relate to Milgram's experiments?

Answers:

1. F 2. d 3. F 4. passive compliance 5. F 6. T 7. There is a big difference between killing someone in hand-to-hand combat and killing someone by lining up images on a video screen. Milgram's research suggests that it is easier for a person to follow orders to kill another human when the victim is at a distance and removed from personal contact.

▶ Attitudes

Survey Question:
■ How are attitudes acquired and changed?

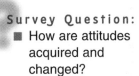

Attitude A learned tendency to respond to people, objects, or institutions in a positive or negative way.

Belief component What a person thinks or believes about the object of an attitude.

Emotional component One's feelings toward the object of an attitude.

Action component How one tends to act toward the object of an attitude.

Direct contact In forming attitudes, the effects of direct experience with the object of the attitude.

Interaction with others In forming attitudes, the influence of discussions with others who hold particular attitudes.

Child rearing In forming attitudes, the effects of parental values, beliefs, and practices.

Group membership As a factor in forming attitudes, social influences associated with belonging to various groups.

Belief + Emotion + Action

What is your attitude toward affirmative action, environmental groups, the death penalty, imported automobiles, k.d. lang, and psychology? The answers can have far-reaching effects on your behaviour. Attitudes are intimately woven into our actions and views of the world. Our tastes, friendships, votes, preferences, and goals are all touched by attitudes.

What specifically is an attitude? An **attitude** is a mixture of belief and emotion that predisposes a person to respond to other people, objects, or institutions in a positive or negative way. Attitudes summarize your evaluation of objects (Petty, Wegener, & Fabrigar, 1997). As a result, they predict or direct future actions.

"Your attitude is showing" is sometimes said. Actually, attitudes are expressed in three ways: through beliefs, emotions, and actions. The **belief component** of an attitude is what a person believes about a particular object or issue. The **emotional component** consists of feelings toward the attitudinal object. The **action component** refers to one's actions toward various people, objects, or institutions. Consider, for example, your attitude toward gun control. You will have beliefs about whether or not gun control would affect rates of crime or violence. You will have emotional responses to guns, finding them either attractive and desirable or threatening and destructive. And you will have a tendency to seek out or avoid gun ownership. The action component of your attitude will probably also include support of organizations that urge or oppose gun control.

As you can see, attitudes orient us to the social world. In doing so, they prepare us to act in certain ways (Olson & Zanna, 1993). (For another example, see Figure 14.7.)

Forming Attitudes

How do people acquire attitudes? Attitudes are acquired in several basic ways. Sometimes, attitudes come from **direct contact** (personal experience) with the object of the attitude—such as opposing pollution when a nearby factory ruins your favourite river. Attitudes are also learned through **interaction with others;** that is, through discussion with people holding a particular attitude. For instance, if three of your friends are volunteers at a local recycling centre, and you talk with them about their beliefs, you will probably come to favour recycling too. **Child rearing** (the effects of parental values, beliefs, and practices) also affects attitudes. For example, if both parents belong to the same political party, chances are two out of three that their children will belong to that party as adults.

Earlier we discussed group forces that operate to bring about conformity. There is little doubt that many of our attitudes are influenced by **group membership** (affiliation with others). In one classic study, for example, groups were formed to discuss the case of a juvenile delinquent. Most participants believed the boy needed love, kindness, and

Issue: Affirmative Action

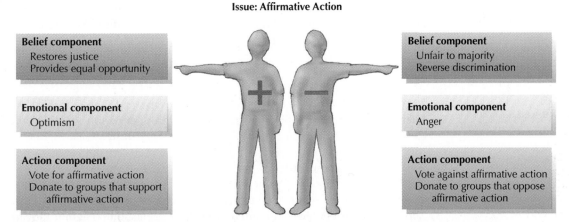

Belief component
Restores justice
Provides equal opportunity

Emotional component
Optimism

Action component
Vote for affirmative action
Donate to groups that support affirmative action

Belief component
Unfair to majority
Reverse discrimination

Emotional component
Anger

Action component
Vote against affirmative action
Donate to groups that oppose affirmative action

▶ **Figure 14.7**

Elements of positive and negative attitudes toward affirmative action.

friendship. To test group pressures on attitudes, a person who advocated severe punishment was added to each group.

How did group members react to the "deviate"? At first they directed almost all of their comments to him. But when he stuck to his position, an interesting thing happened. Soon, he was almost completely excluded from conversation. And later, the deviate was strongly rejected in ratings made by other group members (Schachter, 1951). Group pressures for conformity and the difficulty of holding different or unpopular attitudes can be clearly seen in this outcome.

Attitudes are also influenced by the **mass media** (all media, such as magazines and television, that reach large audiences). As Marshall McLuhan put it, we are "massaged" by the media, meaning we are coaxed and persuaded skillfully. Ninety-nine percent of North American homes have a television set, which is on an average of over seven hours a day. Does the information brought into homes this way have an impact? Perhaps. Frequent viewers mistrust others and overestimate their own chances of being harmed. One possible explanation is that a steady diet of TV violence leads some people to develop a **mean world view,** in which they regard the world as a dangerous and threatening place (Heath & Gilbert, 1996). An alternative explanation, which may be just as likely, is that mistrustful or fearful people choose to watch more television.

As James Olson, at the University of Western Ontario, and Mark Zanna, at the University of Waterloo, have pointed out, some attitudes are simply formed through **chance conditioning** (learning that takes place by chance or coincidence) (Olson & Zanna, 1993). Let's say, for instance, that you have had three encounters in your lifetime with psychologists. If all three were negative, you might take an unduly dim view of psychology and psychologists. In the same way, people often develop strong attitudes toward cities, restaurants, or parts of the country on the basis of one or two unusually good or bad experiences.

Why are some attitudes acted on, while others are not? To answer this question, let's consider an example. Assume that a woman named Lorraine knows that automobiles add to air pollution, and she strongly objects to smog. Why would Lorraine continue to drive to work every day? Probably it is because the immediate consequences of our actions weigh heavily on the choices we make. No matter what Lorraine's attitude may be, it is difficult for her to resist the immediate convenience of driving. Our expectations of how others will evaluate our actions are also important. By taking this factor into account, researchers have been able to predict a variety of choices, including family planning, alcohol use by adolescents, voting on a nuclear power plant initiative, and re-enlistment in the U.S. National Guard (Cialdini, Petty, & Cacippo, 1981). Finally, we must not overlook the effects of longstanding habits (Petty, Wegener, & Fabrigar, 1997).

In short, there are often large differences between attitudes and behaviour—particularly between privately held attitudes and public behaviour. However, barriers to action typically fall when a person holds an attitude with conviction. If you have **conviction** about an issue it evokes strong feelings, you think about it and discuss it often, and you are knowledgeable about it (Abelson, 1988). Attitudes held with passionate conviction often lead to major changes in personal behaviour (Petty, Wegener, & Fabrigar, 1997).

▶ Attitude Change

Although attitudes are relatively stable, they do change. Some attitude change can be understood in terms of **reference groups** (any group a person identifies with and uses as a standard for social comparison). It is not necessary to have face-to-face contact with other people for them to serve as a reference group. It depends instead on whom you identify with or whose attitudes and values you care about.

In the 1930s Theodore Newcomb studied real-life attitude change among students at Bennington College. Most students came from conservative homes, but Bennington was a very liberal school. Newcomb found that most students shifted significantly toward more liberal attitudes during their four years at Bennington. Those who didn't change kept their parents and hometown friends as primary reference groups. This is typified by one stu-

---

Mass media Collectively, all media that reach very large audiences (magazines, for instance, are a medium of mass communication).

Mean world view Viewing the world and other people as dangerous and threatening.

Chance conditioning Conditioning that takes place by chance or coincidence.

Conviction Beliefs that are important to a person and that evoke strong emotion.

Reference group Any group that an individual identifies with and uses as a standard for social comparison.

dent's statement, "I decided I'd rather stick to my father's ideas." Those who did change identified primarily with the campus community. Notice that all students could count the college and their families as *membership* groups. However, one group or the other tended to become their point of reference.

Persuasion

Persuasion A deliberate attempt to change attitudes or beliefs with information and arguments.

Communicator In persuasion, the person presenting arguments or information.

Message In persuasion, the content of a communicator's arguments or presentation.

Audience The person or group toward whom a persuasive message is directed.

Cognitive dissonance An uncomfortable clash between self-image, thoughts, beliefs, attitudes, or perceptions and one's behaviour.

What about advertising and other direct attempts to change attitudes? Are they effective? **Persuasion** is any deliberate attempt to change attitudes or beliefs through information and arguments. Businesses, politicians, and others who seek to persuade us obviously believe that attitudes can be changed. Over US$12 billion is spent yearly on television advertising in the United States and Canada alone. Persuasion can range from the daily blitz of media commercials to personal discussion among friends. In most cases, the success or failure of persuasion can be understood if we consider the **communicator,** the **message,** and the **audience.**

Let's say you have a chance to promote an issue important to you (for or against nuclear power, for instance) at a community gathering. Whom should you choose to make the presentation, and how should that person present it? Research suggests that attitude change is encouraged when the following conditions are met.

1. The communicator is likable, expressive, trustworthy, an expert on the topic, and similar to the audience in some respect.
2. The message appeals to emotions, particularly to fear or anxiety.
3. The message also provides a clear course of action that will, if followed, reduce fear or produce personally desirable results.
4. The message states clear-cut conclusions.
5. The message is backed up by facts and statistics.
6. Both sides of the argument are presented in the case of a well-informed audience.
7. Only one side of the argument is presented in the case of a poorly informed audience.
8. The persuader appears to have nothing to gain if the audience accepts the message.
9. The message is repeated as frequently as possible (Aronson, 1992; Eagly & Chaiken, 1992; Petty, Wegener, & Fabrigar, 1997).

Persuasion. Would you be likely to be swayed by this group's message? Successful persuasion is related to characteristics of the communicator, the message, and the audience.

Once again, the picture gets more complicated when we ask whether what is true in North America is also true in other parts of the world. Chanthika Pornpitakpan of the University of Singapore and June Francis of Simon Fraser University in Vancouver studied how Canadian and Thai students responded to persuasive messages that varied in the strength of the argument and in the perceived expertise of the speaker. They found that Canadian students were more influenced by the strength of the argument, while Thai students responded to the perceived expertise—essentially the reputation—of the person making the argument (Pornpitakpan & Francis, 2001).

Finally, it will not surprise you to learn that someone who is ambivalent on a topic will be easier to persuade than someone who already has a strong opinion. University of Western Ontario researcher Greg Maio and his colleagues found that subjects ambivalent toward Asian people became more favourable to immigration from Hong Kong if they were given a strong pro-immigration message, but not after a weak message. However, the messages had no effect on subjects who were not ambivalent in the first place (Maio, Bell, & Esses, 1996).

Cognitive Dissonance Theory

Cognitions are thoughts. Dissonance means clashing. The influential theory of **cognitive dissonance** states that contradicting or clashing thoughts cause discomfort. That is, we have a need for consistency in our thoughts, perceptions, and images of ourselves (Festinger, 1957; Thibodeau & Aronson, 1992).

What happens if people act in ways that are inconsistent with their attitudes or self-images? Typically, the contradiction makes them uncomfortable. Such discomfort can motivate people to make their thoughts or attitudes agree with their actions (Petty, Wegener, & Fabrigar, 1997). For example, smokers are told on every pack that cigarettes endanger their lives. They light up and smoke anyway. How do they resolve the tension between this information and their actions? They could quit smoking, but it may be easier to convince themselves that smoking is not really so dangerous. To do this, many smokers seek examples of heavy smokers who have lived long lives; they spend their time with other smokers; and they avoid information about the link between smoking and cancer. According to cognitive dissonance theory, we also tend to reject new information that contradicts ideas we already hold. We're all guilty of this "don't bother me with the facts, my mind is made up" strategy at times.

Many people have experienced cognitive dissonance since the terrorist attacks of September 11, 2001. Some of these people believed that North America was not vulnerable to large-scale terrorist attacks of the type suffered by other regions such as Israel, India, and Northern Ireland. To revise that view and accept evidence of our vulnerability may cause cognitive dissonance. To reduce that dissonance, some people have focused on how powerful North Americans are militarily and economically. Similarly, some anti-American people, not willing to accept the image of Americans as victims of brutal violence, have wanted to speak only of a "backlash" against Muslims. Although isolated incidents of Muslims being harassed were reported, a large-scale backlash never happened. Still, saying that it did helps some people deal with their cognitive dissonance. See Table 14.2 for a look at strategies people use to reduce cognitive dissonance.

Acting contrary to one's attitudes doesn't always bring about change. How does cognitive dissonance account for that? The amount of justification for acting contrary to your attitudes and beliefs affects how much dissonance you feel. (**Justification** is the degree to which a person's actions are explained by rewards or other circumstances.) In a classic study, college students did an extremely boring task (turning wooden pegs on a board) for a long time. Afterward, they were asked to help lure others into the experiment by pretending that the task was interesting and enjoyable. Students paid $20 for lying to others did not change their own negative opinion of the task. Those who were paid only $1 later rated the experience as actually being pleasant and interesting. How can we explain these results? Apparently, students paid $20 experienced no dissonance. These students could reassure themselves that anybody would tell a little white lie for $20. Those paid $1 were faced with the conflicting thoughts—"I lied. But I had no good reason to do it." Rather than admit to themselves that they had lied, these students changed their attitude toward what they had done (Festinger & Carlsmith, 1959) (see ▶Figure 14.8).

Justification In cognitive dissonance theory, the degree to which one's actions are justified by rewards or other circumstances.

Table 14.2 Strategies for Reducing Cognitive Dissonance	Celia, who is a college student, has always thought of herself as an environmental activist. Recently, Celia "inherited" a car from her parents, who were replacing the family "barge." In the past, Celia biked or used public transportation to get around. Her parent's old car is an antiquated gas-guzzler, but she has begun to drive it on a daily basis. How might Celia reduce the cognitive dissonance created by the clash between her environmentalism and her use of an inefficient automobile?

STRATEGY	EXAMPLE
Change your attitude	"Cars are not really a major environmental problem."
Add supporting thoughts	"This is an old car, so keeping it on the road makes good use of the resources consumed when it was manufactured."
Change the importance of the dissonant thoughts	"It's more important for me to support the environmental movement politically than it is to worry about how I get to school and work."
Reduce the amount of perceived choice	"My schedule has become too hectic, I really can't afford to bike or take the bus anymore."
Change your behaviour	"I'm only going to use the car when it's impossible to bike or take the bus."

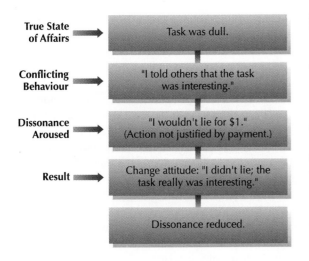

True State
of Affairs → Task was dull.

Conflicting
Behaviour → "I told others that the task
was interesting."

Dissonance
Aroused → "I wouldn't lie for $1."
(Action not justified by payment.)

Result → Change attitude: "I didn't lie; the
task really was interesting."

Dissonance reduced.

▶Figure 14.8

Summary of the Festinger and Carlsmith (1959) study from the viewpoint of a person experiencing cognitive dissonance.

We are especially likely to experience dissonance after we cause an event to occur that we wish hadn't taken place (Cooper & Fazio, 1984). Let's say that you agree to help a friend move to a new apartment. The big day arrives and you feel like staying in bed. Actually, you wish you hadn't promised to help. To reduce dissonance, you may convince yourself that the work will actually be "good exercise," "sort of fun," or that your friend really deserves the help. We often make such adjustments in attitudes to minimize cognitive dissonance.

Before we leave the topic of attitudes, let's see what psychologists have learned about brainwashing and other high-pressure attempts to change attitudes.

▶ Forced Attitude Change—Brainwashing and Cults

Survey Question:

■ Is brainwashing actually possible? How are people converted to cult membership?

If you're a history enthusiast, you may associate brainwashing with techniques used by the Communist Chinese on prisoners during the Korean War. Through various types of "thought reform," the Chinese were able to coerce 16 percent of these prisoners to sign false confessions (Schein et al., 1957). More recently, the mass murder/suicide at Jonestown, the Branch Davidian tragedy at Waco, and the Heaven's Gate group suicide in San Diego have rekindled public interest in forced attitude change.

How does it differ from other persuasive techniques? **Brainwashing,** or forced attitude change, requires a captive audience. If you are offended by a television commercial, you can tune it out. Prisoners in the POW camps in Korea (and later in Vietnam) were completely at the mercy of their captors. Complete control over the environment allows a degree of psychological manipulation that would be impossible in a normal setting.

Brainwashing Engineered or forced attitude change involving a captive audience.

Unfreezing In brainwashing, a loosening of convictions about former values, attitudes, and beliefs.

Change In brainwashing, the point at which a person begins to reject former attitudes and beliefs.

Refreezing In brainwashing, the process of rewarding and strengthening new attitudes and beliefs.

Brainwashing

How does captivity facilitate persuasion? Psychologist James McConnell identified three techniques used in brainwashing: (1) The target person is isolated from other people who would support his or her original attitudes; (2) the target must depend completely on his or her captors for the satisfaction of needs; and (3) the indoctrinator is in a position to reward the target person for changes in attitudes or behaviour.

Brainwashing typically begins with making the target person feel completely helpless. Physical and psychological abuse, lack of sleep, humiliation, and isolation serve to **unfreeze,** or loosen, former values and beliefs. When exhaustion, pressure, and fear become unbearable, **change** occurs as the person abandons former beliefs. Typically, prisoners who reach the breaking point sign a false confession or cooperate to gain relief. When they do, they are suddenly rewarded with praise, privileges, food, or rest. Continued pairing of hope and fear with pressures to conform then serves to **refreeze** (solidify) new attitudes (Schein, Schneier, & Barker, 1961).

How permanent are changes caused by brainwashing? In most cases, the dramatic shift in attitudes brought about by brainwashing is temporary. Most "converted" prisoners who returned home after the Korean War eventually reverted to their original beliefs. Nevertheless, brainwashing can be powerful, as shown by the success of cults in recruiting new members.

Cults

Exhorted by their leader, some 900 members of the Reverend Jim Jones's People's Temple picked up paper cups and drank purple Kool-Aid laced with the deadly poison cyanide. Psychologically, the mass suicide at Jonestown in 1978 is not so incredible as it might

Aftermath of the mass suicide at Jonestown. How do cult-like groups recruit new devotees?

Cult A group that professes great devotion to some person, and follows that person almost without question; cult members are typically victimized by their leaders in various ways.

seem. The inhabitants of Jonestown were isolated in the jungles of Guyana, intimidated by guards and lulled with sedatives. They were also cut off from friends and relatives and totally accustomed to obeying rigid rules of conduct, which primed them for Jones's final "loyalty test." Of greater psychological interest is the question of how people reach such a state of commitment and dependency.

Why do people join groups such as the People's Temple? The People's Temple was a classic example of a cult. A **cult** is a group in which the leader's personality is more important than the beliefs he or she preaches. Cult members give their allegiance to this person, who is regarded as above criticism, and they follow his or her dictates without question. Almost always, cult members are victimized by their leaders in one way or another.

Psychologist Margaret Singer has found that to recruit new members, cults use a powerful blend of guilt, manipulation, isolation, deception, fear, and escalating commitment. In this respect, cults employ high-pressure indoctrination techniques not unlike those used in brainwashing (Isser, 1991; Singer & Addis, 1992). In the United States alone, an estimated 2 to 5 million people have succumbed to the lure of cults (Robinson, Frye, & Bradley, 1997).

RECRUITMENT   Some people studied by Singer were seriously distressed when they joined a cult. Most, however, were simply undergoing a period of mild depression, indecision, or alienation from family and friends (Hunter, 1998). Cult members try to catch potential converts at a time of need—especially when a sense of belonging will be attractive to converts. For instance, many people were approached just after a romance had broken up, or when they were struggling with exams, or were trying to become independent from their families (Sirkin, 1990). At such times, people are easily persuaded that joining the group is all they need to do to be happy again (Hunter, 1998; Schwartz, 1991).

CONVERSION   *How is conversion achieved?* Often it begins with intense displays of affection and understanding ("love bombing"). Next comes isolation from non-cult members and drills, discipline, and rituals (all-night meditation or continuous chanting, for instance). These rituals wear down physical and emotional resistance, discourage critical thinking, and generate feelings of commitment (Galanti, 1993).

Many cults make clever use of the foot-in-the-door technique, described earlier. At first, recruits make small commitments (to stay after a meeting, for example). Then, larger commitments are encouraged (to stay an extra day, to call in sick at work, and so forth). Making a major commitment is usually the final step. The new devotee signs over a bank account or property to the group, moves in with the group, and so forth. Making such major public commitments creates a powerful cognitive dissonance effect. Before long, it becomes virtually impossible for converts to admit they have made a mistake.

Once in the group, members are cut off from family and friends (former reference groups), and the cult can control the flow and interpretation of information to them. Members are isolated from their former value systems and social structures. Conversion is complete when they come to think of themselves more as group members than as individuals. At this point obedience is nearly total (Schwartz, 1991; Wexler, 1995).

Behind the "throne" from which Jim Jones ruled Jonestown was a sign bearing these words: "Those who do not remember the past are condemned to repeat it." If we are to take the Reverend Jones at his word, then we should remember that cults are but one example of the danger of trading independence for security. Cults are merely the most visible sign of how we all can be influenced by sophisticated psychological coercion and by our need for approval from others.

Knowledge builder

ATTITUDES AND PERSUASION

Relate

Describe an attitude that is important to you. What are its three components?

Which of the various sources of attitudes best explain your own attitudes?

Who belongs to your most important reference group?

Imagine that you would like to persuade voters to support an initiative to preserve a small wilderness area by converting it to a park. Using research on persuasion as a guide, what could you do to be more effective?

How would you explain cognitive dissonance theory to a person who knows nothing about it?

Learning Check

1. Attitudes have three parts: a _____ component, an _____ component, and an _____ component.
2. Which of the following is associated with attitude formation? *a.* group membership *b.* mass media *c.* chance conditioning *d.* child rearing *e.* all of the preceding *f. a* and *d* only
3. In presenting a persuasive message, it is best to give both sides of the argument if the audience is already well informed on the topic. T or F?

4. Much attitude change is related to a desire to avoid clashing or contradictory thoughts, an idea summarized by _____ _____ theory.
5. Brainwashing differs from other persuasive attempts in that brainwashing requires a _____ _____.
6. Which statement about brainwashing is false?
   a. The target person is isolated from others.
   b. Attitude changes brought about by brainwashing are usually permanent.
   c. The first step is unfreezing former values and beliefs.
   d. Cooperation with the indoctrinating agent is rewarded.

Critical Thinking

7. Students entering a college gym are asked to sign a banner promoting water conservation. Later, the students shower at the gym. What effect would you expect signing the banner to have on how long students stay in the showers?
8. Cognitive dissonance theory predicts that false confessions obtained during brainwashing are not likely to bring about lasting changes in attitudes. Why?

Answers:

1. belief, emotional, action 2. *e* 3. T 4. cognitive dissonance theory 5. captive audience 6. *b* 7. Cognitive dissonance theory predicts that students who sign the banner will take shorter showers, to be consistent with their publicly expressed support of water conservation. This is exactly the result observed in a study done by social psychologist Elliot Aronson. 8. Because there is strong justification for such actions. As a result, little cognitive dissonance is created when a prisoner makes statements that contradict his or her beliefs.

▶ Prejudice—Attitudes That Injure

Survey Question:
■ What causes prejudice and intergroup conflict?

Prejudice A negative emotional attitude held against members of a particular group of people.

Discrimination Treating members of various social groups differently in circumstances where their rights or treatment should be identical.

Scapegoating Blaming a person or a group for the actions of others or for conditions not of their making.

Love and friendship bind people together. Prejudice, which is marked by suspicion, fear, or hatred, has the opposite effect. **Prejudice** is a negative emotional attitude held toward members of a specific social group. Prejudices may be reflected in the policies of police departments, schools, or government institutions. In such cases, prejudice is referred to as *racism, sexism, ageism,* or *heterosexism,* depending on the group affected. Because it is so prevalent and damaging, let's focus on racism.

Both racial prejudice and racism lead to **discrimination,** or unequal treatment of people who should have the same rights as others. Discrimination frequently prevents people from doing things they should be able to do, such as buying a house, getting a job, or attending a high-quality school. For example, in many cities, black motorists have been stopped by police for DWB—"Driving While Black." For many law-abiding citizens, being detained in this way is a painful reminder that racial discrimination is still common (Harris, 1999).

Becoming Prejudiced

How do prejudices develop? One major theory suggests that prejudice is a form of **scapegoating** (blaming a person or a group for the actions of others or for conditions not of their making). Scapegoating, you may recall, is a type of displaced aggression in which hostilities triggered by frustration are redirected at "safe" targets. Remember the jumpers and people with Latah mentioned at the beginning of the chapter? Perhaps the teasing and startling that produce these phenomena could be understood as hostility redirected at safe targets—women in male-dominated Malaysian society or shy men in a lumber camp full of rugged loggers.

One interesting test of the scapegoating hypothesis was conducted at a summer camp for young men. The men were given a difficult test they were sure to fail. Additionally, completing the test caused them to miss a trip to the theatre, which was normally the high point of their weekly entertainment. Attitudes toward Mexicans and Japanese were measured before the test and after the men had failed the test and missed the movie. Subjects in this study, all European Americans, consistently rated members of these two groups lower after being frustrated (Miller & Bugelski, 1970).

At times, the development of prejudice (like other attitudes) can be traced to direct experiences with members of the rejected group. A child who is repeatedly bullied by members of a particular racial or ethnic group might develop a lifelong dislike for all members of the group. The tragedy is that once prejudices are established, they prevent us from accepting more positive experiences that could reverse the damage (Wilder, Simon, & Faith, 1996).

Distinguished psychologist Gordon Allport (1958) concluded that there are two important sources of prejudice. **Personal prejudice** occurs when members of another racial or ethnic group are perceived as a threat to one's own interests. For example, members of another group may be viewed as competitors for jobs. **Group prejudice** occurs when a person conforms to group norms. Let's say, for instance, that you have no personal reason for disliking out-group members. Nevertheless, your friends, acquaintances, or co-workers expect it of you.

As an example of how membership in a group can promote prejudice, consider a study by Serge Guimond (2000). Guimond assessed attitudes of Anglophone and Francophone students at a Canadian military college in the students' first and fourth years at the college. He found that during their training, both groups increasingly identified with their groups and increased their in-group favouritism. This is particularly interesting because the data were obtained for the same people over a period of years—so we know that the individuals involved changed their views during their training.

The Prejudiced Personality

Other research suggests that prejudice can be a general personality characteristic. Theodore Adorno and his associates (1950) carefully probed what they called the *authoritarian personality* (ah-thor-ih-TARE-ee-un). These researchers started out by studying anti-Semitism. In the process, they found that people who are prejudiced against one group tend to be prejudiced against all out-groups.

What are the characteristics of the prejudice-prone personality? First, recent Canadian work suggests that prejudiced people are, to put it bluntly, not too bright. Todd Morrison and his colleagues at Queen's University in Kingston found that academic achievement was negatively correlated with both *homonegativism* (dislike of homosexuals) and gender-based occupational stereotyping (believing that there are "women's jobs" and "men's jobs") (Morrison et al., 1997).

Secondly, the **authoritarian personality** is marked by rigidity, inhibition, prejudice, and oversimplification. Authoritarians also tend to be very *ethnocentric*. **Ethnocentrism** refers to placing one's own group "at the centre," usually by rejecting all other groups. Put more simply, authoritarians consider their own ethnic or racial group superior to others.

In addition to rejecting out-groups, authoritarians are overwhelmingly concerned with power, authority, and obedience. To measure these qualities, the *F scale* was created (the *F* stands for "fascism"). This scale is made up of statements such as the ones that follow—to which authoritarians readily agree (Adorno et al., 1950).

Authoritarian Beliefs

- Obedience and respect for authority are the most important virtues children should learn.
- People can be divided into two distinct classes: the weak and the strong.

Personal prejudice Prejudicial attitudes held toward persons who are perceived as a direct threat to one's own interests.

Group prejudice Prejudice held out of conformity to group views.

Authoritarian personality A personality pattern characterized by rigidity, inhibition, prejudice, and an excessive concern with power, authority, and obedience.

Ethnocentrism Placing one's own group or race at the centre—that is, tending to reject all other groups but one's own.

- If people would talk less and work more, everybody would be better off.
- What this country needs most, more than laws and political programs, is a few courageous, tireless, devoted leaders, in whom the people can put their faith.
- Nobody ever learns anything really important except through suffering.
- Every person should have complete faith in some supernatural power whose decisions are obeyed without question.
- Certain religious sects that refuse to salute the flag should be forced to conform to such patriotic action or else be abolished.

As children, authoritarians were usually severely punished. Most learned to fear authority (and to covet it) at an early age. Authoritarians are not happy people.

Even if we discount the obvious bigotry of the authoritarian personality, racial prejudice runs deep in many nations. Let's probe deeper into the roots of such prejudiced behaviour.

▶ Intergroup Conflict—The Roots of Prejudice

An unfortunate byproduct of group membership is that it often limits contact with people in other groups. Additionally, groups themselves may come into conflict. Both events tend to foster hatred and prejudice toward the out-group. The bloody clash of opposing forces in Israel, Ireland, Africa, and many other places are reminders that intergroup conflict is widespread. Daily, we read of jarring strife between political, religious, or ethnic groups. In many cases, intergroup conflict is accompanied by stereotyped images of out-group members and by bitter prejudice.

What exactly do you mean by a stereotype? **Social stereotypes** are oversimplified images of people who belong to a particular social group. There is a good chance that you have stereotyped images of some of the following categories: redneck, politician, show-off, do-gooder, juvenile delinquent, business executive, housewife, snob, playboy, teenager, slob, spoiled brat, billionaire. In general, the top three categories on which most stereotypes are based are gender, age, and race (Fiske, 1993a).

Stereotypes tend to simplify people into "us" and "them" categories. Actually, aside from the fact that they always oversimplify, stereotypes may be either positive or negative (see ▶Figure 14.9). Table 14.3 on page 554 shows stereotyped images of various national and ethnic groups and their changes over a 34-year period. Notice that many of the qualities listed are desirable. Note, too, that while the overall trend was a decrease in negative stereotypes, belief in the existence of some negative traits increased.

Even though stereotypes sometimes include positive traits, they are mainly used to control people. When a person is stereotyped, the easiest thing for her or him to do is to abide by others' expectations—even if they are demeaning. That's why no one likes to be stereotyped. Being forced into a small, distorted social "box" is limiting and insulting. Stereotypes rob people of their individuality. Without stereotypes there would be far less hate, prejudice, exclusion, and conflict (Fiske, 1993b).

When a prejudiced person meets a pleasant or likable member of a rejected group, the out-group member tends to be perceived as "an exception to the rule," not as evidence against the stereotype. Even when such

Social stereotypes
Oversimplified images of the traits of individuals who belong to a particular social group.

▶Figure 14.9

Racial stereotypes are common in sports. For example, a recent study confirmed that many people actually do believe that white men can't jump. This stereotype implies that black basketball players are naturally superior in athletic ability. White players, in contrast, are falsely perceived as smarter and harder-working than blacks. Such stereotypes set up expectations that distort the perceptions of fans, coaches, and sportswriters. The resulting misperceptions, in turn, help perpetuate the stereotypes (Stone, Perry, & Darley, 1997).

Table 14.3
University Students' Characterization of Ethnic Groups, 1933 and 1967

TRAIT	PERCENT CHECKING TRAIT		TRAIT	PERCENT CHECKING TRAIT		TRAIT	PERCENT CHECKING TRAIT	
	1933	1967		1933	1967		1933	1967
Americans			**Italians**			**Jews**		
Industrious	48	23	Artistic	53	30	Shrewd	79	30
Intelligent	47	20	Impulsive	44	28	Mercenary	49	15
Materialistic	33	67	Musical	32	9	Grasping	34	17
Progressive	27	17	Imaginative	30	7	Intelligent	29	37
Germans			**Irish**			**Blacks**		
Scientific	78	47	Pugnacious	45	13	Superstitious	84	13
Stolid	44	9	Witty	38	7	Lazy	75	26
Methodical	31	21	Honest	32	17	Ignorant	38	11
Efficient	16	46	Nationalistic	21	41	Religious	24	8

Source: M. Karlins, T. L. Coffman, and G. Walters, "On the fading of social stereotypes: Studies in three generations of college students," *Journal of Personality and Social Psychology, 13* (1969): 116.

Symbolic prejudice
Prejudice that is expressed in disguised fashion.

"exceptional" experiences begin to accumulate, a prejudiced person may not change his or her stereotyped belief (Fiske, 1993a; Wilder, Simon, & Faith, 1996).

Some observers believe that today's racism often takes the form of **symbolic prejudice,** which is expressed in a disguised fashion (Brewer & Kramer, 1985). That is, many people realize that crude and obvious racism is socially unacceptable. However, this may not stop them from expressing prejudice in thinly veiled forms when they state their opinions on issues such as affirmative action, bussing, immigration, crime, and so on. It must be noted, however, that not all opposition to policies such as affirmative action is inspired by prejudice. Researchers at the University of Waterloo studied attitudes and beliefs about prejudice, justice, workplace discrimination, and affirmative action. They concluded that while prejudiced people might hide their prejudice under a concern with justice, non-prejudiced people could oppose affirmative action out of a genuine concern that it leads to unfair decisions (Bobocel et al., 2001).

How do stereotypes and intergroup tensions develop? Two experiments, both in unlikely settings and both using children, offer some insight into these problems.

Experiments in Prejudice

What is it like to be discriminated against? In a unique experiment, elementary school teacher Jane Elliot sought to give her pupils direct experience with prejudice. On the first day of the experiment, Elliot announced that brown-eyed children were to sit in the back of the room and that they could not use the drinking fountain. Blue-eyed children were given extra recess time and got to leave first for lunch. At lunch, brown-eyed children were prevented from taking second helpings because they would "just waste it." Brown-eyed and blue-eyed children were kept from mingling, and the blue-eyed children were told they were "cleaner" and "smarter" (Peters, 1971). Eye colour might seem like a trivial basis for creating prejudices. However, people primarily use skin colour to make decisions about the race of another person (Brown, Dane, & Durham, 1998). Surely, this is just as superficial a way of judging people as eye colour is.

At first, Elliot made an effort to constantly criticize and belittle the brown-eyed children. To her surprise, the blue-eyed children rapidly joined in and were soon outdoing her in the viciousness of their attacks. The blue-eyed children began to feel superior, and the brown-eyed children felt just plain awful. Fights broke out. Test scores of the brown-eyed children fell.

How lasting were the effects of this experiment? The effects were short-lived, because two days later the roles of the children were reversed. Before long, the same destructive effects occurred again, but this time in reverse. The implications of this experiment are unmistakable. In less than one day it was possible to get children to hate

Ethnic pride is gradually replacing stereotypes and discrimination. For example, Caribana, an annual festival held in Toronto celebrating Caribbean culture, draws people from all over North America.

Status inequalities
Differences in the power,
prestige, or privileges of two
or more persons or groups.

Equal-status contact
Social interaction that occurs
on an equal footing, without
obvious differences in power
or status.

Superordinate goal
A goal that exceeds or
overrides all others; a goal
that renders other goals
relatively less important.

Mutual interdependence
A condition in which two or
more persons must depend
on one another to meet each
person's needs or goals.

Jigsaw classroom
A method of reducing
prejudice; each student
receives only part of the
information needed to
complete a project or
prepare for a test.

each other because of eye colour and **status inequalities** (differences in power, prestige, or privileges). Certainly the effects of a lifetime of real racial or ethnic prejudice are infinitely more powerful and destructive (Clark et al., 1999).

EQUAL-STATUS CONTACT *What can be done to combat prejudice?* According to Canadian psychologists James Olson and Mark Zanna (1993), several lines of thought suggest that equal-status contact between groups in conflict should reduce prejudice and stereotyping. **Equal-status contact** is social interaction that occurs on an equal footing, without obvious differences in power or status. In various studies, mixed-race groups have been formed at work, in the laboratory, and at schools. The conclusion from such research is that personal contact with a disliked group tends to induce friendly behaviour, respect, and liking. However, these benefits occur only when personal contact is cooperative and on an equal footing (Grack & Richman, 1996).

SUPERORDINATE GOALS Let us now consider a revealing study done with 11-year-old boys. When the boys arrived at a summer camp, they were split into two groups and housed in separate cabins. At first the groups were kept apart to build up in-group friendships. Soon each group had a flag and a name (the "Rattlers" and the "Eagles") and each had staked out its territory. At this point the two groups were placed in competition with each other. After a number of clashes, disliking between the groups bordered on hatred: The boys baited each other, started fights, and raided each other's cabins (Sherif et al., 1961).

Were they allowed to go home hating each other? As an experiment in reducing intergroup conflict, and to prevent the boys from remaining enemies, various strategies to reduce tensions were tried. Holding meetings between group leaders did nothing. When the groups were invited to eat together, the event turned into a free-for-all. Finally, emergencies that required cooperation among members of both groups were staged at the camp. For example, the water supply was damaged so that all the boys had to work together to repair it. Creating this and other superordinate goals helped restore peace between the two groups. (A **superordinate goal** exceeds or overrides other lesser goals.)

Cooperation and shared goals seem to help reduce conflict by encouraging people in opposing groups to see themselves as members of a single, larger group (Gaertner et al., 1990). Superordinate goals, in other words, have a "we're all in the same boat" effect on perceptions of group membership (Olson & Zanna, 1993). Can such goals exist on a global scale? One example might be a desire to avoid nuclear holocaust. Another that comes to mind is the need to preserve the natural environment on a global scale. Politically, such goals may be far from universal. But their superordinate quality is clearly evident.

"JIGSAW" CLASSROOMS Contrary to the hopes of many, integrating public schools often has little positive effect on racial prejudice. In fact, prejudice may be made worse, and the self-esteem of minority students frequently decreases (Aronson, 1992).

If integrated schools provide equal-status contact, shouldn't prejudice be reduced? Theoretically, yes. But in practice, minority group children often enter schools unprepared to compete on an equal footing. The competitive nature of schools almost guarantees that children will not learn to like and understand each other.

With the preceding in mind, social psychologist Elliot Aronson pioneered a way to apply superordinate goals to ordinary classrooms. According to Aronson, such goals are effective because they create **mutual interdependence.** That is, people must depend on one another to meet each person's goals. When individual needs are linked, cooperation is encouraged (Deutsch, 1993).

How has this idea been applied? Aronson has successfully created "jigsaw" classrooms that emphasize cooperation rather than competition. The term *jigsaw* refers to the pieces of a jigsaw puzzle. In a **jigsaw classroom,** each child is given a "piece" of the information needed to complete a project or prepare for a test.

Many schools require students to wear uniforms. Appearance is one of the major reasons why kids treat each other differently. Uniforms help minimize status inequalities and in-group/out-group distinctions. In Long Beach, California, a switch to uniforms was followed by a 91 percent drop in student assaults, thefts, vandalism, and weapons and drug violations (Ritter, 1998).

In a typical session, children are divided into groups of five or six and given a topic to study for a later exam. Each child is given his or her "piece" of information and asked to learn it. For example, one child might have information on Thomas Edison's invention of the light bulb; another, facts about his invention of the long-playing phonograph record; and a third, information about Edison's childhood. After the children have learned their parts, they teach them to others in the group. Even the most competitive children quickly realize that they cannot do well without the aid of everyone in the group. Each child makes a unique and essential contribution, so the children learn to listen to and respect each other.

Does the jigsaw method work? Compared to children in traditional classrooms, children in jigsaw groups are less prejudiced, they like their classmates more, they have more positive attitudes toward school, their grades improve, and their self-esteem increases (Walker & Crogan, 1998; Webb & Farivar, 1994). Such results are quite encouraging. As Kenneth Clark (1965) has said, "Racial prejudice . . . debases all human beings—those who are its victims, those who victimize, and in quite subtle ways, those who are merely accessories."

To summarize, prejudice will be reduced when:

- Members of different groups have equal status within the situation that brings them together.
- Members of all groups seek a common goal.
- Group members must cooperate to reach the goal.
- Group members spend enough time together for cross-group friendships to develop (Pettigrew, 1998).

Sports teams are an excellent example of a situation in which all of these conditions apply. The close contact and interdependent effort required in team sports often creates lifelong friendships and breaks down the walls of prejudice.

Knowledge builder

PREJUDICE AND INTERGROUP CONFLICT

Relate

Mentally scan over the events of the last week. How would they have changed if prejudices of all types ceased to exist?

Think of the most rigid person you know. Does he or she match the profile of the authoritarian personality?

Stereotypes exist for many social categories, even ordinary ones such as "college student" or "unmarried young adult." What stereotypes do you think you face in daily life?

The director of a youth recreation centre is concerned about the amount of conflict she is seeing between boys and girls from different racial and ethnic groups. What advice can you give the director?

Learning Check

1. As a basis for prejudice, _____ is frequently related to frustration and displaced _____.

2. The authoritarian personality tends to be prejudiced against all out-groups, a quality referred to as _____.
3. The stereotypes underlying racial and ethnic prejudice tend to evolve from the superordinate goals that often separate groups. T or F?
4. The term *symbolic prejudice* refers to racism or prejudice that is expressed in disguised or hidden form. T or F?
5. Jane Elliot's classroom experiment in prejudice showed that children could be made to dislike one another by frustrating the students. T or F?
6. Research suggests that prejudice and intergroup conflict may be reduced by _____ interaction and _____ goals.

Critical Thinking

7. In court trials, defence lawyers sometimes try to identify and eliminate prospective jurors who have authoritarian personality traits. Can you guess why?

Answers:

1. scapegoating, aggression 2. ethnocentrism 3. F 4. T 5. F 6. equal-status, superordinate 7. Because authoritarians tend to believe that punishment is effective, they are more likely to vote for conviction.

▶ Aggression—The World's Most Dangerous Animal

Survey Question:
■ How do psychologists explain human aggression?

Aggression Any action carried out with the intention of harming another person.

Ethologist A person who studies the natural behaviour patterns of animals.

For a time, the City Zoo of Los Angeles, California, had on display two examples of the world's most dangerous animal—the only animal capable of destroying the Earth and all other animal species. Perhaps you have already guessed which animal it was. In the cage were two college students, representing the species *Homo sapiens!*

Clearly, humans have some capacity for aggression. It has been estimated that during the 125-year period ending with World War II, 58 million humans were killed by other humans (an average of nearly one person per minute). War, homicide, riots, family violence, assassination, rape, assault, forcible robbery, and other violent acts offer sad testimony to the realities of human aggression. To give you some perspective, the Population Reference Bureau estimates that during that 125-year period, a total of perhaps 7 billion people were born. So, about 1 in every 121 people died due to human aggression (120 out of 121 died of some other cause). How do you feel about that number?

What causes aggression? **Aggression** refers to any action carried out with the intention of harming another person. The complexity of aggression has given rise to a number of potential explanations for its occurrence. Brief descriptions of some of the major possibilities follow.

Instincts

Some theorists argue we are naturally aggressive creatures, having inherited a "killer instinct" from our animal ancestors. Ethologists theorize that aggression is a biologically rooted behaviour observed in all animals, including humans. (An **ethologist** is a person who studies the natural behaviour patterns of animals.) Noted ethologist Konrad Lorenz (1966, 1974) also believed that humans lack certain innate patterns that inhibit aggression in animals. For example, in a dispute over territory, two wolves may growl, lunge, bare their teeth, and fiercely threaten each other. In most instances, though, neither is killed or even wounded. One wolf, recognizing the dominance of the other, will typically bare its throat in a gesture of submission. The dominant wolf could kill in an instant, but it is inhibited by the submissive gesture. In contrast, human confrontations of equal intensity almost always end in injury or death.

The idea that humans are "naturally" aggressive has an intuitive appeal, but many psychologists question it. Many of Lorenz's "explanations" of aggression are little more than loose comparisons between human and animal behaviour. Just labelling a behaviour as "instinctive" does little to explain it. More important, we are left with the question of why some individuals or human groups (the Arapesh, the Senoi, the Navajo, the Inuit, and others) show little hostility or aggression. And, thankfully, the vast majority of humans do not kill or harm others.

Ritualized human aggression. Violent and aggressive behaviour is so commonplace it may be viewed as entertainment. How "natural" is aggressive behaviour?

Biology

Despite problems with the instinctive view, aggression may have a biological basis. Physiological studies have shown that there are brain areas capable of triggering or ending aggressive behaviour. Also, researchers have found a relationship between aggression and such physical factors as hypoglycemia (low blood sugar), allergy, and specific brain injuries and disorders. For both men and women higher levels of the hormone testosterone are associated with more aggressive behaviour (Banks & Dabbs, 1996; Dabbs, Hargrove, & Heusel, 1996; Harris et al., 1996). None of these conditions, however, can be considered a direct cause of aggression. Instead, they probably lower the threshold for aggression, making hostile behaviour more likely to occur (Baron & Richardson, 1994).

Richard Tremblay of the University of Montreal has recently pointed out that physical aggression precedes verbal aggression ontogenetically (that is, in the development of the individual)

(Tremblay, 2000). In fact, Tremblay and his colleagues (1999) report that, in a sample of 511 children, 80 percent had been physically aggressive for the first time by 17 months. Noting that children typically learn to control their aggression by the time they enter school, Tremblay and colleagues challenge the idea that aggression becomes more common as children approach adolescence. Tremblay urges more study of infants' physical aggression. Such research should provide a strong test of the biological perspective on aggression.

The effects of alcohol and other drugs provide another indication of the role of the brain and biology in aggression. A variety of studies show that alcohol is involved in large percentages of murders and violent crimes. Like the conditions already noted, intoxicating drugs seem to lower inhibitions to act aggressively—often with tragic results (Bushman & Cooper, 1990; Ito, Miller, & Pollock, 1996).

To summarize, the fact that we are biologically capable of aggression does not mean that aggression is inevitable or "part of human nature." Twenty eminent scientists who studied the question concluded that "Biology does not condemn humanity to war. . . . Violence is neither in our evolutionary legacy nor in our genes. The same species that invented war is capable of inventing peace" (Scott & Ginsburg, 1994; UNESCO, 1990). Humans are fully capable of learning to inhibit their use of violence (Lore & Schultz, 1993).

Frustration

Step on a dog's tail and you may get nipped. Frustrate a human and you may get insulted. The **frustration–aggression hypothesis** states that frustration tends to lead to aggression (Dollard et al., 1939).

Does frustration always produce aggression? Although the connection is strong, a moment's thought will show that frustration does not always lead to aggression. Frustration, for instance, may lead to stereotyped responding or perhaps to a state of "learned helplessness" (see Chapter 11). Also, aggression can occur in the absence of frustration. This is illustrated by sports spectators who start fights, throw bottles, tear down goal posts, and so forth, after their team has *won.*

In fact, some psychologists distinguish between proactive aggression, which is used in the absence of provocation to achieve some goal, and reactive aggression, which involves a "hot-blooded," angry outburst in response to an actual or perceived threat. At the University of Montreal, Brendgen and colleagues (2001) distinguished between proactively and reactively violent boys at the age of 13. Three years later, they found that the proactively violent boys were most likely to have engaged in delinquent violence (for example, gang fights, stone throwing), while the reactively violent boys were most likely to have engaged in dating violence. Importantly, in both cases, a strong relationship with their mother kept violent 13-year-old boys from turning into violent 16-year-olds.

AVERSIVE STIMULI Frustration probably encourages aggression because it is uncomfortable. Various **aversive stimuli,** which produce discomfort or displeasure, can heighten hostility and aggression (Anderson, Anderson, & Deuser, 1996; Berkowitz, 1990) (see ▶Figure 14.10). Examples include insults, high temperatures, pain, and even disgusting scenes or odours. Such stimuli probably raise overall arousal levels so that we become more sensitive to **aggression cues** (signals that are associated with aggression) (Carlson, Marcus-Newhall, & Miller, 1990). Aversive stimuli also tend to activate ideas, memories, and expressions associated with anger and aggression (Berkowitz, 1990).

Some cues for aggression are internal (angry thoughts, for instance). Many are external: Certain words, actions, and gestures made by others are strongly associated with aggressive responses. A raised middle finger, for instance, is an almost universal invitation to aggression in North America. Weapons serve as particularly strong cues for aggressive behav-

Frustration-aggression hypothesis States that frustration tends to lead to aggression.

Aversive stimulus Any stimulus that produces discomfort or displeasure.

Aggression cues Stimuli or signals that are associated with aggression and that tend to elicit it.

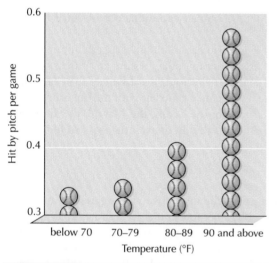

▶**Figure 14.10**

Personal discomfort caused by aversive (unpleasant) stimuli can make aggressive behaviour more likely. For example, studies of crime rates show that the incidence of highly aggressive behaviour, such as murder, rape, and assault, rises as the air temperature goes from warm to hot to sweltering (Anderson, 1989). The results you see here further confirm the heat-aggression link. The graph shows that there is a strong association between the temperatures at major league baseball games and the number of batters hit by a pitch during those games. When the temperature goes over 90°F (32°C), watch out for that fastball! (Reifman, Larrick, & Fein, 1991.)

▶Figure 14.11

Violent behaviour among delinquent boys doesn't appear overnight. Usually, their capacity for violence develops slowly, as they move from minor aggression to increasingly brutal acts. Overall aggression increases dramatically in early adolescence as boys gain physical strength and more access to weapons (Loeber & Hay, 1997).

iour (Berkowitz, 1968). The implication of this **weapons effect** seems to be that the symbols and trappings of aggression encourage aggression. A prime example is the fact that murders are almost three times more likely to occur in homes where guns are kept. Nearly 80 percent of the victims in such homes are killed by a family member or acquaintance. Only 4 percent are murdered by strangers (Kellermann et al., 1993).

Weapons effect The observation that weapons serve as strong cues for aggressive behaviour.

Social learning theory Combines learning principles with cognitive processes, socialization, and modelling to explain behaviour.

Disinhibition The removal of inhibition; results in acting out behaviour that normally would be restrained.

Desensitization A reduction in emotional sensitivity to a stimulus.

Social Learning

One of the most widely accepted explanations of aggression is also the simplest. Social learning theory holds that we learn to be aggressive by observing aggression in others (Bandura, 1973). **Social learning theory** combines learning principles with cognitive processes, socialization, and modelling to explain behaviour. According to this view, there is no instinctive human programming for fist-fighting, pipe-bombing, knife wielding, gun loading, 150-kilometre-an-hour "bean balls," or other violent or aggressive behaviours. Hence, aggression must be learned (see Figure ▶14.11).

York University researchers Paul O'Connell, Debra Pepler, and Wendy Craig observed incidents of bullying on school playgrounds. They found that older boys were more likely to join with the bullies than either younger boys, or older or younger girls. Both younger and older girls were more likely to try to intervene on behalf of the victims (O'Connell, Pepler, & Craig, 1999). They suggested that social learning causes boys to become more likely to participate in bullying, and that reinforcement, in the form of other children standing and watching, was important in this process.

TELEVISED VIOLENCE   Every day, TV provides an endless stream of bad models, especially concerning violence. The average North American has access to nearly 200 hours of violent programs per week. Eighty-one percent of all programs contain violence, which is often quite unrealistic. For instance, an astounding 73 percent of violent characters go unpunished, and 58 percent of violent acts don't lead to painful results. Only 16 percent of all programs show any realistic long-term consequences for violence. For children's programs, the rate falls to just 5 percent (National Television Violence Study, 1995–1996).

How much does TV violence affect children? As Albert Bandura showed in his studies of imitation (Chapter 6), children may learn new aggressive actions by watching violent or aggressive behaviour, or they may learn that violence is "okay." Either way, they are more likely to act aggressively. Heroes on TV are as violent as the villains, and they usually receive praise for their violence.

In addition to teaching new antisocial actions, television may disinhibit dangerous impulses that viewers already have. **Disinhibition** (the removal of inhibition) results in acting out behaviour that normally would be restrained. For example, many TV programs give the message that violence is acceptable behaviour that leads to success and popularity. For some people, this message can lower inhibitions against acting out hostile feelings (Berkowitz, 1984).

Another effect of TV violence is that it tends to lower sensitivity to violent acts. As anyone who has seen a street fight or a mugging can tell you, TV violence is sanitized and unrealistic. The real thing is gross, ugly, and gut wrenching. Even when it is graphic, TV violence is viewed in the relaxed and familiar setting of the home. For at least some viewers, this combination diminishes emotional reactions to violent scenes. When Victor Cline and his associates showed a bloody fight film to a group of boys, they found that heavy TV viewers (averaging 42 hours a week) showed much less emotion than those who watched little or no TV (Cline, Croft, & Courrier, 1972). Television, it seems, can cause a **desensitization** (reduced emotional sensitivity) to violence.

Prosocial behaviour
Behaviour toward others that is helpful, constructive, or altruistic.

Preventing Aggression

What can be done about aggression? Social learning theory implies that "aggression begets aggression." In other words, watching a prize fight or violent television program may increase aggression, rather than drain off aggressive urges. A case in point is provided by psychologist Leonard Eron, who spent 22 years following over 600 children into adulthood. Eron (1987) observes, "One of the best predictors of how aggressive a young man would be at age 19 was the violence of the television programs he preferred when he was eight years old" (see ►Figure 14.12). Others have found that viewers who watch violent videotapes have more aggressive thoughts. As we have noted, violent thoughts often precede violent actions (Bushman & Geen, 1990). Thus, the spiral of aggression might be broken if we did not so often portray it, reward it, and glorify it (Hughes & Hasbrouck, 1996). (See "Buffering Television's Impact.") The world's most peaceful societies actively teach their children to be cooperative, non-violent, and helpful (Bonta, 1997).

Beyond this, the question remains, How shall we tame the world's most dangerous animal? There is no easy answer. For the more immediate future, it is clear that we need more people who are willing to engage in helpful, altruistic, **prosocial behaviour** (actions that are constructive, unselfish, or helpful to others). In the next section we will examine some of the forces that prevent people from helping others and how prosocial behaviour might be promoted.

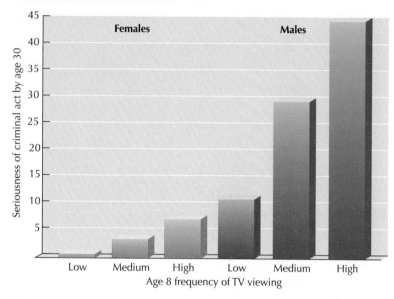

►Figure 14.12

Although TV violence does not cause aggression, it can encourage it. The likelihood of committing criminal acts by age 30 is related to the amount of TV watching a person did when she or he was a child (Eron, 1987). (Graph copyright 1987 by the American Psychological Association, Inc. Reprinted by permission of the author.)

USING PSYCHOLOGY Buffering Television's Impact

Other than pulling the plug, what can parents do about television's negative effects on children? Actually, quite a lot. Children typically model parents' TV viewing habits, and they are guided by parents' reactions to programs. Parents can make a big difference if they do the following (Eron, 1986; Huesmann, 1986; Schneider, 1987).

Parents as TV Guides

1. Limit total viewing time so that television does not dominate your child's view of the world. If necessary, set schedules for when watching TV is allowed. Don't use television as a babysitter.

2. Closely monitor what your child does watch. Change channels or turn off the TV if you object to a program. Be prepared to offer games and activities that stimulate your child's imagination and creativity.

3. Actively seek programs your child will enjoy, especially those that model positive behaviour and social attitudes.

4. Watch television with your child so that you can counter what is shown. Help your child distinguish between reality and TV fantasies. Reply to distortions and stereotypes as they appear on screen.

5. Discuss the social conflicts and violent solutions shown on television. Ask your child in what ways the situations are unrealistic and why the violence shown would not work in the real world. Encourage the child to propose more mature, realistic, and positive responses to situations.

6. Show by your own disapproval that violent TV heroes are not the ones to emulate. Remember, children who identify with TV characters are more likely to be influenced by televised aggression.

By following these guidelines you can help children learn to enjoy television without being overly influenced by programs and advertisers. A recent study found that elementary school children are less aggressive when they decrease the amount of time they spend watching TV and playing video games (Robinson et al., 2001).

▶ Prosocial Behaviour—Helping Others

Survey Question:
■ Why are bystanders so often unwilling to help in an emergency?

Does this person need help? What factors determine whether a person in trouble will receive help in an emergency? Surprisingly, more potential helpers tend to lower the chances that help will be given.

Bystander apathy
Unwillingness of bystanders to offer help during emergencies or to become involved in others' problems.

In May 2001, employees in a Montreal office building noticed a young woman lying in the rain, naked from the waist down and apparently in pain. They did nothing for three hours, with their supervisor telling them not to get involved. The supervisor, who was subsequently fired, claimed he thought the woman was a vagrant and that he did not know she was in distress at first. When she had not moved three hours later, he asked employees to call the police. The comatose woman was taken to hospital.

This case evoked memories of the murder of Kitty Genovese in Queens, New York, in 1964. Late one night, tenants of a Queens apartment building watched and listened in horror as she was murdered on the sidewalk outside. From the safety of their rooms, no fewer than 38 people heard the agonized screams as her assailant stabbed her, was frightened off, and returned to stab her again.

Kitty Genovese's murder took over 30 minutes, but none of her neighbours tried to help. None even called the police until after the attack had ended. Perhaps it is understandable that no one wanted to get involved. After all, it could have been a violent lovers' quarrel. Or helping might have meant risking personal injury. But what prevented these people from at least calling the police? And why did the employees in Montreal take so long to help the comatose young woman?

Aren't these just examples of the alienation of city life? News reports treated events such as these as evidence of a breakdown in social ties caused by the impersonality of the city. While it is true that urban living can be dehumanizing, this does not fully explain such **bystander apathy** (unwillingness of bystanders to offer help during emergencies). According to psychologists John Darley and Bibb Latané (1968), failure to help is related to the number of people present. Over the years many studies have shown that the more potential helpers are present, the lower the chances that help will be given (Latané et al., 1981).

Why would people be less willing to help when others are present? In Kitty Genovese's case, the answer is that everyone thought someone else would help. The dynamics of this effect are easily illustrated: Suppose that two motorists have stalled at roadside, one on a sparsely travelled country road and the other on a busy freeway. Who gets help first?

On the freeway, where hundreds of cars pass every minute, each driver can assume that someone else will help. Personal responsibility for helping is spread so thin that no one takes action. On the country road, one of the first few people to arrive will probably stop, since the responsibility is clearly theirs. In general, Darley and Latané assume that bystanders are not truly apathetic or uncaring; they are inhibited by the presence of others.

Bystander Intervention

People must pass through four decision points before giving help. First they must notice that something is happening. Next they must define the event as an emergency. Then they must take responsibility. Finally, they must select a course of action (see ▶Figure 14.13 on page 562). Laboratory experiments have shown that each step can be influenced by the presence of other people.

NOTICING   What would happen if you fainted and collapsed on the sidewalk? Would someone stop to help? Would people think you were drunk? Would they even notice you? Darley and Latané suggest that if the sidewalk is crowded, few people will even see you. This has nothing to do with people blocking each other's vision. Instead, it is related to widely accepted norms against staring at others in public. People in crowds typically "keep their eyes to themselves."

Is there any way to show that this is a factor in bystander apathy? To test this idea, students were asked to fill out a questionnaire either alone or in a room full of people. While the students worked, a thick cloud of smoke was blown into the room through a vent.

Most students left alone in the room noticed the smoke immediately. Few of the people in groups noticed the smoke until it actually became difficult to see through it.

▶ **Figure 14.13**

This decision tree summarizes the steps a person must take before making a commitment to offer help, according to Darley and Latané's model.

Subjects working in groups politely kept their eyes on their papers and avoided looking at others (or the smoke). In contrast, those who were alone scanned the room from time to time.

DEFINING AN EMERGENCY The smoke-filled room also shows the influence others have on defining a situation as an emergency. When subjects in groups finally noticed the smoke, they cast sidelong glances at others in the room. Apparently, they were searching for clues to help interpret what was happening. No one wanted to overreact or act like a fool if there was no emergency. However, as subjects coolly surveyed the reactions of others, they were themselves being watched. In real emergencies, people sometimes "fake each other out" and underestimate the need for action because each person attempts to appear calm. In short, until someone acts, no one acts.

TAKING RESPONSIBILITY Perhaps the most crucial step in helping is assuming responsibility. In this case, groups limit helping by causing a **diffusion of responsibility** (spreading responsibility among several people).

Can we prove that people in groups are less likely to help others? In fact, it isn't too difficult. For example, working at York University, David Wiesenthal, Douglas Austrom, and Irwin Silverman approached people in the student pub to ask for a donation to charity. Students sitting by themselves gave more, on average, than students in groups. In a second study, students in small classes gave more when approached in the classroom than did students in large classes (Wiesenthal, Austrom, & Silverman, 1983).

Is diffusion of responsibility always bad? Funny you should ask—because, no, it isn't, as shown by Glen Whyte of the Rotman School of Management at the University of Toronto. Whyte (1991) studied a phenomenon known as *escalation of commitment.* This is seen when an enterprise—typically, a business—is about to fail. The person or persons who initiated the enterprise will escalate their commitment—they will invest more money in it, even when it has become clear that the enterprise has no chance of success. Whyte asked: Is such escalation less likely to happen if the enterprise was initiated by a group decision, rather than by an individual? The answer is yes. In that case, people are more likely to "pull the plug" rather than waste more resources in a futile attempt to save the business. Once again we see that most aspects of human psychology have something going for them!

People do help in some emergencies. How are these different? It is not always clear what makes the difference. Helping behaviour is complex and influenced by many variables. One naturalistic experiment staged in a New York City subway gives a hint of the kinds of things that may be important. When a "victim" (actor) "passed out" in a subway car, he received more help when carrying a cane than when carrying a liquor bottle. More important, however, was the fact that most people were willing to help in either case (Piliavin, Rodin, & Piliavin, 1969).

To better answer the question, we need to consider some factors not included in Darley and Latané's account of helping.

Who Will Help Whom?

Many studies suggest that when we see a person in trouble, it tends to cause *heightened arousal* (Dovidio, 1984). This aroused, keyed-up feeling can motivate us to give aid, but only if the rewards of helping outweigh the costs. Higher costs (such as great effort, personal risk, or possible embarrassment) almost always decrease helping (Foss, 1986). In addition to general arousal, potential helpers may also feel **empathic arousal.** This means

Diffusion of responsibility Spreading the responsibility to act among several people; reduces the likelihood that help will be given to a person in need.

Empathic arousal Emotional arousal that occurs when you feel some of another person's pain, fear, or anguish.

they empathize with the person in need or feel some of the person's pain, fear, or anguish. Helping is much more likely when we are able to take the perspective of others and feel sympathy for their plight (Eisenberg, 1991).

Empathic arousal is especially likely to motivate helping when the person in need seems to be similar to ourselves (Eisenberg & Miller, 1987). In fact, a feeling of connection to the victim may be one of the most important factors in helping. This, perhaps, is why being in a good mood also increases helping. When we are feeling successful, happy, or fortunate, we may also feel more connected to others (Dovidio, 1984). In summary, there is a strong **empathy-helping relationship:** We are most likely to help someone in need when we "feel for" that person and experience emotions such as empathy, sympathy, and compassion (Batson, 1990).

Is there anything that can be done to encourage prosocial behaviour? People who see others helping are more likely to offer help themselves. Also, persons who give help in one situation tend to perceive themselves as helpful people. This change in self-image encourages them to help in other situations. One more point is that norms of fairness encourage us to help others who have helped us (Dovidio, 1984). For all these reasons, helping others not only assists them directly, it encourages others to help too.

"DE-VICTIMIZE" YOURSELF   If you should find yourself in need of help during an emergency, what can you do to avoid being a victim of bystander apathy? The work we have reviewed here suggests that you should make sure that you are noticed, that people realize there's an emergency, and that they need to take action. Being noticed can be promoted in some situations by shouting "Fire!" Bystanders who might run away from a robbery or an assault may rush to see where the fire is. At the very least, remember not to just scream. Instead, you should call out "Help" or "I need help right now." Whenever possible, define your situation for bystanders. Say, for instance, "I'm being attacked, call the police." Or, "Stop that man, he has my purse." You can also directly assign responsibility to a bystander by pointing to someone and saying, "You, call the police" or "I'm injured, I need you to call an ambulance" (Cummins, 1995).

A LOOK AHEAD   The Psychology in Action section of this chapter returns to the topic of prejudice for some further thoughts about how to promote tolerance. Don't miss this interesting conclusion to our discussion of social psychology.

> **Empathy-helping relationship** Observation that we are most likely to help someone else when we feel emotions such as empathy and compassion.

Knowledge builder

AGGRESSION AND PROSOCIAL BEHAVIOUR

Relate

Most people have been angry enough at some time to behave aggressively. Which concepts or theories do you think best explain your own aggressive actions?

An elderly woman is at the side of the road, trying to change a flat tire. She obviously needs help. You are approaching her in your car. What must happen before you are likely to stop and help her?

Learning Check

1. The position of ethologists is that there is no biological basis for aggression. T or F?
2. Higher levels of testosterone are associated with more aggressive behaviour. T or F?
3. Frustration and aversive stimuli are more likely to produce aggression when cues for aggressive behaviour are present. T or F?

4. Social learning theory holds that exposure to aggressive models helps drain off aggressive energies. T or F?
5. Heavy exposure to television results in lowered emotional sensitivity to violence. T or F?
6. _____ behaviour refers to actions that are constructive, altruistic, or helpful to others.
7. Seeing that a person in need is similar to ourselves tends to increase empathic arousal and the likelihood that help will be given. T or F?

Critical Thinking

8. If televised violence contributes to aggressive behaviour in our society, do you think it is possible that television could also promote prosocial behaviour?

Answers:
1. F 2. T 3. T 4. F 5. T 6. Prosocial 7. T 8. Yes, TV could be used to promote helping, cooperation, charity, and brotherhood in the same way that it has encouraged aggression. Numerous studies show that prosocial behaviour on TV increases prosocial behaviour by viewers.

PSYCHOLOGY IN ACTION

MULTICULTURALISM— LIVING WITH DIVERSITY

?

Survey Question:
- What can be done to lower prejudice and promote social harmony?

Multiculturalism Giving equal status, recognition, and acceptance to different ethnic and cultural groups.

Individuating information Information that helps define a person as an individual, rather than as a member of a group or social category.

Just-world beliefs Belief that people generally get what they deserve.

Today's society is more like a "tossed salad" than a cultural "melting pot." Rather than expecting everyone to be alike, psychologists believe that we must learn to respect and appreciate our differences. **Multiculturalism,** as this is called, gives equal status to different ethnic, racial, and cultural groups. It is a recognition and acceptance of human diversity (Fowers & Richardson, 1996).

BREAKING THE PREJUDICE HABIT   Most people publicly support policies of equality and fairness. Yet, many still have lingering biases and negative images of people who belong to ethnic groups other than their own. How can we make sense of such conflicting attitudes? Patricia Devine, a social psychologist, has shown that a decision to forsake prejudice does not immediately eliminate prejudiced thoughts and feelings. Non-prejudiced people may continue to respond emotionally to members of other ethnic groups. Quite likely this reflects lingering stereotypes and prejudices learned in childhood (Devine et al., 1991).

For many people, becoming less prejudiced begins with sincerely accepting values of tolerance and equality. People who value tolerance feel pangs of guilt or self-criticism when they have intolerant thoughts or feelings (Zuwerink et al., 1996). This motivates them to try to alter their own biased reactions (Dovidio & Gaertner, 1999). But doing so is not easy. Typically, it requires repeated efforts to learn to think, feel, and act differently. Nevertheless, many people have succeeded in overcoming the "prejudice habit" (Devine et al., 1991). If you would like to be more tolerant, the following points may be helpful to you.

Beware of Stereotyping   Stereotypes make the social world more manageable. For years, social psychologists have argued that placing people in categories almost always causes them to appear more similar than they really are. As a result, we tend to see out-group members as very much alike, even when they are as varied as our friends and family. On this view, non-prejudiced persons work hard to actively inhibit stereotyped thoughts and to emphasize fairness and equality (Devine, 1990). The implication is that a good way to tear down stereotypes is to get to know individuals from various racial, ethnic, and cultural groups.

Seek Individuating Information   When are we most tempted to apply stereotypes? Typically it is when we have only minimal information about a person. Stereotypes help us guess what a person is like and how she or he will act. Unfortunately, these inferences are usually wrong.

One of the best antidotes for stereotypes is **individuating information** (information that helps us see a person as an individual, rather than as a member of a group) (Click, Zion, & Nelson, 1988). Anything that keeps us from placing a person in a particular social category tends to negate stereotyped thinking. When you meet individuals from various backgrounds, focus on the person, not the label attached to her or him.

Don't Fall Prey to Just-World Beliefs   Do you believe that the world is basically fair? Even if you don't, you may believe that the world is sufficiently just so that people generally get what they deserve. It may not be obvious, but such beliefs can directly increase prejudiced thinking.

As a result of discrimination, social conditions, and circumstances (such as recent immigration), minorities may occupy lower socioeconomic positions. **Just-world beliefs** (belief that people generally get what they deserve) can lead us to assume that minority group members wouldn't be in such positions if they weren't inferior in some way. This bit of faulty thinking amounts to blaming people who are *victims* of prejudice and discrimination for their plight.

Be Aware of Self-Fulfilling Prophecies   If you hold strong stereotypes about members of various groups, a vicious cycle can be set up. When you meet someone who is different from yourself, you may treat her or him in a way that is consistent with your stereotypes.

Self-fulfilling prophecy
An expectation that prompts people to act in ways that make the expectation come true.

If the other person is influenced by your behaviour, she or he may act in ways that seem to match your stereotype. This creates a self-fulfilling prophecy and reinforces your belief in the stereotype. (A **self-fulfilling prophecy** is an expectation that prompts people to act in ways that make the expectation come true.)

Remember, Different Does Not Mean Inferior   Some conflicts between groups cannot be avoided. What can be avoided is unnecessary social competition (rivalry among groups, each of which regards itself as superior to others). The concept of social competition refers to the fact that some people seek to enhance their self-esteem by identifying with a "superior" group. However, people who have genuine self-esteem don't need to treat others as inferior in order to feel good about themselves. Similarly, it is not necessary to degrade other groups in order to feel positive about one's own group identity (Messick & Mackie, 1989). In fact, each ethnic group has strengths that members of other groups could benefit from emulating. For instance, African Americans, Asians, and Latinos emphasize family networks that help buffer them from some of the stresses of daily life (Suinn, 1999).

Understand That Race Is a Social Construction   From the viewpoint of modern genetics, the concept of race has absolutely no meaning. Members of various groups are so varied genetically and human groups have intermixed for so many centuries, that it is impossible to tell, biologically, to what "race" any given individual belongs. Thus, race is an illusion based on superficial physical differences and learned ethnic identities. Certainly people act as if different races exist. But this is a matter of social labelling, not biological reality. To assume that any human group is biologically superior or inferior to another is simply wrong. In fact, the best available evidence suggests that all people are descended from the same ancient ancestors. The origins of our species lie in Africa, about 100 000 years ago. Biologically, we are all brothers and sisters under the skin (Cavalli-Sforza, 1991; Segall, Lonner, & Berry, 1998).

Look for Commonalities   We live in a society that puts a premium on competition and individual effort. One problem with this is that competing with others fosters desires to demean, defeat, and vanquish them. When we cooperate with others we tend to share their joys and suffer when they are in distress (Lanzetta & Englis, 1989). If we don't find ways to cooperate and live in greater harmony, everyone will suffer. That, if nothing else, is one thing that we all have in common. Everyone knows what it feels like to be different. Greater tolerance comes from remembering those times.

TOLERANCE AND CULTURAL AWARENESS   Living comfortably in a multicultural society means getting to know a little about other groups. Getting acquainted with a person whose cultural background is different from your own can be a wonderful learning experience. No one culture has all the answers or the best ways of doing things. Multicultural populations enrich a community's food, music, arts, and philosophy. Likewise, learning about different racial, cultural, and ethnic groups can be personally rewarding.

Knowledge builder

MULTICULTURALISM

Relate

Which strategies for breaking the prejudice habit do you already use? How could you apply the remaining strategies to become more tolerant?

Learning Check

1. Multiculturalism refers to the belief that various subcultures and ethnic groups should be blended into a single emergent culture. T or F?
2. Patricia Devine found that many people who hold non-prejudiced beliefs still have prejudiced thoughts and feelings in the presence of minority group individuals. T or F?

3. Individuating information tends to be a good antidote for stereotypes. T or F?
4. Just-world beliefs are the primary cause of social competition. T or F?

Critical Thinking

5. Why is it valuable to learn the terms by which members of various groups prefer to be addressed (for example, Native, Aboriginal, Indigenous, or Indian)?

Answers:

1. F 2. T 3. T 4. F 5. Because labels might have negative meanings that are not apparent to persons outside the group. Labels may have historical associations with periods of oppression or exploitation. Such associations may reasonably be expected to cause distress. Members of any particular group are, obviously, best qualified to say which labels have such an effect on their group and thus should be avoided.

Psychologist's Journal

EPILOGUE

The technological advances of the last 20 years have dramatically changed what is humanly possible. For example, as we write this, the International Space Station is being assembled in orbit by a shuttle crew. Yet, as a species we still have much in common with people who lived many hundreds of years ago. Although we might like to think otherwise, we cannot count on technology to solve all of our problems. The threat of war, social conflict, crime, prejudice, infectious disease, overpopulation, environmental damage, famine, homicide, economic disaster—these and most other major dilemmas facing us are behavioural. Will the human family endure? It's a psychological question.

At the beginning of this book we described psychology as a journey of self-discovery. It is our sincere hope that you have found enough relevance and value here to kindle a lifelong interest in psychology. As your personal journey continues, one thing is certain: Many of your greatest challenges and most treasured moments will involve other people. That's why it's important to keep adding to your understanding of human behaviour. Psychology's future looks exciting. What role will it play in your life?

CHAPTER IN REVIEW

Major Points

▶ Social psychology studies how we behave, think, and feel in social situations.

▶ We are attracted to other people for reasons that are fairly universal.

▶ To understand social behaviour we must know what roles people play, their status, the norms they follow, and the attributions they make.

▶ Everyone is affected by pressures to conform, obey, and comply. There are times when it is valuable to resist such pressures.

▶ Attitudes subtly affect nearly all aspects of social behaviour.

▶ To persuade others, you must be aware of your role as a communicator, the nature of the audience, and messages that will appeal to them.

▶ Prejudice is reduced by equal-status contact and mutual interdependence.

▶ Aggression is a fact of life, but humans are not inevitably aggressive.

▶ We can encourage helping and altruism by removing barriers to prosocial behaviour.

▶ Multicultural harmony can be attained through conscious efforts to be more tolerant of others.

Summary

Why Do People Affiliate? What Factors Influence Interpersonal Attraction?

• Affiliation is tied to needs for approval, support, friendship, and information. Also, affiliation can reduce anxiety.

• Social comparison theory holds that we affiliate to evaluate our actions, feelings, and abilities.

• Interpersonal attraction is increased by frequent contact, beauty, competence, and similarity.

• Mate selection is characterized by a large degree of similarity on many dimensions.

• Self-disclosure follows a reciprocity norm: Low levels of self-disclosure are met with low levels in return; moderate self-disclosure elicits more personal replies.

• In comparison with liking, romantic love involves higher levels of emotional arousal, and it is accompanied by mutual absorption between lovers.

• Evolutionary psychology attributes human mating patterns to the differing reproductive challenges faced by men and women since the dawn of time.

How Does Group Membership Affect Individual Behaviour?

• Social roles are particular behaviour patterns associated with social positions.

- Higher status within groups is associated with special privileges and respect.
- Group structure refers to roles, communication pathways, and power within a group. Group cohesiveness is the degree of attraction among group members.
- Norms are standards of conduct enforced (formally or informally) by groups.
- Attribution theory describes how we perceive the causes of behaviour.
- The fundamental attributional error is to think that internal causes explain the actions of other people. In contrast, we tend to attribute our own behaviour to external causes.

What Have Social Psychologists Learned about Conformity, Obedience, Compliance, and Self-Assertion?

- Social influence refers to alterations in behaviour brought about by the behaviour of others.
- The famous Asch experiments demonstrated that various group pressure and group sanctions encourage conformity.
- Groupthink refers to compulsive conformity in group decision making.
- Obedience to authority in Milgram's studies decreased when the "teacher" and "learner" were close to one another, when the authority was absent, and when others refused to obey.
- Three strategies for gaining compliance are the foot-in-the-door technique, the door-in-the-face approach, and the low-ball technique.
- Many people show a surprising level of passive compliance to unreasonable requests.
- Self-assertion, as opposed to aggression, involves clearly stating one's wants and needs to others.

How Are Attitudes Acquired and Changed?

- Attitudes are learned dispositions made up of a belief component, an emotional component, and an action component.
- Attitudes may be formed by direct contact, interaction with others, child-rearing practices, and group pressures. Peer group influences, reference group membership, the mass media, and chance conditioning also appear to be important in attitude formation.
- Effective persuasion occurs when characteristics of the communicator, the message, and the audience are well matched.
- In general, a likable and believable communicator who repeats a credible message that arouses emotion in the audience and states clear-cut conclusions will be persuasive.
- Maintaining and changing attitudes is closely related to cognitive dissonance and our needs to be consistent in our thoughts and actions.

Is Brainwashing Actually Possible? How Are People Converted to Cult Membership?

- Brainwashing is a form of forced attitude change. It depends on control of the target person's total environment.
- Three steps in brainwashing are unfreezing, changing, and refreezing attitudes and beliefs.
- Many cults recruit new members with high-pressure indoctrination techniques involving isolation, displays of affection, rituals, intimidation, and escalating commitment.

What Causes Prejudice and Intergroup Conflict?

- Prejudice is a negative attitude held toward members of various out-groups. One theory attributes prejudice to scapegoating. A second account says that prejudices may be held for personal reasons (personal prejudice) or simply through adherence to group norms (group prejudice).
- Prejudiced individuals tend to have an authoritarian personality.
- Intergroup conflict gives rise to hostility and the formation of social stereotypes. Status inequalities tend to build prejudice. Equal-status contact tends to reduce it.
- Superordinate goals are a key to reducing intergroup conflict.
- On a smaller scale, jigsaw classrooms (which encourage cooperation through mutual interdependence) have been shown to combat prejudice.

How Do Psychologists Explain Human Aggression?

- Ethological explanations of aggression attribute it to inherited instincts. Biological explanations emphasize brain mechanisms and physical factors related to thresholds for aggression.
- According to the frustration-aggression hypothesis, frustration and aggression are closely linked.
- Frustration is only one of many aversive stimuli that can arouse a person and make aggression more likely. Aggression is especially likely to occur when aggression cues are present.
- Social learning theory has focused attention on the role of aggressive models in the development of aggressive behaviour.

Why Are Bystanders So Often Unwilling to Help in an Emergency?

- Four decision points that must be passed before a person gives help are: noticing, defining an emergency, taking responsibility, and selecting a course of action.
- Helping is less likely at each point when other potential helpers are present.
- Helping is encouraged by general arousal, empathic arousal, being in a good mood, low effort or risk, and perceived similarity between the victim and the helper.

- For several reasons, giving help tends to encourage others to help too.

What Can Be Done to Lower Prejudice and Promote Social Harmony?

- Multiculturalism is an attempt to give equal status to different ethnic, racial, and cultural groups.

- Greater tolerance can be encouraged by neutralizing stereotypes with individuating information; by looking for commonalities with others; and by avoiding the effects of just-world beliefs, self-fulfilling prophecies, and social competition.
- Cultural awareness is a key element in promoting greater social harmony.

PSYCHOLOGY ON THE NET

If you have difficulty finding any of the sites listed here, visit http://www.psychologyjourney.nelson.com for an updated list of Internet addresses and direct links to relevant sites.

Center for Evolutionary Psychology   A primer on evolutionary psychology, a reading list, and links. http://www.psych.ucsb.edu/research/cep/

FacePrints   This site examines our perceptions of facial attractiveness. http://www.psych.nmsu.edu/~vic/faceprints/

Facial Attractiveness: A PsyQuest   Discusses research on facial attractiveness. http://cc6.cumber.edu/ psych/w/Facial%20Attractiveness/ Facial%20Attractiveness%20Home.htm.

Implicit Association Test   Online tests that purportedly reveal the unconscious roots of prejudice. http://buster.cs.yale.edu/implicit/

Information about Cults and Psychological Manipulation   http://www.csj.org/

Social Psychology Network   A comprehensive site with many links to information about social psychology. http://www.socialpsychology.org/

Violence on Television   Discusses research and implications of watching violence on television. http://www.apa.org/pubinfo/violence.html

InfoTrac College Edition   For recent articles on the Psychology in Action feature, use Key Words search for MULTICULTURALISM. For recent articles on coercive attitude change, use Key Words search for CULTS and BRAINWASHING.

INTERACTIVE LEARNING

Psychology: An Interactive Journey   Remember that Chapter 14 of the CD-ROM that came with this text has practice tests, flashcards, interactive exercises, a crossword puzzle, and other valuable materials to enhance your learning experience.

PsychNow!   8a. Helping Others, 8b. Attribution, 8c. Social Influence, 8d. Attitudes and Prejudice, 8e. Aggression, 8g. Gender and Stereotyping.

Psyk.trek   12. Social Psychology.

Chart Your Progress

The questions that follow are only a sample of what you need to know. If you miss any of the items, you should review the entire chapter, do the exercises on the CD, and review the Knowledge Builders. Another way to prepare for tests is to get more practice with *WebTutor*, the *Study Guide*, or the *Practice Quizzes* that are available with this text.

1. The pattern known as homogamy shows the powerful effect that _____ has on interpersonal attraction.
   a. physical beauty
   b. similarity
   c. competence
   d. mutual absorption

2. The fact that men tend to prefer younger, more physically attractive partners is predicted by
   a. evolutionary psychology
   b. the overdisclosure hypothesis
   c. social comparison theory
   d. Rubin's studies of mutual absorption

3. A common error we all make is to attribute the actions of others to internal causes. This is known as the fundamental
   a. reciprocity norm
   b. role conflict
   c. social comparison
   d. attributional error

4. Groupthink is an example of the danger that lies in powerful pressures for group
   a. cohesion
   b. conformity
   c. attribution
   d. reciprocity

5. In Milgram's experiments, the lowest level of obedience occurred when subjects
   a. saw another person refuse to obey
   b. were in the same room with the "learner"
   c. were fact to face with the "learner"
   d. received orders over the phone

6. Which compliance technique involves getting a person committed to act and then making the terms of acting less desirable?
   a. foot in the door
   b. low ball
   c. door in the face
   d. groupthink

7. The three parts of an attitude are
   a. internal, external, group
   b. conviction, attribution, absorption
   c. status, norm, cohesion
   d. belief, emotion, action

8. The amount of cognitive dissonance a person feels is related to how much _____ exists for his or her actions.
   a. reciprocity
   b. justification
   c. chance conditioning
   d. reference

9. One of the reasons that superordinate goals tend to reduce prejudice is that they require cooperation and
   a. social stereotyping
   b. ethnocentrism
   c. unfreezing
   d. equal-status contact

10. The point of view most at odds with the idea that humans are instinctively aggressive is
    a. social learning theory
    b. the frustration-aggression hypothesis
    c. ethology
    d. the aversive stimuli effect

11. People are more likely to help another who is in trouble if
    a. many other helpers are present
    b. a diffusion of responsibility occurs
    c. they experience empathic arousal
    d. desensitization has taken place

12. One of the best antidotes for stereotypes is
    a. accepting just-world beliefs
    b. individuating information
    c. accepting self-fulfilling prophecies
    d. honest social competition

Answers: 1. b 2. a 3. d 4. b 5. d 6. b 7. d 8. b 9. d 10. a 11. c 12. b

Glossary

Ablation Surgical removal of tissue.

Abstract principles Concepts and ideas removed from specific examples and concrete situations.

Accommodation (perceptual) Changes in the shape of the lens of the eye.

Accommodation (Piaget) The modification of existing mental patterns to fit new demands (that is, mental schemes are changed to accommodate new information or experiences).

Acetylcholine The neurotransmitter released by neurons to activate muscles.

Achieved role A role that is assumed voluntarily.

Acquired immune deficiency syndrome (AIDS) A frequently fatal disease caused by HIV infection. In AIDS, the immune system is weakened, allowing other infections to attack the body.

Acquired strategies Learned tactics for swiftly solving the problems encountered in one's area of expertise.

Acquisition The period in conditioning during which a response is reinforced.

Acromegaly Enlargement of the arms, hands, feet, and face caused by excess growth hormone late in the human growth period.

Action component How one tends to act toward the object of an attitude.

Action potential The nerve impulse.

Activation As reflected by facial expressions, the degree of arousal a person is experiencing.

Activation-synthesis hypothesis An attempt to explain how dream content is affected by motor commands in the brain that occur during sleep, but are not carried out.

Actor-observer bias The tendency to attribute the behaviour of others to internal causes while attributing one's own behaviour to external causes (situations and circumstances).

Acute stress disorder A psychological disturbance lasting up to one month following stresses that would produce anxiety in anyone who experienced them.

Adaptive behaviours Actions that aid attempts to survive and adapt to changing conditions.

Adjustment disorder An emotional disturbance caused by ongoing stressors within the range of common experience.

Adrenal cortex The outer layer of the adrenal glands; produces hormones that affect salt intake, reactions to stress, and sexual development.

Adrenal glands Endocrine glands that arouse the body, regulate salt balance, adjust the body to stress, and affect sexual functioning.

Adrenal medulla The inner core of the adrenal glands; a source of epinephrine and norepinephrine.

Adrenaline A hormone produced by the adrenal glands that tends to arouse the body.

Affectional needs Emotional needs for love and affection.

Afterimage Visual sensation that persists after a stimulus is removed.

Aggression Any action carried out with the intention of harming another person.

Aggression cues Stimuli or signals that are associated with aggression and that tend to elicit it.

Agoraphobia (without panic) People fear that something extremely embarrassing will happen to them if they leave the house or enter unfamiliar situations.

Alarm reaction First stage of the G.A.S., during which bodily resources are mobilized to cope with a stressor.

Alcohol Common name for ethyl alcohol, the intoxicating element in fermented and distilled liquors.

All-or-nothing thinking Classifying objects or events as absolutely right or wrong, good or bad, acceptable or unacceptable, and so forth.

Alpha waves Large, slow brain waves associated with relaxation and falling asleep.

Altered state of consciousness (ASC) A condition of awareness distinctly different in quality or pattern from waking consciousness.

Alzheimer's disease An age-related disease characterized by memory loss, mental confusion, and (in its later stages) a nearly total loss of mental abilities.

Ambiguous stimuli Patterns that allow more than one perceptual organization.

Ambivalence Mixed positive and negative feelings or simultaneous attraction and repulsion.

Amphetamine psychosis A severe disruption of psychological functioning caused by abuse of amphetamines.

Amphetamines A class of synthetic drugs having stimulant effects on the nervous system.

Ampulla An enlarged area in a semicircular canal containing a crista.

Amygdala A part of the limbic system associated with fear responses.

Anagrams Test A test of creativity in which subjects try to make as many new words as possible from the letters in a given word.

Anal stage The psychosexual stage corresponding roughly to the period of toilet training (ages one to three years).

Anal-expulsive personality A disorderly, destructive, cruel, or messy person.

Anal-retentive personality A person who is obstinate, stingy, or compulsive, and who generally has difficulty "letting go."

Androgen Any of a number of male sex hormones.

Androgyny The presence of both "masculine" and "feminine" traits in a single person (as masculinity and femininity are defined within one's culture).

Anhedonia An inability to feel pleasure.

Animal model In research, an animal whose behaviour is used to discover principles that may apply to human behaviour.

Anorexia nervosa Active self-starvation or a sustained loss of appetite that has psychological origins.

Anosmia Loss or impairment of the sense of smell.

Antecedents Events that precede a response.

Anterograde amnesia Loss of the ability to form or retrieve memories of events that occur after an injury or trauma.

Anthropomorphic fallacy The error of attributing human thoughts, feelings, or motives to animals, especially as a way of explaining their behaviour.

Antidepressants Mood-elevating drugs.

Antipsychotics Drugs that, in addition to having tranquillizing effects, tend to reduce hallucinations and delusional thinking. (Also called major tranquillizers.)

Antisocial personality A person who lacks a conscience, is emotionally shallow, impulsive, selfish, and tends to manipulate others.

Anxiety Apprehension, dread, or uneasiness similar to fear but based on an unclear threat.

Anxiety disorder Disruptive feelings of fear, apprehension, or anxiety, or distortions in behaviour that are anxiety related.

Anxiety reduction hypothesis Explains the self-defeating nature of avoidance responses as a result of the reinforcing effects of relief from anxiety.

Aphasia A speech disturbance resulting from brain damage.

Apparent-distance hypothesis An explanation of the moon illusion stating that the horizon seems more distant than the night sky.

Applied research Scientific study undertaken to solve immediate practical problems.

Approach–approach conflict Choosing between two positive, or desirable, alternatives.

Approach–avoidance conflict Being attracted to and repelled by the same goal or activity.

Arousal The overall level of activation in the body and

nervous system of a person or animal.

Arousal theory Assumes that people prefer to maintain ideal, or comfortable, levels of arousal.

Artificial intelligence Any artificial system (often a computer program) that is capable of human-like problem solving or intelligent responding.

Ascribed role A role that is assigned to a person; a role one has no choice about playing.

Assertiveness training Instruction in how to be self-assertive and self-confident.

Assimilation In Piaget's theory, the application of existing mental patterns to new situations (that is, the new situation is assimilated to existing mental schemes).

Association cortex All areas of the cerebral cortex that are not primarily sensory or motor in function.

Astigmatism Defects in the cornea, lens, or eye that cause some areas of vision to be out of focus.

Astrology False system based on the belief that human behaviour is influenced by the position of stars and planets.

Asymptomatic Refers to having a disease while lacking obvious symptoms of illness.

Attention–rejection As reflected by facial expressions, the degree of attention given to a person or object.

Attitude A learned tendency to respond to people, objects, or institutions in a positive or negative way.

Attribution The process of making inferences about the causes of one's own behaviour and that of others.

Audience The person or group toward whom a persuasive message is directed.

Auditory ossicles The three small bones that link the eardrum to the cochlea.

Authenticity In Carl Rogers's terms, the ability of a therapist to be genuine and honest about his or her own feelings.

Authoritarian parents Parents who enforce rigid rules and demand strict obedience to authority.

Authoritarian personality A personality pattern characterized

by rigidity, inhibition, prejudice, and an excessive concern with power, authority, and obedience.

Authoritative parents Parents who supply firm and consistent guidance combined with love and affection.

Autonomic nervous system (ANS) The system of nerves that connects the brain with the internal organs and glands.

Autonomic system Nerves carrying information to and from the internal organs and glands.

Autonomy versus shame and doubt A conflict between growing self-control and feelings of shame or doubt.

Aversion therapy Suppressing an undesirable response by associating it with aversive (painful or uncomfortable) stimuli.

Aversive stimulus A stimulus that is painful or uncomfortable.

Avoidance learning Learning to make a response in order to postpone or prevent discomfort.

Avoidance-avoidance conflict Choosing between two negative, or undesirable, alternatives.

Axon Fibre that carries information away from the cell body of a neuron.

Axon terminals Branching fibres at the ends of axons.

Babbling The repetition by infants of meaningless language sounds (including both vowel and consonant sounds).

Barbiturate One of a large group of sedative drugs that depress activity in the nervous system.

Barnum effect The tendency to consider a personal description accurate if it is stated in very general terms.

Base rate The basic rate at which an event occurs over time; the basic probability of an event.

Basic emotions The first distinct emotions to emerge in infancy.

Basic needs The first four levels of needs in Maslow's hierarchy; lower needs tend to be more potent than higher needs.

Basic research Scientific study undertaken without concern for immediate practical application.

Basic suggestion effect The tendency of hypnotized persons

to carry out suggested actions as if they were involuntary.

Behaviour modification The application of learning principles to change human behaviour, especially maladaptive behaviour.

Behaviour therapy Any therapy designed to actively change behaviour.

Behavioural assessment Recording the frequency of various behaviours.

Behavioural contract A formal agreement stating behaviours to be changed and consequences that apply.

Behavioural dieting Weight reduction based on changing exercise and eating habits, rather than temporary self-starvation.

Behavioural genetics The study of inherited behavioural traits and tendencies.

Behavioural medicine The study of behavioural factors in medicine, physical illness, and medical treatment.

Behavioural personality theory Any model of personality that emphasizes learning and observable behaviour.

Behavioural risk factors Behaviours that increase the chances of disease, injury, or premature death.

Behaviourism School of psychology that emphasizes the study of overt, observable behaviour.

Behaviouristic Any approach that emphasizes overt, observable behaviour and the effects of learning and conditioning.

Belief component What a person thinks or believes about the object of an attitude.

Bem Sex Role Inventory (BSRI) A list of 60 personal traits including "masculine," "feminine," and "neutral" traits; used to rate one's degree of androgyny.

Beta waves Small, fast brain waves associated with being awake and alert.

Biased sample A subpart of a larger population that does not accurately reflect characteristics of the whole population.

Binge drinking Consuming five or more drinks in a short time.

Binocular depth cue A depth cue that requires two eyes.

Biochemical abnormality A disturbance of the body's chemical systems, especially in brain chemicals or neurotransmitters.

Biofeedback Information given to a person about his or her ongoing bodily activities; aids voluntary regulation of bodily states.

Biological predisposition The presumed hereditary readiness of humans to learn certain skills, such as how to use language, or a readiness to behave in particular ways.

Biological rhythm Any repeating cycle of biological activity, such as sleep and waking cycles or changes in body temperature.

Biopsychologist A psychologist who studies the relationship between behaviour and biological processes, especially activity in the nervous system.

Bipolar disorders Emotional disorders involving both depression and mania or hypomania.

Bipolar I disorder A mood disorder in which a person has episodes of mania (excited, hyperactive, energetic, grandiose behaviour) and also periods of deep depression.

Bipolar II disorder A mood disorder in which a person is mostly depressed (sad, despondent, guilt-ridden) but has also had one or more episodes of mild mania (hypomania).

Birth injury Any injury or damage that occurs to an infant during delivery.

Bisexual A person romantically and erotically attracted to both men and women.

Blind spot An area of the retina lacking visual receptors.

Bottom-up processing Organizing perceptions by beginning with low-level features.

Brainstem The lower brain, including the cerebellum, medulla, pons, and reticular formation.

Brainstorming Method of creative thinking that separates the production and evaluation of ideas.

Brainwashing Engineered or forced attitude change involving a captive audience.

Branching program A computer program that gives learners corrective information and exercises based on the nature of their errors.

Brief psychodynamic therapy A modern therapy based on psychoanalytic theory but designed to produce insights more quickly.

Brightness The intensity of lights or colours.

Brightness constancy The apparent (or relative) brightness of objects remains the same as long as they are illuminated by the same amount of light.

Broca's area A language area related to grammar and pronunciation.

Bulimia nervosa Excessive eating (gorging) usually followed by self-induced vomiting and/or taking laxatives.

Burnout A job-related condition of mental, physical, and emotional exhaustion.

Bystander apathy Unwillingness of bystanders to offer help during emergencies or to become involved in others' problems.

Caffeine A natural drug with stimulant properties; found in coffee and tea and added to artificial beverages and medicines.

Caffeinism Excessive consumption of caffeine, leading to dependence and a variety of physical and psychological complaints.

Camouflage Designs that break up figure-ground organization.

Cannon-Bard theory States that activity in the thalamus causes emotional feelings and bodily arousal to occur simultaneously.

Carcinogen A substance capable of causing cancer.

Cardinal trait A personality trait so basic that all of a person's activities relate to it.

Caregiving styles Identifiable patterns of parental caretaking and interaction with children.

Case study An in-depth focus on all aspects of a single person.

Catatonic schizophrenia Schizophrenia marked by stupor, rigidity, unresponsiveness, posturing, mutism, and sometimes agitated, purposeless behaviour.

Causation The act of causing some effect.

Central nervous system The brain and spinal cord.

Central traits The core traits that characterize an individual personality.

Cephalocaudal From head to toe.

Cerebellum A brain structure that controls posture and coordination.

Cerebral cortex The outer layer of the cerebrum.

Cerebral hemispheres The right and left halves of the cerebrum.

Cerebrum The two large hemispheres that cover the upper part of the brain.

Chance conditioning Conditioning that takes place by chance or coincidence.

Change In brainwashing, the point at which a person begins to reject former attitudes and beliefs.

Character Personal characteristics that have been judged or evaluated; a person's desirable or undesirable qualities.

Chemical senses Senses, such as smell and taste, that respond to chemical molecules.

Child rearing In forming attitudes, the effects of parental values, beliefs, and practices.

Chromosomes Thread-like "coloured bodies" in the nucleus of each cell that are made up of DNA.

Chronic insomnia Insomnia that persists for more than three weeks.

Chronological age A person's age in years.

Circadian rhythms Cyclical changes in bodily functions and arousal levels that vary on a schedule approximating a 24-hour day.

Clairvoyance The purported ability to perceive events at a distance or through physical barriers.

Classical conditioning A form of learning in which reflex responses are associated with new stimuli.

Client-centred therapy A non-directive therapy based on insights gained from conscious thoughts and feelings; emphasizes accepting one's true self.

Clinical method Studying psychological problems and therapies in clinical settings.

Clinical psychologist A psychologist who specializes in the treatment of psychological and behavioural disturbances or who does research on such disturbances.

Clinical study An intensive investigation of a single person, especially one suffering from some injury or disease.

Close analogy A comparison of a target concept and a very similar concept that improves understanding of the target concept.

Cocaine A crystalline drug derived from coca leaves; used as a central nervous system stimulant and local anesthetic.

Cochlea The snail-shaped organ that makes up the inner ear.

Coefficient of correlation A statistical index ranging from +1.00 to −1.00 that indicates the direction and degree of correlation.

Cognition The process of thinking or mentally processing information (images, concepts, words, rules, and symbols).

Cognitive behaviourism An approach that combines behavioural principles with cognition (perception, thinking, anticipation) to explain behaviour.

Cognitive dissonance An uncomfortable clash between self-image, thoughts, beliefs, attitudes, or perceptions and one's behaviour.

Cognitive interview Use of various cues and strategies to improve the memory of eyewitnesses.

Cognitive learning Higher-level learning involving thinking, knowing, understanding, and anticipation.

Cognitive map Internal images or other mental representations of an area (maze, city, campus, and so forth) that underlie an ability to choose alternative paths to the same goal.

Cognitive psychology The study of thinking, knowing, understanding, problem solving, creativity, and information processing.

Cognitive therapy A therapy directed at changing the

maladaptive thoughts, beliefs, and feelings that underlie emotional and behavioural problems.

Cognitive view Holds that distorted thinking causes people to magnify ordinary threats and failures, leading to anxiety and distress.

Colour blindness A total inability to perceive colours.

Colour weakness An inability to distinguish some colours.

Common traits Personality traits that are shared by most members of a particular culture.

Communicator In persuasion, the person presenting arguments or information.

Community health campaign A community-wide education program that provides information about how to lessen risk factors and promote health.

Community mental health centre A facility offering a wide range of mental health services, such as prevention, counselling, consultation, and crisis intervention.

Comparative psychologist A psychologist primarily interested in studying and comparing the behaviour of different species, especially animals.

Compensation Counteracting a real or imagined weakness by emphasizing desirable traits or seeking to excel in the area of weakness or in other areas.

Competence The degree of general ability or proficiency a person displays.

Compliance Bending to the requests of a person who has little or no authority or other form of social power.

Compulsion An act an individual feels driven to repeat, often against his or her will.

Computer simulations Computer programs that mimic some aspect of human thinking, decision making, or problem solving.

Computer-assisted instruction (CAI) Learning aided by computer-presented information, exercises, and feedback.

Concentrative meditation Mental exercise based on attending to a single object or thought.

Concept A generalized idea representing a class of related objects or events.

Concept formation The process of classifying information into meaningful categories.

Conception The union of an ovum and a sperm cell.

Conceptual rule A formal rule for deciding if an object or event is an example of a particular concept.

Concrete operational stage Period of intellectual development during which children become able to use the concepts of time, space, volume, and number, but in ways that remain simplified and concrete, rather than abstract.

Condensation Combining several people, objects, or events into a single dream image.

Conditioned aversion A learned dislike or conditioned negative emotional response to a particular stimulus.

Conditioned emotional response An emotional response that has been linked to a previously non-emotional stimulus by classical conditioning.

Conditioned response A learned response elicited by a conditioned stimulus.

Conditioned stimulus A stimulus that evokes a response because it has been repeatedly paired with an unconditioned stimulus.

Conditioned taste aversion A learned aversive response to a specific food.

Conditioning chamber An apparatus designed to study operant conditioning in animals; a Skinner box.

Conditions of worth Internal standards used to judge the value of one's thoughts, actions, feelings, or experiences.

Conduction deafness Poor transfer of sounds from the eardrum to the inner ear.

Cones Visual receptors for colours and daylight visual acuity.

Conflict A stressful condition that occurs when a person must choose between incompatible or contradictory alternatives.

Conformity Bringing one's behaviour into agreement or harmony with norms or with the behaviour of others in a group.

Confrontation In existential therapy, the process of confronting clients with their own values and with the need to take responsibility for the quality of their existence.

Congenital problems Problems or defects that originate during prenatal development in the womb.

Conjunctive concept A class of objects that have two or more features in common. (For example, to qualify as an example of the concept an object must be both red and triangular.)

Connector neuron A nerve cell that serves as a link between two others.

Connotative meaning The subjective, personal, or emotional meaning of a word or concept.

Conscience The part of the superego that causes guilt when its standards are not met.

Conscious Region of the mind that includes all mental contents a person is aware of at any given moment.

Consciousness Mental awareness of sensations, perceptions, memories, and feelings.

Consequences Effects that follow a response.

Consequences Test A test of creativity in which subjects try to list as many consequences as possible that would follow if some basic change were made in the world.

Conservation In Piaget's theory, mastery of the concept that the weight, mass, and volume of matter remains unchanged (is conserved) even when the shape or appearance of objects changes.

Consistency With respect to child discipline, the maintenance of stable rules of conduct.

Consolidation Process by which relatively permanent memories are formed in the brain.

Constructive processing Reorganizing or updating memories on the basis of logic, reasoning, or the addition of new information.

Continuous reinforcement A schedule in which every correct response is followed by a reinforcer.

Control Altering conditions that influence behaviour in predictable ways.

Control group In a controlled experiment, the group of subjects exposed to all experimental conditions or variables *except* the independent variable.

Control questions In a polygraph exam, questions that almost always provoke anxiety.

Convergence The simultaneous turning inward of the two eyes.

Convergent thinking Thinking directed toward discovery of a single established correct answer; conventional thinking.

Conversion disorder A bodily symptom that mimics a physical disability but is actually caused by anxiety or emotional distress.

Conviction Beliefs that are important to a person and that evoke strong emotion.

Cooing Spontaneous repetition of vowel sounds by infants.

Cooperative play Play in which two or more children must coordinate their actions; if children don't cooperate, the game ends.

Coping statements Reassuring, self-enhancing statements that are used to stop self-critical thinking.

Cornea Transparent membrane covering the front of the eye.

Corpus callosum The bundle of fibres connecting the cerebral hemispheres.

Correlation The existence of a consistent, systematic relationship between two events, measures, or variables.

Correlational method Making measurements to discover relationships between events.

Correlational study A non-experimental study designed to measure the degree of relationship (if any) between two or more events, measures, or variables.

Corticalization An increase in the relative size of the cerebral cortex.

Counselling psychologist A psychologist who specializes in the treatment of milder emotional and behavioural disturbances.

Counsellor A mental health professional who specializes in helping people with problems not involving serious mental disorder (e.g., marriage counsellors, career counsellors, or school counsellors).

Counterirritation Using mild pain to block more intense or long-lasting pain.

Courtesy bias The tendency to give "polite" answers—especially the tendency to alter answers so as not to hurt an interviewer's feelings.

Covert behaviour A response that is internal or hidden from view.

Covert reinforcement Using positive imagery to reinforce desired behaviour.

Covert sensitization Use of aversive imagery to reduce the occurrence of an undesired response.

Cranial nerves Major nerves that leave the brain without passing through the spinal cord.

Crisis intervention Skilled management of a psychological emergency.

Crista A floating structure that responds to fluid movement within the semicircular canals.

Critical period During development, a period of increased sensitivity to environmental influences. Also, a time during which certain events must take place for normal development to occur.

Critical situations Situations during childhood that are capable of leaving a lasting imprint on personality.

Critical thinking An ability to evaluate, compare, analyze, critique, and synthesize information.

Cross-stimulation effect In group problem solving, the tendency of one person's ideas to trigger ideas from others.

Crystal intelligence The extent to which a person has acquired his or her culture's accumulated knowledge.

CT scan Computed tomography scan; a computer-enhanced X-ray image of the brain or body.

Cue External stimuli that guide responses, especially by signalling the presence or absence of reinforcement.

Cult A group that professes great devotion to some person, and follows that person almost without question; cult members are typically victimized by their leaders in various ways.

Cultural psychologist A psychologist who studies the ways in which culture affects human behaviour.

Cultural relativity The idea that behaviour must be judged relative to the values of the culture in which it occurs.

Cultural values The importance and desirability of various objects and activities as defined by people in a given culture.

Culturally skilled therapist A therapist who has the awareness, knowledge, and skills necessary to treat clients from diverse cultural backgrounds.

Culture-fair test A test (such as an intelligence test) designed to minimize the importance of skills and knowledge that may be more common in some cultures than in others.

Curve of forgetting A graph that shows the amount of memorized information remembered after varying lengths of time.

Cyclothymic disorder Moderate manic and depressive behaviour that persists for two years or more.

Dark adaptation Increased retinal sensitivity to light.

Data Observed facts or evidence (*data*: plural; *datum*: singular).

Data reduction system Any system that selects, analyzes, or condenses information.

Death, freedom, isolation, meaninglessness The universal challenges of existence, including an awareness that everyone will die; the responsibility that comes with freedom to choose; the fact that each person is ultimately isolated and alone in his or her private world; and the reality that meaning must be created in life.

Declarative memory That part of long-term memory containing specific factual information.

Deductive thought Thought that applies a general set of rules to specific situations; for example, using the laws of gravity to predict the behaviour of a single falling object.

Deep lesioning Use of an electrode (electrified wire) to destroy small areas deep within the brain.

Deep sleep Stage 4 sleep; the deepest form of normal sleep.

Defence mechanism A habitual and often unconscious psychological process used to reduce anxiety.

Delta waves Large, slow brain waves that occur in deeper sleep (stages 3 and 4).

Delusion A false belief held against all contrary evidence.

Delusional disorder A psychosis marked by severe delusions of grandeur, jealousy, persecution, or similar preoccupations.

Dementia Serious mental impairment in old age caused by physical deterioration of the brain.

Demonology In medieval Europe, the study of demons and the treatment of persons "possessed" by demons.

Dendrites Neuron fibres that receive incoming messages.

Denial Protecting oneself from an unpleasant reality by refusing to perceive it or believe it.

Denotative meaning The exact, dictionary definition of a word or concept; its objective meaning.

Dependent variable In an experiment, the condition (usually a behaviour) that is affected by the independent variable.

Depressant A substance that decreases activity in the body and nervous system.

Depression A state of despondency marked by feelings of powerlessness and hopelessness.

Depressive disorders Emotional disorders primarily involving sadness and depression.

Deprivation In development, the loss or withholding of normal stimulation, nutrition, comfort, love, and so forth; a condition of lacking.

Depth cues Perceptual features that impart information about distance and three-dimensional space.

Depth perception The ability to see three-dimensional space and to accurately judge distances.

Description In scientific research, the process of naming and classifying.

Desensitization Reducing fear or anxiety by repeatedly exposing a person to emotional stimuli while the person is deeply relaxed.

Determinism The idea that all behaviour has prior causes that would completely explain one's choices and actions if all such causes were known.

Detoxification In the treatment of alcoholism, the withdrawal of the patient from alcohol.

Developmental level An individual's current state of physical, emotional, and intellectual development.

Developmental milestone A significant turning point or marker in personal development.

Developmental psychologist A psychologist interested in human growth and development from birth until death.

Developmental psychology The study of progressive changes in behaviour and abilities from conception to death.

Developmental task Any personal change that must take place for optimal development.

Deviant communication Patterns of communication that cause guilt, anxiety, confusion, anger, conflict, and emotional turmoil.

Deviation IQ An IQ obtained statistically from a person's relative standing in his or her age group; that is, how far above or below average the person's score was relative to other scores.

Diet The types and amounts of food and drink regularly consumed over a period of time.

Difficult child A child who is temperamentally moody, intense, and easily angered.

Diffusion of responsibility Spreading the responsibility to act among several people; reduces the likelihood that help will be given to a person in need.

Digit-span test A test of attention and short-term memory in which a string of numbers is recalled.

Direct contact In forming attitudes, the effects of direct experience with the object of the attitude.

Direct observation Assessing behaviour through direct surveillance.

Discipline A framework of guidelines for acceptable behaviour.

Discovery learning Learning based on insight and understanding.

Discrimination Treating members of various social groups differently in circumstances where their rights or treatment should be identical.

Discriminative stimuli Stimuli that precede rewarded and non-rewarded responses in operant conditioning.

Disease-prone personality A personality type associated with poor health, marked by persistent negative emotions.

Dishabituation A reversal of habituation.

Disinhibition The removal of inhibition; results in acting out behaviour that normally would be restrained.

Disjunctive concept A concept defined by the presence of at least one of several possible features. (For example, to qualify an object must be either blue *or* circular.)

Disorganized schizophrenia Schizophrenia marked by incoherence, grossly disorganized behaviour, bizarre thinking, and flat or grossly inappropriate emotions.

Displaced aggression Redirecting aggression to a target other than the actual source of one's frustration.

Displacement Directing emotions or actions toward safe or unimportant dream images.

Dissociative amnesia Loss of memory (partial or complete) for important information related to personal identity.

Dissociative disorder Temporary amnesia, multiple personality, or depersonalization.

Dissociative fugue Sudden travel away from home, plus confusion about one's personal identity.

Dissociative identity disorder The presence of two or more distinct personalities (multiple personality).

Distant analogy A comparison emphasizing the similarity on some dimension between a target concept and a very different concept.

Distractors False items included with a correct item to form a test of recognition memory (for example, the wrong answers on a multiple-choice test).

Disturbed family environment Stressful or unhealthy family relationships, communication patterns, and emotional atmosphere.

Disturbed verbal communication Speech that is disorganized, garbled, or unintelligible.

Disuse Theory that memory traces weaken when memories are not periodically used or retrieved.

Divergent thinking Thinking that produces many ideas or alternatives; a major element in original or creative thought.

DNA Deoxyribonucleic acid, a molecular structure that contains coded genetic information.

Dominant gene A gene whose influence will be expressed each time the gene is present.

Dominant hemisphere A term usually applied to the side of a person's brain that produces language.

Door-in-the-face effect The tendency for a person who has refused a major request to subsequently be more likely to comply with a minor request.

Dopamine An important transmitter substance found in the brain—especially in the limbic system, an area associated with emotional response.

Double approach-avoidance conflict Being simultaneously attracted to and repelled by each of two alternatives.

Double-blind experiment An arrangement in which both subjects and experimenters are unaware of whether subjects are in the experimental group or the control group.

Dream processes Mental filters that hide the true meanings of dreams.

Dream symbols Images in dreams whose personal or emotional meanings differ from their literal meanings.

Drill and practice A basic CAI format, typically consisting of questions and answers.

Drive The psychological expression of internal needs or valued goals (for example, hunger, thirst, or a drive for success).

Drug interaction A combined effect of two drugs that exceeds the addition of one drug's effects to the other.

Drug tolerance A reduction in the body's response to a drug.

Drug-dependency insomnia Insomnia that follows withdrawal from sleeping pills.

Dysthymic disorder Moderate depression that persists for two years or more.

Easy child A child who is temperamentally relaxed and agreeable.

Echo A brief continuation of sensory activity in the auditory system after a sound is heard.

Educational simulations Computer programs that simulate real-world settings or situations to promote learning.

Effector cells Cells in muscles and glands that are capable of producing some type of response.

Ego The executive part of personality that directs rational behaviour.

Ego ideal The part of the superego representing ideal behaviour; a source of pride when its standards are met.

Egocentric thought Thought that is self-centred and fails to consider the viewpoints of others.

Eidetic imagery The ability to retain a "projected" mental image long enough to use it as a source of information.

Elaborative rehearsal Rehearsal that links new information with existing memories and knowledge.

Electra conflict A girl's sexual attraction to her father and feelings of rivalry with her mother.

Electrical stimulation of the brain (ESB) Direct electrical stimulation and activation of brain tissue.

Electroconvulsive shock An electric current passed directly through the brain, producing a convulsion.

Electroconvulsive therapy (ECT) A treatment for severe depression, consisting of an electric shock passed directly through the brain, which induces a convulsion.

Electrode Any device (such as a wire, needle, or metal plate) used to electrically stimulate nerve tissue or to record its activity.

Electroencephalograph (EEG) A device that records electrical activity in the brain.

Emotion A state characterized by physiological arousal, and changes in facial expression, gestures, posture, and subjective feelings.

Emotional appraisal Evaluating the personal meaning of a stimulus or situation.

Emotional attachment An especially close emotional bond that infants form with their parents, caregivers, or others.

Emotional component One's feelings toward the object of an attitude.

Emotional expression Outward signs that an emotion is occurring.

Emotional feelings The private, subjective experience of having an emotion.

Emotional intelligence Emotional competence, including empathy, self-control, self-awareness, and other skills.

Emotional tone The underlying emotional state an individual is experiencing at any given moment.

Emotion-focused coping Managing or controlling one's emotional reaction to a stressful or threatening situation.

Empathic arousal Emotional arousal that occurs when you feel some of another person's pain, fear, or anguish.

Empathy A capacity for taking another's point of view; the ability to feel what another is feeling.

Empathy-helping relationship Observation that we are most likely to help someone else when we feel emotions such as empathy and compassion.

Empirical evidence Facts or information based on direct observation or experience.

Empirical perception A perception strongly influenced by prior experience.

Encoding Changing information into a form that allows it to be manipulated in thought.

Encoding failure Failure to store sufficient information to form a useful memory.

Encounter group A group experience that emphasizes intensely honest interchanges among participants regarding feelings and reactions to one another.

Endocrine system Glands whose secretions pass directly into the bloodstream or lymph system.

Endogenous depression Depression that appears to be produced from within (perhaps by chemical imbalances in the brain), rather than as a reaction to life events.

Endorphins Chemicals that are similar in structure and pain-killing effect to opiate drugs such as morphine.

Engram A "memory trace" in the brain.

Enkephalins Opiate-like brain chemicals that regulate reactions to pain and stress.

Enrichment Deliberately making an environment more novel, complex, and perceptually or intellectually stimulating.

Environment ("nurture") The sum of all external conditions affecting development, especially the effects of learning.

Epinephrine An adrenal hormone that tends to arouse the body; epinephrine is associated with fear. (Also known as adrenaline.)

Episodic drive A drive that occurs in distinct episodes.

Episodic memory A subpart of declarative memory that records personal experiences that are linked with specific times and places.

Equal-status contact Social interaction that occurs on an equal footing, without obvious differences in power or status.

Ergotism A pattern of psychosis-like symptoms that accompanies poisoning by ergot fungus.

Erogenous zone Any body area that produces pleasurable sensations.

Eros Freud's name for the "life instincts."

Escape Reducing discomfort by leaving frustrating situations or by psychologically withdrawing from them.

Escape learning Learning to make a response in order to end an aversive stimulus.

Estrogen A female sex hormone.

Estrus Changes in the sexual drives of animals that create a desire for mating; particularly used to refer to females in heat.

Ethnocentrism Placing one's own group or race at the centre—that is, tending to reject all other groups but one's own.

Ethologist A person who studies the natural behaviour patterns of animals.

Evaluation fears Fears of being inadequate, embarrassed, ridiculed, or rejected.

Evolutionary psychology Study of the evolutionary origins of human behaviour patterns.

Excitement phase The first phase of sexual response, indicated by initial signs of sexual arousal.

Exemplars Stored representations of individual experiences.

Existential therapy An insight therapy that focuses on the elemental problems of existence, such as death, meaning, choice, and responsibility; emphasizes making courageous life choices.

Existentialism A system of thought that focuses on the elemental problems of existence, such as death, meaning, choice, and responsibility.

Exorcism The practice of driving off an "evil spirit," especially from the body of a person who is "possessed."

Expectancy An anticipation concerning future events or relationships.

Experiment A formal trial undertaken to confirm a fact or principle.

Experimental group In a controlled experiment, the group of subjects exposed to the independent variable or experimental condition.

Experimental method Investigating behaviour through controlled experimentation.

Experimental subjects Humans or animals whose behaviour is investigated in an experiment.

Experimenter effect Changes in subjects' behaviour caused by the unintended influence of an experimenter's actions.

Expert systems Computer programs designed to respond as a human expert would; programs based on the knowledge and rules that underlie human expertise in specific topics.

Expert witness A person recognized by a court of law as being qualified to give expert testimony on a specific topic.

Explicit memory A memory that a person is aware of having; a memory that is consciously retrieved.

Expressive behaviours Behaviours that express or communicate emotion or personal feelings.

External cause A cause of behaviour that is assumed to lie outside a person.

External eating cue Any external stimulus that tends to encourage hunger or to elicit eating.

External frustration Distress caused by external conditions that hinder progress toward a goal.

Extinction The weakening of a conditioned response through removal of reinforcement.

Extracellular thirst Thirst caused by a reduction in the volume of fluids found between body cells.

Extraneous variables Conditions or factors excluded from influencing the outcome of an experiment.

Extrasensory perception (ESP) The purported ability to perceive events in ways that cannot be explained by known capacities of the sensory organs.

Extrinsic motivation Motivation based on obvious external rewards, obligations, or similar factors.

Extrovert A person whose attention is directed outward; a bold, outgoing person.

Eye movement desensitization and reprocessing (EMDR) A technique for reducing fear or anxiety; based on holding upsetting thoughts in mind while rapidly moving the eyes from side to side.

Facet traits Personality traits that characterize the Big Five personality dimensions and are part of them as well. Each of the big five factors has its unique set of facet traits.

Facial blend A mix of two or more basic facial expressions.

Facial feedback hypothesis States that sensations from facial expressions help define what emotion a person feels.

Factor analysis A statistical technique used to correlate multiple measurements and identify general underlying factors.

Fallacy of positive instances The tendency to remember or notice information that fits one's expectations, while forgetting discrepancies.

False positive A false sense of recognition.

Familial retardation Mild retardation associated with homes that are intellectually, nutritionally, and emotionally impoverished.

Family therapy Technique in which all family members participate, both individually and as a group, to change destructive relationships and communication patterns.

Feature detector A sensory system highly attuned to a specific stimulus pattern.

Feedback Information returned to a person about the effects a response has had; also known as knowledge of results.

Feeding system Areas in the hypothalamus that initiate eating when stimulated.

Feeling of knowing A feeling that allows people to predict beforehand whether they will be able to remember something.

Fetal damage A congenital problem; that is, damage or injury that occurs to the fetus during prenatal development.

Figure-ground organization Part of a stimulus appears to stand out as an object (figure) against a less prominent background (ground).

Five-factor model Proposes that there are five universal dimensions of personality.

Fixation The tendency to repeat wrong solutions or faulty responses, especially as a result of becoming blind to alternatives.

Fixed interval schedule A reinforcer is given only when a correct response is made after a set amount of time has passed since the last reinforced response. Responses made during the time interval are not reinforced.

Fixed ratio schedule A set number of correct responses must be made to get a reinforcer. For example, a reinforcer is given for every four correct responses.

Flashbulb memories Memories created at times of high emotion that seem especially vivid.

Flat affect An extreme lack of emotional expressiveness.

Flexibility In tests of creativity, flexibility is indicated by the number of different types of solutions produced.

Fluency In tests of creativity, fluency refers to the total number of solutions produced.

Fluid intelligence The ability to reason and to solve problems, especially unfamiliar ones.

fMRI scan Functional magnetic resonance imaging that records brain activity.

Foot-in-the-door effect The tendency for a person who has first complied with a small request to be more likely later to fulfill a larger request.

Formal operations stage Period of intellectual development characterized by thinking that includes abstract, theoretical, and hypothetical ideas.

Fovea An area at the centre of the retina containing only cones.

Frame of reference A mental perspective used for judging and evaluating events.

Framing In thought, the terms in which a problem is stated or the way that it is structured.

Fraternal twins Twins conceived from two separate eggs. Fraternal twins are no more alike genetically than other siblings.

Free association In psychoanalysis, the technique of having a client say anything that comes to mind, regardless of how embarrassing or unimportant it may seem.

Free choice The ability to freely make choices that are not controlled by genetics, learning, or unconscious forces.

Free will The idea that human beings are capable of freely making choices or decisions.

Frequency theory Holds that tones up to 4000 hertz are converted to nerve impulses that match the frequency of each tone.

Frontal lobes A brain area associated with movement, the sense of smell, and higher mental functions.

Frustration A negative emotional state that occurs when one is prevented from reaching a goal.

Frustration-aggression hypothesis States that frustration tends to lead to aggression.

Fully functioning person A person living in harmony with her or his deepest feelings, impulses, and intuitions.

Functional fixedness A rigidity in problem solving caused by an inability to see new uses for familiar objects.

Functionalism School of psychology concerned with how behaviour and mental abilities help people adapt to their environments.

Fundamental attributional error The tendency to attribute the behaviour of others to internal causes (personality, likes, and so forth).

Galvanic skin response (GSR) A change in the electrical resistance (or inversely, the conductance) of the skin, due to sweating.

Gate control theory Proposes that pain messages pass through neural "gates" in the spinal cord.

General adaptation syndrome (G.A.S.) A series of bodily reactions to prolonged stress; occurs in three stages: alarm, resistance, and exhaustion.

Generalized anxiety disorder The person is in a chronic state of tension and worries about work, relationships, ability, or impending disaster.

Generativity versus stagnation A conflict in which stagnant self-interest is countered by interest in guiding the next generation.

Genes Specific areas on a strand of DNA that carry hereditary information.

Genetic abnormality Any abnormality in the genes, including missing genes, extra genes, or defective genes.

Genetic disorders Problems caused by defects in the genes or by inherited characteristics.

Genital stage Period of full psychosexual development, marked by the attainment of mature adult sexuality.

Gestalt psychology A school of psychology emphasizing the study of thinking, learning, and perception in whole units, not by analysis into parts.

Gestalt therapy An approach that focuses on immediate experience and awareness to help clients rebuild thinking, feeling, and acting into connected wholes; emphasizes the integration of fragmented experiences.

Giantism Excessive bodily growth caused by too much growth hormone.

Giftedness The possession of either a high IQ or special talents or aptitudes.

Glucagon-like peptide 1 A substance in the brain that terminates eating.

Goal The target or objective of motivated behaviour.

Goodness of fit With respect to caregiving, the degree to which parents and children have compatible temperaments.

Grammar A set of rules for combining language units into meaningful speech or writing.

Graphology False system based on the belief that handwriting can reveal personality traits.

Grasping reflex A neonatal reflex consisting of grasping objects placed in the palms.

Group cohesiveness The degree of attraction among group members or their commitment to remaining in the group.

Group intelligence test Any intelligence test that can be administered to a group of people with minimal supervision.

Group membership As a factor in forming attitudes, social influences associated with belonging to various groups.

Group prejudice Prejudice held out of conformity to group views.

Group sanctions Rewards and punishments (such as approval or disapproval) administered by groups to enforce conformity among members.

Group structure The network of roles, communication pathways, and power in a group.

Group therapy Psychotherapy conducted in a group setting to make therapeutic use of group dynamics.

Groupthink A compulsion by members of decision-making groups to maintain agreement, even at the cost of critical thinking.

Growth hormone A hormone, secreted by the pituitary gland, that promotes bodily growth.

Growth needs In Maslow's hierarchy, the higher-level needs associated with self-actualization.

Guided imagery Intentional visualization of images that are calming, relaxing, or beneficial in other ways.

Gustation The sense of taste.

Habit A deeply ingrained, learned pattern of behaviour.

Habituation A decrease in perceptual response to a repeated stimulus.

Hair cells Receptor cells within the cochlea that transduce vibrations into nerve impulses.

Halfway house A community-based facility for individuals making the transition from an institution (mental hospital, prison, and so forth) to independent living.

Hallucination An imaginary sensation, such as seeing, hearing, or smelling something that does not exist in the external world.

Hallucinogen A substance that alters or distorts sensory impressions.

Halo effect The tendency to generalize a favourable first impression to unrelated personal characteristics.

Handedness A preference for the right or left hand in most activities.

Hardy personality A personality style associated with superior stress resistance.

Hashish Resinous material scraped from the leaves of the hemp plant; hashish has a high concentration of THC.

Health psychology Study of how behavioural principles can be used to prevent illness and promote health.

Health-promoting behaviour Any practice that tends to maintain or enhance good health.

Heredity ("nature") The transmission of physical and psychological characteristics from parents to offspring through genes.

Heterosexual A person romantically and erotically attracted to members of the opposite sex.

Heuristic Any strategy or technique that aids problem solving, especially by limiting the number of possible solutions to be tried.

Hierarchy A rank-ordered series of higher and lower amounts, levels, degrees, or steps.

Hierarchy of human needs Abraham Maslow's ordering of needs, based on their presumed strength or potency.

Higher-order conditioning Classical conditioning in which a conditioned stimulus is used to reinforce further learning; that is, a CS is used as if it were a US.

Hippocampus A brain structure associated with emotion and the transfer of information from short-term memory to long-term memory.

Homeostasis A steady state of bodily equilibrium.

Homogamy Marriage of two people who are similar to one another.

Homosexual A person romantically and erotically attracted to same-sex persons.

Honesty test A paper-and-pencil test designed to detect attitudes, beliefs, and behaviour patterns that predispose a person to dishonest behaviour.

Hormone A glandular secretion that affects bodily functions or behaviour.

Hue Classification of colours into basic categories of red, orange, yellow, green, blue, indigo, and violet.

Human growth sequence The pattern of physical development from conception to death.

Human immunodeficiency virus (HIV) A sexually transmitted virus that disables the immune system.

Human nature Those traits, qualities, potentials, and behaviour patterns most characteristic of the human species.

Humanism An approach that focuses on human experience, problems, potentials, and ideals.

Humanistic Any system of thought focused on subjective experience and human problems and potentials.

Hyperopia Difficulty focusing nearby objects (farsightedness).

Hyperthyroidism Faster metabolism and excitability caused by an overactive thyroid gland.

Hypnic jerk A reflex muscle twitch throughout the body that often occurs as one is falling asleep.

Hypnosis An altered state of consciousness characterized by narrowed attention and increased suggestibility.

Hypnotic susceptibility One's capacity for becoming hypnotized.

Hypochondriac A person who complains about illnesses that appear to be imaginary.

Hypochondriasis A preoccupation with fears of having a serious disease. Ordinary physical signs are interpreted as proof of disease, but no physical abnormality can be found.

Hypopituitary dwarfism Shortness and smallness caused by too little growth hormone.

Hypothalamus An area in the brain that regulates motivation and emotion.

Hypothesis The predicted outcome of an experiment or an educated guess about the relationship between variables.

Hypothetical possibilities Suppositions, guesses, or projections.

Hypothyroidism Slower metabolism and sluggishness caused by an underactive thyroid gland.

Hysteria Wild emotional excitability sometimes associated with the development of apparent physical disabilities (numbness, blindness, and the like) without known physical cause.

Icon A mental image or visual representation.

Id The primitive part of personality that remains unconscious, supplies energy, and demands pleasure.

Ideal self An idealized image of oneself (the person one would like to be).

Identical twins Twins who develop from a single egg and therefore have identical genes.

Identification Feeling emotionally connected to a person and seeing oneself as like him or her.

Identity versus role confusion A conflict concerning the need to establish a personal identity.

Illogical thought Thought that is intuitive, haphazard, or irrational.

Illusion A misleading or distorted perception.

Image Most often, a mental representation that has picture-like qualities; an icon.

Imagery rehearsal Mentally rehearsing and changing a nightmare in order to prevent it from reoccurring.

I-message A message that states the effect someone else's behaviour had on you.

Imitation An attempt to match one's own behaviour to another person's behaviour.

Immune system System that mobilizes bodily defences against invading microbes and other disease agents.

Implicit memory A memory that a person does not know exists; a memory that is retrieved unconsciously.

Impossible figure A stimulus pattern that cannot be organized into a stable perception.

In-basket test A testing procedure that simulates the individual decision-making challenges that executives face.

Incentive value The value of a goal above and beyond its ability to fill a need.

Incongruence State that exists when there is a discrepancy between one's experiences and self-image or between one's self-image and ideal self.

Incongruent person A person who has an inaccurate self-image or whose self-image differs greatly from the ideal self.

Independent variable In an experiment, the condition being investigated as a possible cause of some change in behaviour. The values that this variable takes are chosen by the experimenter.

Individual intelligence test A test of intelligence designed to be given to a single individual by a trained specialist.

Individual traits Personality traits that define a person's unique individual qualities.

Individuating information Information that helps define a person as an individual, rather than as a member of a group or social category.

Inductive thought Thinking in which a general rule or principle is gathered from a series of specific examples; for instance, inferring the laws of gravity by observing many falling objects.

Industry versus inferiority A conflict in middle childhood centred on lack of support for industrious behaviour, which can result in feelings of inferiority.

Information bits Meaningful units of information, such as numbers, letters, words, or phrases.

Information chunks Information bits grouped into larger units.

Informational view Perspective that explains learning in terms of information imparted by events in the environment.

Initiative versus guilt A conflict between learning to take initiative and overcoming feelings of guilt about doing so.

Insanity A legal term that refers to a mental inability to manage one's affairs or to be aware of the consequences of one's actions.

Insecure-ambivalent attachment An anxious emotional bond marked by both a desire to be with a parent or caregiver and some resistance to being reunited.

Insecure-avoidant attachment An anxious emotional bond marked by a tendency to avoid reunion with a parent or caregiver.

Insight A sudden mental reorganization of a problem that makes the solution obvious.

Insomnia Difficulty in getting to sleep or staying asleep.

Instructional games Educational computer programs designed to resemble games in order to motivate learning.

Instrumental behaviours Behaviours directed toward the achievement of some goal; behaviours that are instrumental in producing some effect.

Integrity versus despair A conflict in old age between feelings of integrity and the despair of viewing previous life events with regret.

Intelligence An overall capacity to think rationally, act purposefully, and deal effectively with the environment.

Intelligence quotient (IQ) An index of intelligence defined as a person's mental age divided by his or her chronological age and multiplied by 100.

Interaction with others In forming attitudes, the influence of discussions with others who hold particular attitudes.

Interactive CD-ROM instruction Computerized multimedia instruction.

Interference The tendency for new memories to impair retrieval of older memories, and the reverse.

Internal cause A cause of behaviour that is assumed to lie within a person—for instance, a need, preference, or personality trait.

Internal images Mental images or visual depictions used in memory and thinking.

Internal representation Any image, concept, precept, symbol, or process used to mentally represent information during thought.

Interpersonal attraction Social attraction to another person.

Interview (personality) A face-to-face meeting held for the purpose of gaining information about an individual's personal history, personality traits, current psychological state, and so forth.

Intimacy versus isolation The challenge of establishing intimacy with others, versus feeling a sense of isolation.

Intracellular thirst Thirst triggered when fluid is drawn out of cells due to an increased concentration of salts and minerals outside the cell.

Intra-cranial stimulation Direct electrical stimulation and activation of brain tissue.

Intrauterine environment The physical and chemical environment within the uterus during prenatal development.

Intrinsic motivation Motivation that comes from within, rather than from external rewards; motivation based on personal enjoyment of a task or activity.

Introspection To look within; to examine one's own thoughts, feelings, or sensations.

Introvert A person whose attention is focused inward; a shy, reserved, timid person.

Intuition Quick, impulsive thought that does not make use of formal logic or clear reasoning.

Intuitive thought Thinking that makes little or no use of reasoning and logic.

Inverted U function A curve, roughly in the shape of an upside-down U, that relates performance to levels of arousal.

Ion channels Gaps through the axon membrane.

Irrelevant questions In a polygraph exam, neutral, non-threatening, or non-emotional questions.

James-Lange theory States that emotional feelings follow bodily arousal and come from awareness of such arousal.

Jigsaw classroom A method of reducing prejudice; each student receives only part of the information needed to complete a project or prepare for a test.

Justification In cognitive dissonance theory, the degree to which one's actions are justified by rewards or other circumstances.

Just-world beliefs Belief that people generally get what they deserve.

Keyword method As an aid to memory, using a familiar word or image to link two items.

Kinesics Study of the meaning of body movements, posture, hand gestures, and facial expressions; commonly called body language.

Kinesthetic image Any mental representation based on produced, remembered, or imagined muscular sensations.

Kinesthetic senses The senses of body movement and positioning.

Knowledge of results During learning, feedback about the correctness of responses or other aspects of performance.

Language Words or symbols, and rules for combining them, that are used for thinking and communication.

Large-group awareness training Any of a number of programs (many of them commercialized) that claim to increase self-awareness and facilitate constructive personal change.

Latency According to Freud, a period in childhood when psychosexual development is more or less interrupted.

Latent dream content The hidden or symbolic meaning of a dream, as revealed by dream interpretation and analysis.

Latent learning Learning that occurs without obvious reinforcement and that remains unexpressed until reinforcement is provided.

Lateralization Differences between the two sides of the body—especially differences in the abilities of the brain hemispheres.

Law of effect Responses that lead to desirable effects are repeated; those that produce undesirable results are not.

Leaderless group discussion A test of leadership that simulates group decision making and problem solving.

Learned helplessness A learned inability to overcome obstacles or to avoid punishment; learned passivity and inaction to aversive stimuli.

Learning Any relatively permanent change in behaviour that can be attributed to experience.

Learning theorist A psychologist interested in the ways that learning shapes behaviour and explains personality.

Lens Structure in the eye that focuses light rays.

Leptin A substance released by fat cells that inhibits eating.

Lexigram A geometric shape used as a symbol for a word.

Libido In Freudian theory, the force, primarily pleasure oriented, that energizes the personality.

Life change units (LCUs) Numerical values assigned to each life event on the SRRS.

Life skills training A program that teaches stress reduction, self-protection, decision making, self-control, and social skills.

Life stages Widely recognized periods of life corresponding to broad phases of development.

Lifestyle disease A disease related to health-damaging personal habits.

Light sleep Stage 1 sleep, marked by small irregular brain waves and some alpha waves.

Liking A relationship based on intimacy, but lacking passion and commitment.

Limbic system A system in the forebrain that is closely linked with emotional response.

Lobes of the cerebral cortex Areas on the cortex bordered by major fissures or defined by their functions.

Lock-and-key theory Holds that odours are related to the shapes of chemical molecules.

Logical consequences Reasonable consequences that are defined by parents.

Logical thought Drawing conclusions on the basis of formal principles of reasoning.

Long sleeper A person who averages nine hours of sleep or more per night.

Long-term memory (LTM) The memory system used for relatively permanent storage of meaningful information.

Looking chamber An experimental apparatus used to test infant perception by presenting visual stimuli and observing infant responses.

Loudness The intensity of a sound; determined by the amplitude of sound waves.

Low-ball technique A strategy in which commitment is gained first to reasonable or desirable terms, which are then made less reasonable or desirable.

Lucid dream A dream in which the dreamer feels awake and capable of normal thought and action.

Maintenance rehearsal Silently repeating or mentally reviewing information to hold it in short-term memory.

Major depressive disorder A mood disorder in which the person has suffered one or more intense episodes of depression.

Major mood disorders Disorders marked by lasting extremes of mood or emotion and sometimes accompanied by psychotic symptoms.

Maladaptive behaviour Behaviour that makes it difficult to adapt to the environment and meet the demands of day-to-day life.

Management techniques Combining praise, recognition, approval, rules, and reasoning to enforce child discipline.

Manifest dream content The surface, "visible" content of a dream; dream images as they are remembered by the dreamer.

Mantra A flowing word or sound repeated silently during concentrative meditation.

Marijuana The leaves and flowers of the hemp plant *Cannabis sativa*.

Mass media Collectively, all media that reach very large audiences (magazines, for instance, are a medium of mass communication).

Massed practice A practice schedule in which studying continues for long periods, without interruption.

Mastery training Reinforcement of responses that lead to mastery of a threat or control over one's environment.

Maternal influences The aggregate of all psychological effects mothers have on their children.

Maturation The physical growth and development of the body and nervous system.

Mean world view Viewing the world and other people as dangerous and threatening.

Mechanical solution A problem solution achieved by

trial and error or by a fixed procedure based on learned rules.

Medical therapies Any bodily therapy, such as drug therapy, electroshock, or psychosurgery.

Meditation A mental exercise for producing relaxation or heightened awareness.

Medulla The structure that connects the brain with the spinal cord and controls vital life functions.

Melatonin Hormone released by the pineal gland in response to daily cycles of light and dark.

Memory The mental system for receiving, encoding, storing, organizing, altering, and retrieving information.

Memory cue Any stimulus associated with a particular memory. Memory cues usually enhance retrieval.

Memory decay The fading or weakening of memories assumed to occur when memory traces become weaker.

Memory structure Patterns of associations among bits of information stored in memory.

Memory task Any task designed to test or assess memory.

Memory traces Physical changes in nerve cells or brain activity that take place when memories are stored.

Mental age The average mental ability people display at a given age.

Mental disorder A significant impairment in psychological functioning.

Mental hospitalization Placing a person in a protected, therapeutic environment staffed by mental health professionals.

Mental retardation The presence of a developmental disability, a formal IQ score below 70, or a significant impairment of adaptive behaviour.

Mental rotation The ability to change the position of an image in mental space.

Mesmerize To hypnotize.

Message In persuasion, the content of a communicator's arguments or presentation.

Metabolic disorder Any disorder in metabolism (the rate of energy production and use in the body).

Metabolic rate The rate at which energy is consumed by bodily activity.

Meta-needs In Maslow's hierarchy, needs associated with impulses for self-actualization.

Micro-electrode An electrode small enough to record the activity of a single neuron.

Microsleep A brief shift in brain-wave patterns to those of sleep.

Microstressor Any distressing, day-to-day annoyance; also called a *hassle*.

Mild punishment Punishment that has a relatively weak effect—especially punishment that only temporarily slows responding.

Minnesota Multiphasic Personality Inventory-2 (MMPI-2) One of the best-known and most widely used objective personality questionnaires.

Minor tranquillizers Drugs (such as Valium) that produce relaxation or reduce anxiety.

Mirror technique Observing another person re-enact one's own behaviour, like a character in a play; designed to help persons see themselves more clearly.

MMPI-2 profile A graphic representation of an individual's scores on each of the primary scales of the MMPI-2.

Mnemonic Any kind of memory system or aid.

Model A person who serves as an example in observational learning.

Monocular depth cue A depth cue that can be sensed with one eye.

Mood A low-intensity, long-lasting emotional state.

Mood disorder Major disturbances in mood or emotion.

Moon illusion The apparent change in size that occurs as the moon moves from the horizon (large moon) to overhead (small moon).

Moral anxiety Apprehension felt when thoughts, impulses, or actions conflict with the superego's standards.

Moro reflex Neonatal reflex evoked by sudden loss of support or the sounding of a loud noise; in response, the arms are extended and then brought toward each other.

Morphemes The smallest meaningful units in a language, such as syllables or words.

Motherese (or parentese) A pattern of speech used when talking to infants, marked by a higher-pitched voice, short, simple sentences, repetition, slower speech, and exaggerated voice inflections.

Motivation Internal processes that initiate, sustain, and direct activities.

Motor cortex A brain area associated with control of movement.

Motor neuron A nerve cell that carries motor commands from the CNS to muscles and glands.

MRI scan Magnetic resonance imaging; a computer-enhanced three-dimensional representation of the brain or body, based on the body's response to a magnetic field.

Müller-Lyer illusion Two equal-length lines tipped with inward or outward pointing V's appear to be of different lengths.

Multiculturalism Giving equal status, recognition, and acceptance to different ethnic and cultural groups.

Multiple approach-avoidance conflict Being simultaneously attracted to and repelled by each of several alternatives.

Multistable figure A visual figure that oscillates between alternative subjective forms even though the figure itself does not change.

Mutual absorption With regard to romantic love, the nearly exclusive attention lovers give to one another.

Mutual interdependence A condition in which two or more persons must depend on one another to meet each person's needs or goals.

Myelin A fatty layer coating some axons.

Myopia Difficulty focusing distant objects (nearsightedness).

Native perception A perceptual experience based on innate processes.

Natural clinical test A natural event that provides data on a psychological phenomenon.

Natural consequences The effects that naturally tend to follow a particular behaviour.

Natural selection Darwin's theory that evolution favours those plants and animals best suited to their living conditions.

Natural setting The environment in which an organism typically lives.

Naturalistic observation Observing behaviour as it unfolds in natural settings.

Need An internal deficiency that may energize behaviour.

Need for achievement The desire to excel or meet some internalized standard of excellence.

Need for power The desire to have social impact and control over others.

Need to affiliate The desire to associate with other people.

Negative after-potential A drop in electrical charge below the resting potential.

Negative attention seeking Using misbehaviour to gain attention.

Negative correlation A statistical relationship in which increases in one measure are matched by decreases in the other.

Negative reinforcement Occurs when a response is followed by an end to discomfort or by the removal of an unpleasant event.

Negative self-statements Self-critical thoughts that increase anxiety and lower performance.

Neonate A term used for newborn infants during the first weeks following birth.

Nerve A bundle of neuron fibres.

Nerve deafness Deafness caused by damage to the hair cells or auditory nerve.

Network model A model of memory that views it as an organized system of linked information.

Neurilemma A layer of cells that encases many axons.

Neurogenesis The production of new brain cells.

Neuron An individual nerve cell.

Neuropeptide Y A substance in the brain that initiates eating.

Neuropeptides Brain chemicals, such as enkephalins and endorphins, that regulate the activity of neurons.

Neurosis An outdated term once used to refer to anxiety disorders, somatoform disorders, dissociative disorders, and some forms of depression.

Neurotic anxiety Apprehension felt when the ego struggles to control id impulses.

Neurotransmitter Any chemical released by a neuron that alters activity in other neurons.

Neutral stimulus A stimulus that does not evoke a response.

Nicotine A potent stimulant drug found primarily in tobacco; nicotine is a known carcinogen.

Night terror A state of panic that occurs during NREM sleep.

Nightmare A bad dream that occurs during REM sleep.

Non-homeostatic drive A drive that is relatively independent of physical deprivation cycles or bodily need states.

Nonsense syllables Invented three-letter words used to test learning and memory.

Norepinephrine An adrenal hormone that tends to arouse the body; norepinephrine is associated with anger. (Also known as noradrenaline.)

Norm An accepted (but often unspoken) standard of conduct for appropriate behaviour.

Normal curve A bell-shaped curve with a large number of scores in the middle, tapering to very few extremely high and low scores.

NREM sleep Non-rapid eye movement sleep characteristic of stages 2, 3, and 4.

Obedience Conformity to the demands of an authority.

Object permanence Concept, gained in infancy, that objects continue to exist even when they are hidden from view.

Objective test A test that gives the same score when different people correct it.

Observation Gathering data directly by recording facts or events.

Observational learning Learning achieved by watching and imitating the actions of another or noting the consequences of those actions.

Observational record A detailed summary of observed events or a videotape of observed behaviour.

Observer bias The tendency of an observer to distort observations or perceptions to match his or her expectations.

Observer effect Changes in behaviour brought about by an awareness of being observed.

Obsession Recurring irrational or disturbing thoughts or mental images that a person cannot prevent.

Obsessive-compulsive disorder An extreme preoccupation with certain thoughts and compulsive performance of certain behaviours.

Occipital lobes Portion of the cerebral cortex where vision registers in the brain.

Oedipus conflict A boy's sexual attraction to his mother, and feelings of rivalry with his father.

Olfaction The sense of smell.

Operant conditioning A type of learning that occurs when the behaviour of a person or an animal changes in response to the consequences of actions.

Operant extinction The weakening or disappearance of a non-reinforced operant response.

Operant reinforcer Any event that reliably increases the probability or frequency of responses it follows.

Operant stimulus discrimination The tendency to make an operant response when stimuli previously associated with reward are present and to withhold the response when stimuli associated with non-reward are present.

Operant stimulus generalization The tendency to respond to stimuli similar to those that preceded operant reinforcement.

Operational definition Defining a scientific concept by stating the specific actions or procedures used to measure it. For example, "hunger" might be defined as "the number of hours of food deprivation."

Opponent-process theory Theory of colour vision based on three coding systems (red or green, yellow or blue, black or white).

Oral stage The psychosexual stage (roughly birth to one year of age) when infants are preoccupied with the mouth as a source of pleasure and means of expression.

Oral-aggressive personality A person who uses the mouth to express hostility by shouting, cursing, biting, and so forth. Also, one who actively exploits others.

Oral-dependent personality A person who wants to passively receive attention, gifts, love, and so forth.

Organ of Corti Centre part of the cochlea, containing hair cells, canals, and membranes.

Organic mental disorder A mental or emotional problem caused by brain diseases or injuries.

Organic psychosis A psychosis caused by brain injury or disease.

Organismic valuing A natural, undistorted, full-body reaction to an experience.

Organized knowledge Orderly and highly refined information about a particular topic or skill.

Orgasm A climax and release of sexual excitement.

Originality In tests of creativity, originality refers to how novel or unusual solutions are.

Otolith organs Vestibular structures sensitive to movement, acceleration, and gravity.

Oval window A membrane on the cochlea connected to the third auditory ossicle.

Overdisclosure Self-disclosure that exceeds what is appropriate for a particular relationship or social situation.

Overgeneralization Blowing a single event out of proportion by extending it to a large number of unrelated situations.

Overlearning Study or learning that continues after initial mastery of skills or information.

Overly permissive parents Parents who give little guidance, allow too much freedom, or do not require the child to take responsibility.

Overt behaviour An action or response that is directly observable.

Pain disorder Pain that has no identifiable physical cause and appears to be of psychological origin.

Palmistry False system that claims to reveal personality traits and to predict the future by "reading" lines on the palms of the hands.

Panic disorder (with agoraphobia) A chronic state of anxiety and brief moments of sudden panic. The person fears that these panic attacks will occur in public places or unfamiliar situations.

Panic disorder (without agoraphobia) The person is in a chronic state of anxiety and also has brief moments of sudden, intense, unexpected panic.

Paranoid psychosis A delusional disorder centred especially on delusions of persecution.

Paranoid schizophrenia Schizophrenia marked by a preoccupation with delusions or by frequent auditory hallucinations related to a single theme, especially grandeur or persecution.

Paraprofessional An individual who works in a near-professional capacity under the supervision of a more highly trained person.

Parapsychology The study of extranormal psychological events, such as extrasensory perception.

Parasympathetic branch A part of the autonomic system that quiets the body and conserves energy.

Parasympathetic rebound Excess activity in the parasympathetic nervous system following a period of intense emotion.

Parasympathetic system A branch of the ANS that quiets the body.

Parental responsiveness Caregiving that is based on sensitivity to a child's feelings, needs, rhythms, and signals.

Parietal lobes Area of the brain where bodily sensations register.

Part learning Separately studying subparts of a larger body of information (such as sections of a textbook chapter).

Partial hospitalization An approach in which patients receive treatment at a hospital during the day, but return home at night.

Partial reinforcement A pattern in which only a portion of all responses are reinforced.

Partial reinforcement effect Responses acquired with partial reinforcement are more resistant to extinction.

Passive compliance Passively bending to unreasonable demands or circumstances.

Paternal influences The aggregate of all psychological effects fathers have on their children.

Peer counsellor A non-professional person who has learned basic counselling skills.

Perception The mental process of organizing sensations into meaningful patterns.

Perceptual expectancy (or set) A readiness to perceive in a particular manner, induced by strong expectations.

Perceptual features Basic elements of a stimulus, such as lines, shapes, edges, or colours.

Perceptual habits Well-established patterns of perceptual organization and attention.

Perceptual hypothesis An initial guess regarding how to organize (perceive) a stimulus pattern.

Perceptual learning Changes in perception that can be attributed to prior experience; a result of changes in how the brain processes sensory information.

Perceptual reconstruction A mental model of external events.

Performance intelligence Intelligence measured by solving puzzles, assembling objects, completing pictures, and other nonverbal tasks.

Peripheral nervous system All parts of the nervous system outside the brain and spinal cord.

Peripheral vision Vision at the edges of the visual field.

Personal frustration Distress caused by personal characteristics that impede progress toward a goal.

Personal prejudice Prejudicial attitudes held toward persons who are perceived as a direct threat to one's own interests.

Personality A person's unique and relatively stable behaviour pattern.

Personality disintegration A shattering of the coordination among thoughts, actions, and emotions normally found in personality.

Personality disorder A maladaptive personality pattern.

Personality questionnaire A paper-and-pencil test consisting of questions that reveal aspects of personality.

Personality theorist A psychologist who studies personality traits, dynamics, and theories.

Personality theory A system of concepts, assumptions, ideas, and principles used to understand and explain personality.

Personality trait A stable, enduring quality that a person shows in most situations.

Personality type A style of personality defined by a group of related traits.

Persuasion A deliberate attempt to change attitudes or beliefs with information and arguments.

PET scan Positron emission tomography; a computer-generated colour image of brain activity, as revealed by the consumption of radioactive sugar.

Phallic personality A person who is vain, exhibitionistic, sensitive, and narcissistic.

Phallic stage The psychosexual stage (roughly ages three to six years) when a child is preoccupied with the genitals.

Pharmacotherapy The use of drugs to alleviate the symptoms of emotional disturbance.

Phobia An intense and unrealistic fear of some specific object or situation.

Phonemes The basic speech sounds of a language.

Phonological storage Storing a word in memory on the basis of its sound.

Photoreceptor A sensory receptor for light.

Phototherapy A treatment for seasonal affective disorder that involves exposure to bright, full-spectrum light.

Phrenology False and antiquated system based on the belief that personality traits are revealed by the shape of the skull.

Physical attractiveness A person's degree of physical beauty, as defined by his or her culture.

Physical dependence Physical addiction, as indicated by the presence of drug tolerance and withdrawal symptoms.

Physiological changes (in emotion) Alterations in heart rate, blood pressure, perspiration, and other involuntary responses.

Pictorial depth cues Features found in painting, drawings, and photographs that import information about space, depth, and distance.

Pineal gland Gland in the brain that helps regulate body rhythms and sleep.

Pinel, Philippe The French physician who initiated humane treatment of mental patients in 1793.

Pinna The visible, external part of the ear.

Pitch Higher or lower tones; related to the frequency of sound waves.

Pituitary gland The "master gland" whose hormones influence other endocrine glands.

Place theory Theory that higher and lower tones excite specific areas of the cochlea.

Placebo An inactive substance given in the place of a drug in psychological research.

Placebo effect Changes in behaviour due to expectations that a drug (or other treatment) will have some effect.

Plateau phase The second phase of sexual response during which physical arousal is further heightened.

Play Any activity done for sheer enjoyment.

Pleasantness–unpleasantness As reflected by facial expressions, the degree to which a person is experiencing pleasure or displeasure.

Pleasure principle A desire for immediate satisfaction of wishes, desires, or needs.

Polygenic characteristics Personal traits or physical properties that are influenced by many genes working in combination.

Polygraph A device for recording heart rate, blood pressure, respiration, and galvanic skin response; commonly called a "lie detector."

Pons An area on the brainstem that acts as a bridge between the medulla and other structures.

Population An entire group of animals or people belonging to a particular category (for example, all college students or all married women).

Positive correlation A statistical relationship in which increases in one measure are matched by increases in the other (or decreases correspond with decreases).

Positive reinforcement Occurs when a response is followed by a reward or other positive event.

Positive self-regard Thinking of oneself as a good, lovable, worthwhile person.

Post-traumatic stress disorder A psychological disturbance lasting more than one month following stresses that would produce anxiety in anyone who experienced them.

Power assertion The use of physical punishment or coercion to enforce child discipline.

Preadaptation Gradual matching of sleep-waking cycles to a new time schedule.

Precognition The purported ability to accurately predict future events.

Preconscious An area of the mind containing information that can be voluntarily brought to awareness.

Prediction An ability to accurately forecast behaviour.

Prefrontal lobotomy An antiquated surgery in which portions of the frontal lobes were destroyed or disconnected from other brain areas.

Prejudice A negative emotional attitude held against members of a particular group of people.

Premack principle Any high-frequency response can be used to reinforce a low-frequency response.

Preoperational stage Period of intellectual development during which children begin to use language and think symbolically, yet remain intuitive and egocentric in their thought.

Presbyopia Farsightedness caused by aging.

Pressure A stressful condition that occurs when a person must meet urgent external demands or expectations.

Primary appraisal Deciding if a situation is relevant to oneself and if it is a threat.

Primary caregiver A person primarily responsible for the care of an infant; usually the infant's mother or father.

Primary emotions According to Robert Plutchik's theory, the most basic emotions are fear, surprise, sadness, disgust, anger, anticipation, joy, and acceptance.

Primary motives Innate motives based on biological needs.

Primary reinforcers Non-learned reinforcers; usually those that satisfy physiological needs.

Priming Facilitating the retrieval of an implicit memory by using cues to activate hidden memories.

Private self-consciousness Preoccupation with inner feelings, thoughts, and fantasies.

Proactive interference The tendency for old memories to interfere with the retrieval of newer memories.

Proactive maternal involvement Sensitive caregiving in which the mother actively seeks to interact with her child and to provide educational experiences.

Problem-focused coping Directly managing or remedying a stressful or threatening situation.

Procedural memory Long-term memories of conditioned responses and learned skills.

Productivity The capacity of language to generate new ideas and possibilities.

Programmed instruction Any learning format that presents information in small amounts, gives immediate practice, and provides continuous feedback to learners.

Progressive part method Breaking information into a series of short units and then learning increasingly longer groups of units.

Progressive relaxation A method for producing deep relaxation of all parts of the body.

Projection Attributing one's own feelings, shortcomings, or unacceptable impulses to others.

Projective tests Psychological tests making use of ambiguous or unstructured stimuli.

Prosocial behaviour Behaviour toward others that is helpful, constructive, or altruistic.

Prototype An ideal model used as a prime example of a particular concept.

Proximodistal From the centre of the body to the extremities.

Pseudo-memory A false memory that a person believes is real or accurate.

Pseudo-psychology Any false and unscientific system of beliefs and practices that is offered as an explanation of behaviour.

Psi phenomena Events that seem to lie outside the realm of accepted scientific laws.

Psyche The mind, mental life, and personality as a whole.

Psychiatric nurse A nurse with specialized training in mental health.

Psychiatric social worker A mental health professional trained to apply social science principles to help patients in clinics and hospitals.

Psychiatrist A medical doctor with additional training in the diagnosis and treatment of mental and emotional disorders.

Psychoactive drug A substance capable of altering attention, memory, judgment, time sense, self-control, mood, or perception.

Psychoanalysis A Freudian therapy that emphasizes the use of free association, dream interpretation, resistances, and transference to uncover unconscious conflicts.

Psychoanalyst A mental health professional (usually a medical doctor) trained to practise psychoanalysis.

Psychoanalytic dream theory A theory that emphasizes internal conflicts, motives, and unconscious forces.

Psychoanalytic theory Freudian theory of personality that emphasizes unconscious forces and conflicts.

Psychodrama A therapy in which clients act out personal conflicts and feelings in the presence of others who play supporting roles.

Psychodynamic Pertaining to internal motives, conflicts, unconscious forces, and other dynamics of mental life.

Psychodynamic theory Any theory of behaviour that emphasizes internal conflicts, motives, and unconscious forces.

Psychokinesis The purported ability to mentally alter or influence objects or events.

Psycholinguist A specialist in the psychology of language and language development.

Psychological dependence Drug dependence that is based primarily on emotional or psychological needs.

Psychological situation A situation as it is perceived and interpreted by an individual, not as it exists objectively.

Psychological trauma A psychological injury or shock, such as that caused by violence, abuse, neglect, separation, and so forth.

Psychologist A person highly trained in the methods, factual knowledge, and theories of psychology.

Psychology The scientific study of human and animal behaviour.

Psychoneuroimmunology Study of the links among behaviour, stress, disease, and the immune system.

Psychopathology The scientific study of mental, emotional, and behavioural disorders; also refers to abnormal behaviour.

Psychosexual stages The oral, anal, phallic, and genital stages, during which various personality traits are formed.

Psychosis A withdrawal from reality marked by hallucinations and delusions, disturbed thought and emotions, and personality disorganization.

Psychosocial dilemma A conflict between personal impulses and the social world.

Psychosomatic disorders Illnesses in which psychological factors contribute to bodily damage.

Psychosurgery Any surgical alteration of the brain designed to bring about desirable behavioural or emotional changes.

Psychotherapy Any psychological treatment for behavioural or emotional problems.

Psychotic disorder A severe mental disorder characterized by a retreat from reality, hallucinations and delusions, and social withdrawal.

Public self-consciousness Intense awareness of oneself as a social object.

Punisher Any event that decreases the probability or frequency of responses it follows.

Punishment Any event that follows a response and decreases its likelihood of occurring again.

Random assignment The use of chance (for example, flipping a coin) to assign subjects to experimental and control groups.

Random search strategy Trying possible solutions to a problem in a more or less random order.

Rapid eye movements (REMs) Swift eye movements during sleep.

Rapid smoking Prolonged smoking at a forced pace; used to produce discomfort in aversion therapy for smoking.

Rating scale A list of personality traits or aspects of behaviour on which a person is rated.

Rational-emotive behaviour therapy (REBT) An approach that states that irrational beliefs cause many emotional problems and that such beliefs must be changed or abandoned.

Rationalization Justifying personal behaviour by giving reasonable and "rational" but false reasons for it.

Reaction formation Preventing dangerous impulses from being expressed in behaviour by exaggerating opposite behaviour.

Readiness A condition that exists when maturation has advanced enough to allow the rapid acquisition of a particular skill.

Reality principle Delaying action (or pleasure) until it is appropriate.

Reality testing Obtaining additional information to check on the accuracy of perceptions.

Recall To supply or reproduce memorized information with a minimum of external cues.

Receptive meditation Mental exercise based on widening attention to become aware of

everything experienced at any given moment.

Receptor sites Areas on the surface of neurons and other cells that are sensitive to neurotransmitters or hormones.

Recessive gene A gene whose influence will be expressed only when it is paired with a second recessive gene.

Reciprocal inhibition The presence of one emotional state can inhibit the occurrence of another, such as joy preventing fear or anxiety inhibiting pleasure.

Reciprocity A reciprocal interchange or return in kind.

Recitation As a memory aid, repeating aloud information one wishes to retain.

Recoding Reorganizing or modifying information to assist storage in memory.

Recognition memory An ability to correctly identify previously learned information.

Reference group Any group that an individual identifies with and uses as a standard for social comparison.

Reflection In client-centred therapy, the process of rephrasing or repeating thoughts and feelings expressed by clients so they can become aware of what they are saying.

Reflex An innate, automatic response to a stimulus (for example, an eye-blink).

Reflex arc The simplest behaviour, in which a stimulus provokes an automatic response.

Refreezing In brainwashing, the process of rewarding and strengthening new attitudes and beliefs.

Refusal skills training Program that teaches youths how to resist pressures to begin smoking. (Can also be applied to other drugs and health risks.)

Regression Retreating to an earlier stage of development or to earlier, less demanding habits or situations.

Rehearsal Silently repeating or mentally reviewing information to improve memory.

Reinforcement Any event that increases the probability that a particular response will occur.

Reinforcement value The subjective value a person attaches

to a particular activity or reinforcer.

Relational concept A concept defined by the relationship between features of an object or between an object and its surroundings (for example, "greater than," "lopsided").

Relaxation response The pattern of internal bodily changes that occurs at times of relaxation.

Relearning Learning again something that was previously learned. Used to measure memory of prior learning.

Relevant questions In a polygraph exam, questions to which only a guilty person should react.

Reliability The ability of a test to yield nearly the same score each time it is given to the same person.

REM behaviour disorder A failure of normal muscle paralysis, leading to violent actions during REM sleep.

REM rebound The occurrence of extra rapid eye movement sleep following REM sleep deprivation.

REM sleep Sleep marked by rapid eye movements and a return to stage 1 EEG patterns.

Reminding system Pain based on small nerve fibres; reminds the brain that the body has been injured.

Replicate To reproduce or repeat.

Representative sample A small, randomly selected part of a larger population that accurately reflects characteristics of the whole population.

Representativeness heuristic A tendency to select wrong answers because they seem to match pre-existing mental categories.

Repression Unconsciously pushing unwanted memories out of awareness.

Research method A systematic approach to answering scientific questions.

Resistance A blockage in the flow of free association; topics the client unconsciously resists thinking or talking about.

Resolution The fourth phase of sexual response, involving a return to lower levels of sexual tension and arousal.

Respondent reinforcement Reinforcement that occurs when an unconditioned stimulus closely follows a conditioned stimulus.

Response Any identifiable behaviour.

Response chain A linked series of separate actions that lead to reinforcement.

Response cost Removal of a positive reinforcer after a response is made.

Response-contingent consequences Reinforcement, punishment, or other consequences that are applied only when a certain response is made.

Response-contingent reinforcement Reinforcement given only when a particular response is made.

REST Restricted Environmental Stimulation Therapy.

Resting potential The electrical charge of a neuron at rest.

Reticular activating system (RAS) A part of the reticular formation that activates the cerebral cortex.

Reticular formation A network of neurons in the brainstem, associated with attention, alertness, and some reflexes.

Retina The light-sensitive layer of cells at the back of the eye.

Retinal disparity Small discrepancies in images on the right and left retinas.

Retrieval Recovering information from storage in memory.

Retroactive interference The tendency for new memories to interfere with the retrieval of old memories.

Retrograde amnesia Loss of memory for events that preceded a head injury or other amnesia-causing event.

Reversibility of thought Recognition that relationships involving equality or identity can be reversed (for example, if A = B, then B = A).

Reversible figure A stimulus pattern in which figure-ground organization can be reversed.

Reward Anything that produces pleasure or satisfaction; a positive reinforcer.

Rhodopsin The light-sensitive pigment in the rods.

Rods Visual receptors for dim light that produce only black-and-white sensations.

Role conflict Trying to occupy two or more roles that make conflicting demands on behaviour.

Role model A person who serves as a positive example of desirable behaviour.

Role reversal Taking the role of another person to learn how one's own behaviour appears from the other person's perspective.

Role-playing The dramatic enactment or re-enactment of significant life events.

Romantic love Love that is associated with high levels of interpersonal attraction, heightened arousal, mutual absorption, and sexual desire.

Rooting reflex Neonatal reflex elicited by a light touch to the cheek, causing the infant to turn toward the object and attempt to nurse.

Rorschach Technique A projective test composed of 10 standardized inkblots.

Rote learning Learning that takes place mechanically, through repetition and memorization, or by learning rules.

Run of luck A statistically unusual outcome (as in getting five heads in a row when flipping a coin) that could still occur by chance alone.

Satiety system Areas in the hypothalamus that terminate eating.

Saturation The degree of a colour's purity.

Savings score The amount of time saved (expressed as a percentage) when relearning information.

Scaffolding The process of adjusting instruction so that it is responsive to a beginner's behaviour and supports the beginner's efforts to understand a problem or gain a mental skill.

Scapegoating Blaming a person or a group for the actions of others or for conditions not of their making.

Schachter's cognitive theory States that emotions occur when physical arousal is labelled or interpreted on the basis of experience and situational cues.

Schedule of reinforcement A rule or plan for determining which responses will be reinforced.

Schizophrenia A psychosis characterized by delusions, hallucinations, apathy, and a "split" between thought and emotion.

Scientific method Testing the truth of a proposition by careful measurement and controlled observation.

Scientific observation An empirical investigation that is structured to answer questions about the world.

Scientist-practitioner model A view that holds that clinical psychologists should be skilled both as scientists and as therapists.

Seasonal affective disorder Depression that occurs only during fall and winter; presumably related to decreased exposure to sunlight.

Secondary appraisal Deciding how to cope with a threat or challenge.

Secondary elaboration Making a dream more logical and complete while remembering it.

Secondary motives Motives based on learned needs, drives, and goals.

Secondary reinforcer A learned reinforcer; often one that gains reinforcing properties by association with a primary reinforcer.

Secondary traits Traits that are inconsistent or relatively minor.

Secure attachment A stable and positive emotional bond.

Selective attention Giving priority to a particular incoming sensory message.

Selective combination In problem solving, the ability to connect seemingly unrelated items of information.

Selective comparison The ability to relate a present problem to similar problems solved in the past or to prior experience.

Selective encoding The ability to select information relevant to a problem while ignoring useless or distracting information.

Selective perception Perceiving only certain stimuli among a larger array of possibilities.

Self A continuously evolving conception of one's personal identity.

Self-actualization The process of fully developing one's personal potential.

Self-actualizer One who is living creatively and making full use of his or her potentials.

Self-assertion A direct, honest expression of feelings and desires.

Self-awareness Consciousness of oneself as a person.

Self-concept A person's perception of his or her own personality traits.

Self-confidence Belief that one can successfully carry out an activity or reach a goal.

Self-defeating bias A distortion of thinking that impairs behaviour.

Self-disclosure The process of revealing private thoughts, feelings, and one's personal history to others.

Self-esteem Regarding oneself as a worthwhile person; a positive evaluation of oneself.

Self-evaluation Positive and negative feelings held toward oneself.

Self-fulfilling prophecy An expectation that prompts people to act in ways that make the expectation come true.

Self-help group A group of people who share a particular type of problem and provide mutual support to one another.

Self-hypnosis A state of hypnosis attained without the aid of a hypnotist; autosuggestion.

Self-image Total subjective perception of oneself.

Self-recording Self-management based on keeping records of response frequencies.

Self-reference effect Memory works better when you encode for meaning and emphasize personal relevance of the material.

Self-regulated learning Active, self-guided learning.

Self-reinforcement Praising or rewarding oneself for having made a particular response (such as completing a school assignment).

Semantic differential A measure of connotative meaning obtained by rating words or concepts on several dimensions.

Semantic memory A subpart of declarative memory that records impersonal knowledge about the world.

Semantics The study of meanings in language.

Semicircular canals Fluid-filled canals containing the sensory organs for balance.

Senescence Aging; the latter years of life.

Sensation A sensory impression; also, the process of detecting physical energies with the sensory organs.

Sensation and perception psychologist A psychologist who studies the sense organs and the process of perception.

Sensation seeking A personality characteristic of persons who prefer high levels of stimulation.

Sensitivity group A group experience consisting of exercises designed to increase self-awareness and sensitivity to others.

Sensorimotor stage Stage of intellectual development during which sensory input and motor responses become coordinated.

Sensory adaptation A decrease in sensory response to an unchanging stimulus.

Sensory analysis Separation of sensory information into important elements.

Sensory coding Codes used by the sense organs to transmit information to the brain.

Sensory conflict theory Explains motion sickness as the result of a mismatch between information from vision, the vestibular system, and kinesthesis.

Sensory deprivation Any major reduction in the amount or variety of sensory stimulation.

Sensory gating Alteration of sensory messages in the spinal cord.

Sensory localization The principle that the type of sensation experienced is related to the area of the brain activated.

Sensory memory The first stage of memory, which holds an exact record of incoming information for a few seconds or less.

Sensory neuron A nerve cell that carries information from the senses toward the CNS.

Separation anxiety Distress displayed by infants when they are separated from their parents or principal caregivers.

Serial position effect The tendency for the greatest number of memory errors to occur in the middle portion of a list.

Set point The proportion of body fat that tends to be maintained by changes in hunger and eating.

Severe punishment Intense punishment; punishment capable of suppressing a response for long periods.

Sex drive The strength of one's motivation to engage in sexual behaviour.

Sexual and gender identity disorders Any of a wide range of difficulties with sexual identity, deviant sexual behaviour, or sexual adjustment.

Sexual orientation One's degree of emotional and erotic attraction to members of the same sex, opposite sex, or both sexes.

Sexual script An unspoken mental plan that defines a "plot," dialogue, and actions expected to take place in a sexual encounter.

Sexually transmitted disease (STD) A disease that is typically passed from one person to the next by intimate physical contact. Sometimes known as a venereal disease.

Shape constancy The perceived shape of an object is unaffected by changes in its retinal image.

Shaping Gradually moulding responses to a final desired pattern.

Short sleeper A person averaging five hours of sleep or less per night.

Short-term memory (STM) The memory system used to hold small amounts of information for relatively brief time periods.

Shyness A tendency to avoid others plus uneasiness and strain when socializing.

Signal In early language development, any behaviour, such as touching, vocalizing, gazing, or

smiling, that allows non-verbal interaction and turn-taking between parent and child.

Similarity The extent to which two people are alike in background, age, interests, attitudes, beliefs, and so forth.

Single-blind experiment An arrangement in which subjects remain unaware of whether they are in the experimental group or the control group, although the researcher knows.

Single-word stage In language development, the period during which a child first begins to use single words.

Situational context The social situation, behavioural setting, or general circumstances in which an action takes place.

Situational determinants External conditions that strongly influence behaviour.

Situational test Simulating real-life conditions so that a person's reactions may be directly observed.

Size constancy The perceived size of an object remains constant, despite changes in its retinal image.

Size-distance invariance The strict relationship between the distance an object lies from the eyes and the size of its image.

Skin receptors Sensory organs for touch, pressure, pain, cold, and warmth.

Skin senses The senses of touch, pressure, pain, heat, and cold.

Sleep apnea Repeated interruption of breathing during sleep.

Sleep deprivation Being prevented from getting desired or needed amounts of sleep.

Sleep hormone A sleep-promoting substance found in the brain and spinal cord.

Sleep patterns The order and timing of daily sleep and waking periods.

Sleep spindles Distinctive bursts of brain-wave activity that indicate a person is asleep.

Sleep stages Levels of sleep identified by brain-wave patterns and behavioural changes.

Sleep-deprivation psychosis A major disruption of mental

and emotional functioning brought about by sleep loss.

Sleeptalking Speaking that occurs during NREM sleep.

Slow-to-warm-up child A child who is temperamentally restrained and unexpressive.

Social anxiety A feeling of apprehension in the presence of others.

Social comparison Making judgments about ourselves through comparison with others.

Social development The development of self-awareness, attachment to parents or caregivers, and relationships with other children and adults.

Social influence Changes in a person's behaviour induced by the presence or actions of others.

Social learning theory An explanation of personality that combines learning principles, cognition, and the effects of social relationships.

Social motives Learned motives acquired as part of growing up in a particular society or culture.

Social non-conformity Failure to conform to societal norms or the usual minimum standards for social conduct.

Social phobia An intense, irrational fear of being observed, evaluated, embarrassed, or humiliated by others in social situations.

Social psychologist A psychologist particularly interested in human social behaviour.

Social psychology The scientific study of how individuals behave, think, and feel in social situations.

Social Readjustment Rating Scale **(SRRS)** A scale that rates the impact of various life events on the likelihood of illness.

Social reinforcement Praise, attention, approval, and/or affection from others.

Social reinforcers Reinforcers, such as attention and approval, provided by other people.

Social role Expected behaviour patterns associated with particular social positions (such as daughter, worker, student).

Social skills Proficiency at interacting with others.

Social smile Smiling elicited by social stimuli, such as seeing a parent's face.

Social stereotypes Oversimplified images of the traits of individuals who belong to a particular social group.

Social support Close, positive relationships with other people.

Solitary play Playing alone.

Soma The main body of a neuron or other cell.

Somatic system Nerves linking the spinal cord with the body and sense organs.

Somatic therapy Any bodily therapy, such as drug therapy, electroconvulsive therapy, or psychosurgery.

Somatization disorder Afflicted persons have numerous physical complaints. Typically, they have consulted many doctors, but no organic problems can be identified.

Somatoform disorder Physical symptoms that mimic disease or injury for which there is no identifiable physical cause.

Somatosensory area A receiving area for bodily sensations.

Somesthetic senses Sensations produced by the skin, muscles, joints, viscera, and organs of balance.

Somnambulism Sleepwalking; occurs during NREM sleep.

Sound wave Cyclic, wave-like movement of air molecules.

Source traits Basic underlying traits of personality; each source trait is reflected in a number of surface traits.

Spaced practice A practice schedule that alternates study periods with brief rests.

Specific phobia An intense, irrational fear of specific objects, activities, or situations.

Spinal nerves Major nerves that carry sensory and motor messages in and out of the spinal cord.

"Split-brain" operation Cutting the corpus callosum.

Spontaneous recovery The reappearance of a learned response after its apparent extinction.

Spontaneous remission The disappearance of a psychological disturbance without the aid of therapy.

Stage ESP The simulation of ESP for the purpose of entertainment.

Stage hypnosis Use of hypnosis to entertain; often, merely a simulation of hypnosis for that purpose.

Stage of exhaustion Third stage of the G.A.S., at which time the body's resources are exhausted and damage occurs.

Stage of resistance Second stage of the G.A.S., during which bodily adjustments to stress stabilize, but at a high physical cost.

Stanford–Binet Intelligence Scale A widely used individual test of intelligence; a direct descendant of Alfred Binet's first intelligence test.

State-dependent learning Memory influenced by one's bodily state at the time of learning and at the time of retrieval. Improved memory occurs when the bodily states match.

Statistical abnormality Abnormality defined on the basis of an extreme score on some dimension, such as IQ or anxiety.

Status An individual's position in a social structure, especially with respect to power, privilege, or importance.

Status inequalities Differences in the power, prestige, or privileges of two or more persons or groups.

Stem cells Immature cells that differentiate into various types of mature cells in the body, including neurons.

Stereocilia Bristle-like structures on hair cells.

Stereoscopic vision Perception of space and depth caused chiefly by the fact that the eyes receive different images.

Stimulant A substance that increases activity in the body and nervous system.

Stimulation deafness Damage caused by exposing the hair cells to excessively loud sounds.

Stimulus Any physical energy that has some effect on an organism and that evokes a response.

Stimulus control Linking a particular response with specific stimuli.

Stimulus discrimination The learned ability to respond differently to similar stimuli.

Stimulus drives Drives based on needs for exploration, manipulation, curiosity, and stimulation.

Stimulus generalization The tendency to respond to stimuli similar but not identical to a conditioned stimulus.

Stimulus motives Innate needs for stimulation and information.

Storage Holding information in memory for later use.

Stress The mental and physical condition that occurs when a person must adjust or adapt to the environment.

Stress disorder A significant emotional disturbance caused by stresses outside the range of normal human experience.

Stress inoculation Use of positive coping statements to control fear and anxiety.

Stress management The application of behavioural strategies to reduce stress and improve coping skills.

Stress reaction The physical response to stress, consisting mainly of bodily changes related to autonomic nervous system arousal.

Stressor A specific condition or event in the environment that challenges or threatens a person.

Stress-vulnerability model Attributes psychosis to a combination of environmental stress and inherited susceptibility.

Structuralism The school of thought concerned with analyzing sensations and personal experience into basic elements.

Structured interview An interview that follows a prearranged plan, usually a series of planned questions.

Subcortex All brain structures below the cerebral cortex.

Subjective discomfort Personal, private feelings of discomfort, unhappiness, or emotional distress.

Subjective experience Reality as it is perceived and interpreted, not as it exists objectively.

Subjective well-being General life satisfaction combined with frequent positive emotions and relatively few negative emotions.

Sublimation Working off frustrated desires or unacceptable impulses in substitute activities that are constructive or accepted by society.

Substance-related disorder Abuse of or dependence on a mood- or behaviour-altering drug.

Successive approximations A series of steps or ever-closer matches to a desired response pattern.

Sucking reflex Neonatal reflex elicited by touching the mouth, whereupon the infant makes rhythmic sucking movements.

Sudden infant death syndrome (SIDS) The sudden, unexplained death of an apparently healthy infant.

Superego A judge or censor for thoughts and actions.

Superordinate goal A goal that exceeds or overrides all others; a goal that renders other goals relatively less important.

Superstitious behaviour A behaviour repeated because it seems to produce reinforcement, even though it is actually unnecessary.

Support group A group formed to provide emotional support for its members through discussion of stresses and shared concerns.

Suppression A conscious effort to put something out of mind or to keep it from awareness.

Surface traits The visible or observable traits of one's personality.

Survey method Using questionnaires and surveys to poll large groups of people.

Symbolic prejudice Prejudice that is expressed in disguised fashion.

Symbolization The process of bringing an experience into awareness.

Sympathetic branch A part of the ANS that activates the body at times of stress.

Sympathetic system A branch of the ANS that arouses the body.

Synapse The microscopic space between two neurons, over which messages pass.

Syntax Rules for ordering words when forming sentences.

Systematic desensitization A reduction in fear, anxiety, or aversion brought about by planned exposure to aversive stimuli.

Target behaviours Actions or other behaviours (such as speech) that a therapist selects as the focus for behaviour modification efforts.

Taste aversion An active dislike for a particular food.

Taste bud The receptor organ for taste.

Telegraphic speech In language development, the formation of simple two-word sentences that "telegraph" (communicate) a simple idea.

Telepathy The purported ability to directly know another person's thoughts.

Temperament The hereditary aspects of personality, including sensitivity, activity levels, prevailing mood, irritability, and adaptability.

Temporal lobes Areas that include the sites where hearing registers in the brain.

Temporary insomnia A brief episode of insomnia.

Tension-release method A procedure for systematically achieving deep relaxation of the body.

Teratogen Radiation, a drug, or other substance capable of altering fetal development in ways that cause birth defects.

Test anxiety High levels of arousal and worry that seriously impair test performance.

Test battery A group of tests and interviews given to the same individual.

Thalamus A brain structure that relays sensory information to the cerebral cortex.

Thanatos The death instinct postulated by Freud.

THC Tetrahydrocannabinol, the main active chemical in marijuana.

Thematic Apperception Test (TAT) A projective test consisting of 20 different scenes and life situations about which respondents make up stories.

Theory A system of ideas designed to interrelate concepts and facts in a way that summarizes existing data and predicts future observations.

Theory of mind A child's current state of knowledge about the mind, including his or her understanding of desires, beliefs, thoughts, intentions, feelings, and so forth.

Therapeutic alliance A caring relationship that unites a therapist and a client in working to solve the client's problems.

Therapy placebo effect Improvement caused not by the actual process of therapy but by a client's expectation that therapy will help.

Thought stopping Use of aversive stimuli to interrupt or prevent upsetting thoughts.

Threat An event or situation perceived as potentially harmful.

Thyroid gland Endocrine gland that helps regulate the rate of metabolism.

Tip-of-the-tongue state The feeling that a memory is available but not quite retrievable.

Token economy A therapeutic program in which desirable behaviours are reinforced with tokens that can be exchanged for goods, services, activities, and privileges.

Token reinforcer A tangible secondary reinforcer such as money, gold stars, poker chips, and the like.

Tokens Symbolic rewards, or secondary reinforcers (such as plastic chips, gold stars, or points) that can be exchanged for real reinforcers.

Top-down processing Applying higher-level knowledge to rapidly organize sensory information into a meaningful perception.

Trait profile A graph of the scores obtained on several personality traits.

Trait theorist A psychologist interested in classifying, analyzing, and interrelating traits to understand personality.

Trait-situation interaction The influence that external settings or circumstances have on the expression of personality traits.

Tranquillizer A drug that lowers anxiety and reduces tension.

Transducer A device that converts energy from one system into energy in another.

Transference The tendency of patients to transfer to a therapist feelings that correspond to those the patient had for important persons in his or her past.

Transformation The mental ability to change the shape or form of a substance (such as clay or water) and to perceive that its volume remains the same.

Transformation rules Rules by which a simple declarative sentence may be changed to other voices or forms (past tense, passive voice, and so forth).

Trepanning In modern usage, any surgical procedure in which a hole is bored in the skull; historically, the chipping or boring of holes in the skull to "treat" mental disturbance.

Trichromatic theory Theory of colour vision based on three cone types: red, green, and blue.

Trust versus mistrust A conflict about learning to trust others and the world.

Tryptophan A sleep-promoting amino acid.

Turn-taking In early language development, the tendency of parent and child to alternate in the sending and receiving of signals or messages.

Tympanic membrane The eardrum.

Type A personality A personality type with an elevated risk of heart disease; characterized by time urgency, anger, and hostility.

Type B personality All personality types other than Type A; a low cardiac-risk personality.

Unanimity Being unanimous or of one mind; agreement.

Unconditional positive regard Unshakable love and approval given without qualification.

Unconditioned response An innate reflex response elicited by an unconditioned stimulus.

Unconditioned stimulus A stimulus innately capable of eliciting a response.

Unconscious The region of the mind that is beyond awareness—especially impulses and desires not directly known to a person.

Uncritical acceptance The tendency to believe generally positive or flattering descriptions of oneself.

Understanding In psychology, understanding is achieved when the causes of a behaviour can be stated.

Undifferentiated schizophrenia Schizophrenia lacking the specific features of catatonic, disorganized, or paranoid types.

Unfreezing In brainwashing, a loosening of convictions about former values, attitudes, and beliefs.

Unstructured interview An interview in which conversation is informal and topics are taken up freely as they arise.

Unusual Uses Test A test of creativity in which subjects try to think of new uses for a common object.

Vacillation Wavering in intention or feelings.

Validity The ability of a test to measure what it purports to measure.

Validity scales Scales that tell whether test scores should be invalidated for lying, inconsistency, or "faking good."

Variable Any condition that changes or can be made to change; a measure, event, or state that may vary.

Variable interval schedule A reinforcer is given for the first correct response made after a varied amount of time has passed since the last reinforced response. Responses made during the time interval are not reinforced.

Variable ratio schedule A varied number of correct responses must be made to get a reinforcer. For example, a reinforcer is given after three to seven correct responses; the actual number changes randomly.

Verbal intelligence Intelligence measured by answering questions involving vocabulary, general information, arithmetic, and other language- or symbol-oriented tasks.

Vestibular senses The senses of balance, position in space, and acceleration.

Vicarious classical conditioning Classical conditioning brought about by observing another person react to a particular stimulus.

Vicarious desensitization A reduction in fear or anxiety that takes place vicariously ("second-hand") when a client watches models perform the feared behaviour.

Virtual reality exposure Use of computer-generated images to present fear stimuli. The virtual environment responds to a viewer's head movements and other inputs.

Visible spectrum That part of the electromagnetic spectrum to which the eyes are sensitive.

Visual acuity The sharpness of visual perception.

Visual cliff An apparatus that looks like the edge of an elevated platform or cliff.

Visual pigments Light-sensitive chemicals found in the rods and cones.

Waiting-list control group People who receive no treatment as a test of the effectiveness of psychotherapy.

Waking consciousness A state of normal, alert awareness.

Warning system Pain based on large nerve fibres; warns that bodily damage may be occurring.

Weapon focus The tendency of crime victims to fix their attention on an attacker's weapon.

Weapons effect The observation that weapons serve as strong cues for aggressive behaviour.

Wechsler Adult Intelligence Scale-Third Edition (WAIS-III) An adult intelligence test that rates both verbal and performance intelligence.

Wechsler Intelligence Scale for Children-Third Edition (WISC-III) An intelligence test for children that rates both verbal and performance intelligence.

Weight cycling Repeated swings between losing and gaining weight.

Wellness A positive state of good health; more than the absence of disease.

Wernicke's area A brain area related to language comprehension.

Whole learning Studying an entire package of information (such as a complete poem) at once.

Wish fulfillment Freudian belief that many dreams express unconscious desires.

Withdrawal of love Withholding affection to enforce child discipline.

Withdrawal symptoms Physical illness and discomfort following the withdrawal of a drug.

Working memory Another name for short-term memory, especially as it is used for thinking and problem solving.

Yerkes-Dodson law A summary of the relationships among arousal, task complexity, and performance.

You-message Threatening, accusing, bossing, lecturing, or criticizing another person.

Zone of proximal development Refers to the range of tasks a child cannot yet master alone, but that she or he can accomplish with the guidance of a more capable partner.

References

Abbott, A., & Concar, D. (1992, August). A trip into the unknown. *New Scientist*, 30–34.

Abelson, R. P. (1988). Conviction. *American Psychologist, 43*(4), 267–275.

Abi-Dargham, A., et al. (1998). Increased striatal dopamine transmission in schizophrenia. *American Journal of Psychiatry, 155*(6), 761–767.

Aboud, F. E., & Mendelson, M. J. (1998). Determinants of friendship selection and quality: Developmental perspectives. In W. M. Bukowski & A. F. Newcomb (Eds.), *The company they keep: Friendship in childhood and adolescence. Cambridge studies in social and emotional development.* New York: Cambridge University Press.

Abrams, R. (1997). *Electroconvulsive therapy.* New York: Oxford University Press.

Abramson, R. (1993, January 8). EPA officially links passive smoke, cancer. *Los Angeles Times*, p. A27.

Adair, J. G., Pavio, A. & Ritchie, P. (1996). Psychology in Canada. *Annual Review of Psychology, 47*, 341–370.

Adams, J. (1988). *Conceptual blockbusting.* New York: Norton.

Adams, R. J., & Courage, M. L. (1998). Human newborn color vision: Measurement with chromatic stimuli varying in excitation purity. *Journal of Experimental Child Psychology, 68*(1), 22–34.

Adams, R. J., Courage, M. L., & Mercer, M. E. (1995). Systematic measurement of human neonatal color vision. *Vision Research, 34*(13), 1691–1701.

Adelmann, P. K., & Zajonc, R. B. (1989). Facial efference and the experience of emotion. *Annual Review of Psychology, 40*, 249–280.

Ader, R., & Cohen, N. (1993). Psychoneuroimmunology: Conditioning and stress. In L. W. Porter and M. R. Rosenzweig (Eds.), *Annual Review of Psychology, 44*, 53–85.

Adlaf, E. M., Gliksman, L., Demers, A., & Newton-Taylor, B. (2001). The prevalence of elevated psychological distress among Canadian undergraduates: Findings from the 1998 Canadian Campus Survey. *Journal of American College Health, 50*, 67–72.

Adolph, K. E. (1997). Learning in the development of infant locomotion. *Monographs of the Society for Research in Child Development, 62*(3), 1–140.

Adorno, T. W., Frenkel-Brunswik, E., Levinson, D. J., & Sanford, R. N. (1950). *The authoritarian personality.* New York: Harper.

Aguiar, A., & Baillargeon, R. (1998). 8.5-month-old infants' reasoning about containment events. *Child Development, 69*, 636–653.

Aguiar, A., & Baillargeon, R. (1999). 2.5-month-old infants' reasoning about when objects should and should not be occluded. *Cognitive Psychology, 39*, 116–157.

Ahissar, M. (1999). Perceptual learning. *Current Directions in Psychological Science, 8*(4), 124–128.

Akerstedt, T. (1990). Psychological and psychophysiological effects of shift work. *Scandinavian Journal of Work, Environment & Health, 16*(Suppl 1), 67–73.

Akerstedt, T., Hume, K., Minors, D., & Waterhouse, J. (1993). Regulation of sleep and naps on an irregular schedule. *Sleep, 16*(8), 736–743.

Alarcon, R. D. (1995). Culture and psychiatric diagnosis: Impact on DSM-IV and ICD-10. *Psychiatric Clinics of North America, 18*(3), 449–465.

Alberti, R., & Emmons, M. (1995). *Your perfect right.* San Luis Obispo, CA: Impact.

Alberto, P. A., & Troutman, A. C. (1998). *Applied behavior analysis for teachers.* Englewood Cliffs, NJ: Prentice Hall.

Alcock, J. E. (1990). *Science and supernature: A critical appraisal of parapsychology.* Buffalo, NY: Prometheus.

Alden, L. E., & Wallace, S. T. (1995). Social phobia and social appraisal in successful and unsuccessful social interactions. *Behaviour Research & Therapy, 33*(5), 497–505.

Alfeld-Liro, C., & Sigelman, C. K. (1998). Sex differences in self-concept and symptoms of depression during the transition to college. *Journal of Youth & Adolescence, 27*(2), 219–244.

Alicke, M. D., Yurak, T. J., & Vredenburg, D. S. (1996). Using personal attitudes to judge others. *Journal of Research in Personality, 30*(1), 103–119.

Alloy, L. B., & Clements, C. M. (1998). Hopelessness theory of depression. *Cognitive Therapy & Research, 22*(4), 303–335.

Alloy, L. B., Peterson, C., Abramson, L. Y., & Seligman, M. E. (1984). Attributional style and the generality of learned helplessness. *Journal of Personality & Social Psychology, 46*, 681–687.

Allport, G. W. (1958). *The nature of prejudice.* Garden City, NY: Anchor Books, Doubleday.

Allport, G. W. (1961). *Pattern and growth in personality.* New York: Holt, Rinehart, and Winston.

Alonso, J., Black, C., Norregaard, J. C., Dunn, E., Andersen, T. F., Espallargues, M., Bernth-Petersen, P., & Anderson, G. F. (1998). Cross-cultural differences in the reporting of global functional capacity: An example in cataract patients. *Medical Care, 36*(6), 868–878.

Alva, S. A. (1993). Differential patterns of achievement among Asian-American adolescents. *Journal of Youth and Adolescence, 22*(4), 407–423.

Alvarado, N. (1994). Empirical validity of the Thematic Apperception Test. *Journal of Personality Assessment, 63*(1), 59–79.

Alvino, J., & the Editors of *Gifted Children Monthly.* (1996). *Parents' guide to raising a gifted child.* New York: Ballantine.

Amabile, T. M. (1983). *The social psychology of creativity.* New York: Springer-Verlag.

Amar, P. B. (1993). Biofeedback and applied psychophysiology at the crossroads. *Biofeedback & Self-Regulation, 18*(4), 201–209.

Anderson, B. L., Kiecolt-Glaser, J. K., & Glaser, R. (1994). A biobehavioral model of cancer stress and disease course. *American Psychologist, 49*(5), 389–404.

Anderson, C. A. (1989). Temperature and aggression. *Psychological Bulletin, 106*, 74–96.

Anderson, C. A., Anderson, K. B., & Deuser, W. E. (1996). Examining an affective aggression framework. *Personality & Social Psychology Bulletin, 22*(4), 366–376.

Anderson, J. R. (1990). *Cognitive psychology.* New York: Freeman.

Anderson, J. R. (1995). *Cognitive psychology.* New York: Freeman.

Anderson, J. R., Reder, L. M., & Lebiere, C. (1996). Working memory: Activation limitations on retrieval. *Cognitive psychology, 30*(3), 221–256.

Anderson, R. H., Anderson, K., Flemming, D. E., & Kinghorn, E. (1984). A multidimensional test of the attributional reformulation of learned helplessness. *Bulletin of the Psychonomic Society, 22*, 211–213.

Andrews, J. D. (1989). Integrating visions of reality. *American Psychologist, 44*(5), 803–817.

Annett, M., & Manning, M. (1990). Arithmetic and laterality. *Neuropsychologia, 28*(1), 61–69.

Anshel, M. H. (1995). Effect of chronic aerobic exercise and progressive relaxation on motor performance and affect following acute stress. *Behavioral Medicine, 21*(4), 186–196.

Anthony, W. A., Cohen, M., & Kennard, W. (1990). Understanding the current facts and principles of mental health systems planning. *American Psychologist, 45*(11), 1249–1252.

Arbuthnott, K., & Campbell, J. I. D. (2000). Cognitive inhibition in selection and sequential retrieval. *Memory and Cognition, 28*(3), 331–340.

Archer, J. (1996). Sex differences in social behavior. *American Psychologist, 51*(9), 909–917.

Arena, J. G., Bruno, G. M., Hannah, S. L., & Meador, K. J. (1995). A comparison of frontal electromyographic biofeedback training, trapezius electromyographic biofeedback training, and progressive muscle relaxation therapy in the treatment of tension headache. *Headache, 35*(7), 411–419.

Arendt, J. (1994). Clinical perspectives for melatonin and its agonists. *Biological Psychiatry, 35*(1), 1–2.

Arendt, R., Singer, L., Angelopoulos, J., Bass-Busdiecker, O., & Mascia, J. (1998). Sensorimotor development in cocaine-exposed infants. *Infant Behavior & Development, 21*(4), 627–640.

Aronoff, J., Barclay, A. M., & Stevenson, L. A. (1988). The recognition of threatening facial stimuli. *Journal of Personality & Social Psychology, 54*(4), 647–655.

Aronson, E. (1969). Some antecedents of interpersonal attraction. In W. J. Arnold & D. Levine (Eds.), *Nebraska Symposium on Motivation.* Lincoln: University of Nebraska Press.

Aronson, E. (1992). *The social animal.* San Francisco: W. H. Freeman.

Arthur, W., Jr., & Graziano, W. G. (1996). The five-factor model, conscientiousness, and driving accident involvement. *Journal of Personality, 64*(3), 593–618.

Ary, D. V., Duncan, T. E., Biglan, A., Metzler, C. W., et al. (1999). Development of adolescent problem behavior. *Journal of Abnormal Child Psychology, 27*(2), 141–150.

Asch, S. E. (1956). Studies of independence and conformity: A minority of one against a unanimous majority. *Psychological Monographs, 70*(416).

Asendorpf, J. B., & Wilpers, S. (1998). Personality effects on social relationships. *Journal of Personality and Social Psychology, 74*(6), 1531–1544.

Ash, D. W., & Holding, D. H. (1990). Backward versus forward chaining in the acquisition of a keyboard skill. *Human Factors, 32*(2), 139–146.

Ashton, W. A., & Fuehrer, A. (1993). Effects of gender and gender role identification of participant and type of social support resource on support seeking. *Sex Roles, 28*(7–8), 461–476.

Aslin, R. N., & Smith, L. B. (1988). Perceptual development. *Annual Review of Psychology, 39*, 435–473.

Assanand, S., Pinel, J. P. J., & Lehman, D. R. (1998). Personal theories of hunger and eating. *Journal of Applied Social Psychology, 28*(11), 998–1015.

Attenburrow, M. E. J., Cowen, P. J., & Sharpley, A. L. (1996). Low dose melatonin improves sleep in healthy middle-aged subjects. *Psychopharmacology, 126*(2), 179–181.

Ayers, L., Beaton, S., & Hunt, H. (1999). The significance of transpersonal experiences, emotional conflict, and cognitive abilities in creativity. *Empirical Studies of the Arts, 17*(1), 73–82.

Ayllon, T. (1963). Intensive treatment of psychotic behavior by stimulus satiation and food reinforcement. *Behavior Research and Therapy, 1*, 53–61.

Ayllon, T., & Azrin, N. H. (1965). The measurement and reinforcement of behavior of psychotics. *Journal of the Experimental Analysis of Behavior, 8*, 357–383.

Ayotte, J., Peretz, I., & Hyde, K. (2002). Congenital amusia: A group study of adults afflicted with a music-specific disorder. *Brain, 125*(2), 238–251.

Azrin, N. H., Hutchinson, R. R., & McLaughlin, R. (1965). The opportunity for aggression as an operant reinforcer during aversive stimulation. *Journal of Experimental Analysis of Behavior, 8*, 171–180.

Bachman, J. G., & Johnson, L. D. (1979). The freshmen. *Psychology Today, 13*, 78–87.

Baddeley, A. (1990). *Human memory.* Needham Heights, MA: Allyn and Bacon.

Baddeley, A. (1996). *Your memory: A user's guide.* North Pomfret: Trafalgar Square.

Baer, J. M. (1993). *Creativity and divergent thinking.* Hillsdale, NJ: Erlbaum.

Bahrke, M. S., Yesalis, C. E., & Brower, K. J. (1998). Anabolic-androgenic steroid abuse and performance-enhancing drugs among adolescents. *Child & Adolescent Psychiatric Clinics of North America, 7*(4), 821–838.

Bailey, J. M., & Pillard, R. C. (1991). A genetic study of male sexual orientation. *Archives of General Psychiatry, 48*(12), 1089–1096.

Bailey, J. M., Pillard, R. C., Neale, M. C., & Agyei, Y. (1993). Heritable factors influence sexual orientation in women. *Archives of General Psychiatry, 50*(3), 217–223.

Baillargeon, R. (1991). Reasoning about the height and location of a hidden object in 4.5- and 6.5-month-old infants. *Cognition, 38*(1), 13–42.

Baillargeon, R., & DeVos, J. (1992). Object permanence in young infants: Further evidence. *Child Development, 62*(6), 1227–1246.

Baillargeon, R., De Vos, J., & Graber, M. (1989). Location memory in 8-month-old infants in a nonserach AB task. *Cognitive Development, 4*, 345–367.

Baisden, R. H. (1995). Therapeutic uses for neural grafts: Progress slowed but not abandoned. *Behavioral & Brain Sciences, 18*(1), 47–48, 90–107.

Balch, W. R., & Lewis, B. S. (1996). Music-dependent memory. *Journal of Experimental Psychology: Learning, Memory, & Cognition, 22*(6), 1354–1363.

Balk, D. E., et al. (1998). TAT results in a longitudinal study of bereaved college students. *Death Studies, 22*(1), 3–21.

Ballard, M. E., & West, J. R. (1996). Mortal Kombat: The effects of violent videogame play on males' hostility and cardiovascular responding. *Journal of Applied Social Psychology, 26*(8), 717–730.

Banaji, M. R., & Prentice, D. A. (1994). The self in social contexts. *Annual Review of Psychology, 45*, 297–332.

Bandura, A. (1971). *Social learning theory.* New York: General Learning Press.

Bandura, A. (1973). *Aggression: A social learning analysis.* Englewood Cliffs, NJ: Prentice-Hall.

Bandura, A. (1986). *Social foundations of thought and action: A social cognitive theory.* Englewood Cliffs, NJ: Prentice-Hall.

Bandura, A., & Rosenthal, T. L. (1966). Vicarious classical conditioning as a function of arousal level. *Journal of Personality & Social Psychology, 3*, 54–62.

Bandura, A., Blanchard, E. B., & Ritter, B. (1966). Relative efficacy of desensitization and modeling approaches for inducing behavioral, affective, and attitudinal changes. *Journal of Personality & Social Psychology, 13*(3), 173–199.

Bandura, A., Ross, D., & Ross, S. A. (1963). Vicarious reinforcement and imitative learning. *Journal of Abnormal and Social Psychology, 67*, 601–607.

Bandura, A., & Walters, R. (1959). *Adolescent aggression.* New York: Ronald.

Bandura, A., & Walters, R. (1963). *Social learning and personality development.* New York: Holt.

Banks, A., & Gartrell, N. K. (1995). Hormones and sexual orientation: A questionable link. *Journal of Homosexuality, 28*(3–4), 247–268.

Banks, T., & Dabbs, J. M., Jr. (1996). Salivary testosterone and cortisol in delinquent and violent urban subculture. *Journal of Social Psychology, 136*(1), 49–56.

Barber, T. X. (1970). *Suggested ("hypnotic") behavior: The trance paradigm versus an alternative paradigm.* Harding, MA: Medfield Foundation, Report No. 103.

Barker, E. A. (1993, Spring). Evaluating graphology. *Skeptical Inquirer, 17*, 312–315.

Barnet, A. B., & Barnet, R. J. (1998). *The youngest minds.* New York: Touchstone.

Baron, R. A., & Byrne, D. (1997). *Social psychology.* Boston: Allyn & Bacon.

Baron, R. A., & Richardson, D. R. (1994). *Human aggression.* New York: Plenum.

Barowsky, E. I., Moskowitz, J., & Zweig, J. B. (1990). Biofeedback for disorders of initiating and maintaining sleep. *Annals of the New York Academy of Sciences, 602*, 97–103.

Barrett, D. (1993). The "committee of sleep": A study of dream incubation for problem solving. *Dreaming, 3*(2), 115–122.

Barrett, R. J. (1985). Behavioral approaches to individual differences in substance abuse. In M. Galizio & S. A. Maisto (Eds.), *Determinants of substance abuse treatment: Biological, psychological, and environmental factors.* New York: Plenum.

Barron, E. (1958). The psychology of imagination. *Scientific American, 199*(33), 150–170.

Barsalou, L. W. (1992). *Cognitive psychology.* Hillsdale, NJ: Lawrence Erlbaum.

Barsky, S. H., Roth, M. D., Kleerup, E. C., et al. (1998). Histopathologic and molecular alterations in bronchial epithelium in habitual smokers of marijuana, cocaine, and/or tobacco. *Journal of the National Cancer Institute, 90*(16), 1198–1205.

Bartlett, J. C., & Searcy, J. (1993). Inversion and configuration of faces. *Cognitive psychology, 25*(3), 281–316.

Bartz, W. (1990). The basics of critical thought. Personal communication.

Batejat, D. M., & Lagarde, D. P. (1999). Naps and modafinil as countermeasures for the effects of sleep deprivation on cognitive performance. *Aviation, Space, & Environmental Medicine, 70*(5), 493–498.

Bath, H. (1996). Everyday discipline or control with care. *Journal of Child & Youth Care, 10*(2), 23–32.

Batson, C. D. (1990). How social an animal? The human capacity for caring. *American Psychologist, 45*(3), 336–346.

Baum, A., & Posluszny, D. M. (1999). Health psychology. *Annual Review of Psychology, 50,* 137–163.

Baumeister, R. F. (1994). Self-esteem. *Encyclopedia of human behavior,* Vol. 4. San Diego, CA: Academic.

Baumrind, D. (1991). The influence of parenting style on adolescent competence and substance use. *Journal of Early Adolescence, 11*(1), 56–95.

Beach, F. A. (1965). *Sex and behavior.* New York: Wiley.

Beck, A. T. (1985). Cognitive therapy of depression: New perspectives. In P. Clayton (Ed.), *Depression.* New York: Raven.

Beck, A. T. (1991). Cognitive therapy. *American Psychologist, 46*(4), 368–375.

Beck, A. T., Brown, C., Berchick, R. J., Stewart, B. L., et al. (1990). Relationship between hopelessness and ultimate suicide. *American Journal of Psychiatry, 147*(2), 190–195.

Beck, A. T., & Greenberg, R. L. (1974). *Coping with depression.* New York: Institute for Rational Living.

Becker, J. T., & Morris, R. G. (1999). Working memory(s). *Brain & Cognition, 41*(1), 1–8.

Beebe, B., Gerstman, L., Carson, B., Dolins, M., Zigman, A., Rosenweig, H., Faughey K., & Korman, M. (1982). Rhythmic communication in the mother-infant dyad. In M. Davis (Ed), *Interaction rhythms, periodicity in communicative behavior.* New York: Human Sciences Press.

Beilin, H. (1992). Piaget's enduring contribution to developmental psychology. *Developmental Psychology, 28*(2), 191–204.

Bellani, M. L., Furlani, F., Gnecchi, M., & Pezzotta, P. (1996). Burnout and related factors among HIV/AIDS health care workers. *AIDS Care, 8*(2), 207–221.

Bellezza, F. S., Six, L. S., & Phillips, D. S. (1992). A mnemonic for remembering long strings of digits. *Bulletin of the Psychonomic Society, 30*(4), 271–274.

Bellisle, F. (1999). Glutamate and the UMAMI taste. *Neuroscience & Biobehavioral Reviews, 23*(3), 423–438.

Belsky, J. (1996). Parent, infant, and social-contextual antecedents of father-son attachment security.

Developmental Psychology, 32(5), 905–913.

Bem, D. J., & Honorton, C. (1994). Does psi exist? Replicable evidence for an anomalous process of information transfer. *Psychological Bulletin, 115*(1), 4–18.

Bem, S. L. (1975). Sex-role adaptability: One consequence of psychological androgyny. *Journal of Personality & Social Psychology, 31,* 634–643.

Bem, S. L. (1981). Gender schema theory. A cognitive account of sex typing. *Psychological Review, 88,* 354–364.

Benbow, C. P. (1986). Physiological correlates of extreme intellectual precocity. *Neuropsychologia, 24*(5), 719–725.

Benenson, J. F., Aikins-Ford, S., & Apostolaris, N. H. (1998). Girls' assertiveness in the presence of boys. *Small Group Research, 29*(2), 198–211.

Benloucif, S., Bennett, E. L., Rosenzweig, M. R. (1995). Norephinephrine and neural plasticity: The effects of xylamine on experience-induced changes in brain weight, memory, and behavior. *Neurobiology of Learning & Memory, 63*(1), 33–42.

Benoit, S. C., & Thomas, R. L. (1992). The influence of expectancy in subliminal perception experiments. *Journal of General Psychology, 119*(4), 335–341.

Ben-Shakhar, G., Bar-Hillel, M., Bilu, Y., Ben-Abba, E., & Flug, A. (1986). Can graphology predict occupational success? Two empirical studies and some methodological ruminations. *Journal of Applied Psychology, 71*(4) 645–653.

Ben-Shakhar, G., & Dolev, K. (1996). Psychophysiological detection through the guilty knowledge technique: Effect of mental countermeasures. *Journal of Applied Psychology, 81*(3), 273–281.

Benson, H. (1977). Systematic hypertension and the relaxation response. *New England Journal of Medicine, 296,* 1152–1156.

Bergin, A. E. (1991). Values and religious issues in psychotherapy and mental health. *American Psychologist, 46*(4), 394–403.

Berkowitz, L. (1968). The frustration-aggression hypothesis revisited. In L. Berkowitz (Ed.), *Roots of aggression: A re-examination of the frustration-aggression hypothesis.* New York: Atherton.

Berkowitz, L. (1984). Some effects of thoughts on anti- and prosocial influences of media events: A cognitive-neoassociation analysis. *Psychological Bulletin, 95,* 410–427.

Berkowitz, L. (1988). Frustrations, appraisals, and aversively stimu-

lated aggression. *Aggressive Behavior, 14*(1), 3–11.

Berkowitz, L. (1990). On the formation and regulation of anger and aggression. *American Psychologist, 45*(4), 494–503.

Berman, S. L., Kurtines, W. M., Silverman, W. K., & Serafini, L. T. (1996). The impact of exposure to crime and violence on urban youth. *American Journal of Orthopsychiatry, 66*(3), 329–336.

Berne, E. (1964). *Games people play.* New York: Grove.

Bernstein, H. J., et al. (1998). Patient attitudes about ECT after treatment. *Psychiatric Annals, 28*(9), 524–527.

Bernstein, I. L. (1978). Learned taste aversions in children receiving chemotherapy. *Science, 200,* 1302–1303.

Bernthal, P. R., & Insko, C. A. (1993). Cohesiveness without groupthink: The interactive effects of social and task cohesion. *Group & Organization Management, 18*(1), 66–87.

Berscheid, E. (1994). Interpersonal relations. *Annual Review of Psychology, 45,* 79–129.

Bersoff, D. M. (1999). Why good people sometimes do bad things: Motivated reasoning and unethical behavior. *Personality & Social Psychology Bulletin, 25*(1), 28–39.

Bertsch, G. J. (1976). Punishment of consummatory and instrumental behavior: A review. *Psychological Record, 26,* 13–31.

Best, J. B. (1999). *Cognitive psychology.* Pacific Grove: Brooks/Cole.

Betancur, C., Velez, A., Cabanieu, G., le Moal, M., et al. (1990). Association between left-handedness and allergy: A reappraisal. *Neuropsychologia, 28*(2), 223–227.

Bexton, W. H., Heron, W., & Scott, T. H. (1954). Effects of decreased variation in the sensory environment. *Canadian Journal of Psychology, 8,* 70–76.

Beyerstein, B. L., & Beyerstein, D. F. (1992). *The write stuff: Evaluations of graphology.* Buffalo, NY: Prometheus.

Bierley, C., McSweeney, F. K., & Vannieuwkerk, R. (1985). Classical conditioning of preferences for stimuli. *Journal of Consumer Research, 12,* 316–323.

Biglan, A., Ary, D., Yudelson, H., & Duncan, T. E. (1996). Experimental evaluation of a modular approach to mobilizing antitobacco influences of peers and parents. *American Journal of Community Psychology, 24*(3), 311–339.

Bigler, E. D., Johnson, S. C., Anderson, C.V., & Blatter, D. D. (1996). Traumatic brain injury and memory: The role of hippocampal atrophy. *Neuropsychology, 10*(3), 333–342.

Binder, V. (1976). Behavior modification: Operant approaches to therapy. In V. Binder, A. Binder, & B. Rimland (Eds.), *Modern therapies.* Englewood Cliffs, NJ: Prentice-Hall.

Binks, P. G., Waters, W. F., & Hurry, M. (1999). Short-term total sleep deprivation does not selectively impair higher cortical functioning. *Sleep, 22*(3), 328–334.

Biondi, M., & Zannino, L. (1997). Psychological stress, neuroimmunomodulation, and susceptibility to infectious diseases in animals and man. *Psychotherapy & Psychosomatics, 66*(1), 3–26.

Birch, J., & McKeever, L. M. (1993). Survey of the accuracy of new pseudoisochromatic plates. *Ophthalmic & Physiological Optics, 13*(1), 35–40.

Blackmore, S. (1991). Near-death experiences: In or out of the body? *Skeptical Inquirer, 16*(Fall), 34–45.

Blackmore, S. (1993). *Dying to live.* Buffalo, NY: Prometheus.

Blackwell, R. T., Galassi, J. P., Galassi, M. D., & Watson, T. E. (1985). Are cognitive assessments equal? A comparison of think aloud and thought listing. *Cognitive Therapy and Research, 9,* 399–413.

Blanchard, E. B., Eisele, G., Vollmer, A., & Payne, A. (1996). Controlled evaluation of thermal biofeedback in treatment of elevated blood pressure in unmedicated mild hypertension. *Biofeedback & Self Regulation, 21*(2), 167–190.

Blanchard, R., & Ellis, L. (2001). Birth weight, sexual orientation and the sex of preceding siblings. *Journal of Biosocial Science, 33*(3), 451–467.

Blanchette, I. & Dunbar, K. (2001). Analogy use in naturalistic settings: The influence of audience, emotion, and goals. *Memory and Cognition, 29*(5), 730–735.

Bland, R. C. (1997). Epidemiology of affective disorders: A review. *Canadian Journal of Psychiatry, 42,* 367–377.

Bloom, B. (1985). *Developing talent in young people.* New York: Ballantine.

Bloom, J. W. (1998). The ethical practice of Web Counseling. *British Journal of Guidance & Counselling, 26*(1), 53–59.

Bloom, K., Russell, A., & Wassenberg, K. (1987). Turn taking affects the quality of infant vocalizations. *Journal of Child Language, 14*(2), 211–227.

Blumberg, M. S., & Wasserman, E. A. (1995). Animal mind and the argument from design. *American Psychologist, 50*(3), 133–144.

Bobocel, D. R., Davey, L. M., Son-Hing, L. S., & Zanna, M. P. (2001). The concern for justice and reactions to affirmative action: Cause or rationalization? In R. Cropanzano (Ed.), *Justice in the workplace: From theory to practice*, Vol. 2. Mahwah, NJ: Erlbaum.

Boergers, J., Spirito, A., & Donaldson, D. (1998). Reasons for adolescent suicide attempts. *Journal of the American Academy of Child & Adolescent Psychiatry*, 37(12), 1287–1293.

Bogaert, A. F. (2000). Birth order and sexual orientation in a national probability sample. *Journal of Sex Research*, 37(4), 361–368.

Bohan, J. S. (1990). Social constructionism and contextual history: An expanded approach to the history of psychology. *Teaching of Psychology*, 17(2), 82–89.

Bohannon, J. N., & Stanowicz, L. B. (1988). The issue of negative evidence: Adult responses to children's language errors. *Developmental Psychology*, 24(5), 684–689.

Bohart, A. C., & Tallman, K. (1996). The active client: Therapy as self-help. *Journal of Humanistic Psychology*, 36(3), 7–30.

Bohart, W. (1995). The person-centered therapies. In A. S. Gurman & S. B. Messer (Eds.), *Essential psychotherapies*. New York: Guilford.

Bohr, Y. (2000). *Children with physical disabilities: Friendship, self-concept and the role of social attributions*. Dissertation Abstracts International, Section A: Humanities and Social Sciences. Vol. 60(10–A), 3602.

Boivin, D. B. (2000). Influence of sleep-wake and circadian rhythm disturbances in psychiatric disorders. *Journal of Psychiatry and Neuroscience*, 25(5), 446–458.

Boivin, D. B., Czeisler, C. A., & Waterhouse, J. W. (1997). Complex interaction of the sleep-wake cycle and circadian phase modulates mood in healthy subjects. *Archives of General Psychiatry*, 54(2), 145.

Bolles, R. C. (1979). *Learning theory*. New York: Holt, Rinehart & Winston.

Bond, R., & Smith, P. B. (1996). Culture and conformity: A meta-analysis of studies using Asch's (1952b, 1956) line judgment task. *Psychological Bulletin*, 119(1), 111–137.

Bond, T., & Wooten, V. (1996). The etiology and management of insomnia. *Virginia Medical Quarterly*, 123(4), 254–255.

Bongard, S., al'Absi, M., & Lovallo, W. R. (1998). Interactive effects of trait hostility and anger expression on cardiovascular reactivity in young men. *International Journal of Psychophysiology*, 28(2), 181–191.

Bonta, B. D. (1997). Cooperation and competition in peaceful societies. *Psychological Bulletin*, 121(2), 299–320.

Book, H. E., & Luborsky, L. (1998). *Brief psychodynamic psychotherapy*. Washington, DC: American Psychological Association.

Booker, J. M., & Hellekson, C. J. (1992). Prevalence of seasonal affective disorder in Alaska. *American Journal of Psychiatry*, 149(9), 1176–1182.

Borlongan, C.V., Sanberg, P. R., Freeman, T. B. (1999). Neural transplantation for neurodegenerative disorders. *Lancet, 353*(Suppl 1), S29–30.

Borman, W. C., Hanson, M. A., & Hedge, J. W. (1997). Personnel psychology. *Annual Review of Psychology*, 48, 299–337.

Bornstein, M. H. (1995). Parenting infants. In M. H. Bornstein (Ed.), *Handbook of parenting*. Mahwah, NJ: Erlbaum.

Bornstein, R. F. (1996). Sex differences in dependent personality disorder prevalence rates. *Clinical Psychology: Science & Practice*, 3(1), 1–12.

Borod, J. C., Cicero, B. A., Obler, L. K., et al. (1998). Right hemisphere emotional perception. *Neuropsychology*, 12(3), 446–458.

Borrie, R. A. (1990–91). The use of restricted environmental stimulation therapy in treating addictive behaviors. *International Journal of the Addictions*, 25(7A-8A), 995–1015.

Botella, C., et al. (1998). Virtual reality treatment of claustrophobia. *Behaviour Research & Therapy*, 36(2), 239–246.

Botvin, G. J., et al., (1997). School-based drug abuse prevention with inner-city minority youth. *Journal of Child & Adolescent Substance Abuse*, 6(1), 5–19.

Botvin, G. J., Schinke, S., & Orlandi, M. A. (1995). School-based health promotion: Substance abuse and sexual behavior. *Applied & Preventive Psychology*, 4(3), 167–184.

Bouchard, T. J., Jr. (1983). Twins—Nature's twice-told tale. *Yearbook of science and the future*, 66–81. Chicago: Encyclopedia Britannica.

Bouchard, T. J., Lykken, D. T., McGue, M., Segal, N. L., & Tellegen, A. (1990). Sources of human psychological differences: The Minnesota study of twins reared apart. *Science, 250*, 223–228.

Boutros, N. N., & Bowers, M. B., Jr. (1996). Chronic substance-induced psychotic disorders. *Journal of Neuropsychiatry & Clinical Neurosciences*, 8(3), 262–269.

Bower, B. (1990, November 17). Gone but not forgotten. *Science News, 138*, 312–314.

Bower, G. H. (1973, October). How to . . . uh . . . remember. *Psychology Today*, 63–70.

Bower, G. H. (1981). Mood and memory. *American Psychologist, 36*, 129–148.

Bower, G. H., & Springston, F. (1970). Pauses as recoding points in letter series. *Journal of Experimental Psychology, 83*, 421–430.

Bowers, K. S., & Farvolden, P. (1996). Revisiting a century-old Freudian slip—From suggestion disavowed to the truth repressed. *Psychological Bulletin, 119*(3), 355–380.

Bowers, K. S., & Woody, E. Z. (1996). Hypnotic amnesia and the paradox of intentional forgetting. *Journal of Abnormal Psychology, 105*(3), 381–390.

Boyatzis, C. J., Matillo, G. M., & Nesbitt, K. M. (1995). Effects of "The Mighty Morphin Power Rangers" on children's aggression with peers. *Child Study Journal, 25*(1), 45–55.

Bradley, R. H., Caldwell, B. M., Rock, S. L., Ramey, C. T., et al. (1989). Home environment and cognitive development in the first 3 years of life: A collaborative study involving six sites and three ethnic groups in North America. *Developmental Psychology, 25*(2), 217–235.

Braffman, W., & Kirsch, I. (1999). Imaginative suggestibility and hypnotizability. *Journal of Personality & Social Psychology, 77*(3), 578–587.

Brannon, L. (1996). *Gender*. Boston: Allyn & Bacon.

Bransford, J. D., & McCarrell, N. S. (1977). A sketch of cognitive approach to comprehension: Some thoughts about understanding what it means to comprehend. In P. N. Johnson-Laird & P. C. Wason (Eds.), *Thinking: Readings in cognitive science*. Cambridge: Cambridge University Press.

Bransford, J., Sherwood, R., Vye, N., & Rieser, J. (1986). Teaching thinking and problem solving. *American Psychologist, 41*(10), 1078–1089.

Brant, C. (1990). Native ethics and rules of behaviour. *Canadian Journal of Psychiatry, 35*(6), 534–539.

Brant, C. (1995). Communication patterns in Indians: Verbal and non-verbal. *Annals of Sex Research, 6*(4), 259–269.

Braun, A. R., Balkin, T. J., & Herscovitch, P. (1998). Dissociated pattern of activity in visual cortices and their projections during human rapid eye movement sleep. *Science, 279*(5347), 91–95.

Braungart, J. M., Plomin, R., DeFries, J. C., & Fulker, D. W. (1992). Genetic influence on tester-rated infant temperament as assessed by Bayley's Infant Behavior Record. *Developmental Psychology, 28*(1), 40–47.

Brawman-Mintzer, O., & Lydiard, R. B. (1996). Generalized anxiety disorder: Issues in epidemiology. *Journal of Clinical Psychiatry, 57*(Suppl 7), 3–8.

Brebner, J. (1998). Happiness and personality. *Personality & Individual Differences, 25*(2), 279–296.

Brendgen, M., Bowen, F., Rondeau, N., & Vitaro, F. (1999). Effects of friends' characteristics on children's social cognitions. *Social Development, 8*(1), 41–51.

Brendgen, M., Vitaro, F., Tremblay, R. E., & Lavoie, F. (2001). Reactive and proactive aggression: Predictions to physical violence in different contexts and moderating effects of parental monitoring and caregiving behavior. *Journal of Abnormal Child Psychology, 29*(4), 293–304.

Brenner, V., & Fox, R. A. (1998). Parental discipline and behavior problems in young children. *Journal of Genetic Psychology, 159*(2), 251–256.

Bressi, C., Albonetti, S., & Razzoli, E. (1998). "Communication deviance" and schizophrenia. *New Trends in Experimental & Clinical Psychiatry, 14*(1), 33–39.

Brewer, K. R., & Wann, D. L. (1998). Observational learning effectiveness as a function of model characteristics. *Social Behavior & Personality, 26*(1), 1–10.

Brewer, M. B., & Kramer, R. K. (1985). The psychology of intergroup attitudes and behavior. *Annual Review of Psychology, 36*, 219–243.

Bridges, K. M. B. (1932). Emotional development in early infancy. *Child Development, 3*, 324–334.

Brooks, L. (1987). Decentralized control of categorization: The role of prior processing episodes. In U. Neisser (Ed.), *Concepts and conceptual development: Ecological and intellectual factors in categorization*. New York: Cambridge University Press.

Broughton, R., Billings, R., Cartwright, R., et al. (1994). Homicidal somnambulism: A case report. *Sleep, 17*, 253–264.

Brown, A. M. (1990). Development of visual sensitivity to light and color vision in human infants: A critical review. *Vision Research, 30*(8), 1159–1188.

Brown, B. (1980). Perspectives on social stress. In H. Selye (Ed.), *Selye's guide to stress research*, Vol. 1. New York: Van Nostrand Reinhold.

Brown, B. R., Jr., Baranowski, M. D., Kulig, J. W., & Stephenson, J. N. (1996). Searching for the Magic Johnson effect: AIDS, adolescents, and celebrity disclosure. *Adolescence, 31*(122), 253–264.

Brown, G. M. (1994). Light, melatonin and the sleep-wake cycle. *Journal of Psychiatry & Neuroscience, 19*(5), 345–353.

Brown, R. L., Leonard, T., Saunders, L. A., & Papasouiotis, O. (1997). A two-item screening test for alcohol and other drug problems. *Journal of Family Practice, 44*(2), 151–160.

Brown, R., & McNeill, D. (1966). The "tip of the tongue" phenomenon. *Journal of Verbal Learning and Verbal Behavior, 5*, 325–337.

Brown, T. D., Dane, F. C., & Durham, M. D. (1998). Perception of race and ethnicity. *Journal of Social Behavior & Personality, 13*(2), 295–306.

Brownell, K. D., Greenwood, M. R. C., Stellar, E., & Shrager, E. E. (1986). The effects of repeated cycles of weight loss and regain in rats. *Physiology and Behavior, 38*, 459–464.

Bruch, M. A., Berko, E. H., & Haase, R. F. (1998). Shyness, masculine ideology, physical attractiveness, and emotional inexpressiveness. *Journal of Counseling Psychology, 45*,(1), 84–97.

Bruck, M., Hembrooke, H., & Ceci, S. J. (1997). Children's reports of pleasant and unpleasant events. In J. Don Read & D. Stephen Lindsay (Eds.), *Recollections of trauma: Scientific evidence and clinical practice*. New York: Plenum Press.

Bruins Slot, L. A., & Colpaert, F. C. (1999). Recall rendered dependent on an opiate state. *Behavioral Neuroscience, 113*(2), 337–344.

Bruner, J. (1983). *Child's talk*. New York: Norton.

Bryan, J. H., & Walbek, N. H. (1970). Preaching and practicing generosity: Children's actions and reactions. *Child Development, 41*, 329–353.

Bryant, D. M., & Maxwell, K. L. (1999). The environment and mental retardation. *International Review of Psychiatry, 11*(1) 56–67.

Buchanan, R. W., et al. (1998). Positive and negative symptom response to clozapine in schizophrenic patients. *American Journal of Psychiatry, 155*(6), 751–760.

Buchwald, A. (1965, June 20). Psyching out. *The Washington Post*.

Buck, L. A. (1990). Abnormality, normality and health. *Psychotherapy, 27*(2), 187–194.

Buckelew, S. P., et al. (1998). Biofeedback/relaxation training and exercise interventions for fibromyalgia. *Arthritis Care & Research, 11*(3), 196–209.

Buckhout, R. (1974). Eyewitness testimony. *Scientific American, 231*, 23–31.

Budney, A. J., Novy, P. L., & Hughes, J. R. (1999). Marijuana withdrawal among adults seeking treatment for marijuana dependence. *Addiction, 94*(9), 1311–1322.

Buehler, R., Griffin, D., and MacDonald, H. (1997). The role of motivated reasoning in optimistic time predictions. *Personality and Social Psychology Bulletin, 23*(3), 238–247.

Bugental, J. F. T., & Sterling, M. M. (1995). Existential-humanistic psychotherapy: New perspectives. In A. S. Gurman & S. B. Messer (Eds.), *Essential psychotherapies*. New York: Guilford.

Bukowski, W. F., Sippola, L. K., & Newcomb, A. F. (2000). Variations in patterns of attraction of same- and other-sex peers during early adolescence. *Developmental Psychology, 36*(2), 147–154.

Burchinal, M. R., Roberts, J. E., Riggins, R., Zeisel, S. A., Neebe, E., & Bryant, D. (2000). Relating quality of center-based child care to early cognitive and language development longitudinally. *Child Development, 71*(2), 339–357.

Burgess, C. A., & Kirsch, I. (1999). Expectancy information as a moderator of the effects of hypnosis on memory. *Contemporary Hypnosis, 16*(1), 22–31.

Burgner, D., & Hewstone, M. (1993). Young children's causal attributions for success and failure. *British Journal of Developmental Psychology, 11*(2), 125–129.

Burns, D. D., & Persons, J. (1982). Hope and hopelessness: A cognitive approach. In L. E. Abt & I. R. Stuart (Eds.), *The newer therapies: A sourcebook*. New York: Van Nostrand Reinhold.

Burtt, H. E. (1941). An experimental study of early childhood memory: Final report. *Journal of General Psychology, 58*, 435–439.

Bushman, B. J., & Cooper, H. M. (1990). Effects of alcohol on human aggression. *Psychological Bulletin, 107*(3), 341–354.

Bushman, B. J., & Geen, R. G. (1990). Role of cognitive-emotional mediators and individual differences in the effects of media violence on aggression. *Journal of Personality & Social Psychology, 58*(1), 156–163.

Bushnell, L. W., Sai, F., & Mullin, L. T. (1989). Neonatal recognition of the mother's face. *British Journal of Developmental Psychology, 7*(1), 3–15.

Buss, A. H. (1980). *Self-consciousness and social anxiety*. San Francisco: Freeman.

Buss, A. H. (1986). A theory of shyness. In W. H. Jones, J. M. Cheek, & S. R. Briggs (Eds.), *Shyness: Perspectives on research and treatment*. New York: Plenum.

Buss, D. M. (1985). Human mate selection. *American Scientist, 73*, 47–51.

Buss, D. M. (1994). *The evolution of desire*. New York: Basic.

Buss, D. M., Larsen, R. J., Western, D., & Semmelroth, J. (1992). Sex differences in jealousy. *Psychological Science, 3*, 251–255.

Butler, R., & Harlow, H. F. (1954). Persistence of visual exploration in monkeys. *Journal of Comparative Physiological Psychology, 47*, 258–263.

Buyer, L. S. (1988). Creative problem solving: A comparison of performance under different instructions. *Journal of Creative Behavior, 22*(1), 55–61.

Byrd, K. R. (1994). The narrative reconstructions of incest survivors. *American Psychologist, 49*(5), 439–440.

Cabanac, M., & Duclaux, P. (1970). Obesity: Absence of satiety aversion to sucrose. *Science, 168*, 496–497.

Cahill, S. P., Carrigan, M. H., & Frueh, B. C. (1999). Does EMDR work? and if so, why? *Journal of Anxiety Disorders, 13*(1–2), 5–33.

Calle, E. E., Thun, M. J., Petrelli, J. M., Rodriguez, C., & Heath, C. W. (1999). Body-mass index and mortality in a prospective cohort of U. S. adults. *New England Journal of Medicine, 341*(15), 1097–1105.

Calvert, S. L., & Cocking, R. R. (1992). Health promotion through mass media. *Journal of Applied Developmental Psychology, 13*(2), 143–149.

Camara, W. J., & Schneider, D. L. (1994). Integrity tests. *American Psychologist, 49*(2), 112–119.

Camatta, C. D., & Nagoshi, C. T. (1995). Stress, depression, irrational beliefs, and alcohol use and problems in a college student sample. *Alcoholism: Clinical & Experimental Research, 19*(1), 142–146.

Cameron, L. D., & Nicholls, G. (1998). Expression of stressful experiences through writing. *Health Psychology, 17*(1), 84–92.

Campbell, J. B., & Hawley, C. W. (1982). Study habits and Eysenck's theory of extraversion-introversion. *Journal of Research in Personality, 16*, 139–146.

Campfield, L. A., Smith, F. J., Rosenbaum, M., & Hirsch, J. (1996). Human eating: Evidence for a physiological basis using a modified paradigm. *Neuroscience & Biobehavioral Reviews, 20*(1), 133–137.

Campos, A., & Perez, M. J. (1997). Mnemonic images and associated pair recall. *Journal of Mental Imagery, 21*(3–4), 73–82.

Camras, L. A., Sullivan, J., & Michel, G. (1993). Do infants express discrete emotions? *Journal of Nonverbal Behavior, 17*(3), 171–186.

Canadian Centre on Substance Abuse. (1999). *Canadian profile, 1999 highlights*. Document retrieved March 4, 2002, from http://www.csa.ca/Profile/cp99high.htm.

Canadian Foundation for the Study of Infant Deaths. (2001). *Rate of SIDS in Canada per 1000 live births: 1990–2000*. Document retrieved March 6, 2002, from http://www.sidscanada.org/statistics.html.

Canadian Psychological Association (2002). *The cost-effectiveness of psychological interventions*. Ottawa: Author. Document retrieved July 2, 2002, from http://www.cpa.ca/documents/Cost-Effectiveness.pdf.

Canli, T., Desmond, J. E., Zhao, Z., Glover, G., et al. (1998). Hemispheric asymmetry for emotional stimuli detected with fMRI. *Neuroreport, 9*(14) 3233–3239.

Cann, A., Holt, K., & Calhoun, L. G. (1999). The roles of humor and sense of humor in responses to stressors. *Humor: International Journal of Humor Research, 12*(2), 177–193.

Cannon, T. D. (1998). Neurodevelopmental influences in the genesis and epigenesis of schizophrenia. *Applied & Preventive Psychology, 7*(1), 47–62.

Cannon, T. D., et al., (1998). The genetic epidemiology of schizophrenia in a Finnish twin cohort. *Archives of General Psychiatry, 55*(1), 67–74.

Cannon, W. B. (1932). *The wisdom of the body*. New York: Norton.

Cannon, W. B. (1934). Hunger and thirst. In C. Murchinson (Ed.), *Handbook of general experimental psychology*. Worcester, MA: Clark University Press.

Cannon, W. B., & Washburn, A. L. (1912). An exploration of hunger. *American Journal of Physiology, 29*, 441–454.

Cantor, N., & Kihlstrom, J. (1987). *Personality and social intelligence*. Englewood Cliffs, NJ: Prentice Hall.

Caplan, N., Choy, M. H., & Whitmore, J. K. (1992). Indochinese refugee families and academic achievement. *Scientific American*, Feb., 36–42.

Caplan, P. J. (1995). *They say you're crazy*. Reading, MA: Addison-Wesley.

Capner, M., & Caltabiano, M. L. (1993). Factors affecting the progression towards burnout. *Psychological Reports, 73*(2), 555–561.

Carducci, B. J., & Stein, N. D. (1988, April). *The personal and situational pervasiveness of shyness in college students: A nine-year comparison.* Paper presented at the meeting of the Southeastern Psychological Association, New Orleans.

Carli, L. L., Ganley, R., & Pierce-Otay, A. (1991). Similarity and satisfaction in roommate relationships. *Personality & Social Psychology Bulletin, 17*(4), 419–426.

Carlson, J. G., et al. (1998). Eye movement desensitization and reprocessing (EDMR) treatment for combat-related posttraumatic stress disorder. *Journal of Traumatic Stress, 11*(1) 3–24.

Carlson, M., Marcus-Newhall, A., & Miller, N. (1990). Effects of situational aggression cues: A quantitative review. *Journal of Personality & Social Psychology, 58*(4), 622–633.

Carlson, N. R. (1994). *Physiology of behavior* (5th ed.). Boston: Allyn & Bacon.

Carlson, N. R. (1998). *Physiology of behavior* (6th ed.). Boston: Allyn & Bacon.

Carlson, R. W. (1993). From rules to prototypes: Adapting expert systems to the nature of expertise in clinical information processing. *Computers in Human Service, 9*(3–4), 339–350.

Carnegie Corporation of New York. (1994). *Starting points: Meeting the needs of our youngest children.* New York: The Carnegie Corporation.

Carney, R. N., & Levin, J. R. (1998). Do mnemonic memories fade as time goes by? *Contemporary Educational Psychology, 23*(3), 276–297.

Carney, R. N., Levin, J. R., & Stackhouse, T. L. (1997). The face-name mnemonic strategy from a different perspective. *Contemporary Educational Psychology, 22*(3), 399–412.

Carroll, J. M., & Russell, J. A. (1996). Do facial expressions signal specific emotions? Judging emotion from the face in context. *Journal of Personality & Social Psychology, 70*(2), 205–218.

Carson, R. C., Butcher, J. N., & Mineka, S. (1997). *Abnormal psychology and modern life.* Reading, MA: Addison-Wesley.

Carter, R. (1998). *Mapping the mind.* Berkeley, CA: University of California Press.

Carter, W. E. (Ed.). (1980). *Cannabis in Costa Rica: A study of chronic marihuana use.* Philadelphia: Institute for the Study of Human Issues.

Cartwright, R., & Lamberg, L. (1992). *Crisis dreaming.* New York: HarperCollins.

Casey, M. B., Nuttall, R., Pezaris, E., & Benbow, C. P. (1992). The influence of spatial ability on gender differences in mathematics college entrance test scores across diverse samples. *Developmental Psychology, 31*(4), 697–705.

Caspi, A., & Herbener, E. S. (1990). Continuity and change: Associative marriage and the consistency of personality in adulthood. *Journal of Personality & Social Psychology, 58*(2), 250–258.

Casto, S. D., DeFries, J. C., & Fulker, D. W. (1995). Multivariate genetic analysis of Wechsler Intelligence Scale for Children—Revised (WISC—R) factors. *Behavior Genetics, 25*(1), 25–32.

Catalano, R., Novaco, R., & McConnell, W. (1997). A model of the net effect of job loss on violence. *Journal of Personality & Social Psychology, 72*(6), 1440–1447.

Cattell, R. B. (1965). *The scientific analysis of personality.* Baltimore: Penguin.

Cattell, R. B. (1973, July). Personality pinned down. *Psychology Today,* 40–46.

Cautela, J. R., & Bennett, A. K. (1981). Covert conditioning. In R. J. Corsini (Ed.), *Handbook of innovative psychotherapies* (pp. 189–204). New York: Wiley.

Cautela, J. R., & Kearney, A. J. (1986). *The covert conditioning handbook.* New York: Springer.

Cavalli-Sforza, L. L. (1991, November). Genes, peoples, and languages. *Scientific American,* 104–110.

CBC. (1999). *The National online: PTSD.* Document retrieved April 9, 2002, from http://www.tv.cbc.ca/national/pgminfo/ptsd/wounds.html.

Ceci, S. J., & Bruck, M. (1993). Suggestibility of the child witness: A historical review and synthesis. *Psychological Bulletin, 113*(3), 403–439.

Ceci, S. J., & Bruck, M. (1995). *Jeopardy in the courtroom: A scientific analysis of children's testimony.* Washington: American Psychological Association.

Cecil, H., Evans, R. J., & Stanley, M. A. (1996). Perceived believability among adolescents of health warning labels on cigarette packs. *Journal of Applied Social Psychology, 26*(6), 502–519.

Chabris, C. F., Steele, K. M., Bella, S. D., et al. (1999). Prelude or requiem for the "Mozart effect"? *Nature, 400*(6747), 826–828.

Chakos, M. H., Alvir, J. M. J., Woerner, M., & Koreen, A. (1996). Incidence and correlates of tardive dyskinesia in first episode of schizophrenia. *Archives of General Psychiatry, 53*(4), 313–319.

Chan, G. C., Hinds, T. R., Impey, S., & Storm, D. R. (1998). Hippocampal neurotoxicity of Delta-sup-9-tetrahydrocannabinol. *Journal of Neuroscience, 18*(14), 5322–5332.

Chan, R. W., Raboy, B., & Patterson, C. J. (1998). Psychosocial adjustment among children conceived via donor insemination by lesbian and heterosexual mothers. *Child Development, 69*(2), 443–457.

Chandler, M. J., & Lalonde, C. (1998). Cultural continuity as a hedge against suicide in Canada's First Nations. *Transcultural Psychiatry, 35,* 191–219.

Chandrasena, R., Beddage, V., & Fernando, M. L. D. (1991). Suicide among immigrant psychiatric patients in Canada. *British Journal of Psychiatry, 159,* 707–709.

Chapin, F. S. (1939). Social participation and social intelligence. *American Sociological Review, 4,* 157–166.

Charlesworth, W. R., & LaFreniere, P. (1983). Dominance, friendship, and resource utilization in preschool children's groups. *Ethology and Sociobiology, 4*(3), 175–186.

Cheadle, A., Psaty, B. M., Diehr, P., Koepsell, T., et al. (1992–93). An empirical exploration of a conceptual model for community-based health-promotion. *International Quarterly of Community Health Education, 13*(4), 329–363.

Cheek, J., & Buss, A. H. (1979). Scales of shyness, sociability and self-esteem and correlations among them. Unpublished research, University of Texas. (Cited by Buss, 1980.)

Chen, K., & Kandel, D. B. (1995). The natural history of drug use from adolescence to the mid-thirties in a general population sample. *American Journal of Public Health, 85*(1), 41–47.

Chen, Z., Lawson, R. B., Gordon, L. R., & McIntosh, B. (1996). Groupthink: Deciding with the leader and the devil. *Psychological Record, 46*(4), 581–590.

Cheng, H., Cao, Y., & Olson, L. (1996). Spinal cord repair in adult paraplegic rats: Partial restoration of hind limb function. *Science, 273*(5274), 510.

Chess, S., & Thomas, A. (1986). *Know your child.* New York: Basic.

Chicoine, A., Proteau, L., & Lassonde, M. (2000). Absence of interhemispheric transfer of unilateral visuomotor learning in young children and individuals with agenesis of the corpus callosum. *Developmental Neuropsychology, 18,* 73–94.

Chisholm, K. (1998). A three year follow-up of attachment and indiscriminate friendliness in children adopted from Romanian orphanages. *Child Development, 69,* 1092–1106.

Chisholm, K., Carter, M. C., Ames, E. W., & Morison, S. J. (1995). Attachment security and indiscriminately friendly behavior in children adopted from Romanian orphanages. *Development & Psychopathology, 7*(2), 283–294.

Chomsky, N. (1975). *Reflections on language.* New York: Pantheon.

Chomsky, N. (1986). *Knowledge of language.* New York: Praeger.

Christensen, A., & Jacobson, N. S. (1994). Who (or what) can do psychotherapy. *Psychological Science, 5*(1), 8–14.

Christensen, D. (1999). Mind over matter. *Science News, 156,* 142–143.

Christianson, S., Saisa, J., & Silfvenius, H. (1995). The right hemisphere recognises the bad guys. *Cognition & Emotion, 9*(4), 309–324.

Cialdini, R. B., Eisenberg, N., Green, B. L., et al. (1998). Undermining the undermining effect of reward on sustained interest. *Journal of Applied Social Psychology, 28*(3), 249–263.

Cialdini, R. B., Petty, R. E., & Cacippo, T. J. (1981). Attitude and attitude change. *Annual Review of Psychology, 32,* 357–404.

Cialdini, R. B., Vincent, J. E., Lewis, S. K., Catalan, J., Wheeler, D., & Darby, B. L. (1975). A reciprocal concessions procedure for inducing compliance. The door-in-the-face technique. *Journal of Personality & Social Psychology, 21,* 206–215.

Cinciripini, P. M., Wetter, D. W., & McClure, J. B. (1997). Scheduled reduced smoking. *Addictive Behaviors, 22*(6), 759–767.

Clark, K. B. (1965). *Dark ghetto.* New York: Harper & Row.

Clark, R., Anderson, N. B., Clark, V. R., & Williams, D. R. (1999). Racism as a stressor for African Americans. *American Psychologist, 54*(10), 805–816.

Click, P., Zion, C., & Nelson, C. (1988). What mediates sex discrimination in hiring decisions? *Journal of Personality & Social Psychology, 55*(2), 178–186.

Cline, V. B., Croft, R. G., & Courrier, S. (1972). Desensitization of children to television violence. *Journal of Personality & Social Psychology, 27,* 360–365.

Cohen, D., & Gunz, A. (2002). As seen by the other… Perspectives on the self in the memories and emotional perceptions of Easterners and Westerners. *Psychological Science, 13*(1), 55–59.

Cohen, N. L., Waltzman, S. B., & Fisher, S. G. (1993). A prospective, randomized study of cochlear implants. *New England Journal of Medicine, 328*(4), 233–237.

Cohen, S., & Lichtenstein, E. (1990). Partner behaviors that support quitting smoking. *Journal of Consulting & Clinical Psychology, 58*(3), 304–309.

Cohen, S., Tyrrell, D. A., & Smith, A. P. (1993). Negative life events, perceived stress, negative affect, and susceptibility to the common cold. *Journal of Personality and Social Psychology, 64*(1), 131–140.

Cole, J. (1995). *Pride and a daily marathon.* Cambridge, MA: MIT Press.

Cole, J., & Paillarrd, J. (1995). Living without touch and peripheral information about body position and movement: Studies with deafferented subjects. In J. L. Bermudez & A. J. Marcel (Eds.), *The body and the self.* Cambridge, MA: MIT Press.

Cole, P. H. (1998). Affective process in psychotherapy: A Gestalt therapist's view. *Gestalt Journal, 21*(1), 49–72.

Colin, A. K., Moore, K., & West, A. N. (1996). Creativity, oversensitivity, and rate of habituation. EDRA: *Environmental Design Research Association, 20*(4), 423–427.

Collins, A. M., & Quillian, M. R. (1969). Retrieval time from semantic memory. *Journal of Verbal Learning and Verbal Behavior, 8,* 240–247.

Collins, W. A., & Gunnar, M. R. (1990). Social and personality development. *Annual Review of Psychology, 41,* 387–416.

Comperatore, C. A., Lieberman, H. R., Kirby, A. W., & Adams, B. (1996). Melatonin efficacy in aviation missions requiring rapid deployment and night operations. *Aviation, Space, & Environmental Medicine, 67*(6), 520–524.

Condon, W. S., & Sander, L. W. (1974). Synchrony demonstrated between movements of the neonate and adult speech. *Child Development, 45*(2), 456–462.

Connolly, D. A., & Lindsay, D. S. (2001). The influence of suggestions on children's reports of a unique experience versus an instance of a repeated experience. *Applied Cognitive Psychology, 15*(2), 205–223.

Considine, R. V., Sinha, M. K., Heiman, M. L., Kriauciunas, A., et al. (1996). Serum immunoreactive-leptin concentrations in normal-weight and obese humans. *New England Journal of Medicine, 334*(5), 292–295.

Consumer Reports. (1995, November). Mental health: Does therapy help? 734–739.

Conway, M. (2000). On sex roles and representations of emotional experience: Masculinity, femininity and emotional awareness. *Sex Roles, 43,* 687–698.

Conway, M. A., Cohen, G., & Stanhope, N. (1992). Very long-term memory for knowledge acquired at school and university. *Applied Cognitive Psychology, 6*(6), 467–482.

Cooper, G. D., Adams, H. B., & Scott, J. C. (1988). Studies in REST: I. Reduced Environmental Stimulation Therapy (REST) and reduced alcohol consumption. *Journal of Substance Abuse Treatment, 5*(2), 61–68.

Cooper, J., & Fazio, R. H. (1984). A new look at dissonance theory. *Advances in Experimental Social Psychology, 17,* 226–229.

Cooper, R. P., Abraham, J., Berman, S., & Staska, M. (1997). The development of infants' preference for motherese. *Infant Behavior and Development, 20*(4), 477–488.

Coopersmith, S. (1968). Studies in self-esteem. *Scientific American, 218,* 96–106.

Cordova, D. I., & Lepper, M. R. (1996). Intrinsic motivation and the process of learning. *Journal of Educational Psychology, 88*(4), 715–730.

Coren, S. (1992). *The left-hander syndrome.* New York: Free Press.

Coren, S. (1996). *Sleep thieves.* New York: Free Press.

Coren, S. (1999). Do people look like their dogs? *Anthrozoos, 12*(2), 111–114.

Coren, S., & Halpern, D. F. (1991). Left-handedness: A marker for decreased survival fitness. *Psychological Bulletin, 109*(1), 90–106.

Coren, S., Ward, L. M., & Enns, J. T. (1994). *Sensation and perception.* Ft. Worth: Harcourt Brace.

Corey, M. S., & Corey, G. (1996). *Groups: Process and practice.* Pacific Grove, CA: Brooks/Cole.

Cormier, J. F., & Thelen, M. H. (1998). Professional skepticism of multiple personality disorder. *Professional Psychology: Research and Practice, 29*(2), 163–167.

Corrigan, P. W. (1997). Behavior therapy empowers persons with severe mental illness. *Behavior Modification, 21*(1), 45–61.

Corrigan, P. W., & Penn, D. L. (1999). Lessons from social psychology on discrediting psychiatric stigma. *American Psychologist, 54*(9), 765–776.

Corteen, R. S., & Williams, T. M. (1986). Television and reading skills. In T. M. Williams (Ed.), *The impact of television: A natural experiment in three communities.* Orlando, FL: Academic.

Costa, P. T., & McCrae, R. R. (1992). Multiple uses for longitudinal personality data. *European Journal of Personality, 6*(2), 85–102.

Costello, T. W., & Costello, J. T. (1992). *Abnormal psychology.* New York: HarperCollins.

Coursey, R. D., Ward-Alexander, L., & Katz, B. (1990). Cost-effectiveness of providing insurance benefits for posthospital psychiatric halfway house stays. *American Psychologist, 45*(10), 1118–1126.

Courtois, C. A. (1999). *Recollections of sexual abuse.* New York: Norton Professional Books.

Covell, K., Grusec, J. E., & King, G. (1995). The intergenerational transmission of maternal discipline and standards for behavior. *Social Development, 4*(1), 32–43.

Cowles, J. T. (1937). Food tokens as incentives for learning by chimpanzees. *Comparative Psychology,* Monograph, 14(5, Whole No. 71).

Cox, W. E. (1994). Exceptional evidence of ESP by a reputed sensitive. *Journal of the Society for Psychical Research, 60*(836), 16–28.

Coyne, J. C., & Downey, G. (1991). Social factors and psychopathology. In M. R. Rosenzweig and L. W. Porter (Eds.), *Annual Review of Psychology, 42,* 401–425.

Craig, T. Y., & Kelly, J. R. (1999). Group cohesiveness and creative performance. *Group Dynamics, 3*(4), 243–256.

Craik, F. I. M. (1970). The fate of primary items in free recall. *Journal of Verbal Learning and Verbal Behavior, 9,* 143–148.

Craik, F. I., & Lockhart, R. S. (1972). Levels of processing: A framework for memory research. *Journal of Verbal Learning and Verbal Behavior, 11*(6), 671–684.

Crandall, C. S., Preisler, J. J., & Aussprung, J. (1992). Measuring life event stress in the lives of college students: The Undergraduate Stress Questionnaire (USQ). *Journal of Behavioral Medicine, 15*(6), 627–662.

Cravatt, B. F., Prospero-Garcia O., Siuzdak G., Gilula, N. B., et al. (1995). Chemical characterization of a family of brain lipids that induce sleep. *Science, 268*(5216), 1506–1509.

Crawley, S. B., & Sherrod, K. B. (1984). Parent-infant play during the first year of life. *Infant Behavior & Development, 7,* 65–75.

Cregler, L. L., & Mark, H. (1985). Medical complications of cocaine abuse. *New England Journal of Medicine, 315*(23), 1495–1500.

Crencavage, L. M., & Norcross, J. C. (1990). Where are the commonalities among the therapeutic common factors? *Professional Psychology: Research & Practice, 21*(5), 372–378.

Cronbach, L. (1990). *Essentials of psychological testing.* Reading, PA: Addison-Wesley.

Crowe, L. C., & George, W. H. (1989). Alcohol and human sexuality: Review and integration. *Psychological Bulletin, 105*(3), 374–386.

Csikszentmihalyi, M. (1997). *Creativity.* New York: HarperCollins.

Culertson, F. M. (1997). Depression and gender. *American Psychologist, 52*(1), 25–31.

Cull, W. L., Shaughnessy, J. J., & Zechmeister, E. B. (1996). Expanding understanding of the expanding-pattern-of-retrieval mnemonic. *Journal of Experimental Psychology: Applied, 2*(4), 365–378.

Cumming, S., Hay, P., Lee, T., & Sachdev, P. (1995). Neuropsychological outcome from psychosurgery for obsessive-compulsive disorder. *Australian & New Zealand Journal of Psychiatry, 29*(2), 293–298.

Cummins, D. D. (1995). *The other side of psychology.* New York: St. Martins.

Cynader, M. S. (1994). Mechanisms of brain development and their role in health and well-being. *Daedalus, 123*(4), 155–165.

Czeisler, C. A., Kronauer, R. E., Allan, J. S., et al., (1989). Bright light induction of strong (Type O) resetting of the human circadian pacemaker. *Science, 244*(June), 1328–1333.

Czeisler, C. A., Richardson, G. S., Zimmerman, J. C., Moore-Ede, M. C., & Weitzman, E. D. (1981). Entrainment of human circadian rhythms by light-dark cycles: A reassessment. Photochemistry, *Photobiology, 34,* 239–247.

Dabbs, J. M., Jr., Hargrove, M. F., & Heusel, C. (1996). Testosterone differences among college fraternities. *Personality & Individual Differences, 20*(2), 157–161.

Darley, J. M., & Latané, B. (1968). Bystander intervention in emergencies: Diffusion of responsibility. *Journal of Personality & Social Psychology, 8,* 377–383.

Darling, C. A., Davidson, J. K., & Passarello, L. C. (1992). The mystique of first intercourse among college youth: The role of partners, contraceptive practices, and psychological reactions. *Journal of Youth & Adolescence, 21*(1), 97–117.

Darou, W. G., Kurtness, J., & Hum, A. (2000). The impact of conducting research with a First Nation. *Canadian Journal of Counselling, 34*(1), 43–54.

Darwin, C. (1872). *The expression of emotion in man and animals.* Chicago: The University of Chicago Press.

DasGupta, B. (1992). Perceived control and examination stress. *Psychology: A Journal of Human Behavior, 29*(1), 31–34.

Davanloo, H. (1995). Intensive short-term dynamic psychotherapy. *International Journal of Short-Term Psychotherapy, 10*(3–4), 121–155.

Davidson, P. R., & Parker, K. C. H. (2001). Eye movement desensitization and reprocessing (EMDR): A meta-analysis. *Journal of Consulting and Clinical Psychology, 69*, 305–316.

Davis, C., & Scott-Robertson, L. (2000). A psychological comparison of females with anorexia nervosa and competitive male bodybuilders: Body shape ideals in the extreme. *Eating Behaviors, 1*(1), 33–46.

Davis, J. R., Vanderploeg, J. M., Santy, P. A., Jennings, R. T., et al. (1988). Space motion sickness during 24 flights of the Space Shuttle. *Aviation, Space, & Environmental Medicine, 59*(12), 1185–1189.

Davis, M. H., & Harvey, J. C. (1992). Declines in major league batting performance as a function of game pressure. *Journal of Applied Social Psychology, 22*(9), 714–735.

Dawson, M. E. (1990). Where does the truth lie? A review of the polygraph test: Lies, truth, and science. *Psychophysiology, 27*(1), 120–121.

De Benedittis, G., Lorenzetti, A., & Pieri, A. (1990). The role of stressful life events in the onset of chronic primary headache. *Pain, 40*(1), 65–75.

de Bono, E. (1970). *Lateral thinking: Creativity step by step.* New York: Harper & Row.

de Bono, E. (1992). *Serious creativity.* New York: HarperCollins.

de Jong, T., & van Joolingen, W. R. (1998). Scientific discovery learning with computer simulations of conceptual domains. *Review of Educational Research, 68*(2), 179–201.

de Luccie, M. F., & Davis, A. J. (1991). Father-child relationships from the preschool years through mid-adolescence. *Journal of Genetic Psychology, 152*(2), 225–238.

De Raad, B. (1998). Five big, Big Five issues. *European Psychologist, 3*(2), 113–124.

Dean-Church, L., & Gilroy, F. D. (1993). Relation of sex-role orientation to life satisfaction in a healthy elderly sample. *Journal of Social Behavior & Personality, 8*(1), 133–140.

Deaux, K., Dane, F., & Wrightsman, L. S. (1993). *Social psychology in the '90s.* Monterey: Brooks/Cole.

Deese, J., & Hulse, S. J. (1967). *The psychology of learning* (3rd ed.). New York: McGraw-Hill.

Deffenbacher, J. L., & Suinn, R. M. (1988). Systematic desensitization and the reduction of anxiety. *Counseling Psychologist, 16*(1), 9–30.

DeGood, D. E. (1975). Cognitive factors in vascular stress responses. *Psychophysiology, 12*, 399–401.

Degreef, G., Ashtari, M., Bogerts, B., et al. (1992). Volumes of ventricular system subdivisions measured from magnetic resonance images in first-episode schizophrenic patients. *Archives of General Psychiatry, 49*(7), 531–537.

DeKlyen, M., Biernbaum, M. A., Spelz, M. L., & Greenberg, M. T. (1998). *Developmental Psychology, 34*(2), 264–275.

Denmark, F. L. (1994). Engendering psychology. *American Psychologist, 49*(4), 329–334.

Dennis, M., Fletcher, J. M., Rogers, T., Hetherington, R., & Francis, D. J. (2002). Object-based and action-based visual perception in children with spina bifida and hydrocephalus. *Journal of the International Neuropsychological Society, 8*(1), 95–106.

Dennis, M., Rogers, T., & Barnes, M. A. (2001). Children with spina bifida perceive visual illusions but not multistable figures. *Brain and Cognition, 46*(1–2), 108–113.

Derzon, J. H., & Lipsey, M. W. (1999). A synthesis of the relationship of marijuana use with delinquent and problem behaviors. *School Psychology International, 20*(1), 57–68.

Deutsch, M. (1993). Educating for a peaceful world. *American Psychologist, 48*(5), 510–517.

Devine, P. G. (1990). Stereotypes and prejudice: Their automatic and controlled components. *Journal of Personality & Social Psychology, 56*(1), 5–18.

Devine, P. G., Monteith, M. J., Zuerink, J. R., & Elliot, A. J. (1991). Prejudice with and without compunction. *Journal of Personality & Social Psychology, 60*(6), 817–830.

Devoto, A., Lucidi, F., Violani, C., & Bertini, M. (1999). Effects of different sleep reductions on daytime sleepiness. *Sleep, 22*(3), 336–343.

Dewhurst, S. A., & Conway, M. A. (1994). Pictures, images, and recollective experience. *Journal of Experimental Psychology: Learning, Memory, and Cognition, 20*, 1088–1098.

Dickinson, D. J., & O'Connell, D. Q. (1990). Effect of quality and quantity of study on student grades. *Journal of Educational Research, 83*(4), 227–231.

Diefenbach, D. L. (1997). Portrayal of mental illness on prime-time television. *Journal of Community Psychology, 25*(3), 289–302.

Diekstra, R. F., & Garnefski, N. (1995). On the nature, magnitude, and causality of suicidal behaviors: An international perspective. *Suicide & Life-Threatening Behavior, 25*(1), 36–57.

Diener, E., Suh, E. M., Lucas, R. E., & Smith, H. L. (1999). Subjective well-being: Three decades of progress. *Psychological Bulletin, 125*(2), 276–302.

Dies, R. R. (1995). Group psychotherapies. In A. S. Gurman & S. B. Messer (Eds.), *Essential psychotherapies.* New York: Guilford.

Dieter, J. N. I., & Emory, E. K. (1997). Supplemental stimulation of premature infants. *Journal of Pediatric Psychology, 22*(3), 281–295.

Dietz, T. L. (1998). An examination of violence and gender role portrayals in video games. *Sex Roles, 38*(5–6), 425–442.

Digman, J. M. (1990). Personality structure: Emergence of the five-factor model. *Annual Review of Psychology, 41*, 417–440.

Dillard, J. P. (1991). The current status of research on sequential-request compliance techniques. *Personality & Social Psychology Bulletin, 17*(3), 283–288.

Dinkmeyer, D. Sr., McKay, G. D., & Dinkmeyer, D., Jr. (1997). *The parent's handbook.* Circle Pines, MN: American Guidance Service.

Dion, K. K., & Dion, K. L. (1993). Individualistic and collectivistic perspectives on gender and the cultural context of love and intimacy. *Journal of Social Issues, 49*(3), 53–69.

Dion, K. K., Pak, A. W., & Dion, K. L. (1990). Stereotyping physical attractiveness: A sociocultural perspective. *Journal of Cross Cultural Psychology, 21*(2), 158–179.

Dobelle, W. H. (2000). Artificial vision for the blind by connecting a television camera to the visual cortex. *American Society of Artificial Internal Organs, 46*, 3–9.

Docherty, N. M., et al. (1998). Communication disturbances and family psychiatric history in parents of schizophrenic patients. *Journal of Nervous & Mental Disease, 186*(12), 761–768.

Doctor, R. M., & Doctor, J. N. (1994). Stress. *Encyclopedia of human behavior,* Vol. 4, 311–323. San Diego, CA: Academic.

Doidge, N. (1997). Empirical evidence for the efficacy of psychoanalytic psychotherapies and psychoanalysis. *Psychoanalytic Inquiry,* Suppl., 102–150.

Dollard, J., et al. (1939). *Frustration and aggression.* New Haven: Yale University Press.

Dollard, J., & Miller, N. E. (1950). *Personality and psychotherapy: An analysis in terms of learning,*

thinking and culture. New York: McGraw-Hill.

Domhoff, G. W. (1999). Drawing theoretical implications from descriptive empirical findings on dream content. *Dreaming: Journal of the Association for the Study of Dreams, 9*(2–3), 201–210.

Domingo, R. A., & Goldstein-Alpern, N. (1999). "What dis?" and other toddler-initiated, expressive language-learning strategies. *Infant-Toddler Intervention, 9*(1), 39–60.

Dong, C. J., Swindale, N. V., Zakarauskas, P., Hayward, V., & Cynader, M. S. (2000). The auditory motion aftereffect: Its tuning and specificity in the spatial and frequency domains. *Perception and Psychophysics, 62*(5), 1099–1111.

Dorfman, J., Shames, J., & Kihlstrom, J. F. (1996). Intuition, incubation, and insight. In G. Underwood (Ed.), *Implicit cognition.* New York: Oxford University Press.

Dosher, B. A., & Ma, J. (1998). Output loss or rehearsal loop? *Journal of Experimental Psychology: Learning, Memory, & Cognition, 24*(2), 316–335.

Douvan, E. (1997). Erik Erikson: Critical times, critical theory. *Child Psychiatry & Human Development, 28*(1), 15–21.

Dovidio, J. F. (1984). Helping behavior and altruism: An empirical and conceptual overview. In L. Berkowitz (Ed.), *Advances in experimental social psychology,* Vol. 17. New York: Academic.

Dovidio, J. F., & Gaertner, S. L. (1999). Reducing prejudice: Combating intergroup biases. *Current Directions in Psychological Science, 8*(4), 101–105.

Dragoi, V., & Staddon, J. E. R. (1999). The dynamics of operant conditioning. *Psychological Review, 106*(1), 20–61.

Dretzke, Beverly J., & Levin, Joel R. (1996). Assessing students' application and transfer of a mnemonic strategy. *Contemporary Educational Psychology, 21*(1), 83–93.

Drigotas, S. M., Rusbult, C. E., Wieselquist, J., & Whitton, S. W. (1999). Close partner as sculptor of the ideal self: Behavioral affirmation and the Michelangelo phenomenon. *Journal of Personality & Social Psychology, 77*(2), 293–323.

Druckman, D., & Bjork, R. A. (1994). *Learning, remembering, believing: Enhancing human performance.* Washington, DC: National Academy Press.

DSM-IV: Diagnostic and statistical manual of mental disorders (4th ed.). (1994). Washington, DC: American Psychiatric Association.

Dubbert, P. M. (1995). Behavioral (life-style) modification in the prevention and treatment of hypertension. *Clinical Psychology Review, 15*(3), 187–216.

Dubow, E. F., Huesmann, L. R., & Eron, L. D. (1987). Childhood correlates of adult ego development. *Child Development, 58*(3), 859–869.

Dugas, M. J., et al. (1998). Worry themes in primary GAD, secondary GAD, and other anxiety disorders. *Journal of Anxiety Disorders, 12*(3), 253–261.

Dunbar, K. (2000). How scientists think in the real world: Implications for science education. *Journal of Applied Developmental Psychology, 21*(1), 49–58.

Duncker, K. (1945). On problem solving. *Psychological Monographs, 58*(270).

Durham, M. D., & Dane, F. C. (1999). Juror knowledge of eyewitness behavior. *Journal of Social Behavior & Personality, 14*(2), 299–308.

Durso, F. T., Rea, C. B., & Dayton, T. (1994). Graph-theoretic confirmation of restructuring during insight. *Psychological Science, 5*(2), 94–98.

Dutton, D. G., & Aron, A. P. (1974). Some evidence for heightened sexual attraction under conditions of high anxiety. *Journal of Personality & Social Psychology, 30*, 510–517.

Dyer, F. J. (1993). Clinical presentation of the lead-poisoned child on mental ability tests. *Journal of Clinical Psychology, 49*(1), 94–101.

Dywan, J., & Bowers, K. S. (1983). The use of hypnosis to enhance recall. *Science, 222*, 184–185.

Eagly, A. H., & Chaiken, S. (1992). *The psychology of attitudes.* San Diego, CA: Harcourt Brace Jovanovich.

Eastwood, J. D., Smilek, D., & Merikle, P. M. (2001). Differential attentional guidance by unattended faces expressing positive and negative emotion. *Perception and Psychophysics, 63*(6), 1004–1013.

Ebbinghaus, H. (1885). *Memory: A contribution to experimental psychology.* Translated by H. A. Ruger & C. E. Bussenius, 1913. New York: New York Teacher's College, Columbia University.

Eckerman, D. A. (1999). Scheduling reinforcement about once a day. *Behavioural Processes, 45*(1–3), 101–114.

Edwards, D. J. A. (1998). Types of case study work. *Journal of Humanistic Psychology, 38*(3), 36–70.

Eich, E. (1995). Mood as a mediator of place dependent memory. *Journal of Experimental Psychology: General, 124*(3), 293–308.

Eich, E., Rachman, S., & Lopatka, C. (1990). Affect, pain, and autobiographical memory. *Journal of Abnormal Psychology, 99*(2) 174–178.

Eisenberg, N. (1991). Meta-analytic contributions to the literature on prosocial behavior. *Personality & Social Psychology Bulletin, 17*(3), 273–282.

Eisenberg, N., & Miller, P. A. (1987). The relation of empathy to prosocial and related behaviors. *Psychological Bulletin, 101*(1), 91–119.

Ekman, P. (1993). Facial expression and emotion. *American Psychologist, 48*(4), 384–392.

Ekman, P., Friesen, W. V., & Bear, J. (1984, May). The international language of gestures. *Psychology Today*, 64–69.

Ekman, P., Levenson, R. W., & Friesen, W. V. (1983). Autonomic nervous system activity distinguishes among emotions. *Science, 221*, 1208–1210.

Ekman, P., & Rosenberg, E. (1997). *What the face reveals.* New York: Oxford University Press.

Eliot, L. (1999). *What's going on in there?* New York: Bantam.

Ellis, A. (1973, February). The no cop-out therapy. *Psychology Today, 7*, 56–60, 62.

Ellis, A. (1979). The practice of rational-emotive therapy. In A. Ellis & J. Whiteley (Eds.), *Theoretical and empirical foundations of rational-emotive therapy.* Monterey, CA: Brooks/Cole.

Ellis, A. (1987). A sadly neglected cognitive component in depression. *Cognitive Therapy & Research, 11*(1), 121–145.

Ellis, A. (1995). Changing rational-emotive therapy (RET) to rational emotive behavior therapy (REBT). *Journal of Rational-Emotive & Cognitive Behavior Therapy, 13*(2), 85–89.

Ellis, H. C., & Hunt, R. R. (1992). *Fundamentals of Cognitive psychology.* Madison, WI: Brown & Benchmark.

Emmons, K. M., et al. (1998). Predictors of smoking among US college students. *American Journal of Public Health, 88*(1), 104–107.

Enns, J. T., & Coren, S. (1995). The box alignment illusion. *Perception & Psychophysics, 57*(8), 1163–1174.

Eppley, K. R., Abrams, A. I., & Shear, J. (1989). Differential effects of relaxation techniques on trait anxiety: A meta-analysis. *Journal of Clinical Psychology, 45*(6), 957–974.

Erdelyi, M. H., & Appelbaum, A. G., (1973). Cognitive masking: The disruptive effect of an emotional stimulus upon the perception of contiguous neutral items. *Bulletin of the Psychonomic Society, 1*, 59–61.

Ericsson, K. A., & Charness, N. (1994). Expert performance. *American Psychologist, 49*(8), 725–747.

Ericsson, K. A., & Chase, W. G. (1982). Exceptional memory. *American Scientist, 70*, 607–615.

Erikson, E. H. (1963). *Childhood and society.* New York: Norton.

Ernst, E. (1994). Is acupuncture effective for pain control? *Journal of Pain & Symptom Management, 9*(2), 72–74.

Eron, L. D. (1986). Interventions to mitigate the psychological effects of media violence on aggressive behavior. *Journal of Social Issues, 42*(3), 155–169.

Eron, L. D. (1987). The development of aggressive behavior from the perspective of a developing behaviorism. *American Psychologist, 42*, 435–442.

Eronen, S., & Nurmi, J. (1999). Life events, predisposing cognitive strategies and well-being. *European Journal of Personality, 13*(2), 129–148.

Erwin, E. (1996). *A final accounting? Philosophical and empirical issues in Freudian psychology.* Cambridge, MA: MIT Press.

Espy, K. A., Kaufmann, P. M., & Glisky, M. L. (1999). Neuropsychological function in toddlers exposed to cocaine in utero: A preliminary study. *Developmental Neuropsychology, 15*(3), 447–460.

Esser, J. K. (1998). Alive and well after 25 years: A review of groupthink research. *Organizational Behavior & Human Decision Processes, 73*(2–3), 116–141.

Esterling, B. A., L'Abate, L., Murray, E. J., & Pennebaker, J. W. (1999). Empirical foundations for writing in prevention and psychotherapy: Mental and physical health outcomes. *Clinical Psychology Review, 19*(1), 79–96.

Everson, C. A. (1998). Physiological consequences of sleep deprivation. *Journal of Musculoskeletal Pain, 6*(3), 93–101.

Everson, S. A., Goldberg, D. E., & Salonen, J. T. (1996). Hopelessness and risk of mortality and incidence of myocardial infarction and cancer. *Psychosomatic Medicine, 58*(2), 113.

Eyer, Diane E. (1994). Mother-infant bonding: A scientific fiction. *Human Nature, 5*(1), 69–94.

Eysenck, H. J. (1967, June). New ways in psychotherapy. *Psychology Today*, 40.

Eysenck, H. J. (1994). The outcome problem in psychotherapy: What have we learned? *Behaviour Research & Therapy, 32*(5), 477–495.

Eysenck, H. J. (Ed.). (1981). *A model for personality.* New York: Springer-Verlag.

Eysenck, M. W., & Keane, M. T. (1995). *Cognitive psychology.* Hove, East Sussex, UK: Erlbaum.

Fairclough, S. H., & Graham, R. (1999). Impairment of driving performance caused by sleep deprivation or alcohol. *Human Factors, 41*(1), 118–128.

Faith, M. S., Wong, F. Y., & Carpenter, K. M. (1995). Group sensitivity training: Update, meta-analysis, and recommendations. *Journal of Counseling Psychology, 42*(3), 390–399.

Fantz, R. L. (1961, May). The origin of form perception. *Scientific American*, 71.

Farah, M. J. (1988). Is visual imagery really visual? Overlooked evidence from neuropsychology. *Psychological Review, 95*(3), 307–317.

Farah, M. J., Weisberg, L. L., Monheit, M. A., & Peronnet, F. (1989). Brain activity underlying mental imagery. *Journal of Cognitive Neuroscience, 1*(4), 302–316.

Farberman, R. K. (1997). Public attitudes about psychologists and mental health care: Research to guide the American Psychological Association public education campaign. *Professional Psychology: Research and Practice, 28*, 128–136.

Farrimond, T. (1990). Effect of alcohol on visual constancy values and possible relation to driving performance. *Perceptual & Motor Skills, 70*(1), 291–295.

Farthing, G. W. (1992). *The psychology of consciousness.* Englewood Cliffs, NJ: Prentice Hall.

Fava, G. A., et al. (1998). Prevention of recurrent depression with cognitive behavioral therapy. *Archives of General Psychiatry, 55*(9), 816–820.

Feingold, A. (1992). Gender differences in mate selection preferences. *Psychological Bulletin, 111*, 304–341.

Feldhusen, J. F. (1995). Creativity: A knowledge base, metacognitive skills, and personality factors. *Journal of Creative Behavior, 29*(4), 255–268.

Feldhusen, J. F., & Goh, B. E. (1995). Assessing and accessing creativity: An integrative review of theory, research, and development. *Creativity Research Journal, 8*(3), 231–247.

Feldman, R. S., & Meyer, J. (1996). *Fundamentals of neuropsychopharmacology.* Sunderland, MA: Sinauer Associates.

Felmlee, D. H. (1998). "Be careful what you wish for . . .": A quantitative and qualitative investigation of "fatal attractions." *Personal Relationships, 5*(3), 235–253.

Fenton, G. W. (1998). Neurosurgery for mental disorder. *Irish Journal of Psychological Medicine, 15*(2), 45–48.

Fernald, A. (1989). Intonation and communicative intent in mothers' speech to infants: Is the melody the message? *Child Development, 60*(6), 1497–1510.

Fernald, A., & Mazzie, C. (1991). Prosody and focus in speech to infants and adults. *Developmental Psychology, 27*(2), 209–221.

Ferster, C. B., Nurnberger, J. I., & Levitt, E. B. (1962). The control of eating. *Journal of Mathematics, 1*, 87–109.

Festinger, L. (1954). A theory of social comparison processes. *Human Relations, 7*, 117–140.

Festinger, L. (1957). *A theory of cognitive dissonance.* Stanford, CA: Stanford University Press.

Festinger, L., & Carlsmith, J. M. (1959). Cognitive consequences of forced compliance. *Journal of Abnormal and Social Psychology, 58*, 203–210.

Fichten, C. S. (2002). Personal communication.

Fichten, C. S., and Sunerton, B. (1983). Popular horoscopes and the "Barnum Effect." *The Journal of Psychology, 114*, 123–134.

Finke, R. A. (1990). *Creative imagery: Discoveries and inventions in visualization.* Hillsdale, NJ: Erlbaum.

Finkelstein, P., Wenegrat, B., & Yalom, I. (1982). Large group awareness training. *Annual Review of Psychology, 33*, 515–539.

Finkenauer, C., Luminet, O., Gisle, L., et al. (1998). Flashbulb memories and the underlying mechanisms of their formation. *Memory & Cognition, 26*(3), 516–531.

Fischer, S., & Greenberg, R. (1996). *Freud scientifically appraised.* New York: John Wiley.

Fisher, R. P., & Geiselman, R. E. (1987). Enhancing eyewitness memory with the cognitive interview. In M. M. Gruneberg, P. E. Morris, & R. N. Sykes (Eds.), *Practical aspects of memory: Current research and issues.* Chinchester, UK: Wiley.

Fiske, S. T. (1993a). Social cognition and social perception. In L. W. Porter & M. R. Rosenzweig (Eds.), *Annual Review of Psychology, 44*, 155–194.

Fiske, S. T., (1993b). Controlling other people. *American Psychologist, 48*(6), 621–628.

Flavell, J. H. (1992). Cognitive development: Past, present, and future. *Developmental Psychology, 28*(6), 998–1005.

Flavell, J. H. (1999). Cognitive development: Children's knowledge about the mind. *Annual Review of Psychology, 50*, 21–45.

Fleming, J. (1974, January). Field report: The state of the apes. *Psychology Today, 46.*

Flynn, J. R. (1987). Massive IQ gains in 14 nations: What IQ tests really measure. *Psychological Bulletin, 101*(2), 171–191.

Foa, E. B., Franklin, M. E., Perry, K. J., & Herbert, J. D. (1996). Cognitive biases in generalized social phobia. *Journal of Abnormal Psychology, 105*(3), 433–439.

Fobair, P. (1997). Cancer support groups and group therapies. *Journal of Psychosocial Oncology, 15*(3–4), 123–147.

Fochtmann, L. J. (1995). Intractable sneezing as a conversion symptom. *Psychosomatics, 36*(2), 103–112.

Fones, C. S. L., et al. (1998). Social phobia: An update. *Harvard Review of Psychiatry, 5*(5), 1998, 247–259.

Fontenelle, D. H. (1989). *How to live with your children.* Tucson, AZ: Fisher Books.

Ford, C. V. (1995). Dimensions of somatization and hypochondriasis. *Neurologic Clinics, 13*(2), 241–253.

Ford, M. E. & Tisak, M. S. (1983). A further search for social intelligence. *Journal of Educational Psychology, 75*, 196–206.

Foreyt, J. P. (1987). The addictive disorders. In G. T. Wilson, C. M. Franks, P. C. Kendall, & J. P. Foreyt (Eds.), *Review of behavior therapy: Theory and practice,* Vol. II. New York: Guilford.

Forgays, D. G., & Belinson, M. J. (1986). Is flotation isolation a relaxing environment? *Journal of Environmental Psychology, 6*(1), 19–34.

Foss, R. D. (1986). Using social psychology to increase altruistic behavior: Will it help? In M. J. Saks & L. Saxe (Eds.), *Advances in applied social psychology,* Vol. 3. Hillsdale, NJ: Erlbaum.

Foster, C. A., et al. (1998). Arousal and attraction. *Journal of Personality & Social Psychology, 74*(1), 86–101.

Foster, G., & Ysseldyke, J. (1976). Expectancy and halo effects as a result of artificially induced teacher bias. *Contemporary Educational Psychology, 1*, 37–45.

Fouts, R., Fouts, D., & Schoenfield, D. (1984). Sign language conversational interaction between chimpanzees. *Sign Language Studies, 42*, 1–12.

Fowers, B. J., & Richardson, F. C. (1996). Why is multiculturalism good? *American Psychologist, 51*(6), 609–621.

Fowles, D. C. (1992). Schizophrenia: Diathesis-stress revisited. *Annual Review of Psychology, 43*, 303–336.

Foxhall, K. (1999, September). State legislatures address key issues for psychology. *APA Monitor, 22.*

Foxhall, K. (2000, January). Suddenly, a big impact on criminal justice. *APA Monitor,* 36–37.

Foxx, R. M. (1998). A comprehensive treatment program for inpatient adolescents. *Behavioral Interventions, 13*(1), 67–77.

Franche, R., & Dobson, K. S. (1992). Self-criticism and interpersonal dependency as vulnerability factors to depression. *Cognitive Therapy & Research, 16*(4), 419–435.

Frankenburg, W. K., & Dodds, J. B. (1967). The Denver Developmental Screening Test. *The Journal of Pediatrics, 1*, 181–191.

Frazier, J. A., Giedd, J. N., Hamburger, S. D., & Albus, K. E. (1996). Brain anatomic magnetic resonance imaging in childhood-onset schizophrenia. *Archives of General Psychiatry, 53*(7), 617–624.

Freedman, J. L. (1984). Effect of television violence on aggressiveness. *Psychological Bulletin, 96*, 227–246.

Freedman, J. L., & Fraser, S. C. (1966). Compliance without pressure: The foot-in-the-door technique. *Journal of Personality & Social Psychology, 4*, 195–202.

Freeman, A., & Reinecke, M. A. (1995). Cognitive therapy. In A. S. Gurman & S. B. Messer (Eds.), *Essential psychotherapies.* New York: Guilford.

Freeman, W. J. (1991, February). The physiology of perception. *Scientific American,* 78–85.

French, C. C., Fowler, M., McCarthy, K., & Peers, D. (1991). A test of the Barnum effect. *Skeptical Inquirer, 15*(4), 66–72.

Freud, S. (1900). *The interpretation of dreams.* London: Hogarth.

Freud, S. (1949). *An outline of psychoanalysis.* New York: Norton.

Fried, P. A., O'Connell, C. M., & Watkinson, B. (1992). 60- and 72-month follow-up of children prenatally exposed to marijuana, cigarettes, and alcohol. *Journal of Developmental & Behavioral Pediatrics, 13*(6), 383–391.

Fried, P., Watkinson, B., James, D., & Gray, R. (2002). Current and former marijuana use: Preliminary findings of a longitudinal study of effects on IQ in young adults. *Canadian Medical Association Journal, 166*, 887–891.

Friedman, M., & Rosenman, R. (1983). *Type A behavior and your heart.* New York: Knopf.

Friedman, R. C., et al. (1998). Private psychotherapy patients of psychiatrist psychoanalysts. *American Journal of Psychiatry, 155*, 1772–1774.

Furumoto, L., & Scarborough, E. (1986). Placing women in the history of psychology. *American Psychologist, 41*, 35–42.

Gabrieli, J. D. E. (1998). Cognitive neuroscience of human memory. *Annual Review of Psychology, 49*, 87–115.

Gaertner, S. L., Mann, J. A., Dovido, J. E., et al. (1990). How does cooperation reduce intergroup bias? *Journal of Personality & Social Psychology, 59*(4), 692–704.

Gagnon, J. H. (1977). *Human sexualities.* Glenview, IL: Scott, Foresman.

Galambos, N. L., & Tilton-Weaver, L. C. (1998). Multi-risk behavior in adolescents and young adults. *Health Reports,* Autumn 1998. Statistics Canada, Catalogue No. 82–003–XIE.

Galanti, G. (1993). Cult conversion, deprogramming, and the triune brain. *Cultic Studies Journal, 10*(1), 45–52.

Galati, D., Scherer, K. R., & Ricci-Bitti, P. E. (1997). Voluntary facial expression of emotion: Comparing congenitally blind with normally sighted encoders. *Journal of Personality & Social Psychology, 73*(6), 1363–1379.

Gallagher, S., & Cole, J. (1995). Body image and body schema in a deafferented subject. *Journal of Mind & Behavior, 16*(4), 369–389.

Gammage, K. L., Carron, A. V., & Estabrooks, P. A. (2001). Team cohesion and individual productivity: The influence of the norm for productivity and the identifiability of individual effort. *Small Group Research, 32*(1), 3–18.

Ganellen, R. J. (1996). Comparing the diagnostic efficiency of the MMPI, MCMI-II, and Rorschach. *Journal of Personality Assessment, 67*(2), 219–243.

Gardner, M. (1993). The false memory syndrome. *Skeptical Inquirer, 17*(4), 370–375.

Gardner, R. A., & Gardner, B. T. (1989). *Teaching sign language to chimpanzees.* Albany, NY: State University of New York Press.

Gardner, R. M., & Bokenkamp, E. D. (1996). The role of sensory and nonsensory factors in body size estimations of eating disorders subjects. *Journal of Clinical Psychology, 52*(1), 3–15.

Garland, A. F., & Zigler, E. (1993). Adolescent suicide prevention. *American Psychologist, 48*(2), 169–182.

Garnets, L., & Kimmel, D. (1991). Lesbian and gay male dimensions in the psychological study of human diversity. *Psychological perspectives on human diversity in America.* Washington, DC: American Psychological Association.

Gaston, L., et al. (1998). Alliance, technique, and their interactions in predicting outcome of behavioral, cognitive, and brief dynamic therapy. *Psychotherapy Research, 8*(2), 190–209.

Gates, A. I. (1958). Recitation as a factor in memorizing. In J. Deese (Ed.), *The psychology of learning.* New York: McGraw-Hill.

Gatz, M. (1990, July–August). Interpreting behavioral genetic results. *Journal of Counseling & Development, 68*, 601–605.

Gauthier, J., Cote, G., & French, D. (1994). The role of home practice in the thermal biofeedback treatment of migraine headache. *Journal of Consulting & Clinical Psychology, 62*(1), 180–184.

Gazzaniga, M. S. (1970). *The bisected brain.* New York: Plenum.

Gazzaniga, M. S. (1995). On neural circuits and cognition. *Neural Computation, 7*(1), 1–12.

Geiselman, R. E., Fisher, R. P., MacKinnon, D. P., & Holland, H. L. (1986). Eyewitness memory enhancement with the cognitive interview. *American Journal of Psychology, 99*, 385–401.

Gersh, R. D. (1982, June 20). *Learning when not to shoot.* Santa Barbara News Press.

Gershon, E. S., et al. (1998). Closing in on genes for manic-depressive illness and schizophrenia. *Neuropsychopharmacology, 18*(4), 233–242.

Gerwood, J. B. (1998). The legacy of Viktor Frankl. *Psychological Reports, 82*(2), 673–674.

Geschwind, N. (1979). Specializations of the human brain. *Scientific American, 241*, 180–199.

Gewirtz, J. C., & Davis, M. (1998). Application of Pavlovian higher-order conditioning to the analysis of the neural substrates of fear conditioning. *Neuropharmacology, 37*(4–5), 453–459.

Gibson, B., & Werner, C. M. (1994). The airport as a behavior setting: The role of legibility in communicating the setting program. *Journal of Personality and Social Psychology, 66*, 1049–1060.

Gibson, E. J., & Walk, R. D. (1960). The "visual cliff." *Scientific American, 202*(4), 67–71.

Gibson, H. B., & Heap, M. (1991). *Hypnosis in therapy.* Hillsdale, NJ: Erlbaum.

Gick, M. L., & Holyoak, K. J. (1980). Analogical problem solving. *Cognitive Psychology, 12*(3), 306–355.

Gierl, M. J., & Rogers, W. T. (1996). A confirmatory factor analysis of the Test Anxiety Inventory using Canadian high school students. *Educational & Psychological Measurement, 56*(2), 315–324.

Gilbert, D. G., Gilbert, B. O., & Schultz, V. L. (1998). Withdrawal symptoms: Individual differences and similarities across addictive behaviors. *Personality & Individual Differences, 24*(3), 351–356.

Gilbert, D. G., Stunkard, M. E., Jensen, R. A., & Detwiler, F. R. J. (1996). Effects of exam stress on mood, cortisol, and immune functioning. *Personality & Individual Differences, 21*(2), 235–246.

Gill, S. T. (1991). Carrying the war into the never-never land of psi. *Skeptical Inquirer, 15*(1), 269–273.

Gillam, B. (1980). Geometrical illusions. *American Psychologist, 242*, 102–111.

Gillberg, M., & Akerstedt, T. (1998). Sleep loss performance: No "safe" duration of a monotonous task. *Physiology & Behavior, 64*(5), 599–604.

Ginott, H. G. (1965). *Between parent and child: New solutions to old problems.* New York: Macmillan.

Girodo, M. (1978). *Shy? (You don't have to be!).* New York: Pocket Books.

Glass, A. L., Holyoak, K. J., & Santa, J. L. (1979). *Cognition.* Reading, MA: Addison-Wesley.

Glik, D. C., Kronenfeld, J. J., & Jackson, K. (1996). Predictors of well role performance behaviors. *American Journal of Health Behavior, 20*(4), 218–228.

Glisky, M. L., Williams, J. M., & Kihlstrom, J. F. (1996). Internal and external mental imagery perspectives and performance on two tasks. *Journal of Sport Behavior, 19*(1), 3–18.

Gloaguen, V., et al. (1998). A meta-analysis of the effects of cognitive therapy in depressed patients. *Journal of Affective Disorders, 49*(1), 59–72.

Globus, G. (1987). *Dream life, wake life: The human condition through dreams.* Albany, NY: State University of New York Press.

Gobet, F., & Simon, H. A. (1996). Recall of random and distorted chess positions: Implications for the theory of expertise. *Memory & Cognition, 24*(4), 493–503.

Goel, V., & Grafman, J. (1995). Are the frontal lobes implicated in "planning" functions? Interpreting data from the Tower of Hanoi. *Neuropsychologia, 33*(5), 623–642.

Goering, P., Wasylenki, D., & Durbin, J. (2000). Canada's mental health system. *International Journal of Law & Psychiatry, 23*, 345–359.

Gold, P. E. (1987, March–April). Sweet memories. *American Scientist, 75*, 151–155.

Goldberg, L. R. (1993). The structure of phenotypic personality traits. *American Psychologist, 48*(1), 26–34.

Goldfried, M. R., Greenberg, L. S., & Marmar, C. (1990). Individual psychotherapy: Process and outcome. *Annual Review of Psychology, 41*, 659–688.

Goldiamond, I. (1971). Self-control procedures in personal behavior problems. In M. S. Gazzaniga & E. P. Lovejoy (Eds.), *Good reading in psychology.* Englewood Cliffs, NJ: Prentice-Hall.

Goldman, H. H. (1998). Deinstitutionalization and community care. *Harvard Review of Psychiatry, 6*(4), 219–222.

Goldstein, E. (1997). False memory syndrome. *American Journal of Family Therapy, 25*(4), 307–317.

Goldstein, E. B. (1999). *Sensation and perception.* Belmont, CA: Wadsworth.

Goldstein, M. J. (1985). The UCLA family project. Presented at NIMH High-Risk Consortium, San Francisco. Cited by Mirsky & Duncan, 1986.

Goldstone, R. L. (1998). Perceptual learning. *Annual Review of Psychology, 49*, 585–612.

Goleman, D. (1982, March). Staying up: The rebellion against sleep's gentle tyranny. *Psychology Today,* 24–35.

Goleman, D. (1995). *Emotional intelligence.* New York: Bantam.

Good, M. (1995). A comparison of the effects of jaw relaxation and music on postoperative pain. *Nursing Research, 44*(1), 52–57.

Goodale, M. A. (1996). Visuomotor modules in the vertebrate brain. *Canadian Journal of Physiology and Pharmacology, 74*, 390–400.

Goodale, M. A., & Milner, A. D. (1992). Separate visual pathways for perception and action. *Trends in Neuroscience, 15*, 20–25.

Goodale, M. A., Milner, A. D., Jakobson, L. S., & Carey, D. P. (1991). A neurological dissociation between perceiving objects and grasping them. *Nature (London), 349*, 154–156.

Goodall, J. (1990). *Through a window: My thirty years with the chimpanzees of the Gombe.* Boston: Houghton Mifflin.

Goode, E. (1996). Gender and courtship entitlement: Responses to personal ads. *Sex Roles, 34*(3–4), 141–169.

Goodman, G. (1984). SASHA tapes: Expanding options for help-intended communication. In D. Larson (Ed.), *Teaching psychological skills.* Monterey, CA: Brooks/Cole.

Gopnik, A., Meltzoff, A. N., & Kuhl, P. K. (1999). *The scientist in the crib.* New York: William Morrow.

Gordon, T. (1970). *P. E. T. parent effectiveness training: A tested new way to raise children.* New York: Peter H. Wyden.

Gorman, J. M. (1996). *The essential guide to mental health.* New York: St. Martin's Griffin.

Gottesman, I. I. (1991). *Schizophrenia genesis: The origins of madness.* New York: W. H. Freeman & Company.

Gottlieb, G. (1998). Normally occurring environmental and behavioral influences on gene activity: From central dogma to probabilistic epigenesis. *Psychological Review, 105*(4), 792–802.

Gould, E., Reeves, A. J., & Gross, C. G. (1999). Neurogenesis in the neocortex of adult primates. *Science, 286*(5439), 548.

Gould, M. S., et al. (1998). Psychopathology associated with suicidal ideation and attempts among children and adolescents. *Journal of the American Academy of Child & Adolescent Psychiatry, 37*(9), 915–923.

Grack, C., & Richman, C. L. (1996). Reducing general and specific heterosexism through cooperative contact. *Journal of Psychology & Human Sexuality, 8*(4), 59–68.

Graffin, N. F., Ray, W. J., & Lundy, R. (1995). EEG concomitants of hypnosis and hypnotic susceptibility. *Journal of Abnormal Psychology, 104*(1), 123–131.

Graham, S. (1992). Most of the subjects were White and middle class. *American Psychologist, 47*, 629–639.

Graziottin, A. (1998). The biological basis of female sexuality. *International Clinical Psychopharmacology, 13*(Suppl 6), S15–S22.

Greene, D., & Lepper, M. R. (1974, September). How to turn play into work. *Psychology Today,* 49.

Greenfield, P. M., & Savage-Rumbaugh, E. S. (1993). Comparing communicative competence in child and chimp: The pragmatics of repetition. *Journal of Child Language, 20*(1), 1–26.

Greenglass, E. R., Burke, R. J., & Konarski, R. (1998). Components of burnout, resources, and gender-related differences. *Journal of Applied Social Psychology, 28*(12), 1088–1106.

Greenwald, A. G., Spangenberg, E. R., Pratkanis, A. R., & Eskenazi, J. (1991). Double-blind tests of subliminal self-help audiotapes. *Psychological Science, 2*(2), 119–122.

Gregory, R. L. (1990). *Eye and brain: The psychology of seeing.* Princeton, NJ: Princeton University Press.

Griffin, D. R. (1984). Animal thinking. *American Scientist, 72*, 456–463.

Grobstein, P., & Chow, K. L. (1975). Perceptive field development and individual experience. *Science, 190*, 352–358.

Groce, N. E. (1985). *Everyone Here Spoke Sign Language: Hereditary Deafness on the Island of Martha's Vineyard, Massachusetts.* Harvard University Press: Cambridge.

Grolnick, W. S., Cosgrove, T. J., & Bridges, L. J. (1996). Age-graded change in the initiative of positive affect. *Infant Behavior & Development, 19*(1), 153–157.

Groth-Marnat, G., & Schumaker, J. (1995). Psychologists in disease prevention and health promotion: A review of the cost effectiveness literature. *Psychology: A Journal of Human Behavior, 32*(1), 1–10.

Gruder, C. L., Mermelstein, R. J., Kirkendol, S., et al. (1993). Effects of social support and relapse prevention training as adjuncts to a televised smoking-cessation intervention. *Journal of Consulting & Clinical Psychology, 61*(1), 113–120.

Gruner, C. R., & Tighe, M. R. (1995). Semantic differential measurements of connotations of verbal terms and their doublespeak facsimiles in sentence contexts. *Psychological Reports, 77*(3, Pt 1) 778.

Guimond, S. (2000). Group socialization and prejudice: The social transmission of intergroup attitudes and beliefs. *European Journal of Social Psychology, 30*(3), 335–354.

Gump, B. B., & Kulik, J. A. (1997). Stress, affiliation, and emotional contagion. *Journal of Personality & Social Psychology, 72*(2), 305–319.

Gur, R. E., et al. (1998). A follow-up magnetic resonance imaging study of schizophrenia. *Archives of General Psychiatry, 55*(2), 145–152.

Gustavsson, J. P., et al. (1997). Stability and predictive ability of personality traits across 9 years. *Personality & Individual Differences, 22*(6), 783–791.

Haas, L. J., Benedict, J. G., & Kobos, J. C. (1996). Psychotherapy by telephone: Risks and benefits for psychologists and consumers. *Professional Psychology: Research & Practice, 27*(2), 154–160.

Haber, R. N. (1970, May). How we remember what we see. *Scientific American*, 104–112.

Hadjistavropoulos, T., & Genest, M. (1994). The underestimation of the role of physical attractiveness in dating preferences: Ignorance or taboo? *Canadian Journal of Behavioural Science, 26*(2), 298–318.

Hadwin, A. F., Kirby, J. R., & Woodhouse, R. A. (1999). Individual differences in notetaking, summarization and learning from lectures. *Alberta Journal of Educational Research, 45*(1), 1–17.

Haffenden, A. M., & Goodale, M. A. (1998). The effect of pictorial illusion on prehension and perception. *Journal of Cognitive Neuroscience, 10*(1), 122–136.

Haffenden, A. M., & Goodale, M. A. (2000). Independent effects of pictorial displays on perception and action. *Vision Research, 40*, 1597–1607.

Haier, R. J., Siegel, B. V., Nuechterlein, K. H., Hazlett, et al. (1988). Cortical glucose metabolic rate correlates of abstract reasoning and attention studied with positron emission tomography. *Intelligence, 12*, 199–217.

Hall, C. (1966). *The meaning of dreams.* New York: McGraw-Hill.

Hall, C. (1974). What people dream about. In R. L. Woods & H. B. Greenhouse (Eds.), *The new world of dreams: An anthology.* New York: Macmillan.

Hall, C., Domhoff, G. W., Blick, K. A., & Weesner, K. E. (1982). The dreams of college men and women in 1950 and 1980: A comparison of dream contents and sex differences. *Sleep, 5*(2), 188–194.

Hall, R. C. W., Platt, D. E., & Hall, R. C. W. (1999). Suicide risk assessment. *Psychosomatics, 40*(1), 18–27.

Hall, R. I. (1999). A study of policy formation in complex organizations: Emulating group decision-making with a simple artificial intelligence and a system model of corporate operations. *Journal of Business Research, 45*, 157–171.

Halonen, J. S. (1986). *Teaching critical thinking in psychology.* Milwaukee, WI: Alverno Productions.

Halpern, D. F. (1997). Sex differences in intelligence: Implications for education. *American Psychologist Special Issue: Intelligence & Lifelong Learning, 52*(10), 1091–1102.

Hamer, D., & Copeland, P. (1998). *Living with our genes.* New York: Anchor.

Hamill, J. A. (1995). Dexterity and sexuality: Is there a relationship? *Journal of Homosexuality, 28*(3–4), 375–396.

Hamilton, V. L., & Sanders, J. (1995). Crimes of obedience and conformity in the workplace. *Journal of Social Issues, 51*(3), 67–88.

Hamm, J., Matheson, W. R., & Honig, W. K. (1997). Mental rotation in pigeons (Columba livia)? *Journal of Comparative Psychology, 111*(1), 76–81.

Hammer, J. C., Fisher, J. D., Fitzgerald, P., & Fisher, W. A. (1996). When two heads aren't better than one: AIDS risk behavior in college-age couples. *Journal of Applied Social Psychology, 26*(5), 375–397.

Hammer, L. B., Grigsby, T. D., & Woods, S. (1998). The conflicting demands of work, family, and school among students at an urban university. *Journal of Psychology, 132*(2), 220–226.

Haney, M., Ward, A. S., Comer, S. D., Foltin, R. W., & Fischman, M. W. (1999). Abstinence symptoms following oral THC administration to humans. *Psychopharmacology, 141*(4), 385–394.

Hannon, K. (1996, May 13). Upset? Try cybertherapy. *U. S. News and World Report*, pp. 81–83.

Hansel, C. E. M. (1980). *ESP and parapsychology: A critical reevaluation.* Buffalo, NY: Prometheus.

Harding, R. W., et al. (1998). Road rage and the epidemiology of violence. *Studies on Crime & Crime Prevention, 7*(2), 221–238.

Hare, R. D. (1996). Psychopathy: A clinical construct whose time has come. *Criminal Justice and Behavior, 23*, 25–54.

Harland, R. E., & Coren, S. (2001). Individual differences in divergent thinking as a function of variations in sensory status. *Creativity Research Journal, 13*(3/4), 385–391.

Harlow, H. F., & Harlow, M. K. (1962). Social deprivation in monkeys. *Scientific American, 207*, 136–146.

Harlow, J. M. (1868). Recovery from the passage of an iron bar through the head. *Publications of the Massachusetts Medical Society, 2*, 327–347.

Harma, M., Laitinen, J., Partinen, M., & Suvanto, S. (1994). The effect of four-day round trip flights over 10 time zones on the circadian variation of salivary melatonin and cortisol in airline flight attendants. *Ergonomics, 37*(9), 1479–1489.

Harris, D. A. (1999, June). *Driving while black.* American Civil Liberties Union Special Report.

Harris, J. A., Rushton, J. P., Hampson, E., & Jackson, D. N. (1996). Salivary testosterone and self-report aggressive and pro-social personality characteristics in men and women. *Aggressive Behavior, 22*(5), 321–331.

Harris, J. R., & Liebert, R. M. (1991). *The child.* Englewood Cliffs, NJ: Prentice Hall.

Harris, L. J. (1993a). Do left-handers die sooner than right-handers? *Psychological Bulletin, 114*(2), 203–234.

Harris, L. J. (1993b). "Left-handedness and life span": Reply to Halpern and Coren. *Psychological Bulletin, 114*(2), 242–247.

Harrison, L. F., & Williams, T. M. (1986). Television and cognitive development. In T. M. Williams (Ed.), *The impact of television: A natural experiment in three communities.* Orlando, FL: Academic.

Harsch, N., & Neisser, U. (1989, November). *Substantial and irreversible errors in flashbulb memories of the* Challenger *explosion.* Poster presented at the meeting of the Psychonomic Society, Atlanta, GA.

Hart, B., & Risley, T. R. (1999). *The social world of children learning to talk.* Baltimore, MD: Paul H. Brookes.

Hartung, C. M., & Widiger, T. A. (1998). Gender differences in the diagnosis of mental disorders. *Psychological Bulletin, 123*(3), 260–278.

Harvey, C. A., Curson, D. A., Pantelis, C., & Taylor, J. (1996). Four behavioural syndromes of schizophrenia. *British Journal of Psychiatry, 168*(5), 562–570.

Hatfield, E., & Sprecher, S. (1995). Men's and women's preferences in marital partners in the United States, Russia, and Japan. *Journal of Cross-Cultural Psychology, 26*(6), 728–750.

Hathaway, S. R., & McKinley, J. C. (1989). *MMPI-2: Manual for administration and scoring.* Minneapolis, MN: University of Minnesota Press.

Hauri, P., & Linde, S. (1990). *No more sleepless nights.* New York: Wiley.

Hausfather, A., Toharia, A., LaRoche, C., & Engelsmann, F. (1997). Effects of age of entry, day-care quality and family characteristics on preschool behavior. *Journal of Child Psychology and Psychiatry and Allied Disciplines, 38*, 441–448.

Hawkins, M. J., Gray, C., & Hawkins, W. E. (1995, December 3). Gender difference of reported safer sex behaviors within a random sample of college students. *Psychological Reports, 77*(Pt 1), 963–968.

Hay, I., Ashman, A. F., & Van Kraayenoord, C. E. (1998). Educational characteristics of students with high or low self-concept. *Psychology in the Schools, 35*(4), 391–400.

Hayes, C. (1951). *The ape in our house.* New York: Harper & Row.

Hayne, H., & Rovee-Collier, C. (1995). The organization of reactivated memory in infancy. *Child Development, 66*(3), 893–906.

Health Canada. (2001). *Applicant's Quick Guide.* Document retrieved March 13, 2002, from http://www.hc-sc.gc.ca/hecs-sesc/ocma/applicants_qg.pdf.

Heath, L., & Gilbert, K. (1996). Mass media and fear of crime. *American Behavioral Scientist, 39*(4), 379–386.

Hebb, D. O. (1949). *The organization of behavior: A neuropsychological theory.* New York: Wiley.

Hebb, D. O. (1966). *A textbook of psychology.* Philadelphia: Saunders.

Heckhausen, J. (1987). Balancing for weaknesses and challenging developmental potential. *Developmental Psychology, 23*(6), 762–770.

Heermann, J. A., Jones, L. C., & Wikoff, R. L. (1994). Measurement of parent behavior during interactions with their infants. *Infant Behavior & Development, 17*(3), 311–321.

Heimann, M., & Meltzoff, A. N. (1996, March). Deferred imitation in 9- and 14-month-old infants. *British Journal of Developmental Psychology, 14*, 55–64.

Heine, S. J., & Lehman, D. R. (1999). Culture, self-discrepancies, and self-satisfaction. *Personality & Social Psychology Bulletin, 25*(8), 915–925.

Heine, S. J., Lehman, D. R., Markus, H. R., & Kitayama, S. (1999). Is there a universal need for positive self-regard? *Psychological Review, 106,* 766–794.

Heinrich, R. K., Corbine, J. L., & Thomas, K. R. (1990, November–December). Counseling Native Americans. *Journal of Counseling and Development, 69,* 128–133.

Heinrichs, R. W. (1993). Schizophrenia and the brain. *American Psychologist, 48*(3), 221–233.

Heinze, H. J., Hinrichs, H., Scholz, M., Burchert, W., & Mangun, G. R. (1998). Neural mechanisms of global and local processing. *Journal of Cognitive Neuroscience, 10*(4), 485–498.

Hellerstein, D. J., et al., (1998). A randomized prospective study comparing supportive and dynamic therapies. *Journal of Psychotherapy Practice & Research, 7*(4), 261–271.

Hellige, J. B. (1990). Hemispheric asymmetry. *Annual Review of Psychology, 41,* 55–60.

Hellige, J. B. (1993). *Hemispheric asymmetry.* Cambridge, MA: Harvard University Press.

Henderson, L. (1997). Mean MMPI profile of referrals to a shyness clinic. *Psychological Reports, 80*(2), 695–702.

Henderson, N. D. (1982). Human behavior genetics. *Annual Review of Psychology, 33,* 403–440.

Hendrick, S. S., & Hendrick, C. (1993). Lovers as friends. *Journal of Social & Personal Relationships, 10*(3), 459–466.

Henningfield, J. E., & Heishman, S. J. (1995). The addictive role of nicotine in tobacco use. *Psychopharmacology, 117*(1), 11–13.

Hepper, P. G., McCartney, G. R., & Shannon, E. A. (1998). Lateralised behaviour in first trimester human foetuses. *Neuropsychologia, 36*(6), 531–534.

Herbert. T. B., & Cohen, S. (1993). Depression and immunity. *Psychological Bulletin, 113*(3), 472–486.

Herrnstein, R., & Murray, C. (1994). *The bell curve.* New York: Free Press.

Herron, R. E., Hillis, S. L., Mandarino, D. W., & Orme-Johnson, D. W. (1996). The impact of the Transcendental Meditation Program on government payments to physicians in Quebec. *American Journal of Health Promotion, 10,* 208–216.

Higbee, K. L., Clawson, C., DeLano, L., & Campbell, S. (1990). Using the link mnemonic to remember errands. *Psychological Record, 40*(3), 429–436.

Hilgard, E. R. (1968). *The experience of hypnosis.* New York: Harcourt Brace Jovanovich.

Hilts, P. J. (1995). *Memory's ghost.* New York: Simon & Schuster.

Hirt, M., & Pithers, W. (1991). Selective attention and levels of coding in schizophrenia. *British Journal of Clinical Psychology, 30*(2), 139–149.

Hixon, M. D. (1998). Ape language research: A review and behavioral perspective. *Analysis of Verbal Behavior, 15,* 17–39.

Hobson, J. A. (1999). Order from chaos. In R. Conlan (Ed.), *States of mind.* New York: Wiley.

Hobson, J. A., Pace-Schott, E. F., Stickgold, R., & Kahn, D. (1998). To dream or not to dream? *Current Opinion in Neurobiology, 8*(2), 239–244.

Hochstenbach, J., Mulder, T., van Limbeek, J., Donders, R., & Schoonderwaldt, H. (1998). Cognitive decline following stroke. *Journal of Clinical & Experimental Neuropsychology, 20*(4), 503–517.

Hodapp, R. M. (1994). Mental retardation. *Encyclopedia of human behavior,* Vol. 3, 175–185.

Hoffman, D. D. (1999). *Visual intelligence.* New York: Norton.

Hogben, M. (1998). Factors moderating the effect of televised aggression on viewer behavior. *Communication Research, 25*(2), 220–247.

Holden, C. (1980, November). Twins reunited. *Science, 80,* 55–59.

Holmes, D. S. (1984). Meditation and somatic arousal reduction: A review of the experimental evidence. *American Psychologist, 39*(1), 1–10.

Holmes, D. S., Solomon, S., Cappo, B. M., & Greenberg, J. L. (1983). Effects of transcendental meditation versus resting on physiological and subjective arousal. *Journal of Personality & Social Psychology, 44,* 1245–1252.

Holmes, T., & Masuda, M. (1972, April). Psychosomatic syndrome. *Psychology Today, 71.*

Hopson, J. L. (1986, June). The unraveling of insomnia. *Psychology Today,* 43–49.

Horgan, J. (1995, November). Get smart, take a test: A long-term rise in IQ scores baffles intelligence experts. *Scientific American,* 2–14.

Horn, J. M., Loehlin, J. C., & Willerman, L. (1979). Intellectual resemblance among adoptive and biological relatives: The Texas adoption project. *Behavior Genetics, 9,* 177–207.

Horn, O., Paradis, G., Potvin, L., Macaulay, A. C., & Desrosiers, S. (2001). Correlates and predictors of adiposity among Mohawk children. *Preventive Medicine: An International Journal Devoted to Practice and Theory, 33*(4), 274–281.

Horne, J. A., & Reyner, L. A. (1996). Counteracting driver sleepiness: Effects of napping, caffeine, and placebo. *Psychophysiology, 33*(3), 306–309.

Horvath, A. O., & Goheen, M. D. (1990). Factors mediating the success of defiance- and compliance-based interventions. *Journal of Counseling Psychology, 37*(4), 363–371.

Hosch, H. M., & Cooper, D. S. (1982). Victimization as a determinant of eyewitness accuracy. *Journal of Applied Psychology, 67,* 649–652.

Howard, K. I., Kopta, S. M., Krause, M. S., & Orlinsky, D. E. (1986). The dose-effect relationship in psychotherapy. *American Psychologist, 41,* 159–164.

Howes, C. (1997). Children's experiences in center-based child care as a function of teacher background and adult:child ratio. *Merrill-Palmer Quarterly, 43*(3), 404–425.

Hsia, Y., & Graham, C. H. (1997). Color blindness. In A. Byrne, D. R. Hilbert, et al. (Eds.), *Readings on color, Vol. 2: The science of color.* Cambridge, MA: The MIT Press.

Hubble, M. A., Duncan, B. L., & Miller, S. D. (Eds.). (1999). *The heart and soul of change: What works in therapy.* Washington, DC: American Psychological Association.

Hubel, D. H. (1979a). The visual cortex of normal and deprived monkeys. *American Scientist, 67,* 532–543.

Hubel, D. H. (1979b, September). The brain. *Scientific American, 241,* 45–53.

Hubel, D. H., & Wiesel, T. N. (1979). Brain mechanisms of vision. *Scientific American, 241,* 150–162.

Huebner, R. (1998). Hemispheric differences in global/local processing revealed by same-different judgements. *Visual Cognition, 5*(4), 457–478.

Huesmann, L. R. (1986). Psychological processes promoting the relation between exposure to media violence and aggressive behavior by the viewer. *Journal of Social Issues, 42*(3), 125–139.

Huesmann, L. R., Eron, L., Klein, L., Brice, P., & Fischer, P. (1983). Mitigating the imitation of aggressive behaviors by changing children's attitudes about media violence. *Journal of Personality & Social Psychology, 44,* 899–910.

Huesmann, L. R., Moise, J. F., & Podolski, C. (1997). The effects of media violence on the development of antisocial behavior. In D. M. Stoff et al. (Eds.), *Handbook of antisocial behavior.*

Hughes, J. N., & Hasbrouck, J. E. (1996). Television violence: Implications for violence prevention. *School Psychology Review, 25*(2), 134–151.

Hughes, J. R., Oliveto, A. H., Liguori, A., Carpenter, J., & Howard, T. (1998). Endorsement of DSM-IV dependence criteria among caffeine users. *Drug & Alcohol Dependence, 52*(2), 99–107.

Humphries, S. A., Johnson, M. H., & Long, N. R. (1996). An investigation of the gate control theory of pain using the experimental pain stimulus of potassium iontophoresis. *Perception & Psychophysics, 58*(5), 693–703.

Hunsley, J., Lee, C. M., & Aubry, T. (1999). Who uses psychological services in Canada? *Canadian Psychology, 40,* 232–240.

Hunt E. (1995, July–August). The role of intelligence in modern society. *American Scientist, 83,* 356–368.

Hunter, E. (1998). Adolescent attraction to cults. *Adolescence, 33*(131), 709–714.

Hyman, R. (1996a). Evaluation of the military's twenty-year program on psychic spying. *Skeptical Inquirer, 20*(2), 21–23.

Hyman, R. (1996b). The evidence for psychic functioning: Claims vs. reality. *Skeptical Inquirer, 20*(2), 24–26.

Hyman, S. (1999). Susceptibility and "Second Hits." In R. Conlan (Ed.), *States of mind.* New York: Wiley.

Iacono, W. G., & Lykken, D. T. (1997). The validity of the lie detector. *Journal of Applied Psychology, 82*(3), 426–433.

Ickes, W. (1993). Traditional gender roles: Do they make, then break, our relationships? *Journal of Social Issues, 49*(3), 71–86.

Institute of Medicine. (1990). *Broadening the base of treatment for alcohol problems.* Washington, DC: National Academy Press.

Isaac, R. J., & Armat, V. C. (1990). *Madness in the streets: How psychiatry & the law abandoned the mentally ill.* New York: Free Press.

Isaak, M. I., & Just, A. (1995). Constraints on thinking in insight and invention. In R. J. Sternberg & J. E. Davidson (Eds.), *The nature of insight.* Cambridge, MA: MIT Press.

Isabella, R. A. (1993). Origins of attachment. *Child Development, 64*(2), 605–621.

Isabella, R. A., & Belsky, J. (1991). Interactional synchrony and the origins of infant–mother attachment. *Child Development, 62,* 373–384.

Isenberg, P. L., & Schatzberg, A. F. (1976). Psychoanalytic contribution to a theory of depression. In

J. O. Cole, A. F. Schatzberg, & S. H. Frazier (Eds.), *Depression: Biology, psychodynamics, and treatment.* New York: Plenum.

Isser, N. (1991). Why cultic groups develop and flourish. *Cultic Studies Journal, 8*(2), 104–121.

Ito, T. A., Miller, N., & Pollock, V. E. (1996). Alcohol and aggression. *Psychological Bulletin, 120*(1), 60–82.

Ivey, A. E., & Galvin, M. (1984). Microcounseling: A metamodel for counseling, therapy, business, and medical interviews. In D. Larson (Ed.), *Teaching psychological skills.* Monterey, CA: Brooks/Cole.

Izard, C. E. (1977). *Human emotions.* New York: Plenum.

Izard, C. E. (1990). Facial expressions and the regulation of emotions. *Journal of Personality & Social Psychology, 58*(3), 487–498.

Izard, C. E., Fantauzzo, C. A., Castle, J. M., Haynes, O. M., Rayias, M. F., & Putnam, P. H. (1995). The ontogeny and significance of infants' facial expressions in the first 9 months of life. *Developmental Psychology, 31*(6), 997–1013.

Jackson, T., Towson, S., & Narduzzi, K. (1997). Predictors of shyness. *Social Behavior & Personality, 25*(2), 149–154.

Jacobsen, P. B., Bovbjerg, D. H., Schwartz, M. D., et al., (1993). Formation of food aversions in cancer patients receiving repeated infusions of chemotherapy. *Behavior Research & Therapy, 31*(8), 739–748.

Jaeger, J. J., Lockwood, A. H., Van Valin, R. D., Jr., Kemmerer, D. L., et al. (1998). Sex differences in brain regions activated by grammatical and reading tasks. *Neuroreport: An International Journal for the Rapid Communication of Research in Neuroscience, 9*(12), 2803–2807.

Jahn, R. G. (1982). The persistent paradox of psychic phenomena. *Proceedings of the IEEE, 70*(2), 136–166.

James, W. (1890). *The principles of psychology.* New York: Dover.

Janes, L. M., & Olson, J. M. (2000). Jeer pressures: The behavioral effects of observing ridicule of others. *Personality and Social Psychology Bulletin, 26*(4), 474–485.

Jang, K. L., et al. (1998). Heritability of facet-level traits in a cross-cultural twin sample: Support for a hierarchical model of personality. *Journal of Personality and Social Psychology, 74,* 1556–1565.

Jang, K. L., & Livesley, W. J. (1998). Support for a hierarchical model of personality. *Journal of Personality and Social Psychology, 74*(6), 1556–1565.

Janis, I. L. (1989). *Crucial decisions.* New York: Free Press.

Janowiak, J. J., & Hackman, R. (1994). Meditation and college students' self-actualization and rated stress. *Psychological Reports, 75*(2), 1007–1010.

Janus, S. S., & Janus, C. L. (1993). *The Janus report.* New York: Wiley.

Jarvik, E. M. (1964). Ciba found. In H. Steinberg et al. (Eds.), *Symposium of animal pharmacology drug action.*

Jarvik, M. E. (1995). "The scientific case that nicotine is addictive": Comment. *Psychopharmacology, 117*(1), 18–20.

Jeeves, M. A. (1994). Callosal agenesis—A natural split brain: An overview. In M. Lassonde & M. A. Jeeves (Eds.), *Callosal agenesis: A natural split brain?* (pp. 285–299). New York: Plenum Press.

Jellinek, E. M. (1960). *The disease concept of alcoholism.* New Haven: Hill House.

Jenkins, J. G., & Dallenbach, K. M. (1924). Oblivescence during sleep and waking. *American Journal of Psychology, 35,* 605–612.

Jerabek, I., & Standing, L. (1992). Imagined test situations produce contextual memory enhancement. *Perceptual & Motor Skills, 75*(2), 400.

Johnson, J. G., & Sherman, M. F. (1997). Daily hassles mediate the relationship between major life events and psychiatric symptomatology. *Journal of Social & Clinical Psychology, 16*(4), 389–404.

Johnson, K. E., & Mervis, C. B. (1997). Effects of varying levels of expertise on the basic level of categorization. *Journal of Experimental Psychology: General, 126*(3), 248–277.

Johnson, M. H., Breakwell, G., Douglas, W., & Humphries, S. (1998). The effects of imagery and sensory detection distractors on different measures of pain. *British Journal of Psychology, 37*(2), 141–154.

Johnson, S. M., & White, G. (1971). Self-observation as an agent of behavioral change. *Behavior Therapy, 2,* 488–497.

Johnson, S. P., & Nanez, J. E. (1995). Young infants' perception of object unity in two-dimensional displays. *Infant Behavior & Development, 18*(2), 133–143.

Johnsrude, I. S., Owen, A. M., Zhao, W. V., & White, N. M. (1999). Conditioned preference in humans. *Learning & Motivation, 30*(3), 250–264.

Jolicoeur, P., & Dell'Acqua, R. (1999). Attentional and structural constraints on visual encoding. *Psychological Research/Psychologische Forschung* Special Issue: Vision and visual cognition. *62*(2–3), 154–164.

Jones, E. E., & Nisbett, R. E. (1971). The actor and observer: Divergent perceptions of the causes of behavior. In E. E. Jones, D. E. Kanouse, H. H. Kelley, R. E. Nisbett, S. Valins, & B. Weiner (Eds.), *Attribution: Perceiving the causes of behavior.* Morristown, NJ: General Learning Press.

Jones, L., & Petruzzi, D. C. (1995). Test anxiety: A review of theory and current treatment. *Journal of College Student Psychotherapy, 10*(1), 3–15.

Jones, M. K., & Menzies, R. G. (1998). Danger ideation reduction therapy (DIRT) for obsessive-compulsive washers. *Behaviour Research & Therapy, 36*(10), 959–970.

Jones, R. T., Corbin, S. K., Sheehy, L., & Bruce, S. (1995). Substance refusal: More than "just say no." *Journal of Child & Adolescent Substance Abuse, 4*(2) 1–26.

Jones, S. S., Collins, K., & Hong, H. W. (1991). An audience effect on smile production in 10-month-old infants. *Psychological Science, 2,* 45–49.

Jourard, S. M. (1974). *Healthy personality.* New York: Macmillan.

Jouvet, M. (1999). *The paradox of sleep.* Boston: MIT Press.

Joy, L. A., Kimball, M. M., & Zabrack, M. L. (1986). Television and aggressive behavior. In T. M. Williams (Ed.), *The impact of television: A natural experiment involving three towns.* New York: Academic.

Julien, R. M. (1998). *A primer of drug action.* San Francisco: Freeman.

Jurma, W. E., & Powell, M. L. (1994). Perceived gender roles of managers and effective conflict management. *Psychological Reports, 74*(1), 104–106.

Jussim, L., & Eccles, J. S. (1992). Teacher expectations. *Journal of Personality & Social Psychology, 63*(6), 947–961.

Juster, H. R., Heimberg, R. G., Frost, R. O., & Holt, C. S. (1996). Social phobia and perfectionism. *Personality & Individual Differences, 21*(3), 403–410.

Kagan, J. (1971). *Change and continuity in infancy.* New York: Wiley.

Kagan, J. (1989). Temperamental contributions to social behavior. *American Psychologist, 44*(4), 668–674.

Kagan, J. (1999). Born to be shy? In R. Conlan (Ed.), *States of mind.* New York: Wiley.

Kahneman, D., & Tversky, A. (1972). Subjective probability: A judgment of representativeness. *Cognitive psychology, 3,* 430–454.

Kahneman, D., & Tversky, A. (1973). On the psychology of prediction. *Psychological Review, 80,* 237–251.

Kahneman, D., Slovic, P., & Tversky, A. (1982). *Judgment under uncertainty: Heuristics and biases.* Cambridge: Cambridge University Press.

Kaitz, M., Zvi, H., Levy, M., Berger, A., et al. (1995). The uniqueness of mother–own-infant interactions. *Infant Behavior & Development, 18*(2), 247–252.

Kakigi, R., Matsuda, Y., & Kuroda, Y. (1993). Effects of movement-related cortical activities on pain-related somatosensory evoked potentials. *Acta Neurologica Scandinavica, 88*(5), 376–380.

Kalal, D. M. (1999). Critical thinking in clinical practice: Pseudoscience, fad psychology, and the behavioral therapist. *The Behavior Therapist, 22*(4), 81–84.

Kallberg, V. P. (1992). *The effect of reflector posts on driving behaviour and accidents on two-lane rural roads in Finland (Report 59/1992).* Helsinki: The Finnish National Road Administration Technical Development Centre.

Kamin, L. J. (1981). *The intelligence controversy.* New York: Wiley.

Kamphaus, R. W. (1993). *Clinical assessment of children's intelligence.* Needham Heights, MA: Allyn and Bacon.

Kandel, E. (1999). Of learning, memory, and genetic switches. In R. Conlan (Ed.), *States of mind.* New York: Wiley.

Kaplan, P. S. (1998). *The human odyssey.* Pacific Grove, CA: Brooks/Cole.

Kaplan, P. S., Goldstein, M. H., Huckeby, E. R., & Cooper, R. P. (1995). Habituation, sensitization, and infants' responses to motherese speech. *Developmental Psychobiology, 28*(1), 45–57.

Kapleau, P. (1966). *The three pillars of Zen.* New York: Harper & Row.

Karlberg, L. Krakau, I., & Unden, A. (1998). Type A behavior intervention in primary health care reduces hostility and time pressure. *Social Science & Medicine, 46*(3), 397–402.

Karlins, M., Coffman, T. L., & Walters, G. (1969). On the fading of social stereotypes: Studies in three generations of college students. *Journal of Personality & Social Psychology, 13*(1), 1–16.

Karon, B. P., & Widener, A. J. (1997). Repressed memories and World War II: Lest we forget! *Professional Psychology: Research & Practice, 28*(4), 338–340.

Karon, B. P., & Widener, A. (1998). Repressed memories: The real story. *Professional Psychology: Research & Practice, 29*(5), 482–487.

Kasper, M. E., Rogers, R., & Adams, P. A. (1996). Dangerousness and command hallucinations. *Bulletin* of the American Academy of Psychiatry & the Law, 24(2), 219–224.

Kasser, T., & Ryan, R. M. (1996). Further examining the American dream: Differential correlates of intrinsic and extrinsic goals. Personality & Social Psychology Bulletin, 22(3), 280–287.

Kassin, S. M., Ellsworth, P. C., & Smith, V. L. (1989). The "general acceptance" of psychological research on eyewitness testimony: A survey of the experts. American Psychologist, 44, 1089–1098.

Kaufman, A. S. (2000). Intelligence tests and school psychology: Predicting the future by studying the past. Psychology in the Schools, 37(1), 7–16.

Kaufman, L., & Kaufman, J. H. (2000). Explaining the moon illusion. Proceedings of the National Academy of Sciences, 97(1), 500–505.

Kazdin, A. E. (1975). Behavior modification in applied settings. Homewood, IL: Dorsey Press.

Kebbell, M. R., & Wagstaff, G. F. (1998). Hypnotic interviewing: The best way to interview eyewitnesses? Behavioral Sciences & the Law, 16(1), 115–129.

Kellehear, A. (1993). Culture, biology, and the near-death experience. Journal of Nervous & Mental Disease, 181(3), 148–156.

Keller, M. C., & Young, R. K. (1996). Mate assortment in dating and married couples. Personality & Individual Differences, 21(2), 217–221.

Kellermann, A. L., Rivara, F. P., Rushforth, N. B., Banton, J. G., et al. (1993). Gun ownership as a risk factor for homicide in the home. New England Journal of Medicine, 329(15), 1084–1091.

Kelley, H. H. (1950). The warm-cold variable in first impressions of persons. Journal of Personality, 18, 431–439.

Kellner, C. H. (1998). ECT in the media. Psychiatric Annals, 28(9), 528–529.

Kelly, I. W. (1998). Why astrology doesn't work. Psychological Reports, 82, 527–546.

Kelly, I. W. (1999, November–December). "Debunking the debunkers": A response to an astrologer's debunking of skeptics. Skeptical Inquirer, 37–43.

Kelly, I. W., & Saklofske, D. H. (1994). Psychology and pseudoscience. Encyclopedia of human behavior, Vol. 3, 611–618.

Kelly, T. H., Foltin, R. W., Emurian, C. S., & Fischman, M. W. (1990). Multidimensional behavioral effects of marijuana. Progress in Neuro-Psychopharmacology & Biological Psychiatry, 14(6), 885–902.

Kelman, H. C., & Hamilton, V. L. (1989). Crimes of obedience. New Haven, CT: Yale University Press.

Kemp, M. (1998). Why is learning American Sign Language a challenge? Accident Analysis & Prevention, 143(3), 255–259.

Kennedy, P. R., & Bakay, R. A. (1998). Restoration of neural output from a paralyzed patient by a direct brain connection. Neuroreport, 9(8), 1707–1711.

Kenneth, M., Carpenter, K. M., & Hasin, D. S. (1998). Reasons for drinking alcohol. Psychology of Addictive Behaviors, 12(3), 168–184.

Kenrick, D. T., & MacFarlane, S. W. (1986). Ambient temperature and horn honking: A field study of the heat/aggression relationship. Environment and Behavior, 18(2), 179–191.

Kessler, R. C. (1997). The effects of stressful life events on depression. Annual Review of Psychology, 48, 191–214.

Kety, S. S. (1979, September). Disorders of the human brain. Scientific American, 241, 202–214.

Kiecolt-Glaser, J. K., & Glaser, R. (1992). Psychoneuroimmunology: Can psychological interventions modulate immunity? Journal of Consulting & Clinical Psychology, 60(4), 569–575.

Kihlstrom, J. F. (1985). Hypnosis. Annual Review of Psychology, 36, 385–418.

Killen, J. D., & Fortmann, S. P. (1997). Craving is associated with smoking relapse. Experimental & Clinical Psychopharmacology, 5(2) 137–142.

Kim, A., Martin, D., & Martin, M. (1989). Effects of personality on marital satisfaction. Family Therapy, 16(3), 243–248.

Kim, S. (2000, December). Bogglers. Discover, 98.

Kimball, M. M. (1986). Television and sex-role attitudes. In T. M. Williams (Ed.), The impact of television: A natural experiment in three communities. Orlando, FL: Academic.

Kimble, G. A. (1989). Psychology from the standpoint of a generalist. American Psychologist, 44(3), 491–499.

Kimmel, D. C. (1990). Adulthood and aging. New York: Wiley & Sons.

Kimura, D. (1996). Sex, sexual orientation and sex hormones influence human cognitive function. Current Opinion in Neurobiology, 6, 259–263.

Kimura, D. (1999). Sex differences in the brain. Scientific American, 10, Summer Quarterly, 26–31.

King, K. B. (1997). Psychologic and social aspects of cardiovascular disease. Annals of Behavioral Medicine, 19(3), 264–270.

King, L., & Napa, C. (1998). What makes a life good? Journal of Personality and Social Psychology, 75(1) 156–165.

King, L. A., Richards, J. H., & Stemmerich, E. (1998). Daily goals, life goals, and worst fears. Journal of Personality, 66(5), 713–744.

Kipnis, D. (1987). Psychology and behavioral technology. American Psychologist, 42, 30–36.

Kirouac, G., & Hess, U. (1999). Group membership and the decoding of nonverbal behavior. In P. Philippot, R. S. Feldman, & E. J. Coats (Eds.), The social context of nonverbal behavior: Studies in emotion and social interaction. New York: Cambridge University Press.

Kirsch, I., & Lynn, S. J. (1995). The altered state of hypnosis. American Psychologist, 50(10), 846–858.

Kirsch, I., & Lynn, S. J. (1999). Automaticity in clinical psychology. American Psychologist, 54(7), 504–515.

Kirsch, I., Montgomery, G., & Sapirstein, G. (1995). Hypnosis as an adjunct to cognitive behavioral psychotherapy: A meta-analysis. Journal of Consulting and Clinical Psychology, 63, 214–220.

Kirsch, I., & Sapirstein, G. (1998). Listening to Prozac but hearing placebo: A meta-analysis of antidepressant medication. Prevention & Treatment, 1, np.

Kirsh, S. J. (1998). Seeing the world through Mortal Kombat-colored glasses. Childhood: A Global Journal of Child Research, 5(2), 177–184.

Kisilevsky, B. S., & Low, J. A. (1998). Human fetal behavior. Developmental Review, 18(1), 1–29.

Kitayama, S., Markus, H. R., Matsumoto, H., & Norasakkunkit, V. (1997). Individual and collective processes in the construction of the self. Journal of Personality & Social Psychology, 72(6), 1245–1267.

Klaus, M. H., & Kennell, J. H. (1982). Parent–infant bonding. St. Louis: Mosby.

Klebanoff, M. A., Levine, R. J., DerSimonian, R., Clemens, J. D., & Wilkins, D. G. (1999). Maternal serum paraxanthine, a caffeine metabolite, and the risk of spontaneous abortion. New England Journal of Medicine, 341(22), 1639–1644.

Klein, S. B., Loftus, J., & Kihlstrom, J. F. (1996). Self-knowledge of an amnesic patient. Journal of Experimental Psychology: General, 125(3), 250–260.

Kleinke, C. L., Peterson, T. R., & Rutledge, T. R. (1998). Effects of self-generated facial expressions on mood. Journal of Personality and Social Psychology, 74(1), 272–279.

Kleinknecht, R. A. (1986). The anxious self: Diagnosis and treatment of fears and phobias. New York: Human Sciences Press.

Knesper, D. J., Belcher, B. E., & Cross, J. G. (1989). A market analysis comparing the practices of psychiatrists and psychologists. Archives of General Psychiatry, 46(4), 305–314.

Koenig, S. M. (1996). Central sleep apnea. Virginia Medical Quarterly, 123(4), 247–250.

Koepke, J. E., & Bigelow, A. E. (1997). Observations of newborn suckling behavior. Infant Behavior & Development, 20(1), 93–98.

Kohn, A. (1987, September). Art for art's sake. Psychology Today, 52–57.

Kohn, A. (1988, March 21). Shock therapy makes a comeback. Los Angeles Times, Part II, p. 5.

Kolb, B., & Whishaw, I. Q. (1998). Brain plasticity and behavior. Annual Review of Psychology, 49, 43–64.

Kolbe, L. J., Collins, J., & Cortese, P. (1997). Building the capacity of schools to improve the health of the nation. American Psychologist, 52(3), 256–265.

Kolers, P. A. (1975). Specificity of operations in sentence recognition. Cognitive Psychology, 7(3), 289–306.

Konner, M. (1991). Childhood. Boston: Little, Brown.

Kopta, M. S., Lueger, R. J., Saunders, S. M., & Howard, K. I. (1999). Individual psychotherapy outcome and process research. Annual Review of Psychology, 50, 441–469.

Kosslyn, S. M. (1983). Ghosts in the mind's machine. New York: Norton.

Kosslyn, S. M. (1985, May). Stalking the mental image. Psychology Today, 23–28.

Kosslyn, S. M., et al. (2000). Hypnotic visual illusion alters color processing in the brain. American Journal of Psychiatry, 157(8), 1279–1284.

Kosslyn, S. M., Ball, T. M., & Reiser, B. J. (1978). Visual images preserve metric spatial information: Evidence from studies of image scanning. Journal of Experimental Psychology: Human Perception and Performance, 4, 47–60.

Kosslyn, S. M., Seger, C., Pani, J. R., & Hillger, L. A. (1990). When is imagery used in everyday life? A diary study. Journal of Mental Imagery, 14(3–4), 131–152.

Kosslyn, S. M., Thompson, W. L., & Alpert, N. N. (1995). Topographical representation of mental images in primary visual cortex. Nature, 378(6556), 496.

Kotkin, M., Daviet, C., & Gurin, J. (1996). The Consumer Reports mental health survey. American Psychologist, 51(10), 1080–1082.

Kottler, J. A., & Brown, R. W. (1999). Introduction to therapeutic counseling. Monterey, CA: Brooks/Cole.

Kozlowski, L. T., Goldberg, M. E., Yost, B. A., White, E., et al. (1998). Smokers' misperceptions of light and ultra-light cigarettes may keep them smoking. *American Journal of Preventive Medicine, 15*(1), 9–16.

Krakow, B., Kellner, R., Pathak, D., & Lambert, L. (1996). Long-term reduction of nightmares with imagery rehearsal treatment. *Behavioural & Cognitive Psychotherapy, 24*(2), 135–148.

Krakow, B., & Neidhardt, J. (1992). *Conquering bad dreams and nightmares.* New York: Berkley Books.

Krantz, L. (1995). *Jobs rated almanac.* New York: Wiley.

Kratofil, P. H., Baberg, H. T., & Dimsdale, J. E. (1996). Self-mutilation and severe self-injurious behavior associated with amphetamine psychosis. *General Hospital Psychiatry, 18*(2), 117–120.

Kring, A. M., & Gordon, A. H. (1998). Sex differences in emotion. *Journal of Personality & Social Psychology, 74*(3), 686–703.

Kroon, M. B., Van Kreveld, D., & Rabbie, J. M. (1992). Group versus individual decision making: Effects of accountability and gender on groupthink. *Small Group Research, 23*(4), 427–458.

Kropp, P., et al. (1997). Behavioral treatment in migraine. *Functional Neurology, 12*(1), 17–24.

Krosnick, J. A. (1999). Survey research. *Annual Review of Psychology, 50*, 537–567.

Krueger, J., Ham, J. J., & Linford, K. M. (1996). Perceptions of behavioral consistency: Are people aware of the actor-observer effect? *Psychological Science, 7*(5), 259–264.

Kruger, L., & Liebeskind, J. C. (Eds.). (1984). *Advances in pain research and therapy.* New York: Raven Press.

Kubovy, M., & Holcombe, A. O. (1998). On the lawfulness of grouping by proximity. *Cognitive psychology, 35*(1), 71–98.

Kunkel, M. A. (1993). A teaching demonstration involving perceived lunar size. *Teaching of Psychology, 20*(3), 178–180.

Kunzendorf, R. G. (1989). Afterimages of eidetic images: A developmental study. *Journal of Mental Imagery, 13*(1), 55–62.

Kusseling, F. S., Shapiro, M. F., Greenberg, J. M., & Wenger, N. S. (1996). Understanding why heterosexual adults do not practice safer sex: A comparison of two samples. *AIDS Education & Prevention, 8*(3), 247–257.

La Berge, S. P. (1981, January). Lucid dreaming: Directing the action as it happens. *Psychology Today,* 48–57.

La Berge, S. P. (1985). *Lucid dreaming.* Los Angeles: Tarcher.

Laan, E., Everaerd, W., van der Velde, J., & Geer, J. H. (1995). Determinants of subjective experience of sexual arousal in women. *Psychophysiology, 32*(5), 444–451.

Labov, W. (1973). The boundaries of words and their meanings. In C. J. N. Bailey & R. W. Shuy (Eds.), *New ways of analyzing variation in English.* Washington, DC: Georgetown University Press.

Lacayo, A. (1995). Neurologic and psychiatric complications of cocaine abuse. *Neuropsychiatry, Neuropsychology, & Behavioral Neurology, 8*(1), 53–60.

Lachman, M. E., & Weaver, S. L. (1998). The sense of control as a moderator of social class differences in health and well-being. *Journal of Personality & Social Psychology, 74*(3) 763–773.

Lacks, P., & Morin, C. M. (1992). Recent advances in the assessment and treatment of insomnia. *Journal of Consulting and Clinical Psychology, 60*(4), 586–594.

Ladouceur, R., & Dube, D. (1997). Monetary incentive and erroneous perceptions in American roulette. *Psychology: A Journal of Human Behaviour, 34*(3–4), 27–32.

Ladouceur, R., & Gaboury, A. (1988). Effects of limited and unlimited stakes on gambling behavior. *Journal of Gambling Behavior, 4*(2), 119–126.

Lal, S. K. L., et al. (1998). Effect of feedback signal and psychological characteristics on blood pressure self-manipulation capability. *Psychophysiology, 35*(4), 405–412.

Lalonde, R., & Badescu, R. (1995). Exploratory drive, frontal lobe function and adipsia in aging. *Gerontology, 41*(3), 134–144.

Lam, R. W., Goldner, E. M., & Grewal, A. (1996). Seasonality of symptoms in anorexia and bulimia nervosa. In R. W. Lam (Ed.), *Seasonal affective disorder and beyond: Light treatment for SAD and non-SAD conditions.* Washington: American Psychiatric Press.

Lam, R. W., Lee, S. K., Tam, E. M., Grewal, A., & Yatham, L. N. (2001). An open trial of light therapy for women with seasonal affective disorder and comorbid bulimia nervosa. *Journal of Clinical Psychiatry, 62*(3), 164–168.

Lamb, M. R., & Yund, E. W. (1996). Spatial frequency and attention. *Perception & Psychophysics, 58*(3), 363–373.

Lambert, M. J. (1999). Are differential treatment effects inflated by researcher therapy allegiance? *Clinical Psychology: Science & Practice, 6*(1), 127–130.

Lambert, M. J., & Cattani-Thompson, K. (1996). Current

findings regarding the effectiveness of counseling. *Journal of Counseling & Development, 74*(6), 601–608.

Lance, C. E., LaPointe, J. A., & Stewart, A. M. (1994). A test of the context dependency of three causal models of halo rater error. *Journal of Applied Psychology, 79*(3), 332–340.

Langer, E. J., & Abelson, R. P. (1974). A patient by any other name: Clinician group difference in labeling bias. *Journal of Consulting and Clinical Psychology, 42*(1), 4–9.

Langer, E. J., & Piper, A. I. (1987). Prevention of mindlessness. *Journal of Personality & Social Psychology, 53*, 280–287.

Langlois, S., & Morrison, P. (2002). Suicide deaths and suicide attempts. *Health Reports, 13*, 9–22 (Statistics Canada, Catalogue No. 82–003–XIE). Document retrieved July 5, 2002, from http://estat.statcan.ca/Estat/Content/English/articles/health-reports/hr13–2.pdf.

Lanzetta, J. T., & Englis, B. G. (1989). Expectations of cooperation and competition and their effects on observers' vicarious emotional responses. *Journal of Personality & Social Psychology, 56*(4), 543–554.

Larner, A. J., Moss, J., Rossi, M. L., & Anderson, M. (1994). Congenital insensitivity to pain. *Journal of Neurology, Neurosurgery & Psychiatry, 57*(8), 973–974.

Larsen, R. J., & Kasimatis, M. (1990). Individual differences in entrainment of mood to the weekly calendar. *Journal of Personality & Social Psychology, 58*(1), 164–171.

Larson, C. A., & Carey, K. B. (1998). Caffeine. *Professional Psychology: Research & Practice, 29*(4), 373–376.

Larson, D. E. (Ed.). (1990). *Mayo Clinic family healthbook.* New York: Morrow.

Lassonde, M. (1994). Disconnection syndrome in callosal agenesis. In M. Lassonde & M. A. Jeeves (Eds.), *Callosal agenesis: A natural split brain?* (pp. 275–284). New York: Plenum Press.

Latané, L., Nida, S. A., & Wilson, D. W. (1981). The effects of group size on helping behavior. In J. P. Rushton & R. M. Sorrentino (Eds.), *Altruism and helping behavior: Social, personality and developmental perspectives.* Hillsdale, NJ: Erlbaum.

Lattal, K. A., Reilly, M. P., & Kohn, J. P. (1998). Response persistence under ratio and interval reinforcement schedules. *Journal of the Experimental Analysis of Behavior, 70*(2), 165–183.

Laumann, E., Michael, R., Michaels, S., & Gagnon, J. (1994). *The social organization of sexuality.* Chicago: University of Chicago Press.

Lavallee, A. C. (1999). Capuchin (Cebus apella) tool use in a captive naturalistic environment. *International Journal of Primatology, 20*(3), 399–414.

Lawler, K. A., Kline, K. A., Harriman, H. L., & Kelly, K. M. (1999). Stress and illness. In V. J. Derlega et al. (Eds.), *Personality: Contemporary theory and research.* Chicago: Nelson-Hall.

Lay, C., & Verkuyten, M. (1999). Ethnic identity and its relation to personal self-esteem. *Journal of Social Psychology, 139*(3), 288–299.

Lazarus, R. S. (1981, July). Little hassles can be hazardous to health. *Psychology Today,* 12–14.

Lazarus, R. S. (1991a). Progress on a cognitive-motivational-relational theory of emotion. *American Psychologist, 46*(8), 819–834.

Lazarus, R. S. (1991b). Cognition and motivation in emotion. *American Psychologist, 46*(4), 352–367.

Lazarus, R. S. (1993). From psychological stress to the emotions: A history of changing outlooks. In L. W. Porter and M. R. Rosenzweig (Eds.), *Annual Review of Psychology, 44*, 1–21.

Lazgrove, S., et al. (1998). An open trial for EMDR as treatment for chronic PTSD. *American Journal of Orthopsychiatry, 68*(4), 601–608.

Leavens, D. A., & Hopkins, W. D. (1998). Intentional communication by chimpanzees. *Developmental Psychology, 34*(5), 813–822.

Leclerc, G., Lefrancois, R., Dube, M., Hebert, R., & Gaulin, P. (1998). The self-actualization concept: A content validation. *Journal of Social Behavior & Personality, 13*, 69–84.

Lecomte, D., & Fornes, P. (1998). Suicide among youth and young adults, 15 through 24 years of age. *Journal of Forensic Sciences, 43*(5), 964–968.

LeDoux, J. (1996). *The emotional brain: The mysterious underpinnings of emotional life.* New York: Simon & Schuster.

LeDoux, J. (1999). The power of emotions. In R. Conlan (Ed.), *States of mind.* New York: Wiley.

Lee, C. C. (1991). New approaches to diversity. In C. C. Lee & B. L. Richardson (Eds.), *Multicultural issues in counseling.* Alexandria, VA: American Association for Counseling and Development.

Lee, M., Zimbardo, P. G., & Bertholf, M. (1977, November). Shy murderers. *Psychology Today.*

Lee, T. D., & Carnahan, H. (1990). When to provide knowledge of results during motor learning: Scheduling effects. *Human Performance, 3*(2), 87–105.

Leenaars, A. A. (1995). Suicide. In H. Wass & R. A. Neimeyer (Eds.), *Dying.* Washington, DC: Taylor & Francis.

Leeper, R. W. (1935). A study of a neglected portion of the field of learning: The development of sensory organization. *Pedagogical Seminary and Journal of Genetic Psychology, 46,* 41–75.

Lefcourt, H. M., & Thomas, S. (1998). Humor and stress revisited. In W. Ruch et al. (Eds.), *The sense of humor.* Berlin: Walter De Gruyter.

Leibel, R. L., Rosenbaum, M., & Hirsch, J. (1995). Changes in energy expenditure resulting from altered body weight. *New England Journal of Medicine, 332*(10), 621–628.

Lenzenweger, M. F., Cornblatt, B. A., & Putnick, M. (1991). Schizotypy and sustained attention. *Journal of Abnormal Psychology, 100*(1), 84–89.

Lenzenweger, M. F., & Gottesman, I. I. (1994). Schizophrenia. In V. S. Ramachandran (Ed.), *Encyclopedia of human behavior.* San Diego, CA: Academic.

Leonard, C. M. (1997). Language and the prefrontal cortex. In N. A. Krasnegor, G. R. Lyon, et al. (Eds.), *Development of the prefrontal cortex: Evolution, neurobiology, and behavior.* Baltimore: Paul H. Brookes.

Leor, J., Poole, W. K., & Kloner, R. A. (1996). Sudden cardiac death triggered by earthquake. *New England Journal of Medicine, 334*(7), 413.

Lepper, M. R., Keavney, M., & Drake, M. (1996). Intrinsic motivation and extrinsic rewards. *Review of Educational Research, 66*(1), 5–32.

Leslie, K., & Ogilvie, R. (1996). Vestibular dreams: The effect of rocking on dream mentation. *Dreaming: Journal of the Association for the Study of Dreams, 6*(1), 1–16.

Lettvin, J. Y. (1961). Two remarks on the visual system of the frog. In W. Rosenblith (Ed.), *Sensory communication.* Cambridge, MA: MIT Press.

LeVay, S. (1993). *The sexual brain.* Cambridge, MA: MIT Press.

Levesque, M. F., & Neuman, T. (1999). Human trials to begin. *Spinal Cord Society Newsletter, 246,* 3–4.

Levi, A. M. (1998). Are defendants guilty if they were chosen in a lineup? *Law & Human Behavior, 22*(4), 389–407.

Levine, J. M., & Moreland, R. L. (1990). Progress in small group research. *Annual Review of Psychology, 41,* 485–634.

Levine, M., Toro, P. A., & Perkins, D. V. (1993). Social and community interventions. In L. W. Porter and M. R. Rosenzweig (Eds.), *Annual Review of Psychology, 44,* 525–558.

Levine, S. C., Huttenlocher, J., Taylor, A., & Langrock, A. (1999). Early sex differences in spatial skill. *Developmental Psychology, 35*(4), 940–949.

Levinger, G. (1986). Editor's page. *Journal of Social Issues, 42*(3).

Levinson, A. (1999, February 22). Memory champ an absent-minded lady. *Tucson Daily Star,* pp. A1, A8.

Levy, D. A. (1989). Social support and the media: Analysis of responses by radio psychology talk show hosts. *Professional Psychology: Research & Practice, 20*(2), 73–78.

Levy, J., & Reid, M. (1976). Cerebral organization. *Science,* 337–339.

Lewis, J. E., & Maler, L. (2001). Neuronal population codes and the perception of object distance in weakly electric fish. *Journal of Neuroscience, 21*(8), 2842–2850.

Lewis, M. (1995, January–February). Self-conscious emotions. *American Scientist, 83,* 68–78.

Lewis, M., & Brooks-Gunn, J. (1979). *Social cognition and the acquisition of self.* New York: Plenum.

Lewy, A. J., et al. (1998). Morning vs. evening light treatment of patients with winter depression. *Archives of General Psychiatry, 55*(10), 890–896

Lichtenstein, E. (1982). The smoking problem: A behavioral perspective. *Journal of Consulting and Clinical Psychology, 50,* 804–819.

Light, P. (1997). Computers for learning. *Journal of Child Psychology & Psychiatry & Allied Disciplines, 38*(5), 497–504.

Lightsey, O. R., Jr. (1996). What leads to wellness? The role of psychological resources in well-being. *Counseling Psychologist, 24*(4), 589–759.

Lilienfeld, S. (1998). Pseudoscience in contemporary clinical psychology. *The Clinical Psychologist, 51*(4), 3–9.

Lilienfeld, S. O. (1999, September/ October). Projective measures of personality and psychopathology. *Skeptical Inquirer,* 32–39.

Lindemann, B. (1996). Taste reception. *Physiological Reviews, 76*(3), 719–748.

Lindsay, D. S. (1998). Depolarizing views on recovered memory experiences. In S. J. Lynn, K. M. McConkey, et al. (Eds.), *Truth in memory.* New York: The Guilford Press.

Lindsay, E. W., Mize, J., & Pettit, G. S. (1997). Differential pay patterns of mothers and fathers of sons and daughters. *Sex Roles, 37*(9–10), 643–661.

Linton, M. (1979, July). I remember it well. *Psychology Today,* 81–86.

Lipman, J. J., Miller, B. E., Mays, K. S., Miller, M. N., et al. (1990). Peak B-endorphin concentration in cerebrospinal fluid: Reduced in chronic pain patients and increased during the placebo response. *Psychopharmacology, 102*(1), 112–116.

Lipps, G., & Yiptong-Avila, J. (1999). *From home to school: How Canadian children cope. Initial analyses using data from the second cycle of the school component of the National Longitudinal Survey of Children and Youth.* Culture, Tourism and the Centre for Education Statistics, Catalogue No. 89F0117XIE.

Lipschitz, D. S., Kaplan, M. L., Sorkenn, J., & Chorney, P. (1996). Childhood abuse, adult assault, and dissociation. *Comprehensive Psychiatry, 37*(4), 261–266.

Lipsey, M. W., & Wilson, D. B. (1993). The efficacy of psychological, educational, and behavioral treatment. *American Psychologist, 48*(12), 1181–1209.

Liu, X., Matochik, J. A., Cadet, J., et al. (1998). Smaller volume of prefrontal lobe in polysubstance abusers. *Neuropsychopharmacology, 18*(4), 243–252.

Liu, Yijun, Gao, Jia-Hong, Lui, Ho-Ling, & Fox, Peter T. (2000). The temporal response of the brain after eating revealed by functional MRI. *Nature, 405*(6790), 1058–1062.

Lobo, L. L., & Tufik, S. (1997). Effects of alcohol on sleep parameters of sleep-deprived healthy volunteers. *Sleep, 20*(1), 52–59.

Loeber, R., & Hay, D. (1997). Key issues in the development of aggression and violence from childhood to early adulthood. In J. T. Spence (Ed.), *Annual Review of Psychology, 48,* 371–410.

Loehlin, J. C., McCrae, R. R., Costa, P. T., & John, O. (1998). Heritabilities of common and measure-specific components of the Big Five personality factors. *Journal of Research in Personality, 32*(4), 431–453.

Loewen, R., & Pliner, P. (1999). Effects of prior exposure to palatable and unpalatable novel foods on children's willingness to taste other novel foods. *Appetite, 32*(3), 351–366.

Loftus, E. (1993). Psychologists in the eyewitness world. *American Psychologist, 48*(5), 550–552.

Loftus, E. (1994). The repressed memory controversy. *American Psychologist, 49*(5), 443–444.

Loftus, E., & Ketcham, K. (1991). *Witness for the defense.* New York: St. Martin's Press.

Loftus, E., & Loftus, G. (1980). On the permanence of stored information in the human brain. *American Psychologist, 35,* 409–420.

Loftus, E., & Palmer, J. C. (1974). Reconstruction of automobile destruction: An example of interaction between language and memory. *Journal of Verbal Learning and Verbal Behavior, 13,* 585–589.

Loftus, G. R., & Mackworth, N. H. (1978). Cognitive determinants of fixation location during picture viewing. *Journal of Experimental Psychology: Human Perception and Performance, 4,* 565–572.

Lohr, J. M., Tolin, D. F., & Lilienfeld, S. O. (1998). Efficacy of eye movement desensitization and reprocessing. *Behavior Therapy, 29*(1), 123–156.

Long, D. M. (1991). Fifteen years of transcutaneous electrical stimulation for pain control. *Stereotactic & Functional Neurosurgery, 56*(1), 2–19.

Long, V. O. (1989). Relation of masculinity to self-esteem and self-acceptance in male professionals, college students, and clients. *Journal of Counseling Psychology, 36*(1), 84–87.

López, S. R., & Guarnaccia, P. J. J. (2000). Cultural psychopathology. *Annual Review of Psychology, 51,* 571–598.

Lore, R. K., & Schultz, L. A. (1993). Control of human aggression. *American Psychologist, 48*(1), 16–25.

Lorenz, K. (1966). *On aggression.* Translated by M. Kerr-Wilson. New York: Harcourt Brace Jovanovich.

Lorenz, K. (1974). *The eight deadly sins of civilized man.* Translated by M. Kerr-Wilson. New York: Harcourt Brace Jovanovich.

Lovaas, O., & Simmons, J. (1969). Manipulation of self-destruction in three retarded children. *Journal of Applied Behavior Analysis, 2,* 143–157.

Low, K. G., & Feissner, J. M. (1998). Seasonal affective disorder in college students: Prevalence and latitude. *Journal of American College Health, 47*(3), 135–137.

Luborsky, L., et al. (1997). The psychotherapist matters. *Clinical Psychology: Science & Practice, 4*(1), 53–65.

Luce, G. G. (1965). *Current research on sleep and dreams.* Health Service Publication, No. 1389. U. S. Department of Health, Education and Welfare.

Luiselli, J. K. (1994). Behavioral medicine. *Encyclopedia of human behavior,* Vol. 1, 359–363.

Luria, A. R. (1968). *The mind of a mnemonist.* New York: Basic.

Luster, T., & Dubow, E. (1992). Home environment and maternal intelligence as predictors of verbal intelligence. *Merrill-Palmer Quarterly, 38*(2), 151–175.

Luxem, M., & Christophersen, E. (1994). Behavioral toilet training in early childhood: Research, practice, and implications. *Journal* of *Developmental & Behavioral Pediatrics, 15*(5), 370–378.

Lykken, D. T. (1995). *The antisocial personalities.* Hillsdale, NJ: Erlbaum.

Lykken, D. T. (1998). *A tremor in the blood: Uses and abuses of the lie detector.* New York: Plenum.

Lykken, D. T., McGue, M., Tellegen, A., & Bouchar, T. J. (1992). Emergenesis. *American Psychologist, 47,* 1565–1567.

Lyubomirsky, S., & Tucker, K. L. (1998). Implications of individual differences in subjective happiness for perceiving, interpreting, and thinking about life events. *Motivation & Emotion, 22*(2), 155–186.

Lyznicki, J. M., Doege, T. C., Davis, R. M., & Williams, M. A. (1998). Sleepiness, driving, and motor vehicle crashes. *Journal of the American Medical Association, 279*(23), 1908–1913.

Maas, J. (1999). *Power sleep.* New York: HarperCollins.

Mabry, J. H. (1998). Something for the future. *Analysis of Verbal Behavior, 15,* 129–130.

Macdougall, J. P. (1999). *Deafness and sign language in a Yukatec Maya community: Communication and cultural inclusion.* Honour's thesis, Department of Anthropology, McGill University.

Macdougall, J. C. (2000). Access to justice for deaf Inuit in Nunavut: The role of "Inuit sign language." *Canadian Psychology, 42*(1), 61–73.

MacHovec, F. (1994). Near-death experiences: Psychotherapeutic aspects. *Psychotherapy in Private Practice, 13*(3), 99–105.

MacQueen, G. M., Tipper, S. P., Young, L. T., Joffe, R. T., & Levitt, A. J. (2000). Impaired distractor inhibition on a selective attention task in unmedicated, depressed subjects. *Psychological Medicine, 30*(3), 557–564.

Maddi, S. R., Kahn, S., & Maddi, K. L. (1998). The effectiveness of hardiness training. *Consulting Psychology Journal: Practice & Research, 50*(2), 78–86.

Madigan, S., & O'Hara, R. (1992). Short-term memory at the turn of the century. *American Psychologist, 47*(2), 170–174.

Madon, S., Jussim, L., & Eccles, J. (1997). In search of the powerful self-fulfilling prophecy. *Journal of Personality and Social Psychology, 72*(4), 791–809.

Magee, W. J., Eaton, W. W., & Wittchen, H. (1996). Agoraphobia, simple phobia, and social phobia in the national comorbidity survey. *Archives of General Psychiatry, 53*(2), 159–168.

Magnusson, A., & Axelsson, J. (1993). The prevalence of seasonal affective disorder is low among descendants of Icelandic emigrants in Canada. *Archives of General Psychiatry, 50,* 947–951.

Maguire, E. A., Frackowiak, R. S. J., & Frith, C. D. (1997). Recalling routes around London: Activation of the hippocampus in taxi drivers. *The Journal of Neuroscience, 17*(8), 7103.

Maier, N. R. F. (1949). *Frustration.* New York: McGraw-Hill.

Maio, G. R., Bell, D. W., & Esses, V. M. (1996). Ambivalence in persuasion: The processing of messages about immigrant groups. *Journal of Experimental Social Psychology, 32*(6), 513–536.

Malnic, B., Hirono, J., & Buck, L. B. (1999). Combinatorial receptor codes for odors. *Cell, 96*(5), 713.

Mamuza, J. (2001). *Do actuarial assessments fall victim to base rate neglect?* Dissertation Abstracts International, Section B: The Sciences & Engineering. Vol. 61(10-B), 5617.

Mandler, J. M., & McDonough, L. (1998). On developing a knowledge base in infancy. *Developmental Psychology, 34*(6), 1274–1288.

Mangun, G. R. (1995). Neural mechanisms of visual selective attention. *Psychophysiology, 32*(1), 4–18.

Manschreck, T. C. (1996). Delusional disorder: The recognition and management of paranoia. *Journal of Clinical Psychiatry, 57*(3, Suppl), 32–38.

Mansouri, A., & Adityanjee. (1995). Delusion of pregnancy in males: A case report and literature review. *Psychopathology, 28*(6), 307–311.

Mantyla, T. (1986). Optimizing cue effectiveness: Recall of 600 incidentally learned words. *Journal of Experimental Psychology: Learning, Memory, and Cognition, 12*(1), 66–71.

Maquet, P., et al. (2000). Experience-dependent changes in cerebral activation during human REM sleep. *Nature Neuroscience, 3*(8), 831–836.

Marks, D. F. (1990). Comprehensive commentary, insightful criticism. *Skeptical Inquirer, 14*(3), 413–418.

Marks, D. F., & Kammann, R. (1979). *The psychology of the psychic.* Buffalo, NY: Prometheus.

Markus, H. R., & Kitayama, S. (1998). The cultural psychology of personality. *Journal of Cross-Cultural Psychology, 29*(1), 63–87.

Markus, H., Kitayama, S., & Vanden-Bos, G. R. (1996). The mutual interactions of culture and emotion. *Psychiatric Services, 47*(3), 225–226.

Markus, H., & Nurius, P. (1986). Possible selves. *American Psychologist, 41,* 954–969.

Marlatt, G. A., Baer, J. S., Dononovan, D. M., & Kivlahan, D. R. (1988). Addictive behaviors: Etiology and treatment. *Annual Review of Psychology, 39,* 223–252.

Martens, R., & Trachet, T. (1998). *Making sense of astrology.* Amherst, MA: Prometheus.

Martin, P.Y., & Benton, D. (1999). The influence of a glucose drink on a demanding working memory task. *Physiology & Behavior, 67*(1), 69–74.

Martin, S. (1995, January). Field's status unaltered by the influx of women. *APA Monitor,* p. 9.

Maslach, C. (1982). *Burnout: The cost of caring.* Englewood Cliffs, NJ: Prentice-Hall.

Maslow, A. H. (1954). *Motivation and personality.* New York: Harper.

Maslow, A. H. (1967). Self-actualization and beyond. In J. F. T. Bugental (Ed.), *Challenges of humanistic psychology.* New York: McGraw-Hill.

Maslow, A. H. (1969). *The psychology of science.* Chicago: Henry Regnery.

Maslow, A. H. (1970). *Motivation and personality.* New York: Harper & Row.

Maslow, A. H. (1971). *The farther reaches of human nature.* New York: Viking.

Masse, L. C., & Tremblay, R. E. (1997). Behavior of boys in kindergarten and the onset of substance use during adolescence. *Archives of General Psychiatry, 54*(1), 62.

Masters, W. H., & Johnson, V. E. (1966). *Human sexual response.* Boston: Little, Brown.

Masters, W. H., & Johnson, V. E. (1970). *The pleasure bond: A new look at sexuality and commitment.* Boston: Little, Brown.

Matheny, K. B., Brack, G. L., McCarthy, C. J., & Penick, J. M. (1996). The effectiveness of cognitively-based approaches in treating stress-related symptoms. *Psychotherapy, 33*(2), 305–320.

Matias, R., & Cohn, J. F. (1993). Are max-specified infant facial expressions during face-to-face interaction consistent with differential emotions theory? *Developmental Psychology, 29*(3), 524–531.

Maticka-Tyndale, E., & Herold, E. S. (1997). The scripting of sexual behaviour: Canadian university students on spring break in Florida. *Canadian Journal of Human Sexuality, 6*(4), 317–328.

Matossian, M. K. (1982). Ergot and the Salem witchcraft affair. *American Scientist, 70,* 355–357.

Matson, J. L., Sevin, J. A., Fridley, D., & Love, S. R. (1990). Increasing spontaneous language in three autistic children. *Journal of Applied Behavior Analysis, 23*(2), 223–227.

Matsuda, L. A., Lolait, S. J., Brownstein, M. J., Young, A. C., & Bonner, T. I. (1990). Structure of a cannabinoid receptor and functional expression of the cloned cDNA. *Nature, 346*(6284), 561–564.

Matthews, D. B. (1990). A comparison of burnout in selected occupational fields. *Career Development Quarterly, 38*(3), 230–239.

Mauer, M. H., Burnett, K. F., Ouellette, E. A., Ironson, G. H., et al. (1999). Medical hypnosis and orthopedic hand surgery. *International Journal of Clinical & Experimental Hypnosis, 47*(2), 144–161.

May, M. (1996). Resistance: Friend or foe? *American Journal of Psychotherapy, 50*(1), 32–44.

Mayer, J. D., & Hanson, E. (1995). Mood-congruent judgment over time. *Personality & Social Psychology Bulletin, 21*(3) 237–244.

Mayer, R. E. (1995). *Thinking, problem solving, and cognition.* New York: Freeman.

McBride, W. J., Murphy, J. M., & Ikemoto, S. (1999). Localization of brain reinforcement mechanisms. *Behavioural Brain Research, 101*(2), 129–152.

McCann, S. L., & Stewin, L. L. (1988). Worry, anxiety, and preferred length of sleep. *Journal of Genetic Psychology, 149*(3), 413–418.

McCarley, R. W. (1998). Dreams: Disguise of forbidden wishes or transparent reflections of a distinct brain state? In R. M. Bilder, F. F. LeFever, et al. (Eds.), *Neuroscience of the mind on the centennial of Freud's Project for a Scientific Psychology.* New York: New York Academy of Sciences.

McCartney, K., Bernieri, F., & Harris, M. J. (1990). Growing up and growing apart: A developmental meta-analysis of twin studies. *Psychological Bulletin, 107*(2), 226–237.

McCarty, R. (1998, November). Making the case for animal research. *APA Monitor,* 18.

McClelland, D. C. (1961). *The achieving society.* New York: Van Nostrand.

McClelland, D. C. (1965). Achievement and entrepreneurship. *Journal of Personality & Social Psychology, 1,* 389–393.

McClelland, D. C. (1975). *Power: The inner experience.* New York: Irvington.

McClelland, D. C., & Cheriff, A. D. (1997). The immunoenhancing effects of humor on secretory IgA and resistance to respiratory infections. *Psychology & Health, 12*(3), 329–344.

McClelland, D. C., & Pilon, D. A. (1983). Sources of adult motives in patterns of parent behavior in early childhood. *Journal of Personality & Social Psychology, 44, 564–574.

McCormick, R. (1996). Culturally appropriate means and ends of counselling as described by the First Nations people of British Columbia. International Journal for the Advancement of Counselling, 18, 163–172.

McCormick, R. (2000). Aboriginal traditions in the treatment of substance abuse. Canadian Journal of Counselling, 34, 25–32.

McCrae, R. R. (1987). Creativity, divergent thinking, and openness to experience. Journal of Personality & Social Psychology, 52(6), 1258–1265.

McCrae, R. R., & Costa, P. T. (1990). Personality in adulthood. New York: Guilford.

McCrae, R. R., & Costa, P. T. (1997). Personality trait structure as a human universal. American Psychologist, 52(5), 509–516.

McDaniel, M. A., & Schlager, M. S. (1990). Discovery learning and transfer of problem-solving skills. Cognition & Instruction, 7(2), 129–159.

McGinnis, J. M., & Foege, W. H. (1993). Actual causes of death in the United States. Journal of the American Medical Association, 270(18), 2207–2212.

McGregor, I., & Little, B. R. (1998). Personal projects, happiness, and meaning. Journal of Personality and Social Psychology, 74(2), 494–512.

McIntosh, D. N. (1996). Facial feedback hypotheses. Motivation & Emotion, 20(2), 121–147.

McIntosh, W. D., Harlow, T. F., & Martin, L. L. (1995). Linkers and nonlinkers: Goal beliefs as a moderator of the effects of everyday hassles on rumination, depression, and physical complaints. Journal of Applied Social Psychology, 25(14), 1231–1244.

McKean, K. (1985, April). Of two minds: Selling the right brain. Discover, 30–40.

McKean, K. J. (1994). Using multiple risk factors to assess the behavioral, cognitive, and affective effects of learned helplessness. Journal of Psychology, 128(2), 177–183.

McKenna, M. W., & Ossoff, E. P. (1998). Age differences in children's comprehension of a popular television program. Child Study Journal, 28(1), 52–68.

McKim, M. K., Cramer, K. M., Stuart, B. & O'Connor, D. L. (1999). Infant care decisions and attachment security: The Canadian Transition to Child Care Study. Canadian Journal of Behavioural Science, 31, 92–106.

McKim, W. A. (1997). Drugs and behavior. Upper Saddle River, NJ: Prentice Hall.

McKnight, J. D., & Glass, D. C. (1995). Perceptions of control, burnout, and depressive symptomatology. Journal of Consulting & Clinical Psychology, 63(3), 490–494.

McLaughlin, S., & Margolskee, R. F. (1994, November–December). The sense of taste. American Scientist, 82, 538–545.

McLennan, J. (1992). "University blues": Depression among tertiary students during an academic year. British Journal of Guidance & Counselling, 20(2), 186–192.

McLoyd, V. (1998). Socioeconomic disadvantage and child development. American Psychologist, 53(2), 185–204.

McManus, I. C., Sik, G., Cole, D. R., Muellon, A. F., et al. (1988). The development of handedness in children. British Journal of Developmental Psychology, 6(3), 257–273.

McMullan, W. E., & Stocking, J. R. (1978). Conceptualizing creativity in three dimensions. The Journal of Creative Behavior, 12, 161–167.

McNelles, L., & Connelly, J. (1999). Intimacy between adolescent friends: Age and gender differences in intimate affect and intimate behaviors. Journal of Research on Adolescence, 9(2), 143–159.

McRoberts, C., Burlingame, G. M., & Hoag, M. J. (1998). Comparative efficacy of individual and group psychotherapy. Group Dynamics, 2(2), 101–117.

Medin, D. L., & Ross, B. H. (1992). Cognitive psychology. Fort Worth: Harcourt Brace Jovanovich.

Meichenbaum, D. (1993). Changing conceptions of cognitive behavior modification: Retrospect and prospect. Journal of Consulting and Clinical Psychology, 61, 202–204.

Meier, R. P. (1991). Language acquisition by deaf children. American Scientist, 79(1), 60–70.

Meleshko, K. G. A & Alden, L. E. (1993). Anxiety and self-disclosure: Toward a motivational model. Journal of Personality & Social Psychology, 64(6), 1000–1009.

Meltzoff, A. N., & Moore, M. K. (1983). Newborn infants imitate adult facial gestures. Child Development, 54, 702–709.

Meltzoff, J. (1998). Critical thinking about research. Washington, DC: American Psychological Association.

Melzack, R. (1974). Shutting the gate on pain. Science Year: The World Book science annual. Palo Alto, CA: Field.

Melzack, R. (1993). Pain: Past, present and future. Canadian Journal of Experimental Psychology, 47(4), 615–629.

Melzack, R. (1999, August). From the gate to the neuromatrix. Pain (Suppl 6), S121–S126.

Melzack, R., Coderre, T. J., Katz, J., & Vaccarino, A. L. (2001). Central neuroplasticity and pathological pain. In B. A. Sorg and I. R. Bell (Eds.), The role of neuroplasticity in chemical tolerance: Annals of the New York Academy of Sciences, 933, 157–174.

Melzack, R., & Wall, P. D. (1996). The challenge of pain. Harmondworth, UK: Penguin.

Mendolia, M., Moore, J., & Tesser, A. (1996). Dispositional and situational determinants of repression. Journal of Personality & Social Psychology, 70(4), 856–867.

Menzies, R. G., & Clarke, J. C. (1993). A comparison of in vivo and vicarious exposure in the treatment of childhood water phobia. Behaviour Research and Therapy, 31(1), 9–15.

Mercer, J. G., Beck, B., Burlet, A., et al. (1998). Leptin (ob) mRNA and hypothalamic NPY in food-deprived/refed Syrian hamsters. Physiology & Behavior, 64(2), 191–195.

Merckelbach, H., & Muris, P. (1997). The etiology of childhood spider phobia. Behaviour Research & Therapy, 35(11), 1031–1034.

Merenda, P. F. (1996). BASC: Behavior Assessment System for Children. Measurement & Evaluation in Counseling & Development, 28(4), 229–232.

Merikle, P. M., & Skanes, H. E. (1992). Subliminal self-help audiotapes: A search for placebo effects. Journal of Applied Psychology, 77(5), 772–776.

Mermelstein, R. (1986). Social support and smoking cessation and maintenance. Journal of Consulting & Clinical Psychology, 54(4), 447–453.

Merritt, J. M., Stickgold, R., Pace-Schott, E., Williams, J., et al. (1994). Emotion profiles in the dreams of men and women. Consciousness & Cognition, 3(1), 46–60.

Mesquita, B., & Frijda, N. H. (1992). Cultural variations in emotions. Psychological Bulletin, 112(2), 179–204.

Messick, D. M., & Mackie, D. M. (1989). Intergroup relations. Annual Review of Psychology, 40, 45–81.

Metcalfe, J. (1986). Premonitions of insight predict impending error. Journal of Experimental Psychology: Learning, Memory, and Cognition, 12, 623–634.

Metzner, R. (1998). Hallucinogenic drugs and plants in psychotherapy and shamanism. Journal of Psychoactive Drugs, 30(4), 333–341.

Mewhinney, D. M., Herold, E. S., & Maticka-Tyndale, E. (1995). Sexual scripts and risk-taking of Canadian university students on spring break in Daytona Beach, Florida. Canadian Journal of Human Sexuality, 4(4), 273–288.

Meyers, M. M., Fifer, W. P., Schaeffer, L., Sahni, R., et al. (1998). Effects of sleeping position and time after feeding on the organization of sleep/wake states in prematurely born infants. Sleep, 21(4), 343–349.

Michalko, M. (1998). Cracking creativity. Berkeley, CA: Ten Speed Press.

Michel, D. E., & Chesky, K. S. (1995). A survey of music therapists using music for pain relief. Arts in Psychotherapy, 22(1), 49–51.

Michotte, A. (1963). The perception of causality. New York: Methuen/Basic.

Mielke, H. W. (1999, January–February). Lead in the inner cities. American Scientist, 87, 62–73.

Mikulincer, M., & Nachshon, O. (1991). Attachment styles and patterns of self-disclosure. Journal of Personality & Social Psychology, 61(2), 321–331.

Milgram, S. (1963). Behavioral study of obedience. Journal of Abnormal and Social Psychology, 67, 371–378.

Milgram, S. (1965). Some conditions of obedience and disobedience to authority. Human Relations, 18, 57–76.

Milgram, S., Bickman, L., & Berkowitz, L. (1969). Note on the drawing power of crowds of different size. Journal of Personality & Social Psychology, 13, 79–82.

Miller, A. H. (1998). Neuroendocrine and immune system interactions in stress and depression. Psychiatric Clinics of North America, 21(2), 443–463.

Miller, D. T., Turnbull, W., & McFarland, C. (1988). Particularistic and universalistic evaluation in the social comparison process. Journal of Personality & Social Psychology, 55(6), 908–917.

Miller, G. (1956). The magical number seven, plus or minus two: Some limits on our capacity for processing information. Psychological Review, 63, 81–87.

Miller, G. A. (1999). On knowing a word. Annual Review of Psychology, 50, 1–19.

Miller, L. C. (1990). Intimacy and liking: Mutual influence and the role of unique relationships. Journal of Personality & Social Psychology, 59(1), 50–60.

Miller, L. K. (1976). The design of better communities through the application of behavioral principles. In W. E. Craighead, A. E. Kazdin, & M. J. Mahone (Eds.), Behavior modification: Principles, *issues, and applications.* Boston: Houghton-Mifflin.

Miller, M. A., & Rahe, R. H. (1997). Life changes scaling for the 1990s. *Journal of Psychosomatic Research, 43*(3), 279–292.

Miller, N. E. (1944). Experimental studies of conflict. In J. McV. Hunt (Ed.), *Personality and the behavior disorders,* Vol. I, 431–465. New York: Ronald Press.

Miller, N. E. (1985). The value of behavioral research on animals. *American Psychologist, 40,* 423–440.

Miller, N. E., & Bugelski, R. (1970). The influence of frustration imposed by the in-group on attitudes expressed toward out-groups. In R. I. Evans & R. M. Rozelle (Eds.), *Social psychology in life.* Boston: Allyn & Bacon.

Miller, T. Q., Smith, T. W., Turner, C. W., & Guijarro, M. L. (1996). Meta-analytic review of research on hostility and physical health. *Psychological Bulletin, 119*(2), 322–348.

Miller, T. Q., Turner, C. W., Tindale, R. S., Posavac, E. J., et al. (1991). Reasons for the trend toward null findings in research on Type A behavior. *Psychological Bulletin, 110*(3), 469–485.

Millon, T. (1981). *Disorders of personality: DSM-III: Axis II.* New York: Wiley.

Milner, A. D., & Goodale, M. A. (1995). *The visual brain in action.* Oxford: Oxford University Press.

Milner, B. (1965). Memory disturbance after bilateral hippocampal lesions. In P. Milner & S. Glickman (Eds.), *Cognitive processes and the brain* (pp. 97–111). Princeton, NJ: Van Nostrand.

Milton, J., & Wiseman, R. (1997). *Guidelines for extrasensory perception research.* Hertfordshire, England, UK: University of Hertfordshire Press.

Milton, J., & Wiseman, R. (1999). A meta-analysis of mass-media tests of extrasensory perception. *British Journal of Psychology, 90*(2), 235–240.

Mineka, S., & Hamida, S. B. (1998). Observational and nonconscious learning. In W. T. O'Donohue et al. (Eds.), *Learning and behavior therapy.* Boston: Allyn & Bacon.

Minton, H. L. (2000). Psychology and gender at the turn of the century. *American Psychologist, 55*(6), 613–615.

Miranda, J. (1992). Dysfunctional thinking is activated by stressful life events. *Cognitive Therapy & Research, 16*(4), 473–483.

Mirsky, A. F., & Duncan, C. C. (1986). Etiology and expression of schizophrenia. *Annual Review of Psychology, 37,* 291–319.

Mischel, W. (1968). *Personality and assessment.* New York: Wiley.

Mischel, W., & Shoda, Y. (1998). Reconciling processing dynamics and personality dispositions. *Annual Review of Psychology, 49,* 229–258.

Mishara, B. (1999). Suicide in the Montreal subway system: Characteristics of the victims, antecedents, and implications for prevention. *Canadian Journal of Psychiatry, 44,* 690–696.

Mitchell, D. (1987, February). Firewalking cults: Nothing but hot air. *Laser,* 7–8.

Mitchell, D. B. (1989). How many memory systems? Evidence from aging. *Journal of Experimental Psychology: Learning, Memory, and Cognition, 15*(1), 31–49.

Mogg, K., Bradley, B. P., Hyare, H., & Lee, S. (1998). Selective attention to food-related stimuli in hunger. *Behaviour Research & Therapy, 36*(2), 227–237.

Mohanty, S., Pati, N. C., & Kumar, R. (1998). Effects of token economy on the rate of envelope making in the persons with mental retardation. *Social Science International, 14*(1–2), 84–97.

Moller, L. C., & Serbin, L. A. (1996). Antecedents of toddler gender segregation: Cognitive consonance, gender-typed toy preferences, and behavioral compatibility. *Sex Roles, 35,* 445–460.

Mombaerts, P. (1999). Molecular biology of odorant receptors in vertebrates. *Annual Review of Neuroscience, 22,* 487–509.

Monahan, J. (1992). Mental disorder and violent behavior. *American Psychologist, 47*(4), 511–521.

Money, J. (1987). Sin, sickness, or status? *American Psychologist, 42*(4), 384–399.

Montgomery, G. (1989, March). The mind in motion. *Discover,* 58–68.

Montplaisir, J., Petit, D., Lorrain, D., Gauthier, S., & Nielsen, T. (1995). Sleep in Alzheimer's disease: Further considerations on the role of brainstem and forebrain cholinergic populations in sleep-wake mechanisms. *Sleep, 18,* 145–148.

Moody, R. (1975). *Life after life.* Covinda, GA: Mockingbird.

Moore, T. E., (1995). Subliminal self-help auditory tapes: An empirical test of perceptual consequences. *Canadian Journal of Behavioural Science, 27*(1), 9–20.

Moore-Ede, M. C., Sulzman, F. M., & Fuller, C. A. (1982). *The clocks that time us.* Cambridge, MA: Harvard University Press.

Moreno, J. L. (1953). *Who shall survive?* New York: Beacon.

Morgenstern, J., Labouvie, E., McCrady, B. S., et al. (1997). Affiliation with Alcoholics Anonymous after treatment. *Journal of Consulting & Clinical Psychology, 65*(5), 768–777.

Moriarty, T. (1975, April). A nation of willing victims. *Psychology Today,* 43–50.

Morisse, D., Batra, L., Hess, L., & Silverman, R. (1996). A demonstration of a token economy for the real world. *Applied & Preventive Psychology, 5*(1), 41–46.

Moritz, A. P., & Zamchech, N. (1946). Sudden and unexpected deaths of young soldiers. *American Medical Association Archives of Pathology, 42,* 459–494.

Morrison, T. G., McLeod, L. D., Morrison, M. A., Anderson, D., & O'Connor, W. E. (1997). Gender stereotyping, homonegativity, and misconceptions about sexually coercive behavior among adolescents. *Youth and Society, 28*(3), 351–382.

Moss, K. (1989). Performing the light-switch task in lucid dreams: A case study. *Journal of Mental Imagery, 13*(2), 135–137.

Mottron, L., Belleville, S., & Stip, E. (1996). Proper name hypermnesia in an autistic subject. *Brain and Language, 53*(3), 326–350.

Mottron, L., Belleville, S., & Stip, E., & Morasse, K. (1998). Atypical memory performance in an autistic savant. *Memory, 6*(6), 593–607.

Muris, P., & Merckelbach, H. (1999). Traumatic memories, eye movements, phobia, and panic. *Journal of Anxiety Disorders, 13*(1–2), 209–223.

Murray, J. B. (1995). Evidence for acupuncture's analgesic effectiveness and proposals for the physiological mechanisms involved. *Journal of Psychology, 129*(4), 443–461.

Mussen, P. H., Conger, J. J., Kagan, J., & Geiwitz, J. (1979). *Psychological development: A life span approach.* New York: Harper & Row.

Nagy, Z., Esiri, M. M., Jobst, K. A., & Morris, J. H. (1996). Clustering of pathological features in Alzheimer's disease. *Dementia, 7*(3), 121–127.

Naitoh, P., Kelly, T. L., & Englund, C. E. (1989). *Health effects of sleep deprivation.* U. S. Naval Health Research Center Report, No. 89–46.

Naka, M. (1998). The variables affecting the reliability of eyewitness testimony. *Japanese Journal of Psychonomic Science, 16*(2), 100–106.

Nantais, K. M., & Schellenberg, E. G. (1999). The Mozart effect: An artifact of preference. *Psychological Science, 10*(4), 370–373.

Naranjo, C. (1970). Present-centeredness: Technique, prescription, and ideal. In J. Fagan & I. L. Shepherd (Eds.), *What is Gestalt therapy?* New York: Harper & Row.

Natale, V., & Cicogna, P. (1996). Circadian regulation of subjective alertness in morning and evening types. *EDRA: Environmental Design Research Association, 20*(4), 491–497.

Nathan, P. E., & Langenbucher, J. W. (1999). Psychopathology. *Annual Review of Psychology, 50,* 79–107.

National television violence study. (1995–1996). Studio City, CA: Mediascope, Inc.

Navarro, M. (1995, December 9). Drug sold abroad by prescription becomes widely abused in U. S. *The New York Times,* pp. 1, 9.

Neath, I. (1998). *Human memory.* Pacific Grove, CA: Brooks/Cole.

Needles, D. J., & Abramson, L. Y. (1990). Positive life events, attributional style, and hopefulness: Testing a model of recovery from depression. *Journal of Abnormal Psychology, 99*(2), 156–165.

Neisser, U., Boodoo, G., Bouchard, T. J., et al. (1996). Intelligence: Knowns and unknowns. *American Psychologist, 51*(2), 77–101.

Nelson, C. A. (1999). How important are the first 3 years of life? *Applied Developmental Science, 3*(4), 235–238.

Nelson, T. O. (1987). Predictive accuracy of the feeling of knowing across different tasks and across different subject populations and individuals. In M. M. Gruneberg, P. E. Morris, & R. N. Sykes (Eds.), *Practical aspects of memory: Current research and issues.* Chichester, UK: Wiley.

Nesca, M., & Koulack, D. (1994). Recognition memory, sleep and circadian rhythms. *Canadian Journal of Experimental Psychology, 48*(3), 359–379.

Neter, E., & Ben-Shakhar, G. (1989). The predictive validity of graphological inferences: A meta-analytic approach. *Personality and Individual Differences, 10*(7), 737–745.

Neuman, G. A., & Baydoun, R. (1998). An empirical examination of overt and covert integrity tests. *Journal of Business & Psychology, 13*(1), 65–79.

Newman, B. M., & Newman, P. R. (1987). The impact of high school on social development. *Adolescence, 22*(87), 525–534.

Newman, R. (1994, August). Electronic therapy raises issues, risks. *APA Monitor,* 25.

Nickelson, D. W. (1998). Telehealth and the evolving health care system. *Professional Psychology: Research & Practice, 29*(6), 527–535.

Nickerson, R. S., & Adams, M. J. (1979). Long-term memory for a common object. *Cognitive psychology, 11,* 287–307.

Nielsen, D. M., & Metha, A. (1994). Parental behavior and adolescent self-esteem in clinical and non-clinical samples. *Adolescence, 29*(115), 525–542.

Nijstad, B. A., Stroebe, W., & Lodewijkx, H. F. M. (1999). Persistence of brainstorming groups: How do people know when to stop? *Journal of Experimental Social Psychology, 35*(2), 165–185.

Nikles, C. D., Brecht, D. L., Klinger, E., & Bursell, A. L. (1998). *Journal of Personality & Social Psychology, 75*(1) 242–255.

Nist, S. L., Sharman, S. J., & Holschuh, J. L. (1996). The effects of rereading, self-selected strategy use, and rehearsal on the immediate and delayed understanding of text. *Reading Psychology, 17*(2), 137–157.

Nixon, M. (1990). Professional training in psychology. *American Psychologist, 45*(11), 1257–1262.

Njeri, I. (1991, January 13). Beyond the melting pot. *Los Angeles Times*, pp. E1, E8.

Noble, P. (1997). Violence in psychiatric in-patients. *International Review of Psychiatry, 9*(2–3), 207–216.

Noice, H., & Noice, T. (1999). Long-term retention of theatrical roles. *Memory, 7*(3), 357–382.

Nori, G. (1998). Glucagon and the control of meal size. In G. P. Smith et al. (Eds.), *Satiation: From gut to brain.* New York: Oxford University Press.

Norlander, T., Anonymous, & Archer, T. (1998). Effects of flotation rest on creative problem solving and originality. *Journal of Environmental Psychology, 18*(4), 399–408.

Norlander, T., Bergman, H., & Archer, T. (1999). Primary process in competitive archery performance: Effects of flotation REST. *Journal of Applied Sport Psychology, 11*(2), 194–209.

Norman, G. R., & Brooks, L. R. (1997). The non-analytical basis of clinical reasoning. *Advances in Health Sciences Education, 2*(2), 173–184.

Normann, R. A., Maynard, E. M., Rousche, P. J., & Warren, D. J. (1999). A neural interface for a cortical vision prosthesis. *Vision Research, 39*(15), 2577–2587.

Norris, R. M., & Weinman, J. A. (1996). Psychological change following a long sail training voyage. *Personality & Individual Differences, 21*(2), 189–194.

North, C. S. (1987). *Welcome silence.* New York: Simon & Schuster.

Nurnberger, J. I., & Zimmerman, J. (1970). Applied analysis of human behaviors: An alternative to conventional motivational inferences and unconscious determination in therapeutic programming. *Behavior Therapy, 1*, 59–69.

Nyberg, L., & Tulving, E. (1996). Classifying human long-term memory: Evidence from converging dissociations. *European Journal of Cognitive Psychology, 8*(2), 163–183.

Oatley, K., & Jenkins, J. M. (1992). Human emotions: Function and dysfunction. In M. R. Rosenzweig and L. W. Porter (Eds.), *Annual Review of Psychology, 45*, 55–85.

O'Connell, P., Pepler, D., & Craig, W. (1999). Peer involvement in bullying: Insights and challenges for intervention. *Journal of Adolescence, 22*(4), 437–452.

Ohayon, M. M., Guilleminault, C., & Priest, R. G. (1999). Night terrors, sleepwalking, and confusional arousals in the general population. *Journal of Clinical Psychiatry, 60*(4), 268–276.

Olds, M. E., & Fobes, J. L. (1981). The central basis of motivation: Intracranial self-stimulation studies. *Annual Review of Psychology, 32*, 523–574.

Oliver, M. B., & Hyde, J. S. (1993). Gender differences in sexuality. *Psychological Bulletin, 114*(1), 29–51.

Oliwenstein, L. (1993, May). The gene with two faces. *Discover*, 26.

Ollendick, T. H., & King, N. J. (1991). Origins of childhood fears. *Behaviour Research & Therapy, 29*(2), 117–123.

Olson, J. M., & Zanna, M. P. (1993). Attitudes and attitude change. In L. W. Porter and M. R. Rosenzweig (Eds.), *Annual Review of Psychology, 44*, 117–154.

Olson, R. L., & Roberts, M. W. (1987). Alternative treatments for sibling aggression. *Behavior Therapy, 18*(3), 243–250.

Olson, S. L., Bates, J. E., & Kaskie, B. (1992). Caregiver-infant interaction antecedents of children's school-age cognitive ability. *Merrill-Palmer Quarterly, 38*(3), 309–330.

Olthof, A., Sutton, J. E., Slumskie, S. W., D'Addetta, J., & Roberts, W. A. (1999). In search of the cognitive map: Can rats learn an abstract pattern of rewarded arms on the radial maze? *Journal of Experimental Psychology: Animal Behavior Processes, 25*, 352–362.

Ones, D., Viswesvaran, C., & Schmidt, F. L. (1993). Comprehensive meta-analysis of integrity test validities. *Journal of Applied Psychology, 78*(4), 679–703.

Orlock, C. (1993). *Inner time.* New York: Birch Lane Press.

Ormerod, B. K., & Galea, L. A. (2001). Reproductive status influences cell proliferation and cell survival in the dentate gyrus of adult female meadow voles: A possible regulatory role for estradiol. *Neuroscience, 102*, 369–379.

Ornstein, R. (1997). *The right mind.* San Diego, CA: Harcourt Brace.

Osgood, C. E. (1952). The nature and measurement of meaning. *Psychological Bulletin, 49*, 197–237.

Ost, L. (1996). One-session group treatment of spider phobia. *Behaviour Research & Therapy, 34*(9), 707–715.

O'Sullivan, J. J., & Quevillon, R. P. (1992). 40 years later: Is the Boulder model still alive? *American Psychologist, 47*(1), 67–70.

"Outline for cultural formulation and glossary of culture bound-syndromes." (1994). *DSM-IV: Diagnostic and statistical manual of mental disorders* (4th ed.). Washington, DC: American Psychiatric Association.

Overmier, J. B., & LoLordo, V. M. (1998). Learned helplessness. In W. T. O'Donohue et al. (Eds.), *Learning and behavior therapy.* Boston: Allyn & Bacon.

Oyama, T., & Ichikawa, S. (1990). Some experimental studies on imagery in Japan. *Journal of Mental Imagery, 14*(3–4), 185–195.

Oyewumi, L. K. (1998). Jet lag and relapse of schizoaffective psychosis despite maintenance clozapine treatment. *British Journal of Psychiatry, 173*, 268.

Pagano, R. R. (1981). *Understanding statistics.* St. Paul, MN: West.

Pagano, R. R., & Warrenburg, S. (1983). Meditation. In R J. Davidson, G. E. Schwartz, & D. Shapiro (Eds.), *Consciousness and self-regulation* (pp. 153–210). New York: Plenum.

Palfai, T., & Jankiewicz, H. (1991). *Drugs and human behavior.* Dubuque, IA: Wm. C. Brown.

Palinkas, L. A., Suedfeld, P., & Steel, G. D. (1995). Psychological functioning among members of a small polar expedition. *Aviation and Space Environmental Medicine, 66*, 943–950.

Palm, K., & Gibson, P. (1998). Recovered memories of childhood sexual abuse: Clinicians' practices and beliefs. *Professional Psychology: Research & Practice, 29*(3), 257–261.

Palmer, S. E. (1992). Common region: A new principle of perceptual grouping. *Cognitive Psychology, 24*(3), 436–447.

Papa, F. J., Aldrich, D., & Schumacker, R. E. (1999). The effects of immediate online feedback upon diagnostic performance. *Academic Medicine, 74*(Suppl 10), S16–S18.

Papps, F., Walker, M., Trimboli, A., & Trimboli, C. (1995). Parental discipline in Anglo, Greek, Lebanese, and Vietnamese cultures. *Journal of Cross-Cultural Psychology, 26*(1), 49–64.

Park, D. C., Smith, A. D., & Cavanaugh, J. C. (1990). Metamemories of memory researchers. *Memory & Cognition, 18*(3), 321–327.

Parke, R. D. (1995). Fathers and families. In M. H. Bornstein (Ed.), *Handbook of parenting*, Vol. 3. Mahwah, NJ: Erlbaum.

Parks, C. A. (1998). Lesbian parenthood: A review of the literature. *American Journal of Orthopsychiatry, 68*(3), 376–389.

Paterson, S. P., & Hoffer, G. E. (1994). The impact of airbag adoption on relative personal injury and absolute collision insurance claims. *Journal of Consumer Research, 20*(4), 657–662.

Patrick, C. J., Bradley, M. M., & Lang, P. J. (1993). Emotion in the criminal psychopath: Startle reflex modulation. *Journal of Abnormal Psychology, 102*(1), 82–92.

Patrick, C. J., & Iacono, W. G. (1989). Psychopathy, threat, and polygraph test accuracy. *Journal of Applied Psychology, 74*(2), 347–355.

Patten, B. M. (1990). The history of memory arts. *Neurology, 40*(2), 346–352.

Patterson, C. H. (1989). Foundations for a systematic eclectic psychotherapy. *Psychotherapy, 26*(4), 427–435.

Patterson, G. R. (1982). *Coercive family process.* Eugene, OR: Castilia Press.

Paulhus, D. P., & Landolt, M. A. (2000). Paragons of intelligence: Who gets nominated and why. *Canadian Journal of Behavioural Science, 32*(3), 168–177.

Paunonen, S. V., & Ashton, M. C. (2001). Big Five factors and facets and the prediction of behavior. *Journal of Personality and Social Psychology, 81*, 524–539.

Pavlov, I. P. (1927). *Conditioned reflexes.* Translated by G. V. Anrep. New York: Dover.

Pavot, W., & Diener, E. (1993). Review of the satisfaction with life scale. *Psychological Assessments, 5*(2), 164–172.

Peeters, M. C. W., Buunk, B. P., & Schaufeli, W. B. (1995). A microanalysis exploration of the cognitive appraisal of daily stressful events at work. *Anxiety, Stress & Coping: An International Journal, 8*(2), 127–139.

Pendergast, M. (1995). *Victims of memory: Incest accusations and shattered lives.* Hinesburg, VT: Upper Access.

Penfield, W. (1957, April 27). Brain's record of past a continuous movie film. *Science News Letter*, p. 265.

Penfield, W. (1958). *The excitable cortex in conscious man.* Springfield, IL: Charles C. Thomas.

Penfield, W., & Perot, P. (1963). The brain's record of auditory and visual experience. *Brain, 86,* 595–696.

Pennebaker, J. W., & Francis, M. E. (1996). Cognitive, emotional, and language processes in disclosure. *Cognition & Emotion, 10*(6), 601–626.

Pepler, D. J., & Craig, W. M. (1995). A peek behind the fence: Naturalistic observations of aggressive children with remote audiovisual recording. *Developmental Psychology, 31*(4), 548–553.

Pepler, D. J., Craig, W. M., & Roberts, W. L. (1998). Observations of aggressive and nonaggressive children on the school playground. *Merrill-Palmer Quarterly, 44*(1), 55–76.

Perin, C. T. (1943). A quantitative investigation of the delay of reinforcement gradient. *Journal of Experimental Psychology, 32,* 37–51.

Perkins, D. (1995). *Outsmarting IQ: The emerging science of learnable intelligence.* New York: Free Press.

Perkins, K. A. (1995). Individual variability in responses to nicotine. *Behavior Genetics, 25*(2), 119–132.

Perls, F. (1969). *Gestalt therapy verbatim.* Lafayette, CA: Real People.

Perry, C., Orne, M. T., London, R. W., & Orne, E. C. (1996). Rethinking per se exclusions of hypnotically elicited recall as legal testimony. *International Journal of Clinical & Experimental Hypnosis, 44*(1), 66–81.

Perry, D. G., Perry, L. C., & Weiss, R. J. (1989). Sex differences in the consequences that children anticipate for aggression. *Developmental Psychology, 25*(2), 312–319.

Peters, W. A. (1971). *A class divided.* Garden City, NY: Doubleday.

Petersen, S. E., Fox, P. T., Posner, M. I., Mintun, M., et al. (1988). Positron emission tomographic studies of the cortical anatomy of single-word processing. *Nature, 331*(6157), 585–589.

Peterson, B. E., & Klohnen, E. C. (1995). Realization of generativity in two samples of women at midlife. *Psychology & Aging, 10*(1), 20–29.

Peterson, L. R., & Peterson, M. J. (1959). Short-term retention of individual verbal items. *Journal of Experimental Psychology, 58,* 193–198.

Peterson, S. E. (1992). The cognitive functions of underlining as a study technique. *Reading Research & Instruction, 31*(2), 49–56.

Petitto, L. A., & Marentette, P. F. (1991). Babbling in the manual mode: Evidence for the ontogeny of language. *Science, 251,* 1493–1496.

Petri, H. (1996). *Motivation.* Pacific Grove, CA: Brooks/Cole.

Pettigrew, T. F. (1998). Intergroup contact theory. *Annual Review of Psychology, 49,* 65–85.

Pettit, G. S., Brown, E. G., Mize, J., & Lindsey, E. (1998). Mothers' and fathers' socializing behaviors in three contexts. *Merrill-Palmer Quarterly, 44*(2), 173–193.

Petty, R. E., Wegener, D. T., & Fabrigar, L. R. (1997). Attitudes and attitude change. *Annual Review of Psychology, 48,* 609–647.

Phillips, J. L. (1969). *Origins of intellect: Piaget's theory.* San Francisco: Freeman.

Piaget, J. (1951, original French, 1945). *The psychology of intelligence.* New York: Norton.

Piaget, J. (1952). *The origins of intelligence in children.* New York: International University Press.

Piccione, C., Hilgard, E. R., & Zimbardo, P. G. (1989). On the degree of stability of measured hypnotizability over a 25-year period. *Journal of Personality & Social Psychology, 56*(2), 289–295.

Pierce, J. P. (1991). Progress and problems in international public health efforts to reduce tobacco usage. *Annual Review of Public Health, 12,* 383–400.

Pike, J. L., et al. (1997). Chronic life stress alters sympathetic, neuroendocrine, and immune responsivity to an acute psychological stressor in humans. *Psychosomatic Medicine, 59*(4), 447–459.

Piliavin, I. M., Rodin, J., & Piliavin, J. A. (1969). Good samaritanism: An underground phenomenon? *Journal of Personality & Social Psychology, 13,* 289–299.

Pillow, D. R., Zautra, A. J., & Sandler, I. (1996). Major life events and minor stressors: Identifying mediational links in the stress process. *Journal of Personality & Social Psychology, 70*(2), 381–394.

Pinel, J. P. J., Assanand, S., & Lehman, D. R. (2000). Hunger, eating, and ill health. *American Psychologist, 55*(10), 1105–1116.

Pines, A. M. (1998). A prospective study of personality and gender differences in romantic attraction. *Personality & Individual Differences, 25*(1), 147–157.

Pinsof, W. M., Wynne, L. C., & Hambright, A. B. (1996). The outcomes of couple and family therapy. *Psychotherapy, 33*(2), 321–331.

Pisacreta, R. (1998). Superstitious behavior and response stereotypy prevent the emergence of efficient rule-governed behavior in humans. *Psychological Record, 48*(2), 251–274.

Pliner, P., & Haddock, G. (1996). Perfectionism in weight-concerned and -unconcerned women. *International Journal of Eating Disorders, 19*(4), 381–389.

Pliner, P., & Stallberg-White, C. (2000). "Pass the ketchup, please": Familiar flavors increase children's willingness to taste novel foods. *Appetite, 34*(1), 95–103.

Plomin, R., & Rende, R. (1991). Human behavioral genetics. In M. R. Rosenzweig & L. W. Porter (Eds.), *Annual Review of Psychology, 42,* 161–190.

Plowright, C. M. S., Landry, F., Church, D., et al. (2001). A change in orientation: Recognition of rotated patterns by bumble bees. *Journal of Insect Behavior, 14*(1), 113–127.

Plug, C., & Ross, H. E. (1994). The natural moon illusion: A multifactor angular account. *Perception, 23*(3), 321–333.

Plutchik, R. (1980). *Emotion.* New York: Harper & Row.

Plutchik, R. (1990). Emotions in psychotherapy: A psychoevolutionary perspective. In R. Plutchik & H. Kellerman (Eds.), *Emotion.* San Diego, CA: Academic Press.

Plutchik, R. (1994). *The psychology and biology of emotion.* New York: HarperCollins.

Pogatchnik, S. (1990, January 26). Kids' TV gets more violent, study finds. *The Los Angeles Times,* pp. F1, F27.

Polce-Lynch, M., Myers, B. J., Kilmartin, C. T., Forssmann-Falck, R., & Kliewer, W. (1998). Gender and age patterns in emotional expression, body image, and self-esteem. *Sex Roles, 38*(11–12), 1025–1048.

Pollner, M. (1998). The effects of interviewer gender in mental health interviews. *Journal of Nervous & Mental Disease, 186*(6), 369–373.

Pollock, V. E., Briere, J., Schneider, L., Knop, J., et al. (1990). Childhood antecedents of antisocial behavior. *American Journal of Psychiatry, 147*(10), 1290–1293.

Pope, H. G., Gruber, A. J., & Yurgelun-Todd, D. (1995). The residual neuropsychological effects of cannabis. *Drug & Alcohol Dependence, 38*(1), 25–34.

Pope, H. G., Katz, D. L., & Hudson, J. I. (1993). Anorexia nervosa and "reverse anorexia" among 108 male bodybuilders. *Comprehensive Psychiatry, 34*(6), 406–409.

Pope, H. G., & Yurgelun-Todd, D. (1996). The residual cognitive effects of heavy marijuana use in college students. *Journal of the American Medical Association, 275*(7), 521–527.

Porac, C., Friesen, I. C., Barnes, M. P., & Gruppuso, V. (1998). Illness and accidental injury in young and older adult left- and right-handers: Implications for genetic theories of hand preference. *Developmental Neuropsychology, 14*(1), 157–172.

Pornpitakpan, C., & Francis, J. N. P. (2001). The effect of cultural differences, source expertise, and argument strength on persuasion: An experiment with Canadians and Thais. *Journal of International Consumer Marketing, 13*(1), 77–101.

Port, R. L., & Seybold, K. S. (1995). Hippocampal synaptic plasticity as a biological substrate underlying episodic psychosis. *Biological Psychiatry, 37*(5), 318–324.

Potashkin, B. D., & Beckles, N. (1990). Relative efficacy of Ritalin and biofeedback treatments in the management of hyperactivity. *Biofeedback & Self-Regulation, 15*(4), 305–315.

Potkay, C. R., & Allen, B. P. (1986). *Personality: Theory, research, and applications.* Monterey, CA: Brooks/Cole.

Potvin, L., Champagne, F., & Laberge-Nadeau, C. (1988). Mandatory driver training and road safety: The Quebec experience. *American Journal of Public Health, 78,* 1206–1209.

Poulin, J., & Walter, C. (1993). Social worker burnout. *Social Work Research & Abstracts, 29*(4), 5–11.

Poulton, R. G., & Andrews, G. (1996). Change in danger cognitions in agoraphobia and social phobia during treatment. *Behaviour Research & Therapy, 34*(5–6), 413–421.

Powell, A. L., & Thelen, M. H. (1996). Emotions and cognitions associated with bingeing and weight control behavior in bulimia. *Journal of Psychosomatic Research, 40*(3), 317–328.

Premack, A. J., & Premack, D. (1972, October). Teaching language to an ape. *Scientific American,* 92–99.

Premack, D. (1983). Animal cognition. *Annual Review of Psychology, 34,* 351–362.

Premack, D., & Premack, A. J. (1983). *The mind of an ape.* New York: Norton.

Pressley, M. (1987). Are key-word method effects limited to slow presentation rates? An empirically based reply to Hall and Fuson (1986). *Journal of Educational Psychology, 79*(3), 333–335.

Pressley, M., Symons, S., McDaniel, M., A., Snyder, B., et al. (1988). Elaborative interrogation facilitates acquisition of confusing facts. *Journal of Educational Psychology, 80*(3), 268–278.

Pressman, J. D. (1998). *Last resort: Psychosurgery and the limits of medicine.* New York: Cambridge University Press.

Puca, R. M., & Schmalt, H. (1999). Task enjoyment: A mediator between achievement motives and performance. *Motivation & Emotion, 23*(1), 15–29.

Pursch, J. A. (1983, June 12). Cocaine can give you the business. *Los Angeles Times*, Part VII, p. 12.

Quinn, P. C., & Bhatt, R. S. (1998). Visual pop-out in young infants. *Infant Behavior & Development, 21*(2), 273–288.

Quitkin, F. M. (1999). Placebos, drug effects, and study design: A clinician's guide. *American Journal of Psychiatry, 156*(6), 829–836.

Rader, P. E., & Hicks, R. A. (1987, April). *Jet lag desynchronization and self-assessment of business related performance.* Paper presented at the Western Psychological Association meeting in Long Beach, CA.

Rafaeli, A., & Klimoski, R. J. (1983). Predicting sales success through handwriting analysis: An evaluation of the effects of training and handwriting sample content. *Journal of Applied Psychology, 68*, 212–217.

Raison, C. L., Klein, H. M., & Steckler, M. (1999). The moon and madness reconsidered. *Journal of Affective Disorders, 53*(1), 96–106.

Ralevski, E. (2001). *A study of the relationship between creativity and psychopathology.* Dissertation Abstracts International, Section B: The Sciences and Engineering. Vol. 61(12–B), 6751.

Ramachandran, V. S. (1992a). Filling in gaps in perception. *Current Directions in Psychological Science, 1*(6), 199–205.

Ramachandran, V. S. (1992b, May). Blind spots. *Scientific American*, 86–91.

Ramachandran, V. S. (1995). 2–D or not 2–D—that is the question. In R. Gregory, J. Harris, P. Heard, & D. Rose (Eds.), *The artful eye.* Oxford: Oxford University Press.

Ramanaiah, N. V., Detwiler, F. R. J., & Byravan, A. (1995, December). Sex-role orientation and satisfaction with life. *Psychological Reports, 77*(3, Pt 2), 1260–1262.

Ramirez-Valles, J., Zimmerman, M. A., & Newcomb, M. D. (1998). Sexual risk behavior among youth. *Journal of Health & Social Behavior, 39*(3), 237–253.

Randall-Simpson, J. A., Wainwright, P. E., Hoffman-Goetz, L., & Levesque, S. (1994). Effects of different weight loss treatments on weight cycling and metabolic measures in male mice. *Physiology and Behavior, 56*(1), 197–201.

Randi, J. (1980). *Flim-flam!* New York: Lippincott & Crowell.

Rathus, S., Fichner-Rathus, L., Nevid, J., & McKenzie, S. (2001). *Essentials of human sexuality.* Toronto: Pearson.

Rauscher, F. H., & Shaw, G. L. (1998). Key components of the Mozart effect. *Perceptual & Motor Skills, 86*(3, Pt 1), 835–841.

Redelmeier, D. A., & Tibshirani, R. J. (1999). Why cars in the next lane seem to go faster. *Nature, 401*(6748), 35.

Reed, J. D., & Bruce, D. (1982). Longitudinal tracking of difficult memory retrievals. *Cognitive Psychology, 14*, 280–300.

Reed, S. K. (1996). *Cognition: Theory and applications* (3rd ed.). Pacific Grove, CA: Brooks/Cole.

Regan, P. C. (1998). Of lust and love. *Personal Relationships, 5*(2), 139–157.

Regeser López, S., & Guarnaccia, P. J. J. (2000). Cultural psychopathology: Uncovering the social world of mental illness. *Annual Review of Psychology, 51*, 571–598.

Reiff, S. Katkin, E. S., & Friedman, R. (1999). Classical conditioning of the human blood pressure response. *International Journal of Psychophysiology, 34*(2), 135–145.

Reifman, A. S., Larrick, R. P., & Fein, S. (1991). Temper and temperature on the diamond: The heat-aggression relationship in major league baseball. *Personality & Social Psychology Bulletin, 17*(5), 580–585.

Reisner, A. D. (1996). Repressed memories: True and false. *Psychological Record, 46*(4), 563–579.

Reiss, M., Tymnik, G., Koegler, P., Koegler, W., & Reiss, G. (1999). Laterality of hand, foot, eye, and ear in twins. *Laterality, 4*(3), 287–297.

Renner, M. J., & Mackin, R. S. (1998). A life stress instrument for classroom use. *Teaching of Psychology, 25*(1), 46–48.

Rescorla, R. A. (1987). A Pavlovian analysis of goal-directed behavior. *American Psychologist, 42*, 119–126.

Reynolds, S., Stiles, W. B., Barkham, M., & Shapiro, D. A. (1996). Acceleration of changes in session impact during contrasting time-limited psychotherapies. *Journal of Consulting & Clinical Psychology, 64*(3), 577–586.

Reznick, J. S., & Goldfield, B. A. (1992). Rapid change in lexical development in comprehension and production. *Developmental Psychology, 28*(3), 406–413.

Rhine, J. B. (1953). *New world of the mind.* New York: Sloane.

Ricci, L. C., & Wellman, M. W. (1990). Monamines: Biochemical markers of suicide? *Journal of Clinical Psychology, 46*(1), 106–116.

Rice, M. E. (1997). Violent offender research and implications for the criminal justice system. *American Psychologist, 52*(4), 414–423.

Richards, L., Rollerson, B., & Phillips, J. (1991). Perceptions of submissiveness: Implications for victimization. *Journal of Psychology, 125*(4), 407–411.

Richelle, M. N. (1995). *B. F. Skinner: A reappraisal.* Hillsdale: Erlbaum.

Ricketts, M. S., & Galloway, R. E. (1984). Effects of three different one-hour single-session treatments for test anxiety. *Psychological Reports, 54*, 113–119.

Rideout, B. E., Dougherty, S., & Wernert, L. (1998). Effect of music on spatial performance: A test of generality. *Perceptual & Motor Skills, 86*(2), 512–514.

Rideout, B. E., & Taylor, J. (1997). Enhanced spatial performance following 10 minutes exposure to music: A replication. *Perceptual & Motor Skills, 85*(1), 112–114.

Rieber, R. W. (1999). Hypnosis, false memory and multiple personality. *History of Psychiatry, 10*(37, Pt 1), 3–11.

Rieke, M. L., & Guastello, S. J. (1995, June). Unresolved issues in honesty and integrity testing. *American Psychologist*, 458–459.

Rinck, M. (1999). Memory for everyday objects: Where are the digits on numerical keypads? *Applied Cognitive Psychology, 13*(4), 329–350.

Ring, K. (1980). *Life at death.* New York: Coward, McCann & Geoghegan.

Ritter, J. (1998, October 15). Uniforms changing the culture of the nation's classrooms. *USA Today*, pp. 1A, 2A.

Roan, S. (1992, September 1). Forever set in your ways at 30? *Los Angeles Times*, pp. E1, E2.

Roberts, R. (1989). Passenger fear of flying: Behavioural treatment with extensive in-vivo exposure and group support. *Aviation, Space, & Environmental Medicine, 60*(4), 342–348.

Roberts, S. M. (1995). Applicability of the goodness-of-fit hypothesis to coping with daily hassles. *Psychological Reports, 77*(3, Pt 1), 943–954.

Robins, R. W., Gosling, S. D., & Craik, K. H. (1998, July–August). Psychological science at the crossroads. *American Scientist, 86*, 310–313.

Robins, R. W., Gosling, S. D., & Craik, K. H. (1999). An empirical analysis of trends in psychology. *American Psychologist, 54*(2), 117–128.

Robinson, A., & Clinkenbeard, P. R. (1998). Giftedness. *Annual Review of Psychology, 49*, 117–139.

Robinson, B., Frye, E. M., & Bradley, L. J. (1997). Cult affiliation and disaffiliation. *Counseling & Values, 41*(2), 166–173.

Robinson, T. N., Wilde, M. L., Navracruz, L. C., Haydel, K. F.,

and Varady, A. (2001). Effects of reducing children's television and video game use on aggressive behavior. *Archives of Pediatrics and Adolescent Medicine, 155*(1), 17–23.

Robinson-Riegler, B., & McDaniel, M. (1994). Further constraints on the bizarreness effect: Elaboration at encoding. *Memory & Cognition, 22*(6), 702–712.

Robson, P. (1984). Prewalking locomotor movements and their use in predicting standing and walking. *Child Care, Health & Development, 10*, 317–330.

Roediger, H. L. (1990). Implicit memory. *American Psychologist, 45*(9), 1043–1056.

Roediger, H. L., & McDermott, K. B. (1995). Creating false memories: Remembering words not presented on lists. *Journal of Experimental Psychology: Learning, Memory, and Cognition, 21*(4), 803–814.

Rogers, C. R. (1959). A theory of therapy, personality, and interpersonal relationships, as developed in the client-centered framework. In S. Koch (Ed.), *Psychology: A study of a science,* Vol. 3. New York: McGraw-Hill.

Rogers, C. R. (1961). *On becoming a person: A therapist's view of psychotherapy.* Boston: Houghton Mifflin.

Rogers, C. R. (1980). *A way of being.* Boston: Houghton Mifflin.

Rogers, T. B., Kuiper, N. A., & Kirker, W. S. (1977). Self-reference and the encoding of personal information. *Journal of Personality and Social Psychology, 35*(9), 677–688.

Rogerson, J. (1997). Canine fears and phobias: A regime for treatment without recourse to drugs. *Applied Animal Behaviour Science, 52*(3–4), 291–297.

Rohsenow, D. J., & Smith R. E. (1982). Irrational beliefs as predictors of negative affective states. *Motivation and Emotion, 6*, 299–301.

Rollman, G. B. (1998). Culture and pain. In S. S. Kazarian et al. (Eds.), *Cultural clinical psychology.* New York: Oxford University Press.

Roos, P. E., & Cohen, L. H. (1987). Sex roles and social support as moderators of life stress adjustment. *Journal of Personality & Social Psychology, 52*, 576–585.

Rosch, E. (1977). Classification of real-world objects: Origins and representations in cognition. In P. N. Johnson-Laird & P. C. Wason (Eds.), *Thinking: Reading in cognitive science.* Cambridge: Cambridge University Press.

Rose, R. J. (1995). Genes and human behavior. *Annual Review of Psychology, 46*, 625–654.

Rosen, L. A., Booth, S. R., Bender, M. E., McGrath, M. L., et al. (1988). Effects of sugar (sucrose) on children's behavior. *Journal of Consulting & Clinical Psychology*, *56*(4), 583–589.

Rosenbaum, J. F., Biederman, J., Gersten, M., Hirshfeld, D. R., et al. (1989). Behavioral inhibition in children of parents with panic disorder and agoraphobia: A controlled study. *Annual Progress in Child Psychiatry & Child Development*, 294–315.

Rosenbaum, J. F., Biederman, J., Hirshfeld, D. R., Bolduc, E. A., et al. (1991). Further evidence of an association between behavioral inhibition and anxiety disorders. *Journal of Psychiatric Research*, *25*(1–2), 49–65.

Rosenberg, L. B. (1994, July). *The effect of interocular distance upon depth perception when using stereoscopic displays to perform work within virtual and telepresent environments*. USAF AMRL Technical Report (Wright-Patterson), AL/CF-TR-1994–0052. 30 p.

Rosenman, R. H., Brand, R. J., Jenkins, C. D., Friedman, M., Straus, R., & Wurm, M. (1975). Coronary heart disease in the Western Collaborative Group Study: Final follow-up experience of 8 1/2 years. *Journal of the American Medical Association, 233*, 872–877.

Rosenman, R. H. and Friedman, M. (1983). Relationship of Type A behavior pattern to coronary heart disease. In H. Selye (Ed)., *Selye's guide to stress research*, Vol. 2. New York: Scientific and Academic Editions.

Rosenthal, N. E. (1993). *Winter blues: Seasonal affective disorder*. New York: Guilford Press.

Rosenthal, R. (1965). Clever Hans: A case study of scientific method. *Introduction to Clever Hans: (The horse of Mr. Von Osten)*. O. Pfungst. New York: Holt, Rinehart & Winston.

Rosenthal, R. (1973, September). The Pygmalion effect lives. *Psychology Today*, 56–63.

Rosenthal, R. (1994). Science and ethics in conducting, analyzing, and reporting psychological research. *Psychological Science, 5*, 127–134.

Rosenthal, T. L. (1993). To soothe the savage breast. *Behavior Research & Therapy, 31*(5), 439–462.

Rosenthal, T. L., & Rosenthal, R. (1980). *The vicious cycle of stress reaction*. Copyright, Renate and Ted Rosenthal, Stress Management Clinic, Department of Psychiatry, University of Tennessee College of Medicine, Memphis, Tennessee.

Rosenthal, T. L., & Steffek, B. D. (1991). Modeling methods. In F.

H. Kanfer & A. P. Goldstein (Eds.), *Helping people change*. Elmsford, NY: Pergamon.

Rosenzweig, M. R. (1999). Continuity and change in the development of psychology around the world. *American Psychologist, 54*(4), 252–259.

Ross, D. C., Jaffe, J., Collins, R. L., Page, W., & Robinette, D. (1999). Handedness in the NAS/NRC Twin Study. *Laterality, 4*(3), 257–264.

Rothbaum, B. O., Hodges, L., & Kooper, R. (1997). Virtual reality and tactile augmentation in the treatment of spider phobia. *Journal of Psychotherapy Practice & Research, 6*(3), 219–226.

Rothbaum, B. O., Hodges, L. F., Kooper, R., Opdyke, D., et al. (1995). Effectiveness of computer-generated (virtual reality) graded exposure in the treatment of acrophobia. *American Journal of Psychiatry, 152*(4), 626–628.

Rothbaum, B. O., Hodges, L., Watson, B. A., Kessler, G. D., et al. (1996). Virtual reality exposure therapy in the treatment of fear of flying: A case report. *Behaviour Research & Therapy, 34*(5–6), 477–481.

Rothstein, M. G., Burke, R. J., & Bristor, J. M. (2001). Structural characteristics and support benefits in the interpersonal networks of women and men in management. *International Journal of Organizational Analysis, 9*(1), 4–25.

Rotter, J. B., & Hochreich, D. J. (1975). *Personality*. Glenview, IL: Scott, Foresman.

Rowe, D. C., Chassin, L., Presson, C., & Sherman, S. J. (1996). Parental smoking and the "epidemic" spread of cigarette smoking. *Journal of Applied Social Psychology, 26*(5), 437–454.

Rubin, D. C. (1985, September). The subtle deceiver: Recalling our past. *Psychology Today*, 38–46.

Rubin, K. H. (1998). Social and emotional development from a cultural perspective. *Developmental Psychology, 34*(4), 611–615.

Rubin, V., & Comitas, L. (Eds.). (1975). *Ganja in Jamaica*. The Hague: Mouton.

Rubin, Z. (1973). *Liking and loving: An invitation to social psychology*. New York: Holt.

Ruscio, J., Whitney, D. M., & Amabile, T. M. (1998). Looking inside the fishbowl of creativity. *Creativity Research Journal, 11*(3), 243–263.

Russell, T. G., Rowe, W., & Smouse, A. D. (1991). Subliminal self-help tapes and academic achievement: An evaluation. *Journal of Counseling and Development, 69*(Mar–Apr), 359–362.

Russo, M. B., et al. (1998). Conversion disorder presenting as mul-

tiple sclerosis. *Military Medicine, 163*(10), 709–710.

Russo, N. F. (1990). Forging research priorities for women's mental health. *American Psychologist, 45*(3), 368–373.

Rutter, M. (1995). Maternal deprivation. In M. H. Bornstein (Ed.), *Handbook of parenting*, Vol. 4. Mahwah, NJ: Erlbaum.

Ryan, R. M, & Deci, E. L. (2000). Self-determination theory and the facilitation of intrinsic motivation, social development, and well-being. *American Psychologist, 55*(1), 68–78.

Sacks, O. (1990). *Seeing voices*. New York: Harper Perennial.

Sadker, M., & Sadker, D. (1994). *Failing at fairness: How America's schools cheat girls*. New York: Scribner's.

Sahelian, R. (1998). *5–HTP*. Wakefield, RI: Moyer Bell.

Sainte-Hilaire, M. H., Sainte-Hilaire, J. M., & Granger, L. (1986). Jumping Frenchmen of Maine. *Neurology, 36*(9), 1269–1271.

Salive, M. E., Guralnik, J. M., & Glynn, R. J. (1993). Left-handedness and mortality. *American Journal of Public Health, 83*(2), 265–267.

Salovey, P., & Mayer, J. (1997). *Emotional development and emotional intelligence*. New York: Basic.

Salovey, P., & Singer, J. A. (1989). Mood congruency effects in recall of childhood versus recent memories. *Journal of Social Behavior & Personality, 4*(2), 99–120.

Sampson, E. E. (1993). Identity politics. *American Psychologist, 48*(12), 1219–1230.

Sanders, P., & Rosenfield, M. (1998). Counselling at a distance. *British Journal of Guidance & Counselling, 26*(1), 5–10.

Sansone, R. A., Sansone, L. A., & Righter, E. L. (1998). Panic disorder. *Journal of Women's Health, 7*(8), 983–989.

Santor, D. A., Messervey, D., & Kusumakar, V. (2000). Measuring peer pressure, popularity, and conformity in adolescent boys and girls: Predicting school performance, sexual attitudes, and substance abuse. *Journal of Youth and Adolescence, 29*(2), 163–182.

Sarason, I. G. (1981). Test anxiety, stress, and social support. *Journal of Personality, 49*, 101–114.

Saudino, K. J., et al. (1997). Can personality explain genetic influences on life events? *Journal of Personality & Social Psychology, 72*(1), 196–206.

Saunders, T., Driskell, J. E., Johnston, J. H., & Salas, E. (1996). The effect of stress inoculation training on anxiety and perform-

ance. *Journal of Occupational Health Psychology, 1*(2), 170–186.

Savage-Rumbaugh, E. S., Murphy, J., Sevcik, R. A., Brakke, K. E., et al. (1993). Language comprehension in ape and child. *Monographs of the Society for Research in Child Development, 58*(3–4), v-221.

Savage-Rumbaugh, S., & Lewin, R. (1996). *Kanzi*. New York: Wiley.

Savage-Rumbaugh, S., Sevcik, R. A., Brakke, K. E., Rumbaugh, D. M., et al. (1990). Symbols: Their communicative use, comprehension, and combination by bonobos (Pan paniscus). *Advances in Infancy Research, 6*, 221–278.

Saxe, L. (1991). Lying. *American Psychologist, 46*(4), 409–415.

Saxe, L. (1994). Detection of deception: Polygraph and integrity tests. *Current Directions in Psychological Science, 3*(3), 69–73.

Saxe, L., Dougherty, D., & Cross, T. (1985). The validity of polygraph testing. *American Psychologist, 40*, 355–366.

Scarr, S. (1998). American child care today. *American Psychologist, 53*(2), 95–108.

Schachter, S. (1951). Communication, deviation, and rejection. *Journal of Abnormal and Social Psychology, 46*, 190–207.

Schachter, S. (1959). *Psychology of affiliation*. Stanford, CA: Stanford University Press.

Schachter, S., & Wheeler, L. (1962). Epinephrine, chlorpromazine and amusement. *Journal of Abnormal and Social Psychology, 65*, 121–128.

Schacter, D. L. (1996). *Searching for memory*. New York: Basic.

Schacter, D. L. (1999). The seven sins of memory. *American Psychologist, 54*(3), 194–201.

Schacter, D. L., Norman, K. A., & Koutstaal, W. (1998). The cognitive neuroscience of constructive memory. *Annual Review of Psychology, 49*, 289–318.

Schafer, M., & Crichlow, S. (1996). Antecedents of groupthink: A quantitative study. *Journal of Conflict Resolution, 40*(3), 415–435.

Schaller, S. (1991). *A man without words*. New York: Summit.

Scheck, M. M., Schaeffer, J. A., & Gillette, C. (1998). Brief psychological intervention with traumatized young women. *Journal of Traumatic Stress, 11*(1) 25–44.

Schein, E. H., Hill, W. F., Lubin, A., & Williams, H. L. (1957). Distinguishing characteristics of collaborators and resistors among American prisoners of war. *Journal of Abnormal and Social Psychology, 55*, 197–201.

Schein, E. H., Schneier, I., & Barker, C. H. (1961). *Coercive persuasion*. New York: Norton.

Schick, T., & Vaughn, L. (1995). *How to think about weird things: Critical thinking for a new age*. Mountain View, CA: Mayfield.

Schlosberg, H. (1954). Three dimensions of emotion. *Psychological Review, 61*, 81–88.

Schmidt, L. A., & Fox, N. A. (1995). Individual differences in young adults' shyness and sociability. *Personality & Individual Differences, 19*(4), 455–462.

Schmitt, D. P., & Buss, D. M. (1996). Strategic self-promotion and competitor derogation. *Journal of Personality & Social Psychology, 70*(6), 1185–1204.

Schneider, C. (1987). *Children's television: The art, the business, and how it works*. Chicago: NTC Business Books.

Schneider, H. G., & Shugar, G. J. (1990). Audience and feedback effects in computer learning. *Computers in Human Behavior, 6*(4), 315–321.

Schooler, C., Flora, J. A., & Farquhar, J. W. (1993). Moving toward synergy: Media supplementation in the Stanford Five-City Project. *Communication Research, 20*(4), 587–610.

Schredl, M. (1995). Creativity and dream recall. *Journal of Creative Behavior, 29*(1), 16–24.

Schreiber, E. H., & Schreiber, D. E. (1999). Use of hypnosis with witnesses of vehicular homicide. *Contemporary Hypnosis, 16*(1), 40–44.

Schreiber, F. R. (1973). *Sybil*. Chicago: Regency.

Schroeder, J. E. (1995). Self-concept, social anxiety, and interpersonal perception skills. *Personality & Individual Differences, 19*(6), 955–958.

Schunk, D. H. (1990). Goal setting and self-efficacy during self-regulated learning. Special issue: Self-regulated learning and academic achievement. *Educational Psychologist, 25*(1), 71–86.

Schwartz, B., & Robbins, S. J. (1995). *Psychology of learning & behavior*. New York: Norton.

Schwartz, L. L. (1991). The historical dimension of cultic techniques of persuasion and control. *Cultic Studies Journal, 8*(1), 37–45.

Schweickert, R. (1993). A multinomial processing tree model for degradation and redintegration in immediate recall. *Memory & Cognition, 21*(2), 168–175.

Sclafani, A., & Springer, D. (1976). Dietary obesity in adult rats: Similarities to hypothalamic and human obesity syndromes. *Psychology and Behavior, 17*, 461–471.

Scott, J. P., & Ginsburg, B. E. (1994). The Seville statement on violence revisited. *American Psychologist, 49*(10), 849–850.

Scott, L., & O'Hara, M. W. (1993). Self-discrepancies in clinically anxious and depressed university students. *Journal of Abnormal Psychology, 102*(2), 282–287.

Scroppo, J. C., Drob, S. L., Weinberger, J. L., & Eagle, P. (1998). Identifying dissociative identity disorder: A self-report and projective study. *Journal of Abnormal Psychology, 107*(2), 272–284.

Seal, D. W., & Palmer-Seal, D. A. (1996). Barriers to condom use and safer sex talk among college dating couples. *Journal of Community & Applied Social Psychology, 6*(1), 15–33.

Sears, R. R., Maccoby, E. E., & Levin, H. (1957). *Patterns of child rearing*. Evanston, IL: Row, Peterson.

Seckel, A. (2000). *The art of optical illusions*. London: Carlton Books.

Segall, M. H., Lonner, W. J., & Berry, J. W. (1998). Cross-cultural psychology as a scholarly discipline. *American Psychologist, 53*(10), 1101–1110.

Seligman, M. E. P. (1972). For helplessness: Can we immunize the weak? In *Readings in Psychology Today* (2nd ed.). Del Mar, CA: CRM.

Seligman, M. E. P. (1989). *Helplessness*. New York: Freeman.

Seligman, M. E. P. (1994). *What you can change and what you can't*. New York: Knopf.

Seligman, M. E. P. (1995). The effectiveness of psychotherapy. *American Psychologist, 50*(12), 965–974.

Seligman, M. E. P. (1998). Why therapy works. *APA Monitor, 29*(12), 2.

Selye, H. (1956, 1976). *The stress of life*. New York: Knopf.

Senden, M. V. (1960). *Space and sight*. Translated by P. Heath. Glencoe, IL: Free Press.

Serbin, L. A., & O'Leary, K. D. (1975, December). How nursery schools teach girls to shut up. *Psychology Today*, 57–58, 102–103.

Seybolt, D. C., & Wagner, M. K. (1997). Self-reinforcement, gender-role, and sex of participant in prediction of life satisfaction. *Psychological Reports, 81*(2) 519–522.

Shaffer, D. R. (1999). *Developmental psychology*. Pacific Grove, CA: Brooks/Cole.

Shaffer, J. B., & Galinsky, M. D. (1989). *Models of group therapy*. Englewood Cliffs, NJ: Prentice Hall.

Shafir, E. (1993). Choosing versus rejecting: Why some options are both better and worse than others. *Memory and Cognition, 21*, 546–556.

Shafton, A. (1995). *Dream reader*. Albany, NY: SUNY Press.

Shapiro, F. (1995). *Eye movement desensitization and reprocessing*. New York: Guilford.

Sharma, T., et al. (1998, August). Brain changes in schizophrenia.

British Journal of Psychiatry, 173, 132–138.

Shaw, G. L. (1999). *Keeping Mozart in mind*. San Diego, CA: Academic.

Shaywitz, S. E., & Gore, J. C. (1995). Sex differences in functional organization of the brain for language. *Nature, 373*(6515), 607.

Sheehan, P. W., & Statham, D. (1989). Hypnosis, the timing of its introduction, and acceptance of misleading information. *Journal of Abnormal Psychology, 98*(2), 170–176.

Sheehy, M., & Cournos, F. (1992). What is mental illness? In F. I. Kass, J. M. Oldham, & H. Pardes (Eds.), *The Columbia University College of Physicians and Surgeons complete home guide to mental health*. New York: Sharpe Communications/Henry Holt.

Sheldon, K. M., & Elliot, A. J. (1999). Goal striving, need satisfaction, and longitudinal well-being. *Journal of Personality and Social Psychology, 76*(3), 482–497.

Sheldon, K. M., Ryan, R. M., Rawsthorne, L. J., & Ilardi, B. (1997). Trait self and true self: Cross-role variation in the Big-Five personality traits and its relations with psychological authenticity and subjective well-being. *Journal of Personality & Social Psychology, 73*(6), 1380–1393.

Shepard, R. N. (1975). Form, formation, and transformation of internal representations. In R. L. Solso (Ed.), *Information processing and cognition: The Loyola Symposium*. Hillsdale, NJ: Erlbaum.

Sherif, M., Harvey, O. J., White, B. J., Hood, W. R., & Sherif, C. W. (1961). *Intergroup conflict and cooperation: The Robbers Cave experiment*. University of Oklahoma, Institute of Group Relations.

Shneidman, E. (1987a, March). At the point of no return. *Psychology Today*, 54–58.

Shneidman, E. S. (1987b). Psychological approaches to suicide. In G. R. VandenBos & B. K. Bryant (Eds.), *Cataclysms, crises, and catastrophes: Psychology in action*. Washington, DC: American Psychological Association.

Shore, L. A. (1990, Fall). Skepticism in light of scientific literacy. *Skeptical Inquirer, 15*, 3–4.

Shurkin, J. N. (1992). *Terman's kids*. Boston: Little, Brown.

Shweder, R. A. (1999). Why cultural psychology? *Ethos, 27*(1), 62–73.

Siau, Keng L. (1996). Group creativity and technology. *Journal of Creative Behavior, 29*(3), 201–216.

Siegel, S. (1999). Drug anticipation and drug addiction. The 1998 H. David Archibald Lecture. *Addiction, 94*, 1113–1124.

Siegel, S., Baptista, M. A. S., Kim, J. A., McDonald, R. V., & Weise-Kelly, L. (2000). Pavlovian psy-

chopharmacology: The associative basis of tolerance. *Experimental and Clinical Psychopharmacology, 8*, 273–276.

Siegler, R. S. (1989). Mechanisms of cognitive development. *Annual Review of Psychology, 40*, 353–379.

Silva, C. E., & Kirsch, I. (1992). Interpretive sets, expectancy, fantasy proneness, and dissociation as predictors of hypnotic response. *Journal of Personality & Social Psychology, 63*(5), 847–856.

Silverman, I., Choi, J., Mackewn, A., Fisher, M., Moro, J., & Olshansky, E. (2000). Evolved mechanisms underlying wayfinding: Further studies on the hunter-gatherer theory of spatial sex differences. *Evolution and Human Behavior, 21*, 201–213.

Silverman, K., Evans, S. M., Strain, E. C., & Griffiths, R. R. (1992). Withdrawal syndrome after the double-blind cessation of caffeine consumption. *New England Journal of Medicine, 327*(16), 1109–1114.

Simon, L. (1998). *Genuine reality: A life of William James*. Ft. Worth: Harcourt-Brace.

Simonet, S., & Wilde, G. J. S. (1997). Risk: Perception, acceptance and homeostasis. *Applied Psychology: An International Review, 46*(3), 235–252.

Simons, D. J., & Levin, D. T. (1998). Failure to detect changes to people during a real-world interaction. *Psychonomic Bulletin & Review, 5*(4), 644–649.

Simpson, D. D., Joe, G. W., Fletcher, B. W., Hubbard, R. L, & Anglin, M. D. (1999). A national evaluation of treatment outcomes for cocaine dependence. *Archives of General Psychiatry, 57*(6), 507–514.

Sinclair, L., & Kunda, Z. (2000). Motivated stereotyping of women: She's fine if she praised me but incompetent if she criticized me. *Personality and Social Psychology Bulletin, 26*(11), 1329–1342.

Singer, L. T., Arendt, R., Fagan, J., Minnes, S., et al. (1999). Neonatal visual information processing in cocaine-exposed and non-exposed infants. *Infant Behavior & Development, 22*(l), 1–15.

Singer, M. T., & Addis, M. E. (1992). Cults, coercion, and contumely. *Cultic Studies Journal, 9*(2), 163–189.

Singh, N. N., McKay, J. D., & Singh, A. N. (1998). Culture and mental health: Nonverbal communication. *Journal of Child & Family Studies, 7*(4), 403–409.

Single, E., Rehm, J., Robson, L. & Van Troung, M. (2000). The relative risks and etiologic fractions of different causes of death and disease attributable to alcohol, tobacco and illicit drug use in Canada. *Canadian Medical Association Journal, 162*(12), 1669–1675.

Sirkin, M. I. (1990). Cult involvement: A systems approach to assessment and treatment. *Psychotherapy, 27*(1), 116–123.

Sison, C. E., Alpert, M., Fudge, R., & Stern, R. M. (1996). Constricted expressiveness and psychophysiological reactivity in schizophrenia. *Journal of Nervous & Mental Disease, 184*(10), 589–597.

Skeels, H. M. (1966). Adult status of children with contrasting early life experiences. *Monograph of the Society for Research in Child Development, 31*(3).

Skinner, B. F. (1938). *The behavior of organisms*. Englewood Cliffs, NJ: Prentice-Hall.

Skipton, L. H. (1997). The many faces of character. *Consulting Psychology Journal: Practice & Research. 49*(4), 235–245.

Skrandies, W., Reik, P., & Kunze, C. (1999). Topography of evoked brain activity during mental arithmetic and language tasks: Sex differences. *Neuropsychologia, 37*(4), 421–430.

Slaby, A. E., Garfinkel, B. D., & Garfinkel, L. F. (1994). *No one say my pain*. New York: Norton.

Slater, A., Mattock, A., Brown, E., & Bremner, J. G. (1991). Form perception at birth: Cohen and Younger (1984) revisited. *Journal of Experimental Child Psychology, 51*(3), 395–406.

Sledge, W. H., Tebes, J., Rakfeldt, J., & Davidson, L. (1996). Day hospital/crisis respite care versus inpatient care: I. Clinical outcomes. *American Journal of Psychiatry, 153*(8), 1065–1073.

Sleek, S. (1995, November). Online therapy services raise ethical questions. *APA Monitor, 9.*

Sleek, S. (1998, November). How are psychologists portrayed on screen? *APA Monitor, 11.*

Slotkin, T. A. (1998). Fetal nicotine or cocaine exposure: Which one is worse? *Journal of Pharmacology and Experimental Therapeutics, 285*(3), 931–945.

Smith, A. P., Clark, R., & Gallagher, J. (1999). Breakfast cereal and caffeinated coffee: Effects on working memory, attention, mood and cardiovascular function. *Physiology & Behavior, 67*(1), 9–17.

Smith, C. (1995). Sleep states and memory processes. *Behavioural Brain Research, 69*(1–2), 137–145.

Smith, C., Carey, S., & Wiser, M. (1985). On differentiation: A case study of the development of the concepts of size, weight, and density. *Cognition, 21*(3), 177–237.

Smith, E. E. (1989). Concepts and induction. In M. I. Posner (Ed.),

Foundations of cognitive science. Cambridge, MA: The MIT Press.

Smith, J. C. (1986, September). Meditation, biofeedback, and the relaxation controversy: A cognitive-behavioral perspective. *American Psychologist,* 1007–1009.

Smith, R. W., & Kounios, J. (1996). Sudden insight: All-or-none processing revealed by speed-accuracy decomposition. *Journal of Experimental Psychology: Learning, Memory, & Cognition, 22*(6), 1443–1462.

Smith, W. P., Compton, W. C., & West, W. B. (1995). Meditation as an adjunct to a happiness enhancement program. *Journal of Clinical Psychology, 51*(2), 269–273.

Snowden, P. L., & Christian, L. G. (1999). Parenting the young gifted child: Supportive behaviors. *Roeper Review, 21*(3), 215–221.

Snyderman, M., & Rothman, S. (1987). Survey of expert opinion on intelligence and aptitude testing. *American Psychologist, 42*(2), 137–144.

Sobel, E., Shine, D., DiPietro, D., & Rabinowitz, M. (1996). Condom use among HIV/infected patients in South Bronx, New York. *AIDS, 10*(2), 235–236.

Solowij, N., Michie, P. T., & Fox, A. M. (1995). Differential impairments of selective attention due to frequency and duration of cannabis use. *Biological Psychiatry, 37*(10), 731–739.

Somberg, D. R., Stone, G., & Claiborn, C. D. (1993). Informed consent: Therapists' beliefs and practices. *Professional Psychology: Research & Practice, 24*(2), 153–159.

Spangenberg, J. J., & Lategan, T. P. (1993). Coping, androgyny, and attributional style. *South African Journal of Psychology, 23*(4), 195–203.

Speca, M., Carlson, L. E., Goodey, E., & Angen, M. (2000). A randomized, wait-list controlled clinical trial: The effect of a mindfulness meditation-based stress reduction program on mood and symptoms of stress in cancer outpatients. *Psychosomatic Medicine, 62,* 613–622.

Spence, J. T. (1984). Masculinity, femininity, and gender-related traits. In B. A. Maker & W. B. Maker (Eds.), *Progress in experimental personality research: Normal personality processes,* Vol. 13. New York: Academic.

Sperry, R. W. (1968). Hemisphere deconnection and unity in conscious awareness. *American Psychologist, 23,* 723–733.

Sperry, R. W. (1995). The riddle of consciousness and the changing scientific worldview. *Journal of*

Humanistic Psychology, 35(2), 7–33.

Spiegler, M. D., & Guevremont, D. C. (1998). *Contemporary behavior therapy*. Pacific Grove, CA: Brooks/Cole.

Sprafka, J. M., Folsom, A. R., Burke, G. L., et al. (1990). Type A behavior and its association with cardiovascular disease prevalence in Blacks and Whites: The Minnesota Heart Survey. *Journal of Behavioral Medicine, 13*(1), 1–13.

Sprecher, S. (1998). Insiders' perspectives on reasons for attraction to a close other. *Social Psychology Quarterly, 61*(4), 287–300.

Springer, S. P., & Deutsch, G. (1998). *Left brain, right brain*. New York: Freeman.

Squire, L. R., Knowlton, B., & Musen, G., (1993). The structure and organization of memory. In L. W. Porter & M. R. Rosenzweig (Eds.), *Annual Review of Psychology, 44,* 453–495.

Squire, L. R., & Zola-Morgan, S. (1988). Memory: Brain systems and behavior. *Trends in Neurosciences, 11*(4), 170–175.

Stalheim-Smith, A., & Fitch, G. K. (1993). *Understanding human anatomy and physiology*. St. Paul, MN: West.

Stallberg-White, C., & Pliner, P. (1999). The effect of flavor principles on willingness to taste novel foods. *Appetite, 33*(2), 209–221.

Stamm, B. H. (1998). Clinical applications of telehealth in mental health care. *Professional Psychology: Research & Practice, 29*(6), 536–542.

Stanovich, K. E. (1996). *How to think straight about psychology* (4th ed.). New York: HarperCollins.

Stanovich, K. E. (1998). *How to think straight about psychology* (5th ed.). New York: Longman.

Star, The. (1983, October 11). "Horoscopes really true, says psychologist."

Statistics Canada. (2000). *Statistical report on the health of Canadians* (Catalogue No. 82–570–X1E). Document retrieved May 27, 2002, from http://www.statcan.ca/english/freepub/82–570–XIE/free.htm.

Statistics Canada (2001). You snooze, you lose? Sleep patterns in Canada. *Canadian Social Trends,* Catalogue No. 11–008. Ottawa: Author. Document retrieved February 26, 2002, from http://www.statcan.ca/english/indepth/11–008/feature/star2000059000s4a02.pdf.

Statistics Canada website: http://www.statcan.ca/english/pgdb/People/Population/demo28d.htm (accessed June 18, 2002).

Statistics Canada website: http://www.statcan.ca/english/pgdb/

People/Health/health36.htm (accessed March 1, 2002).

Staum, M. J., & Brotons, M. (1992). The influence of auditory subliminals on behavior. *Journal of Music Therapy, 29*(3), 130–185.

Steblay, N. M. (1992). A meta-analytic review of the weapon focus effect. *Law and Human Behavior, 16,* 413–424.

Steele, K. M., Bass, K. E., & Crook, M. D. (1999). The mystery of the Mozart effect: Failure to replicate. *Psychological Science, 10*(4), 366–369.

Steele, K. M., Brown, J. D., & Stoecker, J. A. (1999). Failure to confirm the Rauscher and Shaw description of recovery of the Mozart effect. *Perceptual & Motor Skills, 88*(3, Pt 1), 843–848.

Steen, R. G. (1996). *DNA and destiny: Nature and nurture in human behavior*. New York: Plenum.

Stefanis, C., Dornbush, R. L., & Fink, M. (1977). *Hashish: A study of long-term use*. New York: Raven.

Stein, M. B., Forde, D. R., Anderson, G., & Walker, J. W. (1997). Obsessive-compulsive disorder in the community: An epidemiologic survey with clinical reappraisal. *American Journal of Psychiatry, 154,* 1120–1126.

Stein, M., Miller, A. H., & Trestman, R. L. (1990). Depression and the immune system. In R. Ader, N. Cohen, & D. L. Felten (Eds.), *Psychoneuroimmunology II*. New York: Academic Press.

Stein, M. I. (1974). *Stimulating creativity*, Vol. 1. New York: Academic.

Steinberg, L. D., Catalano, R., & Dooley, P. (1981). Economic antecedents of child abuse and neglect. *Child Development, 52,* 975–985.

Stephan, W., Berscheid, E., & Walster, E. (1971). Sexual arousal and heterosexual perception. *Journal of Personality & Social Psychology, 20*(1), 93–101.

Stephens, K., Kiger, L., Karnes, F. A., & Whorton, J. E. (1999). Use of nonverbal measures of intelligence in identification of culturally diverse gifted students in rural areas. *Perceptual & Motor Skills, 88*(3, Pt 1), 793–796.

Stephens, T., & Joubert, N. (2001). The economic burden of mental health problems in Canada. *Chronic Diseases in Canada, 22,* 18–23.

Steriade, M., & McCarley, R. W. (1990). *Brainstem control of wakefulness and sleep*. New York: Plenum.

Sterman, M. B. (1996). Physiological origins and functional correlates of EEG rhythmic activities: Implications for self-regulation.

Biofeedback & Self Regulation, *21*(1), 3–33.

Stern, D. (1982). Some interactive functions of rhythm changes between mother and infant. In M. Davis (Ed.), *Interaction rhythms, periodicity in communicative behavior*. New York: Human Sciences Press.

Sternberg, R. J. (1996). *Successful intelligence*. New York: Simon & Schuster.

Sternberg, R. J., & Davidson, J. D. (1982, June). The mind of the puzzler. *Psychology Today*.

Sternberg, R. J., & Lubart, T. I. (1995). *Defying the crowd*. New York: The Free Press.

Sternberg, W. F., Bailin, D., Grant, M., & Gracely, R. H. (1998). Competition alters the perception of noxious stimuli in male and female athletes. *Pain, 76*(1–2), 231–238.

Stewart, A. J., & Ostrove, J. M. (1998). Women's personality in middle age. *American Psychologist, 53*(11), 1185–1194.

Stewart, J. V. (1996). *Astrology: What's really in the stars*. Amherst, NY: Prometheus.

Stiles, W. B., et al. (1998). Relations of the alliance with psychotherapy outcome. *Journal of Consulting & Clinical Psychology, 66*(5), 791–802.

Stiles, W. B., Shapiro, D. A., & Elliott, R. (1986). Are all psychotherapies equivalent? *American Psychologist, 41*, 165–180.

Stockhorst, U., Klosterhalfen, S., & Steingrueber, H. (1998). Conditioned nausea and further side-effects in cancer chemotherapy. *Journal of Psychophysiology, 12*(Suppl 1), 14–33.

Stolerman, I. P., & Jarvis, M. J. (1995). The scientific case that nicotine is addictive. *Psychopharmacology, 117*(1), 2–10.

Stone, J., Perry, Z. W., & Darley, J. M. (1997). "White men can't jump." *Basic and Applied Social Psychology, 19*(3), 291–306.

Stoney, S., & Wild, M. (1998). Motivation and interface design: Maximising learning opportunities. *Journal of Computer Assisted Learning, 14*(1), 40–50.

Storck, L. E. (1997). Cultural psychotherapy. *Group, 21*(4), 331–349.

Strack. F., Martin, L. L., & Stepper, S. (1988). Inhibiting and facilitating conditions of facial expressions: A non-obtrusive test of the facial feedback hypothesis. *Journal of Personality & Social Psychology, 54*, 768–777.

Strange, J. R. (1965). *Abnormal psychology*. New York: McGraw-Hill.

Straus, M. A., & Mouradian, V. E. (1998). Impulsive corporal punishment by mothers and antisocial behavior and impulsiveness

of children. *Behavioral Sciences & the Law, 16*(3), 353–374.

Strickler, E. M., & Verbalis, J. G. (1988, May–June). Hormones and behavior: The biology of thirst and sodium appetite. *American Scientist*, 261–267.

Strongman, K. T. (1996). *The psychology of emotion*. New York: Wiley.

Strupp, H. H. (1989). Psychotherapy: Can the practitioner learn from the researcher? *American Psychologist, 44*(4), 717–724.

Sturges, J. W., & Sturges, L. V. (1998). In vivo systematic desensitization in a single-session treatment of an 11-year-old girl's elevator phobia. *Child & Family Behavior Therapy, 20*(4), 55–62.

Suedfeld, P. (1990). Restricted environmental stimulation and smoking cessation. *International Journal of Addictions, 25*(8), 861–888.

Suedfeld, P., & Borrie, R. A. (1999). Health and therapeutic applications of chamber and flotation restricted environmental stimulation therapy (REST). *Psychology & Health, 14*(3), 545–566.

Suinn, R. M. (1975). *Fundamentals of behavior pathology* (2nd ed.). New York: Wiley.

Suinn, R. M. (1999, March). Scaling the summit: Valuing ethnicity. *APA Monitor, 2.*

Suls, J., & Swain, A. (1994). Type A-Type B personalities. *Encyclopedia of human behavior*, Vol. 4, 427–436. San Diego, CA: Academic.

Sumerlin, J, R. (1997). Self-actualization and hope. *Journal of Social Behavior & Personality, 12*(4), 1101–1110.

Sumerlin, J. R., & Bundrick, C. M. (1996). Brief Index of Self-Actualization: A measure of Maslow's model. *Journal of Social Behavior & Personality, 11*(2), 253–271.

Susman-Stillman, A., Kalkose, M., Egeland, B., & Waldman, I. (1996). Infant temperament and maternal sensitivity as predictors of attachment security. *Infant Behavior & Development, 19*(1), 33–47.

Swan, G. E., & Denk, C. E. (1987). Dynamic models for the maintenance of smoking cessation: Event history analysis of late relapse. *Journal of Behavioral Medicine, 10*(6), 527–554.

Swanson, M. W., Streissguth, A. P., Sampson, P. D., & Carmichael-Olson, H. (1999). Prenatal cocaine and neuromotor outcome at four months: Effect of duration of exposure. *Journal of Developmental & Behavioral Pediatrics, 20*(5), 325–334.

Swartz, C. M. (1993). ECT or programmed seizures? *American Journal of Psychiatry, 150*(8), 1274–1275.

Swayze, V. W. (1995). Frontal leukotomy and related psychosurgical procedures in the era before antipsychotics (1935–1954): A historical overview. *American Journal of Psychiatry, 152*(4), 505–515.

Swets, J., Bjork, R. A., Cook, T. D., Davison, G. C., et al. (1988). *Enhancing human performance: Issues, theories, and techniques*. Washington, DC: National Academy Press of the United States National Research Council.

Swim, J. K., & Sanna, L. J. (1996). He's skilled, she's lucky: A meta-analysis of observers' attributions for women's and men's successes and failures. *Personality & Social Psychology Bulletin, 22*(5), 507–519.

Takei, N., Sham, P., O'Callaghan, E., Murray, G. K., et al. (1994). Prenatal exposure to influenza and the development of schizophrenia. *American Journal of Psychiatry, 151*(1), 117–119.

Talley, P. F., Strupp, H. H., & Morey, L. C. (1990). Matchmaking in psychotherapy: Patient-therapist dimensions and their impact on outcome. *Journal of Consulting & Clinical Psychology, 58*(2), 182–188.

Tallis, F. (1996). Compulsive washing in the absence of phobic and illness anxiety. *Behaviour Research & Therapy, 34*(4), 361–362.

Tamis-LeMonvda, C. S., & Bornstein, M. H. (1994). Specificity in mother-toddler language-play relations across the second year. *Developmental Psychology, 30*(2), 283–292.

Tang, S., & Hall, V. C. (1995). The overjustification effect: A meta-analysis. *Applied Cognitive Psychology, 9*(5), 365–404.

Tannenbaum, S. I., & Yukl, G. (1992). Training and development in work organizations. In M. R. Rosenzweig & L. W. Porter (Eds.), *Annual Review of Psychology, 43*, 399–441.

Tardif, T. Z., & Sternberg, R. J. (1988). What do we know about creativity? In R. J. Sternberg (Ed.), *The nature of creativity*. New York: Cambridge University Press.

Tart, C. T. (1986). Consciousness, altered states, and worlds of experience. *Journal of Transpersonal Psychology, 18*(2), 159–170.

Tavris, C. (1992). *The mismeasure of woman*. New York: Touchstone/ Simon & Schuster.

Taylor, S. E. (1990). Health psychology. *American Psychologist, 45*(1), 40–50.

Taylor, S. E., Kemeny, M. E., Reed, G. M., Bower, J. E., & Gruenewald, T. L. (2000). Psychological resources, positive illusions,

and health. *American Psychologist, 55*(1), 99–109.

Teasdale, N., Bard, C., Fleury, M., et al. (1994). Bimanual interference in a deafferented patient and control subjects. In S. P. Swinnen et al. (Eds.), *Interlimb coordination: Neural, dynamical, and cognitive constraints*. San Diego: Academic Press.

Teng, E., & Squire, L. R. (1999). Memory for places learned long ago is intact after hippocampal damage. *Nature, 400*(6745), 675–677.

Teplin, L. A., Abram, K. M., & McClelland, G. M. (1994). Does psychiatric disorder predict violent crime among released jail detainees? *American Psychologist, 49*(4), 335–342.

ter Riet, G., de Craen, A. J. M., de Boer, A., & Kessels, A. G. H. (1998). Is placebo analgesia mediated by endogenous opioids? A systematic review. *Pain, 76*(3), 273–275.

Terborg, J. R. (1998). Health psychology in the United States. *Applied Psychology: An International Review, 47*(2), 199–217.

Terman, L. M., & Merrill, M. A. (1937, revised 1960). *Stanford-Binet Intelligence Scale*. Boston: Houghton Mifflin.

Terman, L. M., & Oden, M. (1959). *The gifted group in mid-life, Vol. 5: Genetic studies of genius*. Stanford, CA: Stanford University Press.

Thase, M. E., & Kupfer, D. L. (1996). Recent developments in the pharmacotherapy of mood disorders. *Journal of Consulting & Clinical Psychology, 64*(4), 646–659.

Thelen, E. (1995). Motor development. *American Psychologist, 50*(2), 79–95.

Thibodeau, R., & Aronson, E. (1992). Taking a closer look: Reasserting the role of self-concept in dissonance theory. *Personality and Social Psychology Bulletin, 18*(5), 591–602.

Thompson, R. F. (1991). Are memory traces localized or distributed? *Neuropsychologia, 29*(6), 571–582.

Thorndike, E. L. (1920). Intelligence and its use. *Harper's Magazine, 140*, 227–235.

Tierny, J. (1987, September/ October). Stitches: Good news; Better health linked to sin, sloth. *Hippocrates*, 30–35.

Tiffany, S. T., Martin, E. M., & Baker, T. B. (1986). Treatments for cigarette smoking: An evaluation of the contributions of aversion and counseling procedures. *Behavior Research & Therapy, 24*(4), 437–452.

Till, B. D., & Priluck, R. L. (2000). Stimulus generalization in classical conditioning: An initial investigation and extension. *Psychology & Marketing, 17*(1), 55–72.

Timmerman, I. G. H., Emmelkamp, P. M. G., & Sanderman, R. (1998). The effects of a stress-management training program in individuals at risk in the community at large. *Behaviour Research & Therapy, 36*(9), 863–875.

Tipper, S. P., & Cranston, M. (1985). Selective attention and priming: Inhibitory and facilitatory effects of ignored primes. *Quarterly Journal of Experimental Psychology: Human Experimental Psychology, 37A*(4), 591–611.

Tolman, E. C., & Honzik, C. H. (1930). Introduction and removal of reward and maze performance in rats. *University of California Publications in Psychology, 4,* 257–275.

Tolman, E. C., Ritchie, B. F., & Kalish, D. (1946). Studies in spatial learning: II. Place learning versus response learning. *Journal of Experimental Psychology, 36,* 221–229.

Tomes, H. (1998, December). Diversity: psychology's life depends on it. *APA Monitor, 28.*

Toneatto, T., Sobell, L. C., Sobell, M. B., & Rubel, E. (1999). Natural recovery from cocaine dependence. *Psychology of Addictive Behaviors, 13*(4), 259–268.

Torrey, E. F. (1988). *Surviving schizophrenia: A family manual.* New York: Harper & Row.

Torrey, E. F. (1996). *Out of the shadows.* New York: John Wiley & Sons.

Townsend, J. M., & Wasserman, T. (1998). Sexual attractiveness. *Evolution & Human Behavior, 19*(3), 171–191.

Trehub, S. E., Unyk, A. M., Kamenetsky, S. B., et al. (1997). Mothers' and fathers' singing to infants. *Developmental Psychology, 33,* 500–507.

Trehub, S. E., Unyk, A. M., & Trainor, L. J. (1993a). Adults identify infant-directed music across cultures. *Infant Behavior & Development, 16*(2), 193–211.

Trehub, S. E., Unyk, A. M., & Trainor, L. J. (1993b). Maternal singing in cross-cultural perspective. *Infant Behavior & Development, 16*(3), 285–295.

Tremblay, R. E. (2000). The development of aggressive behaviour during childhood: What have we learned in the past century? *International Journal of Behavioral Development, 24*(2), 129–141.

Tremblay, R. E., Japel, C., Perusse, D., et al. (1999). The search for the age of "onset" of physical aggression: Rousseau and Bandura revisited. *Criminal Behavior and Mental Health, 9*(1), 8–23.

Troll, L. E., & Skaff, M. M. (1997). Perceived continuity of self in

very old age. *Psychology & Aging, 12*(1), 162–169.

Truax, S. R. (1983). Active search, mediation, and the manipulation of cue dimensions: Emotion attribution in the false feedback paradigm. *Motivation and Emotion, 7,* 41–60.

Truchlicka, M., McLaughlin, T. F., & Swain, J. C. (1998). Effects of token reinforcement and response cost on the accuracy of spelling performance with middle-school special education students with behavior disorders. *Behavioral Interventions, 13*(1), 1–10.

Trut, L. N. (1999). Early canid domestication. *American Scientist, 87,* 160–169.

Tulley, M., & Chiu, L. H. (1995). Student teachers and classroom discipline. *Journal of Educational Research, 88*(3), 164–171.

Tulving, E. (1972). Episodic and semantic memory. In E. Tulving & W. Donaldson (Eds.), *Organization of memory.* New York: Academic Press.

Tulving, E. (1989). Remembering and knowing the past. *American Scientist, 77*(4), 361–367.

Tulving, E., & Schacter, D. L. (1990). Priming and human memory systems. *Science, 247*(4940), 301–306.

Tulving, E., Schacter, D. L., McLachlan, D. R., & Moscovitch, M. (1988). Priming of semantic autobiographical knowledge: A case study of retrograde amnesia. *Brain & Cognition, 8*(1), 3–20.

Turkheimer, E. (1998). Heritability and biological explanation. *Psychological Review, 105*(4), 782–791.

Turkheimer, E., & Parry, C. D. H. (1992). Why the gap? *American Psychologist, 47*(5), 646–655.

Turkington, C. (1986, August). Pot and the immune system. *APA Monitor, 22.*

Turner, S. J. M. (1997). The use of the reflective team in a psychodrama therapy group. *International Journal of Action Methods, 50*(1), 17–26.

Turton, M. D., O'Shea, D., Gunn, I., Beak, S. A., et al. (1996). A role for glucagon-like peptide-1 in the central regulation of feeding. *Nature, 379*(6560), 69–74.

Tutkun, H., Yargic, L. I., & Sar, V. (1995). Dissociative identity disorder. *Dissociation: Progress in the Dissociative Disorders, 8*(1), 3–9.

Tversky, A., & Kahneman, D. (1981). The framing of decisions and the psychology of choice. *Science, 211,* 453–458.

Tversky, A., & Kahneman, D. (1982). Judgments of and by representativeness. In D. Kahneman, P. Slovic, & A. Tversky (Eds.), *Judgment under uncertainty: Heuristics*

and biases. Cambridge: Cambridge University Press.

Tye-Murray, N., Spencer, L., & Woodworth, G. G. (1995). Acquisition of speech by children who have prolonged cochlear implant experience. *Journal of Speech & Hearing Research, 38*(2), 327–337.

Tzeng, M. (1992). The effects of socioeconomic heterogamy and changes on marital dissolution for first marriages. *Journal of Marriage and Family, 54,* 609–619.

Ulett, G. A. (1992). 3000 years of acupuncture: From metaphysics to neurophysiology. *Integrative Psychiatry, 8*(2), 91–100.

Ulrich, R. E., Stachnik, T. J., & Stainton, N. R. (1963). Student acceptance of generalized personality interpretations. *Psychological Reports, 13,* 831–834.

Underwood, B. J. (1957). Interference and forgetting. *Psychological Review, 64,* 49–60.

UNESCO. (1990). The Seville statement on violence. *American Psychologist, 45*(10), 1167–1168.

Utts, J. M. (1996). Response to Ray Hyman's report of September 11, 1995, "Evaluation of program on anomalous mental phenomena." *Journal of Scientific Exploration, 10*(1), 59–61.

Valins, S. (1966). Cognitive effects of false heart-rate feedback. *Journal of Personality & Social Psychology, 4,* 400–408.

Valins, S. (1967). Emotionality and information concerning internal reactions. *Journal of Personality & Social Psychology, 6,* 458–463.

Van Goozen, S. H. M., Cohen-Kettenis, P. T., Gooren, L. J. G., & Frijda, N. H. (1995). Gender differences in behaviour: Activating effects of cross-sex hormones. *Psychoneuroendocrinology, 20*(4), 343–363.

van Lawick-Goodall, J. (1971). *In the shadow of man.* New York: Houghton Mifflin.

van Rooij, J. J. F. (1994). Introversion-extraversion: Astrology versus psychology. *Personality & Individual Differences, 16*(6), 985–988.

Van Wyk, P. H., & Geist, C. S. (1995). Biology of bisexuality: Critique and observations. *Journal of Homosexuality, 28*(3–4), 357–373.

Vandenberg, S. G., & Kuse, A. R. (1978). Mental rotations, a group test of three-dimensional spatial visualization. *Perceptual and Motor Skills, 47*(2), 599–604.

VandenBos, G. R., & Bryant, B. K. (1987). Preface. In G. R. VandenBos & B. K. Bryant (Eds.), *Cataclysms, crises, and catastrophes: Psychology in action.* Washington, DC: American Psychological Association.

Vane, J. R., & Guarnaccia, V. J. (1989). Personality theory and personality assessment measures: How helpful to the clinician? *Journal of Clinical Psychology, 45*(1), 5–19.

Vargha-Khadem, F., Gadian, D. G., Watkins, K. E., Connelly, A., et al. (1997). Differential effects of early hippocampal pathology on episodic and semantic memory. *Science, 277*(5324), 376–380.

Vastag, B. (2001). Stem cells step closer to the clinic: Paralysis partially reversed in rats with ALS-like disease. *Journal of the American Medical Association, 285,* 1691–1693.

Velakoulis, D., & Pantelis, C. (1996). What have we learned from functional imaging studies in schizophrenia? *Australian & New Zealand Journal of Psychiatry, 30*(2), 195–209.

Viegener, B. J., Perri, M. G., Nezu, A. M., et al. (1990). Effects of an intermittent, low-fat, low-calorie diet in the behavioral treatment of obesity. *Behavior Therapy, 21*(4), 499–509.

Vitaro, F., Brendgen, M., & Tremblay, R. E. (2000). Influence of deviant friends on delinquency: Searching for moderator variables. *Journal of Abnormal Child Psychology, 28*(4), 313–325.

Vogler, R. E., & Bartz, W. R. (1982). *The better way to drink.* New York: Simon and Schuster.

Vogler, R. E., & Bartz, W. R. (1992). *Teenagers and alcohol.* Philadelphia: Charles Press.

Vogler, R. E., Weissbach, T. A., Compton, J. V., & Martin, G. T. (1977). Integrated behavior change techniques for problem drinkers in the community. *Journal of Consulting and Clinical Psychology, 45,* 267–279.

Volkmann, J., Schnitzler, A., Witte, O. W., & Freund, H. J. (1998). Handedness and asymmetry of hand representation in human motor cortex. *Journal of Neurophysiology, 79*(4), 2149–2154.

Volkow, N. D., Gillespie, H., Mullani, N., & Tancredi, L. (1996). Brain glucose metabolism in chronic marijuana users at baseline and during marijuana intoxication. *Psychiatry Research: Neuroimaging, 67*(1), 29–38.

Volpicelli, J. R., Ulm, R. R., Altenor, A., & Seligman, M. E. P. (1983). Learned mastery in the rat. *Learning and Motivation, 14,* 204–222.

Voyer, D. (1995). Effect of practice on laterality in a mental rotation task. *Brain and Cognition, 29*(3), 326–335.

Vygotsky, L. S. (1962). *Thought and language.* Cambridge, MA: MIT Press.

Vygotsky, L. S. (1978). *Mind in society. The development of higher mental processes.* M. Cole, V. John-Steiner, S. S. Scribner, & E. Souberman (Eds.). Cambridge, MA: Harvard University Press.

Wadden, T. A., Vogt, R. A., Foster, G. D., & Anderson, D. A. (1998). Exercise and the maintenance of weight loss. *Journal of Consulting and Clinical Psychology, 66*(2), 429–433.

Waid, W. M., & Orne, M. T. (1982, July/August). The physiological detection of deception. *American Scientist, 70,* 402–409.

Wakefield, J. C. (1992). The concept of mental disorder. *American Psychologist, 47*(3), 373–388.

Wakeling, A. (1996). Epidemiology of anorexia nervosa. *Psychiatry Research, 62*(1), 3–9.

Walker, I., & Crogan, M. (1998). Academic performance, prejudice, and the Jigsaw classroom. *Journal of Community & Applied Social Psychology, 8*(6), 381–393.

Walker, R. E., & Foley, J. M. (1973). Social intelligence: Its history and measurement. *Psychological Reports, 33,* 839–864.

Wallach, M. A. (1985). Creativity testing and giftedness. In F. D. Horowitz & M. O'Brien (Eds.), *The gifted and talented: Developmental perspectives* (pp. 99–123). Washington, DC: American Psychological Association.

Wallach, M. A., & Kogan, N. (1965). *Modes of thinking in young children.* New York: Holt.

Walsh, J., & Uestuen, T. B. (1999). Prevalence and health consequences of insomnia. *Sleep, 22*(Suppl 3), S427–S436.

Walsh, J. K., & Schweitzer, P. K. (1999). Ten-year trends in the pharmacological treatment of insomnia. *Sleep, 22*(3), 371–375.

Walsh, M. F., & Flynn, T. J. (1995). A 54-month evaluation of a popular very low calorie diet program. *Journal of Family Practice, 41*(3), 231–236.

Walsh, R. (1984). An evolutionary model of meditation research. In D. H. Shapiro & R. N. Walsh (Eds.), *Meditation: Classic and contemporary perspectives.* New York: Aldine.

Walster, E. (1971). Passionate love. In B. I. Murstein (Ed.), *Theories of attraction and love.* New York: Springer.

Walton, C. E., Bower, M. L., & Bower, T. G. (1992). Recognition of familiar faces by newborns. *Infant Behavior & Development, 15*(2), 265–269.

Wampold, B. E., et al. (1997). A meta-analysis of outcome studies comparing bona fide psychotherapies. *Psychological Bulletin, 122*(3), 203–215.

Ward, C. A. (1989). The cross-cultural study of altered states of consciousness and mental health. In C. A. Ward (Ed.), *Altered states of consciousness and mental health.* Newbury Park, CA: Sage.

Ward, P. B., Catts, S. V., Fox, A. M., Michie, P. T., et al. (1991). Auditory selective attention and event-related potentials in schizophrenia. *British Journal of Psychiatry, 158,* 534–539.

Warwick-Evans, L. A., Symons, N., Fitch, T., & Burrows, L. (1998). Evaluating sensory conflict and postural instability: Theories of motion sickness. *Brain Research Bulletin, 47*(5), 465–469.

Washabaugh, W. (1980). The manufacturing of a language. *Sign Language Studies, 29,* 291–330.

Washabaugh, W. (1981). Sign language in its social context. *Annual Review of Anthropology, 10,* 237–252.

Watson, D. L., & Tharp, R. G. (1996). *Self-directed behavior: Self-modification for personal adjustment* (4th ed.). Monterey, CA: Brooks/Cole.

Watson, J. B. (1913). Psychology as the behaviorist views it. *Psychological Review, 20,* 158–177.

Watson, J. B. (1994). Psychology as the behaviorist views it. [Special Issue: The centennial issue of the *Psychological Review.*] *Psychological Review, 101*(2), 248–253.

Weaver, C. A. (1993). Do you need a "flash" to form a flashbulb memory? *Journal of Experimental Psychology: General, 122*(1), 39–46.

Webb, N. M., & Farivar, S. (1994). Promoting helping behavior in cooperative small groups in middle school mathematics. *American Educational Research Journal, 31*(2), 369–395.

Webb, W. B. (1994). Sleep as a biological rhythm: A historical view. *Sleep, 17*(2), 188–194.

Wechsler, H., Molnar, B. E., Davenport, A. E., & Baer, J. S. (1999). College alcohol use: A full or empty glass? *Journal of American College Health, 47*(6), 247–252.

Weekley, J. A., & Jones, C. (1997). Video-based situational testing. *Personnel Psychology, 50*(1), 25–49.

Weems, C. F. (1998). The evaluation of heart rate biofeedback using a multi-element design. *Journal of Behavior Therapy & Experimental Psychiatry, 29*(2), 157–162.

Weinberg, R. A. (1989). Intelligence and IQ. *American Psychologist, 44*(2), 98–104.

Weiner, I. B. (1996). Some observations on the validity of the Rorschach Inkblot Method. *Psychological Assessment, 8*(2), 206–213.

Weiner, I. B. (1997). Current status of the Rorschach Inkblot Method. *Journal of Personality Assessment, 68*(1), 5–19.

Weintraub, M. I. (1983). *Hysterical conversion reactions.* New York: SP Medical & Scientific Books.

Weisburd, D. E. (1990). Planning a community-based mental health system: Perspective of a family member. *American Psychologist, 45*(11), 1245–1248.

Weiss, B., Dodge, K. A., Bates, J. E., & Pettit, G. S. (1992). Some consequences of early harsh discipline. *Child Development, 63*(6), 1321–1335.

Weiss, J. (1990, March). Unconscious mental functioning. *Scientific American,* 103–109.

Weiss, J. M. (1972). Psychological factors in stress and disease. *Scientific American, 26,* 104–113.

Weiten, W. (1998). Pressure, major life events, and psychological symptoms. *Journal of Social Behavior & Personality, 13*(1), 51–68.

Weitzenhoffer, A. M. and Hilgard, E. R. (1959). *Stanford Hypnotic Susceptibility Scale, Forms A and B.* Palo Alto, CA: Consulting Psychologists Press.

Wells, G. L. (1993). What do we know about eyewitness identification? *American Psychologist, 48*(5), 553–571.

Wells, N. (1994). Perceived control over pain: Relation to distress and disability. *Research in Nursing & Health, 17*(4), 295–302.

Welte, J. W., Barnes, G. M., Hoffman, J. H., & Dintcheff, B. A. (1999). Trends in adolescent alcohol and other substance use. *Substance Use & Misuse, 34*(10), 1427–1449.

Werner, C. M., & Makela, E. (1998). Motivations and behaviors that support recycling. *Journal of Environmental Psychology, 18*(4), 373–386.

Wertheimer, M. (1959). *Productive thinking.* New York: Harper & Row.

West, T. G. (1991). *In the mind's eye.* Buffalo, NY: Prometheus.

Westen, D. (1998). The scientific legacy of Sigmund Freud: Toward a psychodynamically informed psychological science. *Psychological Bulletin, 124*(3), 333–371.

Wexler, M., Kosslyn, S. M., & Berthoz, A. (1998). Motor processes in mental rotation. *Cognition, 68*(1), 77–94.

Wexler, M. N. (1995). Expanding the groupthink explanation to the study of contemporary cults. *Cultic Studies Journal, 12*(1), 49–71.

Whatley, M. A., Webster, J. M., Smith, R. H., & Rhodes, A. (1999). The effect of a favor on public and private compliance. *Basic & Applied Social Psychology, 21*(3), 251–259.

Wheeler, R. J., & Frank, M. A. (1988). Identification of stress buffers. *Behavioral Medicine, 14*(2), 78–89.

White, B. L., & Watts, J. C. (1973). *Experience and environment,* Vol. I. Englewood Cliffs, NJ: Prentice-Hall.

Whittal, M. L., Agras, W. S., & Gould, R. A. (1999). Bulimia nervosa: A meta-analysis of psychosocial and pharmacological treatments. *Behavior Therapy, 30*(1), 117–135.

Whyte, G. (1991). Diffusion of responsibility: Effects on the escalation tendency. *Journal of Applied Psychology, 76*(3), 408–415.

Wichstrom, L. (1995). Social, psychological and physical correlates of eating problems. *Psychological Medicine, 25*(3), 567–579.

Wickett, J. C., Vernon, P. A., & Lee, D. H. (2000). Relationships between factors of intelligence and brain volume. *Personality and Individual Differences, 29*(6), 1095–1122.

Widiger, T. A., & Sankis, L. M. (2000). Adult psychopathology. *Annual Review of Psychology, 51,* 377–404.

Widiger, T. A., & Trull, T. J. (1991). Diagnosis and clinical assessment. In M. R. Rosenzweig & L. W. Porter (Eds.), *Annual Review of Psychology, 42,* 109–133.

Wiesenthal, D. L., Austrom, D., & Silverman, I. (1983) Diffusion of responsibility in charitable donations. *Basic and Applied Social Psychology, 4*(1), 17–27.

Wilder, D. A., Simon, A. F., & Faith, M. (1996). Enhancing the impact of counterstereotypic information. *Journal of Personality & Social Psychology, 71*(2), 276–287.

Wilding, J., & Valentine, E. (1994a). Memory champions. *British Journal of Psychology, 85*(2), 231–244.

Wilding, J., & Valentine, E. (1994b). Mnemonic wizardry with the telephone directory: But stories are another story. *British Journal of Psychology, 85*(4), 501–509.

Wilgosh, L. (1991). Underachievement in culturally different gifted children. *European Journal for High Ability, 2*(2), 166–173.

Wilhelm, J. L. (1976). *The search for superman.* New York: Simon & Schuster.

Wilkinson, G., Piccinelli, M., Roberts, S., Micciolo, R., & Fry, J. (1997). Lunar cycle and consultations for anxiety and depression in general practice. *International Journal of Social Psychiatry, 43*(1), 29–34.

Wilkinson, R. B. (1997). Interactions between self and external reinforcement in predicting depressive symptoms. *Behaviour Research & Therapy, 35*(4), 281–289.

Williams, B. A. (1984, November 30). U. S. approves implants to aid the totally deaf. *Santa Barbara News Press,* Part C, p. 6.

Williams, C. C., & Collins, A. (2002). Factors associated with insight among outpatients with serious mental illness. *Psychiatric Services, 53*(1), 96–98.

Williams, R. (1989). *The trusting heart: Great news about Type A behavior.* New York: Random House.

Williams, R. J., Odaibo, F. S., & McGee, J. H. (1999). Incidence of fetal alcohol syndrome in northern Manitoba. *Canadian Journal of Public Health, 90*(3), 192–194.

Williams, R. J., & Schmidt, G. G. (1993). Frequency of seasonal affective disorder among individuals seeking treatment at a northern Canadian mental health center. *Psychiatry Research, 46,* 41–45.

Williams, R. L., et al. (1964). Sleep patterns in young adults: An EEG study. *Electroencephalography and Clinical Neurophysiology,* 376–381.

Williams, R. L., & Long, J. D. (1991). *Toward a self-managed life style.* Boston: Houghton Mifflin.

Willinger, M., Hoffman, H. J., & Hartford, R. B. (1994). Infant sleep position and risk for sudden infant death syndrome. *Pediatrics, 93*(5), 814–819.

Willoughby, T., Wood, E., Desmarais, S., Sims, S., & Kalra, M. (1997). Mechanisms that facilitate the effectiveness of elaboration strategies. *Journal of Educational Psychology, 89*(4), 682–685.

Wilson, G. T. (1987). Chemical aversion conditioning as a treatment for alcoholism: A re-analysis. *Behaviour Research and Therapy, 25*(6), 503–516.

Wilson, R. R. (1986). *Don't panic: Taking control of anxiety attacks.* New York: Harper & Row.

Wilson, T. L., & Brown, T. L. (1997). Reexamination of the effect of Mozart's music on spatial-task performance. *Journal of Psychology, 131*(4), 365–370.

Wise, R. A., & Rompre, P. P. (1989). Brain dopamine and reward. *Annual Review of Psychology, 40,* 191–225.

Withers, N. W., Pulvirenti, L., Koob, G. F., & Gillin, J. C. (1995). Cocaine abuse and dependence. *Journal of Clinical Psychopharmacology, 15*(1), 63–78.

Witherspoon, W. (1994, July 28). Disorder consumed her life. *Los Angeles Times,* p. C1.

Wolfe, J. B. (1936). Effectiveness of token rewards for chimpanzees. *Comparative Psychology Monographs, 12*(5), Whole No. 60.

Wolitzky, D. L. (1995). The theory and practice of traditional psychoanalytic psychotherapy. In A. S. Gurman & S. B. Messer (Eds.), *Essential psychotherapies.* New York: Guilford.

Wolpe, J. (1974). *The practice of behavior therapy* (2nd ed.). New York: Pergamon.

Wolpe, J., & Plaud, J. J. (1997). Pavlov's contributions to behavior therapy. *American Psychologist, 52*(9), 966–972.

Wolpin, M., Marston, A., Randolph, C., & Clothier, A. (1992). Individual difference correlates of reported lucid dreaming frequency and control. *Journal of Mental Imagery, 16*(3–4), 231–236.

Wolsko, C., Park, B., Judd, C. M., & Wittenbrink, B. (2000). Framing interethnic ideology: Effects of multicultural and color-blind perspectives on judgments of groups and individuals. *Journal of Personality & Social Psychology, 78*(4), 635–654.

Wolters, C. A. (1998). Self-regulated learning and college students' regulation of motivation. *Journal of Educational Psychology, 90*(2), 224–235.

Wong, J. L., & Whitaker, D. J. (1993). Depressive mood states and their cognitive and personality correlates in college students. *Journal of Clinical Psychology, 49*(5), 615–621.

Woo, E. (1995, January 20). Teaching that goes beyond IQ. *Los Angeles Times,* pp. A1, A22, A23.

Wood, J. M., & Bootzin, R. R. (1990). The prevalence of nightmares and their independence from anxiety. *Journal of Abnormal Psychology, 99*(1), 64–68.

Wood, J. M., Bootzin, R. R., Kihlstrom, J. F., & Schacter, D. L. (1992). Implicit and explicit memory for verbal information presented during sleep. *Psychological Science, 3*(4), 236–239.

Wood, N. L., & Cowan, N. (1995). The cocktail party phenomenon revisited. *Journal of Experimental Psychology: General, 124*(3), 243–262.

Woods, B. T. (1998). Is schizophrenia a progressive neurodevelopmental disorder? *American Journal of Psychiatry, 155,* 1661–1670.

Woods, S. C., Schwartz, M. W., Baskin, D. G., & Seeley, R. J. (2000). Food intake and the regulation of body weight. *Annual Review of Psychology, 51,* 255–277.

Woods, S. C., Seeley, R. J., Porte, D. (1998). Signals that regulate food intake and energy homeostasis. *Science, 280*(5368), 1378–1383.

Woodward, J., & Goodstein, D. (1996). Conduct, misconduct and the structure of science. *American Scientist, 84,* 479–490.

Woody, S. R. (1996). Effects of focus of attention on anxiety levels and social performance of individuals with social phobia. *Journal of Abnormal Psychology, 105*(1), 61–69.

Worthen, J. B., & Marshall, P. H. (1996). Intralist and extralist sources of distinctiveness and the bizarreness effect. *American Journal of Psychology, 109*(2), 239–263.

Wright, D. B. (1993). Recall of the Hillsborough disaster over time: Systematic biases of "flashbulb" memories. *Applied Cognitive Psychology, 7*(2), 129–138.

Wulf, G., Shea, C. H., & Matschiner, S. (1998). Frequent feedback enhances complex motor skill learning. *Journal of Motor Behavior, 30*(2), 180–192.

Wyatt, J. W., Posey, A., Welker, W., & Seamonds, C. (1984). Natural levels of similarities between identical twins and between unrelated people. *The Skeptical Inquirer, 9,* 62–66.

Yadama, G. N., & Drake, B. (1995). Confirmatory factor analysis of the Maslach Burnout Inventory. *Social Work Research, 19*(3), 184–192.

Yalom, I. D. (1980). *Existential psychotherapy.* New York: Basic.

Yank, G. R., Bentley, K. J., & Hargrove, D. S. (1993). The vulnerability-stress model of schizophrenia. *American Journal of Orthopsychiatry, 63*(1), 55–69.

Yarmey, A. D., Yarmey, M. J., & Yarmey, A. L. (1996). Accuracy of eyewitness identification in showups and lineups. *Law & Human Behavior, 20*(4), 459–477.

Yee, A. H., Fairchild, H. H., Weizmann, F., & Wyatt, G. E. (1993). Addressing psychology's problems with race. *American Psychologist, 48*(11), 1132–1140.

Yewchuk, C. (1999). Savant syndrome: Intuitive excellence amidst general deficit. *Developmental Disabilities Bulletin, 27*(1), 58–76.

Yontef, G. M. (1995). Gestalt therapy. In A. S. Gurman & S. B. Messer (Eds.), *Essential psychotherapies.* New York: Guilford.

Yoshida, M. (1993). Three-dimensional electrophysiology atlas created by computer mapping of clinical responses elicited on stimulation of human subcortical structures. *Stereotactic & Functional Neurosurgery, 60*(1–3), 127–134.

Zadra, A., & Pihl, R. (1997). Lucid dreaming as a treatment for recurrent nightmares. *Psychotherapy and Psychosomatics, 66,* 50–55.

Zeidner, M. (1995). Adaptive coping with test situations: A review of the literature. *Educational Psychologist, 30*(3), 123–133.

Zellner, D. A., Harner, D. E., & Adler, R. L. (1989). Effects of eating abnormalities and gender on perceptions of desirable body shape. *Journal of Abnormal Psychology, 98*(1), 93–96.

Zgodzinski, D. (1996, February). Cybertherapy. *Internet World,* 50–53.

Zhang, D. (1995). Depression and culture: A Chinese perspective. *Canadian Journal of Counselling, 29*(3), 227–233.

Zigler, E. (1995). Can we "cure" mild mental retardation among individuals in the lower socioeconomic stratum? *American Journal of Public Health, 85*(3), 302–304.

Zimbardo, P. G., Pilkonis, P. A., & Norwood, R. M. (1978). The social disease called shyness. In *Annual editions, personality and adjustment 78/79.* Guilford, CT: Dushkin.

Zimmerman, B. J. (1996a). Enhancing student academic and health functioning: A self-regulatory perspective. *School Psychology Quarterly, 11*(1), 47–66.

Zimmerman, J. D. (1996b). A prosocial media strategy. *American Journal of Orthopsychiatry, 66*(3), 354–362.

Zimmerman, S., & Zimmerman, A. M. (1990). Genetic effects of marijuana. *International Journal of Addictions, 25*(1A), 19–33.

Zinbarg, R. E., Barlow, D. H., Brown, T. A., & Hertz, R. M. (1992). Cognitive-behavioral approaches to the nature and treatment of anxiety disorders. In M. R. Rosenzweig & L. W. Porter (Eds.), *Annual Review of Psychology, 43,* 235–267.

Zohar, D. (1998). An additive model of test anxiety: Role of exam-specific expectations. *Journal of Educational Psychology, 90*(2), 330–340.

Zuckerman, M. (1990). The psychophysiology of sensation seeking. *Journal of Personality, 58*(1), 313–345.

Zuckerman, M. (1996). Item revisions in the Sensation Seeking Scale Form V (SSS-V). *EDRA: Environmental Design Research Association, 20*(4), 515.

Zuckerman, M., Eysenck, S., & Eysenck, H. J. (1978). Sensation seeking in England and America: Cross-cultural, age, and sex comparisons. *Journal of Consulting and Clinical Psychology, 46,* 139–149.

Zuwerink, J. R., Devine, P. G., Monteith, M. J., & Cook, D. A. (1996). Prejudice toward Blacks: With and without compunction? *Basic & Applied Social Psychology, 18*(2), 131–150.

Credits

About the Authors. page vi: photos courtesy of (top to bottom) Dennis Coon, Patrick Brown, Rajesh Malik, and Sue McKenzie.

Chapter 1. page 1: © Corel; 3: Jeff Greenberg/Photo Edit; 4 (bottom): CP Picture Archive/Tom Hanson; 4 (top left): © Photodisc; 4 (top right): © EyeWire; 5 (top): Susan Kuklin/Photo Researchers; 5 (bottom): © Richard T. Nowitz/Corbis/Magma; 6: Archives of the History of American Psychology – The University of Akron; 7 (top): Archives of the History of American Psychology – The University of Akron; 7 (bottom): Archives of the History of American Psychology – The University of Akron; 8: © Nina Leen/Timepix; 9 (top left): Archives of the History of American Psychology, University of Akron; 9 (top right): Archives of the History of American Psychology – The University of Akron; 9 (bottom left): Archives of the History of American Psychology – The University of Akron; 9 (bottom centre): Archives of the History of American Psychology – The University of Akron; 9 (bottom right): Archives of the History of American Psychology – The University of Akron; 10: Archives of the History of American Psychology – The University of Akron; 12: McGill University Archives; 14: © Photofest; 19:

© Hugo Van Lawick/NGS Image Collection; 29: © Bettmann/Corbis/Magma; 30: block quotation reprinted with permission of author and publisher from R. E. Ulrich, T. J. Stachnik, and N. R. Stainton, "Student acceptance of generalized personality interpretations," *Psychological Reports, 13* (1963), 831–834; 33: Mary Stangolis/Nelson; 34: CP Picture Archive/Nikos Giakoumidis.

Chapter 2. page 40: © Corel; 48: CP Picture Archive/Boris Spremo; 50: Huntington Magnetic Resonance Center, Pasadena, California; 51 (both): Washington University School of Medicine, St. Louis; 53: Courtesy of Richard Haier, University of California, Irvine; 54: Figure 2.17 from *Left Brain, Right Brain*, Revised Edition, by S. P. Springer and G. Deutsch, copyright 1981, 1985, 1989, 1993, 1998. Reprinted with the permission of W. H. Freeman and Company; 59: Shaywitz et al., 1995, NMR Research/Yale Medical School; 64: © Hulton-Deutsch Collection/Corbis/Magma; 68: Courtesy of Wendy Yano; 69: © Superstock.

Chapter 3. page 75: © Katherine Strain; 76: Andrew Syred/Science Photo Library; 78: © Photodisc; 79 (left): Dr. M. A. Ansary/Science Photo Library; 79 (right): © David H. Wells/Corbis/Magma; 83 (left): Courtesy of Cindy Howard; 83 (group of six): From A. N. Meltzoff & M. K. Moore, "Imitation of facial and manual gestures by human neonates," *Science, 198* (1977), 75–78; 84: Courtesy of David Linton; 84: drawings in Figure 3.5 from "The Origin of Form Perception," by Robert L. Fantz; 85: Courtesy of Carolyn Rovee-Collier/Rutgers University; 86: Figure 3.8 after K. M. B. Bridges, 1932. Reprinted by permission of the Society for Research in Child Development, Inc.; 88 (left): © Ann Brown/Super-

Stock; 88 (right): Dan Grogan Photography; 91: Courtesy of George Brown College; 96: © Photodisc; 97 (left): © Tony Freeman/PhotoEdit; 97 (right): © Farrell Grehan/Corbis/Magma; 103: © PhotoEdit; 106: © Photodisc.

Chapter 4. page 114: © Angela Cluer; 120: Omikron/Photo Researchers; 123: © Photodisc; 125: © Photodisc; 128: Susumu Nishinaga/Science Photo Library; 130: Richard Costano, Discover Magazine, 1993; 134: NASA; 138 (top): © Yvaral, *Marilyn Numerisee #420,* © Yvaral 1990, courtesy of Circle Gallery; 138 (bottom): © Mark Richards/PhotoEdit; 140: © Index Stock Imagery; 143: © 1994 by N. E. Thing Enterprises. All rights reserved. Reprinted by permission of Andrews McMeel Universal Press Syndicate; 145 (top): © Dennis Coon; 145 (bottom right): © *Concave and Convex,* by M. C. Escher © 2001 Cordon Art – Baarn, Holland. All rights reserved; 146 (bottom): © Dennis Coon; 148 (top left): National Archives of Canada/Pittaway & Jarvis/C-000686; 148 (top right): based on National Archives of Canada/Pittaway & Jarvis/C-000686; 148 (bottom): Richard Nowitz/Phototake; 151: Figure 4.49 from M. H. Erdelyi and A. G. Applebaum (1973), Cognitive masking: The disruptive effect of an emotional stimulus upon the perception of contiguous neutral items, *Bulletin of the Psychonomic Society, 1,* 59–61. Reprinted by permission.

Chapter 5. page 165: © Corel; 167: © Arne Hodalic/Corbis/Magma; 168: © Index Stock Imagery; 176: © David H. Wells/Corbis/Magma; 180: Mary Stangolis/Nelson; 182 (both): Mary Stangolis/Nelson; 189: Illustration courtesy of The National Library of Medicine; 190: CP Picture Archive/AP Photo/E. Pablo Kos-

micki; 191: Mary Stangolis/Nelson; 197 (top): "Marijuana and the Brain," *Science News, 143*; 197 (bottom): © "Beware Marijuana," courtesy of Dr. Lester Grinspoon, Harvard Medical School; 200: © Index Stock Imagery.

Chapter 6. page 208: © Corel; 219: boxed text after B. F. Skinner, *The Behavior of Organisms.* © 1938. D. Appleton-Century Co., Inc. Reprinted by permission of The B. F. Skinner Foundation; 220: © Yale Joel/TimePix; 227: © Frank Conaway/IndexStock; 229: © Frank Siteman/Index Stock Imagery; 236 (top): © Branson Reynolds/Index Stock Imagery; 236 (series, bottom): Dr. Albert Bandura; 238: © Getty Images; 240: © Photodisc.

Chapter 7. page 247: © Corel; 248: © Photodisc; 252: From Wilder Penfield, *The Excitable Cortex in Conscious Man*, 1958. Courtesy of the author and Charles C. Thomas Publisher, Springfield, Illinois; 258: © Larry Day; 265: © Paul Conklin/PhotoEdit; 267 (left): © Rick Martin/San Jose Mercury News; 267 (right): Associated Press/Carmen Taylor; 271: © E. Tulving (1989), "Remembering and knowing the past," *American Scientist, 77*(4), 361–367; 271: © Al Grotell; 274: CP Picture Archive/Dave Buston; 277: © Photodisc.

Chapter 8. page 283: © Ken Phipps; 285: © Dennis Coon; 289: Mary Stangolis/Nelson; 300: © Laura Dwight/Corbis/Magma; 302: Table 8.4 courtesy of the Psychological Corporation; 306: CP Picture Archive/Maclean's Photo/Phil Snel; 309: © Hulton Archive.

Chapter 9. page 324: © Ken Phipps; 326: CP Picture Archive/Ryan Remiorz; 329: "Hyper Rat" photograph courtesy of Neal E. Miller, Rockefeller

Subject Index

Index of Names